A HISTORY OF THE MEDITERRANEAN AIR WAR 1940–1945
Volume Five: From The Fall of Rome to the End of the War 1944–1945

A HISTORY OF THE
MEDITERRANEAN AIR WAR
1940–1945

Volume Five:
From The Fall of Rome to the End of the War
1944–1945

Christopher Shores and Giovanni Massimello
with Russell Guest, Frank Olynyk,
Winfried Bock and Andrew Thomas

GRUB STREET • LONDON

Published by
Grub Street
4 Rainham Close
London SW11 6SS

Copyright © Grub Street 2021
Copyright text © Christopher Shores, Giovanni Massimello, Russell Guest,
Frank Olynyk, Winfried Bock and Andrew Thomas 2021

A CIP record for this title is available from the British library

ISBN-13: 978-1-911621-97-3

Maps by Jeff Jefford
Front cover illustration by Barry Weekley

Printed and bound by Finidr, Czech Republic

CONTENTS

PREAMBLE

It is perhaps useful to our readers to summarize at this point where our Mediterranean Air War series has reached. Volume 3 has explained the developments and changes in command which had led to the formation during February 1943 of the Mediterranean Air Command under the leadership of Air Chief Marshal Sir Arthur Tedder coupled with the division within that command principally of the North West African Strategic, Tactical and Coastal Air Forces. That volume then concluded with the expulsion of Axis forces from the entirety of the southern coastline of the Mediterranean, equating effectively to that of North Africa.

Volume 4 then dealt with the invasions and occupations of Sicily, southern Italy, Sardinia and Corsica, culminating in the fall of Rome to the Allies at the beginning of June 1944. This current volume deals largely with the balance of the tactical operations in central and northern Italy, concluding with the end of the war at the start of May 1945.

As has been explained within this volume it remains our intention to devote Volume 6 in due course to the strategic operations of the US 15th Air Force and 205 Group, RAF, from the formation of the former of these commands during the autumn of 1943. Where operations were undertaken as an adjunct to those of the Tactical Air Force and were not specifically in compliance with the Allied Combined Bombing Offensive, but were of a nature which we have described as "long-range tactical", we will frequently cross-reference these between Volumes 5 and 6 in order that readers may more readily be able to follow the chronology of our coverage.

But herein lies something of an anomaly which requires some further explanation. The logic of our chronology would appear to have followed the conclusion of operations in North Africa (Volume 3 – May 1943) with the invasions of Sicily and Italy as set out in Volume 4 (May 1943-June 1944). This, however, leaves us with a specific series of operations which impinge on the main Allied lines of advance. To leave these out, or to place them in a separate appendix form would seem to break the line of our chronology.

Specifically, we refer to the events affecting the eastern basin of the Mediterranean generally described as the Aegean area. When the establishment of the Mediterranean Air Command, referred to above, took place in February 1943, there was a separate command responsible for this area entitled Headquarters, RAF Middle East. Initially we considered including coverage of this area within Volume 4 in order to maintain the chronological consistency but here we were brought to a halt by a mundane matter. Briefly, we were running out of space if the book, already likely to be large in any event, were not to be rendered difficult to use in practice. We then considered the course we have actually taken of dealing with this area at the start of Volume 5, allowing the text thereof to flow into the main narrative at the 'fall of Rome' point.

In selecting this course of action there were several other aspects which seemed to us to favour it despite the break in the chronology which thereby resulted. Throughout most of 1943 RAF Middle East was fighting its own war and was not a part of the Mediterranean Air Command – although there was provision for Middle East Command and Coastal Air Force to call upon each other's assistance at times of need. Further, the operations in the Balkans and Greece were already bringing elements of both Mediterranean Allied Tactical Air Force and Coastal Air Force into this area, and occasionally also pulling in Strategic Air Force, albeit in its XII Bomber Command form.

In conclusion, we present to you in Volume 5 an opening section dealing with RAF, Middle East and its opponents from May 1943 to the beginning of June 1944 incorporating such other elements of the Allied air forces as may be appropriate. This is followed by a major section containing a number of chapters dealing with the campaigns in Italy from June 1944 to May 1945, and also incorporating details relative to the formation and operations of the Balkan Air Force over the same period, together with the invasion of southern France during the period August-September 1944.

*

Readers of the earlier volumes in this series (notably *Air War for Yugoslavia, Greece and Crete*) will be aware that the spring and summer months of 1941 saw very considerable aerial combat as the Axis powers (both German and Italian) swept southwards to invade and capture Yugoslavia, Greece, Crete and the other islands of the eastern Mediterranean not already in Italian hands.

Thereafter this area of the ocean remained for many months one of great danger for the Royal Navy and of difficulty for the squadrons of the Royal Air Force. This was not to change greatly during the next two years and little activity was to be seen here. Importantly, the Luftwaffe employed airfields in Greece and some of the larger islands for refuelling and re-arming bombers targeted with Alexandria, Cairo, the Suez Canal Zone and other North African locations. Occasional raids were launched in the opposite directions but apart from regular reconnaissance sorties by all the air forces involved, activity was slight. Indeed, given the level of operations taking place all along the African coast and over Malta this is not surprising given the facilities available much of the time.

As Volume 3 indicates, by the spring of 1943 the growing strength of the Allied forces was at last offering the opportunity to pay a little more attention to the area in question. Even so, the Allies had only just consolidated their occupation of Tunisia which, with Algeria and French Morocco, was becoming the main USAAF base area for equipment, servicing and pre-combat training – not only for the Americans but also for the rapidly re-growing French forces. Of more immediate concern was the forward planning for the potential invasions of Sicily and Italy and consideration of the future intentions about the islands of Sardinia and Corsica. Coupled with these matters was the continuation of protection to a growing stream of supply convoys sailing through the Straits of Gibraltar now not only to this main battle area, but also heading towards Suez as a shorter route to the Far East. With all this before the Allied commanders, it is of little surprise that the Aegean remained very much a backwater of the war at this stage.

As shown in the Allied Order of Battle on pages 152–157 in Volume 4, the whole area of the Aegean and Balkans came under the control of Headquarters, RAF Middle East rather than under the relatively new Mediterranean Allied Air Force. The largest part of this sub-command was 201 Group, essentially a naval co-operation and anti-submarine force, supported by four rather small groups based at various points all along the Libyan and Egyptian coastlines and equipped mainly with fighters – most of them obsolescent Hurricanes.

HQ Air Defence Eastern Mediterranean could, of course, seek any immediate reinforcement from within the command beyond which *in extremis* it could call upon Coastal Air Force and HQ Malta. Also, in the area at this time were the heavy bombers of the US IX Air Force and the other 'heavies' of 205 Group but all these units were operating for the Strategic Air Force. However, RAF Middle East was being reinforced to provide a limited element capable of providing some offensive striking power by the arrival from Malta of a single squadron (227) of Beaufighter VIcs. In May 1943 it was this unit which provided the only real offensive element. A further new arrival was 454 Squadron which had just completed re-equipment with Baltimores to become a light bomber unit. The command did have some more Beaufighters on detachments, but these were essentially defensive units with Mark If night-fighters of 46 Squadron.

Due to the unusual division of this volume effectively into two separate elements we have, in the interests of clarity, divided the main contents into two sections which we have entitled Parts I and II. This has allowed each part to be sub-divided into somewhat more logical chronological chapters.

NB: The authors have been keeping a running total of amendments and corrections to Volumes 1–4 which will be collated together and appear in Volume 6.

PART I–THE AIR WAR OVER THE AEGEAN

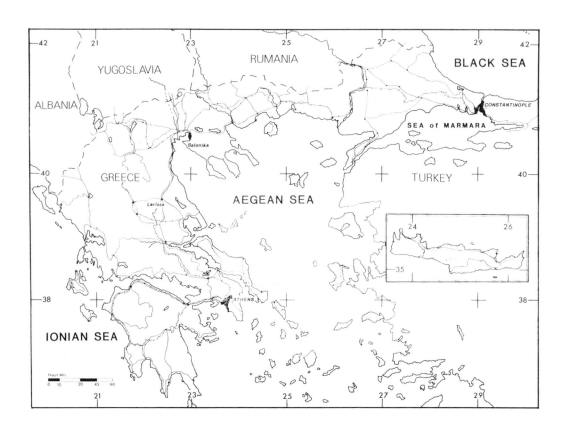

CHAPTER 1

EARLY MOVES IN THE AEGEAN

Monday, 15 May 1943

On 1 January 1943 the Oberkommando der Luftwaffe (OKL) had established a new high command, Luftwaffe Kommando Süd-Ost (LKS) under Gen Otto Hoffmann von Waldau, RK, who became responsible for the coordination of operations in the south-eastern area of the front. On 17 May he was flying to his new headquarters at Salonika when the Do 215B piloted by Lt Hermann Köhler crashed near Petrič, Bulgaria, killing all aboard. Five days later von Waldau was replaced by Gen Martin Fiebig.

German Casualties

Flugber./LKS	Do 215B WNr 182 crashed nr Petri, N Salonika; Lt Hermann Köhler, two crew members and two passengers: Gen d.Fl Otto Hoffmann von Waldau (LKS CO) and Hptm Fhr Wolf von Gummingen all KiA

Friday, 21 May 1943

At 0645 the 1./Luftwaffe Reg 2 reported that five Ju 52/3mW floatplanes had left Phaleron at 0645 and subsequently landed at Milos at 0855. At 1300 they made the return journey, this time escorted by Ar 196 floatplanes. Three of 227 Squadron's Beaufighters were on a sweep over the Aegean when the Ju 52/3ms and five Ar 196s were spotted near Milos island where Flg Off A.J.Phillips claimed one of the latter shot down and hits were thought to have been achieved on two of the trimotors. 1./JagdRegt reported further that one Ju 52 had been shot down and others damaged; at 1423 one of these landed at Kalamaki 30% damaged; one Beaufighter failed to return and it appeared from the German transports that the Beaufighter had collided with an Arado and crashed into the sea.

British Claims

227 Sqn	Plt Off A.J.Phillips/Flg Off E.Gittins	Beaufighter VI JL533 'K'	Ar 196	nr Milos island	1255-1720
227 Sqn	Plt Off A.J.Phillips/Flg Off E.Gittins	Beaufighter VI JL533 'K'	2 Ju 52/3ms Dmgd	nr Milos island	1255-1720

British Casualties

227 Sqn	Beaufighter VI JL314 'R' left 1255, shot down near Milos island, believed from German data to have collided with a Ju 52; Flt Lt J.E.Atkins/Plt Off R.W.Wellington MiA

German Claims

SAGr 126	Obfw Müller	Ar 196	Beaufighter	off Crete	1345

German Casualties

Seetransportst. 1	Ju 52/3mW 30% damaged by collision with Beaufighter, crash-landed on Kalamaki a/f

Monday, 24 May 1943

German Casualties

6./TG 4	Ju 52/3m force-landed on Skyros, out of fuel, 80% damaged
7.Seenotst.	Do 24T-2 WNr 0058 CM+1X crashed 13km E Antikythera; Fw Willi Gebhard WiA and four KiA

Tuesday-Wednesday, 25/26 May 1943

Early in the morning, a Rhodes-based S.79 of 253ª Squadriglia, 104° Gruppo AS, flown by Cap Enrico

Marescalchi, attacked and claimed to have torpedoed a destroyer along the coast between Ras Hashifa and Ras El Daba.

Thursday, 27 May 1943

The commanding officer of 227 Squadron, Wg Cdr Mackenzie, shot down a Ju 88C-6 long-range fighter of 11./ZG 26.

British Claims					
227 Sqn	Wg Cdr R.M.Mackenzie/Plt Off A.L.Craig	Beaufighter VIf EL467 'B'	Ju 88	Aegean	0827-1340
227 Sqn	Flg Off J.R.S.Modera/Plt Off A.K.Hodge	Beaufighter VIf EL460 'U'	Ju 88 Damaged	Aegean	0827-1340

German Casualties	
11./ZG 26	Ju 88C-6 WNr 360188 3U+DV shot down by Beaufighters nr Milos; Fw Erich Borner and two KiA

Saturday, 29 May 1943

Beaufighters of 227 Squadron again swept over the Aegean when a Ju 52/3m and an Ar 196 of 1./SAGr 126 were intercepted near Kythnos (Thermin) at 1115, the transport flying on the route, Milos-Athens, and were both shot down. The pilot of the Junkers survived but one passenger was killed and three of those aboard were wounded. The Arado was set on fire and landed on the sea, running aground; there it was strafed by the Beaufighters and the observer was killed.

British Claims					
227 Sqn	Flg Off A.J.Phillips/Flt Lt E.Gittins	Beaufighter VI JL533 'K'			
227 Sqn	Flg Off J.R.S.Modera/Plt Off A.K.Hodge	Beaufighter VI EL460 'U'			
227 Sqn	Sgt H.E.Thomas/Sgt R.C.Howes	Beaufighter VI EL522 'S'	Ju 52/3m	near Kythnos	1115
227 Sqn	Sgt A.D.May/Sgt C.G.Roskin	Beaufighter VI JL708 'A'			
227 Sqn	Flg Off A.J.Phillips/Flt Lt E.Gittins	Beaufighter VI JL533 'K'			
227 Sqn	Flg Off J.R.S.Modera/Plt Off A.K.Hodge	Beaufighter VI EL460 'U'			
227 Sqn	Sgt H.E.Thomas/Sgt R.C.Howes	Beaufighter VI EL522 'S'	Ar 196	near Kythnos	1115
227 Sqn	Sgt A.D.May/Sgt C.G.Roskin	Beaufighter VI JL708 'A'			

German Casualties	
Seetransportst. 1	Ju 52/3m WNr 7103 shot down nr Kythnos en route Milos-Athens; Obgfr Georg Hiepe safe, three WiA, one passenger (Marine) KiA
1./SAGr 126	Ar 196A-3 WNr 0298 D1+JH force-landed and strafed nr Kythnos en route Milos-Athens; Fw Michalek safe/Lt Josef Müller KiA

Friday, 4 June 1943

British Casualties	
227 Sqn	Beaufighter VI EL460 'U' shot down by Flak off Stampalita Island near harbour 1915; Sgt J.A.Lewis/Sgt J.A.J.Roff MiA

German Casualties	
3./SAGr 126	Ar 196 WNr 1036 D1+AL shot down by partisans bombing Stampalia harbour; Uffz Hermann Nitzsche/Lt Horst Stolzenberg MiA

Sunday, 6 June 1943

During a mid-morning reconnaissance off the Palestine coast near St Jean a Cant.Z.1007bis of 195ª Squadriglia was intercepted and shot down by a 46 Squadron night-fighter that happened to be on patrol, the whole Italian crew being lost.

At 1300 two more Cants from the same unit set off to search for the missing aircraft and its crew. 127 Squadron at St Jean scrambled two Hurricanes at 1610 (local time) followed by two Spitfires at 1615. At 1640 (based on the surviving Italian crew timing being intercepted at 1540, presumably Italian time) one of the two Cants was intercepted off the Palestine coast by one of the two Spitfires piloted by Flt Sgt James who made three attacks in all and claimed a Cant damaged. On its way back past Cyprus this aircraft was intercepted by a detachment from 238 Squadron on Cyprus and shot down. Again, the crew were lost. The third Cant.Z.1007 appears to have also been attacked by the 238 Squadron Hurricanes. This one was damaged but managed to make its way back to base with two members of the crew wounded.

British Claims

46 Sqn	Flt Lt O.Hooker/Sgt E.H.Chambers	Beaufighter 'E'	Cant.Z.1007	in sea off St Jean	0934–1054
127 Sqn	Flt Sgt G.M.James	Spitfire V ES335	Cant Z.1007 Damaged	off St Jean	1640
238 Sqn	Plt Off R.W.Bunyon	Hurricane IIb	Cant.Z.1007	Cyprus	1730
238 Sqn	Flt Sgt H.D.Rayment	Hurricane IIb			
238 Sqn	Plt Off R.W.Bunyon	Hurricane IIb	Cant Z.1007 Damaged	Cyprus	1730
238 Sqn	Flt Sgt H.D.Rayment	Hurricane IIb			

German Casualties

IV./TG 3	Ju 52/3m WNr 3168 damaged by fighters; gunner KiA, crew safe

Italian Casualties

195ª Sq, 90º Gr, 30º St BT	Cant.Z.1007 left 0710, failed to return; pilot Ten Arrigo Zorzut, co-pilot Serg Primo Saccomandi and four MiA
195ª Sq, 90º Gr, 30º St BT	Cant.Z.1007 MM 24758 left 1300 to search for missing aircraft, shot down off Cyprus by Spitfires; pilot Ten Alessandro Marri, co-pilot Ten Mario Silvestro and four KiA
195ª Sq, 90º Gr, 30º St BT	Cant.Z.1007 left 1300 to search for missing aircraft, damaged by Beaufighter and Spitfires, landed at base at 1820; pilot and three safe, co-pilot M.llo Francesco Nunnari and gunner Serg Magg De Bernardini WiA

Tuesday, 8 June 1943

On take-off from Misurata West at 1640 to provide anti-submarine cover to convoy 'Paper' a 38 Squadron Wellington's starboard tyre burst, but the pilot managed to avoid a crash and continued with his patrol. Upon return he jettisoned the six 250lb depth charges being carried and prepared to land. While in the circuit the port engine's propeller fell off the aircraft and a belly landing resulted, the crew being unhurt – and somewhat fortunate!

British Casualties

38 Sqn	Wellington VIII LB113 'U' left Misurata West 1640 on anti-submarine cover to convoy 'Paper', crash-landed on return; Flt Lt R.M.Pugh and five safe
454 Sqn	Baltimore III AH 371 crashed on take-off believed caused when a dinghy, being used by the pilot as a cushion, inflated and pushed him off the controls; Flt Lt E.G.Bamkin and three KiA
74 Sqn	Hurricane IIb left 0820 on patrol over a single RN cruiser, coolant leak, pilot baled out; Plt Off H.B.Prendergast rescued by the cruiser HMS *Abdiel* within 5 minutes

Saturday, 12 June 1943

Spitfires of 123 Squadron and 103 MU scrambled to intercept a Bf 109G of 2.(F)/123 fitted with long-range tanks. This was shot down by Plt Off Watton in a Spitfire V. The pilot, Oblt Justus Lindemann, was captured and reported that he had fallen to a Hurricane. A 2.(F)/123 Ju 88 was also intercepted at 1023 over Alexandria, but evaded and returned safely to base.

Left: On 12 June Plt Off John Watton of 123 Squadron brought down a high-flying reconnaissance Bf 109 the pilot of which was captured.

Right: A Spitfire Vc of 123 Squadron wearing the rarely seen 'XE' unit code letters.

Saturday-Sunday, 12/13 June 1943

During an anti-shipping patrol from Berka between 1940 and 0345, Flt Sgt H.A.Taylor, flying a 38 Squadron Wellington carrying bombs and a torpedo, encountered two small ships of an estimated 300 tons each. He bombed the first one and strafed the second, the latter firing back and hitting the Wellington in the torpedo air chamber. This exploded, blowing off the bomb-bay doors and the torpedo, setting the aircraft on fire; this was extinguished. The aircraft reached Derna where it crash-landed. The 21-year-old Taylor received an immediate DFM. Six weeks later Taylor and his crew were lost without trace on another Aegean reconnaissance mission.

British Casualties	
38 Sqn	Wellington VIII LB 146 'D' left 1940 from Berka, bombed a ship, damaged by Flak, reached Derna where it crash-landed; Flt Sgt H.A.Taylor and crew safe

Tuesday, 15 June 1943

On this date, the German submarine *U-97* (Kaptlt Hans-Georg Trox) torpedoed and sank the large British tanker *Athelmonarch* (8,995 tons) near Haifa in the eastern Mediterranean. Consequently, an intensive hunt for the submarine was launched.

British Claims					
103 MU	Flt Lt T.P.M.Cooper-Slipper	Spitfire IX	Ju 188 Damaged	45m N Aboukir	1215-1315

Tuesday-Wednesday, 15/16 June 1943

During the early hours of 16 June, Flg Off Dowden and his radar operator, Sgt Stevens, claimed a Ju 88 shot down in the Castel Benito area, although on this occasion no loss of a Luftwaffe aircraft in such circumstances has been discovered.

British Claims					
89 Sqn	Flg Off D.J.Dowden/Sgt R.F.Stevens	Beaufighter VIf V8514	Ju 88	Castel Benito	0208

British Casualties	
458 Sqn	Wellington VIII LB195 on anti-submarine convoy cover, lost from radar plot 0020; Sgt E.B.Bottomley and five MiA

Wednesday, 16 June 1943

At 1437 on this day Flt Sgt David Barnard in Hudson 'T' of 459 Squadron found the *U-97* off Lydda and dropped four depth charges, one of which achieved a direct hit on the vessel's decking and two more alongside. The submarine went down by the stern within minutes, leaving 21 survivors. The explosion nearly eliminated the Hudson as well, blowing it 400ft in the air; Barnard just managed to coax the damaged aircraft home to base where it was classified damaged beyond repair. For this effort, which was also only his third operational sortie, he was immediately awarded a DFM.

Later on this day, Flg Off Olley of 46 Squadron's detached flight at St Jean claimed a Cant.Z.1007bis over the Khelidosia Rocks. His victim appears to have been an aircraft of 90° Gruppo BT which ditched in the Gulf of Antalya, Turkey, following which the Italian crew were interned.

British Claims					
46 Sqn (St Jean Det)	Flg Off A.G.Olley/Flt Sgt E.W.Baldwin	Beaufighter VIf X8165 'G'	Cant.Z.1007bis	Khelidosia Rocks	1525-1816

British Casualties	
459 Sqn	Hudson V FH311 'T' damaged by explosion of depth charge which had struck *U-97* and sunk it, landed at base damaged Cat II; Flt Sgt D.T.Barnard and crew safe
336 Sqn	Hurricane II AP885 left 1805 on convoy patrol, ditched 1850; Sgt C.H.Stavropoulos rescued

German Casualties	
Wekusta 27	Ju 88D-1 trop WNr 430800 crashed in sea NE Rhodes after engine failure; Fw Werner Janicke, Wd Insp Kurt Dilcher and two injured
3.(F)/123	Ju 88D-1 trop WNr 430733 lost, crashed in night-landing accident S Tatoi a/f; Uffz Walter Schafer and two KiA
II./StG 3	Ju 87B-3 trop WNr 100376 lost nr Argos; Ofhr Jakob Keil/Uffz Richard Schwenken WiA
II./StG 3	Ju 87B-3 trop WNr 100276 lost nr Argos; Uffz Leopold Dolesal/Gefr Johannes Hanneken WiA
II./StG 3	Ju 87B-3 trop WNr 100371 lost nr Argos; Uffz Wilhelm Westerwelle/Uffz Reinhold Keser KiA

Italian Casualties	
90° Gr BT	Cant.Z.1007bis hit in combat, ditched in Antalya Gulf, Turkey; T.Col Grimaldo Casalnuovo, S.Ten Salvatore Marino and four interned

Saturday-Sunday, 19/20 June 1943

Italian Casualties	
252ª Sq, 104° Gr AS	S.79 left Rhodes 0045, force-landed in Turkey; Ten Gennaro Grasso, Serg Magg Giordano Prampolini and three interned

Sunday, 20 June 1943

British Casualties	
7 SAAF Sqn	Hurricane IIC HL709 left from Derna to patrol a convoy, ditched off Benghazi near a destroyer 1130; Lt D.S.J.W.King KiA

Monday, 21 June 1943

Late in the evening four Baltimores of 454 Squadron on a shipping strike attacked and Flt Lt M.J.Moore (in AG689) sank an 80-ton caique in Vronti Bay, Scarpanto island. They then saw a 1,000-ton cargo vessel, and tried to attack but were driven off by intense Flak.

British Casualties	
15 SAAF Sqn	Baltimore IIIA 329 'J' left 1138 on convoy escort off Palestine, both engines failed, belly-landed 5–7m NE Tel Aviv 1420; Capt L.D.Liddle and three injured
38 Sqn	Wellington VIII HF603 ditched off Alexandria on convoy escort; Flg Off J.Bullock and one rescued, four KiA

Wednesday, 23 June 1943

RAF bombers attacked Salonika-Sedes airfield destroying ten aircraft and damaging 15 more. The German report on the raid noted that the raiders were too high for fire from the 37mm Flak to reach them.

German Casualties	
I./TG 4	Ju 52/3m WNr 10133 lost Tatoi-Gadurra; crew (two WiA) rescued by 7.Seenotstaffel

Thursday, 24 June 1943

The B-24 raid on Salonika-Sedes, already mentioned in Volume 4, caused destruction or damage to several German aircraft and casualties to aircrews.

German Casualties	
I./LG 1	Ju 88C-6 WNr 360157 20% damaged by bombs at Salonika-Sedes
I./LG 1	Ju 88A-4 WNr 2558 destroyed, WNr 1400445 60%, 140125 15%, 1038 55%, 1715 20%, 140050 45%, 8767 25% damaged by bombs at Salonika-Sedes; pilots Oblt Hans Schweigel, Lt Herbert Zschinger, Lt Ernst Schofer and four crew members injured
II./LG 1	Pilots Obfw Ernst Reggmann, Fw Paul Drobinski, Uffz Josef Vesely, Uffz Max Killat, Uffz Erwin Fischer, Uffz Gottfried Wagner, Uffz Wilhelm Rumpf and 13 crew members injured by bombs at Salonika-Sedes
IV./LG 1	Ju 88A-4 WNr 2429 25% damaged, Ju 88C-6 WNr 0157 15% damaged, Caudron C 445 WNr 490 destroyed, Kl 35 WNr 1764 80% damaged, W 34 WNr 211 15% damaged by bombs at Salonika-Sedes; nine crew members injured
I./TG 4	Ju 52/3m WNr 10041 destroyed by bombs at Salonika-Sedes

Sunday, 27 June 1943

Twenty-four B-24s of 98th Bomb Group raided Eleusis and 22 from 376th Bomb Group attacked Kalamaki. During these raids the gunners claimed seven fighters shot down. At Eleusis in total four aircraft were destroyed, one badly damaged and 22 lightly damaged. At Kalamaki two aircraft were destroyed, three damaged and a pilot killed, with 14 ground crew also killed.

Four Beaufighters of 252 Squadron, led by Sqn Ldr Ernest R.Meade, strafed and bombed in the Levkas canal the Italian cargo ship *Quirinale* (3,779 tons), which was beached near Preveza. (See also Vol. 4.)

US Claims (all times are GMT)

343rd BS/98th BG	gunner S/Sgt Milton P.Remley	B-24D 41-11840 'P'	Bf 109	Eleusis	1105
344th BS/98th BG	gunner S/Sgt John A.Givens	B-24D 4x-xx106 'I'	Bf 109 Probable	Eleusis	1105
344th BS/98th BG	gunner S/Sgt John R.Rielly	B-24D 4x-xx106 'I'	Bf 109	Eleusis	1105
344th BS/98th BG	gunner S/Sgt Robert C.Coleman	B-24D 41-24197 'A'	Bf 109	Eleusis	1105
344th BS/98th BG	gunner T/Sgt Paul A.Eshelman	B-24D 41-24197 'A'	Bf 109 Probable	Eleusis	1105
344th BS/98th BG	gunner S/Sgt Harry J.Baughn	B-24D 41-24197 'A'	Bf 109 Damaged	Eleusis	1105
344th BS/98th BG	gunner Flt Off A L.Anderson	B-24D 42-40663	Bf 109 Probable	Eleusis	1105
514th BS/376th BG	gunner S/Sgt C.H.Phillips	B-24D 41-11935 '60/E'	Bf 109	Kalamaki	1030–1140
514th BS/376th BG	gunner S/Sgt G.R.Unger	B-24D 41-11935 '60/E'	Bf 109	Kalamaki	1030–1140
515th BS/376th BG	gunner T/Sgt K.D.Calhoun	B-24D 41-24031 '94/S'	Bf 109	Kalamaki	1030–1140
514th BS/376th BG	gunner S/Sgt W.T.Minyard	B-24D 41-11935 '60/E'	Bf 109	Kalamaki	1030–1140
514th BS/376th BG	gunner M/Sgt G.T.Ouellette	B-24D 41-24035 '72/J'	Bf 109 Probable	Kalamaki	1030–1140
514th BS/376th BG	gunner Sgt C.Valentine	B-24D 41-24252 '70/W'	Bf 109 Probable	Kalamaki	1030–1140
514th BS/376th BG	gunner S/Sgt W.W.Smith	B-24D 42-40649 '73/H'	Bf 109 Probable	Kalamaki	1030–1140

German Casualties

II./ZG 26	Ju 88C-6 WNr 360414 destroyed and Ju 88C-6 80% WNr 360084 damaged by bombs on Eleusis a/f
Stab/LG 1	He 111 WNr 7083 destroyed by bombs on Eleusis a/f
I./LG 1	Ju 88A-4 WNr 7088 destroyed, Ju 88A-4 WNr 550042 80% and Ju 88A-4 WNr 8767 25% damaged by bombs on Eleusis a/f
Eins./KG 100	He 111H-3 WNr 7646 15% and He 111H-6 WNr 7997 20% damaged by bombs on Eleusis a/f
IV./JG 27	Bf 109F-4 WNr 8090 30% damaged by bombs on Kalamaki a/f
IV./JG 27	Uffz Horst Rüdiger killed by bombs on Kalamaki a/f
I./StG 3	Ju 87D-3 WNr 1445 15% damaged by bombs on Kalamaki a/f
Fl.Kom./Ln.Regt 40	Ju 52/3m WNr 6138 destroyed and Ju 52/3m WNr 3273 damaged by bombs on Kalamaki a/f
Fl.Kom./Ln.Regt 40	Fi 156 WNr 5984 destroyed by bombs on Kalamaki a/f
Fl.Kom./Ln.Regt 40	He 111 WNr 7458 damaged by bombs on Kalamaki a/f

Italian Casualties

unstated	Cant.Z.1007 destroyed by bombs on Kalamaki a/f

Tuesday, 29 June 1943

German Casualties

Wekusta 26	Ju 88 D-1 WNr 430766 5M+K reported missing on a mission to Malta; Uffz Kurt Fischer and three MiA

Wednesday, 30 June 1943

134 Squadron scrambled a section of Spitfires from Bersis at 1836 pursuing a Ju 88. This aircraft was intercepted 10–12 miles north of Apollonia where the guns of both Spitfires failed. Flt Sgt J.Farrow, the leader, was distracted by sand flying around the cockpit which caused him to collide with the Ju 88, slightly damaging his Spitfire, and presumably the German aircraft also, although no claims were submitted on either side.

British Casualties

134 Sqn	Spitfire Vb EP960 scrambled at 1836, collided with Ju 88 10–12m N Apollonia 1925, landed at Savoia; Flt Sgt J.Farrow safe

Flt Lt Spencer Whiting of 94 Squadron in Hurricane IIc KX875 'C' escorting a Beaufort of 16 SAAF Squadron shortly before he participated in the ill-fated Operation Thesis.

Friday, 2 July 1943

The Kommodore of JG 27 Maj Gustav Rödel claimed a Beaufighter shot down at an unknown time and in unknown circumstances. Two Ultra intercepts shed some light on this matter. The first records that the Germans had encountered two Beaufighters, one being shot down by fighters. The second added that a single Bf 109 on a ferry flight to Argos from Greece that had departed at 0421 contacted two Beaufighters and one was shot down. The allied aircraft involved is not known.

Mid-afternoon two Spitfire IXs of 80 Squadron took off with others from 103 MU to intercept one of the high-flying pressurised Ju 86s of 2.(F)/123. Contact was made at a height of 44,000 feet and the intruder was forced down to 31,000 feet. Here it caught fire and disintegrated, falling into the sea. One of the 80 Squadron aircraft then suffered engine failure and Plt Off Pratley had to bale out.

British Claims

80 Sqn	Flg Off J.Hunter	Spitfire Vc EE839			
80 Sqn	Plt Off G.T.Pratley	Spitfire Vc EE840	Ju 86	N El Alamein	1545
103 MU	Flg Off H.Freckelton	Spitfire IX BS342			
103 MU	Flg Off H.R.Rowlands	Spitfire IX JL228			

British Casualties

80 Sqn	Spitfire Vc EE840 engine trouble, pilot baled over sea after combat; Plt Off G.T.Pratley safe

German Claims

Stab JG 27	Maj Gustav Rödel		Beaufighter	NW Milos	0421-c0530

German Casualties

2.(F)/123	Ju 86R-1 WNr 02922 4U+IK shot down by Spitfires near Alexandria; Lt Franz Stock/Uffz Heinz-Udo Kannenberg MiA
6./LG 1	Ju 88A-4 WNr 888786 bombed Michaniona, south of Salonika, collided with Ju 88A-4 WNr 141126; Obfw Josef Pfreng and three KiA
6./LG 1	Ju 88A-4 WNr 141126 collided with Ju 88A-4 WNr 888786; Hptm Heinz Frank KiA, one WiA, two safe

Monday, 5 July 1943

British Casualties	
134 Sqn	Spitfire Vb JG876 scrambled 1145, vectored after e/a, engine failed at 32,000ft, belly-landed at base, damaged Cat II; Flt Sgt W.T.K.Pate safe

German Casualties	
Kdo.Fl.H. Ber. 7/VI	Kl 35 WNr 3055 destroyed by sabotage at Kastelli airfield

Thursday, 8 July 1943

British Casualties	
680 Sqn	Spitfire IV BP928 engine failed on return from a PR sortie, pilot baled out off Lebanese coast but not rescued; Capt D.R.C.Main MiA

Friday, 9 July 1943

IV./JG 27 now based on Crete reported the unit's first engagement there when seven Bf 109s were scrambled, intercepting a reported 23 Liberators. Pilots claimed two bombers shot down and Flak a third, while one of the Messerschmitts was hit and force-landed, significantly damaged.

The evening report from LKS, intercepted by Ultra, noted a raid on Maleme by 23 Liberators from 1333 to 1409. The bombs fell east and west of the airfield, for the most part in the water, and one bomb hit the landing area, causing slight damage.

US Casualties				
567th BS/389th BG	B-24D 42-40779 'P' shot down by e/a, crashed into sea SE Crete; 1/Lt Arthur J.Scates and nine KiA [41]			

German Claims				
12./JG 27	Oblt Ernst-Georg Altnorthoff	B-24	28km W Cap Spatha	1553
12./JG 27	Fw Hans Fahrenberger	B-24	78km SW Cap Spatha	1557
Flak		B-24	Cap Spatha	1604

German Casualties	
12./JG 27	Bf 109G-6 WNr 15324 hit in combat with B-24s, force-landed, 60% damaged; Oblt Ernst-Georg Altnorthoff safe

NB: The numbers in square brackets after the US Casualties refer to the relevant USAAF Mission Air Crew Report.

Saturday, 10 July 1943

A 454 Squadron Baltimore crew, searching for E-boats off Crete, encountered two Bf 109s between Crete and Gavdos island at 2052. These had been scrambled and reported meeting a Boston at 1950 (CET time), 50km south-east of Gavdos. The leading Messerschmitt pilot made two attacks before departing for Crete, his aircraft reportedly pouring smoke from the rear fuselage and losing height. His wingman made four attacks, after the last of which the fighter climbed to 600 feet emitting smoke from the engine and then crashed in flames into the sea. The leader returned claiming a damaged Boston.

During the day another 203 Squadron's Baltimore, which had also been E-boat hunting, attacked Italian vessels off Crete. Ultra noted the details as occurring at 1200 when three aircraft machine-gunned the Italian torpedo-boat *MS 12*, one aircraft was shot down and another claimed as a probable. *MS 12* was hit and beached, with one member of the crew dead and four wounded.

British Claims					
454 Sqn	Flg Off D.W.Lewis	Baltimore IV FA390	Bf 109 Damaged	NE Gavdos island and Crete	2055
454 Sqn	Flg Off D.W.Lewis	Baltimore IV FA390	Bf 109	NE Gavdos island and Crete	2100

British Casualties	
203 Sqn	Baltimore III AG917 left 1115 on strike against E-boats off Crete, shot down by Flak; Lt H.W.Nottingham DoW, three KiA

German Casualties	
12./JG 27	Bf 109G WNr 15460 Yellow 8 shot down 1750, 50km SE Gavdos; Uffz Karl Schafferus KiA

Italian Claims				
Flak		Beaufighter	Palaiochora, Crete	1217
Flak		Beaufighter Probable	Palaiochora, Crete	1218

Monday, 12 July 1943

British Casualties

38 Sqn — Wellington VIII HX656 'E' left Berka 1315 on patrol of convoy 'Brewery' in Gulf of Sirte, engine failed, ditched 1855; Wg Cdr F.R.Worthington and crew rescued by HMS *Wishart* at 1910

Tuesday, 13 July 1943

German Casualties

I./TG 4 — Ju 52/3m WNr 2832 G6+AL crashed at Tatoi; Uffz Waldemar Siegmann, four crew and one ground serviceman KiA

Wednesday-Thursday, 14/15 July 1943

British Casualties

38 Sqn — Wellington VIII HZ395 'B' hit by Flak at Levkas Channel, damaged in bomb-bay doors and hydraulic system, landed safely 0145; Plt Off E.J.Mostyn and crew safe

During an armed recce of western Greece, Beaufighters of 252 Squadron overfly Cant.Z.501 '184-3' moored in Preveza harbour.

Wednesday, 21 July 1943

Sgt Lound of 94 Squadron crashed on take-off at Savoia, resulting in six Hurricanes being burnt out and one damaged Cat II. The squadron armoury also caught fire and was destroyed.

British Claims					
80 Sqn	Flt Sgt H.F.Ross	Spitfire IX ES140 'P'	Ju 88	15m N Apollonia	1826

British Casualties	
134 Sqn	Hurricane IIb HW295 crashed into sea on convoy patrol 40m WSW Benghazi 1140; Flt Sgt F.Bullock MiA
134 Sqn	Hurricane IIb KW812 left 1300, crash-landed at base 1550, damaged Cat II; Flg Off T.D.Sanderson safe
94 Sqn	Hurricane IIc HW235 crashed 0540, swung off runway, crashed into parked Hurricanes, six a/c burnt out and another damaged; Sgt H.F.Lound safe

German Casualties	
2.(F)/123	Ju 88 D-1 trop WNr 430792 4U+XK shot down by Spitfire nr Benghazi; Obfw Erwin Freudig and three KiA

Thursday, 22 July 1943

Ten Hurricanes of 134 Squadron took off at 0945 from Bersis to transfer to Bu Amud to take part in a 'special operation', one suffered engine failure (camshaft drive sheared) on take-off and force-landed.

British Casualties	
134 Sqn	Hurricane IIb HM113 engine failed on take-off 0945 from Bersis, force-landed on edge of a/f, damaged Cat II; Sgt L.A.J.Dennahy safe

OPERATION THESIS

Within little more than ten days the invasion of Sicily was well underway and the Axis air forces were virtually driven from skies over the island. Under such pressure there was little call on the forces in the eastern Mediterranean other than to carry out some convoy protection duties and anti-submarine patrolling. Much of these requirements were being fulfilled by units of 201 Group and the escorted bombers of the Strategic Air Force. For the defensive fighter units along the North African shore calls were few and far between.

It was against this background that plans were brought forward to make some profitable usage of the squadrons of HQ Air Defence Eastern Mediterranean (ADEM) although under what plans and under whose authority subsequent official and semi-official records have proved to be remarkably reticent, so it is therefore perhaps best to begin with such background as is available.

Grp Capt Max Aitken commanded 219 Group at the time of Operation Thesis. Several of the squadrons under his command participated in this attack.

As shown in the RAF Middle East Order of Battle (and particularly that of ADEM) set out in the later pages of Vol. 4 of this series, the multifarious units of 201 Group may be seen to have been spread out throughout the North African area from Palestine in the east to the Libyan/Tunisian frontier to the west. Located in this same general area were four fighter-equipped groups which had all been formed quite recently by the amalgamations of wings which had been left behind following the Alamein battle and the advance westwards which had followed.

Three had been created during December 1942 and one more at the beginning of May 1943. The first so formed was 209 Group set up at Ramleh, Palestine, at Middle East Command responsible for the defence of Cyprus and the eastern Mediterranean, under the command of Grp Capt R.C.F.Lister. 212

Group was then formed at Gazala under Air HQ Egypt for coastal protection and the air defence of Cyrenaica, commanded by Grp Capt J.Grandy, while the third of the new units, 219 Group, formed at the Seagull Camp in the Alexandria area for the general defence of Egypt. This unit was commanded by Grp Capt The Hon W.J.Max Aitken, DSO, DFC.

During April 1943 209 Group moved to Haifa while at the start of May 210 Group was formed as the fourth such new unit at Governor's Palace, Tripoli, close to the Libyan/Tunisian border where it was tasked with the defence of the Tripolitanian province and the protection of coastal shipping. The command here rested in the hands of Air Cdr A.H.Wait.

RAF Order of Battle for Operation Thesis

209 Group

| 127 Sqn | St Jean | Sqn Ldr P.W.Lovell | Hurricanes |
| 46 Sqn Det | Haifa | Wg Cdr G.A.Reid | Beaufighters |

210 Group

3 SAAF Sqn	Mellaha	Maj E.M.Baker	Hurricanes
33 Sqn	Misurata	Sqn Ldr G.May	Hurricanes
213 Sqn	Idku	Sqn Ldr S.N.R.Whitney, DSO	Hurricanes
274 Sqn	Mellaha	Sqn Ldr J.R.R.Wells, DFC	Hurricanes
80 Sqn	Savoia	Sqn Ldr J.Curry, DFC	Spitfires

212 Group

7 SAAF Sqn	Derna	Maj C.A.van Vliet, DFC	Hurricanes
41 SAAF Sqn	Bu Amud	Maj W.J.B.Chapman	Hurricanes
94 Sqn	Savoia	Sqn Ldr A.V.Clowes	Hurricanes
123 Sqn	Bu Amud	Sqn Ldr K.N.T.Lee, DFC	Hurricanes
134 Sqn	Bersis	Sqn Ldr W.H.Stratton, DFC	Hurricanes
237 Sqn	Bersis	Sqn Ldr E.T.Smith, DFC	Hurricanes

219 Group

74 Sqn	LG 106	Sqn Ldr J.C.F.Hayter, DFC	Hurricanes
238 Sqn	El Gamil	Sqn Ldr H.P.Cochrane, DFC	Hurricanes
335 Sqn	LG 108	Sqn Ldr G.Panagalos	Hurricanes
336 Sqn	LG 219	Sqn Ldr D.C.Cloete	Hurricanes
451 Sqn	LG 108	Sqn Ldr J.Paine	Hurricanes

Rather oddly, given the absolute preponderance of fighter aircraft and units in ADEM, the greater part of the command structure was placed in the hands of officers with very little recent experience of flying or operating such aircraft. Both Lister and Wait had spent time on the North-West Frontier of India between the wars as too had Air Cdr T.A.Langford-Salsbury, AFC, commander of the predominant 201 Group. Even the Commander-in-Chief, Air Vice-Marshal R.E.Saul, was not noted for such experience. Of the other two group commanders, John Grandy had been involved in an element of fighter training for several years prior to the outbreak of war in 1939 but had been shot down and wounded during September 1940. On recovery from this experience he was to serve in a variety of staff, developmental and airfield command roles in Fighter Command until posted to the Middle East in early 1943.

Max Aitken was an entirely different case, however. Having joined the Auxiliary Air Force in the thirties, he had taken a very active role in part of the Battle of Britain, subsequently becoming one of the early specialist night-fighters. Having started the war with an early promotion to flight lieutenant, by 1943 he had risen to the fairly exalted rank of group captain and had been awarded a DSO, DFC and Czech War Cross. Further, he had been credited with having shot down nine or ten German aircraft. Tellingly, perhaps, he was also the son and heir of the Canadian newspaper mogul, Lord Beaverbrook, at that time Minister of Aircraft Production, and personal friend of the Prime Minister, Winston Churchill. There seems little doubt that Aitken proved able to employ the family relationship to his advantage when he deemed it appropriate.

Given this apparent pedigree it may seem a little odd that he should have been given command of the most easterly of the new groups, furthest away from the enemy. However, granted his apparent dual position at the head of the Fighter Tactics Branch, it seems more than likely that he had been positioned near command headquarters where he was well-placed to provide guidance to AVM Saul.

It will be noted that despite the considerable number of fighter squadrons on hand for the groups by July 1943 there were no officers of wing commander rank capable of carrying out the duties of wing leader should any operations involve two or more squadrons together. This would appear to have indicated an assumption that the duties of the units to hand were likely to be of a limited nature only. Thus, it was that in mid-July, with the Sicily operation clearly well-established, orders went out to prepare for the launch of a quite major attack mainly by the ADEM units on the Axis-held island of Crete. It has been mentioned above and in earlier volumes that during the previous two years there had been a number of commando-style attacks on this island and Rhodes to attack airfields there. These had on at least two occasions led to numbers of local civilians subsequently being executed for providing aid to Allied troops temporarily on the islands for these purposes.

The force to be dispatched was subsequently established as 11 squadrons of Hurricanes amounting to 93 aircraft. The breakdown of these numbers may be indicative; they were joined by one squadron of 12 Spitfires (80 Squadron) seven Beaufighters (drawn from 227 Squadron) and eight Baltimores (454 Squadron).

The Hurricanes were to be sent off in three waves between 0700–0715, each aircraft fitted with long-range tanks, the presence of which were vital given the maximum distance to be covered during the two-way return flight; each wave was also to be led by two Beaufighters for navigational purposes plus one extra leading the initial wave flown by Wg Cdr Mackenzie who was thus the senior officer actually taking part in the attack.

The whole formation was to be provided with a top cover by 80 Squadron's Spitfires while 454 Squadron's Baltimores were to bomb from medium altitude in an effort to inflict heavier damage on more substantial radio or radar sites than could be achieved by the strafing of the fighters which had no facility to carry bombs on this occasion.

The numbers of Hurricanes required from each squadron for the planned operation which was to be launched on 23 July were in eight cases to be nine aircraft each while in a further three cases the number was six. There appears to have been some anomalies which, however, have proved generally explicable. The two Greek squadrons, 335 and 336 were linked with a single figure of 12 (e.g. six aircraft each) although 335 alone was listed as providing eight. In the case of 123 Squadron the commanding officer, Sqn Ldr Lee (certainly one of the most experienced pilots to be involved on the day) seems to have acted as a single wing leader (though without promotion); this squadron led by Lee contributed ten aircraft to the force.

It is also worth noting that the numbers of Hurricanes may be divided by three to create sections of three aircraft 'vics' rather than the more practical and favoured 'finger four' which had become employed to a considerably greater extent by 1943. Adequate availability of Hurricanes to meet the quantities set out appear also to have been demonstrated by several initial mishaps during the run-up to the due date. On the 21st, whilst taking off from Savoia, Loud's Hurricane swung off the runway and crashed into 94 Squadron's parked aircraft, six of which were burnt out and a seventh damaged. Yet two days later the squadron had nine aircraft ready for Thesis; that same day one aircraft of 134 Squadron on a convoy patrol and a second was damaged crash-landing after a similar sortie. Next day this squadron lost a further aircraft in force-landing due to engine failure.

210 Group's pilots were visited by Air Cdr Wait at this time to receive a 'pep-talk' regarding the pending operation. With events such as those of the last few days it becomes probable that Thesis was not receiving a high level of secrecy and that the Germans on Crete were probably well aware that something unusual was likely to occur of which early information was desirable. Consequently on the evening of the 21st a reconnaissance Ju 88D of 2.(F)/123 was intercepted by two of 80 Squadron's Spitfires over the Benghazi area and was shot down into the sea by Flt Sgt Ross. He watched as a Walrus set out in an effort to pick up the crew but the latter could not be found, Obfw Erwin Freudig and his crew having been killed (see page 18).

Friday, 23 July 1943

From 0700 the British formations began taking off, led around the eastern end of Crete by the first of 227 Squadron's Beaufighters. As he reached the area Wg Cdr Mackenzie spotted a lone Arado 196 floatplane at

One of the Hurricanes of the Greek-manned 335 Squadron that participated in Operation Thesis during which it lost two aircraft shot down by Flak over Crete.

which he fired, claiming possibly to have damaged it. A following pilot also did the same but made no claim; interception of an Ultra report by the British subsequently provided confirmation that the Luftwaffe aircraft had indeed escaped undamaged.

The RAF pilots had been ordered not to attack the Cretan airfields as their Flak defences were known to be extremely strong. However, it was confirmed that in the circumstances it was desirable to kill as many enemy personnel as possible. Tents and similar such targets should be attacked but efforts should be made to avoid as far as possible inflicting any damage to Cretans or their property. Effectively this guidance gave the fighter pilots very little of any worth to attack, though the Flak defences proved at least as dangerous as had been anticipated. Although some flights saw very little worth expending ammunition on, some Axis troops were seen and a relatively small number were killed or wounded.

As the Hurricane pilots made their hasty way back southwards 13 of their number had been lost including the aircraft flown by Sqn Ldr Lee who became one of the POWs, nine pilots were killed, and four suffered wounds.

But this was not the worst of it for at the eastern end of the island as the Hurricanes cleared the area, they were followed in by the Baltimores of 454 Squadron, the Australian crews finding the Flak ferocious and ready for them. It appears from the reports of the few surviving crew members that the bombers went in at low, rather than at medium altitude, and that they approached in flights of two aircraft rather than as a single formation. Several saw the lead aircraft flown by the unit commander, Sqn Ldr Folkard, hit first and crashing into the sea offshore as the second aircraft was seen to be hit but to fly away. Within minutes four more bombers had fallen with the loss of all their crews. Meanwhile the second aircraft to have been hit had escaped at low level over Kastelli and through the mountains. The pilot, Flt Sgt Akhurst, managed to fly the crippled aircraft back to undertake a successful ditching off the Libyan coast near Derna. He survived unhurt, also saving the lives of his crew members for which he would receive the squadron's first medal, a DFM. For 454 Squadron the day ultimately proved to be the worst for casualties throughout the rest of the war.

It remained only quite early in the morning as 80 Squadron's 12 Spitfires acted as withdrawal cover during which two pilots encountered 15 returning Hurricanes six miles south-west of Gavdos but little else. Landfall was made by this pair to the west of Gavdos from where they flew north-westwards to Cape Lithinos and back. Flg Off Waterhouse had not gone on the sortie and was returning to join the other pilots when he was vectored

During Operation Thesis Flt Sgt F.W. Farfan was one of three 123 Squadron pilots shot down. However, he evaded capture and eventually returned to Egypt in September, though for security reasons was not allowed to pass details to his colleagues.

onto a Ju 88. This proved to be another aircraft of 2.(F)/123, this time flown by Uffz Christian Dieroff and this Waterhouse shot down into the sea in flames; again the German crew were all killed.

In little more than three hours the German Flak gunners had claimed ten British aircraft down which they identified as seven Hurricanes, one Defiant, one Beaufighter, and one Boston (the latter clearly one of the Baltimores). Subsequently an unsigned report, widely believed to have emanated from Max Aitken, concluded:

"On the face of it the material damage to the enemy was probably in no way commensurate with the total loss of 13 Hurricanes and five Baltimores together with other aircraft casualties and damage. On the other hand it is undeniable that the unpalatable medicine administered to the enemy, coupled with the fine tonic effect on 212 and 219 Group squadrons, made the operation a success on balance."

We leave it with the readers to draw their own conclusion as to what credence may be given to the comments on this fiasco. Suggestions have been made that many of the losses were to an extent due to the level of inexperience of several of the pilots involved. In considering this possible criticism it is suggested that readers consider the Order of Battle presented above and note the number of unit commanders who had already received awards for gallantry, success in combat and leadership. Might the question to be asked alternatively was why so little consideration should have been given to the advice and proven experience which these individuals had perhaps been well-placed to provide?

British Claims

227 Sqn	Wg Cdr R.M.Mackenzie/Flg Off A.L.Craig	Beaufighter VI EL516 'Y'	Ar 196 Damaged	N Maleme	0855
80 Sqn	Flg Off J.C.R.Waterhouse	Spitfire Vc JK142	Ju 88	50m N El Hania	0755–0920

British Casualties

238 Sqn	Hurricane IIc HW483 'P' left 0705 to strafe eastern Crete; Flt Sgt H.D.R.Rayment MiA
238 Sqn	Hurricane IIc KZ130 'J' left 0705 to strafe eastern Crete; Flt Sgt P.A.George MiA
238 Sqn	Hurricane IIc HL657 'D' left 0705 to strafe eastern Crete damaged by Flak; Sqn Ldr H.P.Cochrane WiA
94 Sqn	Hurricane IIc KW935 'A' left 0710 shot down by Flak SW Alikianou, crash-landed in trees on side of a mountain; Sgt W.G.Imrie KiA
123 Sqn	Hurricane IIc KZ141 left 0715, damaged by Flak, crash-landed on Crete; Sqn Ldr K.N.T.Lee POW
123 Sqn	Hurricane IIc HW538 left 0715, shot down into sea by Flak; Flg Off J.D.LeMare KiA
123 Sqn	Hurricane IIc KW964 left 0715, shot down over Crete by ground fire; Flt Sgt F.W.Farfan evaded and returned in September
134 Sqn	Hurricane IIb HW299 left 0720, hit by Flak, force-landed on Crete 0900–0920; Flg Off W.A.P.Manser POW
134 Sqn	Hurricane IIb HW372 left 0715, hit by Flak 0900–0920; Sgt D.A.Horsley MiA
134 Sqn	Hurricane IIb HW605 left 0720, hit by Flak 0900–0920 pilot wounded in the leg, landed at base; Flg Off I.L.Lowen WiA
134 Sqn	Hurricane IIb HV905 left 0715, hit by Flak 0900–0920 pilot wounded in the lung, landed at base; Flg Off W.H.Wright WiA
237 Sqn	Hurricane IIc HV508 left 0715, hit by Flak over Gavdos island, landed at base damaged Cat II; Flg Off A.W.B.Davies WiA
335 Sqn	Hurricane IIC KZ130 left 0710, shot down near Kalo Horio Lasithou, Mirabello Bay; Flt Sgt V.Doucas KiA
335 Sqn	Hurricane IIc left 0710, shot down near Tymbaki; Flt Sgt M.Leitmer KiA
336 Sqn	Hurricane IIc BP125(or BP232) left 0710, lost a long-range tank on way to Crete, continued with mission, out of fuel on return trip, force-landed on Crete; Wt Off E.Athanasakis killed resisting arrest by the Germans after crash-landing
336 Sqn	Hurricane IIc HL607 left 0710, shot down over Crete; Wt Off S.Skantzikas POW, murdered by the Gestapo after the Great Escape
41 SAAF Sqn	Hurricane IIb HV492 left 0710, shot down by Flak near Tymbaki; Lt W.J.K.Bliss MiA
41 SAAF Sqn	Hurricane IIb left 0710, oil tank hit by Flak, engine seized when base was reached, crash-landed; Lt C.George safe
454 Sqn	Baltimore III AG995 hit by Flak, crash-landed near Heraklion; Sqn Ldr L.F.Folkard and two WiA/POW, one KiA

454 Sqn	Baltimore III AG869 left 0730 as one of a pair to attack central section Crete, neither seen nor heard from after take-off; Wt Off F.P.Bayly and three KiA
454 Sqn	Baltimore III FA224 left 0730 as one of a pair to attack central section Crete, neither seen nor heard from after take-off; Flt Sgt G.W.Harnett and three KiA
454 Sqn	Baltimore III FA247 left 0730 to attack Crete, sent SOS at 0850 from a position S Crete, W Hierapetra, but not heard from or seen again; Plt Off L.D.Blomley and three KiA
454 Sqn	Baltimore IV FA409 left 0730 hit by Flak, last seen W Hierapetra; Flg Off C.A.Irvine and two POW, one KiA
454 Sqn	Baltimore IV FA390 'A' hit by Flak at Kastelli, flew away from Crete and ditched near Derna; Flt Sgt R.G.Akhurst and two safe, one WiA

German Claims

Flak		Defiant	Hierapetra	0754
Flak		Hurricane	Dafnes	0818
Flak		Hurricane	1km S Gurnes	0819
Flak		Hurricane	Crete	0825
Flak		Beaufighter	S Crete	0825
Flak		Hurricane	Ibatsiana (?)	0827
Flak		Hurricane	Paximadia Island	0830
Flak		Hurricane	Kastelli	0850
Flak		Boston	Crete	0900
Flak		Hurricane	Crete	1000

German Casualties

| 2.(F)/123 | Ju 88D-1 WNr 430800 4U+GK left 0234, lost on a mission to Tobruk; Uffz Christian Dieroff and three MiA |

Monday, 26 July 1943

British Casualties

| 38 Sqn | Wellington VIII MP627 'C' reported missing from offensive reconnaissance of the Aegean; Flg Off H.A.Taylor DFM and five MiA |

Thursday, 29 July 1943

British Claims

| 335 Sqn | Plt Off E.Hajioannou | Hurricane IIb BP606 | Ju 88 Damaged | off l/g 121 | 1700–1800 |

British Casualties

| 252 Sqn | Beaufighter VIf EL369 left 1255, shot down by land-based Breda AA fire Ionian sea area; Flt Lt J.H.Manley/Sgt J.F.King KiA |

German Casualties

| Eins.Gr Ju 88 | Ju 88 KQ+KR shot up by Hurricanes, crashed on landing at Larissa; Lt Adolf Kukeil and three KiA |

The RAF had the unending task of convoy patrols such as on 29 July 1943 when 203 Squadron Baltimore II AG803 'V' covered shipping off the Libyan coast.

Friday, 30 July 1943

Around midday a pair of 227 Squadron Beaufighters were engaged by a pair of MC.202s of the 395ª Squadriglia, 154º Gruppo CT, over Alimnia Island, west of Rhodes, one of them force-landing on return to base. The Italian pilots each claimed one shot down, in both cases identifying their victims as Beauforts, only one of which was hit.

On the other side of the Grecian peninsula a heavy strafing attack was made on the Preveza seaplane base during the early afternoon by Beaufighters of 272 Squadron. Claims made included two He 115s, and a Do 18 destroyed and at least four more Do 18s damaged. In the absence of any Luftwaffe Do 18s in the Mediterranean it is likely that the British pilots were actually firing on Cant.Z.501 flyingboats. It is equally likely that the two aircraft claimed as He 115s were both Cant.Z.506B floatplanes, both of which failed to return from reconnaissance missions, one of 82º Gruppo RM and one of 93º Gruppo RM. (see also Vol. 4).

British Casualties					
227 Sqn	Beaufighter VI JL539 'G' shot up over Alimnia 1405 by two MC.202s; force-landed on return, Cat II damaged; Plt Off P.F.L.Glynn/Sgt T.J.Barrett safe				

Italian Claims					
395ª Sq, 154º Gr CT	Serg Antonio Brombin	MC.202	Beaufort	Alimnia Island	1217
395ª Sq, 154º Gr CT	Ten Luigi Matelli	MC.202	Beaufort	Alimnia Island	1217

Saturday, 31 July 1943

British Claims					
227 Sqn	Flg Off C.B.Feight/Sgt G.A.Brown	Beaufighter VIf EL516 'Y'	Ar 196 Damaged	off Milos	1225
227 Sqn	Flt Sgt W.C.Budd/Flt Sgt R.E.Jobling	Beaufighter VIf JL619 'X'	Ar 196 Damaged	off Milos	1225

Italian Casualties	
192ª Sq, 87º Gr, 30º St BT	Cant.Z.1007bis '192-6' crash-landed at Rhodes; pilot M.llo Antonio Valdes and three WiA, co-pilot Serg Magg Germano Lunghi, one crew and German Maj Rudolf Rossbacher KiA

Tuesday, 3 August 1943

The Admiral Aegean records note that two Ar 196s from 2./SAG 125 on return from convoy escort were attacked at 1540 by four Beaufighters at Chania, one being shot down, and a second aircraft damaged. One of the attackers was claimed damaged.

Throughout the summer of 1943 Greek-manned Blenheim Vs of 13 (Hellenic) Squadron flew convoy protection patrols from Libyan bases.

British Claims					
227 Sqn	Flg Off W.Y.McGregor/Flg Off C.E.Turner	Beaufighter VI EL239 'N'	Ar 196	1m E Chania	1230
227 Sqn	Plt Off C.A.Feight/Sgt G.A.Brown	Beaufighter VI JL541 'Q'			
227 Sqn	Flt Sgt W.C.Budd/Flt Sgt R.E.Jobling	Beaufighter VI EL476 'R'	Ar 196 Damaged	Chania	1230
46 Sqn	Plt Off W.Jenkinson/Flt Sgt R.Kendall	Beaufighter VI V8766 'U'	Cant.Z.506	Aegean area	daylight

German Casualties	
2./SAGr 125	Ar 196 WNr 0240 7R+AK shot down and crashed in sea 15km NE Chania; Obfw Karl-Heinz Stienkemeier/Lt Wolfgang Zacharias KiA

Friday, 6 August 1943

On a sweep 336 Squadron lost a Hurricane to engine failure 17 miles off Bardia. The pilot was seen in a dinghy and contact was maintained despite rough seas. A Walrus from Gambut attempted to land at 2030 but could not find the dinghy, and during the night it sank. Wt Off Xanthacos using his shirt as a sail, landed safely near Buq Buq at 1950 next day.

The crew of the Italian tug-boat *Porto Fassone* claimed to have shot down a British reconnaissance aircraft in flames in the channel at Santa Maura on Levkas Island, on the west coast of Greece. No such loss has been discovered.

British Claims				
103 MU	Flt Lt J.G.West	Spitfire IX	Ju 86 Damaged	15m N Apollonia

British Casualties	
336 Sqn	Hurricane IIc BP645 left 0745 on a sweep, engine failed, pilot baled out off Bardia 0930; Wt Off G.Xanthacos safe
ASR Flight Gambut	Walrus X9582 landed off Bardia to rescue a 336 Sqn pilot, could not take off due to bad weather and sank

German Casualties	
2.(F)/123	Ju 86R-1 4U+OK damaged by Spitfires on reconnaissance of Benghazi

Italian Claims			
AA	Tug-boat *Porto Fassone*	reconnaissance a/c	Levkas Island

Thursday 12 August 1943

Two Hurricane pilots from 336 Squadron, Wt Off D.Soufrilas (in KX927) and Sgt D.Sarsonis (in HW614) spotted a submarine 120 miles north of landing ground 121 at 0905 and strafed the conning tower as it dived.

Flt Lt Tom Freer of 227 Squadron bombed and sank an 80-ton caique at 1310 in a small bay on the west coast of Paros Island.

British Claims					
103 MU	Flt Lt J.G.West	Spitfire IX	Bf 109 Damaged	Nile Delta	1752–1900

Friday-Saturday, 13/14 August 1943

The crew of a 38 Squadron Wellington reported having torpedoed and sunk a 2,000-ton ship escorted by a destroyer, the Flak from which wounded the rear gunner.

British Casualties	
38 Sqn	Wellington VIII HZ417 'S' left 2040, bombed Syros Harbour and then sank a ship, hit by Flak, rear gunner wounded; Flt Sgt H.Van Der Pol and four safe, Sgt C.R.Edbrooke WiA

Saturday, 14 August 1943

British Claims					
103 MU	Flg Off G.H.Purdy	Spitfire IX	Ju 88 Damaged	Nile Delta	1830–1930

German Casualties	
2.(F)/123	Ju 88T-1 WNr 430548 4U+IK shot down by Spitfires, Alexandria; Lt Hans Peters and two KiA

Tuesday, 17 August 1943

British Casualties

272 Sqn	Beaufighter VI EL390 'C' hit by Flak at Argostoli, belly-landed at base, Cat II damaged; Flg Off C.P.Johns/Sgt T.W.Hollinshead safe
38 Sqn	Wellington VIII MP783 returned from patrol with engine on fire; Flg Off C.B.Urwin and four WiA, one KiA

Thursday, 19 August 1943

227 Squadron sent four Beaufighters to reconnoitre Rhodes. These were attacked off the island by two MC.202s, one of which departed for the island after an ineffectual attack. The other made nine passes on all four Beaufighters, slightly damaging one.

Italian Claims

396ª Sq, 154° Gr CT	unidentified pilot	MC.202	Beaufort	off Rhodes	1205

Tuesday, 24 August 1943

Two long-range reconnaissance Bf 109Gs were pursued over the North African coast by both Spitfires and Hurricanes, one of the Messerschmitts being claimed shot down into the sea by Flt Lt J.G.West, DFM, of 103 MU.

British Claims

103 MU	Flt Lt J.G.West	Spitfire IX JK980	Bf 109G	NW Ras el Hillal c1000–1100

Friday, 27 August 1943

15 SAAF Squadron flew the first South African Air Force reconnaissance over the Aegean Islands on this date with a Baltimore.

Monday-Tuesday, 30/31 August 1943

British Casualties

162 Sqn	Wellington IC HF365 left Gambut 1943 to investigate enemy radar in the vicinity of Corfu, FTR; Flt Lt J.M.J.Fryer and five MiA, two washed ashore in Africa and buried

Italian Claims

AA	e/a	Zante

Tuesday, 31 August 1943

German Casualties

2.(F)/123	Ju 88D-1trop WNr 430960 4U+6K lost at Cyprus; Uffz Helmut Danders and three KiA

During the summer of 1944 specially modified Spitfire IXs of the High Altitude Flight were attached to 94 Squadron at Savoia. Flying JK980 seen here, Flt Lt J.G.'Shorty' West (3rd from right) claimed a reconnaissance Bf 109G though his victim has not been traced.

CHAPTER TWO

STRIKE AND COUNTERSTRIKE IN THE DODECANESE

September review

During the month the Beaufighter night-fighters of 46 Squadron supported operations in the Dodecanese, flying night intruders over Rhodes and engaging in some ground strafing too. For these operations the unit had a detachment in Cyprus at Lakatamia though their effectiveness was somewhat limited due to the extreme range to the target areas. September also saw the maritime patrol Hudsons of 459 Squadron temporarily re-roled into light bomber duties and began operations in support of the campaign in the Aegean. Day and night attacks on enemy ports and airfields in Greece and Crete were made to cover the British landings on the islands of Kos and Leros in the Dodecanese.

Thursday, 2 September 1943

British Casualties	
227 Sqn	Beaufighter VI JL522 'Z' left 1028 to attack 80-ton caique off Kos, struck mast, crashed c1300; Flg Off W.Y.McGregor POW, DoW/Flg Off C.E.Turner POW

German Claims		
Flak 45	Beaufighter	Kos

From St Jean in Palestine the Spitfire PR IVs of 680 Squadron conducted extensive reconnaissance of the Aegean Islands ahead of the British landings; BR416 'X' is shown.

With a cover of USAAF P-38s overhead, Hudson III FH428 'R' of 459 RAAF Squadron patrols low over the sea off the coast of Crete.

Saturday, 4 September 1943

British Claims

252 Sqn	Sqn Ldr K.L.Faulkner/Flt Sgt T.R.Lumsden	Beaufighter VI JL508	}	Ju 88 Damaged	convoy 'Riband'	0615–1125
252 Sqn	Flt Sgt D.DeVilliers/Flt Sgt W.P.Fryer	Beaufighter VI JL585				

British Casualties

7 SAAF Sqn	Spitfire Vb ER335 scrambled, heard to give a Tally Ho about 70m NE Port Said 1750, FTR; Lt H.F.P.Boyer KiA					

German Claims

2.(F)/123	unstated			Spitfire	20km off African coast	1540

German Casualties

2.(F)/123	Bf 109G-4 WNr 19201 engine failure, ditched S Crete; pilot rescued					

Monday, 6 September 1943

German Casualties

1./TG 4	Ju 52/3m WNr 6590 ditched nr Kea Island; crew rescued by Do 24 KO+KA from 7.Seenotstaffel

Thursday, 9 September 1943

The Luftwaffe attacked the Italian destroyer *Monzambano* (Cap Corv Alberto Cuomo) near Zante at 1300; one Ju 87 was claimed being shot down.

The RAF reinforced its presence on Cyprus, when 213 Squadron flew into Paphos from Idku in Egypt with 12 Hurricane IIcs.

German Casualties

6./StG 3	Ju 87D-3 trop WNr 110530 S7+GP shot down by Italian ship's AA 10km E Ithaki; Fw Fritz Wente/Uffz Max Klüsch WiA
2./StG 3	Ju 87D-3 WNr 1499 S7+PK engine failure, crashed W Araxos; Uffz Walter Obermeit/Uffz Herbert Freybote KiA

SOME RAMIFICATIONS OF THE ITALIAN ARMISTICE

In September 1943 a considerable part of the Axis garrison forces in Yugoslavia and Greece (as well as of the Aegean and Adriatic Islands) were provided by the Italian air force and army, thereby raising a number of new considerations:

A) In Yugoslavia and Greece there was already intense guerrilla action which was now aimed virtually entirely against the Germans until the partisans discovered which elements of the Italian forces would continue to fight on with the Germans, and seek to join the new Repubblica Sociale Italiana (RSI) forces which immediately began to form in the Fascist-held areas of Italy. Other Italian forces went over to the Allies, and other elements simply lay down their weapons and ceased operations entirely. Being already well aware of the potential threats from the partisans and those Italian forces prepared to fight them, the Germans moved considerable forces, including aviation, into Yugoslavia. As within Italy itself no doubt intending any Italian forces encountered would be persuaded to remain loyal, or be obliterated.

B)   The armistice in the Aegean area awakened once again in Churchill's mind the opportunity to seize some or all of the main Aegean Islands (notably Rhodes and Crete especially).

C)   The rapid evacuation of Sardinia and Corsica at much the same time reduced the call on Coastal Air Force in the western part of the area, notably in Sicily and southern Italy.

D)   The Americans were totally opposed to Churchill's proposals and brought no aid at all – or so it seemed. However, the arrival of increased Luftwaffe presence in Yugoslavia, Albania and Greece gave the USAAF considerable concern regarding the threat posed by this factor to Bari, Foggia and other locations planned to be employed as the main base area for the Strategic Air Force. Therefore, the US bombers launched a series of heavy raids against Axis airfields. These frequently coincided with RAF Middle East's operations over the Aegean. At this time calls from Tito, now the guerrilla commander in much of Yugoslavia, were frequently being acceded to, these leading to an increase in the number of raids on targets on western and coastal Yugoslavia by both DAF to the northern sector and by Coastal from south Italy and Sicily.

E)   Meanwhile, the main Allied thrust northwards coincided with these various activities leading to the Anzio landings and eventually to the advance to Rome. During this period more Allied units (mainly RAF) were withdrawn for Normandy while elements from the USAAF and RAF were sent to the China/Burma/India area.

Friday, 10 September 1943

Two Beaufighters from 227 Squadron were ordered to provide escort for two motor launches at Castelrosso, aware that an Italian ship or boat might appear but which they were not to attack but could approach to inform the launches. Both launches left the harbour at 1925. Three minutes later a Cant.Z.506 landed in the harbour, fired two red Very lights and then attempted to take off. Flt Sgt W.C.Budd (in JM242 'Q') made three dummy attacks on the floatplane to persuade it not to depart, and it went back into the harbour, but when 300 yards from the motor launches two of the crew climbed out onto the engine cowling. The launches at 1941 signalled "thanks for your co-operation" and the Beaufighters departed.

A detachment of 15 SAAF Squadron was sent to Gambut to assist 13 (Hellenic) Squadron. The squadron also began bombing targets in the Aegean, the forerunner of more offensive tactics on a larger scale than the squadron had hitherto been allowed to employ; during the month many caiques were attacked and offensive reconnaissances made into the Aegean.

British Casualties	
15 SAAF Sqn	Baltimore IV FA547 'N' on return from a convoy escort crashed and burnt out on landing at LG 07 1240; Capt E.A.Endler WiA, two safe; Lt M.B.Hall KiA
German Casualties	
2.(F)/123	Bf 109G-4 WNr 14902 4U+2K lost on sea recce, believed crashed near Kastelli; Lt Heinz Gruttke KiA

Saturday, 11 September 1943

A 15 SAAF Squadron Baltimore on patrol, flown by Lt S.Meijer, bombed a 300-ton steamer at Gavdos Island at 1100; one direct hit struck the bridge and exploded, leaving it burning. The German staff of Admiral Aegean recorded that the ship was its vessel *GP-3* which sank.

On this date the Luftwaffe began bombing Kos when two Ju 88s attacked at 0440, while Ju 87s attacked gun positions on Rhodes and the W/T station.

147ª Squadriglia RM, based at Leros, had eight Cant.Z.506s and four Cant.Z.501s in its inventory; three 506s were based at Rhodes. On this day one of these (MM 45427), flown by S.Ten Giovanni Russo with a crew of four and two passengers, managed to fly to Alexandria but the two others were lost.

Italian Casualties	
147ª Sq RM	2 Cant.Z.506s MM 45428 and 45374 lost at Rhodes

Sunday, 12 September 1943

Over the south-eastern Aegean, the crew of a 15 SAAF Squadron Baltimore, flown by Lt Strydom, spotted two Ar 196s escorting a Do 24 off Cape Sidero. One Arado broke off to attack the Baltimore, the crew of which returned fire; tracers were seen to hit the fuselage of both the Arado and the flying boat. This was the squadron's only engagement with enemy aircraft in the month.

In support of the Kos landings, 38 B-24s of IX Bomber Command raided Kalymnos and Maritza on Rhodes.

British Claims

15 SAAF Sqn	Lt Strydom	Baltimore IV FA440 'S'	Do 24 Damaged	30km SE Makra	1045
15 SAAF Sqn	Lt Strydom	Baltimore IV FA440 'S'	Ar 196 Damaged	30km SE Makra	1045

German Casualties

7.Seenotst.	Do 24T-2 WNr 0036 CM+IB damaged

Monday, 13 September 1943

British Claims

252 Sqn	Flt Sgt D.DeVilliers/Flt Sgt W.P.Fryer	Beaufighter VI V8347	Ju 88	90km W Cape Arnauti	1300
252 Sqn	Flt Sgt A.B.McKeown/Sgt A.Dixon	Beaufighter VI JL621			
103 MU	Flg Off D.G.McQueen	Spitfire IX	Ju 88	100m WNW Alexandria	

Italian Co-Belligerent Claims

396ª Sq, 154º Gr CT	Ten Giuseppe Morganti	MC.202	Ju 88	off Rhodes

German Casualties

2.(F)/123	Ju 88A-4 WNr 882517 4U+HK lost between Rhodes and Scarpanto; Lt Klaus Delfs and three MiA
2.(F)/123	Ju 88T-1 WNr 430879 4U+7K missing off Alexandria; Lt Werner Schiller and two KiA
Wekusta 27	Ju 88A-4 WNr 140437 5M+Y lost W Cyprus; Fw Fritz Wolters, Met Dr Christian Theusner and two MiA
Eins.Gr Ju 88	Ju 88 K5+UE shot down by AA, Kythera; Obfw Schumacher and three KiA
FlKomp./Ln 40	Ju 52/3m WNr 3273 TH+UE hit by Italian AA, crash-landed on Corfu; Fw Werner Öhme and three POW

Tuesday, 14 September 1943

Beaufighter V8578 of 46 Squadron, flown by Sqn Ldr W.A.Cuddie, was the first RAF aircraft to land on Kos at 0640, off-loading three 'passengers' and 'special equipment' before departing safely 50 minutes later. Later in the day 7 SAAF Squadron landed on Kos.

Wednesday, 15 September 1943

By mid-September the British 234th Infantry Brigade under Major General F.G.R.Brittorous from Malta, and Special Boat Service (SBS) and Long-Range Desert Group (LRDG) detachments had secured the islands of Kos, Kalymnos, Samos, Leros, Symi, and Stampalia, supported by ships of the British and Greek navies and a Spitfire squadron on Kos. The Germans quickly mobilized in response. Generalleutnant Friedrich-Wilhelm Müller, the commander of the 22nd Infantry Division at Crete, was ordered on 23 September to take Kos and Leros.

Leros was occupied by British forces on 15 September and from first light, a standing patrol of two Spitfires of 7 SAAF Squadron was maintained over Kos to cover the arrival on that island of transport aircraft and ships bringing in equipment and reinforcements.

These activities soon brought out the Luftwaffe reconnaissance aircraft and at midday a Ju 88 of 2.(F)/123 was intercepted and shot down in the Derna area by a Spitfire IX pilot of 80 Squadron.

Shells from a 252 Squadron Beaufighter track towards a Junkers Ju 88 A-4 of Wekusta 26 which was shot down; its crew survived and were captured.

On the night of 14/15 September this particular 216 Squadron Dakota III FD831 was flown into Kos and for which Sqn Ldr Christopher Forsythe received the DSO and his navigator, Flt Sgt John Whitelaw the DFM.

British Claims

80 Sqn	Sgt J.Stephen	Spitfire IX EN399	Ju 88	30m off coast Bersis-Toretta	1200

German Casualties

2.(F)/123	Ju 88T-1 WNr 430817 4U+IK shot down 100km N Derna; pilot Obfw Alfred Nitsch (RK) and radio op Obfw Herbert Richter rescued by HMS *Aldenham*, POW, observer Oblt Peter Schug (St.Kpt) KiA
FlK X K	Fi 156C-3 WNr 110050 DO+VJ lost Valona-Jannina; Fw Heinz Findeisen MiA

Thursday, 16 September 1943

On the morning of the 16th another reconnaissance Ju 88 from 2.(F)/123 flew over Kos, where it was claimed to have been badly hit by fire from the 20mm AA guns of the RAF Regiment. Two Spitfires from 7 SAAF Squadron then intercepted it, and chased it towards Rhodes, Lts Taylor and Cheesman shooting the aircraft down not far from Rhodes.

During the day a Cant.Z.506B, now operating in a Co-Belligerent role, was undertaking a flight from Leros to Stampalia to pick up some personnel from the former island. Having reached a point 5km from Stampalia the Italian crew reported that their aircraft was attacked by a pair of heavy fighters, identified as Bf 110s (but actually Ju 88C-6 aircraft of 11./ZG26), which were escorting a convoy. Tenente Addonizio's crew claimed to have shot down one of the attackers and to have severely damaged a second before their own aircraft was heavily hit, requiring a forced landing on the sea following which it was destroyed by fire; the crew were later safely recovered.

Despite these details extensive research has failed to record any German claims or losses and it remains likely therefore that in practice any such encounter on this occasion was not considered sufficiently noteworthy for inclusion by the Luftwaffe in any subsequent report.

British Claims

7 SAAF Sqn	Lt J.W.Taylor	Spitfire Vc JK466	} Ju 88	30m off Rhodes	0755
7 SAAF Sqn	Lt A.E.F.Cheesman	Spitfire Vc JK140			

Italian Co-Belligerent Claims

147ª Sq RM	gunner	Cant.Z.506B	Bf 110	Stampalia	
147ª Sq RM	gunner	Cant.Z.506B Dmgd	Bf 110	Stampalia	

Italian Co-Belligerent Casualties

147ª Sq RM	Cant.Z.506B '147-1' ditched near Stampalia; pilot Ten Luciano Addonizio, co-pilot M.llo Luciano Storari and three rescued

German Claims

11./ZG 26	crew	Ju 88C	Cant Z.506B	Stampalia

German Casualties

2.(F)/123	Ju 88T-1 trop WNr 430424 4U+RK shot down by Spitfires off Rhodes; Uffz Heinz Hanke and three MiA
2./SAGr 125	Ar 196A-3 WNr 0346 damaged by strafing at Suda

Friday, 17 September 1943

During the mid-afternoon period a German convoy was approaching Naxos when it was attacked by a small force of Beaufighters drawn from 227 and 252 Squadrons led by Sqn Ldr Keith Faulkner of the latter unit. Escorting Ar 196s of 1./SAGr 126 engaged, but one of them was shot down and seen to land by a ship which took off the crew of two. This was the U-Jäger *UJ 2104*. Three of the Beaufighters were hit and damaged by flak and crash-landed at base with one navigator dead.

At Kos during the early evening and at the conclusion of another day of patrols, two Spitfire pilots saw several formations of Luftwaffe aircraft below including nine Ju 52/3ms that were seen in a suitable location to be attacked off Stampalia. Lt Ray Burl claimed one of them shot down but his Spitfire was hit and damaged and forced to break off and return to base escorted by the second aircraft.

To the north of this action the destroyers HMS *Hurworth* and *Croome* landed a communications party of 300 troops and stores at Leros where the arrivals were promised the full co-operation of the Italian garrison.

Over Cephalonia in the Adriatic, Italian bases under attack by German troops claimed to have shot down a Ju 87 and a Bf 110, the latter a tactical reconnaissance aircraft of NAGr 2.

British Claims

227 Sqn	Plt Off P.F.L.Glynn/Sgt T.J.Barrett	Beaufighter VI JL766 'G'	Ar 196 Damaged	Scarpanto Strait	1550
252 Sqn	Sqn Ldr K.L.Faulkner/Flt Sgt G.V.Goodes	Beaufighter VI JM250	Ar 196	W Tholos Island	1235–1840
7 SAAF Sqn	Lt R.P.Burl	Spitfire Vc	Ju 52/3m	Stampalia	1705–1745

British Casualties

227 Sqn	Beaufighter VI JL766 'G' damaged by Arado 196 1550, crash-landed at base; Plt Off P.F.L.Glynn/Sgt T.J.Barrett safe
15 SAAF Sqn	Baltimore III FA649 left 1325, crashed at Stampalia Island 1815; Lt S.Meijer and three KiA
252 Sqn	Beaufighter VI JM 250 starboard engine shot out by Flak from *UJ 2104*, but landed safely at base; Sqn Ldr K.L.Faulkner/Flt Sgt G.V.Goodes safe
252 Sqn	Beaufighter VI V8335 damaged by Flak from *UJ 2104*, which killed the observer, crash-landed at Nicosia; Flt Lt D.Delcour safe/Flt Sgt T.R.Lumsden KiA

German Casualties

IV./JG 27	Bf 109G-6 WNr 15321 crashed N Kythnos; Uffz Kurt Nern KiA
1./SAGr 126	Ar 196A-3 WNr 0185 D1+EH shot down attacking convoy 6km NE Kos; Uffz Fritz Schaar/Uffz Herbert Schneider rescued by *UJ 2104*, captured next day, POW
1./SAGr 126	Ar 196A-3 WNr 1017 D1+MH shot down during convoy escort 6km NE Kos; Uffz Kurt Dehl/Fw Benno Unsin WiA
3./NAGr 2	Bf 110 WNr 5394 J8+GL shot down by Italian Flak off Corfu; Lt Karl Puff and two MiA
1./StG 3	Ju 87D-3 WNr 1127 S7+GH, shot down by Flak 1km SW Lixourion; Fw Karl-Heinz Fischer/Uffz Otto Pietsch WiA
7.Seenotst.	Do 24T-3 WNr 3211 KO+KA damaged at Phaleron; Hptm Hans Lösch and five WiA

Saturday, 18 September 1943

During the early hours the German convoy composed of the MVs *Paula* (3,754 tons) and *Pluto* (1,156 tons) with the escorting *UJ 2104* was intercepted again. This time by a Royal Navy surface force comprising HMS *Faulkner*, *Eclipse* and the Greek *Vassilissa Olga*. They sank *Paula* and *Pluto* and forced the escort vessel to beach on Stampalia where the crew, including the Ar 196 crew rescued the previous day, were captured.

7 SAAF Squadron's Lts Burl and Fisher were up on early patrol when at 0720 they claimed the destruction of a Ju 88 near Kos. A Ju 88C of 11./ZG 26 was reported lost to Spitfires north-west of Rhodes, but a claim for a damaged Ju 88 was made by 252 Squadron when four Beaufighters off the north-west coast of Rhodes at about this time were attacked by a lone Ju 88, which was shot up and damaged. By 1030 the German reconnaissance crews had established that there were at least 12 Spitfires and seven transport aircraft on Antimachia airfield. Later in the morning at 1100 a bombing attack on Kos was made by seven Ju 88s, two of which were claimed shot down. Later in the day at around 1500 a third raid was mounted by Bf 109s of IV./JG 27. Following this Panzer Armee 2's daily report stated: "Two Ju 88s attacked by Spitfires north of Kos in the morning. 11 Spitfires and five Douglas on the ground. Three Douglas destroyed, two damaged by strafing, three Spitfires shot down, two 109s lost."

Three C-47s (Dakotas) of 216 Squadron were actually destroyed on the ground and another damaged. A Spitfire that was just taking off was shot down by Bf 109s and Lt A.E.F.Cheesman of 7 SAAF Squadron was killed. Four Spitfires on patrol attacked, Capt Kirby and Lt Taylor each claiming a Bf 109 shot down although Lt

A.G.Turner was shot down and killed, crashing into the sea. At least two Bf 109s were lost: Obfw Morgenstern was killed and Uffz Dettmar captured.

During the day Wg Cdr R.C.Love arrived to take command of 243 (F) Wing despite it only comprising the 7 SAAF Squadron aircraft at the time.

To the west, Regia Aeronautica aircraft started operating at this time over Greece and Albania. It was reported that five RE 2002 fighter-bombers of 5° Stormo Tuffatori went to Corfu to attack German shipping; there they were engaged with Ar 196 floatplanes, one Italian aircraft, flown by Ten Valenza, being shot down in flames. Early in the morning near Mathraki Island off Corfu a crew in a 141ª Squadriglia RM Cant.Z.506 floatplane was attacked and shot down by three Ar 196 floatplanes; S.Ten Coletta and crew survived. (see also Vol. 4 p.376.)

British Claims

252 Sqn	Sqn Ldr H.G.Hubbard/Flg Off G.E.Jones	Beaufighter VI JL621	}		
252 Sqn	Flg Off J.G.Barrett/Plt Off A.S.Haddon	Beaufighter VI X8158	Ju 88 Damaged	NW Rhodes	0615-1115
252 Sqn	Flt Sgt D.de Villiers/Flt Sgt W.P.Fryer	Beaufighter VI JL595	}		
252 Sqn	Flt Sgt L.J.Passow/Flt Sgt A.Underwood	Beaufighter VI JL406			
7 SAAF Sqn	Lt R.P.Burl	Spitfire Vc JK140 'O'	} Ju 88	N Giali, near Kos	0720
7 SAAF Sqn	Lt D.R.Fisher	Spitfire Vc JG881 'R'			
7 SAAF Sqn	Lt A.A.Ground	Spitfire Vc	Ju 88	48km W Kos	1100
7 SAAF Sqn	Lt O.J.Kelly	Spitfire Vc	Ju 88	48km W Kos	1100
7 SAAF Sqn	Lt. P.P.van Deventer	Spitfire Vc	Ju 88 Probable	48km W Kos	1100
7 SAAF Sqn	Capt H.E.Kirby	Spitfire Vc JK466	Bf 109E	Salino	1510
7 SAAF Sqn	Lt J.W.Taylor	Spitfire Vc	Bf 109G	Antimachia	1520
AA	2909 Sqn RAF Rgt		Ju 88	Kos	
AA	2909 Sqn RAF Rgt		Bf 109	Kos	

British Casualties

7 SAAF Sqn	Spitfire Vc JK140 'O' force-landed at Kos 0730; Lt. R.P.Burl safe
7 SAAF Sqn	Spitfire Vc JK881 'R' shot down just after take-off from Antimachia l/g on Kos 1510; Lt A.E.F.Cheesman KiA
7 SAAF Sqn	Spitfire Vc JK140 missing from combat with Bf 109s over Antimachia l/g on Kos 1515; Lt A.G.Turner KiA
216 Sqn	4 Dakota IIIs (FD832, FD892, FD893 and FD921) destroyed by air attack at Antimachia l/g on Kos

German Claims

SAGr 126	unstated	Ar 196	RE 2002	Corfu	
SAGr 126	unstated	Ar 196	Cant.Z.506S	SE Mathraki Island	0730
11./JG 27	Fw Heinz Keller		Spitfire/C-47	5-6km N Kos a/f	1508
11./JG 27	FhjUffz Manfred Hientzsch		Spitfire	8km NW Kos	1512
11./JG 27	Fw Heinz Keller		Spitfire	8km NNW Kos	1513

German Casualties

10./JG 27	Bf 109G-2 WNr 10463 White 1 lost in combat with Spitfires at Kos; Obfw Wilhelm Morgenstern MiA
10./JG/27	Bf 109G-6 WNr 18470 White 5 lost in combat with Spitfires at Kos; Uffz Gustav Dettmar POW
Eins.Gr Ju 88	Ju 88 K5+LL shot down by Spitfires 50km W Kalymnos; Fw Paul Epp and crew KiA
11./ZG 26	Ju 88C-6 WNr 360091 3U+JV shot down NW Rhodes; Obfw Heinz Gründling and two KiA
11./ZG 26	Ju 88C-6 WNr 750453 3U+PV lost at Leros; Lt Hans Sukowski and two crew MiA

Sunday, 19 September 1943

At 0840 a pair of Spitfires took off to intercept five Ju 88s and ten Bf 109s attacking Antimachia airfield. Lt Burl made attacks on one of each of these aircraft but his own fighter was then hit and damaged, obliging him to make a force-landing. Shortly thereafter Lt Seel shot down Uffz Torge who was killed, but Seel suffered a similar fate, falling victim to Lt Hetzler; a further Spitfire was claimed by Lt Bösler but this was not confirmed. The Italian torpedo-boat *MS 12* was sunk at Stampalia by German bombers.

During the day LKS confirmed that an Ar 196 of SAGr 126 was shot down near Corfu by fire from an Italian MTB. Over the Mediterranean in the Mersa Matruh area a reconnaissance Bf 109G of 2.(F)/123 was lost, presumably to engine failure as no Allied claim was made, Uffz Josef Hofmeister being killed.

Another 141ª Squadriglia Cant.Z.506B was shot down off Otranto by a Ju 52/3m at 0705, and a RE 2002 was lost. (see also Vol. 4 p.379.)

7 SAAF Sqn	Lt R.P.Burl	Spitfire Vc JK466	Ju 88 Damaged	Kos	0850-
7 SAAF Sqn	Lt R.P.Burl	Spitfire Vc JK466	Bf 109 Damaged	Kos	0850-
7 SAAF Sqn	Lt I.M.Seel	Spitfire Vc JK677	Bf 109	west end of Kos	0915
AA	2909 Sqn RAF Rgt		Bf 109 Damaged	Kos	
AA	2909 Sqn RAF Rgt		Bf 109 Damaged	Kos	

British Casualties

252 Sqn	Beaufighter VI JL621 on return from convoy escort crashed 2.5m from Limassol a/f; Flt Sgt N.Smyth/Sgt J.D.Bulman WiA
7 SAAF Sqn	Spitfire Vc JK466 shot down by Bf 109 west end of Kos, crash-landed 0850; Lt R.P.Burl safe
7 SAAF Sqn	Spitfire Vc JK677 shot down by Bf 109 3-5m W Antimachia 0915; Lt I.M.Seel KiA
216 Sqn	Dakota I FD806 ditched in sea off Kerme Ora, Turkey while on mission to Kos; Wt Off R.A.Pacquet and crew interned briefly

German Claims

unstated	Ju 52/3m crew		Cant.Z.506B	off Otranto	0705
12./JG 27	Lt Hans Hetzler		Spitfire	1km WSW Kos	0817
12./JG 27	Oblt Dietrich Bösler		Spitfire (unconfirmed)	Kos	

German Casualties

2.(F)/123	Bf 109G-6/R3 WNr 19938 4U+IK lost near Mersa Matruh; Uffz Josef Hofmeister KiA
10./JG 27	Bf 109G-6 WNr 20235 Red 7 shot down by Spitfire at Kos; Uffz Walter Torge KiA
1./SAGr 126	Ar 196A-3 WNr 0298 D1+JH attacked Italian motor-boat *MS 33* at Corfu, shot down by AA; Obfw Wilhelm Gerwins/Obfw Theodor Harings KiA

Monday, 20 September 1943

Shortly after dawn a pair of He 111s of Einsatz II./KG 100 attacked Antimachia, bombing from 2,000 feet. At the same time Flt Lt I.G.Astbury arrived overhead in a Beaufighter night-fighter of 89 Squadron bringing in a passenger from St Jean, Palestine, but flew off when fired on by airfield defences. He then spotted the intruders and promptly attacked and shot down the Heinkel of Uffz Nowotny who was captured with his crew. The second bomber was damaged by AA fire from the airfield.

Six additional Spitfires were flown in to reinforce 7 SAAF Squadron. Further south six Beaufighters of 227 and 252 Squadrons attacked barges in Vronti Bay, Scarpanto but lost one aircraft and crew to Flak. On Rhodes the Germans reported a bombing raid on Maritza airfield that damaged two Bf 109Gs of IV./JG 27.

British Claims

AA			He 111	Kos	0630
89 Sqn	Flt Lt I.G.Astbury/Wt Off W.Busby	Beaufighter VI V8508 'R'	He 111	Kos	0640

British Casualties

227 Sqn	Beaufighter VI JL642 'C' shot down by Flak attacking barges in Vronti Bay, Scarpanto about 1420; Flt Sgt W.D.Webster/Sgt E.S.Taylor MiA

German Casualties

Eins./KG 100	He 111H-11 WNr 8450 6N+AP shot down by AA over Kos; Uffz Joachim Nowotny and three POW
Eins./KG 100	He 111H-11 WNr 8011 6N+EP damaged by AA at Kos; one crew WiA
II./TG 4	Hptm Johannes Casper (St.Kpt) KiA, Lt Kurt Dittmann and two WiA by artillery shots at Symi

Monday-Tuesday, 20/21 September 1943

Half an hour before midnight a 38 Squadron Wellington departed on an armed recce from Berka III but crashed on take-off killing the crew. 252 Squadron's Flg Off F.A.Cohan strafed and set a Ju 52/3m on fire. During the early hours of the morning a mixed formation of Beaufighters from 46, 227 and 252 Squadrons attacked Maritza airfield where 227 Squadron lost one aircraft, shot down with its crew by Flak.

British Claims

252 Sqn	Flg Off F.A.Cohan/Sgt L.J.Barton	Beaufighter EL398	Ju 52/3m (on ground)	Maritza a/f	0334-0755

British Casualties

227 Sqn	Beaufighter VI JL640 'F' left 0329 to strafe Maritza, shot down by Flak over Peragno North, Rhodes 0445; Flt Sgt R.S.Neighbour/Flt Sgt C.G.Hoskin KiA
38 Sqn	Wellington XI MP644 'L' left 2330 on armed recce, crashed on take-off, the load exploded; Flg Off H.E.Bazell and five KiA

Tuesday, 21 September 1943

At midday a Baltimore of 454 RAAF Squadron was shot down by Flak off the coast of Scarpanto Island and the crew was captured.

In the southern Adriatic II./StG 3 lost two Ju 87s. One blew up in the air off Cephalonia when its own bomb load exploded, killing instantly the 6.Staffel commander and Knights Cross holder, Hptm Herbert Stry. The other suffered an engine failure, but the crew survived.

British Claims				
AA	2909 Sqn RAF Rgt		2 Bf 109s Damaged	Kos
AA	2909 Sqn RAF Rgt		Bf 109 Probable	Kos
AA	2909 Sqn RAF Rgt		Ju 88 Probable	Kos
British Casualties				
454 Sqn	Baltimore IV FA574 'S' left 0800, hit by Flak, ditched off Diafani, Scarpanto Island around 1200; Flt Sgt P.S.Kennedy and two POW, one KiA			
German Claims				
Flak		a/c	Rhodes	night
German Casualties				
6./StG 3	Ju 87D-3 WNr 110285 S7+CP either hit by Flak or bomb exploded prematurely, nr Cephalonia; Hptm Herbert Stry (St.Kpt, RK) /Uffz Fritz Strassburger KiA			
4./StG 3	Ju 87D-3 WNr 110287 S7+EH engine failed near Cephalonia, ditched; Fw Walter Grunert/Obgfr Franz Vaculka rescued			

Wednesday, 22 September 1943

Approximately 50 B-24s of 98th and 376th Bomb Groups made the last raid by the US 9th Air Force before their transfer to the 12th and relocation of the 9th AF HQ to England. The US bombers struck airfields on Rhodes and Greece.

Off the northern coast of Crete near Suda Bay an Ar 196A-3 of 1./SAGr 126 attacked a Co-Belligerent Cant.Z.506 but was shot down by return fire from the gunner and the crew was lost.

The Ju 88s of II./KG 6 began transferring to Heraklion from France, with 4.Staffel being the advanced element.

Italian Co-Belligerent Claims				
147ª Sq RM	gunner	Cant.Z.506	Ar 196	Crete-Phaleron
German Casualties				
1./SAGr 126	Ar 196A-3 WNr 0324 D1+AH shot down by Cant.Z.506 Suda-Phaleron; Uffz Manfred Binias/Uffz Heinz Greller WiA			
5./StG 3	Ju 87D-3 WNr 1479 S7+JN engine failed Cephalonia, crashed; Oblt Edmund Pflugmacher/Uffz Ewald Bartels KiA			

Wednesday-Thursday, 22/23 September 1943

That night the destroyer HMS *Eclipse* landed 1,200 personnel and additional stores on Leros before departing southwards on an anti-shipping sweep. Having sailed to the Scarpanto Strait, at 0130 *Eclipse* intercepted and sank the MV *Donizetti* (2,428 tons) close inshore under Cape Prasonisi on the southern tip of Rhodes; she also damaged the escorting German destroyer *TA10* (ex-French *La Pomone*) that beached itself. Unfortunately, the *Donizetti* was carrying 1,800 Italian POWs from Rhodes and 1,584 of them lost their lives.

A German convoy consisting of three steamers escorted by two submarine chasers, was attacked while on passage to Crete. The steamer *Ditmarschen* (1,171 tons) was torpedoed and sunk in an attack by four Wellingtons from 38 Squadron. Only Flg Off F.J.Collins, in Wellington XI HZ396 'E' reported a flash which might have been a strike. The others did not observe the results of their drop. Accurate medium to heavy A/A was encountered, but all aircraft were able to return to base although Collins' was slightly damaged, by 0655, on the 23rd. The rest of the convoy reached Candia, without further losses.

Thursday-Friday, 23/24 September 1943

For the second night in a row, the RAF bombed both aerodromes on Rhodes. On this night 7 Halifaxes of 462 and five Liberators of 178 Squadrons destroyed on Maritza airfield, an Italian aircraft. They also claimed two Ju 52s, all "confirmed" from bomb damage assessment photographs.

Liberator II AL536 'N' of 178 Squadron was among those used to bomb Maritza airfield on Rhodes on the night of 23/24 September when flown by Plt Off Cramer. The raid caused significant damage.

Friday, 24 September 1943

During the early evening a Beaufighter of 227 Squadron flown by Grp Capt Max Aitken and carrying AVM Richard Saul, AOC Air Defences, Eastern Mediterranean, arrived at Kos for a staff visit; they departed the following morning.

British Casualties	
227 Sqn	Beaufighter XI JL915 collided on take-off when it swung and crashed into JM239; Flg Off J.P.Timmons/Sgt S.G.C.Palmer KiFA
227 Sqn	Beaufighter XI JM239 struck by JL915 when waiting to take off; Flt Sgt W.C.Budd/Wt Off G.B.Grennan KiFA
7 SAAF Sqn	Spitfire Vc BR530 crashed on landing; Lt A.L.Basson safe

German Casualties	
2./NAGr 2	Bf 109G-4 WNr 19725 Black 4, lost at Corfu; Lt Ernst Raspe MiA
III./StG 151	Ju 87D-3 WNr 1135 shot down by AA; Lt Hans Robel KiA/radio op safe

Saturday, 25 September 1943

During a reconnaissance of Corfu by a pair of Co-Belligerent Macchi C.205s of 4° Stormo, they made an inconclusive attack on three Ar 196s that were seen. The Macchis were in turn attacked by a pair of Bf 109Gs of IV./JG 27 one of which was shot down by Cap Emanuele Annoni, though the pilot baled out and was rescued by one of the floatplanes. (see also Vol. 4 p.388)

Later in the day Heraklion airfield in eastern Crete was bombed by five Baltimores of 454 RAAF Squadron and five Venturas of 459 RAAF Squadron without loss.

From their base at Lakatamia, Cyprus, four Beaufighters each from 227 and 252 Squadrons attacked the destroyer *TA 10*, still beached on southern Rhodes after the action with HMS *Eclipse* two days earlier.

Saturday-Sunday, 25/26 September 1943

German Claims				
Flak		bomber	3km W of Cap Punda	2205
Flak		bomber	Glyfada	2206

Sunday, 26 September 1943

II./KG 6 had begun to transfer to the Aegean four days earlier from Le Culot in France, the 4.Staffel arriving at Heraklion on Crete the previous day.

At 0700 the destroyers HMS *Intrepid* and the Greek *Vassilissa Olga* arrived in Portolago, Leros. Two hours later eight Ju 88s of the newly arrived 4./KG 6, escorted by Bf 109s III./JG 27, and Ju 88s of 11./ZG 26 dive-bombed the ships in the face of heavy anti-aircraft fire. The Greek vessel was sunk and *Intrepid* badly damaged. At least one Ju 88 was damaged and crashed north of Athens with the loss of its crew. In a strafing attack on Portolago the Ju 88s of 11./ZG 26 attacked and sank two Cant. Z.501s of 147ª Squadriglia RM. A repeat attack was mounted from Larissa by 5./KG 6 in the late afternoon when the bombers again struck *Intrepid* which sank in the harbour; both ships suffered heavy loss of lives. On Kos 7 SAAF Squadron were given just a two-minute warning of the afternoon raid and over Leros two Spitfire pilots saw five Ju 88s and four Bf 109s. One bomber was attacked and shot down by Lt Inggs.

Flt Lt D.J.Harcourt in Walrus W2709 of 294 Squadron landed and rescued a 213 Squadron Hurricane pilot from a position west-south-west of Paphos. Plt Off Temple-Murray's dinghy failed and he was seen swimming, so Flt Lt G.Carrick, the leader of the sweep dropped him his dinghy, he climbed aboard and was rescued within half an hour.

British Claims					
7 SAAF Sqn	Lt V.C.Inggs	Spitfire Vc	Ju 88	N Leros	1700

British Casualties	
7 SAAF Sqn	Spitfire damaged in oil cooler, by Bf 109 or Ju 88; Capt E.A.Rorvik safe
213 Sqn	Hurricane IIC HV444 left 0930 on a sweep over Aegean NW Cyprus, engine failed, ditched 25m off Paphos 1120; Plt Off P.T.P.Temple-Murray rescued by 294 Sqn Walrus flown by Flt Lt D.J.G.Harcourt

Italian Co-Belligerent Casualties	
147ª Sq RM	2 Cant.Z.506Bs destroyed at Leros

German Casualties	
I./TG 4	Ju 52/3m WNr 3160 collided with a Ju 88 at Athens Tatoi, 30% damaged; one passenger KiA
2.(F)/123	Ju 88D-1 WNr 430719 4U+LK collided with a Ju 52/3m at Athens Tatoi, 95% damaged; Lt Karl Dittmann and three WiA
4./KG 6	Ju 88A-14 WNr 144523 left 0640, crashed possibly due to AA damage 25km N Athens; Uffz Richard Ohnacker and three KiA
5./KG 6	Ju 88A-4 WNr 885875 3E+GM shot down in the afternoon by Spitfires off Portolago; Uffz Heinz Radünz and three MiA
Lw Kdo Südost	FW 58 WNr 3001 P4+OA lost Salonika-Tirana; Oblt Heinrich Banke, Obstlt Georg Berstorff and two passengers MiA, returned later
Fl X FlK	Do 17Z WNr 1210 crashed SE Tatoi; Fw Lorenz Bantel and crew KiA

Monday, 27 September 1943

7 SAAF Squadron Spitfire Vc JG895 'K' at Tingaki on Kos in late September when the unit was heavily in action but was eventually overwhelmed.

During the day the Ju 88s of 6./KG 6 arrived at Larissa. In the late morning 23 Ju 88s of KG 6 with an escort of six Bf 109s of 9./JG 27 attacked Antimachia airfield on Kos. The two Spitfires of 7 SAAF Squadron on standing patrol intervened and claimed one bomber shot down and two damaged; they landed at the auxiliary strip at Lampi. With the raid in progress, two more Spitfires attempted to take off but both were shot down and the pilots killed shortly after they became airborne. An Ultra intercept noted that during the day 23 Ju 88s glide-bombed Antimachia, where fire from one Spitfire hit a Ju 88 which returned to base having survived 30–40 machine-gun and cannon hits.

Later in the afternoon Bf 109s came in ahead of an attack by four He 111s and three Ju 88s on Leros. They were engaged by a patrol of 7 SAAF Squadron Spitfires that went for the escorting Bf 109s, one of which might have been shot down before the Spitfire pilot was forced to bale out. He was rescued by an Italian caique. The commanding officer of 7 SAAF Squadron, Maj Corrie van Vliet, also claimed a Bf 109 shot down. A German pilot was also picked up by a caique but apparently dived overboard when an Ar 196 alighted nearby. With the emergency strip at Lampi located, that evening 24 Ju 88s bombed the strip rendering it unusable and forcing the four Spitfires there to return to Antimachia. With 7 SAAF Squadron reduced to just four serviceable aircraft the officer commanding 243 Wing requested urgent reinforcement of at least six Spitfires.

British Claims

7 SAAF Sqn	Lt A.A.Ground	Spitfire Vc	} Ju 88	Antimachia	1215
7 SAAF Sqn	Lt D.R.Fisher	Spitfire Vc			
7 SAAF Sqn	Lt A.A.Ground	Spitfire Vc	Ju 88 Damaged	Antimachia	1215
7 SAAF Sqn	Lt D.R.Fisher	Spitfire Vc	Ju 88 Damaged	Antimachia	1215
7 SAAF Sqn	Maj C.A.van Vliet	Spitfire Vc	Bf 109	20km off Kos	1715
7 SAAF Sqn	Lt A.L.Basson	Spitfire Vc JK667	Bf 109	Kos	c1715

British Casualties

7 SAAF Sqn	Spitfire Vc JG844 attacked by Bf 109s at 1115, shot down 12m from Antimachia; Lt J.H.Hynd KiA
7 SAAF Sqn	Spitfire Vc JG567 attacked by Bf 109s at 1115, shot down 10m S Kos; Lt K.W.Prescot KiA
7 SAAF Sqn	Spitfire Vc JK667 attacked by Bf 109s at 1715, shot down, pilot baled out; Lt A.L.Basson rescued
7 SAAF Sqn	Spitfire Vc JK671 damaged on the ground by strafing of Antimachia by Bf 109s

German Claims

9./JG 27	Uffz Hannes Löffler	Spitfire	10km NW Kos a/f	1118
9./JG 27	Obfw Fritz Gromotka	Spitfire	1–2km N Kos a/f	1120
9./JG 27	Obfw Fritz Gromotka	Spitfire	NW Kos a/f	1517
9./JG 27	Obfw Johannes Scheit	Spitfire	6km N Kos a/f	1520

German Casualties

IV./JG 27	Bf 109G-6 WNr 15975 destroyed in combat at Rhodes; pilot safe
Verb.Kdo.(S)1	Hs 45 WNr 848 H4+LZ lost; Obfw Wilhelm Lagemann and one MiA
Verb.Kdo.(S)1	DFS 230 WNr 127233 LE+13 lost; Uffz Emil Stratmann and two MiA

Monday-Tuesday, 27/28 September 1943

462 Squadron sent ten Halifaxes to illuminate (two aircraft) and bomb (eight aircraft) at Larissa airfield. One illuminator suffered engine failure, the other was hit by three bursts of heavy Flak, sent out of control and spun down. This was claimed by the Larissa Flak defences, but the pilot regained control and landed safely at Berka. Another aircraft crashed on landing and burst into flames. Luck stayed with the crew and they all got out with only one minor injury.

Elsewhere, at Rhodes a Beaufighter of 46 Squadron was lost during a night-intruder sortie.

British Casualties

462 Sqn	Halifax II BB412 left 1920 to illuminate Larissa a/f, hit by heavy Flak over the target, landed safely at Berka 0315; Sgt J.C.Broomfield and five safe
462 Sqn	Halifax II BB321 'S' left 2000 to illuminate Larissa a/f, on return in landing circuit an engine cut, crash-landed; Flg Off R.H.V.Thomas and four safe, one WiA
46 Sqn	Beaufighter XI JL909 left 1830 on intruder mission over Rhodes, FTR; Flg Off G.E.C.Norman/Flg Off E.S.Marsh MiA

German Claims

Flak	Larissa	4-engined a/c	Olympia	2312
Flak	Larissa	4-engined a/c	20km WNW of Larissa	2232

Sqn Ldr J.C.F.'Spud' Hayter (4th from left) and pilots of 74 Squadron at Nicosia before taking off for Kos. Soon after arriving Flg Off J.R.Lewis (standing from right) damaged a Ju 88 but Plt Off A.G.A.Anderson (standing 2nd from right) died when he force-landed. The next day over Kos Flt Sgt W.J.Wilson (5th from left) claimed two Ju 88s destroyed and another damaged.

Tuesday, 28 September 1943

Kos was attacked by surprise by 24 Ju 88s which came in at low level, avoiding interception and inflicting further serious damage. However, at 1500 three pilots of 7 SAAF Squadron did manage to intercept 15 Ju 88s with an escort of Bf 109s which were attacking Lampi strip. Here Capt E.A.Rorvik and Lt J.W.Taylor were shot down by Maj Düllberg and two other pilots of III./JG 27 who claimed three Spitfires between them without loss.

Meanwhile during the day, nine pilots of 74 Squadron had left Cyprus for Kos, eight of them arriving after one had baled out en route. Thus, at evening there remained just nine serviceable Spitfires left on the island together with three more classified as "serviceable within 48 hours".

British Claims

74 Sqn	Flg Off J.R.Lewis	Spitfire Vc ER483 'J'	Ju 88 Damaged	N Kos	1630

British Casualties

74 Sqn	Spitfire Vc ES204 engine trouble, force-landed 10m SE Castelrosso 1215; Flt Lt A.G.A.Anderson KiA
7 SAAF Sqn	Spitfire Vc EE786 shot down by Bf 109 near Kos 1515; Capt E.A.Rorvik KiA
7 SAAF Sqn	Spitfire Vc shot down by Bf 109 near Kos 1515; Lt J.W.Taylor baled out safely

German Claims

Stab III./JG 27	Maj Ernst Düllberg		Spitfire	30km S Kardámaina	1608
9./JG 27	Obfw Johannes Scheit		Spitfire	4km W Kos a/f	1610
9./JG 27	Obfw Fritz Gromotka		Spitfire	N Giali	1615

German Casualties

8./JG 27	Bf 109G-6 WNr 15993 engine trouble SE Athens, pilot baled out; Uffz Otto Mühlbauer MiA
9./JG 27	Bf 109G-6 WNr 160068 engine trouble nr Kos, pilot baled out; Uffz Jacob Herweg rescued by Italian ship
15./KG 53	Do 17Z WNr 2789 A1+DZ reported lost over Adriatic Sea; Lt Šime Fabijanović, Oblt Marin Perović and two deserted to Allies

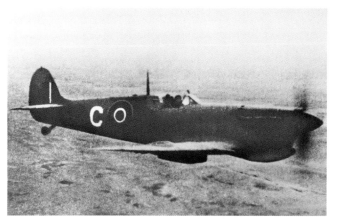

A 74 Squadron Spitfire over Kos where, although making several claims, they suffered heavy losses before evacuating piecemeal to Cyprus.

Wednesday, 29 September 1943

Early in the morning 18 Ju 88s with an escort of a dozen Bf 109s once again attacked Antimachia airfield on which the RAF Regiment gunners claimed one bomber destroyed. The strip was extensively damaged by over 40 bombs. In the air two 7 SAAF Squadron pilots claimed a Ju 88 destroyed and another damaged, whilst a pilot from 74 Squadron claimed a pair of Ju 88s destroyed, though there was no significant damage to the bombers. Later in the afternoon the airfield was again attacked with little opposition other than by the AA gunners that claimed another bomber. Several more men were killed and many wounded on the ground.

British Claims

46 Sqn	Flt Sgt R.Lindsay/Flt Sgt C.Gardner	Beaufighter VI JL905 'D'	e/a Damaged		Calato, Rhodes	2330
7 SAAF Sqn	Lt A.A.Ground	Spitfire Vc	} Ju 88		Antimachia	1050
7 SAAF Sqn	Lt D.R.Fisher	Spitfire Vc				
7 SAAF Sqn	Lt A.A.Ground	Spitfire Vc	} Ju 88 Damaged		Antimachia	1050
7 SAAF Sqn	Lt D.R.Fisher	Spitfire Vc				
74 Sqn	Flt Sgt W.J.Wilson	Spitfire Vc	2 Ju 88s		Antimachia	1100
74 Sqn	Flt Sgt W.J.Wilson	Spitfire Vc	Ju 88 Damaged		Antimachia	1100
AA	2909 Sqn RAF Rgt		2 Ju 88s			

German Casualties

5./KG 6	Ju 88A-14 WNr 144684 on return from afternoon raid on Kos, engine failure, force-landed at Larissa; Lt Hans Berstecher and one WiA, two safe
II./StG 3	Ju 87D destroyed by bombs at Argos; Lt Klaus Reich KiA

Thursday, 30 September 1943

There was now some respite for the airmen on Kos as the Luftwaffe did not attack during the day. However, in the early afternoon, during a *Freie Jagd* carried out by Bf 109s of III./ JG 27, Maj Ernst Düllberg promptly shot down an unfortunate Walrus amphibian biplane. This aircraft, on loan to HQ RAF Middle East, was flown from Cyprus to Leros, before its fateful flight to Kos. It was flown by Flt Lt Frank Rashleigh of HQ RAF ME with Sgt Clifford Platt as navigator. Rashleigh had been ordered to the Aegean Islands to join Flt Lt Balfour – second-in-command of a special unit established to ascertain the possibilities of Aboukir, Castelrosso, Kos and Leros being used as bases for transport and mail services between Egypt and the Dodecanese Islands. Flt Lt Balfour had arrived at Leros on 24 September 1943 to ascertain the possibility of using Italian floatplanes that were reported as being stationed there. The aircraft also carried Maj Patrick G.O.Landon of 9 (Field) Squadron

Flying a Walrus over the Aegean Flt Lt Frank Rashleigh, who had previously won a DFC when flying a Swordfish, had the misfortune to be intercepted and shot down by a Bf 109 flown by Maj Ernst Düllberg, Kommandeur of III./JG 27.

Royal Engineers to assist them. He had twice been mentioned in dispatches. The Naval Walrus lent specifically for this mission, was attacked and shot down by Bf 109s of III.JG 27 five miles south-east of Leros, but no trace of the aircraft or crew was ever found.

Further north off the island of Samos the German ship *Taganrog* (574 tons, ex-Spanish *Vicente*) was bombed and sunk.

243 Wing on Kos signalled the headquarters of Air Defences Eastern Mediterranean (ADEM) requesting the remainder of 74 Squadron be sent to Kos as soon as the landing ground was serviceable. Three non-operational Spitfires of 7 SAAF Squadron were flown out to Cyprus.

British Casualties					
HQ RAF ME	Walrus shot down by Bf 109 between Leros and Kos; Flt Lt F.E.G.Rashleigh DFC/Sgt C.Platt and Maj P.G.O.Landon (passenger) KiA				
94 Sqn	Hurricane IIc KX485 left 1835 on practice flight from Savoia, baled out into the sea; Flt Sgt A.E.Stott rescued				
German Claims					
Stab III./JG 27	Maj Ernst Düllberg		Walrus	Leros Straights	1440

Friday, 1 October 1943

Ultra recorded that two Bf 109s were scrambled from Crete at 1627 and that a pilot reported two Bostons shot down, landing again at 1700. A few days later another intercept provided further details. From one aircraft a crew member baled out after an engine was set on fire and the other aircraft force-landed, presumably on Crete. Two Bf 109s crash-landed there during the day because of engine trouble.

The Italian destroyer *Euro* was badly damaged and later sunk by German bombers at Partheni harbour at Leros.

British Claims					
203 Sqn	gunner Sgt J.E.Flaherty	Baltimore IV 'T'	Bf 109 Damaged	Suda Bay	1610–1700
British Casualties					
203 Sqn	Baltimore IV 'T' damaged in both wings and turret by Bf 109 Suda Bay to Antikythera Straits from 1610 to 1700, reached base and landed safely 1800, a/c written off; Plt Off F.L.Mitchell and two safe, one WiA				
German Claims					
11./JG 27	Fw Heinrich Bartels		2 Beauforts u/c	Suda Bay Crete	c1700

Saturday, 2 October 1943

During the day the bulk of III./JG 27 transferred to Gadurra on Rhodes to provide the fighter cover for the invasion of Kos, which was scheduled for the next day. The transfers were uneventful, except when at 1700 eight Bf 109s from 8. and 9.Staffel/JG 27 departed Kastelli on Crete, for Gadurra. On the way they encountered a single English twin-engine machine. Oblt Kurt Hammel reached it first and shot it down on the easternmost point of Crete. The Bf 109s then landed at Gadurra, where at dusk three Ju 52/3ms arrived with 21 groundcrew.

Ultra reported on this date that six Bf 109s of 11. and 12./JG 27 were at Maleme.

British Casualties					
683 Sqn	Spitfire XI EN670 left 1000 for Larissa, on return refuelled at Brindisi, encountered violent thunderstorm after leaving for Malta; Flt Lt J.B.Burnet KiA				
15 SAAF Sqn	Baltimore IIIA FA360 'X' left 1550, missing from block patrol of Kaso Straights, NE coast of Crete; Lt A.A.Lewin and three KiA				
German Claims					
8./JG 27	Oblt Kurt Hammel		Beaufort	Eastern point of Crete	1722

Sunday, 3 October 1943

On 3 October, at 0500, the Germans effected amphibious and airborne landings on Kos, Operation *Eisbär*, reaching the outskirts of the island's capital later that day. The British withdrew under cover of night and surrendered the next day. The seaborne force was comprised of seven transports, two destroyers, and seven landing craft, E-boats and caiques. By 1030 there were 1500 German troops ashore and communication with the island ceased.

The fall of Kos was a major blow to the Allies, since it deprived them of vital air cover. Grounded SAAF personnel had to make their escape by whatever means could be found. Lt Cecil Golding for example crossed to Turkey in a tiny native coracle. The squadron reassembled in North Africa and counted the cost of its brief but bloody excursion. Six officers had been killed and 15 other ranks were missing; on the other hand, 12 enemy aircraft had been shot down.

Wg Cdr G.A.Reid, the commander of 46 Squadron, and two crews of 89 Squadron who were on detachment to the latter unit at Idku for night intruding took off at 0700 on a shipping strike on a corvette near Rhodes. "Fierce opposition" was encountered and both 89 Squadron's aircraft were damaged. Sgt R.S.Trevett the observer in Flt Lt R.Wright's aircraft, was wounded in one eye. For navigating the aircraft back to base in this condition he was awarded an immediate DFM. On the return flight six Ar 196s attacked and shot down the Beaufighter flown by Wg Cdr Reid, who was killed. 46 Squadron's ORB states that he was shot down by Flak, whereas the 89 Squadron's ORB makes it quite clear that he was shot down by an Ar 196. Flg Off C.H.A.Foster, pilot of the other 89 Squadron crew, claimed an Arado as probably destroyed during this encounter.

UJ 2102 reported being attacked at 0745 by seven Beaufighters, four of which were probably on an early patrol of 46 Squadron, during which a Ju 87 was claimed shot down. A midday patrol of 46 and 227 Squadron aircraft claimed two more Ju 87s shot down at Kos.

Two nights later Flg Off C.H.A.Foster of 89 Squadron undertook an intruder sortie over Rhodes, the unit's last sortie in the Mediterranean theatre prior to moving to Ceylon.

British Claims

46 Sqn	Sqn Ldr T.P.K.Scade/Flg Off H.V.Doodson	Beaufighter VI EL475	} Ju 87	Kos	0400-0845
46 Sqn	Flg Off J.A.Horsfall/Sgt J.R.Colley	Beaufighter VI JL909			
46 Sqn	Wt Off A.Boswell/Sgt H.B.Lawn	Beaufighter VI JL905			
46 Sqn	Flg Off J.E.C.Atkins/Flt Sgt D.Mayo	Beaufighter VI JM238			
89 Sqn	Flg Off C.H.A.Foster/Sgt B.R.Connor	Beaufighter VI	Ar 196 Probable	near Rhodes	c0830
227 Sqn	Sqn Ldr J.R.H.Lewis/Flg Off G.J.Matthews	Beaufighter VI JM277 'E'	} Ju 87	Giali on Kos Island	1235
46 Sqn	Flg Off J.S.Holland/Sgt H.E.Bruck	Beaufighter VI JL910			
227 Sqn	Flg Off A.G.Deck/Sgt J.Templeton	Beaufighter VI JL939 'G'	} Ju 87	Tilos Island	1235
227 Sqn	Sqn Ldr J.R.H.Lewis/Flg Off G.J.Matthews	Beaufighter VI JM277 'E'			
227 Sqn	Flg Off A.G.Deck/Sgt J.Templeton	Beaufighter VI JL939 'G'	} Ju 87 Damaged	Kos	1235
227 Sqn	Lt A.E.Hounsom/Sgt W.H.Duncan	Beaufighter VI JM648 'N'			
46 Sqn	Flg Off J.S.Holland/Sgt H.E.Bruck	Beaufighter VI JL 910			

The splash on the right marks the demise of one of the Beaufighters shot down in the attack on shipping during the German landings on Kos.

252 Sqn	Sqn Ldr H.G.Hubbard/Flg Off G.E.Jones	Beaufighter VI EL528			
252 Sqn	Flt Sgt D.G.R.Ward/Flt Sgt P.Bernard	Beaufighter VI JD911	Ar 196 Damaged	Kos	1255–1735
252 Sqn	Flt Sgt J.A.Evans/Flt Sgt F.Hawthorne	Beaufighter VI JM267			

British Casualties

227 Sqn	Beaufighter VI JM760 'B' left 0510 to attack German shipping off Kos, shot down by Flak; Plt Off P.F.L.Glynn/Sgt T.J.Barrett KiA
46 Sqn	Beaufighter VI JM238 left 0700, attacked German ship off Kos, shot down by Ar 196; Wg Cdr G.A.Reid KiA/Flg Off W.R.Peasley rescued by Turkish vessel
46 Sqn	Beaufighter VI JL907 left 1325, attacked German ship off Kos, shot down and blew up; Sqn Ldr W.A.Cuddie/Flg Off L.E.M.Coote KiA
46 Sqn	Beaufighter VI JL903 'N' left 1325, attacked German ship off Kos, shot down and ditched off Turkish coast and spent 8 hours paddling to Turkey; Wt Off E.W.Ledwidge/Flt Sgt J.T.Rowley safe
46 Sqn	Beaufighter VI JM264 left 1325 for Kos, attacked German ship off Kos, shot down and ditched off Turkish coast and paddled to Turkey, Flt Sgt C.Holmes/Flt Sgt M.W.Bell safe
89 Sqn	Beaufighter VI damaged; Flt Lt R.Wright safe/Sgt R.S.Trevett WiA
89 Sqn	Beaufighter VI damaged; Flg Off C.H.A.Foster/Sgt B.R.Connor safe

German Claims

2./SAGr 125?	unstated	Ar 196	Beaufighter	Kos	0745
2./SAGr 125?	unstated	Ar 196	2 Beaufighters	near Rhodes	1400
Flak	*UJ 2102*		Beaufighter	Kos	1425

German Casualties

II./StG 3	Ju 87D-3 trop WNr 110288 hit by AA, crashed into sea nr Kos 1157; crew rescued
1./StG 3	Ju 87D-3 WNr 1113 S7+FH shot down by AA 9km ENE Kos; Uffz Jordan Stifter/Gefr Arthur Aschenbach KiA
1./StG 3	Ju 87D-4 WNr 1072 S7+LH ditched off Symi Island; Gefr Walter Kneissl/Fw Rudolf Fischmann rescued
I./TG 4	Ju 52/3m WNr 6965 G6+KL destroyed by bombs at Heraklion; Uffz Albert Kring and one KiA, one WiA

Order of Battle of Luftwaffe in Greece, Crete and Dodecanese as of 3 October 1943 (from Ultra)

II./KG 6	Ju 88	Larissa
II./KG 51	Ju 88	Sedes
Staffel KG 100	He 111	probably Eleusis
Staffel LG 1	Ju 88	probably Eleusis
2.(F)/123		Tatoi, Kastelli, Gadurra
1.(F)/122		Kastelli
Wekusta 27		Tatoi, Kastelli
Stab StG 3		Eleusis
I./StG 3	Ju 87	Megara
II./StG 3	Ju 87	Argos
Stab JG 27		possibly Kalamaki
III./JG 27		Argos
9./JG 27		probably Gadurra
IV./JG 27		Argos and possibly Kalamaki, small detachments at Maleme, Kastelli and possibly Heraklion
11./ZG 26	Ju 88C	Eleusis
2./NAGr 2		Jannina, Argos
3./NAGr 2		Devoli and possibly Larissa
2./SAGr 125		possibly Suda Bay and Phaleron
SAGr 126		Skaramanga

Sunday-Monday, 3/4 October 1943

462 Squadron attacked Heraklion airfield on Crete.

German Claims

| Flak | | | Bomber | NE Rethymon | 2207 |

Monday, 4 October 1943

Five Ju 88s attacked an Allied ship at Leros at 1645 claiming a direct hit. One merchant ship was damaged.

Thirty-five B-25s of 321st Bomb Group bombed Argos at 1055, two to three aircraft were claimed destroyed. Two pilots of III./JG 27 were killed in the raid, Uffzs Bauer and Herweg. III./JG 27 repeated its cover of Kos, this time flying nine missions totalling 33 sorties and 63 hours. Unlike the previous day, engine trouble forced six Bf 109s to abort during the day. 12./JG 27 was recruited to join one of the patrols due to III./JG 27 running short of serviceable Bf 109s.

It was on this date that German forces completed the occupation of Kos, recording that 600 British and 2,500 Italians were taken prisoner, while 40 guns and 22 partly destroyed aircraft were captured.

A bomber claim was made by Maj Gustav Rödel against a bombing raid on Kos but there are conflicting sources as to what day this actually happened. The Americans did not raid Kos or the nearby Rhodes until the 7th, 9th and 10th of October.

British Claims					
203 Sqn	Sgt Viney	Baltimore IV	He 115 Damaged	12km S Milos	1358
US Casualties					
96th FS/82nd FG	P-38G 43-2456 lost 2m S Argos a/d, probably engine trouble at 1150; 2/Lt Stanley S.Hand KiA [923]				
German Claims					
Stab/JG 27	Maj Gustav Rödel		B-24	10km SW Kos a/f	1220
German Casualties					
2./NAGr	Bf 109G-4 WNr 19778 destroyed by bombs at Argos				
9./JG 27	Uffz Rudi Bauer and Uffz Jakob Herweg killed by bombs at Argos				
Flugber.X.Kps	FW 58 WNr 1228 70% damaged by bombs at Tatoi				

Tuesday, 5 October 1943

During this day the 37th Fighter Squadron of the 14th Fighter Group had deployed to Gambut for a new venture – assisting the RAF in the Aegean campaign.

The 321st Bomb Group's Mitchells bombed Salonika-Sedes airfield mid-morning; this attack caused little damage to the airfield – two aircraft slightly damaged and an ammunition dump partly destroyed – but personnel casualties were heavy: 31 Germans killed, 39 seriously wounded and 78 slightly so. However, the airfield was expected to be serviceable again by midday of the 6th. Such delays in regaining serviceability in raids that caused little damage were almost always due to unexploded bombs having to be dealt with.

Meanwhile, the B-24s of 98th and 376th Bomb Groups, escorted by 24 P-38s of the 82nd Fighter Group bombed Greek airfields. The 376th reported that 20 to 25 FW 190s with red noses and Bf 109s coloured silver attacked after a bomb run in formations of two to seven concentrating from 3 to 9 o'clock at all levels. Enemy aircraft fired heavy cannon at long range pressing attacks to within 100 yards.

At 1145 15 Bf 109s were scrambled by III. and IV./JG 27, the pilots of which claimed to have shot down eight of the Liberators and two 'possibles' for the loss of two pilots. The American gunners claimed 11 fighters destroyed, but three Liberators were downed – with 18 parachutes seen to open.

Oblt Werner Küffner had made the first claim at 1215 at Erimokastron, a town which had its name changed to Thespies in 1934. Fw Heinrich Bartels then made two claims, before Lt Emil Clade made the first claim for III.Gruppe at 1243 20km north-west of Levadhia, for a Liberator that exploded on impacting the ground. Five minutes later Uffz Rudolf Moycis made the next claim 10km west of Amfissa, also reporting that it exploded on impact. A further five minutes elapsed until Obfw Fritz Gromotka claimed one Liberator 10km south-west of Lidhorikion. Two minutes on, Maj Düllberg made the last claim, 10km west of Lidhorikion, north of Gromotka's claim (see also Vol. 4 p.399).

Earlier in the morning Uffz Heckmann had claimed one aircraft shot down which he identified as a Baltimore or Beaufighter. There seems little doubt that it was one of the former and that this was an aircraft of 203 Squadron reported missing from a photo-reconnaissance sortie over the central Aegean area.

In the morning 29 Ju 88s, 34 Ju 87s and 4 He 111s attacked Portolago Bay; Ju 88s of II./KG 6 sank the Italian mine-layer *Legnano*, and the steamers *Prode* (1,244 tons) and *Porto di Roma* (470 tons). Returning with no bombs Oblt Sicheritz (promoted on the first of the month) and Fw Vogelsang encountered a destroyer off Naxos and could only strafe it with their forward-firing 20mm cannon.

The Staffelkapitän of 7./JG 27 Lt Emil Clade in his Bf 109G-6 'Weisse 2' was involved in many actions over the Aegean in late 1943.

British Casualties

203 Sqn	Baltimore IV FA557 'P' left 0710, lost over the Aegean sea; Wt Off H.W.Robinson and three MiA

US Claims

344th BS/98th BG	gunner S/Sgt Clarence H.Weckesser	B-24D 4x-xx733/J	Bf 109F	over sea near Athens	1405
343rd BS/98th BG	gunner S/Sgt Paul A.Whorlow	B-24D 4x-xx014/R	Bf 109	Eleusis	1405
343rd BS/98th BG	gunner S/Sgt Charles R.Hooper	B-24D 4x-xx014/R			
344th BS/98th BG	gunner S/Sgt Edward H.Underwood	B-24D 41-23795/I	Bf 109	over sea near Athens	1415
512th BS/376th BG	gunner Sgt A.L.Collier	B-24D 42-72843/24/U	Bf 109	Eleusis a/d	
512th BS/376th BG	gunner Sgt McKenna	B-24D 42-72768/36	FW 190	Eleusis a/d	
512th BS/376th BG	gunner S/Sgt F.E.Dunham	B-24D 42-72852/39	FW 190	Eleusis a/d	
512th BS/376th BG	gunner S/Sgt Butler	B-24D 42-72852/39	FW 190	Eleusis a/d	
513th BS/376th BG	gunner T/Sgt R.G.Byers	B-24D 42-72782/47/A	Bf 109	Eleusis a/d	
513th BS/376th BG	gunner T/Sgt W.E.Larzelere	B-24D 42-72782/47/A	Bf 109	Eleusis a/d	
515th BS/376th BG	gunner Sgt Gerard W.Brand	B-24D 41-24258/23	Bf 109	Eleusis a/d	
514th BS/376th BG	gunner S/Sgt P.J.Ridolphi	B-24D 42-40206/64	Bf 109	Eleusis a/d	

US Casualties

515th BS/376th BG	B-24D 41-24035 *The Gremlin* shot down by Bf 109s NW Athens at 1125; 2/Lt Charles Petty and seven KiA, two POW [1096]
514th BS/376th BG	B-24D 41-24310 *Eight Ball Patches* shot down by Bf 109s NW Athens 1125; 2/Lt Frank Buehl and seven POW, two KiA [1097]
513th BS/376th BG	B-24D 42-72902 *Patches* shot down by fighters off Eleusis; Capt Paul J.Fallon and five returned, two KiA, two POW [930]
98th BG	B-24D classified as severely damaged on return

German Claims

7./JG 27	Uffz Theo Heckmann	Beaufighter	29km SW Naxos	0810
Flak		B-24	Mt Parnassus	1211
12./JG 27	Oblt Werner Küffner	B-24	5km N Erimokastron	1215
11./JG 27	Fw Heinrich Bartels	B-24	Petromogula	1223
11./JG 27	Fw Heinrich Bartels	B-24	Iliki Sea N Thebes	1233
7./JG 27	Lt Emil Clade	B-24	20km NW Levadhia	1243
7./JG 27	Uffz Rudolf Moycis	B-24	8m W Amfissa	1248
9./JG 27	Obfw Fritz Gromotka	B-24	10km SW Lidhorikion	1253
Stab III./JG 27	Maj Ernst Düllberg	B-24	20km W Lidhorikion	1255

German Casualties

7./JG 27	Bf 109G-6 WNr 17005 combat Argos area; Lt Emil Clade baled out safe
7./JG 27	Bf 109G-6 WNr 160074 White 8 combat Atalanta/Thebes area; Uffz Karl Schaffhauser MiA, returned later
9./JG 27	Bf 109G-6 WNr 130330 Yellow 6 combat N Gulf of Patras; Uffz Alfred Kluss MiA
II./StG 3	2 Ju 87D-3 trops WNr 1445 and 110268 damaged by Greek partisans at Argos

Wednesday, 6 October 1943

A strafing attack on Araxos airfield by 36 P-38s of the 82nd Fighter Group brought forth claims for seven aircraft destroyed on the ground. This appears to have led to a rather considerable set of overclaims, Axis records indicating the actual loss of one Italian aircraft destroyed and one soldier wounded.

Of considerably more significance was the agreement of General Eisenhower to authorize a degree of direct support to the British forces in the Aegean. At this stage this included two heavy bomber groups of B-24s which moved to Benghazi and six squadrons of P-38s which moved virtually at once to Gambut. The latter, which comprised the three squadrons of the 1st and those of the 14th Fighter Groups, were very much what RAF Middle East desired, but unfortunately they were subject to the rider that they were to return to Tunisia for continued escort operations after the 10th. Also provided, however, was 603 Squadron of coastal Beaufighters which would arrive by the 11th and one squadron of B-25s (the USAAF's 321st Bomb Group's 'G' Squadron armed with 75mm cannons).

The first mission of I./StG 3 against the Royal Navy was flown on this day, on receipt of news of the presence of a strike force of cruisers and destroyers withdrawing down the Scarpanto Strait. The Stukas started in Megara at 1020. After 95 minutes they reached the British surface force striking deep in the Scarpanto Strait. After the heavy and sustained attacks the Stukas of I./StG3 returned to Megara where they landed at 1345.

British Casualties

227 Sqn	Beaufighter VI JM648 'N' left 1305 to escort convoy 'Nostril', ditched 1517; Flg Off B.J.Beare/Sgt C.E.Humphreys rescued
227 Sqn	Beaufighter VI EL516 'Y' left 1305 to escort convoy 'Nostril', ditched 1805; Sgt R.H.Carter/Sgt H.J.Harris rescued

US Claims

82nd FG	claimed 7 aircraft on ground at Araxos
99th BG	claimed 4 e/a destroyed

Thursday, 7 October 1943

The British force comprising two cruisers, HMS *Sirius* and *Penelope*, and four destroyers arrived off Leros at 0530 and found no signs of an invasion. Then, at 0630 they picked up HMS *Unruly*'s enemy report. At 0800 off Stampalia, the force intercepted and sank six landing craft, one armed trawler and one ammunition ship, and then withdrew. Sailing on the Scarpanto route *Sirius* force was attacked by 39 Ju 87s of StG 3, 35 Ju 88s of LG 1 together with II./KG 51, along with four He 111s. Eighteen Ju 87s of II./StG3 took off on this day at 0810 (CET time) and immediately pursued the warships which were sighted at 0955. The cruiser and the destroyers were attacked and the Stukas badly damaged – HMS *Penelope* by a SC 50 bomb on the stern and several near misses, but the warship continued at 22 knots. The casualties aboard were two officers and 22 ratings killed and 29 wounded. On the return flight from this attack a Ju 88 ditched, reportedly due to engine failure. The Stukas arrived back in Megara at 1215. During the attack the Stuka with the call-sign S7+OL was shot down by ships' guns. German air-sea rescue service picked up the pilot Lt Wolfgang Wendel and his wireless operator Fw Georg Scheller injured south-west of Rhodes.

The first patrols by the American Lightnings were flown on this date. Eight P-38s of 1st Fighter Group's 71st Squadron took off from Gambut at 0815 to cover the British force from 1030 to 1130, when the convoy reported five Ju 88s, one Bf 109 and one FW 190 to the south-west. One flight of P-38s led by Maj Hanes made two attacks 10 miles south of the convoy, while Lt Taylor's flight attacked from 12 o'clock high. The Ju 88s took no evasive action and the combat lasted 15 minutes. A Ju 88 crashed into the water, the crew baling out. Another Ju 88 left trailing black smoke from one engine. Then more P-38s of 1st Fighter Group covered the convoy during the morning. Their place was taken during the afternoon by 14th Fighter Group. Eight P-38s of 49th Squadron took off from Gambut at 1120 to cover the British force and the pilots sighted a submarine on the surface but not the warships. Then eight P-38s of 37th Squadron patrolled the convoy from 1410 to 1440, replaced by eight Lightnings of 48th Squadron from 1440 to 1510, and again by P-38s of 37th Squadron from 1510 to 1540.

Two waves of B-24s of the 98th Bomb Group bombed Kastelli airfield on Crete late in the morning, without significant effect. A B-24 was believed shot down from an expenditure of 640 rounds of 88mm and 163 rounds of 10.5cm Flak. The Germans reported that the B-24 was last seen on fire but was not observed to crash. Other

B-24s of the 376th Bomb Group bombed Maritza on Rhodes in the late morning also without causing significant damage. An aircraft was reported in the sea south-east of Rhodes at 1228 GMT.

The Italian merchant ship *Ivorea* (3,276 tons) was damaged beyond repair by bombs at Partheni.

British Claims					
203 Sqn	Flg Off Maconie	Baltimore IV FA399 'X'	Ju 88C Damaged	SE Kythnos	1155
British Casualties					
603 Sqn	Beaufighter VI JL761 'E' left 1130 to escort RN force, between Scarpanto and Rhodes, shot down by Bf 109s; Flt Sgt J.P.Hey/ Flt Sgt E.A.Worrall MiA				
US Claims					
71st FS/1st FG	unspecified	P-38	Ju 88	NW Scarpanto Straits	0815–1355
71st FS/1st FG	unspecified	P-38	Ju 88 Damaged	NW Scarpanto Straits	0815–1355
US Casualties					
71st FS/1st FG	P-38 left Gambut 0815, after combat headed for Cyprus low on fuel, crash-landed at Nicosia 1355; Lt Taylor unhurt				
German Claims					
11./JG 27	Oblt Alfred Burk		Beaufighter	50–60km off Scarpanto	1130
4./KG 6	Lt Karl-Georg Schmidt crew (?)	Ju88A-4	P-38		1600
German Casualties					
III./JG 27	Bf 109G-6 WNr 160062 50% damaged at Gadurra				
IV./JG 27	Bf 109G-6 WNr 18461 engine failure, crashed nr Tanagra; pilot baled out, rescued				
I./StG 3	Ju 87D-3 trop WNr 1376 S7+OL shot down by AA 30km NE Scarpanto; Lt Wolfgang Wendel/Fw Georg Scheller rescued				
4./KG 6	Ju 88A-4 3E+BM left 0742 from Heraklion to reconnaissance Kos area, damaged by P-38s, landed at base; Lt Karl-Georg Schmidt and three safe				
4./KG 6	Ju 88A-4 WNr 888872 3E+KM shot down by AA N Scarpanto; Uffz Siegfried Hermann and three MiA				
II./KG 6	Ju 88A-4 WNr 300130 60% damaged by bombs at Heraklion				

Thursday-Friday, 7/8 October 1943

462 Squadron bombed Heraklion, damaging at least one Ju 88. Of more significance Sgt S.A.Heard in Halifax BB415 was attacked by a twin-engine fighter believed to be a Ju 88 at 2238 over the SW coast of Crete. Three attacks were made, all from a relatively long range and no fire was observed from the attacking aircraft.

German Casualties	
4./KG 6	Ju 88A-4 WNr 144572 35% damaged by bombs at Heraklion

Friday, 8 October 1943

Six patrols were flown by the 14th Fighter Group on this date. Eight P-38s took off at 0905 to cover the British force that had also been escorted by the group the preceding day. The 1st Fighter Group flew two missions to cover the ships, on the second of which the 71st Squadron encountered Ju 88s and Lt Russell Williams claimed one shot down, while another was claimed damaged. In fact these were He 111s from KG 100. *ML 351* shot down a Ju 88 in a raid on Leros.

Thirty-eight B-24s of XII Bomber Command raided Tatoi and Eleusis airfields and targets on Rhodes, Heraklion and Maritza. Forty-eight B-25s of the 321st Bomb Group refuelled at Grottaglie before flying on to repeat the raid on Eleusis. They were escorted by 24 P-38s of the 82nd Fighter Group which also undertook some convoy escort work. Over the Gulf of Corinth Bf 109s of III. and IV./JG 27 were engaged, the Lightning pilots claiming two of these shot down and four damaged for the loss of two of their own aircraft.

Fw Heinrich Bartels of 11./JG 27 claimed regularly during the autumn fighting over the Aegean and central Mediterranean.

The B-25s suffered the loss of two of their number to fighters as well, while 26 of the bombers sustained damage to some degree or another. The Luftwaffe pilots claimed three twin-engined bombers, one of which was incorrectly identified as a Manchester. A B-24 was also claimed together with eight P-38as, all for the loss of one Messerschmitt. All the returning US pilots and gunners, the latter of whom claimed eight of the interceptors shot down, reported being attacked by both Bf 109s and FW 190s, plus two Bf 110s.

Eleven Bf 109s of I./NAGr 12 flew to Tirana during the day but at once the unit lost two aircraft which crashed while landing. On this date III./JG 53, which now had no aircraft, was ordered to re-equip at Vicenza, 7.Staffel at once, 8. and 9.Staffeln following over the next ten days.

US Claims

95th FS/82nd FG	2/Lt Robert W.Muir	P-38	Bf 109	Gulf of Corinth	1140–1515
95th FS/82nd FG	1/Lt J.D.Stoughtenborough	P-38	Bf 109	Gulf of Corinth	1140–1515
95th FS/82nd FG	1/Lt Claud E.Ford	P-38	Bf 109 Damaged	Gulf of Corinth	1140–1515
95th FS/82nd FG	2/Lt George M.Magee	P-38	Bf 109 Damaged	Gulf of Corinth	1140–1515
95th FS/82nd FG	2/Lt Robert W.Muir	P-38	Bf 109 Damaged	Gulf of Corinth	1140–1515
95th FS/82nd FG	2/Lt John H.Tennery	P-38	Bf 109 Damaged	Gulf of Corinth	1140–1515
445th BS/321st BG	gunners	B-25s	8 Bf 109s	Gulf of Corinth	1140–1515
71st FS/1st FG	2/Lt Russell E.Williams	P-38	Ju 88	Leros area	1600
71st FS/1st FG	unspecified	P-38	Ju 88 Damaged	Leros area	1600

US Casualties

445th BS/321st BG	B-25C 42-64590 shot down by Bf 109 at mouth of Livadhostra Bay in Gulf of Corinth 1345, attempted to ditch but exploded on hitting the water; 2/Lt Joel T.Hartmeister and one crew evaded with the partisans, one POW and three KiA [1307]
445th BS/321st BG	B-25C 42-64675 *Poochie* shot down in Gulf of Patras by fighters, made a safe water landing 1405; 1/Lt James B.Fisher Jr, six crew and observer Capt Clarence H.Corning of 97th FS/82nd FG POW [927 & 1301]
95th FS/82nd FG	P-38G 43-2332 shot down in Gulf of Corinth by Bf 109 and FW 190, 1345; 2/Lt Clayton A.Bennett rescued by Greek patriots [925 A]
95th FS/82nd FG	P-38G 42-13062 shot down in Gulf of Corinth by Bf 109 and FW 190, 1345; 2/Lt James P.Shawver KiA [925 B]

German Claims

8./JG 27	Obfw Hans Niederhöfer	P-38	5km W Kiriaki	1347
7./JG 27	Uffz Theo Heckmann	P-38	4km W Khosyta	1348
Stab JG 27	Maj Gustav Rödel	Mitchell	20km SE Levadhia	1348
11./JG 27	Fw Heinrich Bartels	P-38	30km S Levadhia	1350
11./JG 27	Fw Heinrich Bartels	P-38	7km SSW Cap Vourlias	1352
9./JG 27	Obfw Fritz Gromotka	B-25	8km NNW Cap Pappas	1353
8./JG 27	Fw Alfred Stückler	P-38	15km S Antikyra	1355
11./JG 27	Fw Heinrich Bartels	P-38	5km W Cap Velanidhia	1355
8./JG 27	Obfw Hans Niederhöfer	P-38	15km SW Khosyta	1357
Stab JG 27	Maj Gustav Rödel	P-38	N Patras	1400
8./JG 27	Fw Alfred Stückler	Manchester	40km SW Pytheia	1405
8./JG 27	Obfw Kurt Hoppe	B-25	15km N Araxos	1410

German Casualties

8./JG 27	Bf 109G-6 WNr 13997 combat with P-38, crashed 20–30m S Khosyta; Lt Werner Gützmann MiA
Eins./KG 100	He 111H-6 WNr 7824 damaged in combat W Kos; crew safe
Eins./KG 100	He 111H-11 WNr 8001 damaged in combat W Kos; crew safe
II./KG100	3 He 111Hs (WNr 7116, 8445 and 7937) damaged by bombs at Eleusis
II./KG 100	2 Ju 88A-4s (WNr 4578 and 140054) damaged by bombs at Eleusis

Saturday, 9 October 1943

During the nights of the 7th/8th and 8th/9th another Royal Navy strike force swept through the area seeking to intercept German forces attempting to reach the Dodecanese from the Piraeus. No sightings were made until the morning of the 9th when at 0515 the RN force was seen heading south-east between Scarpanto and Rhodes, making for Alexandria to refuel. By now the P-38s were in the area, providing strong defensive patrols almost all the time. In these circumstances Stab of StG 3 were able to calculate that their two Gruppen of Stukas potentially enjoyed a window of opportunity of some two hours when both units could join to inflict a major attack on the ships in the area south of Rhodes. It does appear, however, that at this stage the Germans were not aware of the almost permanent presence of the escorting American fighters.

Ju 87s of I./StG 3 from the Megara air base succeeded in sinking HMS *Panther* at 1205 leaving 33 dead. They later seriously damaged HMS *Carlisle* which received four direct hits and several near misses that caused extensive structural damage and flooding. The starboard shaft and propeller was blown off and the port shaft was buckled. The attack left 20 of the ship's company killed and 17 wounded. She was taken in tow to Alexandria by HMS *Rockwood* but was considered to be beyond economical repair and was converted to serve as a harbour depot ship.

Thus, it was that the time planned for arrival over the target was set at midday or thereabouts following fairly long flights to the area. In the event this coincided with the point at which the six P-38s of the 1st Fighter Group completed their patrol and turned for Gambut to refuel while a flight from the 37th Squadron of the 14th Fighter Group approached to take over. Consequently the departing P-38 pilots failed to encounter the I.Gruppe Ju 87s that were able to launch a heavy attack on the British ships. This was seen to be underway by the 37th Squadron pilots as they approached, struggling to gain altitude, allowing the I.Gruppe Stukas to complete their attack and to depart for Megara, having suffered the loss of just one of their aircraft to the ships' defensive fire.

It was at this point at about 1215 that II.Gruppe approached from the north-west right in front of 37th Squadron's flight, jettisoning their bombs and diving to escape as the P-38s attacked with results which are now described below. The combat report subsequently submitted by Maj William Leverette, commanding officer of the squadron, was succinct in providing a clear and precise account of the engagement insofar as the USAAF was concerned:

"At 1030 hours I departed with nine P-38s from Gambut. Shortly after take-off two planes were forced to return because of engine trouble, leaving four P-38s of my Red Flight, and three of Lt Wayne Blue's Flight. We went all the way on the deck to stay under German radar on Crete, and sighted the British warships at almost exactly noon, fifteen minutes before our scheduled rendezvous. The ships were approximately 15 miles east of Cape Valoca, on the Isle of Scarpanto. I contacted them on their frequency and was told that they were under attack. I could see that the cruiser was smoking from the stern. Before we could get within firing range of the Stukas several of them made dive-bombing runs on the British warships. At least one hit was scored on a destroyer, which broke in two and sank immediately. I led my P-38s up to 6,000 feet and began a counter-clockwise circle around the ships, just out of range of any nervous anti-aircraft gunners. As I reached 8,000 feet and was about halfway through the first circuit Lt Homer Sprinkle, the number four man in my flight called out: 'Bogies at one o'clock!' There was a cloud of them in the distance. They were slightly higher and approaching the ships from the north-west. I immediately added power to speed up the climb and I changed course to pass slightly behind the bogies in order to make a positive identification as to the type of enemy aircraft. It quickly became clear that they were Junkers 87 Stuka gull-winged dive-bombers, probably out of Crete or the airfield at Scarpanto. There were 25 or 30 of them in three flights.

"As we closed on the Stukas – it was about 1215 – I told Lieutenant Blue to hold up his flight momentarily in case there were more enemy aircraft – possibly fighters following the Stukas. With my flight I immediately closed on the left rear quarter of the Stuka formation. The obvious plan of attack was to get in close to the Stukas and clobber them with short, accurate bursts from our .50-calibre machine guns. Before the Germans knew we were there, I attacked the nearest enemy airplane ahead of me. I fired a short burst with the .50s from about 20 degrees. Smoke poured from the left side of the Stuka's engine. The Stuka pilot who still had bombs aboard jettisoned them as soon as the shooting started. Several of my pilots also reported later that a number of Stukas jettisoned their fixed main landing gear as well. As soon as I saw smoke coming from the first Stuka I broke to my left and attacked a second Stuka from his rear and slightly below. After I fired a short burst from about 200 yards this aeroplane rolled over and spiralled steeply downwards. I broke away to the left again and turned back towards the formation of Stukas. As I did, I saw both Stukas I had already fired on strike the water. Even though each Stuka had a rear gunner armed with 7.92mm machine guns on a flexible mount, I am sure that neither of the rear gunners had fired at me. I attacked a third Stuka from a slight angle off its left rear. I opened fire at this aeroplane just as the rear gunner fired at me. The gunner immediately ceased firing, and I saw the pilot jump out of the aeroplane, although I did not see his parachute open. The gunner did not get out. I continued on into the enemy formation and attacked another Stuka – my fourth – from an angle of 30 degrees.

"I observed cannon and machine-gun fire hit the Stuka's engine, and I saw large pieces of cowling and other parts fly off. The engine immediately began smoking profusely, and the Stuka nosed down. I broke away upwards to my left and then re-entered the enemy formation. Another Stuka was nearly dead ahead, I opened fire again with my cannon and machine guns from an angle of about 15. The canopy and various parts of this Stuka flew off, and a large flame shot out of the engine and from along the left wing root. The gunner jumped out of the aeroplane as I passed it. Continuing into the formation, I approached a sixth Stuka from below and to his left rear, but on a crossing course that would take me over to his right rear, heading slightly away from it. I was closing so fast, the only way to bring my guns to bear was to roll the P-38 tightly left, to an almost inverted attitude. As my guns lined up on the Stuka momentarily, I opened fire at very close range and observed concentrated strikes on the upper right side of the engine. The engine immediately began to smoke, and I broke away slightly to my left. My element leader, Lt Troy Hanna, saw this aeroplane hit the water. I attacked the seventh Stuka from straight behind and slightly below. The rear gunner fired at me briefly, but he stopped as soon as I fired a short burst of my own. As the Stuka nosed slightly down, I closed to minimum range and fired a short burst into the bottom of the engine and fuselage. Some Ju 87s were thought to have wooden props, and this one acted as though its prop had been shattered and completely shot away. The Stuka abruptly and uncontrollably pitched downwards and I was instantly looking broadside at a nearly vertical Stuka directly in front of me. I was nearly committed to passing underneath him, so I intuitively jammed the control yoke forward as hard as I could. I heard and felt a large thump as I went past him. Looking back, I saw a falling object that at first I feared was my left tail. But the tail was still in place. The falling object was probably the pilot or gunner catapulted out of this seat by the negative G force of the plunging airplane.

"In the dogfights, lasting approximately 15 minutes, fifteen 87s (and one Ju 88) were shot from the skies by the attacking flight and the top cover had accounted for another Ju 87 which brought the grand total to seventeen. We engaged the Ju 87s until they passed over the south coast of Rhodes at approximately 1230 hours. Later on the ground the damage to the edge of my propeller blades proved to be very light. We reasoned that my props had cut into the tail of the German's rudder and fin. Fortunately, he fell faster than I did, or I would have plowed headlong into him."

Apparently it was only the fact that the Lightnings were running out of fuel and ammunition which caused the American pilots not to continue the slaughter. As can be seen, the P-38 pilots had over-claimed considerably as so often happened in combats between fighters and dive-bombers. One of the first claims to be submitted was that made by 2/Lt Wayne Blue for a Ju 88 which was described as featuring a "blacked-out nose" which caused it to be described as possibly a reconnaissance machine. Actually, it was a 252 Squadron Beaufighter that the US pilots reported had attempted to attack the trio of P-38s maintaining top cover over the rest of the 37th's formation, and the "Ju 88" was claimed by the leader of the flight, 2/Lt Blue. Three Beaufighters of 252 Squadron were also over the area, lending further escort to the stricken HMS *Carlisle*, when Flt Sgt Piece's aircraft was attacked in error by a 37th Squadron P-38 which inflicted sufficient damage to cause the pilot to crash land on return to base at Lakatamia.

Events on this date may also have reflected some degree of inexperience amongst the pilots of this US unit. Apart from Maj Leverette himself, every other pilot making claims during this engagement was still a 2nd Lieutenant and only one pilot (Lt Blue) had been credited with any claims prior to 9 October. Claims made against the Stukas had amounted to 16 destroyed, two probables and three damaged whereas actual losses had totalled seven of the dive-bombers. The situation had indeed been favourable to the Americans, allowing confirmations to be set at three destroyed for 2/Lt Sprinkle, five for 2/Lt Hanna and a remarkable seven for Maj Leverette.

A further attack on Greek targets – Athens, Argos, and Salonika – was made by more than 110 XII Bomber Command B-17s while 37 B-24s raided Rhodes and Heraklion. In the evening eight 82nd Fighter Group P-38s provided cover for four B-25Gs of 'G' Squadron (it will be recalled a detachment from the 321st Bomb Group) on a shipping strike over the Corfu-Dubrovnik area where at 1620 a Ju 88 of Einsatz Kampfgruppe – an operational training unit – was shot down by 2/Lt Robert Williams north of Kerkyra. Finally, as P-38s landed in the Gambut area at the end of an evening patrol, they found a fierce sandstorm in progress and had to divert to other fields where two of the unit's aircraft crash-landed.

Above: A formation of Ju 87D Stukas from StG 3 returning from a mission over the Aegean. Left: Smoke pours from the cruiser HMS *Carlisle* after being struck by four bombs dropped by Stukas of I./StG 3 causing heavy casualties.

British Claims

227 Sqn	Sgt J.A.Swift/Sgt G.F.Austin	Beaufighter VI JM276 'C'	Ar 196 Damaged	convoy 'Credential'	0830

British Casualties

252 Sqn   Beaufighter VI JM230 left 1340 to cover convoy 'Credential', damaged by a P-38, crash-landed at base 1543; Flt Sgt A.W.Piece/ Sgt J.P.Hopgood safe

US Claims

37th FS/82nd FG	2/Lt Wayne L.Blue	P-38G	Ju 88	10-20m E Scarpanto-W Rhodes	1217-1230
37th FS/82nd FG	Maj William L.Leverette	P-38G '81' *Stingaree*	7 Ju 87s	10-20m E Scarpanto-W Rhodes	1217-1230

37th FS/82nd FG	Maj William L.Leverette	P-38G '81' *Stingaree*	2 Ju 87s Damaged	10–20m E Scarpanto-W Rhodes	1217-1230
37th FS/82nd FG	2/Lt Harry T.Hanna	P-38G	5 Ju 87s	10–20m E Scarpanto-W Rhodes	1217-1230
37th FS/82nd FG	2/Lt Harry T.Hanna	P-38G	Ju 87 Damaged	10–20m E Scarpanto-W Rhodes	1217-1230
37th FS/82nd FG	2/Lt Homer L.Sprinkle	P-38G	3 Ju 87s	10–20m E Scarpanto-W Rhodes	1217-1230
37th FS/82nd FG	2/Lt Homer L.Sprinkle	P-38G	Ju 87 Probable	10–20m E Scarpanto-W Rhodes	1217-1230
37th FS/82nd FG	2/Lt Robert L.Margison	P-38G	Ju 87	10–20m E Scarpanto-W Rhodes	1217-1230
37th FS/82nd FG	2/Lt Elmer H.LaRue	P-38G	Ju 87 Probable	10–20m E Scarpanto-W Rhodes	1217-1230
97th FS/82nd FG	2/Lt Robert B.Williams Jr	P-38G	Ju 88	30m S Dubrovnik	1625

German Casualties

Eins.Gr Ju 88	Ju 88A-4 WNr 8830 K5+JL shot down by P-38 off N point Kerkyra, Corfu; Hptm Helmut Schüler (St.Kpt) and three KiA
2./StG 3	Ju 87D-4 WNr 110461 S7+AK shot down by ships' AA 30km S Cap Prasonisi; Uffz Siegfried Martens/Obfw Ernst Kröger MiA
3./StG 3	Ju 87D-4 WNr 2376 S7+OL shot down by ships' AA SW Rhodes; Lt Wolfgang Wendel/Fw Georg Scheller WiA
4./StG 3	Ju 87D-3 trop WNr 100375 S7+GM lost 40km SW Rhodes in combat with P-38; Lt Rudolf Metzger/Uffz Hans Sonnemann KiA
4./StG 3	Ju 87D-3 WNr 100378 S7+BC hit by P-38, force-landed at Rhodes, pilot safe, radio operator Obfw Hans Birkner DoW
5./StG 3	Ju 87D-3 WNr 1007 S7+HN hit by P-38, ditched SW Rhodes; Lt Otto Hecht/Hans Krajacic WiA, rescued
5./StG 3	Ju 87D-3 trop WNr 100380 S7+DN lost SW Rhodes in combat with P-38; Uffz Heinrich Manger/Gefr Erfried Prenissl MiA
5./StG 3	Ju 87D-3 trop WNr 110535 S7+AN lost SW Rhodes in combat with P-38; Hptm Peter von Heydebrandt (St.Kpt)/Uffz Herbert Bluschle MiA
6./StG 3	Ju 87D-3 trop WNr 110322 S7+FP lost SW Rhodes in combat with P-38; Uffz Josef Rose/Gefr Franz Neumann MiA
6./StG 3	Ju 87D-3 trop WNr 100374 S7+KP lost SW Rhodes in combat with P-38; Lt Horst Skambraks/Uffz Georg Peters MiA
6./StG 3	Ju 87D-3 trop WNr 110336 S7+MP lost SW Rhodes in combat with P-38; Lt Heinz Spielmann KiA/Fw Rudolf Malina WiA
I./StG 3	Ju 87D-4 trop WNr 1123 damaged by bombs at Heraklion
II./StG 3	Ar 66 WNr 1851 damaged by bombs at Argos
II./KG 6	Ju 88A-4 WNr 144697 20% damaged by bombs at Larissa
NAGr 2	Bf 109G-2 WNr 19962 destroyed by bombs at Larissa
NAGr 2	W 34 WNr 3176 destroyed by bombs at Larissa

Sunday, 10 October 1943

Sixty B-17s of 2nd, 99th, 301st and 97th Bomb Groups attacked Tatoi at 1200. Nineteen Bf 109s scrambled against this raid. Maj Rödel of Stab/JG 27 claimed one bomber and Oblt Schlang another, while Oblt Burk of 11./JG 27 claimed a third. The 99th Group recorded the loss of one B-17F. Oblt Dietrich Bösler, the commander of 12./JG 27, was shot down and killed in this fight by the bomber gunners. A Ju 88 of Einsatz KGr crashed on take-off at Tatoi, Oblt Georg Denkmann and crew being killed; the pilot was Fw Toni Rauch.

Six P-38s attacked the ships in Cattaro Bay at 0705, German tanker *John Knudsen*'s Flak detachment claimed one shot down, but the merchant vessel *Potestas* took on water from a near miss. No fighter losses were reported by the USAAF.

Nachtschlachtgruppe 7 was formed on this date at Zagreb. Maj Theodor Blaich was named commander. The Stab flew Ju 87s, 1./NSGr 7 was formed from Störkampfstaffel SüdOst and 2./NSGr 7 from Nahaufklärungsstaffel Kroatien, flying to the end of the year a mix of Hs 126s, Do 17s and He 46s.

US Casualties

348th BS/99th BG	B-17F 42-30446, bombing Tatoi a/f, hit by Flak, left formation, shot down by Bf 109s, crashed 15m inland on south side of Gulf of Corinth, five baled out near Perachora 1215-1230; 2/Lt Samuel B.Gilmore and four KiA, five POW/evaded [924]
352nd BS/301st BG	B-17F 42-30108, ditched 60m W of Cephalonia, Greece, due to bad weather on return flight from Tatoi; Lt Bowman and eight rescued, one KiA

German Claims

Flak	Tanker *John Knudsen*	P-38	Cattaro Bay	0705
11./JG 27	Oblt Alfred Burk	B-17	20km NW Megara	1204
Stab/JG 27	Oblt Josef Schlang	B-17	25km W Corinth	1215
Flak		B-17	Eleusis	1240
Stab/JG 27	Maj Gustav Rödel	B-17	Lamia	1250

German Casualties

12./JG 27	Bf 109G-6 WNr 18468 shot down in combat with B-17 nr Megara; Oblt Dietrich Bösler KiA
II./KG 51	Ju 88A-4 WNr 300154 lost at Salonika; Fw Herbert Schmidt and three KiA
II./KG 51	Ju 88A-4 WNr 550062 lost at Salonika; Uffz Franz Malcher and three KiA
1./Eins.Gr Ju 88	Ju 88A-4 WNr 0183 K5+AH crashed at Tatoi after combat with fighters; Fw Anton Rauch and three KiA, one WiA
2.(F)/123	2 Ju 88D-1s (WNrn 430865 and 430773) destroyed on the ground by bombs at Tatoi
2.(F)/123	5 Ju 88D-1 trops (WNrn 430090, 430772, 430625, 430575 and 1543) damaged by bombs at Tatoi
I./TG 4	Ju 52/3m WNr 3124 30% damaged by bombs at Tatoi
Flugber.X.Kps	Fi 156 WNr 4465 50% damaged by bombs at Tatoi

Monday, 11 October 1943

ML 835 was lost at 1700 after ten hours of bombing at Leros; the crew was safe.

German Casualties

II./KG 6	Ju 88A-4 WNr 82254 crashed E Larissa; Lt Gerhard Neubauer and two KiA, one WiA

Monday-Tuesday, 11/12 October 1943

462 Squadron lost a Halifax and the entire crew in what may have been an operational accident, as a fire was seen by another aircraft burning on the sea 90 miles south of Crete at 0216, and given no German Flak claims at this time it is possible that this was the missing aircraft.

British Casualties

462 Sqn	Halifax II BB417 left Terria 2040, failed to return from a raid on Maritza a/f; Flt Sgt M.F.Hall and five KiA

Tuesday, 12 October 1943

The Italian merchant vessel *Bucintoro* (1,273 tons) was sunk by aerial attack at Portolago, Leros.

British Casualties

227 Sqn	Beaufighter XI JM242 'Q' left 1605 on convoy patrol, engine trouble, ditched 1744, crew in dinghy, Lt A.E.Hounsom/Sgt W.H. Duncan rescued

Tuesday-Wednesday, 12/13 October 1943

At 0330 Germans began landing on Naxos (Ultra).

British Casualties

462 Sqn	Halifax II BB333 left 2351, crashed 7 minutes later and blew up; Flt Sgt K.E.M.Marsh and five KiA

Wednesday, 13 October 1943

British Claims

46 Sqn	Plt Off W.Jenkinson/Plt Off L.Charles	Beaufighter VI JL905	Ju 88 Damaged	8m S Castelrosso	1745
46 Sqn	Plt Off W.Jenkinson/Plt Off L.Charles	Beaufighter VI JL905	Cant.Z.506B no claim*	Castelrosso	1735
	*Friendly aircraft shot up in error. It was being used as an air ambulance. Attack aborted when colours of the day were fired and Red Cross seen. The floatplane landed at Castelrosso but then sank due to damage; Sqn Ldr Tom Balfour, Wt Off Skinner, Flt Sgt Allen, Cpl Fulton and the Italian doctor S.Ten Ubaldo Raffone safe.				

Italian Co-Belligerent Casualties

147ª Sq RM	Cant.Z.506B '147-1' damaged by Beaufighter, crash-landed at Castelrosso; Sqn Ldr T.Balfour and crew safe

German Casualties

II./StG 3	Ju 87D-3 trop WNr 100418 damaged by bombs at Maritza airfield
I./TG 4	Ju 52/3m destroyed by bombs at Tatoi; four men KiA

When taking off from LG 91 near Alexandria for a patrol on 13 October, Baltimore IV FA417 'N' 454 RAAF Squadron flown by Flt Sgt Curry hit a bump and crashed back onto the runway; the crew escaped injury.

Thursday, 14 October 1943

Thirty-six B-25s of 321st Bomb Group and 30 P-38s of 82nd Fighter Group returned to Argos at 0900, destroying one Bf 108 and damaging one Bf 109. Twenty-one Bf 109s were scrambled and one was shot down. Losses on the ground were a Bf 108 liaison aircraft of II./StG 3 50% damaged, ten groundmen killed and 30 wounded.

2.(H)/14 and 4.(H)/12 were incorporated into NAGr 11 on this date (according to Ultra).

British Claims					
46 Sqn	Flg Off J.S.Holland/Sgt H.E.Bruck	Beaufighter VI T5170	Ju 88 Damaged	over convoy	0705–1135
US Claims					
95th FS/82nd FG	Maj Hugh M.Muse	P-38	Bf 109	Argos	0745–1130
US Casualties					
95th FS/82nd FG	P-38G 42-12945 combat with 4 Bf 109s at 1000, last seen flying W Argos a/d; 2/Lt Stephen A.Plutt MiA [974]				
95th FS/82nd FG	P-38F 43-2105 probable mechanical failure, last seen 10–15 minutes off Italy on way to target; 2/Lt Harold I.Smith MiA [974]				
German Claims					
Flak			P-38	W Argos	0959
German Casualties					
III./JG 27	Bf 109G-6 WNr 17001 shot down in combat W Argos; pilot baled out safely				
5./KG 6	Ju 88A-14 WNr 144344 3E+CN hit by Flak 30km E Leros, landed in Turkey; Lt Egon Ruhland and three interned				
5./KG 6	Ju 88A-4 hit by Flak over Leros, landed safely; pilot and two crew safe, Uffz Michael Müller KiA				
II./StG 3	Bf 108 WNr 834 50% damaged at Argos a/f by bombs				

Friday, 15 October 1943

B-25s raided Salonika-Sedes and Megalo Mikra. At Salonika a Ju 88 from II./KG 51 was destroyed and four were damaged; in addition a Klemm 35 was destroyed.

A Baltimore of 454 Squadron on a convoy escort was mistakenly attacked and badly damaged by a Beaufighter at 1200.

British Casualties					
454 Sqn	Baltimore IV FA590 badly damaged off Castelrosso at 1200 hours by a Beaufighter; Flg Off D.W.Lewis and three safe				
German Casualties					
II./KG 51	Ju 88A-4 WNr 8878 destroyed and 3 (WNrn 300374, 300146 and 694) damaged by bombs at Sedes				
II./KG 51	Ju 88A-14 WNr 4062 25% damaged by bombs at Sedes				
II./KG 51	Kl 35 WNr 3040 destroyed by bombs at Sedes				
II./TG 4	Ju 52/3m WNr 3318 30% damaged by bombs at Megara; Uffz Markschlägel safe				
5./KG 6	Ju 88A-4 WNr 300367 hit by AA, crash-landed at Paros; Lt Werner Unverfehrt and three safe				

Saturday, 16 October 1943

A Do 24 was lost on a sea rescue: the flyingboat landed near Amorgos to pick up survivors of German MV *Kari* (1,925 tons, ex-French *S.te Colette*, sunk by HMS *Torbay*), but on taking off the aircraft dug a wingtip into the water and crashed. The crew was picked up by *UJ 2110*.

Seven aircraft attacked *LS 5* off Kos and the boat had to be run aground at about 1515.

German Casualties	
7.Seenotst.	Do 24T-2 WNr 0071 VH+SK crashed 10km W Amorgos; crew (two WiA) and 18 survivors of *Kari* rescued by *UJ 2110*

Sunday, 17 October 1943

HMS *Sirius* proceeding from Alexandria to the Aegean with HMS *Eclipse*, *Pathfinder* and *Belvoir* was hit by a bomb on the quarter deck in a raid by Ju 88s at 1830 and returned to Alexandria. Her casualties were 14 men killed and 30 wounded.

British Claims					
252 Sqn	Sgt W.Davenport/Sgt C.P.Grainger	Beaufighter VI EL403	2 Ju 88s Damaged	convoy 'Datum'	1547-2100
British Casualties					
252 Sqn	Beaufighter VI EL403 left 1547, damaged by return fire from Ju 88s; Sgt W.Davenport/Sgt C.P.Grainger safe				
227 Sqn	Beaufighter VI JL735 'W' left 0450 on convoy patrol, engine trouble, ditched; Sgt R.S.Reid safe/Sgt H.C.Seymour KiA, pilot rescued by Walrus W2709 flown by Wt Off F.E.Tutton				
German Claims					
1./SAGr 126	crew	Ar 196	Beaufighter	S Rhodes	
1./SAGr 126	crew	Ar 196	Beaufighter Probable	S Rhodes	
German Casualties					
II./KG 51	Ju 88A-4 WNr 300369 crashed into sea NW Heraklion; Lt Norbert Marawitzek and one WiA, two KiA				
7.Seenotst.	Do 24T-3 WNr 3211 KO+KA destroyed N Chania; Uffz Mathias Schneider and one WiA, rest of crew safe				

Monday, 18 October 1943

Eleven Ju 88s of KG 6 attacked Castelrosso harbour, one bomber broke away due to engine trouble and two were shot down. Presumably Oblt Hammel was leading the ASR escort when he came across a 46 Squadron Beaufighter and shot it down.

Thirty-six B-25s of the 321th Bomb Group, escorted by 12 P-38s of the 95th Squadron of the 82nd Fighter Group, targeted the marshalling yards of Skopje, while 12 P-38s each of the 96th and 97th Squadrons dropped bombs on a rail bridge and signal building 6km south-east of the town between 1220 and 1245. Seeing a motorized column near the city, the 82nd Fighter Group launched a second mission with 28 aircraft, back over Vardar valley four hours later. The raid caused significant damage to the infrastructure and left 30 civilians and three German soldiers dead. Two pairs of Bulgarian Bf 109s from 3/6 IO fighter unit were scrambled from Bozhurishte but failed to make contact with the intruders. This was, however, the first involvement of the Bulgarian air force in this theatre which was to become an important part of the strategic activities of the US heavy bombers from now on. While mention will continue to be made of activities which impinge on Tactical Air Force operations, it is our intention that detailed coverage of such matters will essentially be reserved to Volume 6 of this series.

British Claims					
213 Sqn	Flt Lt H.R.Rowlands	Hurricane IIc HL912 'C'	Ju 88	20m from Castelrosso	0933
213 Sqn	Plt Off R.Jackson	Hurricane IIc HL889 'X'	Ju 88	20m from Castelrosso	0933
213 Sqn	Wt Off P.C.Haslam	Hurricane IIc KW934 'I'	Ju 88	N Ro Island	0933

British Casualties				
46 Sqn	Beaufighter XI JM249 shot down by Bf 109 off Castelrosso; Flg Off J.S.Holland rescued/Sgt H.E.Bruck DoW			

US Casualties				
97th FS/82nd FG	P-38G 43-2552 strafing 8m W Skopje, hit ammunition dump which exploded and resulted in a/c crashing 1635; 2/Lt John Homan Jr MiA [990]			

German Claims				
8./JG 27	Oblt Kurt Hammel	Beaufighter	SW Castelrosso	1120

German Casualties				
4./KG 6	Ju 88A-14 WNr 144323 3E+CM lost on mission to Castelrosso; Uffz Karl-Heinz Lilienthal and three MiA			
6./KG 6	Ju 88A-14 WNr 144358 3E+AP lost on mission to Castelrosso; Uffz Heinz Walther and three MiA			

Monday-Tuesday, 18/19 October 1943

At 2309 the German merchant ship *Sinfra* (4,470 tons, ex-French) was sited by Flt Sgt Peighton, flying Wellington MP640 of 38 Squadron; Peighton dropped his torpedo that missed astern and homed other aircraft to the scene. The first two to arrive were Sqn Ldr John M.Milburn (in HZ378 'A') and Flt Sgt D.A.Mitchell (in MH655 'K'), both of whom launched their torpedoes. The weapon dropped by Milburn apparently hit the ship aft of amidships but the other appeared to miss. Mitchell's aircraft was then hit by Flak and the navigator was wounded. *Sinfra* sank off Suda Bay. About 2,300 Italian prisoners were aboard plus 300 Germans, some 2,000 of whom were lost. 38 Squadron's crews noted that the fire could be seen from 30 miles away.

British Casualties	
38 Sqn	Wellington VIII MP655 'K' left 2030 on offensive sweep, hit by Flak while attacking a ship E Antikythera, navigator being wounded, landed safely; Flt Sgt D.A.Mitchell and four safe, Flg Off G.Bird WiA

Tuesday, 19 October 1943

A Do 24 of 7.Seenotstaffel was lost. This aircraft had previously picked up 33 survivors and landed to rescue more when it was attacked by a Beaufighter of 227 Squadron; it was later taken in tow by *Fl.B 435* but sank.

British Claims					
227 Sqn	Flt Lt J.Watters/Wt Off F.Burrow	Beaufighter JM407 'G'	Ar 196	20m NE Cap Spatha	1250
227 Sqn	unstated	Beaufighter	Do 24 on the sea	20m NE Cap Spatha	1250

German Casualties	
7.Seenotst.	Do 24T-3 WNr 3214 KO+KD strafed and sunk by Beaufighters, NE Cape Spatha, Crete; pilot and one safe, two WiA

Wednesday, 20 October 1943

British Claims				
227 Sqn	Plt Off A.C.Gibbard/Sgt B.H.L.Blake	Beaufighter VI JL900 'S'	Ju 88	1810-1820

German Casualties	
1.(F)/122	Ju 88D-1 WNr 430213 F6+AH shot down 120km S Rhodes by Beaufighter; Oblt Walter Panchyrz and three MiA, rescued by Ar 196s on 23 October
Eins.Gr Ju 88	Ju 88A-4 WNr 0141 hit by Flak, crash-landed at Eleusis; Fw Hermann Reisinger and three WiA

Thursday, 21 October 1943

The 82nd Fighter Group returned to Skopje on this date, a dozen P-38s each from the 95th and 97th Squadrons being dispatched to dive-bomb the locomotive sheds. Less than ten Bulgarian Bf 109s scrambled and claimed one Lightning 45km north-east of Scutari.

On this day III./JG 27 transferred to Podgorica to counter raids in Serbo-Croat and Northern Greece areas.

German Casualties	
1.(F)/122	Ju 88A-4 trop WNr 5745 F6+PH lost u/k cause SW Rhodes; Uffz Kurt Backenhausen and three MiA
Flber.X.Kps	Fi 156C-3 trop WNr 8083 BP+MH lost SW Patiopoulo

Friday, 22 October 1943

After midday eight P-38s strafed Antimachia airfield on Kos. Stampalia Island was captured by the Germans. A heavy air raid occurred in the morning, parachutists were dropped and landed by seaplane. LKS reported losses of two Bf 109s and one Ju 88.

German Claims

Flak		P-38	8km NW Eleusis	1225
Flak		P-38	NW Eleusis	1226
Flak		B-26	Eleusis	

German Casualties

III./JG 27	Bf 109G-6 WNr 140014 shot down in combat S Tanagra; Uffz Karl Stumpf KiA
III./JG 27	Bf 109G-6 WNr 20556 shot down in combat W Thebes; Fw Johann Sahl KiA
6./KG 6	Ju 88A-4 WNr 550094 3E-NP ditched near Naxos; Oblt Wolfgang Faber and three MiA
I./StG 3	Ju 87D-3 trop WNr 2700 80% damaged by bombs at Maritza

Saturday, 23 October 1943

British Casualties

227 Sqn	Beaufighter VI JM277 'E' lost on return from convoy patrol near base at Lakatamia; Sgt T.C.Morfitt/Sgt H.Jackson KiA

German Casualties

II./StG 3	Ju 87D-3 trop WNr 110531 damaged by Flak at Calino Island; crew safe
II./TG 4	Ju 52/3m WNr 7616 G6+LS lost Podgorica-Belgrade; Stfw Walter Risch and four MiA

Sunday, 24 October 1943

Four Ar 196s rescued a Baltimore crew shot down at Gavdos.

British Casualties

13(H) Sqn	Baltimore IV FA483 'B' left 1007, shot down near Gavdos Island and ditched; Flg Off N.Coskinas and one rescued by Ar 196s, POW, two KiA
94 Sqn	Hurricane IIc HL841 on convoy patrol, ditched off Benghazi; Flg Off M.P.Northmore KiA
680 Sqn	Spitfire IV BR414 left 0700 from Nicosia on photo reconnaissance of Dodecanese Islands, flew into a hill near Bodrum in Turkey; Plt Off G.L.L.Hay KiA

German Claims

Flak		Baltimore	5km S Gavdos	1051

German Casualties

3./Eins.KG Ju 88	Ju 88A-4 WNr 1267 K5+AL lost Samos-Leros, presumed engine failure; Lt Werner Kley and three MiA
2./Eins.KG Ju 88	Ju 88A-4 WNr 5716 K5+FJ lost Samos-Leros, presumed engine failure; Lt Alfons Firlus and three MiA

Tuesday, 26 October 1943

Thirty-six B-25s of the 321st Bomb Group and 12 P-38s attacked airfields at Salonika-Sedes and Megalo-Mikra at about 1245. *ML 579* was destroyed by bombs at Lipsos; two officers and two of the crew were killed, the remaining 13 being rescued. The Italian *MAS 534* and the torpedo-boat *MS 15* were sunk by German bombers at Leros.

British Claims

47 Sqn	Flg Off J.B.Fletcher/Flg Off T.E.Jones Beaufighter 'J'		Ju 52/3m floatplane S Amorgos	1534
47 Sqn	Flg Off J.B.Fletcher/Flg Off T.E.Jones Beaufighter 'J'		Ar 196 Damaged S Amorgos	1534

US Claims

'G' Sqn/321st BG	Flt Off James L.Peplinski	B-25G 42-6458	} Ju 52/3m Probable S Amorgos	1520–1530	
'G' Sqn/321st BG	Flt Off Charles F.Keith	B-25G 42-32487 *Black Magic*			
'G' Sqn/321st BG	2/Lt Angelo M.C.Durante	B-25G 42-64587 *Red Nosed Beckie*			
'G' Sqn/321st BG	Flt Off James L.Peplinski	B-25G 42-6458	} Ju 52/3m Damaged S Amorgos	1520–1530	
'G' Sqn/321st BG	Flt Off Charles F.Keith	B-25G 42-32487 *Black Magic*			
'G' Sqn/321st BG	2/Lt Angelo M.C.Durante	B-25G 42-64587 *Red Nosed Beckie*			

US Casualties

'G' Sqn/321st BG	B-25G 42-64580 starboard engine shot out by Ar 196 S Amorgos 1530, regained base safely; Flt Off James L.Peplinski and crew safe

German Casualties

Transportst. (See) 1	Ju 52/3m See WNr 6162 destroyed by fighters Phaleron-Stampalia; crew safe
Transportst. (See) 1	Ju 52/3m See WNr 6922 damaged by fighters Phaleron-Stampalia; crew safe, one WiA
2./SAGr 126	Ar 196A-3 WNr 0382 D1+DK escorted Ju 52/3ms, shot down in combat with Beaufighter 8km NW Stampalia; Uffz Heinrich Leifeld/Lt Hans Klindert KiA
II./KG 51	2 Ju 88A-4s WNrn 300271 and 300375 damaged on ground by bombs at Salonika/Sedes
Eins.Gr Ju 88	Ju 88A-4 WNr 0140 80% damaged by own Flak at Eleusis

Wednesday, 27 October 1943

LCTs *104* and *115* on passage to Castelrosso from Haifa were attacked by 12 Stukas within sight of the island at 1800 and LCT *115* was sunk. There were 22 naval but no military casualties.

British Claims

227 Sqn	Sgt G.Fowkes/Sgt E.A.Webber	Beaufighter VI LX998 'N'	} Ju 88 Damaged	7m S convoy 'Extend'	1430
227 Sqn	Flt Sgt K.G.Thomas/Sgt J.Thorogood	Beaufighter VI EL301 'Y'			
46 Sqn	Wt Off A.Boswell/Sgt H.B.Lawn	Beaufighter VI JL894			
46 Sqn	Flg Off B.F.Wild/Flt Sgt R.Gibbon	Beaufighter VI EL475			
46 Sqn	Flt Lt D.R.Arundel/Flt Sgt J.McDermot	Beaufighter VI JL898	} 3 Ju 88s Damaged	Castelrosso	1015
46 Sqn	Flg Off J.A.Horsfall/Sgt J.R.Colley	Beaufighter VI JM248			

German Claims

Flak			Blenheim	Kos	

Wednesday-Thursday, 27/28 October 1943

British Casualties

38 Sqn	Wellington XIII HZ603 left Nicosia 1827 to reconnaissance Aegean, nothing heard after take-off; Flt Sgt C.D.Duberry and six KiA

Thursday, 28 October 1943

British Casualties

15 SAAF Sqn	Baltimore IV FA525 'J' left 1400, from Scarpanto to Crete, last seen 1548 10m SE Scarpanto; Lt R.M.Tucker and three KiA
15 SAAF Sqn	Baltimore IV FA458 'F' left 1400 on recce from Scarpanto to Crete, last seen 1548 10m SE Scarpanto; Lt I.M.Meiring and three KiA
15 SAAF Sqn	Baltimore IV FA659 'G' left 1400 on recce from Scarpanto to Crete, last seen 1548 10m SE Scarpanto; Capt P.A.Van Velzen and three KiA

German Claims

8./JG 27	Oblt Kurt Hammel	Maryland	S Chalki Island	1433
8./JG 27	Ofhr Alexander Ottnad	Maryland	S Chalki Island	1434
8./JG 27	Gefr Friedrich Ullrich	Maryland	NW of Rhodes	1435

German Casualties

8./JG 27	Bf 109G-6 WNr 140044 crashed N Chalki; Obfw Hans Niederhöfer WiA

Thursday-Friday, 28/29 October 1943

German Casualties

II./StG 3	Ju 87D-3 trop WNr 110497 destroyed by bombs at Maritza

Friday, 29 October 1943

British Claims

47 Sqn	Flg Off J.A.Unwin/Sgt K.R.Farmer	Beaufighter 'F'	Ar 196 Damaged	SE Naxos	1025

British Casualties

| 47 Sqn | Beaufighter X JM255 'W' shot down by Ar 196 SE Naxos at 1025; Flg Off J.Dixon/Flg Off G.A.Terry MiA | | | |

German Claims

| 2./SAGr 126 | Obfw Hahlbohm | Ar 196 | Beaufighter | Naxos |
| Flak | ships | | Beaufighter | |

German Casualties

| 7.Seenotst. | Do 24T-2 WNr 0032 CH+EX lost nr Naxos, possibly related to the sinking of *Ingeborg* by HMS *Unsparing*; Uffz Hans Lieber and one rescued, four KiA | | | |

Saturday, 30 October 1943

At 1059 Beaufighters of 227 Squadron were vectored onto a plot at sea level. A lone Ju 88 was indeed found there and at 1112 they attacked the Ju 88 of Lt Walter Plattner from 2.(F)/123. Flg Off Kendall fired three short bursts while closing to 300 yards, as the Ju 88 gunner shot back. Flg Off Mazur then attacked closing to 400 yards and firing a burst while the Ju 88 broke hard to starboard. Mazur then attacked from dead astern with a burst at 300 yards and the Ju 88 broke again. This time Mazur could follow and fired again. Hits were observed mid-way up the fuselage, silencing the gunner. Finally, Kendall attacked and although the Ju 88 was still taking evasive action a five-second burst from 200 yards hit both engines and the front of the fuselage, whereupon the Ju 88 dived straight into the sea. The successful crews landed at 1245.

HMS *Aurora* (12th Cruiser Squadron), HMS *Petard*, *Beaufort* and *Belvoir* while proceeding towards the Rhodes Channel were bombed at 1532 by two Ju 88s without suffering damage, and again by 13 Ju 88s in Turkish waters where *Aurora* was hit by a 500kg bomb abaft the after funnel. Extensive damage to the after structure included armament fires caused by the detonation of ammunition; 47 personnel were killed and 30 wounded. *Belvoir* received slight damage from a hit by an unexploded bomb. The crews of the Ju 88s thought their bombs had missed.

Dornier Do 24 flying boats were extensively used for air-sea rescue and transport work throughout the Aegean Islands though when looking for survivors from a sunken ship CH+EX of 7.Seenotstaffel was lost.

The tail of 227 Squadron Beaufighter VIc EL467 'B' shows the damage after being attacked by a Bf 109G flown by Fw Hannes Löffler near Castelrosso, not a MC.202 as reported by the crew.

Four more Beaufighters from 227 Squadron left at 1600 to provide cover to the 'Nettle' convoy. This patrol at 1800 hours sighted two groups each of four Ju 88s in vic formations at 14,000 feet west of Castelrosso. One group was reportedly carrying bombs and the other acting as escorts. The Beaufighters attacked. Flg Off B.J.Beare/Sgt C.E.Humphreys selected a Ju 88 at 12,000ft and fired from 150 to 30 yards causing it to burst into flames and explode. A second Ju 88 at 10,000ft was attacked from the starboard quarter, firing from 200 to 50 yards; the starboard engine caught fire and the aircraft crashed into the sea in a mass of flames. Beare then attacked a third Ju 88 from head on at 4,000ft and again the starboard engine caught fire and also this aircraft crashed into the sea in flames. Plt Off W.Yurchison/Plt Off P.M.Wroath attacked a Ju 88 at 9,000ft shooting from 400 to 300 yards, the fuselage caught fire and the Ju 88 crashed in flames into the sea. Flt Lt W.R.Kemp/Flg Off C.S.Wyles attacked four Ju 88s at 11,000ft and opened fire at 400 yards but while firing he stalled the aircraft and on pulling out at 11,500ft was attacked by a Ju 88 from astern which shot away the rudder controls, the hydraulic system and badly holed the fuselage. Flg Off Weares' guns jammed and he was unable to return fire. Four German aircraft were reported to have been seen burning in the sea and another flying towards Rhodes at 10,500ft in a shallow dive with the starboard engine on fire. An unidentified crew from 11./ZG 26 claimed one Beaufighter shot down, which appeared to be that flown by Kemp but he too limped back to base where he crash-landed at 2030. 227 Squadron reported four fires on the sea and four parachutes in the air and estimated the latter would land about 4m west of Castelrosso.

As a matter of fact four Ju 88s from the Einsatz Gruppe led by Hptm Gunther Fischer (attached from 1./LG 1) left Eleusis at 1410 and attacked at 1700. Two Ju 88s were shot down; it would appear that Beare and Yurchison shot down one Ju 88 each and the three seen with their starboard engine on fire made it to Rhodes and landed.

227 Sqn	Flg Off P.A.Mazur/Flg Off K.Stakes	Beaufighter VI X7819 'V'	} Ju 88		convoy 'Nostril'	1122
227 Sqn	Flg Off J.M. Kendall/Flg Off R.Mackay	Beaufighter VI HL478 'F'				
227 Sqn	Plt Off W.Yurchison/Plt Off P.M.Wroath	Beaufighter VI JL939 'G'	Ju 88	5-10m E Castelrosso		1800
227 Sqn	Flt Lt W.R.Kemp/Flg Off C.S.Wyles	Beaufighter VI JM268 'N'	Ju 88 Probable	5-10m E Castelrosso		1800
227 Sqn	Flg Off B.J.Beare/Sgt C.E.Humphreys	Beaufighter VI JL900 'S'	3 Ju 88s	5-10m E Castelrosso		1800, 1803
						& 1805

British Casualties

213 Sqn	Hurricane IIC HV587 left 1150 on convoy escort, engine failed 1210, pilot baled out; Plt Off L.P.Geoffrion rescued
47 Sqn	Beaufighter VI JM317 'S' shot down by Flak at Naxos 1545; Flg Off J.E.Hayter/Wt Off T.J.Harper (603 Sqn) evaded
227 Sqn	Beaufighter VI JM268 'N' shot up by Ju 88C E Castelrosso 1800, crash-landed at base; Flt Lt W.R.Kemp/Flg Off C.S.Wyles safe
227 Sqn	Beaufighter VIc EL467 'B' damaged by MC.202 near Castelrosso 1615, landed at base safely, Sgt E.C.James/Sgt E.L.Linfield safe
252 Sqn	Beaufighter VI X8159 left 1350, shot up by fighter, landed safely at base 1855; Sgt F.P.Stanger/Sgt J.Poulton safe

US Casualties

'G' Sqn 446th BS/321st BG	B-25G 42-64579 *Flying Caisson* shot down by Flak 2m NW Naxos harbour 1555; 2/Lt Gordon J.Black and five KiA [1137]

German Claims

Flak			Beaufighter	Naxos	1445
9./JG 27	Uffz Hannes Löffler		Beaufighter	S Castelrosso	1515
11./ZG 26	unstated	Ju 88C	Beaufighter	Castelrosso	1700

German Casualties

2.(F)/123	Ju 88A-4 WNr 300142 4U+GK lost S Rhodes; Lt Walter Plattner and three MiA
1./Eins.Gr Ju 88	Ju 88A-4 WNr 0231 K5+AB shot down by fighters W Castelrosso; Lt Wilhelm Glaser and three KiA
3./Eins.Gr Ju 88	Ju 88A-4 WNr 3932 K5+BL shot down by fighters W Castelrosso; Uffz Erich Grimmer and three KiA
4./KG 6	Ju 88A-14 WNr 144458 3E+HM shot down by AA eastern Mediterranean; Fw Johann Vogelsang and three MiA

Sunday-Monday, 31 October/1 November 1943 (see also Vol. 4)

216 Squadron carried Greek paratroops (the Greek Sacreda Squadron) to drop onto Samos, but an aircraft encountered difficulties, running out of fuel while attempting to reach Nicosia, forcing the crew to bale out over Turkey.

British Casualties

216 Sqn	Dakota III FD829 ran out of fuel returning from paratroop drop on Samos, crew baled out over Turkey; Flt Lt B.Smith DFC and five interned

Appreciation of Events for October 1943

The month opened with the German domination of the skies over the Aegean firmly established from airfields in Crete, Rhodes and the Greek mainland, from where they were able to neutralize British airfields in Kos. That island itself was subsequently invaded by German forces and was occupied on the 3rd; with it was lost the last hope of staging a frontal assault on Rhodes for which the Kos airfield was considered to be a prerequisite. It was decided to maintain the precarious foothold inside the 'Iron Ring' for as long as possible and the pursuance of this policy developed into a struggle between the Royal Navy and the Luftwaffe.

In the face of these adverse conditions, HMS *Sirius* and *Penelope* with destroyers sunk a convoy off Stampalia in daylight on the 7th and withdrew at the cost of a bomb-damaged *Penelope*. After carrying out a similar sweep two days later, HMS *Panther* was sunk and HMS *Carlisle* seriously damaged whilst leaving the Scarpanto Strait under heavy air attack. The escorting Lightnings inflicted casualties but it was evident that fighter protection could not be maintained on an adequate scale so far from Allied air bases and so close to the enemy's. Most fortunately, Turkey did not object to Allied use of her territorial waters for maintaining destroyers in a position of comparative safety during the day from which they could operate with some confidence under the cover of darkness. (Ultra reported that Hitler had specifically forbidden any attacks inside Turkish territorial waters, which was of more relevance.)

Monday, 1 November 1943 (see also Vol. 4)

In line with the reclassification and renaming of Stuka units throughout the Luftwaffe as Schlacht units, on this date II./StG 3 at Maritza became II./SG 3, its 27 Ju 87D-3s on strength being appropriately reclassified.

British Casualties	
203 Sqn	Baltimore V FW301 left 0930 missing from reconnaissance sortie; Flt Sgt C.J.Withers and three MiA

German Casualties	
II./TG 4	Ju 52/3m WNr 3224 shot down by fighters 6km S Podgorica; Flg Xaver Resch, six crew and twelve passengers KiA
2./NAGr 2	Bf 109G-6 WNr 15506 crashed W Megara; Hptm Horst Scheibel (St.Kpt) KiA

Tuesday-Wednesday, 2/3 November 1943 (see also Vol. 4)

178 Squadron sent three Liberators to bomb Heraklion, in conjunction with 462 Squadron's Halifaxes. These two heavy bomber squadrons were the main such units operating in support of Aegean operations and almost always operated together and attacked the same targets. From the occupation of Kos by the Allies in mid-September, their routine operations became attacking airfields, either those on Crete or those on Rhodes, with occasional raids on those in mainland Greece.

German Casualties	
2./KG 100	He 111H-13 WNr 7937 6N+CN lost u/k cause; Fw Wilhelm Wehlam and three MiA

Wednesday, 3 November 1943 (see also Vol. 4)

Forty-eight B-25s of the 321st Bomb Group, escorted by P-38s, targeted Araxos and Eleusis airfields, German records identifying the attackers as 50 Marauders which they categorised as dropping 'a few' bombs. They also reported that this represented the first use of Marauders over Balkan targets, most of which apparently missed the airfields. On this occasion 14 Bf 109s of III./JG 27 were scrambled at 0743. Lt Culemann underwrote the faulty recognition by claiming his victim as a Marauder although the Flak defences got it right, claiming another of the bombers as a B-25. The same formation then bombed Araxos, destroyed two Italian aircraft and slightly damaged two German ones.

US Claims					
447th BS/321st BG	gunner S/Sgt Harold H.Dexter	B-25C 42-64546	} Bf 109 Probable	Eleusis	0805
447th BS/321st BG	gunner S/Sgt Boyd F.Tracey	B-25C 42-64600			
447th BS/321st BG	gunner Sgt Harry B.Harmer	B-25C 41-30557	Bf 109 Probable	Eleusis	0805
447th BS/321st BG	gunner S/Sgt William R.Henry	B-25C 42-64695	Bf 109 Damaged	Eleusis 0805	0805

US Casualties	
445th BS/321st BG	B-25C 42-32486 *Censored* shot down by Flak W Eleusis 0805; 2/Lt Gail G.Miller and five KiA [1198]
447th BS/321st BG	B-25C 42-64600 *Lady Luck* damaged by Bf 109 Eleusis-Araxos 0805, returned safely; 2/Lt Harry A.Fraser Jr and six safe
447th BS/321st BG	B-25C 42-64546 *Jessie James* damaged by Bf 109 Eleusis-Araxos 0805, returned safely; 1/Lt Ellwood H.Beeson and five safe, Lt Devlin picked up by 283 Sqn

German Claims				
Flak		B-25	2km SW Eleusis	0800
Stab III./JG 27	Lt Hans-Gunnar Culemann	Marauder	SW Eleusis	0805

Friday, 5 November 1943

The morning was opened by a sweep over Rhodes by six Beaufighters of 227 Squadron which brought a scramble by four Bf 109s of 8./JG 27, the pilots of which then gave chase, shooting down four of the British aircraft within about three minutes. Two Beaufighters got away, one after their aircraft had been hit twice, but all eight aircrew of the aircraft shot down were killed.

Some four to five hours later three torpedo-carrying aircraft of 47 Squadron escorted by four more from 603 Squadron launched an attack on three merchant vessels in Lavrion Bay. Here, however, the Flak was deadly and two of the attackers were shot down, including that flown by Wg Cdr J.A.Lee-Evans, DFC, after he had dropped his torpedo. On this occasion both crews survived being shot down and became POWs.

3./SAGr 126 transferred to Skaramanga to support Operation *Tragic*, the Germans' next planned invasion of an occupied Aegean Island, which had been delayed for some days due to bad weather.

British Casualties

227 Sqn	Beaufighter VI JL900 'S' shot down by Bf 109 N Rhodes 0950–1000; Flt Lt J.P.Tremlett/Flt Sgt R.E.Jobling KiA
227 Sqn	Beaufighter VI EL478 'F' shot down by Bf 109 N Rhodes 0950–1000; Flt Sgt J.A. Swift/Flt Sgt G.F.Austin KiA
227 Sqn	Beaufighter VI JL939 'G' shot down by Bf 109 N Rhodes 0950–1000; Plt Off W.Yurchison /Plt Off P.M.Wroath KiA
227 Sqn	Beaufighter VI JM276 'C' shot down by Bf 109 N Rhodes 0950–1000; Flg Off P.A.Mazur/Fg Off K.Stakes KiA
47 Sqn	Beaufighter X 'D' shot down by Flak attacking shipping in Lavrion Bay 1500; Wg Cdr J.A.Lee-Evans/Flt Lt D.Hedon POW
47 Sqn	Beaufighter X 'B' shot down by Flak attacking shipping in Lavrion Bay 1500; Flt Lt T.C.Graham/Flg Off J.H.K.Langdon POW

German Claims

8./JG 27	Gefr Heinrich Pothmann	Beaufighter	SW Gadurra	0825
8./JG 27	Fw Alfred Stückler	Beaufighter	SW Gadurra	0827
8./JG 27	Ofhr Alexander Ottnad	Beaufighter	SW Gadurra	0828
8./JG 27	FhjUffz Friedrich Ullrich	Beaufighter	S Gadurra	0828
Flak		Beaufighter	NW Launion	1246
Flak		Beaufighter	NW Launion	1246
Flak		Beaufighter	3km SE Launion	1250

German Casualties

II./SG 3	Ju 87D-3 WNr 100385 destroyed by bombs at Maritza

Friday-Saturday, 5/6 November 1943

The General der Schlachtflieger, Obstltn Dr Ernst Kupfer, was killed when his aircraft crashed into mountains in northern Greece.

German Casualties

Gen.d.Schl.Fl	He 111 H-6 WNr 7455 flew into mountains 60km N Salonika, NE Lake Dorian; Obfw Willi Reeg, three crew and Obstltn Dr Ernst Kupfer (General der Schlachtflieger) KiA

Saturday, 6 November 1943

Four Beaufighters of 47 Squadron and four of 603 Squadron attacked barges in Naussa Bay, also reporting encountering eight Ar 196s and five Bf 109s. Pilots from III./JG 27 had been flying regular patrols all morning, during the latest of which pilots from 7.Staffel reported encountering six of the British fighters over some German ships. A dogfight commenced during which two 47 Squadron aircraft were shot down, one disappearing in a fight with Bf 109s while the second was seen to go down in flames, apparently the victim of an Arado. One of the 603 Squadron aircraft ditched after claiming one Ar 196 shot down – apparently once more victim of a Messerschmitt – he and his navigator then being picked up by HMS *Unrivalled*. One further Beaufighter was damaged by an Arado and crash-landed at Gambut on return. In their ten-minute battle with the RAF, the Luftwaffe pilots seemed to have achieved four victories without loss – although the Flak gunners laid claim to three more of these.

Ultra reports indicated that two German ships, *GA 45* and *GA 42*, escorting an Operation *Tragic* invasion convoy, were sunk by aircraft during this day's attacks.

British Claims

603 Sqn	Plt Off K.I.E.Hopkins/Wt Off K.V.Roget	Beaufighter X LX998 'Y'	Ar 196	Yanni Bay Paros	1415
603 Sqn	Plt Off R.M.Giles/Flt Sgt L.Coulstock	Beaufighter X LZ148 'H'	Ar 196 Damaged	Yanni Bay Paros	1415

British Casualties

39 Sqn	Beaufighter X LZ142 'Y' lost in bad weather transferring from Grottaglie to Sidi Amor; Wt Off J.R.Power/Flt Sgt W.D.Paul MiA
47 Sqn	Beaufighter X JM403 'F' shot down by Ar 196 N Langeri Bay Paros 1415; Flg Off L.Rossner/Flt Sgt H.K.Levy KiA
47 Sqn	Beaufighter X JM352 'R' shot down by Bf 109 at Port Naussa, Paros 1415; Sqn Ldr C.A.Ogilvie/Flg Off M.O'Connor evaded
603 Sqn	Beaufighter X LX998 'Y' shot down by Bf 109, ditched 5m S Amorgos 1415; Plt Off K.I.E.Hopkins/Wt Off K.V.Roget rescued by HMS *Unrivalled*
603 Sqn	Beaufighter X LX985 'M' damaged by Ar 196 at Yanni Bay Paros 1415, crash-landed at Gambut; Flt Sgt T.Truesdale WiA/Flt Sgt E.Oldfield safe

German Claims					
Flak			Beaufighter	3km N Naussa	1316
Flak			Beaufighter	5km SW Naussa	1317
Flak			Beaufighter	7km N Paros	1318
7./JG 27	Uffz Karl Höchtl		Beaufighter	SE Tripodo	1320
7./JG 27	Uffz Paul Martin		Beaufighter	SE Naussa	1325
I./SAGr 126	unstated	Ar 196	Beaufighter	Paros	
I./SAGr 126	unstated	Ar 196	Beaufighter	Paros	

German Casualties	
4./SAGr 126	Ar 196A-3 WNr 384 shot down by Beaufighter NW Amorgos; pilot safe, Uffz Walter Kleinknecht KiA

Sunday, 7 November 1943

British Claims				
227 Sqn	Flg Off B.J.Beare/Sgt C.Humphreys	Beaufighter VI JL619 'X'	Ju 88 Damaged	1026

German Casualties	
I./TG 4	Ju 52/3m WNr 3320 crashed into mountain on take-off from Rhodes; Oblt Heinz Petzold, three crew and nine passengers KiA

Sunday-Monday, 7/8 November 1943

Flg Off R.W.Adams and his crew had an exciting time when they left to attack shipping in Naxos harbour. They sighted a ship in the harbour and attacked at about 0100, the first strike missed and in the second attack a bomb hit the ship. Defending Flak struck the Wellington in the starboard engine and a shell entered the cabin, without injuring the crew. The starboard engine's propeller would not feather due to damage, height could not be maintained, and the Wellington ditched some fifteen minutes later 1½ miles south-east of Syphnos Island. When the aircraft failed to return the crew were reported as missing and the casualty signals were sent by 38 Squadron to the relevant authorities and the next of kin were informed the crew were missing. However, the crew were all uninjured and after three to four hours paddled ashore onto an island, from where on about 13 November, some five days after being shot down, they managed to communicate to British forces on Leros that they were safe. Leros informed the RAF and telegrams were sent to the next of kin informing them the crew were safe on Leros. When Leros fell to the Germans and no further word was received in Egypt, the crew were reclassified as missing believed prisoners of war and further notifications were sent to the next of kin. Then on 7 December the crew reached Cyprus and were back in allied hands. The next of kin then received further telegrams reporting the crew as safe. A terrible ordeal for the next of kin was over with a happy ending. A report in the Australian archives from the one Australian crew member sets out the details of what happened, including that the crew never actually landed on Leros and were never in enemy hands, but does not elaborate on how they managed to get away.

British Casualties	
38 Sqn	Wellington XIII MP705 left 1900 to bomb Naxos, SOS sent from S Milos 2345, FTR, crew reported safe on Leros on 14 Nov, then all reported captured when Leros fell, all reclassified safe in Middle East on 5 December; Flg Off R.W.Adams and five POW

Monday, 8 November 1943

Four Bf 109s of 7./JG 27 took off at 0950 to provide cover for landing ships heading for Paros Island. At 1135 Lt Clade claimed a Beaufighter shot down south of Syphnos, which was probably a Baltimore of 454 Squadron reported missing on a reconnaissance sortie. A few hours later, a 603 Squadron Beaufighter crew claimed an Ar 196 shot down. Unusually this was believed to have fallen to the fire of a single hand-held Vickers 'K' machine gun installed in the small rear fuselage-observation blister – mainly for the encouragement of the navigator. SAGr 126 reported subsequently that the radio-operator of an Arado floatplane had been killed north-west of Amorgos while the aircraft itself returned badly damaged.

British Claims					
603 Sqn	Plt Off R.M.Giles/Flt Sgt L.Coulstock*	Beaufighter X LZ148 'H'	Ar 196	NW Amorgos	1427
	* shot down by the navigator				

British Casualties					
454 Sqn	Baltimore IV FA523 'W' left 0721, reconnaissance of Naxos, last seen 1030; Plt Off V.M.Clarkson and three MiA				

German Claims					
7./JG 27	Lt Emil Clade		Beaufighter	10km S Syphnos	1035

German Casualties					
4./SAGr 126	Ar 196A-3 WNr 0384 damaged in combat NW Amorgos; Uffz Walter Napierski WiA/Uffz Walter Kleinknecht KiA				
II./SG 3	Ju 87D-3 Trop WNr 100399 left Rhodes for Argos in Greece, 15% damaged in aerial combat; crew safe				

Tuesday, 9 November 1943

Bf 109s of JG 27 were kept extremely busy during the day in providing cover to the convoy 'Tragic' making for Amorgos, amounting to 22 sorties. German records indicate that 11 Beaufighters carrying torpedoes attacked the convoy south of Amorgos, one of these being claimed shot down, although no losses were recorded on this occasion. The pilots were from 603 Squadron and they did encounter two Ar 196s of 2./SAGr 125, four of them jointly shooting down one of these and claiming to have inflicted damage on the other to the north-east of Stampalia.

German records also noted that six Hurricanes had strafed a fuel depot at Kastelli in Crete at 1140 where seven tons of fuel were burned. Locally based infantry shot down one aircraft which was one of the now rarely seen Hurricanes, in this case from 336 Squadron.

British Claims					
603 Sqn	Plt Off R.A.McKendrick/Flg Off P.V.Langler	Beaufighter X LX951 'E'			
603 Sqn	Flt Sgt W.A.Encott/Plt Off W.B.P.Pritchard	Beaufighter X LX783 'K'	Ar 196	NE Stampalia	1535
603 Sqn	Wt Off F.M.Cox/Wt Off N.S.Ferguson	Beaufighter X LZ139			
603 Sqn	Flt Sgt E.T.Lynch/Sgt C.C.Sykes	Beaufighter X LX242 'C'			
603 Sqn	Plt Off R.A.McKendrick/Flg Off P.V.Langler	Beaufighter X LX951 'E'			
603 Sqn	Flt Sgt W.A.Encott/Plt Off W.B.P.Pritchard	Beaufighter X LX783 'K'	Ar 196 Damaged	NE Stampalia	1535
603 Sqn	Wt Off F.M.Cox/Wt Off N.S.Ferguson	Beaufighter X LZ139			
603 Sqn	Flt Sgt E.T.Lynch/Sgt C.C.Sykes	Beaufighter X LX242 'C'			

British Casualties		
336 Sqn	Hurricane IIc KZ599 left 1200 shot down by ground fire at Pesa Alagni 20km SSW Heraklion 1248; Flt Lt S.Diamantopoulos POW	

US Casualties		
154th CMS	F-5A 42-13100 PR mission over Greece, last heard from 1648 on return flight; 2/Lt George Castings Jr POW [1310] or 15th PS/3rd PG	

German Claims					
Flak			Hurricane	2km S Melessos	1248

German Casualties		
2./SAGr 125	Ar 196A-3 WNr 0429 7R+IK lost to fighter NE Stampalia; Obfw Adolf Sontowski/Lt z.S. Konrad Schulze MiA	
2./SAGr 125	Ar 126A-3 WNr 0332 D1+AM shot down by AA 10km E Leros; crew rescued	

Wednesday, 10 November 1943

At 0920 four Bf 109s of 8./JG 27 took off to escort ships from Rhodes. The pilots of one Rotte (pair) saw aircraft identified as Beaufighters and Uffz Gerhard Albert shot down one, actually a 454 Squadron Baltimore, at 1115 but was then shot down in return by the Baltimore's crew and was killed.

At 1135 four more Bf 109s took off, followed by another four at 1230. These pilots intercepted more Beaufighters – nine from 603 Squadron and three from 47 Squadron – which attacked barges in the Amorgos-Leros area. One of the 47 Squadron aircraft was shot down at once by Gefr Pothmann of 8.Staffel at 1335, and a second was hit by Obfw Gromotka of 9.Staffel at 1340 and crash-landed in the sea with one engine on fire; Pothmann and Gromotka reported seeing 13–15 Beaufighters in total and claimed both their victories in the Scarpanto area.

British Claims					
47 Sqn	Flt Sgt E.Daden/Sgt W.Lorains	Beaufighter 'S'	Ar 196 Damaged on the water	SW Kos	1534

British Casualties

47 Sqn	Beaufighter X LZ148 'H' shot down by Bf 109 near Scarpanto 1430–1445; Flg Off J.S.Hayden KiA/Sgt J.McMaster rescued
603 Sqn	Beaufighter X LB275 'L' shot down by Bf 109 near Scarpanto 1450; Flt Sgt W.A.Eacott/Wt Off W.B.F.Pritchard POW
454 Sqn	Baltimore IV FA669 'O' left 0820 on photo reconnaissance of Stampalia and Kos, last heard from 1120; Flt Sgt J.H.Joiner and two MiA, one KiA washed ashore on Stampalia Island

German Claims

8./JG 27	Uffz Gerhard Albert	Beaufighter unconfirmed	1115
8./JG 27	Gefr Heinrich Pothmann	Beaufighter	N Scarpanto	1335
9./JG 27	Obfw Fritz Gromotka	Beaufighter	WSW Scarpanto	1340

German Casualties

8./JG 27	Bf 109G-6 WNr 27174 lost in combat with Beaufighters over Leros; Uffz Gerhard Albert KiA
I./SG 3	Ju 87D-4 trop WNr 110591 S7+KH hit by AA over Kos, force-landed, burnt out; Gefr Walter Kneisel/Uffz Otto Baierl WiA

Wednesday-Thursday, 10/11 November 1943

Two Halifaxes dropped supplies to partisans on Crete, and six more aircraft did the same on Leros and Samos. Ten Halifaxes and two Liberators bombed Maritza airfield, while four Wellingtons, four Hudsons and six Baltimores attacked Antimachia.

German Claims

Flak	B-24	Maritza

German Casualties

8./LG 1	Ju 88A-4 WNr 550394 L1+JS on night recce of Turkish coast, reported overdue between Kos and Leros 0330; Oblt Otto Dobrawa KiA, three MiA

Friday, 12 November 1943 (see also Vol. 4)

German operations prior to a landing on Leros commenced with considerable air actions. At 1230 the Germans recorded that a convoy was attacked by 11 aircraft, one of which was claimed shot down, although no relevant Allied losses have been noted. During the day pilots of III./JG 27 operating from Rhodes undertook eight missions escorting 26 Ju 52/3ms and nine Ju 88s to drop paratroops in the area during one of which one of the former aircraft from I./TG 4 was brought down in the sea near the island with the loss of three killed and a fourth wounded. By 1500 the Germans established footholds in the north and east with a parachute battalion landing in the neck of the island. Two landing craft were sunk and two damaged in the first assault.

Six Beaufighters from 603 Squadron escorted two torpedo-carrying Beaufighters (Torbeaus) from 47 Squadron and two B-25Gs from the 310th Bomb Group to attack a convoy off the north-west coast of Crete. The convoy consisted of two freighters (of 2,000 tons and 3,000 tons) escorted by seven vessels and seven Ar 196s. Behind them came what 603 Squadron's records report as "a small boat full of men astern". British pilots claimed to have damaged both Arados and scored strikes on one merchant ship and two escorts.

47 Squadron also recorded that three Arados were approaching the convoy and two were overhead; it seems that it was the latter pair which were attacked by the British pilots. Meanwhile the B-25 crews attacked the ships first, claiming damage to one merchant ship. They were followed by the Torbeaus, the pilots of both of which dropped their torpedoes but missed. Behind them in turn came the aircraft of 603 Squadron but as they did so those of 47 Squadron were attacked from the port side by an Arado, the crew of which failed to open fire as almost the entire Allied formation broke towards it with the sole exception of the Beaufighter flown by Flg Off Greentree which broke to starboard and was not seen again.

British Claims

603 Sqn	Flt Lt J.Watters/Wt Off F.Burrow	Beaufighter X LZ145 'G'			
603 Sqn	Flt Sgt M.B.Yates/Sgt J.M.S.Walley	Beaufighter X LZ123 'S'			
603 Sqn	Plt Off R.H.Giles/Flt Sgt L.Coulstock	Beaufighter LZ241	2 Ar 196s Damaged	off Cap Spatha	1325
603 Sqn	Sgt A.Rooks/Flg Off M.J.R.Thom	Beaufighter LX949 'F'			
603 Sqn	Flt Sgt P.G.Spooner/Flg Off F.H.Pritchett	Beaufighter LZ272 'B'			
603 Sqn	Sgt J.N.Bowen/Sgt P.B.McGregor	Beaufighter 'X'			
13(H) Sqn	Flg Off Assinikis/Sgt E.Hayball	Baltimore IV FA512 'F'	Ar 196 Damaged	N Canae harbour	1305

German Fallschirmjäger make final preparations before boarding the Ju 52/3m transport that would drop them onto Leros on 12 November.

British Casualties

47 Sqn	Beaufighter TX LX912 'T' attacking shipping, shot down by fighter and/or Flak NW Crete 1325; Flg Off A.G.Greentree/Sgt G.H.Freeman MiA

German Claims

Ships' Flak		Beaufighter	Cap Spatha	1230

German Casualties

11./ZG 26	Ju 88C-6 WNr 750908 3U+JV lost u/k cause nr Leros; Uffz Gregor Merva and one MiA, one KiA
5./KG 51	Ju 88A-4 WNr 300385 landing gear damaged, presumed by AA, crashed on landing at Gadurra; Lt Wolf Pätz and one WiA
1./SG 3	Ju 87D-4 trop WNr 110598 S7+CH, force-landed on Paros Island; Uffz Joachim Kurth/Uffz Karl Zimmermann safe
5./SG 3	Ju 87D-3 WNr 110594 S7+RN shot down by AA 1km S Antimachia; Lt Jürgen Wellmann/Uffz Richard Köhlmann KiA
11./SG 3	Ju 87D-3 WNr 1223 damaged over Leros, crash-landed at Maritza; crew safe
1./SAGr 126	Ar 196A-3 damaged by Beaufighter nr Paros Island; crew safe
1./SAGr 126	Ar 196A-3 WN 0377 D1+EH damaged by AA nr Leros; crew safe
2./SAGr 126	Ar 196A-3 WNr 0224 hit by fighters, force-landed E Leros; crew rescued
2./SAGr 126	Ar 196A-3 WNr 0341 damaged by AA nr Leros; crew safe
1./TG 30	He 111 H-6 WNr 7748 S3+FH missing over Mediterranean, unknown reason; Obfw Gerhard Rosenberg and four MiA
Stab./TG 30	He 111 H-6 WNr 7173 S3+AM missing over Mediterranean, unknown reason; Oblt Gunther Köntges, four crew and Obstlt Karl-Heinz Schellmann (Gr.Kdr) MiA

Friday-Saturday, 12/13 November 1943

Four Wellingtons bombed the landing grounds on Kos. Kos was also bombed by 15 SAAF Squadron Baltimores, one of which was presumed by the squadron to have been lost to a night-fighter. Frequent encounters with night-fighters were reported by the RAF bombers over Crete, Kos and Rhodes, and 15 SAAF Squadron's pilots became over time increasingly annoyed that higher authority insisted that no such aircraft were operating in this area! However, in this case the Baltimore lost was claimed by Flak gunners, who identified it as a Boston.

British Casualties

15 SAAF Sqn	Baltimore IV FA446 'L' left 2140 for night bombing Kos, possibly shot down by a night-fighter; Lt R.H.Yaldwyn and three MiA

German Claims

Flak		Boston	SE Kos	2240

Saturday, 13 November 1943

Two Hurricanes from 336 Squadron shot up the German radar station at Lentas on the south coast of Crete and the German Flak defences claimed one Hurricane shot down.

British Claims

47 Sqn	Flg Off W.W.Thwaites/Flg Off J.E.Lovell		Beaufighter X LZ125 'W'	Ju
88 Damaged	Partheni, Leros	1600		
47 Sqn	Flg Off W.W.Thwaites/Flg Off J.E.Lovell		Beaufighter X LZ125 'W'	Ju
88 Damaged	Leros	1615		

British Casualties

47 Sqn	Beaufighter X LZ127 shot down 5m SW Leros 1002 by 2 Bf 109s; Flg Off E.L.Clary Jr/Flt Sgt W.E.Finbow MiA
47 Sqn	Beaufighter X LX928 'D' shot down San Nicola Bay Leros 1530 by return fire from Ju 88s; Sqn Ldr S.Muller-Rowland/Flt Sgt J.D.Anderson interned in Turkey
603 Sqn	Beaufighter X LX977 'Z' engine failure returning from a sweep, ditched in bad weather 1042; Wt Off F.M.Cox/Wt Off N.S.Ferguson MiA
336 Sqn	Hurricane IIc KZ490 left 0852, hit by Flak, force-landed on Crete; Flt Sgt G.Tzouvalis

Flg Off E.L.Clary Jr of 47 Squadron who with his navigator, Flt Sgt W.E.Finbow, was shot down off Leros, probably by Lt Emil Clade of 7./JG 27.

POW

US Claims

379th BS/310th BG	gunner Cpl Charles E.Nithman	B-25G 488	Bf 109	5–7m NW Kos	1020
379th BS/310th BG	gunner Cpl Charles E.Nithman	B-25G 488	2 Bf 109s Damaged	5–7m NW Kos	1020

German Claims

7./JG 27	Lt Emil Clade		Beaufighter	N Lèvita	0855
Flak			a/c	Crete	morning

German Casualties

2./TG 4	Ju 52/3m WNr 6763 shot up at Leros after dropping paratroops; Lt Helmut Günther and one KiA, one WiA, one safe
6./TG 4	Ju 52/3m WNr 6799 G6+FP shot down by AA at Leros; Fw Günther Voigt and one MiA, two rescued, one POW, 12 paratroopers MiA (aircraft salvaged in 2003 by Greek navy)
Seetransportst. 1	Ju 52/3m See WNr 6941 G6+HS destroyed by storm at Kalamaki
3./LG 1	Ju 88A-4 WNr 300615 L1+AL damaged by fighters near Leros; pilot safe, Uffz Udo Lange and two WiA

Sunday, 14 November 1943

The RAF diverted attention from the attack on Leros by undertaking strafing missions over Crete. Hurricanes had the range to get to Crete but not to the Leros area, so if the single-seater fighter force was to do anything to help, then all it could do was to attack Crete. As with previous operations of a similar nature the raids achieved very little and cost very much. The Greeks of 336 Squadron sent four Hurricanes to strafe Crete in the early morning, where all four were shot down. 94 Squadron also sent eight Hurricanes in the early afternoon losing another three aircraft, precisely matching the German claims for seven shot down, two by infantry weapons.

The crews of two 46 Squadron Beaufighters shared in the destruction of a Heinkel He 111H which was shot down north of Leros with the loss of one crew member.

Heinkel He 111H WNr 8611 6N+EW flown by Uffz Walter Pink tries to evade the fire from Flt Lt D.J.Crerar's Beaufighter off the coast of Leros on 14 November.

Beaufighter XIs of 46 Squadron detached to Lakatamia, Cyprus were supporting operations off Leros when they encountered Uffz Pink's He 111 on 14 November 1943.

British Claims

46 Sqn	Flt Lt D.J.A.Crerar/Plt Off L.Charles Beaufighter X JL913 'E'	} He 111	10m E Leros	1425
46 Sqn	Flg Off B.J.Wild/Flt Sgt R.W.Gibbon Beaufighter XI JL898			

British Casualties

336 Sqn	Hurricane IIc KZ628 left 0825 to strafe Crete, shot down by Flak, ditched off the coast; Flg Off E.Caridis POW
336 Sqn	Hurricane IIc KZ408 left 0825 to strafe Crete, shot down by Flak; Flg Off C.Psilolignos KiA
336 Sqn	Hurricane IIc KZ672 left 0825 to strafe Crete, shot down by Flak, crash-landed; Sgt G.Mademlis POW
336 Sqn	Hurricane IIc LD130 left 0825 to strafe Crete, shot down by Flak; Sgt D.Sarsonis KiA
94 Sqn	Hurricane IIc KZ144 'N' left 1200 to strafe Alikianos, Crete, last seen in cloud, possibly lost to fighters; Capt I.Beran RYAF, MiA
94 Sqn	Hurricane IIc BP198 'R' left 1200 to strafe Alikianos, Crete, last seen in cloud, possibly lost to fighters; 2/Lt R.Matejic RYAF, MiA
94 Sqn	Hurricane IIc HL902 'B' left 1200 to strafe RDF station at Elafos on Crete, shot down by Flak 1335; Flg Off J.S.Hay KiA
46 Sqn	Beaufighter VI MJ248 'R' shot down by Bf 109 near Leros 1430; Flg Off J.A.Horsfall/Flt Sgt J.R.Colley MiA
46 Sqn	Beaufighter VI JL994 'S' shot down by Bf 109 near Leros 1430; Wt Off R.Lindsay/Flt Sgt A.C.A.Gardener MiA

US Claims

446th BS/321st BG	gunner T/Sgt V.L.Fontenot	B-25C 42-64599 *Old 99*	Bf 109 Probable	Sofia area	1245
445th BS/321st BG	gunner Sgt J.W.Rose	B-25C 41-13207 *Oh 7*	} Bf 109 Damaged	Sofia area	1245
445th BS/321st BG	gunner Sgt Warren G.Woogerd				
447th BS/321st BG	gunner S/Sgt William R.Mercer	B-25C 42-64694 *Yankee Girl*	Bf 109	Sofia area	1245
447th BS/321st BG	gunner Sgt Hillard J.Manning	B-25C 42-64694 *Yankee Girl*	Bf 109	Sofia area	1245

German Claims

Flak		Hurricane	Episkopi	0906
Flak		Hurricane	15km N Episkopi	0906
Flak		Hurricane	Kentri	0909
Flak		Hurricane	6km W Hierapetra	0916
Flak		Hurricane	14km S Hierapetra	0918

Flak			Hurricane	N Stamion Bay	1251
Flak			Hurricane	Megara Scaraphia	1254
Stab III./JG 27	Maj Ernst Düllberg		Beaufighter	NW Leros	1335
8./JG 27	Ofhr Alexander Ottnad		Beaufighter	NW Gaidaros	1336
German Casualties					
Eins./KG 100	He 111H-11 WNr 8011 6N+EP shot down N Leros; Uffz Walter Pink and one safe, one WiA, gunner Gefr Helmut Grundke KiA				
III./JG 27	Bf 109G WNr 17001 lost in combat W Argos; pilot baled				
II./TG 2	Ju 52/3m WNr 7607 4V+BT shot down by AA nr Leros; pilot and one safe, two KiA. Aircraft recovered from sea 3 October 2003				
II./TG 2	Ju 52/3m WNr 4046 damaged by AA nr Leros; Oblt Walter Bordelle and two safe, one KiA				
6./TG 4	Ju 52/3m WNr 640187 damaged by AA nr Leros; pilot and two safe, one KiA				

Sunday-Monday, 14/15 November 1943

British Casualties	
38 Sqn	Wellington XI MP655 left to bomb Heraklion, last heard from S Crete 0400; Flt Sgt N.V.Whiteman and five MiA

Monday, 15 November 1943

Forty-nine B-25s of 321st Bomb Group and 49 from 340th Bomb Group, escorted by P-38s of 82nd Fighter Group, left for Kalamaki. Bad weather turned back the complete 321st Group formation and four B-25s of the 340th. However, at least 14 Axis aircraft were claimed destroyed on the ground, photographic evidence appearing to confirm these. About 12 Bf 109s attacked over Kalamaki but were driven off without loss to the bombers. Forty-six B-24s of 98th and 376th Bomb Group bombed Athens Eleusis airfield at 1100–1105.

On this date and on two days later pilots of IV./JG 27 made 21 claims but actually shot down nothing. Bartels claimed seven of these dubious claims, Kirschner six, Hackl three and Kühn two.

British Claims					
227 Sqn	Flt Lt A.G.Deck/Plt Off G.W.Ridley	Beaufighter VI LX133 'G'	MC.202 Damaged	E Leros	1402
US Claims					
94th FS/1st FG	2/Lt Jack P.Muffitt	P-38	FW 190 ?	Eleusis a/d	1105
96th FS/82nd FG	2/Lt George P.Brown	P-38	Ju 87	Kalamaki	1300
95th FS/82nd FG	Maj Hugh M.Muse	P-38	Bf 109 Damaged	Kalamaki	1300
95th FS/82nd FG	2/Lt Earl O.Chapman	P-38	Bf 109 Damaged	Kalamaki	1300
82nd FG	2/Lt Francis J.McGrath	P-38	2 Bf 109s Damaged	Kalamaki	1300
97th FS/82nd FG	2/Lt Raymond K.Cooke	P-38	Bf 109 Damaged	Kalamaki	1300
96th FS/82nd FG	2/Lt George P.Brown	P-38	FW 190 Damaged	Kalamaki	1300
German Claims					
Flak			P-38	Mt Parnas	1113
Stab IV./JG 27	Hptm Joachim Kirschner		Mitchell	S Lebadeia	1124
Stab IV./JG 27	Hptm Joachim Kirschner		P-38	W Arachoba	1128
12./JG 27	Fw Heinz Hackl		P-38	S Algra Spitia	1130
Stab IV./JG 27	Hptm Joachim Kirschner		P-38	W Arachoba	1132
12./JG 27	Fw Heinz Hackl		P-38	S Amfissa	1135
11./JG 27	Fw Heinrich Bartels		P-38	SE Kalamaki	1310
11./JG 27	Fw Heinrich Bartels		P-38	SE Kalamaki	1310
10./JG 27	Obfw Horst Ziller		P-38	Gaidarousi	1310
11./JG 27	Fw Heinrich Bartels		P-38	SE Kalamaki	1311
11./JG 27	Fw Heinrich Bartels		P-38	SE Kalamaki	1312
11./JG 27	Uffz Günther Kühn		P-38	20km SE Kalamaki	1314
12./JG 27	Fw Heinz Hackl		P-38	Flebes	1315
Flak			Spitfire	3km S Durazzo	1315
10./JG 27	Lt Gerhard Suwelack		P-38	SW Aegina	1316
Stab IV./JG 27	Hptm Joachim Kirschner		P-38	E Aegina	1317

German Casualties

III./JG 27	FW 58 WNr 3575 destroyed by bombs at Kalamaki
8./JG 27	Bf 109G-6 WNr 160302 crash-landed on Tatoi a/f, 90% damaged; Gefr Heinrich Pothmann safe
III./JG 27	FW 58 WNr 3575 destroyed by bombs at Kalamaki
5./KG 100	2 Do 217E-4s WNrn 1148 and 5613 destroyed by bombs at Kalamaki a/f
5./KG 100	6 Do 217E-5s (WNrn 4572, 4710, 5411, 5618, 5639 and 5658) damaged by bombs at Kalamaki a/f
I./TG 4	Fi 156 WNr 652 20% damaged by bombs at Kalamaki a/f
Stab St G3	He 111H-6 WNr 4179 20% damaged by bombs at Eleusis
I./LG 1	Ju 88A-4 WNr 550055 50% damaged by bombs at Kalamaki; Fw Hans Bialucha WiA
7./LG 1	Ju 88A-4 WNr 5547 L1+GR hit by Flak near Leros; pilot and two safe, gunner WiA
Stab/SG 3	Ju 87D-3 trop WNr 11592 S7+BA damaged by fighters, force-landed 4km S Kalamaki; pilot safe/Gefr Günther Hürtner WiA
II./SG 3	Ju 87D-5 WNr 130962 crash-landed on Maritza a/f, 40% damaged; crew safe
Eins.KGr	Ju 88 Hptm Karl von der Fecht (Gr.Kdr) wounded by bombs at Eleusis

Tuesday, 16 November 1943

At midday three pilots of III./JG 27 set off to patrol over Leros in the Levitha-Calino area where two more of this unit's Bf 109s were already present, having taken off about an hour earlier. Here both flights spotted Beaufighters identified as seven-ten in number. These were in fact seven aircraft of 47 and one of 603 Squadron which strafed and sank Siebel Ferry *SF 105*, east of Levitha. The Messerschmitt pilots attacked, claiming three Beaufighters shot down; two further claims were made a few hours later by pilots of 11./ZG 26 heavy fighters. Three of the British aircraft were lost – apparently all to the pilots of the Bf 109s. Meanwhile six more Beaufighters of 603 Squadron had also swept over Leros, spotting two Ar 196s north-east of Amorgos, one of which was claimed shot down and a second damaged, although no such losses were recorded by German floatplane crews.

Somewhat later B-25s of the US XII Bomber Command undertook a raid on Eleusis and Sibenik airfields without any significant success, although the Germans recorded that over 100 Allied aircraft appeared over the former airfield where two Ju 88s were damaged on the ground. Two escorting P-38s were claimed shot down, one by the Flak defences and one by Hptm Kirschner of IV./JG 27, the latter south-west of Amfissa, but no US losses were actually recorded.

British Claims

603 Sqn	Plt Off C.B.Megone/Flg Off S.W.Piner	Beaufighter X LZ239 'J'			
603 Sqn	Sgt A.Rooks/Flg Off M.J.R.Thom	Beaufighter X LZ278	Ar 196	NW Amorgos	1105
603 Sqn	Sgt J.N.Bowen/Sgt P.B.McGregor	Beaufighter X LZ139			
603 Sqn	Flt Sgt E.T.Lynch/Sgt C.C.Sykes	Beaufighter X LZ138			
603 Sqn	Plt Off C.B.Megone/Flg Off S.W.Piner	Beaufighter X LZ239 'J'			
603 Sqn	Sgt A.Rooks/Flg Off M.J.R.Thom	Beaufighter X LZ278	Ar 196 Damaged	NW Amorgos	1105
603 Sqn	Sgt J.N.Bowen/Sgt P.B.McGregor	Beaufighter X LZ139			
603 Sqn	Flt Sgt E.T.Lynch/Sgt C.C.Sykes	Beaufighter X LZ138			

British Casualties

47 Sqn	Beaufighter X LX883 'I' shot down by Bf 109 near Leros 1340; Flg Off A.G.Bond KiA/Sgt A.R.Cottle POW, escaped
47 Sqn	Beaufighter X LX923 'C' shot down by Bf 109 near Leros 1340; Flg Off J.B.Fletcher/Sgt J.Dale KiA
47 Sqn	Beaufighter X LZ125 'S' shot down by Bf 109, near Leros 1340; Flg Off W.W.Thwaites/Flg Off J.E.Lovell KiA
126 Sqn	Spitfire Vc JK950 left 1350 to bomb bridge NE Bicak, hit by Flak, pilot baled out 1m W Kneta, E Kravasta at 1,000ft parachute opened as he hit the sea; Sqn Ldr W.T.Page KiA

German Claims

Stab III./JG 27	Maj Ernst Düllberg		Beaufighter	E Levitha	1230
7./JG 27	Lt Emil Clade		Beaufighter	NNW Kos	1235
8./JG 27	Ofhr Alexander Ottnad		Beaufighter	S Tyranisia	1248
Flak			P-38	Eleusis	
Stab IV./JG 27	Hptm Joachim Kirschner		P-38	NW Amfissa	1320
11./ZG 26	Obfw Steinstrass	Ju 88C	Beaufighter	N Amorgos	1420
11./ZG 26	Obfw Walter Regel	Ju 88C	Beaufighter	W Kos	1425

5./KG 51   Ju 88A-4 WNr 800632 9K+CN lost at Leros; Lt Martin Franke and three MiA

3./LG 1   Ju 88A-4 WNr 883621 L1+EL crashed on take-off at Tanagra; Uffz Otto Dietrichkeit and three KiA

I./TG 4   Fi 156 WNr 652 20% damaged by bombs at Kalamaki

Tuesday-Wednesday, 16/17 November 1943

British Casualties

216 Sqn   Dakota I FD790 on supply mission to Leros forced to ditch off Bodrum on the Turkish coast; Flt Lt P.E.Henn and crew
                 interned, returned 24 November

Wednesday, 17 November 1943

Eighty-one B-25s of 321st and 340th Bomb Groups, escorted by 44 P-38s of 82nd Fighter Group, attacked Kalamaki, reportedly leaving seven aircraft burning on the ground. Seven Bf 109s of III./JG 27 scrambled at 1207, joined by others of IV.Gruppe. Lt Culemann of the former unit claimed one 'Marauder' shot down while the enthusiastic pilots of IV.Gruppe, led by Kirschner again, claimed five B-25s and three P-38s, Flak gunners adding two more of the bombers. The escorting P-38 pilots reported seeing a B-25 being shot down by two fighters near the target; one B-25 was actually lost. The 340th Bomb Group war diary reported:

"Today the 340th lost a bomber over the target in the daytime to enemy fighter opposition. That is the first time such an event happened in the combat history of this group. Six men were in the plane, which was a 486th [Squadron] ship piloted by 2/Lt John D.O'Leary, a recent replacement. On our side of the ledger gunners in the 487th Squadron knocked down three Me-109's who attacked in the target vicinity. The objective was Kalamaki airdrome again, and for the second time we bombed brilliantly. Surely the 340th Group never had three such excellent days consecutively in all its history as it has these past three days. Without a doubt our boys have greatly lessened the air strength for weeks, perhaps months, to come in the Athens area."

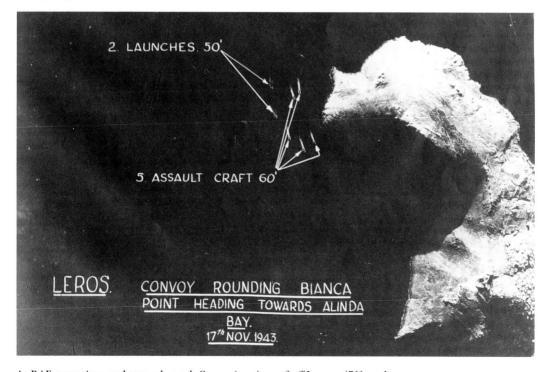

An RAF reconnaissance photograph reveals German invasion craft off Leros on 17 November.

Ultra's intercept of the German final report on the Kalamaki and Eleusis raids recorded:

"Kalamaki: eight aircraft destroyed, including one Ju 88 and three Ju 52s all from TG 4 plus one from II./TG 2, three Do 217s plus two Do 217s 30% damaged, five slightly damaged, some damage to the landing area, splinter damage to buildings and four men killed.

"Eleusis: three Ju 88s and one He 111 destroyed, two Ju 88s 85% damaged, four Ju 88s, two He 111s and two small aircraft slightly damaged. Two Ju 88s and one He 111 very slightly damaged. Three ammunition shelters blown up, several huts destroyed and other buildings splinter damaged."

Ju 87 Stukas pull out of their dives when attacking British positions on Leros.

US Claims

447th BS/321st BG	gunner Sgt Argyle H.Smith	B-25C 41-13181	Bf 109	Kalamaki	1250
487th BS/340th BG	gunner Dillingham	B-25C	Bf 109	Kalamaki	1250
487th BS/340th BG	gunner Casey	B-25C	Bf 109	Kalamaki	1250
487th BS/340th BG	gunner Bradley	B-25C	Bf 109	Kalamaki	1250
97th FS/82nd FG	2/Lt Hiram C.Pitts	P-38	Bf 109	Kalamaki	1250

US Casualties

486th BS/340th BG	B-25C 42-64540 '6N' last seen Athens Kalamaki, crashed near Koropi 1254; 2/Lt John D.O'Leary evaded, four KiA, one POW [1826]
487th BS/340th BG	B-25C '7P' shot up by fighters Athens Kalamaki, hydraulics damaged, ran off the runway on landing; Lt Pirnie and crew safe

German Claims (see also Vol. 4 p.440)

2./NAGr 12	Lt Hans-Georg Mett	Spitfire	10km NW Semeni estuary	1056
Stab IV./JG 27	Hptm Joachim Kirschner	P-38	SW Piraeus	1248
11./JG 27	Lt Wolfgang Hohls	B-25	W Krapias	1249
11./JG 27	Fw Heinrich Bartels	B-25	NE Kalamaki	1250
Stab III./JG 27	Lt Hans-Gunnar Culemann	Marauder	S Athens	1250
Flak		B-25	SW Koroni	1250
Flak		B-25	Athens	1251
11./JG 27	Fw Heinrich Bartels	B-25	NE Kalamaki	1252
11./JG 27	Fw Heinrich Bartels	P-38	E Marathon	1258
11./JG 27	Uffz Günther Kühn	P-38	SE Kalamaki	1300
Stab IV./JG 27	Hptm Joachim Kirschner	B-25	W Disporia Island	1303

German Casualties (see also Vol. 4 p.440)

4./SG 3	Ju 87D-3 WNr 110323 100% forced to ditch 4km N Kastello, NW coast of Rhodes; Obgfr Walter Ortner/Hubert Enkel and a passenger KiA
III./JG 27	Bf 109G-6 WNr 20304 50% damaged in combat, crash-landed on Kalamaki a/f; pilot safe
III./JG 27	Bf 109G-6 WNr 140164 35% damaged in combat crash-landed on Kalamaki a/f; pilot safe
12./JG 27	Bf 109G-6 WNr 140... shot down W Aegina; Lt Hans Hetzler WiA
II./TG 2	Ju 52/3m WNr 500139 destroyed by bombs at Kalamaki
I./TG 4	Ju 52/3m WNr 5419 destroyed by bombs at Kalamaki
II./TG 4	2 Ju 52/3ms WNrn 3326 and 3327 destroyed by bombs at Kalamaki
II./KG 51	2 Ju 88A-14s WNrn 144076 and 14736 80% damaged by bombs at Eleusis

5./KG 100	2 Do 217Es WNrn 5613 and 1148 destroyed and 6 (WNrn 5658, 3618, 5411, 5639, 4572, 4719) damaged by bombs at Kalamaki
Eins.St./KG 100	He 111H-6 WNr 7461 destroyed and WNr 7160 20% damaged by bombs at Eleusis
Eins.St./KG 100	He 111H-11 WNr 8445 destroyed and He 111H-11 WNr 7922 15% damaged by bombs at Eleusis
NAGr 12	2 a/c lost (probably Bf 109s)

Thursday, 18 November 1943

US medium and light bombers attacked Larissa airfield where two Ju 52/3ms were damaged on the ground at 1244.

German Casualties	
SAGr 126	Ar 196A-3 WNr 100430 on search for missing Ju 88, lost W Budwar; Uffz Paul Rogge/Lt Friedrich Kellner KiA
Eins.St./KG 100	2 He 111H-6s WNrn 7116 and 7824 damaged by bombs at Eleusis
transport unit	2 Ju 52/3ms damaged on the ground at Larissa

Thursday-Friday, 18/19 November 1943

Two Liberators from 178 Squadron undertook minelaying in Heraklion harbour on Crete and another two laid mines across the Khalkis Straight. 462 Squadron as a diversion bombed Heraklion airfield. The surviving Liberator of the two mining Heraklion noted heavy opposition including being coned by searchlights. The pilot Flt Lt P.G.Brown was awarded an immediate DFC and his navigator Flt Sgt B.J.McCowan an immediate DFM; their joint citation stated:

"This officer and airman were pilot and navigator respectively of an aircraft detailed for a minelaying mission one night in November 1943. When approaching the target the aircraft was illuminated by several searchlights and the harbour defences opened fire with great intensity. Defying the barrage, Flt Lt Brown flew on and released his mines with accuracy. Throughout the operation, Flt Sgt Mc-Cowan displayed exceptional coolness and his skilful efforts were of great assistance to his pilot. In hazardous circumstances Flt Lt Brown and Flt Sgt McCowan displayed a high degree of courage and determination."

British Casualties	
178 Sqn	Liberator III BZ891 'K' left 0145 minelaying near Crete, seen falling in flames 0437, crashed at Glydia; Sqn Ldr R.J.S.Wootten and six KiA

German Claims				
Flak		B-24	Heraklion	0344
Flak		B-24	Heraklion	0350

Friday, 19 November 1943

HMS *Phoebe* left Alexandria in company with French destroyers *Le Fantasque* and *Le Terrible* at 0600. During the approach to the Aegean this force was shadowed from 1515 and attacked at 1620 by 20 Ju 88s during which *Phoebe* and *Le Fantasque* were near missed but without damage. Again at 1711 the destroyers were attacked but again suffered no damage.

British Claims					
227 Sqn	Flt Lt A.G.Deck/Plt Off G.W.Ridley	Beaufighter VI LX133 'G'	Ju 88 Damaged	180m S Castelrosso	1720

British Casualties	
249 Sqn	Spitfire Vc BP978 'O' left 0900, hit a tree strafing and crashed in flames near Fier Albania; Flt Sgt K.L.Dale KiA
454 Sqn	Baltimore IV FA672 engine failure on patrol, last heard from 20m S Crete; Sgt B.Frost and three KiA

German Claims				
Flak	MG 42 100 JD		Spitfire	Fier	0930

Sunday, 21 November 1943

British Casualties

74 Sqn	Spitfire Vc JL329 left 1515 on offensive sweep over Rhodes, force-landed in Turkey near Castelrosso; Sgt W.J.Wilson interned

Monday, 22 November 1943

A Fi 156 Storch with two German NCOs aboard deserted and landed at Ras el Hillal where they were captured.

British Casualties

15 SAAF Sqn	Baltimore IV FA687 'A' left 0830 on reconnaissance Stampalia and Scarpanto, on return collided with No. 3 whilst flying at 20 feet 150km S of Crete 1159, ditched; Maj C.R.Brinton safe, Lt Truscott severely injured, two safe, all rescued next day
15 SAAF Sqn	Baltimore IV FA656 'K' left 0830 on reconnaissance Stampalia and Scarpanto, on return collided with the leader whilst flying at 20 feet 1159, scraped the water but managed to fly home damaged; Lt Fairburn and three safe

German Casualties

2.(F)/122	Ju 88A-4 WNr 550728 4U+NK on reconnaissance of Cyprus FTR; Uffz Karl Heinz Risken and three KiA

Tuesday, 23 November 1943

II./SG 3 at Maritza sent a report regarding flying personnel losses in operations over the Leros area from 26 September to 11 November 1943. These were reported to have been one officer and two NCOs dead, three officers, four NCOs and two men missing, plus two NCOs wounded. Later, from 12 to 16 November, one officer and one NCO dead, one officer wounded.

German Casualties

2.(F)/122	Ju 88D-1WNr 430758 destroyed by bombs at Kalamaki

Wednesday, 24 November 1943

British Casualties

13(H) Sqn	Baltimore IV 423 'H' left 1235 on convoy patrol, caught fire 1550, force-landed on the coast 1557; Flt Sgt B.Zafiropoulis and three safe

Friday, 26 November 1943

British Casualties

47 Sqn	Beaufighter X LX987 'D' engine trouble off Stampalia 1330, presumed ditched; Flg Off F.J.Gregory/Flg Off A.G.Wood KiA

Saturday, 27 November 1943

German Casualties

1./NAGr 12	Bf 109G-6 R+FO White 3 hit by Chetniks, force-landed 12m SE Valona; Obfw Franz Bischofe MiA
7.Seenotst.	Do 24T-3 WNr 3236 KO+IF ditched nr Samos; Fw Josef Pfaffendorf and three KiA, two WiA

Monday, 29 November 1943

During a morning patrol over Kos, a Baltimore of 454 Squadron was intercepted and shot down by Fw Löffler.

In the early evening, an Allied convoy in the Bizerta area, escorted by Hurricanes of 3 SAAF and 41 SAAF Squadrons, was attacked by Ju 88s of III./LG 1. One of these was claimed shot down at 1715 by Lt Dowden of the latter unit and Capt Yeats of the former. Yeats and Capt Geldenhuys claimed a second as a probable at the same time. Before these engagements had actually taken place, two more sections of Hurricanes had been launched by 33 Squadron at 1715 to reinforce the South Africans. Arriving to see one of these bombers become separated, they attacked and shot it down after a long chase by Plt Offs Hodgson and Bateson. (This report represents a slight correction on that set out in Vol. 4.)

British Claims

33 Sqn	Plt Off F.J.Bateson	Hurricane IIc xx511	} Ju 88	70m NW Benghazi	1715-
33 Sqn	Plt Off J.S.Hodgson	Hurricane IIc xx958			

3 SAAF Sqn	Capt R.C.Yeats	Hurricane IIc KZ776 'J'	} Ju 88	90m NW Benghazi	1740
41 SAAF Sqn	Lt W.A.Dowden	Hurricane IIc KZ495 'S'			
3 SAAF Sqn	Capt R.C.Yeats	Hurricane IIc KZ776 'J'	} Ju 88 Probable	90m NW Benghazi	1740
3 SAAF Sqn	Capt M.Geldenhuys	Hurricane IIc KZ286 'W'			
British Casualties					
454 Sqn	Baltimore IV FA602 'D' left 0655, sent a sighting report of shipping near the east coast of Greece 0950, FTR; Flg Off K.E.Adamson and three MiA				

German Claims				
9./JG 27	Fw Hannes Löffler	Baltimore	E Kos	0945
German Casualties				
7./LG 1	Ju 88A-4 WNr 800928 L1+CR shot down by fighters N Benghazi; Obfw Otto Piasta and three MiA			
8./LG 1	Ju 88A-4 WNr 300354 L1+GS shot down by fighters N Benghazi; Fw Theodor Cöster and three MiA			

Tuesday, 30 November 1943

German Casualties	
Verb.St 58	Bf 110G-3 WNr 5497 damaged by partisans NE Agram

THE CAIRO CONFERENCE

The Cairo Conference, codenamed 'Sextant', was a top-level meeting held from 22–26 November 1943 between President Roosevelt, Prime Minister Winston Churchill and Generalissimo Chiang Kai-shek to agree the Allied long-term position for the war against Japan. Having then conferred with Marshal Stalin in Tehran, the two western leaders returned to Cairo for a further bilateral conference. Held between 2 and 7 December this was to decide the future conduct of the war in Europe.

On conclusion of the main business of appointing Eisenhower as Allied Supreme Commander for the forthcoming invasion of Western Europe, the Combined Chiefs of Staff (CCS) reconvened to consider other relevant matters. The advances of the Allies from Africa through Sicily to Italy had required several changes to organisation and command. Now, however, it was felt that there should be a unified command for the Mediterranean and that the air forces should be similarly united to ensure the full co-ordination of the theatre's far-flung air resources.

There had previously been the Mediterranean Air Command under ACM Sir Arthur Tedder for the co-ordination of operations among the Northwest African and Middle East air forces. With the increasing consolidation of these forces there arose the question as to the advantage in maintaining the status quo.

A paper was presented that placed the air and sea commanders on the same level with the commander of the 15th Army Group, all under the Commander-in-Chief of Allied Force. The new Mediterranean Allied Air Force would direct operations through a single combined operational staff to assure cohesion in planning and action by the USAAF and RAF elements.

The CCS that directed the new organisation of Allied forces in the Mediterranean should become effective on 10 December 1943, though in fact MAAF was not activated until ten days later. However, from 10 December under the Air Commander-in-Chief Mediterranean fell all air organisations in the theatre, viz: all USAAF and RAF elements including RAF Malta, and RAF Middle East, French and Italian units operating within the area, and those forces later assigned to it. The CCS further directed that the Commander-in-Chief Allied Force should furnish the 15th Air Force with necessary logistical and administrative support "… in performance of Operation Point Blank as the air operation of first priority". In the event of "a strategic or tactical emergency" C-in-C Allied Force might, at his discretion, use the 15th Air Force for purposes other than its primary mission. This was conditional on his informing the CCS and the commanding general US Strategic Air Forces in Europe if and when such a command was created.

On 20 December ACM Sir Arthur Tedder became Air C-in-C with Lt Gen Carl A.Spaatz as his operational deputy who also assumed the duties of commanding general of USAAF in the theatre. These assignments were temporary as the decision on the transfer of Tedder and Spaatz to England and the appointment of Lt Gen Ira C.Eaker to the command of MAAF had already been reached. The MAAF would later evolve to include new formations, such as the Balkan Air Force, to co-ordinate operations in new areas as they arose.

Wednesday, 1 December 1943

British/US Claims (see also Vol. 4)

249 Sqn	Flg Off J.W.Brooks	Spitfire Vc JK366 'H'	} Ju 52/3m	5m N Shegas, Albania	1530
92nd/81st FG	1/Lt Robert H.Wagner	P-39N		11km SE Alessio	1530

British Casualties

38 Sqn	Wellington XIII MP708 engine failure on patrol, ditched off Haifa; Sgt R.S.Ledger KiA

German Casualties

8./TG 4	Ju 52/3m WNr 10149 G6+DS shot down by fighters S Alessio; Obfw Walter Brädler and one safe, one crew and three passengers WiA, three passengers KiA (see also Vol. 4)

Friday, 3 December 1943

Six Bf 109s of III./JG 27 were scrambled from Kalamaki at 0843 to pursue a reconnaissance aircraft which was identified as a Beaufighter near Cap Sunion at 0950. This was very likely the Baltimore of 454 Squadron which was probably shot down by Lt Bauer. Initially it was claimed that he had shot up and damaged this aircraft and killed the rear gunner at which point the guns of his Messerschmitt jammed. Consequently, no confirmation of a victory was given until later; it is presumed that this subsequently occurred when the sole survivor was picked up.

British Casualties

454 Sqn	Baltimore I FW282 'P' left 0655 shot down by 2 Bf 109s N Antikythera; Flt Lt W.A.H.J.Horsley POW, three KiA

German Claims

7./JG 27	Lt Ludwig Bauer		Beaufighter	Cap Sunion	0950

Saturday, 4 December 1943

At 0815 two Bf 109s of 9./JG 27 were scrambled after a reconnaissance Baltimore of 454 Squadron which was shot down almost at once by Obfw Gromotka in the Kea Island area.

47 Squadron sent out a patrol of six Beaufighters, but two returned early. The remaining four sighted an Arado on the water at 1350 with three more circling above. One of the airborne Arados was shot down and sank immediately and the one on the water also sank, the crew taking to their dinghy. The pilots of the escorting Ar 196s claimed two Beaufighters damaged.

The German *Schnellboot* (torpedo-boat) *S 511* (ex-Italian *MAS 522*) was sunk by air attack off Makronisos.

British Claims

249 Sqn	Wg Cdr E.N.Woods	Spitfire Vc MA701 'EN-W'	Ju 87	over Podgorica	1210
47 Sqn	Sgt G.R.Willis/Sgt D.P.Thompson	Beaufighter X LX898 'W'	Ar 196 on sea	5-6m N Levitha	1350
47 Sqn	Sgt G.R.Willis/Sgt D.P.Thompson	Beaufighter X LX898 'W'	Ar 196	5-6m N Levitha	1350
252 Sqn	Sqn Ldr H.G.Hubbard/Flg Off G.E.Jones	Beaufighter VI JM250	} Ar 196 on sea	near Leros	1425-1917
252 Sqn	Flt Sgt D.A.Pitt/Sgt H.Roe	Beaufighter VI JM235			
252 Sqn	Flt Lt F.A.Cohan/Flt Sgt L.J.Barton	Beaufighter VI JL757			
252 Sqn	Flt Sgt A.W.Squires/Sgt W.H.Boon	Beaufighter VI JL896			

British Casualties

454 Sqn	Baltimore I FA584 'R' last signal received 0926, shot down by two Bf 109s, ditched east of Kea: Flt Lt D.V.Paul and two POW, one KiA

German Claims

9./JG 27	Obfw Fritz Gromotka		Baltimore	near Kea Island	0832
SAGr 126	crews		2 Beaufighters Damaged	near Leros Island	

German Casualties

13./SG 151	Ju 87D-1 WNr 2244 shot down by fighters, force-landed NW Podgorica and burnt out; Uffz Siegfried Robbe/Obgfr Willi Rössler WiA (to be added to Vol. 4)
2./SAGr 126	Ar 196A-3 WNr 0302 D1+DH strafed and sank 10km NE Levitha Island; Lt Friedrich Brunswig KiA/Lt Eberhard Ahrends safe
2./SAGr 126	Ar 196A-3 WNr 1015 D1+MK strafed by Beaufighter and sank 5km NE Levitha Island; Uffz Karl Steinbrecher WiA/Lt Eberhard Ahrends KiA
3./SAGr 126	Ar 196A-3 WNr 0306 D1+KL shot down off Portolago Bay, Leros; Obfw Walter Schindler/Obfw Otto Albrecht KiA

Monday, 6 December 1943

Although heavy raids were aimed at Greek airfields, again poor weather conditions rendered it difficult for the bombers to find their targets in many cases. Action began at about 1050 as 45 B-24s raided Eleusis and 56 B-17s targeted Kalamaki; P-38s from the 82nd Fighter Group provided cover for both these formations. Twenty-one Bf 109s of III./JG 27 scrambled. Against the first of these raids Obfw Gromotka of 9.Staffel claimed one B-24, while Flak gunners claimed two more plus a P-38; the 376th Bomb Group did indeed lose two bombers and the 82nd Group one P-38.

The escorting US fighters claimed four German fighters shot down and the pilot of a third was wounded, plus three probables while gunners in the Liberators added three more fighters and two probables. One pilot of 7./JG 27 was shot down and killed, a second Messerschmitt crash-landing at Kalamaki and a third force-landed with the pilot having been wounded; during the morning's engagements three more of the defenders were damaged although the pilots of all these suffered no harm. About an hour after the initial scramble ten more Bf 109s got into the air, intercepting 38 of the B-17s. Two of the latter were then claimed shot down by Maj Düllberg and Lt Dr Peter Werfft.

Apart from the claims in the air the Luftwaffe also lost two Ju 88Ds of 1.(F)/122 destroyed by bombs on the ground where 11 of JG 27's Bf 109s were damaged – all to a fairly light degree.

In the Aegean the ship *Isis* was reportedly shot up and set on fire by Beaufighters.

US Claims

96th FS/82nd FG	1/Lt Leslie E.Anderson	P-38G	2 Bf 109s	Athens	1150–1230
96th FS/82nd FG	2/Lt Clarence Dolezal	P-38G	Bf 109 Probable	Athens	1150–1230
97th FS/82nd FG	2/Lt Gene A.Chalfield	P-38G	FW 190	Athens	1150–1230
97th FS/82nd FG	1/Lt William R.Clark	P-38G	Bf 109	Athens	1150–1230
95th FS/82nd FG	2/Lt J.D.Stoutenborough	P-38G	Bf 109 Probable	Athens	1150–1230
96th FS/82nd FG	2/Lt Clements W.Turner	P-38G	Bf 109 Probable	Athens	1150–1230
98th & 376th BGs	gunners	B-24Ds	2 Bf 109s	Athens	ca 1200
98th & 376th BGs	gunners	B-24Ds	2 Bf 109s Probable	Athens	ca 1200
98th & 376th BGs	gunners	B-24Ds	2 Bf 109s Damaged	Athens	ca 1200
98th & 376th BGs	gunners	B-24Ds	FW 190	Athens	ca 1200
97th & 301st BGs	gunners	B-17Fs	6 Bf 109s	Kalamaki	ca 1250
97th & 301st BGs	gunners	B-17Fs	4 Bf 109s Probable	Kalamaki	ca 1250
97th & 301st BGs	gunners	B-17Fs	4 Bf 109s Damaged	Kalamaki	ca 1250
97th & 301st BGs	gunners	B-17Fs	2 FW 190s Damaged	Kalamaki	ca 1250

US Casualties

96th FS/82nd FG	P-38G 43-2531 combat over Athens, engine on fire, pilot baled out 3m NW Desfina Greece 1230; 2/Lt Edwin R.English POW [1469]
514th BS/376th BG	B-24D 42-72844 hit by Flak over Eleusis 1145, crew baled out; 1/Lt William Metzger Jr and five evaded, three POW [1478]
341st BS/97th BG	B-17F 42-0381 damaged by Flak nr Athens, returned to base; pilot and seven safe, two baled: navigator 2/Lt William J.Brown POW, engineer S/Sgt Frederick H.Herreilers KiA [2069]

German Claims

9./JG 27	Obfw Fritz Gromotka	B-24	E Thebes	1140
Flak		B-24	Eleusis	1150
Flak		B-24	Tatoi	1210
Flak		P-38	Thermopolyae	1211
Flak		B-17	Mt Hymettos	1246
9./JG 27	Lt Dr Peter Werfft	B-17	Kalamaki	1247
Flak		B-17	40km S Wula Peninsula	1253
Stab III. JG 27	Maj Ernst Düllberg	B-17	E Milos	1255

German Casualties

7./JG 27	Bf 109G-6 WNr 140029 White 5 shot down by 4-engined bombers N Thebes; Uffz Wilhelm Hensel KiA
7./JG 27	Bf 109G-6 WNr 15488 crash-landed after combat with P-38, 70% damaged; Lt Horst Kizina WiA
III./JG 27	3 Bf 109G-6s WNrn 18264, 20288 and 140238 damaged in combat, landed at Kalamaki; pilots safe
III./JG 27	8 Bf 109G-6s WNrn 15461, 15479, 140179, 17011, 20566, 10502, 140090, 15998 damaged by bombs at Kalamaki
10./JG 27	Bf 109G-6 WNr 140307 damaged in combat, force-landed 5km N Metkovic; Lt Günther Potrafke WiA
1.(F)/122	2 Ju 88D-1s WNrn 430897 and 430765 damaged by bombs at Kalamaki
I./LG 1	Ju 88A-4 destroyed and 3 damaged by bombs at Kalamaki 1145

Tuesday, 7 December 1943

At 1625, *S 55* (Oblt z.S Weber) and *S 36*, two *Schnellboote* heading from Leros to Athens, were attacked by three Beaufighters ten sea miles south of Samos. *S 55* received many hits, whereas *S 36* was hit by one 20mm cannon shell. Some hours later the German crews picked up two British airmen from a rubber dinghy. This was the crew of a 47 Squadron Beaufighter.

British Claims

252 Sqn	Flt Sgt A.W.Squires/Sgt W.H.Boon	Beaufighter VI EL523	Ar 196 Damaged	0452-1023
252 Sqn	Flt Sgt A.Taylor/Flt Sgt J.S.L.Reynolds	Beaufighter VI JM257	Ar 196 Damaged*	0452-1023
	* by the observer			

British Casualties

47 Sqn	Beaufighter X JL898 'W' left 1504, attacked E-boats near Leros, hit by Flak, attempted to return on one engine, last seen over Trageia at 1725; Flg Off D.Nicol/Wt Off G.Ball POW

Wednesday, 8 December 1943

US 'heavies' were over Greece again on this day to attack the main Athens airfields, B-24s of 98th and 337th Bomb Groups hitting Tatoi while the B-17s of 97th and 301st Bomb Groups targeted Eleusis; once more the escort was provided by 82nd Fighter Group P-38s. Before and just after midday the bombers appeared and in quick succession various batteries of naval and coastal Flak defences claimed one P-38 and five B-17s. On this occasion claims were moderately accurate, two of the big bombers and one P-38 were indeed lost. On the ground at Tatoi one Ju 52/3m of I./TG 4 was destroyed and four were damaged together with a 2.(F)/123 Ju 88. At Eleusis a Ju 88 and a Klemm trainer were destroyed and four Ju 88s were also damaged.

Beaufighters of 252 Squadron were out very early, sweeping to the west of Cyprus but here one aircraft flew into the sea and exploded, the pilot being killed. It appears to have been the victim of the Flak (identified as a Baltimore), claimed at 0916. At early evening Fw Hackl of 12./JG 27 claimed a Beaufighter shot down but Lt Kunkel of the same Gruppe's 11.Staffel was reported shot down and killed.

British Casualties

252 Sqn	Beaufighter VI JL899 left 0458 on offensive sweep, crashed into the sea W Cyprus; Flt Sgt P.J.Martin/Sgt J.Hamilton KiA
74 Sqn	Spitfire Vc EP814 left 0840 from El Adem to Mersa Matruh to escort a VIP York, collided near destination 1040; Flg Off D.Leeke KiA
74 Sqn	Spitfire Vc JL302 left 0840 from El Adem to Mersa Matruh to escort a VIP York, collided near destination 1040; Flg Off A.M.Parker baled out

US Claims

97th FS/82nd FG	Maj Harry L.Smith Jr	P-38	2 Bf 109s Damaged	Athens	1200

US Casualties

95th FS/82nd FG	P-38G 42-13210 took off to escort bombers to Athens, dropped out, returned to base to be repaired, took off 1007 and never heard from again; 2/Lt Josef A.Porterfield KiA [1466]
353rd BS/301st BG	B-17F 42-3137 bombing Athens Eleusis a/f, direct Flak hit in bomb bay over Eleusis 1245; 1/Lt Jack A.Scott and five POW, three KiA [1481]

German Claims

Flak		Baltimore	30km E Sideron Bay	0916
Flak		P-38	Mount Parnas	1144
Flak	Marine Abt 720	B-17	ENE Megalo	1235
Flak	Marine Abt 720	B-17	Megalo-Petko	1236
Flak	Coastal Defence boat GA-02	B-17		
Flak		B-17	15km W Maguela	1238
12./JG 27	Fw Heinz Hackl	Beaufighter	S Ston, Pelješac	1535

German Casualties

11./JG 27	Bf 109G-6 WNr 140235 engine failure; crashed nr Metkovic; Lt Richard Kunkel KiA
2.(F)/123	Ju 88 D-1 WNr 881207 15% damaged by bombs at Tatoi
I./TG 4	Ju 52/3m WNr 6690 destroyed and 3 Ju 52/3ms (WNrn 3160, 640209 and 7749) damaged by bombs at Tatoi

Friday, 10 December 1943

German Claims			
Flak		e/a	Heraklion

Saturday, 11 December 1943

British Casualties	
1435 Sqn	Spitfire IX EN352 'V' left 1015, investigated aircraft heading for Bari, which turned out to be P-38s, one of which shot at him, causing a crash-landing 1055; Wt Off T.V.Pigot safe

Sunday, 12 December 1943

British Casualties	
15 SAAF Sqn	Baltimore IV FA527 'F' left 1215 on reconnaissance around Rhodes, FTR; 1/Lt C.G.Heher and three MiA

Monday, 13 December 1943

At 0759 two Bf 109s were scrambled and intercepted a 454 Squadron Baltimore which Maj Düllberg shot down south of Georgios Island.

British Casualties	
454 Sqn	Baltimore I FW315 'O' left 0634 on shipping reconnaissance of Western Aegean, FTR; Plt Off D.Todhunter and three MiA

German Claims				
Stab III./JG 27	Maj Ernst Düllberg		Baltimore	S Georgios Island	0818

Tuesday, 14 December 1943

More than 150 heavies escorted by all three Lightning groups bombed Tatoi, Eleusis and Kalamaki airfields. Piraeus docks were also bombed. The Germans had received prior warning of the incoming attacks and all air-worthy aircraft were flown out, resulting in only nine being damaged on the ground, including three Ju 88s, three Bf 109s and one Ju 52; one ship was claimed sunk in the harbour.

Twenty-three Bf 109s of III./JG 27 were scrambled at 1000 to intercept a reported 80 B-17s and 28 P-38s, Maj Düllberg claiming a B-17 east of Tatoi at 1030, but this was the only claim made by the defending fighters to which were added three more by the Flak; just one bomber was reported lost by the 2nd Bomb Group. However, the raid was manifestly a complete failure.

Although the Flak had also claimed B-17s, it seems certain that Düllberg was victor over the single Luftwaffe bomber loss since P-38 pilots of the 14th and 82nd Fighter Groups reported seeing the bomber in the course of being shot down by hostile fighters. Despite the evidence apparently being to the contrary, the 14th Fighter Group claimed one Bf 109 shot down and one probable. It seems that the probable was later confirmed and the victories were credited to Maj Leverette and Maj Burton E.McKenzie.

Uffz Rolf Steinberg of 9./JG 27 was reported missing and Gefr Ullrich crash-landed after his Messerschmitt had been hit in the engine by fire from a P-38 and was later classified as a write-off. Total claims by the ever enthusiastic bomber gunners amounted to ten.

A Cant.Z.506B was being used by the Luftwaffe as a medical plane by 2./ SAGr 125. On this day the pilot was Serg Domenico Sancristoforo, an Italian who joined the Luftwaffe after the armistice, the radio-operator was Uffz Werner Schmidt of 2./SAGr 126 while four German groundmen were carried as passengers; they ran into a patrol of Beaufighters from 47 Squadron that shot down their floatplane, killing all aboard.

British Claims					
47 Sqn	Sgt G.R.Willis/Sgt D.P.Thompson	Beaufighter X 'E'	} He 115	S Stampalia	1525
47 Sqn	Sgt K.Thomas/Sgt W.N.Hartley	Beaufighter X 'J'			
US Claims					
2nd & 97th BGs	gunners	B-17Fs	4 e/a	Athens area	
2nd & 97th BGs	gunners	B-17Fs	e/a Probable	Athens area	
2nd & 97th BGs	gunners	B-17Fs	e/a Damaged	Athens area	

US Casualties

96th BS/2nd BG	B-17F 42-5050 shot down by Flak/fighters near Korpi 20km E Athens 1055; 2/Lt Walter R.Ward and eight baled (two evaded, seven POW), one KiA in a/c [1482]

German Claims

Flak		B-17	Kalamaki	1051
Stab III./JG 27	Maj Ernst Düllberg	B-17	E Tatoi	1055
Flak		B-17	SW Marathon	1055
Flak		B-17	SW Marathon	1058

German Casualties

9./JG 27	Bf 109G-6 WNr 140079 Yellow 2 shot down by P-38 near Paramythia; Uffz Rolf Steinberg WiA
8./JG 27	Bf 109G-6 WNr 18507 damaged by P-38 crash-landed at Kalamaki; Gefr Friedrich Ullrich safe
2./SAGr 125	Cant.Z.506B flying from Scarpanto to Crete, shot down by four Beaufighters; Serg Domenico Sancristoforo, five crew and passengers KiA (see also Vol. 4)
I./TG 4	Ju 52/3m WNr 10135 damaged by bombs at Kalamaki
Wekusta 27	Ju 88A-4 WNr 142431 damaged by bombs at Tatoi
16./Fl.Verb.G 2	Fi 156 WNr 1440 damaged by bombs at Tatoi

Wednesday, 15 December 1943

603 Squadron undertook the first sorties in the Middle East armed with rocket projectiles during this day but pilots saw no targets and returned with the projectiles unfired.

German Claims

12./JG 27	Fw Heinz Hackl	B-26	10km S Lagosta Island	1115
Flak		P-47	Ploče	1304

Saturday, 18 December 1943

British Casualties

603 Sqn	Beaufighter X LZ278 left 1120 on offensive sweep, crashed on take-off; Sgt K.J.Tennant/Sgt A.Burgess safe

German Claims

Flak		Beaufighter	Heraklion

Monday, 20 December 1943

Eleusis airfield was again attacked, this time by 109 B-17s escorted by two groups of P-38s. German records indicate that the attack took place at 1239–1245 and that eight aircraft were damaged on the ground; 26 Bf 109s of III./JG 27 had been scrambled from Kalamaki at 1200. Eventual claims by Flak and fighters were for nine bombers and two P-38s, but the initial claims were for ten bombers and three P-38s.

US Claims

2nd BG	gunners	B-17s	10 Bf 109s	Eleusis a/f	1240
HQ 14th FG	Lt Col Oliver B.Taylor	P-38 '56'	Bf 109	Eleusis a/f	1240
HQ 14th FG	Lt Col Oliver B.Taylor	P-38 '56'	Bf 109 Probable	Eleusis a/f	1240
HQ 14th FG	Lt Col Oliver B.Taylor	P-38 '56'	Bf 109 Probable	Eleusis a/f	1240
37th FS/14th FG	2/Lt Kenneth L.Stahl	P-38	Bf 109 Damaged	Eleusis a/f	1240
HQ 14th FG	2/Lt Richard D.Wilhelm	P-38	Bf 109	Eleusis a/f	1240
49th FS/14th FG	2/Lt Robert E.Hoke	P-38 '58'	Bf 109	Eleusis a/f	1240
49th FS/14th FG	2/Lt Herbert C.Schoener	P-38 '57'	Bf 109	Eleusis a/f	1240
49th FS/14th FG	2/Lt Robert K.Seidman	P-38 'ML'	3 Bf 109s	Eleusis a/f	1240
49th FS/14th FG	2/Lt Robert K.Seidman	P-38 'ML'	Bf 109 Damaged	Eleusis a/f	1240
49th FS/14th FG	Flg Off Jack Lenox Jr	P-38 'HS'	Bf 109 Probable	Eleusis a/f	1240
49th FS/14th FG	Flg Off Jack Lenox Jr	P-38 'HS'	Bf 109 Damaged	Eleusis a/f	1240
94th FS/1st FG	1/Lt Donald D.Kienholz	P-38	FW 190	Eleusis a/f	1250

US Casualties

20th BS/2nd BG	B-17F 41-24345 hit by Flak, crashed 32m WNW Eleusis 1229; 2/Lt William A.Slaughter and nine evaded, one POW [1514]
96th BS/2nd BG	B-17F 42-5776 *Eager Beaver* hit by Flak or fighters over target 1238; some of the crew baled out; 1/Lt David G.Rohrig and three KiA, five POW, one evaded [1518]

96th BS/2nd BG	B-17F 42-80197 *Hangar Queen* hit by Flak or fighters over target 1245, crash-landed on Corfu 1300; 2/Lt Orville L.Doughty and nine POW [1517]

German Claims

Stab III./JG 27	Maj Ernst Düllberg	B-17	Eleusis	1238
9./JG 27	Lt Dr Peter Werfft	B-17	NW Megara	1241
7./JG 27	Lt Emil Clade	B-17	NNE Megara	1245
Stab III. JG 27	Maj Ernst Düllberg	B-17	Corfu	1250
9./JG 27	Fw Hannes Löffler	B-17	NNW Megara	1250
9./JG 27	Lt Dr Peter Werfft	P-38	NE Megara	1252
8./JG 27	Gefr Heinrich Pothmann	P-38	NW Megara	1300
Flak		4 B-17s	Athens raid	

German Casualties

7./ JG 27	Bf 109G-6 WNr 160028 shot down by B-17 5km S Eleusis; Fw Rudi Dietz KiA

Tuesday, 21 December 1943

German Casualties

7.Seenotst.	Do 24T-3 WNr 1033 KK+LC lost presumably in an accident at the seaplane base at Mikra near Salonika; Obfw Wilhelm Lange, five crew and three passengers MiA
3./SAGr 126	Ar 196A-3 WNr 0251 D1+EL 10% damaged; crew safe

Wednesday, 22 December 1943

On this date 603 Squadron actually fired their rockets for the first time when three rocket-equipped Beaufighters, two with 60lb warheads and one with 25lb warheads, with one other aircraft armed only with cannons, attacked a caique on the north side of Amorgos Island and left it apparently in a sinking condition. They then attacked another in Mykonos harbour, claiming damage to that as well.

Thursday, 23 December 1943

Four Beaufighters from 603 Squadron attacked four Ar 196s moored on the water at Samos. Sgt Harman reported that he had blown one apart with a rocket projectile.

When landing at Kythera Island in the southern Peloponnese on 23 December, this Do 24T DJ+ZM ran ashore and was wrecked.

Four 227 Squadron Beaufighters ran into a convoy on either this or the previous day north-west of Crete near Kythera and claimed to have sunk a 200-ton ship also damaging two more. One British aircraft was indeed shot down by Flak and a second damaged.

British Claims					
603 Sqn	Sgt E.G.Harman/Sgt L.E.Hopkin	Beaufighter X LZ239 'J'	Ar 196	Samos	0942

British Casualties	
227 Sqn	Beaufighter VI JM226 'J' shot down by Flak near Tsoumalia, Greece 1130 attacking shipping; Flg Off J.M.Kendall/Flg Off R.Mackay KiA
227 Sqn	Beaufighter VI JL908 'P' damaged by Flak near Tsoumalia, Greece 1130 attacking shipping, landed safely, a/c written off Cat III; Wg Cdr J.K.Buchanan/Wt Off R.C.Howes safe

German Claims				
Flak	Net Layer *Pireaus*	Beaufighter	Monemvasia	1036

German Casualties	
3./SAGr 126	Ar 196A-3 WNr 0251 D1+EL destroyed by enemy fire at Samos; crew safe
7.Seenotst.	Do 24T-2 WNr 087 DJ+ZM crashed on landing Kythera Island, ran ashore, hit a house; Obfw Walter Steinig and two WiA, three KiA

Saturday, 25 December 1943
Three Allied aircraft strafed a Do 24 in Kythera harbour and inflicted some damage to it.

British Claims					
454 Sqn	Wt Off D.McMurray	Baltimore FA406	Bf 109 Damaged	S Milos	1140-1600

Sunday, 26 December 1943

German Claims			
Flak		e/a	Stampalia
Flak		e/a	Stampalia

Wednesday, 29 December 1943
The Greek 336 Squadron had been provided with one Spitfire to begin conversion training from the unit's Hurricanes, however on this date it crashed killing the pilot.

British Casualties	
336 Sqn	Spitfire V EE806 left 0935 on local flight, spun in for reasons unknown 5m from LG 121 at 1000, completely wrecked; Plt Off S.Christakos KiFA

Friday, 31 December 1943
A 454 Squadron Baltimore was shot up by two Bf 109s just south of Polygandros but during this engagement its turret guns failed. At 1154 just after leaving Kythera Channel the Baltimore was attacked by two more Bf 109s. Flt Lt Railton's guns failed again and until 1202 a Bf 109 sat right on the Baltimore's tail and filled it with holes although failing to shoot it down. This second attack had been made by Fw Moycis who was subsequently – but incorrectly – credited with shooting the Baltimore down.

British Casualties	
454 Sqn	Baltimore IV FA450 left 0825, shot up by Bf 109s just S Polygandros and off Kythera Channel 1202, landed at base 1405; Flt Lt W.Railton and two safe, Sgt A.H.White WiA

German Claims				
7./JG 27	Fw Rudolf Moycis	Baltimore	W Crete	1103

Monday, 3 January 1944
Eight Beaufighters of 47 Squadron swept over Suda Bay where they were attacked by Bf 109s of III./JG 27, the pilot of one of which shot one down.

221 Squadron Wellington XII JA416/L flown by Wg Cdr M.J.A.Shaw on an anti-shipping patrol from Malta on 3 January 1944.

British Casualties				
47 Sqn	Beaufighter TFX LX919 'X' shot down Canae Bay W Maleme 1632; Wt Off R.J.Barrett/Sgt W.H.Fairfield MiA			

German Claims				
7./JG 27	Lt Horst Kizina	Beaufighter	NW Maleme	1540

Thursday-Friday, 6/7 January 1944

A 38 Squadron Wellington was on a related area patrol over convoy 'Parcel' during the night in an area north-east of Benghazi. Another Wellington from the same squadron was on a close area patrol nearby when a message was received from the convoy that a fire was seen in the sky, and neither Wellington returned. It was presumed that they had collided at 2105. There were no survivors.

British Casualties	
38 Sqn	Wellington XI MP679 'U' left 1708 on convoy escort and based on convoy's radar and visual siting of fire and smoke presumed to have collided with HZ727 about 100m N Benghazi at 2101; Plt Off W.H.Bowen and five MiA
38 Sqn	Wellington XI HZ727 'B' left 1655 on convoy escort and based on convoy's radar and visual siting of fire and smoke presumed to have collided with MP679 about 100m N Benghazi at 2101; Flg Off K.R.Munro and five MiA

Monday, 10 January 1944

The torpedo boat *S 55* was sunk by aerial attack west of Korcula.

Tuesday, 11 January 1944

Sixteen P-38s of the 1st Fighter Group escorted B-17s raiding Piraeus harbour. Here the patrol boats *GA 08* and *GA 09* and the minesweeper *M 1226* (ex-Italian *RD 9*) were all destroyed by the bombers and heavy civilian casualties were inflicted. Here the Lightnings' pilots claimed two Bf 109s shot down and a FW 190 probably so, while six more Messerschmitts were claimed destroyed by the bombers' gunners.

US Claims					
94th FS/1st FG	1/Lt Ralph A.Theissen	P-38	Bf 109	Piraeus harbour	1305–1315
27th FS/1st FG	1/Lt Francis J.Maron	P-38	Bf 109	5m S Piraeus	1310
27th FS/1st FG	1/Lt Thomas E.Rafael	P-38	FW 190 Probable	Athens	1315

5th Wing	gunners	B-17F	6 Bf 109s	Athens area
5th Wing	gunners	B-17F	2 Bf 109s Probable	Athens area

US Casualties

346th BS/99th BG	B-17F 42-5470 collided with P-38 in cloud E of Trikolonoi 1237; 1/Lt Joseph M.Donahue and six KiA, three evaded [1820]

German Casualties

III./JG 27	one Bf 109 lost and one damaged

Tuesday-Wednesday, 11/12 January 1944

British Casualties

104 Sqn	Wellington XLN721 'N' left Foggia 1907 to bomb Pireaus harbour, FTR; Wt Off D.W.Bowell and four MiA

Wednesday, 12 January 1944

A Beaufighter of 46 Squadron engaged in an early morning combat off the Nile Delta with a Ju 88. Listening Service believed it later force-landed, which indeed it had.

British Claims

46 Sqn	Flt Sgt S.M.Kent/Flt Sgt L.W.Cooper Beaufighter VIb MM928	Ju 88 Damaged	NW Damietta Point	0158

German Casualties

2.(F)/123	Ju 88D-1 4U+CK damaged by 46 Sqn Beaufighter off Nile Delta and belly-landed at Gadurra on Rhodes; crew safe

Wednesday-Thursday, 12/13 January 1944

British Casualties

38 Sqn	Wellington XI JA177 'T' left 2220, damaged by Flak while mining off Rhodes, force-landed on return at Gambut 0455, Cat II damaged; Flg Off D.S.Kirkland and crew safe

Thursday, 13 January 1944

227 Squadron's Wg Cdr Buchanan led four Beaufighters on a sweep of the Greek coast from Hydra to Spetses, just off the Greek mainland. In the sea between Hydra and the mainland a sighting was made of vessels thought possibly to be an R boat and two trawlers and these were attacked. These were in fact the German patrol boats *GA 62*, *67* and *72*. The attack left all three vessels on fire and out of control but none of them sank. They did shoot back however, hitting Buchanan's aircraft in the starboard cannon area, wounding Sqn Ldr W.R.Kemp in the ankle and shooting down Flg Off Morgan's aircraft.

British Casualties

227 Sqn	Beaufighter VI JM235 'G' left 1020, hit by Flak nr Hydra, returned; Wg Cdr J.K.Buchanan/Wt Off R.C.Howes safe
227 Sqn	Beaufighter VI JM233 'U' left 1020, hit by Flak nr Hydra, returned; Sqn Ldr W.R.Kemp WiA, Sgt F.L.Tyrell safe
227 Sqn	Beaufighter VI JM274 'T' left 1020, hit by Flak, ditched 2m from port on Hydra Island 1527; Flg Off L.F.Morgan/Sgt R.A.W.Ferguson POW

German Claims

Marine Flak	GA 62, 67 & 72		Beaufighter	Hydra Island

Friday-Saturday, 14/15 January 1944

British Casualties

162 Sqn	Wellington Ic HX724 left 2230 on RDF investigation ops over eastern Aegean, starboard engine failed on return flight, crash-landed near Burg el Arab; Flt Lt P.Griffin and six safe

Sunday, 16 January 1944

British Casualties

603 Sqn	Beaufighter X LZ 138 'N' hit by debris from ship attacked in Khios harbour, headed south, ditched off Panaghia Island; Flt Lt G.W.MacDonald/Flg Off S.W.Piner KiA

Saturday, 22 January 1944

British Casualties

47 Sqn	Beaufighter TFX LX863 'A' left 1235 escorting four Mitchells on a sweep of the Aegean, engine trouble, ditched S Crete 1343; navigator escaped the aircraft, rescued by a HSL from Tobruk; Flg Off D.B.Hume KiA/Flt Sgt E W.Peggram rescued

Sunday, 23 January 1944

British Casualties

227 Sqn	Beaufighter VI JL905 'Q' hit by Flak attacking shipping at Koroni 1016, FTR; Flg Off R.B.Hutchison/Flt Sgt L.Sawle MiA
227 Sqn	Beaufighter VI EL270 'N' hit by Flak at Kalamata 1030, tail damaged, crashed on return; Flg Off K.S.Judd KiA/Sgt A.G.Thomas safe

Monday, 24 January 1944

Two patrols each of two Baltimores from 15 SAAF Squadron undertook their usual reconnaissance sorties. The first pair left Matruh West at 0926 and covered the area from Rhodes eastwards to Crete, while at 1054 the second pair went from Scarpanto westwards to Crete. The first pair, Lt Smetherham (in FA482 'W') and Lt Emmett (in FA614 'K'), were attacked north-east of the north-western tip of Crete at 1126 by three Bf 109s which made one pass and left. Shortly after, at 1135 four Bf 109s attacked about 15 miles off the north-western most point of Crete. Both Baltimores climbed into cloud and became separated. Baltimore 'K' emerged from cloud and was attacked by a Messerschmitt that fired one burst from 1,500 yards and broke away. Both Baltimores then returned to base. The second pair, Lt Fairburn (in FA529 'D') and Lt Davis (in FA671 'Z') also encountered two Bf 109s but no combat resulted. During the first combats Uffz Büsen of 7./JG 27 claimed a Baltimore shot down but no Allied casualties were recorded.

British Casualties

459 Sqn	Ventura FB544 'B' left 0202 on escort to convoy 'Tryst' W Derna, on return flight engine failed, set course for El Adem, crash-landed 0610; Flt Sgt C.Daking and three safe
603 Sqn	Beaufighter X LZ531 'R' left 1135 on armed recce, attacked caique off Monemvasia 1414, damaged by Flak, crash-landed at base 1630; Flg Off B.G.Wilson/Flg Off P.C.Denay safe

German Claims

7./JG 27	Uffz Franz Büsen		Baltimore	40km S Gadurra	1026

Wednesday, 26 January 1944

Wg Cdr Buchanan led four Beaufighters on a sweep, attacked at 1055 the sailing vessel *Spiridon*, a 80–100-ton caique moored at Gythion, which exploded. They then flew west across the peninsula, and on the west side of the peninsula (the east side of the Messanian Gulf) attacked another caique at 1117 anchored in Limeni Bay surrounded by 1,200ft high hills. In the attack one aircraft, apparently unable to pull out of its steep dive in time, went straight into the sea.

British Casualties

227 Sqn	Beaufighter VI JL708 'E' left 0848, attacked ship 1118 in Limeni Bay but dived into the sea; Flg Off A.H.Will/Flg Off B.Findlay KiA

Thursday, 27 January 1944

The crews of four 603 Squadron Beaufighters engaged three Ju 52/3m floatplanes, escorted by three-four Ar 196s, claiming the whole formation shot down off Mykonos at 1315. A subsequent Ultra intercept confirmed that all the transports and three escorting Arados were lost.

British Claims

603 Sqn	Flt Lt A.P.Pringle/Flg Off A.E.Ross	Beaufighter X LZ133 'H'	Ju 52/3m See	Mykonos	1315
603 Sqn	Flt Sgt J.R.Edgar/Flt Sgt N.W.Wood	Beaufighter X LZ281 'K'	Ju 52/3m See	Mykonos	1315
603 Sqn	Wt Off P.G.Spooner/Flt Sgt A.C.B.Noble	Beaufighter X LZ242 'C' }	Ju 52/3m See	Mykonos	1315
603 Sqn	Flt Sgt A.Rooks/Flg Off M.J.R.Thom	Beaufighter X LZ144 'B' }			
603 Sqn	Flt Lt A.P.Pringle/Flg Off A.E.Ross	Beaufighter X LZ133 'H'	Arado 196	Mykonos	1315

603 Sqn	Flt Sgt J.R.Edgar/Flt Sgt N.W.Wood	Beaufighter X LZ281 'K'	Arado 196	Mykonos	1315
603 Sqn	Wt Off P.G.Spooner/Flt Sgt A.C.B.Noble	Beaufighter X LZ242 'C'	} Arado 196	Mykonos	1315
603 Sqn	Flt Sgt A.Rooks/Flg Off M.J.R.Thom	Beaufighter X LZ144 'B'	}		

British Casualties

603 Sqn	Beaufighter TFX LZ144 'B' engine damaged by Ar 196, ditched 40m S of Gavdos Island; Flt Sgt A.Rooks/Flg Off M.J.R.Thom MiA

German Casualties

Seetransportst. 3	Ju 52/3m See WNr 6987 8A+GL TE+DZ shot down by Beaufighters off Mykonos; Uffz Kurt Werner and two KiA, two survived
Seetransportst. 1	Ju 52/3m See WNr 7126 8A+GJ DE+TS shot down by Beaufighters off Mykonos and ditched; Obfw Heinrich Selhorn-Timm, three crew KiA and 11 passengers lost
Seetransportst. 1	Ju 52/3m See shot down by Beaufighters off Mykonos; Hans Cremer and crew rescued
1./SAGr 126	Ar 196A-3 WNr 0154 D1+AH shot down by Beaufighters W Mykonos; Gefr Horst Pfützner/Lt Wolfgang Reichel MiA
1./SAGr 126	Ar 196A-3 WNr 0328 D1+CH shot down by Beaufighters W Mykonos; Fw Gustav Zobel/Uffz Herbert Thürner MiA
1./SAGr 126	Ar 196A-3 WNr 0297 D1+FH damaged by Beaufighters W Mykonos, ditched off Delos; crew rescued

Friday, 28 January 1944

Lt J.Biggs, the observer in Lt I.Davis' 15 SAAF Squadron Baltimore, took this remarkable photo of a Bf 109G when attacked by it over Rhodes on 28 January; it was driven off damaged.

The German ship *Seerose* (211 tons) was sunk at Mykonos by four Beaufighters from 47 Squadron. Baltimores of 15 SAAF Squadron undertook their usual reconnaissances. The pair flying from Scarpanto to Crete saw nothing, but the pair covering the Rhodes area ran into Bf 109s. Lt Fairburn (in 'W') and Lt Minne (in 'K') were attacked during a rainstorm at 1005 by two Bf 109s, fire from which hit the turret of 'K'. The gunner in 'W' fired back and claimed damage to one fighter near the pilot's seat after which the Bf 109 maintained station 800 yards on the port quarter while the second fighter made six attacks, badly damaging both the South African aircraft before breaking away at 1020.

British Claims

15 SAAF Sqn	crew	Baltimore IV FA482 'W'	Bf 109 Damaged	E Rhodes	1005

British Casualties

| 15 SAAF Sqn | Baltimore IV FA482 'W' left 0800 to reconnaissance Rhodes harbour, attacked by 2 Bf 109s E Rhodes 1005, landed at base damaged by 122 holes, Cat II; Lt Fairburn and three safe |
| 15 SAAF Sqn | Baltimore IV FA614 'K' left 0800 to reconnaissance Rhodes harbour, attacked by 2 Bf 109s E Rhodes 1005, landed at base, damaged Cat II; Lt Minne and two safe, Lt Kay slightly WiA |

Friday-Saturday, 28/29 January 1944

Bad weather caused losses to both sides.

British Casualties

| 17 SAAF Sqn | Ventura V FP586 'U' left 1930 from St Jean to escort convoy 'Rose' from Haifa to Famagusta in Cyprus, lost in bad weather; Lt H.A.Schonken and three MiA |

German Casualties

| Kurierstaffel OKM* | Ju 52/3m See WNr 5452 PD+AK lost when struck mountain in bad weather NW Jagodina in Serbia; Obfw Hubert Krause and one KiA, one WiA, six passengers KiA |
| | *Ober Kommando Marine = Naval High Command Courier Squadron |

Saturday, 29 January 1944

Lts Davis and Emmett of 15 SAAF Squadron reconnoitred Rhodes harbour and, if they thought tactical surprise would be achieved by flying the sortie an hour later than the previous day, they were to be disappointed as they were intercepted by two Bf 109s off Rhodes; the Baltimores were subject to the same number of attacks as on the previous day. This time the gunners claimed to have damaged both the Bf 109s while sustaining only one 20mm cannon shell hit in a propeller blade.

During the day 76 OTU Wellingtons from Aqir joined the searches for the missing 17 SAAF Ventura, and one of these also disappeared without trace.

British Claims

15 SAAF Sqn	Lt I.Davis gunner 2/Lt van der Walt	Baltimore IV FA302 'R'	Bf 109 Damaged	Rhodes	1126
15 SAAF Sqn	Lt Emmet gunner Lt Furstenberg	Baltimore IV FA639 'L'			
15 SAAF Sqn	Lt I.Davis gunner 2/Lt van der Walt	Baltimore IV FA302 'R'	Bf 109 Damaged	Rhodes	1128

British Casualties

232 Sqn	Spitfire IX LZ950 scrambled from Lakatamia, encountered severe electrical storm, crashed near Kambia Village; Flg Off H.R.Davis KiA
15 SAAF Sqn	Baltimore FA302 'R' attacked by 2 Bf 109s, one 20mm cannon shell hit starboard propeller blade, landed safely at base; Lt I.Davis and crew safe
76 OTU	Wellington III HF754 lost on ASR search for 17 SAAF Ventura FP586; Flt Sgt S.Begg and 4 MiA

Sunday, 30 January 1944

During the early evening 47 Squadron dispatched two Torbeaus and six rocket carriers under an escort of six 603 Squadron aircraft which all attacked a convoy off Milos, confirmed by the war diary of the German 21.UJ.Flo, as containing a 2,500-ton merchant ship, an 800-ton sloop and two 500-ton escorts, all under a top cover of three Arado 196s. Sqn Ldr C.D.Pain in Beaufighter 'A' of 603 Squadron strafed a Flak ship without obvious results.

British Claims

603 Sqn	Flt Sgt M.B.Yates/Flt Sgt J.M.S.Walley	Beaufighter X LZ272 'F'	Ar 196 Damaged	Milos	1730
603 Sqn	Flt Sgt A.Gow/Flt Sgt A.H.Power	Beaufighter X LX932 'Y'			

British Casualties

47 Sqn	Beaufighter TFX ND203 'D', left 1455 shot down by Flak off Milos 1730, headed home but ditched 1832; Flt Sgt I.Davies/Flt Sgt C.A.Melling rescued by Swedish Red Cross ship *Mongabarra*, then POW?
603 Sqn	Beaufighter X LZ331 'A' left 1430 on shipping sweep, damaged by Flak off Milos 1730, crash-landed on return at Gambut II; Sqn Ldr C.D.Pain/Flg Off J.M.Scott safe
603 Sqn	Beaufighter X LZ272 'F' left 1430 on shipping sweep, damaged by Flak off Milos 1730, crash-landed on return at El Adem 1955; Flt Sgt M.B.Yates/Flt Sgt J.M.S.Walley safe
603 Sqn	Beaufighter X LZ242 'C' left 1430 on shipping sweep, possibly damaged by Flak off Milos 1730, crashed on landing at Gambut III; Flt Sgt K.J.Tennant/Flt Sgt A.Burgess safe

German Claims

Flak		e/a	nr Milos

Monday, 31 January 1944

During the early afternoon eight Beaufighters of 252 Squadron became engaged over the eastern Aegean with a reported three Ju 88s and two Bf 109s. As no claims were submitted by any pilots of III./JG 27 it is suggested that the combat was actually between aircraft of 252 Squadron and 11./ZG 26.

British Claims

252 Sqn	Flt Lt R.H.R.Meyer/Flt Sgt P.Grieve	Beaufighter VIf LZ287	Ju 88	Stampalia	1310-1715

British Casualties

252 Sqn	Beaufighter VIf LZ341 left 1310, dived into sea, shot down by a Ju 88 at Stampalia; Flg Off D.A.L.Hall/Sgt A.K.Cowie KiA
252 Sqn	Beaufighter VIf LZ377 left 1310, dived into sea, possibly shot down by Ju 88 at Stampalia; Flt Sgt F.A.Stevenson/Sgt C.Thompson interned in Turkey

German Claims

11./ZG 26	gunner Uffz Friedrich Stoll	Ju 88C 3U+EV	Beaufighter	Stampalia	1400

1L./ZG 26	Ju 88C-6 WNr 360053 3U+EV shot down SW Stampalia; Uffz Franz Gruber/Uffz Friedrich Stoll safe, Uffz Hans Schmidt KiA

Tuesday, 1 February 1944

The *TA 416* war diary reported an attack on Leros by six Mitchells during the late morning. Flak gunners claimed to have shot one down and hit a second which flew away south, smoking.

The American records show that a merchant vessel with two escorts was seen two miles off Portolago Bay on the west coast of Leros, and as the Mitchells passed over the ships Lt Slater's aircraft was hit by Flak, dived into the sea and exploded. Lt Lavender's aircraft was hit while over the ships but maintained formation until it ditched with one survivor. No mention of the presence of fighters was made in the American records.

During this same midday period Baltimores of 15 SAAF Squadron also undertook a raid on Rhodes where one of these aircraft was attacked and damaged by six Bf 109s. This may have been the engagement recorded by Gefr Gerhard Siegling who claimed a "B-25" while two Bf 109s were claimed damaged in return. However, it may have been one of the Mitchells that he had attacked.

Later in the afternoon Beaufighters of 39 Squadron were also in the area but engaged with Ju 88s, one of which brought down one of the British aircraft into the sea on fire with a second crash-landing on return to base due to damage suffered. During one of these attacks *UJ 2124* was sunk by bombs.

British Claims

15 SAAF Sqn	Capt M.J.Andendorff/gnr Flt Sgt Bouwer	Baltimore IV FA302 'R'	2 Bf 109s Damaged	Rhodes	1140
15 SAAF Sqn	Lt Van Beerden/gnr Flt Sgt Williams	Baltimore IV FA639 'L'			

British Casualties

15 SAAF Sqn	Baltimore IV FA639 'L' left 0911, attacked by 6 Bf 109s over Rhodes, damaged by 20mm hits in starboard wing root and nacelle 1140 landed at base 1353; Lt Van Beerden and crew safe

US Casualties

379th BS/310th BG	B-25C 42-64770 lost attacking shipping in Portolago Bay, shot down by Flak and crashed 4m off Leros at 1257; 2/Lt Edmund M.Slater and five KiA [2815]
379th BS/310th BG	B-25C 42-64840 lost, last seen 2m off Leros 1257; 2/Lt James F.Lavender and five KiA, one POW [2814]

Germans Claims

7./JG 27	Gefr Gerhard Siegling	B-25	W Kalymnos	1230
Flak		B-25	Leros	

German Casualties

12./TG 1	S.82 MM 61219, crashed on Samos; Obfw Helmut Buchholz and three KiA

Tuesday-Wednesday, 1/2 February 1944

British Casualties

38 Sqn	Wellington XIII JA105 'Y' left 2006, damaged by Flak over Rhodes, on return flaps were inoperative and at 0215 aircraft ground-looped at the end of the runway in order to stop overshooting; Flg Off R.H.Pugh and five safe

Wednesday, 2 February 1944

German Claims

2.(F)/123	crew	Spitfire	SE Port Said	0207

Wednesday-Thursday, 2/3 February 1944

Two convoys were running at this time: one (Allied) was sailing from Malta to Port Said and Alexandria, while a second (German) was making for Rhodes. This comprised the merchant vessel *Leda* with four or five escorts.

At 2120 ten Wellingtons of 38 Squadron made a torpedo attack near Amorgos during which *Leda* (4,500 tons) carrying 2,210 troops from Samos to Rhodes, blew up. The war diary of *R 195* reported that Flak shot down one aircraft at 2103 and a second at 2150. Crew believed that a third attacker hit the mast of *Leda* and may have been destroyed. In fact, two Wellingtons were shot down and a third damaged.

British Casualties

38 Sqn	Wellington XI MP569 left 1800 on shipping strike near Amorgos Island, last heard from when SOS sent 2050 heading for Turkey; Flt Sgt L.R.Taylor and five KiA
38 Sqn	Wellington XIII JA108 'H' left 1800 on shipping strike near Amorgos Island, dropped torpedo in the face of heavy Flak, crashed into the sea in flames; Plt Off C.G.Barnett and three KiA, two POW
38 Sqn	Wellington XI MP582 'J' left 1805 on shipping strike near Amorgos Island bombed ship from 5,000ft, damaged by Flak, landed safely Cat II damaged; Flg Off R.W.Parkes and five safe

German Claims

| Marine Flak | | 2 Wellingtons | Amorgos | 2103 & 2150 |

Thursday, 3 February 1944

With daylight four Ju 88s of 2.(F)/123 searched for the Allied convoy, being assisted in their task by more aircraft from 3.(F)/33 at Kalamaki which arrived at Tatoi. Several sightings were reported, but as Obfw Röhrich of 2.(F)/123 returned to base he flew over Cyprus apparently inadvertently. Here his Ju 88T was intercepted by a pair of Spitfires from a detachment of 154 Squadron being maintained on the island by 127 Squadron and was shot down. The pilot was killed but his two crewmen baled out successfully, one of them claiming to have damaged one of the Spitfires.

British Claims

| 154 Sqn | Flt Lt A.R.Boyle | Spitfire IX MA447 | } Ju 88 | Cyprus | 1107 |
| 154 Sqn | Plt Off D.J.P.Matthews | Spitfire IX MA583 | | | |

British Casualties

| 24 SAAF Sqn | Marauder II FB478 'T' left Gambut 1225 to bomb shipping in Suda Bay, shot down by a direct Flak hit 1415; Lt Col J.N.Robbs and one POW, four KiA |
| 227 Sqn | Beaufighter VIf T5170 'O' ditched due to technical failure W of Benghazi 1036, rescued by Walrus 1220; Wt Off K.F.Wright/ Flt Sgt G.L.Jones safe |

German Casualties

| 2.(F)/123 | Ju 88T-1 WNr 430939 4U+BK shot down by Spitfires over Cyprus; Obfw Lothar Röhrich KiA, two POW |

Friday 4 February 1944

A Ventura of 17 SAAF Squadron attacked a submarine but was shot down by Flak from Oblt Dierk Lührs' *U-453*, the crew of which reported that at 1944, south of Cyprus, the Ventura (misidentified as a Mosquito) made a first attack using the Leigh Light. He then dropped four bombs in a second attack, but the port engine then caught fire after being hit by Flak. The aircraft was seen by the Germans to crash into the sea about 1km away, killing all four aircrew. The bombs landed off the port side, causing no damage. This U-boat crew had already shot down a 500 Squadron Hudson during the previous April and now had brought down a second victim. The vessel would be sunk on 21 May 1944 in the Ionian Sea north-east of Cape Spartivento, by depth charges from the British destroyers HMS *Termagant* and *Tenacious* and the British escort destroyer HMS *Liddesdale*, with only one of the 52 crew being killed.

British Casualties

| 17 SAAF Sqn | Ventura V FP635 'Y' left 1643 from St Jean, shot down S Cyprus 1944 by *U-453*; Lt A.De Yong and three KiA |

Saturday, 5 February 1944

16 SAAF Squadron became fully operational on Beaufighters.

Monday, 7 February 1944

At 1140 (CET time) on this day three low-level attacks on Khios harbour by six "Blenheims" were recorded, severely damaging the Swedish Red Cross cargo ship *Viril* (933 tons), while also two motor-torpedo boats and six small civil craft suffered some damage.

According to 47 Squadron's ORB this attack occurred when six Beaufighters attacked Khios harbour at 1230, approaching from the south at 1,700ft, crossing the island and diving on the harbour, in which they reported a 1,000-ton vessel alongside the west quay and 20 caiques along the north-west and west quays. Wg Cdr

Filson-Young, leading the formation and Flg Off J.Macklem attacked the vessel, as the other four pilots attacked the caiques. The formation made three runs, noting the vessel was set on fire in the forward hatch and heavy black smoke was pouring from amidships. On the third run Flt Sgt Willis's navigator, Flt Sgt D.Thompson, saw red crosses on the side of the vessel and informed his pilot who radioed the rest of the formation, but too late to stop the third run. The attack was then broken off, 47 Squadron's records noting that six caiques were reported sunk in a subsequent PRU report, but this contained no mention of the vessel.

British Claims

454 Sqn	Flt Lt D.W.Lewis/gnr Flg Off G.S.Hissey	Baltimore FW330	Bf 109 Damaged	Syros	0700–1310

British Casualties

252 Sqn	Beaufighter VIf LZ345 left 0812, strafed caique, stalled onto the sea due to down draught, crew seen in water; Flg Off C.H.Mason/Sgt J.R.Smith evaded via Turkey, returned February 1944
252 Sqn	Beaufighter VIf LZ375 left 0812, strafed caique, struck the mast due to down draught, returned damaged; Flg Off D.E.Lendrum/Plt Off D.C.Rooke safe
454 Sqn	Baltimore FA534 'W' left 0930 on convoy escort, radio failure in bad weather, ran out of fuel, crash-landed near Magrun 1510; Lt A.T.Dryden and three safe

Tuesday, 8 February 1944

The German ship *SS Petrella* (4,785 tons, ex-Italian *Capo Pino*, ex-French *Aveyron*) carrying 3,173 Italian POWs who had been captured at Crete, was sunk by HMS *Sportsman* off Suda at 0634; 2,670 prisoners lost their lives.

Wednesday, 9 February 1944

At 1105 the crews of four Beaufighters of 252 Squadron on a shipping search sighted off Cap Zulufi, 20km south-west Patmos, a small convoy covered by two Ar 196s. The British aircraft were then bounced by three Bf 109s from III./JG 27 and three of them failed to return. III./JG 27 claimed six Beaufighters on this date: the first three by Culemann, Appel and Kaiser, following which Culemann, Büsen and Kaiser added three more; three of these were not confirmed, however.

British Casualties

252 Sqn	Beaufighter VIf LZ287 'E' shot down by Bf 109 1313, Ikaria between Patmos and Levitha Island; Flt Lt R.H.R.Meyer/Flt Sgt P.Grieve KiA
252 Sqn	Beaufighter VIf LZ141 'A' shot down by Bf 109 1314, 5–10m NE Patmos; Plt Off F.P.Stanger/Flt Sgt J.S.L.Reynolds KiA
252 Sqn	Beaufighter VIf LZ271 'D' shot down by Bf 109 1313, between Patmos and Levitha Island; Flt Sgt A.W.Squires/Flt Sgt W.H.Boon KiA

German Claims

7./JG 27	Lt Hans-Gunnar Culemann	Beaufighter	S Patmos	1202
7./JG 27	Uffz Franz Büsen	Beaufighter	2km NW Patmos	1206
9./JG 27	Uffz Josef Kaiser	Beaufighter	3km off Levitha	1207

Thursday-Friday, 10/11 February 1944

While on patrol Wellington pilot Flt Sgt J.E.Bunyan saw the exhaust smoke of a Ju 52/3m. The rear gunner fired and the aircraft was seen going down to 100ft above the sea. Bunyan followed it down and shot it down in flames. The war diary of Sturmdivision Rhodes reported that a Ju 52/3m was lost.

British Claims

38 Sqn	Flt Sgt J.E.Bunyan *by rear gunner Sgt W.H.Cooksey	Wellington XI HZ304 'S'	Ju 52/3m*	W Khalkis	2235

German Casualties

13./TG 1	Ju 52/3m WNr 6984 shot down 25km SE Tilos; Uffz Hans Post and one KiA, two WiA

Friday, 11 February 1944

Two Baltimore crews of 15 SAAF Squadron saw three Ar 196s, five Ju 88s and one Ju 52/3m in the Rhodes area and one Bf 109 taking off. The Arados struck without effect following which four Ju 88s attacked, two engaging each Baltimore. Despite this, Maj Cormack's crew claimed a Ju 88 destroyed when the gunner Flt Sgt J.M.Julian claimed to have shot it down into the sea pouring black smoke. Three more Bf 109s then took off from Rhodes and attacked but Lt van Amerongen's gunner, Flt Sgt Etchell, although wounded, claimed hits on one of these, his Baltimore suffering some damage. Julian was awarded an immediate DFM citing that he had shot down a Ju 88, probably a Bf 109 and damaged two more of the latter.

A 47 Squadron formation bombed and strafed five caiques at Syphnos, claiming three sunk.

British Claims						
127 Sqn	Wt Off C.D.Bell	Hurricane IIc PM101 'O'	Ju 88 Damaged	SW Cyprus	0648-0826
15 SAAF Sqn	Maj C.Cormack/gnr Flt Sgt J.M.Julian	Baltimore IV FA554 'K'	Ju 88	off Rhodes	0945
15 SAAF Sqn	Maj C.Cormack/gnr Flt Sgt J.M.Julian	Baltimore IV FA554 'K'	Bf 109 Probable	off Rhodes	0945
15 SAAF Sqn	Maj C.Cormack/gnr Flt Sgt J.M.Julian	Baltimore IV FA554 'K'	2 Bf 109s Damaged	off Rhodes	0945
15 SAAF Sqn	Lt A.J.van Amerongen/gnr Flt Sgt Etchell	Baltimore V FA476 'W'	Bf 109 Damaged	off Rhodes	0950

British Casualties	
227 Sqn	Beaufighter VIf JL585 'A' shot down by Flak and crashed on ditching E of Spetses harbour 1205; Wt Off K.F.Wright KiA/Flt Sgt G.L.Jones interned in Turkey
15 SAAF Sqn	Baltimore V FA476 'W' damaged in tail plane, fin and starboard engine by Bf 109 off Rhodes 0945-0955, landed safely at base; Lt A.J.van Amerongen and two safe
24 SAAF Sqn	Marauder II FB435 'L' left Gambut 1155 to bomb Calato l/g, ran out of fuel, belly-landed 3-400 yards short of the runway 1620; Lt G.A.Bowles and crew safe

Friday-Saturday, 11/12 February 1944

Five Beaufighter Xs were loaned to 46 Squadron by 252 Squadron for an intruder sortie. Four went off at night to Rhodes. The war diary of the German Sturmdivision Rhodes confirmed that three Ju 52/3ms were lost over Gadurra to night-fighters.

Seven Wellingtons of 38 Squadron, five with torpedoes, undertook a sweep during which four crews saw a merchant vessel and four escorts five miles south of Kos between 0130 and 0205. Three torpedoes were dropped but no results were observed. Sqn Ldr Milburn's Wellington was badly hit and it was last heard from as the pilot was attempting to force land; which he did off Turkey. After a short internment the crew were back in Cairo on 11 March, and a month later Milburn was awarded a DSO.

British Claims					
46 Sqn	Sqn Ldr J.R.Blackburn/Flg Off M.G.Keys	Beaufighter X LZ462 'J'	2 Ju 52/3ms	Calato	2015-0030
46 Sqn	Sqn Ldr J.R.Blackburn/Flg Off M.G.Keys	Beaufighter X LZ462 'J'	Ju 52/3m Damaged	Calato	2015-0030
46 Sqn	Flt Lt D.J.A.Crerar/Plt Off L.Charles	Beaufighter X LZ335 'P'	Ju 52/3m	Maritza	2015-0100

British Casualties	
38 Sqn	Wellington XIII HZ977 'L' left 2030, attacked M/V 5m S Kos, damaged by Flak from 4 escorts, ditched off Bodrum, Turkey, crew paddled ashore 0615; Sqn Ldr J.M.Milburn and five interned, back in Cairo on 11 March

German Casualties	
14./TG 1	Ju 52/3m WNr 130949 IZ+LY shot down by night fighters SW Rhodes; Gerhard Kneschke and four MiA
15./TG 1	Ju 52/3m WNr 501164 IZ+HZ shot down by night fighters SW Rhodes; Obfw Emil Armhorst and three MiA
15./TG 1	Ju 52/3m WNr 130941 IZ+LZ shot down by night fighters SW Rhodes; Gefr Willi Hess and two MiA

Saturday, 12 February 1944

8. and 9./JG 27 prepared to depart the Aegean, leaving only 7.Staffel there, with three Bf 109s at Kalamaki and five at Gadurra.

Luftwaffe Order of Battle

3.(F)/2	Larissa	(9)
1./SAGr 126	Volos	(4)
2.(F)/123	Tatoi	(2)
X Flk	Kifissia	
1.(F)/122	Kalamaki	(3)
7./JG 27	Kalamaki	(3)
11./ZG 26	Eleusis	(8)
Stab 126 + 1./126 & 2./126	Skaramanga	(13)
3./SAGr 126	Leros	(6)
7./JG 27	Gadurra	(5)
4./SAGr 126	Suda	(6)

Saturday-Sunday, 12/13 February 1944

15 SAAF Squadron launched several aircraft on night-intruder sorties to Rhodes-Calato airfield, but one aircraft crashed on take-off. Venturas of 17 SAAF Squadron also took part – a rather different role from the unit's usual anti-submarine operations – but lost a crew during this raid.

British Casualties

15 SAAF Sqn	Baltimore IV 'M' left 2033 on intruder sortie to Rhodes, crashed shortly after take-off; Lt Wolk and three WiA
17 SAAF Sqn	Ventura V FP593 'X' left 2010 for night raid on Maritza a/f, shot down; Lt F.Bluck and three MiA

Sunday, 13 February 1944

The PRU Spitfire BR430 took off from Tocra at 1330 for a photo reconnaissance of Candia and Piraeus. Strong winds were encountered and the pilot, Sgt Vincent Alwyn McCarthy, was instructed to return at 1345. At 1412 the aircraft had been correctly on track to Candia 164 miles from base, after which nothing further was heard and no distress calls were received. The Spitfire did not return to base and at 1720, with the aircraft overdue, air-sea rescue action was initiated but no trace of the missing aircraft or pilot was found. Flt Sgt McCarthy was a member of 680 Squadron, attached to 682 Squadron and is commemorated on the Malta Memorial.

Four Beaufighters from 47 Squadron left on patrol, but two had to return unserviceable, the remaining two were attacked north of Milos by three Bf 109s and one was shot down.

In Egypt, at Idku the Hurricanes of 213 Squadron were replaced by a mixture of Spitfire Mk Vc and IX aircraft that were flown until the early summer.

British Casualties

682 Sqn	Spitfire PR IVT BR430 on sortie Crete-Greece area 1300, FTR; Flt Sgt V.A.McCarthy MiA
47 Sqn	Beaufighter X LZ240 'L' on sweep over the central Aegean, attacked by three Bf 109s, shot down N Milos; Flg Off J.A.Unwin/ Flt Sgt K.R.Farmer KiA
15 SAAF Sqn	Baltimore IV FA639 'L' left 0731 on recce, hit by Flak off Rhodes harbour, landed 1258 at LG 08; Maj M.G.Howson and two safe, 2/Lt J.A.Breet KiA

German Claims

8./JG 27	Gefr Walter Appel	Beaufighter	4km N Milos	1207
8./JG 27	Gefr Walter Appel	Beaufighter	W Milos	1209

During an attack on Rhodes on 13 February, Baltimore IV FA639 'L' of 15 SAAF Squadron flown by Maj Howson was hit by Flak which killed his air gunner 2/Lt J.A.Breet instantly.

Monday, 14 February 1944

German Casualties	
14./TG 1	Ju 52/3m WNr 130942 IZ+BY hit obstacle 2km S Gadurra, destroyed; Uffz Friedrich Eicker and three injured
6./TG 4	Ju 52/3m left Rhodes for Tatoi and presumed lost shortly after take-off, as some of the crew were washed ashore in Turkey; Uffz Karl Schaaf and four KiA, one rescued

Tuesday-Wednesday, 15/16 February 1944

British Casualties	
459 Sqn	Ventura V FB545 left Gambut to escort convoy 'Rubble' in extremely bad weather, radar plot lost 20 minutes after take-off, FTR; Flg Off L.A.Caldow and three MiA

Wednesday, 16 February 1944

During a sortie off the coast of the Peloponnese by Beaufighters of 227 Squadron, Flak from positions near the port of Nauplia struck one aircraft that crashed into the sea. One of those lost was flown by Wg Cdr J.K.Buchanan DSO, DFC and Bar who was probably the most notable of all Beaufighter strike pilots. He was on his fifth operational tour at this time, an outstanding record by itself. When added to this was the fact that he had shot down ten enemy aircraft, shared in the destruction of four more, destroyed one on the ground and also led many damaging attacks on shipping, and had, before flying Beaufighters completed 230 bomber sorties flying Blenheims and Wellingtons, it will be seen what a great loss he was. Last seen sitting on a floating fuel tank from his shot-down aircraft, twiddling his moustache and making rude signs at the rest of the formation, he was not found until many days later, by which time he had died from hunger, thirst and exposure.

British Casualties	
16 SAAF Sqn	Beaufighter LZ333 'N' left 1205, engine trouble probably from Flak damage, near Zakinthos 1432, headed for Taranto, last heard from at 1437; Lt W.P.Ridley/Lt J.A.S.Louw POW
227 Sqn	Beaufighter VI FL467 'J' shot down by Flak off coast near Nauplia 1120; Wg Cdr J.K.Buchanan DSO, DFC, KiA/Wt Off R.C.Howes rescued/LAC E.Eliav KiA

Wednesday-Thursday, 16/17 February 1944

British Casualties	
162 Sqn	Wellington Ic HF831 left 1922 on RDF investigation of Crete, flew into a mountain in bad weather near Bathiako on Crete; Plt Off J.W.Morris and six KiA

Friday, 18 February 1944

British Claims					
24 SAAF Sqn	Lt G.R.Bell/gnr Sgt J.P.L.Snyman	Marauder II FB507 'W'	Bf 109 Damaged	Rhodes harbour	1530

British Casualties	
16 SAAF Sqn	Beaufighter TFX LZ481'V' left 0945, shot down by Flak attacking a motor vessel N Hydra 1205; Lt T.J.Simpson/Capt J.F.A.Steyn KiA

German Claims				
7./JG 27	Fw Otto Hemmersbach	B-26	10km E Gadurra	1445

Saturday, 19 February 1944

The patrol boat *GA 52* was sunk by aircraft near Hydra.

German Casualties	
15./TG 1	Ju 52/3m WNr 130866 thought to have crashed on fire in Salamina Bay (Gulf of Athens); Obfw Arthur Reger and four MiA

Sunday, 20 February 1944

454 Squadron undertook the unit's first reconnaissance of the west coast of mainland Greece, whereupon Sqn Ldr Don Beaton decided to make this event noteworthy by strafing four Ju 52/3ms he spotted on Araxos airfield.

British Claims

454 Sqn	Sqn Ldr D.Tableton	Baltimore IV FW303	4 Ju 52/3ms Dmgd	Araxos airfield	0824–1303
15 SAAF Sqn	Lt L.G.Van Renan/gnr Wt Off Hammond	Baltimore IV FA302 'R'	Ju 88	20km E Rhodes	1020
15 SAAF Sqn	Lt L.G.Van Renan/gnr Wt Off Hammond	Baltimore IV FA302 'R'	Bf 109	20km E Rhodes	1023
15 SAAF Sqn	Lt L.G.Van Renan/gnr Wt Off Hammond	Baltimore IV FA302 'R'	Bf 109 Damaged	20km E Rhodes	1025

British Casualties

15 SAAF Sqn	Baltimore IV FA554 'K' shot down by Bf 109 20km E of Lindos, on E coast of Rhodes 1025; Lt P.C.de B.Otto and two MiA, one POW

German Claims

7./JG 27	Uffz Günter Striebel		Baltimore	20km SE Rhodes	0910

Monday, 21 February 1944

The war diary of the Heeresgruppe E recorded that a Lufthansa Ju 52/3m disappeared near Skopelos; engine failure was believed to have been the cause.

British Claims

451 Sqn	Flt Lt W.W.B.Gale	Spitfire IX MA418	} Ju 88	130m N Port Said	0730
451 Sqn	Flg Off G.H.Purdy	Spitfire IX BS339			

British Casualties

24 SAAF Sqn	Marauder II FB453 'N' left 1315, encountered severe icing off Crete, spun into the sea 1510; Lt A.M.Shepherd and five KiA

German Casualties

2.(F)/123	Ju 88T-1 WNr 430921 4U+RK shot down by Hurricanes N Port Said; Fw Adalbert Langer and two KiA
6./TG 4	Ju 52/3m crashed between Rhodes and Tatoi; Gefr Walter Pleninger KiA
Lufthansa	Ju 52/3m WNr 6561 D-AWAS *Joachim Blankenburg* lost in Mediterranean

Tuesday, 22 February 1944

The German torpedo boats *TA 15* and *TA 17* were tasked to escort the transports *Agathe* (1,549 tons ex-Italian *Aprilia*) and *Lisa* (5,343 tons, ex-Italian *Livenza*) to Crete. The convoy left Piraeus on 19 February and made a stop in Milos. On the 22nd, south of Milos, *Lisa* was shadowed by Baltimores of 454 Squadron; some Ar 196s, four Ju 88s and two Bf 109s of 7./JG 27 were sent to protect the convoy. A Baltimore was shot down north-north-west Heraklion by Lt Culemann at 1225 who flew over the ships waggling his wingtips. Then six torpedo-carrying Beaufighters and two anti-Flak aircraft of 47 Squadron, escorted by eight more Beaufighters from 227 Squadron and two from 603 Squadron, plus eight B-25s, attacked *Lisa* ten miles north of Heraklion. During this initial attack 47 Squadron crews torpedoed and claimed to have sunk *Lisa*, loaded with 1,750 tons of fuel and 660 tons of ammunition, and left a motor-torpedo boat on fire, while one Ar 196 was claimed shot down by Flg Off Somerville of this unit. 227 Squadron's pilots reported meeting five Ju 88s, four Bf 109s and four Ar 196s with one Beaufighter shot down by an Arado and a second hit. Then a second Beaufighter went down in flames.

At 1300 four Mitchells flew near the vessels at very low altitude, the Bf 109s giving chase to these, but at that moment some 20 Beaufighters appeared at similarly low altitude. The fighting was heavy and in a few seconds rockets were launched, one of these hitting *TA 15*, one member of the crew being killed and 15 wounded. *Lisa* had indeed been hit by a torpedo, although this did not explode – fortunate for those aboard as she was full of fuel. However, she was taken in tow but would sink next morning in Heraklion harbour.

British Claims

227 Sqn	Sqn Ldr D.B.Bennett/Flt Sgt T.R.Bignold	Beaufighter VI EL530 'C'	Ar 196 Damaged	N Heraklion	1415
603 Sqn	Flt Lt A.P.Pringle/Flg Off A.E.Ross	Beaufighter X LX533 'R'	Ar 196 Damaged	N Heraklion-Dia	1420
603 Sqn	Wt Off P.G.Spooner/Flt Sgt A.C.B.Noble	Beaufighter X LX872 'D'	Ar 196 Damaged	N Heraklion-Dia	1420
47 Sqn	Flg Off R.Somerville/Flt Sgt H.Laing	Beaufighter X 'O'	Ar 196	N Heraklion-Dia	1420

British Casualties

454 Sqn	Baltimore V FW329 'W' left 1104 to shadow convoy N Heraklion; Flt Sgt B.E.Rawlings and three MiA
16 SAAF Sqn	Beaufighter X LZ237 'O' left 1045 on shipping strike, ditched S of Zante Island en route; Lt N.A.Smith/Lt C.H.Clark, seen in dinghy, never found, MiA

227 Sqn	Beaufighter X X8103 'D' shot down by Ar 196 near convoy N Heraklion, ditched SW of convoy 1420; Flt Sgt S.B.Appleton/Flt Sgt J.Fenton KiA
227 Sqn	Beaufighter X EL228 'P' attacked convoy nr Dia Island, shot down by Bf 109 1220; Flt Sgt R.F.Scarlett/Flg Off G.S.Hartley KiA
227 Sqn	Beaufighter X JL731 'Q' attacked convoy nr Dia Island, shot down by Bf 109 1220; Flg Off J.C.Corlett KiA/Flg Off G.Williams POW

German Claims

7./JG 27	Lt Hans-Gunnar Culemann		Baltimore	NNW Heraklion	1225
7./JG 27	Lt Hans-Joachim Hayessen		Beaufighter	1km NW Dia Island	1320
4./SAGr 126	unstated	Ar 196	Beaufighter	Dia Island	1320
7./JG 27	Lt Hans-Joachim Hayessen		Beaufighter	18km E Dia Island	1327
Naval Flak	TA 15		Beaufighter		
Naval Flak	TA 17		Beaufighter		

German Casualties

1./SAGr 126	Ar 196 damaged by Beaufighter during shipping escort 10km N Heraklion; crew safe
4./SAGr 126	2 Ar 196s damaged

Luftwaffe Order of Battle Kdo Süd-Ost

Stab/JG 27	Jafü Balkan	Niš	Obstlt Gustav Rödel
IV./JG 27	Jafü Balkan	Niš	Hptm Otto Meyer
III./JG 77	Jafü Balkan	Mizil	Maj Kurt Ubben
10./JG 301	Jafü Balkan	Taxerul-Nou	n.n
III./JG 27	Jafü Griechenland	Kalamaki	Maj Ernst Düllberg
11./ZG 26	Jafü Griechenland	Eleusis	n.n.

Tuesday-Wednesday, 22/23 February 1944

British Casualties

38 Sqn	Wellington XI MP643 'P' left 1930 on offensive recce of Aegean, bombed Candia harbour as alternate, seen falling in flames near target; Flg Off R.H.Pugh and five KiA

Wednesday, 23 February 1944

British Casualties

15 SAAF Sqn	Baltimore IV FA471 'W' shot down by Bf 109 N of Dia 0820; Lt C.P.Peachey and three MiA
227 Sqn	Beaufighter VI JL757 'B' left 1200 to meet convoy 'Raven', port engine cut, turned for home, crash-landed on a beach 1433; Flg Off E.J.Powers/Flt Sgt R.J.Roll safe

German Claims

7./JG 27	Lt Hans-Joachim Hayessen	Baltimore	E Dia	0728

Thursday, 24 February 1944

Five Marauders of 24 SAAF Squadron raided Portolago Bay, Leros, and were reportedly attacked by Bf 109s and FW 190s. One Marauder was damaged and crashed on landing.

British Claims

24 SAAF Sqn	gunner	Marauder II	Bf 109	Portolago Bay	1420-1440
24 SAAF Sqn	gunner	Marauder II 'M'	Bf 109	Portolago Bay	1420-1440
24 SAAF Sqn	gunner	Marauder II 'K'			
24 SAAF Sqn	gunner	Marauder II 'M'	Bf 109 Damaged	Portolago Bay	1420-1440
24 SAAF Sqn	gunner	Marauder II 'K'			

British Casualties

24 SAAF Sqn	Marauder II FB478 'B' left 1150 to attack shipping in Portolago Bay, damaged by Bf 109 off Leros, crash-landed at base 1700; Lt H.A.Puntis and four safe, one WiA

Friday, 25 February 1944

Four Marauders of 24 SAAF Squadron raided Portolago Bay again, reporting that Bf 109s and FW 190s attacked and one Marauder was shot down in flames. On return the crews claimed two fighters shot down and one more probably.

British Claims					
24 SAAF Sqn	four crews	Marauder II	Bf 109	15m S Kos	1405
24 SAAF Sqn	Capt A.F.Shuttleworth	Marauder II 'S'	Bf 109	15m S Kos	1405
24 SAAF Sqn	gnr Flt Sgt Glass	Marauder II 'M'	Bf 109 Probable	15m S Kos	1405

British Casualties	
24 SAAF Sqn	Marauder II FB491 'F' left 1150 to attack shipping in Portolago Bay, shot down off Leros 1407 by 7 Bf 109s and 2 FW 190s, ditched; Capt F.Ribbink and five KiA
47 Sqn	Beaufighter X 'X' left 1255 for a sweep around Scarpanto, attacked schooner 1504, hit by Flak from it, ditched 1540 60m S of western point of Crete; Flg Off R.Euler/Flt Sgt C.A.Boffin rescued on 29 February by RN

German Claims				
7./JG 27	Uffz Rudolf Moycis	B-26	10km W Leros	1252
7./JG 27	Uffz Werner Pflüger	B-26	8km W Kos	1305

German Casualties	
7./JG 27	Bf 109G-6 WNr 15888 White 5 shot down SW Kos; Uffz Werner Pflüger KiA
16./TG 1	Ju 52/3m WNr 501125 crashed 7km N Heraklion; Uffz Hans Heidricks WiA, two drowned, one DoW

Sunday, 27 February 1944

Four aircraft of 227 Squadron undertook a sweep of the west coast of Greece, losing one Beaufighter to the Flak position they had just attacked. The remaining three crews then attacked a tug which they thought they had probably sunk off Missolonghi.

British Claims					
454 Sqn	Flg Off R.Crouch/gnr Wt Off C.H.Manning	Baltimore III FA468	Bf 109 Damaged	Antikythera	0825

British Casualties	
454 Sqn	Baltimore III FA499 'U' left 0750 on reconnaissance to west coast of Greece, after issuing distress calls, ditched about 100km N Benghazi 1320; Flg Off A W.Dawe and three MiA
454 Sqn	Baltimore III FA468 'R' left 0825, shot up by 2 Bf 109s off Antikythera, crash-landed at Derna 1245 with 26 cannon shell hits, w/o; Flg Off R.Crouch and three safe
227 Sqn	Beaufighter VI EL509 'K' left 0920 on sweep of west coast of Greece, attacked Flak positions at Missolonghi 1157, shot down, ditched; Flg Off W.M.Davies/Flt Sgt G.A.Brown KiA

German Claims				
7./JG 27	Uffz Johann Penz	Baltimore		1224
Flak 6./GR 522	Obgfr Rudolf Tautz	e/a	nr Cap Rodoni	

Monday, 28 February 1944

Four Spitfire Vs from 335 Squadron were scrambled at 1415 after an unidentified aircraft and, much to their surprise, the pilots actually sighted a Ju 88, which evaded into cloud. This was the first enemy aircraft the pilots of this unit had seen since re-equipping with Spitfires the previous December.

At 1127 *TA 16* (ex-Italian *Castelfidardo*, Kptlt Jürgen Quaet-Faslem) was called to go to the rescue of an Ar 196 forced to land between Ikaria and Samos. It was found and the crew were taken aboard with various materials; an attempt was then made to tow the aircraft but one float was then damaged and it overturned. Consequently, it had to be destroyed with the vessel's 20mm guns.

German Casualties	
1./SAGr 126	Ar 196 WNr 0375 sunk near Leros; crew safe
1./SAGr 126	Ar 196 WNr 0216 engine trouble, ditched between Ikaria and Samos, sank in tow; crew rescued by T-boat

Tuesday, 29 February 1944

3 SAAF Squadron, who five days earlier, to their total joy, had completed re-equipment with Spitfire IXs and now, to their equal joy, achieved their fourth success since May 1943, shooting down a Ju 88 off Derna.

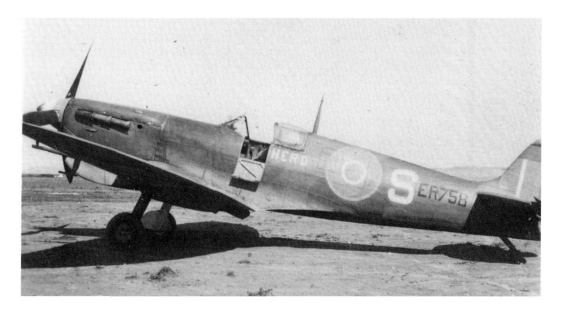

On 28 February four Spitfire Vbs of the Greek-manned 335 Squadron scrambled after a Ju 88. ER758/S, named 'Hero', was usually flown by Flt Lt Karamolegos.

Indignation would follow three days later when higher authority ordered ten Spitfire IXs to be sent to 7 SAAF Squadron in exchange for the latter's Spitfire Vs.

454 Squadron had sited a German convoy near Hydra, and during the day four separate crews encountered the convoy's air cover of Ju 88s and Ar 196s, which they evaded as required without too much difficulty, unlike when the air cover was Bf 109s which would soon continue to inflict heavy losses on the Baltimores.

British Claims					
3 SAAF Sqn	Lt H.A.Geater	Spitfire IX MH971 'H'	} Ju 88	12m SE Derna	0840-0845
3 SAAF Sqn	Lt H.T.R.du Preez	Spitfire IX MH612 'F'			
German Casualties					
2.(F)/123	Ju 88T-1 WNr 430926 4U+WK shot down by Spitfires near Derna; Lt Kurt Fischer and two KiA				

Wednesday-Thursday, 1/2 March 1944

British Casualties	
38 Sqn	Wellington XIII HZ866 'F' on minelaying mission to Milos; Plt Off J.E.Bunyan and one POW, four MiA
38 Sqn	Wellington XIII MP742 'D' left evening on shipping strike in the Aegean, lost without trace; Plt Off W.D.C.Boyd and five MiA

Thursday-Friday, 2/3 March 1944

British Casualties	
17 SAAF Sqn	Ventura V FP653 'C' left 2100 on sea search, around midnight got lost, eventually crashed in Turkey; Capt P.N.Murray and five interned

Friday, 3 March 1944

Both reconnaissance flights of 454 Squadron over the Aegean failed to return, the squadron records reporting: "We were not prepared for the severe shock we suffered today." Since 1 November 1943 the squadron had lost ten aircraft to Bf 109s.

British Casualties

454 Sqn	Baltimore V FW300 'A' left 0708 to reconnoitre N Crete, shot down by 2 Bf 109s, ditched S Milos ca 1036; Flt Sgt A.W.J.Kempnich, Flt Sgt F.J.Brown and Flt Sgt J.D.Seymour got into the dinghy, Wt Off J.F.Stapleton was killed in the crash. After five days Kempnich attempted to swim to Antiparos Island but disappeared, the other two drifted ashore next day
454 Sqn	Baltimore IV FA601 left 0742 to reconnaissance Suda Bay, FTR; Flg Off F.N.Scott and three KiA

German Claims

7./JG 27	Uffz Hans Giese	Baltimore	Cape Spatha, Crete	0907
7./JG 27	Lt Hans-Gunnar Culemann	Baltimore	50km S Milos	0935

Friday-Saturday, 3/4 March 1944

The German merchant ship *Sifnos* (397 tons, ex-Greek *Mira*) was sunk by aircraft from 38 Squadron (Flg Off A.G.Lidstrom) during a midnight patrol between Suda Bay and Milos Island. Aboard this vessel there were 90 Italian POWs, 12 Germans and 12 tons of materials; rescued were 31 Italians, 12 Germans and the Greek crew. The Wellington that hit the ship was damaged and the crew just managed to return to base.

British Casualties

38 Sqn	Wellington XIII JA403 'S' left 1940 on shipping strike, damaged by Flak, starboard engine failed, managed to land at Gambut Cat II damaged; Flg Off A.G.Lidstrom and five safe
459 Sqn	Ventura V FP517 'E' left 1705 on anti-submarine search, at 2033 signalled starboard engine failed and 5 minutes later ditched 10m SW Cape Greco Cyprus; Flg Off A.H.Ringland and three MiA

German Casualties

2.(F)/123	Ju 88D-1 crashed 8km NE Gadurra on return from a sortie to Port Said; Fw Robert Götz and three KiA

Saturday, 4 March 1944

British Casualties

24 SAAF Sqn	Marauder II FB480 'O' left 1400 to bomb Suda Bay, hit by Flak, dropped out of formation, shot down by a Bf 109, ditched, bounced and burst into flames off north coast of Crete 1611; Lt E.J.Thornhill-Cook and five KiA

German Claims

7./JG 27	Uffz Rudolf Moycis	B-26	N Crete	1507

Saturday-Sunday, 4/5 March 1944

British Claims

227 Sqn	Flt Lt J.S.Holland/Flt Sgt J.Templeton	Beaufighter XI JM237 'N'	Ju 52/3m	100m W Cap Matapan	2245-0315

German Casualties

15./TG 1	Ju 52/3m WNr 130765 IZ+FZ lost between Maleme and Eleusis; Obgfr Hugo Lübke and three MiA
13./TG 1	Ju 52/3m WNr 131070 attacked by night fighter, tried to avoid it but lost formation. Flying above coast where *Agathe* was sailing, was shot down when the vessel's Flak opened up at 2205; Obfw Berthold Schröder and two KiA, one survived

Sunday, 5 March 1944

German Casualties

4./SAGr 126	Ar 196A-4 WNr 0121 D1+GL damaged by bombs at Leros

Sunday-Monday, 5/6 March 1944

Grp Capt Max Aitken borrowed a 46 Squadron Beaufighter to undertake a lone intruder sortie over Crete.

British Claims

219 Grp	Grp Capt J.W.M.Aitken/Flt Lt G.A.Muir	Beaufighter X LZ330 'F'	Ju 52/3m	Heraklion area	2020
219 Grp	Grp Capt J.W.M.Aitken/Flt Lt G.A.Muir	Beaufighter X LZ330 'F'	Ju 52/3m Damaged	Heraklion area	2025
219 Grp	Grp Capt J.W.M.Aitken/Flt Lt G.A.Muir	Beaufighter X LZ330 'F'	Ju 52/3m	N Dia Island	2030
219 Grp	Grp Capt J.W.M.Aitken/Flt Lt G.A.Muir	Beaufighter X LZ330 'F'	Ju 52/3m Probable	N Crete	2040
227 Sqn	Sqn Ldr D.B.Bennett/Flt Sgt T.R.Bignold	Beaufighter VIf EL530 'C'	Ju 88	Cape Spatha	0116

German Casualties

15./TG 1	Ju 52/3m WNr 131078, between Eleusis and Maleme, force-landed in sea near Polyaigos Island; crew rescued, radio operator DoW

Monday, 6 March 1944

The crew of a reconnaissance Baltimore of 15 SAAF Squadron spotted the *Agathe* in Scala Bay, Milos, with two destroyers and four armed schooners. Six Marauders took off to attack the shipping at Santorini Island but as they rounded Crete to the west they were intercepted at 1245 on the way to the target by a reported nine Bf 109s and three FW 190s. Three Marauders were shot down before reaching the target, which was bombed at 1325; the fourth to fall was reported by survivors to have shot down one fighter. The tail gunner of one survivor claimed to have shot down an FW 190 which he reported had blown up. One turret gunner claimed a Bf 109 in flames and two others were seen smoking. 7./JG 27 did not report any losses or serious damage but claimed six of the bombers shot down with two claims not confirmed. After this raid Middle East Command was ordered not to send out bombers again without fighter escorts. When 24 SAAF Squadron recommenced operations a month later, 94 Squadron Spitfires with 90-gallon long-range tanks were the escort.

British Claims

24 SAAF Sqn	Capt H.Braithwaite/gnr Lt A.Berger	Marauder II FB508 'T'	Bf 109	Milos	1305
24 SAAF Sqn	Capt H.Braithwaite/gnr Flt Sgt R.E.Harrison	Marauder II FB508 'T'	FW 190	Milos	1305
24 SAAF Sqn	Capt A.F.Shuttleworth/gnr Flt Sgt R.Pines	Marauder II 'M'	Bf 109	Milos	1305
24 SAAF Sqn	Capt A.F.Shuttleworth/gnr Flt Sgt R.Pines	Marauder II 'M'	2 Bf 109 Probables	Milos	1305
24 SAAF Sqn	Lt G.R.Bell/gnr Lt C.W.Heaven	Marauder II FB507 'W'	Bf 109	S Milos	1400–1425

British Casualties

24 SAAF Sqn	Marauder II FB481 'E' shot down by fighters off Milos 1305, crash-landed in Turkey; Lt L.L.Doveton and co-pilot interned, four baled out and drowned
24 SAAF Sqn	Marauder II FB496 'V' shot down by fighters 4m S of west coast of Milos 1305; Lt G.A.Bowles and five KiA
24 SAAF Sqn	Marauder II FB504 'L' shot down by fighters 4 miles S of west coast of Milos 1305; Capt G.Frolich and five KiA
24 SAAF Sqn	Marauder II FB507 'W' shot down SW Antikythera 1429; Lt G.R.Bell and five KiA
24 SAAF Sqn	Marauder II FB508 'T' damaged by Bf 109s at Milos, reached base and landed 1625, Cat I damaged; Capt H.Braithwaite and crew safe

German Claims

7./JG 27	Lt Hans-Gunnar Culemann	B-26	SW Milos Island	1210
7./JG 27	Uffz Gerhard Siegling	B-26	S Folegandros Island	1215
7./JG 27	Fw Karl Schaffhauser	B-26	SE Folegandros Island	1216
7./JG 27	Lt Hans-Joachim Hayessen	B-26	SW Antikythera	1324

German Casualties

4./SAGr 126	Ar 196A-3 WNr 623053 D1+PN destroyed by bombs at Scarpanto, Pigadia harbour
4./SAGr 126	Ar 196A-5 WNr 0433 D1+DN 70% damaged by bombs at Scarpanto, Pigadia harbour
4./SAGr 126	Ar 196A-5 WNr 0187 D1+EN 30% damaged by bombs at Scarpanto, Pigadia harbour

Monday-Tuesday, 6/7 March 1944

British Casualties

46 Sqn	Beaufighter X LZ335 'P' left 0135 to intrude over Kos and Maritza, FTR; Flg Off A.Taylor/Flg Off R.T.Peace KiA
38 Sqn	Wellington XIII MP804 'L' left to mine Rhodes harbour, flew into the sea just off the target; Flg Off C.F.Bull DFC and three KiA, two reported safe in friendly hands

Tuesday-Wednesday, 7/8 March 1944

British Claims

38 Sqn	Flg Off C.B.Urwin*	Wellington XIII JA358 'H'	2 Ju 52/3ms	Suda Bay-Antikythera	1805–0055
	*probably by the rear gunner Flt Sgt P.Varese			

British Casualties

500 Sqn	Ventura V FP546 believed on convoy escort, crashed into the sea off Oran in bad weather; Flg Off F.S.Knighton and three MiA

German Casualties

15./TG 1	Ju 52/3m WNr 131079 left Eleusis for Crete, shot down near Polyaigos Island (Milos); most of the crew rescued, engineer WiA, went down with the aircraft

Friday, 10 March 1944

Luftwaffe Order of Battle

3./FGr 2	Larissa	(6)
1 Schw 1./SAGr 126	Volos	(2)
2.(F)/123	Tatoi	(7)
Stab FGr 4		(1)
X.Fl K	Kifissia	
11./ZG 26	Eleusis	(10)
Stab 126 + 2./SAGr	Skaramanga	(1) + (7)
3./SAGr 126	Leros	(7)
1 Schw 7./JG 27	Gadurra	(4)
1./SAGr 126	Maleme	(4)
4./SAGr 126	Suda	(4)

Sunday, 12 March 1944

British Casualties

16 SAAF Sqn	Beaufighter X NE248 'D' left 1340, shot down by fighters or Flak, SE Makra Island 1540; Maj J.E.Bell KiA/Lt N.H.Stead POW

Monday, 13 March 1944

KTB Heeresgruppe E reported that the three aircraft missing had been shot down by a night-fighter and that three more aircraft had been heavily damaged.

British Claims

252 Sqn	Flg Off E.A.T.Taylor/Flt Sgt D.C.Dick	Beaufighter X LZ147	2 Ju 52/3ms	10–15m E Scarpanto	1550–2025

German Claims

7./JG 27	Uffz Günter Striebel		Beaufighter	50km W Cap Tenaron	0810

German Casualties

1.(F)/122	Ju 88D-1 WNr 430897 F6+CH on reconnaissance Crete-Sicily-North Africa, lost u/k cause; Fw Kurt Backenhausen and three MiA
13./TG 1	Ju 52/3m WNr 501217 shot down into sea S Rhodes; Fw Gustav Dickentmann and three KiA
16./TG 1	Ju 53/3m WNr 10099 IZ+DQ shot down by night-fighter S Rhodes; Uffz Joachim Kleindick, Oblt Hans Griebner (St.Kpt) and two KiA

Wednesday-Thursday, 15/16 March 1944

Flt Lt Holland and Flt Sgt Templeton of 227 Squadron intruded along the Crete coast from Cape Spatha to Suda Bay and return. At Cape Spatha on the return leg, Holland thought he spotted an aircraft and made a tight turn to starboard towards it. In so doing his starboard wingtip struck the sea. Following the application of full opposite rudder and maximum power he managed to drag the wing out of the water and set course for base at Tocra. The starboard engine failed on the trip, but a successful landing was made. Damage was extensive to the starboard engine nacelle, the undercarriage doors on that side were smashed, one propeller blade was bent back three feet and the other two bent back by two feet.

British Casualties

227 Sqn	Beaufighter VIf X8103 'O' left 0245 for Crete, damaged by striking sea; Flt Lt J.S.Holland/Flt Sgt J.Templeton safe

German Casualties

6./TG 4	Ju 52/3m WNr 7170 lost Athens-Kifissia; Oblt Karl Neff and three KiA, one WiA

Sunday, 19 March 1944

On this day the Kriegsmarine was authorised to fire at night on any aircraft, including those of the Luftwaffe, on the assumption that aircraft will either not fly by night or will fire identification rockets. This would allow every aircraft by night to be considered hostile.

Tuesday, 21 March 1944

3 RAAF Squadron attacked and sank two German Siebel ferries: *SF 277* and *SF 278*.

Capt Du Toit, the father of the 16 SAAF Squadron pilot lost on this day, personally went to Greece in late 1944 and traced the remains of the aircraft and crew.

British Casualties	
16 SAAF Sqn	Beaufighter X LZ378 'L' left 1105, damaged by splinters from own rockets attacking F boat off Navarino at 1306, crashed 2m NE Kyparissia, Greece; Lt L.W.M.Du Toit/Lt C.J.De Jager KiA

Thursday, 23 March 1944

British Casualties	
41 SAAF Sqn	Spitfire IX MH776 engine failed on submarine search, ditched off Sidi Barrani 1747; Lt A.Thompson KiA
336 Sqn	Spitfire V ER797 left 1030 from Bu Amud on convoy patrol, crashed into the sea; Flg Off J.Papacostas KiA

Saturday, 25 March 1944

German Casualties	
16./TG 1	Ju 52/3m WNr 7176 IZ+CZ crashed in the sea on the way to Milos-Eleusis; Uffz Robert Vogt and three MiA

Thursday, 30 March 1944

British Casualties	
227 Sqn	Beaufighter JL913 'N' left 1610 to cover convoy 'Rump', lost to engine problems; Sgt P.E.Davies/Sgt R.W.Beach KiA
227 Sqn	Beaufighter JL626 'J' left 1630 on shipping strike to Kalamata harbour, hit by Flak, reached within 5m of base before ditching; Flt Sgt L.Hibbert/Flt Sgt H.Parker safe, rescued by a destroyer 1715 the following day
603 Sqn	Beaufighter X NE263 'C' left 0600 on sweep, hit by Flak at Naxos, hydraulics shot out, crash-landed at base 1200; Flt Sgt J.N.Bowen/Flt Sgt P.B.McGregor safe

Thursday-Friday, 30/31 March 1944

Intruder missions by the strike Beaufighters were quite common by this time, but at Maleme on this night Flt Lt Pringle of 603 Squadron added a 'twist' by firing rocket projectiles at the aerodrome.

Friday, 31 March 1944

German Casualties	
13./TG 1	Ju 52/3m WNr 501111 ditched 1km off Rhodes; Obfw Hans Beck MiA, crew rescued
5./TG 4	Ju 52/3m WNr 10042 G6+GN crashed Amonte-Abeiro (Rhodes); Obfw Bruno Nawrocki and four KiA

Friday-Saturday, 31 March/1 April 1944

Sqn Ldr J.R.C.Young/Flt Lt J.M.Ritchie were scrambled from Reghaia at 0245 to intercept a raid, and were vectored into a group of six aircraft. However, two of their initial contacts showed IFF and were not attacked. Eventually a contact was made that was not showing IFF and was identified as an aircraft with a flat tail and two rudders. Believing this to be a Do 217 Young attacked and shot the aircraft down in flames. As soon as it caught fire, he identified the aircraft as a Ventura with British markings. The unfortunate victims were a crew from 500 Squadron returning from an anti-submarine patrol over convoy 'Tennant' and all were killed.

British Claims					
153 Sqn	Sqn Ldr J.R.C.Young/Flt Lt J.M.Ritchie	Beaufighter VIf ND207	Ventura	off Algerian coast	0450

500 Sqn   Ventura V FP633 'R' left 0004 on anti-sub escort to convoy 'Tennant', shot down by a Beaufighter from 153 Sqn about 0445; Flg Off V.C.Pockson and four KiA

Saturday, 1 April 1944

German Casualties

14./TG 1   Ju 52/3m WNr 640990 crash-landed u/k reason, adjacent to Gadurra a/f, Rhodes; crew safe

Sunday, 2 April 1944

British Casualties

454 Sqn   Baltimore V FW404 'W' left 0448 to reconnaissance over Leros, nothing further heard; Flg Off H.E.Jarvis and three MiA

Monday-Tuesday, 3/4 April 1944

British Casualties

46 Sqn   Beaufighter X LZ369 'U' left 1830 to intrude to Rhodes and Kos, FTR; Flt Sgt V.S.Lacey/Flt Sgt R.E.Brown MiA

252 Sqn   Beaufighter X LZ464 left 2150 to intrude to Rhodes, FTR; Flg Off R.W.Densham/Flg Off K.N.Bradford MiA

Wednesday, 5 April 1944

227 Squadron sent four Beaufighters on a sweep along the Greek coast from Katakolo to Koroni. A caique of approximately 100 tons was attacked by bombing and strafing in Katakolo harbour. The last aircraft in struck the caique's mast and crashed into a hillside, the crew being killed.

British Casualties

227 Sqn   Beaufighter XI JL730 'O' left 1255 on sweep, struck ship's mast in Katakolo harbour and crashed; Flg Off R.J.Owen/Flt Sgt L.A.Everett KiA

Thursday, 6 April 1944

While covering convoy 'Extended' near Benghazi from 0755, a section of 335 Squadron consisting of Flg Off A.Coundouris (in Spitfire Vb AB339) and Sgt A.Antonopoulis (in Spitfire Vc JG785) sighted and fired at a low-flying Ju 188 which, according to the unit's ORB, was much too fast for them.

Thursday-Friday, 6/7 April 1944

British Casualties

38 Sqn   Wellington XIII MP796 'J' left 2208 on a shipping sweep of western coast of the Peloponnese peninsula between Monemvasia and Spetses; Flt Lt A.H.Green and five MiA. The pilot's body was washed ashore and buried

Saturday, 8 April 1944

A Beaufighter of 603 Squadron ditched and only the injured observer, Sgt John Foster, managed to get out and into the dinghy. After drifting for three days he washed ashore on Syrna Island. Eight days later he was found and rescued by a commando patrol.

British Casualties

603 Sqn   Beaufighter X NE282 'B' left 1120 on strike on vessels in Karlovasi harbour, Samos, left engine seen smoking and ditched; Sgt H.Lacey MiA/Sgt J.Foster rescued

Saturday-Sunday, 8/9 April 1944

British Casualties

38 Sqn   Wellington XIII HZ598 'P' left 0022 on mining sortie to Milos Island, shot down by Flak off the harbour; Flg Off J. Normandale and two POW, three KiA

Sunday, 9 April 1944

Luftwaffe Order of Battle – defence units

Eleusis	11./ZG 26	Ju 88C	(14)
Kalamaki	7./JG 27	Bf 109G	(4)
Maleme	7./JG 27	Bf 109G	(4)
Gadurra	7./JG 27	Bf 109G	(4)

German Casualties	
4./SAGr. 126	Ar 196A-5 WNr 0439 D1+JH on approach to landing at Leros, collided with a radio mast and crashed; Obgfr Alfred Stübinger/Uffz Hans Bollacke KiA

Tuesday, 11 April 1944

UJ 2114 was sunk in Piraeus by bombs.

British Casualties	
603 Sqn	Beaufighter X NE421 'L' left 1350 on sweep, last seen with starboard engine on fire off Seriphos, crashed and exploded; Wt Off E.T.Lynch/Sgt C.C.Sykes KiA

Wednesday, 12 April 1944

German Casualties	
3.(F)/33	Ju 188F-1 WNr 280072 8H+KL crashed into Pireaus harbour, Athens; Oblt Bernhard Beyer and three KiA

Thursday, 13 April 1944

British Casualties	
603 Sqn	Beaufighter X LZ370 'N' left 0640 on sweep of Gulf of Laconia, shot down by Bf 109 W Cape Matapan; Flt Sgt R.T.Gosling/ Sgt S.A.West KiA
603 Sqn	Beaufighter X LZ272 'F' left 0640 on sweep of Gulf of Laconia, severely damaged by two Bf 109s, landed 1120; Flt Sgt C.J.Gould/Wt Off T.J.Harper safe
16 SAAF Sqn	Beaufighter X 'R' attacked a caique off Koroni, damaged by own rocket splinters, ditched 1355; Lt A.M.Kenyon/Lt P.D.van der Berg KiA

German Claims				
7./JG 27	Uffz Günter Striebel	Beaufighter	50km W Cape Matapan	0810

Saturday, 15 April 1944

The German ships *UJ 2141* with *GK 92* and the Greek motor vessel *Sokrates* left Kythera at 1320 but were attacked by four Beaufighters which sunk the submarine chaser. The ships' Flak claimed some hits on the attackers.

Sunday, 16 April 44

Spitfires from 94 and 41 SAAF Squadrons escorted 24 SAAF Squadron Marauders to Heraklion where one bomber was hit by Flak and dropped out of the formation. Two Spitfires of 41 SAAF Squadron were detailed to escort it and these were attacked by two Bf 109s at 1210 without any result.

Air Vice-Marshal William F.Dickson who assumed command of the Desert Air Force during April 1944.

British Casualties	
24 SAAF	Marauder II FB422 'L' left 1015, damaged by Flak Heraklion, attacked by 2 Bf 109s, landed at base 1327 with over 200 hits; Lt H.R.Dyer and four safe, one WiA and one KiA
24 SAAF	Marauder II 'N' left 1015, damaged by Flak Heraklion, reached base; Maj D.E.Chin and five crew safe, one WiA

Friday, 21 April 1944

Three sections of Spitfires from 336 Squadron scrambled from Mersa Matruh after two hostile aircraft. One of these was intercepted at 7,000ft about 50 miles off the coast and dived gently weaving, at which point it was shot down, the crew of three all being killed. The Greek pilots regarded the tactics employed by the German pilot to be a mistake, as flying straight and level would have enabled the Ju 88 to pull away from Spitfire Vs.

British Claims					
336 Sqn	Flg Off G.Tsotsos	Spitfire Vb LZ807	} Ju 88	70m N Mersa Matruh	1325
336 Sqn	Plt Off D.Soufrilas	Spitfire Vc JL352			

German Casualties	
2.(F)/123	Ju 88D-1 WNr 430625 4U+FK shot down in combat W Mersa Matruh; Uffz Helmut Arndt and three KiA

Monday, 24 April 1944

Two Spitfires of 41 SAAF Squadron scrambled at 1140 and intercepted a reconnaissance Ju 88 which was approaching the Nile delta at sea level. No return fire was encountered by the interceptors, Lt de Klerk, in a specially stripped-down Spitfire, being thought to have put the gunner out of action. The Ju 88 crew from 2.(F)/123 claimed a Spitfire shot down, but in fact neither was hit.

Spitfires of 336 Squadron were also scrambled from their base at Mersa Matruh, but one of the unit's fighters ran out of fuel on the return flight causing the pilot to bale out off the coast where he was rescued 90 minutes later by an HSL.

British Claims					
41 SAAF Sqn	Lt I.I.de Klerk	Spitfire IX MA407 'T'	} Ju 88 Damaged	off Idku	1210–1220
41 SAAF Sqn	Lt J.C.Silberbauer	Spitfire IX ME780 'E'			

British Casualties	
16 SAAF Sqn	Beaufighter X 'R' last light cover to convoy, became lost returning to base; Lt A.E.Wallem/Lt A.R.L.Stewart MiA
336 Sqn	Spitfire V EF655 scrambled 1125, ran out of fuel 40m off Mersa Matruh 1220, pilot baled out; Flg Off A.Moulopoulos rescued

German Claims			
2.(F)/123	crew	Spitfire	1120

Tuesday, 25 April 1944

On this day pilots of 41 SAAF Squadron were rather more effective, intercepting and shooting down another very low-level reconnaissance Ju 88. This time both pilots were in the special lightweight Spitfires.

British Claims					
41 SAAF Sqn	Lt M.H.Hartogh	Spitfire IX MA257 'X'	} Ju 88	NW Idku	1800
41 SAAF Sqn	Lt J.C.Silberbauer	Spitfire IX LZ894 'V'			

German Casualties	
2.(F)/123	Ju 88D-1 WNr 430575 4U+HK lost in combat with Spitfires nr Alexandria; Fw Joachim Lüdtke and three KiA

Saturday, 29 April 1944

British Claims					
213 Sqn	Sgt E.A.Stringer	Spitfire IX MA526 'V'	Ju 88	5m S Cape Greco Cyprus	0722

German Casualties	
2.(F)/123	Ju 88A-4 WNr 300134 4U+BK shot down by Spitfire over Cyprus 0730; Obfw Helmuth Jonas and three crewmembers rescued by 294 Sqn Walrus Z1782 flown by Flt Sgt H.G.C.King and made POW

Monday, 1 May 1944

Luftwaffe Order of Battle

3.(F)/2	Larissa	(4)
7./JG 27	Argos	(4)
7./JG 27	Gadurra	(7)
1./SAGr 126	Volos	(4)
3./SAGr 126	Leros	(9)
4./SAGr 126	Suda	(9)
11./ZG 26	Eleusis	(13)
3.(F)/33	Tatoi	(4)
Stab FGr 4	Tatoi	(1)
2.(F)/123	Tatoi	(8)

Thursday, 4 May 1944

The pressure on the remaining German garrison on Crete increased when 24 SAAF Squadron Marauders and 15 SAAF Squadron Baltimores, escorted by 94 Squadron Spitfires, bombed Maleme.

Saturday, 6 May 1944

German Casualties

2./NAGr 12   Bf 109G-8 shot down by partisans of II Herzegovina Brigade, crash-landed Dabarski Polje; Fw Scutemann POW (?)

Sunday, 7 May 1944

At 1005 Plt Off Dixon of 213 Squadron intercepted a Ju 88T of 2.(F)/123 flying 10m south-east of Nicosia at 30,000ft. The pilot, Obfw Heinz Hagmann, later described how he and his crew reached Rhodes. Basically, they landed undamaged, being of the view that the Spitfire's cannons had jammed. Dixon reported having made two attacks, having seen hits on the starboard wing. On the second attack he had to pull up sharply to avoid a collision, stalled and spun off 5,000ft before regaining control but also losing sight of the Ju 88.

Sqn Ldr Russ Foskett, the commander of 94 Squadron, flying Spitfire Vc MH558/GO-C during an attack on Rhodes on 5 May.

Yugoslav partisans of the 11th Herzegovina Brigade sit on a battered Bf 109G-8 of 2./NAGr 12 after Fw Seutemann had crash-landed it near Dabarski Polje on 6 May.

British Claims

| 213 Sqn | Plt Off J.M.Dixon | Spitfire IX MA526 'V' | Ju 88 Damaged | SE Tymbou, Cyprus | 1005 |

Sunday-Monday, 7/8 May 1944

British Casualties

| 24 SAAF Sqn | Marauder II FB508 'T' left 2035 on night raid on Maleme a/f, presumed shot down by Flak; Lt R.O.D.Brooksbank and five KiA |
| 38 Sqn | Wellington XI HE419 'Q' left 2300 to mine Khalkis, shot down by Marine Flak near Nea Artaki 0115; Flt Sgt E F.Maidment and five KiA |

German Claims

| Flak | | Baltimore | 2141 |

Tuesday-Wednesday, 9/10 May 1944

British Claims

| 46 Sqn | Flt Sgt K.C.Bottle/Sgt N.Mayer | Beaufighter VIf KW122 | Ju 88* | ca 140m N Benghazi | 0701 |
| | * claimed damaged, confirmed destroyed when the crew was rescued from their dinghy four days later |

German Casualties

| Wekusta 27 | Ju 88A-4 WNr 430480 Q5+F left Tatoi, shot down by Beaufighter, ditched S Peloponnese; Fw Werner Janicke and two POW, rescued by ship after four days, one MiA |

Sunday, 14 May 1944

Four Beaufighters from 603 Squadron spotted a convoy escorted by three Arados and two Bf 109s between Syros and Tenos. The Messerschmitts approached at which the Beaufighters turned south-east and departed.

After chasing for three minutes, the Bf 109s returned to the convoy. Shortly thereafter, south of Anafi Island, three more Arados were seen, apparently strafing a mine. In the subsequent engagement one Arado was claimed destroyed and the other two damaged. An aircraft from 4./SAGr 126 was lost.

Wt Off Peter Haslam, who was with the 213 Squadron detachment at Idku, was scrambled at 0642 after a lone aircraft plotted on radar. He 'Tallyhoed' at 0656 50 miles north-west of Idku; nothing further was heard from him. The strong presumption can be made that he intercepted a 2.(F)/123 Ju 88 and they either collided or shot each other down, as the radar plots of both aircraft disappeared simultaneously at the time Haslam reported contact.

British Claims

603 Sqn	Flt Sgt W.G.Harrison/Flt Sgt J.W.H.Dibbs	Beaufighter X 379 'M'	} Ar 196	S Anafi Island	1540–2100
603 Sqn	Flt Lt D.G.Simpson/Flt Sgt F.S.Bunn	Beaufighter X 361 'Y'			
603 Sqn	Flt Lt D.G.Simpson/Flt Sgt F.S.Bunn	Beaufighter X 361 'Y'	Ar 196 Damaged	S Anafi Island	1540–2100
603 Sqn	Flt Sgt T.Cook/Flt Sgt A.T.Blow*	Beaufighter X 465 'R'	} Ar 196 Damaged	S Anafi Island	1540–2100
603 Sqn	Flg Off W.Tame/Flg Off W.G.King	Beaufighter X 246 'K'			
	*claim made by Flt Sgt A.T.Blow				

British Casualties

213 Sqn	Spitfire IX MH991 scrambled 0642, reported contact with e/a 50m NW Idku 0656, not heard from again; Wt Off P.C.Haslam KiA

German Casualties

2.(F)/123	Ju 88D-1WNr 430836 4U+QK lost nr Sidi Barrani probably in combat with Spitfire; Uffz Rudolf Schmidt and three POW
4./SAGr 126	Ar 196A-3 WNr 0264 D1+KH lost to Beaufighter N Dia Island; Uffz Josef Meidel/Obgfr Max Kakarutt MiA
4./SAGr 126	2 Ar 196A-3s damaged by fighters S Anafi; crews safe

Sunday-Monday, 14/15 May 1944

British Casualties

38 Sqn	Wellington XIII JA200 'K' left 2340, missing from reconnaissance of central Aegean Sea; Flg Off J.F.H.Jolly and five KiA

Monday, 15 May 1944

Four Beaufighters of 603 Squadron led by Flt Lt A.P.Pringle attacked the landing ground at Paros, which was under construction, in the face of intense Flak that shot down two aircraft and damaged the others. Four Bf 109s that appeared were successfully avoided by the survivors.

Ju 188Fs such as 8H+AL of 2.(F)/33 were active flying reconnaissance sorties over the Aegean throughout the spring and summer of 1944.

British Casualties

603 Sqn	Beaufighter X NE607 'K' left 1520, shot down by Flak attacking Paros a/f; Plt Off E.G.Harman/Flt Sgt L.E.Hopkin KiA
603 Sqn	Beaufighter X LZ404 'Q' left 1520, shot down by Flak attacking Paros a/f; Flt Sgt J.E.Paddison/Flt Sgt J.C.Rhodes KiA
603 Sqn	Beaufighter X 'R' left 1520 damaged by Flak attacking Paros a/f; Flt Lt A.P.Pringle/Flg Off A.E.Ross safe
603 Sqn	Beaufighter X 'C' left 1520 damaged by Flak attacking Paros a/f; Flt Sgt J.Edgar/Flt Sgt H.W.Wood safe

German Claims

Flak	3 Beaufighters	Paros	1716, 1717, 1718

German Casualties

3.(F)/33	Ju 188F-I WNr 280084 8H+AL left Kalamaki, lost over Mediterranean; Lt Wolfgang Klein and three KiA

Tuesday, 16 May 1944

British Casualties

252 Sqn	Beaufighter X NE579 'C' shot down by Flak from landing craft 25m WNW Chalki Island 0623; Flg Off D.C.Lendrum/Flg Off D.C.Rooke MiA
252 Sqn	Beaufighter X NE554 'Q' damaged by Flak 25m WNW Chalki Island 0623, crash-landed at base 0825; Flt Lt C.W.Fowler safe/ Flt Sgt A.E.Potter WiA

Wednesday, 17 May 1944

On this day the first two Mustang IIIs were delivered to 213 Squadron at Idku. It became only the second RAF squadron in the Mediterranean to receive them and they were flown alongside the Spitfires for the next month.

Monday, 22 May 1944

The 332nd Fighter Group was transferred from the 12th Air Force to the 15th Air Force, under the operational control of the 306th Fighter Wing, commanded by Brig Gen Dean C.Strother.

Thursday, 25 May 1944

Luftwaffe Order of Battle (fighter units)

7./JG 27	Scutari (Albania)	(minus 2 Schw: 12–7)
1 Schw 7./JG 27	Araxos	
1 Schw 7./JG 27	Kalamaki	

British Casualties

252 Sqn	Beaufighter X LZ518 'C' strafing lighter SW Alimnia Bay ca 0845, failed to pull out of dive, hit rising ground west of the bay, cartwheeled into sea in flames; Flg Off E.A.T.Taylor/Flt Sgt D.C.Dick KiA

Saturday, 27 May 1944

Operations for the Liberators of the newly formed 31 SAAF Squadron from Jebel Hamza, Egypt over the Aegean and Crete began on this date with an attack on a German garrison at Kastelli Pediata in eastern Crete. This mission was repeated four days later.

Tuesday, 30 May 1944

British Casualties

336 Sqn	Spitfire V ES262 left 1035, collided with another Spitfire, crashed 15m SE Mersa Matruh 1050; Flt Sgt K.Christakos b/o WiA
336 Sqn	Spitfire V EE809 left 1035, collided with another Spitfire, crashed 15m SE Mersa Matruh 1050; Flg Off E.Souvleros KiA

Wednesday, 31 May 1944

94 Squadron Spitfires were escorting 24 and 15 SAAF Squadrons bombing Kastelli. Four Bf 109s of a detachment from 13./JG 27 were scrambled.

Above: In an attempt to capture Marshal Tito on 25 May the Germans began Operation Rösselsprung that commenced with a parachute and glider-borne assault by the 500th SS Parachute Battalion; one of the DFS 230 gliders is seen after depositing its troops near Drvar. Left: A ship moored in Trieste harbour is hit on the stern by bombs dropped from a Wellington of 221 Squadron during a night attack on 25 May.

British Claims					
94 Sqn	Fl Lt H.MacLachlan	Spitfire IX MH698 'Y'	Bf 109G	3m off Kastelli	0925–1200
94 Sqn	Flg Off F.H.W.Harrington	Spitfire IX MA508 'B'	Bf 109G Damaged	Kastelli, Crete	0925–1200

German Claims				
Flak		e/a	Hierapetra	2133

Thursday, 1 June 1944

On this day a big combat occurred between 24 Beaufighters from 252, 227, 16 and 603 Squadrons, 12 Marauders of 24 SAAF Squadron and 18 Baltimores of 15 SAAF Squadron, covered by 13 Spitfires of 94 Squadron and 4 Mustangs of 213 Squadron, against a large German force involved in the protection of a convoy sailing from Piraeus to Crete, composed of the freighters *Gertrud* (1,960 tons, ex-Danish *Gerda Toft*), *Tanais* (1,545 tons, ex-Greek *Hollywood*) and *Sabine* (2,252 tons, ex-Italian *Salvatore*). The ships were escorted by four torpedo boats (*TA 14, 16, 17* and *19*), three *U-Jägern* (submarine chasers *UJ 2101, 2105* and *2110*) and two mine sweepers (*R 34* and *R 211*) while the aerial protection was provided by four Bf 109s, four Ju 88s and four Ar 196s of 4./SAGr 126. At the end of the attacks, carried on about 25 miles north of Crete, *Sabine* was sunk, together with *UJ 2101* and *2105*, while *TA 16*, heavily damaged, and *Gertrud*, towed by *TA 19*, were forced to try and recover in Heraklion harbour where they were sunk the next day by British Wellingtons, Baltimores and Marauders. These losses were considered, as reported in the German naval staff operations war diary "extremely serious to our shipping in the Aegean, especially as regards Crete supplies". Lt R.Richards of 16 SAAF Squadron was awarded with a DFC for his attack on the *Gertrud*, his camera recording at least four hits with RPs. In the aerial clashes one Bf 109 and three Ar 196s were shot down and one floatplane was badly damaged, while the attackers lost four Beaufighters and a Baltimore.

British Claims					
252 Sqn	Flg Off J.A.T.MacIntosh/Flt Sgt R.H.Alderton	Beaufighter X NE479 'E'	Ar 196 Damaged	25–30m N Heraklion	1905
227 Sqn	Flt Sgt F.G.W.Sheldrick/Flt Sgt R.E.Ash	Beaufighter X JL897 'V'	Ar 196	25–30m N Heraklion	1905
603 Sqn	Flg Off R.Hartley/Flg Off D.Vaughan	Beaufighter X NE595 'S'	Ar 196 Probable	25–30m N Heraklion	1905
603 Sqn	Flg Off R.Hartley/Flg Off D.Vaughan	Beaufighter X NE595 'S'	Ar 196 Damaged	25–30m N Heraklion	1905
15 SAAF Sqn	Lt R.J.Jooste/gunner 2/Lt A.H.Harper	Baltimore V 648 'K'	} Bf 109	25–30m N Heraklion	1905
15 SAAF Sqn	Capt M.J.Adendorff/gunner Lt A.H.Burnard	Baltimore V 468 'R'			

Capt E.A.Barrett and Lt A.J.Haupt prepare to ditch their stricken Beaufighter into the Mediterranean after combat with Arado Ar 196 floatplanes during a convoy attack.

British Casualties

252 Sqn	Beaufighter X NE293 'M' shot down over convoy 25–30m N Heraklion 1910–1915; Wg Cdr B.G.Meharg/Flt Lt E.H.G.Thompson POW
603 Sqn	Beaufighter X LZ517 'F' shot down over convoy by Ar 196 N Heraklion 1910; Flt Sgt R.M.Atkinson/Flt Sgt D.F.Parsons KiA
227 Sqn	Beaufighter X JM235 'W' shot down over convoy by Ar 196 N Heraklion 1910; Flg Off J.W.A.Jones POW/Flg Off R.A.R.Wilson evaded
16 SAAF Sqn	Beaufighter X NE641 'G' shot down over convoy by Ar 196 N Heraklion 1910, ditched; Capt E.A.Barrett/Lt A.J.Haupt POW
454 Sqn	Baltimore V FW399 left 1020, presumed shot down by fighters about 1320; Wt Off G.W.Liels and three MiA

German Claims

Flak	*Tanais*		1 bomber	btwn Milos and Crete	
Flak	*TA 16*		4 e/a		
4./SAGr 126	Obfw Günther Knorth/Lt Böckling	Ar 196A-5	Beaufighter	off Heraklion	1810
4./SAGr 126	Obfw Kurt Chalupka/Oblt Schäfer	Ar 196A-5	Beaufighter	off Heraklion	1810
2./SAGr 126	Ofhr Friedrich Rupp/Oblt Richter	Ar 196A-5	Beaufighter	off Heraklion	1811
4./SAGr 126	Uffz Hässler/Uffz Busse	Ar 196A-5	Beaufighter	off Heraklion	1812

German Casualties

2./SAGr 126	Ar 196A-5 WNr 623004 D1+EK damaged in combat N Heraklion; Obfw Kurt Chalupka/Oblt Schäfer rescued

Friday, 2 June 1944

German Claims

Flak		B-26	Heraklion	1745

German Casualties

Wekusta 27	Ju 88A-4 left Athens Tatoi and ditched S of Greece; crew rescued

Friday-Saturday, 2/3 June 1944

British Casualties

38 Sqn	Wellington XIII HZ726 'A' left 2119 to bomb Heraklion harbour, Crete, crashed on return 4m NE Tocra; Flt Lt S.D.Meadowcroft and two KiA, three survived

Saturday, 3 June 1944

On 3 June 1944 Marshal Tito, the Yugoslav partisan leader of choice, was flown with elements of his staff, from a strip at Kupresko Polje due to the German offensive. Tito was installed in a villa at Bari, to be met with Air Marshal Sir John Slessor and Brigadier Fitzroy MacLean where they developed the future policy for support of the partisans. Earlier, the CCS had approved the formation of the Balkan Air Force under AVM William Elliot who was also given the responsibility for the co-ordination of all other trans-Adriatic activity including land, sea and special operations.

Saturday-Sunday, 3/4 June 1944

British Casualties

31 SAAF Sqn	Liberator VI EW197 'C' shot down attacking shipping in Heraklion harbour, Crete; Capt H.van B.Duckitt and five KiA
38 Sqn	Wellington JA296 'K' left 2010 to attack Khalkis harbour in Greece, shot down by Flak and ditched; Flt Sgt L.W.Cook and one POW, four KiA

Sunday, 4 June 1944

From their base near Foggia Spitfires of 73 Squadron were dispatched in pairs throughout the day as cover for the withdrawal of a force of British commandos and partisan forces from the island of Brac. At about 0840 one pair spotted three fighters identified as Bf 109s and two of these were claimed shot down. (See also Vol. 4)

British Claims

73 Sqn	Wt Off P.Strange	Spitfire Vc JK191	Bf 109G	SW Brac	0840
73 Sqn	Wt Off P.Strange	Spitfire Vc JK191	Bf 109G Damaged	SW Brac	0840
73 Sqn	Flt Sgt A.D.Rowe	Spitfire Vc ES142	Bf 109G	SW Brac	0840

Air Vice-Marshal William Elliot (left) was given command of the Balkan Air Force to co-ordinate the increasingly intense air operations over Yugoslavia and Greece.

German Casualties

2./NAGr 12	Bf 109G-8 WNr 710007 Black 1 shot down by Spitfire 3km SW Nerenice; Lt Heinz-Hasso Wagner MiA

Sunday-Monday, 4/5 June 1944

On the night of 4/5 June nine 31 SAAF Squadron Liberators attacked the landing ground at Gadurra on Rhodes shortly after which they moved to Italy to join 205 Group. Their operations thereafter will be described in Volume 6.

British Claims

46 Sqn	Flt Sgt A.M.Webster/Flt Sgt F.E.Treble	Beaufighter VIf ND473 'O'	Ju 52, 2 damaged on grnd Kos a/f	2257-0354

Monday, 5 June 1944

On the Italian mainland at this time 324 Wing, accompanied by 225 Squadron, moved to Tre Cancelli airfield at Anzio, finding it very dusty. On the same day 40 SAAF Squadron moved to Aquino while on the 6th the 324th Fighter Group went to La Banca. From Tre Cancelli 324 Wing was to undertake a considerable number of bomber escort sorties, but it was the squadrons of 251 and 322 Wings which were meeting such elements of the Luftwaffe as were still about. In their role as replacements of the USAAF's Spitfire groups following the latter's departure to re-equip with P-51s and transfer to the 15th Air Force, they were able to gain several successes.

British Casualties (see also Vol. 4)

237 Sqn	Spitfire IX MK346 left 1600 on sweep of Lake Bolsena to Viterbo area, hit by Flak, pilot wounded in thigh, crash-landed 20 miles north of the front line safely at 1815; Sgt L.P.Pearson WiA by troops when still in the a/c, managed to evade, returned on 15 June. Later awarded the only MM to a Rhodesian airman
237 Sqn	Spitfire IX MK604 left 1845 on sweep of Lake Bolsena to Viterbo area, hit by Flak near Lake Bolsena, force-landed; Plt Off A.C.Coulson POW

US Casualties

443rd BS/320th BG	B-26 42-43309 '57' *Gotta Match* left 0939 to bomb road bridge S Rieti 1034, damaged by Flak, crash-landed 5m N Anzio about 1200; 1/Lt John S.MacKinnon and five safe

German Casualties

2./NAGr 11	Bf 109G-6 damaged in combat 10km NE Terni; Uffz Heinz Gniostko WiA

PART II — ITALY AND THE BALKANS FROM JUNE 1944

CHAPTER 1

WITHER NEXT? THE CONTINUING CAMPAIGN IN ITALY

Monday-Tuesday, 5/6 June 1944

British Claims				
255 Sqn	Wt Off G.R.Smith/Plt Off H.S.Taffs	Beaufighter VIf	Ju 88 Damaged	0515
British Casualties				
38 Sqn	Wellington XIII JA196 'V' on minelaying sortie of Khalkis, FTR; Flg Off J.B.Rain and five KiA			

This is the time when Rome fell to the Allied forces. It is from this point onwards that the operations of units over the Aegean and eastern Adriatic became increasingly enmeshed with those based on the Italian mainland. It is here therefore that our narrative merges the activities of all the tactical air force units where Volume 4 concluded until the end of the war.

Hptm Jürgen Harder, Kommandeur of I./JG 53, examines work on his Bf 109G-6 'gunboat' at Bologna in early June just before the Gruppe departed for Rumania.

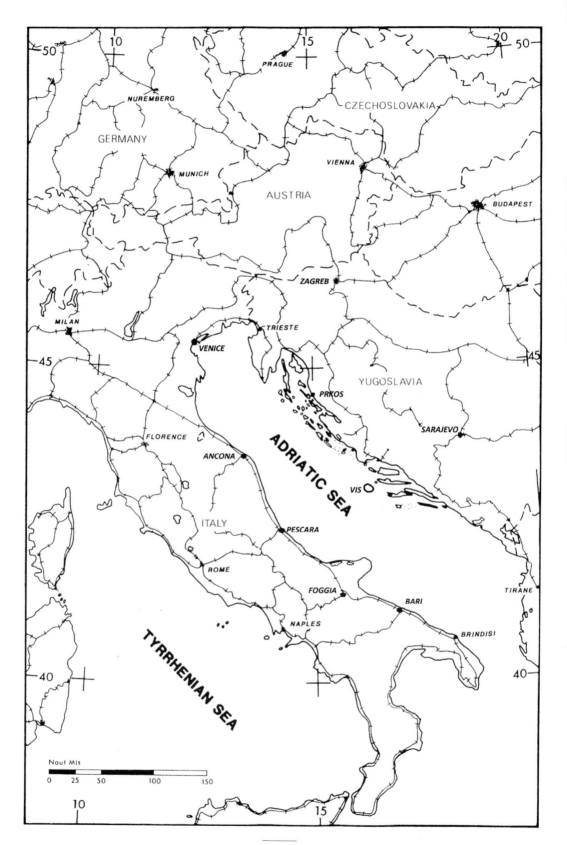

ADVANCE ON THE CAPITAL CITY

Tuesday, 6 June 1944

Over Libya in the early morning two Spitfires of 3 SAAF Squadron scrambled to intercept a Ju 52/3m. Before they could find it Sqn Ldr Russell Foskett of 94 Squadron had already intercepted in rain and low cloud and forced it to land near Tmimi at about 0700.

In Italy it was again a day of losses to Flak. 208 Squadron lost an aircraft near Rieti, 243 Squadron also lost a pilot during an evening sweep, Flt Lt Colin Chrystall failing to return, last seen after damaging two trucks by strafing at 1835. Earlier, at about 1640, two Spitfires from 243 watched as a Walrus landed and picked up Lt P.J.S.Louw from 242 Squadron downed due to engine failure north of Grosseto rocks. The sea was too rough for it to take off so it began to taxi to base.

Two further Spitfires went down lost over Yugoslavia, one to Flak and one to engine failure. 154 Squadron pilots claimed eight motor transports destroyed and eleven damaged around Rome.

The American fighter-bomber units were hard hit by Flak, with the 27th Fighter Bomber Group losing five P-40s; the 79th Fighter Group also lost four of its P-47s to Flak on this date and another pilot from the 57th flew into a tree. The 324th lost one P-40 to bad weather, one to Flak and another when its target exploded, causing it to crash.

British Claims

94 Sqn	Sqn Ldr R.G.Foskett	Spitfire IX MA766 'F'	Ju 52/3m	nr Tmimi	ca 0700

British Casualties

243 Sqn	Spitfire IX MK773 left 1735 on sweep, strafed 6 trucks at Castellina Marittima, last seen 1835; Flt Lt Colin Chrystall POW
242 Sqn	Spitfire IX 'M' engine failure 1½ miles off Grosseto rocks, pilot baled out; Lt P.J.S.Louw safe, rescued by Walrus Z1784 of 284 Sqn flown by Wt Off I.A.Paterson that could not take off due to the sea state, all picked up by HSL. Walrus was abandoned
208 Sqn	Spitfire Vb ER863 left 1320 for recce of Rieti area, last seen nr Guercino at 9,000ft; Plt Off K.A.Bayliss KiA
238 Sqn	Spitfire IX MK400 'Z' left 1040 on fighter sweep of Piombino area, damaged by Flak, force-landed on the beach N of base 1300; Lt P.M.van Rensberg safe
253 Sqn	Spitfire Vc MH567 left 1515, hit by Flak train; crashed 7m SE of Veliki Radic, Yugoslavia; Wt Off J.M.G.L.Lavoie KiA
73 Sqn	Spitfire Vc JK454 left 1705, glycol leak 12m W Knin; Flt Lt V.H.Twomey baled, rescued by partisans
40 SAAF Sqn	Spitfire V left 1930 to recce Terni-Rieti area, landed at Nettuno due to bad weather when a Thunderbolt landed on top of a/c; Capt R.K.Dunkerley (on completion of last operation of his tour) DoW on 11 June

US Casualties

522nd FS/27th FBG	P-40F 41-14559 'Y' *Boris* shot down by ground fire 5m N Vetralla 1145; 2/Lt Jesse A.Harris Jr returned [5449]
522nd FS/27th FBG	P-40F 42-10452 'F' *GI Gibrone* shot down by ground fire in Lake Bolsena area; 2/Lt Laurence J.Flory Jr KiA [5448]
523rd FS/27th FBG	P-40F 41-19812 'L' shot down by ground fire W Terni 1310; 2/Lt Ralph S.Hansman KiA [5646]
523rd FS/27th FBG	P-40F damaged by ground fire W Terni 1310; 2/Lt Robert F.Boissevain safe
523rd FS/27th FBG	P-40F 'S' hit by Flak 1710, pilot baled; Lt Abraham I.Gottlieb returned on 9 June
87th FS/79th FG	P-47D 43-25654 hit by Flak, crashed S Lake Bracciano 1940; 2/Lt Charles L.Landers POW [5450]
87th FS/79th FG	P-47D hit by Flak, last seen S Capranica 1940; pilot evaded and returned on 9 June
87th FS/79th FG	P-47D hit by Flak, last seen S Capranica 1940; Lt John T.Boone WiA
84th FS/79th FG	P-47D lost; Lt Bell rescued by 293 Sqn RAF
64th FS/57th FG	P-47D hit tree while strafing 0900; 2/Lt Richard K.Nevett returned
315th FS/324th FG	P-40 '60' lost in bad weather, last seen 0720; 2/Lt Jerome J.Lennon returned
316th FS/324th FG	P-40 '86' lost due to target explosion 0900; Flt Off Harris F.Crawford KiA
316th FS/324th FG	P-40 '70' shot down by Flak 0920; 1/Lt Arthur E.Martone evaded, returned on 10 June

German Claims

Flak		P-40	Alatri	0645
Flak		2 Spitfires	Viterbo	0825 & 0827
Flak		P-40	East area W Tuzla	0830
Flak		Spitfire	Bradini	1120
4./Flak Regt Hermann Göring		P-47	Viterbo	1150
6./Flak Regt Hermann Göring		P-40	W Terni	1310

German Claims

Flak	P-40	Bracciano	1332
3./Flak 717	2 Spitfires	Bracciano	1400-1415
Flak	P-51		1705
2./Flak 865	Spitfire	NE Sarajevo	1830
Flak	Dragonfly		1900
Flak	P-51		1942
Flak	2 P-47s	Bracciano	1943 & 1947
Flak	P-40		1950
Flak	4 P-47s	Sutri	2003-2012

German Casualties

5.(K)/LG 1	Ju 88A-4 WNr 301505 L1+AN hit by AA SW Rome; Obfw Helmut Heidlauf and one WiA, two safe
3./KG 77	Ju 88A-17 WNr 801416 3Z+MK engine failure, ditched 50km S Marseille; Lt Hans-Werner Grosse and two WiA, one MiA
2.(F)/122	Me 410B-3 F6+QK damaged in crash-landing at Perugia; Oblt von der Daele and one safe
Wekusta 26	Ju 88A-4 WNr 301546 5M+H lost during recce mission near Elba Island; Obfw Heinz Burkhardt and three MiA

ROME HAS FALLEN – SO WHERE NOW?

The fall of Rome had no sooner made the headlines in the Allied newspapers than it was thrust right into the background by the Normandy invasion of 6 June. From then on, the Italian campaign would receive little publicity, and quickly began to take on the appearance of a sideshow. With the occupation of the city the 5th and 8th Armies now began to fan out again, 5th Army heading north-north-west in a line Rome-Leghorn, advancing on Civitavecchia, Viterbo and the Arno river, airfields and the port facilities at Leghorn being the prime objectives. 8th Army turned north-eastwards towards Terni, Foligno, Perugia and ultimately, Florence. As the Germans had fallen back generally, V Corps on the east coast had also moved on, and its left flank would soon make contact with the right flank of the main body of the 8th Army.

As the respective areas of the two Allied armies began to diverge, once more the tactical air units returned to their original roles, XII TAC covering 5th Army and DAF providing similar facilities to 8th Army in the centre and V Corps in the east, although both tactical commands maintained their close liaison and co-operation. From Corsica 87th Fighter Wing, which was controlling 251 and 322 Wings and the 57th Fighter Group, was responsible for attacking the west coast sea communications and those on the land above the Pisa-Rimini line, and was also working closely with the mediums of XII Bomber Command. The Desert Air Force (DAF) which had been commanded by Air Vice-Marshal William F.Dickson since April 1944, carried out similar duties up the east coast, though it was about to be relieved of further operations over Yugoslavia by the creation of Balkan Air Force, commanded by Air Vice-Marshal William Elliot.

This new command comprised mainly ex-Coastal Air Force units no longer required for air defence duties, although a few of the DAF's squadrons would subsequently join it. It was to take over all MAAF's tactical responsibilities over the eastern side of the Adriatic.

As the advance from Rome continued towards Viterbo and Rieti, there remained many targets for the fighter-bombers. The aircraft of 239 Wing spent much of the first two weeks of June flying armed reconnaissances generally in formations of six aircraft, during which much motor transport was destroyed. 244 Wing flew some escorts to the Kittyhawks, also undertaking a fair amount of strafing, together with escorts to the Baltimores of 223 and 13 (Hellenic) Squadrons. 417 Squadron was now regularly carrying 500lb bombs, joining the Kittyhawks in their armed reconnaissances, now led by a new commanding officer, Sqn Ldr 'Sandy' Kallio, his broken leg now healed. (see Vol. 4).

Units were now moving northwards fast in the wake of the armies; 239 Wing began shifting to Guidonia on the 10th, and two days later 92 Squadron moved to Fabrica, the rest of 244 Wing going to Littorio; 324 Wing moved to Tarquinia and the 86th Fighter-Bomber Group to Ciampino; all these airfields were on the outskirts of Rome. At the same time the 86th was joined by the 99th Fighter Squadron which was now attached to this group for a few weeks while the 324th Fighter Group with which it had been flying, went to Montalto di Castro. The 111th Tactical Reconnaissance Squadron flew to Galera on the 11th; however, the stay here was short, the unit moving to Voltone on the 18th, while next day the 86th Fighter-Bomber Group also moved again, this time going to Orbetello. In 324 Wing 43 Squadron bade farewell to Sqn Ldr Patrick Laing-Meason at this time, his tour having ended. He was replaced by Sqn Ldr A.H.Jupp from 72 Squadron.

The tactical reconnaissance units were also keeping well up with the advance, 225 Squadron going to Galera on the 12th, with 208 Squadron making four moves during the month, to Aquino, Osa, Falerium and Orvieto. The DAF bombers were also moving, 18 and 114 Squadrons going initially to an airstrip at Nettuno, then to Tarquinia where they were joined by 13 and 55 Squadrons, all four units at last being together, from there continuing their night interdiction sorties. Further east 7 SAAF Wing moved partially to Marcianise.

Most captured airfields proved too badly damaged to use initially, but US construction engineers soon worked wonders in refurbishing them at the rate of one every five days. The whole of 12th Air Force was being further weakened at this stage, however. From XII Fighter Command's 87th Fighter Wing in Corsica the second American Spitfire group, the 52nd, its presence freed by the arrival on that island of the two RAF Spitfire Wings (251 and 332), had now also converted to P-51s and joined the 15th Air Force. At this point the 332nd Fighter Group exchanged its P-40s for P-47s. This was an all-Negro unit, and consequently in late June the 99th Squadron joined it on a permanent basis, going with it to the 15th for bomber escort duties. XII Fighter Command had also lost the 81st Fighter Group which had accompanied the 33rd Fighter Group to India.

This period also saw a significant equipment exchange which was not to the satisfaction of some of the US pilots – initially at any rate. All early versions of the P-51 and A-36A were now out of production and replacements were becoming in short supply. This had resulted in the P-40s which had been left behind in North Africa by the 33rd Fighter Group on that unit's departure to join the US 10th Air Force in India, divided between the 27th and 86th Fighter-Bomber Groups. At first one squadron in each group was re-equipped with these aircraft, while these two units released 14 A-36s to the 111th Tactical Reconnaissance Squadron. All the remaining aircraft were then handed to the 86th Fighter-Bomber Group to continue operations on the Warhawks pending the arrival of more modern aircraft.

Pilots expressed themselves less than delighted with the P-40s ("most of them are in poor shape") although it was known that early replacements were likely to be forthcoming. These were anticipated to be either P-51s or P-47s, but the growing likelihood that it would be the latter brought forth further complaints: "Today was a mournful day in the eyes of everyone. These aircraft have been a source of pride for the squadron for more than a year and there is much doubt on the part of the pilots on whether any other airplane can do the type of work as well as the A-36." "There is still much weeping and wailing about flying the P-47 and not the P-51 that everyone hoped we would get." Fair to say that a little over a month later the 86th recorded: "The pilots are liking the P-47 more every day."

During this unsettled period of operations, the last sorties by A-36As had been undertaken by pilots of the 27th Fighter-Bomber Group during the opening weeks of the year; the P-47s were soon fully established on operations by the time of the capture of Rome.

On 11 June the air echelon of the 47th Bomb Group (L) and the 79th Fighter Group moved to Corsica, the P-47s of the latter unit being based at Serraglia ready to support landings which were shortly to be made on the island of Elba.

Tuesday-Wednesday, 6/7 June 1944

British Casualties			
114 Sqn	Boston IIIA BZ355 left 2147 for Viterbo-Bracciano area, disappeared without trace; Flt Sgt René M.P.E.Salmon (Belgian) and three MiA		
55 Sqn	Baltimore V FW313 'Z' left 0120 on armed recce of Avezzano-Rieti and Terni areas; Capt M.M.Djonlic and three MiA		
German Claims			
Flak	Boston	Viterbo	0043

Wednesday, 7 June 1944

The 57th Fighter Group suffered five losses during three missions, though at least three of the pilots involved were safe, two of them returning later in the day, together with a pilot who had baled out on 14 May.

Meanwhile, on the 3rd 145 Squadron had moved to Venafro and from here on the 6th the unit escorted a big formation of 108 B-26s and 144 B-25s to bomb roads and bridges in the Viterbo-Terni area. Next day (7th), however, the Spitfire flown by the unit's commanding officer, Sqn Ldr Duke, was hit in the engine by ground fire when he was leading a section of four to strafe motor transports in the Rieti area. He baled out into Lake Bracciano from 2,000 feet but was lucky to avoid drowning when struggling out of his parachute harness. Fortunately for him, the Germans had already evacuated the area and he was rescued and taken care of by some Italians until the advancing US troops arrived. Duke had just received a second Bar to his DFC at this time.

213 Sqn	Flt Lt C.D.A.Smith	Spitfire IX MH342 'M'			
213 Sqn	Flg Off R.H.Garwood	Spitfire IX MA528 'F'			
213 Sqn	Lt V.Vorster	Spitfire IX BS339 'G'	Ju 188 Damaged	50m NE Rosetta	1318-1412
213 Sqn	2/Lt J.W.Moor	Spitfire IX BS354 'J'			
15 SAAF Sqn	crew	Baltimore V	Bf 109	W Rhodes	1905

British Casualties

145 Sqn	Spitfire VIII JG241 glycol leak due to small-arms fire, pilot baled out over Lake Bracciano 0930; Sqn Ldr N.F.Duke safe, rescued by Italian civilians from the lake and then by US Army
451 Sqn	Spitfire IX MH769 presumed damaged by Flak strafing near Vetralla, pilot forced to bale out 15m off Corsica 1145; Flg Off G.C.W.O'Neil safe, rescued by Walrus R6549 of 284 Sqn flown by Flg Off T.H.Humphrey/Sgt A.J.Hesseltine
417 Sqn	Spitfire VIII JG321 left 1155, hit by Flak, crashed in Allied lines; Wt Off G.M.Horter slightly WiA
253 Sqn	Spitfire Vc BR380 left 1800 from Vis, engine failed 1815, pilot baled out 8m W Lukavici Island; Sgt V.Woods picked up next day by HSL

US Casualties

64th FS/57th FG	P-47D 42-75010 lost on dive-bombing mission NE Orvieto 0645; 2/Lt Ernest H.Newhouse baled and returned [5825]
65th FS/57th FG	P-47D 42-76008 shot down by small-arms fire 1015; 2/Lt William J.Fournier KiA [5788]
65th FS/57th FG	P-47D 42-76013 flew into ground while strafing SW Volterra 1015; Flt Off William Swartz KiA [5787]
66th FS/57th FG	P-47D hit by Flak 0910, crash-landed E Porretta; 2/Lt George F.Deckert returned
66th FS/57th FG	P-47D hit by Flak nr Lake Bolsena 0910; 2/Lt Charles W.Turner returned on 12 June
86th FS/79th FG	P-47D hit by Flak, last seen near Perugia 1010; Lt Edward M.Walsh evaded and returned next day
301st FS/332nd FG	P-47D 42-75824 crashed into sea off San Benedetto, probably due to engine trouble 1025; 2/Lt Carroll N.Langston KiA [5639]
379th BS/310th BG	B-25J 43-4059 lost to Flak near Bologna 1702; 2/Lt Benton F.Eichorn and five KiA, one evaded and returned [5826]

German Claims

Flak		P-47	Valentano	0922
Flak		P-47	Tuscania	0928
Flak		P-47	Montalto	1016
Flak		P-47	Gambassi	1120
Flak		P-47	Viterbo	1235
Flak		P-40	Bracciano	1450
Flak		B-25	Verniana	1700
Flak		P-47	Montefiascone	2010

Wednesday-Thursday, 7/8 June 1944

For close air support in Italy DAF employed control procedures codenamed 'Rover' that had been tested in North Africa and then refined with the benefit of experience, initially during the Battle of the River Sangro in late 1943. It depended on each major army formation having a forward roving observation post with direct VHF R/T to nearby fighter-bombers. Alongside each army forward observation officer (FOO) was a trained pilot who could be in radio contact with a six-aircraft Cab Rank overhead. The basic Rover David procedure ensured that a list of fixed targets was briefed to pilots before take-off so that if after 20 minutes over the front line they had not been used by the FOO to offer immediate battlefield support, they could depart to attack the pre-briefed target, typically a road junction or local HQ building. Cab Ranks came on task every 30 minutes. There were variations on this that were given discrete designators, and the US version was Rover Joe.

British Claims

255 Sqn	Flt Sgt D.Fisher/Wt Off J.Walsh	Beaufighter VIf	Ju 88 or 188	20m S.ta Maria di Leuca	0426

British Casualties

46 Sqn	Beaufighter VIf MM906 'A' left 1830 to intrude to Rhodes and Kos, shot down by Flak, crashed on Kos; Flt Sgt A.Lord/Sgt T.L.Dawes KiA

German Casualties

11./ZG 26	Ju 88C-6 WNr 751001 3U+OV lost off S.ta Maria di Leuca; Obfw Heinrich Schiller and one POW, one KiA

Thursday, 8 June 1944

451 Squadron, which was to fly 623 sorties during June, including 11 major bomber escort missions, commenced a run of success on this date, when Wg Cdr Morris (Wing Leader 251 Wing) and Flt Lt Sutton, un-

dertaking an evening reconnaissance, caught Ju 88 of 1.(F)/122 flying low over the Cortona-Poggibonsi area. They carried out several attacks and it fell in flames and exploded.

On this day gunners of the Flak Regiment Hermann Göring claimed the unit's 180th aircraft shot down, an indication of the sheer volume of Flak the Germans were now able to utilise.

Thursday-Friday, 8/9 June 1944

On 9 June Baltimore V FW366/G flown by Sqn Ldr Don Beaton led a formation of four aircraft from 454 RAAF Squadron for a bombing raid on an oil refinery at Navarino in the southern Peloponnese; each aircraft dropped one 500lb and two 250lb GP bombs from 8,000 feet.

British Claims					
255 Sqn	Flt Lt R.S.Pinks/Plt Off M.Noble	Beaufighter VIf	Ju 88	off S.ta Maria di Leuca	0428

British Casualties	
39 Sqn	Beaufighter TFX NE385 'W' left 2245 to attack MTBs between Genoa and La Spezia, two reports received 0052 and 0114, nothing further heard; Flg Off J.L.Griffiths/Flg Off B.J.Atkin KiA
39 Sqn	Beaufighter TFX LZ143 'S' left 0145 on Rover patrol from La Spezia to Elba, nothing heard after take-off; Sqn Ldr T.H.Curlee/Sgt R.Adam spent 2 ½ days in dinghy, then rescued by ASR Walrus off Capraia Island
39 Sqn	Beaufighter X LZ338 'O' left 0205 on Rover patrol from La Spezia to Leghorn, unwittingly flew over a convoy, damaged by Flak, crash-landed at base; Flt Sgt V.J.Kyrke-Smith safe/Flt Sgt S.S.Campbell WiA

German Claims				
Flak		bomber	Stavros	2255

Friday, 9 June 1944

At about noon four 451 Squadron pilots intercepted three Bf 109s over Poggibonsi and all were claimed shot down. Flg Off Kemp saw four more at lower altitude but was unable to contact the other pilots due to the radio being jammed with transmissions and had to let them escape. The formation was led by Flt Lt Don McBurnie, DFM, in MK145.

British Claims					
253 Sqn	Flt Sgt T.H.Harrison	Spitfire Vc JK307	Ju 52/3m (on ground)	Banja Luka a/f	0840-1110
451 Sqn	Flt Lt R.J.Robert	Spitfire IX MJ733 'H'	Bf 109	3m SW Colle Val D'Elsa	1224
451 Sqn	Flt Lt R.H.Sutton	Spitfire IX MJ941 'V'	Bf 109	4m W Poggibonsi	1225
451 Sqn	Flg Off T.H.S.James	Spitfire IX MH772 'B'	Bf 109	N Greve in Chianti	1230

British Casualties	
241 Sqn	Spitfire VIII JP563 left 0500 on weather recce, attacked shipping off Ovindoli, crash-landed in no man's land 0630; 2/Lt A.E.Goodman returned
241 Sqn	Spitfire VIII JF451 left 1040 on patrol of Rieti, Terni and Spoleto, hit by 20mm Flak while strafing trucks, attempted to crash land near Spoleto 1130, burst into flames, crashed and turned over; Flt Lt J.B.L.Jones KiA
13(H) Sqn	Baltimore IV FA490 'D' crashed on take-off from Biferno 1423 on bombing raid, bombs exploded; Flt Lt G.Liakeas and three KiA
2 SAAF Sqn	Spitfire IX bombing bridge at Teramo, hit by Flak, crash-landed at base, Cat II damaged; Capt R.Gray safe
237 Sqn	Spitfire IX MJ943 left 1900, strafed truck which exploded, crash-landed near Pommerance; Flg Off J.Crook evaded

US Casualties	
315th FS/324th FG	P-40F 41-19988 '44' shot down by Flak attacking gun positions S Grotte di Castro 1125; 1/Lt Paul M.Bull POW [5833]
86th FS/79th FG	P-47D hit house while strafing, crashed in Foligno-Spoleto area 1900; 2/Lt Stuart L.Bartlett KiA
301st FS/332nd FG	P-47D 42-75800 lost u/k cause, possibly engine trouble; 2/Lt Cornelius G.Rogers KiA [5758]
332nd FG	P-47D damaged; Capt Playford slt WiA
332nd FG	P-47D damaged

German Claims				
Flak		P-47	Silvi	1005
Flak		P-40	Latera	1122
3./Flak 945		P-40	Bolsena	1124
Flak		P-40	Casa	1129
Flak		Spitfire	Casa	1130
Flak		P-40	Valentano	1131
Flak		P-40	Piansano	1132
Flak		P-47	Montefalco	1337
Flak		P-40		1956
Flak		Spitfire	Riparbella	1021

German Casualties	
I./JG 77	Bf 109G-6 WNr 162449 White 11 lost in combat with fighters S Florence; Lt Hans Tomschegg MiA
I./JG 77	Bf 109G-6 WNr 163513 Black 5 shot down by enemy fighters nr Empoli; Obfhr Josef Czibulski MiA
I./JG 77	2 Bf 109G-6s badly damaged in combat S Florence; pilots safe
2./NAGr 11	Bf 109G-6 WNr 162057 White 5 crashed at Castiglione; Uffz Martin Ringel WiA

| Seenot 6 | Cant.Z.506B shot down into Adriatic 60km SE Trieste; Uffz Rudolf Streb and one WiA, one KiA and two safe* |
| | *shot down by a P-38 of the 1st FG of the 15th AF |

Friday-Saturday, 9/10 June 1944

British Casualties	
13 Sqn	Baltimore V FW311 'P' left 2040, damaged by heavy Flak NW Aquila, hydraulics damaged, belly-landed at base 2214; Sqn Ldr T.N.Staples DFM and three safe

German Casualties	
5./NJG 6	Bf 110G-4 crash-landed at Perugia; Fw Pata and one safe
II./NJG 6	Bf 110G-4 crash-landed at Perugia; Lt Mahr safe

Saturday, 10 June 1944

Pilots of 242 Squadron strafed Foligno airfield, claiming four single-engine 'flamers' and three Me 210s destroyed. Two of the strafers ran low on fuel, but just managed to make Allied lines before crash-landing.

British Casualties	
243 Sqn	Spitfire IX MH559 damaged by Flak near Leghorn, belly-landed on return 1135, Sgt H.J.Bennison safe
242 Sqn	Spitfire IX 'P' belly-landed south of the lines out of fuel; Flt Lt A.P.Skinner safe
242 Sqn	Spitfire IX 'M' belly-landed south of the lines out of fuel; Lt D.Muller safe
249 Sqn	Spitfire Vc JK266 while strafing target at Barmash, Albania, it exploded causing glycol leak, pilot headed west but baled out at 0900; Wt Off A.L.Fox evaded, back on 2 August

US Casualties	
87th FS/79th FG	P-47D crashed in a valley N Rome while strafing, 1015; 2/Lt Damon E.Atkins KiA
379th BS/310th BG	B-25J 43-4098 lost to Flak nr Calafuria 1147; 1/Lt Ernest J.Kulik evaded and returned, five KiA [5828]
379th BS/310th BG	B-25J badly damaged by Flak nr Calafuria railroad bridge; 1/Lt Truman R.Coble and crew safe
525th FBS/86th FBG	A-36A 42-84083 *Dottie* hit by small-arms fire, crashed 3m N Civitavecchia 1010, pilot baled but parachute failed to open; 1/Lt Carl E.Correll Jr KiA [12928]
347th FS/350th FG	P-39Q 44-2454 lost over Elba u/k cause; 1/Lt James K.Levy KiA [6169]

German Claims		
Flak	B-25	1140

Sunday, 11 June 1944

British Casualties	
232 Sqn	Spitfire IX MK424 shot down by Flak at Poggibonsi, S Cecina 1010; Lt T.D.Bremner baled and evaded
238 Sqn	Spitfire IX MJ836 'F' left 1035 to sweep Leghorn-Florence area, reported Flak 1115, then flew into a thunderstorm and disappeared; Flg Off K.C.Smyth POW
237 Sqn	Spitfire IX MH541 left 0930 for Florence-Poggibonsi area, damaged by Flak, reached Allied lines, crash-landed near Rome; Plt Off B.Rainsford safe

Monday, 12 June 1944

British Claims					
237 Sqn	Plt Off J.Malloch	Spitfire IX MK402	} Ju 52 (on ground)	Pistoia a/f	1900-2100
237 Sqn	Flt Lt I.Ipsen	Spitfire IX MK713			

British Casualties	
232 Sqn	Spitfire IX MH767 'Q' engine cut on patrol 1115, force-landed Empoli, squadron strafed aircraft after pilot left the scene; Wt Off S.J.Donnellan evaded, returned on 18 July
243 Sqn	Spitfire IX MK771 left 1500, strafing at Rovinate struck power lines, crashed; Flt Sgt J.M.Brigham KiA
154 Sqn	Spitfire IX MJ689 left 0855 on fighter sweep Trasimeno area, presumed hit by Flak, engine cut on return W Pianosa, spun into the sea; Wt Off S.E.Boxall KiA

US Casualties

523rd FS/27th FBG	P-40F 41-14580 'Y' shot down by Flak 0645; 2/Lt Aubry Turner KiA [5789]			
95th BS/17th BG	B-26 '55' damaged by Flak, crashed on landing; 1/Lt R.L.Benner and six safe			
438th BS/319th BG	B-26 42-95780 crash-landed in Sardinia; crew safe			

German Claims

Flak		Spitfire	Montefino	0545
Flak		Spitfire	Teramo	0650
Flak		P-40	Santa	0702
Flak		Spitfire	Teramo	1932

German Casualties

2.(F)/122	Me 410B-3 F6+KK crash-landed on Forlì a/f, 95% damaged; Lt Kurt Neumann and one safe

Monday-Tuesday, 12/13 June 1944

British Claims

255 Sqn	Flt Sgt T.W.Burnett/Flg Off R.B.Booth	Beaufighter VIf	Ju 88	160m SE Grottaglie	0230-0510

Tuesday, 13 June 1944

Four Spitfires each from 451 and 238 Squadrons on an early mission saw an Me 410 of 2.(F)/122 flying up valley near Pontremoli, which was shot down by two of the pilots from the former unit. Capt I.N.L.Taylor DFC, of 40 SAAF Squadron, was hit by Flak and crashed at high speed.

British Claims

451 Sqn	Flt Lt G.R.Jones	Spitfire IX MJ579 'X'	Me 410	Villafranca-Pontremoli	0717
451 Sqn	Flg Off R.J.Mercer	Spitfire IX MJ733 'H'			

British Casualties

154 Sqn	Spitfire IX MJ826 left 1615 to strafe in central sector, damaged by Flak, force-landed; Flg Off F.Cooper POW, escaped after 14 hours and evaded, returned on 19 June
40 SAAF Sqn	Spitfire Vc EF738 left 1100, shot down by Flak nr Orvieto; Capt I.N.L.Taylor KiA
2 SAAF Sqn	Spitfire shot down by Flak, pilot baled out near Spoleto; Lt B.D.Shelver POW
1435 Sqn	Spitfire IX MA419 'N' scrambled 1645, engine failed 25m NE of base 1655, pilot baled out; Sgt F.W.Morris rescued safe
238 Sqn	Spitfire IX MH533 'S' left 0605 to sweep Leghorn-Pisa area, damaged by Flak, pilot baled out 10m NE Gorgona; Flg Off J.N.Hannan safe, rescued by HSL

US Claims

111th TRS	Lt Karlson	F-6	Ju 88 (?)	Leghorn-La Spezia area

US Casualties

523rd FS/27th FBG	P-40L 42-10820 'B-G' crash-landed SW Asciano 0740; 2/Lt Ivan W.Gugeler returned [5786]
523rd FS/27th FBG	P-40L 'B' hit by Flak 1140, pilot baled; Lt Robert F.Boissevain returned
448th BS/321st BG	B-25 43-27640 left 1020 to attack Sassoferrato RR bridge, damaged by Flak, crew baled out over base on Corsica; 1/Lt William A Green and four safe, two KiA

French Casualties

GB 1/22	Marauder damaged by Flak nr Pérouse; bombardier Sous Lt Lenormand KiA, pilot and crew safe

German Claims

Flak 362. Inf.Div.	Hptm Doil	e/a	near Siena	
Flak		P-40	Monteramo	0735
Flak		P-40	Campello	1047
Flak		P-40	Terraia	1141
Flak		P-40		1210
Flak		P-40	Terraia	1745

German Casualties

2.(F)/122	Me 410B-3 F6+FK intercepted low over La Spezia, returned shot up and crashed in flames; Obfw Jackstadt and crew safe

Tuesday-Wednesday, 13/14 June 1944

British Casualties

108 Sqn	Beaufighter VIf MM947 'K' left 2130 on intruder mission, nothing further heard; Flt Lt H.R.Smith/Flt Sgt C.F.Adams MiA

German Casualties

4./KG 26	Ju 88A-17 WNr 8229175 1H+CH ditched NW Corsica due to engine failure; Lt Werner Mörath and three POW
16./TG 1	Ju 52/3m WNr 501122 IZ+CQ ditched between Eleusis and Rhodes; Fw Walter Gallina and four KiA

Wednesday, 14 June 1944

Six Spitfires of 451 Squadron provided top cover to 36 B-25s of 310th Bomb Group with 12 of 237 Squadron as close escort. Eight Bf 109s were seen diving and were chased, but four more were then spotted above these. Wg Cdr Morris hit one of the latter and it was last seen diving inverted. Later confirmed, seen to crash by the bomber force.

Lt Begbie and Lt Phipps were one of a pair from 16 SAAF Squadron that intercepted a Ju 88 at 0940 at 2,000ft while the Beaufighters were protecting convoy 'Stubbs' about 170 miles SE of Malta. Begbie's Beaufighter was shot down by the rear gunner of the German aircraft and ditched, only the observer being rescued by a RN corvette.

Meanwhile far away on the east side of Italy, Flt Lt G.R.Gould, DFC, of 241 Squadron was engaged with German aircraft, claiming a pair of Bf 109s shot down over the Adriatic. These were the squadron's first victories.

During the period 11th-14th, while 251 Wing had been meeting much success, 322 Wing's fortunes had been less acceptable, six Spitfires being lost to Flak, at least one from each squadron in the wing. However, five of the pilots had been able to crash land or bale out. Over western Corsica the commanding officer of Groupe de Chasse (GC) 2/7 (also known as 326 Squadron), Cdr Henri Hoarau de La Source achieved a rare victory for the French squadrons when he claimed an FW 190.

Left: When escorting B-25s near Pistoia Wg Cdr Teddy Morris, leader of 251 Wing, claimed a Bf 109 for his penultimate personal success.

Right: As was the privilege of his rank, Wg Cdr Morris carried his initials 'TM' in place of unit code letters on his Spitfire IX.

251 Wg	Wg Cdr E.J.Morris	Spitfire IX MK187 'TM'	Bf 109	N Pistoia	1030
241 Sqn	Flt Lt G.R.Gould	Spitfire VIII JG419	Bf 109	Adriatic Sea	2033
241 Sqn	Flt Lt G.R.Gould	Spitfire VIII JG419	Bf 109 b/o	Adriatic Sea	2034

British Casualties

3 RAAF Sqn	Kittyhawk IV FX775 left 1900, bombed a target near Chiusi, shot down by Flak, belly-landed; Flt Sgt R.E.R.Fountain evaded, returned 17 June
154 Sqn	Spitfire IX MT677 hit in engine by Flak near Pianosa ca 2000, pilot baled out over sea; Flg Off D.C.Dunn rescued by 284 Sqn Walrus X9503 flown by Flg Off G.M.Gallagher. Unable to take off they were towed back by an HSL
242 Sqn	Spitfire IX MH561 'Z' went low over Casciano Val di Pesa to investigate a target, not seen again, believed lost to Flak; Sgt J.R.Tanner POW
243 Sqn	Spitfire IX MJ950 hit by Flak between Cecina and Guardistallo 1510, force-landed; Sgt E.E.East safe
237 Sqn	Spitfire IX MK521 left 1730, hit by Flak and force-landed in Allied lines near Lake Bolsena 1910; Plt Off P.Sutton safe
2 SAAF Sqn	Spitfire L.IXc MH957 'D' left 0600, shot down by Flak nr Ascoli; Lt R.D.McKenzie baled, evaded, returned next day
16 SAAF Sqn	Beaufighter X LZ397 'M' left 0725 to escort convoy 'Stubbs' half way between Benghazi and Malta, shot down by return fire from a Ju 88, ditched 0950; Lt F.W.Begbie KiA/Lt P.M.E.Phipps rescued by a RN corvette

US Casualties

100th FS/332nd FG	P-47D 42-74973 engine trouble 1620; 2/Lt Roger D.Brown safe, returned [6922]
316th FS/324th FG	P-40 '96' engine trouble; Lt Holder baled safely
523rd FS/27th FBG	P-40 'N' shot down by Flak N River Tiber 1155, pilot baled; 1/Lt Lawrence E.Eastman returned on 15 June
34th BS/17th BG	B-26B 42-95954 lost in transit flight between Naples and Villacidro, Sardinia 1609; 1/Lt John E.Lee, two crew and nine passengers (Maj Robert D.Fast, Capt Thomas P.Edgar Jr and seven Red Cross personnel) KiA [5824]
444th BS/320th BG	B-26 '90' left 1030 to attack ships in Leghorn harbour, damaged by Flak, crash-landed at base 1355; Lt Garland Burke and five safe

French Claims

GC 2/7 (326 Sqn)	Cdt Henry Hoarau de La Source	Spitfire IX	FW 190	50m W Cargèse	

German Claims

Flak		P-47	Montepulciano	1215
12./Flak Regt Hermann Göring		Spitfire	Bolgheri	1645
Flak		P-40	Seggiano	1816
Flak		P-40	Ripabianca	2030
1.-4./Flak 365		Spitfire		2035
Flak		P-40	S.Angelo	2040
Flak		P-47	Montepulciano	2046

German Casualties

Wekusta 26	Ju 88A-4 WNr 301154 5M+F lost in Elba area; Oblt Hans Haarbauer and three MiA
II./JG 77	Bf 109 lost in combat N Pistoia; pilot safe
2./NAGr 12	Bf 109G-6 WNr 5119 162063 Red 2 lost in combat Pescara-Vieste; Obfw Heinrich Hassler MiA
2./NAGr 12	Bf 109G-6 WNr 5119 162056 Black 9 lost in combat Pescara-Vieste; FjFw Walter Pannhausen MiA
2./NAGr 13	FW 190A-3 WNr 130340 shot down by fighters near Ajaccio; Oblt Walter Erhard KiA

Thursday, 15 June 1944

Operating from Corsica, 243 Squadron fought 322 Wing's first engagement with the Italian fighters of the Aeronautica Nazionale Repubblicana (ANR), the air force of the Repubblica Sociale Italiana (RSI). On an afternoon sweep by eight Spitfires over Piacenza 20 hostile aircraft were met, identified as MC.205s and Fiat G.55s. Wg Cdr Lovell claimed a Macchi shot down while Wt Off Davoren claimed one of the Fiats; three more Macchis were claimed damaged. 92 Squadron lost one Spitfire strafing south-west of Perugia. Two G.55s were lost by the 1° Gruppo C on this occasion which seem clearly the victims of the British pilots.

British Claims

243 Sqn	Wt Off P.J.Davoren	Spitfire IX MK625 'J'	G.55 c/l	30m W Piacenza	1510
243 Sqn	Lt J.H.Burls	Spitfire IX MA243 'R'	MC.205 Damaged	Albinea	1510
243 Sqn	Flt Lt M.L.Burke	Spitfire IX MK406 'N'	MC.205 Damaged	S Reggio Emilia	1510
243 Sqn	Flt Lt C.S.Bamberger	Spitfire IX MJ991 'G'	MC.205 Damaged	30m W Piacenza	1510
322 Wg	Wg Cdr A.D.J.Lovell	Spitfire IX MH667 'AD-L'	MC.205 b/o	N La Spezia	1535

Above: A G.55 of ANR 2° Gruppo C. Two Fiat
G.55 Centauro fighters of the ANR 1° Gruppo
Caccia were lost to British fighters on 15 June.
Right: The leader of 322 Wing, Wg Cdr Tony
Lovell, here receiving the American DFC,
destroyed a Fiat G.55 on 15 June, though he
misidentified his victim as a MC.205.

British Casualties

92 Sqn	Spitfire VIII JF290 left 1000, shot down by Flak while strafing SW Perugia; Lt J.D.H.Harding KiA

US Casualties

314th FS/324th FG	P-40L 42-11033 '20' last seen NE Seggiano 1920; 2/Lt Jeremiah F.Hammond baled, evaded and returned on 21 June [6041]
111th TRS	P-51C 42-103457 hit by Flak SW Cortona 1920; 2/Lt Arthur S.Kazarian KiA [6043]
111th TRS	P-51C damaged by Flak when circling site of Kazarian's crash; Lt (Jg) Harold J.Eckardt (USN VCS-8 on attachment) landed safely
438th BS/319th BG	B-26 42-95988 crashed in Sardinia; Capt Artur N.Riegel and five KiA

German Claims

Flak	Regt Mitte	Spitfire		1047
Flak	3rd Flak Brigade	P-47		1912
Flak		P-51	Camaldoli	1925
Flak		P-51	Terraia	1930

German Casualties

2./NAGr 11	Bf 109G-8 WNr 710052 White 7 lost in combat near Civitavecchia; Obfhr Bernd-Heinz Franzmann MiA

Italian ANR Casualties

3ª Sq, 1° Gr C	G.55 MM 91087 shot down; S.Ten Fausto Morettin baled out but DoW
1ª Sq, 1° Gr C	G.55 crash-landed; S.Ten Giovanni Sajeva safe

ESTABLISHMENT OF THE BALKAN AIR FORCE

All available units were brought into the fray over Yugoslavia and along the coast now strafing, bombing and escorting supply-dropping aircraft filled the skies. Early in June enemy fighters again appeared but two Spitfires of 73 Squadron were quickly dispatched over Brac on the 4th. Three days later Balkan Air Force was formed under the command of Air Vice-Marshal W.Elliot who opened his headquarters at Bari.

The new air force was formed from a nucleus initially known as Special Operations Air Force which had encompassed 324 Wing at Brindisi and was initially allocated eight squadrons and one flight, a strength which very rapidly increased. Even before BAF was formed air support had made all the difference at Drvar and within a week the Germans were on the defensive again. A small ground detachment, known as 2 Balkan Air Terminal Service (2 BATS), was sent to join Tito and to find landing strips into which supplies could be flown and from which casualties could be evacuated.

By 3 June one such strip had been discovered at Kupresko Polje, and immediately a Russian Dakota (licence built as the Lisunov Li 2) flew in and lifted Tito together with the British and Russian missions to attend a conference at Bari. Tito's staff and 118 wounded were brought out by C-47s of the 60th Troop Carrier Group. The purpose of the conference was to arrange much closer air support for the partisans. To this end a Soviet air force detachment of 12 Li 2 transports and 12 Yak 9 fighters arrived at Bari to operate over Yugoslavia under Balkan Air Force command. 2 BATS stayed in Yugoslavia to find other suitable landing strips while radio specialists were moved into the offshore islands to report on enemy shipping movements. As a result of their reports very heavy losses were to be inflicted by Wellingtons of 221 Squadron, Hurricanes of 6 Squadron and Beaufighters of 39 Squadron, a detachment of which had just arrived at Grottaglie from Sardinia.

Meanwhile the fighter-bombers, joined by Desert Air Force units, began a campaign against rail traffic on the Zagreb-Belgrade-Skopje line and on the Brod-Sarajevo-Mostar line, which ran along the coast; during the first month no less than 262 locomotives were to be destroyed or damaged. Flak over Yugoslavia was, however, extremely heavy and units operating here were to suffer regular losses to this cause. In mid-June 87 Squadron moved north to re-join 323 Wing which now for the first time in many months had all four of its fighter squadrons – 32, 73, 87 and 253 – together again. On the last day of the month four Spitfires of 73 Squadron spotted 15 aircraft on Sarajevo airfield, including some Dornier bombers; these were strafed and eight claimed probably destroyed for the loss of one Spitfire.

The strength of Balkan Air Force now began to rise rapidly. On 13 June the Baltimore-equipped 13 (Hellenic) Squadron was transferred from 232 Wing of DAF to 254 Wing at Biferno, joined next day by the Beaufighters of 39 Squadron, the whole of which unit had now arrived from Sardinia. 213 Squadron arrived to join the same wing from Egypt, flying Mustang IIIs for long-range activities over Yugoslavia and to escort the Baltimores, Venturas and Beaufighters. 73 Squadron moved to Canne early in the month on attachment to 281 Wing, 32, 249 and 253 Squadrons moving to this base during the month. 73 Squadron remained only until mid-July when it flew back to Foggia to convert to Spitfire IXs.

In the middle of the month the Germans launched a heavy assault on the partisan II Corps in Montenegro, air support being given by about two dozen Ju 87s and some Fi 156s and Hs 126s, with a little fighter cover. Heavy fighting ensued, the partisans counter-attacking under close support by BAF units and driving back the Germans who suffered heavy losses. On 20 July Mustangs of 213 Squadron engaged a formation of 12 Hs 126s and seven Bf 109s while on a sweep over the battle area, claiming to have shot down one of each and also two probables. Other fighter units also occasionally met enemy aircraft and by the end of the month three more had been shot down. To support the forces in Montenegro partisans in the north of the country increased their activities south of Drvar, gaining control of the roads from Knin to Zara and Sibenik.

As may have been noted a number of the units to be allocated to BAF had already commenced operations before an actual formation of the new command had taken place. This latter event took place with effect from 31 July when the initial Order of Battle was established:

334 (Special Duties) Wing
148 (SD) Squadron	Halifax IIa and V; Lysander IIIa
1586 (Polish) Flight (SD)	Halifax IIa/II, Liberator III
1° Gruppo Trasporti Notturno	S.82
88° Gruppo Trasporti Notturno	Cant.Z.1007

281 Wing
249, 253 Squadrons	Spitfire Vc
32 Squadron	Spitfire Vc, Vb, VIII, IX
102° Gruppo Caccia	Macchi C.202
155° Gruppo Caccia	Macchi C.205

254 Wing
13 (Hellenic) Squadron	Baltimore IV, V
39 Squadron	Beaufighter X
213 Squadron	Mustang III

On temporary SD duties with BAF were:

60th Troop Carrier Group, USAAF (10th, 11th, 12th and 28th Squadrons)	C-47
One detached flight of 267 Squadron	Dakota
Attached force of	12 Dakotas (PS.84) and 12 Yak 9s of the Soviet air force

Further units arrived during August – by this time urgently needed – which included 16 SAAF and 19 SAAF Squadrons both from Egypt where they had been training on rocket-firing Beaufighter Xs. The former was the long-serving 227 Squadron, renumbered and now mainly crewed by South Africans. Meanwhile 6 Squadron and its Hurricanes moved up to Canne.

Order of Battle of Italian Co-Belligerent fighter units by 15 June 1944

Raggruppamento Caccia		T.Col Duilio Fanali
4° Stormo Caccia	P-39	Magg Luigi Mariotti
9° Gruppo		Cap Emanuele Annoni
96ª Squadriglia		Ten Otello Gensini
97ª Squadriglia		Ten Giuseppe Ferazzani
10° Gruppo		Magg Ranieri Piccolomini
84ª Squadriglia		Ten Alessandro Mettimano
90ª Squadriglia		Ten Carlo Tommasi
12° Gruppo		Cap Eugenio Salvi
73ª Squadriglia		Cap Eugenio Salvi
91ª Squadriglia		Ten Mario Mecatti

51° Stormo Caccia		MC.205	T.Col Duilio Fanali
20° Gruppo			Cap Paolo Spadaccini
	356ª Squadriglia		Cap Giuseppe Bentivoglio
	360ª Squadriglia		Ten Tullio Martinelli
21° Gruppo			Cap Remo Dezzani
	386ª Squadriglia		Ten Arrigo Bagajoli
	351ª Squadriglia		Ten Giovanni Franchini
155° Gruppo			Cap Manlio Biccolini
	361ª Squadriglia		Ten Enrico Manfredini
	378ª Squadriglia		Ten Giuseppe Scarinci
5° Stormo Caccia		MC.202	Magg Mario Bacich
8° Gruppo			Cap Ippolito Lalatta
	92ª Squadriglia		Ten Giuseppe Pesce
	93ª Squadriglia		Ten Gioacchino Bissoli
101° Gruppo			Cap Umberto Cerretani
	208ª Squadriglia		Ten Edoardo Migliore
	238ª Squadriglia		Ten Mario Parodi
102° Gruppo			Cap Antonio Montuori
	209ª Squadriglia		Cap Antonio Montuori
	239ª Squadriglia		Cap Mario Spreafico

Friday, 16 June 1944

Flt Lt Bruce Ingalls of 417 Squadron was shot down by Flak and killed while strafing vehicles on this date; he had been credited with seven victories.

After their brief introduction to operations bombing targets in the Aegean, 31 SAAF Squadron began moving to Italy to join 205 Group.

British Casualties

417 Sqn	Spitfire VIII JF715 left 0955, shot down by Flak at Collestrada SE Lake Trasimeno; Flt Lt B.J.Ingalls KiA
601 Sqn	Spitfire VIII MJ389 left 0830, last seen near Perugia a/f, presumed hit by Flak, crashed, wreck and body found by army units next day; Sgt E.T.Lascelles KiA
253 Sqn	Spitfire Vc JK279 ; left 0500 on offensive sweep Bosan-Prijedor-Bosanski Petrovac; hit by Flak over Stari Majdan, Yugoslavia, belly-landed; Plt Off J.Melville evaded
39 Sqn	Beaufighter X LZ486 'X' left 1455 on armed recce Gulf of Fiume, presumed shot down by Flak W Novalja; Flt Sgt J.A.Spence/Flt Sgt N.E.J.Barnes MiA
7 SAAF Sqn	Spitfire IX MJ666 hit by Flak strafing near Città di Castello and Umbertide; Lt D.J.Lindsay baled out

US Casualties

523rd FS/27th FGB	P-40F 41-19996 shot down by Flak 0950 S Pienza; 2/Lt Edward F.Jones evaded and returned [6068]

German Claims

2./Flak 865		Spitfire	Prijedor	0558
9./Flak Regt 5		Spitfire	Collestrada	0912
Flak Regt 5		Spitfire	Perugia	0917
Flak		Spitfire	Bastia Umbra	0922
Flak		Spitfire	Passignano	1005
Flak		Spitfire		1050
Flak		Spitfire		1052
10./Flak Regt 5		Spitfire	Umbertide	1235
Flak		P-47	Populonia	1325
Flak		Spitfire		1455
Flak		Spitfire	Sarnano	1645
Flak		Beaufighter	Novalja Island	1815

Friday-Saturday, 16/17 June 1944

British Casualties

17 SAAF Sqn   Ventura V JS890 left on anti-submarine patrol S Sardinia, flew into a hill at Cap Serrat on return; Lt T.F.Borgen and three
                       KiA

Saturday, 17 June 1944

On 13 June P-47s of the 79th Fighter Group had commenced a three-day series of attacks on the Isle of Elba, strafing docks, gun positions and other similar targets; the American pilots would claim ten barges, 12 vehicles and two ships during the next four days. On the morning of the 17th landings went ashore on the island comprised almost entirely of French troops spearheaded only by a British Commando force. The air support was organised by the 87th Fighter Wing and amounted to 24 dive-bombing missions and 48 patrols. Elements of the Armée de l'Air equipped with Spitfires and P-47s took part but little hostile reaction was encountered initially.

While Elba was temporarily the focus of attention, away to the east the crew of a reconnaissance Baltimore of 454 Squadron spotted a German convoy

The ever-present risk from Flak was brought home on 16 June when Flt Lt Bruce Ingalls, a successful pilot with 417 Squadron, was shot down and killed.

(GK 91) comprising three small cargo vessels – *Aspasia, Ioannis Kutifari, Maria Vol* and a motor yacht – which were sailing north-west of Falconera from Chania to Piraeus under an aerial escort of four Ar 196s. Two of these floatplanes at once gave chase to the reconnaissance aircraft but were unable to catch it. The convoy was subsequently attacked off Cape Maleas by eight Beaufighters drawn equally from 227 and 16 SAAF Squadrons and the yacht was sunk. However, the two escorting Arados of 4./SAGr 126 engaged the attackers and claimed one shot down very low above the waves. Two Beaufighters were lost during this engagement and one more crash-landed on return, falling to ships' Flak and/or the Arados. Both the German floatplanes were shot down by the Beaufighters, their crews being rescued by the convoy's vessels.

Having earlier departed the Union, by this date the ground and air parties of 25 SAAF Squadron had reassembled at Pomigliano under their commanding officer, Lt Col H.G. (Lawrie) Shuttleworth, DFC, a veteran of the East African campaign. The unit was equipped with Ventura II aircraft which were the Lend-Lease equivalent of the USAAF's B-34 Lexington. These had previously been employed on maritime duties in South Africa but were now no longer required in this capacity; and were therefore about to commence re-training for the light bomber role.

British Claims

227 Sqn	Flg Off G.H.Snape/Flt Sgt J.G.Purnell	Beaufighter X JL910 'S'	Ar 196	off Cape Maleas	1100
227 Sqn	Wt Off N.R.Davis/Flt Sgt J.Sefton	Beaufighter X JL619 'X'	Ar 196	off Cape Maleas	1100

227 Sqn	Flt Sgt K.W.Abbott/Plt Off D.Buxton	Beaufighter X JL697 'V'	Ar 196	off Cape Maleas	1100
227 Sqn	Flt Sgt D.H.Robertson/Flt Sgt L.Evans	Beaufighter X EL598 'M'	Ar 196 Damaged	off Cape Maleas	1100
16 SAAF Sqn	Lt J.R.D.Strange/Lt A.E.Diack	Beaufighter X 'S'	Ar 196 Damaged	off Cape Maleas	1100

British Casualties

39 Sqn	Beaufighter X NE415 'L' left 0625, flew into ground strafing train NW Salonika; Flg Off P.H.Greenburgh/Flg Off A.Oakes MiA
16 SAAF Sqn	Beaufighter X NE590 'X' left 0907, shot down by Flak and/or Ar 196, ditched 3m off Cape Maleas 1106; Maj R.Munton-Jackson/Lt Hutton safe in dinghy, rescued
16 SAAF Sqn	Beaufighter X NE551 'Z' left 0907, shot down at 1104, crashed into the sea in flames 400 yards S of convoy N Cape Maleas; Capt K.G.Muir/Lt J.H.Strydom KiA
227 Sqn	Beaufighter X JL697 'V' hydraulics shot out, crash-landed at base; Flt Sgt K.W.Abbott/Plt Off D.Buxton safe
417 Sqn	Spitfire VIII JF882 engine failed during patrol, pilot baled out into Allied lines; Flt Lt B.N.M.Delarminat WiA

US Casualties

316th FS/324th FG	P-40 '45' shot down by Flak N Cecina 0622; Flt Off Alfred F.Pompay KiA
441st BS/320th BG	B-26B 42-96022 '19' *Bobo the Strong boy* lost for u/k cause on transit flight from La Senia, Algeria to Decimomannu, Sardinia; 1/Lt Jack E.Dillon and three crew plus nine passengers (eight of which were French soldiers) MiA [6039]

German Claims

Flak			P-40	Cecina	0625
Flak	*GK 91* convoy ships		2 Beaufighters	off Cape Maleas	ca 1000
4./SAGr 126	Uffz Busse/Obgfr Schramm	Ar 196-5	Beaufighter	E Agios Georgios	1006

German Casualties

4./SAGr 126	Ar 196A-3 WNr 623010 D1+AN shot down off Cape Maleas; Uffz Paduch/Lt Böckling WiA
4./SAGr 126	Ar 196A-3 WNr 100505 D1+FN damaged by Beaufighters off Cape Maleas, landed at base; Uffz Rudolf Busse WiA/Obfw Schramm safe

Sunday, 18 June 1944

Portoferraio was taken on this date, the rest of Isle of Elba falling swiftly next day. Over southern France French-flown P-47Ds led by Cne Pierre Gouachon-Noireault, who had achieved some success in 1940, destroyed a He 111.

Sous Lt George Gauthier was one of the French P-47D pilots of GC II/5 who combined to destroy an He 111 near Montpellier.

British Casualties				
14 Sqn	Marauder FK123 'J' left 0847, badly damaged off Sette Nouville by two Bf 109s 1100; Flg Off M.C.Hogg and three safe, two WiA			

US Casualties				
316th FS/324th FG	P-40L 42-108670 '92' last seen W Cecina 1440, lost u/k cause; 2/Lt Wesley H.Hunt KiA [6081]			

French Claims				
GC 2/5	Cne Pierre Gouachon-Noireault	⎫		
GC 3/6	Sous Lt Georges Gauthier	⎬ He 111	Montpellier/Ayres	
GC 2/5	Lt Henry Ducru			
GC 2/5	Sgt Pierre Bernard	⎭		

German Claims				
Flak		Hudson	Rhodes	1948

Monday, 19 June 1944

Only on this date did elements of the Luftwaffe appear over Elba when a pair of tactical reconnaissance Bf 109s of NAGr 11 approached from the direction of Piombino. These were intercepted and both were shot down by 242 Squadron's Wt Off Eric Doherty, one of the unit's most successful pilots. Five minutes later Control issued a warning that further hostile aircraft were approaching and as one of these appeared from out of cloud Doherty shot this down as well under the impression that it was an FW 190. Unfortunately, it was a P-39 of the 350th Fighter Group, the pilot of which was killed. The other American pilots initially thought the Airacobra had been shot down by an FW 190.

Plt Off Bill Davenport and Flt Sgt Cecil Grainger of 252 Squadron became POWs after ditching their Beaufighter due to Flak damage off Nisiros on the afternoon of 19 June.

British Claims					
242 Sqn	Wt Off E.S.Doherty	Spitfire IX 'J'	2 Bf 109s	E Piombino	2015
242 Sqn	Wt Off E.S.Doherty	Spitfire IX 'J'	FW 190 (P-39!)	5m E Pianosa	2020

British Casualties					
252 Sqn	Beaufighter X NE546 'Q' shot down by Flak from *TA 19* and ditched at SW Nisiros 1600; Plt Off W.Davenport/Flt Sgt C.P.Grainger POW				

US Casualties					
347th FS/350th FG	P-39 shot down by 'FW 190' at Elba 2020, turned out to be RAF Spitfire; 2/Lt Elbert R.Carpenter KiA				

German Casualties					
2./NAGr 11	Bf 109G-6 WNr 163805 White 1 lost in combat between Elba and Piombino; Uffz Otto Hübner MiA				
2./NAGr 11	Bf 109G-8 WNr 200028 White 5 lost in combat between Elba and Piombino; Gfr Erich Pieczkowski MiA				

Monday-Tuesday, 19/20 June 1944

Early in the morning a reconnaissance aircraft – an Me 410 of 2.(F)/122 – was intercepted west of Isle of Elba by one of the 350th Group's P-39 from the 347th Squadron. This intruder was attacked and damaged by Lt Sharock.

US Claims

347th FS/350th FG	Lt M.W.Sharock	P-39	Me 410 Damaged	W tip of Elba	0522-0545

German Casualties

2.(F)/122	Me 410 F6+EK badly damaged by two P-39s of 347th FS/350th FG, landed at Bergamo; Oblt von Daele/Uffz Blaschek safe

Tuesday, 20 June 1944

On this date responsibility for the air defence of Elba passed to Coastal's 63rd Fighter Wing which was also operating units from Corsica. The island was not, however, to be used as an air base, its occupation having been undertaken primarily as a boost to French morale.

US Casualties

84th BS/47th BG	A-20G 42-9206 lost nr Rome, unknown cause; 2/Lt Leo J.Rusk and one KiA [6024]
87th FS/79th FG	P-47D hit by Flak, crashed in Genoa harbour 1515; pilot slightly WiA

French Casualties

GC 2/3	P-47D hit by Flak during raid on a bridge nr Pisa 1315, pilot baled between Italy and Corsica; Lt Marill rescued by Walrus X9471 from 284 Sqn flown by Sqn Ldr J.S.Barnett. They were towed back to Bastia by HSL 2595

When Sqn Ldr Jack Te Kloot of 249 Squadron attacked these oil storage tanks in Albania on 20 June, the explosion blackened the underside of his aircraft.

Mid-June Overview

When the Elba landings were taking place, on the mainland 5th Army had entered Grosseto and 8th had taken Foligno. By the 20th the Americans had occupied Civitavecchia and Viterbo as well, while the French on their right flank reached the southern bank of the Orcia river. In central Italy 8th Army had reached a line running from Lake Trasimeno to Chiusi, just to the north of Perugia, and on the east coast V Corps had occupied Pedaso. It was in the centre that the Germans decided to try and fight a strong delaying action where 8th Army would soon become involved in a fierce battle around the lake.

At this time the weather had deteriorated somewhat and would remain indifferent for most of the rest of June. On the 17th the whole of 244 Wing had commenced a move to join 92 Squadron at Fabrica where it was also to be joined by some Seafires and their pilots of 807 and 809 Squadrons led by Lt Cdr George Baldwin, DSC. Although known collectively as 4 Naval Fighter Wing, the Seafires were in practice parcelled out on attachment to several of the RAF squadrons to gain experience in ground-attack work.

The swift Allied advance to and beyond Rome quickly provided much confirmation of the claims for Axis transport destroyed. On one stretch of the Forlì road where 117 had been claimed, 122 were found to have been totally destroyed. During the first week of June the Germans had been forced almost wholly onto the roads due to the great damage inflicted on the railways and in this particular period they had lost over 1,000 motor transports totally destroyed. Since the start of Operation Diadem in May until 22 June more than 5,000 vehicles had been claimed destroyed by the air forces with about an equal number damaged.

The evidence indicated that in an advance the fighter-bombers were more profitably employed against the supply lines than in direct support, and that Cab Rank operations were only really desirable when static positions were being attacked.

During mid-June 244 Wing's Spitfire VIII squadrons practised dropping bombs from their aircraft ready for future fighter-bomber operations. Having considered themselves to be the premier fighter wing in Italy, the pilots were a little taken aback at this turn of events but the truth was that opposition in the air had markedly decreased since the fall of Rome and there were few signs that it would resume. To retain squadrons purely for the odd strafing mission in such circumstances would clearly be a waste of resources.

It was not, however, the fall of Rome that led to the disappearance of the Luftwaffe. The initial withdrawal up to early June 1944 was for the Defence of the Reich with III. and IV./JG 27 leaving Greece for Germany during April and May 1944, followed in early June by I./JG 4, leaving just a Staffel of III.JG 27 in Greece. By the end of May the defence of the Romanian oilfields was in the hands of I./JG 53, III./JG 77 and II./JG 51, while Italy was defended by I. and II./JG 77. As the Eastern Front was perceived as more critical than Italy the Gruppen of Schlachtgeschwader 4 were also withdrawn; these were sent to Russia

Seafires from 4 Naval Fighter Wing led by Lt Cdr George Baldwin were based at Castiglione and Perugia in early July to allow his pilots to gain some combat experience.

following Soviet attacks into the Balkan region and ahead of the massive main Russian offensive, Operation Bagration, which commenced on 22 June.

For the Luftwaffe in Italy, the main impact of the invasion of Normandy was the almost instant cessation of operations by the Kampfgeschwader bomber units based in southern France, Italy and Greece. Except for some small-scale convoy operations, LG 1, KG 100, KG 26 and KG 77 no longer undertook any major raids. The bombers were based in southern France and flew north to Normandy, as there were no available bases closer to the invasion area. They remained based in this region prior to the invasion of southern France in August. As will be seen, the response to Operation Dragoon in August was limited with only elements of three Gruppen opposing these new landings.

The new Western Front proved a deadly whirlpool into which Luftwaffe bomber units were rapidly sucked before swiftly disappearing almost without trace. By September some bomber Gruppen from the Eastern Front began operating into Greece and the Aegean but in the transport role. Thus, by the end of June Luftwaffe fighter units in the Mediterranean area comprised I. and II./JG 77 in Italy, JGr 200 in southern France and II./JG 51 in Yugoslavia. All other fighter units had gone.

To supplement, and later replace, these the Germans began supplying the ANR with the Bf 109G. Training for their pilots was provided in the Reich. The first unit to re-equip was the 2° Gruppo Caccia and by mid-June its conversion to the Bf 109G was almost complete. 1° Gruppo Caccia that had been engaging the 15th Air Force formations alongside JG 77 since early 1944 was now becoming considerably weakened but would remain *in situ* in Italy until the end of October. It then withdrew to Germany to reform and re-equip with Bf 109Gs. However, operations of these two Gruppi were hampered by the fiasco which was the German attempt to conscript the ANR units into the Luftwaffe. This halted operations from August to October as did the impounding of fuel supplies.

Amongst the Allied air forces at this time other changes were taking place. On 17 June 241 Squadron left 7 SAAF Wing to join 318 Squadron at San Vito. Here it was now the only DAF fighter squadron on the east coast. Two days later 225 Squadron moved forward to Voltone, but in 244 Wing 145 Squadron had a veritable exodus of its more experienced pilots, Flt Lt J.Wooler, DFC, Flg Off J.C.Stirling, DFC, and Flt Lt C.R.Parbury all ending their tours. Flt Lt R.F.Starnes, DFC, was posted in from 72 Squadron to take over one of the vacant flight commander posts, but on the 24th he was to be shot down while on a strafing sortie and had to bale out into Axis territory. He returned safely on 18 July.

Wednesday, 21 June 1944

251 Wing continued its run of good fortune during its more northerly operations from Corsica, but it was now 238 Squadron which seemed to enjoy all the success. On the 21st, during the second mission of the day, the squadron strafed Azzano d'Asti airfield where four Bf 109s, a Do 217, a He 111 and an Fi 156 were all claimed destroyed, three of them by Sqn Ldr Wilson, an ex-Desert Gladiator pilot; the remaining claims were by Plt Off H.Nice and Lt P.M.van Rensberg. The ANR lost four aircraft on the ground at Cervere which is some 45km further to the south-west!

3 SAAF Wing noted the retirement of 21 SAAF Squadron's Baltimore III FA383 'W' *Wacky Wabbitt* after 174 raids totalling 395 operational hours, plus another 30 hours non-operational flights. Corporal W.R.Janson, the crew chief, was proud of the fact that she had never failed to take off on a briefed mission.

British Claims				
238 Sqn	Sqn Ldr A.Wilson	Spitfire IX MK783 'L'	2 Bf 109s (on ground)	Azzano d'Asti
238 Sqn	Sqn Ldr A.Wilson	Spitfire IX MK783 'L'	Do 217 (on ground)	Azzano d'Asti
238 Sqn	Plt Off H.H.Nice	Spitfire IX MK143 'G'	He 111 (on ground)	Azzano d'Asti
238 Sqn	Lt P.M.van Rensberg	Spitfire IX MJ909 'V'	2 Bf 109s (on ground)	Azzano d'Asti
238 Sqn	Lt P.M.van Rensberg	Spitfire IX MJ909 'V'	Fi 156 (on ground)	Azzano d'Asti
British Casualties				
241 Sqn	Spitfire IX MA811 left 0500 to strafe Ancona-Pesaro road, hit in coolant system by Flak, crash-landed 0545; Flg Off J.S.B.Reynolds MiA, returned to unit on 25 June			
US Casualties				
87th FS/79th FG	P-47D hit by Flak, crashed at Pisa 1210; 1/Lt Edward H.Ryan Jr returned			
German Claims				
Marine Flak		Hudson	Rhodes	1527

German Casualties

2./NAGr 11	Bf 109G-6 WNr 410568 White 2 shot down by fighters 20km N Pisa; Obfw Hans Stölting KIA

Italian ANR Casualties

Gr.Compl. C	1 CR.42, 2 Ca.309s and 1 Ca.133 destroyed on ground at Cervere

Wednesday-Thursday, 21/22 June 1944

A C-47 crashed during a supply-dropping mission into Albania.

US Casualties

28th TCS/60th TCG	C-47 42-23405 lost over Albania, unknown cause 0230; Capt Robert H.Snyder and five KiA [16192]

Thursday, 22 June 1944

232 Squadron, again from 251 Wing, escorted B-25s to the Leghorn area but Flak was both intense and accurate, at least eight Mitchells being shot down.

Four Spitfires of 241, 242, 237 and 249 Squadrons were also shot down by Flak during the day. The 241 Squadron aircraft was flown by Flt Lt Steedman who later rose to become Air Chief Marshal Sir Alasdair Steedman. On a flight over the Florence-Leghorn area by eight 154 Squadron Spitfires, one section was described as being heavily weighted down with gold braid, since Grp Capt Hugo (in Spitfire IX MK603) was leading a visiting Wg Cdr (J.R.H.Gayner, DFC, in MK119) as his No. 2, a Grp Capt (J.M.Thompson, DSO, DFC, in MK467) as No. 3 and a US Colonel (Earl E.Bates in MJ943) as No. 4.

On this date 112 Squadron flew its last 24 Kittyhawk sorties following which Mustangs began to arrive at last.

Plt Off Ian Smith of 237 (Rhodesia) Squadron survived being shot down by Flak near the port of La Spezia. After the war he became the prime minister of Rhodesia.

British Casualties

241 Sqn	Spitfire VIII JF561 left 0510 on weather recce of Ancona-Frosinone area, hit by Flak, crash-landed 0615; Flt Lt A.M.S.Steedman MiA; evaded and returned by 6 July
242 Sqn	Spitfire IX MA626 'B' left 0600, shot down by Flak and crash-landed when strafing motor transports 5m S Siena; Plt Off W.J.T.Young POW
237 Sqn	Spitfire IX MK620 left 1630, shot down by Flak N La Spezia; Plt Off I.Smith baled, evaded to November 1944
249 Sqn	Spitfire Vc ES311 left 0955, pilot wounded in leg by Flak at Peqin, u/c collapsed on landing at Brindisi; Sgt R.S.Perry WiA
5 SAAF Sqn	Kittyhawk IV FX624 left 0700 on armed recce, shot down by 20mm Flak SSW Arezzo 0750; Lt D.N.Vernon baled out, evaded

US Casualties

379th BS/310th BG	B-25J 43-4043 shot down by Flak over Leghorn 1910; 2/Lt W.Bombeck and four safe, one KiA
379th BS/310th BG	B-25J 43-4036 shot down by Flak over Leghorn 1916; 2/Lt D.G.Howlett and four safe, one KiA
487th BS/340th BG	B-25J 43-27656 '7C' shot down by Flak nr Leghorn 1923; 2/Lt Thomas V.Casey and two KiA, one POW, two evaded [6070]
380th BS/310th BG	B-25J 43-4018 hit by Flak in right wing nr Leghorn 1930, crashed into sea; 1/Lt Frank Peterson and five KiA [6090]
381st BS/310th BG	B-25J 43-4042 hit by Flak in bomb-bay section nr Leghorn 1930, crashed into sea; 1/Lt James V.Quitta and two KiA, two POW, one rescued [6089]
381st BS/310th BG	B-25J 43-4087 shot down by Flak Leghorn area 1935; 1/Lt Robert F.Killian and two evaded, three POW [6040]
381st BS/310th BG	B-25J 43-4054 hit by Flak, belly-landed at Alesan, Corsica 2040; 1/Lt Glenn T.Black and one WiA, five safe
381st BS/310th BG	B-25J 43-27507 nose gear collapsed on landing 2040; 2/Lt Charles Prasse and three safe, two WiA
100th FS/332nd FG	P-47 42-26812 lost in Corsica 0915; 2/Lt Samuel Jefferson KiA [6078]
100th FS/332nd FG	P-47 42-75798 lost 12m N Finale Ligure 0945; Capt Robert B.Tresville KiA [6079]
100th FS/332nd FG	P-47 lost over Italy; 2/Lt Charles B.Johnson KiA

Flak		Recce Spitfire	Ancona	0550
III./FAS 2		P-51	SE Buonconvento	0645
3./Flak 750		Kittyhawk	Castiglione	0750
Flak		B-25	Florence	1914
Flak		B-25	Prato	1925
1.-4./Flak 354		5 B-25s		1926-1947

One of the mounting list of losses to Flak suffered by 249 Squadron was New Zealander Flt Lt Clive Jacobsen who was killed near Kicevo on 23 June and is now buried in Belgrade War Cemetery.

Friday, 23 June 1944

239 Wing began moving to Falerium where it was to become involved in Cab Rank operations again as 8th Army started its attack on the German defences in the Lake Trasimeno area.

Effective from this date the 86th Fighter Bomber Group was re-designated as the 86th Fighter Group, its squadrons also receiving new identities.

French-flown Spitfires of GC 1/7 'Provence' and GC 2/7 'Nice' flew some missions and one was shot down by Flak near Pisa, Sous-lieutenant Guy Antoine Bouttier being killed.

A P-39 of GC 3/6 'Roussillon' was lost due to a failure of a fuel tank off Djidjelli, Algeria, the pilot, Second-maître Marpaud, baling out and being rescued some hours later.

Two Spitfires of 1435 Squadron on an ASR patrol sighted two Bf 109s at low level off the Albanian coast. The section leader Flt Sgt Miller broke away and shot down the wingman. The leader got away.

British Claims

1435 Sqn	Flt Sgt T.A.Miller	Spitfire IX MH609 'E'	Bf 109	NE Brindisi-Albanian coast	1925-2020

British Casualties

92 Sqn	Spitfire VIII JF290 left 1700, strafed goods wagons at Fano, pilot baled out into the sea, seen in dinghy but not rescued; Lt W.F.Steenkamp KiA
249 Sqn	Spitfire Vc ES299 left 0520 on road strafing, attacked a train S of Orese, hit by Flak, pilot baled; Flt Lt C.F.Jacobsen KiA as POW

French Casualties

GC 1/7	Spitfire V 836 on armed recce La Spezia-Leghorn, shot down by light Flak 4km N Pisa 0630; Sous Lt Guy Antoine Bouttier KiA
GC 3/6	P-39 42-13372 lost due to fuel tank failure; 2nd-Mtr Marpaud baled out, rescued

German Claims

Flak	278 Inf Div		multi-engined a/c	E Kuesti	
Flak			P-47		1117
Flak			Spitfire	Greece	
Flak			Hudson		2157

German Casualties

1./NAGr 12	Bf 109G-6 WNr 19979 White 7 lost in combat with Spitfire 80km NW Valona; Obfw Artur Geyer MiA

Saturday, 24 June 1944

During the second mission of the day of GC 2/5 'La Fayette' against a rail bridge south of Ovada, as the P-47s were starting their bombing run, 14 Bf 109s and eight Fiat G.55s of ANR 2° Gruppo Caccia dived out of clouds and surprised them. The French pilots all managed to evade the attack and after some aerobatics and many bursts fired by both sides, both formations broke away without any loss on either side. The 11 P-47s landed at 1855 at Alto, only two, flown by Capitaine Thierry and Sergent-chef Lesieur, having suffered some light damage. Ten Drago and Serg Magg Cavagliano claimed one Thunderbolt shot down each.

324 Wing moved to Grosseto; Flt Lt R.W. 'Paddy' Turkington was posted to 241 Squadron at San Vito from 72 Squadron. 12 SAAF Squadron moved with its Marauders to Pescara, joined by Baltimores of 13 (Hellenic) Squadron.

British Claims

41 SAAF Sqn	Capt R.P.Burl	Spitfire IX LZ984 'V'	Ju 88	bn Cyprus and Turkey	1814-1937

British Casualties

1435 Sqn	Spitfire Vc LZ929 left 0805, shot down by ground fire strafing Kelcyre, pilot baled 4m W Cerevode; Wt Off T.V.Pigot POW
145 Sqn	Spitfire VIII JG186 left 1425, shot down strafing Arezzo-Florence area, pilot baled out in enemy territory 1530; Flt Lt R.F.Starnes evaded, returned on 18 July

US Casualties

66th FS/57th FG	P-47D left 1430, engine began cutting so returned to Alto, Corsica, crashed while attempting to land; Flt Off Julius H.Coburn KiFA
319th FS/325th FG	P-51C 42-103552 hit by Flak between Pesaro and Fano 0.5m off shore 1503; 2/Lt Howard F.Welch KiA [6178]

French Casualties

GC 2/5	P-47 damaged by Bf 109s S Ovada; Sgt Chef Lesieur safe
GC 2/5	P-47 damaged by Bf 109s S Ovada; Cne Thierry safe

German Claims

Stab/JG 77	FhjFw Gottfried Fährmann		P-51	20km NE Pesaro	1034
Flak			Spitfire	Fano	1435
Flak			P-51	Fano	1501
Flak			P-40	Fano	1505

German Casualties

2.(F)/123	Ju 88T-1 WNr 430925 4U+KK shot down by Spitfires E Cyprus; Uffz Fritz Schmidt and two KiA

Italian ANR Claims

4ª Sq, 2° Gr C	Ten Ugo Drago	Bf 109G-6	P-47	Varazze-Genoa	1755
4ª Sq, 2° Gr C	Serg Magg Carlo Cavagliano	Bf 109G-6	P-47	Varazze-Genoa	1755

Sunday, 25 June 1944

Four Spitfires escorted Baltimores to Fano, where over the target a lone Bf 109 dived on two of them shooting down both. One pilot managed to bale out into the Adriatic and was later picked up by a Walrus of 293 Squadron. I./JG 77 carried out a *Freie Jagd* patrol over the area of Rimini between 1428-1605. Two of the unit's veterans, Hptm Lothar Baumann and Oblt Bruno Kolthoff, claimed a Spitfire each.

British Casualties

241 Sqn	Spitfire IX MA811 left 1420 escorting bombers to Rimini, shot down by Bf 109 15m NNE Senigallia 1535; Flg Off D.G.English MiA
241 Sqn	Spitfire VIII JF701 left 1420 escorting bombers to Rimini, shot down by Bf 109 off Rimini 1545, Plt Off J.Johnstone baled out, rescued by 293 Sqn Walrus K8549 flown by Wt Off K.G.Hall/Wt Off M.D.Kelly

US Casualties

522nd FS/27th FBG	P-47D 42-26680 'red O' lost to Flak 3m NE Fucecchio 1100; 2/Lt Erwin Ginsberg POW [6066]

German Claims

1./Flak 507			P-47	Vinci	1109
2./Flak 921			P-47	Vinci	1115
Flak			P-51	Fano	1443
Stab I./JG 77	Hptm Lothar Baumann		Spitfire	ESE Rimini	1525
Stab I./JG 77	Oblt Bruno Kolthoff		Spitfire	off Rimini	1528

Sunday-Monday, 25/26 June 1944

British Claims

108 Sqn	Wt Off C.E.Baldry/Flg Off J.Watson	Beaufighter VIf BT300 'G'	He 177	Bron-Valence	2240-0330

Monday, 26 June 1944

While 8th Army was heavily engaged in the centre advancing slowly towards Arezzo, in the west the Americans took Piombino on 25 June and Cecina on 1 July, while the French were in Siena on the 3rd. On 26 June 239 Wing carried out a successful attack in the Trasimeno area, Sqn Ldr R.H.Bayly and Flt Sgt A.T.Field of 3 RAAF Squadron gaining direct hits on a field headquarters, destroying it and killing the commanding officer of one of the main units of the Hermann Göring Division.

Twelve Spitfires of 72 Squadron swept over Bologna airfield but here Flt Lt Mayes' Spitfire was hit by Flak and he had to bale out. Further west 238 Squadron Spitfires, led by Flt Lt G.W.Small, encountered several Bf 109s and Macchis during the afternoon, Flg Offs Hannan and Nice each claiming one of the former shot down, two more being claimed damaged. Nice reported Italian markings on his 109 and indeed the aircraft were Italian, with a MC.205 being lost and two more damaged of 1° Gruppo Caccia.

Four Spitfires of 73 Squadron saw an airfield near Zagreb, at Borongai, known to the Germans as Agram, with approximately 50 enemy aircraft visible. They strafed and claimed eight destroyed and two damaged, including an FW 190, Do 217s and Ju 87s. A few miles to the west they saw another airfield at Lučko and strafed it, claiming two Do 215s destroyed and one damaged. These claims were accurate as although Nachtschlachtgruppe 7 only reported three of their aircraft damaged, they reported eight (five Ju 87s, a Do217, a MC.202 and a FW 190) as burnt out.

British Claims

238 Sqn	Flg Off J.N.Hannan	Spitfire IX MK783 'L'	Bf 109	nr Bologna	1510-1905
238 Sqn	Flg Off H.H.Nice	Spitfire IX MK486 'M'	Bf 109	nr Bologna	1510-1905
238 Sqn	Flg Off G.C.N.Johnson	Spitfire IX MH979 'P'	Bf 109 Damaged	nr Bologna	1510-1905
238 Sqn	Flg Off T.H.Cockerill	Spitfire IX MK458 'Z'	Bf 109 Damaged	nr Bologna	1510-1905

British Casualties

3 RAAF Sqn	Kittyhawk IV FX830 left 1800, hit by Flak and crash-landed S of Todi; Wt Off E.C.Jennings back 28 June
72 Sqn	Spitfire IX MK353 'Z' left 0600, hit by heavy Flak over Bologna a/f, baled near Fiorenzuola 0705; Flt Lt G.H.Mayes POW
2 SAAF Sqn	Spitfire IX MK231 'I' engine cut while bombing railway sheds near Fano; Capt N.M.Phillips baled, POW
73 Sqn	Spitfire Vc ER914 left 1500, lost to Flak attacking a/f between Karlovac and Zagreb; Flt Lt F.C.Bremner KiA
14 Sqn	B-26B Marauder 41-18039 'Z' left 1052 from Alghero on patrol, crashed into the sea 0.5m W Asinara Island, off Sardinia; Lt M.J.W.Brummer and five KiA

US Casualties

66th FS/57th FG	P-47D 42-75770 hit telegraph pole near Lugo 1245; 2/Lt William C.Burt KiA [6323]

German Claims

Flak		Spitfire	Buiano	0708
Flak		Spitfire	Fano	0932
Flak		P-47	Bilane	1106
Flak		Spitfire	Bihac	1218
Flak		Spitfire	Rudes	1604
Flak		Spitfire	Prectev	1610
Flak		P-51	Salvaro	1952

Italian ANR Casualties

3ª Sq, 1° Gr C	MC.205 '3-2' shot down at Monte San Pietro; Serg Gianni Arrigoni KiA

Monday-Tuesday, 26/27 June 1944

British Casualties

55 Sqn	Baltimore V FW441 'S' left 2115 on recce Pistoia-Bologna road, shot down by Flak NW Florence 2225; Flg Off I.C.Campbell and three evaded
55 Sqn	Baltimore V FW344 'U' left 2124 on recce Pistoia-Bologna road, probably shot down by Flak, crashed at Marzabotto; Capt S.D.Zarkov and three MiA

German Claims

Flak		B-26	Marzabotto	2220

Tuesday, 27 June 1944

Twelve Spitfires from 238 Squadron caught eight 'Bf 109s' marshalled at the end of the runway at Reggio Emilia about to take off. The pilots attacked and Flt Lt E.C. 'Mouse' House, a veteran of 450 Squadron in the desert, claimed three destroyed on the ground; two others were claimed damaged by House and his No. 2, Wt Off E.W.Taylor, the latter being slightly damaged by Flak. Actually, the aircraft were G.55s of ANR 1° Gruppo Caccia, who lost two fighters and had another damaged. During the afternoon a Seafire of 879 Squadron attached to 4 SAAF Squadron was shot down by Flak and Sub Lt Gowan baled out but evaded and later returned. It was the first of the attached RN aircraft to be lost.

British Claims

238 Sqn	Flt Lt E.C.House	Spitfire IX MK239 'LS'	3 Bf 109s (on ground)	Reggio Emilia	0755-1020
238 Sqn	Flg Off H.H.Nice	Spitfire IX MH727 'MH'	Bf 109 Dmgd (on ground)	Reggio Emilia	0755-1020

British Casualties

1 SAAF Sqn	Spitfire IXc MH609 hit by Flak S Rimini strafing; Lt J.R.Spencer baled out, POW
1 SAAF Sqn	Spitfire IX left 1945, damaged by heavy Flak strafing 10m NW Perugia; Lt H.B.Harrison safe
1 SAAF Sqn	Spitfire IX left 1945, damaged by heavy Flak strafing 10m NW Perugia; Lt C.W.L.Boyd safe
879 Sqn (4 SAAF)	Seafire L2C MB243 left 1415, shot down by Flak near Sant Angelo 1510, pilot baled out; Sub Lt R.A.Gowan evaded, returned on 10 July
73 Sqn	Spitfire Vc ES342 left 1500, shot down by Flak; crashed on the Banja Luka a/d, Yugoslavia, after destroying a Ju 87 on the ground; 2nd Lt R.H.Van den Bergh safe, rescued by partisans
15 SAAF Sqn	Baltimore V FW518 'R' damaged by Flak over Heraklion, Crete; Capt F.E.Wood and crew safe

US Casualties

346th FS/350th FG	P-39Q 44-3126 'K' failed to recover from spin 5m S Capri; 2/Lt Flamer S.Lent KiA [14572]

German Claims

1.(F)/123	Obfw Beise (Schubert?)		Spitfire	1550
2.-4./Flak 237			Spitfire	Anghiari	2039

Italian ANR Casualties

1° Gr C	2 G.55s destroyed and one damaged on ground at Reggio Emilia; no casualties of pilots

Tuesday-Wednesday, 27/28 June 1944

British Claims

600 Sqn	Plt Off N.L.Jefferson/Plt Off Spencer	Beaufighter VIf MM945 'J'	Ju 88 Damaged	Bologna area	0255

Wednesday, 28 June 1944

24 SAAF Squadron at last returned from Egypt on the 28th, flying to Pescara to take its place in 3 SAAF Wing which was thereby brought back to full strength. Two days earlier 223 Squadron had moved to Pescara which meant that all the day bombers of DAF were now located at this base.

Lt Col R.A.Blackwell, officer commanding 24 SAAF Squadron (right), with the commander of 3 SAAF Wing, Col Jack Mossop, after the squadron had re-joined the wing.

Thursday, 29 June 1944

Twelve Spitfires of 451 Squadron, led by Sqn Ldr Kirkham, swept over Bologna during the morning, the pilots spotting aircraft taking off – four at first, then a further four followed by another three then a lone one. The Allied pilots gave chase but in doing so three became separated from the rest of the unit. This trio saw three Bf 109s 25 miles north-east of Bologna which they attacked, claiming two shot down and one probable, but one of the Spitfires was lost. Flt Sgt Vinter claimed a Bf 109 which exploded in the air and Flg Off Bray an FW 190 which he forced to crash land, while Flg Off Sidney also claimed an FW 190 from which black smoke poured and which he claimed as a probable. Flt Lt Alec Arnel's aircraft appeared to have been hit and he baled out. All the Axis aircraft on this occasion appear to have been Bf 109s.

At midday 92 Squadron then sent three Spitfires and three Seafires from the 807 Squadron attachment to escort 12 Baltimores of 21 SAAF Squadron to attack Cesena marshalling yards where a reported 25-30 Bf 109s and FW 190s attacked; these interceptors included ten Messerschmitts from 2° Gruppo Caccia of the ANR up over Forlì with other Messerschmitts of II./JG 77. The Italian unit lost one Bf 109 which blew up, while the only claim made by the escorts was for an FW 190 damaged; the victim may well have been the aircraft shot down by Vinter of 451 Squadron a little earlier in the morning.

During this second raid one of the Baltimores was damaged by two or three Messerschmitts and crash-landed at Tortoreto on return to base. Here the crew were found to be under the impression that their aircraft had been hit by light Flak, "some guns" were recorded by 92 Squadron's ORB. Probably they had been attacked by Cap Bellagambi of the 2° Gruppo who claimed a Boston in the same area at 1300. But, recorded 92, they were lucky to extricate themselves from persistent attacks. At the same time and location two other Italian pilots claimed a Spitfire and a Thunderbolt, meanwhile at 1237 Fw Leo Siwa of 5./JG 77 also claimed a Spitfire in the Rimini area, while over Ferrara and Poggio Renatico two of I./JG 77's aircraft and their pilots were shot down, in each case being involved in combats with Spitfires.

At early evening, A-20s of the US's 47th Bomb Group were escorted by Spitfires to the Arezzo area where much Flak was encountered and the second 'box' of bombers was hard hit and three of the A-20s went down. Five claims for American fighter-bombers were also made during the same evening period against actual losses of four P-47s, a single P-40 and another A-20.

At evening 232 Squadron on Corsica sent off a final sweep over Genoa and towards Nice, an area where the presence of Arado 196 floatplanes had been reported. No such enticing prey was to be found but two FW 190s were reported seen near Monaco. Flg Off Genillard claimed one of these shot down in flames with a second claimed to have been damaged. No such casualties have been found in Luftwaffe records although it is possible that the victims may have been tactical reconnaissance aircraft of a NAGr unit.

Elsewhere during the day Spitfires of 73 Squadron had been dispatched eastwards to attack targets in Yugoslavia where they dive-bombed Sarajevo airfield and claimed to have destroyed eight aircraft plus another seven damaged. However, one of the unit's aircraft was hit by Flak, the pilot's parachute then becoming tangled around the tail, following which the aircraft crashed and he was killed. On the way out they strafed and destroyed six locomotives.

British Claims

451 Sqn	Flg Off H.J.Bray	Spitfire IX MH547 'D'	FW 190	3m E Poggio Renatico	0900
451 Sqn	Flt Sgt J.F.Vinter	Spitfire IX MK444 'S'	Bf 109	3m E Finale Emilia	0900
451 Sqn	Flg Off E.J.Sidney	Spitfire IX MH7621 'M'	FW 190 Probable	20m NE Bologna	0900
807 att 92 Sqn	Sub Lt D.S.Robinson	Seafire L.IIc MA992			
807 att 92 Sqn	Sub Lt J.V.Morris	Seafire L.IIc MB313	FW 190 Damaged	Cesena	1155-1320
92 Sqn	Lt V.Boy	Spitfire VIII JF484			
232 Sqn	Flg Off A.Genillard	Spitfire IX MJ442 'H'	FW 190	Cap D'Antibes	2015
232 Sqn	Lt G.W.Dibb	Spitfire IX MJ895 'W'			
232 Sqn	Flt Lt F.Rothwell	Spitfire IX MJ952 'K'	FW 190 Damaged	Cap D'Antibes	2015

British Casualties

451 Sqn	Spitfire IX MJ733 engine failure in dogfight, pilot baled SE Bologna 0900; Flt Lt A.F.Arnell POW
21 SAAF Sqn	Baltimore IV left 1110 to bomb Cesena marshalling yards, damaged by 2 or 3 Bf 109s, crash-landed at Tortoreto l/g., Cat II damaged; Lt van Niekerk and two safe, one WiA

| 92 Sqn | Spitfire VIII JF303 left 1155, damaged in Cesena area by Bf 109s, landed at base; Flt Lt B.Garner safe |
| 73 Sqn | Spitfire Vc JL193 left 0845, hit by Flak attacking Sarajevo a/d, parachute tangled on the tail, crashed and blew up; Sgt C.D.Woodruff KiA |

US Casualties

64th FS/57th FG	P-47D 42-75863 hit by Flak, crashed 5m NW Bologna 1645; 2/Lt Samuel A.Martin POW [6324]
99th FS/332nd FG	P-40L 42-10799 lost over Italy u/k cause, last seen 1745 SW Cesena; 2/Lt Floyd A.Thompson POW [6447]
85th BS/47th BG	A-20J 43-22097 hit by Flak, crashed ca 40m W Ancona; 2/Lt John I.Craw and one POW, one KiA [6463]
85th BS/47th BG	A-20J 43-9638 '44' hit by Flak, last seen 1845 Sansepolcro area; 1/Lt Frederick H.Stephenson and one KiA, two evaded [6461]
85th BS/47th BG	A-20J 43-22094 hit by Flak, last seen 1845 Sansepolcro area; 2/Lt Vasil V.Vantz KiA, two evaded [6462]
524th FBS/27th FBG	P-47 42-26357 shot down by direct 88mm hit, Sansepolcro area 1915, pilot baled out, parachute fouled on tail; 1/Lt Wallace S.McDaniel KiA [6448]

Top: During an evening raid on Arezzo on 29 June the US 47th Bomb Group lost three A-20J Havocs; this one, 43-22070 '36', was not one of these. Above: Further to the north near Forlì on 29 June Cap Mario Bellagambi, the commander of the ANR 5ª Sq, 2° Gr Caccia, claimed a Boston, though none were in fact lost.

5./JG 77	Fw Leo Sliwa		Spitfire	Rimini	1237
Flak			2 P-40s	Formignano	1740 & 1754
Flak			Boston	Bibbiena	1850
Flak 182			Boston	Poppi	1853
1./2./4./Flak 182			Boston	La Casetta	1855
1./2./4./Flak 182			Boston	Poppi	1856
Flak			P-47		1900
Flak			Boston	Bibbiena	1901
Flak			P-47	Sansepolcro	1908
Flak			P-47	Anghiari	1909

German Casualties

1./JG 77	Bf 109 WNr 163201 White 9 lost in combat over Ferrara 1145-1315; Lt Richard Heller KiA
2./JG 77	Bf 109 WNr 162998 Red 11 lost in combat with Spitfires over Poggio Renatico 0845-0930; Fw Heinrich Wolters KiA
2./NAGr 13	FW 190A-4 WNr145656 left Cuers, shot down in combat over the sea, 5km S Nice; Obfw Wilhelm Stockburger KiA

Italian ANR Claims

5ª Sq, 2° Gr C	Cap Mario Bellagambi	Bf 109G-6	Boston	Cesena-Forlì	1300
5ª Sq, 2° Gr C	Serg Magg Attilio Sanson	Bf 109G-6	P-47	Cesena-Forlì	1300
4ª Sq, 2° Gr C	M.llo Renato Mingozzi	Bf 109G-6	Spitfire	Cesena-Forlì	1300

Italian ANR Casualties

6ª Sq, 2° Gr C	Bf 109G blew up; M.llo Romano Bolzoni KiA

Thursday-Friday, 29/30 June 1944

Six Ventura bombers and one flare dropper from 459 Squadron based at St Jean, Palestine, attacked shipping in Rhodes harbour. One aircraft was lost.

British Casualties

459 Sqn	Ventura V JT838 'A' prob hit by Flak and ditched off Castelrosso; Flg Off K.Pond and crew MiA

German Claims

Flak		Ventura	Rhodes

Friday, 30 June 1944

Twelve P-47s of 79th Fighter Group on a sortie were bounced by 12 Bf 109s of II./JG 77 over Bazzano; in the ensuing fight one Bf 109 was claimed destroyed and another damaged.

232 Squadron at 1600 flew a sweep during the afternoon over the Florence-Bologna area. Eight Bf 109s were seen near Bologna, one of which was reported to have a green and pink diamond painted on the fuselage – clearly an ANR aircraft. They claimed one destroyed, and one damaged, with the destroyed being seen to crash land in a dry riverbed, hit a horse and cart and then end up in the water. The pilot was not seen to emerge.

Six Spitfires of 2 SAAF Squadron were west of Arezzo at 8,000ft at about 1830 when they were attacked by seven Thunderbolts with yellow tails and yellow stripes on their wings and the leader opened fire. Four of the Spitfires took evasive action and waggled their wings and the Thunderbolts departed.

Four Spitfires of 73 Squadron flew to Sarajevo airfield where 15 Axis aircraft were seen, including Do 217s. Pilots claimed eight probables and six locomotives.

On Malta, 185 Squadron had two Spitfires scrambled at 0920 and another at 0950. This latter was flown by the squadron commander, who was eventually vectored onto a Ju 188 flying at sea level.

Flt Sgt Scarlett and his 294 Squadron crew with their Walrus in which they rescued Flg Off Pleonis of 335 Squadron, who had ditched during a convoy escort on 30 June.

Ground crew work on Spitfire Vc JK723 'GN-V' at Grottaglie following an emergency landing after Flak had shot away the rudder cables over Yugoslavia on 30 June. It was flying again by mid July.

British Claims

185 Sqn	Sqn Ldr T.W.Willmott	Spitfire IX MA464	Ju 188 Damaged	80-100m E Malta	1020
232 Sqn	Wt Off R.P.Tutill	Spitfire IX MJ641	Bf 109 Damaged	WSW Bologna	1600
232 Sqn	Wt Off T.W.Green	Spitfire IX MK743 'P'	Bf 109	Budrio WSW Bologna	1705
249 Sqn	Lt R.Briggs	Spitfire Vc JK725	Ju 52/3m	E Skopje	1545-1845

British Casualties

21 SAAF Sqn	Baltimore V FW457 left 0940 to bomb Faenza M/Y, two bombs collided on release and exploded, a/c blew up 1125, crashed in flames; Lt E.G.Elliot-Wilson and three KiA
335 Sqn	Spitfire VB ER524 left 1730 from Savoia to cover convoy 'Cropper', engine trouble, pilot baled out off Libyan coast 1816; Flg Off G.Pleonis rescued by 294 Sqn Walrus W3107 flown by Flt Sgt L.Scarlett ca1845

US Claims

87th FS/79th FG	Lt Benjamin Cassidy	P-47D	Bf 109	nr Bazzano	0915
87th FS/79th FG	Lt David Shuttleworth	P-47D	Bf 109 Probable	nr Bazzano	0915

German Claims

II./JG 77	Uffz Schummer		P-47	0920
Flak			Spitfire	Senigallia	1310
Flak			Spitfire	Bihac	1832

German Casualties

II./JG 77	2 Bf 109s damaged in combat
II./TG 4	Ju 52/3m WNr 10047 shot down by Spitfires 10km E Skopje; Uffz Walter Jordt and three KiA

Italian ANR Claims

6ª Sq, 2° Gr C	M.llo Artidoro Galetti	Bf 109G	Spitfire	Bologna	1715

Italian ANR Casualties

6ª Sq, 2° Gr C	Bf 109G hit by Spitfire, force-landed near Budrio; Serg Virginio Stella WiA
6ª Sq, 2° Gr C	Bf 109G hit by Spitfire, crash-landed; Ten Giovanni Mancini safe

Friday-Saturday, 30 June/1 July 1944

By the end of June the whole of the 79th Fighter Group was firmly ensconced in Corsica. It had been a busy month for the unit, though somewhat less so than in May. Some 307 motor transports (M/T) had been claimed in flames, 253 destroyed and others damaged, together with hits on 51 bridges. Losses were down somewhat, with nine P-47s and three pilots lost but a staggering 51 more had been damaged. Claims against opposing aircraft totalled two shot down, one probably destroyed and three damaged.

The 57th Fighter Group had been equally busy flying about ten missions a day through most of the month, including some sorties during the invasion of Elba, as already noted. After the initial heavy losses suffered in early June, only three more P-47s had been lost during the latter part of the month.

British Claims

255 Sqn	Flg Off R.E.Reynolds/Flg Off M.A.Wingham	Beaufighter	Ju 88		0025
46 Sqn	Sqn Ldr H.StG Bond/Plt Off J.Lamb	Beaufighter VI MM972	Do 24 on water	Portolago	0100
46 Sqn	Sqn Ldr H.StG Bond/Plt Off J.Lamb	Beaufighter VI MM972	Ar 196 on water	Portolago	0100
46 Sqn	Sqn Ldr H.StG Bond/Plt Off J.Lamb	Beaufighter VI MM972	Do 24 Dmgd on water	Portolago	0100
46 Sqn	Sqn Ldr H.StG Bond/Plt Off J.Lamb	Beaufighter VI MM972	Ar 196 Dmgd on water	Portolago	0100

German Casualties

Wekusta 26	Ju 88T-1 WNr 430910 5M+D lost over Ancona-Tremiti area; Uffz Helmut Krause and three MiA
7.Seenotst.	Do 24T-3 WNr 2103 J9+AA strafed and sunk in Portolago Bay, Leros; Fw Ludwig Gosepath and two WiA, three safe

July Overview

244 Wing was on the move yet again, this time to Perugia, while 324 Wing moved to Piombino and 255 Squadron with the 111th Tac Recce Squadron to Follonica. Both fighter wings were greatly involved in escort missions now, both to bombers and fighter-bombers, whereas 244 Wing's units continued practising bomb dropping. 601 Squadron, which had only recently stopped fighter-bombing activities itself on conversion to Spitfire VIIIs, was ready first, attacking rail and bridge targets with 500lb bombs from 5 July. On this date 112 Squadron flew its first Mustang sorties, though a number of bomb hang-ups were experienced initially.

Losses to Flak continued at a somewhat reduced level during July. To the east 7 SAAF Wing had lost three Spitfires during June, but only one more would fail to return during the first half of the new month. The unit was still split up, with 4 SAAF Squadron at Cisterna during most of June, moving to Orvieto early in July, while 2 SAAF Squadron went to Foiano. These two units each had a few of the Royal Navy Seafires and their pilots attached to them at this time. Maj Brown of the 57th Fighter Group had to bale out on the 6th, and two days later this unit, 601 Squadron and 417 Squadron each lost aircraft to Flak. The 57th would lose four more Thunderbolts during the next week, though all the pilots returned safely.

It was at night that the Luftwaffe was now appearing, however. Following the withdrawal of the fighters and the Jabos soon to go, a night ground-attack unit, Nachtschlachtgruppe 9, had been dispatched to Italy in order that the Wehrmacht would not be left totally without air support of any kind. The Gruppe was equipped with the Junkers Ju 87D, a development of the famous but out-dated Stuka dive-bomber. Fitted for night operations, it now had an increased armament which included wing-mounted cannons. These aircraft were first engaged by the patrolling Beaufighters of 600 Squadron early in July, when attempting to attack columns of advancing Polish troops on the east coast, near Ancona. 600 and 255 Squadrons between them would account for ten of these new opponents by the middle of the month.

While 241 Squadron had been so vigilant in its defensive patrolling in the east, much support had been provided for the forces on the ground around Ancona by the tactical reconnaissance Spitfire Vs of 318 Squadron. During the advance and the fighting for the town the Polish pilots undertook 425 reconnaissances, 82 artillery spotting and 176 ground-strafing sorties, mainly directed against motorised columns. Many of these latter flights were carried out after the German defenders suddenly broke and retreated in broad daylight, presenting many easy targets. Throughout this period not one aircraft was lost, and only a single pilot was wounded by ground fire. No sooner was the town secure, however, than A Flight was ordered to join 208 Squadron at Castiglione to undertake some special reconnaissance missions for the 5th Army.

Elsewhere the XII TAC fighter-bombers were making their presence felt in no uncertain manner in their task of interdiction in the Po Valley. Particularly involved were the five groups of P-47s, the 47th Bomb Group and the RAF Spitfires of 251, 322 and 324 Wings. The mediums also continued their attacks in the area, often escorted by the above-mentioned fighter units. The bombing was particularly effective now, and by 23 July every main bridge over the river between Ostiglia and Cremona had been destroyed. Three days later every bridge east of Torre Beretti was reported destroyed or damaged to the point of being impassable.

The fighter-bombers also attacked bridges, but without notable success on most occasions, though this was not always the case. On one sortie P-47s from the 79th Fighter Group were ordered to attack a bridge after two squadrons of mediums had failed to damage it. 24 Thunderbolts dropped a total of 48 500lbs of bombs, claiming nearly 20 direct hits and more than 20 near misses; the bridge was subsequently reported to be unserviceable.

Other fighters took a heavy toll of rolling stock, and also concentrated on cutting the tracks. During the last three weeks of July a total of 221 such cuts were achieved. The communications targets were not the only areas targeted, however, and at this time 57th Bombardment Wing B-25s made frequent attacks on coastal and airfield targets in the South of France as well as flying odd missions as far afield as Austria and Yugoslavia.

Saturday, 1 July 1944

The month opened with a significant success for US pilots of the 57th Fighter Group. Eleven pilots of the 66th Squadron of that unit, while returning from attacking bridges in the Ferrara area, sighted south of Reggio a formation of ten fighters identified as Bf 109s; four more were seen flying somewhat higher. All the Messerschmitts appeared to have a red, green and white vertical design on the fuselages, and appeared to have clipped wingtips, although at this stage of the war they were certainly not Bf 109Es. These were obviously ANR aircraft of 1° Gruppo Caccia. The Americans attacked the top four, claiming four shot down in flames, two of them by 2/Lt Howard Cleveland, while 2/Lt Johnson claimed also two damaged. The other ten Bf 109s then fought with the rest of the P-47s, as the main group of Italian fighters became engaged. The US pilots claimed two more shot down and a third damaged; three of their own aircraft were damaged.

The first hostiles to be attacked were in fact six MC.205s of the 1° Gruppo's 2ª Squadriglia which were providing top cover, two of them being shot down. Five G.55s of the 3ª Squadriglia were then engaged and three of these aircraft were shot down. Two of the Italian pilots were lost and two wounded while one baled out safely. In return one P-47 was claimed shot down although none were actually lost. One of the successful Thunderbolt pilots, 2/Lt Richard Johnson, had long been extremely interested in aircraft and on this occasion had recognised the G.55. "I knew they were not 109s. I said G.55s. No one except for myself and one other had ever even heard of them." One of the successful pilots, Lt Stephen Bettinger, would later claim five MiG 15 jets shot down over Korea during 1952.

During the late morning of 1 July six MC.205s of the ANR 2ª Squadriglia, 1° Gruppo Caccia were involved in a combat with P-47Ds of the 57th Fighter Group suffering severe losses.

A little later in the morning the ANR's 2° Gruppo Caccia scrambled 12 Bf 109s to patrol as far south as Bologna, this formation intercepting 11 more P-47s of 79th Fighter Group's 85 Squadron which were also involved in bridge bombing. Four Italian pilots dived to the attack, claiming one Thunderbolt shot down. Again, no US aircraft was lost but two of the American pilots claimed damage to two of the attackers, Cap Mancini being killed.

During the day the USAAF 1 Emergency Rescue Squadron (1 ERS) B Flight acquired a Stinson L-5 Sentinel, which it used for searches of crash sites on land.

On 1 July a new unit was established by the Italian Co-Belligerent Air Force, the Stormo Baltimore, so composed:

Stormo Baltimore	Martin M.187	T.Col Giuseppe Noziglia
		T.Col Renato Roveda (from 11 August)
28° Gruppo		Magg Carlo Emanuele Buscaglia
19ª Squadriglia		Ten Vittorio Sanseverino
260ª Squadriglia		Cap Umberto Scapellato
132° Gruppo		Magg Massimiliano Erasi
253ª Squadriglia		Cap Enrico Marescalchi
281ª Squadriglia		Cap Michele Avalle
		Cap Giulio Cesare Graziani (from 16 August)

British Casualties

4 SAAF Sqn	Spitfire IX left 1910 for dive-bombing mission, wing struck a drum on the side of the runway, damaged Cat III; Lt P.J.Welman safe
14 Sqn	B-26B Marauder 41-18017 'G' *Devil's Playmate* left 0515 on low level coastal recce of Venice-Ancona area, nothing heard after take-off; Flg Off N.Cornish and five MiA
352 Sqn	Spitfire Vc JG920 caught fire in mid-air and crashed attempting to force land; Flt Sgt Z.Halambek KiA
73 Sqn	Spitfire Vb JK660 left 1350, hit by Flak near Zagnel, crash-landed at base; Flg Off W.Ritchie safe

US Claims

66th FS/57th FG	2/Lt Howard W.Cleveland	P-47D '86'	2 Bf 109s	8m S Reggio l/g	1115
66th FS/57th FG	2/Lt Stephen L.Bettinger	P-47D '88'	Bf 109	8m S Reggio l/g	1115
66th FS/57th FG	2/Lt Richard L.Johnson	P-47D '89'	Bf 109	8m S Reggio l/g	1115
66th FS/57th FG	2/Lt Richard L.Johnson	P-47D '89'	2 Bf 109s Damaged	8m S Reggio l.g	1115
66th FS/57th FG	2/Lt Thomas D.Davis Jr	P-47D '02'	Bf 109	8m S Reggio l/g	1115
66th FS/57th FG	2/Lt Claude G.Rahn	P-47D '93'	Bf 109	8m S Reggio l/g	1115
85th FS/79th FG	Lt Eugene L Kleiderer Jr	P-47D	Bf 109 Damaged		1150
85th FS/79th FG	2/Lt Cecil T.Bush	P-47D ⎫	Bf 109 Damaged		1150
85th FS/79th FG	1/Lt Richard W.Long	P-47D ⎭			

US Casualties

65th FS/57th FG	P-47D hit by Flak, ditched in sea near Borgo; Lt Teron E.Wright picked up safely, returned
66th FS/57th FG	P-47D '02' damaged by Bf 109 S Reggio Cat I; 2/Lt Thomas D.Davis Jr safe
66th FS/57th FG	P-47D '91' damaged by Bf 109 S Reggio Cat II; Lt William R.Hill safe
66th FS/57th FG	P-47D '88' damaged by Bf 109 S Reggio Cat II; 2/Lt Stephen L.Bettinger safe

French Casualties

GB 1/19	Marauder '62' damaged by Flak over La Spezia; Cne Chaboureau and three safe, two WiA

German Casualties

1./(F) 123	Ju 88T-1 WNr 430950 4U+MH on photo mission crashed nr Lugo 2330 for u/k reason; Obfw Robert Strehl and three KiA
16./TG 1	Ju 52/3m WNr 501126 IZ+EK lost 25km E Hydra 0110; Obgfr Gottfried Pritsche and three MiA

Italian ANR Claims

1° Gr C	Serg Magg Mario Veronesi	MC.205	P-47	SW Reggio Emilia	1116
6ª Sq, 2° Gr C	M.llo Artidoro Galetti	Bf 109G	P-47	SE Bologna	1155

Italian ANR Casualties

2ª Sq, 1° Gr C	MC.205 shot down by P-47 over Mancasale 1115; Serg Magg Luigi Boscaro KiA
2ª Sq, 1° Gr C	MC.205 shot up by P-47 1115, force-landed; S.Ten Elio Pezzi WiA
3ª Sq, 1° Gr C	G.55 shot down by P-47 1115; Cap Giulio Torresi KiA
3ª Sq, 1° Gr C	G.55 shot down by P-47 1115; M.llo Romano Spazzoli baled out WiA
3ª Sq, 1° Gr C	MC.205 shot down by P-47 1117; Ten Alessandro Beretta baled out safely
6ª Sq, 2° Gr C	Bf 109G-6 < I hit in combat with P-47, crashed near Minerbio 1155; Cap Massimino Mancini KiA

Sunday, 2 July 1944

At the start of the month 39 Squadron's Beaufighters were based at Alghero in Sardinia but a detachment of the unit's aircraft was at Grottaglie in Italy from where the squadron's crews were patrolling over the Adriatic and into the Balkans. By mid-month the whole unit would have staged through Grottaglie to a new base at Biferno where it joined the Balkan Air Force.

Meanwhile the crews based in Italy commenced a new type of patrol, the first of which was undertaken on this date. Now two of the unit's Beaufighters would proceed on shipping reconnaissance over the northern Adriatic accompanied by a single 14 Squadron Marauder. The latter was then to cruise approximately five miles off the shore where if shipping were to be spotted the crew were to advise the Beaufighter crews via VHF radio, allowing the latter to attack with rockets and cannon fire. Now on the first such operation a pair of Beaufighters flown by Flg Off R.H.Pitman/Flt Sgt N.W.Mitchell (in NE528 'W') and Wt Off L.W.Mickelborough/Flt Sgt E.M.Potts (in NE549 'G') claimed to have sunk a 60-ton schooner.

British Claims

241 Sqn	Plt Off D.F.White	Spitfire VIII JF557 'RZ-L'	Bf 109 Damaged	Ancona	2040

British Casualties

24 SAAF Sqn	Marauder II FB517 'F' left 0942 to bomb Pesaro, hit by Flak over Pesaro harbour, force-landed at Fermo; Lt A.W.R.Woods and crew safe
13 (H) Sqn	Baltimore V FW294 'R' left 1600 to bomb Lugo marshalling yards, crashed on landing at Pescara 1830; Flg Off J.Katsaros and two safe, one WiA

German Casualties

2./NSGr 9	Ju 87D-3 WNr 1244 crashed at Forlì on return from mission; Obgfr Walter Buttner/Uffz Eugen Pendel KiA
Wekusta 27	Ju 88D-1 WNr 430840 lost in the western Peloponnese area to AA; Oblt Hermann Wacker and three MiA
	LKS reports one Ju 88 missing

OPERATIONS OVER THE ADRIATIC

Operations in this theatre and along the coastline of Yugoslavia and Greece had opened in a fairly small way late in 1943. In September the Germans had occupied the islands of Corfu, Cephalonia and Zante in order to strengthen their hold on Yugoslavia. These moves were well in hand during the following month when in response Allied units from Coastal and Tactical Air Forces could be spared to operate on occasions over this area and in support of Marshal Tito's partisan forces in Yugoslavia.

Late in October several of the Malta Spitfire squadrons, which now came under Coastal Air Force control, moved to Grottaglie (as already mentioned) and here they formed 286 Wing as part of 242 Group. In November 249 Squadron from this wing moved up to Brindisi, flying a number of missions over the Valona and Durazzo areas of Albania, some of these being fighter-bomber sorties. A few hostile aircraft were encountered in these localities, the squadron claiming several successes during December 1943 and January 1944 before returning to Grottaglie. From Montecorvino on the west coast meanwhile 73 Squadron from 323 Wing had occasionally staged through to operate along the same Albanian coast. Early in December this wing moved across to Foggia to provide local defence.

In January 1944 334 Wing was formed at Brindisi for special operations, dropping arms and supplies to the Yugoslav partisans; this unit incorporating 148 and 624 Squadrons (the latter still conducting some of its activities over southern France from Bône), with 1586 (Polish) Flight, the 62nd Troop Carrier Group, USAAF, plus 36 Cant.Z.1007s and Savoia S.82s of the Stormo Notturno of the Italian Co-Belligerent Air Force. At the same time the island of Vis off the coast of Yugoslavia, which had fallen undefended into Allied hands, was strongly reinforced by commandos and US troops, who were ordered to hold it at all costs; airfield facilities were developed for its use initially as an advanced landing ground and refuelling base.

Operations during January began to get more fully established, Spitfires from 126, 185, 249 and 1435 Squadrons undertaking more strafing and fighter-bomber sorties along the coast and over southern Yugoslavia where several losses were suffered to Flak. 1435 Squadron had a particularly successful month, engaging in three combats during which four Bf 109s were claimed shot down (see Vol. 4). In February 73 Squadron was joined at Foggia by 32 Squadron which was relieved from defensive duties in the western Mediterranean area and at once began to escort the former unit's fighter-bombers over the Dalmatian Islands.

At Grottaglie 6 Squadron, now equipped with rocket-firing Hurricanes, arrived to begin operations with an early March strike on a headquarters in Durazzo. Thereafter the unit was to concentrate on shipping targets in the Adriatic. In this role it was to be joined by the torpedo-dropping Wellingtons of 221 Squadron which soon began anti-shipping and bombing sorties attacking vessels, Siebel ferries and Yugoslav ports. In April a detachment of Spitfires from 87 Squadron moved from Catania on attachment to 286 Wing, operating with the squadrons there for a few weeks. Strafing of traffic in coastal waters was the favoured target at this time and a substantial amount of it was undertaken, occasional engagements with German aircraft also occurring. Here again 1435 Squadron achieved most success, claiming a Bf 109 early in April and another three on 11 May, an aircraft identified as a Dornier 217 also being claimed on the 7th. A pair of Fi 156s and another Bf 109 fell to other units during this period.

More units continued to arrive during May, 253 Squadron re-joining 323 Wing at Foggia after a spell in Corsica, and 25 SAAF Squadron arrived at Pomigliano to work up its Venturas as light bombers for Adriatic operations. At dawn on 25 May came a crisis however, as German forces attacked Tito's headquarters at Drvar with paratroops and glider-borne units, supported by bombers and fighter aircraft. All available Allied air support was given by both Strategic and Tactical Forces and by Coastal. On the very first day four Spitfires of 73 Squadron, while strafing vehicles in the Bihac area spotted an airfield on which were at least 20 aircraft. As the British pilots approached an Hs 126 was seen in the air and was shot down, more of these aircraft, together with Ju 87s, Fi 156s and Italian Macchi fighters, then being strafed. On reporting this find six more Spitfires were sent out, refuelling at Vis en route in order to repeat the attack.

Next day the squadron returned, Sqn Ldr J.H.Chase, the commanding officer, leaving a Ju 87 in flames, but being shot down by Flak. 253 Squadron also visited the area, claiming two Hs 126s while aircraft of 249 Squadron on patrol claimed to have shot down two more of these aircraft and destroyed another pair on the ground.

Sunday-Monday, 2/3 July 1944
252 Squadron sent eight Beaufighters out on night armed reconnaissance of the Aegean. Sqn Ldr I.B.Butler/ Plt Off N.Johns (in NE254 'E') sighted a convoy in the channel at the north-eastern end of Rhodes. After being

joined by Flt Lt C.A.Wyatt/Flt Sgt R.A.Barrett (in NE499 'P') he attacked but missed. As he was drawing the Flak, Wyatt made four dummy runs before releasing eight rockets, scoring multiple hits on a merchant ship, setting it on fire. Three other Beaufighters joined the attack, but with no apparent results. One reported evading an attack by a twin-engine aircraft at 2245 at the western tip of Rhodes. The German freighter *Agathe* sank next morning.

British Claims					
255 Sqn	Sqn Ldr H.P.E.Patten/Sgt E.Blundell	Beaufighter VIf	Ju 88	66m NW Penna Point	2235-0110
British Casualties					
55 Sqn	Baltimore V FW299 'Y' left 2200 on armed recce of Arezzo-Fano-Rimini-Sansepolcro area; Lt C.A.Harris and two KiA, one POW				
256 Sqn	Mosquito XIII HK399 left 2205 from Alghero on intruder to Lyon area, shot down by Flak at Faramans NE Lyons; Wt Off T.D.De Renzy POW/Wt Off R.F.Cottrell KiA				
German Claims					
Flak			Mosquito	20km NE Lyon	0030
German Casualties					
Wekusta 26	Ju 88A-4 WNr 550435 5M+G on night recce to Ancona, lost nr Adria; Lt Werner Scheibel and three MiA				

Monday, 3 July 1944

The units on Corsica continued to meet active opposition over northern Italy at this time, 237 Squadron engaging 20 Bf 109s when escorting B-25s over the Po Valley. On this occasion these were probably Luftwaffe-flown aircraft of I./JG 77 one of which was shot down by Flg Off Moubray, from which Lt Kolb baled out. From Algeria Spitfires of C Flight of the Mosquito-equipped 256 Squadron (previously the Gibraltar Defence Flight) shot down a Ju 88, the crew of which unsuccessfully tried to set fire to the aircraft before being taken prisoner.

British Claims					
237 Sqn	Flg Off D.M.Moubray	Spitfire IX MH981	Bf 109	Po Valley	1030-1255
256 Sqn	Sgt T.M.Ninan	Spitfire VIII JG166	Ju 88	Arzew Bay	1330-1415
256 Sqn	Wt Off K.A.Hadley	Spitfire VIII JF584			
British Casualties					
1 SAAF Sqn	Spitfire IXc MA510 left 2000, shot down by Flak S Forlì; Capt D.R.Judd seen to bale out but KiA				
1 SAAF Sqn	Spitfire IXc LZ861 'A' left 1120, hit by Flak on return from sweep 11km SW Sarsina, pilot baled out San Donato area, broke ankle on landing; Lt L.H.Brown evaded, returned on 2 August				
417 Sqn	Spitfire VIII JG272 left 0535, attacked a road 2-3m SE Sansepolcro, shot down by heavy Flak; Plt Off R.W.McLaren KiA				
7 SAAF Sqn	Spitfire LIXc MH971 shot down by Flak nr Bagno, pilot baled out; Lt W.H.Matthews returned two days later				
US Casualties					
488th BS/340th BG	B-25J 43-27702 '8L' shot down by Flak nr Ferrara 1135; 2/Lt James E.Cooper and three KiA, three POW [6457]				
486th BS/340th BG	B-25J 43-27728 '6E' damaged by Flak nr Ferrara 1135, crash-landed at base; 1/Lt R.W.Pike and five safe				
1st ERS	L-5 collided with Walrus in Corsica; 2/Lt Carl R.Mingle and one KiA				
German Claims					
Flak			Spitfire	Sorbano	
Flak			Mitchell*	Francolino nr Ferrara	1130
Flak			Mitchell	Francolino nr Ferrara	1130
	* The Germans noted the markings on the wreck as being 8L				
German Casualties					
2./JG 77	Bf 109G-6 WNr 162294 Red 4 shot down by Spitfires nr Lagnasco; Lt Hans Kolb baled, WiA				
4./SG 4	FW 190F-8 WNr 930850 struck ground at Savigliano; Hptm Hans-Horst Graf KiA				
1.(F)/33	Ju 88T-1 WNr 1407 8H+GH reported lost 25m N Oran due to engine failure; Obfw Helmut Knapp and two POW				
	LKS reports two Ju 88s missing and one Bf 109 lost in air combat				

Monday-Tuesday, 3/4 July 1944

This night saw the first claims to be made by RAF night-fighters against the Nachtschlachtsgruppe.

British Claims

600 Sqn	Wt Off H.Ewing/Flt Sgt J.T.Chenery	Beaufighter VIf V8898 'V'	Ju 87 Damaged	SE Lake Trasimeno	2204
600 Sqn	Wt Off H.Ewing/Flt Sgt J.T.Chenery	Beaufighter VIf V8898 'V'	Ju 87	NE Lake Trasimeno	2241

British Casualties

38 Sqn	Wellington XIII HZ633 'J' left 2100 to mine Partheni Bay Leros, shot down by Flak; Flg Off K.J.A.Moderwell and five KiA

German Claims

Flak		Wellington	Leros	0030

German Casualties

2./NSGr 9	Ju 87D-5 WNr 141010 reportedly collided near Florence; Uffz Ewald Kapahnke/Gefr Wilhelm Happe KiA
2./NSGr 9	Ju 87D-5 WNr 140994 reportedly collided near Florence; Uffz Adolf Jägers KiA

Tuesday, 4 July 1944

On this day Flg Off Daly of 417 Squadron was lost over Fano, and a Marauder of 3 SAAF Wing was shot down over Faenza marshalling yards.

Twelve Marauders of 21 SAAF Squadron raided Faenza marshalling yards and Forlì; seven unidentified single-engined fighters attacked at 0855 with no results.

British Claims

603 Sqn	Wt Off L.F.Sykes/Sgt W.H.Foxley	Beaufighter TFX NE304 'W'	Ju 52/3m See	off Syros	1755-2245
603 Sqn	Flt Sgt E.F.Pennie/Flt Sgt G.W.Hinde	Beaufighter TFX NE246 'K'			

British Casualties

417 Sqn	Spitfire VIII JF836 left 0835, hit by Flak 5m S Fano; Flg Off J.R.Daly KiA
3 RAAF Sqn	Kittyhawk IV FX704 left 1205 on armed recce, dive-bombed motor transports near Arezzo, hit by Flak in dive; Flt Sgt A.T.Field KiA
3 RAAF Sqn	Kittyhawk IV FX808 left 1205 hit by 88mm Flak near San Giovanni reached Allied lines, crash-landed; Flt Sgt J.M.Turkington returned next day
24 SAAF Sqn	Marauder III HD433 'T' left 1010 to bomb Faenza marshalling yards, hit by Flak before target, believed to have ditched; Capt G.S.Brink and two KiA, three POW
24 SAAF Sqn	Marauder III left 1010 to bomb Faenza marshalling yards, hit by Flak, landed at base with Cat III damage; crew safe
249 Sqn	Spitfire Vc LZ873 left 1250 to strafe roads north of Pholrina, FTR; Sgt R.Penny POW

German Claims

Flak	Marauder	Tombe	1150
Flak	Marauder	near Tombe	1200

Left: A Ju 52/3mW of 5./TG 4 under attack off Syros by a 603 Squadron Beaufighter flown by Flt Sgt Pennie. Right: A Ju 52/3mW blazes after being strafed in harbour by Beaufighters of 603 Squadron on 4 July.

Tuesday-Wednesday, 4/5 July 1944

British Casualties	
252 Sqn	Beaufighter X NE591 'N' left 2021 on shipping sweep, attacked MV off Leros, damaged by Flak, crash-landed at base 0137; Flg Off D.M.Reid/Sgt R.C.Ray safe
US Casualties	
97th BS/47th BG	A-20B 41-3489 left 2203, crashed and burnt out nr Pontedera 2245; 2/Lt William H.Graves and four KiA [6458]
German Casualties	
1./NSGr 9	Ju 87D-5 WNr 140999 E8+OH shot down by AA nr Loreto; Oblt Rolf Begemann POW/Uffz Hermann Lehr MiA
1./NSGr 9	Ju 87D-5 E8+CH damaged by AA nr Loreto; Fw Pieper and gunner safe

Wednesday, 5 July 1944

Six 450 Squadron Kittyhawks were off at 1200 to dive bomb in the Forlì-Cesena area. As the leader Flt Lt Goldman pulled out of his dive at 1,500ft he spotted aircraft approaching at 1,400ft. Goldman got his formation together and headed south at 10,000ft. The aircraft were identified as 20 Bf 109s approaching from the east and 12 FW 190s from above and behind. One Bf 109 made a diving dead-astern attack on White Section. The Kittyhawks broke into the attack and Goldman fired at the 109 from 150 yards, scoring hits on the starboard wing before it dived away into clouds. Three 109s then attacked Yellow Section from out of the sun, hitting Yellow 2 in the tail, and then the German aircraft departed. The 109s were from II./JG 77 and Hptm Franz Hrdlicka and Uffz Joachim Schemel both claimed to have shot down a 'P-47' when on a patrol from Bologna to Rimini, although the site of the fight was given as north-east of Arezzo, which is well to the south-west.

The 14 Squadron Marauder and 39 Squadron Beaufighter joint shipping patrols struck again with a 1,500-ton motor vessel being left severely damaged by Flt Lt I.D.Charles/Flg Off J.P.J.Browne (in NE410 'K') and Flt Sgt D.C.McMurchy/Flt Sgt L.S.Morgan (in NE598 'S').

232 Squadron was on the way to escort the 340th Bomb Group on a raid but found that the bombers had arrived early at the rendezvous and had gone on alone. They had been intercepted and were heard on the radio calling for help. The Spitfires arrived to find their charges under attack reportedly by FW 190s and Bf 109s, the latter bearing ANR markings. The British pilots dived to the rescue, two pilots claiming one fighter shot down while a third claimed damage to another. This was later upgraded to destroyed and the ANR indeed lost two Bf 109s in combat with Spitfires.

40 SAAF Squadron's commanding officer, Lt Col W.A.'Tiny' Nel, was awarded the DSO at this time, becoming the SAAF's most highly decorated pilot to date. On 5 July this unit moved to Castiglione del Lago airfield but five days later the second in command, Maj D.W.Maree, DFC, was killed in a flying accident in a Harvard.

British Claims					
450 Sqn	Flt Lt W.E.Goldman	Kittyhawk IV FX815 'B'	Bf 109 Damaged	Cesenatico	1200-1335
232 Sqn	Wt Off T.Armstrong	Spitfire IX MK137	FW 190	Modena area	1815-1820
232 Sqn	Flt Sgt M.J.Rimes	Spitfire IX MJ442			
232 Sqn	Wt Off E.A.McCann	Spitfire IX MJ737	Bf 109 Damaged	Modena area	1815-1820
British Casualties					
450 Sqn	Kittyhawk IV FX844 'R' left 1200, attacked by Bf 109 SE Forlì landed at base damaged Cat II; 2/Lt T.C.Nel safe				
603 Sqn	Beaufighter TFX NE379 'M' left 1320 on sweep of central Aegean, ditched 10m SE Melos 1530; Flt Sgt C.H.Dean/Flt Sgt D.W.Taylor KiA				
US Claims					
487th BS/340th BG	gunners	B-25J	Bf 109 Probable	Ostiglia	1810
US Casualties					
487th BS/340th BG	B-25 attacked Ostiglia rail bridge 1810, damaged by fighters, landed at base; crew safe				
64th FS/57th FG	P-47D hit by Flak on dive-bombing mission, engine failed on return, pilot baled out over the sea; Maj Robert C.Brown rescued by a Walrus				
French Casualties					
GC 2/3	P-47D left 1400, hit by Flak, force-landed nr Marina di Pisa; Lt Lombardo POW				
GC 2/3	P-47D left 1830, hit by Flak, pilot baled nr Palaia; Sgt Laurent Lacassie hidden by Italian peasants, returned on 22 July				

5./JG 77	Hptm Franz Hrdlicka	P-47	N Arezzo	1308
5./JG 77	Uffz Joachim Schemel	P-47	N Arezzo	1309
Flak		Thunderbolt	N Leghorn	1500

German Casualties

5./JG 77	Bf 109G-6 WNr 162560 combat 5km S Pieve Santo Stefano; Uffz Joachim Schemel baled out, WiA
6./TG 4	Ju 52/3m WNr 10108 G6+NP lost Heraklion-Kalamaki; FhjFw Josef Rössler and one returned, one KiA, one MiA
	LKS reports three Bf 109s lost in combat and one Ju 52/3m missing

Italian ANR Casualties

5ª Sq, 2° Gr C	Bf 109G lost in combat with Spitfires; Ten Elvio Palermi KiA
6ª Sq, 2° Gr C	Bf 109G lost in combat with Spitfires; Serg Magg Pietro Secchi KiA

Wednesday-Thursday, 5/6 July 1944

British Casualties

13 Sqn	Baltimore V FW544 'G' on armed recce against shipping form Cervia to Marina di Ravenna, overturned on landing and wrecked; Flt Sgt E.A.Day and two safe, one WiA

German Casualties

1./NSGr 9	Ju 87 D-5 WNr 140999 E8+OH shot down by Allied AA near Loreto; Oblt Rolf Begemann POW/Uffz Hermann Lehr KiA
1./NSGr 9	Ju 87 D-5 E8+CH damaged by Allied AA near Loreto; Fw Pieper and gunner safe

Thursday, 6 July 1944

Six Hurricanes of 6 Squadron escorted by Spitfires of 32 Squadron fired 27 rocket projectiles and sank the 5,000-ton MV *Italia* moored alongside a quay in the Arsa Channel.

British Casualties

253 Sqn	Spitfire Vc JK427 hit by Flak strafing, crash-landed 2m E of Otak, Yugoslavia; Flt Lt N.L.Delaney POW
4 SAAF Sqn	Seafire L2C NM919 crashed on landing as Very pistol fell jamming the rudder 1345, damaged Cat II; Sub Lt C.B.Taylor safe

US Casualties

325th FS/86th FG	A-36A 42-84057 failed to pull out from strafing a truck NW Pisa 1325; 2/Lt Russell E.Jefferson KiA [6469]
325th FS/86th FG	A-36A 42-84149 strafing NW Pisa 1325, damaged by own bomb blasts, crashed on landing; 2/Lt Carl F.Hernandez safe
524th FS/27th FBG	P-47D 42-26378 last seen S Bologna 1215; Flt Off Stephen E.Fletcher KiA [6459]
87th FS/79th FG	P-47D hit by Flak, ditched at sea; Lt Thomas M.Baker rescued by ASR
66th FS/57th FG	P-47D '76' left 0540, hit by Flak bombing Piacenza-Fidenza railway, ditched near base 0650; 2/Lt Howard W.Cleveland rescued by Walrus X9503 of 284 Sqn flown by Lt K.B.Walker

French Casualties

GC 2/3	P-47D damaged by Flak nr Mantua, pilot baled E Campiglia Marittima 1810; Lt Seguin safe

Thursday-Friday, 6/7 July 1944

The outstanding achievement of the RAF night fighters during the series of interceptions in July was undoubtedly that of Flg Off Bruce Bretherton and his radar operator, Flg Off T.E. Johnson during the night of the 6th/7th. Readers of earlier volumes may well recall that this pilot had previously flown as a night intruder with 73 Squadron, operating in a Hurricane over the North African coast during June 1943. He had joined 255 Squadron early in 1944 to begin his second tour and was now flying in Beaufighter VIf ND254 which carried the individual identification letters YD-E. They took off initially to patrol over Ancona at 2145. After around 90 minutes they detected an intruder north-east of Ancona, shooting it down in flames at

During a remarkable sortie on the night of 6/7 July, Flg Offs B.A.Bretherton (right) and T.E.Johnson in a 255 Squadron Beaufighter destroyed three Ju 87s near Ancona.

2315. Half an hour later they were vectored onto another Ju 87 by 'Adieu' control and attacked, reporting that it crashed into a hillside near the town. At 0010 Johnson picked up a third 'bogey' on the Beaufighter's own A.I. set and Bretherton closed on this at 10,000ft. At first, he thought his opponent was a twin-engined type, but closer inspection showed it apparently to be another Ju 87 which was carrying bombs. The rear gunner appeared to have spotted the night fighter, for the Junkers suddenly dived away, jettisoning its bombs as it did so. For a moment Bretherton lost it, but he was able to regain contact swiftly, and he fired four bursts, closing from a range of 500 to 300 feet. Smoking heavily, the dive-bomber went vertically into the ground where it burst into flames.

British Claims

255 Sqn	Flg Off B.A.Bretherton/Flg Off T.E.Johnson Beaufighter VIf ND254 'E'	Ju 87		NW Ancona	2315
255 Sqn	Flg Off B.A.Bretherton/Flg Off T.E.Johnson Beaufighter VIf ND254 'E'	Ju 87		Ancona	2345
255 Sqn	Flg Off B.A.Bretherton/Flg Off T.E.Johnson Beaufighter VIf ND254 'E'	Ju 87		SW Ancona	0015
255 Sqn	Sqn Ldr J.F.McLaren/Flg Off A.W.Tozer	Beaufighter VIf	Ju 87 Damaged	Ancona area	2307-0255
255 Sqn	Flt Sgt T.C.Griffiths/Flt Sgt E.R.Kimberley	Beaufighter VIf	Ju 87	Ancona area	0135-0450

British Casualties

221 Sqn	Wellington XIII MP759 left Grottaglie on armed recce of northern Adriatic 2100, believed to have lost power on take-off run, jettisoned bomb load to lighten aircraft, the bomb fusing switches were found to have been switched to the live position for unknown reasons, 13 of them exploded, destroying the aircraft; Flg Off K.F.Pattison and five KiA

US Claims

417th NFS	2/Lt Thomas A.Hill/2/Lt H. H.Heinecke	Beaufighter VIf	Ju 88 Damaged	23m W Calvi	0320

German Casualties

2./NSGr 9	Ju 87D-3 WNr 100355 shot down by night-fighter nr Loreto; Uffz Erich Ackermann/Uffz Hermann Kasper WiA
2./NSGr 9	Ju 87D-3 WNr 100382 E8+NK shot down by night-fighter nr Loreto; Lt Fritz Itzstein/Gefr Wilhelm Rumholz WiA
2./NSGr 9	Ju 87D damaged by night-fighter nr Loreto; Obfw Wilhelm Böwing safe/Fw Johannes Nawroth WiA
	LKS reports two night ground-attack a/c lost and one damaged

Friday, 7 July 1944

The 57th Fighter Group had a rare find when the 65th Squadron was operating in the Fidenza area. Here an old Caproni Ca 133 trimotor bomber-transport was met in the air and was attacked by Lt Hare. The aircraft blew up in mid-air when subjected to the impact of the P-47's eight .50-in machine guns. The pilots of 86th Fighter Group shot down a lone Bf 109 in the circuit of Ferrara aerodrome, and destroyed another on the ground as well as a high-wing silver monoplane as it taxied into a hangar.

British Casualties

6 Sqn	Hurricane IV KX804 'M' left 1850 and attacked two Siebel ferries in the Plannitsa Channel, shot down by Flak, exploded on the sea; Sgt R.McCafferty KiA
2 SAAF Sqn	Spitfire IX MJ195 'H' left 1300 on armed recce of Faenza area, strafed a staff car, damaged by intense Flak, returned to base, crashed on landing 1440, Cat III damaged; Capt C.N.Shone WiA

US Claims

65th FS/57th FG	1/Lt James C.Hare	P-47D	Ca 133 (German)	River Po	1630
526th FS/86th FG	1/Lt Saunders	A-36	monoplane on ground	Ferrara a/f	
526th FS/86th FG	1/Lt Bishop	A-36	Bf 109	Ferrara a/f	
526th FS/86th FG	1/Lt Sellars	A-36	Bf 109 on ground	Ferrara a/f	

US Casualties

445th BS/321st BG	B-25 43-27714 left 1045 to attack Sasso RR bridge, damaged by Flak, landed safely at base; 1/Lt Albert F.Hardman Jr and four safe, one KiA

German Casualties

2./NAGr 11	Bf 109 damaged in action by enemy fighter; pilot safe
	LKS reports one Bf 109 damaged in air combat, eight a/c destroyed on ground and four damaged

Italian ANR Casualties

2° Gr C	Bf 109G shot down in combat with 'Bostons' nr Forli; Serg Renato Saletti KiA

Friday-Saturday, 7/8 July 1944

British Claims

255 Sqn	Flg Off R.E.Reynolds/ Plt Off M.A.Wingham	Beaufighter VIf KW154 'R'	2 Ju 87s	Ancona/SEAncona	2310-0215
600 Sqn	Sqn Ldr J.RA.Bailey/Flt Sgt N.Wint	Beaufighter VIf ND165 'N'	Ju 88	15m SE Elba	0020
600 Sqn	Flg Off F.H.Jeffrey/Flg Off J.R.Brewer	Beaufighter VIf ND320 'R'	Ju 87	Lake Trasimeno	0208

German Casualties

1./NSGr 9	Ju 87D-5 WNr 141029 E8+HH lost nr Osimo; Uffz Erwin Mokrus/Gefr Hans Wagner MiA
2./NSGr 9	Ju 87D-3 WNr 1266 lost nr Mondolfo; Obgfr Fritz von Bork/Obgfr Ulrich Tröster KiA
2./NSGr 9	Ju 87D-5 WNr 141722 damaged nr Castelfidardo; pilot safe/Uffz Artur Ballok WiA
6.(F)/122	Ju 88 WNr 301500 SM+R lost 15m NW Elba; Obfw Emil Braitsch and three MiA
	LKS reports three attack a/c lost in combat

Saturday, 8 July 1944

The idea of how dangerous the new dive-bombing activity was was brutally brought home with 601 Squadron losing an aircraft strafing Rimini, while one from 417 Squadron was also lost strafing. When undertaking a bombing sortie, Lt F.M.du Toit of 145 Squadron was unable to release his bomb despite violent endeavours to shake it free. As he landed it finally fell off and exploded directly beneath his Spitfire, which overturned and burst into flames, killing the pilot.

British Claims

94 Sqn	Flt Lt H.McLachlan	Spitfire IX MH698 'Y'	Bf 109G	NE Gavdos	1030-1255
94 Sqn	Flt Lt R.J.Howley	Spitfire IX MA508 'B'	Bf 109G	5m SE Gavdos	1030-1300

British Casualties

601 Sqn	Spitfire IXc MH622 left 1955, shot down by Flak while strafing Rimini airfield; Lt J.E.Sharpe baled over sea, KiA
145 Sqn	Spitfire VIII JF568 bomb hang-up, fell off on landing and exploded destroying the aircraft 1040; Lt François Meyer du Toit KiA
417 Sqn	Spitfire VIII JG337 'X' left 0520 crashed while strafing a truck; Flg Off G.S.Kimber KiA
223 Sqn	Baltimore ..575 'S' left 0825 to bomb various dumps, hit by Flak, belly-landed at base, damaged Cat II; Lt T.Ryan and two safe, one slt WiA

US Casualties

64th FS/57th FG	P-47 strafing train at 2000, damaged by debris, on return flight pilot baled out; rescued

German Claims

5./JG 51	Uffz Hans Langer		Spitfire	off Crete	1105
5./JG 51	Obfw Emil Reinhardt		Spitfire	off Crete	1108

Sunday, 9 July 1944

239 Wing began moving forward to Crete airfield which was 120 miles north of the former base and very close indeed to the front. From here the fighter-bombers were to undertake a very busy week of Cab Rank operations, from 10th-16th, in support of XIII Corps advancing on Arezzo. At this time 92 and 145 Squadrons also began bomb dropping operationally. The latter unit's pilots had recently gained two more decorations, Flg Off Ekbery being awarded a DFC at the end of June and Flt Lt W.A.R.MacDonald a similar award in early July.

13 (Hellenic) Squadron began to transfer to Biferno from Pescara due to its leaving 3 SAAF Wing DAF and joining 254 Wing Balkan Air Force, commencing operations in this new role on 14 July.

US Casualties

65th FS/57th FG	P-47D left 0830 to bomb railway between Ferrara and Padua, last seen in cloud 0900; Lt Harold W.Lancaster KiA
316th FS/324th FG	P-40 '82' possibly hit by Flak, last seen 0835; Lt Bert E.Holder returned

German Casualties

	LKS reports one Bf 109 lost in combat

Sunday-Monday, 9/10 July 1944

British Casualties

38 Sqn	Wellington XIII HZ706 'K' left 2214 on armed recce of Aegean, caught fire after take-off, crash-landed 2219; Plt Off H.V.Tomlinson and five safe

Monday, 10 July 1944

Meanwhile in Corsica 251 Wing moved to St Catherine from where it now began undertaking sorties over southern France as well as over Italian targets. It was in the latter area that combats continued to occur, however. On the 10th 12 Spitfires of 154 Squadron from 322 Wing escorted 36 B-26s of the 320th Bomb Group to attack the Marzabotto rail bridge. After bombing the target the formation was intercepted by about 15 Bf 109s of 2° Gruppo C. Flt Lt Boyle fired at two, reporting strikes on both but failed to observe any results; he was credited with both damaged, with one other pilot also claiming a third damaged. Although claims were made by ANR pilots for two Spitfires shot down, all the British fighters returned safely. The Allied formation did lose one of the bombers but one of the Messerschmitts was also lost, it would appear possibly to the fire of one of the Spitfires.

On 10 July when assessing the prospects for Operation Dragoon, Air Marshal Sir John Slessor, C-in-C RAF Mediterranean and Middle East said "... the Luftwaffe can be virtually ignored".

During an attack on a rail bridge near Marzabotto, Flak destroyed the port wing of B-26C Marauder 42-107566 '06' of the US 441st Bomb Squadron which crashed with the loss of its crew.

British Claims

32 Sqn	Flt Lt P.Quine	Spitfire VIII JF898 ⎫	Ghibli (German mkgs)	5m S Grado	1630
32 Sqn	Flt Lt R.D.Riddell	Spitfire IX MA693 ⎭			
154 Sqn	Flt Lt A.R.Boyle	Spitfire IX MK119 'C	2 Bf 109s Damaged	SW Bologna	1750
154 Sqn	Flg Off F.Cooper	Spitfire IX MK467 'F'	Bf 109 Damaged	15m La Spezia	1755

British Casualties

73 Sqn	Spitfire VC JK519 'W' left 1525 on sweep of Gospic area, damaged by Flak, force-landed 12m SE Gospic; Sgt K.Wilson safe
601 Sqn	Spitfire IX MH786 left 1015 bombing road 1m SE Leghorn, engine failed, pilot baled out near Castel Fiorentino into Allied lines; Lt D.W.Lee safe

US Casualties

441st BS/320th BG	B-26C 42-107566 '06' left 1448 to attack railroad bridge N Marzabotto, shot down by Flak S Marzabotto 1730; 1/Lt Murray B.Wiginton Jr and five KiA [6454]

Italian ANR Claims

4ª Sq, 2° Gr C	Ten Raffaele Valenzano	Bf 109	Spitfire	S Modena	1715
4ª Sq, 2° Gr C	Serg Magg Carlo Cavagliano	Bf 109	Spitfire	S Modena	1715

Monday-Tuesday, 10/11 July 1944

British Claims

255 Sqn	Sqn Ldr J.F.McLaren/Flg Off A.W.Tozer	Beaufighter VIf	Ju 87	5m E Osimo	0035-0315
600 Sqn	Sqn Ldr J.R.A.Bailey/Flt Sgt N.Wint	Beaufighter VIf ND165 'N'	Ju 87	15m NW Lake Trasimeno	0130

1./NSGr 9   Ju 87D-5 WNr 141025 E8+GH shot down by night fighter N Ancona 0230; Ofhr Klaus Wolff-Rothermel/Gefr Hans Lankes POW

                  LKS reports one attack a/c missing

Tuesday, 11 July 1944

At 0930 a dozen Spitfires from 238 Squadron escorted 16 French B-26s from GB 1/19 'Gascogne' and GB 2/20 'Bretagne' in an attack on a fuel depot near Piacenza; over a dozen German and Italian Bf 109s were scrambled from Ghedi and Villafranca. One of the Spitfire pilots was a Rhodesian, Flg Off Rodney Simmonds who was flying his own aircraft as part of Blue Section which carried his personal Zulu warrior emblem on the nose and who recalled:

"Shortly after 0011 we spotted enemy fighters flying in pairs but made up of two distinct formations flying at about 20,000 feet. They positioned behind the bombers and my section was ordered to get rid of our fuel tanks and go for the first group of bandits. Thus began what was actually my one and only aerial contact with the Huns in the whole of my two tours of ops. With my colleague Philip van Rensburg (SAAF) we managed to catch up with a couple of 109s before they regained cloud cover and got in a quick squirt. Philip claimed he hit his chap in the wing root and claimed a 'probable'. I fired a couple of short bursts but I wasn't so sure about mine so only claimed a 'damaged'. However, it was later established that both 109s that Philip and I fired on were in fact shot down; one of the chaps spotted mine spinning down in flames, the pilot having taken to his parachute. I was later able to contact the pilot that I had encountered, a Feldwebel Albert Ulrich in Baden Baden and we corresponded for years."

The South African's victim was Uffz Richard Kurz of 4.JG 77 who was wounded. However, in spite of their efforts, two Italian pilots shot down the Marauder flown by Lt Cornet, from which only four baled out, and damaged another.

Top: Escorting French bombers on 11 July Rhodesian pilot Flg Off Rodney Simmonds of 238 Squadron hit a Bf 109 near the target, claiming it damaged. Above left: Flg Off Simmonds in fact shot down the Bf 109G of 6./JG 77 flown by Fw Albert Ulrich who baled out. Above right: When he claimed Fw Ulrich's Messerschmitt, Rodney Simmonds was flying his usual Spitfire IX 'KC-T'.

238 Sqn	Lt P.M.van Rensberg	Spitfire IX MH567 'K'		Bf 109 Probable	Piacenza	1110
238 Sqn	Lt P.M.van Rensberg	Spitfire IX MH567 'K'		Bf 109 Damaged	Piacenza	1110
238 Sqn	Flg Off R.G.S.Simmonds	Spitfire IX MH529 'T'		Bf 109 Damaged	Piacenza	1110
238 Sqn	Flg Off J.Stockden	Spitfire IX MK113 'E'		Bf 109 Damaged	Piacenza	1110
41 SAAF Sqn	Capt R.P.Burl	Spitfire IX LZ894 'V'	}	Ju 88 Damaged	over Turkey	1908
41 SAAF Sqn	Lt P.B.Brokensha	Spitfire IX MA257 'X'	}			

US Casualties

86th FS/79th FG	P-47D 42-28075 crashed during night flight; 2/Lt Sam Rospo Jr KiA

French Claims

GB 2/20	gunner	B-26	Bf 109	Piacenza	1110
GB 2/20	gunners	B-26	2 Bf 109s Probable	Piacenza	1110

French Casualties

GC 2/7 (326 Sqn)	Spitfire V left 0550 on recce, engine failed, pilot baled into sea NE Gorgona Island c 0630; Sgt-Chef Courteville WiA, picked up by HSL 2601 after 27 hours in his dinghy
GB 2/20	Marauder '37' left 0830, shot down by Italian Bf 109 nr Piacenza; pilot Lt Cornet, copilot Adj Despinoy and two KiA, three baled out
GB 2/20	Marauder 42-107776 '34' damaged by Italian Bf 109; pilot Sous Lt Viala, copilot Sgt Chef Pierre Hentges and four safe

German Casualties

4./JG 77	Bf 109G WNr 163189 Black < shot down in combat with Spitfires, Isola Dovarese; Uffz Richard Kurz WiA
6./JG 77	Bf 109G shot down in combat; Fw Albert Ulrich baled out safely

Italian ANR Claims

5ª Sq, 2° Gr C	Cap Mario Bellagambi	Bf 109	B-26	Piacenza	1110
5ª Sq, 2° Gr C	Serg Leo Talin	Bf 109	B-26	Piacenza	1110

Tuesday-Wednesday, 11/12 July 1944

The commander of 256 Squadron Wg Cdr P.M.Dobree-Bell was scrambled at 0155 to patrol a line 40m NE Oran as 'bandits' were approaching convoy 'Queenie'. He was vectored to the coast of Spain and back before being put onto a contact at extreme low level. While turning in behind the contact at 50 feet Dobree-Bell flew into the slipstream of a Ju 88, which caused him to strike the sea with the starboard propeller of the Mosquito. This knocked off the spinner and set the engine on fire. Understandably he lost the contact but managed to regain base and made a successful single-engine landing.

British Casualties

256 Sqn	Mosquito XIII HK398 scrambled 0155 to patrol convoy 'Queenie', flew in slipstream of Ju 88 at 50ft, struck the sea, returned to base with starboard engine on fire, landed safely 0600; Wg Cdr P.M.Dobree-Bell/Flt Lt J.H.Smithes safe
162 Sqn	Wellington X LP238 left 1930 on special mission over Eastern Aegean, engine caught fire, ditched near the coast; Flg Off H.Painter and six POW by Bulgarian forces, then released when Bulgaria changed sides, returned to Egypt by mid September

German Casualties

9./KG 26	Ju 88A-17 WNr 550285 1H+ET lost Cap Tenes-Cap Ivi area; Uffz Werner Achilles and three MiA
	LKS reports three Ju 88s lost

Wednesday, 12 July 1944

In the early hours of this day the 489th Squadron of 340th Bomb Group was directed to fly a bombing mission against the railroad bridge in Ferrara. It was known to be a 'hot' target, well defended by German guns. A B-25J called *Flack Fodder II* was specially equipped as a camera ship and was to follow behind the other bombers to photograph the target after the formation's bombs were dropped. The bomber formations encountered a flight of about 16 German fighters. A group of six or eight fighters broke away to attack the lone camera ship that was trailing far behind the tight bomber formations. The gunners aboard *Flak Fodder II* acquitted themselves well: one German fighter was confirmed shot down and a second was judged as a probable. Later this day this same B-25J was assigned another mission to hit the railroad bridge at Chiavari. Over the sea the bomber developed engine trouble and had to ditch; T/Sgt Harold Winjum and S/Sgt Wallace MacRitchie apparently misunderstood the pilot's instructions and parachuted from the aircraft. The crew who stayed with the aircraft when it ditched were rescued. Neither Winjum nor MacRitchie were ever found.

British Casualties

40 SAAF Sqn	Spitfire Vb EP205 left 1620 on Arty recce W Arezzo, last seen in cloud at 5,000ft 1750; Lt P.Naylor KiA

US Claims

489th BS/340th BG gunner	T/Sgt Harold E.Winjum	B-25J 43-4071	FW 190	Ferrara	1005
489th BS/340th BG gunner	Sgt Harry Yohe	B-25J 43-4071	FW 190 Probable	Ferrara	1005
489th BS/340th BG gunner	Sgt Bob Hertel	B-25J 43-4071			

US Casualties

316th FS/324th FG	P-40 '16' hit by Flak, last seen 2000; Lt Oscar W.Sparks returned
489th BS/340th BG	B-25J 43-4071 '9B' *Flak Fodder II* left to attack Chiavari rail bridge, engine failure, ditched 1940; 1/Lt John L.Mitchell Jr and four rescued by a 1 ERS OA-10 Catalina 0800 next day, two KiA [6611]

German Casualties

6./JG 77	Bf 109G-6 WNr 441320 hit in combat, belly-landed near Ferrara; Fw Albert Ulrich WiA

Italian ANR Claims

6ª Sq, 2° Gr C	Ten Giovanni Mancini	Bf 109G	A-20	Comacchio	
6ª Sq, 2° Gr C	M.llo Giuseppe Desideri	Bf 109G	P-47		

Italian ANR Casualties

4ª Sq, 2° Gr C	Bf 109G crashed into Adriatic; Ten Alfredo Fissore KiA

Wednesday-Thursday, 12/13 July 1944

During the summer of 1944 the Ju 88A-17s of KG 77 fitted with FuG 200 radar conducted torpedo-bombing operations over the Mediterranean from La Jasse/Salon en Provence.

British Casualties

18 Sqn	A-20J 43-9646 '32' left 0040 to strafe Rimini-Bologna road, hit by Flak near Florence, crashed near Poggio Cerette just inside the French Corp's front line 0200; Flt Lt D.S.Barnes DFM and one KiA, two WiA. Note: this was a 47th BG aircraft on loan, fitted with 4 x .50 machine guns firing 12° downwards. The squadron ORB described it as an A-20G with an A-20J nose

German Casualties

7./KG 77	Ju 88A-4 WNr 801367 3Z+GR damaged by AA, ditched off Cap Ivi near Oran 0430; Uffz Wilhelm Trepper and three POW
9./KG 77	Ju 88A-4 3Z+AT engine fire on return from attack off Oran, force-landed in Spain; Uffz Kurt Langendorf and three interned

Lt Kurt Becker (left), Fw Francke (centre) and Obgfr Supsch (right) of II./KG 77 prepare for another sortie from Salon en Provence in mid 1944.

Thursday, 13 July 1944

During the attacks in support of 8th Army the bombers were meeting increasingly heavy Flak defences, as the Germans strove to make up for their lack of air cover in other ways. A good example of this occurred on this day when the two Marauder squadrons of 3 SAAF Wing, escorted by Spitfires of 7 SAAF Wing, set out to bomb a rail junction at Montevarchi, south of Florence. Flak was encountered from the moment the German lines were crossed and continued ceaselessly all the way to the target. Suddenly the Marauder flown by Lt Col Miles Barnby, commanding officer of 12 SAAF Squadron, was seen to blow up violently. The next moment the remains of this aircraft, together with the two which had been flanking it in the formation, were seen to fall and crash in flames, only two parachutes being observed. Three more of this unit's aircraft were badly damaged during this raid and had to crash land away from base, only half of the aircraft dispatched arriving back at their own airfield. At this time 12 SAAF Squadron had a number of Belgian personnel (from the Congo colony) serving with the unit, and one of these, Cdt Franz Burniaux, was promoted to command in Barnby's stead. This was not the only ill-fated mission for the squadron at this time, the unit suffering a series of adverse fortunes. Indeed, the very next day an attack on a stores dump west of Florence was again met by heavy Flak.

223 Squadron took off to raid a petrol dump but on crossing the front lines near Volterra at 1020 encountered the most severe Flak attack they had ever experienced. One aircraft was hit in both engines, turned back and the wounded pilot Lt G.L.Woodhead was forced to belly land at Perugia airfield with bombs still on board. Two of the crew, Sgts H.Drake and T.G.Ling baled out prior to this and suffered no further injuries, nor did the navigator Lt A.J.Cassidy who remained on board. Ten of the twelve Baltimores were hit, with one landing using the elevator trim tabs as the elevator controls had been shot away.

British Casualties

4 SAAF Sqn	Spitfire IX MJ368 left 1425 hit by Flak in the starboard wing, engine seized, force-landed in Allied lines near a 239 Wing a/f 1505, damaged Cat III; Capt R.D.B.Morton safe
4 SAAF Sqn	Spitfire IX MK348 'Q' left 1800, probably hit in the glycol tank by Flak, pilot forced to bale out over Lake Trasimeno 1850; Lt F.A.O'Connor POW
2 SAAF Sqn	Spitfire L.IXc MJ904 tail severely damaged by Flak, pilot baled nr Lake Trasimeno; Lt K.B.Borcherds safe
40 SAAF Sqn	Spitfire Vb left 1030 on Arty recce in Radda area, hit by Flak, lost coolant, crash-landed in Allied lines; Capt P.H.Donnelly safe

12 SAAF Sqn	Marauder II FB437 'Y' left 0745, premature bomb explosion when bombs dropped and two bombs collided just below the aircraft N Montevarchi 0915; Lt J.C.Webb and five KiA
12 SAAF Sqn	Marauder II FB487 'B' left 0745, destroyed in explosion of above B-26, crashed W of Montevarchi 0915; Lt Col M.Barnby and four KiA, one POW
12 SAAF Sqn	Marauder II FB461 'N' left 0745, damaged in explosion of above B-26, crash-landed on Perugia a/f colliding with a Spitfire; Lt G.M.Leslie and three WiA, copilot Lt J.F.Pienaar KiA, one DoW
12 SAAF Sqn	Marauder II FB518 'L' damaged in explosion of above B-26, rear gunner baled out over the target; Capt B.L.Redding and four safe, one POW
12 SAAF Sqn	Marauder 'P' damaged by Flak; pilot and four safe, observer Lt K.T.F.Ryan WiA
223 Sqn	Baltimore V FW634 'B' left 0915 on bombing raid, hit by Flak near Volterra 1020, belly-landed on Perugia l/g; Lt G.L.Woodhead WiA, three safe
3 RAAF Sqn	Kittyhawk IV FX713 left 1735 to bomb guns near Arezzo, hit by Flak, pilot baled out into Allied lines; Flt Lt I.H.Roediger returned next day

US Claims

86th FS/79th FG	Capt George W.Ewing Jr	P-47D	FW 190	nr Occhiobello	0905-1145

US Casualties

27th FS/1st FG	P-38J 43-28790 shot down by Flak, crashed 4km SE Mortegliano; Flt Off Thomas E.Wood KiA [6806]
27th FS/1st FG	P-38J 43-28783 shot down by Flak, crashed 2km NW Mortegliano 1045; 2/Lt George F.Eldred KiA [6805]
27th FS/1st FG	P-38J 44-23200 shot down by Flak, crashed 10km SW Mortegliano; 2/Lt Leo E.Lemons KiA [6804]
95th FS/82nd FG	P-38J 43-28813 shot down by Flak, last seen 6m N Porto Marghera 1040; 2/Lt Lester J.Henry POW [6909]
86th FS/79th FG	P-47D 42-76015 'X53' shot down by Bf 109s 5m N Viareggio; 2/Lt Robert M.Ryan Jr evaded, returned later [6616]
86th FS/79th FG	P-47D 42-25290 crashed 10m NE Corte, Corsica; 1/Lt Robert L.Patin KiA [7066]
314th FS/324th FG	P-40F '12' hit by Flak crashed in friendly territory; Capt James F.Kirkendall baled and returned
32nd PRS/5th PRG	F-5B 42-68212 lost over Italy; 2/Lt Richard L.Luce KiA [6460]

German Claims

Flak		Marauder	Montevarchi	0943

Marauder III FB487 'B' of 12 SAAF Squadron flown by Lt Col Barnby's crew falls away in flames after the bomb load of a neighbouring aircraft prematurely detonated on being released.

Friday, 14 July 1944

When attacking an ammunition dump near Florence on 14 July the Marauders of 12 SAAF Squadron endured an intense Flak barrage that damaged three aircraft including FB425 'Z' seen here on the right.

The flurry of activity in the north was due to a sustained series of attacks on the Po bridges which were launched during the second week in July by the medium bombers of the 42nd and 57th Bomb Wings under the codename 'Mallory Major'. The plan for this attack had been ready for some time but its implementation had been delayed by the hope that the armies might achieve a swift advance to the Po, and by bad weather. Twenty-one bridges were to be attacked, five of them rail crossings only, two joint road and rail, and the rest road only. Half of these were of a permanent nature, the others being pontoon bridges, and they were spread between Piacenza and the east coast. Bridges over the Trebbia river were also to be attacked between Piacenza and Genoa, as were other bridges over various streams, rivers and gullies.

While the mediums were responsible for the initial cutting of the bridges, fighter-bombers were subsequently involved to disrupt the attempts to reopen them. The first attacks were made on 12 July, the operation lasting just four days. By the end of this period 12 bridges had been seriously damaged or totally demolished, with eight more disrupted less permanently. Only one bridge of very strong construction remained open and even on this the railway track had been torn up by bombs: 'Mallory Major' had achieved its objective.

At the same time as this operation was underway, DAF was much involved in support of the 8th Army in the Trasimeno area as the troops advanced on Arezzo. During the seven days from 10th-16th July 900 sorties were made by 239 Wing Kittyhawks and Mustangs against artillery positions and road concentrations, Baltimores, Marauders and Spitfire fighter-bombers adding their weight to the assault while other Spitfires attacked roads and supply dumps to the rear.

1 SAAF Squadron had now followed the example of the 244 Wing units and had joined the other three squadrons of 7 SAAF Wing in bomb-dropping operations. No opposing aircraft were to be seen at this time.

During an attack on an ammunition dump north-west of Florence 12 SAAF Squadron Marauder crews spent half an hour flying through very intense, heavy and accurate Flak, which broke up the formation and caused damage to three aircraft. Possibly with the previous day's tragedy still so deeply etched on their minds, some of the 12 SAAF Squadron's Marauder crews became confused and three gunners baled out into Axis territory in the mistaken belief that their aircraft had been mortally hit. A fourth man was injured when a Marauder, which had been damaged during the attack, crash-landed at Pescara on return.

Baltimores of 21 SAAF Squadron took off at 0847 to bomb Tavola marshalling yards. Lt Batley's aircraft suffered engine trouble and returned alone. At 1105 his Baltimore was attacked and badly hit by two fighters over Accumoli but managed to return to base. The crew reported that the attacking aircraft had yellow wing-tips and were thought to be Mustangs.

A detachment of French fighter pilots from GC 1/5 'Champagne' was loaned to 256 Squadron's C Flight, the Spitfire Flight at La Senia, to help out with readiness periods. The pilots involved were Cne Marin La Meslee, Adj Jérémie Bressieux, Sgt Chef Simon, Lt Gustave Giraud and Sgt Chef Gigot.

British Claims

232 Sqn	Wt Off E.A.McCann	Spitfire IX MK296	Ital.Bf 109 Damaged	Parma area	1040

British Casualties

112 Sqn	Mustang III FB287 'J' left 0815 on dive-bombing mission, one bomb hung up, pilot tried for 2 hours to shake it off but could not, instructed to bale out over land with aircraft pointing out to sea, did so, landed safely on land, while aircraft blew up on impact with the sea; Flg Off R.H.Newton safe
145 Sqn	Spitfire VIII JF472 left 1155 to bomb roads nr Perugia, glycol leak after bombing, crash-landed 1230; Sub Lt A.Foley (att 809 Sqn) WiA, helped by Italian civilians, returned on 18 July
4 SAAF Sqn	Spitfire IX MJ675 hit by 40 or 37mm Flak in starboard wing and engine, pilot baled W Arezzo 1905, Lt H.G.Chapman POW
39 Sqn	Beaufighter X LZ480 'O' left 1522 on sweep of railway lines west of Belgrade, shot down by Flak, crashed N Vincovci 1730; Flg Off L.A.Chandler/Flg Off J.H.Lamb KiA
21 SAAF Sqn	Baltimore IV 565 'W' left formation with engine trouble, on return flight attacked by two Mustangs and shot up, force-landed at Tortorella; Lt Batley and crew safe
24 SAAF Sqn	Marauder left 0920 on bomb raid, damaged by Flak and force-landed at Castiglione damaged Cat II; five safe, one WiA
12 SAAF Sqn	Marauder left 0950 on bomb raid, damaged by Flak and force-landed at Castiglione damaged Cat II; six safe
12 SAAF Sqn	Marauder II FB 475 'R' left 0950 on bomb raid, damaged by Flak, force-landed at Lucera, damaged Cat II; Lt R.van der Westhuizen and four safe, one WiA
12 SAAF Sqn	Marauder II FB425 'Z' left 0950 on bomb raid, damaged by Flak, landed safely; Lt Parsons and two safe, three crew baled out over the target
73 Sqn	Spitfire Vb ER550 left 1335, shot down by ground fire 15m N of Imotski, pilot baled out but hung up on the tail; Plt Off F.C.Hampton MiA

US Claims

317th FS/325th FG	Maj Herschel H.Green	P-51	Bf 109G	20m SW Ferrara	1055
HQ 325th FG	Maj Charles E.Caple	P-51	Bf 109G Damaged	Porto Marghera area	1055
340th BG	gunners	B-25J	Bf 109 Probable	Cento-Portomaggiore	1056
340th BG	gunners	B-25J	FW 190 Probable	Cento-Portomaggiore	1056

US Casualties

314th FS/324th FG	P-40L 42-10436 crashed Lake Bolsena; 2/Lt Roland J.Fischer KiA
65th FS/57th FG	P-47D shot down by Flak 0930; pilot rescued

French Casualties

GC 2/5	P-47D hit by Flak nr Pietrasanta, returned to Corsica but crashed on fire nr Alto; Sgt Leboucher DoW 23 July

German Claims

Stab/JG 77	Obstlt Johannes Steinhoff		B-25 Damaged	
Stab/JG 77	Uffz Gerhard Hanff		B-25 Damaged	
Flak			Spitfire	S Arezzo	1930

German Casualties

4./JG 77	Bf 109G badly damaged in combat nr Modena; FhjFw Erich Fährmann baled safely
Stab/JG 77	Bf 109G 30% damaged in combat; Obstlt Johannes Steinhoff safe
1./JG 77	Bf 109G-6 WNr 163175 White 8 shot up in combat nr Carpi; Oblt Kurt Hammel (St.Kpt) WiA
	LKS reports one Bf 109 missing, one lost and one damaged in combat

Italian ANR Claims

4ª Sq, 2° Gr C	Ten Ugo Drago	Bf 109G	Boston	E Parma
5ª Sq, 2° Gr C	Serg Leo Talin	Bf 109G	Boston	E Parma
4ª Sq, 2° Gr C	Serg Magg Carlo Cavagliano	Bf 109G	Spitfire	E Parma

5ª Sq, 2° Gr C   Bf 109G shot down 20m SW Ferrara; Serg Magg Luigi Santuccio KiA

Friday-Saturday, 14/15 July 1944

During the early evening of 14 July Wt Off Towey's crew of 459 Squadron flew Ventura V JS937 'B' to bomb Rhodes harbour on the unit's final operation with this type.

British Casualties

459 Sqn   Ventura V JT836 left Nicosia at 2000 to bomb Calato a/f on Rhodes, FTR; Flg Off I.M.Yeates and three MiA

Saturday, 15 July 1944

At 0705 Sqn Ldr Spencer Whiting led four Mustangs from Biferno to sweep the rail line Vukovar–Osijek where they shot up two trains in the latter area. At 0815 the British pilots sighted six Bücker Bü 131s of 1.PŠ near Borovo, claiming four destroyed. The actual losses were one destroyed, one force-landed in Hungarian territory and three damaged. The Mustangs continued along the railway, two more trains being reported disabled before the aircraft turned towards Sarajevo. Passing Rajlovac an hour later, they spotted seven aircraft on the ground and one pair attacked and set fire to a Do 17E parked outside the hangars, while a second pair strafed the burned-out wreck of an ancient Do Y which had been placed there as a decoy. The airfield commander, Pukovnik (Puk: Col) Zlatko Šintić, reported that one of the attackers departed trailing white smoke, but in fact all the Mustangs returned safely at 1000.

Only 324 Wing had not yet assumed the fighter-bomber role in Italy and was not to do so for some time yet, for on this date its four squadrons moved to join 251 and 322 Wings in Corsica.

British Claims

213 Sqn	Sqn Ldr S.R.Whiting	Mustang III FB337 'A'	2 Bü 131s	Vukovac	0835
213 Sqn	Wt Off D.E.Cooke	Mustang III FB322 'W'	Bü 131	Vukovac	0835
213 Sqn	Flg Off R.Anthony	Mustang III FB302 'B'	Bü 131	Vukovac	0835
213 Sqn	Sqn Ldr S.R.Whiting	Mustang III FB337 'A'	Do 17 (on ground)	Sarajevo	0900
213 Sqn	Flg Off R.Anthony	Mustang III FB302 'B'			
213 Sqn	Wt Off D.E.Cooke	Mustang III FB322 'W'	Do 217 (on ground)	Sarajevo	0900
213 Sqn	Wt Off K.A.L.Ford	Mustang III FB313			

British Casualties

1435 Sqn   Spitfire Vc LZ929 'R' left 1115, strafed trucks on road S Yanina, hit by return fire, pilot baled; Wt Off E.A.Rushmere safe, returned in August

6 Sqn   Hurricane IV KZ575 'F' left 1030 on armed recce of Plannitsa Channel, attacked shipping at Senj, hit by Flak, pilot baled nr Kornat; Wt Off R.Y.Ulrich safe, rescued by partisan fishing boat, returned two days later

US Casualties

522nd FS/27th FBG	P-47D 42-26550 shot down by Flak; 2/Lt Paul R.Joyce KiA
64th FS/57th FG	P-47D left 0745, escort to bombing of rail bridge 0850, presumed engine failure or hit by Flak, ditched; Lt Bruce H.Hale rescued, returned
66th FS/57th FG	P-47D left 1600 to bomb bridge 1650, hit by light Flak, on return pilot baled out 2m off base; 2/Lt Louis J Pernicka rescued by 284 Sqn Walrus R6549 flown by Lt K.B.Walker, returned
527th FS/86th FG	P-47D 42-28052 lost u/k cause 1530; Flt Off Douglas V.Neale evaded [7063]
488th FS/340th BG	B-25J 43-27551 '8H' left 1650 to bomb Pontelagoscuro rail bridge nr Ferrara 1844, damaged by Flak, landed safely; 1/Lt T.E.Jones and four safe, one DoW
486th BS/340th BG	3 B-25Js damaged by Flak, belly-landed at base; crews safe but one WiA

Croatian casualties

1.PŠ	Bücker Bü 131 shot down by Mustangs near Borovo 0815; pupil Ustasha Mirko Hamader KiA
1.PŠ	Bücker Bü 131 damaged by Mustangs near Borovo 0815, crash-landed in Hungary
1.PŠ	3 Bücker Bü 131s damaged by Mustangs near Borovo 0815
3.LJ	Do 17E destroyed by fire on ground by Mustangs 0915

Above: Whilst leading a sweep over Yugoslavia in Mustang III FB337 'A' on 15 July, Sqn Ldr Spencer Whiting of 213 Squadron claimed two Bü 131 trainers shot down. Left: On 15 July a formation of Bücker Bü 131 trainers from the Croat 1 Pilot School were attacked near Borovo by Mustangs of 213 Squadron, suffering several losses.

Saturday-Sunday, 15/16 July 1944

British Casualties	
55 Sqn	Baltimore V FW364 'W' left 2130 on armed recce against Hermann Göring Division NE Arezzo; Lt. J.E.Andrews and two KiA, one POW

Sunday, 16 July 1944

Two days after its most recent losses to Flak, 12 SAAF Squadron flew eastwards to attack strong points near Ancona, and here Lt Cedric Dutton's aircraft was seen to fall out of control, the whole crew being killed. Fortunately for the South Africans, this would prove to be the last casualty of the month, though on the 25th an aircraft of the sister squadron, 24 SAAF, crash-landed at Pescara after one engine had been knocked out by Flak during an attack on marshalling yards at Faenza.

Although DAF's bombers were so active at this time, they had been weakened on 12 July by the withdrawal of the most recently

A B-26G Marauder, 42-107777 '53' of the French bomber unit GB 1/32 'Bourgogne' runs in on its target during a mission on 16 July.

arrived Baltimore unit, 13 (Hellenic) Squadron, which returned to Biferno to become a part of the newly formed Balkan Air Force. This posting would allow the Greek personnel to operate more directly over their own homeland.

British Casualties	
249 Sqn	Spitfire Vc LZ822 left 0930 strafing Bihac-Otocac area, glycol leak, pilot baled out 1030; Flt Lt D.Sinclair paddled ashore, POW
213 Sqn	Mustang III FB313 hit by Flak, crash-landed near Sisak ca 0800; 2/Lt J.W.Moor evaded, returned on 16 August
213 Sqn	Mustang III FB314 hit by Flak, crash-landed near Sisak ca 0800; Plt Off A.R.Botherstone POW?
12 SAAF Sqn	Marauder II FB459 'K' shot down by Flak over target 3m S Ancona 0955, three parachutes seen; Lt H.C.Dutton and J.A.Ferreira shot attempting to escape, three KiA, Lt I.Margowski evaded, returned on 19 July

US Casualties	
314th FS/324th FG	P-40F 41-19736 crashed; 2/Lt William Aynes KiA

Italian Co-Belligerent Casualties	
351ª Sq, 21° Gr, 51° St	MC.205 MM 92189 shot down near Susak Island, pilot baled out; Ten Giovanni Franchini (Sq CO) rescued by partisans
239ª Sq, 102° Gr, 5° St	MC.205 MM 91835 left 0910, ran out of fuel, ditched near Vis; Ten Silvio Leonesio baled, DoW
239ª Sq, 102° Gr, 5° St	MC.202 MM 9529 left 0910, ran out of fuel, ditched near Vis; S.Ten Aldo Dagnino WiA, rescued by partisans

German Claims		
Flak	Spitfire	Sibenik

German Casualties	
2./NAGr 11	Bf 109G shot down at Florence by own Flak; Oblt Karl-Otto Holzapfel (St.Kpt) WiA

On 16 July SAAF Marauders bombed the railway and strong points near Ancona, though the attack cost 12 SAAF Squadron one aircraft to Flak.

Sunday-Monday, 16/17 July 1944

A Dakota of 267 Squadron was detailed to carry out a special operational flight of infiltrate and evacuate in Yugoslavia to Tito's headquarters. On board were Maj Randolph Churchill, the son of Sir Winston Churchill, and the novelist Captain Evelyn Waugh who was then a commando. During this night, at the landing strip at Bosnanski Dubica in Yugoslavia, the Dakota attempted to go around again and performed normal overshoot procedures rapidly gaining height at first, but then losing height rapidly and crashing just beyond the flare path. Seven aboard were killed and ten survived; among them Randolph Churchill and Evelyn Waugh, who were injured. Another passenger, Air Commodore Guy L.Carter, Senior Air Staff Officer of the Balkan Air Force and former commander of 211 Group of the Desert Air Force in 1942, died of injuries two days later.

British Casualties	
108 Sqn	Mosquito NFXIII MM441 'T' left Alghero 2359 for Toulouse area, failed to return; Flt Sgt M.H.Gill/Flt Sgt K.R.E.Spencer MiA
267 Sqn	Dakota III (C-47A) KG472 stalled, crashed at partisan l/g nr Bosnanski Dubica, Yugoslavia; Capt H.W.Solms, three crew and four passengers KiA, ten survived WiA
153 Sqn	Beaufighter VIf MM871 left 0013 on intruder to Lyon area, aircraft abandoned on return flight off southern coast of France; Flt Sgt G.K.Hug rescued/Sgt B.Lansley MiA

Monday, 17 July 1944

During the day pilots of 451 Squadron, one of the units of 251 Wing, saw their commanding officer, Sqn Ldr Wally Gale, shot down while on a special Tac R on the state of the Arno river bridges only a week after he had arrived to take over the unit; he was replaced by Sqn Ldr G.W.Small.

The Germans began a determined offensive in Montenegro which prompted increased attacks on enemy lines of communication, the pressure on the partisans continuing into August with fighter support.

British Casualties	
451 Sqn	Spitfire IX MK267 shot down by ground fire over River Arno bridge; Sqn Ldr W.W.B.Gale KiA
6 Sqn	Hurricane IV KZ243 left 1840, set on fire by Flak SE Druvenik, jettisoned RPs, landed at Vis; Lt J.Bosch safe
6 Sqn	Hurricane IV KX883 'E' left Vis 0500, engine cut while on runway, retracted undercarriage causing severe damage; Flt Lt R.B.Davidson safe
US Casualties	
315th FS/324th FG	P-40L 42-10980 lost, pilot baled 2m offshore of Volturno river; Lt Norman A.Olson returned
527th FS/86th FG	P-47D 42-26693 shot down by Flak 4m NW Pisa 2045; 1/Lt Frank E.Myrick KiA [7069]
527th FS/86th FG	P-47D 42-26679 crash-landed at sea; Flt Off Sylvan J.Kapner returned

Monday-Tuesday, 17/18 July 1944

During the Lake Trasimeno operations, 8th Army once again enjoyed the support of 208 Squadron. This unit had moved to Castiglione del Lago to join 40 SAAF Squadron; this airfield was a pleasant one, situated on the western edge of the lake from where the length of the tactical reconnaissance (TacR) and artillery reconnaissance (ArtyR) sorties which were being undertaken by these units were considerably shortened. These reconnaissance pilots spotted for many artillery 'shoots' at this time, mainly against opposing gun pits, and here DFCs were awarded to two of the 208 Squadron flight commanders, Flt Lts Peter Perry and Basil Champreys. Further east, 318 Squadron continued to fly similar operations over the approaches to Ancona.

With XII TAC meanwhile, the 324th Fighter Group became the last unit in this particular command to convert to P-47s, exchanging its faithful P-40s for these new aircraft during July. Immediately re-armament had been completed this unit also moved to Corsica, flying over to this island on the 19th. By the middle of this month however, the advance, which had begun with Diadem, had lost its momentum; it was time for the Allied commanders to review the whole situation in the Mediterranean again.

British Casualties	
18 Sqn	Boston III W8391 'J' take-off accident, landed in the sea off Tarquinia; Sgt B.J.Monsey and two KiA, one WiA

Operation Dragoon

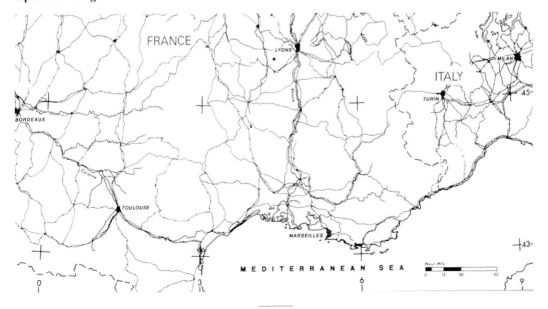

CHAPTER 2

OPERATION DRAGOON – THE AMERICAN CHOICE

Mid July 1944 found the whole Allied position and strategy in the Mediterranean in a state of flux. The landing in Normandy had been successful and the beachhead area had been secured. So far, as the US High Command was concerned, north-west and western France now formed the only theatres of major importance, so they desired that all possible strength be diverted there so that the full weight of Allied manpower and material might be concentrated to destroy the German Wehrmacht on its own frontiers. Indeed, it had originally been the US demand to launch an invasion of southern France at the same time as that in the north-west. Only a shortage of landing craft at the requisite time and place had frustrated their primary wish.

To them Italy was now a mere sideshow; the US 15th Air Force bases in the Foggia area were secure and playing a full part in the Combined Bomber Offensive, while a substantial number of Axis divisions were tied down in central and northern Italy and in Yugoslavia to protect the southern approaches to the Reich. All that was necessary in the American view was to leave sufficient forces to man a static line to the north of Rome and to continue to pin down this Axis strength as the main battle was fought in France.

It was at this stage that British policy regarding the Italian campaign really diverged from that of the Americans. With memories of the slaughter of 1914-18 still clearly in their minds, the British war leaders were as unwilling as ever to enter upon a major continental war if a suitable strategic alternative could be found. They also doubted the capacity of the French ports so far in Allied hands along the western Atlantic coast to supply and maintain so vast an army on French soil. Further, the deep and basic distrust of Soviet ambitions in Eastern Europe and the Balkans reinforced the urgent desire to do all possible to re-establish as strong a British presence and influence in this part of the world as could possibly be achieved.

It was the dream of Winston Churchill to break free of the mountains of Italy, drive north-eastwards into southern Austria and on to the plains of Hungary. From here the heartlands of Germany would, in his view, be at the mercy of the Allies while the great bulk of the Wehrmacht was held in the east by the Red Army and in the west by the Anglo-American forces in France. The Americans had little sympathy for this plan, considering it to be unnecessarily complicated and risky; they felt its practicability was questionable and also suspected it to be more closely linked with British Imperial pretentions than with the earliest possible defeat of Germany (and subsequently of Japan). With no strategic interests in the Balkans and Eastern Europe they were quite prepared to leave the war in the East to the Russians – a view which they probably subsequently had cause to regret!

Shortage of landing craft, coupled with British arguments generally had caused the landings in southern France to be postponed, but by July planning was well advanced for such a venture. It was agreed nonetheless that some US forces would remain in Italy to take part in a new offensive there – at least until such time as its outcome was known.

Mid-August was selected for Operation Anvil (soon re-named Dragoon) with landings to take place in the St Tropez area of the French Riviera. Corsica was to be the main base from which air support for this operation was to be launched; already a substantial air force was gathered there. On 18 July the headquarters of XII TAC moved to this island followed next day by the main headquarters of Mediterranean Allied Tactical Air Force (MATAF). A supplementary headquarters was left in Italy to advise the Allied army group there, but support for the whole of the Italian front – both 5th and 8th Armies – now devolved onto DAF.

Even as the air units involved began their re-dispositions, nine infantry divisions were withdrawn from 5th Army to join the revitalised 7th Army (descendant of the force which had shared in the Sicilian landings) for the Anvil landings. Included amongst these were the French mountain divisions of the Expeditionary Corps which had proved invaluable during recent actions; their absence from the Italian front would be sorely felt. Units of 8th Army moved to take over their sector as they pulled out of the line on 22 July.

While these changes were taking place the soldiers at the front continued their steady advance towards the River Arno. The continual defensive actions fought by Kesselring's hard-pressed units – particularly those around Lake Trasimeno – had taken much of the initial drive out of the Allied thrust and the initial rush following the capture of Rome had now slowed down greatly. Despite this, US forces in the west took Pontedera on 18 July and Leghorn (on the coast) next day. At the same time Laterina was taken by 8th Army units while on the far east coast 18th Polish II Corps had entered Ancona on the 8th. Within five more days the Americans would reach the south bank of the Arno, opposite Pisa but the main focus for the rest of July was to centre upon Florence, major city of the Arno. Both 5th and 8th Armies were now moving on this objective city down each bank of the river.

During this period operations around Florence were getting well underway as the main part of DAF began its attack. Since the withdrawal of units for Operation Dragoon (as it had now been dubbed), the Allies were left with only 21 effective divisions in Italy, and these were faced by 26 German and six Italian Fascist divisions in strong defensive positions. The Allies were strong in armour but weak in infantry due to the manpower demands of other fronts; further, the mountainous nature of the central Italian terrain prevented the exploitation of the armoured advantage.

This apparent disparity against the Allies was resolved to their overall advantage by the massive preponderance of air power which they possessed, and the much greater mobility that this permitted them to enjoy. Indeed, air power was now quite the strongest and most effective weapon on this front. Although now seldom challenged in the air, however, the Allied aircrews were acquiring an increasingly healthy respect for the German Flak which could at times inflict some severe blows. For the fighter-bombers the multiple-barrelled 20mm and 37mm light Flak was the deadliest enemy while the mediums were always wary of the concentration of 88mm heavy Flak, particularly when this was of the radar-laid variety.

Throughout the period 20 July–4 August Kittyhawks of 239 Wing and Spitfires of 7 SAAF Wing ranged over the front bombing and strafing strongpoints, guns, vehicle columns and troop concentrations as well as railways and coastal shipping. At the height of the advance Cab Rank operations in direct contact with the ground forces were flown and at this time gun pits were the prime targets at the army's request.

At first 244 Wing and some of the Spitfire IXs of 7 SAAF Wing continued with their patrols, sweeps, bomber and fighter-bomber escorts but as the two-week period rolled on more and more of their activities became involved with bomb dropping and strafing during armed reconnaissances. 1 SAAF Squadron was perhaps the last of the 'pure' fighter squadrons to begin this way of life, dropping its first bombs against live targets on 1 August. Possibly because of their newness to such operations it was the Spitfire VIII units which tended to suffer the greatest proportion of losses at this time. 601 Squadron lost one Spitfire and its pilot on 18 July and two days later a second fell to Flak; on this occasion Flg Off H.G.Proudman managed to bale out. On the 26th a Spitfire of 417 Squadron was lost in similar circumstances, Flt Sgt J.T.Macleod also baling out although in his case to become a prisoner of war.

Amongst the other wings, 239 lost two Mustangs and a Kittyhawk while 7 SAAF Wing lost four of its aircraft, two by 2 SAAF Squadron and one each from 3 SAAF Squadron, which had just arrived, and 4 SAAF Squadron. 40 SAAF Squadron also lost three of its TacR Spitfires. During the latter part of July the Seafires which had been attached to 244 and 7 SAAF Wings returned to their aircraft carriers.

The Kittyhawks and Mustangs of 239 Wing had already moved to Creti airfield from where they had provided support for units of 8th Army's XIII Corps attacking the town of Arezzo. Situated very close to the front, the average sortie from this strip lasted just about 40 minutes. Ground crews at their dispersals were able to see their squadron's aircraft actually making their bombing and strafing attacks on the German positions. XIII Corps expressed considerable satisfaction with the level of support received from the wing during this period and Arezzo fell to its forces on 16 July.

Thus, as the Allied armies in Italy prepared for their next moves forward from the line which now stretched almost due west-east from the south bank of the Arno to Ancona, DAF was now solely responsible for the support of further operations on the ground. However, in order to allow its units to concentrate upon these duties, XII TAC in Corsica was directed to concentrate its activities over Italy to the north of DAF's area of operations throughout the last two weeks of July. During this period XII TAC's fighter-bombers would not yet be required to operate over southern France and were therefore able to take up the good work begun by the medium bombers a few weeks earlier. Attacking bridges, rolling stock, viaducts, marshalling yards and other rail and communications targets between the Apennines and the River Po, the P-47s and A-20s were quickly to achieve considerable success.

Dispositions of the Mediterranean Tactical Air Force at this crucial time were as follows:

ITALY

Desert Air Force

285 (Reconnaissance) Wing

The wing had temporarily lost 225 Squadron, which had moved to Corsica with XII TAC, but still had two squadrons on the west side of Italy. 208 and 40 SAAF Squadrons were both at Castiglione del Lago, from where operations were being flown in support of both 5th and 8th Army units. A flight of photo-reconnaissance Spitfire XIs from 682 Squadron, on loan from the Photographic Reconnaissance Wing, was also based in the west, while in the east the recently arrived 318 Squadron was operating in support of the fellow Poles of II Corps in the Ancona area, initially from San Vito, and then from Tortorella and Fermo.

239 Wing

This veteran close-support wing, still six squadrons strong, was at Creti in the centre of the front, ready to operate in direct support of the forces advancing on Florence. 112 and 260 Squadrons were now both operational on Mustang IIIs, with 250, 450, 3 RAAF and 5 SAAF Squadrons continuing to fly the faithful Kittyhawks, though all units were now equipped with the latest Mark IVs.

244 Wing

The air-superiority Spitfire VIII wing had recently moved forward to Perugia, somewhat to the east of Lake Trasimeno. From here the four squadrons could operate either east or west and were also well-placed to cover and support the main drive on Florence. So little opposition was now to be met in the air over the front, that this premier fighter wing had recently undertaken its first fighter-bomber sorties and was to fly increasing numbers of close support and strafing missions as the summer wore on. The wing still comprised 92, 145, 417 and 601 Squadrons.

7 SAAF Wing

Like the squadrons of 244 Wing, 1 SAAF Squadron had also begun to practise the carriage and dropping of bombs, though it had not yet undertaken any sorties of this nature over the front. 7 SAAF Squadron had by now become fully into the ways of fighter-bomber operations, having joined the wing's other two veteran fighter-bomber units in these duties. The wing had recently moved to Foiano della Chiana to support the drive on Florence, and all four squadrons, 1 SAAF, 2 SAAF, 4 SAAF and 7 SAAF, were now fully equipped with Spitfire IXs. This move left 241 Squadron as the only fighter unit available for operations over the east coast. Until recently operating as a part of 7 SAAF Wing, this unit had moved to join 318 Squadron at San Vito during June, and had now just moved again, this time to Fermo. From this base, patrols by its Spitfire VIIIs were to be made over Ancona and the Polish troops in the line.

232 Wing

All squadrons of the wing were now involved almost entirely on night interdiction sorties. Nos. 13 and 55 Squadrons with Baltimores, 18 and 114 Squadrons with Bostons, were all in the process of moving from Tarquinia to Cecina. Although losses on the nocturnal sorties undertaken by the bombers were generally light, averaging one or two per month at the most, the sudden and unexpected Flak concentration could still sometimes take an unpleasant toll. During the night of 26/27 June 55 Squadron had lost two Baltimores while attacking targets on the Pistoia-Bologna road; generally, however, to lose two bombers in one night was extremely unusual on these operations.

3 SAAF Wing

Desert Air Force's other bomber wing was temporarily weakened at this juncture. Although 12 SAAF and 24 SAAF Squadrons were available at Pescara with their Marauders, aircraft with which they were now thoroughly familiar, and 223 Squadron was also a part of this wing, the fourth squadron, 21 SAAF, had just stood down from operations to exchange its faithful Baltimores for Marauders also. However, during July 223 Squadron would be joined at Pescara by a new Baltimore unit, 454 (RAAF) Squadron, from Egypt. At the same time 15 SAAF Squadron – also with Baltimores – arrived from the same place, taking up station at nearby Falconara. These two units were eventually to be joined by a third squadron to form a new Baltimore wing – No 253 – for daylight operations. In the interim both these units began day formation bombing attacks over the front under the operational control of 287 Fighter Wing, Coastal Air Force. Although administered by a Coastal wing and indeed escorted by Spitfires from that wing's squadrons, these new Baltimore units nevertheless operated as a part of Desert Air Force, attacking the latter's tactical targets.

Also available to DAF were the Beaufighter VIf night-fighters of 600 Squadron, which were to move from Rosignano to Follonica during the month, together with detachments of these aircraft from 255 Squadron on attachment to DAF; these were to operate variously from Falconara, Pomigliano and Rosignano.

CORSICA

On the island were the 27th, 57th, 79th, 86th and 324th Fighter Groups, all now fully equipped with Republic P-47D Thunderbolts, each group comprising three squadrons. They were joined by three RAF fighter wings, all equipped with Spitfire IXs. These comprised:

251 Wing: 237, 238 and 451 Squadrons
322 Wing: 154, 232, 242 and 243 Squadrons
324 Wing: 43, 72, 93 and 111 Squadrons

The other elements of XII TAC were the 47th Bombardment Group (Light) with its four squadrons of A-20 Havocs, four squadrons (groupes) of the Forces Aeriennes Françaises Libres (one equipped with Spitfires), plus two tactical reconnaissance squadrons and one night-fighter unit. Of the former, 225 Squadron, RAF, had now supplemented its Spitfire Vs with a few Mark IXs, while the 111th Tactical Reconnaissance Squadron still had its F-6B Mustangs. These cannon-armed aircraft had managed to shoot down a number of German aircraft at Salerno and Anzio. All these units were under the operational direction of the resident US 87th Fighter Wing.

57th Bombardment Wing
All three B-25-equipped Bombardment Groups (Medium) of this wing, the 310th, 321st and 340th, were now based in Corsica, although these still operated directly under US 12th Air Force and MATAF command, rather than as a part of XII TAC. Also, on the island were two F-5 Lightning-equipped photo-reconnaissance squadrons and the 350th Fighter Group, equipped with P-39s and P-47s. This latter unit was stationed here for air defence purposes, and was a part of XII Fighter Command, the US contingent in Coastal Air Force. Before the landings began the 14th and 82nd Fighter Groups with their P-38 Lightnings were to arrive on attachment to XII TAC from the 15th Air Force.

SARDINIA

42nd Bombardment Wing
Enjoying the same semi-independent status as the 57th Wing, this element's three B-26-equipped groups – 17th, 319th and 320th – and the French Groupe 2/20 'Bretagne', were equally well-placed to operate over both southern France and northern Italy. The defence of the island was fully in the hands of units of Coastal Air Force, including the US 414th Night Fighter Squadron, another unit equipped with reverse Lease-Lend Beaufighter VIfs.

Additionally, due to the large number of air transport formations recalled to the United Kingdom during early 1944, only the US 51st Troop Carrier Wing now remained, comprising three troop carrier squadrons, the 60th, 62nd and 64th. In consequence Troop Carrier Command had now been dissolved, and these C-47 units brought under the direct command of MATAF within 12th Air Force.

Tuesday, 18 July 1944
Three Hurricanes from 6 Squadron left on an armed reconnaissance of the Korcula-Pelješac Channel, attacked and sank a 60-ft schooner at Podobuce, then attacked a 60-ft barge at Trstenik, without result. The leader Flt Lt Walker was hit by Flak from Zuljana and ditched a quarter of a mile off shore. Two hours later he was rescued by a Catalina.

Left: On 18 July Flt Lt C.S.Vos of 213 Squadron led a section that destroyed a Ju 52/3m on the ground at Skopje airfield. Right: Through the mid summer the obsolescent He 46Es of Stormkampf Staffel Kroatien flew night anti-partisan operations over the Yugoslav mountains.

On this date Flt Lt Vos led a section of four Mustangs of 213 Squadron on an offensive sweep strafing road and rail targets around Skopje. The airfield at Shijak was attacked and a Ju 52/3m destroyed.

British Claims

213 Sqn	Flt Lt C.S.Vos	Mustang III FB335	}			
213 Sqn	Lt H.B.Helm	Mustang III FB315	} Ju 52 (on ground)	Skopje	1200-1420
213 Sqn	Flg Off S.Chappell	Mustang III FB324	}			

British Casualties

601 Sqn	Spitfire IX MK376 left 1130 to bomb railway, hit by heavy Flak over Mercato Saraceno 1145; Sgt M.Ord KiA
4 SAAF Sqn	Spitfire IXc MK174 'L' left 1845 to dive bomb road in the Romano area, hit by Flak, pilot baled 16km SE Florence 1900; Capt P.C.R.Burger KiA
4 SAAF Sqn	Spitfire IXc MK634 'W' left 1910 to dive bomb road near Bibbiena, shot down by 88mm Flak 32km N Arezzo 1930, pilot baled; Lt A.I.Bristol evaded, returned on 9 August
6 Sqn	Hurricane IV KZ404 'D' left on armed recce of Korcula-Pelješac Channel, hit by Flak nr Zuljana, ditched; Flt Lt A.E.Walker DFC rescued by Catalina

US Casualties

316th FS/324th FG	P-40 shot down by friendly P-51 or by Flak; 2/Lt George L.Porter WiA

Wednesday, 19 July 1944

The Ancona area was to prove a most fruitful hunting ground for the sole day-fighter squadron in the east during July. The day after the town had fallen to the Poles (19 July), a standing patrol was instated by 241 Squadron, this being undertaken by a pair of Spitfire VIIIs. Almost at once a pair of reconnaissance Bf 109s appeared, and one of these was swiftly sent crashing to the ground by Flt Lt Turkington as the pilot baled out.

Operating so much further north than the DAF units, the XII TAC fighters had more opportunities at this time to meet the small numbers of Axis fighters defending northern Italy. A few FW 190s of the Schlacht-gruppen were still around, though now these seldom operated in the attack role, supplementing the Italian Bf 109s in fighter defence operations instead. The RAF Spitfires achieved a few successes against these during the month; late in the afternoon of 19 July 154 Squadron escorted bombers over the Piacenza-La Spezia area where over 30 Bf 109s and FW 190s were seen. Flt Lt Wilson chased an FW 190 which he claimed shot down, while Flg Off Dobson-Smyth attacked a Bf 109 from which the pilot baled out as soon as he was hit. This latter aircraft may have been from 2° Gruppo, pilots of this unit reporting a combat with a formation of Bos-tons and their escorts over Reggio Emilia on this date. P-47s of the 57th Fighter Group also flew two escort missions during the day, one of these at the same time as 154 Squadron. 65th Squadron aircraft escorted 36 B-26s over Italy first, the 64th Squadron then escorting 310th Bomb Group B-25s to Ferrara. The recognition of some of the ANR pilots seems to have left something to be desired, and during 1944 they frequently appear to have identified B-26s as Bostons.

That evening during a high level patrol off northern Corsica, Flt Lt J.A.Ormerod of 72 Squadron chased an Me 410 for 100 miles before shooting it down near Piacenza.

Pilots of two Beaufighters from 39 Squadron claimed to have destroyed four locomotives in the Vincovci-Novska area but an aircraft was lost to Flak. Four more aircraft from this unit attacked the chrome mine at Dhomokos, but on return an aircraft belly-landed at Foggia due to hydraulic failure probably caused by Flak, which had slightly wounded the observer.

During the 19th 92 Squadron detached a flight to the west coast to counter enemy reconnaissance aircraft.

British Claims

241 Sqn	Flt Lt R.W.Turkington	Spitfire VIII JG404 'Y'	Bf 109	S Senigallia	0520-0600
154 Sqn	Flt Lt A.F.Wilson	Spitfire IX MK629 'V'	FW 190	La Spezia area	1803
154 Sqn	Flg Off W.E.Dobson-Smyth	Spitfire IX MK535 'Y'	Bf 109	La Spezia area	1805
72 Sqn	Flt Lt J.A.Ormerod	Spitfire IX MJ718	Me 410 Damaged	20m NNW Corsica	1935-2100

British Casualties

39 Sqn	Beaufighter X NE615 'X' left 0750 on sweep of Vincovci-Novska area, hit by Flak, crash-landed 0915; Flg Off A.T.Patterson/ Flt Sgt H.W.McDonald evaded
39 Sqn	Beaufighter X NE383 'F' left 1127 to attack chrome mine at Dhomokos, probably damaged by Flak, belly-landed at Foggia 1530; Flg Off A.A.Settle safe/Flg Off H.V.Webb WiA
603 Sqn	Beaufighter TFX NE595 'S' left 1620 on a sweep, shot down by Flak off Fiscardo, Cephalonia 1855; Flt Sgt H.E.Yorke evaded/Flt Sgt J.G.Shaw KiA

US Claims

85th FS/79th FG	Lt Martin J.Granberg	P-47D	FW 190 Damaged	Ostiglia area	1700-1910
85th FS/79th FG	Lt William J.Stalter	P-47D	FW 190 Damaged	Ostiglia area	1700-1910
86th FS/79th FG	unstated	P-47D	Bf 109	NE Cremona	1700-2000

German Claims

Flak			Beaufighter*	Port Fiscardo, Cephalonia	1745
	*identified as being 'S' of 603 Sqn			

German Casualties

2.(F)/122	Me 410 F6+FK damaged by e/a, crash-landed at Piacenza; Lt Galle and Gerstner safe
	LKS reports three Bf 109s lost and one damaged in combat

Italian ANR Claims

4ª Sq, 2° Gr C	M.llo Giovanni Cavagnino	Bf 109G	A-20	Parma
4ª Sq, 2° Gr C	Serg Luigi Marin	Bf 109G	A-20	Parma
4ª Sq, 2° Gr C	Serg Sergio Mazzi	Bf 109G	A-20	Parma

Italian ANR Casualties

2° Gr C	Bf 109G damaged in combat, force-landed at Reggio Emilia; pilot safe

Wednesday-Thursday, 19/20 July 1944

British Casualties

18 Sqn	Boston III W8345 'P' left 2255 on armed recce of Florence-Bologna-Faenza region, an engine failed, crashed into a building in Modena; Flt Sgt W.F.Worsley and one KiA, two evaded and returned on 5 November

US Claims

417th NFS	2/Lt Robert W.Inglis/Flt Off Theodore F.Hearne	Beaufighter VIf ND262	u/i e/a	10m E Montecristo	2310-2325

US Casualties

417th NFS	Beaufighter VIf ND262 lost E Montecristo 2329; 2/Lt Robert W.Inglis/Flt Off Theodore E.Hearne KiA [7068]

German Casualties

6.(F)/122	Ju 88A-4 WNr 301547 F6+EP lost on sea reconnaissance W Italy-Corsica; Uffz Konrad Metz and three MiA

Thursday, 20 July 1944

Fliegerführer Kroatia had received instructions to provide air support for the up-coming offensive against the bridgehead held by Tito's partisan forces over the Lim river in the Andrijevica area north-east of Podgorica. This operation had commenced two days earlier and on this date 213 Squadron provided two strong sweeps each by four of its new Mustangs over the area. The first of these went off at dawn, not seeing any opposing aircraft but using their time to strafe some m/t. The second sweep departed at 1119 led by Sqn Ldr Spencer Whiting. The pilots of these reported encountering seven Bf 109s which were escorting 12 Hs 126 army co-operation aircraft; the fighters were from II./JG 51 which had taken off from Medosevac while the Henschels, which were from III./LLG 1, were on their way from Krusevac to attack targets near Andrijevica. The Mustang pilots attacked the Messerschmitts from behind and below, reporting that after four or five minutes their opponents appeared to be anxious to break, allowing the RAF pilots to claim one shot down, two probably so and two damaged. During the engagement the Mustangs became separated into two sections, one of which headed for base. Sqn Ldr Whiting then led the first section in a search for the Henschels, which were sighted at 1205 still in their initial formation of four vics each of three aircraft in line astern. In the attack which followed Whiting and his wingman, Wt Off Cooke, attacked the rear vic and that ahead of it, claiming one destroyed and three damaged.

At 1900 Lt Giraud and Sgt Chef Gigot were airborne on a dusk patrol off Algeria in two of 256 Squadron's Spitfire IXs, having been attached from GC I/5 to gain experience on the type. At 1950 20m north of Cape Kramis, Gigot's engine failed. He crossed the coast and force-landed about 10m north-east of La Passet aerodrome. After a run of 20 yards the Spitfire hit a tree, burst into flames and Gigot was flung out and killed.

Lt Bergmann, the commander of the 5./JG 51 detachment normally based on Crete was killed in a take-off accident from Gadurra airfield on Rhodes.

After Sqn Ldr Spencer Whiting (centre), the commanding officer of 213 Squadron, had claimed a Bf 109 and an Hs 126 shot down over Yugoslavia on 20 July, adding to his success a few days earlier, his ground crew adorned his aircraft with four swastikas.

The Walrus amphibians of 293 Squadron such as L2217 'P' parked at Pomigliano, Naples, conducted rescues of aircrew from the Mediterranean and Adriatic throughout 1944.

British Claims

213 Sqn	Sqn Ldr S.R.Whiting	Mustang III FB337 'A'	Bf 109	Rozaj	1200
213 Sqn	Sqn Ldr S.R.Whiting	Mustang III FB337 'A'	Bf 109 Probable	Rozaj	1200
213 Sqn	Wt Off D.E.Cooke	Mustang III FB322 'W'	Bf 109 Probable	Rozaj	1200
213 Sqn	Wt Off J.G.P.Watkins	Mustang III FB329 'L'	2 Bf 109s Damaged	Rozaj	1200
213 Sqn	Sqn Ldr S.R.Whiting	Mustang III FB337 'A'	Hs 126	NE Rozaj	1205
213 Sqn	Sqn Ldr S.R.Whiting	Mustang III FB337 'A'	Hs 126 Damaged	NE Rozaj	1205
213 Sqn	Wt Off D.E.Cooke	Mustang III FB322 'W'	2 Hs 126s Damaged	NE Rozaj	1205

British Casualties

601 Sqn — Spitfire IX MK481 left 0625 to bomb road junction W Pesaro, hit by Flak, pilot baled off Fano 0655; Flg Off H.G.Proudman rescued by Walrus L2170 of 293 Sqn flown by Lt J.V.Peters

256 Sqn C Flight — Spitfire VIII JF591 left 1900 on dusk patrol, engine failed 20m N Cape Kramis at 20,000ft, crashed 10m NE La Passet 2010; Sgt Chef Gigot (GC 1/5 attached) KiA

US Casualties

523rd FS/27th FBG — P-47D 42-27952 'C' shot down by Flak; Flt Off Nile F.Timmermann KiA [7040]

438th BS/319th BG — B-26C 42-107554 shot down by Flak, last seen 1833, crashed 2m SW Ostiglia, nr Quistello; 1/Lt George E.Marple and five POW, one evaded [6683]

440th BS/319th BG — B-26B 42-95793 '85' collision with a/c '81' (which did not crash), crashed 5m S Cape Corse 1922; 1/Lt Clifton A.Collins and five KiA [6613]

34th BS/17th BG — B-26B 42-96021 '22' badly damaged by Flak, crashed nr Bosco di Corniglia; 1/Lt James M.Baker and five KiA, one POW, one evaded [6682]

34th BS/17th BG — B-26B '06' damaged by Flak, crash-landed at base; 1/Lt O.J.Boudreau and five safe

German Claims

Flak		Marauder *	Bosco di Corniglia	1840
Flak		Marauder **	Quistello	1900

*Identified as being from the 34th BS/17th BG

**Identified as being from the 438th BS/319th BG

Stab II./JG 51	Bf 109G-6 WNr 162435 Black < +- shot down E Rozaj by Mustangs; Gefr Eduard Wolkersdorfer KiA			
5./JG 51	Bf 109G-6 WNr 17012 Red 13 crashed on take-off from Gadurra a/f, Rhodes; Lt Götz Bergmann KiA			
2./NAGr 11	Bf 109G-8 WNr 200452 White 3 lost 10km S Modena; Oblt Helmut Kaeber baled out			
11./LLG 1	Hs 126B-1 WNr 4051 H4+NV damaged by fighters 35km W Novi Pazar; pilot safe/Obgfr Heinrich Knittel WiA			
	LKS reports one Bf 109 lost in combat and one Ju 88 missing			

Friday, 21 July 1944

Early in the day on the central front 244 Wing had enjoyed one brief flash of its more normal role when Sqn Ldr Cox and Lt Manne of 92 Squadron scrambled at dawn to intercept and shoot down a reconnaissance Ju 188.

After some frustrations with mounting standing patrols Flt Lt Turkington and his wingman from 241 Squadron were just completing a dusk patrol in the same area when two more Bf 109s were spotted. This time Turkington was able to claim one destroyed with the other falling to Lt R.V.Lyon.

British Claims

92 Sqn	Sqn Ldr G.J.Cox	Spitfire VIII JF895	} Ju 188	SE Perugia airfield	0530-0715
92 Sqn	Lt E.Manne	Spitfire VIII JF396			
241 Sqn	Flt Lt R.W.Turkington	Spitfire VIII JG351 'U'	Bf 109	8m NE Senigallia	2048
241 Sqn	Lt R.V.Lyon	Spitfire VIII JG494 'Y'	Bf 109	W Ancona	2048

British Casualties

603 Sqn	Beaufighter X LZ465 'R' left 1720, shot down by ships' Flak E Mykonos; Flt Sgt D.Joyce/ Flt Sgt K.F.Thomas KiA
39 Sqn	Beaufighter X NE598 'S' left 0715, hit by Flak, crash-landed W of Ceprat; Flg Off W.P.Clifford/Flt Sgt S.Williams POW
39 Sqn	Beaufighter X NE322 'T' left 0715, hit by Flak, managed to reach Brindisi before crash-landing; Flt Sgt H.W.Mullens/Flt Sgt R.G.Robson safe
32 Sqn	Spitfire Vc MA345 left 1730 to bomb target at Bihac, hit by Flak 1930, force-landed nr Knin; Flt Lt P.Quine KiA
6 Sqn	Hurricane IV LD167 'H' left 1810 on armed recce, attacked shipping at Senj, shot down by Flak, ditched 13m SW Senj; Lt D.M.A.Hunter KiA

US Casualties

523rd FS/27th FBG	P-47D damaged by Flak crashed 8m E Ancona 0710; 1/Lt Lawrence E.Eastman rescued

Dakota transports of 267 Squadron regularly flew into improvised airstrips in Yugoslavia to support partisan operations, such as here on 21 July.

1./NAGr 11	Bf 109G-6 WNr 163609 Black 2 shot down S Fabriano; Uffz Heinz Möbius KiA
1./NAGr 11	Bf 109G-6 WNr 163617 Black 1 shot down S Fabriano; Oblt Ernst Nagler MiA
Stab (F)/122	Ju 188D-2 WNr 290183 F6+HM shot down by Spitfires at Castagni; Oblt Fritz Müller, Maj Gunther Pannwitz (Gr.Kdr) and three KiA
7./TG 4	Ju 52/3m WNr 500177 G6+OR reportedly shot down by Flak 15km S Antimilos; Lt Walter Peters KiA, one WiA, one MiA, one safe
	LKS reports two Bf 109s and one Ju 188 missing and one Bf 109 lost in combat, one Ju 52/3m lost in ops

Italian ANR Casualties

| 5ª Sq, 2° Gr C | Bf 109G lost in combat; Serg Magg Luigi Feliciani KiA |

Friday-Saturday, 21/22 July 1944

US Casualties

| 10th TCS/60th TCG | C-47 41-18388 shot down by e/a over Yugoslavia 2335; 2/Lt Morris N.Houser and three KiA, one evaded [14290] |

German Claims

| Stab III./NJG 6 | Hptm Leopold Fellerer | Bf 110G-4 | C-47 | W Brod | 2342 |

Saturday, 22 July 1944

During the evening a pair of Spitfires of 185 Squadron were scrambled from Malta after a Ju 188 that they hit and which subsequently crashed. It was a far from one-sided fight, however, as the Junkers crew had fought back effectively and both Spitfires were also shot down.

Above: Shortly before midnight on 21 July a US C-47 Dakota on a mission into Yugoslavia was shot down near Brod by a Bf 110G-4 night-fighter of III./NJG 6. Right: Hptm Leopold Fellerer, Kommodore of III./NJG 6, achieved a rare night victory over Yugoslavia when he shot down the US C-47.

| 185 Sqn | Plt Off P.S.Ballantine | Spitfire IX MA464 ⎫ | Ju 188 | 90m from Comiso | 1845-2005 |
| 185 Sqn | Lt R.J.Rowe | Spitfire IX MA249 ⎭ | | | |

British Casualties

260 Sqn	Mustang III FB270 left 1635 to attack railway trucks near Ravenna, shot down by Flak; Plt Off R.Glen KiA
185 Sqn	Spitfire IX MA249 scrambled 1845, intercepted Ju 188, shot down by return fire 90m off Malta; Lt R.J.Rowe baled and rescued by an HSL after one night in water
185 Sqn	Spitfire IX MA464 scrambled 1845, intercepted Ju 188, shot down by return fire 90m off Malta; Plt Off P.S.Ballantine safe
223 Sqn	Baltimore V FW542 'Y' left 1355 to bomb Ravenna marshalling yards, bad weather prevented all but one a/c bombing, on attempting to climb to avoid cloud, spun into the sea and blew up 30m off Ancona; Flt Sgt R.I.Hyslop and three KiA

German Casualties

| 1.(F)/33 | Ju 188F-1 8H+EL attacked by two Spitfires, ditched by Cephalonia; Lt Kaspar Kähn and three safe |
| | LKS reports one Ju 188 and one Ju 52/3m lost in combat |

Saturday-Sunday, 22/23 July 1944

British Casualties

| 38 Sqn | Wellington XIII JA359 'A' left 1952 to bomb Kastelli a/f, starboard engine failed, ditched 2m off the coast between Tolmietta and Ras Aemer; Flt Lt A.Donati and five crew paddled ashore, rescued next day |

Sunday, 23 July 1944

The Ar 196A-5 of 3./SAGr 126 sinking after being shot into the sea off Mykonos by Flt Lt Deck and Flt Sgt Warner of 603 Squadron.

British Claims

| 603 Sqn | Flt Lt A.G.Deck/Flt Sgt H.J.Warner | Beaufighter X 413 'P' | Ar 196 | 10m W Mykonos | 1036 |

British Casualties

603 Sqn	Beaufighter X NE494 'A' left 0625, damaged by an Ar 196 W Mykonos, ditched; Flg Off C.M. De Bounevialle/Flt Sgt A.E.Potter rescued by a Greek caique, evaded to Turkey and returned
603 Sqn	Beaufighter TFX NE610 'X' left 0625, attacked a convoy off Mykonos, hit by Flak, FTR; Flg Off D.K.Jenkinson rescued after six days in dinghy/Flt Sgt J.J.Rogers KiA
603 Sqn	Beaufighter X NE340 'H' left 0625, attacked a convoy off Mykonos, hit by Flak in starboard engine, ditched; Wt Off L.F.Sykes/Sgt W.H.Foxley rescued
39 Sqn	Beaufighter X NE249 'Z' left 1055 on day intruder from Lamia to Larissa, damaged by Flak, crash-landed on return in the Biferno Valley; Flt Sgt V.J.Kyrke-Smith/Flt Sgt S.S.Campbell safe
417 Sqn	Spitfire VIII JG248 left 1345 on armed recce crashed on landing 1345; Plt Off N.H.Gerrand severely injured DoI 26 July
32 Sqn	Spitfire Vc JK759 left 1400 on strafe, hit by Flak, pilot baled out 1445; Flg Off J.A.Wall safe

US Casualties

| 381st BS/310th BG | B-25J 43-27721 damaged by Flak; 1/Lt K.L.Gimson and five safe, tail gunner KiA |

3./SAGr 126	Ar 196A-5 WNr 0451 D1+?L shot down by Beaufighter E Mykonos during convoy escort 0815; Lt Hans-Georg Weigel/Uffz Karl Rathenow WiA	
	LKS reports one Ar 196 lost in combat	

Monday, 24 July 1944

Patrols by 241 Squadron were continued, and before long the squadron was again rewarded for its vigilance. Once more a pair of Bf 109s was engaged during the evening of the 24th, and this time one was shot down by Flg Off Walton, but in return the Bf 109s shot down Plt Off Bennett.

Having recovered from his wounds, suffered on 27 March, Wt Off Bobby Bunting had re-joined 93 Squadron in Corsica. The squadron's Spitfires were conducting last-light patrols over the French Riviera. During one of these, when over the sea to the south of Nice, Bunting intercepted an Me 410 with an escorting pair of FW 190s, one of which he managed to shoot down. He was the last pilot to become an ace when flying a Spitfire in the Mediterranean theatre.

A notable success was achieved by the Kittyhawk pilots of 239 Wing during the day when aircraft of 450 Squadron bombed a tank repair depot near Florence, the result of which was a massive explosion. It was subsequently reported that 55 vehicles had been destroyed in the blast including 15 tanks.

British Claims					
93 Sqn	Wt Off B.Bunting	Spitfire IX MA583	FW 190	5-7m S Nice	2012
241 Sqn	Flg Off J.E.Walton	Spitfire VIII JF333	Bf 109 Damaged	10-15m N Ancona	2040
British Casualties					
5 SAAF Sqn	Kittyhawk IV FX733 left 0930, hit by Flak, pilot baled out into Allied lines; Lt P.W.Bennee safe, returned next day				
241 Sqn	Spitfire VIII JG484 left 1950, shot down by Bf 109 about 6m off Fano 2055; Plt Off D.G.Bennett KiA				
6 Sqn	Hurricane IVKZ223 'J' left 1405, shot down by Flak lost attacking two schooners at Krk Island; Sgt G.Taylor KiA, found and buried by partisans				
17 SAAF Sqn	Ventura V JT893 missing from shipping recce off Spanish coast; Lt F.Youngleson and four MiA				
German Claims					
Flak			a/c		
1./NAGr 11	Obfw Lober		Spitfire	20km E Fano	2055
German Casualties					
5./TG 4	Ju 52/3m WNr 501162 G6+RN lost Tatoi-Gadurra, crashed neat Mykonos 2130; Lt Ernst-Rudolf Köhler and two KiA, one safe				
	LKS records a TacR FW 190 shot down in combat and one Ju 52/3m missing				

Tuesday, 25 July 1944

British Casualties	
4 SAAF Sqn	Spitfire IXc MH955 left 1755, shot down by Flak or struck the ground attacking motor transports 8km NW Pisa; Lt E.Williams KiA
13 (H) Sqn	Baltimore V FW333 'B'left 0630 to bomb steel works at Zenica, short on fuel, diverted to Vis, crash-landed; Flg Off P.Frangoyannis and three safe
US Casualties	
321st BG	B-25 damaged by Flak, crashed on landing, crew safe
German Casualties	
3./JG 4	Bf 109G-6 WNr 160756 Yellow 4 left Maniago and deserted to Allies landing at Caserta; Uffz René Darbois deserted
	LKS reports one Bf 109 lost

Italian ANR Claims					
3ª Sq, 1° Gr C	Ten Gian Mario Zuccarini	MC.205	P-47	Mantua-Modena	1100
2ª Sq, 1° Gr C	Serg Magg Tommaso Morabito	MC.205	P-47 Probable	Mantua-Modena	1100

Wednesday, 26 July 1944

Two pilots of 1435 Squadron were scrambled from Hal Far in the morning, intercepting a Ju 88 at the southeast of the island flying at 25,000 feet. Both pilots attacked repeatedly and after six passes the reconnaissance aircraft of 2.(F)/123 disintegrated.

The ANR pilots of 2° Gruppo were twice engaged in combat on this day. Firstly with 15th Air Force aircraft, and then with P-47s south of Piacenza, three of these being claimed shot down in flames by Cap Miani, Ten Drago and Serg Magg Ancillotti.

During a morning escort to 310th Bomb Group B-25s over northern Italy, the P-47s of the 86th Squadron, 79th Fighter Group were bounced by at least 11 Bf 109s. The Messerschmitt pilots seriously mishandled their opportunity and became involved in a long dogfight with the big Thunderbolts. The US pilots claimed six, these following an earlier sortie during which an FW 190 was claimed shot down and two fighters damaged, all without loss. Later in the day the group's other two squadrons, the 85th and 87th, strafed Valence airfield in southern France, claiming 13 aircraft destroyed on the ground, seven more probably and eight damaged. One P-47 was lost.

Flying a Bf 109G Serg Magg Rolando Ancillotti of the ANR 4ª Squadriglia, 2° Gruppo Caccia claimed a P-47 south of Piacenza on 26 July; his aircraft was then hit and he was forced to bale out.

British Claims

1435 Sqn	Flg Off F.W.T.Read	Spitfire IX MH704 'H'	} Ju 88	160m SE Malta	0800-0935
1435 Sqn	Plt Off S.C.Stephens	Spitfire IX EN518 'C'			

British Casualties

417 Sqn	Spitfire VIII JF874 left 0630 on armed recce of Route G, engine caught fire possibly due to Flak, pilot baled out; Flt Sgt J.T.MacLeod POW
237 Sqn	Spitfire IX MH553 left 0730 for a standing patrol N of Corsica, reported engine running rough 0750, a French merchant ship reported an aircraft exploding at this time and place, FTR; Sgt M.McKenzie KiA

US Claims

86th FS/79th FG	Maj George W.Ewing Jr	P-47D	FW 190	Ostiglia area	0845-1130
86th FS/79th FG	Lt Edward M.Walsh	P-47D	FW 190 Damaged	Ostiglia area	0845-1130
86th FS/79th FG	Lt Eugene O.Gilmore	P-47D	Bf 109 Probable	Ostiglia area	0845-1130
86th FS/79th FG	1/Lt Charles T.Hancock	P-47D	2 Bf 109s	Brescia area	1510-1800
86th FS/79th FG	1/Lt Charles T.Hancock	P-47D	Bf 109 Damaged	Brescia area	1510-1800
86th FS/79th FG	1/Lt Billy M.Head	P-47D	2 Bf 109s	Brescia area	1510-1800
86th FS/79th FG	2/Lt Richard W.Hilgard	P-47D	Bf 109	Brescia area	1510-1800
86th FS/79th FG	Lt Robert B.Steiner	P-47D	Bf 109	Brescia area	1510-1800

86th FS/79th FG	Lt Warren H.Tallent	P-47D		Bf 109 Damaged	Brescia area	1510-1800

US Casualties

87th FS/79th FG	P-47D 42-27962 'X90' shot down while strafing Valence airfield 1605; 1/Lt George W.Vaccaro KiA [7335]
448th FS/321st BG	B-25J 43-27631 left 0900 to bomb bridge at Verona, shot down by Flak 1047, crashed NE Verona; 1/Lt Wyndham E.Brown III and three POW, two returned [7065]
448th FS/321st BG	B-25J 43-4051 left 0900 to bomb bridge at Verona, shot down by Flak 1100, crashed nr Peschiera; 1/Lt Orin E.Olson and three KiA, three POW [7064]
448th BS/321st BG	B-25 43-27668 left 0900 to bomb bridge at Verona, damaged by Flak, landed at base; 2/Lt Walter W.Ready and four safe, one KiA

German Claims

Flak			Mitchell	S Brescia	1050
Flak			Mitchell	S Lake Garda	1100

German Casualties

2.(F)/123	Ju 88D-1 WNr 881543 4U+HK shot down by Spitfires E Malta; Uffz Hans Bräustedt and three KiA

Italian ANR Claims

NC* 2° Gr C	Cap Carlo Miani	Bf 109G	P-47	S Piacenza	1730
4ª Sq, 2° Gr C	Ten Ugo Drago	Bf 109G	P-47	S Piacenza	1730
4ª Sq, 2° Gr C	Serg Magg Rolando Ancillotti	Bf 109G	P-47	S Piacenza	1730
	*NC stands for 'Nucleo Comando' Italian equivalent to Staff Flight				

Italian ANR Casualties

4ª Sq, 2° Gr C	Bf 109G hit in combat, pilot baled out; Serg Magg Rolando Ancillotti safe

Wednesday-Thursday, 26/27 July 1944

British Casualties

13 Sqn	Baltimore V FW317 'Z' left 2217 for armed recce Florence-Bologna area, presumed shot down by Flak, crashed at Fiorenzuola 2318; Flt Lt D.D.Laird and three KiA
256 Sqn	Mosquito XIII MM533 scrambled 2310, pilot reported contact NW Corsica 2341, nothing further heard; Flt Sgt T.J.Tucker/Flt Sgt F.L.Smith KiA
256 Sqn	Mosquito XIII HK436 scrambled 2345, last plotted NE Corsica 0057; Wt Off R.O.Clee/Flg Off W.H.Hoskins KiA

German Casualties

1./NSGr 9	Ju 87D-5 WNr 141738 E8+EH lost u/k cause; Uffz Richard Schwobe/Gefr Günter Schlichting MiA
3./NSGr 9	Ju 87D D3+CK force-landed at Reggio 2300; Fw Hans-Joachim Deutsch/Obgfr Erwin Kaufmann WiA
3./NSGr 9	Ju 87D-3 WNr 212291 force-landed at Barco; Fw Otto Brinkmann safe/Obgfr Franz Till WiA
3./NSGr 9	Ju 87D-3 WNr 1369 hit a power line on landing; Obfw Otto Gieger/Obgfr Karl Gabauer KiA
	LKS reports one ground-attack a/c missing

Thursday, 27 July 1944

At Ancona two more days passed and then the 241 Squadron dawn patrol on the 27th also struck lucky; on this occasion both Messerschmitts failed to return, claimed by Flg Offs Monard and Hawkes. At dusk that same day another pair ventured over Ancona, but these were prepared for interception. When 241 Squadron's pilots attacked, the Germans turned on them and shot down Lt Goodman's Spitfire before escaping unscathed.

The pilots of 86th Fighter Group claimed three Ju 52/3ms destroyed on the ground for the loss of a Thunderbolt, whose pilot was rescued uninjured by a Walrus.

The 1° Gruppo Caccia now joined 2° Gruppo in opposing the Allied raids for a brief period, Magg Adriano Visconti leading his unit to attack a bomber formation.

British Claims

241 Sqn	Flg Off D.S.Monard	Spitfire VIII JF412 'N'	Bf 109	nr Loreo	0505-0620
241 Sqn	Flg Off W.D.C.Hawkes	Spitfire VIII JF357 'Z'	Bf 109	Marina di Ravenna	0505-0620
213 Sqn	Sqn Ldr S.R.Whiting	Mustang III FB322			
213 Sqn	Lt H.B.Helm	Mustang III HB921	Ju 52/3m on ground	Nis	0830-1150
213 Sqn	2/Lt S.W.Pienaar	Mustang III FB342			

British Casualties

241 Sqn	Spitfire VIII JF357 left 2000, shot down by Bf 109 N Ancona 2030; Lt A.E.Goodman POW
451 Sqn	Spitfire IX MJ941 engine failed on bomber escort, crash-landed S Bagnasco 1210; Flg Off J.H.Poate POW
213 Sqn	Mustang III FB318 left 0830, hit by Flak, crash-landed 3m NE Unosevac; Plt Off A.A.Smailes POW
2 SAAF Sqn	Spitfire LIXe MJ754 'R' hit by Flak, burst into flames 19km behind Axis lines near Veghereto; Lt D.J.S.Jansen van Rensberg baled out, evaded and returned 27 August

US Casualties

526th FS/86th FG	P-47D hit by Flak 1220, pilot baled out over sea 3-5m S Portofino; Lt Walter C.Taylor rescued by Walrus W2757 of 293 Sqn flown by Lt A.G.Riley
97th BS/47th BG	A-20B 41-3166 lost u/k cause, crashed off shore from Savona ca 1100; 1/Lt Oransdale R.Welch and one KiA, two POW [7463]

French Casualties

GB 1/22	Marauder damaged by Flak S Turin

German Claims

Flak		a/c	Portofino	
Flak		a/c Probable	Portofino	
1./NAGr 11	Fw Menzel	Spitfire	10km NW Fano	2030

German Casualties

2./NAGr 11	Bf 109G-6 damaged in combat 3km NE Lugo; Obfw Egon Keich WiA
SanFlugber. 7	Ju 52/3m destroyed by strafing
SanFlugber. 7	Fi 156 destroyed by strafing
	LKS records two TacR Bf 109s shot down in combat, one Ju 52/3m and two Fi 156s destroyed on ground

Thursday-Friday, 27/28 July 1944

Following its heavy losses early in July, NSGr 9 had been absent from the front during the middle of the month. Its aircraft began re-appearing over Ancona in some force towards the end of July and one was shot down by Flg Off Reynolds of 255 Squadron during the night of 27/28th.

British Claims

255 Sqn	Flg Off R.E.Reynolds/Plt Off M.Wingham	Beaufighter VIf	Ju 87	Ancona	2101-2345
600 Sqn	Flt Sgt L.W.Waitman/Flt Sgt J.G.Goss	Beaufighter VIf ND162 'E'	Ju 87	6m SE Colle Val d'Elsa	2245

British Casualties

13 Sqn	Baltimore V FW428 'X' left 2140 on armed recce Arezzo-Ravenna-Forlì, on return flight mistakenly fired on by Beaufighter pursuing a Ju 87, hit in port engine and hydraulics damaged, belly-landed 2255, written off; Lt C.A.Musto and three safe

US Casualties

414th NFS	Beaufighter KW164 lost over southern Spain 2200; 2/Lt William J.Barrons/Flt Off Harry E.Sharp KiA [7332]
86th BS/47th BG	A-20B 41-3374 lost u/k cause, crashed nr Bettola 0200; 1/Lt Fredric E.Durland and three KiA [8257]

German Casualties

1./NSGr 9	Ju 87D-5 WNr 140755 lost to night-fighter nr Cerasolo; Uffz Werner Waissnor KiA/Gefr Hermann Koch WiA
2./NSGr 9	Ju 87D WNr 110459 E8+DK lost to night-fighter nr Pontedera 2324; Uffz Kurt Urban/Uffz Gottfried Lässig MiA
2./NSGr 9	Ju 87D-5 WNr 2008 lost W Modena; Obgfr Franz Spörr/Flg Gustav Leumann WiA
	LKS reports three ground-attack a/c lost in combat

Friday, 28 July 1944

British Casualties

252 Sqn	Beaufighter X NE255 'C' attacked shipping 17m N Suda Bay 2257, hit by Flak, attempted to ditch 15-17m N Suda Bay, caught fire in the air and blew up when hit the sea; Flt Lt C.A.Wyatt/Flt Sgt R.A.Barrett KiA
242 Sqn	Spitfire IX MH321 'N' left 1810, crashed into the sea; Lt P.J.S.Louw MiA
40 SAAF Sqn	Spitfire Vc EF732 left 1145 on recce, hit by Flak, crash-landed at Impruneta 5m S Florence 1330; Lt J.H.du Plessis KiA
13 (H) Sqn	Baltimore V FW452 'D' left 0745 to bomb Sarajevo railway workshops, hit by Flak, crew baled NNE of target; Flt Lt A.Angelidis and one evaded, two POW

Friday-Saturday, 28/29 July 1944

38 Squadron's Flg Off L.Trigg, one of four crews on armed recce of the Aegean, found a merchant ship and an escort vessel just before midnight. He attacked the estimated 800-1,200-ton ship by dropping seven bombs

from 50 feet, presumably with delayed-action fuses, and claimed it sunk. Another of the squadron's crews failed to return from attempting to mine Lavrion in south-eastern Greece.

British Casualties	
55 Sqn	Baltimore V FW547 'F' left 0015 on armed recce to Borgo-Rimini-Florence area, crashed into Mt Cesana for u/k reason; Lt H.Thistleton and three KiA
38 Sqn	Wellington XIII MF186 'D' left 1926 to mine Lavrion and failed to return; Flg Off M.D.Zimmermann and five KiA

Saturday, 29 July 1944

The stay at Fermo for 241 Squadron was now already over, and on the 29th the squadron flew back to Falconara. No sooner had the aircraft landed and refuelled, however, then a scramble was ordered. Turkington and one other pilot got into the air to find a pair of reconnaissance Bf 109s once again. Turkington attacked at once as these approached, claiming one shot down and the other probably suffering the same fate. In ten days the squadron had claimed six confirmed, one probable and one damaged for two Spitfires shot down on a quiet front; it was a most notable feat. For his important part in this successful series of engagements, 'Paddy' Turkington received a Bar to his DFC and was at the same time posted to command 601 Squadron in 244 Wing.

The 526th Fighter Squadron of the 86th Group strafed airfields near Milan claiming 23 aircraft (including four-engined Ju 52/3ms, FW 190s and Bf 109s) destroyed and more than 10 damaged.

British Claims					
9 SAAF Sqn	Lt Joubert	Spitfire IX LZ994 'V' ⎱	Ju 88	40m W Limassol, Cyprus	1608-1738
9 SAAF Sqn	Lt A.B.Reteif	Spitfire IX MA257 'X' ⎰			
241 Sqn	Flt Lt R.W.Turkington	Spitfire VIII JF351 'U'	Bf 109	20m NE Rimini airfield	2020-2100
241 Sqn	Flt Lt R.W.Turkington	Spitfire VIII JF351 'U'	Bf 109 Probable	10-12m NE Pesaro	2020-2100
British Casualties					
2 SAAF Sqn	Spitfire IX bombing motor transports N Prato, hit by Flak, belly-landed at base Cat II damage; Lt J.Meintjies safe				
2 SAAF Sqn	Spitfire IX left 1830 to attack gun positions nr Subiaco, damaged by Flak Cat II; Lt Powell safe				
US Casualties					
65th FS/57th FG	P-47D 42-75745 lost; 2/Lt Joseph T.Markham KiA				
German Casualties					
1./NAGr 11	Bf 109G-6 WNr 162050 Black 6 shot down by Spitfire 30km E Rimini; Lt Wilhelm Metz MiA				
2./NAGr 13	Bf 109G WNr 200628 on recce mission to Corsica, engine failed; Ofhr Bruno-Georg Braun POW				
3.(F)/33	Ju 188F-1 8H+EL attacked by Spitfire over Cephalonia, FTR; Lt Kaspar Kähn and three rescued				
	LKS reports one Ju 188 missing, one Bf 109 lost and one damaged in combat				
Italian ANR Casualties					
Gr Aerosil	4 S.79s and a Cant.Z.1018 destroyed on the ground at Lonate Pozzolo				

Saturday-Sunday, 29/30 July 1944

British Claims					
600 Sqn	Flt Lt D.A.Thompson/Flg Off G.Beaumont	Beaufighter VIf MM876 'X'	Ju 87	Sarsina, SE Florence	2340
German Casualties					
3.(F)/33	Ju 188F-1 WNr 280070 8H+IL lost S Cyprus u/k reason; Uffz Eberhard Hübner and three MiA				

Sunday, 30 July 1944

A dozen Spitfires of 232 Squadron escorted B-26s of the 17th Bomb Group on a morning raid; the bombers made three passes over the target at 1027 but did not bomb for unknown reasons. They then encountered ANR fighters near Torriglia at 1030 in an attack that lasted 10 minutes. 2/Lt Wilcox's Marauder was shot up sufficiently that it later crash-landed at its base on Corsica with one crew member wounded. 1° Gruppo had sent up 18 MC.205s at 0955 followed soon after by 19 Bf 109s from 2° Gruppo both formations engaging the 17th BG and 232 Squadron in the area north of Genoa from 1030. A "Boston" was claimed collectively by pilots of 1° Gruppo. Five Marauders lagged behind the formation and 232 Squadron's Blue Section attacked a formation of 12 Bf 109s that were attacking these bombers; this was followed immediately by a clash with six Fiat G.55s in the Novi Ligure-Piacenza area. In the fight with 232 Squadron, Ten Beretta claimed a Spitfire

shot down; one of the 232 Squadron aircraft was indeed damaged by a cannon hit in the tail unit. The aircraft of Serg Magg Morabito was hit and claimed damaged by Wt Off McCann who identified it as a Fiat G.55. In fact it was a Macchi MC.205 that was fatally damaged and crashed near Sampierdarena killing the pilot.

The ANR pilots of 2° Gruppo made no claims in this action, but lost two Messerschmitts, one of which was shot down in flames near Torriglia by the 17th Bomb Group who reported one enemy aircraft believed damaged but last seen going down in flames, with the loss of M.llo Giuseppe Desideri. Serg Sergio Mazzi was shot down near Bobbio by Flg Off True and baled out safely but was captured by partisans. During the month of July alone 2° Gruppo had lost nine pilots in action.

Twelve P-47s from the 57th Fighter Group escorted 36 B-25s from the 310th Bomb Group to attack a bridge around midday but one Thunderbolt flown by 2/Lt Hain of the 66th Squadron was hit by Flak, his aircraft blowing up as he tried to make a belly-landing at 1215.

During a fight with ANR fighters on 30 July Wt Off Eddie McCann of 232 Squadron claimed a G.55 damaged. However, he appears to have actually destroyed an MC.205 of 1° Gruppo Caccia.

British Claims

232 Sqn	Plt Off L.True	Spitfire IX BS309 'A'	Bf 109	N Genoa	1030-1040
232 Sqn	Wt Off E.A.McCann	Spitfire IX MK296 'V'	G.55 Damaged	N Genoa	1030-1040

US Casualties

34th BS/17th BG	B-26 '04' damaged by enemy aircraft, crash-landed at Corsica; 2/Lt C.I.Wilcox and five safe, one WiA
66th FS/57th FG	P-47D 42-26373 hit by Flak, belly-landed nr Portalbera but blew up 1215; 2/Lt Calvin S.Hain Jr KiA [7333]

German Claims

Flak			a/c	Genoa	1200

German Casualties

1./Kroat Legion	Do 17Z-5 WNr 2899 Z8+AH deserted to Allies, crash-landed nr Cerignola; Lt Albeiu Vouk and four safe
	LKS reports one Do 17 and one Bf 109 missing, one Bf 109 lost in combat

Italian ANR Claims

1° Gr C	Ten Alessandro Beretta	MC.205	Spitfire	Novi Ligure-La Spezia	1030
1° Gr C	unstated	MC.205	Boston	Novi Ligure-La Spezia	1030

Italian ANR Casualties

2ª Sq, 1° Gr C	MC.205 hit in combat, crashed nr Sampierdarena; Serg Magg Tommaso Morabito KiA
4ª Sq, 2° Gr C	Bf 109G crashed nr Bobbio; Serg Sergio Mazzi baled out, captured by partisans
6ª Sq, 2° Gr C	Bf 109G crashed nr Torriglia; M.llo Giuseppe Desideri KiA

Sunday-Monday, 30/31 July 1944

Flg Off Bretherton chased a Ju 88 into the sea, last seen taking violent evasive action from 80 feet behind, at 15 feet above sea level, radar plot disappeared and wreckage was seen.

British Claims

255 Sqn	Flg Off B.A.Bretherton/Flt Lt W.T.Cunningham	Beaufighter VIf KW190 'A'	Ju 88	25m NW Ancona	0200-0440

Monday, 31 July 1944

The German navy reported that during July its marine Flak units had shot down 40 Allied aircraft in, or near, Italy. One of the French casualties on this date, missing in action, was the famous writer Antoine de Saint-Exupéry, author of *The Little Prince*.

A Cant.Z.1007bis of the Italian Co-Belligerent Air Force displaying the new Italian roundels, though the black rings of the previous fascist insignia are still visible. These aircraft were mainly employed on supply-dropping missions as on 31 July when one was lost over Montenegro.

British Claims					
213 Sqn	2/Lt S.W.Pienaar	Mustang III FB335 'S'	} S.79	5m S Otocac	0600-0746
213 Sqn	Flt Lt C.S.Vos	Mustang III FB328 'V'			

British Casualties
213 Sqn	Mustang III HB916 shot down by Flak 9m W Rajic 0950; Flg Off R.Anthony MiA

US Casualties
522nd FS/27th FBG	P-47D 42-26445 *Darling Jo* shot down by Flak 3m NW Castano Primo 1100, crashed SW Gallarate a/d; Flt Off Rafael Y.Mylly KiA [11400]

French Casualties
GC 2/3	P-47D left 0800, shot down by Flak nr Amarins (Vaucluse), pilot baled but parachute did not open; Cne Jallier (CO 5eme Esc) KiA
GR 2/33	F-5B 42-68273 left 0840, lost at sea off Toulon, probably shot down by heavy Flak while crossing the coast; Cdt Antoine de Saint-Exupéry MiA

Italian Co-Belligerent Casualties
190ª Sq, 88° Gr	Cant.Z.1007 failed to return from supply-dropping mission to Kolasin; pilot Serg Magg Francesco Genitali, copilot Serg Magg Rolando Vitelli and three MiA

German Claims	
Flak	2 a/c

German Casualties
5./TG 1	S.82 WNr 61829 crashed during transfer flight nr Vicenza 1600; Uffz Werner Schmuhl and six KiA
II./TG 1	3 Ju 52/3ms destroyed at Gallarate by strafing
1./KG 26	Ju 88A-17 WNr 550911 3Z+BH ditched 20km S Marseille; two safe, two WiA
8./KG 26	Ju 88A-17 WNr 550899 1H+ES ran out of fuel, ditched off coast at Beziers; pilot and two rescued, one KiA
8./KG 26	Ju 88A-17 WNr 801595 1H+FT missing off Cap Corbelin; Uffz Karl-Heinz Ugries and three MiA
	LKS reports three Ju 88s missing, three Ju 52/3ms and three S.82s destroyed on ground

Italian ANR Casualties
Gr Aerosil	S.79 III MM 21746 'B1-00' en route to Eleusis, shot down near Agram 0700; pilot Ten Francesco Pandolfo baled out WiA, copilot M.llo Sesto Moschi, three crew and German liaison officer Hptm Helferich KiA
Gr Aerosil	S.79 III B2-04 crash-landed at Villafranca; Ten Gianfranco Neri and crew safe

July into August

Operations were not always without loss and the Flak in the Po Valley was becoming increasingly fierce. The 79th Fighter Group lost three P-47s and their pilots during July for example, while on the 17th 451 Squadron, one of the units of 251 Wing, saw their commanding officer, Sqn Ldr W.W.B.Gale, shot down when reconnoitring a bridge over the Arno.

At this time operations around Florence were getting well underway as the main part of DAF began its attacks. Since the withdrawal of units for Operation Dragoon, the Allies were left with only 21 effective divisions in Italy, and these were faced by 26 German and six Italian Fascist divisions in strong defensive positions. The Allies were strong in armour and weak in infantry due to the manpower demands of other fronts, as stated earlier, but the mountainous nature of the central Italian terrain prevented the exploitation of the armoured advantage.

An unusual event late in July was a visit by HM King George VI to several bases during a tour of inspection of the Italian front. Travelling under the pseudonym of General Collingwood, he was escorted by Spitfires of 1 SAAF Squadron in an Avro York aircraft to Naples on the 23rd. Next day he went aboard a Dakota and was again escorted by the South Africans to Viterbo. On the 27th he arrived at Foiano to inspect 7 SAAF Wing. He also visited 239 Wing, 208 Squadron at Castiglione and A Flight of 318 Squadron on this date. Immediately after this event, 208 was on the move forward again flying up to Malignano, near Siena.

A number of other events occurring within DAF at this time may be swiftly summarized. On 19 July Sqn Ldr G.B.Johns, DFC, took over from Sqn Ldr Jandrell as commanding officer of 260 Squadron, while next day Sqn Ldr L.N.Ahern, DFC, 112 Squadron's commander ended his tour and was replaced by another experienced fighter-bomber pilot, Sqn Ldr A.P.Q.Bluett, DFC. A few days later 239 Wing was taken over by Grp Capt Brian Eaton, DSO, DFC, an Australian pilot who had previously served with distinction with 3 RAAF Squadron.

In 244 Wing 601 Squadron's commander, Sqn Ldr J.H.Nicholls, DFC, ended his second tour and was replaced by Sqn Ldr Turkington who came from 241 Squadron at Falconara as has just been related. On 23 July 92 Squadron welcomed Plt Off E.S.Doherty, DFM, who arrived from 242 Squadron in Corsica, having enjoyed a most distinguished career as a fighter pilot with his previous unit. Four days later Flg Off G.R.S.McKay was posted to 145 Squadron from 601 Squadron to become a flight commander, while at the same time Flg Off R.J.Mackenzie was posted the other way to lead one of 601's flights. The wing was joined by two new units at this time; 87 and 185 Squadrons had both been serving in Italy as part of Coastal Air Force in the Foggia area. Now both were advised that they were to join DAF, and on the 23rd 87's pilots flew to Perugia, moving on to Falconara to fly their first DAF mission on the 25th, an escort to Marauders. Both these units were at this stage equipped with Spitfire Vs.

Towards the end of July 3 SAAF Squadron had arrived in Italy from Egypt and was ordered to join 7 SAAF Wing at once, commencing fighter-bomber operations with its Spitfire Vs on arrival. Within this wing Maj 'Piggy' Boyle ended his tour with 4 SAAF Squadron on the 26th, Maj J.H.Faure, DFC, arriving to take over early in August. Among the tactical reconnaissance units, while the US 111th Squadron had moved to Corsica in mid-July, a detachment of its P-51s still remained in Italy for the time being, based at Santa Maria. On 1 August 40 SAAF Squadron moved to Malignano where a few days later Lt Col R.H.Rogers, DFC, arrived to take over command from Lt Col Nel.

The men of 208 Squadron give 'three cheers' to King George VI during his visit to Castiglione on 27 July.

Above: During the mid-summer of 1944 the leader of 239 Wing, Lt Col Laurie Wilmot SAAF, used Mustang III FB260 decoratively wearing his initials as his personal mount. It also carried his rank pennant beneath the cockpit. Right: Lt Col Laurie Wilmot (right) the 239 Wing leader discusses a sortie with Flt Lt Ken Richards of 3 RAAF Squadron.

On 4 August 8th Army forces took the southern part of Florence, South African armoured forces being first into the city; they were soon followed by elements of 5th Army. With the Poles and Co-Belligerent Italian troops now well-entrenched at Ancona, a short lull descended on the whole front while the Allies began re-grouping for the next assault. This was intended to thrust across the Arno and drive on towards the formidable defences which stretched across the country roughly from Pisa to Rimini, 20 miles to the north.

This line had still been unfinished at the time of the fall of Rome, and it was to allow works here to progress that Kesselring had fought his series of delaying actions at Lake Trasimeno, Arezzo and Florence. It was now his intention to hold the Allies on this, the Gothic Line, until winter brought an effective end to the present advance.

Tuesday, 1 August 1944

The first fortnight of August consisted of intensive patrols over southern France by RAF Spitfires in preparation for the landings planned for the 15th of the month.

Six MC.205s and six G.55s of 1° Gruppo took off at 0950 to intercept medium bombers and escorts over Mantua-Verona area; pilots engaged Bostons and P-47s and claimed one twin-engined bomber destroyed and a fighter damaged.

Four rocket-armed Beaufighters from 252 Squadron left Berka on an anti-shipping recce of the west coast of Greece. This mission resulted in a pair of brutal encounters between the aircraft and two F boats. On reaching the Greek coast they split into two pairs as prearranged. The leader Sqn Ldr I. B.Butler/Flt Sgt I.P.Cowl (in NR254 'B') with Wt Off C.G.Davis /Sgt G.N.Waller (in NT895 'H') proceeded south to Oxia Island, on the northern side of the entry into the Gulf of Patras, where they sighted two F boats and attacked. Butler's attack failed due to the fact that the F boat gained the shelter of high ground on the coast. He then circled the site, in time to see Davis who had attacked the other F boat, ditch. Butler then saw a dinghy with one man in it headed for the shore with another man swimming behind. Flak was intense throughout and Butler who had been hit in the port wing and tail returned to base. Meanwhile Flg Off J.A.T.Macintosh/Plt Off R.H.Alderton (in LZ135 'R') and Plt Off J.D.Clark/Flt Lt E.A.C.Young (in LZ530 'K') on hearing of the other pair's attack returned to the Oxia area and saw a dinghy now with two men in it, still heading for land and one F boat much closer to the shore. They attacked. Macintosh went in first firing two rockets and his cannon but was hit by Flak and damaged in the starboard wing root. Plt Off Clark then attacked but was also hit by Flak, reporting he was damaged and would head for Italy. Macintosh joined up and began to escort Clark towards Italy but soon after at 0900 about 25 miles to the south-west Clark's Beaufighter dived into the sea killing the Canadian pilot and his observer. When Davis and Waller in their dinghy eventually reached the coast, Davis managed to evade but Waller was captured.

British Casualties					
145 Sqn	Spitfire VIII JF578 'F' left 0635, hit by Flak San Lorenzo SW Bologna; Lt J.M.G.Anderson safe with partisans, returned on 1 October				
2 SAAF Sqn	Spitfire IXc MK485 'H' left 0630 to bomb a bridge near Bologna, hit by heavy Flak in coolant system 20m N of Florence, pilot baled out but not seen to land due to cloud; Lt J.H.Meintjies POW				
112 Sqn	Mustang III FB317 'T' left 1535 on dive-bombing mission, engine cut on take-off, crashed; Lt A.H.Jones KiA				
252 Sqn	Beaufighter X NT895 'H' left 0535 from Berka on recce of west coast of Greece, attacked F boats S Oxia in Gulf of Patras 0836, shot down by Flak, ditched; Wt Off C.G.Davis evaded/Sgt G.N.Waller POW				
252 Sqn	Beaufighter X LZ530 'K' left 0535 from Berka on recce of west coast of Greece, attacked F boat off Oxia, damaged by Flak, dived into the sea 0900; Plt Off J.D.Clark/Flt Lt E.A.C.Young KiA				
US Casualties					
87th FS/79th FG	P-47D 42-27953 shot down by Flak nr Villafranca 1200; 1/Lt Noel Sonnichsen KiA [7328]				
German Claims					
Flak			Thunderbolt		
Italian ANR Claims					
1° Gr C	unstated pilots	MC.205/G.55	Boston	Mantua-Verona	0950-
1° Gr C	unstated pilots	MC.205/G.55	P-47 Damaged	Mantua-Verona	0950-
Italian ANR Casualties					
3ª Sq, 1° Gr C	G.55 shot down; Serg Domenico Balduzzo baled out, WiA				

Tuesday-Wednesday, 1/2 August 1944

Flt Sgt Roberts of 256 Squadron obtained a success when scrambled from Alghero, shooting down a reconnaissance Ju 88. He had only been on the squadron for three days, having been one of four crews posted in from 108 Squadron in the general restructuring and moving of night-fighter squadrons occurring at this time. The remaining African-based elements of 256 Squadron were currently in transit to Alghero.

British Claims					
600 Sqn	Flt Lt D.A.Thompson/Flg Off G.Beaumont	Beaufighter VIf MM876 'X'	Ju 87	15-20m NW Arezzo	2213
600 Sqn	Flt Lt D.A.Thompson/Flg Off G.Beaumont	Beaufighter VIf MM876 'X'	Ju 87 Damaged	NE Florence	2255
256 Sqn	Flt Sgt R Roberts/Flt Sgt J.R.Hebdige	Mosquito XII HK435	Ju 88	N Algiers	0140
255 Sqn	Flg Off R.E.Reynolds/Plt Off M.A.Wingham	Beaufighter VIf	Ju 88	15m NE Ancona	0335-0445

When attacking an F boat off the coast of Greece on 1 August this 252 Squadron Beaufighter X, NT895 'H', was hit by Flak and forced to ditch.

British Casualties

18 Sqn	Boston III Z2241 left 2241 to bomb targets of opportunity in the Po Valley, attacked motor transport at Polesella 0015, damaged by Flak, landed safely at base, damaged Cat II; Plt Off H.Cole-Baker and three safe

US Claims

417th NFS	2/Lt Lloyd G.Moldrew/Flt Off Ed H.Bowman	Beaufighter VIf	Ju 88 Damaged	Chanoines airfield	2338

German Casualties

6.(F)/122	Ju 88A-4 WNr 300219 F6+NP lost on night recce over the Adriatic to Ancona area; Uffz Franz Wentzlaff and crew MiA
3./NSGr 9	Ju 87D-3 WNr 432614 lost SE Florence; Fw Werner Hensel returned/Uffz Heinrich Laufenberg KiA
8./KG 26	Ju 88A-17 WNr 801349 3Z+LP 100% lost nr Cap Corbellin on night raid; Lt Fritz Richert and three MiA
13./TG 3	S.82 WNr 60665 crashed east of Lonate a/f at Busto Arsizio, reason unknown; Obfw Robert Matlock and two WiA
	LKS reports two Ju 88s and two ground-attack a/c missing

Wednesday, 2 August 1944

British Casualties

241 Sqn	Spitfire VIII JF403 left 0530 on shipping recce, engine failure or Flak at River Po mouth, crash-landed; Plt Off J.L.Herd MiA
154 Sqn	Spitfire IX MK739 left 1725, fired on by US P-47s, force-landed 1900; Wt Off W.Wright safe
260 Sqn	Mustang III FB285 left 1120 to bomb bridge N Florence, hit by Flak, pilot baled out; Capt J.B.Davis POW

US Casualties

85th FS/79th FG	P-47D 42-26814 shot down by Flak nr Orio al Serio 1135; 2/Lt Vincent I.Millican KiA [12208]
66th FS/57th FG	P-47D 42-26374 crashed 1000; 2/Lt Gordon H.Jones KiA [7324]

French Casualties

GC 2/7	Spitfire IX MA254 left 1325 on scramble from Ajaccio, crashed into the sea 1355; Sous Lt Laurent KiA

German Claims

Flak	Jabo a/c	La Spezia
Flak	Jabo a/c	Palmaria-S La Spezia
Marine Flak	4-engined a/c	Venice

Italian ANR Casualties

2ª Sq, 1° Gr C	G.55 shot down by friendly fire, crashed nr Lonigo; Serg Magg Paolo Cimatti KiA

Wednesday-Thursday, 2/3 August 1944

British Claims

600 Sqn	Plt Off N.L.Jefferson/Plt Off E.Spencer	Beaufighter VIf MM945 'J'	Ju 87	5-10m SW Arezzo	2235
600 Sqn	Wt Off R.L.Crooks/Sgt R.Charles	Beaufighter VIf V8896 'A'	Ju 87	15m NE Pisa	0300

British Casualties

18 Sqn	Boston III HK871 'M' left 0157 on armed recce of Po Valley, crashed and exploded at Polesella; Flt Lt J.D.R.B.Carruthers and three KiA
55 Sqn	Baltimore V FW553 'J' left on armed shipping recce off River Po mouth; Flt Sgt J.Dean and three KiA

US Claims

417th NFS	1/Lt William R.Williamson/2/Lt Dan B.Cordell	Beaufighter VIf	Ju 188	27m NW Cap Corse	0110

German Casualties

3./NSGr 9	Ju 87D-3 WNr 331120 E8+PK shot down by night-fighter SW Arezzo 0300; Obfw Hans Wolfsen/Gefr Hans Wilk MiA
1./NSGr 9	Ju 87D-5 WNr 131613 E8+DH shot down SW Arezzo 2235; Uffz Herbert Fietz/Fw Karl Razinski MiA
Stab I./NSGr 9	Ju 87D-5 WNr 131150 E8+BB shot down nr Città di Castello 2244; Uffz Helmut Krüger/Obgfr Günter Tschirch MiA
6.(F)/122	Ju 88D-1 WNr 430145 F6+CP lost off Cap Corse 2317; Uffz Rudolf Beck and three MiA
4.(F)/122	Ju 88T-1 WNr 43075 F6+OM crashed at Vercelli; Uffz Rudolf Klemm KiA, three safe
	LKS reports two Ju 88s and three ground-attack a/c missing

Thursday, 3 August 1944

The Hurricanes on 6 Squadron were active overnight though that flown by Flt Lt Walker was hit and he baled out. He got ashore on the island of Galoila where he survived for four days before again being picked up by a Catalina. On being hauled aboard the crewman exclaimed: "Not you again!" It was the same crew as had come to his aid a fortnight earlier.

British Claims

72 Sqn	Flt Lt E.Galitzine	Spitfire IX MM763 }			
72 Sqn	Lt K.D.Davidson	Spitfire IX MK171 }	Do 24	taking off Lake Berre	1155

British Casualties

249 Sqn	Spitfire Vc ER718 left 1000 to bomb bridge N of Sarande, hit by Flak, pilot baled out 10m W Himare 1120; Flg Off P.F.Noble rescued by Greek destroyer
40 SAAF Sqn	Spitfire IX MH975 left 1640 on Arty recce, shot down by Flak Montelupo-Signa area W Florence; Lt N.G.Boys KiA
6 Sqn	Hurricane IV KX803 'E' left 2145 on night mission to attack targets at Cres Island, sent Mayday call, pilot baled out off Galoila Island, Yugoslavia; F/Lt A.E.Walker rescued by a US 1 ERS OA-10 Catalina

US Casualties

85th FS/79th FG	P-47D shot down by Flak 1705; 2/Lt James L.Greene KiA
523rd FS/27th FBG	P-47D 42-28131 shot down by Flak 1055, crashed 1.8km S Ghedi a/d; 2/Lt Claude E.Belt KiA [7330]

Italian Co-Belligerent Casualties

92ª Sq, 21° Gr, 51° St	MC.205 MM 92178 '21-18' shot down by Flak nr Poljice, pilot baled out; Serg Magg Filippo Baldin helped by partisans, returned

German Claims

Flak Legion San Marco	Leg Guido Pizzato		e/a	nr Turkovici

Thursday-Friday, 3/4 August 1944

British Claims

600 Sqn	Flg Off A.MacDonald/Sgt J.Towell	Beaufighter VIf ND162 'E'	Ju 87	SW Arezzo	2245
255 Sqn	Flg Off B.A.Bretherton/Flt Lt W.T.Cunningham	Beaufighter VIf	Ju 88	NW Ancona	2355-0235

British Casualties

38 Sqn	Wellington XIII MF153 left 2030 on armed recce of Aegean Sea, shot down by ships' Flak, crashed on Kea Island 0047; Plt Off E.T.Hughes and four KiA, one POW
13 Sqn	Baltimore V FW292 'Y' left 2153 on armed recce Borgo Pace-Fano-Rimini-Forlì and River Po mouth, hit by 40mm fire, landed safely, Cat II damaged; Capt J.H.G.Klompie and three safe

German Claims

Ships' Flak		a/c	N Kea

Friday, 4 August 1944

A Fiat test pilot, M.llo Serafino Agostini, carrying Ten Francesco Gentile, an Allied agent parachuted behind German lines two months earlier, flew a brand-new G.55 (MM 91150) from Mirafiori airfield, near Turin, to Piombino, defecting to the Allies. It was the first aircraft to this type falling intact into Allied hands.

Flown by Lt E.V.Woods of 24 SAAF Squadron, Marauder 'G' bombs the Cavarzere bridge near Rovigo on 4 August.

British Casualties

213 Sqn   Mustang III FB322 left 0900, shot down by Flak 1m NNW Ilovice 1015; 2/Lt S.W.Pienaar KiA

43 Sqn   Spitfire IX MH929 left 0915 on B-26 escort, last seen climbing into cloud over Calvi Bay 0920; Flt Lt R.V.Griffiths MiA

Friday-Saturday, 4/5 August 1944

On that night, eight S.79s of Gruppo Aerosiluranti 'Buscaglia' of Italian ANR took off from Eleusis airfield for a mission against an Allied convoy of 30 merchant ships escorted by four warships NW of Tolemaide (today

Ad Dirsyah, Libya). Due to the bad weather, only three S.79s, flown by Tens Adriano Merani, Luigi Morselli and Domenico De Lieto, found and attacked the convoy, claiming three hits on the merchant ship *Samsylarna* (7,210 tons) which sank.

Italian ANR Casualties	
Gruppo Aerosil	S.79 left to attack convoy off Libya, lost near Crete on return; pilot M.llo Enrico Jasinski, copilot Serg Magg Luigi Bernardi and three MiA
Gruppo Aerosil	S.79 MM 22293 'B2-09' left to attack convoy off Libya, ditched out of fuel near Argos; pilot Ten Marcello Perina, copilot Ten Gianfranco Neri and three safe

Saturday, 5 August 1944

Allied troops entered the city of Florence but to the north across the rugged mountains of northern Italy the enemy had established the Gothic Line which was clearly going to be difficult to break.

Two pilots of 241 Squadron were airborne searching for a German pilot reported to have ditched off Rimini. However, almost at once Sgt Etchells' aircraft became uncontrollable and he was obliged to ditch and get into his dinghy about nine miles north of Pesaro, close to the German pilot. A Walrus of 293 Squadron was sent out at once finding Etchells (but not the German). However, the sea was rough and the Walrus pilot decided that he should try and taxi his aircraft across the Adriatic. Cover to the rescue was undertaken by 87 Squadron based at Falconara but by now the Walrus had run aground and the pilot of the Spitfire was ordered to strafe and destroy the little amphibian. At this stage Etchells decided to try and swim but, unable to do the same, the crew members of the Walrus remained where they were and became POWs; Etchells, however, was intercepted by a high-speed launch and returned safely to Italy.

While these rescue attempts were underway a Wellington of 221 Squadron had taken off at 0930 searching for a submarine reported about 25km west of Dhermi on the Albanian coast. At 1500 hours two Bf 109s appeared from behind hills to the east: one of these attacked from below and to the starboard, the other from the port side. The first burst of fire hit the port engine causing it to seize up. The Wellington pilot, Sgt Bray, headed his aircraft away and made for Brindisi on one engine where on landing at 1611 he discovered that the tyres had been hit and consequently the undercarriage collapsed. Interestingly, 221 Squadron made no report of this although a 14 Squadron Marauder arrived on the scene during the attack causing the Messerschmitts to depart. (Nineteen days later Bray and his crew failed to return from a sortie, never to be traced.)

British Casualties	
112 Sqn	Mustang III FB296 'R' left 1750, shot down by Flak SE Florence 1820; Sgt K.R.Mann KiA
4 SAAF Sqn	Spitfire IX MH537 left 0615 on weather recce Argenta-Ravina-Rimini area, met 20mm Flak fire, disappeared 0730; Lt B.D.Jenkins KiA
241 Sqn	Spitfire VIII JF351 left 0615, reported aircraft uncontrollable, ditched, got into dinghy 9m N Pesaro ca 0700; Sgt K.Etchells rescued by Walrus, then by HSL
293 Sqn	Walrus L2223 landed at 0900 to rescue 241 Sqn pilot, sea too rough to take off, became beached, strafed and destroyed by 87 Sqn; Sgt P.F.Lydford/Wt Off J.A.Slater POW
40 SAAF Sqn	Spitfire Vc left 1420 shot down by Flak NW Florence; Lt W.R.Sobey baled out, POW
German Casualties	
4.(F)/122	Ju 88D-1 WNr 430796 F6+HM crashed 10km E Ravenna; Lt Josef Mader and three KiA
	LKS reports one Ju 88 missing, four S.82s destroyed and two damaged on ground

Saturday-Sunday, 5/6 August 1944

British Casualties				
17 SAAF Sqn	Ventura GRV FP662 'T' left 2231, lost presumed to bad weather on shipping sweep between Genoa and Via Reggio, contact lost 0330; Lt J.M.Mathieson and four MiA			
272 Sqn	Beaufighter X NE492 'D' left 0025, attacked convoy off Cap Mele, on return trip engine failed, crashed at base; Flg Off C.L.Reynolds/Flt Sgt A.Davies safe			
US Claims				
414th NFS	2/Lt Roy E.Patten/Capt John E.Patterson	Beaufighter VIf	Ju 88	0155
German Claims				
Marine Flak			a/c	over convoy

German Casualties	
Stab/KG 26	Ju 88A-17 WNr 550483 3Z+DP shot down 0130 by Beaufighter, ditched; Uffz Walter Pabst MiA, three POW

Sunday, 6 August 1944

Thirty-six B-25Js of 310th Bomb Group carried out their first bombing mission to southern France, their target being a railway bridge at Avignon; at least three bombers suffered damages on this sortie. As Nick Beale quotes on his remarkable website ghostbombers.com:

> "The imminence of Allied landings brought the diversion of 12th Air Force units from Italian to French targets and so JGr 200 found itself in action against tactical bombers. The Gruppe's first operation of this day was a scramble by ten Bf 109s to intercept a formation of B-25s which were attacking the bridge at Avignon. While part of the German formation reported combat with escorting fighters, three Messerschmitts got through to the Mitchells. […] No claims appear have been made on either side, but at 0932 Allied Signal Intelligence heard a fighter force-landing at base with engine trouble."

Flt Lt Don McBurnie in MK444 led a sweep of 451 Squadron over the Toulon-Marseille area and gave cover to medium bombers hitting the Rhône bridges; he was awarded a DFC soon afterwards at the end of his tour, as was Flg Off Bray.

US Casualties			
381st BS/310th BG	B-25J 43-3995 on bombing mission to Avignon, damaged by Bf 109; 1/Lt G.K.McDonald and five safe		
381st BS/310th BG	B-25J 43-27253 on bombing mission to Avignon, damaged by Flak/Bf 109; landed safely at Calvi; 2/Lt O.L.J.Twedt and four safe, copilot 2/Lt R.C.Eichten WiA		
381st BS/310th BG	B-25J 43-4034 on bombing mission to Avignon, damaged by Bf 109; landed safely at Calvi; 2/Lt S.J.Larkin, and five safe		
French Casualties			
GC 2/3	P-47D strafed Les Milles, hit by ground fire; Lt de Chanterac WiA, POW		
German Claims			
Flak	Les Milles	Jabo a/c	over a/f

Sunday-Monday, 6/7 August 1944

British Casualties			
272 Sqn	Beaufighter X NE552 'O' left 0217 on recce of coast Genoa to Monaco, FTR; Sqn Ldr J.B.Coates/Flt Sgt M.H.Rogers KiA		
German Claims			
Flak		a/c	over convoy
Flak		a/c Probable	over convoy

Monday, 7 August 1944

From 0925, Plan de Dieu and Caritat airfields were shot up by Thunderbolts of the 79th Fighter Group, which claimed a He 111 and a Ju 52/3m destroyed; in fact they appear to have inflicted slight damage on two Ju 88s and wounded one man of the airfield's Flak crews.

Twelve Bf 109s from JGr 200 were scrambled from 0846-0851 in response to a raid by B-25s of the 310th Bomb Group on the rail bridge at Avignon. All the Messerschmitts took off from Les Milles: four from 1.Staffel, three from 2. and five from 3., with the interception taking place at 0935. The 86th Fighter Group was escorting the bombers and the 527th Squadron's diary reported:

> "Excitement! On an escort mission today – B-25s – sixteen Mes attacked the bombers but were driven off without breaking up their formation. Lts Mauck and Saunders each got strikes on the 'Jerrys', each claiming one damaged."

The bombers claimed damage to a Bf 109 and the 525th Fighter Squadron's pilots did also engage, claiming one probable and two damaged near Cheval Blanc, 17km north of Salon. Radio talk revealed to Allied Signals Intelligence that at 0940 (local time) "an aircraft was shot down; its nationality could not be determined". At 1000 hours, Thunderbolts of the 522nd Fighter Squadron sighted a Bf 109 which they chased into the ground 4.5km north-east of Salon en Provence, without firing a shot; the victory was awarded to the squadron collectively.

The 1./JGr. 200 lost two Bf 109 G-6s that day: its Staffelkapitän, Hptm Georg Seckel baled out with injuries that put him in hospital for the next two weeks; Uffz Walter Cöster (who had survived being shot down on 14 July) was killed. It was probably Cöster's demise that Uffz Walter Lang recalled while in captivity:

"One fellow who had just escaped from the partisans and come back to the Staffel crashed the following day in the 'red 9'. We used to say: 'Flyers get more out of life, but those who don't fly live longer.'"

The German pilots did claim some compensatory success: one P-47 shot down by Seckel for his 40th victory; and two B-25s damaged. One of the latter was subsequently awarded to Obgfr Horst Rippert as a full kill. In fact the Americans reported no loss or damage to any participating aircraft with the exception of a P-47 rendered Cat III by Flak, its pilot returning safely nevertheless.

With Hptm Georg Seckel of 1.Staffel (acting as Gruppe Kommandeur) and Lt Arndt-Richard Hupfeld in hospital and the 2.Staffel's Kurt Bell apparently fetching new aircraft, JGr 200 was now without any Staffelkapitäne in its zone of operations.

In Egypt, one of the only three Typhoons sent to the Middle East for trials, crashed at 107MU on this date, killing Flt Lt Francis R.Barker DFC who had previously completed a tour on 145 Squadron's Spitfires.

British Casualties

145 Sqn	Spitfire VIII JF467 left 1515, hit by Flak causing glycol leak, crash-landed at Falconara a/f; Sgt A.Garth safe					
253 Sqn	Spitfire Vc JK732 left 1000 on offensive sweep, strafed train between Sisak and Brod, hit by Flak 5m W Sas, crash-landed; Wt Off A.E.W.Day evaded					
107 MU	Typhoon Ib R8891 crashed 28m E Cairo; Flt Lt F.R. Barker DFC KiA					

US Claims

527th FS/86th FG	Lt Warren R.Mauck	P-47	Bf 109 Damaged	Avignon	0935
527th FS/86th FG	Lt Newton L.Saunders	P-47	Bf 109 Damaged	Avignon	0935
525th FS/86th FG	Capt Lemuel W.Purdom III	P-47	Bf 109 Damaged	Cheval Blanc 12m N Salon	c0945
525th FS/86th FG	2/Lt William P.Curtin	P-47	Bf 109 Probable	Cheval Blanc 12m N Salon	c0945
525th FS/86th FG	Lt John V.Jordan	P-47	Bf 109 Damaged	Cheval Blanc 12m N Salon	c0945
522nd FS/27th FG	Squadron claim	P-47Ds	Bf 109	3m NE Salon	1000

US Casualties

| 379th BS/310th BG | B-25J 43-27744 on bombing mission to Avignon, damaged by Flak; Capt W.J.Schneider, co-pilot Maj R.B.Allison and five safe | | | | |
| ?? | P-47 badly damaged by Flak, pilot safe | | | | |

German Claims

3./JGr. 200	Obgfr Horst Rippert		B-25		0935
3./JGr. 200	Hptm Georg Seckel		P-47		0940
3./JGr. 200	Ofw Eduard Isken		B-25		0940
Flak			Jabo a/c	Italy	

Monday-Tuesday, 7/8 August 1944

British Claims

255 Sqn	Wt Off C.V.James/Sgt J.J.McGibbon	Beaufighter VIf	Ju 188	30m NE Ancona-6m N Rimini	0130-0430

German Casualties

6./(F)/122	Ju 188F-1 WNr 280229 F6+FP crashed at Borella 0410; Uffz Günther Rüssmann and three KiA
	LKS reports one Ju 188 missing

Tuesday, 8 August 1944

Six Spitfires from 241 Squadron escorted Marauders to Rovigo. The pilots met a formation of about 20 Bf 109s and drove them off. These were actually 16 Bf 109s of 2° Gruppo ANR which made some inconclusive pass, while four fighters broke away and attacked 12 SAAF Squadron, their crews claiming one damaged in return for very slight damage to a Marauder.

The American medium bombers returned to southern France, escorted by French Thunderbolts. The 310th Bomb Group was attacked, recording: "Some of the men flew to Avignon today and it was rough." Their target was once again the railway bridge and the Germans scrambled 12 Bf 109s, meeting the incoming force over the sea, off L'Espiguette, at 0940. They rapidly became engaged. MAAF Signals Intelligence heard one victory being called in at 0940. The French summarised the action as follows:

"Thirteen P-47s of GC 2/3 and 1/4 on bomber escort mission. Attacked by 12 Me 109s west of Is-tres. Seven P-47s maintained the escort, six accepted combat. Results: two Mes destroyed, one P-47 failed to return."

Sgt Seeten of Groupe de Chasse 1/4 'Navarre' was missing in action while Sgt Galano of GC 2/3 'Dauphiné' belly-landed and found refuge with partisans. GC 2/3's Adjutant Le Guennec claimed a Bf 109 over the Étang de Scamandre and Lt Dugit-Gros and Capitaine Faure-Doré of the same unit shared a Bf 109 over Arles.

A Messerschmitt got past the escorts and came at the bombers from 6 o'clock, causing some damage. The Mitchells were over the target area from just before 1000 and their gunners claimed the fighter as a probable. The B-25J of the 488th Bomb Squadron flown by 1/Lt James C.Burrhus was hit by Flak and went down in flames north-east of the target with between three and five parachutes being seen to open. Another aircraft was seen to be falling behind when the formation turned away after bombing, as the diary of the 381st Bomb Squadron relates:

"One aircraft, piloted by 1/Lt Joe W.Maywald, failed to return. 2/Lt Woodson J.Williams was severe-ly injured by 20mm fire from attacking enemy aircraft and was taken to the 35th Station Hospital. Maywald's bombardier, 2/Lt Erwin E.Carman, had been injured on the run-in and with the aircraft losing power, the pilot was forced to land on an open field. The entire crew was taken prisoner but they escaped and were able to contact American forces following the invasion. All were back in Ghisonaccia by 22 August, except the gunner Sgt Andrew W.Citara who was taken sick and had a brief spell in hospital before re-joining his squadron on the 27th. Apart from the two shot down, 11 bombers were reported as holed by Avignon's intense, accurate heavy Flak."

Ultra reported that JGr 200 had flown one operation with 12 Bf 109s scrambled. Reported successes: three Thunderbolts shot down, two Thunderbolts effectively shot up. Losses: two Bf 109s shot down, of which one belly-landed, pilot wounded; one pilot baled out, slightly wounded.

Late in the evening the light-bomber units based at Cecina airfield were preparing for their usual night-fly-ing activities. Shortly before this a routine event happened when a crew from 4 Aircraft Dispatch Unit took off in a 114 Squadron Boston to ferry it to No.51 R&SU to be repaired, but it crashed five minutes after take-off. The initial casualty report on the pilot – who was Australian and thus the report is in the Australian National Archives – stated the reasons for the crash were unknown and that it was an accident. This classification was later changed to 'Flying Battle', which generally means that the aircraft was on an operational sortie (which it was not) or its loss was caused by enemy action. If so, the only likely candidates were Bf 109s from NAGr 11 on a tactical-reconnaissance mission.

British Claims					
12 SAAF Sqn	crew	Marauder	Bf 109 Damaged	nr Rovigo railway bridge	1000
73 Sqn	Wt Off E.F.F.Potvin	Spitfire IX MA751	2 Bf 109Gs	NE Vis, over sea	1530

British Casualties

4 ADU — Boston III W8353 left Cecina a/f 1710 to be ferried to the RSU, crashed 5km N Cecina 1715; Plt Off R.A.Clark WiA, Sgt I.T.Clarke KiA

US Claims

340th BG	gunner	B-25J	Bf 109 Probable	Avignon	1000-1015

US Casualties

314th FS/324th FG — P-40 42-26568 '13' crashed due to bomb explosion; 2/Lt Lewis J.Milton K

488th BS/340th BG — B-25J 43-4013 '8F' left 0727 to bomb Avignon rail bridge, shot down by Flak 0918; 1/Lt James C.Burrhus Jr and two KiA, one POW, two evaded [7331]

488th BS/340th BG — B-25J 43-27522 '8N' left 0727 to bomb Avignon rail bridge, hit by Flak 0918, force-landed in sea; Flt Off E.J.Ritter and five rescued by 1530

381st BS/310th BG — B-25J 43-27494 '11' hit by Flak Avignon 0957, landed at base; 2/Lt Frederick W.Watson and four safe, copilot 2/Lt W.J.Wil-liams DoW next day [15823]

381st BS/310th BG — B-25J 43-27527 '12' shot down by Flak southern France 1012, crash-landed at Barjols; 1/Lt Joe W.Maywald DFC and five captured, post invasion persuaded guards to surrender to US forces [7304]

428th BS/310th BG — B-25J 43-3529 mission to Avignon, starboard engine damaged by Bf 109 1000-1015; 1/Lt T.J.Werling and crew safe

French Claims

GC 2/3	Lt Henri Dugit-Gros	}	Bf 109	Arles
GC 2/3	Cne Jean Clément Faure-Doré	}		
GC 2/3	Adj Alain Le Guennec		Bf 109	Étang de Scamandre

French Casualties

GC 2/3	P-47D left 0930, shot down by Bf 109, crashed nr Vauvert (Gard); Sgt Chef Galano hidden by a local farmer
GC 1/4	P-47D shot down by Flak nr Carpi 1815, pilot baled; Sgt Seeten recovered by Italian partisans, died later fighting with them
GC 2/7	Spitfire V disappeared during shipping recce 1540 NW Ajaccio; Adj Jean Doudies MiA

German Claims

3./JGr. 200	Obgfr Horst Rippert		P-47	0940
JGr. 200	Ofw Eduard Isken		P-47	0940
JGr. 200	Ofw Eduard Isken		P-47	0940
Flak			a/c	Imperia
Flak			a/c	Venice

German Casualties

3./JGr 200	Bf 109G-6 WNr 163835 shot down in combat; Uffz Walter Cöster KiA
3./JGr 200	Bf 109G-6 WNr 440559 hit in combat, pilot baled out; Hptm Georg Seckel WiA
4./(F)/122	Ju 188D-1 WNr 290172 F6+EM shot down by friendly fire near Venice; Fw Gerhard Freytag and crew KiA
	LKS reports one Ju 188 missing, one Bf 109 destroyed and one damaged in air combat

Tuesday-Wednesday, 8/9 August 1944

At 0255 Flg Off Bretherton, who had taken off from Bergamo-Orio al Serio at 0100 to make a reconnaissance south of Ancona, intercepted a Ju 88. The pilot, Oberfahnrich Albrecht, was no novice, having completed 44 sorties over the front, and he changed course every two minutes. Despite this Bretherton was able to get in two short bursts which set the fuselage and port wing alight. He was met by accurate return fire, and as he approached from astern to administer the coup de grace, the Junkers throttled back. The gunner continued to fire at him as he overshot and Bretherton had to make several more passes before the pilot finally ditched his burning aircraft in the sea. Three members of the crew, Albrecht included, survived and were subsequently picked up. He confirmed that his Staffel had lost five aircraft in recent operations, including his own. He also mentioned that the Gruppen-kommandeur, Maj Bannwitz, had been killed some three weeks earlier; the Staffel had apparently lost 100 crews since the start of the year. Bretherton's sortie had been to try to locate artillery positions from the gun flashes for which Flt Lt Wlodzimierz Bereżecki of 318 Squadron was aboard to assist as an observer.

The recent run of success for the RAF night fighters now again brought a lull of night activity over Anco-na, and indeed was to be the last occasion on which 255 Squadron was to make a confirmed claim for many months. 600 Squadron was soon to take up the battle with NSGr 9 as will subsequently be related. Flg Off Bretherton's extraordinary success in gaining six victories in little more than a month made him the highest-scoring night-fighter in the Mediterranean for some time, though he was run close by 600 Squadron's Sqn Ldr Bailey who had claimed five since the spring, and by his own unit's Flg Off Reynold with four claims in less than a month.

153 Squadron lost an aircraft when Flt Lt Boardman, who had been scrambled after a reconnaissance aircraft, reported contact and that he had damaged the enemy aircraft before all contact was lost. Boardman and his navigator Plt Off Mordan were never found. The squadron records lamented next day that news had come through that Boardman had been promoted to squadron leader, back dated to 1 July 1944, and that the damaged aircraft on his last sortie had brought his score to four Ju 88s destroyed, one probable and another aircraft damaged.

British Claims

255 Sqn	Flg Off B.A.Bretherton/Flg Off W.T.Cunningham	Beaufighter VIf	Ju 88	N Ancona	0255
153 Sqn	Flt Lt H.S.Boardman/Plt Off J.R.Mordan	Beaufighter VIf ND314	e/a Damaged	85m NW Alghero	c0315

British Casualties

153 Sqn	Beaufighter VIf ND314 lost 85m NW Alghero, Sardinia; Flt Lt H.S.Boardman/Plt Off J.R.Mordan KiA
18 Sqn	Boston IV BZ463 'B' left 2235 on armed recce of Adriatic coast roads, crashed near Cesena; Flg Off A.R.Gaskell and three KiA

German Casualties

6.(F)/122	Ju 88A-4 WNr 550209 F6+DP 40m NW Ancona 0305; Uffz Helmut Pfützner and two survivors POW, one KiA
4.(F)/122	Ju 188D-2 WNr 290172 F6+EM shot down near Venice by German naval Flak; Fw Gerhard Freytag and four KiA
	LKS reports one Ju 88 missing

Wednesday, 9 August 1944

319th Bomb Group attacked Bergamo-Orio al Serio airfield. As a result of this the group estimated three twin-engined aircraft destroyed and six damaged plus a single-engined aircraft damaged. One B-26 ran out of fuel and crashed on the return flight.

British Casualties

260 Sqn	Mustang III FB256 left 1920, damaged by Flak, engine seized, pilot baled out into Allied lines; Plt Off J.Maddison safe
112 Sqn	Mustang III FB340 'Z' left at 1045, swung on take-off, crashed into a Kittyhawk III; Sgt D.C.Goodwin injured
213 Sqn	Mustang III FB324 left 1700, strafed train, shot down by Flak W Pristina 1820; 2/Lt L.J.Leach KiA
601 Sqn	Spitfire IX MH767 'Q' left 1030 to bomb gun positions, shot down by Flak at Pontassieve, 7m SE Florence; Sgt L.A.Holt KiA

US Casualties

523rd FS/27th FBG	P-47D 42-28090 shot down by Flak 1730, crashed 3km E Villanova, nr Casale Monferrato; 2/Lt Leslie H.Nave KiA [8258]
314th FS/324th FG	P-47D 42-27080 shot down by Flak, crashed nr Audincourt, NE Besançon, France, 1825; 2/Lt Charles W.Neely POW [8767]
100th FS/332nd FG	P-51C 43-24910 lost, last seen 10m S Banja Luka 1000; 2/Lt Alphonso Simmons KiA [7327]
95th BS/17th BG	B-26C 42-107788 '51' shot down by Flak nr Bergamo 0830; 2/Lt Robert E.Shank and three POW, two KiA, one evaded [7329]
437th BS/319th BG	B-26C 42-107546 left 0637 to attack Bergamo-Orio al Serio a/f, ran out fuel, crashed into mountains 20 m NE of base 1152; 2/Lt Harrell O.Quattlebaum and five KiA

Wednesday-Thursday, 9/10 August 1944

German Casualties

	LKS reports one Ju 88 missing

Thursday, 10 August 1944

Twenty Bf 109s of 2° Gruppo ANR were scrambled against Allied formations south of Milan. No contact. Shortage of aviation fuel throughout the Third Reich now began to have a serious effect on operations and the reduction in training also led to a decreasing spiral of effectiveness, the Italians flying their last operation for over two months during this day, as the Luftwaffe commandeered their fuel.

During one of 94 Squadron's escort operations, Capt D.Stanic claimed the first victory by a Yugoslav pilot in the RAF. It was also 94 Squadron's 31st and last victory of the war. In the same action Sqn Ldr Foskett made his final claim when he damaged a Bf 109 over Crete. The Yugoslavs were all posted away at the end of the month and 94 Squadron concentrated on Spitfire Vs before being withdrawn from operations in September pending a move to Greece.

British Claims

94 Sqn	Capt D.Stanic	Spitfire IX MA526	Bf 109	Crete	0655-0925
94 Sqn	Sqn Ldr R.G.Foskett	Spitfire IX MJ328	Bf 109 Damaged	Crete	0655-0925
94 Sqn	Lt R.Manoljovic	Spitfire IX MH558	Bf 109 Damaged	Crete	0655-0925
241 Sqn	Flg Off D.S.Monard	Spitfire VIII JF395 ⎫	Me 410	30m N Falconara	2020
241 Sqn	Plt Off D.F.White	Spitfire VIII JF362 ⎭			

British Casualties

249 Sqn	Spitfire Vc MA332 left 0625 strafing roads, hit by Flak, flew into ground N of Decani nr Pec; Flt Lt O.B.Andrews KiA
249 Sqn	Spitfire Vc JK660 left 0620 strafing roads, hit in drop tank by ground fire W of Rudnik, caught fire, went into the ground and burned; Lt R.Briggs KiA
253 Sqn	Spitfire Vc JK168 left 0905 to bomb Jablanica railway station, hit by Flak in oil tank, crash-landed on Vis 1110; Sgt H.Holdcroft slightly WiA
417 Sqn	Spitfire VIII JF951 left 1235 on weather recce NW Florence, engine failed, pilot baled out at Montebelluna; Plt Off J.E.R.Locks evaded, returned on 25 October

US Casualties

66th FS/57th FG	P-47D 42-26963 lost over Mediterranean; 2/Lt James R.Lord KiA [8767]

2.(F)/122	Me 410B-3 WNr 170087 F6+IK shot down by Spitfires; Lt Dietrich Stämmler/Uffz Arthur Karsch MiA
	LKS reports 1 Me 410 missing and 1 Bf 109 lost in air combat

Friday, 11 August 1944

Late that afternoon, 93 Squadron Spitfires participated in an attack to destroy a Giant Würzburg radar station near Marseille before the landings in southern France. Also taking part were eight P-47s of 'White' and 'Red' flights from 527th Fighter Squadron. Their pilots encountered very bad haze with an overcast at 10,000ft, 500ft thick and extending 5 miles inland. They had to get beneath this to attack but 'White' leader, 2/Lt James R.Whiting saw his wingman, 2/Lt Arnold Landan continue above the layer as the other P-47s descended. Whiting called on Landan to re-join but got no response. The formation made a 360° turn, taking them over Marseille and attracting heavy-calibre Flak which demanded evasive action before they could dive on the target from north-north-east. Whiting reported that:

> "As 'Red' flight went into their dive, I noticed a P-47 spinning down, pouring out black smoke. It was directly under the Flak from the islands. I went into my bombing dive and broke right… and saw a large spot on the water burning and pouring off large quantities of black smoke. This is approximately 6 miles south of Marseille… I did not hear from 2/Lt Arnold Landan again although I tried to raise him…"

Jagd Gruppe 200 scrambled twice with 16 sorties in all, six of its Bf 109s contacting Allied aircraft.

Obfw Eduard Isken claimed his 41st kill, a P-47 at 1812. This encounter shows the risks run by a pilot new to combat when faced by a highly experienced adversary: Isken was likely able to take advantage of the layer of overcast – and perhaps the distraction afforded by the Flak – to stalk and ambush him unseen.

6 Squadron was moved to the Balkan Air Force's 281 Wing (Grp Capt A.H.Boyd DSO DFC) at Canne; the other units in the wing were now 32, 249, 253 and 352 Squadrons.

British Casualties	
13 (H) Sqn	Baltimore IV FA642 'Y' left 0915 to bomb Debar, Macedonia, on return overshot the runway at Brindisi, crashed; Flg Off E.Economidis and three KiA
213 Sqn	Mustang III FB335 left 0825, strafed Kruševac a/f, hit by Flak, pilot baled out at 5,000ft between Lučice and Užice; Flg Off S.Chappell KiA
249 Sqn	Spitfire Vc JK214 left 0925, strafed M/T W Mt Lakasion, hit by Flak in radiator, pilot baled out; Sgt A.W.Gordon rescued by partisans, returned
232 Sqn	Spitfire IX MJ641 left 1145 on bomber escort to Cap Benet, glycol leak, pilot baled out 75m S Cap Benet 1310; Lt J.K.Anderson rescued by HSL
US Casualties	
315th FS/324h FG	P-47D 42-27085 lost over Italy, pilot baled; 2/Lt Jerome J.Lennon returned
527th FS/86th FG	P-47D 42-27095 '89' lost u/k cause 6m S Marseille 1815; 2/Lt Arnold Landan KiA [8254]
German Claims				
2./JGr. 200	Obfw Eduard Isken	P-47	near Marseille	1812

Friday-Saturday, 11/12 August 1944

Two Wellingtons, code letters A and B, from 38 Squadron left on an armed recce of the shipping channels between Crete and Milos. At 0200 a radar contact was made by A on a single vessel at a position 25 to 30 miles south of Milos; ten minutes later gunfire was seen followed by a large ball of fire burning on the sea and Flt Sgt Jones and his crew in B failed to return.

British Casualties	
38 Sqn	Wellington XIII MF145 'B' left 2150 with another aircraft on a recce over the Aegean, believed to have attacked a ship and been shot down by Flak; Flt Sgt R.H.G.Jones and five crew MiA

Saturday, 12 August 1944

The last of the rare encounters for the RAF component in XII TAC occurred on 12 August, and again it was enjoyed by 322 Wing. Spitfires of 232 Squadron were escorting B-25s and B-26s to attack a radar station in the Cap Benet area of the French Riviera during the morning when Bf 109s attacked. Two were claimed shot down by Plt Off Frewer and Wt Off McCann, although Lt G.W.Dibb failed to return. The combat was with JGr 200 which lost Uffz Kurt Kubeit killed near Carnoules about 20km south-east of Brignoles. The Messerschmitt was reported crashing into the sea but cannot be reconciled from German records. Two Spitfires were despatched at midday to look for Lt Dibb but without success; overall though 232 Squadron's mission had been so successful that none of the B-25 units reported so much as a sighting of enemy aircraft.

The Germans made at least three reports on the day's actions, the first speaking of a Spitfire probably shot down and another damaged. Later this became one destroyed (by 2 Staffel's Eduard Isken, for his 42nd victory) and one probable; ultimately, however, Isken and 3.JGr 200's Obgfr Horst Rippert were credited with a Spitfire each. Since no other Spitfires were in fact lost, it is likely that both men had fired at Dibb's aircraft.

In the early evening 42 P-47s of the 27th Fighter Group attacked Miramas marshalling yards near Istres and were engaged by six hostiles after leaving the target area. Amongst these were three Bf 109s of 1./JGr 200 that had scrambled at 1805hrs, the pilots claiming two intercepting fighters shot down and two more damaged, but at a cost of two of their own, reportedly to Flak. The 15th Air Force's 332nd Fighter Group lost five P-51s to Flak over the French coastal area during the day.

British Claims					
232 Sqn	Plt Off A.V.Frewer	Spitfire IX MJ818 'L'	Bf 109	Hyères Islands	1030
232 Sqn	Wt Off E.A.McCann	Spitfire IX MJ737	Bf 109	Hyères Islands	1030
British Casualties					
232 Sqn	Spitfire IX MJ442 'R' shot down by Bf 109 Cap Benet-Hyères Islands area 1045; Lt G.W.Dibb KiA				
US Claims					
522nd FS/27th FG	1/Lt Clarence A.Gary	P-47D	FW 190	Istres, France	1630-1930
522nd FS/27th FG	Squadron claim	P-47Ds	Bf 109	Istres, France	1630-1930
522nd FS/27th FG	unstated	P-47D	Bf 109 Damaged	Istres, France	1630-1930
524th FS/350th FG	Lt Hendrickson	P-47D	Bf 109 Damaged	Toulon area	1645-1945
US Casualties					
522nd FS/27th FBG	P-47D 42-26442 hit by Flak, crashed southern France 1915; 2/Lt Norbert W.Herriges KiA [8092]				
524th FS/27th FBG	P-47D hit by Flak southern France 0710, pilot baled; 2/Lt Cedric S.Lussier WiA, returned on 13 August				
346th FS/350th FG	P-47D 42-28376 lost over Mediterranean; 2/Lt John E.Diemer KiA [14556]				
302nd FS/332nd FG	P-51 shot down by Flak, pilot baled out near Narbonne Plage 1045-1100; 2/Lt Alexander Jefferson POW				
99th FS/332nd FG	P-51 shot down by Flak near Toulon 1045-1100; 2/Lt Joseph E.Gordon KiA				
99th FS/332nd FG	P-51 shot down by Flak strafing a radar station near Montpellier 1045-1100, pilot baled out; 2/Lt Richard D.Macon WiA POW				
302nd FS/332nd FG	P-51 shot down by Flak, ditched off Narbonne Plage 1045-1100; 2/Lt Robert H.Daniels Jr POW				
100th FS/332nd FG	P-51C 42-103918 shot down by Flak 10km SE Marseille 1047; 1/Lt Langdon E.Johnson KiA [7469]				
German Claims					
2./JGr 200	Obfw Eduard Isken		Spitfire	NE Hyères Islands	1030
3./JGr 200	Uffz Horst Rippert		Spitfire	Hyères Islands	1031
1./JGr 200	Fhr Johannes Brandau		P-47	5km S St Maximin	1820
2./JGr 200	Obfw Eduard Isken		P-47	N St Maximin	1828
3./JGr 200	Fw Herbert Guth		P-47	5km S St Maximin	1933
Flak			Spitfire		
Flak			P-47		
German Casualties					
3./JGr 200	Bf 109G-6 WNr 166257 Yellow 2 2km S Carnoules in combat 1047; FjFw Kurt Kubeit KiA				
1./JGr 200	Bf 109G-6/U-4 WNr 441525 White 11 E Aix-en-Provence in combat 1800; Fhr Johannes Brandau KiA				
3./JGr 200	Bf 109G-6 WNr 165609 Yellow 5 8km NE Aix-en-Provence in combat 1840; Uffz Martin Hermanitz KiA				

Saturday-Sunday, 12/13 August 1944

The Ju 88A-17s of I./KG 77 were very active flying reconnaissance missions from bases in southern France. Many wore the 'Wellenmuster' camouflage as seen here.

After the morning's sightings the reconnaissance effort for the night and evening was intense: Luftflotte 2 reported shipping for one division in Ajaccio and warned that a landing was to be expected in the South of France or Liguria "in the near future". The Allies plotted radio traffic from a total of 10 long-range reconnaissance sorties from southern France, noting that eight aircraft, drawn from both 6./KG 77 and 1./F 33, patrolled the sea between Corsica and France but between midnight and dawn, eight aircraft of 6./KG 77 were up, controlled from Istres and "further shipping was seen approaching Corsica from the south-west". In its return records on the 13th, 6./KG 26 reported one aircraft missing with its crew and one 60% damaged in a crash.

British Casualties	
458 Sqn	Wellington XIV HF400, on return hang-up bomb exploded on landing at Alghero 0605; Flg Off C.Fereday and six WiA, Wt Off G.W.Duncan DoW on 17 August and Wt Off J.B.O'Connell DoW on 27 September
German Casualties	
Stab/KG 26	Ju 88A-4 WNr 88804 3Z+KP missing over the Mediterranean; Lt Hans-Karl Krampf and three MiA

Sunday, 13 August 1944

Just after 1100 hours P-38s strafed and bombed Montélimar without warning, damaging two Ju 88s of II./KG 26. The 6. Staffel reported that its own four-barrel machine guns "played a large part in shooting down a Lightning".

Twenty-four P-47s of 324th Fighter Group strafed Les Chandines airfield, claiming one Ju 88, one Bf 110, two He 111s destroyed, and one Ju 88 probable, five Ju 88s and one Bf 110 damaged. Two Ju 88s were damaged at Salon-La Jasse while at St Martin (the German name for Les Chandines), home of 1.(F)/33, a Ju 188 was destroyed and two damaged while one air crewman was killed.

The activities of Luftwaffe reconnaissance aircraft were still a concern to the Allied commanders so on the 13th a second attack was planned on Bergamo-Orio al Serio. Early in the morning all three squadrons of the 57th Fighter Group took off from their airfield at Alto, Corsica, and flew to this area. The 66th Squadron went in first, claiming to have left one trimotor aircraft in flames and damaged some others; also a few vehicles were hit. The 64th went in next, the pilots of this unit seeing the real quarry and reported attacking six Ju 88s, seven Me 410s, three fighters and three gliders. One Me 410 was left in flames with one more thought to have been probably destroyed as was another Me 410, a further Ju 88 and a fighter. Finally, the 65th Squadron also strafed, attacking 20 Ju 88s and an He 111, claiming two Ju 88s and the He 111 damaged.

Meanwhile on the other side of the peninsula preparations were well advanced for the South of France landings, but here too Luftwaffe reconnaissance aircraft were flying over the Italian coastal ports. To counter these the Mustang IIIs of 260 Squadron and a detachment of Spitfire VIIIs from 92 Squadron were ordered to the airfield at Rosignano which was situated on the coast a few miles south of Leghorn. Here they joined 225 Squadron which had flown in here from Corsica at the end of July.

Patrols were flown around the Leghorn area all month, the reconnaissance aircraft being seen on occasions but initially escaped interception. At last on the 13th Plt Offs Young and Stevenson of 92 Squadron caught an Me 410 of 2.(F)/122 near Corsica and shot it down into the sea. Stevenson's aircraft was hit by return fire and he was forced to bale out but was later picked up unharmed.

Over France little opposition to the series of attacks launched early in August was encountered, and even the Flak defences were relatively light, so that casualties remained low. When the landings began the Luftwaffe made a few brief appearances but after a series of sweeps by Allied naval fighter aircraft operating from aircraft carriers of Task Force 88 which was supporting the landings and by XII TAC fighters on the 17th, the surviving units were quickly withdrawn. Virtually no opposing aircraft were seen after 19 August; indeed from 10 August to 11 September claims for German aircraft shot down over southern France by the whole of MATAF totalled only ten and two probables (three of the former being Bf 109s claimed by P-47 pilots of the 79th Fighter Group).

Further DAF support for Operation Dragoon was forthcoming at this time, and on 14 August the Mustangs of 112 Squadron arrived at Rosignano followed next day by the rest of 92 Squadron and the whole of 145 Squadron, all the Spitfires having been fitted with long-range tanks.

RAF Spitfires attacked enemy radar stations two days before the invasion. 242 Squadron lost two pilots, with one of their flight commanders the Australian Nelson Myers being killed and Flg Off Strutt being seen to bale out into the sea; after an international distress signal was sent out and acknowledged by the Germans, an ASR search saw a Do 24 in the area, which picked up Strutt who became a prisoner.

British Claims					
92 Sqn	Plt Off D.A.Stevenson	Spitfire VIII JF414	Me 410	nr Corsica into sea	2005

British Casualties	
92 Sqn	Spitfire VIII JF414 shot down by return fire from Me 410, pilot baled out 2010; Plt Off D.A.Stevenson rescued next morning
242 Sqn	Spitfire IX MH994 'R' left 0945 to strafe Giant Würzburg radar, shot down by Flak, dived into the sea in Gulf of Fos 1040; Flt Lt N.L.Myers KiA
242 Sqn	Spitfire IX 'H' left 0945 to strafe Giant Würzburg radar, shot down by Flak, pilot baled out over Gulf of Fos 1040, picked up by Do 24; Flg Off P.C.J.Strutt POW
450 Sqn	Kittyhawk IV FX536 left 1145, dive-bombed gun positions near Fano, last seen after pulling off target; 2/Lt H.J.Gater KiA
16 SAAF Sqn	Beaufighter X 'F' left 1140 from Canne, attacked 2,300-t motor vessel in Parenzo harbour 1305, damaged by Flak, crash-landed alongside runway at Canne 1440, damaged Cat III; Flt Lt A.S.Wickens/Flg Off J.R.Pygram safe
16 SAAF Sqn	Beaufighter X LZ469 'E' attacked 2,300-t motor vessel in Parenzo harbour, shot down by Flak 1313; Lt G.B.Cruickshank/Lt F.R.Campbell KiA
16 SAAF Sqn	Beaufighter X LZ246 'Z' attacked 2,300-t motor vessel in Parenzo harbour, shot down by Flak, ditched 2m NW Parenzo 1740; Lt Col P.Loock/Lt G.Pettet POW

US Casualties	
85th FS/79th FG	P-47D 42-26995 shot down by Flak off Cape Couronne, France 1845; 1/Lt Robert H.Williams KiA [8094]
87th FS/79th FG	P-47D 42-26371 lost u/k cause 1900 at RR station Calisanne, France; Flt Off Herbert H.Woerpel KiA [8089]
64th FS/57th FG	P-47D 42-75681 damaged by Flak at Bergamo-Orio al Serio 0710, Cat 2; pilot safe
66th FS/57th FG	P-47D 42-26843 damaged by Flak at Bergamo-Orio al Serio 0710, Cat 2; pilot safe
65th FS/57th FG	P-47D 42-26795 damaged by Flak at Bergamo-Orio al Serio 0720, Cat 2; pilot safe
65th FS/57th FG	P-47D 42-75975 damaged by Flak at Bergamo-Orio al Serio 0720, Cat 2; pilot safe
441st BS/320th BG	B-26B 42-43297 '20' *Lady Eve III* left 0454 to attack gun positions near Toulon, shot down by Flak 2-3m E Signes, France 0725; 1/Lt James H.Hipple KiA, one POW, four evaded [7303]
111th TRS	F-6A 42-103200 left 0950, lost over S France; 1/Lt Collis C.Lovely KiA [8742]

German Claims				
Flak	3/22 MbFlak A	2 Blenheim IVs	Parenzo harbour	1245
Flak	3/22 MbFlak A	Blenheim IV	Parenzo harbour	1745

German Casualties	
2.(F)/122	Me 410B-3 WNr 170150 F6+GK shot down by Spitfires 20km W La Spezia, crew baled; Fhr Richard Hesse POW/Obgfr Helmut Seegert MiA
II./KG 26	2 Ju 88 A-17s (WNn 823016 and 823019) damaged at Montélimar by strafing by P-38s
1.(F)/33	Ju 188 destroyed by strafing at St Martin
1.(F)/33	2 Ju 188s damaged by strafing at St Martin
	LKS reports 1 Me 410 and 1 Ju 88 missing, 2 Ju 88s destroyed on ground by bombs; 2 Ju 188s destroyed and 3 damaged plus 1 S.82 and another a/c destroyed on the ground by enemy aircraft

Sunday-Monday, 13/14 August 1944

In a very rare event, intruder crews from England were sent to look for Do 217, He 177 and Ju 290 aircraft based around Toulouse and then land at Maison Blanche in Africa. Sqn Ldr D.S.Handley and Plt Off T.

J.Philips of 151 Squadron had taken off in their Mosquito from Ford, West Sussex at 1750 on 9 August. They left at 0430 on the 14th on the return flight and landed at Ford at 0930. On the way at Leucate on the French coast, they shot up four Ar 196 on the lagoon. One, suspended from a crane, caught fire and fell, damaging another, while the other two were strafed at their moorings. Other crews followed this path over the next week.

Ultra intercepted a signal from Oblt Dietrich Astheimer, 2./SAGr 128 informing Fliegerdiv.2 that at 0630 a 'Marauder' had shot up parked aircraft at Perpignan and although there had been no casualties, the Ar 196 6W+AK had been destroyed by fire, confirming Handley's efforts. After this the Arados were evacuated from southern France.

British Claims

151 Sqn	Sqn Ldr D.S.Handley/Plt Off T.J.Philips	Mosquito HS956	Ar 196	on ground at Leucate	0430-0930
151 Sqn	Sqn Ldr D.S.Handley/Plt Off T.J.Philips	Mosquito HS956	3 Ar 196s Damaged	on ground at Leucate	0430-0930

British Casualties

17 SAAF Sqn	Ventura V JT833 'F' left 2033 to bomb M/T workshop at Cannes, reported returning to base, lost without trace; Lt E.H.Horton and four MiA

German Casualties

I./KG 200	Ju 188A-2 WNr 170492 A3+SD crashed due to engine fire at Fontanella 35km SE Bergamo; Obfw Heinz Kornhoff and two KIA, one WiA
2./SAGr. 128	Ar 196 6W+AK strafed at Leucate and destroyed by fire

Monday, 14 August 1944

The activity over southern France continued as the invasion force approached with P-51s of the 332nd Fighter Group sweeping the Toulon area and strafing from 1000-1020 hours. Just north of the city, at 13,000ft, four enemy aircraft (reported as two Bf 109s and two FW 190s) attacked "coming in very aggressively from 5 o'clock high" on the rear flight of the 99th Squadron. The P-51s turned into their assailants; following one pair down, 2/Lt Rhodes of the 100th Squadron opened fire on a FW 190, blowing off its right wing as his second victory.

JGr 200 claimed two P-51s at 1023. The 332nd Fighter Group reported an aircraft lost and another missing. 2/Lt Robert O'Neil of the 100th Squadron was last seen in a spin over the Toulon area and Lt Clarence Allen

Aircrew of 16 SAAF Squadron sit on the PSP at Biferno with Beaufighter X LZ336 'K' before an attack against a German HQ building in Dubrovnik on 14 August.

was reported to have baled out safely over the island of Elba. O'Neil eventually returned to his unit after having evaded enemy forces in France for almost two weeks.

It may be recalled that the 332nd Fighter Group had but recently been transferred from the 12th to the 15th Air Force. Other operations of a tactical nature undertaken by this or other strategic units while on loan to the

Top: The bridge over the River Po at Pontelagoscuro under attack by SAAF Marauders on 14 August. Above: Three of the crew of 12 SAAF Squadron Marauder II FB471 'G' *Pistol Packin' Mama* died when it was shot down attacking the railway bridge over the River Po at Pontelagoscuro.

———

15th during the Dragoon operations will be referred to in detail as appropriate in Volume 6 in due course. Entries referring to strategic units conducting tactical activity are indicated by a *.

The Allies intended to cripple the Luftwaffe's command and control system on the eve of the landings. At 1650 hours 12 P-38s of the 94th Squadron, 1st Fighter Group, led by Maj La Clare, took off to dive bomb the headquarters of Jafü Süd at La Nerthe, 7 miles north of Avignon. One of the Americans aborted with mechanical trouble, but the remainder were over the target at 1812 and claimed two direct hits on the buildings, six very near misses and five near misses within 100ft. No enemy aircraft were seen but Caritat airfield put up some accurate Flak. The attack's success was

Top: US troops say a final prayer before boarding a CG-4A Hadrian glider prior to taking off on Operation Dragoon on the night of 14 August. Above: Soldiers of the British 2nd Parachute Brigade aboard a C-47 Dakota of the 51st Troop Carrier Wing before being dropped into southern France.

confirmed when, at 1900, the Jafü reported that his *Gefechtsstand* (command post) had been bombed-out by eight Lightnings and that three personnel were killed, three badly wounded and three not severely.

By nightfall, 2./NAGr 13 reported landing craft stretching 50 miles west from Ajaccio roads and at 2235, two convoys were sighted by Luftwaffe aircraft, 100 miles south of Menton. These totalled over 100 landing craft and included strong surface and air escorts.

In the Adriatic, from its detachment at Vis four aircraft from 6 Squadron led by the commanding officer, Sqn Ldr J.H.Brown, attacked four Seibel ferries north of Jablanac during which Flt Lt Langdon-Davies was wounded in the shoulder by Flak and he was evacuated to the mainland.

19 SAAF Sqn	Beaufighter VI JM250 'J' left 1415, attacked ship in Senj harbour, ditched 5m E Senj and 2m S Prvic Island 1520; Wg Cdr J.R.Blackburn/Flt Sgt C.A.Boffin rescued			
213 Sqn	Mustang III HB901 left 1000, hit by Flak, pilot baled out 2m SE Valira 1130; Plt Off D.E.Cooke POW			
12 SAAF Sqn	Marauder II FB471 'G' left 1549 to bomb railway bridge at Pontelagoscuro, met intense accurate Flak 1751, crashed in flames near target, two parachutes seen; Capt C.S.van Heerden and three KiA, two POW			
12 SAAF Sqn	Marauder II FB458 'J' left 1549 to bomb railway bridge Pontelagoscuro, met intense accurate Flak, force-landed at Jesi; Lt J.N.H.Bezuidenhout and five safe			
12 SAAF Sqn	Marauder left 1549 to bomb railway bridge Pontelagoscuro, met intense accurate Flak; force-landed at base; crew safe			
24 SAAF Sqn	Marauder III HD465 'F' left 1600 to bomb railway bridge at Pontelagoscuro 1754, met intense accurate Flak, crashed in flames near target, five parachutes seen; Lt A.J.Cooney and five POW			
24 SAAF Sqn	Marauder left 1600 to bomb railway bridge at Pontelagoscuro 1754, met intense accurate Flak, crash-landed at Falconara damaged Cat II; crew safe			

US Claims

*100th FS/332nd FG	2/Lt George M.Rhodes Jnr	FW 190	N Toulon	1025

US Casualties

*100th FS/332nd FG	P-51 shot down by fighters near de Trets, SE Aix-en-Provence; 2/Lt Robert O'Neil evaded			
*99th FS/332nd FG	P-51 damaged by Flak strafing, pilot reached Elba and baled out; Lt Clarence Allen rescued			

German Claims

2./JGr. 200	Obfw Eduard Isken	P-51	N Toulon	1023
2./JGr. 200	Uffz Gunther Kniestedt	P-51	N Tooulon	1023
Flak	*Cagliari*	Mustang	Parenzo harbour	0645

Monday-Tuesday, 14/15 August 1944

Allied intelligence kept track of what the Germans were up to and thus what they knew of the invasion. 2./KG 77 was active all night (flying five sorties in all) and at 0022hrs shipping was reported 30 miles south of the Hyères Islands. Minutes later radio traffic was intercepted from KG 77 aircraft "closely watching our invasion forces" again reporting the two convoys on their westerly course at 42°15'N/07°25'E, the first consisting of 20 landing craft and the second of 75-100 units, including landing craft with large escort, very heavy AA and air cover.

At 0300 German FlgDiv 2 ordered a maximum effort by KG 26 and 3./KG 100 against shipping in the Toulon-Marseille area. Primary targets would be notified once reconnaissance had taken place, routes for both units were given and the attacks would go in from 0530 to 0615. In the event these raids did not take place.

Tuesday, 15 August 1944

In mid-August 1944 the invasion of southern France was planned principally with US and French landing forces with significant British air and naval support. Following large-scale airborne drops the main amphibious landings would be centred on St Tropez and extended for 30 miles, divided into four landing zones codenamed (east to west) Camel, Delta, Alpha and Sitka. The landing force was formed of the US VI Corps and the French 1st Armoured Division. The US 3rd Infantry Division went in on the left at Alpha (Cavalaire-sur-Mer), the 45th Division was in the centre at Delta (St Tropez) with the 36th Division landing at Camel beach at St Raphael. The US/Canadian First Special Service Force ('The Devil's

With Wildcats parked on its deck, the escort carrier HMS *Pursuer* leads HMS *Attacker* and HMS *Khedive*, plus what are thought to be the two US carriers, towards southern France ahead of Operation Dragoon. In between them is the Force flagship, the cruiser HMS *Royalist*.

Brigade') landed offshore on Sitka to neutralise several islands. The landings were successful and by the end of the day over 60,000 troops and over 6,700 vehicles were safely ashore, including the French division. They were transported in almost 500 ships supported by four battleships, 20 cruisers and 98 destroyers as well as nine escort carriers.

The Western Naval Task Force incorporated seven escort aircraft carriers; five of these were Royal Navy vessels. These would remain until such time as airfields had been secured ashore. The carriers were divided into two task groups, TG 88.1 with five of the vessels under the direct command of Rear Admiral Sir Thomas Troubridge who flew his flag from the anti-aircraft cruiser, HMS *Royalist*, and TG 88.2, formed around the other four carriers which included the two USN ships, all commanded by Rear Admiral Calvin.T.Durgin with his flag on USS *Tulagi*. Each group was screened by two RN AA cruisers and six or seven destroyers. The disposition of vessels and squadrons were as follows:

Task Group 88.1		Task Group 88.2	
HMS *Attacker*		USS *Tulagi*	
879 Sqn	24 Seafire L.III	VOF-1	24 F6F-5
	4 Seafire LRIIC		
HMS *Khedive*		USS *Kasaan Bay*	
899 Sqn	26 Seafire L.III	VF-74	24 F6F-5
HMS *Emperor*		HMS *Hunter*	
800 Sqn	23 Hellcat I	807 Sqn	24 Seafire L.III
700 Sqn	1 Walrus		
		HMS *Stalker*	
HMS *Pursuer*		809 Sqn	24 Seafire L.IIC
881 Sqn	24 Wildcat VI		
HMS *Searcher*			
882 Sqn	28 Wildcat V		

Thus equipped, three of the RN 'escorts', *Attacker*, *Hunter* and *Stalker*, arrived in the Mediterranean towards the end of May to commence a month of training on conclusion of which 28 Seafires were disembarked at Orvieto and Fabrica as 'D' Naval Fighter Wing for attachment to DAF's 244 Wing as already recounted.

The other four British carriers arrived at Malta on 25 July, *Khedive* newly worked-up and ready for its first action while *Emperor*, *Pursuer* and *Searcher* arrived direct from operations in the Atlantic; here they were joined by *Kasaan Bay* and *Tulagi*. The Americans brought with them 75% reserves for their F6F-5s, also putting ashore in Corsica the seven F6F-3(N) night-fighters of VF(N)-74 and five TBM-1C Avengers to provide anti-submarine protection should this be required.

Readers of Volume 3 may recall that the USN set great store on the provision of observer spotting for naval gunfire support and it was this duty which was perceived as being the primary function of the airmen. It is interesting to note that on board USS *Tulagi* was Squadron VOF-1which was the first US Navy unit to have received specialist training for this role as well as its basic fighter training. Meanwhile, a group of four naval aviators from USS *Brooklyn*'s VCS-8 had arrived at Bertaux, Algeria, on 15 January 1944 to commence transition to P-40s. Having been joined by other pilots from USS *Philadelphia*, the whole group converted to P-51s during April. On 21 April they were formally attached to the 111th Tactical Reconnaissance Squadron where they were to fly F-6As (Allison-engined P-51As) and began to fly missions. In July these VCS-8 pilots received ten new P-51Cs which they would subsequently fly during the invasion of southern France. By 30 August land operations were reaching areas outside the range of naval gunfire support and they were disbanded. They then passed the P-51Cs to the 111th Squadron and returned to their ships.

In setting out the level of experience of the RN fighter pilots J.David Brown as head of Naval Historical Branch, recorded:

> "The principal roles of the 224 fighters included fighter patrols, ground attack and interdiction, and bombardment spotting. All RN pilots had been given extensive training in the first two roles, and a

proportion of the pilots and ships had been trained for spotting for the gunnery of bombarding battleships and cruisers. Nos. 800 and 879 Squadrons had specialist tactical reconnaissance pilots trained to provide the 'eyes' of the carrier groups after the first few days of operations. The US Hellcat squadrons had also received extensive ground-attack training and *Tulagi*'s VOF-1 was a specialist spotting unit; both squadrons lacked combat experience."

This description perhaps provides the clue to Admiral Samuel Eliot Morison's comments:

"Escort carriers had been used off Salerno (September 1943) but for a different purpose, to provide combat air patrol over amphibious forces in an area where the Luftwaffe was strong. Here their primary mission was to provide spotting planes for naval gunfire in order to prevent the waste of time and fuel involved when such planes had to be dispatched from the nearest land base. Each carrier had a group of pilots specially trained for that branch of combat aviation. They spotted for *Nevada*, *Texas*, *Philadelphia* and *Montcalm* on D-Day, but for the most part the gunfire support ships preferred to be observed by their own SOCs (biplane floatplanes) and by fast spotting aircraft furnished by XII Tactical.

"The carrier groups, however, had also a second function in Dragoon: armed reconnaissance. While landing fields were being prepared near the beaches and the Air Force was moving up planes and equipment from its Corsican bases, these 'floating fighter strips' acted as bases for fighters to cover the assault area. The Hellcats and Wildcats penetrated 120 miles up the Rhône valley and, armed with bombs, selected their own targets on retiring enemy columns, while the Seafires were used for short-range missions."

It is unlikely that most fighter pilots of all the air forces involved would not have already been fairly familiar with these facts by August 1944!

Because of the heavy operational losses suffered by the Seafires at Salerno there was much initial concern regarding their likely performance here. However, with the benefit of hindsight David Brown had been able to record that "… losses were light". Flak had accounted for the loss of 21 RN and 14 USN aircraft but the balance of the overall total of 60 were written off in landing accidents.

As the great convoy of shipping headed for the Cannes and St Tropez area in the early hours of 15 August the first paratroopers were dropped along the coast to mark landing beaches and overwhelm certain coastal batteries. They were soon followed by 400 more C-47s and then by more aircraft, which towed more than 400 gliders. The vulnerable transports carried out their task unscathed beneath a strong cover of P-38s, P-47s and Spitfires from the 87th Fighter Wing in Corsica, with Mustangs of 112 and 260 Squadrons from Rosignano operating along the coast in a Flak-suppression role.

From early 15 August the US carrier-borne aircraft flew offensive sorties whilst the shorter-range Seafires undertook combat air patrols. At 0546 USS *Tulagi* launched its first VOF-1 Hellcat sortie led by Lt Cdr W.F.Bringle. The cool weather with little wind was less than ideal for operating the Hellcat which preferred at least 28 knots of wind at take-off, and most launches were therefore done by catapult. Foggy conditions around dawn did not help either. The first VF-74 mission that was then launched from USS *Kasaan Bay* at 0602 was led by the commanding officer, Lt Cdr Harry B.Bass, an experienced Pacific veteran on a dive-bombing sortie. They spotted the targeted gun emplacements easily and dropped their 1,000lb (450kg) bombs in attacks from 6,000ft (1,800m) achieving some near misses.

The first section of 809 Squadron was launched from HMS *Stalker* 70 miles offshore in the dark before dawn to cover the landing beaches near St Tropez. Arriving on patrol the section also spotted for the shore bombardment by the French cruiser *Montcalm* sailing two miles offshore. However, the weather was very poor with low cloud all the way into the coast and it was initially impossible to control the bombardment. When the cloud broke it was clear that the landings were going well, albeit in the face of heavy fire in places. There was no sign of any air opposition, though 809 Squadron did lose one Seafire in very unhappy circumstances. Having become separated from his section Sub Lt Morris found himself short of fuel and so landed on HMS *Attacker* 30 miles north of *Stalker*. He was refused fuel and ordered to take off immediately which resulted in him ditching soon afterwards. Fortunately, Morris was picked up by a launch after three hours in the water. He was soon flying again. The perennial Seafire weakness of landing on the small decks of escort carriers was again evident with no fewer than eight incidents that caused aircraft damage through the day.

The four squadrons continued to support the advancing ground forces with ground attacks dropping 500lb bombs and strafing retreating columns. Most pilots flew three or four sorties a day and these were maintained until the 27th when the advance reached Montélimar. Even as the airborne landings were underway, the first landing craft were reaching the beaches and soon after 0800 Allied troops were ashore and consolidating their positions fast in the face of generally light resistance. P-47s flew Cab Rank patrols, sweeping down to blast pillboxes, gun pits and machine-gun nests holding up the infantry. The Spitfire VIIIs of 92 and 145 Squadrons joined XII ASC fighters in patrolling along the coastline as far as the Italian border but nothing was to be seen. Before the day was out the commanding officers of both 111 Squadron from Corsica and 145 Squadron from Rosignano had landed at an improvised airstrip at Ramatuelle within the beachhead and next day other Spitfires were able to land at Cannes. The German Army Group G was ill equipped and undermanned, but nonetheless provided stiff opposition, at least initially.

Inland of the invasion a Mosquito crew from 151 Squadron was making its way from England to Africa when it first encountered a Bf 108 at 0640, which was damaged but escaped due to effective evasive action and then shortly after a Do 24 from Seenot 3 was met east of Châlons and shot down. The first aggressive action was launched at 0710, when JGr 200 scrambled a formation of about a dozen Bf 109s from its 1. and 2.Staffeln. The former was to provide top cover while the latter attacked the landing fleet with WGr 21 mortars. Before they could come near, they ran into the Lightnings of 1st Fighter Group and the German attack was dispersed, suffering three lost or damaged. Aside from some reconnaissance flights, that was the Luftwaffe's total reaction to the invasion.

By 1000 hours, 28 Bf 109s of II./JG 77 had left Ghedi in Italy, bound for Orange-Caritat with the balance of the Gruppe due to follow next day. The transfer was assisted by nine S.82s of II./TG 1 carrying ground crew, spares and other stores. II./JG 77 recorded one aircraft damaged by enemy action and another four in accidents.

After the 15th, no long-range reconnaissance flights from southern France were recorded by Allied listening posts but it was believed that 2.(F)/122 probably began to operate daily from Italy over the approaches to the beachheads.

This Vought OS2U Kingfisher floatplane, seen catapulting from the heavy cruiser USS *Quincy* for bombardment spotting, was among the first Allied aircraft off the Côte d'Azur as Operation Dragoon commenced.

Top: Smoke belches from the forward turret guns of the cruiser USS *Quincy* as it bombards the coast of southern France on D-Day. Above: With 500lb bombs carried underwing, the pilot of VF-74 F6F-5 Hellcat '23' gets the launch signal on the deck of the USS *Kasaan Bay* on the opening day of Operation Dragoon.

Top: The wreckage of German vehicles near St. Maximin la Sainte Baume in Provence after an attack by rocket-firing Hellcats on 15 August.
Above: Seafire III LR880 'HF' of 807 Squadron was flown from HMS *Hunter* by Lt K.M.Evans but tipped onto its nose when landing back on the ship after the sortie.

With the fire crew standing by, Ens William McKeever extricates himself from his VOF-1 F6F-5 Hellcat 58314 '18' after a heavy landing aboard USS *Tulagi* on the evening of 15 August.

British Claims

151 Sqn	Lt J.A.Cramp/Lt J.H.L.Maggs	Mosquito PZ201	Bf 108 Damaged	NW Tabaux, SW Dijon	0640
151 Sqn	Lt J.A.Cramp/Lt J.H.L.Maggs	Mosquito PZ201	Do 24	15m E Châlons	0647

British Casualties

242 Sqn	Spitfire IX 'F' left 1935 on patrol Hyères Islands, engine trouble, belly-landed in the beachhead in France; Flt Lt K.L.Waud safe
807 Sqn	Seafire L.III LR880 arrester wire not fully deployed, tipped on nose landing on HMS *Hunter*; Lt K.M.Evans safe
807 Sqn	Seafire L.III NF443 lost height on launch from HMS *Hunter* and ditched; Lt J.B.Leeming picked up by destroyer
807 Sqn	Seafire L.III NF645 on landing floated into barrier HMS *Hunter*; Sub Lt M.La Page OK
809 Sqn	Seafire L.IIc MB280 short of fuel, landed on HMS *Attacker* to refuel, but was refused fuel and ordered to take off immediately, failed to reach own carrier and ditched; Sub Lt G.C.Morris rescued
809 Sqn	Seafire L.III NF658 on landing bounced and hit barrier HMS *Stalker*; Sub Lt A.O.Fry safe
879 Sqn	Seafire L.IIc LR692 after op sortie, landed on HMS *Attacker*, missed wires and went into barrier; Lt J.G.Hornshaw safe
879 Sqn	Seafire L.IIc LR759 on landing floated into barrier landing on HMS *Attacker*; Sub Lt D.A.Gibson safe
899 Sqn	Seafire L.III NF543 missed wires on landing, crashed into barrier; Sub Lt E.W.Hunt safe
881 Sqn	Wildcat VI could not find HMS *Pursuer* ran out of fuel and ditched 1100; Sub Lt R.P.Gibson rescued
881 Sqn	Wildcat VI could not find HMS *Pursuer* ran out of fuel and ditched 1100; Sub Lt W.T.R.Smith rescued
882 Sqn	Wildcat V JV555 bounced on landing on HMS *Searcher*, floated into the barrier and overturned; Sub Lt P.J.M.Canter safe
882 Sqn	Wildcat V bombardment spotting for the battleships near St Tropez damaged by Flak and ditched two miles south of Lavandou; Sub Lt R.Brierley WiA rescued by PT boat

US Claims

*71st FS/1st FG	2/Lt Robert A.Longworth	P-38	Bf 109	NE Avignon	0730
*27th FS/1st FG	Capt Thomas E.Maloney	P-38	2 Bf 109s	inland of beachhead area	0744

87th FS/79th FG	P-47D 42-27912 lost u/k cause 4.5m SW Nice 1745; 2/Lt James P.Williams KiA [8255]
441st BS/320th BG	B-26C 42-107711 '02' left Decimomannu 0459 to attack targets at Baie de Cavalaire, drifted off course on take-off, crashed into Monte Azza 10m N of base 0500; 1/Lt Paul E.Trunk and seven KiA [7300]
442nd BS/320th BG	B-26C 42-95758 '32' left Decimomannu 0455 to attack targets at Baie de Cavalaire, lost power after take-off, crash-landed 400yds N of runway, burned and exploded; 1/Lt Van W.McDougal safe, Lt Col William A.Adams and five WiA
444th BS/320th BG	B-26B 42-96013 '99' left Decimomannu 0514 to attack targets at Baie de Cavalaire, lost power after take-off, crash-landed 1m N of runway, caught fire; 1/Lt Edward C.Jones Jr and two safe, three WiA
489th BS/340th BG	B-25J 43-4046 *Jersey Bounce* shot down by Flak 2-3km SE St Giles, France, 1420; 1/Lt Baxter Thomas and three evaded, one POW, one KiA [7973]
486th BS/340th BG	B-25J 43-27783 '6T' shot down by Flak, crashed at Rochefort-du-Gard, France 1629; 1/Lt John P.Hoschar and five MiA
488th BS/340th BG	B-25J 43-27713 '8D' *Double Trouble* left to bomb Avignon railway bridge, hit by Flak, crew baled out off southern France 1700; 2/Lt Earl C.Moon and four KiA, gunner S/Sgt Carmen Masciullo rescued by ASR Catalina [7972]
VOF-1	F6F-3 58314 '18' crashed on deck on return from spotting/attack sortie over beaches; Ens William C McKeever safe

2./(F)/122	Me 410B-3 WNr 190124 F6+DK crashed 20km N Mantua; Lt Gerhard Fischer KiA, one safe
Seenot 3	Do 24T-3 WNr 3386 CI+GV shot down by Mosquito on transfer from Marseille to Friedrichshafen; Obfw Christian Sölbrand and three crew KiA, two crew WiA, ten ground crew as passengers KiA
3./JGr 200	Bf 109G-6 Yellow 1, shot down 20km NE Aix-en-Provence; Uffz Hans Ludwig KiA

Tuesday-Wednesday, 15/16 August 1944

US Navy *LST-282* was hit off Cape Dramont during the evening of the 15th by an HS 293 glider bomb delivered by a Do 217 of KG 100. It is still smoking the following day sunk in the shallows of Green Beach near St. Raphael.

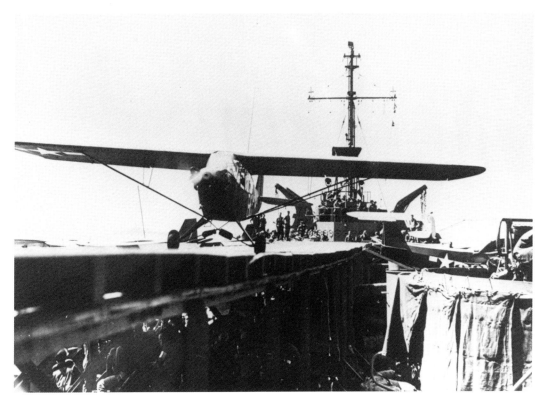

US Army engineers constructed an improvised 'runway' on an LST so as to fly off a US Army Piper Cub for bombardment spotting during the landings.

At least six Do 217s from III./KG 100 attacked between 2038 and 2159, with one hit claimed with a Fritz X and two with Hs 293s. The Allies noted that a small Do 217 force (estimated to be four at most) approached the Camel beach area:

> "… first at about 15,000 feet, then dropped to about 8,000 feet to release their glider bombs… The German control aircraft skilfully operated over the land, thus keeping the LST between it and our jamming ships and compelling them to attempt taking control of a glider bomb approaching head on – the most difficult angle for control. This new German technique foiled no less than twenty-two of our jamming ships: this was the first occasion of its kind recorded – an important point to remember in view of the fact that we had written off the glider bomb as not really a serious menace."

LST 282 was 600 yards off St Raphael heading for shore when she was hit and caught fire. Although beached, she was a total loss and about 40 men aboard were killed. Bombs were also reported to have landed near the attack transport (and floating HQ), USS *Bayfield*.

German guided weapons had sunk their last ship of the war and III./KG 100's work for the night was finished. From 2250-2328, two Fritz X and five Hs 293 carrier aircraft landed at Blagnac. Two Do 217s were reported lost: one plane was shot down by the ships' AA fire, the crew subsequently baling out to be rescued by Spanish fishermen and interned.

When the Dorniers were engaging the fleet, Ju 88s were also due to be in action. I./KG 26 had been ordered to carry out a torpedo attack at St Raphael while II.Gruppe was assigned a target just east of Cap Nègre, where French commandos had come ashore. Effective results were minimal, the crews could not get near the real targets, the transport ships and their war material. These lay within so strong a protective cordon of warships that to break through the massive defensive fire was simply not possible. This attempted torpedo attack was the last in the Mediterranean.

The KG 26 illuminator unit (flare droppers to aid torpedo bombers) were down to four operational crews while 1.(F)/33 had no aircraft with "apparatus" (i.e. FuG 200 radar) available, leaving the Staffel operational only for security cover. Thus, night-reconnaissance capability was somewhat lacking. Preparations for the night's operations by II./KG 26 were disrupted by an air raid warning that lasted for an hour from 1610 local time. Transport and equipment could not move and only four Ju 88s could be made ready for their assigned mission.

British Claims					
600 Sqn	Plt Off R.L.Crooks/Sgt R.Charles	Beaufighter VIf V8837	He 177 Damaged	Leghorn area	2325
British Casualties					
153 Sqn	Beaufighter VIf ND281 left 2025 from Reghaia on patrol over convoy 'Skunk', engine failure, ditched 1m NW Rocher Noir near Algiers 2120, rescued at 2300 by French fishing vessel; Sgt P.A.Drown/Flt Sgt D.A.Norton safe				
German Casualties					
III./KG 100	Do 217K-3 WNr 4733 6N+GT lost in St Raphael area; Fw Helmut Germann and crew baled out safely				
III./KG 100	Do 217M-11WNr 6429 6N+AS missing in St Raphael area; Obfw Rudolf Blab and four interned in Spain				
	LKS records two Do 217s missing				

Wednesday, 16 August 1944

At 0636 2./JGr 200 scrambled three Bf 109s to escort a pair of FW 190s from 2./NAGr 13. They were up for about an hour, photographing Hyères from 20,000 feet. Between 1147 and 1330 another pair of FW 190s of the same unit was up to photograph the area Draguignan-St Raphael-St Tropez-Lavandou. Ofhr Robert Heichele landed his burning FW 190 at Avignon after a fierce air combat, followed minutes later by his wingman, Uffz Högel who had extricated himself safely from the fight.

Ultra revealed that from 1538 to 1625 hours an FW 190 and four Bf 109s of the "same unit" (presumed to be 2./NAGr 13) were on convoy reconnaissance in the "Toulon-Marseille areas" to a total depth of 60km. An hour after they landed 11 of I./JG 77's Bf 109s mounted a *Freie Jagd* looking for low-flying raiders and reconnoitred fires on the Salon-Lézignan railway in what was apparently the last fighter mission of the day.

When dive-bombing a coastal defence battery near Toulon, an 899 Squadron Seafire was shot down by Flak. The Seafires of 879 Squadron were also very active on this day, carrying out 26 sorties.

British Claims					
72 Sqn	Wt Off C.E.B.Wood	Spitfire IX MK134	FW 190 Damaged	Castellana	1250
British Casualties					
1 SAAF Sqn	Spitfire IX left 1445 bombing a railway bridge E Bologna, damaged by Flak, crash-landed near base; Lt H.P.Freeman WiA				
12 SAAF Sqn	Marauder II HD452 'H' left 0820 to bomb Rovigo railway bridge, crashed into sea u/k cause off Pescara; Lt B.J.De Klerk and five KiA				
899 Sqn	Seafire dive-bombed coastal defence battery nr Toulon, hit by Flak; Sub Lt J.G.Barrett baled out but KiA				
807 Sqn	Seafire L.III NF606 hit by ship's Flak S Toulon, caught fire, dived into the sea; Sub Lt L.G.Lloyd KiA				
879 Sqn	Seafire L.II.c LR732 bounced on landing on HMS *Attacker*, crashed into the barrier; Sub Lt G.Calder safe				
809 Sqn	Seafire L.III NF665 on landing hit tail on round down of HMS *Khedive* and broke back; Sub Lt G.H. Brittain safe				
US Casualties					
66th FS/57th FG	P-47D 42-27391 hit by ground fire, crashed into sea; 2/Lt Thomas H.Callan rescued				
315th FS/324th FG	P-47D 42-28062 lost over Italy, pilot baled; 2/Lt Gerald G.Ricks safe				
*99th FS/332nd FG	P-51C 42-103938 lost to Flak 1.5m N Miane 1230; 1/Lt Herbert V.Clark POW [7691]				
German Casualties					
1./JGr 200	Bf 109G-6/U4 White 1 shot down near Valensole by fighters; Uffz Walter Lang POW				
JGr 200	Bf 109 G-6 destroyed by strafing of Pierrelatte l/g N Orange at 1315				
2./NAGr 13	FW 190F-8 WNr 581300 left Avignon East a/f, damaged in combat, force-landed, burnt out; Ofhr Robert Heichele WiA				

Wednesday-Thursday, 16/17 August 1944

Fifteen bombers of KG 26 took off around 0200 to attack St Tropez town and harbour. Also at dusk, six Do 217s of III./KG 100 operated against ships off St Tropez with Hs 293s. Apparently just a successful hit was claimed.

British Casualties	
255 Sqn	Beaufighter VIF MM870 scrambled at 2315 from Foggia Main, engine failed, crashed on landing 2325; Wt Off T.R.Swale/Flt Sgt N.M.Holmes safe

US Casualties

97th BS/47th BG	A-20B 41-3468 '91' lost over Corsica 0330; 1/Lt Neil R.Underwood and three KiA [8091

German Casualties

7./KG 100	Do 217M-11 WNr 6461 damaged in St Raphael area, crashed off Pamplona; Obfw Rudolf Freiburg and four crew interned
	LKS reports one Do 217 lost

Thursday, 17 August 1944

At around 0950 Capt Dave C.Hearrell Jr and 2/Lt Forrest L.White, flying F-6s of the 111th Tactical Reconnaissance Squadron, claimed a Ju 52 destroyed. Then, at Avignon East airfield, Hearrell claimed a FW 190 damaged. A wrecked FW 190 was later found on the airfield and the two Americans had indeed hit a three-motor transport but it was a Savoia Marchetti S.82 of 6./TG 1. The crew of this reported an attack by two fighters between Avignon and Orange. The transport caught fire and its centre engine was apparently blown right off, slightly injuring the pilot, Obgfr Fritz Pauleweit, while the gunner Uffz Otto Meistring was hit in the head by gunfire. After landing at Avignon they were driven 30km to the military hospital at St Audiol. The radio operator, Uffz Heinz Herbstleb, accompanied them in the ambulance and although the two wounded men were delivered successfully, Herbstleb disappeared!

During the morning RN Seafires on patrol strafed the corvette *UJ-6081*. At 1325 six P-47s of the 27th Fighter Group strafed the airfield at Avignon, setting a parked Ju 52 on fire (perhaps an S.82, since two were later found burned out there). One Thunderbolt was hit by local Flak and crashed 2km south of Avignon.

After being hit by Flak, Sub Lt C.A.M.Poublon was forced to ditch his 800 Squadron Hellcat but was quickly picked up.

Late in the day, at 2005, Colonel Daniel Campbell of the 14th Fighter Group claimed an unidentified twin-engine aircraft at Blagnac airdome west of Toulouse. This was a Do 217 III./KG 100 reportedly shot down by Lightnings 15 minutes after take-off.

At 2040 six Ju 88s dropped bombs between St Raphael and St Maxime without causing any damage. First reports spoke of a glider bomb hitting the destroyer USS *Charles F Hughes*, but as it turned out the missile only registered a near miss and the ship was undamaged.

Five of III./KG 100's Do 217s had operated; two aborted the mission while another jettisoned its Hs 293 glider bomb; two claimed near misses. Use of the Fritz X was reported to have been impossible on account of cloud cover, yet the crew of 6N+TR claimed a near miss on a 6-8,000-ton troop transport with this weapon. Just under an hour later another American destroyer, USS *Champlain*, came under attack this time from a low-flying Ju 88 and claimed it shot down thus accounting for a I./KG 26 loss.

At 2215 two of II./KG 26's Ju 88s managed to get off from Valence for radar coverage of the sea area between Nice and Corsica and to the south of Toulon.

British Casualties

241 Sqn	Spitfire VIII JF955 left 1805, strafed a locomotive near Castelfranco, which exploded, causing a/c to crash; Flg Off J.E.Walton KiA
242 Sqn	Spitfire IX 'X' left 1230, on return crashed on landing, written off; Sgt J.R.Collins WiA
4 SAAF Sqn	Spitfire IX MA761 struck tree while strafing, caught fire, pilot baled 1m S Bibbiena 0850; Lt J.G.Booyens POW
16 SAAF Sqn	Beaufighter X LZ336 'K' strafed trucks S Petrovo, damaged by Flak, ditched, seen in dinghy off Croatian coast at about 1020; Lt G.H.W.Downer/Lt J.V.Hall POW
800 Sqn	Hellcat I JV111 'EP' hit by Flak, ditched off coast; Sub Lt C.A.M.Poublon rescued

US Claims

111th RS	Capt Dave C.Hearrell Jr	F-6A	Ju 52/3m	Avignon area	1000
111th RS	2/Lt Forrest L.White	F-6A	Ju 52/3m Damaged	Avignon area	1000
111th RS	Capt Dave C.Hearrell Jr	F-6A	FW 190 Damaged	Avignon area	1000
14th FG	Col Daniel S.Campbell	P-38	twin-engined a/c	W Toulouse	2005

527th FS/86th FG	P-47 '86' strafed railway box car which exploded N of Toulon 1610, pilot baled out; 1/Lt Harry L.Caldwell evaded, returned on 22 August			
522nd FS/27th FBG	P-47D 42-26802 shot down by Flak 1335, crashed nr Avignon; Flt Off Alfred A.Nelson returned on 29 August [8258]			
66th FS/57th FG	P-47D 42-26993 hit by Flak W Nice 1345; Capt Roy C.Emerson KiA [8256]			
66th FS/57th FG	P-47D 42-76744 hit by Flak damaged Cat 2; pilot rescued			
66th FS/57th FG	P-47D 42-26644 hit by Flak damaged Cat 2; pilot rescued			
VF-74	F6F-5 58867 '3' lost u/k cause N Aix 1800; Lt(jg) John D.Frank KiA			
VF-74	F6F-5 58241 '17' lost u/k cause N Aix 1800; Lt Robert J.Johnson KiA			

German Claims

Flak	2.1/Flak Abt 501 (mot)	P-47	2km S Avignon	1525

German Casualties

6./TG 1	S.82 1Z+OP damaged by enemy fighters on Avignon a/f; Obgfr Fritz Paluweit and one WiA, rest of crew safe
3./KG 26	Ju 88A-17 WNr 550919 3Z+AK shot down by ships' Flak off St Raphael; Uffz Walter Leucht and three MiA
III./KG 100	Do 217M-11 WNr. 6461 shot down after take-off by a P-38 near Toulouse Blagnac a/f; crew MiA?

Friday, 18 August 1944

254 Wing of the Balkan Air Force lost its commander when Group Captain John Alexander Powell led a formation of Beaufighters from 19 SAAF Squadron to strafe Banja Luka airfield. His aircraft was hit by Flak over the target and crashed while attempting to force land, Powell and his observer being killed. Another two Beaufighters were lost to Flak, with no survivors. This unit had been 227 Squadron until renamed on 15 August.

352 (Yugoslav) Squadron equipped with Spitfire Vs undertook its first missions on this date, which were to include operating over Yugoslavia on fighter-bombing sorties and providing escorts to 6 Squadron Hurricanes.

Meanwhile, regarding the invasion, the Luftwaffe reorganised itself: essentially Fl.Div 2 was subordinated to Luftflotte 2 with immediate effect and was to move its headquarters to Bergamo South. Its Order of Battle was:

Stab KG 26	Valence
I./KG 26	Orange Plan-de-Dieu
II./KG 26	Valence
1.(F)/33	St Martin
III./KG 100	Toulouse

Over southern France 1/Lt Hubert Nicholson of the 111th Tactical Reconnaissance Squadron destroyed a Ju 88 "on the deck" just south of Orgon, during the morning. Two Bf 109s were seen in the Montélimar area by pilots of the same unit but no contact was made; and at 1430 P-38 pilots of the 14th Fighter Group spotted two Bf 109s attacking a Walrus amphibian, but these flew off as the Americans approached.

Five Do 217s and ten-15 torpedo-carrying Ju 88s were estimated to have been airborne together with ten more Ju 88s as bombers. One Junkers crew attempted to torpedo *FDT 13* (Fighter Direction Tender) in the Delta beach area, but the weapon exploded 250 yards short. Another Ju 88 dropped anti-personnel bombs on the same beach from 6,000 feet. The light cruiser HMS *Colombo* and other ships of Task Force 87 engaged the Ju 88 through gaps in the smoke screen but observed no hits; it was believed that only two hostiles had passed over the task force.

Eleven Ju 88s attacked around St Tropez while five passed over Camel and Delta beaches (Gulf of Fréjus) at 9,000 feet. At 2105 one of these came as close to seriously impeding the Allied effort as any Luftwaffe aircraft was to do. Its anti-personnel bombs straddled the Fighter Direction Ship (FDS) USS *Catoctin*. One hit the after well deck, killing two men and seriously injuring three (two of the seriously wounded died the next day). Twelve others received less serious injuries. *PT 208* was close by and four of its crew were also injured. *Catoctin* was the flagship of Admiral Hewitt, Allied naval commander, and had been the vessel that had put VI Corps commander, Gen Patch, ashore. Fortunately for the Allies a handover was already in progress at the time of the attack and control was not affected. At 2300 FlDiv 2 reported that 11 aircraft (context indicating that they were from KG 26) had taken off and attacked their designated targets. Two of the three setting down at Valence had belly-landed after being shot up; three landed at Montélimar and five at Orange Plan-de-Dieu.

The night's last known operation was a five-hour radar reconnaissance from 0140 by a Ju 88 of II./KG 26 in the sea area south of Marseille and Cannes.

Top: In Italy the Yugoslav-manned 352 Squadron commenced operations on 18 August. Its RAF commander, Sqn Ldr J.E.Proctor (left) and the Yugoslav flight commander are in discussion beforehand with Air Marshal Sir John Slessor (centre). Above: Ground crew prepare the Spitfires of 352 (Yugoslav) Squadron for their first operation at Canne on 18 August; Mk Vc JK608 'C' is nearest.

British Casualties

249 Sqn	Spitfire Vc JK723 'V' hit by Flak, had rudder cables shot away, crash-landed at Vis 2050; Lt H.K.Rachmann safe				
19 SAAF Sqn	Beaufighter VI F X7891 left 0845, strafed Banja Luka airfield, hit by Flak, force-landed, burst into flames; Grp Capt J.A.Powell DSO DFC/Flg Off J.R.F.Reid KiA				
19 SAAF Sqn	Beaufighter VI JL508 'L' left 0845, strafed Banja Luka airfield, hit by Flak, crashed nearby; Flt Sgt H.D.Scott/Sgt W.McDermott KiA				
19 SAAF Sqn	Beaufighter XI JL910 'S' left 0745, strafed train near Prdejci, hit by Flak, last seen climbing to avoid hills into cloud, crashed; Plt Off J.A.Neilson/Flt Sgt B.Gantz KiA				
899 Sqn	Seafire L.III NF661 from *Khedive* attacked motor transports but flew into a hill near Aix-en-Provence; Sub Lt David A.Cary DoW				

US Claims

111th Recce Sqn	1/Lt Hubert L.Nicholson	F-6A	Ju 88	SE Orgon	0925-1230

US Casualties

65th FS/57th FG	P-47D 42-75739 hit high tension wires Durance river 0920; 2/Lt William W.Bateman KiA [8095]
34th BS/17th BG	B-26C 42-107736 '03' *Thunderbird* shot down by Flak off Toulon, France; 1/Lt Charles J.Olson and two KiA, one WiA, three safe [7531]

French Casualties

GB 1/19	Marauder '69' left 1200, shot down by Flak, crashed at sea 20km S Porquerolles; Lt Meunier and six KiA

German Casualties

5./KG 26	Ju 88A-17 shot down at Orgon SE Avignon by US fighter; pilot and three crew safe
5./KG 26	Ju 88A-17 WNr 550918 failed to return from western Mediterranean; Lt Hans-Joachim Weise and three MiA
II./KG 26	Ju 88 belly-landed on Valence a/f after damage by enemy fire; pilot and two safe
3./JGr 200	Bf 109G-6 Yellow 3 shot down on take-off during strafing attack on Avignon South a/f; FhjUffz Alfred Kocken KiA
	LKS reports one Ju 88 missing

Saturday, 19 August 1944

With the German position in Normandy collapsing, orders were given that their 19th Army should withdraw north before it was cut off from friendly forces in northern France and from Germany itself. Thus, one of

The commander of VF-74, Lt Cdr Harry Bass (left), debriefs aboard USS *Kasaan Bay* after his successful sortie when his section brought down a Ju 88. He would be killed the following day.

Dragoon's aims to pin down forces in the south so that they could not reinforce the defence of Normandy had become redundant.

At 0810 three of JGr 200's Bf 109s took off to undertake WGr21 attacks on guerrillas in the Valon area, one of their number being posted missing. Half an hour later the 'Y' Service heard an enemy patrol reporting Allied aircraft in the Rhône Valley area.

Twelve Bf 109s of II./JG 77 that reconnoitred along the coast may well have been the aircraft encountered north of the beachhead by P-47s of the USAAF's 86th Fighter Bomber Group at 0915. JG 77 had sent another Schwarm at midday on a reconnaissance between Digne and Grasse but they broke off in the face of Allied fighters.

During the day, as evidence of a full German withdrawal became evident, Allied carrier-borne aircraft claimed five enemy bombers destroyed (plus one damaged). Two were by VF 74 of Lt Cdr Harry Bass with a Ju 88 in the morning and a Do 217 in the afternoon. A section from VOF-1 led by Lt Cdr John H.Sandor which spotted three He 111s did not have enough fuel to engage them. However, in the evening a section, again led by Sandor, shot down the three He 111s that they encountered.

From HMS *Stalker* a section that bombed and strafed train and station at Avignon encountered Flak and a Seafire was hit in the radiator. Sub Lt D.D.James managed to coax his damaged aircraft to the coast and baled out to be picked up by a destroyer. The squadron log also recorded Sub Lt Morrison had to bale out and was also rescued.

The 881 Squadron Wildcat flown by Sub Lt R.Banks attacked an airfield near Avignon, was hit by Flak that severely damaged the engine, but the pilot managed to ditch in the River Rhône and evade capture. He eventually returned to his ship on 24 August.

882 Squadron lost Sub Lt Fred Sherborne when he crash-landed his aircraft in a field and was harboured by the French Resistance until the Allies took the village of Châteaurenard. As well as some damage to the aircraft from the ground fire, Sherborne suffered a shoulder injury and cuts to his face from fragments of his cockpit canopy and a bullet had grazed his temple. Villagers used a tractor to hide his plane in the nearby Durance river. He was hidden in a hen house for two weeks before the village was secured. He was later feted as a symbol of heroism by the villagers during their victory parade. Sherborne wrote afterwards:

"The invasion of France was going on apace with four losses on our part and an orderly retreat by the Germans. The assault carrier force to which I was attached had carried out numerous sorties. Beachheads were covered, tactical and armed recces were flown off and dive-bombing and strafing were a daily feature in the life of pilots in Nos 7 and 3 Fighter Wings of the Assault Carrier Force. Although the Flak put up was accurate, there was not much of it and to our group who had just left the very heavily guarded and armed convoys and installations of Norway, it was all a very easy piece of work. It was reckoned to be such a 'piece of cake' that one looked upon it all more as training than actual warfare and D plus 4 we had all been lulled into a false sense of security and took to the air with a rather condescending blasé feeling.

"My flight had just dropped bombs on and near gun posts just outside Orange in the face of light AA – not intense. I received one 20mm in my starboard wing, which made little difference, and carried down on the deck for my get away. Once out of range, I climbed up to 4,000 feet to carry out a strafing attack on two a/c which I had noticed on an airfield earlier in the recce.

"As we entered the dive for the high-speed strafe, the 40mm and lighter stuff started coming up and just as I was about to fire my guns my machine, a Wildcat V, was hit by several 20mm. One hit the cockpit, luckily on the armoured glass directly in front of my face. This stopped the main force of the shell, but I received a big piece on my forehead and smaller pieces round my eyes and nose. Just about this time the whizzer stopped turning and there was quiet all round. All of this time I was jinking both to avoid more shells and to make the Jerry think I had not been hit. All of this was at treetops and below. There was of course no hope of baling out nor was there a chance of picking a suitable field for a landing as it would have given my position away completely had I attempted to zoom. I therefore tightened my harness, opened the hood, switched off all the switches and trusted to luck and the hardiness of the machine. This takes some time to relate but it all happened in seconds. Luckily as the speed dropped off, I sensed rather than saw, blood over my eyes making it fairly difficult to see properly, a small field surrounded by bamboos. Straightaway I pushed the nose into those on the near side of the field, hoping that they would slow me down sufficiently, which they did, and I found myself stopped on the ground right side up."

Above: Wildcat V JV368 'SB' of 882 Squadron was hit by Flak and crash-landed near Avignon, though Sub Lt Fred Sherborne evaded capture. Left: Sub Lt Fred Sherborne was treated as a hero by the local French populace and was later feted through the streets.

British Casualties

2 SAAF Sqn	Spitfire LF IX MJ755 'F' bombed gun position, engine cut in circuit on return, crash-landed 3m N Foligno l/g, damaged Cat II; Lt C.F.G.Greenham safe
809 Sqn	Seafire L.IIc LR638 bombed and strafed train and station at Avignon, hit by Flak in radiator, pilot baled out off the coast; Sub Lt D.D.James rescued by a destroyer
809 Sqn	Seafire III possibly damaged nr Avignon, pilot baled out; Sub Lt A.C.S.Morrison rescued by a destroyer
881 Sqn	Wildcat VI JV669 'UR' hit by Flak strafing airfield near Avignon, ditched in Rhône; Sub Lt R.Banks evaded, back on ship on 24 August
882 Sqn	Wildcat V JV384 shot down in attack on target at Caumont-sur-Durance SE Avignon at about 1100; Sub Lt A.Sharpe KiA
882 Sqn	Wildcat V JV368 'SB' hit by 20mm Flak, crash-landed at Châteaurenard near Avignon; Sub Lt F.T.Sherborne evaded

US Claims

526th FS/86th FG	1/Lt Bert Benear	P-47D	Bf 109	0730-0915
526th FS/86th FG	1/Lt Bert Benear	P-47D	Bf 109 Damaged	0730-0915
VF-74	Lt Cdr Harry Brinkley Bass	F6F-5		
VF-74	Lt Leo Horacek Jr	F6F-5		
VF-74	Lt(jg) Edwin W.Castanedo	F6F-5	Ju 88	0805
VF-74	Ens Paul Pavlovich	F6F-5		
66th FS/57th FG	Lt Bobby J.Pridgeon	P-47D	Bf 109	1245-1530

VF-74	Ens Charles W.S.Hulland	F6F-5	}	Do 217	4m NE Issoire	1750
VF-74	Lt(jg) Edwin W.Castanedo	F6F-5				
VOF-1	Lt Rene E.J.Poucel	F6F-5	}	He 111	N Vienne	1815
VOF-1	Ens Alfred R.Wood	F6F-5 58173 '8'				
VOF-1	Ens Alfred R.Wood	F6F-5 58173 '8'		He 111	N Vienne	1815
VOF-1	Ens David E.Robinson	F6F-5	}	He 111	N Vienne	1815
VOF-1	Lt Cdr John H.Sandor	F6F-5				

US Casualties

527th FS/86th FG	P-47D 42-26678 '71' shot down by Flak strafing a tank 3m SE Cavaillon, 13m SE of Avignon 1720; 2/Lt Donald E.Burns KiA [8093]
439th BS/319th BG	B-26C 42-107797 '65' lost over southern France 1132; Maj Harold G.Senften command pilot, 1/Lt Harold T.Novak pilot and five KiA [8007]
439th BS/319th BG	B-26 damaged by Flak; 1/Lt E.W.Wakeland and six safe
380th BS/310th BG	B-25J 43-27780 lost over southern France 1132; 1/Lt Robert E.Keane and five rescued and returned
*27th FS/1st FG	P-38 damaged by target explosion (train), force-landed at sea, pilot got in his dinghy, managed to get ashore into a mine-field, one of which exploded, badly damaging both legs along with other injuries; Capt Thomas E.Maloney WiA rescued by French workers

French Casualties

GB 2/52	B-26C Marauder '77', shot down by Flak off Toulon, crew swam ashore; Cne Lanier-Lachaise, Cdt Lanier, Lt.Col Michel Bouvard (CO 34eme Escadre de Bombardement) and crew POW, returned 27 Aug
GB 2/52	B-26C Marauder damaged by Flak, force-landed at Calvi; pilot and four safe, one WiA

German Casualties

2./KG 26	Ju 88A-17 WNr 800614 3Z+HK shot down by fighters in the Rhône Valley; Obgfr Hans-Werner Hinz and four KiA
4./KG 26	Ju 88A-17 1H+KN shot down by fighters 10km S Lyon; Obfw Alfred Urbanzyk and four crew MiA
5./KG 26	He 111H shot down after take-off from Lyon at Vourles 10km SSE Lyon; four safe, one WiA
II./KG 26	He 111H shot down at Mauves N Valence; four safe, one WiA
Stab II./KG 26	He 111H-6 WNr 110280 1H+EC shot down 20km S Lyon, crash-landed and burnt out; four safe, one WiA
III./KG 100	Do 217 shot down near Issoire, 35km SE Brioude; Uffz Wilhelm Krag, three crew and three passengers KiA
JGr 200	Bf 109G-6 shot down near Valion by P-47

Saturday-Sunday, 19/20 August 1944

British Casualties

13 Sqn	Baltimore V FW342 'Y' left 0110 on armed recce of Genoa-Turin area, believed shot down by Flak S Rapallo 0130; Capt J.H.G.Klompje and three KiA

Sunday, 20 August 1944

A Seafire of 807 Squadron from HMS *Hunter* was hit by Flak attacking targets in southern France and Lt E.V. Speakman was probably badly wounded. Attempting to land he seemed to realise that no air pressure was available and no flaps were operating. Speakman appeared to fall unconscious just on touching down and at full throttle his aircraft broke through the crash-barrier and went over the bow taking three ratings down with it.

The US Navy lost five Hellcats to Flak, with Lt/Cdr Harry B.Bass, commander of VF-74 being killed as the unit diary recorded at the time:

The Ju 88A-17s of I./KG 26 suffered several losses to fighters during 19 August. Here Lt Ulrich Laubis of 3.Staffel sits in the cockpit of his torpedo-armed aircraft at La Jasse.

Bombs dropped from a Seafire of 879 Squadron flown by Sub Lt W.A.Clarke explode around a road junction in Provence on 19 August.

"At the northernmost point of their flight, Bass' division went low looking for targets and over Chamelet, Bass suddenly pushed over steeply and at 200 feet went into a dive. The others couldn't see his target much but thought it to be a motorcycle. Bass went so low on his strafing run that his belly tank hit an object on the ground and tore away, the plane pulled up to 300 feet but never regained proper altitude. It pulled away to port and plummeted to earth, exploding."

The 17th Bomb Group also lost three bombers to Flak. 225 and 93 Squadrons left Calvi and landed at the newly constructed strip at Ramatuelle, southern France, from where the latter carried out patrols, escorts and strafing missions between Lyon and Mâcon.

At 0730 three French Thunderbolts from GC 2/5 on armed reconnaissance between Nice and Torino strafed an airfield near Savigliano destroying a Ju 88 on the ground. Then they encountered three Bf 109s, 90km north-east of Nice, claiming one Messerschmitt destroyed for one P-47 missing. The French unit lost two other P-47s to Flak during the day.

British Claims

151 Sqn	Wt Off L.Cunningham/Flt Sgt T.L.Williams	Mosquito HR297	Bf 109Damaged on ground	SE Nîmes	1700

British Casualties

92 Sqn	Spitfire VIII JF896 left 0730 on escort, shot down by Flak near Bologna, pilot baled in Allied lines nr Folgato; Flt Lt D.Wright safe
93 Sqn	Spitfire IX MA854 left 1010 on beachhead patrol, presumed engine failure, pilot baled out over the sea; Flg Off E.R.Stewart rescued by ASR
12 SAAF Sqn	Marauder II FB519 'K' left 0720 to bomb Budrio marshalling yards, force-landed at Falconara l/g; Lt Foxcroft and crew safe
12 SAAF Sqn	Marauder II FB443 'G' left 0720 to bomb Budrio marshalling yards, stalled on take-off, crashed 0725; Maj R.H.F.Howarth and two KiA, three WiA

Left: When attacking a target, Seafire L IIc MB314 was hit by Flak that caused serious damage and probably wounded Lt Speakman who, when attempting to land on HMS *Hunter*, appeared to fall unconscious. At full throttle the aircraft broke through the barrier and crashed over the bow. Right: Lt Eric Speakman of 807 Squadron who died attempting to land his damaged Seafire on HMS *Hunter*.

807 Sqn	Seafire L.IIc MB314 hit by Flak, crashed on landing on HMS *Hunter*; Lt E.V.Speakman, AF (E), S.T.C.Barter, AF (E), W.G.P.Pierce and AM (2) E.F.Pym KiA

US Casualties

526th FS/86th FG	P-47D 42-27916 lost u/k cause, 5m NE Saluzzo; Flt Off Reginald M.Jorgensen POW [8772]
66th FS/57th FG	P-47D 42-26421 hit by Flak, strafing gun positions 1000, damaged Cat 2; pilot safe
37th BS/17th BG	B-26B 42-96010 '25' shot down by Flak over France 1423; 1/Lt Robert E.Browning and three KiA, three POW [7865]
95th BS/17th BG	B-26C 42-107735 '50' shot down by Flak over France 1438; 1/Lt Joseph L.Albury Jr and five KiA, two evaded [7867]
432nd BS/17th BG	B-26C 42-107728 '84' hit by Flak, last seen 1445 40m NW Calvi, Corsica; Flt Off Beverly D.Draughn and three rescued, three KiA [7866]
VF-74	F6F-5 58333 '23' lost u/k cause nr Balaruc, France, 1100; Lt(jg) William N.Arbuckle KiA
VF-74	F6F-5 58307 '15' damaged by Flak, France, last seen 13m S Casteldaury 1140; Ens Charles W.S.Hulland evaded and returned
VF-74	F6F-5 58109 '1' lost possibly to Flak, 1m N Chamelet, France, 1300; Lt Cdr Harry B.Bass MiA
VOF-1	F6F-5 58279 '10' lost to Flak, 1300; Lt David D.Crockett POW; German commander surrendered the garrison to him on 23rd. Returned to *Tulagi* on 26 August
VOF-1	F6F-5 58300 '14' damaged by Flak, 5m N Carcassonne, 1900; Lt James M.Alston returned

French Claims

GC 2/5	Cne Pierre-Marie de L'Espinay	P-47D	Bf 109	Mondon

French Casualties

GC 2/5	P-47D hit tree while strafing motor transports; Sgt Hallut KiA
GC 2/5	P-47D hit by Flak, force-landed near St Raphael; Cne Jacques de Montravel
GC 2/5	P-47D shot down by Flak in flames, pilot baled; Sous Lt Robert Guillemard

German Casualties

7./JG 77	Bf 109G-6 WNr 165719 Black <+- shot down by fighters on transfer flight from Orange, crashed near Cuneo; Gefr Gerhard Ebert and Uffz Christian Maier, a passenger in the rear of this Bf 109, KiA
5./TG 1	Ju 52/3m WNr 130723 crashed at Courmayeur, 15km W Aosta, near Mont Blanc; Uffz Hans Ibbs and three KiA
6./TG 1	Ju 52/3m WNr 7213 crashed at Courmayeur, 15km W Aosta, near Mont Blanc; Fw Hermann Stiller and three KiA
5./JG 77	Bf 109G-6 WNr 163226 Yellow 12 disorientated after a dogfight, landed in Switzerland; Fw Karl Tanck interned
5./JG 77	Bf 109G-6 WNr 163956 Yellow 3 disorientated after a dogfight, landed in Switzerland; Flg Karl-Friedrich Nehrenheim interned

Sunday-Monday, 20/21 August 1944

The night-fighter F6F-3Ns were fitted with zero length rocket launchers and on the night of the 20th five Hellcats flew an anti-shipping sweep off the mouth of the Rhône, having earlier landed on *Tulagi* to brief and refuel. Unfortunately, on the return flight to Calvi, Ens Marion F.DeMasters was forced to ditch off the Corsican coast and was lost.

US Casualties	
VF (N)-74 det	F6F-3N ditched off coast of Corsica; Ens Marion F.DeMasters MIA

Monday, 21 August 1944

The Fleet Air Arm on HMS *Attacker*, *Stalker* and *Hunter* had another ten Seafires in support of the landings lost or damaged, only two to enemy action. One of these was at dawn when two pairs from 879 Squadron were launched on separate armed reconnaissances. In the first pair, Sub Lt G.Calder's aircraft was hit by light Flak; he successfully force-landed, evaded capture and eventually linked up with advancing US troops. The other pair led by Lt George Ogilvy found some German artillery on a rural road but was hit by Flak and Sub Lt A.I.R.Shaw had to bale out. He briefly became a prisoner but escaped bringing with him two of his captors! He recalled the attack:

> "Our sortie was undoubtedly a failure and we found nothing to report in the next thirty minutes, although, from time to time, we did fly over small areas which were clear of fog. We decided to return to the ship but, no sooner had we set course than we flew over another small patch of countryside that was visible. We looked down and there, before our eyes, was a long column of motorized artillery moving along a tree-lined road. The vehicles stopped hurriedly as we approached. Ignoring the 'one target, one attack' rule I made several firing runs on the column and during the fourth attack my aircraft was struck in the engine. There was a heavy explosion and as I climbed away my windscreen became covered with oil, fumes filled the cockpit and white smoke poured from the exhaust stubs. The smoke soon became black as I struggled to gain altitude and I was lucky to reach about 4,000 feet before the engine burst into flames and then seized solid.
>
> "I called to Ogilvy that I was going to bale out, undid the straps and inverted the aircraft, but it lost momentum and began to nosedive. I found myself caught by the legs, hanging out of the cockpit as the plane hurtled towards the ground. With all the strength I could muster I strained forward until the stick was just within reach. I gave it a 'flip' with the backs of my fingers. The result was immediate and violent. I was literally ejected from the cockpit to find myself tumbling over and over in a wild rush of air.
>
> "After a few seconds everything calmed down and I pulled the ripcord. It came away so easily that I thought, for an unhappy moment, that it had not worked properly. Then there was a sudden jerk and I was floating down in comfort. As I looked around, I saw my Seafire strike the ground with a numbing explosion and, from a small village nearby, I could see soldiers running in my direction. A shot rang out and, assuming that I was being fired at, I used the shroud lines to swing myself about. I landed in a grassy field, quickly gathered up the parachute and headed for some scrub. They knew I was somewhere in the scrub. I raised my head, half turned and found myself the aiming point of half a dozen rifles..."

In a costly day for the squadron five other aircraft were damaged in landing accidents, one of which hit several parked aircraft and critically injured Sub Lt R.A.Gowan who was in the cockpit of one of them.

881 Squadron's Sub Lt Ronald Brittain disappeared when he lost contact with his flight returning from a fighter-bomber sortie. One Wildcat acting as a spotter was hit by 40mm fire with a further twenty aircraft damaged during the day's missions, mainly from ground fire.

The 21st was 882's busiest day of Dragoon with 30 sorties being flown, but Sub Lt N.Wood in a Wildcat failed to return from a raid over southern France but came back later.

Following an urgent request form Army Group G for supplies of anti-tank weapons Luftwaffe Regional Command 6/XI at Salon en Provence agreed that weapons would be airlifted into Orange-Caritat. Some of these aircraft were encountered by a patrol of F6Fs from VOF-1 that destroyed three Ju 52/3ms. This was the last day in support by the two US carriers, their F6Fs having claimed eight aircraft, 825 M/T and 84 locomotives destroyed.

Between 17 and 21 August OA-10 Catalina crews of 1 Emergency Rescue Squadron rescued 21 Allied airmen, making open sea landings in hazardous weather conditions and heavy seas.

Right: Sub Lt A.I.R.Shaw of 879 Squadron parachutes from Seafire IIc LR691 'A-C' after being hit by Flak on 21 August. He was soon captured but subsequently escaped. Below: During a sortie near Orange, Ens Edward Olszewski (left), flying an F6F-5 of VOF-1, claimed two Ju 52/3m transports and indeed two such aircraft from 6./TG 3 were lost. Two days earlier, Ens Archie Wood (right) of the same unit had claimed two He 111s flying in this same aircraft, hence the application of four victory symbols.

3 RAAF Sqn	Kittyhawk IV FX760 left 1705 to bomb guns S Pesaro, hit by intense 20mm Flak in bomb dive, spun in; Wt Off C.T.Halpin KiA
16 SAAF Sqn	Beaufighter X LZ375 'W' left 1755, attacked a power station at Zadvarje, struck the roof of the building, crashed; Lt C.R.Russell/Lt G.W.Stanbury KiA
879 Sqn	Seafire on dawn TacR hit by Flak, force-landed in southern France; Sub Lt G.Calder evaded
879 Sqn	Seafire L.IIc LR710 on landing on HMS *Attacker* bounced over wires, hit LR643, NN128 & LR740; Sub Lt W.A.Clarke safe
879 Sqn	Seafire L.IIc LR691 'AC' hit by Fak, pilot baled out over S France; Sub Lt A.I.R Shaw POW, escaped
879 Sqn	Seafire L.IIc LR760 caught No 5 Wire and hit barrier, HMS *Attacker*; Lt G.Ogilvy safe
807 Sqn	Seafire L.III NF487 bounced into barrier, damaged propeller and wings; Sub Lt M.La Page safe
807 Sqn	Seafire L.III NF645 hook locked up, hit round down of HMS *Hunter*, crashed into barrier; Sub Lt P.M.Lamb safe
809 Sqn	Seafire III NN352 clipped propeller on deck, HMS *Stalker*; Sub Lt G.H.Brittain safe
881 Sqn	Wildcat VI JV668 'UY' lost returning from bombing sortie; Sub Lt R.Brittain KiA
882 Sqn	Wildcat V JV331 failed to return from raid over France; Sub Lt N.Wood evaded

US Claims

VOF-1	Ens Edward W.Olszewski	F6F-5 58173 '8'	2 Ju 52/3ms	N Orange	1615
VOF-1	Ens Richard Van B.Yentzer	F6F-5	Ju 52/3m	N Orange	1615

US Casualties

527th FS/86th FG	P-47D 42-27303 '92' reported wing tank failure and out of fuel, 10m S Cannes 2115; Lt John R.McGehee rescued by a destroyer
527th FS/86th FG	P-47D 42-26964 '94' crash-landed at St Catherines' a/f 2100; Lt James C.Watson, Jr safe
522nd FS/27th FBG	P-47D 42-28054 shot down by Flak 1200, crashed into sea; Lt Harold H.Neale Jr rescued by ASR Catalina
64th FS/57th FG	P-47D 42-26421 hit by Flak, attacking Alessandria M/Y 1015, damaged Cat 2; pilot safe
442nd BS/320th BG	B-26B 42-95752 '29' *Wine Women and Song* left 1600 to attack road bridge N Grizzana Morandi, damaged by Flak, crew baled out 8m E Sassocorvaro 1900, crashed SW Pesaro; 1/Lt Joseph R.Armstrong and three POW, three evaded [7868]
438th BS/319th BG	B-26G 43-34259 left 0814 to bomb road bridge, damaged by Flak, crash-landed at Grosseto 1149; Lt Sturmer and five safe
VOF-1	F6F-5 58263 '8' lost to Flak 5m N Nîmes 1430; Lt(jg) John H.Coyne KiA

German Casualties

6./TG 3	Ju 52/3m WNr 7688 4V+ FP shot up N Orange, force-landed; Uffz Werner Geipel and three MiA
6./TG 3	Ju 52/3m WNr 501336 4V+ DP shot up nr Orange, force-landed and exploded; pilot and one safe, two WiA

Monday-Tuesday, 21/22 August 1944

British Claims

256 Sqn	Flg Off P.D.W.Brunt/Flg Off A.E.Harris	Mosquito XIII MM470	Ju 88 Damaged	Ghedi	0225-0625

Tuesday, 22 August 1944

800 Squadron's Hellcats flew 24 sorties against shore targets while Seafires of 899 Squadron joined the assault on the retreating 11th Panzer Division, concentrating on railway rolling stock.

Cmdt Frans J.Burniaux DFC of the Belgian Congo Air Force, acting commander of 12 SAAF Squadron, became the permanent commander on this day, and was appointed as a lieutenant colonel in the SAAF while he held command.

British Casualties

1 SAAF Sqn	Spitfire IXc MA805 'L' hit by Flak N Bologna, crash-landed; Lt S.Schneider evaded, KiA with partisans on 7 November
2 SAAF Sqn	Spitfire IXc JL370 'B' shot down by 20mm Flak near San Marino, pilot baled out nr Fano; Lt J.B.Miller returned
5 SAAF Sqn	Kittyhawk IV FX729 hit by 20mm Flak in bombing dive 1430; Lt C.W.Nunneley baled out in Ferrara area, evaded, returned on 8 October
241 Sqn	Spitfire VIII JF339 left 0600 on shipping recce, on return engine failed 10m off Fano 0800, pilot baled out; Plt Off G.L.Garnham picked up by Walrus L2170 of 293 Sqn flown by Lt J.V.Peters
899 Sqn	Seafire III NN338, heavy landing on HMS *Khedive*, port undercarriage collapsed; Lt R.B.Haworth safe
800 Sqn	Hellcat I JV102 'EB' undercarriage leg would not lower; Lt J.G.Devitt baled out safely
800 Sqn	Hellcat I JV153 failed to pull out of dive when attacking a train 2m SE Villeneuve-lès-Béziers; Lt R.M.Rogers KiA
800 Sqn	Hellcat I I JV100 taxied over the side of HMS *Emperor*; Lt O.R.Oakes safe
800 Sqn	Hellcat I ditched on operations; Sub Lt C.D.Spencer rescued

US Casualties

525th FS/86th FG	P-47D 42-27272 on return from op, crashed on landing approach to Poretta a/f 1400; 2/Lt Benjamin A.Higginson Jr KiA	
526th FS/86th FG	P-47D 42-27949 on return from op, pilot baled out, parachute partially failed, landed in a swamp near Poretta a/f 2200; Lt Harold J.Ingley retrieved safely	
441st BS/320th BG	B-26 43-34234 '24' left 0825 to bomb bridge at Vergato, damaged by Flak in starboard engine, ditched 50yds off Corsican coast; 1/Lt Robert E Dinwiddie and five safe	
111th TRS	F-6A 43-103428 shot down by Flak in southern France; 2/Lt Richard F.Hoy MiA [8774]	

Tuesday-Wednesday, 22/23 August 1944

A crew of 414th Night Fighter Squadron was ordered to intrude to Ghedi airdrome 10m south-south-west Brescia. The crew were due over the target area at 2130 until 2200, when they were to clear it for the next crew. The last message received at 2225 reported that they were baling out. At this time, their scheduled route would be near the coast south-west of Portofino. It was presumed that they came down in the sea as no trace of them was found.

17 SAAF Squadron had been given the task of undertaking 'Nickel' operations (dropping propaganda leaflets) with the aim of discouraging non-German units of the Wehrmacht from defending the invasion of southern France. After many attempts had been frustrated by bad weather, Lt Col B.R.Mackenzie took off from Alghero at 1950 on such a sortie to the Hendaye-Bayonne area on the French/Spanish border of the Bay of Biscay. Over Spain he encountered an extremely violent electrical storm which damaged his aircraft. With no hydraulics and with the port mainplane of his aircraft severely buckled, Mackenzie reached Gibraltar and crash-landed.

British Casualties		
13 Sqn	Baltimore V FW535 'J' left 2145 on armed recce of Lodi area, crashed near Genivolta 2234; Flt Lt P.D.K.MacGlashan and three KiA	
17 SAAF Sqn	Ventura V JT896 'L' left Alghero 1950 on Nickel-dropping mission to Hendaye-Bayonne area, damaged by electrical storm, crash-landed at Gibraltar; Lt Col B.R.Mackenzie and crew safe	
US Casualties		
414th NFS	Beaufighter VIf MM882 left 1957 from Alghero on night-intruder mission to Ghedi, possibly shot down by Flak; 2/Lt James T.Hope/Flt Off Carmen J.Phillipi KiA [8088]	

Wednesday, 23 August 1944

HMS *Emperor*'s 800 Squadron conducted its last operations over southern France flying 32 sorties against shore targets. Having possibly been hit by Flak, Petty Officer Pilot William MacLean ditched but was picked up. HMS *Emperor* then withdrew to Maddalena to replenish with its Hellcats having flown 252 sorties for the loss of nine to 11 aircraft. The ship then sailed for Alexandria with the remaining ten serviceable Hellcats and four repairable ones.

The result of the invasion of southern France was that little opposition to the series of attacks launched early in August was encountered and even the Flak defences were comparatively light, so that casualties re-mained relatively low. When the landings began the Luftwaffe made a few brief appearances but after a series of sweeps by Allied naval fighter aircraft operating from aircraft carriers of Task Force 88 which was support-ing the landings and by XII TAC fighters on the 17th, the surviving units were quickly withdrawn. Virtually no opposing aircraft were seen after 19 August.

185 Squadron escorted Marauders to Imola, the unit's pilots flying six Mk V and Mk VIII Spitfires, losing two aircraft and a pilot when they collided on landing at Falconara. During the day the squadron also com-menced moving to Loreto.

Magg Carlo Emanuele Buscaglia, the most successful torpedo-bomber Italian pilot, holder of a Medaglia d'Oro al valor militare, crashed on taking off in a Baltimore bomber; he would die of wounds the next day to be replaced as 132° Gruppo commander by T.Col Paolo Moci.

After a day of naval bombardment, on the 23rd the German commander in Toulon summoned the senior Allied prisoner, Lt David Crockett – a descendent of the Davy Crockett of the Alamo fame – who had been shot down three days earlier, and promptly surrendered the entire garrison of 500 men to him! Crockett re-turned to the *Tulagi* on 26 August with some interesting tales to tell.

Top left: Having been shot down over Toulon harbour on 20 August and captured, Lt David Crockett (a descendent of the legendary frontiersman) received the surrender of the port, together with over 500 enemy troops, three days later! Top right: An F6F-5 Hellcat flown by Ens John A.Mooney of VOF-I attacks a train west of the town of Carcassonne during a sortie on 23 August. Above: Based in Sardinia the B-26G Marauders of the 320th Bomb Group were well placed to hit targets in both northern Italy and southern France but when bombing Modigliana on this date Flak brought down one and damaged two others.

Top: Ground crew service the Merlin engine of Spitfire VIII MT714 'F' of 43 Squadron at the recently captured strip at Ramatuelle on the Côte d'Azur. Above: Due to a loose cockpit canopy, P-51C Mustang 42-103578 NJ *Val Gal II* of the 111th Tactical Reconnaissance Squadron flown by Lt Stanley F.Fierstein became the first US aircraft to land in southern France.

British Casualties

450 Sqn	Kittyhawk IV FT357 left 1830 to bomb five 88mm guns, engine trouble, force-landed on Iesi a/f; Flt Lt H.E.Watkins safe
454 Sqn	Baltimore V FW701 'D' left 1530 to bomb fuel dumps at Limestre N Pistoia, shot down by Flak, crashed 1700; Flg Off K.A.Howard and two POW, one KiA
454 Sqn	Baltimore V FW602 'E' left 1510 to bomb fuel dumps at Limestre N Pistoia, hit by Flak, crash-landed in Allied lines, caught fire; Flt Sgt L.W.Gray KiA, three WiA
260 Sqn	P-51C Mustang III FB292 left 1815, pilot wounded by Flak near Bologna, returned to base; Sgt D.Varey WiA
112 Sqn	Mustang III HB895 'N' left 1705, shot down by Flak E Modena 1705; Lt J.C.Hoyle KiA
241 Sqn	Spitfire VIII JF458 left 0615, hit by Flak near Rovigo, crashed; Flg Off D.S.Monard KiA
241 Sqn	Spitfire VIII JF344 left 1730, damaged by Flak, pilot baled out 2-3m S River Po Delta 5m off shore; Flt Lt D.M.Leitch rescued next morning by 293 Sqn Walrus L2170 of Lt J.V.Peters
185 Sqn	Spitfire on transfer from Loreto to Falconara, was struck by another Spitfire after landing; Flg Off G.Cross KiA
185 Sqn	Spitfire on transfer from Loreto to Falconara, on a bomber escort, struck another Spitfire after landing; Flg Off G.M.Buchanan injured
800 Sqn	Hellcat I JV134 'EZ' on landing after a mission crashed through the barrier and hit JV174 'EH'; Sub Lt R.J.Tee safe
800 Sqn	Hellcat I on return from mission ditched near carriers but was not picked up; Petty Officer Pilot W.G.MacLean KiA

US Casualties

522nd FS/27th FBG	P-47D 42-27103 shot down by Flak 1700, crashed nr Narbonne; 2/Lt Ellis G.Heath KiA
444th BS/320th BG	B-26G 43-34240 '97' *Pancho Villa/River Rats/Kiss Me Honey* left 0810, shot down by Flak nr Modigliana 1005; 1/Lt Wilbert L.Weier and five KiA, one returned [7997]
444th BS/320th BG	B-26B 42-95946 '79' left 0810, hit by Flak nr Modigliana 1015, landed at Cecina l/g; 1/Lt Richard N.Driscoll and five safe, one WiA, one baled out and POW [7996]
444th BS/320th BG	B-26B '94' left 0810 damaged by Flak, crashed on landing 1200; 1/Lt Albert D.Stearns and five safe

French Casualties

GC 2/3	P-47D shot down by Flak NE Orange 1830; Sgt Ancelet WiA, POW, released when hospital overrun

Italian Co-Belligerent Casualties

28° Gr. St Baltimore	Baltimore FA638 crashed on taking-off; Magg Carlo Emanuele Buscaglia MOVM, DoW next day

Wednesday-Thursday, 23/24 August 1944

British Casualties

221 Sqn	Wellington XIII HZ883 'X' left 0030 on offensive recce over northern Adriatic, lost u/k cause; Wt Off F.R.W.Bray and five KiA

Thursday, 24 August 1944

During an armed recce north-west of Nîmes 809 Squadron's Sub Lt Ray Rawbone had to force land his Seafire. He unsuccessfully tried to set the aircraft on fire and was then seen by the rest of the patrol to run into a wood. He hid in a barn for several days and then managed to link up with the Maquis, participating in a successful ambush of a German patrol and returned to the ship on 3 September. Sub Lt G.E.Thomas also failed to return to HMS *Hunter* from a ground strafe over southern France but was later found to be safe.

When the carriers withdrew in the evening, 881 Squadron had flown 180 sorties over southern France whilst 882 Squadron had mounted 167 fighter-bomber sorties over the same area in support of the US Army. Royal Navy aircraft from the seven carriers flew 1,673 sorties for the loss of 21 RN and 14 USN aircraft to enemy action. Sixty more were damaged or destroyed in deck-landing accidents.

British Claims

92 Sqn	Flg Off A.D.Taylor	Spitfire VIII JF356	Bf 109 Probable	in sea off La Spezia	1855-1945

British Casualties

4 SAAF Sqn	Spitfire IX MJ121 struck tree while strafing SE Forlì l/g, crash-landed 0855; Lt M.W.V.Odendaal POW, escaped and returned
352 Sqn	Spitfire Vc JK712 damaged by Flak, u/c collapsed on landing at Vis, Cat B damage; Flt Lt Jovanovic safe
454 Sqn	Baltimore V FW658 left to bomb Ravenna wharf, hit by Flak 1815, u/c collapsed on landing; Flg Off G.Hume and three safe
807 Sqn	Seafire L.III NM994 failed to return to HMS *Hunter* from ground strafe over southern France; Sub Lt G.E.Thomas safe
809 Sqn	Seafire IIc MA999 on armed recce, force-landed north-west of Nîmes; Sub Lt A.R.Rawbone linked up with Maquis and returned on 3 September

US Casualties

441st BS/320th BG	B-26B 42-95768 '16' *Becky* left 1505 to bomb Montpellier railway bridge 1723, engine trouble 1805; 2/Lt Harry E.Jenkins and six KiA [7998]

French Casualties

GB 1/22	Marauder damaged by Flak S Bologna; Lt Lamy and five safe

German Casualties

	LKS reports one tactical recce Bf 109 Damaged

Thursday-Friday, 24/25 August 1944

British Claims

255 Sqn	Flt Sgt B.C.Dinham-Peren/Plt Off D.E.Williams	Beaufighter VIf	Ju 88 Probable	15m NE Ancona	0200-0225

British Casualties

55 Sqn	Baltimore V FW390 'K' left 2237, FTR from night intruder to Bologna-Ferrara-Rimini area; Flt Sgt A.G.Kenebel and three KiA
600 Sqn	Beaufighter VIf MM945 'J' crashed E Lake Trasimeno u/k cause; Flg Off N.L.Jefferson/Plt Off E.Spencer KiA

Friday, 25 August 1944

The 8th Army crossed the Metauro river and began its push against the Gothic Line during the evening with the opening of a huge artillery barrage before the armour and infantry advanced the next morning.

British Claims

92 Sqn	Flt Lt L.J.Montgomerie		Spitfire VIII JF339	Bf 109	NW Leghorn	0600-0650

Above: Lt Col Guy Fanneau de Horie flying with GC I/4 died when his P-47D was shot down by Flak near Malataverne on the River Rhône near Montélimar. Right: Rear Adm Calvin Durgin welcomes Lt Cdr William Bringle of VOF-1 back aboard after the latter had 'got his feet wet' when his aircraft was hit by Flak during a spotting mission in the Marseille area.

British Casualties

4 SAAF Sqn	Spitfire IX MH548 'O' shot down by Flak while strafing, pilot baled 16km from Florence 0840; Lt E.D.K.Franck evaded, returned on 9 September
213 Sqn	Mustang III FB366 'C' left 0735, strafed M/T, shot down by Flak 0935, pilot baled out; Sgt A.Liudzius evaded
32 Sqn	Spitfire Vc MA291 left 0905, strafed train NE Kaitsa, hit by Flak, pilot baled; Wt Off R.C.Lamb evaded, returned to Bari in a DC-3 on 4 September
247 Sqn	Spitfire IX BS337 left 1600 to escort B-25s to Marseille, engine cut on return flight, pilot baled out 40m N Calvi, a Walrus and a Catalina attempted to pick him up but could not take off due to rough sea, later rescued by an ASR launch which also recovered the other two crews; Sqn Ldr I.H.R.Shand safe
24 SAAF Sqn	Marauder III HD466 'M' left 1600 to bomb road SSW Faenza, port engine damaged by Flak, on final approach to land at Falconara engine cut, crash-landed 1830; Lt T.F.Sussmann and five safe
114 Sqn	Boston IV BZ490 crashed into sea off Piombino; Wt Off H.L.Dowland and three KiA
15 SAAF Sqn	Baltimore V FW596 'M' bombing marshalling yards Forlì, on landing propellers struck runway, overturned, wrecked; Lt K.D.Sievwright and three WiA
16 SAAF Sqn	Beaufighter X 'M' left 0600 to attack Bulgarian barracks at Prenjasi, engine failed on take-off, crashed and caught fire; Lt Kendall/Lt W.A.Hewett WiA

US Casualties

525th FS/86th BG	P-47D 42-xx971 hit by Flak bombing highway near Pistoia, spun in at 1620; Lt Donovan J.Cooper KiA
314th FS/324th FG	P-47D 42-26982 lost over France; 1/Lt Michael Krasulak KiA
66th FS/57th FG	P-47D 42-27089 hit by Flak at Bologna 1345, damaged Cat 2; pilot safe
85th FS/79th FG	P-47D lost over Italy; 2/Lt Harry W.Mitchell KiA
95th BS/17th BG	B-26C 42-107734 '71' lost SE Bologna 1204; 2/Lt Philip I.Eschbach Jr and four returned, two POW [8768]
12th PRS/ 3rd PRG	F-5A 42-13309 lost over Italy, possibly due to small-arms fire; 1/Lt Jerald B.Jensen MiA [7995]
VOF-1	F6F-5 58173 hit by Flak, ran out of gas 1052; Lt Cdr William F.Bringle returned

French Casualties

GC 1/4	P-47D '92' shot down by Flak at Châteauneuf-du-Rhône ca1530; Lt Pierre Soubeirat KiA
GC 1/4	P-47D '99' shot down by Flak at Malataverne ca1530; Lt Col Guy Fanneau de la Horie KiA
GC 2/5	P-47D shot down by Flak from motor transports NE Donzère 1645; Sous Lt Robert Guillemard crash-landed, killed by German troops
GC 2/5	P-47D badly damaged by Flak 1645, crash-landed at Fréjus; Cne de Montravel safe
GC 2/5	P-47D hit by Flak 1645, returned; Cne Pierre-Marie de L'Espinay safe

Italian Co-Belligerent Casualties

73ª Sq, 12° Gr, 4° St	P-39N 42-18330 crashed at Campo Vesuvio on taking off; Serg Magg Teresio Martinoli KiFA
361ª Sq, 155° Gr, 51° St	MC.205 MM 92211 '155-14' left 0900, crashed nr Saranda, Albania, u/k cause; S.Ten Giovanni Mancina baled out, returned later

German Casualties

2./NAGr 11	Bf 109G-8 WNr 200640 White 3 lost in combat with Spitfire 35km W Pisa; Fw Rolf Rathgeber KiA
	LKS reports 1 Bf 109 lost in combat

Saturday, 26 August 1944

Flt Lt Leighton Montgomerie was scrambled after an Me 410 on a reconnaissance which he failed to intercept. However, as he returned to land, his engine failed and he was critically injured in the subsequent crash; he died in the early hours of the 27th. Sqn Ldr Neville Duke recorded an epitaph in his diary: "Bad news this morning that 'Monty' in 92 has been killed trying to force land short of fuel on the 'drome over at Rosignano. Shame: Montgomery [sic] was one of the better types in life."

While leading a low-level attack at 500 feet up the Rhône Valley against mechanical transport near Montélimar, Lt Charles Jefferson's Seafire was hit by Flak that shot the wing away and it crashed killing him instantly.

British Casualties

92 Sqn	Spitfire IX JF651 scrambled 1630 after Me 410, engine cut, crashed; Flt Lt L.J.Montgomerie badly hurt, DoW 27 August
213 Sqn	Mustang III FB315 left 1420, hit by Flak, crash-landed S Zagreb; Flt Lt C.S.Vos rescued by partisans, returned 1 September
153 Sqn D Flt	Spitfire IX 'H' left Reghaia 1120 for La Senia, crashed off Cap Falconara N Oran; Flg Off J.F.Baird KiA
809 Sqn	Seafire III hit by Flak, wing shot away leading a low-level attack against M/T near Montélimar; Lt C.E.H.Jefferson KiA
809 Sqn	Seafire L.IIc MA988 bounced into barrier landing on HMS *Stalker*, badly damaged; Sub Lt W.S.Donnelly safe
807 Sqn	Seafire L.IIc LR686 crashed into barrier landing on HMS *Hunter*; Sub Lt P.M.Lamb safe

US Casualties

444th BS/320th BG	B-26B 42-95904 '87' left 0850 to bomb coastal defence guns on Île de Ratonneau, collided with # 91 in southern France 1035; 1/Lt Albert Stearns and four KiA, one POW [7999]
99th FS/332nd FG	P-51 crashed nr Krujino, Yugoslavia; 2/Lt Henry A.Wise Jr POW
VOF-1	TBM-1C 25489 '31' burned by own crew Pointe de Sabian; Lt(jg) Curtis M.Ely and two returned

French Casualties

GC 2/5	P-47D crashed while attacking motor transports near Uzès; Sgt Baills KiA
Esc 2S (or 3S)	Latécoère 298 crashed while searching for missing 153 Sqn Spitfire off Cap Falconara

German Casualties

1./NAGr 11	Bf 109G-8 WNr 200646 Black 9 shot down by Spitfire 26km W Pesaro; Obfhr Hubert Kürschner KiA
2./NAGr 11	Bf 109G-6 WNr 163718 White 6 crashed 4km SW Cesena; Uffz Martin Ringel KiA
	LKS reports one Bf 109 lost in combat and two lost on operations; one Ju 52/3m missing

Saturday-Sunday, 26/27 August 1944

British Casualties

36 Sqn	Wellington XIV HF247 'F' left 0103 from Alghero, investigated a radar contact W Bonifacio Straits 0230, on third pass hit the sea and crashed; Flt Sgt A.E.McCormick and two KiA, three rescued by US OA-10 Catalina 1730 next day

Sunday, 27 August 1944

Another day of landing incidents saw the Fleet Air Arm suffering damage to another seven Seafires, continuing to illustrate the difficulties of landing Seafires on small escort carriers. The very short deck area, at the end of which was the crash barrier, combined with the restricted visibility over the nose and relatively fragile landing gear, resulted in enormous attrition. It is quite apparent the accident rate of the purpose-built Grumman Wildcats and Hellcats was far lower than that of Seafires.

In the Adriatic four R/P-armed Hurricane IVs of 6 Squadron escorted by 352 (Yugoslav) Squadron, flew to Zavratnica Bay near Jablanac to attack some Siebel ferries. The commanding officer, Sqn Ldr Brown, dived to lead the attack and was hit by intense and accurate Flak and after he had fired his rockets his aircraft was hit, crashed into a hillside and exploded. He was replaced by Sqn Ldr R.H.Langdon-Davies DFC.

British Casualties

6 Sqn	Hurricane IV KZ243 'Y' left 0535, shot down by Flak attacking Siebel ferry Zavratnica Bay; Sqn Ldr J.H.Brown DFC KiA
807 Sqn	Seafire L.IIc LR749 bounced into barrier landing on HMS *Hunter*; Sub Lt M.La Page safe
807 Sqn	Seafire L.III NF626 hook caught No 3 barrier and into forward lift of HMS *Hunter*, causing major damage; Sub Lt J.E.M.Thornhill safe
807 Sqn	Seafire L.III NF638 crashed into barrier landing on HMS *Hunter*, damaged propeller; Sub Lt L.D.Graham safe
807 Sqn	Seafire L.III NN112 on landing on HMS *Hunter* starboard oleo collapsed and damaged propeller; Lt Cdr A.W.Bloomer safe
807 Sqn	Seafire L.III NN117 on landing on HMS *Hunter* hit barrier and nosed over; Sub Lt W.A.Neal safe
809 Sqn	Seafire L.III NN122 heavy landing on HMS *Stalker*; Sub Lt H.L.Aspinal safe
809 Sqn	Seafire L.IIc MB268 heavy landing on HMS *Stalker*, undercarriage damaged; Sub Lt J.O.Jerromes safe

French Casualties

GC 1/4	P-47D left 1735, hit by Flak, landed 30km SW Turin; Sgt Vincent rescued by Italian partisans, returned to unit 8 September

Sunday-Monday, 27/28 August 1944

With the intentions of 8th Army now clear to the Gothic Line defenders, the Ju 87s of NSGr 9 were once more thrown into the fight, appearing during the nights of late August, the concentration points and supply lines of the assaulting forces being frequently attacked. 600 Squadron once more provided Beaufighters to patrol over the front, the first effective contacts being made during the night of 27/28 August when Flt Lt Thompson shot down one of the dive-bombers.

British Claims

600 Sqn	Flt Lt D.A.Thompson/Flg Off G.Beaumont	Beaufighter VIf ND165 'N'	Ju 87	nr Arezzo	2231

British Casualties

272 Sqn	Beaufighter VI V8888 'H' last seen firing rockets at ships near Finale Ligure 2330; Flt Lt H.Scholefield MiA/Flg Off P.J.Baker KiA

1./NSGr 9   Ju 87D-4 WNr 141039 lost at Fano; Uffz Günther Voss MiA

LKS reports 2 Ju 87s and 1 Ju 52/3m missing

Monday, 28 August 1944

At dusk on 28 August TG 88.1 was released from Operation Dragoon and sailed for Alexandria to replenish, receive new aircraft where necessary and to conduct training pending further operations in the Aegean.

British Claims					
92 Sqn	Wt Off F.R.Newman	Spitfire VIII JF559	Bf 109	La Spezia area	0605-0640

British Casualties

4 SAAF Sqn	Spitfire IX JL163 'U' damaged by Flak while strafing, engine seized 1925, pilot baled out but parachute streamed; Lt P.J.Welman KiA
12 SAAF Sqn	Marauder II FB425 'J' left 0850-0901 to bomb gun positions nr Pesaro, damaged by Flak, crash-landed at Jesi, damaged Cat II; Lt W.R.A.Grosse-Rasgado and five safe
450 Sqn	Kittyhawk IV FX589 left 1735 as leader of six a/c on bombing sortie S Pesaro, hit by Flak, crash-landed 1805 in area held by Polish troops, one of 250lb bombs exploded destroying the a/c; Flg Off S.C.Youl KiA
93 Sqn	Spitfire IX MA631 left 1550, strafed motor transports near Pont du Gard, possibly damaged by Flak, crashed into hill behind Nice; Sgt D.L.Karck KiA

US Casualties

527th FS/86th FG	P-47D '80' hit stack of fuel tanks while strafing, reached base at Poretta, crash-landed; 1/Lt James F.McPherson WiA
523rd FS/27th FBG	P-47D 42-28061 'Z' lost u/k cause, last seen 0805; 2/Lt Alexander R.Cattanach safe
524th FS/27th FBG	P-47D 42-26358 hit by small-arms fire 1700; 1/Lt Calvin D.Mosher KiA
65th FS/57th FG	P-47D 42-26754 hit by Flak 0800, damaged Cat 2; pilot safe
314th FS/324th FG	P-47D '20' possibly hit by Flak, crashed into hill nr Montélimar 1745; 2/Lt William A.Clark Jr KiA
86th FS/79th FG	P-47D 42-26809 shot down by Flak 0720; Capt Roger B.Files safe
86th FS/79th FG	P-47D 42-76613 shot down by Flak S Lyon 0725; 2/Lt Percy E.Brown Jr evaded [8383]
85th FS/79th FG	P-47D 42-26810 shot down by Flak 1630; 2/Lt William W.Ogden evaded
87th FS/79th FG	P-47D 42-27109 shot down by Flak nr Primarotte, France 1825; 2/Lt Philip Bagian evaded [8387]
87th FS/79th FG	P-47D 42-75997 shot down by Flak nr Vienne, France 1825; Flt Off Russell K.Jennings KiA [8381]

Italian Co-Belligerent Casualties

92ª Sq, 8° Gr, 5° St	MC.202 MM 91840 shot down over Albania; Serg Umberto Canali POW

German Casualties

2./NAGr 11	Bf 109G-8 WNr 200300 White 7 lost in combat with Spitfire 10km NE Pescaglia; Obfhr Walter Graab WiA
	LKS reports one Bf 109 and one Ju 52/3m lost in combat; one Bf 109 and one Fi 156 destroyed by bombs on ground

Monday-Tuesday, 28/29 August 1944

This night 600 Squadron enjoyed more successes, three Ju 87s being claimed, two by Plt Off G.W.Judd and one by Wg Cdr Styles DFC, the commanding officer.

Overnight, the US Navy carriers withdrew from Operation Dragoon for redeployment to the Pacific. From USS *Kasaan Bay* VF-74 flew a total of 432 sorties, 289 offensive, 79 combat air patrols and 64 beach patrols on just over 1,000 hours flying. Five aircraft and pilots were lost over enemy territory and 37 aircraft were damaged by enemy fire. The Hellcats of VOF-1 aboard USS *Tulagi* had flown 74 combat air patrols, 96 bombardment spotting and 258 armed-reconnaissance/dive-bombing sorties for the loss of three aircraft. On the credit side, however, the VOF-1 pilots claimed 23 locomotives and 600 assorted vehicles destroyed or damaged, as well as six German aircraft.

Shipping in Trieste harbour as seen from a Beaufighter of 16 SAAF Squadron as it ran in at less than 200 feet during an attack on 28 August.

600 Sqn	Plt Off G.W.Judd/Flg Off J.R.Brewer	Beaufighter VIf V8879 'D'	Ju 87	15m SE Pesaro	2115
600 Sqn	Plt Off G.W.Judd/Flg Off J.R.Brewer	Beaufighter VIf V8879 'D'	Ju 87	60m S Pesaro	2210
600 Sqn	Wg Cdr L.H.Styles/Flg Off H.J.Wilmer	Beaufighter VIf ND170 'F'	Ju 87	15-20m NE Florence	2345

British Casualties

600 Sqn	Beaufighter VIf V8879 'D' damaged by debris from second victim 2210, port engine failed, landed safely to Falconara; Plt Off G.W.Judd/Flg Off J.R.Brewer safe

German Casualties

3./NSGr 9	Ju 87D-3 WNr 100396 E8+KL shot down by Beaufighter E Florence; Fw Otto Brinkmann POW/Uffz Franz Scherzer MiA
1./NSGr 9	Ju 87D-5 ..+GL shot up by Beaufighter; Obfw Toni Fink WiA/Obgfr Egon Zantow safe

Wg Cdr Laurie Styles, the commander of 600 Squadron, after he had claimed a Ju 87 destroyed north-east of Florence as his 4th victory.

CHAPTER 3

THE GOTHIC LINE AND A BITTER WINTER

Tuesday, 29 August 1944

Spitfires of 93 Squadron claimed to have destroyed three locomotives and damaged other trucks, a staff car was wrecked, six trucks set on fire and four others badly damaged.

Sgt Arthur Banks of 112 Squadron took part in an armed reconnaissance of the Ravenna and Ferrara areas. During this sortie, his aircraft was damaged by Flak and he was compelled to make a forced landing. After the aircraft had been destroyed, Banks decided to try and reach the Allied lines. He made contact with a group of Italian partisans, amongst whom, during the following months, he became an outstanding figure, advising and encouraging them in action against the enemy. Early in December 1944, during an attempt at crossing into Allied territory by boat he was captured with a number of partisans, taken to a prison, cruelly tortured and later killed. The young Welshman was later posthumously awarded the George Cross, the only 'Level 1' award made to an airman during the Italian Campaign.

Having completed training for light-bomber duties 25 SAAF Squadron moved to Campomarino landing ground, Biferno, where it joined 254 Wing of the Balkan Air Force alongside the Baltimore-equipped 13 (Hellenic) and the Italian Co-Belligerent 28° and 132° Gruppi.

Above: After Sgt Arthur Banks of 112 Squadron was shot down on 29 August he joined a partisan group for several months. He was later captured and endured brutal treatment before being murdered on 20 December. His stoicism and bravery were later recognised by the award of the George Cross. Left: Mustang III HB936 'A' was the aircraft in which the gallant Sgt Arthur Banks was shot down by Flak near Rovigo.

111 Sqn	Spitfire IX MJ277 'S' left 1500, strafed motor transports, shot down by ground fire; Sgt R.E.D.Parker WiA and POW, when Germans evacuated hospital rescued by Maquis and returned to Allied lines
93 Sqn	Spitfire IX EN342 left 1345, strafing a train at Mâcon hit in neck and leg by Flak, landed safely; Sgt H.C.Fielding WiA
112 Sqn	Mustang III HB366 'A' left 1645 on armed recce, hit by Flak Rovigo area, crash-landed 1900; Sgt A.Banks evaded until captured early December, murdered on 20 December 1944
213 Sqn	Mustang III HB899 left 0830 on bombing mission, crashed shortly after take-off; Sgt A.MacFarlane KiA

US Casualties

524th FS/27th FBG	P-47D 42-26381 shot down by Flak 1430, last seen nr Chateauburg; 1/Lt William F.Kuykendall KiA [8259]
524th FS/27th FBG	P-47D 42-27968 hit by Flak 1530, last seen nr Montélimar; 1/Lt H.L.Nielson MiA, returned 3 September
524th FS/27th FBG	P-47D 42-27259 shot down probably by Flak, last seen 1200; Lt Robert D.Ainsworth MiA
64th FS/57th FG	P-47D 42-75716 hit by Flak 0910, damaged Cat 2; pilot safe
86th FS/79th FG	P-47D 42-26376 shot down by Flak 2m N Valence 1645; 1/Lt Leonard A.Charpentier evaded [8384]
99th FS/332nd FG	P-51C 42-106544 lost over Yugoslavia 0950; 2/Lt Emil G.Clifton POW [8101]

Tuesday-Wednesday, 29/30 August 1944

German Casualties

4.(F)/122	Ju 188D-2 F6+MM on reconnaissance of Palermo harbour, FTR; Uffz Hans Vessen and crew KiA
6./TG 4	Ju 52/3m WNr 641232 G6+KP crash-landed at Heraklion; Fw Ernst Rienth and three KiA
	LKS reports one Ju 188 missing and one Ju 52/3m lost in combat

Wednesday, 30 August 1944

25 SAAF Squadron flew its first operations in support of partisan forces in Yugoslavia when the commanding officer, Lt Col L.H.G.Shuttleworth in Ventura II 6001, led an attack by six aircraft on German barracks in Karlovac and the adjacent marshalling yards, scoring direct hits and starting fires.

25 SAAF Squadron began bombing operations with Ventura Is on 30 August with a raid led by Lt Col Lawrie Shuttleworth.

British Casualties

4 SAAF Sqn	Spitfire IX EN265 'E' left 1615, shot down by Flak dive-bombing sheds at Dicomano 1635; Lt P.O.Dawber (3 SAAF Sqn attached) KiA
16 SAAF Sqn	Beaufighter X JM415 'U' left 0600 to attack guns on Zirje Island, pilot's foot shot off by Flak, ditched 0647, crew rescued by partisans and transported to Vis; Lt D.K.Stewart DoW on 1 September/Lt T.W.Pumphrett evaded
19 SAAF Sqn	Beaufighter VIc EL398 'M' left 1010 strafed train running S Larissa, hit by Flak, crash-landed 1205 near Dhikastom, burnt out; Flt Lt G.H.Calveley/Flt Sgt R.H.E.Collinson KiA
87 Sqn	Spitfire IX JG776 left 1425 to dive bomb near Forlì, last seen in bomb dive; Sgt A.J.Seares KiA, believed body picked up by a Walrus off Cattolica on 31 August
93 Sqn	Spitfire IX MA223 left 1015, hit by Flak strafing near Mâcon, crash-landed in Roybon area; Flg Off R.R.Fisher safe
111 Sqn	Spitfire IX NH252 'C' left 1600 on armed recce N Lyon, shot down by Flak at St Pierre; Wt Off W.J.Cowling WiA, evaded next day
241 Sqn	Spitfire VIII JF540 left 1800 on a shipping recce, flew into a tree while strafing; Flg Off C.J.Nowak MiA
260 Sqn	Mustang III FB305 left 0700 bombing a railway bridge near Forlì, shot down by Flak; Sgt C.McGarry KiA

15th CMS/5th PRG	F-5C 42-67117 *R&R* lost u/k cause over Italy; 2/Lt George A.Hartwick Jr MiA [8097]
301st FS/332nd FG	P-51C 43-25086 '66' lost over Yugoslavia 1100; 2/Lt Charles T.Williams POW [8332]

Wednesday-Thursday, 30/31 August 1944

British Casualties	
272 Sqn	Beaufighter X NT907 'D' left 2355 on shipping strike 4m N of Finale Ligure, FTR; Wt Off W.H.Billing/Flt Sgt H.Thornton KiA
55 Sqn	Baltimore V FW459 'D' left 0308 to attack roads in the Imola-Cesena-Ravenna area; Lt B.J.Marais POW, escaped, three KiA
114 Sqn	Boston IV BZ506 left 0300 to intrude Bologna-Ravenna area, on return crashed on approach to Cecina a/f; Sgt R.W.Gibbs KiA, one MiA, one WiA, Sgt J.A.Bridger (A/G) rescued by 293 Sqn Walrus X9474 flown by Sgt W.J.Bishop/Flg Off A.A.O'Dell

Thursday, 31 August 1944

One of the Ju 87Ds of 2./NSGr 9 stayed over its target area rather too long during the early hours of the 31st and had not cleared Allied territory when dawn broke. It was spotted by Capt Dixon, a pilot of 241 Squadron, who was carrying out an early morning reconnaissance. In short order he wheeled his Spitfire after it and sent it crashing into the ground in flames.

British Claims					
241 Sqn	Capt L.E.Dixon	Spitfire VIII MT634 'U'	Ju 87	Po Valley-E Copparo	0724

British Casualties	
145 Sqn	Spitfire VIII JG338 left 1000, attacking motor transports under direction by Auster of 657 Sqn, shot down by Flak nr Pesaro; Lt R.G.Field KiA
93 Sqn	Spitfire IX MA482 left 0915, strafing roads near Valbonne, shot down by Flak 1020, crash-landed; Sgt R.J.Hulse POW
12 SAAF Sqn	Marauder HD589 'M' hit by Flak on bomb run, on Gothic Line target, spun and blew up 1556; Lt W.R.A.Grosse-Rasgado and five KiA
450 Sqn	Kittyhawk IV FX643 left 1350 on Rover David patrol, hit by Flak, engine trouble, pilot baled out in Allied lines 1445; Flt Lt R.H.Burden safe
352 Sqn	Spitfire Vc BR439 'K' strafed a train near Vis, turned over and crashed; Plt Off Alexandar Vukovic KiA
32 Sqn	Spitfire Vc EP343 left 1250, on strafing near Sjenica-Pozega flew into a hill and exploded; Flt Sgt P.G.Bignell KiA
43 Sqn	Spitfire IX MT680 left 1425 on armed recce, engine caught fire, pilot baled out near base; Flg Off A.W.Guest safe
19 SAAF Sqn	Beaufighter VI NE651 'C' left 0700 to attack railway targets Devedelija-Ulangi, attacked train near Prilep, hit by Flak, on return engine failed, ditched off Termoli 1140; Wt Off A.R.Standen/Flt Sgt A.Chippendale rescued by Italian navy ship
US Casualties	
527th FS/86th FG	P-47D 42-26954 'blue 83' caught fire probably due to Flak, crashed 5km S Villimpenta 1030 pilot baled out; 2/Lt Lloyd D.Kinley POW [8385]
448th BS/321st BG	B-25 43-4027 left 0845 to attack Mira rail bridge, damaged by Flak, crash-landed at base 1220; 1/Lt Robert J.Cottle Jr and three WiA, two safe
488th BS/340th BG	B-25J 43-27504 hit by Flak over Cittadella; 1/Lt Robert.C.Pagh and four safe, one WiA
488th BS/340th BG	B-25J 43-35983 hit by Flak over Cittadella; 1/Lt E.W.McDonald and four safe, one WiA
German Casualties	
2./NSGr 9	Ju 87D damaged by Spitfire E Copparo; Obgfr Harry Fischer WiA/Obgfr Hüssmann safe
	LKS reports one Ju 87 and one Ju 52/3m lost in combat; two Ju 52/3ms destroyed on ground

Thursday-Friday, 31 August/1 September 1944

A 255 Squadron Beaufighter was shot down on an intruder mission to the Danube basin near Belgrade. Ships *Uta* and *Bechelaren*, both Danube river gunboats, shot down one low-flying enemy aircraft claimed as a Vickers Wellington near km 1080 – the distance along the Danube as measured by the Germans – the victim hit the ground and exploded.

British Casualties	
255 Sqn	Beaufighter VIF MM838 left 2040 to intrude over Danube basin in the Belgrade area, shot down by Flak from naval vessels, crashed at Dubovac 2230; Flt Lt J.Summers/Flg Off C.J.Sanders KiA

Friday, 1 September 1944

During early September the last Luftwaffe fighter units, Stab and II./JG 77 departed Italy leaving the fighter defence in the hands of the newly reformed ANR, though the night-attack and reconnaissance units remained. For those units still engaged in the Aegean, accurate and concentrated anti-aircraft fire was now the main threat to ground-attack and light-bomber units.

Launched on 1 September 1944, Operation Ratweek was a series of coordinated attacks on the axis forces' communication lines in the Balkans. These were led by the combined operations units of Yugoslav Partisans, Land Forces Adriatic, the heavy bombers of the 15th Air Force and the Balkan Air Force light and medium bombers.

Left: A 3.(F)/AufklGr 33 Ju 188A crew celebrate 100 missions at the unit's base at Kalamaki near Athens. Below: The Beaufighter VIfs of the 415th and 417th Night Fighter Squadrons dispersed around La Vailon airfield, France between 1 and 25 September.

British Casualties

19 SAAF Sqn	Beaufighter X 'U' left 0755 on shipping sweep, hit by Flak near Katerini, crash-landed S Kymina ca1015; Wt Off N.R.Davis/ Flt Sgt J.Sefton safe, evaded in Italy 12 September
145 Sqn	Spitfire VIII JG274 left 1840, hit by Flak, ditched off coast 15m NW Pesaro; Sgt A.B.Lowe safe, evaded, returned on 2 September
185 Sqn	Spitfire Vc JG928 left 1500, shot down by Flak near Rimini, pilot baled out but hung up on tailplane; Sgt J.Brown KiA
1 SAAF Sqn	Spitfire IX MA475 left on armed recce of roads near Pistoia, pilot got lost, crash-landed on a beach near Ancona, Cat B 2 damaged; Lt R.D.Marshall slightly injured
1 SAAF Sqn	Spitfire IX MH619 left 0855, bombed entrance to railway tunnel, u/c collapsed on landing, Cat II damaged; Lt G.A.Roy safe
241 Sqn	Spitfire VIII JF394 left 1840 on shipping recce to Chioggia, engine trouble, pilot baled out off the River Po delta; Flt Lt J.R.Hamankiewicz MiA
40 SAAF Sqn	Spitfire Vc JK658 left on Arty recce of Pesaro area, shot down by Flak 6m N Ghidolfo; Lt G.Morgan KiA

French Casualties

GC 1/4	P-47D hit by Flak, crashed while diving near Tenda, Italy, 1825; Cne Jean-Marie Auber KiA

German Casualties

7./TG 4	Ju 52/3m WNr 500179 G6+AP ditched between Kalamaki and Maleme; Fw Adolf Herden KiA, two crew rescued
	LKS reports one Ju 52/3m lost in combat and 1 destroyed on ground

Friday-Saturday, 1/2 September 1944

British Casualties

55 Sqn	Baltimore V FW482 'U' left 0304 on armed recce of Forlì-Rimini area; Sgt H.F.L.David POW, Lt D.M.Cameron and two KiA
17 SAAF Sqn	Ventura V JT827 'E' left Alghero on shipping sweep of west coast Italy-south-east France, FTR; Lt C.T.Bain-Marais and four MiA

German Casualties

10./TG 2	Ju 52/3m 8T+OU damaged by own Flak 70km SE Belgrade; Obfw Heinz Meinecke WiA, two safe
6.(F)/122	Ju 188D-2 WNr 150234 F6+BP left Bergamo, crashed nr Casalbuttano; Lt Andreas Finke and one KiA, two WiA

Saturday, 2 September 1944

A Bf 109 bounced a patrol of six Spitfires from 87 Squadron at last light, attacking Wt Off R.C.Hayward who was 500ft below and behind the formation as he had observed an unidentified aircraft flying offshore parallel to the coast. The identity issue was resolved when it attacked him from astern and turned out to be

P-47D Thunderbolt 42-26421 '87' of the 66th Fighter Squadron, 57th Fighter Group was a War Bond machine purchased by Republic employees. It was shot down by Flak near Ferrara on 2 September 1944 with the loss of 2/Lt Thomas D.Davis.

Two bomb-laden Spitfire IXs, MJ532 'G' and MJ250 'Q' taking off from Fano. The latter was damaged by Flak during one such sortie on 2 September resulting in Sgt E.J.Hendrick being wounded.

a Bf 109. Flt Lt Doig came to the rescue and Hayward headed for base, with jammed cannons. A long fight ensued for five to seven minutes with "three dead head on" passes being made without result, before Doig got a 30-degree deflection shot seeing hits on the starboard mainplane. The 109 dived for the sea and was lost in the thick haze. The squadron described the 109 pilot as "the lone wolf of the Luftwaffe". Oblt Joachim Deicke of 6./JG 77 recorded in his logbook leading an interception of Mitchells and Mustang escorts in the Forlì-Cervia area between 1615 and 1715 German time. Gefr Klose was shot down near Cervia, almost certainly the claim by Flt Lt Doig.

The sweep leader of 7 SAAF Wing Lt Col Andrew Bosman in his Spitfire VIIIc JG616 strafed and damaged a Me 210 on Ferrara landing ground.

British Claims

87 Sqn	Flt Lt R.P.Doig	Spitfire IX MH895	Bf 109 Damaged	Rimini	1815-1950

British Casualties

32 Sqn	Spitfire Vc JL131 left 0915 armed recce Sarajevo to Doboj, damaged by Flak, u/c would not lower, crash-landed at base 1240; Flt Sgt R.H.Cross safe
7 SAAF Sqn	Spitfire IXe MH563 port wing torn off by heavy Flak nr Pontepetri-E San Marcello Pistoiese at 300m, pilot baled out but parachute did not open properly; Lt S.P.Griessel KiA
5 SAAF Sqn	Kittyhawk IV FT878 left 1340, hit by Flak, pilot baled out over enemy lines W Coriano, 1410; Lt A.E.Dickson WiA, POW, DoW 9 September
112 Sqn	Mustang III FB297 'X' left 1030, shot down by Flak near Pesaro at 1100; Sgt J.R.Greenaway KiA
72 Sqn	Spitfire IX MK664 left 1005 on armed recce of Rhône Valley, engine trouble, pilot baled out W Grenoble 1035 into American lines; Lt W.D.D.Grieve safe
24 SAAF Sqn	Marauder III HD490 'L' left 1024 to bomb targets near Colle Monte, shot down by Flak, aircraft crashed in flames, six parachutes seen; Lt V.E.Hansel and two landed in Allied lines, two POW, one KiA by ground fire
24 SAAF Sqn	Marauder III FB562 'X' left 1024 to bomb targets near Colle Monte, damaged by Flak, force-landed at Jesi; Lt Oakcroft and four safe, one WiA
24 SAAF Sqn	Marauder III FB510 'C' left 1024 to bomb targets near Colle Monte, damaged by Flak, force-landed at Falconara; Lt B.Clark and four safe, one WiA
24 SAAF Sqn	Marauder III 'O' left 1415 to bomb targets near Rimini, damaged by Flak, force-landed at Jesi, damaged Cat II; Maj D.Liddell and four safe, one WiA
250 Sqn	Kittyhawk IV FX794 left 1850 on armed recce, bombed motor transports at 1905, FTR; Sgt W.M.Docherty KiA
601 Sqn	Spitfire IX MH781 left 1755, bombed and strafed M/Y NW Cattolica, hit by Flak crash-landed at base; Sqn Ldr S.W.Daniel safe

601 Sqn	Spitfire IX MH778 left 1755, bombed and strafed M/Y NW Cattolica, hit by Flak, crashed 3m W Coriano, wreck found by the army on 11 September; Flg Off T.H.Smith KiA
601 Sqn	Spitfire IX MJ984 left 1125 to bomb 88mm guns at Montefiore Conca, no Flak seen, FTR; Sgt R.J.Adams KiA
601 Sqn	Spitfire IX MJ250 left 1415 to bomb and strafe in the Castello Plain area, hit by Flak, landed at base; Sgt E.J.Hendrick WiA
US Casualties	
65th FS/57th FG	P-47D 42-26433 hit by Flak, crashed into sea 0725; Capt James W.Smith rescued
66th FS/57th FG	P-47D 42-26421 shot down possibly by Flak SW Ferrara 0825; 2/Lt Thomas D.Davis KiA [8380]
German Claims	
OKH *	4 Flak claims in Italy
	*OberKommando Heeres Tagesmeldung – Army High Command daily report
German Casualties	
5./JG 77	Bf 109G-6 WNr 412585 Black 11 crashed nr Cervia; Gefr Hans-Günter Klose KiA
	LKS reports one Bf 109 damaged in combat

Sunday, 3 September 1944

Two Spitfires of 145 Squadron took off on anti-reconnaissance patrol along the Adriatic coast. Three Bf 109s were sighted in the Pesaro-Rimini area. The British pilots gave chase and Sqn Ldr Duke shot down one which was lagging, the pilot baling out of the burning aircraft. The other two dived and then climbed to 15,000ft. Here Duke caught them and shot down a second, this pilot also baling out of his burning aircraft; the third escaped. These were Duke's final victories and he remained the most successful Allied fighter pilot in the Mediterranean theatre.

Two aircraft from 40 SAAF Squadron were on an artillery reconnaissance near Rimini, Lt E.C.K.Johnson doing the reconnaissance and Lt F.P.Lee acting as weaver. North-east of Coriano, Lee sighted some aircraft up-sun which he could not identify. Two of these attacked him and he turned into them, distinctly seeing black crosses and recognising them as "long-nosed FW 190s". They attacked again and Lee undertook more evasive action, but as he turned towards them, he saw two other aircraft with white corkscrew spinners attacking him from the other quarter. The lead aircraft was within range and shot at him. Lee's Spitfire was hit in the cockpit, wounding him; and the rudder and almost all aileron controls were shot away. As he began to bale out the "long-nosed FW 190s" attacked again, forcing him to make a steep climbing turn to evade the attack. He now spun off, managed to recover from the spin, but then the engine failed. He then rolled his aircraft over onto its back and baled out west of Cattolica, landing in Allied lines, despite his parachute having been badly damaged when it was hit by a cannon shell when it was still in its pack.

British Claims					
145 Sqn	Sqn Ldr N.F.Duke	Spitfire VIII MT775 'J'	2 Bf 109s	nr Rimini	0645
British Casualties					
601 Sqn	Spitfire VIII MJ410 left 1810 bombing road 3m E Montegrimano, possibly hit by Flak, engine failed, crash-landed near base; Sgt A.W.Harris safe				
40 SAAF Sqn	Spitfire IX shot down by a FW 190 NE Coriano, pilot baled out over Allied lines; Lt F.P.Lee safe				
US Casualties					
523rd FS/27th FBG	P-47D 42-27651 'R' hit by Flak 1100; 1/Lt Raymond C.Knispel MiA				
315th FS/324th FG	P-47D '68' hit while strafing 0955; 2/Lt Douglas W.Mapes KiA				
German Casualties					
1./NAGr 11	Bf 109G-8 WNr 200685 Black 3 shot down in combat NW Imola; Obfw Kurt Holstein WiA				
1./NAGr 11	Bf 109G-8 WNr 200023 Black 1 shot down in combat NE Forlì; Uffz Joachim Müller WiA				
	LKS reports two Bf 109s and one Ju 52/3m lost in air combat; 20 a/c destroyed and four damaged on ground				

Sunday-Monday, 3/4 September 1944

Beaufighters of 600 Squadron intercepted a number of Ju 87s west of Rimini; Burke's victim exploded, and he had to fly through the debris, which damaged his aircraft. Cole's target had been observed strafing, and when shot down hit the ground with a very large explosion. Judd's first victim apparently tried to force land but hit an obstruction and crashed. His second victim went down in flames.

600 Sqn	Plt Off G.W.Judd/Flg Off J.R.Brewer	Beaufighter VIf ND147 'Q'	Ju 87	20m SW Rimini	0008
600 Sqn	Plt Off G.W.Judd/Flg Off J.R.Brewer	Beaufighter VIf ND147 'Q'	Ju 87	6m NW Rimini	0020
600 Sqn	Sqn Ldr P.L.Burke/Flt Lt L.F.S.Whaley	Beaufighter VIf ND172 'B'	Ju 87 Damaged	10m W Rimini	0317
600 Sqn	Flt Sgt W.S.M.Cole/Sgt A.C.Odd	Beaufighter VIf V8891 'M'	Ju 87	20m WSW Rimini	0355
600 Sqn	Sqn Ldr P.L.Burke/Flt Lt L.F.S.Whaley	Beaufighter VIf ND172 'B'	Ju 87	5m SW Rimini	0408
153 Sqn	Flt Sgt P.Manning/Flt Sgt N.Philpott	Beaufighter VIf 'Q'	Ju 88 on ground	Bergamo a/f	2240-0525

German Casualties

2./NSGr 9	Ju 87D shot down by night-fighter nr Borghi; Uffz Kurt Urban DoW/Gefr Erwin Schertel KiA
3./NSGr 9	Ju 87D shot down by night-fighter nr Cattolica; Obfw Wilhelm Böwing/Obgfr Josef Jantos MiA
3./NSGr 9	Ju 87D shot up by night-fighter; pilot safe/Obgfr Rolf Möhrke KiA
3./NSGr 9	Ju 87D shot down by night-fighter nr Fano 2355; Fw Oskar Hug KiA/Obgfr Paul Sonnenberg POW
2./NSGr 9	Ju 87D E8+HK damaged by AA; Lt Volkmar von Grone/Gefr Heinrich Lenz safe

Monday, 4 September 1944

During the day 242 Squadron flew their last operation. Activity by 322 Wing's squadrons then effectively ended and the wing was officially disbanded on 7 November.

British Claims

241 Sqn	Sgt D.L.Lancaster	Spitfire VIII J7F779 'D'	Bf 109	SW Cattolica	1919

British Casualties

450 Sqn	Kittyhawk IV FX789 left 1150, shot down by Flak NW San Pietro near Forlì 1225; Sgt E.W.James POW
2 SAAF Sqn	Spitfire IX MJ280 left 0745, engine cut on way to target, pilot baled out over no man's land 0815; Lt A van der Spuy returned

Sqn Ldr P.L.Burke (left) and his navigator Flt Lt L.F.S.Whaley of 600 Squadron with Beaufighter VIf ND172 'B' showing the damage caused by the exploding Ju 87 they had shot down near Rimini.

4 SAAF Sqn	Spitfire IX JL226 left 1025 to bomb guns at S.Lucia, engine failed on return, pilot baled into Allied lines; Lt W.M.Thompson WiA
72 Sqn	Spitfire IX MK422 left 1740 on armed recce of Chagny-Beaume Road, shot down by Flak, pilot baled out 12m NE Grenoble; Sgt R.H.Fenton safe
12 SAAF Sqn	Marauder II FB502 'Y' left 0850, shot down by Flak W Rimini, blew up; Lt D.H.Moodie and four KiA, one POW
30 SAAF Sqn	Marauder III HD596 'R' left 0856, shot down over target area by Flak, two Bf 109s were also seen in target area; Lt H.R.Gelb and one evaded, one KiA, three POW
24 SAAF Sqn	Marauder III HD590 'X' left 0906 to bomb target 3m SW Rimini, damaged by Flak, crash-landed at base; Lt P.M.J.McGregor and two WiA, three safe
12 SAAF Sqn	Marauder II FB516 'C' left 1400 to bomb target W Rimini, damaged by Flak, crash-landed at base; Maj J.F.O.Davis and five safe

US Casualties

66th FS/57th FG	P-47D 42-75744 lost u/k cause S Borgoforte 0800; 2/Lt Alfred D.Mammarelli KiA [8777]
64th FS/57th FG	P-47D 42-75664 lost u/k cause NW Asti 1305; 1/Lt Edgar N.Peters KiA [8736]
86th FS/79th FG	P-47D 42-26838 shot down by Flak S Frontenard, France 1100; 1/Lt Donald E.Claycomb POW [8778]
523rd FS/27th FBG	P-47D 42-28082 'U' hit by Flak 1130; 1/Lt John C.Newman MiA
523rd FS/27th FBG	P-47D 42-27940 'N' hit by Flak 1330; Flt Off William W.Daniel MiA
316th FS/324th FG	P-47D 42-27647 '92' damaged by target explosion 1745; Flt Off LeRoy W.Saunders KiA

French Casualties

GC 1/4	P-47D shot down by Flak 15km SE Mantua; Lt Racon KiA
GC 1/4	P-47D shot down by Flak 15km SE Mantua; Sgt Allain recovered by Italian partisans, returned to unit 17 March 1945

German Claims

Flak		Spitfire	SW Rimini	1000
Flak		Marauder	S Forlì	1000
Flak		Marauder	Bologna	1100
Flak		Kittyhawk	NW San Pietro	1225

German Casualties

LKS reports one TacR Bf 109 shot down in combat

Monday-Tuesday, 4/5 September 1944

British Claims

255 Sqn	Wt Off D.Fisher/Wt Off J.Walsh	Beaufighter VIf	Ju 188 Damaged	Falconara area	2300-0035
600 Sqn	Flg Off S.W.Rees/Flg Off D.C.Bartlett	Beaufighter VIf ND162 'E'	Ju 87	10m W Rimini	2304
600 Sqn	Flg Off S.W.Rees/Flg Off D.C.Bartlett	Beaufighter VIf ND162 'E'	Ju 87	20m SW Rimini	2315
600 Sqn	Flt Lt A.M.Davidson/Plt Off L.A.Telford	Beaufighter VIf ND320 'R'	Ju 87 Damaged	15m SW Rimini	0235

British Casualties

272 Sqn	Beaufighter X NV203 'A' left 0220 to attack four ships off Sestri Levante, seen to fire RP at ship, then blew up; Flg Off A.F.Reynolds/Flg Off N.F.Young KiA
272 Sqn	Beaufighter X NV142 'O' left 0450, attacked barges in Sestri Levante, made second pass with cannon, hit by Flak, set on fire; Flg Off C.N.West/Flg Off F.G.Burgess KiA

German Casualties

LKS reports one Ju 88 lost

Tuesday, 5 September 1944

The 79th Fighter Group was the first 12th Air Force unit to penetrate German air space with a strafe on Freiburg airfield. One Bf 109 tried to intercept but was claimed shot down. 87th Squadron's pilots claimed four He 111s, two Messerschmitts and a Junkers destroyed on the ground at Mulhouse. At Freiburg a He 111 was claimed destroyed and 12 aircraft damaged.

112 Squadron strafed an airfield near Grado where pilots claimed eight aircraft damaged, including Ju 87s, FW 190s and a Bf 109.

Four Bf 109s attacked a 321st Bomb Group B-25 formation 10 miles north of Ferrara at 1137. They made several aggressive passes from 5 to 7 o'clock and below, breaking away from B-25s at 300 yards. A Bf 109 was claimed damaged – seen going down in smoke. The Bf 109s were from II./JG 77 at Ghedi and they lost two pilots, FhjObfw Maximilian Volke and Gefr Rudolf Burgstaller. Volke crashed about 10 miles west of the combat, likely the victim of the 321st Bomb Group's gunners. Burgstaller may have become separated and was engaged by Spitfires of 601 Squadron, who reported encountering a lone Bf 109 and damaging it. These pilots were the last casualties of the day-fighter arm of the Luftwaffe in Italy, and Max Volke was the last German ace killed in action in the Italian campaign. Three days later II./JG 77 pulled out of Italy, leaving the theatre without any German day-fighter force, solely reliant on the ANR to provide any fighter defence.

British Claims

601 Sqn	Sqn Ldr S.W.Daniel	Spitfire IX MH787 }	Bf 109 Damaged	Bellaria	1055-1205
601 Sqn	Sgt B.Watford	Spitfire IX MK463 }			

British Casualties

87 Sqn	Spitfire IX EN578 left 0850 bombing artillery at Santarcangelo, last seen in bombing dive; Lt D.Mackenzie POW
249 Sqn	Spitfire Vc MA900 left 0900 from Brindisi, hit by Flak Metsovan, pilot baled off the coast 1045; Sgt D.A.Preece safe, rescued by a Cant.Z.506B of 141ª Squadriglia at 1200
352 Sqn	Spitfire Vc JG836 'O' left 0630, hit by Flak bombing a HQ at Marcetica, force-landed at Kulen Vakef; Plt Off Milan Delic rescued by partisans, returned 17 September

US Claims

321st BG	gunners	B-25	Bf 109	10m N Ferrara	1137

US Casualties

65th FS/57th FG	P-47D 42-75648 hit high tension wires E Pavia 1010, crashed 6km SE Melegnano; 1/Lt John A.Wittenberger KiA [8734]
85th FS/79th FG	P-47D 42-27112 shot down by Flak at Colmar, France, 1700; 1/Lt Arthur J.Palmer WiA
314th FS/324th FG	P-47D '24' hit by Flak 8m NW Dijon, France, 1035; 2/Lt John W.Dilworth evaded, returned 14 September
345th FS/350th FG	P-47D 42-28355 hit by Flak nr Bologna 1000; 2/Lt William E.Hardin KiA [8753]
345th FS/350th FG	P-47D 42-28559 hit by Flak nr Bologna 1000, pilot baled out but parachute failed; 2/Lt Earl Calhoun KiA [9782]
443rd BS/320th BG	B-26B 42-95937 '68' *Baby Shoes* left 0755 to bomb road bridge SE Pavia, hit by Flak nr Mortara 1025; Capt Luther K.Moyer KiA, four POW, two evaded [8090]
447th BS/321st BG	B-25G 42-32458 damaged by Flak, returned; 2/Lt James T.Edwards and four safe

French Casualties

GC 1/4	P-47D shot down by Flak nr Rosignano, landed in American-controlled zone; Cne Minot returned

German Claims

OKH	7 Flak claims in Italy

A Jagdpanzer IV knocked out on the Gothic Line.

German Casualties

6./JG 77	Bf 109G WNr 441456 shot down in combat at Mirandola; FhjObfw Maximilian Volke KiA
7./JG 77	Bf 109G WNr 163612 White 7 shot down in combat 5km E Villafranca; Gefr Rudolf Burgstaller KiA
2./NAGr 11	2 Bf 109s destroyed and one damaged on ground
	LKS reports two Bf 109s destroyed and one damaged on ground

Tuesday-Wednesday, 5/6 September 1944

The RAF night-fighters from 46 and 108 Squadrons intercepted various reconnaissance missions over Alexandria but made no claims. However, a Ju 88 was lost when intercepted by night-fighters; it began to vibrate, then exploded and crashed off Alexandria leaving one survivor.

German Casualties

2.(F)/123	Ju 88T-3 WNr 330231 4U+KK left 2110 from Athens to recce Alexandria, intercepted by night-fighters, dived to evade, aircraft began to vibrate and then exploded; Hptm Helmut Weixelbaum (St.Kpt) and 2 KiA. Lt Horst Woldfarth POW – rescued by Walrus Z1757 of 294 Sqn flown by Flg Off R.A.Williams but could not take off, so towed in by HSL

Wednesday, 6 September 1944

Four Beaufighters from 603 Squadron acted as top cover to eight from 252 Squadron on a shipping strike off the Greek coast. Two aircraft attacked and damaged a lone Ar 196 from 2./SAGr 126 apparently flown by Oblt Klaus-Jürgen Rohwer, who is also believed to have claimed a Beaufighter shot down, although none were actually lost. 603 Squadron's records do not list the crews of the four aircraft participating in this sortie, so it has not been possible to name them.

During the early afternoon Flt Lt Smith of 213 Squadron led four of the unit's Mustangs to the Sombor area over an airfield identified as S52, where four Bf 110s were seen. Following the bombing of Novi Sad aerodrome on 5 September where 8./NJG 6 lost two Bf 110Gs, its commander, Oblt Wilhelm Johnen, decided to transfer the remaining eight aircraft to Hodshag auxiliary airfield, about ten miles south of Sombor on the following day. Near the airfield at the end of the transit flight four Bf 110Gs were caught completely off-guard by the Mustangs that attacked from 1,800 feet. One Messerschmitt managed to evade the Mustangs, the remaining three were shot down. The Bf 110 of pilot Uffz Max Loock fell in flames and he was badly injured though his crew of Uffz Fritz Funk and Obgfr Thomas were uninjured. The aircraft of Fw Herbert Hubatsch also caught fire and he too was badly injured whilst his crew of Fw Heinz Krüger and Obgfr Georg Berthold were killed. The third aircraft flown by Oblt Helmut Buder crash-landed with the three crew slightly wounded.

British Claims

603 Sqn	crew	Beaufighter NV264 'A'	Ar 196 Damaged	S Cap Sunion	1315
603 Sqn	crew	Beaufighter NV205 'W'			
213 Sqn	Flt Lt C.D.A.Smith	Mustang III FB303	Bf 110	E Backi, SE Sombor	1450-1720
213 Sqn	Lt V.Vorster	Mustang III FB311			
213 Sqn	Flt Sgt D.E.Firman	Mustang III FB308	Bf 110	a/f E Backi, SE Sombor	1450-1720
213 Sqn	Wt Off S.G.Pickford	Mustang III HB894	Bf 110	a/f E Backi, SE Sombor	1450-1720

British Casualties

601 Sqn	Spitfire IX MH778 left 1755, shot down by Flak 3m NE Coriano, on Coriano-Misano road; Flt Lt T.H.Smith KiA
92 Sqn	Spitfire VIII JF895 left 0800, strafed village N Rimini, presumed lost to ground fire; Plt Off G.H.Meagher POW
3 RAAF Sqn	Kittyhawk IV FX750 left 1250 to bomb guns W of Rimini, returned to base, crashed on landing, bombs exploded; Wt Off J.H.Hedger KiA

German Claims

2./SAGr 126	Oblt Klaus-Jürgen Rohwer	Ar 196	Beaufighter		
Flak			Spitfire	S Ravenna	0900

German Casualties

2./SAGr 126	Ar 196 D1+..K damaged by enemy aircraft
8./NJG 6	Bf 110G-4 2Z+SS shot down in flames over Hodshag auxiliary airfield, Serbia; Uffz Max Loock WiA, two safe
8./NJG 6	Bf 110G-4 W/Nr 730216 2Z+JS shot down in flames over Hodshag auxiliary airfield; Fw Herbert Hubatsch WiA, two KiA
8./NJG 6	Bf 110G hit over Hodshag auxiliary airfield, crash-landed; Oblt Helmut Buder and two WiA
	LKS reports one Ar 196 damaged in combat

Wednesday-Thursday, 6/7 September 1944

British Casualties

272 Sqn — Beaufighter X NE639 'G' left 0245 on shipping strike, last heard from 0325, crashed in mountains S Piacenza; Flt Sgt J.Horsford/Wt Off J.C.Watson KiA

Thursday, 7 September 1944

Lt Col Catton was leading four 19 SAAF Squadron Beaufighters which encountered a He 111 flying in the opposite direction. Before they had a chance to attack a large cloud of dust appeared, caused by the Heinkel striking the ground whilst trying to pass underneath one of the Beaufighters, which subsequently claimed it!

335 Squadron at Bersis began to move to Greece, via a stopover at Canne in Italy.

British Claims

213 Sqn	2/Lt R.E.Rorvik	Mustang III HB894	Hs 126	Danube, SSW Sichevita	0730
19 SAAF Sqn	Wt Off D.H.Robertson/Flt Sgt L.J.Evans	Beaufighter X 'Q'	He 111	S Surdulica	1830

Above: This Spitfire IX, MH660 'V-Y' of 1435 Squadron, was abandoned 40 miles off Vis on 7 September, though Lt Lomax was picked up by a rescue launch. Left: On 7 September this Caproni Ca 313G of the Croat I5 Aviat. Squadron was flown to Glamoüko Polje by Stanko Forkapic, Josip Jirasek and four others when they defected to the partisans.

32 Sqn	Spitfire Vc EF538 left 1015, bombed and strafed motor transports E Gospic, hit by small-arms fire, crash-landed at Brindisi; Flt Lt R.D.Riddell safe
1435 Sqn	Spitfire IX MH660 'Y' left 1145, engine caught fire 50 miles S Vis after glycol leak; Lt R.L.Lomax rescued by ASR launch
39 Sqn	Beaufighter X LX877 'K' left 1830 to attack barges, hit by Flak, ditched off Brac Island 1918; Flt Sgt V.J.Kyrke-Smith/Flt Sgt S.S.Campbell KiA

US Casualties

64th FS/57th FG	P-47D 42-75840 lost 1m from Grosseto airfield; 2/Lt John C.Noesges KiA

German Casualties

	LKS reports 2 a/c lost in air combat

Croatian Casualties

15 AvSq/5 Av Base	Caproni Ca 313G defected to partisans at Glamoüko Polje; Stanko Forkapic, Josip Jirasek and four others safe

Friday, 8 September 1944

Twelve 260 Squadron Mustangs strafed Campoformido airfield; three FW 190s and a Ju 87 were claimed damaged. 213 Squadron undertook a sweep during which they ran into some German aircraft, He 111s towing Gotha 242 gliders. LKS reported that both He 111s and Go 242s were destroyed.

Eight 272 Squadron Beaufighter Xs attacked the Italian liner *Rex* (51,062 tons) at Capodistria, south of Trieste, with 25lb rocket projectiles and cannons. Pilots claimed 59 hits with the rockets (out of 64 carried) and fired 4,000 rounds of cannon at the liner. Later six of 39 Squadron Beaufighters with two more from 16 SAAF Squadron followed up this attack and blasted the already blazing ship again.

The smoking hulk of the liner *Rex* after attack by Beaufighters of 16 SAAF Squadron.

Lt Col Catton of 19 SAAF Squadron led another two Beaufighters from 16 SAAF Squadron on a reconnaissance over the railway between Larissa and Salonika. All three aircraft were hit by Flak, Catton's observer being severely wounded, the pilot of another aircraft belly-landing, the third crashing when a tyre blew on landing due to Flak damage. Light Flak was encountered every two to four miles along the track.

Bulgaria, which had been overrun by the Russian army, re-entered the war on the Allied side at this time. The Bulgarian air force, operating with a mixture of aircraft began to attack German forces to the east of the country. Aircraft used included Ju 87s and Bf 109s as well as more esoteric types, and this led to some unfortunate encounters with the Balkan Air Force in November, as well as the Bulgarians losing Ju 87s to Flak and on one occasion to FW 190s from SG 10.

British Claims

213 Sqn	2/Lt R.E.Rorvik	Mustang III HB894	} Go 242	Grocka, S Danube	0645-0930
213 Sqn	2/Lt J.W.Moor	Mustang III HB292			
213 Sqn	Flt Lt C.D.A.Smith	Mustang III FB303	Go 242	Grocka, S Danube	
213 Sqn	Flt Lt C.D.A.Smith	Mustang III FB303	}		
213 Sqn	Lt V.Vorster	Mustang III FB329			
213 Sqn	2/Lt J.W.Moor	Mustang III HB292	} He 111	Grocka, S Danube	0645-0930
213 Sqn	2/Lt R.E.Rorvik	Mustang III HB894			

British Casualties

93 Sqn	Spitfire IX MA624 left 1415 to patrol W Dijon, strafed motor transports, propeller blade seen to fly off, crashed 1545, burnt out; Flt Sgt J.W.Wagstaffe KiA
19 SAAF Sqn	Beaufighter 'V' left 1025 to recce of railway Larissa-Salonika, hit by Flak, observer killed, returned to base; Lt Col E.G.Catton safe/Flt Lt A.G.Brewis KiA
16 SAAF Sqn	Beaufighter X 'K' left 1025 to recce of railway Larissa-Salonika, hit by Flak, crash-landed at Canne 1425; Capt J.R.D.Strange/Lt A.E.Diack safe
16 SAAF Sqn	Beaufighter X 'J' left 1025 to recce of railway Larissa-Salonika, hit by Flak, crash-landed at Biferno 1412; Lt R.F.Ashdown/Lt G.Dixon safe

US Casualties	
522nd FS/27th FBG	P-47D 42-26429 'M' hit by Flak 3m E Belfort, France 1115; Capt Charles C.Williams POW [8388]
314th FS/324th FG	P-47D 42-27080 '28' hit by Flak nr Adincourt, France, 1825; 2/Lt Charles W.Neely POW [8767]
German Casualties	
3.(Go)/Schlgr 1	2 He 111H-6s (one WNr 7631) shot down by fighters
3.(Go)/Schlgr 1	2 Go 242s (one WNr 220325) shot down by fighters
	LKS reports 56 a/c (of which 32 Ju 52/3ms) destroyed on ground by strafing

Saturday, 9 September 1944

On a morning sortie, 112 Squadron claimed 12 locomotives, a 1,200-ton ship, a He 111 on the ground and various other targets. On an afternoon mission to the Vicenza area this unit strafed and claimed the destruction of three S.79s and a Ju 52/3m, plus five aircraft damaged and another locomotive. Flt Lt Hearn also engaged a Ju 88, and made 112 Squadron's final air combat claim of the war. During the day Sqn Ldr S.R.Whiting, the commanding officer of 213 Squadron, flew his final mission after a lengthy period in command and for which he was later awarded the DSO. Sqn Ldr C.S.Vos became commanding officer.

The official first day of the Bulgarian air force operating on the Allied side, was marked by the loss of a Bf 109 shot down by Flak.

British Claims					
603 Sqn	Flt Lt A.G.Deck/Flg Off C.L.Heide	Beaufighter X NV213 'R'	Ar 196	S Milos	1430-1625
112 Sqn	Flt Lt R.V.Hearn	Mustang III FB309 'Q'	Ju 88	Vicenza-Treviso a/f	1830
British Casualties					
5 SAAF Sqn	Kittyhawk IV FX570 left 1605 on Cab Rank, bombed artillery, shot down by Flak 8km SW Rimini 1650; Lt P.W.Bennee KiA				
21 SAAF Sqn	Marauder III HD409 'F' during bombs being loaded, one exploded while being fused; the pilot Lt F.W.Braill was killed in the cockpit, six ground crew were killed and three injured				
US Casualties					
522nd FS/27th FBG	P-47D 42-27067 'red U' hit smoke stack 2m SE Vesoul, France 1150; 2/Lt Ned O.Hunger KiA [8386]				
524th FS/27th FBG	P-47D 42-26375 hit by Flak 6-8m N Mulhouse 1445; 1/Lt Lester C.Carlyle evaded [8939]				
523rd FS/27th FBG	P-47D 42-27941 hit by Flak between Belfort and Mulhouse 1500; 2/Lt George T.Hebbel evaded [8769]				
66th FS/57th FG	P-47D 42-27269 lost due to Flak or target explosion 1m off shore S Genoa 1930; 1/Lt Vincent J.Bracha evaded [8776]				

After being hit by Flak near Bologna, three of the crew of B-26C Marauder 42-107765 '39' of GB 2/20 'Bretagne' baled out but the remaining crew flew it back to make a wheels-up landing at Foiano.

316th FS/324th FG	P-47D '87' hit by Flak SW Besançon, France, 0900; 2/Lt William R.Richmond evaded and returned 12 September	
314th FS/324th FG	P-47D 42-27976 '17' hit by Flak 10m NNE Mulhouse, France, 1150; 1/Lt Odell J.Johnson POW [8771]	
316th FS/324th FG	P-47D '89' hit by Flak 1730; 2/Lt Merril C.Grey KiA	
380th BS/310th BG	B-25J 43-27735 hit by Flak ditched 0.5-1m SW of Genoa;1/Lt John M.Rock POW-DoW, five KiA [8382]	
12th TCS/60th TCG	C-47 43-48314 '70' both engines cut circling drop zone in central Greece, crashed into mountains; Capt Paul C.Davison and twelve KiA [16195]	

French Casualties

GC 1/5	Spitfire V shot down by Flak while strafing in S France
GB 2/20	B-26C Marauder 42-107765 '39'left 1247, damaged by Flak W Bologna, crash-landed; Adj Jean Lanvario and two safe, three baled and POW
GB 1/22	B-26C Marauder '14' left 1247, damaged by Flak W Bologna, crash-landed; Lt Fourlinie and five safe

Bulgarian Casualties

2/6 Orlyak	Bf 109G-6 shot down by Flak over Nis a/f; Pod Martin Svetkov KiA

German Casualties

4./SAGr 126	Ar 196A-3 WNr 0311 D1+HM shot down by Beaufighter 15km S Milos; Obgfr Heinrich Gruber/Obfhr Werner Rössler MiA
2.(F)/122	Me 410 F6+EK damaged by fighters, crash-landed at Treviso a/f; Obfw Jackstadt/Uffz Schütze safe
Stab JG 77	Fi 156 left Villafranca, damaged by ground fire, presumably from partisans
	LKS reports one Ar 196 missing

Sunday, 10 September 1944

260 Squadron strafed Campoformido airfield again; this time the Bf 109s had departed.

Cannon fire from a Spitfire strikes the Me 410 shot down near Modena on 10 September which was the final victory of WWII for 1 SAAF Squadron.

British Claims

213 Sqn	2/Lt R.E.Rorvik	Mustang III FB337 'A'	He 111	25m S Mirovori	0606-0823
213 Sqn	Flt Lt C.D.A.Smith	Mustang III FB303			
213 Sqn	Flt Lt C.D.A.Smith	Mustang III FB303	Ju 52/3m	E Devdelija	0606-0823
1 SAAF Sqn	Capt D.M.Brebner	Spitfire IX MH901 'G'			
1 SAAF Sqn	Lt T.E.Wallace	Spitfire IX MH532 'H'	Me 410	8m NNE Modena	0720
1 SAAF Sqn	Lt J.B.S.Ross	Spitfire IX EN352 'I'			

British Casualties

6 Sqn	Hurricane IV KZ394 'H' left 1205 on shipping strike, attacked schooner in river near Nin, hit by Flak, pilot baled out 6km W Zaton between Nin and Ugljan, rescued by a Catalina; Sgt M.Gelbhauer safe
16 SAAF Sqn	Beaufighter X 'A' left 1515 to attack M/Y at Polykastron, hit by Flak, crash-landed 2m S of target 1605; Flt Lt A.S.Wickens/ Flg Off J.R.Pygram POW
16 SAAF Sqn	Beaufighter X 'R' left 1515 to attack M/Y at Polykastron, hit by Flak, crash-landed 10m SW Priliep 1620; Lt W.M.Snyman/ Lt R.Ribbink evaded by end of September
213 Sqn	Mustang III FB311 left 0606, shot down by return fire from He 111 25m S Mirovori; Sgt L.W.Brierley MiA
145 Sqn	Spitfire VIII JG250 'P' left 1345, hit by 20mm Flak while strafing NW Coppolo, Cat II damaged; Lt G.E.Milborrow WiA

German Claims

Flak		Mustang	N Polykastron	0721
Flak		Beaufighter	near Polykastron	1650

2.(F)/122	Me 410 WNr 0732 F6+CK belly-landed and burst into flames; Klinka and Misch survived			
1./TG 4	Ju 52/3m WNr 7609 G6+OH shot down 20km N Polykastron 0715; Fw Günther Voigt and three KiA			
	LKS reports one Ju 52/3m MiA and one He 111 damaged in combat			

Sunday-Monday, 10/11 September 1944

British Claims

600 Sqn	Flt Lt D.A.Thompson/Flg Off G.Beaumont	Beaufighter VIf MM876 'X'	Ju 87	10m SW Rimini	0312

Monday, 11 September 1944

Beaufighters of 16 SAAF Squadron led by Capt A.le Roux caught the Italian liner *Giulio Cesare* (21,900 tons) at anchor near Trieste and sank her in the shallow waters.

A special high-flying Spitfire IX, MH946, was delivered to 10 SAAF Squadron at Savoia, Libya from 9 SAAF Squadron. It had been stripped of all paint to enhance performance and was 'silver' overall.

During another patrol by 213 Squadron Mustang pilots submitted claims for three Axis aircraft including an Hs 126. LKS records indicated that a Ju 52/3m and an Fi 156 had been lost in combat. The second of these was the Fi 156 which may in this case have been incorrectly identified for the now-familiar and basically similar high-wing aircraft on this occasion.

British Claims

7 SAAF Wg	Lt Col A.C.Bosman	Spitfire VIII JG616	Bf 110 on ground	a/f nr Verona	0545-
213 Sqn	Flt Lt J.H.Fairbairn	Mustang III HB854	Ju 52/3m	2-3m E Dolovo	0705
213 Sqn	Flt Lt C.S.Vos	Mustang III HB902 ⎫			
213 Sqn	Flg Off F.A.E.Penson	Mustang III HB916 ⎭	Ju 88	2-4m WSW Uzdin	0710
213 Sqn	Sgt D.H.Bell	Mustang III HB888	Hs 126	nr Dolovo	0752

British Casualties

2 SAAF Sqn	Spitfire IXe EN453 'F' dawn strafe of motor transports, shot down by Flak 0750, pilot baled out over Allied lines; Capt H.C.W.Liebenberg returned to sqn 1045
92 Sqn	Spitfire VIII JF704 left 1815 to bomb bridge nr Rimini, shot down by Flak NW Cervia, pilot baled into sea; Capt M.D.Lawton promoted that day, picked up by Walrus X6529 'ZE-T' of 293 Sqn, flown by Sgt D.Newsome. Unable to take off, the Walrus was sunk in error for E boat by RN MTB at dusk 8km SE Rimini. Lawton and Walrus crew were rescued by MTB 633 which was later mined that night. Taken off by another MTB and landed next day, back to sqn

Highly polished Spitfire IXs were delivered to 10 SAAF Squadron at Savoia, Libya for intercepting high-flying German reconnaissance aircraft.

526th FS/86th FG	P-47D hit tree while strafing 1500; 1/Lt Richard P.Marcy KiA [16356]
315th FS/324th FG	P-47D 42-27096 hit by Flak 2m W Beaucourt, France, 1605; 2/Lt Wilford P.McKenzie POW [8935]

German Casualties

Stab./NAGr 12	Bf 109G-8 WNr 201089 Red 4 on recce of Dalmatian Islands, shot down by AA 10km N Vis; Fw Ernst Riepen MiA
9./TG 2	Ju 52/3m WNr 7768 shot down by fighters Padina, NE Belgrade; Lt Rudolf Rahn KiA, three safe
	LKS reports one Bf 109 lost to AA, one Fi 156 and one Ju 52/3m lost in combat

Monday-Tuesday, 11/12 September 1944

British Casualties

13 Sqn	Baltimore V FW358 'G' left 2148 on armed recce of Rapallo-Massa area, shot down by Flak between Borgo Val di Taro and Pontremoli; Flt Lt W.L.Saunders-Knox-Gore and three KiA
55 Sqn	Baltimore V FW497 on armed recce to Mercato Saraceno, undercarriage collapsed on landing due to prior damage; Flt Sgt R.Newstead and three safe
114 Sqn	Boston IV BZ499 left 0244 to bomb target near Rimini, an explosion reported over the target 0346, wreck found in San Marino in March 1945; Flg Off A.J.Jenkins and three KiA

Tuesday, 12 September 1944

The new 5th Army attack had caught the Germans off-guard and by the 12th all initial objectives had been reached. On this date 113 B-26s and 33 B-25s bombed the communications centre of Fiorenzuola very effectively, following which the town fell. Even as these successes were being registered 8th Army launched an all-out assault on the Coriano Ridge positions during the night of 12/13 overrunning the main defences and forcing the defenders to withdraw to Rimini where a week's hard fighting began on the outskirts.

In the afternoon, Beaufighter KV930 of 19 SAAF Squadron took off from Biferno in company with three other aircraft. On his very first mission was Lt Arthur Geater with his navigator Stan Dellow, seconded from the Royal Air Force. At approximately 1705 they reached the northern tip of Ithaki Island. The Beaufighters immediately started their attack but were greeted with strong anti-aircraft fire from a heavily armed Siebel ferry. Geater's Beaufighter was hit, both engines of his aircraft receiving strikes. Oil and thick smoke erupted and

Spitfire IX EN199 'S' of 225 Squadron during a recce sortie over the Arno river valley in September. This aircraft still exists and is preserved in the Malta War Museum.

the pilot took the decision to ditch the aircraft in a 'controlled sea landing' before it became an uncontrolled one. The Siebel ferry had sustained heavy damage according to German records and was eventually beached to avoid sinking. Geater successfully managed to ditch the aircraft and both he and the navigator climbed out and took to their inflatable dinghy. Within 30 minutes the two Allied airmen were saved by Greeks and taken to Ithaki Island, where they were provided with both food and shelter. Arthur Geater's adventure was not to stop there because, whilst he and Dellow were moved in a small fishing boat to another hiding place on the island, they were stopped at sea by a German patrol combing the area to locate the airmen. Stan Dellow could not swim and remained on the boat, Arthur Geater could; he dived into the water and swam to freedom. Stan Dellow survived the war but was caught and spent the rest of the war as a POW. Arthur Geater got away and linked up with the Greek resistance in Ithaki; he eventually managed to return to Italy and re-joined his squadron.

British Claims

213 Sqn	Flt Lt R.H.Garwood	Mustang III HB924	Do 217 Damaged (on ground)	Pančevo a/f, N Belgrade	0745-0800
213 Sqn	Flt Sgt D.E.Firman	Mustang III FB303	Ju 88 Damaged (on ground)	Pančevo a/f, N Belgrade	0745-0800
213 Sqn	Flt Sgt D.E.Firman	Mustang III FB303	Do 217 Probable (on ground)	Pančevo a/f, N Belgrade	0745-0800

British Casualties

185 Sqn	Spitfire VIII JF421 left 0925, a wing came off dive-bombing a railway near Russi, crashed; Sgt A.E.Jeans KiA
19 SAAF Sqn	Beaufighter VI KV930 'V' left 1330, shot down by Flak attacking a Siebel ferry, ditched 1m off Ithaki Island, on west coast of Greece 1505; Lt R.A.Geater evaded, returned to Italy 6 October/Flg Off S.W.G.Dellow POW
39 Sqn	Beaufighter X NE297 'P' left 1345 on shipping Rover, attacked a Siebel ferry, damaged by Flak, crash-landed at Grottaglie 1730; Flt Sgt H.W.Mullens/Flt Sgt R.G.Robson safe
417 Sqn	Spitfire VIII LV754 left 1615 on Cab Rank, dive-bombed Monte Colombo area, believed hit by Flak in bombing dive and exploded; Wt Off L.J.Baxter KiA

US Casualties

523rd FS/27th FBG	P-47D 42-28037 lost possibly to Flak E Belfort, France, 1015; 2/Lt Roy C.Ruble POW [8958]
523rd FS/27th FBG	P-47D 42-26589 shot down by Flak at Belfort, France, 1025; 2/Lt D.H.Chaplin MiA
64th FS/57th FG	P-47D 42-75729 crashed while strafing NW Mortara 1625; 1/Lt Paul E.Rawson KiA [8945]
526th FS/86th FG	P-47D 42-27921 lost u/k cause 1.5km NE Bordighera 1710; 2/Lt Lewis K.Foster KiA [8781]
527th FS/86th FG	P-47D 42-26701 '72' hit by Flak, ditched 10m N Corsica; Lt Goslin rescued
442nd BS/320th BG	B-26B '35' left 0745 to bomb defence positions in Fiorenzuola d'Arda area, damaged by Flak, crashed on landing; 1/Lt Russell G.Estes and five safe

German Claims

OKH	3 Flak claims in Italy

German Casualties

Wekusta 27	Ju 88D-1 WNr 881207 Q5+L damaged at Pančevo a/f by strafing
NASt.Kroat	Do 17 destroyed at Pančevo

Wednesday, 13 September 1944

Twenty-four Marauders from 21 SAAF Squadron attacked the Rimini area. The leader of the last box, Lt G.vd H.Whitehouse, was hit and crashed into the sea 5 miles south-east of Rimini. Three parachutes were seen.

The Mustangs of 249 Squadron flew their first operation from Brindisi when the commanding officer, Sqn Ldr Jack Te Kloot, and 2/Lt Shields flew a sweep along the Vardar Valley into northern Greece shooting up some locomotives. The pair flew another operation that afternoon, though while attacking a large motor transport convoy Shields' aircraft was hit and the pilot was forced to bale out. Luckily he was picked up by partisans and later got back to Italy.

British Claims

213 Sqn	Flt Lt J.H.Fairbairn	Mustang III HB888	S.79 Probable	8m NW Crupija	0725

British Casualties

27 SAAF Sqn	Ventura V JS935 'A' missing from a convoy patrol; Plt Off J.E.Stevens and four KiA
5 SAAF Sqn	Kittyhawk IV FX772 hit by Flak in bombing dive, spun in 32km N Florence 0915; Maj R.L.Morrison MiA
21 SAAF Sqn	Marauder III HD591 'C' left 1510 to attack target 3m SW Rimini, hit by Flak 1625, ditched; Lt G.vd.H.Whitehouse and one POW, two baled out in Allied lines, two MiA
213 Sqn	Mustang III HB888 struck the ground chasing a Ju 52/3m, crashed 6m W of Alibunar 0725; Flt Lt J.H.Fairbairn KiA

249 Sqn	Mustang III HB926 left 1515, struck in glycol system by Flak N of Lamia, pilot baled out 10m SE Agrinon 1710; 2/Lt W.Shields evaded, back in January 1945
92 Sqn	Spitfire VIII JF413 'V' left 0830, shot down by Flak 0930 5m SE Faenza; Lt E.Manne baled out, evaded and returned by 17 September
250 Sqn	Kittyhawk IV FX831 left 1110 to dive bomb strong point, damaged by Flak near Florence 1155, landed safely; Maj J.R.R.Wells WiA
603 Sqn	Beaufighter X NE367 'C' left 1405 on sweep, engine failed, ditched about 60m S Crete 1425; Plt Off A.B.Woodier/Sgt H.Lee rescued by Flg Off J.S.Turner in Walrus Z1776 of 294 Sqn

Italian Co-Belligerent Casualties

386ª Sq, 21° Gr, 51° St	MC.205 MM 92160 hit by Flak, crashed; S.Ten Vittorio Sigismondi KiA

German Claims

Flak		Marauder	W Rimini	1620
OKH	2 Flak claims in Italy			

German Casualties

10./TG 2	Ju 52/3m WNr 501361 lost Nisch-Salonika; Obfw Günther Schmitz and three MiA
3./TG 4	Ju 52/3m WNr 6825 G6+AH crashed 4.5km E Paracin-S Cuprija, Serbia; pilot safe, three KiA
6.(F)/122	Ju 188D-2 WNr 150235 left Bergamo, crashed nr Soprana, S Cuneo, u/k reason; Lt Gottfried Heene and three KiA
	LKS reports one Ju 188 missing

Wednesday-Thursday, 13/14 September 1944

A 2,000-ton ship spotted off Marina di Ravenna was hit and damaged at 0240 by Wt Off M.R.Priest's Wellington (NS253) of 458 Squadron. It was finished off later that night by another aircraft flown by Flt Sgt J.M.Whitten (MP650) from the same squadron at 0438, being last seen ablaze, probably *GK 14* which was sunk by bombs.

A Wellington of 36 Squadron, in taking off from Alghero swung off the runway and ended up in 284 Squadron's dispersal area, where it caught fire and its bombs exploded, destroying four of 284 Squadron's Warwicks.

British Casualties

36 Sqn	Wellington XIV HF407 left on patrol, crashed on take-off, caught fire and blew up; crew safe
284 Sqn	4 Warwick ASR Is BV275, BV362, BV458, BV524 destroyed when Wellington XVI HF407 blew up
14 Sqn	Marauder B-26A FK124 'Z' left 0550 on armed recce, crashed on take-off; Flg Off M.T.Holmes and five KiA

Thursday, 14 September 1944

1 SAAF Squadron's Lt Cecil Boyd was shot down by Flak. He had flown 87 hours on operations in four months and this was the third time he had been shot down and baled out.

British Casualties

241 Sqn	Spitfire VIII JP396 left 1125 as weaver to 40 SAAF Tac R, engine trouble on return, pilot baled out in Allied lines; Sgt M.R Huish safe
1 SAAF Sqn	Spitfire IX EN333 'C' left 1125, hit by Flak, caught fire, pilot baled out in Allied lines; Lt C.Boyd safe
2 SAAF Sqn	Spitfire IX MK662 'C' left 1220, engine failed, crash-landed N Bologna; Lt R.B.McKechnie evaded, returned on 28 September
601 Sqn	Spitfire IX PT397 left 1045, strafed motor transports near Montescuolo, believed hit by Flak, exploded and crashed in flames; Sgt C.Hutchinson KiA
6 Sqn	Hurricane IV LD233 'C' left 0630 on armed recce, shot down by Flak near Murtar; Flg Off F.M.Clarke KiA
352 Sqn	Spitfire Vc JK967 left 1655, hit by Flak, crashed into Cetina river; Plt Off Franjo Kluz KiA
7 SAAF Sqn	Spitfire IX LZ918 hit by ground fire near Fiorenzuola, pilot baled out; Capt A.W.Meikle returned

US Casualties

380th BS/310th BG	B-25J 42-7676 hit by frag bomb from another B-25 0930; 1/Lt Robert E.Keane and four returned, one POW [8773]
37th BS/17th BG	B-26G 43-34247 '48' damaged by Flak, crashed on landing 1215; 2/Lt J.King and two WiA, three safe
12th PRS/3rd PRG	F-5E 44-23230 *Rose Marie* lost u/k cause over Po Valley 1700; 2/Lt James F.Babcock MiA [9669]
447th BS/321st BG	B-25J 43-27701 left 0825 to bomb Le Grazie, damaged by Flak, crashed on landing 1220; 1st Lt Marion E Walker and five safe

Italian Co-Belligerent Casualties

253ª Sq, 132° Gr	Baltimore V FW720 crashed on taking-off from Campo Vesuvio; Ten Silvio Cella and three KiA

The F-5 Lightnings of the US 90th Photo Reconnaissance Wing provided much valuable targeting information for the HQs tasking the Allied medium bombers. F-5E 44-23230 *Rose Marie* was lost over the Po Valley on one such mission.

German Claims				
Flak		Mitchell	S Rimini	1000
Flak		e/a	Isola	
6./Nav Flak Det. 628	StFw Leo Burger	Spitfire	Sumartin, Brac Island	1500
Flak		e/a	Boffalora, S Milan	1825

German Casualties	
II./TG 4	Ju 52/3m WNr 6492 G6+JK lost Salonika-Tatoi; Fw Alfred Manz and three MiA
	LKS reports one Ju 52/3m missing and five destroyed on ground

Thursday-Friday, 14/15 September 1944

British Casualties	
46 Sqn	Beaufighter VIf ND283 'T' left 1950 from Idku to intrude to Calato on Rhodes, and failed to return; Flt Sgt K.C.Bottle/Flt Sgt W.H.Mayor KiA

Friday, 15 September 1944

260 Squadron Kittyhawk pilots strafed Ancona airfield where they fired at one of five S.79s. More than 20 aircraft were then seen under trees and the intruders claimed a Ju 88 and a Ju 52/3m set on fire. Airfields around Athens were attacked by B-17s of the 2nd, 97th, 99th and 463rd Bomb Groups and B-24s of the 376th, 454th, 455th and 456th Bomb Groups causing considerable damage and destroying at least two-dozen aircraft.

The 20° Gruppo of the Italian Co-Belligerent air force received the first Spitfire Vs, in order to replace its war-weary MC.205s.

British Casualties	
601 Sqn	Spitfire IX MH 534 left 1655 to bomb gun positions 5m N San Martino, hit by Flak, pilot baled in Allied lines; Flg Off H.G.Proudman safe
US Casualties	
65th FS/57th FG	P-47D 42-75664 shot down by Flak NE Velezzo Lomellina 0950; Capt Donald W.Bell KiA [8775]

German Claims				
Flak	Lt Platoon Milos/N Flak 720			
Flak	*Achilles*	Martlet	Milos	0830

German Casualties	
15./TG 4	4 Ju 52/3ms (WNrn 641408, 649747, 640164 and 5745) destroyed by bombs at Eleusis
15./TG 4	2 Ju 52/3ms (WNrn 501115 and 7102) destroyed by e/a at Megara
15./TG 4	Ju 52/3m WNr 501411 destroyed by e/a at Tatoi
	LKS reports two transport a/c lost in combat, 24 a/c destroyed on ground and 13 damaged

Saturday, 16 September 1944

Beaufighters of 603 Squadron were on patrol when their crews spotted two Ju 52/3ms and one Ar 196 leaving Portolago Bay on Leros. They attacked but the Germans retreated over the bay where Flak put up an intense barrage. One of the British aircraft was hit by Flak and ditched on the return flight.

185 Squadron moved to Borghetto to join the new 8 SAAF Wing which commenced operations with 3 SAAF, 11 SAAF and 87 Squadrons. 284 Squadron's B Flight on Warwicks became 293 Squadron's E Flight on this date. It was based at Calvi.

Operation Outing I began on this day with the first phase intending to neutralise the outer defence ring formed by the islands of Crete, Scarpanto and Rhodes. During the day Wildcats from HMS *Pursuer* and *Searcher* and 879

Right: The commander of 8 SAAF Wing throughout the autumn fighting was Col S.F.'Rosie' du Toit. Below: Seafire IIc MB270 'A-A' of 879 Squadron flown by Sub Lt W.A.Clarke over HMS *Attacker* near Crete on 16 September.

Squadron's Seafires made strafing attacks on road traffic on Crete and offshore, with four caiques sunk with bombs and six others damaged. The Wildcats also spotted for shore bombardment. However, three of 881's Wildcats were damaged by return fire and another by striking telephone wires, but all returned safely to make emergency landings on HMS *Pursuer*.

British Claims					
603 Sqn	Flt Lt A.G.Deck/Flg Off C.L.Heide	Beaufighter X NV213 'R'	Ar 196	Leros	1450

British Casualties

145 Sqn	Spitfire VIII MT671 left 1835, hit by Flak over San Marino, crashed in flames 1935; Plt Off J.M.Dixon MiA
145 Sqn	Spitfire VIII JF810 left 0945, hit by Flak, crash-landed at base, Cat II damaged; Sgt B.C.Britton safe
213 Sqn	Mustang III HB903 'B' left 0730, lost in bad weather over Belgrade area 0925; 2/Lt J.W.Moor KiA
2 SAAF Sqn	Spitfire IXc MJ367 'V' left 0630 to River Po delta, strafed motor transports, hit by Flak near Lorio 0735, pilot baled; Capt G.H.Wates POW
260 Sqn	Mustang III FB287 left 0630 on armed recce, attacked San Felice rail station, shot down by Flak near Rivale; Sgt N.A.R.Hughes POW
603 Sqn	Beaufighter X NV213 'R' left 1450, attacked aircraft at Leros, hit by Flak, ditched; Flt Lt A.G.Deck/Flg Off C.L.Heide rescued
19 SAAF Sqn	Beaufighter X NV215 'B' left 1407, attacked barracks at Valjevo SW Belgrade, shot down by Flak 1550; Plt Off C.H.Mason/ Plt Off J.S.Peacey (Offical War Photographer) KiA

Below: A Do 17P of the Bulgarian air force's 4/1 Orlyak was badly damaged when attacked by a 213 Squadron Mustang over Lake Ohrid on the Albania/Bulgaria border. **Bottom:** A US Navy blimp dwarfs Spitfire IX MT952 'K' of 451 Squadron parked at Cuers in southern France on 17 September.

881 Sqn	Wildcat V JV677 'UV' starboard wing hit by Flak while strafing Crete; Sub Lt R.P.Gibson safe			
881 Sqn	Wildcat V JV696 'UQ' hit by a 40mm shell while strafing Crete; Sub Lt T.L.M.Brander safe			
881 Sqn	Wildcat V JV706 'UD' damaged by return fire while strafing Crete; Sub Lt D.L.W.Frearson safe			
881 Sqn	Wildcat V JV670 'UO' starboard wing damaged by striking telephone wires while strafing; Mid R.G.Williams safe			
US Casualties				
345th FS/350th FG	P-47D 42-28322 lost to Flak (or mech trouble), crashed 2km W Villafranca Lunigiana 1205; 1/Lt Robert E.Buser KiA [8944]			

German Claims				
Flak		Mustang	San Pietro	0600
Flak	Lt Platoon Milos/N Flak 720	Baltimore	Milos	0945
German Casualties				
II./TG 4	Ju 52/3m lost in combat; Fw Erich Feist and three MiA			
	LKS reports one Ju 53/3m lost in combat			

Sunday, 17 September 1944

Sqn Ldr Jack Te Kloot of 249 Squadron led a sweep to the Prilep area by 15 Mustang IIIs, which included eight from 213 Squadron. Seven miles south-east of Kičevo, a Dornier bomber identified as a Bulgarian Do 217 was sighted. It was indeed Bulgarian, being a Do 17P-1 from 73.jato of 4./1.RO. Green Section jettisoned their bombs and gave chase and Lt Ron Rorvik, SAAF, attacked first and set the Dornier's starboard engine on fire. The Dornier turned into the attackers and pouring smoke and flames from the damaged engine, dived steeply for the cloudbank and was lost to sight. Rorvik claimed a probable "Do 217", though the Bulgarian crew managed to regain control of the heavily damaged aircraft and crash-land shortly after crossing the Bulgarian border.

British Claims					
213 Sqn	2/Lt R.E.Rorvik	Mustang FB337 'A'	Do 217 Probable	20m ENE Ohridsko Lake	1100
British Casualties					
1 SAAF Sqn	Spitfire IX MA529 'O' left 1540 on Cab Rank, dive-bombed near Barco 1620, burst into flames in bombing dive at 6,000ft, no Flak seen; Lt G.A.Roy KiA				
1 SAAF Sqn	Spitfire IX MH664 left 1635 on Cab Rank, dive-bombed 1735, caught fire, crashed 10m NE Florence 1745; Lt D.P.Farrell KiA				
601 Sqn	Spitfire IXb PT490 left 1135 to bomb target 2m N Rimini, dive-bombed, FTR; Sgt M.Young KiA				
Italian Co-Belligerent Casualties					
208ª Sq, 101° Gr, 5° St	MC.202 MM 9101 failed to return; Ten Carlo Graziani MiA				
Bulgarian Casualties					
2/6 Orlyak	Bf 109G-6 '172' shot down by Flak Bela Palanka area at 0830, pilot baled out; Kpt M.G.Petrov WiA				
2/6 Orlyak	Bf 109G-6 possibly damaged by Flak, ran out of fuel and crash-landed; Por A.Barev safe				
4/1 Orlyak	Do 17P-1 heavily damaged in attack by 213 Sqn Mustang, crash-landed in Bulgaria; crew safe				
German Casualties					
11./TG 4	Ju 52/3m WNr 131473 G6+HV lost 45km E Skopje; Fw Wilhelm Oehler and four MiA				
4./MSGr 1	Ju 52/3m WNr 3404 3k+KM destroyed by strafing attack 0650 at Maritza, Rhodes				
1./NSGr 10	Ju 87D-3 WNr 110768 lost near Pančevo, Serbia				
	LKS reports three a/c missing				

Monday, 18 September 1944

Six Spitfires from 73 Squadron led by Maj D.W.Golding strafed Ljubljana airfield and the pilots claimed three Hs 126s, one Cant.Z. and one unidentified twin-engined type in flames. One Bf 109 and one biplane were left smoking; five aircraft were claimed damaged.

British Casualties		
5 SAAF Sqn	Kittyhawk IV FX841 left 1450, hit by ground fire, pilot baled out S Santarcangelo 1730; Lt J. B.Raleigh POW	
185 Sqn	Spitfire IX MK724 left 1205, shot down by Flak nr Verucchio, 16km SW Rimini 1245; Lt R.J.Rowe KiA	
73 Sqn	Spitfire IX MJ116 left 1020 on offensive sweep to Ljubljana a/f; not seen after strafing, probably shot down by Flak; Sgt P.J.Clark POW	
73 Sqn	Spitfire IX ML425 left 1020 on offensive sweep to Ljubljana a/f; probably damaged by Flak, on return flight pilot baled but got caught on the aircraft; Wt Off L.C.Evans KiA	

| 250 Sqn | Kittyhawk IV FT866 shot down by Flak, 11km W Rimini 1645, pilot baled; Lt M.A.Cousins WiA |
| 87 Sqn | Spitfire IX MH676 left 0720, hit by 20mm Flak, reached San Giovanni l/g, crash-landed; Flt Sgt J.R.Harling WiA |

US Casualties

445th BS/321st BG	B-25J 43-27792 *Cuddle Bunny* shot down by Flak, last seen NW Savona 0900, ditched 5m N Rimini; 1/Lt John S.Richardson and five POW, one KiA [8779]
428th BS/310th BG	B-25J 43-27771 *Sharpie* hit by Flak, last seen 5m W Rimini 1405; 1/Lt Louis Shovanek and four safe, one POW [8938]
428th BS/310th BG	B-25J 43-28068 *Little Hiawatha* hit by Flak, last seen 5m W Rimini 1405; 1/Lt Harold G.Iverson and five POW, one KiA [8940]
379th BS/310th BG	B-25J 43-28075 damaged by Flak, last seen off the coast nr Pesaro 1430; 1/Lt Ralph H.Keller and three KiA, two POW [8780]

German Claims

Flak		Kittyhawk	NW Rimini	
Flak		Mitchell	W Rimini	1430
Flak		Mitchell '771'	W Rimini	1500
Flak		Mitchell	nr Rimini	1500

Tuesday, 19 September 1944

With 335 Squadron at Canne pilots carried out their first operation from the European mainland when four Spitfires reconnoitred the Split area.

The Royal Navy carrier force launched aircraft for a dive-bombing attack on Rhodes. Targets included four of the airfields, road transport and shipping in the harbours and coastal waters. On return the pilots claimed two Ju 52/3ms and 68 vehicles destroyed as well as sinking two depot ships and five caïques. A 1,000-ton vessel was left damaged as was a radio station. Later in the evening, near Rhodes, two Beaufighters of 603 Squadron were providing last-light cover to the naval force when they were attacked by Wildcats in error, both Beaufighters having to crash land at base.

British Casualties

| 6 Sqn | Hurricane IV LD169 'P' left 1255 to attack a ship damaged by previous mission, hit by Flak at Zavratnica, flew 75km south towards Vis before ditching 1m NE Rava Island; Wt Off R.Y.Ulrich rescued by rowing boat, then transferred to a partisan launch and returned |

Wildcat VI JV338 'S-X' launches from HMS *Searcher* during attacks on Rhodes through the day.

603 Sqn	Beaufighter X NT893 'P' left 1810, damaged by Wildcats, crash-landed at base 2125; Plt Off C.Goodwin/Flt Sgt H.J.Turner safe				
603 Sqn	Beaufighter X NT912 'H' left 1810, damaged by Wildcats, crash-landed at base 2125; Sgt S.A.Seear/Sgt R.B.Smith safe				
267 Sqn	Dakota III FD865 left 1000 from Capodichino to Cagliari, lost in bad weather; Flg Off C.R.Ryerse, three crew and 17 passengers KiA				
92 Sqn	Spitfire VIII JF505 left 0745 on Rover Paddy of Verucchio area, hit by Flak, abandoned 2m E of Monte Colombo; Flg Off A.D.Taylor baled out into Allied lines, safe				
12 SAAF Sqn	Marauder III HD456 'J' left 1230 to attack tactical targets north-west of Rimini, hit by Flak, force-landed at Jesi; Lt East and four safe, obs Lt R.N.Cullinan severely WiA				

German Casualties					
2./TG 4	Ju 52/3m WNr 3237 G6+LK lost Kalamaki-Heraklion; Uffz Horst Kämmerlig and two MiA, one safe				
	LKS reports one Ju 52/3m destroyed on ground				

Wednesday, 20 September 1944

Two 249 Squadron Mustangs strafed Lianovergi airfield destroying a Ju 52/3m, then continued to Larissa airfield where another Ju 52/3m was claimed destroyed on the ground and a Ju 88 and a Bf 109 damaged, and additionally five locomotives were destroyed.

Seven Spitfires of 253 Squadron strafed motor transports in northern Greece, claiming over 100 vehicles destroyed and another 100 damaged. This devastation was confirmed by photo reconnaissance the next day. Also, next day a section of four returned to strafe in northern Greece, with rather less success.

351 (Yugoslav) Squadron with Hurricane IVs joined 281 Wing, which at this time controlled both the RAF's Greek fighter squadrons and both the Yugoslav squadrons as well.

British Claims					
249 Sqn	Capt R.T.Whittingham	Mustang III KG429	Ju 52/3m (on ground)	Lianovergi	0520-0755
249 Sqn	Flt Lt A.E.Dryden	Mustang III KH422			
249 Sqn	Capt R.T.Whittingham	Mustang III KG429	Ju 52/3m (on ground)	Larissa a/f	0520-0755
249 Sqn	Flt Lt A.E.Dryden	Mustang III KH422			
249 Sqn	Capt R.T.Whittingham	Mustang III KG429	Ju 88 and Bf 109 damaged (on ground)	Larissa a/f	0520-0755
249 Sqn	Flt Lt A.E.Dryden	Mustang III KH422			

British Casualties					
253 Sqn	Spitfire Vc JK771 left 0510 strafing motor transports in northern Greece, damaged by ground fire, landed at base; Flg Off M.Smyth safe				
253 Sqn	Spitfire Vc JK460 left 0510 strafing motor transports in northern Greece, damaged by ground fire, landed at base; Plt Off T.H.Harrison safe				

German Casualties					
1./NAGr 12	Bf 109G-6 WNr 19678 White 2 lost at Mostar; Uffz Helmut Wittenberg KiA				
Seenotgr 70	Do 24T-1 WNr 0090 IM+AC crashed in Suda Bay; Obfw Emil Harder and four KiA, one rescued				

Thursday, 21 September 1944

British Claims					
249 Sqn	Flg Off T.H.Ashworth	Mustang III HB937	Ju 52/3m (on ground)	Larissa l/g	0500-0710
249 Sqn	Sgt A.W.Manning	Mustang III KH422	Ju 52/3m (on ground)	Larissa l/g	0500-0710
213 Sqn	Sgt D.H.Bell	Mustang III HB879	Bf 109 Damaged	16m N Tirana	1620
213 Sqn	Wt Off S.G.Pickford	Mustang III HB854	Bf 109	16m N Tirana	1620

British Casualties					
14 Sqn	Marauder I FK138 'X' left 0445, crashed after take-off due to striking cables; Wt Off F.Elliott and five KiA				
249 Sqn	Mustang III KH422 left 0500, strafed l/g 10m N Larissa, destroyed a Ju 52, hit by Flak, pilot baled out; Sgt A.W.Manning safe, rescued by partisans, flown out by DC 3 a few days later				
238 Sqn	Spitfire IX BS530 left 1515 on armed recce of roads near Savona, hit by Flak; Wt Off S.G.Lee KiA				
237 Sqn	Spitfire IX NH296 left 0935 on armed recce of Cuneo area, shot down by Flak, pilot baled out; Flt Sgt J.Hackett evaded				
253 Sqn	Spitfire Vc JK339 left 0510, last seen strafing two Ju 52/3ms on a/f near Salonika, crashed near Veria, Greece, FTR; Lt B.W.G.Carrick KiA				
253 Sqn	Spitfire Vc JK755 left 0510, strafing motor transports near Veria, Greece, FTR; Sgt W.H.Aldercotte evaded and returned later				

| 253 Sqn | Spitfire Vc JL115 left 0510, strafing motor transports near Khalkedon; Plt Off J.W.Patterson evaded and returned later |
| 253 Sqn | Spitfire Vc JK339 left 0510, strafing motor transports near Khalkedon, hit by Flak, landed at base; Flt Lt R.Slade-Betts WiA |

German Casualties

Stab2./SAGr 126	Ar 196A-5 WNr 623163 D1+NK shot down by ships' AA E Trikkeri; Obfw Herbert Schumann/Lt Hans Kluck WiA
1./NSGr 7	CR.42 WNr 5623 White 12 shot down by own Flak, crashed at Kragujevac, 50% damaged; Obfw Anton Huberth WiA
	LKS reports two Ju 52/3ms destroyed on ground and one Ar 196 lost on ops

Below: Partisans use branches to camouflage 249 Squadron Mustang III HB946 GN-E after it had arrived on a strip named 'Piccadilly Peggy' in northern Greece. Bottom: Sqn Ldr Jack Te Kloot (in bush hat) and other pilots of 249 Squadron after their arrival at Piccadilly Peggy.

Friday, 22 September 1944

Venice harbour photographed from a 682 Squadron Spitfire during a reconnaissance on 22 September.

At first light Sqn Ldr Te Kloot led a pair of 249 Squadron Mustangs to carry out a number of strafing attacks on enemy transport across Salonika before attacking the enemy landing strip at Megara. Diving down, Jack Te Kloot destroyed two Ju 52/3m transports parked there before moving on and strafing a parade before flying back to Brindisi. He noted: "Two Ju 52s destroyed on Megara LG near Athens. Two locos destroyed, three locos damaged. Several oil wagons fired. Three motor transports destroyed, one motor transports damaged. One bullshit parade liquidated."

The other pair failed to return, and though Flt Lt Alf Dryden was killed after being struck by debris from an exploding train, Capt Whittingham, whose Mustang was also damaged, managed to bale out and returned that night. This was the first of a number of attacks using the strip codenamed 'Piccadilly Peggy'.

Sqn Ldr N.F.Duke of 145 Squadron became tour expired and was replaced by Sqn Ldr S.W.F.'Dan' Daniel. One of 145's flight commanders, Flt Lt Frankie Banner, was also tour expired and left.

British Claims

249 Sqn	Sqn Ldr J.Te Kloot	Mustang III KH465	2 Ju52/3ms (on ground)	Megara l/g	0455-0815

British Casualties

185 Sqn	Spitfire IX PT366 left 1425, strafed Cervia-Rimini area, shot down by Flak; Sgt D.W.Medlicott KiA
249 Sqn	Mustang III KH468 left 0455, strafed a train 3m N Kastri 18-10m NW of Lamia 0700, locomotive blew up, FTR; Flt Lt A.E.Dryden KiA
249 Sqn	Mustang III KH425 left 0455, lost coolant after damage by debris, pilot baled out near partisan base; Capt R.T.Whittingham safe, flown back by DC 3 later the same day
250 Sqn	Kittyhawk IV FX509 left 1540, damaged by Flak, crash-landed 200yds S Rimini a/f 1745; Lt A.McG.Brand WiA

US Casualties

347th FS/350th FG	P-47D 42-27264 '7A5' shot down by Flak 5m SW Imola 0800; 1/Lt Leroy Clifton rescued by partisans [9038]
526th FS/86th FG	P-47D 42-27002 *Windy Baby* lost u/k cause, crashed nr Valle Lomellina 1230; Capt Jackson Saunders POW [8963]
526th FS/86th FG	P-47D 42-28042 *Marge* shot down by Flak, last seen nr Breme 1225; 2/Lt Ardel Klemme POW [8964]

Bulgarian Casualties

3/6 Orlyak	Bf 109G-6 '163' shot down by Flak SW Veles 1500; Pod D.D.Sotirov KiA
3/6 Orlyak	Bf 109G-6 damaged by Flak, crash-landed at base; Pod P.E.Pavlov safe

German Claims

Flak		Hurricane	Croatia	
Flak		Thunderbolt	near Valle Lomellina	1325

Friday-Saturday, 22/23 September 1944

Saturday, 23 September 1944

The arrival of British forces to Greece during the month brought with it units of the Royal Air Force. The airfield at Araxos became the first foothold, when it was occupied on 23 September and many airfields around it were secured within a month, including Megara (taken over by parachute landings by 4th Battalion, Parachute Regt).

This gave the RAF capacity to strike at the German forces who were withdrawing in a south to north direction from each side of Greece, with the forces on the east side of Greece near Salonika then withdrawing westwards across northern Greece into Yugoslavia and then northwards to exit the Balkans past the northern point of the Adriatic, all the while the German army fought to keep the Russians from cutting of the Balkans from Europe by reaching the Adriatic.

As well as being under severe pressure from the partisan forces in Yugoslavia, the Germans were also suffering from increasing partisan activity in Greece as well as facing the westward thrust of the Soviet Red Army and their newly acquired Romanian and Bulgarian allies.

In the Aegean, the reduced garrisons on Rhodes, Crete and those islands that had not already been evacuated still required support and German transport units continued operating to resupply them. Whilst much reduced, Allied air operations continued over the Aegean to harass the remnant garrisons and any attempts to supply them. To assist in the retreat from Greece and Yugoslavia from August 1944 onwards, a force of Ju 52/3ms, supplemented by He 111s and occasionally larger aircraft such as Ju 290s, continued to fly in supplies and evacuate the wounded. These were almost exclusively night missions. The small Croatian air arm provided what support it could for their German allies.

The encounters with the Axis aircraft over the Balkans were related to interceptions of these activities. Only the 15th Air Force fighters operating further north over Hungary and Czechoslovakia encountered German fighter aircraft of units mainly tasked with supporting the southern sector of the eastern front against the Russians.

In Italy a night ground-attack capacity was still occasionally used at dusk and dawn, but as winter approached primarily at night. Night and day strategic and tactical reconnaissance were still present. The day-fighter force was now exclusively in the hands of the ANR's Bf 109s.

The Ju 87s, Hs 126s, CR.42s and other types were still used in daylight over the Balkans from August onwards, but not over Italy. Thus, aerial combat for the Allied Tactical Air Forces declined to the end of the war over Italy, constrained to intercepting reconnaissance aircraft in the day, and the Nachtschlacht Ju 87s at night, with a series of encounters with the ANR fighters. Operations over the Balkans resulted in encounters with a low number, but with an incredibly diverse range, of aircraft, from various air arms supporting the Axis powers.

The prime danger to the Allied Tactical Air Forces, as the winter of 1944/45 approached remained the ever-increasing quantities of Flak, particularly in areas with efficient radar coverage and an efficient air-raid-warning system. As the Germans withdrew westwards and northwards, the area they defended decreased in size, and the density of Flak increased. The transport routes, primarily the rail lines through the Brenner Pass became legendary for the volume of Flak produced. Indeed, once the German defensive lines stabilised in northern Italy after the retreat from Rome with the Flak repositioned, the losses to this means increased sharply. Almost equally as dangerous remained the capricious weather, with the single highest one-mission loss to a fighter squadron (namely six aircraft and four pilots from 5 SAAF Squadron), occurring when a patrol of their new Mustangs was caught over Yugoslavia in atrocious weather in December 1944.

24 SAAF Sqn	Marauder III HD580 'T' left 1331 to bomb rail bridge, crash-landed shortly after take-off, caught fire, bombs exploded; Lt D.V.Bartholomew and four KiA, one severely WiA
250 Sqn	Kittyhawk IV FT867 left 1310, hit by intense 20mm Flak, belly-landed on Rimini a/f; Lt C.D.Wollaston safe
252 Sqn	Beaufighter TFX LZ456 'D' left 1140 to attack ship *Orion* S Denusa Island, near Naxos, hit by Flak 1435, FTR; Flt Sgt S.C.Skippen/Flt Sgt J.A.Truscott KiA
252 Sqn	Beaufighter TFX NV200 'N' left 1140 to attack ship *Orion* S Denusa Island, near Naxos, hit by Flak 1435, crash-landed at base; Flt Lt C.W.Fowler/Flg Off R.H.Kemp safe

US Casualties

527th FS/86th FG	P-47D 42-27946 '95' shot down by Flak 5m SW Imola 1705; 2/Lt Paul Lefkow POW [8965]
439th BS/319th BG	B-26C 42-107555 left 0830 to bomb Vigevano railway bridge, shot down by Flak, last seen over target 0951; 2/Lt Earl O.Peterson and two KiA, three returned [8936]
439th BS/319th BG	B-26B 42-95997 left 0830 to bomb Vigevano railway bridge, blew a tyre on take-off, crashed; crew safe
428th BS/310th BG	B-25J 43-27797 damaged by Flak, last seen NW Savona 1045; 2/Lt Fredrick L.Van Dien and three KiA, two safe [8937]
47th BG	A-20 lost over Italy; Flt Off Alvin C.Jones and two POW

German Claims

Flak		Marauder	E Vigevano	1045
Flak		Spitfire	near Castel del Rio	1700
Flak		Thunderbolt	Imola	1730

Saturday-Sunday, 23/24 September 1944

British Casualties

55 Sqn	Baltimore V FW359 'K' left 2159 on armed recce of Savignano-Bologna-Ferrrara-Ravenna area, FTR; Flg Off G.A.White and three KiA

Sunday, 24 September 1944

251 Wing on Corsica ceased operations.

British Casualties

293 Sqn	Warwick ASR I BV449 left 1434 on ASR search off Terracina, last heard from 1537, FTR; Flt Lt A.O.Black and six MiA

Italian Co-Belligerent Casualties

238ª Sq, 101° Gr, 5° St	MC.202 MM 91971 left 0830 on recce over Dholana area, failed to return; Ten Socrate Peroni KiA
238ª Sq, 101° Gr, 5° St	MC.202 MM 9117 left 0830 on recce over Dholana area, failed to return; Ten Crisanto Venditti KiA

Monday, 25 September 1944

249 Squadron continued its sweeps over Greece, and on this occasion the Australian commanding officer Sqn Ldr Jack Te Kloot and his wingman Lt A.J.Malherbe strafed Ju 52/3ms on Athens Tatoi airfield claiming five destroyed. Aside from this they also claimed destroyed two locomotives each with 15 wagons of fuel, a staff car, three more locomotives and two wagons, and finally two motor transports.

British Claims

249 Sqn	Sqn Ldr J.Te Kloot	Mustang III KH465	3 Ju 52/3ms on ground	Tatoi airfield
249 Sqn	2/Lt A.J.Malherbe	Mustang III HB946	2 Ju 52/3ms on ground	Tatoi airfield

British Casualties

112 Sqn	Mustang III FB323 'E' left 0710 bombing roads E of Rimini, shot down by Flak E Cesena 0750; Lt G McFie KiA
260 Sqn	Mustang III FB261 left 1400, hit by Flak near Rimini, pilot baled out off the coast but did not survive; Sgt R.H.Barnes KiA
3 RAAF Sqn	Kittyhawk IV FX664 left 1445, shot down by Flak attacking bridge 2m N San Savio; Wt Off R.Faria KiA
3 RAAF Sqn	Kittyhawk IV FT871 left 1445, hit by Flak attacking bridge 2m N San Savio, crash-landed at base; Flt Sgt S.J.Haggarty safe
352 Sqn	Spitfire Vc ER309 left 1200 to bomb Ljubuski a/f, last seen entering heavy cloud at Vrgorac; Plt Off Leopold Ankon KiA

US Casualties

347th FS/350th FG	P-47D 42-28329 '7B2' shot down by Flak W Piacenza 0700; 1/Lt H.E.McCall POW [8961]
380th BS/310th BG	B-25D 43-3449 lost u/k cause between Sicily and Corsica, last seen 0806; 1/Lt William G.Spackey and one MiA [9311]

German Claims

Flak		Thunderbolt	W Piacenza	0755

Above: On 25 September Adum Romeo and Matja Petrović defected to Topusko airfield in this Croatian Fieseler Fi 167A biplane. Below: Flying Spitfire Vc JK226 'A' from Araxos on 25 September, Flt Lt Derek Rake flew 32 Squadron's first intercept sortie from Greek soil.

German Casualties

LKS reports two a/c lost in combat and one by AA

Croatian Casualties

u/k unit   Fieseler Fi 167A defected to partisans at Topusko airfield; Adum Romeo and Matja Petrović safe

Monday-Tuesday, 25/26 September 1944

US Casualties

414th NFS   Beaufighter VIf ND294 starboard engine failed and feathered, crashed when stalled attempting to force land 4km SSW
Lonate Pozzolo 2205; 2/Lt Franklin M.Andrews/2/Lt Jacob C.Attone KiA [9709]

German Claims

OKH   5 Flak claims in Italy

Tuesday, 26 September 1944

Operation Cablegram commenced on the 26th with a flight of four Seafires on an armed-recce reconnaissance over Rhodes. The commanding officer of 809 Squadron, Lt Cdr H.D.B.Eadon, destroyed a Ju 52/3m during an attack on Calato airfield. Some motor transports were strafed and cover maintained over the minesweepers all day.

46 Squadron now mounted a detachment of Beaufighter night-fighters at Gambut to work over the Aegean under control of the ground control ship HMS *Ulster Queen*, following its successful employment during Operation Dragoon. This small force, aided by a flight from 108 Squadron, intercepted transport aircraft operating at night between Crete and Greece, and was soon very successful, eventually claiming 19 such aircraft in little over a week. A similar attempt at the start of the month, with HMS *Royalist*, had not met with success and further training ensued before this second attempt was made.

Wing Commander Patrick Henry Woodruff of 337 Wing, Balkan Air Force, welcomed 32 Squadron to Greece by leading the unit's aircraft at 0900 on their first sortie.

A superb view of 46 Squadron Beaufighter VIf V8708/S flown by Flg Off B.J.Wild at about the time of the Gambut detachment, showing that the undersides had been painted black in contravention of the camouflage instructions!

36 Squadron, whose Wellingtons had been doing reconnaissances and shipping strikes in the Mediterranean departed for England.

British Claims

809 Sqn	Lt Cdr H.D.B.Eadon	Seafire	Ju 52 on ground	Calato

British Casualties

601 Sqn — Spitfire IX PT378 left 1645, hit by Flak 1m SE Cesano, pilot baled out into sea off Cattolica; Sgt B.Watford rescued by Walrus

3 RAAF Sqn — Kittyhawk IV FX569 left 0725, went down low after motor transports near Bologna-Rimini, crashed near San Pietro SE Bologna; Plt Off F.C.Sanders KiA

208 Sqn — Spitfire IX PT432 left 1155 on TacR as weaver to Bologna, strafed train, shot down by Flak; Sqn Ldr P.M.Bezencenet evaded, returned on 2 October but wounded when shot while crossing the lines

272 Sqn — Beaufighter X PT899 'L' left 0500, attacked a schooner, shot down by Flak; Flt Lt F.H.Foden/Flg Off A.C.Porter KiA

US Casualties

526th FS/86th FG — P-47D 42-27244 *Skeeter II* shot down by Flak 2m E Ostiglia 1145; 1/Lt James F.Sturman POW [8962]

440th BS/319th BG — B-26B 42-95785 *Little Sue* left 1003 to bomb Ostiglia railway bridge, shot down by Flak over target 1143; Capt Thomas L.Burson and three POW, one KiA, one evaded [8941]

37th BS/17th BG — B-26C 42-107535 '28' *Shock Date* shot down by Flak, crashed 15m NW Ancona in Allied lines;1/Lt Jacob Miller and three baled out safe, three b/o WiA

95th BS/17th BG — B-26C 41-34921 '58' *Helen* damaged by Flak, belly-landed at Borgo; 1/Lt R.A.Hildebrandt and five safe

95th BS/17th BG — B-26C 43-34241 '55' damaged by Flak, belly-landed at Borgo; 2/Lt J.C.Limberg and four safe

German Claims

Flak		Marauder	Italian border	
Flak		Thunderbolt	Bologna	1230

Tuesday-Wednesday, 26/27 September 1944

HMS *Ulster Queen* vectored the 46 Squadron Beaufighter VIf of Wt Off Roy Butler onto various radar contacts, of which he shot down three and Wt Off T.K.Phelan claimed another. The report written at the end of the *Ulster Queen*'s operations noted all four aircraft were seen from the ship to fall in flames.

British Claims

46 Sqn	Wt Off R.T.Butler/Wt Off R.F.Graham	Beaufighter VIf ND243 'Q'	Do 24	off W tip of Crete	2250
46 Sqn	Wt Off R.T.Butler/Wt Off R.F.Graham	Beaufighter VIf ND243 'Q'	Ju 52/3m	Crete area	2310
46 Sqn	Wt Off R.T.Butler/Wt Off R.F.Graham	Beaufighter VIf ND243 'Q'	Ju 52/3m floatplane	3m off Trypete	2340
46 Sqn	Wt Off T.K.Phelan/Flt Sgt F.W.K.Baldwin	Beaufighter VIf MM939 'C'	Ju 52/3m floatplane	5m N Maleme	2347

British Casualties

13 Sqn — Baltimore V FW590 'Y' left 1944 on armed recce, seen to explode in the air SE Ferrara; Flt Lt D.A.Smart and three KiA

German Casualties

Seetransportst. 1 — Ju 52/3m See WNr 501197 8A+NJ lost Phaleron to Suda Bay; Obfw Hans Vorberg and three KiA

Seetransportst. 1 — Ju 52/3m See WNr 130716 8A+HJ damaged by night-fighters Phaleron to Suda Bay; Uffz Helmut Reinecke WiA, two safe

Seetransportst. 1 — Ju 52/3m See WNr 641396 8A+BJ missing Phaleron to Suda Bay; Hptm August Meyer and three MiA

unstated unit — Ju 52/3m damaged by strafing at Gadurra

Seenot 70 — Do 24T-1 WNr 3331 1M+RR lost N Crete; Fw Hans Escher, Oblt Hans Glinkermann (St.Kpt) and four MiA

LKS reports three Ju 52/3ms, one Do 24 and one Fi 156 lost

Wednesday, 27 September 1944

After a period of bad weather 249 Squadron's Mustangs were back over Greece again on this day when four of their pilots hit further rail transport before sweeping in on Prokhama airfield as Flg Off Doug McCaig, who hailed from Fiji, recounted many years later:

"Squeezing down the tension, I checked the guns to fire, gunsight on. I saw them in the blink of an eye, a perfect blue silhouette, a Focke-Wulf 190 – I couldn't believe it, PR jobs. The second, just behind showed the tailplane and cockpit canopy. Squeezing the trigger, exploded my .50 in a spray, all four guns roaring. The nearest one was smouldering, the second took my bursts, leaping and jumping all over its engine cowling and cockpit. A whole world of armament was coming up at us, lines of arcing tracer, vicious, bright in the shrouded light."

McCaig was credited with both aircraft probably destroyed, while Flt Sgt Davey destroyed a third. One of the other pair was lost to ground fire, however. In spite of their retreat, the German Flak was as efficient and deadly as ever.

Twelve Venturas of 25 SAAF Squadron mounted a highly effective attack on a German barracks at Koritza, where partisans later reported that at least 200 German troops had been killed and 30 vehicles had been destroyed.

During the day 809 Squadron made further ground attacks on motor transports on Rhodes and conducted a photo-reconnaissance of Syros in the Cyclades Islands, 80 miles south-east of Athens, though low cloud interfered with this mission.

Ten He 111s of 2./KG 4 left Hungary to reinforce the transport aircraft in Greece. Formed as 'Kommando Schumm' in name of Hptm Hans Schumm, commander of 6./KG 4, who assembled his aircraft from various Staffeln. The Kommando's main base was Polykastron, north of Salonika.

British Claims

249 Sqn	Flg Off D.P.F.McCaig	Mustang III KH425	2 FW 190s Probable on ground	Prokhama, Greece
249 Sqn	Flt Sgt C.N.V.Davey	Mustang III HB924 'D'	FW 190 on ground	Prokhama, Greece

British Casualties

2 SAAF Sqn	Spitfire IXc MJ383 hit by Flak, FTR from cloud 5km SW Bologna 0925; Lt S.B.Healey POW
213 Sqn	Mustang III FB651 spun in cloud near Zagreb 1050, FTR; Sgt A.A.Dowling MiA
249 Sqn	Mustang III KH476 left 0545, destroyed 4 locomotives, damaged by Flak, pilot baled out 1m SE Kalivia; Flt Sgt E.Ray KiA
335 Sqn	Spitfire V ER649 left 1505 strafed a train and trucks in the Stofilio-Knin area, hit by Flak, landed at Vis; Wt Off G.Tangalakis WiA
336 Sqn	Spitfire V ER703 left 1400 on sweep of Imotiki-Mostar area, hit by Flak, landed at Vis; Flt Lt J.Kipouros safe
336 Sqn	Spitfire V JK406 left 1400 swung on take-off, tipped onto nose and blew up; Plt Off G.Papaioannou KiA

The Bedford trucks carry the unit code letters 'WU' as 225 Squadron's ground party crosses the River Arno en route to Peretola on 27 September.

German Claims

Flak		Spitfire	S Bologna	1000
Flak		Spitfire	5km S Castel Bolognese	1200

Wednesday-Thursday, 27/28 September 1944

British Claims

46 Sqn	Flg Off G.W.Kirk/Flt Sgt S.Carr	Beaufighter VIf ND243 'Q'	Ju 52/3m see	20m N Candia	2230
46 Sqn	Flt Sgt E.G.Chapman/Flt Sgt W.Briginshaw	Beaufighter VIf MM939 'C'	Ju 52/3m	N Maleme	0015
46 Sqn	Flt Sgt E.G.Chapman/Flt Sgt W.Briginshaw	Beaufighter VIf MM939 'C'	Ju 52/3m Damaged	N Maleme	0025

German Casualties

3./TG 4	Ju 52/3m WNr 3237 G6+KL lost Heraklion-Athens; Uffz Günter Hermann and three MiA, one safe
	LKS reports one Ju 52/3m and one a/c missing

Thursday, 28 September 1944

249 Squadron strafed Sedes airfield; one Ju 52/3m and one Caproni were claimed destroyed, a He 111 and two gliders damaged. A section of 809 Squadron's Seafires attacked a W/T station on Levitha and other aircraft provided bombardment spotting support. One section attacked a twin-engine aircraft but with no results which was fortunate as it was an RAF Beaufighter.

British Claims

249 Sqn	Sqn Ldr J.Te Kloot	Mustang III HB952 'F'	Ju 52/3m on ground	Salonika
249 Sqn	Sqn Ldr J.Te Kloot	Mustang III HB952 'F'	Caproni on ground	Salonika
249 Sqn	Sqn Ldr J.Te Kloot	Mustang III HB952 'F'	He 111 Damaged on ground	Salonika
249 Sqn	Sqn Ldr J.Te Kloot	Mustang III HB952 'F'	Go 242 Damaged on ground	Salonika
249 Sqn	Flt Lt P.F.Noble	Mustang III HB912	3 a/c Damaged on ground	Salonika

British Casualties

25 SAAF Sqn	Ventura I 6001 (AE778) engine failed on take-off from Biferno on a flight to Vis, ditched off shore; Lt Col L.H.G.Shuttle-
	worth and one WiA, Wg Cdr M.A.Johnson DFC and Sqn Ldr the Rev G.A.G.Campbell KiA

Thursday-Friday, 28/29 September 1944

British Claims

46 Sqn	Wt Off D.Griffin/Flt Sgt A.D.Green	Beaufighter VIf ND299 'G'	Ju 52/3m Probable	8m N Trypete	2105
46 Sqn	Wt Off T.K.Phelan/Flt Sgt F.W.K.Baldwin	Beaufighter VIf MM939 'C'	Ju 88	50-60m NE Heraklion	2255
46 Sqn	Wt Off R.T.Butler/Wt Off R.F.Graham	Beaufighter VIf ND243 'Q'	Ju 188	W Melos	0117

US Claims

415th NFS	Capt H.F.Augspurger/2/Lt A.G.Petry	Beaufighter	He 111	Dijon area	0120

German Casualties

2.(F)/123	Ju 88 lost off Cap Sunion; Lt Witt and one MiA, one KiA, one POW
5./KG 27	He 111H-20 WNr 701242 1G+DM shot down 3km N Belgrade, crashed near Semlin 0440; Fw Karl Schott and five KiA, one WiA
2./KG 4	He 111H-20 WNr 701711 shot down by night-fighter off Melos; Uffz Hans-Joachim Schneider and five KiA, one WiA
	LKS reports one He 111 lost in combat, one Ju 52/3m missing and one destroyed on ground plus a Fi 156 lost

Friday, 29 September 1944

The Royal Navy launched Operation Outing II, in the Aegean. HMS *Stalker* had remained on station and a dawn reconnaissance located four Siebel ferries off the west coast of Tenos. A four-aircraft section later dive-bombed them with Sub Lt J.Birtle sinking one, the others later being sunk by the destroyer HMS *Tuscan*.

Later in the day 809 Squadron Seafires spotted for the bombardment of Syros harbour by the cruiser HMS *Black Prince*. The squadron finished the operation with a quartet of Seafires dive-bombing the harbour, hitting ships and a warehouse. The ship then sailed for Alexandria where it arrived the next day.

US Claims

346th FS/350th FG	Maj Andrew R.Schindler	P-47D	FW 190	Pontevillo	1330-1615

During a bombing raid on 29 September Forlì railway station receives a direct hit.

German Casualties

LKS 4	FW 190 on transfer flight after repairs at CANSA at Cameri, shot down nr Fontanella 7km SW Chiari; Obfw Paul Forhne baled out, WiA

Friday-Saturday, 29/30 September 1944

British Claims

46 Sqn	Wt Off D.V.Hammond/Flt Sgt D.A.Harrison	Beaufighter VIf KV920 'L'	Ju 52/3m Damaged	NE Trypete	2135
46 Sqn	Wt Off D.V.Hammond/Flt Sgt D.A.Harrison	Beaufighter VIf KV920 'L'	Ju 52/3m	30m NW Trypete	2145
46 Sqn	Wt Off D.V.Hammond/Flt Sgt D.A.Harrison	Beaufighter VIf KV920 'L'	Ju 52/3m	4m N Maleme	2150
46 Sqn	Flt Sgt H.J.Bays/Flt Sgt C.T.W.Battiste	Beaufighter VIf KW153 'V'	Ju 52/3m Damaged	S coast Melos	0020
108 Sqn	Wt Off J.L.Burleton/Flt Sgt H.W.Graham	Beaufighter VIf MM902 'Y'	Ju 52/3m	N Retimo	0545
108 Sqn	Wt Off J.L.Burleton/Flt Sgt H.W.Graham	Beaufighter VIf MM902 'Y'	Ju 52/3m Damaged	N Retimo	0550

German Casualties

16./TG 1	Ju 52/3m WNr 501138 crash-landed Heraklion-Eleusis; Obfw Siegfried Treichel and four KiA on ground by partisans
15./TG 1	Ju 52/3m WNr 7725 1Z+AW 'P4A' lost Eleusis-Maleme; Uffz Walter Strulick and two MiA, one POW
15./TG 1	Ju 52/3m WNr 640624 lost Eleusis-Maleme; Obfw Erich Sulz and one MiA, one KiA, one WiA
15./TG 1	Ju 52/3m WNr 7785 lost Eleusis-Maleme; Lt Kuno Janssen and three KiA
3./TG 4	Ju 52/3m WNr 640607 missing Heraklion-Eleusis; Uffz Günther Hoffmann and three MiA
16./FlVerb.G 2	Ju 52/3m WNr 130934 shot down by own Flak W Struma, Greece; Fhr Walter Merz and one POW, two KiA

Saturday, 30 September 1944

With the completion of Operation Dragoon, 324 Wing moved into La Jasse just to the north of Marseille in preparation for going back to Italy. Orders were received for a return in the fighter-bomber role in October, the wing's squadrons moving to Peretola near Florence, over the next few days. The last to leave La Jasse was 111 Squadron led by Sqn Ldr P.H.Humphreys who took his unit direct to Peretola, the others staging via Calvi in Corsica.

The night-fighter Mosquitos of 256 Squadron moved from Alghero, Sardinia to Foggia on the Italian east coast from where it began operations over the Balkans on day and night 'Rangers'.

260 Sqn	Mustang III FB284 left 1515 on armed recce Treviso-Vicenza-Mestre area, shot down by Flak; pilot baled out; Sgt G.Chees-brough evaded	
260 Sqn	Mustang III HB910 left 1515 on armed recce Treviso-Vicenza-Mestre area, hit by Flak, crash-landed; Flg Off E.V.Hollins-head POW evaded	

US Casualties

526th FS/86th FG	P-47D 42-26992 '44' *Anastasia II* shot down by Flak 5m S Verona 1635; 2/Lt Lawrence L.Johnston POW [8966]
66th FS/57th FG	P-47D 42-27113 hit by Flak, belly-landed at Florence 1250; 2/Lt David T.Hutton safe

Saturday-Sunday, 30 September/1 October 1944

At 1915 241 Squadron at Rimini airfield was attacked by a reported lone Ju 87 which dropped between 50-60 anti-personnel bombs on the airmen living on site. Unfortunately, there was a queue outside the NAAFI at the time and this was hit, a total of ten men being killed and 15 others wounded. Six of the bombs did not explode and the squadron reported they were of a type they had not seen before.

British Claims

108 Sqn	Flt Sgt J.P.Underwood/Flt Sgt J.I.Hall	Beaufighter VIf MM902 'Y'	Ju 88	NE Dia	2100
46 Sqn	Flt Lt A.J.Bradley/Flt Sgt J.Forrester	Beaufighter VIf ND166 'Z'	Do 24		0310

British Casualties

108 Sqn	Beaufighter VIf V8865 'C' last heard in contact with bogey S Milos 0618, FTR; Wt Off R.T.Knight/Flt Sgt L.H.Harwood MiA
17 SAAF Sqn	Ventura V JT874 'J' port engine failed after taking off, ditched 2m off the coast near Tarquinia; Lt D.I.Clur and four rescued

German Casualties

Seenot 70	Do 24T WNr 3331 1M+RR shot down by night-fighter N Crete; Fw Hans Escher, Oblt Hans Glinkermann (St.Kpt) and four MiA
3./NSGr 9	Ju 87D-3 E8+EL shot down near Riccione; Lt Peter Stollwerk and one safe

Sunday, 1 October 1944

Wg Cdr Hugh 'Chubby' Eliot, DSO DFC, assumed command of 256 Squadron.

British Casualties

92 Sqn	Spitfire VIII JF470 left 1025 to bomb bridge over Savio river, hit twice by Flak, crashed on landing; Maj P.W.Venter WiA

US Casualties

346th FS/350th FG	P-47D 42-28332 *Millie* shot down by Flak nr Castell'Arquato 1110; 2/Lt Shuford M.Alexander Jr POW [9036]
487th BS/340th BG	B-25J left 1510 to bomb Magenta railway bridge, damaged by Flak, returned over lines at low level, further damaged by ground fire, force-landed in Allied lines; 2/Lt Charles F.Donovan WiA, five safe

Sunday-Monday, 1/2 October 1944

Over the Aegean, 46 Squadron's campaign against the German transports with HMS *Ulster Queen* continued with another successful night's operations. Fw Alfred Jobst of 7./KG 27 had departed Athens Kalamaki at 1925 for Heraklion and at about 2040 German time 35km N Heraklion he was attacked by a Beaufighter, both wings set on fire following which he ditched, before he managed with his crew to reach Dia Island.

British Claims

46 Sqn	Wt Off R.T.Butler/Wt Off R.F.Graham	Beaufighter VIf KW160 'A'	He 111	10m W Milos	2225
46 Sqn	Wt Off D.V.Hammond/Flt Sgt D.A.Harrison	Beaufighter VIf KV920 'L'	Ju 88	Antikythera Straits	0445
46 Sqn	Flt Sgt H.J.Bays/Flt Sgt C.T.W.Battiste	Beaufighter VIf MM910 'E'	Ju 52/3m see	10-20m SW Milos	0555
46 Sqn	Flt Sgt H.J.Bays/Flt Sgt C.T.W.Battiste	Beaufighter VIf MM910 'E'	Do 24	sea near Anafi	0615

British Casualties

55 Sqn	Baltimore V FW351 'P' left 2100 on armed recce of upper Savio-Ravenna-Ostiglia-Modena-Bologna; crashed NW Ferrara 2315; 2/Lt R.Nesterovic and three POW
18 Sqn	Boston IV BZ500 'F' left 2210, bombed Faenza marshalling yards 2305, hit by Flak, crash-landed at base; Plt Off E.G.Cooper and three safe
114 Sqn	Boston IV BZ559 left 2202 to recce bombing along Savio river, believed seen in flames 0020; Sgt D.A.Hinchcliffe and three KiA

Above: Many of the successful Aegean night-interception patrols flown by 46 Squadron were controlled by the radar piquet HMS *Ulster Queen*. Below: Seen at Edku with aircrew of 46 Squadron, Beaufighter VIf ND242 'Q' was named *Kampala Queen* and was flown by Wt Offs Butler and Graham when claiming their first four victories.

German Casualties

4./KG 27	He 111H-20 WNr 701243 1G+EM attacked by British night-fighters, ditched 20km N Heraklion; one crew KiA
7./KG 27	He 111H-20 1G+MR shot down by Beaufighter, ditched 35km off Heraklion; Fw Alfred Jobst and two rescued
7./KG 27	He 111H-20 WNr 701674 1G+HR missing over the Aegean, shot down off Crete; Ofw Hans Ospel and four MiA
13./TG 1	Ju 52/3m WNr 501437 shot down by night-fighters; pilot and one crew safe; Obfw Wilhelm Schneck and crew MiA
	LKS records two He 111s missing and one Ju 52/3m lost in combat

Monday, 2 October 1944

324 Wing returned from southern France to Italy but suffered a disaster. According to 208 Squadron's ORB "apparently the Wing was under the impression it was last light here at 1900 when it was 1815". 111 Squadron had landed at Peretola near Florence at 1530, but 43 Squadron arrived over the aerodrome after dark, and Peretola had no night-landing facilities at all. All squadrons on the airfield were instructed to line up their trucks and jeeps on either side of the runway and use their headlights to provide lighting. Disaster struck when after several aircraft had landed safely a 43 Squadron aircraft left the runway and struck 208 Squadron's water bowser, killing the pilot Lt Duchen and fatally injuring the truck driver. Two more Spitfires landed safely then Flt Lt Lowther's Spitfire crashed into the wreckage of the upturned Spitfire and water bowser killing Flg Off Ainslie of 111 Squadron who was aiding the injured driver, and severely injuring Lowther. The duty pilot had attempted to fire red flares to warn of the dangers, but no less than five flares failed to go off. A third Spitfire flown by Lt Dalton avoided the wreckage but went off the runway and struck a 111 Squadron truck, injuring the pilot and severely injuring the driver. The last five Spitfires of 43 Squadron were saved when an American aerodrome at Pisa put its lights on, although two of the five ran out of petrol after landing.

Wt Offs R.T.Butler and R.F.Graham of 46 Squadron achieved a rich run of success against German transport flights to the Aegean islands.

British Casualties

111 Sqn	On duty on Peretola a/f when struck by a landing aircraft; Flg Off H G.Ainslie KiA
208 Sqn	On duty on Peretola a/f when struck by a landing aircraft; LAC H.Griffiths KiA
43 Sqn	Spitfire VIII MT786 'P' crashed on landing at new base at Peretola 1825; Lt M.Duchen KiA
43 Sqn	Spitfire VIII JF887 'U' crashed on landing at new base at Peretola 1825; Flt Lt J.L.Lowther WiA
43 Sqn	Spitfire VIII MT670(?) crashed on landing at new base at Peretola 1825; Lt L.N.Y.Dalton WiA

Monday-Tuesday, 2/3 October 1944

British Claims

46 Sqn	Flt Sgt E.G.Chapman/Flt Sgt W.Briginshaw	Beaufighter VIf KV920 'L'	Do 24 Damaged	Fleves Island	2112
108 Sqn	Wg Cdr J.R.C.Young/Flg Off W.J.Hyatt	Beaufighter VIf MM929 'H'	He 111	W Parapola Isl.	0015

British Casualties

108 Sqn	Beaufighter VIf MM929 'H' damaged in tail by return fire from He 111; Wg Cdr J.R.C.Young/Flg Off W.J.Hyatt safe

German Casualties

7./KG 27	He 111H-20 WNr 701691 1G+CR shot down by night-fighter off Crete; Oblt Claus-Wilhelm Henkel and four MiA
Seenot 70	Do 24T-3 WNr 2112 J9+CA crashed S Milos; Obfw Wilhelm Lange, five crew and 21 troops KiA
	LKS records one He 111 and one Ju 52/3m missing

Tuesday, 3 October 1944

Ten Beaufighters of 603 Squadron, led by Wing Commander Foxley-Norris, took off at midday, accompanied by two of 252 Squadron, to hunt for the German minelayer *Zeus* of 2,423 tons, off the east coast of the mainland of Greece. This vessel, the former Italian merchant ship *Francesco Morosini*, was considered a prime target, for she was playing an important part in the evacuation of the Greek islands. One Beaufighter turned back with engine trouble. The others didn't find *Zeus* but came across a convoy of five small vessels to the east of Athens and attacked. Rockets and cannon fire damaged three of the vessels, but return fire was intense and two Beaufighters were shot down. The pilot of the first, Sgt Desmond Harrison, was killed, but his navigator, Sgt Derek V.Bannister, was later reported to be "safe in friendly hands". The other crew was Flg Off Casimir Marmaduke De Bounevialle and Plt Off A.E.'Gillie' Potter. De Bounevialle ditched with his starboard engine on fire, not far from the position where he had gone down six weeks earlier. The two men were not injured but were picked up by an UJ-boat and taken to Piraeus, ending in a POW camp in Germany.

Capt Oldham of the 86th Fighter Group led a strafe by eight P-47s of Villafranca airfield at 0705, during which four aircraft were claimed destroyed; Oldham's Thunderbolt was hit by Flak, forcing the pilot to crash land on fire and being killed, after some 90 sorties.

British Casualties	
145 Sqn	Spitfire VIII LV731 left 0850, hit by Flak, crash-landed at Rimini a/f 0930; Flt Lt H.Brown-Gaylord safe
145 Sqn	Spitfire VIII JG274 left 0850, hit by Flak, landed at base 0930, Cat II damaged; Sgt A.Garth safe
145 Sqn	Spitfire VIII JF566 left 0905, hit by Flak, baled out off Cervia and rescued by Walrus; Sgt S.L.Piercey safe
4 SAAF Sqn	Spitfire IX MJ788 'V' hit by Flak NE Casola Valsenio 1615, pilot baled out; Capt I.G.Will returned next day
603 Sqn	Beaufighter TFX NT893 left 1200 attacked shipping E Athens, shot down by Flak; Sgt D.Harrison KiA/Sgt D.V.Bannister evaded
603 Sqn	Beaufighter TFX NV205 left 1200 attacked shipping E Athens, shot down by Flak, ditched off west coast Kea Island; Flg Off C.M.De Bounevialle/Plt Off A.E.Potter POW
800 Sqn	Hellcat I JV263 'EC' shot down bombing shipping at Leros; Sub Lt Keith F.Wilson KiA
US Casualties	
525th FS/86th FG	P-47D 42-28604 *Dora Pat III* hit by Flak from Villafranca a/f, crash-landed at Roverbella 0710; Capt Richard G.Oldham KiA [9039]
527th FS/86th FG	P-47D 42-27943 '75' *M'Luv* shot down by Flak 17m S Bologna 1325; 1/Lt John T.Boone KiA [9073]
445th BS/321st BG	B-25J 43-27553 *Evora* left 1205 to bomb road bridge at Galliate, hit by Flak in left engine, crashed 2.5km NE Trecate 1420; 1/Lt Robert R.Frank and five KiA [9028]
445th BS/321st BG	B-25J 43-27740 left 1205 to bomb road bridge at Galliate, hit by Flak in right engine, crashed nr Voghera 1440; Capt Lawrence L.Russell and five POW, one returned [9037]

Tuesday-Wednesday, 3/4 October 1944

British Claims					
600 Sqn	Wg Cdr L.H.Styles/Flg Off H.J.Wilmer	Beaufighter VIf ND170 'F'	Ju 87	SE Cesena	2020
46 Sqn	Flt Lt J.Irwin/Plt Off G.H.Watson	Beaufighter VIf ND166 'Z'	Ju 52/3m	Antikythera Straits	2136
German Casualties					
8./KG 27	He 111H-20 WNr 791694 1G+LS shot down by night-fighters crashed 30km S Athens; Oblt Günther Lacke and four MiA				
8./KG 27	He 111H-20 1G+AD left Salonika 0012, damaged by two night-fighter attacks, landed at Athens Kalamaki 0121; Oblt Günther Jäschke and crew safe				
16./TG 1	Ju 52/3m shot down Maleme-Eleusis; Obfw Günther Raetz and three KiA				
	LKS reports one He 111, one FW 190 and one Ju 52/3m missing				

Wednesday, 4 October 1944

Two 800 Squadron Hellcats, both flown by Netherland's navy pilots, Sub Lt Herman 'Harm' de Witt (in JV126 'E-R') and Sub Lt Gerardus 'Gerry' H.Grewe claimed to have shot down a Junkers Ju 52/3m as it was approaching Maleme, Crete. De Witt then force-landed in Turkey when the undercarriage of his Hellcat proved inoperable. He returned later to Alexandria on release.

Lt T.J.C.Hopkins of 1 SAAF Squadron was killed on 4 October when Spitfire IX MA425 'Y' was shot down by Flak near Livergnano.

British Claims

800 Sqn	Sub Lt H.de Witt	Hellcat I JV126 E-R	} Ju 52/3m	nr Maleme, Crete	
800 Sqn	Sub Lt G.H.Grewe	Hellcat I			

British Casualties

800 Sqn	Hellcat I JV126 'E-R' force-landed in Turkey due to u/c failure; Sub Lt H.de Witt returned when released
1 SAAF Sqn	Spitfire IX MA425 'Y' left 1450, dive-bombed Livergnano 1525, hit by Flak, burst into flames; Lt T.J.C.Hopkins KiA
73 Sqn	Spitfire IX PT617 left 1130 on offensive sweep of Banja Luka area, damaged by Flak near Kalamaki, crash-landed at base 1440; Lt L.D.Westbrook safe
352 Sqn	Spitfire Vc JL325 left 1300, hit by Flak, crash-landed at Teslic; Flt Lt Ratko Jovanovic KiA
6 Sqn	Hurricane IV KX704 'J' left 1130 on armed recce Gulf of Corinth, attacked F boats near Patras, hit by Flak, pilot baled out; Sgt E.Tomlinson evaded, rescued by Greek fishing boat

US Casualties

347th FS/350th FG	P-47D 44-19612 '7A6' shot down by Flak, crashed S Bologna 1045; 2/Lt Grover Howard POW [9308]
347th FS/350th FG	P-47D 42-28314 '7C1' shot down by Flak, crashed S Bologna 1045; 1/Lt Donald A.Ellis POW [9310]
526th FS/86th FG	P-47D crashed 0810; 2/Lt Harry A.Master KiA

German Claims

Flak		Thunderbolt	S Bologna	1130

Wednesday-Thursday, 4/5 October 1944

On intruder sorties over Greece pilots of the night-fighters of 256 Squadron met with considerable success including the new commanding officer, 'Chubby' Eliot, as he recalled in his combat report:

"We observed a Ju 52 with landing light burning in the circuit making its final approach at approx. 400 feet. I gave two short bursts at 500 yards closing to 150 yards with deflection on a beam attack. The e/a burst into flames, crashing just off the end of the runway. Resumed patrol but e/a was still burning vigorously when we came off patrol at 2225."

British Claims

256 Sqn	Wg Cdr H.W.Eliot/Flt Lt D.Ibbotson	Mosquito XIII HK507	Ju 52/3m	Salonika/Sedes a/f	2015-0030
256 Sqn	Sqn Ldr J.M.McEwan/Flt Sgt S.Cole	Mosquito XIII MM527	He 111	Epanom	2110-0115
256 Sqn	Sqn Ldr R.M.Mumford/Flg Off R.B.Joyson	Mosquito XIII HK437	Ju 88	Salonika area	2350

German Claims

Flak	M Abt 720		Liberator	S basin of Khalkis Straits	2310

German Casualties

2./KG 4	He 111H-20 WNr 701676 5J+FK lost nr Athens; Obfw Günther Döring and four MiA
6./KG 27	He 111H-20 WNr 701256 1G+BN crashed after take-off nr Salonika; Uffz Eugen Ott, four crew and 14 passengers KiA
13./TG 1	Ju 52/3m WNr 501124 lost Salonika-Eleusis; Obfw Günther Dörrfeld and three MiA
	LKS records two He 111s lost and one Ju 52/3m missing

Thursday, 5 October 1944

A solo Ju 88 flew over 32 Squadron's airfield at Araxos, and two Spitfires managed to get off from the soggy ground, chased it over the mountains, in and out of cloud, but only managed to claim damage to it. A little after 1700 Flg Off A.H.Davis (in MD349) and Flt Sgt J.F.Vintner (in MT764) flew 451 Squadron's final operations in the Mediterranean. 5 SAAF Squadron, meanwhile, began operations with Mustangs.

British Claims

32 Sqn	Wt Off A.Oates	Spitfire Vc MA751 ⎫	Ju 88 Damaged N Araxos	1250-1410
32 Sqn	Sgt J.T.O'Reilly	Spitfire Vc EF558 ⎭		

British Casualties

73 Sqn   Spitfire IX MK406 left 0645 to patrol Zagreb-Novista area, on return hit by Flak near Sibenik, pilot baled out just E of Zirje into the sea, in dinghy off the coast; Sgt J.M.Shearer rescued

Bulgarian Casualties

2/6 Orlyak   Bf 109G-6 shot down by ground fire Rankovtsi, W Kriva Palanka 1515; Por N.D.Bonchev POW, KiA

3/6 Orlyak   Bf 109G-6 shot down by ground fire Kriva Palanka-Kumanovo 1600; Pod P.A.Bochev believed POW

Friday, 6 October 1944

Having trained in the US, the Brazilian 1° Grupo de Aviação de Caça (1st Fighter Group) arrived at Leghorn. Pilots and ground crewmen then moved by train to Tarquinia, north-west of Rome, to join the 350th Fighter Group; there they took delivery of 31 P-47Ds painted in Brazilian markings modified from the US 'star and bar'. The fighter unit was led by Ten Cor (Lieutenant Colonel) Nero Moura who had 48 pilots among his 350 men, formed into four flights: *Azul* (Blue – A), *Verde* (Green – B), *Vermelha* (Red – C), and *Amarela* (Yellow – D). The Força Expedicionária Brasileira, FEB (Brazilian Expeditionary Force) also included 1ª Equadrilha de Ligação e Observação (ELO – 1st Observation and Liaison Squadron) flying the Piper Super Cub.

The Brazilian 1° Grupo de Aviação de Caça (1st Fighter Group) arrived in Italy and joined the US 350th Fighter Group. P-47D Thunderbolt 42-26756 'A4' flown by 2° Ten.Av Alberto M.Torres is seen during an early sortie over northern Italy.

British Casualties

253 Sqn   Spitfire Vc left 1415 to sweep Korce Albania, strafed motor transports N Mifol, hit by Flak, force-landed; Sgt J.E.H.Lander KiA

Italian Co-Belligerent Casualties

260ª Sq, 28° Gr   Baltimore IV FA581 crashed nr Marigliano; Serg Magg Nicola Nocera and three KiA

German Casualties

14./TG 4   2 Piaggio 108s (GS+FY and G6+AY) destroyed on the ground at Salonika-Sedes

             LKS reports two Piaggio 108s destroyed on ground

The Força Expedicionária Brasileira included 1ª Equadrilha de Ligação e Observação flying the Piper L-4H Grasshopper.

Friday-Saturday, 6/7 October 1944

The KTB of the Heeresgruppe E recorded that a Do 24 crashed at Phaleron with five crew killed. This may well have been the aircraft claimed by Wg Cdr Eliot during the night, his ninth and final victory, as he described:

Flying a Mosquito XIII of 256 Squadron on the night of 6/7 October, Wg Cdr H.W.'Chubby' Eliot shot down a Do 24 south-west of Athens killing all five crew.

> "We sighted an aircraft with nav lights on at 500 feet and closed in from 500 yards and gave a full deflection short burst without seeing any result. The aircraft was observed to be a large three-engined flying boat. We orbited to deliver a second attack with the e/a now on an easterly course at 500 feet without nav lights (!) but very bright exhausts were seen so enabling our Mosquito to intercept and deliver a second attack at 500 yards but with no visible results. We then made further attacks, following the e/a on a southeast course approximately one mile inside the coastline and identified the aircraft as a Do 24. We delivered a long burst from dead astern on the rapidly closing range. Many strikes were observed on and around the port engine. The e/a burst into flames so we banked away and orbited. The e/a attempted to ditch but crashed onto the water's edge and exploded."

British Claims

256 Sqn	Wg Cdr H.W.Eliot/Flt Lt D.Ibbotson	Mosquito XIII HK435	Do 24	Athens area	2135-0200

German Casualties

70.Seenotst.	Do 24T-3 IM+RK shot down by fighters S Kalamaki; Obfw Karl Büge and five KiA

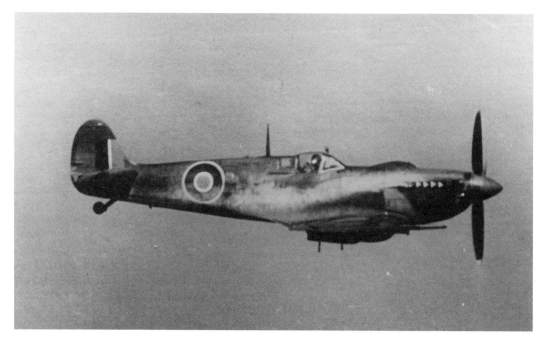

During anti-shipping operations over the Aegean between 6 and 8 October, Seafire LF IIc MB115 'HR' was flown by Lt Cdr L.G.C.Reece, the commanding officer of 807 Squadron.

Saturday, 7 October 1944

32 Squadron strafed Kalamaki where Sqn Ldr G.F.Silvester and his wingman Sgt A.R.Tooze claimed a Ju 52/3m damaged on the ground.

On Royal Navy Operation Picnic 809 Squadron's Seafire of Lt Cdr H.D.B.Eadon reported obtaining a direct bomb hit on a large ship south-west of Lemnos that sank in 20 seconds, but two Seafires were lost to Flak. (On this date the ship *Olympus* of 852 tons was sunk near Stampalia, reportedly by the submarine HMS *Unruly*.)

British Claims

32 Sqn	Sqn Ldr G.F.Silvester	Spitfire Vc ⎫	
32 Sqn	Sgt A.R.Tooze	Spitfire Vc ⎬	Ju 52/3m Damaged (on ground) Kalamaki

British Casualties

16 SAAF Sqn	Beaufighter X NE537 'Y' left 0555 on shipping sweep, formation turned back due to bad weather, port engine caught fire, crash-landed, burnt out 3m N Atri 0756; Lt A.T.Wellington/Lt B.G.MacKenzie KiA
601 Sqn	Spitfire IX PL345 left 0850 to attack strongpoint 8km S Cesena, presumed hit by Flak 0915; Capt R.R.Hart KiA
145 Sqn	Spitfire VIII MT975 left 0945 to attack gun positions near Ravenna, last seen in bomb dive in intense Flak; Sgt J.Lambert KiA
809 Sqn	Seafire LIII NF638 HMS *Stalker*, on armed recce, hit church spire strafing lorries, crashed near Zinopoten, Kos; Sub Lt A.D.Perry DoW
807 Sqn	Seafire LIII NF439 HMS *Hunter*, hit by Flak during ship attack in Petai Channel; Sub Lt Donald Stewart KiA

US Casualties

86th FS/79th FG	P-47D 42-27694 shot down by Flak, crashed nr Cesena 0935; 2/Lt Calvin J.Arnold POW [9071]
319th BG	B-26 xx-7968 lost during transfer flight; Lt Col Charles G.Robinson and two K
86th BS/47th BG	A-20 lost over Italy; crew safe but gunner KiA

German Casualties

	LKS reports three Ju 52/3ms destroyed on ground and one Ju 52/3m missing

Sunday, 8 October 1944

At 1715 three Spitfires from 335 (Hellenic) Squadron landed at Araxos. These were flown by Flt Lt Volonakis (in JG956), Flg Off Mitrakis (in JL159) and Flg Off Margaritis (in JG946) and they became the first Greek airmen to land on Greek soil since 1941.

The escort carriers were maintaining operations. Sub Lt A.C.S.Morrison of HMS *Stalker*'s 809 Squadron scored a direct hit with a 500lb bomb on large MV that sank south-west of Lemnos, while Sub Lt G.H.Brittain (shared with Sub Lt A.R.Rawbone in MB150) sank a small schooner. Rawbone had also attacked railway engines and set wagons on fire, damaging a signal box between Larissa and Salonika. Three German ships were actually lost in this area on this day: *Achilles* (1,150 tons), *Horst* (212 tons) and *Paul* (200 tons). Sub Lt G.S.Macartney's aircraft was hit by Flak; he baled out 10 miles off Cape Drepanon and was picked up an hour later by HMS *Tuscan*.

British Casualties	
249 Sqn	Mustang III HB933 'X' left 1345 to strafe railway targets in Greece, hit by Flak near Polykastron, pilot baled out landing 1m S of Megala Livadia; Flg Off D.P.F.McCaig, evaded, flown out in a DC 3 late in October
809 Sqn	Seafire LIII hit by Flak in attack on Koifus harbour, pilot baled out 10 miles off Cape Drepanon, picked up by HMS *Tuscan*; Sub Lt G.S.Macartney safe
809 Sqn	Seafire LIII caught wire, stalled into deck of HMS *Stalker*; Sub Lt D.D.James safe

Monday, 9 October 1944

British Casualties	
6 Sqn	Hurricane IV hit by Flak at Sarande, pilot reached 2m off Brindisi before baling out; Flt Lt J.W.Grundy safe
19 SAAF Sqn	Beaufighter 'E' left 0845, swung on take-off, got airborne, ditched just offshore; Maj D.P.Tilley/Wt Off A.Powell safe
19 SAAF Sqn	Beaufighter 'R' left 1105, swung on take-off and crashed; Lt R.F.Dickson/Flg Off F.G.Brace safe
809 Sqn	Seafire L.III NF629 engine hit during attack on a railway, landed on HMS *Stalker* with no oil pressure, subsequently pushed overboard; Sub Lt D.Lee-Jones safe
807 Sqn	Seafire L.III NF427 on landing on HMS *Hunter* floated into the barrier and damaged; Sub Lt J.H.Brewer safe
807 Sqn	Seafire L.III NN389 on landing on HMS *Hunter* floated over wires and into barrier; Sub Lt A.C.B.Ford safe
US Casualties	
86th FS/79th FG	P-47D 42-25279 shot down by Flak, pilot baled out off coast nr Cesena 1300; 2/Lt James E.Menifee KiA [9072]
86th FS/79th FG	P-47D 42-75763 shot down by Flak, pilot seen in water off coast nr Cesena 1630; 2/Lt Robert S.Stahl Jr KiA [9070]
86th FS/79th FG	P-47D 42-76611 shot down 1635; pilot MiA
525th FS/86th FG	P-47D 42-xx937 hit by Flak, crashed at Pisa 1535; 2/Lt Aloysius J.Lochowitz DoW on 11 October
German Casualties	
	LKS reports four Ju 52/3ms destroyed on ground

Tuesday, 10 October 1944

213 Squadron's pilots watched Beaufighters of 39 Squadron shooting at a bomber identified as a Do 217 at 0920 – which they missed. Sgt Bell from 213 then hit it and it was finished off by Plt Off Wallace of 39, who claimed it shot down and crash-landed in the Zagreb area; it was also strafed until it burst into flames. It was in fact a Do 17Z from the NASt Kroatian which had been bombing partisans.

A Fi 167 flown by Narednik (Nar: Sgt) Božidar Bartulović (who had claimed eight victories over the Eastern front when attached to the Luftwaffe) was intercepted by RAF Mustangs of 213 Squadron near Sisak. Bartulović reported that five fighters had made attacks on him, setting the aircraft alight and wounding him in the head. His gunner, Satnik (Sat: Flt Lt) Mate Jurković, claimed one of the attackers before both men had to bale out. During the same period, another 'unidentified single-engined biplane' was claimed near Glina by Vos and two other pilots. This was actually a Bü 131 Jungmeister on its way from Zagreb to Bihac that force-landed near the village of Markičevići near Glina; pilot Nar Lojen and passenger Ernest Ceisberger were wounded and captured by the partisans.

British Claims					
39 Sqn	Plt Off I.D.Wallace/Flg Off D.A.Andrews	Beaufighter X NT889 'F'	Do 217	Novo Setke	0925
213 Sqn	Sgt D.H.Bell	Mustang III			
213 Sqn	Sqn Ldr C.S.Vos	Mustang III HB902			
213 Sqn	Sgt D.E.Firman	Mustang III FB337 'A'	Fi 167A	Martinska Ves	1636
213 Sqn	Sgt D.E.Firman	Mustang III FB337 'A'			
213 Sqn	Sqn Ldr C.S.Vos	Mustang III HB902	Bü 131	5m N Glina	1648
213 Sqn	Sgt W.H.Butterworth	Mustang III HB854			

British Casualties

5 SAAF Sqn	Mustang III KH486 left 1430 on strafing sortie, last seen diving to strafe motor transports E Imola 1625, FTR; Capt J.M.Pienaar POW. First SAAF Mustang loss
213 Sqn	Mustang III KH554 left 1430, shot down by return fire from Fi 167A, crash-landed 3m NE Martinska Ves 1637; Sgt W.E.Mould evaded, back on 21 October
19 SAAF Sqn	Beaufighter X NT997 'A' left 1320 to attack shipping, target found in Senj harbour, fired rockets then shot down by Flak; Flt Lt A.R.Vance/Lt A.M.Medalie MiA
19 SAAF Sqn	Beaufighter 'C' attacking shipping in Senj harbour, hit by Flak, returned to base; Lt C.J.Franken safe/Sgt Quick severely WiA

German Claims

Flak		Mustang	near Bologna	1530

German Casualties

NASt. Kroatien	Do 17Z WNr 3240 9H+EL shot down 5km ENE Griz, 55km E Agram; Hptm Georg Stark and one WiA, one KiA, passenger Maj Paul Lube Ia Fl.Führ North Balkans WiA
2./NSGr 7	CR.42 WNr 9199 Black 9 shot down by ground fire 20km S Lapovo; Obfw Walter Bormann KiA
2./NSGr 7	CR.42 WNr 9221 Black 20 shot down by ground fire and Flak near Kalinovac; Obfw Hellmuth Rauer DoW on 15 October
	LKS reports one Do 17 destroyed in combat and three a/c lost to enemy action

Croatian Claims

2.LJ	Nar Božidar Bartulović/Sat Mate Jurković	Fi 167	Mustang III	NE Martinska Ves	1636

Croatian Casualties

2.LJ	Fi 167 WNr 4808 shot down by Mustang NE Martinska Ves 1636; Nar Božidar Bartulović WiA/Sat Mate Jurković baled out
Croat Air Force	Bü 131 force-landed near Markičevići near Glina 1648; pilot Nar Lojen and passenger Ernest Ceisberger WiA, captured by partisans

Tuesday-Wednesday, 10/11 October 1944

108 Squadron was continuing to intrude north of Crete, now controlled by HMS *Colombo*, which had replaced the *Ulster Queen* on the 9th after that ship had to return to port on the 4th with technical problems. On this night Plt Off Baldry was vectored onto a low-level contact and was pursuing it with wheels and flaps down when his wingtip hit the sea and he crashed. HMS *Colombo* rescued him, but his observer was not found.

British Casualties

108 Sqn	Beaufighter VIf ND159 intruding N Candia, last heard 2015 being vectored onto bogey, crashed, pilot rescued by warship; Plt Off C.E.Baldry safe/Flg Off J.Watson MiA

Wednesday, 11 October 1944

HMS *Emperor*'s 800 Squadron attacked shipping off Salonika prior to the Allied re-occupation of Greece. Sub Lt Charles D.Spencer was shot down in flames by Flak.

Wg Cdr Richard Mitchell/Flt Lt S.H.Hatsell, Sqn Ldr Ian McCall/Flt Sgt T.Caulfield and Flt Lt John Pengelly/Flt Sgt C.R.Couchman of 605 Squadron from Fighter Command based at Manston in England, had flown down to Jesi airfield on the 10th. They left Jesi at 0920, from where they set out on a day Ranger mission to the Zagreb area. They attacked two airfields and claimed a Me 110 which caught fire and exploded and what was believed to be a B.71, actually a Do17 and a Ca.311 of the Croatian air force, that caught fire at Zagreb at 1030. Then at Pleso to the north of the city they claimed two Ju 87s, a Bf 109 and a Ju 52/3m at 1035. All three Mosquitos were slightly damaged by return fire.

Lt Cdr M.F.Fell assumed command of the Hellcat-equipped 800 Squadron aboard HMS *Emperor* when it was engaged in operations over the Aegean.

British Claims

605 Sqn	Wg Cdr R.A.Mitchell/Flt Lt S.H.Hatsell	Mosquito VI	Me 110 (on ground)	Zagreb	1030
605 Sqn	Sqn Ldr I.F.McCall/Flt Sgt T.Caulfield	Mosquito VI	B.71 (on ground)	Zagreb	1030
605 Sqn	Flt Lt J.I.Pengelly/Flt Sgt C.R.Couchman	Mosquito VI			
605 Sqn	Wg Cdr R.A.Mitchell/Flt Lt S.H.Hatsell	Mosquito VI	2 Ju 87s (on ground)	Pleso	1035
605 Sqn	Sqn Ldr I.F.McCall/Flt Sgt T.Caulfield	Mosquito VI	Ju 52/3m (on ground)	Pleso	1035
605 Sqn	Flt Lt J.I.Pengelly/Flt Sgt C.R.Couchman	Mosquito VI	Bf 109 (on ground)	Pleso	1035

British Casualties

39 Sqn	Beaufighter X NT889 'F' left 0950 to strafe shipping W Levrera Island, damaged by Flak, lost an engine, crash-landed at Ancona; Plt Off I.D.Wallace/Flg Off D.A.Andrews safe
800 Sqn	Hellcat I JV149 EG shot down in flames attacking enemy shipping in Euripus Channel near Khalkis, Greece; Sub Lt Charles D.Spencer KiA

US Casualties

87th FS/79th FG	P-47D 42-28050 propeller failure, pilot baled out NE Imola 0945; 1/Lt Victor L.Phelps POW [9069]
65th FS/57th FG	P-47D 42-75762 hit by Flak 1445, damaged Cat 2; pilot safe
446th BS/321st BG	B-25J 43-4052 *Lil Butch*, left 1225 to bomb bridge over River Po at Torre Beretti, damaged by Flak target 1400, gunner Sgt D.H.Brown baled out, POW, a/c ditched 10m off Cape Corse; 1/Lt Frederick I.Peterson and four picked up by ASR Service

Some of the pilots of 800 Squadron aboard HMS *Emperor*, left to right: Sub Lt I.D.Scanes, Lt D.C.Hill, Lt T.H.Hoare, Sub Lts C.D.Spencer, J.H.Jellie, R.Hooker and G.Y.Cooper. Behind them is Hellcat I JV149 'E-G' in which Sub Lt Spencer was killed when attacking shipping on 11 October.

| 3/6 Orlyak | Bf 109G-6 damaged by Flak and force-landed; Por B.V.Damev safe | | | |

German Claims

| Flak | | | Thunderbolt | Castel Bolognese | 0945 |
| Flak | 6./720 | | Martlet | off Euboa Island | 1434 |

German Casualties

| 6./KG 27 | He 111H-20 WNr 700894 1G+AP lost on flight from Salonika Sedes to Semlin; Uffz Günther Köhler, four crew and 14 passengers MiA |
| | LKS reports one He 111 missing and five a/c destroyed on ground |

Flt Lt Epaminondas Kotas of 335 Squadron was killed on a sweep over Bugojno-Mostar when JG946 was shot down.

Thursday, 12 October 1944

The wooden-hulled RN minesweeper HMS *MMS-170* under Lt R.H.F.Savage was engaged on sweeping near Gorgona Island off the north-west coast of Italy when it struck a mine killing seven of the crew including the captain, but leaving 12 survivors in the mine-infested water. Walrus W2719 of 293 Squadron flown by Plt Off A.F.G.Stevens with Flt Sgt R.Barnes was scrambled and despite adverse weather and the severe danger from other mines, they alighted and managed to rescue one of the survivors. An ASR launch also entered the minefield and picked up the other three. In the prevailing rough sea the overloaded Walrus was unable to take off so was safely towed back to Leghorn by the ASR launch. Stevens received the DFC for his gallant efforts.

418 Squadron followed the example of 605 by sending Sqn Ldr Gray and Flg Off Thomas to Jesi, on the 11th and from there they intruded over the Ceske, Budojovice and Nemecky Brod area. They claimed eight aircraft destroyed on the ground, another probably destroyed and another nine damaged before returning to Jesi at 0935. After refuelling and a fine lunch, both crews departed Jesi, one aircraft carrying Flt Sgt Caulfield from 605 Squadron, at 1500 and landed at Hunsdon in England at 1925.

British Claims

418 Sqn	Sqn Ldr R.G.Gray/Flt Lt N.J.Gibbons	Mosquito VI	2 Ju W34s (on ground)	Budojovice	0640
418 Sqn	Sqn Ldr R.G.Gray/Flt Lt N.J.Gibbons	Mosquito VI	Ju W34 Dmgd (on ground)	Budojovice	0640
418 Sqn	Flg Off R.D.Thomas/Flt Lt R.W.MacDonald	Mosquito VI	Ju W34 (on ground)	Budojovice	0640
418 Sqn	Sqn Ldr R.G.Gray/Flt Lt N.J.Gibbons	Mosquito VI	4 Ju 87s (on ground)	Nemecky Brod	0715
418 Sqn	Sqn Ldr R.G.Gray/Flt Lt N.J.Gibbons	Mosquito VI	5 Ju 87s Dmgd (on ground)	Nemecky Brod	0715

Spitfire Vc JG946 'L' of 335 Squadron was one of the first three Greek aircraft to return to Greece, but on 12 October it was shot down by Flak.

418 Sqn	Flg Off R.D.Thomas/Flt Lt R.W.MacDonald	Mosquito VI	2 Ju 87s (on ground)	Nemecky Brod	0715
418 Sqn	Flg Off R.D.Thomas/Flt Lt R.W.MacDonald	Mosquito VI	3 Ju 87s Dmgd (on ground)	Nemecky Brod	0715

British Casualties

16 SAAF Sqn	Beaufighter X NT906 'F' left 1155 as one of four on anti-shipping sweep from Khalkis to Volos, attacked small boats in the Oreos Channel 1415, shot down by Flak, turned on its back and dived into the sea; Lt H.L.Harrison MiA/Lt A.R.Henry KiA
112 Sqn	Mustang III FB263 'M' left 0830 to bomb bridge near San Felice, shot down by Flak 0920, pilot baled out; Lt C.J.Liebenberg POW
19 SAAF Sqn	Beaufighter X NV125 'X' left 0915, starboard engine cut en route to target, crash-landed near Ostuni, NW Brindisi 1004, struck an embankment; Lt O.Lloyd KiA/Flg Off A.E.Easterbee WiA
335 Sqn	Spitfire Vc JG946 left 1205, strafed the Mostar-Jablanica road, shot down by Flak; Flt Lt E.Kotas KiA

US Casualties

64th FS/57th FG	P-47D 42-75722 shot down by Flak, west end of Orio a/f 1635; 2/Lt Billy E.Adams KiA [9328]
64th FS/57th FG	P-47D 42-26368 hit by Flak, SE dispersal Orio a/f 1635; 2/Lt George J.Dorval POW [9329]
64th FS/57th FG	P-47D 42-28582 hit by Flak 1340, damaged Cat 3; pilot safe
37th BS/17th BG	B-26G 43-34393 '39' lost u/k cause SE Massa Marittima 1540; 2/Lt Thomas E.Hughes and five KiA [9061]
414th NFS	Beaufighter KW195 *Daisy Mae the Hangar Queen III* on night-intruder mission to western Po Valley, FTR; 1/Lt John A.Prescott/Flt Off Samuel G.Danforth Jr KiA

German Casualties

4./KG 27	He 111H-20 WNr 701232 1G+BM left Sedes for Semlin, presumed flown into a mountain; Obfw Josef Walcher, two crew and seven passengers KiA
	LKS reports two He 111s and one Ju 52/3m missing, plus two a/c destroyed on ground
	Note: no fewer than four He 111s of KG 27 were shot down over Hungary by 15th Air Force fighters on this date

Thursday-Friday, 12/13 October 1944

British Casualties

256 Sqn	Mosquito XIII HK509 left on night intruder Padua area, FTR; Flt Sgt J.McEwan DFM/Flt Sgt S.Cole KiA

Friday, 13 October 1944

Nine Venturas of 25 SAAF Squadron with an escort of three Spitfires mounted a very successful strike on the Greek harbour at Volos resulting in the freighter *Anna* (ex-Italian *Adriana* of 4,353 tons) being left listing and

Above: Three Ventura Is of 25 SAAF Squadron over the Adriatic returning from a raid on 13 October. The furthest aircraft, 'A', has suffered damage to its hydraulics resulting in the undercarriage dropping down. Left: Bombs dropped by Venturas of 25 SAAF Squadron explode on Volos harbour on 13 October which sank or damaged several ships.

on fire, while the F boat/barge *Laudon* and the corvette *Brigitte* were claimed sunk. The quayside was also badly damaged when an ammunition store exploded and a moored seaplane was also sunk. The unit received several congratulatory messages for this attack.

On this day 3 SAAF Squadron began operations in 8 SAAF Wing under the leadership of Maj E.K.Dunning. Until 18 November the squadron operated under Desert Air Force control, but on 19 November, the wing was attached to 22nd TAC of the 12th USAAF in support of the 5th Army.

108 Squadron flew their Beaufighter night-fighters to Araxos, where they would be controlled once more by HMS *Colombo*. It would take a week for 108 to commence operations from Greece, bad weather causing delays.

British Claims					
25 SAAF Sqn	Squadron claim	Ventura II	Ju 52 seaplane sunk	Volos harbour	1225
British Casualties					
272 Sqn	Beaufighter X NT999 'D' left 1510 on armed recce, requested emergency landing but ditched in Lake Lesina 30m from base; Flg Off J.R.Rutland/Sgt J.Rimington safe				
39 Sqn	Beaufighter X LZ460 'I' left 1040 on a shipping Rover, engine failed, ditched 1134; Sqn Ldr P.A.S.Payne/Flt Sgt E.M.Potts rescued by Italian Cant.Z.506 seaplane of 288ª Sq 1517				
39 Sqn	Beaufighter X NT905 'P' left 1040 on a shipping Rover, on return an engine failed, crash-landed at Brindisi 1450; Flg Off E.E.Horwill/Flt Sgt A.Taylor safe				
450 Sqn	Kittyhawk IV FT864 left 0815 attacking bridge near Cesena, shot down by Flak; Sgt N.T.Brooks POW				
601 Sqn	Spitfire IX PT646 left 1500 on Rover, bombed target at Gambettola, hit by Flak, crash-landed at Rimini; Wt Off G.H.Friis WiA				
US Casualties					
525th FS/86th FG	P-47D 42-26862 *Bulldog* / F50 *Lady Esther* lost in bad weather N Genoa 1250; 1/Lt Robert L.Anderson KiA [9200]				
345th FS/350th FG	P-47D shot down by Flak, crashed SE Bologna 1045; 2/Lt William E.Patterson evaded				

Saturday, 14 October 1944

73 Squadron's pilots encountered five enemy aircraft, three of which were CR.42s; two were claimed shot down north of Zagreb, the third escaping in a valley.

As the Germans evacuated Greece, the island of Corfu was liberated by British troops when 40 Commando, Royal Marines landed under cover provided by the Balkan Air Force.

British Claims					
73 Sqn	Wt Off E.F.F.Potvin	Spitfire IX NH271	CR.42	N Zagreb	1400-1710
73 Sqn	Flg Off W.Chumak	Spitfire IX MK444			
73 Sqn	Flt Lt G.A.Martin	Spitfire IX MA484	CR.42	15m N Zagreb	1400-1710
72 Sqn	Sqn Ldr C.I.R.Arthur	Spitfire IX PL319			
72 Sqn	Flt Lt J.N.M.McKinnon	Spitfire IX MK171			
72 Sqn	Flt Lt D.C.Dunn	Spitfire IX PT485			
72 Sqn	Flg Off W.E.C.Bunting	Spitfire IX PL444	Me 410	10m ENE Bergamo	1550
72 Sqn	Flg Off D.G.Crawford	Spitfire IX PK322			
72 Sqn	Sgt S.Degerlund	Spitfire IX PT594			
British Casualties					
250 Sqn	Kittyhawk IV FT926 left 1010, bombed target NW Cesena, FTR; Flg Off L.J.Philpott KiA				
250 Sqn	Kittyhawk IV FT923 left 1010, bombed target NW Cesena, FTR; Sgt T.W.Greene evaded				
450 Sqn	Kittyhawk IV FX538 left to dive bomb a road river bridge, hit by Flak 1615, reached Allied lines, crash-landed; 2/Lt T.C.Nel WiA				
German Casualties					
6.(F)/122	Ju 188D-2 WNr 150500 F6+AP shot down in combat nr Bergamo; Oblt Bodo Freisenhausen survived, two KiA				
1./NSGr 7	CR.42 WNr 9768 White 8 shot down on take-off from Varazdin a/f at 1530; Uffz Ewald Jost KiA				
1./NSGr 7	CR.42 lost, no further details				
3./NSGr 7 (TG2)	Ju 52/3m WNr 3050 8T+GT damaged by partisans and force-landed Gorica; Uffz Günther Christophe and 10 POWs and 2 KiA; POWs later exchanged				
	LKS reports one Ju 188 lost in combat, one ground-attack fighter destroyed in combat and one damaged				

Saturday-Sunday, 14/15 October 1944

Sunday, 15 October 1944

Operation Manna, the liberation of Athens and the Greek mainland, commenced. As the Allies moved further into Greece and especially in the Athens area they soon found the Germans were not the only matters they had to deal with. The political tensions between the communists and other forces within Greece that would result in a full-scale civil war, began to manifest themselves shortly after the Allies landed. The Royal Navy's carrier force sailed from Alexandria as part of Task Force 120 for the occupation of Athens. HMS *Emperor* in company with HMS *Attacker* and *Stalker*, and destroyers *Troubridge, Termagant, Tyrian, Tuscan* and *Garland* then began a further series of strikes in the Aegean, commencing in the area around the island of Rhodes.

A Seafire from 809 Squadron intercepted and shot down a reconnaissance Ju 88 15 miles south of Athens, in the only encounter by the Fleet Air Arm with German aircraft over Greece. The commanding general of the Luftwaffe in Greece, who still carried the title, despite leaving the country concerned, had no battlefield support capability of his own with which to assist his troops' passage north.

The German Order of Battle in Greece was as follows:

Unit	Type	Strength	Serviceabble
3.(F)/33	Ju 188 F-1	2	(0)
	Ju 188 D-2	4	(1)
2.(F)/123	Ju 88 T-3	0	(0)
IV./TG 1	Ju 52	15	(3)
I./TG 4	Ju 52	22	(18)
14./TG 4	Ju 352	1	(1)
II./KG 4	He 111 as transports	20	(20)
III./KG 27	He 111 as transports	7	(3)
Seenotgr. 70	Do 24 T-3	7	(2)
TSt See 1	Ju 52 (See)	3	(2)

A Ju 88 of 2.(F)/123 after being attacked over the Aegean by the Seafire of 809 Squadron flown by Lt D.S.Ogle.

British Claims

809 Sqn	Lt D.S.Ogle	Seafire LR.IIc MB150	Ju 88	15m S Athens	1115
213 Sqn	Sgt A.F.W.W.Hunt	Mustang III HB905	} CR.42*	Zagreb area, 8m SE Sisak	1430-1710
213 Sqn	Flg Off G.F.Allan	Mustang III KH534	}		

*forced down but not destroyed, so strafed on ground

British Casualties

5 SAAF Sqn	Mustang III FB251 left 1215, shot down by Flak 5km N Cesena 1250; Lt G.C.Murray KiA
272 Sqn	Beaufighter X NV470 'B' left 1500, shot down by Flak S Fiume, crashed into sea; Wg Cdr G.R.Park DFC/Flg Off D.L.Edwards KiA
93 Sqn	Spitfire IX MA486 left 1020 on practice flight, last seen near Piombino, presumably became lost, came down in German lines near Parma 1200; Lt J.T.Marais POW
93 Sqn	Spitfire IX left 1020 on practice flight, last seen near Piombino presumably became lost, came down in German lines near Parma 1200; Flg Off R.W.Sloan POW
32 Sqn	Spitfire Vc JK337 left 0745, on returning to base from convoy patrol, engine trouble, crashed on south coast of Gulf of Corinth 1100; Sgt G.E.T.Gooch KiA
32 Sqn	Spitfire Vc JL127 left 1555 on convoy patrol off Athens, apparently ran out of fuel, ditched near Corinth 1737; Sgt T.W.Green KiA
809 Sqn	Seafire L.III NN115 on landing struck round down of HMS *Stalker*, damaged; Sub Lt K.Herring safe

US Casualties

65th FS/57th FG	P-47D 42-26839 hit by Flak 0935, damaged Cat 3; pilot safe
65th FS/57th FG	P-47D 42-76005 hit by Flak 0935, damaged Cat 2; pilot safe

German Casualties

2.(F)/123	Ju 88T 4U+..K shot down nr Anavyssos/Athens; Fw Erich Labus and three KiA
2./NSGr 7	CR.42 lost to Mustangs near Zagreb; no further details
	LKS reports one ground-attack fighter destroyed in combat

Monday, 16 October 1944

British Casualties

213 Sqn	Mustang III FB337 'A' hit in glycol tank by Flak, crash-landed 1130; Sgt S.W.Farley evaded, back on 12 November
249 Sqn	Mustang III KH532 left 1055 on sweep, attacked train at Jasenovac, presumed hit in coolant, pilot baled out 1340 into the Adriatic; Capt R.T.Whittingham rescued by US 1 ERS OA-10 Catalina 1430

An OA-10 Catalina of the US 1st Emergency Rescue Squadron rescued Capt R.T.Whittingham of 249 Squadron from the Adriatic after he had baled out of his Mustang.

1 SAAF Sqn	Spitfire IX MA949 'A' left 0800, met with intense Flak in the Cesena-Lugo area, damaged Cat II; Lt J.B.S.Ross safe				
1 SAAF Sqn	Spitfire IX MA530 'Z' left 0800, met with intense Flak in the Cesena-Lugo area, damaged by debris from a self-propelled railway trolley which blew up while being strafed, landed safely at base; Capt R.J.Barnwell safe				
352 Sqn	Spitfire Vc JK447 left 1400, shot down by Flak at Slevo near Ston, Majr Arkadije Popov KiA				
US Casualties					
85th FS/79th FG	P-47D 42-27003 shot down by Flak, crashed 6m off coast nr Ravenna 1630; 2/Lt Jack L.Slatton rescued				
85th BS/47th BG	A-20J 43-22067 shot down by Flak WSW Medicina 1630; 1/Lt Harland T.Taigan and two KiA [9438]				

Tuesday, 17 October 1944

Two incidents of attacks on friendly forces occurred on this day. Four Mustangs attacked a Partisan Air Force Fi 167 near Vrdovo. The Fi 167 was part of the Squadron Staba NOVJ based at Vis. The aircraft had defected on 25th September. The crew survived, but their passenger Gen-Maj Vlado Ćetković, commander of 8 Corps NOVJ, was killed.

During Operation Manna four Hellcat fighter-bomber pilots of the Fleet Air Arm mistakenly strafed what they thought were German Siebel ferries located off the Greek island of Skopelos, but were actually craft of the Coastal Forces. There were nine casualties – two fatal – on *MTB 397* and *MTB 399*. Three of the craft were damaged.

Two flights of Seafires from 809 Squadron bombed Velos harbour and sank a Do 24 as it was taking off. Later in the day Flg Off M.W.Smyth, flying one of four Spitfires from 253 Squadron was lost over Yugoslavia; the other three circled the dinghy for as long as possible, causing them to arrive back at base low on fuel and after dark. They were diverted to another airfield with lights but all three – Flg Off D.D.S.Evans (in ER976), 2/Lt J.R.Cleverley (in JK876) and Sgt P.J.Blythe (probably in JK868) – crashed on landing.

British Claims					
809 Sqn	Sub Lt G.S.Macartney	Seafire IIc MB133 SS			
809 Sqn	Sub Lt G.C.Morris	Seafire IIc MB269 SA			
809 Sqn	Sub Lt A.C.S.Morrison	Seafire LIII NF607 SG	Do 24	Velos harbour	1015
809 Sqn	Sub Lt A.B.Foley	Seafire LIII NF134 SU			
809 Sqn	Sub Lt D.E.James	Seafire III NN390 SL			
213 Sqn	Flt Lt E.H.MacLellan	Mustang III HB932			
213 Sqn	Flt Sgt A.Liudzius	Mustang III FB512	Fi 167	2m SW Binj	1045
213 Sqn	2/Lt R.E.Rorvik	Mustang III FB307			
213 Sqn	Sgt A.F.W.W.Hunt	Mustang III HB905			
19 SAAF Sqn	Maj C.F.Geere/Lt D.E.J.Ironside	Beaufighter X 'D'			
19 SAAF Sqn	Flg Off A.Ingram/Flg Off R.Pollard	Beaufighter X 'Q'			
19 SAAF Sqn	Flt Sgt F.G.W.Sheldrick/Flt Sgt R.E.Ash	Beaufighter X 'V'	Do 24	10m E Platamon	1051
19 SAAF Sqn	Lt C.J.Franken/Flt Sgt R.V.Smith	Beaufighter X 'K'			
19 SAAF Sqn	Lt J.E.Henry/Flg Off C.W.Thomas	Beaufighter X 'S'			
British Casualties					
40 SAAF Sqn	Spitfire missing Cesena area on Arty Recce, last heard of about to force land NW Cesenatico; Lt D.G.C.Chessman evaded				
19 SAAF Sqn	Beaufighter X 'D' damaged by return fire from Do 24 E Platamon 1050; Maj C.F.Geere/Lt Ironside safe				
253 Sqn	Spitfire Vc ER490 left 1550 on sweep of Metkovic to Mostar railway, strafed train E Domanovici, hit by Flak, glycol leak, pilot baled out off Pelješac Peninsula; Flg Off M.W.Smyth drifted ashore on Hvar Island after 16 hours in dinghy, evaded				
6 Sqn	Hurricane IV KX820 'D' left 0705 on armed recce, attacked 40 motor transports near Durazzo, shot down by Flak, pilot baled out 5m inland from coast; Sgt A.W.Coghlan evaded, back in Italy by 2 November				
13 (H) Sqn	Baltimore V FW852 'Y' left 1005 to bomb Alipasin Most railway station, hit by Flak over target, belly-landed at Canne 1315; Flt Lt E.Hatzakis DFC and three safe				
809 Sqn	Seafire L.III NN133 crashed into barrier on HMS *Stalker*, badly damaged; Sub Lt R.D.Wood safe				
US Casualties					
86th BS/47th BG	A-20K 44-35756 '56' left on intruder mission, flew into a mountain in bad weather 0415, wreck found 8m NE San Pietro on 20 October; 1/Lt Eual J.Ragsdale and three KiA [9989]				
Yugoslav Casualties					
Partisan Air Force	Fi 167A-0 WNr 4807 shot down in error by four RAF Mustangs 2m SW Binj; pilot Miljenko Lipošćak and two slt WiA, Gen-Maj Vlado Ćetković, 8th Corps NOVJ commander, KiA				

A section of Mustangs of 213 Squadron shot down an Fi 167A on 17 October but it was the aircraft that had previously defected and was carrying a senior partisan commander who was killed.

German Claims

Flak	Spitfire	Rimini	1000

German Casualties

13./TG 1	Ju 52/3m WNr 501445 lost Ampelon-Larissa; Fw Reinhold Gotthardt and three KiA
70.Seenotst.	Do 24T-2 WNr 0051 CM+IQ shot down by fighters Volos-Salonika; Lt Johann Zwarte and five KiA
70.Seenotst.	Do 24T-3 J9+EA damaged by fighters Volos-Salonika; pilot and four safe, one KiA
	LKS reports two a/c destroyed by enemy action and one Ju 52/3m lost in operations

Wednesday, 18 October 1944

During this day Seafires concentrated on motor transports in the Larissa area though south of Mount Olympus Sub Lt L.J.B.Baker's aircraft was hit by Flak and the pilot baled out. Nearby a Seafire was also damaged by Flak attacking a railway engine and Sub Lt G.J.T.Moore baled out near Mount Olympus. He too was later reported safe.

The ground party of 32 Squadron was shipped to Athens and took up occupation of Kalamaki on this date, where it began to be joined by the air party from Araxos. Also 335 Squadron ceased operations in order to prepare to move to Greece.

British Casualties

16 SAAF Sqn	Beaufighter X JM353 'E' left 0955 on anti-shipping sweep at Salonika Bay, attacked convoy off Atherida Point, damaged by Flak 1213, force-landed in Greece 1245; Lt R.B.Berry KiA/Flg Off N.M.Wicks WIA evaded
16 SAAF Sqn	Beaufighter X NV211 'K' left 0955 on anti-shipping sweep at Salonika Bay, attacked convoy off Atherida Point, damaged by Flak 1215, force-landed at Brindisi; Lt Kendall/Lt W.A.Hewett safe
16 SAAF Sqn	Beaufighter X NV128 'U' left 0955 on anti-shipping sweep at Salonika Bay, attacked convoy off Atherida Point, damaged by Flak 1215, belly-landed at Canne; Lt H.B.Stopforth/Lt L.S.J.Keeton safe
809 Sqn	Seafire LIIc MA975 HMS *Stalker* damaged attacking railway engine, pilot baled out near Mount Olympus; Sub Lt G.J.T.Moore safe
809 Sqn	Seafire LIII NF134 SU hit by Flak strafing motor transports S of Mount Olympus; Sub Lt L.J.B.Baker baled out safely
418 Sqn	Mosquito FBVI HR351 departed Jesi on day Ranger, shot down or crashed at Planik hill ca 20km W Rijeka; Flt Lt S.H.R.Cotterill/Flt Lt C.G.Finlayson KiA

German Casualties

	LKS reports one ground-attack Bf 109 missing and one Fi 156 lost in combat

Thursday, 19 October 1944

ANR's 2° Gruppo C was involved in a complicated combat following the return of this unit to action. Twenty-two Bf 109s of the three Squadriglie took off from Villafranca and Ghedi to intercept 12 B-26s of 319th Bomb Group raiding Mantua. The incoming bombers were identified by the Italians both as Bostons and "English Marauders". Seven twin-engined bombers were claimed, one each by Magg Miani, Cap Bellagambi

Bf 109Gs of the ANR's 2° Gruppo Caccia were involved in a big combat on the afternoon of 19 October during which Serg Magg Fausto Fornaci (right) claimed two Marauders and Serg Magg Rolando Ancillotti (left) a P-47.

and M.llo Galetti and two each by Serg Magg Fornaci and Serg Magg Sanson. In addition, two P-47s were claimed by Serg Magg Ancillotti and Serg Talin. One Bf 109 was lost and the pilot killed.

94 Squadron flew from Savoia to Kalamaki in Greece where two aircraft crashed on landing; Lt Q.R.. Dummett was killed.

British Casualties

249 Sqn	Mustang III KH428 left 0930 to bomb Amyntaio, on return encountered bad weather NE Tirana 1240; Wt Off C.N.V.Davey KiA
249 Sqn	Mustang III KH530 left 0930 to bomb Amyntaio, on return encountered bad weather NE Tirana 1240, ran out of fuel, pilot baled out; Plt Off R.Andrew reported safe on 22 October
94 Sqn	Spitfire Vc LZ823 left 0800 to transfer to Kalamaki, crashed on landing 1050; Lt Q.R.Dummett KiA
94 Sqn	Spitfire Vc JG831 left 0800 to transfer to Kalamaki, crashed on landing 1050; Flt Sgt H.J.O'Keefe safe
94 Sqn	Spitfire Vc JK797 left 1315 on recce of Larissa area, hit by Flak, force-landed; Flt Lt H.McLachlan returned safely

US Claims

440th BS/319th BG	tail gunner	B-26C	Bf 109	Mantua area	ca 1410
440th BS/319th BG	bombardier	B-26C	Bf 109	Mantua area	ca 1410
440th BS/319th BG	tail gunners	B-26Cs	2 Bf 109 Probables	Mantua area	ca 1410
440th BS/319th BG	top turret gunner	B-26C	Bf 109 Probable	Mantua area	ca 1410
440th BS/319th BG	gunner	B-26C	FW 190 Damaged	Mantua area	ca 1410

US Casualties

440th BS/319th BG	B-26C 41-35041 '93' left 1250 to bomb Mantua railway bridge, shot down by a Bf 109 over target 1416, crew baled out; 1/Lt Floyd W.Roberts and five POW [9307]
440th BS/319th BG	B-26C 42-107565 '88' *Roger the Dodger II* left to bomb Mantua railway bridge, shot down by a Bf 109 over target 1417, crashed NW Curtatone; 1/Lt Donald Treadwell Jr and three KiA, copilot POW [9309]
440th BS/319th BG	B-26C 42-107561 '97' *Tally Ho* left to bomb Mantua railway bridge, shot down by Bf 109s over target 1417, crew baled out; 1/Lt John L.O'Bryant and five POW [9305]
487th BS/340th BG	B-25J '7Z' left 1345 to bomb Magenta railway bridge, shot up by Flak over target; 1/Lt Wilbur C.Lentz safe, 2/Lt Robert H.Meek copilot KiA, three WiA, one safe
381st BS/310th BG	B-25J 43-27576 left to bomb Cameri RR bridge, shot down by Flak, crash-landed nr Nizza Monferrato 1650; 1/Lt Henry L.Collins and four evaded, one POW, one baled out DoW [9443]

Hellcat I JV105 'E-W' of 800 Squadron parked on the deck of HMS *Emperor* off Khios, Greece, on 19 October when the ship had been called to embark a party of Italian POWs for transfer to Egypt.

Italian ANR Claims

NC 2° Gr C	Magg Carlo Miani	Bf 109G	Marauder	Mantua area	ca 1410
5ª Sq, 2° Gr C	Cap Mario Bellagambi	Bf 109G	Marauder	Mantua area	ca 1410
5ª Sq, 2° Gr C	M.llo Artidoro Galetti	Bf 109G	Marauder	Mantua area	ca 1410
5ª Sq, 2° Gr C	Serg Magg Fausto Fornaci	Bf 109G	2 Marauders	Mantua area	ca 1410
5ª Sq, 2° Gr C	Serg Magg Attilio Sanson	Bf 109G	2 Marauders	Mantua area	ca 1410
5ª Sq, 2° Gr C	Serg Magg Rolando Ancillotti	Bf 109G	P-47	Mantua area	ca 1420
5ª Sq, 2° Gr C	Serg Leo Talin	Bf 109G	P-47	Mantua area	ca 1420

Italian ANR Casualties

5ª Sq, 2° Gr C	Bf 109G Yellow 4 damaged in combat with B-26s, exploded in mid-air; Serg Leo Talin KiA

Thursday-Friday, 19/20 October 1944

US Claims

417th NFS	2/Lt Hyrum J.Allen/2/Lt William E.Grinnell	Beaufighter VIf	Ju 188 Probable	10-15m SW Cremona	1930

German Casualties

6.(F)/122	Ju 188D-2 F6+GP lost on night reconnaissance over Adriatic; Obfw Kurt Rautenberg and crew MiA
13./TG 1	Ju 52/3m WNr 5763 G6+BX crashed E Agram; Obfw Stefan Wiener and three rescued, two troops KiA, eight MiA
7.Seenotst.	Do 24T-3 WNr 1033 J9+AA crashed in the Gulf of Salonika; Lt Werner Büchner and two WiA, two KiA
	LKS reports one Ju 188 and one Ju 52/3m missing

Friday, 20 October 1944

British Claims

213 Sqn	Flt Sgt D.A.Stevenson	Mustang III HB898	Ju 52/3m	SE Sombor	0810-1100

British Casualties

4 SAAF Sqn	Spitfire IX MH995 'Q' left 1020 attacking motor transports S Imola, hit by Flak SW Cesena-Forlì 1115, pilot baled out; Capt E.W.Sturgess POW
241 Sqn	Spitfire IX PL323 left 1335 to attack barges in the Loreo, River Po area, reported engine trouble after attack, force-landed; Sgt J.R.Kedie POW
1 SAAF Sqn	Spitfire IX MA638 'C' shot down by Flak SW Forlì 0850, Lt H.M.Fisher KiA
351 Sqn	Hurricane IV LF461 left 1440, hit by Flak near Rudine, Montenegro, crashed in flames on Ston Island; Potporučnik (Plt Off) Stanislav Vouk KiA

US Casualties

522nd FS/27th FBG	P-47D 42-26834 'red F' *Midge III* hit by Flak, crashed 3m W Gallicano, pilot baled 1100; Capt Robert E.Fromm, commanding officer, KiA [9441]
447th FS/321st BG	B-25D 43-3403 *Incendiary Blonde* left 1020 to attack road bridge at Galliate, hit by Flak, crashed 500m W Pieve Albignola 1230; 1/Lt Richard L.Willis and one KiA, two POW, one safe [9442]
448th FS/321st BG	B-25D badly damaged by Flak; 1/Lt Vernon C.Dossey and six safe

German Claims

3.Flak Brigade	3./376 (V) Batterie	Thunderbolt		1055
Flak		Spitfire	Castel San Pietro	1045
Flak		Mitchell	Pieve Albignola	1230
Flak		Spitfire*	area Porto Vire	1400
	* claim recorded as being a 241 Squadron Spitfire			

Saturday, 21 October 1944

Seven Spitfires of 72 Squadron, undertaking an armed reconnaissance over the Venice area, engaged eight Bf 109s of ANR's 2° Gruppo over Lake Garda, pilots claiming one shot down, one probable and one damaged.

19 SAAF Squadron Beaufighters and eight Mustangs from 249 Squadron sank a motor torpedo boat moored at the dock of Olib harbour at 1305. This unfortunately was the partisan ship NB 13 *Partizan*. The encounter report noted that the formation had tried to get the ship to identify itself, which it had failed to do, so the Mustangs strafed it, then Beaufighters followed up with rockets. These all missed but nonetheless the ship burnt out; only three members of the crew were wounded.

112 Squadron went locomotive hunting again during a reconnaissance of northern Italy, the pilots of 11 Mustangs claiming another 28 destroyed. Sgt Jones was shot down into the sea and took to his dinghy. Flg Off Burditt in a 293 Squadron Walrus had originally landed and rescued an American survivor from a 15th Air Force B-24, was then ordered to rescue Capt Meikle of 7 SAAF Squadron, which was done by taxiing over to him. However, the Walrus was damaged by artillery fire and the engine failed, a Catalina was called in to help and picked up all three survivors at 1130, while the Walrus crew stayed with their aircraft. Overnight they were captured, presumably by German vessels.

British Claims

72 Sqn	Flg Off R.B.Hendry	Spitfire IX MJ631	Bf 109	S corner Lake Garda	1010-1140
72 Sqn	Sgt A.Bell	Spitfire IX MK553	Bf 109 Probable	S corner Lake Garda	1010-1140
72 Sqn	Flt Lt E.Galitzine	Spitfire IX PL465	Bf 109 Damaged	S corner Lake Garda	1010-1140
72 Sqn	Lt J.F.Jackson	Spitfire IX PT594	Bf 109 Damaged	S corner Lake Garda	1010-1140

British Casualties

253 Sqn	Spitfire Vc left 1210 on sweep Bishqem-Elbasan area, Albania, shot down by Flak; Flt Lt J.M.Sullivan baled out, evaded, back in Italy by 2 November
7 SAAF Sqn	Spitfire IXe PT375 damaged in glycol system probably by own rockets while strafing 1135 over Adriatic; Capt A.W.Meikle picked up by Catalina 1215
112 Sqn	Mustang III HB925 'Z' left 0630 on long-range recce of northern Italy, shot down by Flak near Udine, pilot baled out off shore, rescued by Walrus and Catalina; Sgt A.W.Jones safe
213 Sqn	Mustang III HB854 contact lost at 1030 2m W Kutina, just prior to strafing a train; Flt Sgt C.Postlethwaite MiA
39 Sqn	Beaufighter X NE724 'W' left 1430 on a shipping Rover of the Gulf of Fiume, damaged by Flak, crash-landed at Canne; Plt Off C.B.Lyon/Flt Sgt D.D.Cathro safe

| 1435 Sqn | Spitfire IX MH654 'X' left 1100, shot down by Flak 16km NE Tirana 1220; Lt S.R.R.Pittard baled out, safe with partisans |
| 293 Sqn | Walrus L2266, landed to rescue a 459th BG survivor, then rescued 7 SAAF and 112 Sqn pilots off Venice, engine failed, could not take off, survivors transferred to a Catalina, all aboard captured; Flg Off H.F.Burditt/Flg Off I.Morgan POW |

US Casualties

| 439th BS/319th BG | B-26C 42-107731 left 0855 to bomb Nervesa railway causeway, hit by Flak, crashed nr Ponte della Priula 1107; 2/Lt Dean H.Rice and five KiA, one POW [9437] |
| 525th FS/86th FG | P-47D '92' lost to Flak; 1/Lt George E.Hill baled and returned |

German Casualties

| 4./KG 4 | He 111H-20 WNr 700028 lost on flight to Rhodes; Hptm Hans Schumm (St.Kpt) and three MiA |

Italian ANR Claims

| 5ª Sq, 2° Gr C | Serg Magg Attilio Sanson | Bf 109G | Spitfire | Lake Garda | 1050- |

Italian ANR Casualties

4ª Sq, 2° Gr C			Bf 109G shot down; Ten Raffaele Valenzano baled out safely
5ª Sq, 2° Gr C			Bf 109G shot down; Serg Guido Minardi baled out safely
5ª Sq, 2° Gr C			Bf 109G crash-landed; Cap Mario Bellagambi safe
5ª Sq, 2° Gr C			Bf 109G damaged; Serg Magg Attilio Sanson safe

Sunday, 22 October 1944

A German train on the Larissa-Salonika line was reportedly attacked near Pyrgetos by four Allied aircraft, identified as Thunderbolts; the defending Flak unit fired 21 rounds of 4cm Flak and claimed two aircraft shot down in flames. These were actually Spitfires of 32 Squadron, a section of which strafed the train at Pyrgetos, encountered "exceptionally heavy" Flak from the train and Flt Sgt I.T.R.James was lost.

British Casualties

112 Sqn	Mustang HB893 'K' strafing tanks SSW Ravenna, shot down by Flak 1615; Lt J.R.Lund KiA
92 Sqn	Spitfire VIII JF894 left 1530 Bologna-Ravenna area, hit by Flak; Maj J.E.Gasson WiA
92 Sqn	Spitfire VIII JF709 left 1530 Bologna-Ravenna area, hit by Flak, reached Allied lines, crash-landed; Wt Off M.Doran safe
32 Sqn	Spitfire Vc MA698 left 1445, strafed train E Pyrgetos, hit by Flak; Flt Sgt I.T.R.James KiA
1435 Sqn	Spitfire IX MH647 'K' left 0745 hit by Flak, attempted to force land W Fushe near Vlore 0840, crashed; Flt Lt J.G.Douglas KiA

German Claims

| Flak | Railway Transport Detachment | 2 P-47s | Pyrgetos | 1520 & 1525 |

German Casualties

1./NAGr 11	Bf 109G-8 WNr 202059 Black 12 crashed 30km W Rovinj, Yugoslavia; Uffz Rolf Thomsen MiA
15./TG 1	Ju 52/3m WNr 7126 lost Polykastron-Pristina; Obfhr Michael Staudinger and three MiA
	LKS reports one recce Bf 109 and one Ju 52/3m missing

Sunday-Monday, 22/23 October 1944

British Claims

| 108 Sqn | Flg Off A.D.Cunningham/Flg Off R.Common | Beaufighter VIf 'W' | He 111 | E Lampinou | 1640-2030 |

Monday, 23 October 1944

Four Spitfires from 94 Squadron led by the wing leader, Wg Cdr Woodruff, flying over Gorgopi airfield on the Larissa plain mid-afternoon, spotted two He 111s and each pair made a single strafing pass that left both of them burning. However, the last man through, Flg Off Jock Maxwell was hit by Flak and crashed on the airfield.

British Claims

94 Sqn	Wg Cdr P.G.Woodruff	Spitfire Vc BR253			
94 Sqn	Wt Off Dorman	Spitfire Vc ER501			
94 Sqn	Flg Off J.Anderson	Spitfire Vc ER867	2 He 111s (on ground)	Gorgopi a/f	1315-1510
94 Sqn	Flg Off J.G.P.Maxwell	Spitfire Vc JI365			

British Casualties

94 Sqn	Spitfire Vc JL362 left 1315 to strafe airfield at Gorgopi SW Polykastron, shot down by Flak; Plt Off J.G.P.Maxwell KiA
32 Sqn	Spitfire Vc JK652 left 0900, strafed train N Pyrgetos, hit by Flak, force-landed N Karitsa; Wt Of R.C.Evans safe
225 Sqn	Spitfire IX MH768 LF-X left 1420 TacR Modena area, hit by Flak 5m S Modena in fuel system, pilot baled out NW Prato in Allied lines; Flg Off L.E.H.Williams WiA

Bulgarian Casualties

2/6 Orlyak	Bf 109G-6 shot down by Flak strafing M/T near Kumanovo; Por K.S.Andonov KiA
2/6 Orlyak	Bf 109G-6 shot down by Flak strafing M/T near Kumanovo; Por G.P.Georgiev POW

German Claims

Flak	Spitfire	Polykastron a/f	1442

German Casualties

8./KG 27	He 111H-20 1G+MS damaged by strafing by Spitfire at Polykastron

Tuesday, 24 October 1944

British Casualties

4 SAAF Sqn	Spitfire IXc MJ926 'KJ-D' left 0840 to dive bomb guns W of Corletto, last seen diving on target 5m NE Faenza 0905; Capt J.V.Rochford KiA
19 SAAF Sqn	Beaufighter X 'F' left 0900 strafed Bjelovar and Kriz area, hit by Flak, crash-landed near Svinjici 1103; Maj D.P.Tilley/Wt Off A.Powell evaded, reported safe on 26 October
249 Sqn	Mustang III HB941 left 1155 on road sweep, attacked motor transports near Shegas, dived into ground; Lt H.K.Rachmann KiA
7 SAAF Sqn	Spitfire IXc EN402 'F' shot down by Flak attacking a train Polesella-W Copparo 0705; Flg Off G.S.Richardson (attached from 93 Sqn) KiA
253 Sqn	Spitfire Vc JL304 left 1135, strafed motor transports in the Tirana-Scutari area, hit by Flak force-landed at Shegas, Albania; Flt Sgt P.Watts evaded
43 Sqn	Spitfire IX PT588 left 0850, hit by Flak S.Bologna, on return pilot baled out near base; Flt Lt J.G.Thompson safe
40 SAAF Sqn	Spitfire IX shot down by Flak near Forlì; Lt A.R.S.Dorning POW

German Claims

Flak	Spitfire*	near Forlì	1630
	*recorded as being a 40 Sqn Spitfire		

Wednesday, 25 October 1944

HMS *Emperor* began her final operation in the Mediterranean theatre for which she had embarked a Swordfish, for spotting duties as well as the Walrus. They were to support Operation Contempt the assault on the island of Milos during which the Hellcats flew 260 bombing sorties. The operation lasted until 5 November. By this date HMS *Attacker* and *Emperor* had provided air cover to the amphibious landing at Mitylene to retake Lesbos. Next day a detachment of Seafires moved ashore to Mitylene for three days. On the 26th HMS *Emperor*'s air group carried out strikes and bombardment spotted for the battleship HMS *King George V* in preparation for the allied occupation of Milos.

British Casualties

272 Sqn	Beaufighter X NE374 'L' left 0430, shot down by Flak, ditched off Piran Point, Slovenia; Flt Lt T.StB.Freer DFC POW/Flt Lt C.P.Holman DFC KiA
256 Sqn	Mosquito XIII MM530 left 1550 on dusk Ranger patrol to Tirana area, hit by Flak strafing motor transports N Verre, on return starboard engine on fire, ditched 30m N Brindisi 1734, rescued by HSL three hours later; Sgt L.R.Misselbrook/Flt Sgt R.D.Turner safe

German Claims

Flak	Beaufighter	nr Salvore Point, off Trieste	0720

German Casualties

16./TG 1	Ju 52/3m WNr 3185 destroyed at Agram; Obfw Max Voss and one KiA
	LKS reports one Ju 52/3m destroyed on ground

Shipping berthed in the port of Trieste is revealed in this reconnaissance photograph taken by a 682 Squadron Spitfire on 25 October.

Friday, 27 October 1944

Sub Lt W.D.Vine of 800 Squadron was shot down in flames when strafing a shore battery. Vine baled out and was picked up by an ASR Walrus.

British Casualties

208 Sqn	Spitfire IX MH695 left 1330 on reconnaissance nr Pavullo, contact lost in heavy cloud; Flg Off J.R.Glass KiA
800 Sqn	Hellcat I JV227 EF shot down when strafing shore battery, pilot baled out, rescued by Walrus L2238 of HMS *Emperor*'s Flight; Sub Lt W.D.Vine safe

Saturday, 28 October 1944

By late October 1944, the Germans had pulled out of mainland Greece and were fighting to keep open the routes for their forces' withdrawal through Yugoslavia to Hungary. Yugoslav partisans, the Soviets and their former Bulgarian and Romanian allies were all trying to stop them. The remnant Luftwaffe Command South East units were supporting the fighting around Belgrade and the German command began to consider what assistance further to the south could be provided, in particular to service the transport units which were flying supplies in and flying out hundreds of Germans wounded every night.

Plans were considered to provide a tactical daylight presence, and after various delays, these materialised into providing a Staffel of FW 190 from II./SG 10 to operate from Skopje in the ground-attack role to assist in keeping the choke point at the neck of Yugoslavia open by striking at the advancing Russian and Bulgarian forces, which in the rugged terrain and the approaching winter was restricted to a relatively few roads, that were, as the Germans well knew having just retreated over them and been subject to attack, vulnerable.

British Casualties				
253 Sqn	Spitfire IX left 1000, suffered glycol leak on strafing, 25m from Brindisi pilot reported he was baling out, but dived straight into the sea, no sign of dinghy; Wt Off R.P.Wilson KiA			
253 Sqn	Spitfire Vc JK275 hit by ground fire, round went through the cockpit missing the pilot; Flg Off R.A.Day safe			
German Claims				
Flak	8./720 Naval Flak Rail Car	Bulgarian Ju 87	Veles railway station	1100

Sunday, 29 October 1944

US Casualties				
85th FS/79th FG	P-47D 42-26535 'X19' *Impatient Virgin* shot down by Flak, ditched off shore nr Porto Garibaldi 1340; 1/Lt Robert B.Bell POW [9676]			
German Claims				
Flak		Thunderbolt	near Porto Garibaldi	1330

Monday, 30 October 1944

Having re-equipped with Spitfires in July, 11 SAAF Squadron moved to Italy where it transferred its Spitfires to 3 SAAF Squadron. It received as replacement 5 SAAF Squadron's Kittyhawks, with 5 SAAF Squadron re-equipping with Mustangs. On this day 11 SAAF Squadron carried out its first operation as a fighter-bomber unit.

HMS *Attacker* withdrew to Alexandria, leaving *Emperor* and 800 Squadron in the Aegean. Its Seafire squadron, 879, had flown 240 operational sorties from 16 September.

British Casualties	
112 Sqn	Mustang III HB908 'W' left 1115 on bombing mission, shot down by Flak 1255 off San Vito; Lt D.F.Prentice POW
213 Sqn	Mustang III HB894 left 1415, ordered his section to return to base because of bad weather, disappeared 50-60m NE Tremiti Islands 1530; 2/Lt R.E.Rorvik KiA
213 Sqn	Mustang III HB952 shot down by Flak in Skopje area 1450; Flt Lt R.H.MacLellan KiA
249 Sqn	Mustang III KH437 left 1345 to strafe roads, encountered bad weather in Skopje area, last seen 10m SW Lagosta Island; Sgt H.G.Pallett KiA
32 Sqn	Spitfire Vc JK667 left 0600, damaged by Flak strafing a train S Gorgopi, force-landed; Flg Off E.C.Clark evaded, returned to unit on 9 November, then spent 10 days in hospital to recover
19 SAAF Sqn	Argus II FS645 (a 254 Wing a/c), crashed into cloud-covered mountain near Santa Lucia/Isernia 45 minutes after take-off at ca 1200; Maj C.F.Geere and Maj S.Fuchs 16 SAAF Adj KiA, Capt A.P.J.Le Roux 16 SAAF Sqn severely injured

Monday-Tuesday, 30/31 October 1944

German Claims				
Flak	3/31 Naval Flak	Wellington	Polykastron station	1906

Tuesday, 31 October 1944

Sqn Ldr Russ Foskett, the Australian commanding officer of 94 Squadron was lost when on an operation over the Aegean. Between the islands of Skiathos and Skopelos his aircraft suffered an engine failure and although he successfully baled out into the sea he did not survive.

The commanding officer of 94 Squadron, Sqn Ldr Russ Foskett, was lost during the day after his Spitfire suffered an engine failure.

Top: Ten Tiberio Biasi of 6ª Squadriglia, 2° Gruppo Caccia was killed in a combat with P-47s of the 350th Fighter Group on 31 October.
Above: Flying Mustang III KH427 'V' on 31 October Flt Lt P.F.Noble shared the destruction of an Fi 156 over Albania which was 249 Squadron's final victory of the war.

Over Albania two Mustangs of 249 Squadron shot down an Fi 156 to make the unit's only air-to-air victory with the type. It took their total to 244 confirmed.

British Claims					
249 Sqn	Flt Lt P.F.Noble	Mustang III KH427 'V'	Fi 156	N Bitol, Albania	0640-0910
249 Sqn	Flg Off J.Dickerson	Mustang III KH575 'Z'			

British Casualties

250 Sqn	Kittyhawk IV FX814 left 1420, presumed shot down by Flak NW Ravenna 1525; Lt M.H.Grusd POW	
94 Sqn	Spitfire Vb ER489 'A' left 0530, strafed a train, on return flight ditched between Skiathos and Skopelos islands; Sqn Ldr R.G.Foskett DFC KiA, body retrieved by a boat from a RN aircraft carrier shortly afterwards, buried at sea later in the day	
19 SAAF Sqn	Beaufighter X NV491 'Z' left 1100, attacked Novi harbour 1240, hit by Flak, attempted to ditch 60m S Novi 1305, crashed and burnt out; Lt J.E.Henry/Flg Off C.W.Thomas KiA	

US Claims					
346th FS/350th FG	1/Lt James B.Dailey Jr	P-47D	Bf 109	W Lonato	1230-1430
346th FS/350th FG	1/Lt James B.Dailey Jr	P-47D	Bf 109 Probable	W Lonato	1230-1430
346th FS/350th FG	1/Lt Robert C.Tomlinson	P-47D	2 Bf 109s	W Lonato	1230-1430
346th FS/350th FG	1/Lt Robert C.Tomlinson	P-47D	Bf 109 Probable	W Lonato	1230-1430
346th FS/350th FG	1/Lt Robert C.Tomlinson	P-47D	Bf 109 Damaged	W Lonato	1230-1430

US Casualties

346th FS/350th FG	P-47D damaged by e/a in tail section, collided on ground at Pisa a/d with P-47 1430; 1/Lt Robert C.Tomlinson safe
347th FS/350th FG	P-47D 42-28557 '7A7' hit by Flak, engine failed, crashed and exploded nr Correggio 1500; 1/Lt John P.Jerue KiA [9665]
87th FS/79th FG	P-47D 42-27960 attacked barges in river NE Caorle, shot down by Flak from barges, crashed off coast S Caorle 1120; 1/Lt Keith S.Croskery KiA [9596]
65th FS/57th FG	P-47D 42-26795 *Jackie VI* not seen leave clouds 15/20m W Siena 1515; 1/Lt George C.Lovato KiA [9597]
64th FS/57th FG	P-47D 42-29003 hit by Flak, crashed 50y off shore of Grosseto l/g 1600; 1/Lt Paul M.Hall rescued, returned

German Claims				
Flak	3.Brigade	P-47	Correggio	1500
Eins.2./NAGr 13	Uffz Gunther Weil	Auster III	W Baccarat	1645

German Casualties

	LKS reports one Bf 109 lost in combat

Italian ANR Claims					
5ª Sq, 2° Gr C	Ten Fausto Filippi	Bf 109G	P-47	nr Lonato	1315-
6ª Sq, 2° Gr C	M.llo Tullio Covre	Bf 109G	P-47	nr Lonato	1315-
5ª Sq, 2° Gr C	Serg Magg Attilio Sanson	Bf 109G	P-47	nr Lonato	1315-

Italian ANR Casualties

5ª Sq, 2° Gr C	Bf 109 crashed nr Desenzano; Ten Enrico Canavese KiA
6ª Sq, 2° Gr C	Bf 109 crashed nr Desenzano; Ten Tiberio Biasi KiA

November 1944

During November Timothy operations were introduced to the 7 SAAF Wing squadrons. These required the fighter-bombers to strafe and bomb parallel to a smoke screen laid down ahead of advancing troops in a variation of close air support. The success of this technique greatly reduced casualties among advancing troops where they were often just a few hundred yards from enemy positions.

Wednesday, 1 November 1944

As far as is known the II./SG 10 detachment finally arrived in Skopje. They promptly encountered the situation that as no German aircraft had been operating by day in the northern Yugoslavian area, their own ground forces considered everything in the air to be hostile and shot at them. An Ultra decrypt noted a signal was issued to railway Flak units in the area that friendly FW 190s would be operating and so the guns must only engage aircraft which attacked or were "uncontestably recognised as hostile".

Ultra also noted a complaint from the detachment commander, tentatively identified as Oblt Berger, that despite firing off the necessary recognition signals, the unit had been continually shot at by the Flak gunners of German units while in transit, three of the Focke-Wulfs incurring enough damage to put them out of action for 48 hours, and to cap this off one was shot down on its approach to land. This left the unit's strength that evening as seven FW 190s, of which three were serviceable, and six pilots. What such a small force was ex-

The pilots of 335 Squadron at Hassani in November 1944, left to right: Plt Offs Kalogeridis, Plionis, Michailidis, Georgopoulos, Flt Lt Voutsinas, Sqn Ldr Doukas (the commanding officer), Plt Offs Vladousis, Fragou and Hatzioannou. The Spitfire has its spinner painted in the Greek national colours.

pected to achieve says more about the lethal combination of lack of capacity and wishful thinking bordering on the delusional prevalent in the German command.

During the day the naval Flak unit protecting the rail line at Skopje claimed a Bulgarian Ju 87 shot down.

British Casualties					
5 SAAF Sqn	Mustang III HB950 left 0730, shot down by Flak 11km NW Padua 0820; Capt K.C.Kelsey KiA				
5 SAAF Sqn	Mustang III HB935 left 1340, shot down by Flak, crash-landed nr Dobrinj 1720; Lt R.W.P.Manning WiA, rescued and evacuated by partisans				
German Claims					
Flak	3/31 Naval Car 5		Bulgarian Ju 87	Skopje railway station	1600
German Casualties					
II./SG 10	FW 190F-8 WNr 931823 shot down by own Flak while landing at Skopje, crashed and caught fire; Uffz Dess KiA				
II./SG 10	3 FW 190Fs damaged by own Flak, landed at Skopje				

Thursday, 2 November 1944

Four FW 190s sortied to attack enemy positions south of Kumanovo but heavy Flak fire over German-held territory forced them to jettison their bombs and shot one of them down, this time the pilot was unharmed. With two FW 190s now destroyed and three badly damaged by friendly fire, Generalmajor Hans Korte, commanding general of the Luftwaffe in Greece and Generaloberst Alexander Löhr (commanding Army Group E) agreed to suspend ground-attack operations "until fire discipline has been restored" in XXII. Armee Korps' area.

Another Ultra stated that Ju 52s were urgently required at Skopje, as the majority of the wounded were there, but with insufficient aircraft on hand to evacuate them.

British Casualties	
6 Sqn	Hurricane IV KZ551 taking off from Vis after a sweep, hit a ridge, belly-landed; pilot safe
US Casualties	
417th NFS	Beaufighter VIf BT287 Sad Sack #2 lost over S France, last seen 10m E Bourg at 2010; 1/Lt Jesse W.Barryhill, 2/Lt Raymond Rodgers and passenger KiA [9942]

Friday, 3 November 1944

5 SAAF Squadron Mustangs strafed an airfield north-west of Zagreb 0655-1010 claiming three Ju 52/3ms destroyed and one Ju 87 and three Ju 52/3ms damaged, all on the ground.

In the afternoon SG 10's detachment clashed west of Kumanovo with 11 Bulgarian Ju 87s, two of which were claimed shot down and three damaged. Only one Ju 87 was in fact lost. A 22-year-old Bulgarian pilot, Lieutenant Stoiu Stoianoff Kafedieff, baled out and was captured by the Germans. From him it was learned that his unit, the 2nd Stuka Polk, was based at Sofia-Vrasdebana and commanded by a Captain Karalvamov. They had flown four operations against vehicle convoys in Macedonia and prior to the mission of 3 November had lost two Ju 87s to Flak at Prilep. Normal serviceability was about 20 aircraft out of 30, since no spares were available; there were no anti-aircraft defences on their airfield, nor any Russian units – in fact they had hardly any contact with the Soviets.

British Claims			
5 SAAF Sqn	Lt J.H.M.Davidson	Mustang III HB947 'A'	Ju 52/3m and Ju 87 Damaged (on ground)
British Casualties			
5 SAAF Sqn	Mustang III HB939 left 0655, hit by Flak WNW Zagreb 0810, crashed on airfield; Lt E.R.Borland KiA		
145 Sqn	Spitfire VIII JG159 left 1435 strafing, intense light Flak caused glycol leak, pilot baled out over Allied lines 1505; Flt Sgt R.M.P.Williams safe		
Bulgarian Casualties			
2nd Stuka Pulk	Ju 87 shot down by FW 190 W Kumanovo; Lieutenant S.S.Kafedieff POW		
German Claims			
II./SG 10	unstated pilots	2 Ju 87s	W Kumanovo
II./SG 10	unstated pilots	3 Ju 87s Damaged	W Kumanovo
German Casualties			
II./SG 10	FW 190 damaged by return fire, crash-landed at Skopje		

Saturday, 4 November 1944

Wt Off John Anthony Ulm crash-landed on Rimini airfield, after being hit by Flak. He was the son of the famous Charles Ulm, the co-pilot of the record-breaking aircraft 'Southern Cross', piloted by Charles Kingsford-Smith, when in 1928 the pair made the first ever crossing of the Pacific by air from America to Australia.

The Italian Co-Belligerent Air Force was very active on this day, carrying out several armed reconnaissance sorties over the Albanian front; three pilots failed to return and five aircraft were lost or badly damaged. Among these was one of the Spitfires recently assigned to 51° Stormo, while two more were badly damaged.

The 800 Squadron Hellcat flown by Sub Lt P.S.Craig was hit by Flak and the engine burst into flames on landing, as HMS *Emperor* completed flying 455 sorties in the Aegean, more than double that achieved by any other carrier.

A P-39 of the Italian Co-Belligerent Air Force 4° Stormo. Two aircraft of this type were lost during a fighter-bomber mission on 4 November.

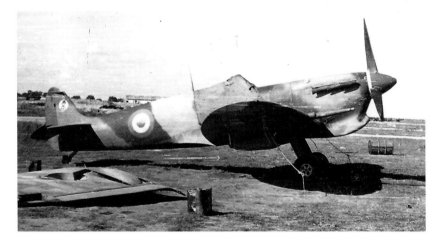

A Spitfire Vc '20-3' freshly delivered to the 20° Gruppo of 51° Stormo Caccia of the Italian Co-Belligerent Air Force at Leverano. On 4 November this unit lost an aircraft while two more were badly damaged.

SG 10's detachment flew six operations totalling 22 sorties against tank and vehicle concentrations in the Podujevo area, claiming "very good hits... considerable casualties and losses in motor transport probable" despite defence by "Flak of all calibres, in part well placed".

British Claims

5 SAAF Sqn	Lt C.G.Begg	Mustang III KH456	Ju 52/3m in flames	Brod-Sarajevo rail line	0810-1135

British Casualties

351 Sqn	Hurricane IV LF453 'B' left 0915, shot down by Flak near Sucevici, 30km N Knin, pilot baled; Capt Milan Karić POW
145 Sqn	Spitfire VIII JF744 left 0840 on Rover Paddy, hit by Flak; crash-landed on Rimini a/f 1030; Wt Off J.A.Ulm safe
145 Sqn	Spitfire VIII MT560 left 0840 on Rover Paddy, hit by Flak, damaged Cat II; Wt Off A.L.Briand safe
800 Sqn	Hellcat I hit by Flak, on landing on HMS *Emperor* engine burst into flames; Sub Lt P.S.Craig safe
272 Sqn	Beaufighter X NE550 'C' left 1445 on armed recce of Fiume area, on return from operations at dusk flew into a hillside 10m S Termoli; Flt Sgt R.E.E.Manktelow /Flt Sgt I.D.Goodwin KiA

US Casualties

346th FS/350th FG	P-47D 42-74984 '6C9' shot down by Flak, crashed W Asti 1445; Capt Zane E.Carlson KiA [14562]
489th BS/340th BG	B-25J 43-27746 '9E' shot down by Flak, crashed at Alessandria 1324; 1/Lt Donald H.Rossler and four KiA, one returned [9711]
488th BS/340th BG	B-25J 43-27770 '8F' left 1205 to bomb Casale Monferrato, hit by Flak, ditched nr Cape Corse 1432; 2/Lt Byron D.King and one KiA, four returned [10778]
442nd BS/320th BG	B-26B-50 42-95992 '39' left 1422 to bomb Cassano d'Adda railroad bridge, tyre blew before take-off, broke up and caught fire, five minutes later the bombs exploded; 1/Lt Charles W.Schane Jr and two WiA, two KiA

Italian Co-Belligerent Casualties

90ª Sq, 10° Gr, 4° St	P-39Q 44-3137 hit by Flak in right wing, pilot baled out 40km S Kukës; Ten Fabio Clauser MiA
90ª Sq, 10° Gr, 4° St	P-39Q hit by Flak, pilot baled out 10km S Kukës; Ten Marco De Ferrari evaded, helped by partisans, returned later
356ª Sq, 20° Gr, 51° St	Spitfire Vc JK803 hit by Flak Durazzo area, failed to return; Ten Alberto Veronese MiA
356ª Sq, 20° Gr, 51° St	Spitfire Vb JK784 hit by Flak Durazzo area, crashed on landing; Ten Arnaldo Laurenti WiA
356ª Sq, 20° Gr, 51° St	Spitfire V EF640 hit by Flak Durazzo area, belly-landed; Serg Magg Mario Donini safe

German Casualties

7./TG 2	Ju 52/3m WNr 641401 8T+PR force-landed 100% destroyed; Oblt Helmut Pixberg, Maj Gerhard Dudeck and three WiA

Sunday, 5 November 1944

Twelve Bf 109s from 2° Gruppo Caccia surprised B-26s of the 320th Bomb Group attacking the line. The pilots claimed three bombers shot down and six damaged; five were subsequently, and correctly, confirmed. The bombers' gunners claimed a number of fighters destroyed.

British Casualties

3 SAAF Sqn	Spitfire IXc MJ680 'E' blew up in bomb dive at Forlì a/f 1415, crashed close NW boundary; 2/Lt H.D.Wheeler KiA
260 Sqn	Mustang III FB248 left 0745 shot down by Flak SE Zagreb; Lt C.B.Susskind baled, safe with partisans, back on 24 November
260 Sqn	Mustang III FB271 left 1300, hit by Flak, pilot baled Zagreb-Brod area; 2/Lt P.J.van der Merwe evaded

450 Sqn	Kittyhawk IV FX842 left 1445, hit by Flak when attacking a strongpoint near Ravenna, blew up at 4,000ft in dive-bombing attack 1540 possibly hit by small-arms fire; Flt Sgt A.Y.Cousins KiA
19 SAAF Sqn	Beaufighter X 'G' left 1020, attacked barracks at Tirana, damaged by Flak, observer wounded, ditched off Brindisi; Lt G.H.Black safe/Sgt Cutler WiA

US Claims

320th BG	gunners	B-26s	3 Bf 109s	Rovereto area
320th BG	gunners	B-26s	2 Bf 109s Probable	Rovereto area
320th BG	gunners	B-26s	FW 190	Rovereto area
320th BG	gunners	B-26s	MC.202	Rovereto area

US Casualties

525th FS/86th FG	P-47D 42-26974 *Sack Time Shirley* blast from own bombs 2.5m SE Vignola 1110; 1/Lt Clifford A.Karrels returned [9708]
526th FS/86th FG	P-47D 42-20125 '42' shot down by Flak crashed 1m NE Lonigo 1500; 1/Lt Raymond J.Huff KiA [9706]
527th FS/86th FG	P-47D 42-26966 '84' shot down by Flak 15m NW Pistoia 1600; 1/Lt Raymond L.Maloney POW [9705]
66th FS/57th FG	P-47D 42-27070 damaged Cat 2 by explosion of ammo dump, crashed between Reggio and Modena; pilot safe
486th BS/340th BG	B-25J 43-27709 '6M' *Schnapps/Yo-Yo* last seen entering cloud bank NW Elba Island en route to bomb Padua East railway bridge, lost over Mediterranean 1020; 1/Lt Richard H.Brandle and five KiA [9703]
444th BS/320th BG	B-26G 42-107532 '86' *Gean* shot down by Messerschmitt nr Riva del Garda 1134; 1/Lt James R.Logsdon and three POW, two KiA [9595]
441st BS/320th BG	B-26G 43-34396 '01' shot down by e/a nr Ala 1128; 2/Lt Truman C.Cole (captured on 25 December nr Udine) and two POW, four KiA [9598]
444th BS/320th BG	B-26B 43-34261 '84' damaged by e/a, reached Corsica then crew baled out 1307; Lt Charles W.Paul Kamanski and four rescued by Walrus W3048 of Flt Lt G.M.Gallacher/Wt Off V.Udberg of 293 Sqn and a HSL
42nd BW	6 B-26s damaged over Rovereto

German Casualties

II./SG 10	FW 190 WNr 930854 force-landed near Novi Pazar, Serbia; Obgfr Franz Antes KiA
	LKS reports one Ju 88 and one Bf 109 lost in combat

Italian ANR Claims

5ª Sq, 2° Gr C	Cap Mario Bellagambi	Bf 109G	B-26	Lake Garda area	ca 1130
4ª Sq, 2° Gr C	Serg Magg Carlo Cavagliano	Bf 109G	B-26	Lake Garda area	ca 1130
6ª Sq, 2° Gr C	Serg Magg Luigi Pacini	Bf 109G	B-26	Lake Garda area	ca 1130
4ª Sq, 2° Gr C	Ten Antonio Camaioni	Bf 109G	B-26	Lake Garda area	ca 1130
4ª Sq, 2° Gr C	Serg Magg Loris Baldi	Bf 109G	B-26	Lake Garda area	ca 1130

Italian ANR Casualties

4ª Sq, 2° Gr C	Bf 109G crash-landed at Villafranca; Ten Antonio Camaioni slightly WiA
4ª Sq, 2° Gr C	Bf 109G crash-landed at Villafranca; S.Ten Emanuele Rosas safe
6ª Sq, 2° Gr C	Bf 109G WNr 162467 crash-landed nr Pescantina Veronese; Serg Magg Rolando Ancillotti safe

Monday, 6 November 1944

On this date, personnel of all three of the RAF's Greek Squadrons (13 [H], 335 and 336) arrived at Athens on a ship and began to establish themselves at Hassani (Kalamaki) airfield. Their aircraft flew over from Italy on the 14th.

On a mission with the 347th Fighter Squadron two Brazilians joined eight US pilots attacking artillery positions south of Bologna when 2° Ten Cordeiro e Silva was shot down becoming the first Brazilian airman to die in Italy.

British Casualties

112 Sqn	Mustang III FB320 'N' left 0700; shot down by Flak at Slovenske Konjice near Maribor 0845; Plt Off R.J.Deeble KiA
5 SAAF Sqn	Mustang III KH487 shot down by Flak Sarajevo marshalling yards 0940; Lt R.R.Linsley KiA
5 SAAF Sqn	Mustang III KH475 damaged Cat II by Flak; Capt W.J.Lombard safe
7 SAAF Sqn	Spitfire IXc EN528 left 1235, hit by Flak, spun in while bombing at 10m NW Forlì 1250; Lt P.J.du Toit KiA
40 SAAF Sqn	Spitfire IX left 1450 on ArtyR, shot down by Flak near Forlì 1600, pilot reported baling out; Lt S.S.M.Gray POW

US Casualties

87th FS/79th FG	P-47D 42-25664 *Betty Jo/Haid Gal* shot down by Flak nr Ravenna 1555; 1/Lt Robert P.Norman POW [9702]
66th FS/57th FG	P-47D 42-27011 hit by Flak between Bologna and Modena 1505, Cat 2 damaged; pilot safe
1° Gr Caça/350th FG	P-47D 42-26782 shot down by Flak 1230; 2° Ten John Richardson Cordeiro e Silva KiA

2/6 Orlyak	Bf 109G-6 failed to return from a combat mission; Por K.I.Kalvachev MiA

Tuesday, 7 November 1944

Eleven Bulgarian Ju 87s dive-bombed and damaged a bridge near Skopje, and in this area Spitfires damaged two locomotives. Eight Bulgarian Bf 109s also strafed in this area, and the 15th Air Force bombers and Lightning escorts were also very active, resulting in a clash with their Russian allies.

Over recent days the RAF had begun to use Wellington bombers in daylight over the less-defended areas of Yugoslavia. On this day 37 Squadron attacked Sarajevo, losing two aircraft, one probably to a pair of NAGr 12 Bf 109s.

Ultra decrypts cited a report that during the night seven He 111s, 15 Ju 52/3ms and one Ju 290, carrying 248 wounded, 30 men and 7.5 tons of equipment, left.

British Casualties

213 Sqn	Mustang III FB505 left 1345 to bomb bridge at Kukës, shot down by Flak E Vavi Dejes; Flt Sgt D.E.Firman KiA
250 Sqn	Kittyhawk IV FT879 left 1350, dive-bombed three houses N Forlì a/f, seen to be on fire in bomb dive, pilot baled out over forward troops too low for parachute to deploy; Sgt J.M.Dick KiA
87 Sqn	Spitfire IX JL353 left Fano 0635 on strafing recce, hit by 20mm Flak between Lavezzola and Alfonsine, pilot baled out nr Lake Comacchio; Flt Sgt R.M.Rayson evaded, returned on 22 November
37 Sqn	Wellington X MF349 'X' left 1411 to raid Sarajevo marshalling yards, presumed shot down by Flak or shot down by Bf 109s of NAGr 12, FTR; Flg Off G.E.Eid and Sgt J.W.Gall reportedly captured by Chetniks and murdered, three evaded
37 Sqn	Wellington X LP603 'R' left 1411 to raid Sarajevo marshalling yards, exploded on touch down presumed due to bomb hang up; Flg Off R.F.Lavack and one safe, two WiA, two KiA

US Casualties

522nd FS/27th FBG	P-47D 42-26432 failed to pull out of dive nr Imola 0935; 2/Lt Donald M.Harris KiA [15841]
85th FS/79th FG	P-47D 42-28311 shot down by Flak NE Imola 1635; 1/Lt Eugene T.Van Houten POW [9704]
347th FS/350th FG	P-47D 42-27197 '7A2' went into spin SW Siena; 1/Lt Paul A.Tarantino KiA [9980]

German Claims

1.Eins./NAGr 12	Lt Haus			
1.Eins./NAGr 12	Uffz Heinrich Voss	Wellington	WSW Sarajevo	1605

Wednesday, 8 November 1944

112 Squadron had set off to attack a target in Yugoslavia and found it obscured by fog, so had diverted to a target near Venice. This target was one which Plt Off 'Knobby' Clark knew well and had the maps and been briefed for. He took charge in the air, led them to it, and they bombed it. They all came out safely, but nobody could give Clark a satisfactory report on how they had left it. He therefore returned to over-fly it to look and the guns were waiting for him. He had gone well over his 200-hour tour when he was killed.

In the early afternoon a formation of B-25s from the 480th Bomb Squadron, 340th Bomb Group was attacked by three Bf 109s near Caorle north-east of Venice, without result.

British Casualties

250 Sqn	Kittyhawk IV FX700 left 1430, attacked bridge S Ravenna, not seen after the attack; Plt Off D.P.Feeny MiA
94 Sqn	Spitfire Vc JK162 left 1200, caught in explosion of strafed train, seen to crash 15-20m SE Skopje 1330; Lt C.G.Boshoff KiA
112 Sqn	Mustang III KH601 'Z' left 1300, shot down by Flak at 1500 near Cavanella d'Adige 17m S Venice; Plt Off G.G.Clark KiA
92 Sqn	Spitfire VIII JF664 left 1505 on Rover Paddy, shot down by Flak or engine failed, pilot baled out into Allied lines at Gambettola; Plt Off S.R Fry safe

US Casualties

523rd FS/27th FBG	P-47D 42-19585 hit by Flak nr Imola 1330; Capt D.L.Staehle baled safely
444th BS/320th BG	B-26C 42-107556 '98' *Cindy the II* left 1146 to bomb railroad bridge at Casale Monferrato, hit by Flak in right engine, crashed nr Balzola 1322; Capt David Q.Hammond Jr and four KiA [9707]

German Claims

Flak	I/12	B-26	Balzola	1222

German Casualties

Wekusta 27	Ju 188F-1 Q5+E missing, reportedly shot down; Uffz Lothar Abel and four MiA

Thursday, 9 November 1944

25 SAAF Squadron flew its final Ventura raid before concentrating on conversion to Marauders. The Ju 52/3m shot down by Lt Begg was the 71st and last victory claimed by pilots of 5 SAAF Squadron.

British Claims					
5 SAAF Sqn	Lt C.G.Begg	Mustang III KH487 'H'	Ju 52/3m	70m S Zagreb	0630-1000

British Casualties	
5 SAAF Sqn	Mustang III KH487 'H' left 0630, hit by fire from Ju 52/3m near Zagreb before shooting it down; Lt C.G.Begg safe
351 Sqn	Hurricane IV LF569 left 1150 to attack a target at Risan, Yugoslavia, became lost in bad weather; Sgt Jovan Pesic MiA
351 Sqn	Hurricane IV LF509 left 1150 to attack warehouses at Trebinje, Yugoslavia, hit by Flak, crash-landed 6m S Bielce; Plt Off Josip Klokocovnik rescued by partisans, returned to unit on 19 November

US Casualties	
86th FS/79th FG	P-47D 44-19589 lost 10m E Rimini 1630; 2/Lt James E.Anderson Jr KiA [13115]

German Casualties	
16./TG 1	Ju 52/3m WNr 501137 IZ+KQ lost Agram-Skopje; Obfw Paul Koslowski and three MiA

Friday, 10 November 1944

Twenty-two Bf 109s from 2° Gruppo Caccia of ANR were scrambled at about 1220 to intercept B-26s of 320th Bomb Group; the bombers were attacked over the Lake Garda area at 1240 and the Italian pilots claimed two B-26s shot down. The pilots of 320th Bomb Group reported that 25 to 30 Bf 109s, G.55s, MC.202s, and FW 190s (majority were Bf 109s) commenced attacking the formation at Desenzano, and continued attacks until the formation reached the River Po on the return. Markings of Bf 109s were dark grey-green with white stripes on the fuselage, from the cockpit back, black crosses with white outlines on the wings. The G.55s and MC.202s were speckled brown and grey fuselages, light bellies, with German insignia. Two Bf 109s had white spinners and clipped wings; the FW 190s were black with German markings. The fighters stayed out of Flak but remained in the area, resuming attacks once the Flak stopped.

At about 1300 P-47Ds of the 57th Fighter Group which were dive-bombing in the Lake Garda area saw a lone Bf 109 attacking some twin-engined bombers. Many US pilots attacked and the Messerschmitt was claimed shot down jointly by five pilots. This was a Bf 109G of 2° Gruppo flown by Serg Pacini, back from the previous attack, who was killed.

British Casualties	
601 Sqn	Spitfire IX PT648, shot down by Flak in the Forlì-Faenza area 1045; Wt Off A.J.Haynes KiA

US Claims					
320th BG	gunners	B-26	Bf 109	Lake Garda area	1230-1300
320th BG	gunners	B-26s	5 Bf 109s Damaged	Lake Garda area	1230-1300
320th BG	gunners	B-26s	FW 190	Lake Garda area	1230-1300
64th FS/57th FG	Capt Frank E.Boyd Jr	P-47D			
64th FS/57th FG	1/Lt Paul M.Hall	P-47D			
64th FS/57th FG	1/Lt Lawrence G.Grace Jr	P-47D	Bf 109	Lake Garda area	1300
64th FS/57th FG	1/Lt John.P.Anderson	P-47D			
64th FS/57th FG	1/Lt George W.Anderson	P-47D			

US Casualties	
64th FS/57th FG	P-47D 42-29067 *Thunderbolt* bombed railway bridge S Ostiglia, shot down by Flak, crash-landed 1030; 1/Lt Warren R.Schultz POW [9710]
524th FS/27th FBG	P-47D 42-19586 hit by Flak 1400; Lt Taylor WiA
446th BS/321st BG	B-25J 43-27732 *Loydale* left 1135 to bomb RR bridge at Ostiglia, hit by Flak, crashed nr Traversetolo 1405; 1/Lt Walton M.Ligon and two KiA, two POW, two evaded [9962]
448th BS/321st BG	B-25J 43-27805 *Desirable* left 1135 to bomb RR bridge at Ostiglia, hit by Flak, crashed nr Pisa 1410; 1/Lt Douglas R.Anderson and two POW, four evaded [9952]
447th BS/321st BG	B-25J 43-28082 *Traveling Comedy* left 1135 to bomb RR bridge at Ostiglia badly damaged by Flak, crash-landed nr Pisa; 1/Lt Gordon A.Ramey and three KiA, one WiA, one POW, one escaped [15275]
447th BS/321st BG	B-25J 43-27492 *Reddie Teddie* left 1135 to bomb RR bridge at Ostiglia damaged by Flak, returned; Capt J.Maurice Wiginton and five safe, one WiA

| 448th BS/321st BG | B-25J 43-4068 *The Dutchess* to bomb ferry terminal at Ostiglia, damaged by Flak, crashed at base 1505; 1/Lt Milford E.Kruse and five safe | | | | |

German Casualties

| 3./NSGr 9 | Ju 87D-5 E8+HL damaged by AA nr Loiano; Obfhr Peter Stollwerk/Uffz Franz Fischer safe | | | | |

Italian ANR Claims

| 4ª Sq, 2° Gr C | Serg Magg Stefano Camerani | Bf 109G | B-26 | Lake Garda area | 1240 |
| 4ª Sq, 2° Gr C | Serg Magg Loris Baldi | Bf 109G | B-26 | Lake Garda area | 1240 |

Italian ANR Casualties

6ª Sq, 2° Gr C	Bf 109G shot down in combat; Serg Luigi Pacini KiA
4ª Sq, 2° Gr C	Bf 109G damaged in combat with B-26s; Serg Magg Loris Baldi safe
2° Gr C	Bf 109G-12 destroyed on the ground at Villafranca by strafing attack

Saturday, 11 November 1944

In another case of fratricide, US P-51s attacked six Spitfires of 43 Squadron near Padua shooting two of them down with the death of one pilot and injury to the other in this tragic event.

Independent operations for 1° Grupo de Caça began when at 0800 eight P-47Ds of the *Vermelha* and *Verde* Flights led by Capts Lafayette and Pamplona mounted an uneventful sweep between Bergamo, Verona and Mantua.

British Casualties

| 43 Sqn | Spitfire IX PT585 left 1230 on sweep, shot down 10m NW Padua by 15th AF P-51s; Flt Lt A.M.Cummings KiA |
| 43 Sqn | Spitfire VIII MT667 left 1230 on sweep, shot down 10m NW Padua by 15th AF P-51s, crash-landed at Rimini l/g; Flt Lt E.W.Creed WiA |

US Casualties

527th FS/86th FG	P-47D 44-19613 '80' shot down by Flak 2m W Oderzo 1200; 2/Lt Francis P.Maleszewski KiA [9999]
428th BS/310th BG	B-25J 43-27719 shot down by Flak 6m E Arco 1230; 2/Lt Jared H.Grossmith and five KiA [9848]
379th BS/310th BG	B-25J 44-28917 shot down by Flak W Casale Monferrato 1340; 1/Lt LaVerle T.Hacking and four POW, two evaded [9851]
414th NFS	Beaufighter lost over Italy due to engine trouble; 1/Lt Reuben Welliver Jr and 2/Lt William F.Pownall KiA [15267]

Sunday, 12 November 1944

To increase the range of its Spitfires 94 Squadron began using Sedes airfield, just outside the city of Salonika some 150 miles to the north, as an advance landing ground for refuelling and rearming. This new area of operations, bordering on some of the smaller Axis allied countries and neutral Turkey was at times to cause 94 Squadron's pilots problems of identity. This was highlighted by the claim on this date regarding an encounter with a Bf 109 which they reported had "<< X markings on the fuselage". The squadron's operations diary recorded that "the 109 may have been Bulgarian".

The Bulgarians too were now operating over the Balkans as at 1105 17 Bf 109Gs of 2./6 and 3./6 Iztrebitel-en orlyak (fighter group), flying for the first time with new Bulgarian markings (pre-war Bulgarian tri-colour) attacked Obilicevo airfield near Pristina and claimed the destruction of no less than 12 German planes – two by 2./6 and ten by 3./6 – one Ju 88C (Captain Krsto A.Atanasov), seven Ju 52s, two Fi 156s, one Bü 133 and one Hs 129. Actual results were far more modest: Maj Maier of the Airfield Command at Pristina reported that an Hs 126 and an Fi 156 had been damaged, a man killed and four more wounded in a low-level attack by six Bf 109s.

After the attack, Bulgarian pilots continued with low-flying armed reconnaissance over the communications in the Skopje-Kacanik-Pristina area. Four aircraft attacked a train near Lipljan but then Captain Atanasov lost contact with the rest of the formation. As he tried to catch up with them, he was attacked by five unidentified Allied single-engine fighters. Atanasov claimed that he managed to shoot one down before he escaped to Bulgaria at treetop height. Allies informed Yugoslav partisans that Spitfires attacked one Bf 109 at 5,000 feet over Gnjilane. Strikes were observed on the right wing and pieces were seen falling off, and it was claimed as damaged (see claim on page 308).

The Bulgarian Bf 109 encountered by 94 Squadron was flown by Capt Krsto Atanasov who claimed a Spitfire destroyed, although none were in fact hit.

Above: On 12 November Flt Lt Roger Howley flew Spitfire Vc JK731 'R' of 94 Squadron in an attack on marshalling yards at Pristina that engaged a Bf 109. The Spitfires got close enough to identify the '<< X' markings on the fuselage that identified it as Bulgarian. Left: A Bf 109G-6 of the Bulgarian 3/6 Orylak, one of which had a brief encounter with Spitfires of 94 Squadron over Kosovo.

At 0820 Bf 109s of 2° Gruppo Caccia ANR took off from Ghedi and were over Villafranca a few minutes later. There ten Bf 109s of the same unit were just taking off to join them when they were attacked by P-47Ds of 350th Fighter Group. Two Italian pilots claimed a P-47 shot down in cooperation.

The Baltimore-equipped 132° Gruppo of the Italian Co-Belligerent Air Force was assigned to the Balkan Air Force's 254th Wing on this day; it would start operating over Yugoslavia on 18 November.

British Claims

94 Sqn	Flt Lt R.J.Howley	Spitfire Vc JK731			
94 Sqn	Flg Off G.S.Hulse	Spitfire Vc EF539	Bf 109 Damaged	N Pristina	1015-1230
94 Sqn	Plt Off G.Barber	Spitfire Vc JK649			
94 Sqn	Flt Sgt N.W.Tickner	Spitfire Vc LZ928			

British Casualties

92 Sqn	Spitfire VIII JF894 left 1025 on weather recce over Fiume area, FTR; Plt Off J.J.Lane MiA
92 Sqn	Spitfire VIII JF466 left 1025 on weather recce over Fiume area, FTR; Wt Off E.Smith MiA
450 Sqn	Kittyhawk IV FX835 left 1205 leading 12 a/c to dive bomb and strafe a target, attacked 1240, on return flight called formation to say he could not make base and crash-landed in own lines; Flt Lt R.H.Burden safe
3 RAAF Sqn	Kittyhawk IV FX576 'B' lost while strafing NW Forlì 0725; Flt Sgt W.T.Dobbie POW

5 SAAF Sqn	Mustang III KH456 shot down by Flak Zagreb-Maribor rail bridge NE Celje 0850-1140; Maj T.C.MacMurray WiA and POW, leg amputated				
5 SAAF Sqn	Mustang III FB289 shot down by Flak 40km NW Zagreb 1040; Lt D.H.R.McLeod evaded and returned in December				
40 SAAF Sqn	Spitfire IX EN461 left 1350 on ArtyR near Faenza, presumed hit by Flak, crash-landed near Forlì 1430; Capt P.H.Donnelly WiA				

US Claims

346th FS/350th FG	Capt F.H.Michel	P-47D	2 Bf 109s Probable	1m NE Villafranca	0720-0915
346th FS/350th FG	Capt F.H.Michel	P-47D	Bf 109 Damaged	1m NE Villafranca	0720-0915
346th FS/350th FG	1/Lt Robert C.Tomlinson	P-47D	Bf 109 Damaged	1m NE Villafranca	0720-0915

US Casualties

345th FS/350th FG	P-47D 42-28346 hit building while strafing 0.5m E S.ta Caterina; 2/Lt Garvin C.Pape [9850]
346th FS/350th FG	P-47D 42-28619 '6A7' failed to recover from spin NW Florence; 2/Lt Carl L.Brazil Jr KiA [12318]
346th FS/350th FG	P-47D damaged in combat; Capt F.H.Michel safe
66th FS/57th FG	P-47D 42-28385 destroyed by own bomb blast 1410; 2/Lt Eugene L.Noyd KiA [9846]
51st TCS/62nd TCG	C-47A 42-24203 'C' *Bar Fly* lost over Mediterranean; 2/Lt Oren E.Leeds and five KiA [9976]

Bulgarian Claims

3/6 Orlyak	Capt Krsto A.Atanasov		Spitfire (!)	near Lipljan

German Claims

Flak	3/31 Naval Railway Car M.7		Spitfire	Priluzzi	1010

Italian ANR Claims

4ª Sq 2° Gr C	S.Ten Amedeo Fagiano	Bf 109G	}		
4ª Sq 2° Gr C	Ten Antonio 'Max' Longhini	Bf 109G	P-47	Villafranca	0820

Sunday-Monday, 12/13 November 1944

US Casualties

86th BS/47th BG	A-20K 44-36271 '71' shot down by heavy Flak near Modena during night armed recce 0130; 2/Lt Ross F.Wright KiA, three evaded [9959]

Partisans of the Goce Delčev Brigade parade through the Yugoslav city of Skopje on 13 November after its capture.

7 SAAF Squadron Spitfire IX JL254 'A' force-landed on the banks of Lake Comacchio after being hit by Flak; however, Lt Buddell evaded capture.

Monday, 13 November 1944

British Casualties	
601 Sqn	Spitfire IXb PL372 left 1100 to attack San Martino, in bomb dive exploded and crashed; Flt Sgt W.F.Waters KiA
92 Sqn	Spitfire VIII JF513 left 0745 engine failure or Flak near Forlì 0820, pilot baled out; Flt Sgt P.G.T.Hoolihan safe
4 SAAF Sqn	Spitfire IXc MH976 'E' left 1245 shot down by Flak during bombing dive S Ravenna 1300; Lt W.M.Thompson seen to bale out and apparently land safely, but KiA
7 SAAF Sqn	Spitfire IXc JL254 left 1155, shot down by ground fire 1235 NE Ravenna, force-landed on beach Lake Comacchio; Lt J.C.Buddell evaded with partisans, returned to sqn on 5 December
US Casualties	
527th FS/86th FG	P-47D '74' hit by Flak nr Tolle 1015, pilot baled out but chute failed; Capt Newton L.Saunders KiA
414th NFS	Beaufighter VIf KV931 lost u/k cause near La Spezia 0546; Capt Franklin W.Chapman POW/2/Lt Floyd P.Foss evaded [9981]
German Casualties	
1./NAGr 12	W 34 WNr 1641 engine trouble, crash-landed nr Travnik, badly damaged; Oblt Emmersdorfer safe

Tuesday, 14 November 1944

The code breakers at Bletchley Park intercepted a message reporting that a Me 410 had been fired on by its own navy Flak as it passed over the Italian coast at the mouth of the River Piave at 1405, being hit in the port engine and the tail. It was fired on again at 1417 near Chioggia by 2cm Flak, despite firing recognition signals on both occasions. At 1455 the aircraft crashed while attempting an emergency landing, the crew were wounded, and the aircraft lost.

German Casualties	
2.(F)/122	Me 410 F6+SK damaged by own Flak at River Piave mouth and Chioggia, crash-landed at Ghedi and destroyed; Fhr Sewald/Obgfr Wachtfeidl WiA

Wednesday, 15 November 1944

Two pilots from 32 Squadron took off at 1025 to strafe the Skopje-Mitrovica road and encountered a lone Ju 52/3m near Skopje which they forced to land.

On 15 November Maj Rupert Frost, the Kommodore of NSGr 9, became the first NSGr pilot to be awarded the Knight's Cross.

Flt Lt Hatzilakos of 336 Squadron poses by his Spitfire Vc MA898 at Grottaglie before departing to Greece later in the day.

On this day the commanding officer of NSGr 9, Maj Rupert Frost was awarded the Knight's Cross, the first Nachtschlacht pilot to be so honoured.

British Claims

32 Sqn	Plt Off A.Oates	Spitfire Vc ER637	} Ju 52/3m	N Mitrovica	1025-1300
32 Sqn	Flg Off E.Evans	Spitfire Vc JK485			

US Casualties

10th TCS/60th TCG	C-47A 43-30649 'yellow 10 L' *One Hung Low* lost in bad weather 1030; 1/Lt Robert M.Arthur and three MiA [10138]

German Casualties

10./TG 2	Ju 52/3m WNr 501373 shot down 18km NE Pristina a/f, force-landed, badly damaged; one crew WiA, rest safe

Thursday, 16 November 1944

Wg Cdr R.N.Lambert DFC assumed command of 272 Squadron.

British Casualties

112 Sqn	Mustang III FB246 'P' crashed on take-off due to mechanical failure, attempted to land but struck 2 Marauder IIIs of 24 SAAF Sqn (HD436 42-96363 and HD451 42-96378) and a petrol bowser; Flg Off J.W.J.Roney DoW

US Casualties

524th FS/27th FBG	P-47D 42-26362 *Jane Scores* hit by Flak nr Suzzara 0917; 2/Lt Henry L.Nielsen POW [9988]
66th FS/57th FG	P-47D 42-27089 shot down by Flak 1030; 1/Lt William C.Tench evaded [9849]
444th BS/320th BG	B-26B 41-18190 '84' *Judy* left 1152 to bomb Santa Margherita rail bridge, hit by Flak nr Ostia Parmense 1400, reached the sea and ditched; 1/Lt Russell W.Jones and five KiA [9847]
441st BS/320th BG	B-26B '15' left 1134 to bomb Sant'Ambrogio di Valpolicella rail, damaged by Flak, reached base at Borgo, crash-landed 1439; 1/Lt Arnsdorff and seven safe

356ª Sq, 20° Gr, 51° St	Spitfire IX805 failed to return; Ten Fiorenzo Jannicelli MiA
378ª Sq, 155° Gr, 51° St	MC.205 MM 9311 hit by Flak over Albania, belly-landed at base; Ten Osvaldo Bartolozzi safe

German Casualties

	LKS reports one Bf 109 lost to enemy action

Thursday-Friday, 16/17 November 1944

US Casualties

417th NFS	Beaufighter VIf KW197 *Lois Mae* last heard from closing on an e/a 25m SE Nice at 2108; 2/Lts Jack DeVore/William Grinnell KiA [10215]

Friday, 17 November 1944

British Casualties

4 SAAF Sqn	Spitfire IXe PT831 'Q' shot down in flames by Flak when strafing N Bologna 1620; Capt M.W.V.Odendaal POW
7 SAAF Sqn	Spitfire IXc JL172 shot down by Flak S Faenza 1530; Lt D.C.Bosch KiA
450 Sqn	Kittyhawk IV FT936 left to bomb a bridge, probably hit in bomb dive by Flak, crashed; Sgt S.R.Moncrieff KiA
417 Sqn	Spitfire VIII MD352 left 1430 to bomb defended house near Forlì, hit by Flak, pilot baled out SW Forlì into Allied lines; Plt Off R.A.Shannon safe

US Casualties

64th FS/57th FG	P-47D 44-20132 flew camera-equipped a/c over target after attack, last seen 1410; Lt Charles R.Neumann KiA [9987]
65th FS/57th FG	P-47D 42-27948 hit by Flak, crashed between Bologna and Castel San Pietro 1120; pilot safe
65th FS/57th FG	P-47D 42-75718 damaged Cat 2 by Flak 1445; pilot safe
437th BS/319th BG	B-25J 43-36122 left 1055 to bomb Tomba railway bridge, shot down by Flak, crashed nr S.Vito al Tagliamento 1254; 1/Lt Benjamin B.Betsill Jr and four KiA, two POW [9991]
488th BS/340th BG	B-25J 43-27504 '8K' right engine on fire; 2/Lt W.Y.Simpson and five rescued

The Spitfire of Flt Lt D.S.V.Rake (right) of 32 Squadron was hit by Flak when he was strafing a train on 18 November; he was rescued by Albanian peasants after force-landing.

Friday-Saturday, 17/18 November 1944

US Casualties	
416th NFS	Beaufighter VIf KV944 left Pisa 1745 on night-intruder mission to Bergamo-Brescia area, nothing heard after take-off, a fire was reported near Bergamo 2115; 2/Lt Joe S.Graham/Flt Off Richard Roop MiA [9993]

Saturday, 18 November 1944

A heavy attack was performed by 15th Air Force heavy bombers on the northern Italy airfields of Campoformido, Vicenza, Villafranca and Aviano. At least seven Luftwaffe aircraft were reportedly destroyed on the ground and 14 damaged, while ANR 2° Gruppo lost six Bf 109Gs at Aviano and had 14 aircraft damaged.

While strafing a train north of Mitrovica, Flt Lt Rake's 32 Squadron aircraft was hit in the cockpit by Flak, which smashed the radio and instrument panel and wounded him in the left arm and right hand. He continued to climb away, but his engine cut and he had to force land. All the time he was losing consciousness and became completely so when his Spitfire turned over on hitting a mound after landing. He came to as he was being rescued from the cockpit by local Albanians. He persuaded them to lend him a horse and set off, whereupon he encountered Bulgarian cavalry and his wounds were dressed by their doctor. He managed to return to his unit on 30 November.

British Casualties	
1 SAAF Sqn	Spitfire IXe PT728 'D' left 1535, engine cut while strafing after bombing strongpoint 16km SW Forlì, hit ridge and crashed 1605; Capt R.B.McKechnie WiA
4 SAAF Sqn	Spitfire IXe MJ739 'Z' left 1350, hit by Flak, crashed SW Forlì, pilot baled out 1430; Lt H.A.Carter safe
253 Sqn	Spitfire IX MH958 left 1345 on armed recce Mostar-Zeljusa-Jablanica; Plt Off R.Woods evaded
112 Sqn	Mustang III KH627 'B' left 0740 shot down by Flak attacking bridge near Sisak, Yugoslavia 0825; 2/Lt J.H.Weeber KiA
32 Sqn	Spitfire Vc ER637 left 1115 to strafe railway between Pristina and Mitrovica, hit by Flak, force-landed and overturned 1230; Flt Lt D.S.V.Rake WiA, returned on 30 November
87 Sqn	Spitfire IX MH902 left 1435 to bomb target near Ferrara, hit by Flak, reported no air pressure, crashed at Rimini 1555; Flt Sgt J.N.Harrison safe
US Casualties	
65th FS/57th FG	P-47D 42-75993 damaged by Flak, engine failed near Modena 0810; 2/Lt Alvie H.Nicholson POW [9990]
66th FS/57th FG	P-47D 44-20119 flew too low when strafing Brescia-Lonato road, wing struck tree 0850; 2/Lt Richard L.Place KiA [9979]
526th FS/86th FG	P-47D 42-27909 '59' *Edith* lost dive-bombing ferry point 0.5m W Ostiglia 0910; 1/Lt Sanford B.Hutchins POW [9983]
525th FS/86th FG	P-47D 42-26855 lost u/k cause at Ghedi a/d 1250; 1/Lt James B.Joslin KiA [9984]
380th BS/310th BG	B-25J 43-27796 hit by Flak, crashed 5m NW Casarsa 1300; Capt Arthur T.Ensley and two evaded, two KiA, one POW [9982]
381st BS/310th BG	B-25J 44-28916 damaged by Flak 1100; 1/Lt Paul G.Galentine Jr and four safe, one KiA
Bulgarian Casualties	
3/6 Orlyak	Bf 109G-6 WNr 1257057 shot down by Flak, pilot baled out NW Pristina; Pod M.Konstantinov, reportedly POW but killled
3/6 Orlyak	Bf 109G-6 damaged by Flak NW Pristina, landed safely at base; Kpt A.D.Kovachev safe

German Claims				
Flak	Obmt Kuhlmann	3/31 Naval Railway Flak Abt	Bf 109	Vučitrn
Flak	Obmt Kuhlmann	3/31 Naval Railway Flak Abt	Bf 109	Vučitrn

German Casualties	
NSGr 9	3 Ju 87Ds destroyed and 4 Ju 87Ds damaged by bombing at Villafranca 0954; one Ju 87D damaged by strafing p.m.
2./NAGr 11	2 Bf 109s destroyed and 3 damaged by bombs
	LKS reports losses on ground to bombs: four Bf 109s destroyed and six damaged, one FW 190 damaged, two Ju 87s destroyed and six damaged, one Fi 156 destroyed, one other aircraft damaged

Saturday-Sunday, 18/19 November 1944

British Casualties	
600 Sqn	Beaufighter VIf KW166 left 1645 on defensive patrol, on return to Falconara crash-landed 1905, burnt out; Flt Sgt W.Westwell KIA/Sgt W.H.Smith WiA.
272 Sqn	Beaufighter X LX787 'S' left 2207 on shipping strike, crashed on take-off; Flt Sgt D.M.Reike/Flt Sgt D.Collins safe

Top: Refresher and theatre orientation flying for new arrivals was the responsibility of 5 Refresher Flying Unit at Perugia that flew Spitfire IXs, including MA545 'A-12'. Above: One of the instructors with 5 RFU was Flt Lt Desmond Ibbotson DFC who was killed in an accident on 19 November.

US Casualties

97th BS/47th BG	A-20K 44-359 left 1845 to bomb target at Anzola W Bologna, last heard from 1923, crashed NNE Florence; 1/Lt Louis L. Surber Jr and three KiA
85th BS/47th BG	A-20J 43-9662, crashed on take-off on mission 0132; 2nd Lt Donald A.Criss and three KiA
414th NFS	Beaufighter VIf MM935 left 1957 on intruder mission over eastern Po Valley, failed to return; 1/Lt John M.Howard/2/Lt John F.Murphy KiA [10217]

Sunday, 19 November 1944

Flt Lt Desmond Ibbotson, DFC and bar, formerly of 601 Squadron and now on 5 RFU, was killed in a flying accident in central Italy. He had claimed 11 opposing aircraft shot down since July 1942.

British Casualties

250 Sqn	Kittyhawk IV FT881 left 0745, strafed train, shot down by Flak 15-20m SE Ljubljana 0950; Lt D.B.Tattersall baled out, evaded
293 Sqn	Walrus I X9565 crashed on take-off from Pianosa Island; Flt Sgt G.Cooper KiA/Wt Off G.W.Blackwell DoW on 20 November
70 Sqn	Wellington X LP179 'W' attacked German forces retreating along the Sjenica-Priboj road, crashed on fire, possibly due to Flak, at Prijopolje; Sgt I.Parry and four KiA
70 Sqn	Wellington X LP641 'C' attacked German forces retreating along the Sjenica-Priboj road, crashed 35m west of Sjenica. Crew baled out over partisan held territory; Sgt A.W.MacDonald and four evaded, flown back to Italy
5 RFU	Spitfire LFIXc MH614 'C-7' left 1515 from Perugia on test flight, dived into the ground near Castelnuovo 1330; Flt Lt D.Ibbotson KiFA

US Casualties

85th FS/79th FG	P-47D 42-27997 shot down by Flak over Yugoslavia 1530; 1/Lt Maurice A.Brash POW [9997]
85th FS/79th FG	P-47D 42-28375 shot down by Flak over Yugoslavia 1530; Lt Joseph V.Lansing MiA
95th BS/17th BG	B-26G 43-34398 '55' hit by Flak nr Zambana 1415; 1/Lt Ollie B.Childs and five POW [11109]

Bulgarian Casualties

6 Orlyak	Bf 109G-6 damaged by Flak strafing a train; Por Damev safe

German Claims

Flak	6./720 Naval Flak		2 Ju 87s	N Priluka	1008 & 1011
Flak	6./720 Naval Flak		Bf 109F Damaged	1km N Kosovo Polje	1031
Flak	3/31 Naval Railway Flak Cars 4,5,10 &12		Wellington	Ucice railway station	1130-1133

German Casualties

	LKS reports three Ju 87s damaged on the ground by strafing

Italian ANR Claims

4ªSq, 2° Gr C	Serg Magg Loris Baldi	Bf 109G	Boston

Sunday-Monday, 19/20 November 1944

US Casualties

84th BS/47th BG	A-20K damaged by Flak crashed near San Benedetto Po 2020; 1/Lt Ernest H.Banker and two evaded and returned, one POW [10008]

Monday, 20 November 1944

Grp Capt H.S.L.'Cocky' Dundas took over from Grp Capt C.B.F.Kingcome as the commander of 244 Wing. 25 SAAF Squadron flew their first Marauder raid when four aircraft led by Maj Freeman, attacked the marshalling yards at Konjic, dropping 40 x 250lb bombs.

British Casualties

241 Sqn	Spitfire IXe PT701 left 0805 to bomb railway line near Rovigo, damaged by own bomb burst, pilot baled out; Flg Off W.D.C.Hawkes POW
241 Sqn	Spitfire IXe FL689 left 0805 to bomb railway line near Rovigo, damaged by own bomb burst, crash-landed at base; Flg Off G.D.Loewenthal WiA
92 Sqn	Spitfire VIII JF616 'H' left 0820, hit by Flak strafing motor transports near Manzano, reported he was baling out; Flg Off H.Mosedale evaded

145 Sqn	Spitfire VIII JG108 left 1310, engine cut on return flight, crash-landed near Cattolica 1445; Sgt C.T.Padden safe
US Casualties	
525th FS/86th FG	P-47D 42-26697 *Yankee Gal/Bets* lost probably to Flak nr Ferrara 0830; 2/Lt Glenn E.Marsh KiA [9985]
Italian Co-Belligerent Casualties	
378ª Sq, 155° Gr, 51° St	MC.205 MM 9370 '155-11' hit by Flak N Alessio, crash-landed nr Shegas; Ten Alberto Ballista (361ª Sq) WiA, helped by partisans, returned

Tuesday, 21 November 1944

Six Spitfire IXs of 72 Squadron carried out their first fighter-bomber operation, promptly losing one to Flak.

British Casualties	
4 SAAF Sqn	Spitfire IXe PT491 'A' left 0710, shot down by Flak 5km E Faenza 0725; Capt I.G.Will KiA
601 Sqn	Spitfire IXe PT606 left 1205, attacked a target S Faenza 1245, pulling out from bomb dive dived into a house; Flt Sgt R.L.Clements KiA
5 SAAF Sqn	Mustang III HB909 left 1345, shot down by Flak 8km S Faenza 1410; Lt B.J.Eaton KiA
72 Sqn	Spitfire IX PT411 left 1140, hit by Flak SE Faenza 1215; Flg Off L.True baled in no man's land, safe
145 Sqn	Spitfire VIII MT777 left 0940 from Fano to bomb in Forlì- Faenza area, on take-off a bomb dropped off and exploded causing aircraft to crash; Flt Sgt R.N.Harding KiA
1 SAAF Sqn	Spitfire IXc EN476 left 1240, bombed target NE Cesena, engine cut in bomb dive, crash-landed in Allied lines; Lt C.W.Boyd safe
US Casualties	
523rd FS/27th FBG	P-47D 42-26560 *Christine* shot down by Flak 9m S Bologna 1030; 2/Lt Thomas E.Thrasher KiA [10042]
66th FS/57th FG	P-47D 44-20141 *Sweet Violet* shot down by small-arms fire SW Avio 1000; 2/Lt Harry T.Leek Jr POW [9961]
64th FS/57th FG	P-47D 42-75708 destroyed by ammo car explosion 1425; 2/Lt Edwin S.Frierson KiA [9960]
French Casualties	
GC 3/6	P-39 shot down by Flak over bridge of Gaiola; Cne Roger Demoulin KiA

German Claims				
Flak	3/31 Naval Railway Car M.7 20mm	Spitfire	Pocega railway station	1445
Flak	1/31 2 Platoon 20mm	Mustang	Drakcic-Samaila	1445
Flak	1/31 2 Platoon 20mm	Mustang Probable	Drakcic-Samaila	1445

Wednesday, 22 November 1944

3 RAAF Squadron flew its first Mustang operation when the commanding officer, Sqn Ldr M.P.Nash in KH630, led five other aircraft on a special mission escorting a Lysander over northern Italy. However, in another case of so-called friendly fire by USAAF fighters, the 'spydropper' was shot down by a P-51 of 325th Fighter Group (belonging to 15th Air Force), and although the leader of the attacking section pulled out, one of his men fired a short burst from long range, hitting the Lysander. 3 RAAF Squadron's attempts to force the Americans away was reported by the 325th, and the 52nd who intervened to attack what they perceived to be Spitfires attacking them! Why such experienced and successful groups made such errors is difficult to explain, especially in not recognising the 3 RAAF aircraft as Mustangs! In two weeks, three RAF aircraft had now been shot down by 15th Air Force Mustangs.

British Casualties	
454 Sqn	Baltimore V FW689 'E' left 1328 to bomb positions 4km S Faenza, hit by Flak, crashed in flames; Flg Off K.R.Thompson and two KiA, one POW
87 Sqn	Spitfire IX PT839 left 1315, bombing target near Florence, hit by Flak, crash-landed in Allied lines near Loiano; Flt Sgt W.H.Bundock WiA
6 Sqn	Hurricane IV KZ574 left to Danilovgrad, crashed near Janjina on Peljesac Peninsula; Wt Off G.Duffey KiA
148 Sqn	Lysander III T1456 left from Fano on Operation Templar, shot down 32km N Venice by USAAF Mustangs; Flg Off J.F.A.Rayns and three KiA
US Casualties	
64th FS/57th FG	P-47D 42-27255 *Mickey* dive-bombed rail track nr Pieve di Coriano, destroyed by own bomb blast 1300; 1/Lt Ralph B.Brad- shaw KiA [9995]
85th FS/79th FG	P-47D 42-26423 *Sweetheart* propeller went out, crashed nr Ponte di Barberino 0940; 1/Lt Frederick J.Moschberger POW [9996]

German Claims

Flak	Feld-Ers Btl 29	e/a	near Capitello

German Casualties

6./FAGr 122	Ju 188D-2 WNr 150258 F6+EP crash-landed 5km S Bergamo and destroyed; Uffz Kurt Schulze and one KiA, one WiA

Thursday, 23 November 1944

British Casualties

213 Sqn	Mustang III KH633 left 0630, strafed M/T E Sarajevo, failed to pull out from diving attack, possibly shot down by Flak; Sgt A.Liudzius KiA

Thursday-Friday, 23/24 November 1944

British Claims

600 Sqn	Wt Off D.B.Smith/Flt Sgt J.B.Dunford	Beaufighter VIf KV972	Ju 87	25m E Lake Comacchio	1645-1850
600 Sqn	Wt Off D.B.Smith/Flt Sgt J.B.Dunford	Beaufighter VIf KV972	Ju 87 Damaged	25m E Lake Comacchio	1645-1850
256 Sqn	Flt Sgt R.Roberts/Flt Sgt J.A.Hebdige	Mosquito XIII MM584	Ju 52/3m	W Butmir	1740

British Casualties

255 Sqn	Beaufighter ND295 left 2250 on scramble from Rosignano, last heard from 16m from base 0045; Flt Lt T.W.Reynolds/Flg Off R.E.Rudling KiA
256 Sqn	Mosquito XIII MM585 left 1857 on night-intruder mission to Sarajevo area, FTR; Plt Off B.Nicholls/Flt Sgt J.G.Marsden KiA
18 Sqn	Boston IV BZ511 'M' on armed recce Faenza area, crashed on landing at Falconara; Flt Sgt J.P.Wilson and one WiA, two safe

German Casualties

1./NSGr 9	Ju 87D WNr 141018 E8+JH shot down by night-fighter E Comacchio; Ofhr Bernhard Buckow/Uffz Artur Berkemeyer KiA
2./TG 3	Ju 52/3m WNr 7767 4V+OK shot down on take-off from Sarajevo
	LKS reports one Ju 87 missing

Saturday, 25 November 1944

British Casualties

6 Sqn	Hurricane IV KZ555 undercarriage collapsed during take-off from strip at Niksic; Flt Sgt I.S.W.H.Lewis safe

US Casualties

523rd FS/27th FBG	P-47D 42-27970 shot down by Flak WNW Argenta 0815; 1/Lt Richard C.Crabtree POW [9994]

Italian Co-Belligerent Casualties

84ª Sq, 10° Gr, 4° St	P-39Q 44-3043 hit by Flak, force-landed nr Valona; Ten Enzo Dall'Asta safe, returned on 7 December

Sunday, 26 November 1944

The three Spitfires lost on this date over Italy were all due to bad weather. The fourth aircraft lost was a Greek Spitfire shot down by Flak over Crete.

British Casualties

272 Sqn	Beaufighter X NV374 'N' left 0655 on armed recce, engine failure, ditched 4m off the coast SE Lignano 0848; Flt Lt D.L. Gaydon/Plt Off R.V.Fawkner-Corbett POW
87 Sqn	Spitfire IX MH833 left 1245 to bomb guns near Florence, encountered solid cloud, force-landed near Fabriano; Flg Off A.M.Griffiths safe
87 Sqn	Spitfire IX PT557 left 1245 to bomb guns near Florence, encountered solid cloud, crashed into mountains and disintegrated; Wt Off D.M.Bell KiA
3 SAAF Sqn	Spitfire IXc MK134 left 1220, on return from dive-bombing, got lost in bad weather, pilot baled out; Capt F.E.Potgieter safe
335 Sqn	Spitfire V EE805 left 1030 on recce of Crete, hit by heavy Flak in the Maleme-Canea area, crashed in flames into a mountain NW Armenoi; Sgt J.Vatimbellas KiA

US Casualties

522nd FS/27th FBG	P-47D 42-27219 hit by Flak 1010; 2/Lt T.E.Norquist WiA

Tuesday, 28 November 1944

Sqn Ldr O.H.Archer, flying a 600 Squadron Beaufighter, shot down a Ju 87 reporting that it spiralled into the ground and blew up. The crew also noted that the pilot was captured and the navigator killed.

British Claims						
600 Sqn	Sqn Ldr O.H.Archer/Flt Lt C.J.Barrington	Beaufighter VIf BT299 'T'	Ju 87		Forlì	1715
US Casualties						
526th FS/86th FG	P-47D 44-19715 *Lady Luck* damaged by own bomb blast, crashed en route home between Bedonia and Borgo Val di Taro					
	1235; 2/Lt Beriger A.Anderson evaded and returned [9998]					
Italian Co-Belligerent Casualties						
91ª Sq, 12° Gr, 4° St	P-39N 42-9377 hit by Flak, force-landed nr Elbasan and set on fire; Ten Silvio Barbasetti di Prun KiA					
90ª Sq, 10° Gr, 4° St	P-39Q 43-3019 hit by Flak, crashed N Podgorica; Serg Magg Natale Molteni KiA					
German Claims						
Flak	1/1 Naval Motor Transport Detachment		e/a		Lake Scutari	1532
Flak			Spitfire		Danilovgrad	
German Casualties						
1./NSGr 9	Ju 87D-5 WNr 131086 E8+DH shot down by fighter nr Forlì; Fw Kaspar Stuber POW/Uffz Alois Adami KiA					

Tuesday-Wednesday, 28/29November 1944

US Claims					
417th NFS	1/Lt Theodore A.Deakyne/1/Lt Robert E.Perkins	Beaufighter VIf	Ju 188	SE St Tropez	2320-2337
German Casualties					
6.(F)/122	Ju 188D WNr 150044 F6+DP FTR from night recce to Ligurian Sea; Fw Hans Krieg and crew MiA				
	LKS reports one Ju 87 and one Ju 88 missing				

Wednesday-Thursday, 29/30 November 1944

US Casualties	
416th NFS	Beaufighter VIf MM917 lost over Pontedera a/f u/k cause 2015; 2/Lts Billie J.Fox/Ralph D.Mulhollen POW [10099]

The P-39N Airacobras of 4° Stormo, Italian Co-Belligerent Air Force, were very active on 30 November, losing two of their number to Flak over the Balkans.

Thursday, 30 November 1944

The Italian Co-Belligerent Air Force was active on this day. The first mission was carried out by four P-39s of 4° Stormo (one returned early), between 0755 and 1015. Ten Francesco Rizzitelli's aircraft was hit by Flak and crashed near Virpazar, north-west of Lake Scutari. A second mission was performed by three P-39s of 4° Stormo between 1015 and 1230. Ten Raffaele Giusto's aircraft was also hit by Flak and he crashed near Lake Scutari but survived. German Flak claimed a P-39 that blew up at 500m and crashed at Mahala, one of three P-39s strafing the Podgorica-Plavnica road, the pilot baling out and evading.

British Casualties					
6 Sqn	Hurricane IV LD162 left 1550 to attack M/T parked nr Danilovgrad, hit by Flak, pilot baled out 5m ENE Danilovgrad; Sqn Ldr R.Slade-Betts met by partisans and later returned				
6 Sqn	Hurricane IV KX821 left 1550 to attack M/T parked nr Danilovgrad, crash-landed in soft ground Niksic; Sgt A.W.Coghlan slt WiA				
US Claims					
417th NFS	2/Lt Robert C.Anderson/2/Lt Thomas L.Welfley	Beaufighter VIf	Ju 188 Damaged		2213-2255
Italian Co-Belligerent Casualties					
91ª Sq, 12° Gr, 4° St	P-39N 42-18787 left 0755, shot down by Flak, crashed nr Virpazar 0930; Ten Francesco Rizzitelli KiA				
90ª Sq, 10° Gr, 4° St	P-39Q 44-3024 hit by Flak, crashed nr Lake Scutari; Ten Raffaele Giusto baled, evaded, back on 13 December				
German Claims					
Flak	1/1 Naval Motor Transport Detachment		P-39	Mahala	0920
Flak	Platoon TMiKW.A		P-39	nr Lake Scutari	1131

BALKAN AIR FORCE DEVELOPMENTS

Throughout November and December Balkan Air Force units concentrated on transport targets in an effort to prevent as many Germans as possible from extricating themselves from the Balkan morass. Meantime the Strategic Air Force contributed to the Allied effort, bombing marshalling yards and troop concentrations, and flying in supplies to the partisans. BAF had been reinforced during early December by the Stormo Baltimore of the Italian Co-Belligerent Air Force, a unit of Baltimore bombers about the strength of two RAF squadrons, which now joined 254 Wing.

Early in December the Spitfires of 73 Squadron had to be released to Greece due to the ELAS crisis, but the Mustang squadrons were now regularly carrying substantial bomb loads of 1,000lb, or even on occasions, double that, during their frequent sorties over Yugoslavia. By the end of the year Russian forces had advanced well into Hungary and had surrounded Budapest. However, the New Year found the weather so bad that few sorties could be made by BAF. 73 Squadron returned from Greece as did 38 Squadron, which now joined 286 Coastal Wing at Grottaglie.

There were several moves and changes in this period; in late November 25 SAAF Squadron exchanged its Venturas for Marauders and in January 39 Squadron was also re-equipped with them, replacing Beau-fighters. These two squadrons flew alongside the Italian Baltimores in 254 Wing. 272 Squadron remained with 323 Wing operating from Foggia, its Beaufighters frequently being escorted by Spitfires from 287 Wing at Falconara and later Rosignano. During February 1945 1435 Squadron moved north to join this wing, and both it and 237 (Rhodesia) Squadron began fighter-bomber and strafing missions over Yugo-slavia. No 272 Squadron's Beaufighters had also been undertaking a number of night shipping strikes, the targets being illuminated for them by flare-dropping Leigh-Light-equipped Wellingtons of 458 Squadron, which operated form Foggia with a detachment at Rosignano. Late in January, however, 458 was sent to Gibraltar to support the Venturas of 22 SAAF Squadron on anti-submarine patrols over the Atlantic. Pre-viously a Special Duties unit in Balkan Air Force, 624 Squadron was reformed with Walrus amphibians, joining 286 Wing at Grottaglie to co-operate with the Royal Navy on mine-spotting duties. In February it sent a detachment for these duties to Foggia and to Hassani in Greece. The generally improved situation also allowed for the release of 267 Squadron which left Bari during February and moved with its Dakotas to the Far East. 216 Squadron had also been maintaining a detachment at Bari, particularly for missions

During December the 414th Night-Fighter Squadron re-equipped with the P-61B Black Widow such as 42-39682, seen here parked at Rosignano.

into Greece. These too now left, returning to flying normal scheduled services between North Africa and Europe.

Friday, 1 December 1944
December saw the arrival of Northrop P-61Bs to begin the re-equipment of the 12th Air Force night-fighter units. The first 'Black Widows' replaced the Beaufighter with the 414th Night-Fighter Squadron at Pontedera near Pisa. With the P-61 it began more offensive activities providing defensive cover for the 5th Army and intruders into enemy territory. It also continued defensive patrols including patrolling ports and escorting shipping through vulnerable areas.

British Claims					
600 Sqn	Wt Off H.G.Baits/Flt Sgt A.Lothian	Beaufighter VIf KV972 'G'	Ju 87 Probable	Faenza	1703
600 Sqn	Wt Off H.G.Baits/Flt Sgt A.Lothian	Beaufighter VIf KV972 'G'	Ju 87 Damaged	Faenza	1705

British Casualties	
5 SAAF Sqn	Mustang III FB275 left 1330 on armed recce of Ravenna-Padova-Vicenza area, left wing struck tree while strafing truck, crashed 13km S Vicenza 1430; Lt C.J.Coetzer KiA
111 Sqn	Spitfire IX PL157 'F' scrambled 1550 on a plot that turned out to be friendly, on landing approach struck a truck working on extending the runway, crashed 1635; Lt J.A.Anderson inj, truck driver killed
249 Sqn	Mustang III HB884 left 1120 on weather recce, lost in severe weather, pilot baled out N Vis 1410; Sgt W.M.Monkman rescued

US Claims				
527th FS/86th FG	1/Lt George E.Hill		Ju 88	nr Lodi	1420-1630

German Casualties	
4.(F)/122	Ju 88T-3 WNr 330227 F6+FM hit on op to Milan; one crew WiA

Saturday, 2 December 1944
With the reduction of U-boat activity, having been withdrawn from operations at the end of November, 27 SAAF Squadron was split into two elements. One ferried the Venturas back to the Union whilst the other prepared to re-equip with the Warwick GR V – the first in this theatre.

British Casualties	
15 SAAF Sqn	Baltimore V FW741 left 0948 to bomb harbour installations at Pola, badly damaged by heavy Flak, crash-landed at Fano l/g; Lt R.J.Jooste DFC and three safe
24 SAAF Sqn	Marauder III HD436 'S' left 1256 to bomb Bjelovar, mission aborted due to bad weather, crashed on landing 1640; Lt P.J.Kemp and five safe
7 SAAF Sqn	Spitfire IX MA640 left 1510 to bomb and strafe target, presumed crashed 1536; Capt N.G.Nisbet POW
249 Sqn	Mustang III KH472 left 1320 on armed recce, bombed bridge near Bioce, not seen after bombing; Sgt F.J.Wood POW
250 Sqn	Kittyhawk IV FX793 left 1020 last seen near target in Ravenna-Ferrara area; Sgt J.V.Funnell KiA
40 SAAF Sqn	Spitfire IX left 0900, damaged by Flak near Faenza, force-landed on Forlì l/g, airframe Cat A, engine Cat III damaged; Lt Col R.H.Rogers DFC safe

Sunday, 3 December 1944
On this day the Baltimore-equipped 28° Gruppo of the Italian Co-Belligerent Air Force was incorporated into the Balkan Air Force.

Ten Giannino Balboni climbs into a Baltimore of the Co-Belligerent 28° Gruppo that was incorporated into the Balkan Air Force on 3 December.

Monday, 4 December 1944

British Casualties

43 Sqn	Spitfire IX PT542 left 1400, shot down by Flak, spun in in flames; Flt Sgt G.R.Leigh KiA
5 SAAF Sqn	Mustang III FB274 left 1005, shot down by Flak near Brod 1200; Lt F.N.Lock POW
72 Sqn	Spitfire IX PL322 left 1445 to attack gun positions, shot down by Flak, pilot baled out into V Corps lines; Sgt N.E.Milner safe
417 Sqn	Spitfire VIII JF932 left 0940 on Rover David, bombed a target and then strafed roads, damaged by Flak, pilot baled out into sea SE Russi; Plt Off J.Waslyk rescued
250 Sqn	Kittyhawk IV FX616 left 1420, bombed bridge near Mezzano, hit by Flak, reached Allied lines, pilot baled out; Sgt C.H. Jones safe

US Casualties

87th FS/79th FG	P-47D 42-29054 shot down by Flak, pilot baled nr Lugo 0930; 1/Lt Ronald M.Faison POW [10388]
525th FS/86th FG	P-47D 42-26830 *The Chief* lost probably to Flak, crashed nr Casalecchio 1125; 2/Lt Samuel C.McArthur KiA [10224]
526th FS/86th FG	P-47D '58' shot down by Flak 1240, pilot baled out; Lt Douglas W.Leader WiA

Monday-Tuesday, 4/5 December 1944

British Casualties

256 Sqn	Mosquito XIII MM565 on intruder to Sarajevo area, starboard engine cut on taking off 2030, crashed; Flt Sgt R.J.Board/Flt Sgt R.J.Thomas safe
18 Sqn	Boston IV BZ502 'T' left 1730 on weather recce over Yugoslavia, sent a report one hour after take-off, not heard from again; Flg Off S.Downes and three MiA

Tuesday, 5 December 1944

British Casualties	
335 Sqn	Spitfire V JK185 left 1045 to bomb target near Yoryoupolis, Crete, shot down by Flak; Flt Lt E.Tingos KiA

Wednesday, 6 December 1944

Six of ten Mustangs of 5 SAAF Squadron on armed reconnaissance were lost over Yugoslavia in bad weather. This was the worst single loss by a fighter squadron during the Balkan campaign.

British Casualties	
5 SAAF Sqn	Mustang IVa KH736 disappeared in bad weather 1245; Capt W.J.Lombard KiA
5 SAAF Sqn	Mustang III HB931 'X' disappeared in bad weather 1245; Lt T.F.Hart KiA
5 SAAF Sqn	Mustang III KH576 disappeared in bad weather; Lt C.G.Begg KiA
5 SAAF Sqn	Mustang III KH607 pilot baled out in bad weather 1245; Lt E.W.Hall KiA
5 SAAF Sqn	Mustang III FB301 pilot baled out in bad weather; Lt G.D.Kilpin POW
5 SAAF Sqn	Mustang III FB256 pilot baled out in bad weather nr Lovinac; Lt A.E.Burnett rescued by Yugoslav partisans, evacuated by Beaufighter and returned to unit later in December
253 Sqn	Spitfire VIII JF485 left 0950 on armed recce, hit by debris after attacking fuel carrier, lost oil pressure, pilot baled out SW Kiseliak 1135; Sgt L.V.Judd safe, returned on 10 December

Thursday, 7 December 1944

Six Beaufighters from 272 Squadron, escorted by four Spitfires from 237 Squadron, left at 1100 on an armed reconnaissance. They sighted, attacked and sank a barge on the River Livenza at 1300; then they attacked six barges on a canal nearby at San Giorgio di Livenza at 1320, claiming three more sunk. Light Flak was seen and a Beaufighter reported an oil leak. Two minutes later it crash-landed to the south-west of Caorle. The crew were last seen sitting on the wing and waving, before evading.

British Casualties	
272 Sqn	Beaufighter X NV201 'B' hit by Flak attacking barges, crash-landed 3m SW Caorle 1322; Flg Off J.R.Rutland/Flt Sgt E.M.Potts evaded

Saturday, 9 December 1944

The 66th Fighter Squadron of the 57th Group recorded its costliest day in the war to date when it lost four aircraft. Two were shot down by Flak near Padua in the morning, only Capt Callan surviving as a POW. A third Thunderbolt flew into a tree while strafing, possibly having been hit by Flak. Lt Dodds was the fourth, hit by Flak and crash-landing just north of the bomb line in enemy territory but successfully evading.

272 Squadron lost a crew when Flg Off John C.Horlock and Wt Off Frank H.Rapley were hit by light Flak near Monfalcone. After being hit Horlock attempted to force land in a field but the aircraft blew up when it skidded along the ground. Rapley survived and tried to rescue Horlock but was forced out of the burning machine and became a POW.

Lt Col L.H.G.Shuttleworth left 25 SAAF Squadron assuming command of 15 SAAF Squadron and was succeeded by Lt Col C.Cormack DFC.

In the middle of the day a He 111H arrived at San Severo flown by the head of the Hungarian General Staff Technical Branch on behalf of the Hungarian resistance movement. He brought with him his family, a member of the resistance who was an escaped Dutch POW and a mechanic. They had left Papa at 0900 coasting out from Yugoslavia south of Zara and on being intercepted lowered the wheels and approaching San Severo were surrounded by 30 fighters! This aircraft was later shipped to the US as 'FE-1600'.

British Casualties	
272 Sqn	Beaufighter X NT971 'V' left 0845 on armed recce, shot down by Flak at 1045; Flg Off J.C.Horlock KiA/Wt Off F.H.Rapley POW
US Casualties	
66th FS/57th FG	P-47D 42-27683 *Jeeter* shot down by Flak W Cittadella 1040; 1/Lt Charles S.Dehmer KiA [10381]
66th FS/57th FG	P-47D 42-28358 *Hell'n-Marie* shot down by Flak 10km NE Padua 1045; Capt Thomas H.Callan POW [10382]

66th FS/57th FG	P-47D 42-26953 *Jeanie* flew into a tree, possibly hit by Flak 1415; 1/Lt Robert C.Lown KiA [10386]
66th FS/57th FG	P-47D 42-29041 shot down by Flak 1500, crash-landed just north of bomb line; 1/Lt Wayne S.Dodds evaded and returned [10383]
346th FS/350th FG	P-47D 44-19583 '6O4' shot down by Flak, crashed nr Castelfranco Emilia 1000; 1/Lt Forrest W.McCargo KiA [10776]

German Casualties

| 2.Fliegerschuldiv. | He 111H-16 WNr 8433 2B+DC defected to Italy flown by Maj Domokos Hadnagy with a senior member of the Hungarian resistance |

Saturday-Sunday, 9/10 December 1944

British Casualties

| 114 Sqn | Boston IV BZ465 left 2000 on armed recce in the area Imola-Ferrara-Lugo, presumed shot down; Sqn Ldr J.L.Steele DFC and two KiA, Flg Off H.R.Honeker POW |

Sunday, 10 December 1944

Cap Bellagambi led 21 Bf 109s of 2° Gruppo Caccia to intercept medium bombers over the Po Valley, the raiders being 18 aircraft of the 319th Bomb Group newly converted from B-26s to B-25s. The first claim for one of the US aircraft was made by Bellagambi himself, following which three more Mitchells were claimed by a trio of other Italian pilots; these probably actually managing to damage them rather than to shoot them down. One of the four against which claims had been made (probably that claimed by Bellagambi) crashed north-west of Lake Garda. A P-47 escort from the 57th Fighter Group arrived in time to drive off the intercep-tors but only managed to claim damage to one Messerschmitt. However, gunners in the B-25s claimed one shot down, one probable and three damaged; on this occasion four of the Messerschmitts did indeed suffer damage during this interception.

Elsewhere, another P-47 pilot of the 86th Fighter Group reported shooting down a reconnaissance Me 410. This was an aircraft of 2./(F)/122 which was lost with its crew south-south-west of Villafranca.

272 Squadron's Beaufighters were active again, strafing barges on the River Livenza from the coast to Oderzo, claiming four sunk and seven others damaged. Wg Cdr R.N.Lambert, leading the flight was hit and

Serg Magg Guido Mazzanti (left) and Ten Luigi De Masellis with a Bf 109G of the ANR 5ª Squadriglia, 2° Gruppo Caccia. De Masellis claimed a B-25 destroyed on 10 December and Mazzanti a B-26 on 3 March 1945.

wounded by Flak. He summoned his navigator for assistance. Flg Off A.E.Easterbee came forward, rendered first aid and essentially flew the aircraft back to Fano, where Lambert, with Easterbee operating the throttles, belly-landed on soft ground next to the runway. Lambert was hospitalised and Sqn Ldr R.K.H.Johnson took over the squadron.

British Casualties

260 Sqn	Mustang III KH501 shot down by Flak 12km W Udine 1217; 2/Lt W.J.Ashworth POW
417 Sqn	Spitfire VIII JG243 left 1140 on Rover David collided over target and exploded; Plt Off R.A.Shannon KiA
417 Sqn	Spitfire VIII JG329 left 1140 on Rover David collided over target and exploded; Wt Off 2 R.W.Rideout KiA
601 Sqn	Spitfire IX PT603 left 1135, bombed target 1m NE Faenza, hit by Flak, reached base when caught fire and pilot baled over Forlì l/g; Sgt J.Hodgson safe
250 Sqn	Kittyhawk IV FX802 left 1415 to bomb target near Ferrara, hit by Flak, reached Rimini l/g, belly-landed; Sgt B.E.Jarmey safe
6 Sqn	Hurricane IV KZ905 left from Bari on ferry flight to Hassani Greece, ran low on fuel in very bad weather, force-landed on Levkas Island 1410, burnt to prevent possibility of falling into the hands of ELAS partisans; Flt Lt J.W.E.Grundy safe
6 Sqn	Hurricane IV KX405 left from Bari on ferry flight to Hassani Greece, ran low on fuel in very bad weather, force-landed on Levkas Island 1410, burnt to prevent possibility of falling into the hands of ELAS partisans; Flg Off J.C.Brand safe
272 Sqn	Beaufighter X NV120 'G' left 1200 on armed recce, hit by Flak at Oderzo, pilot WiA, observer flew to Fano, crash-landed 1520; Wg Cdr R.N.Lambert WiA/Flg Off A.E.Easterbee safe

US Claims

65th FS/57th FG	Lt Benjamin J.Atwood	P-47D	Bf 109 Damaged	SW corner Lake Garda	1115
439th BS/319th BG	gunner Sgt Throop	B-25J	Bf 109	N Salò	1115
439th BS/319th BG	gunner Sgt Sennett	B-25J	Bf 109	N Salò	1115
439th BS/319th BG	gunner Sgt Zubenko	B-25J	Bf 109	N Salò	1115
439th BS/319th BG	gunner Sgt Borel	B-25J	Bf 109 Probable	N Salò	1115
439th BS/319th BG	gunner Sgt Williams	B-25J	Bf 109 Damaged	N Salò	1115
439th BS/319th BG	gunner Sgt R.Rochon	B-25J	Bf 109 Damaged	N Salò	1115
439th BS/319th BG	gunner Sgt H.E.Oyster	B-25J	Bf 109 Damaged	N Salò	1115
527th FS/86th FG	Capt Jesse R.Core III	P-47D '73'	Me 410	SW Villafranca	1145

US Casualties

66th FS/57th FG	P-47D 42-28605 *Little David/Battle Baby* hit by Flak SW Thiene, crashed and exploded 0930; 2/Lt Eugene F.Smith KiA [10373]
527th FS/86th FG	P-47D 42-28371 '72' damaged by ammunition car explosion 25m SW Brescia 0855; 2/Lt Bruce W.Fulton POW [10370]
526th FS/86th FG	P-47D 42-29026 '64' hit trees while strafing motor transports S Padua 1520; 1/Lt Charles E.Williams KiA
526th FS/86th FG	P-47D 44-19603 hit by Flak crashed nr Bologna 1532; 1/Lt Richard D.Lawrence evaded [10371]
428th BS/310th BG	B-25J 44-28937 *Donna-Marie II* hit by Flak, crashed nr Valle d'Astico 1104; 1/Lt Lee McAllister Jr KiA, five POW [10777]
380th BS/310th BG	B-25J 43-27693 *El Lobo III* hit by Flak, crashed N Tregnago 1105; 1/Lt William B.Berry and two evaded, one POW, two KiA [10387]
439th BS/319th BG	B-25J 43-36216 left 0944 to bomb San Michele railway bridge, shot down by e/a 1115, crashed NW Lake Garda; 1/Lt Herbert Herman and one KiA, four POW [10384]
439th BS/319th BG	B-25J 43-36111 damaged Cat 2 by e/a; crew safe
439th BS/319th BG	B-25J damaged Cat 1 by e/a; crew safe
446th BS/321st BG	B-25J 43-27895 *Haulin' Ass* left 0950 to bomb barracks at Bologna, hit by Flak, crashed SW Pavullo 1149; 1/Lt Frederick C.Ritger evaded, three POW, two KiA [10385]

German Casualties

2.(F)/122	Me 410B-3 WNr 190161 F6+ZK lost in combat 6km SSW Villafranca; Lt Kurt Neumann/Uffz Franz Meister KiA

Italian ANR Claims

5ª Sq, 2° Gr C	Cap Mario Bellagambi	Bf 109G	B-25	Lake Iseo	1100
5ª Sq, 2° Gr C	Ten Luigi De Masellis	Bf 109G	B-25	Lake Iseo	1100
4ª Sq, 2° Gr C	Ten Mario Giorio	Bf 109G	B-25	Lake Iseo	1100
5ª Sq, 2° Gr C	M.llo Renato Mingozzi	Bf 109G	B-25	Lake Iseo	1100

Italian ANR Casualties

4ª Sq, 2° Gr C	Bf 109G Black 15 lost, pilot baled out NW Lake Garda; Ten Raffaele Valenzano slt WiA
5ª Sq, 2° Gr C	Bf 109G damaged in combat; Cap Mario Bellagambi safe
4ª Sq, 2° Gr C	Bf 109G-14 damaged in combat, force-landed at Orio al Serio; Serg Magg Loris Baldi safe
4ª Sq, 2° Gr C	Bf 109G damaged in combat; S.Ten Emanuele Rosas safe

Sunday-Monday, 10/11 December 1944

British Casualties	
272 Sqn	Beaufighter X NV388 'U' left 0057 on armed recce, on return flew into a hillside on the Italian coast E Termoli, burnt out; Flt Sgt D.W.Lane/Flt Sgt B.W.R.Morgan KiA

Monday, 11 December 1944

Twelve Marauders of 30 SAAF Squadron raided railyards W Faenza in the morning.

A Hungarian civil register's M-24 Courier was flown to Italy by a Polish engineer living in Hungary.

With its civilian registration overpainted by crude US-style markings, MSrE M-24 Courier HA-NAN was flown to Italy by Denes Szucs, a Polish engineer living in Hungary.

British Casualties	
5 SAAF Sqn	Mustang III FB247 left 1150, shot down by Flak strafing trains, crashed into a river N Sarajevo 1350; Lt W.N.Spence KiA
213 Sqn	Mustang III KH534 shot down by Flak strafing in Brod Doboj area 1120, pilot baled out but parachute did not open; Flg Off G.F.Allan KiA
253 Sqn	Spitfire IX MJ248 attacking M/T N Sarajevo, crash-landed S of town; Flt Sgt F.Weatherall safe
72 Sqn	Spitfire IX PL465 'T' left 1300 to dive bomb artillery, shot down by Flak 12m NW Forlì l/g; Sgt C.B.Griffin WiA, rescued by 10th Hussars
417 Sqn	Spitfire VIII JF952 left 1430, bombed target 1455, hit by Flak, pilot baled out; Plt Off H.C.Murray POW
30 SAAF Sqn	Marauder III HD509 'S' left 0940 to bomb guns NW Faenza, hit by Flak, crew baled out into Allied lines 4m S Forlì 1045; Lt A.G.Scott and three safe, two WiA
Hungarian Casualties	
Civil register	M-24 Courier HA-NAN defected to Italy by Denes Szucs

Wednesday, 13 December 1944

US Casualties	
524th FS/27th FBG	P-47D 42-28065 shot down by Flak nr Pontedera a/f 0850; 2/Lt Wallace B.Turner KiA
347th FS/350th FG	P-47D 42-28914 '7D3' damaged by own bomb blast, crashed 1m SE Piadena 0915; 2/Lt William K.Redmon Jr POW [10779]

Wednesday-Thursday, 13/14 December 1944

British Casualties

458 Sqn	Wellington XIV NB864 on armed recce, when weather deteriorated, diverted to land at Jesi, but overshot and flew into a mountain 10-12m SW Jesi; Wt Off G.G.Simons and five KiA

Thursday, 14 December 1944

British Casualties

1 SAAF Sqn	Spitfire IXc BS309 left 1405, on take-off a 500lb bomb dropped off and exploded; Lt B.D.Mair KiA
7 SAAF Sqn	Spitfire IXe PT591 'V' damaged at dispersal by bomb from 1 SAAF Sqn Spitfire
7 SAAF Sqn	Spitfire IX MA687 damaged at dispersal by bomb from 1 SAAF Sqn Spitfire

US Casualties

527th FS/86th FG	P-47D '81' damaged by own bomb blast nr Pistoia 0930; 1/Lt Manuel A.Pidcock baled and returned [10370]
526th FS/86th FG	P-47D '63' damaged by Flak 1120, ditched nr Marina di Pisa; 2/Lt George T.Sewell rescued [10370]
97th BS/47th BG	A-20K 44-570 lost u/k cause, crashed 8km SSE Mirandola 1919; 1/Lt Robert J.MacMullin and three POW [10775]

Friday, 15 December 1944

British Casualties

43 Sqn	Spitfire IX PT546 left 1225 to bomb target near Forlì, hit by Flak, crash-landed N Forlì 1330; Flt Lt B.H.Thomas DFC safe
145 Sqn	Spitfire VIII MT932 left 0900, hit by Flak in starboard fuel tank which streamed fuel, crashed; Flt Sgt A.Marquis KiA
92 Sqn	Spitfire VIII JG121 left 1525, bombing Bagnacavallo near Ravenna, shot down by Flak, crashed near target; Flg Off E.E.McCann KiA
450 Sqn	Kittyhawk IV FX562 left 0825, dive-bombed a target 4m WNW Imola 1000, hit by Flak, set on fire; Flg Off A.O.Ellis KiA
500 Sqn	Baltimore IV FA665 'W' hit by Flak near Castel Bolognese crash-landed 3m N Cervia; Flt Sgt A.J.Snow and one safe, Wt Off J.N.Messenger KiA, Flt Sgt J.J.Hedley DoW

US Claims

417th NFS	Maj Clarence R.McCray/1/Lt Robert D.Hamilton	Beaufighter VIf V8899 'V'	Ju 188 Damaged	2310-0005

US Casualties

523rd FS/27th FBG	P-47D 42-26824 damaged by previous a/c bomb blast 1540; 2/Lt John P.Mackey KiA
347th FS/350th FG	P-47D 42-27307 '7D3' damaged by Flak, pilot baled 1520; Lt Lorn K.Nichols safe

In mid-December the Beaufighter Xs of 39 Squadron arrived at Hassani near Athens from where they flew operations for the next month.

Saturday, 16 December 1944

Mustang IIIs of 260 Squadron strafed Aviano airfield where at least 12 Bf 109s and FW 190s were claimed damaged.

US Casualties

527th FS/86th FG	P-47D 42-27022 '91' *Audrey* damaged by own bomb blast, crashed nr Imola 0930; 1/Lt W.Clifford Adler POW [10789]

Sunday, 17 December 1944

British Casualties

450 Sqn	Kittyhawk IV FX796, left 0935 to bomb bridge at Lugo 12m W Ravenna, hit by Flak in bomb dive 1015, caught fire and crashed; Flt Lt R.A.Hast KiA
250 Sqn	Kittyhawk IV FX683 left 0945, shot down by Flak near Faenza, W Ravenna; Flg Off W.Davidson KiA
22 SAAF Sqn	Ventura V JS924 (6460) left Gibraltar on ASR search for a missing B-17, failed to return; Lt J.W.M.Treu and four MiA
260 Sqn	Mustang III KH639 left Fano 1420 on armed recce, take-off accident, struck parked Thunderbolts, one bomb exploded causing several American casualties and several Thunderbolts damaged; Sgt L.W.W.Hooper KiA

US Casualties

526th FS/86th FG	P-47D 42-27938 damaged by small arms or bomb blast, crashed 5m E Varese 1030; 2/Lt Arthur E.James returned [10788]
345th FS/350th FG	P-47D 42-29025 shot down by Flak, crashed W Carrara 0955; 1/Lt Robert G.Johnson Jr KiA [10774]
345th FS/350th FG	P-47D 42-75755 shot down by Flak, crashed W Carrara 0955; 2/Lt Elwood W.Lawson KiA [10774]

Monday, 18 December 1944

In mid-December a detachment of half a dozen Hurricanes from 6 Squadron was sent to Niksic in Montenegro from where attacks were made on targets around Danilovgrad and Spuz where they destroyed a vital rail bridge. During another attack on the 18th the Hurricanes reprised their 'flying can opener' role from the desert when they hit a group of the much-feared Tiger tanks, destroying one and damaging two others. The operation was successfully repeated the following day, but after this 6 Squadron's tank busting days were now finally over.

US Casualties

Air Crew Rescue	B-25C 42-491 *Durmitor* on supply dropping near Glina, last heard from 1415, lost over Yugoslavia; 1/Lt John Sullivan, four crew and Capt Justin J.McGowan of the OSS MiA [10787]

German Casualties

3./NAGr 7	CR.42 Yellow 17 shot down by AA near Pitomaca; Fw Hans Kruschel KiA
3.(F)/33	Ju 188D-2 WNr 150536 lost nr Agram; Obfw Robert Hoffmann and two KiA, one safe

Tuesday, 19 December 1944

British Casualties

237 Sqn	Spitfire IX PT715 left 1100 on shipping recce, believed lost near Falconara in bad weather; Flg Off W.J.Little KiA
352 Sqn	Spitfire Vc JK329 'A' left 1000, shot down by Flak nr Brezovo Polje 1100; Maj Mileta Protić KiA

Italian Co-Belligerent Casualties

253ª Sq, 132° Gr St B	Baltimore V FW425 crashed on return from bombing mission; Ten Nazzareno Biagiola and three KiA

Wednesday, 20 December 1944

British Casualties

213 Sqn	Mustang III KH637 shot down by Flak at Niksic 0905, pilot baled out; Wt Off F.A.O.Ralph safe
213 Sqn	Mustang III KH513 damaged by Flak near Ninsec 1230 and force-landed; Flt Lt J.A.Mulcahy-Morgan safe?
213 Sqn	Mustang III HB879 left 1110; crashed into the sea soon after take-off; Sgt D.H.Bell safe

US Casualties

66th FS/57th FG	P-47D 42-29319 shot down by Flak, crashed nr Trento 1005, pilot baled; 1/Lt Harry J.Gogan POW [10773]
154th TRS	P-38J 42-104219 left Bari on weather recce, engine failure, pilot baled 50m S Linz 1115; 1/Lt John C.Johnson POW [10634]

Italian ANR Casualties

4ª Sq, 2° Gr C	Bf 109G engine trouble; Serg Magg Loris Baldi baled out

The P-47D Thunderbolts of the 345th Fighter Squadron, 350th Fighter Group suffered a number of losses to ground fire over Italy during December, including three on the 21st.

Thursday, 21 December 1944

British Casualties	
145 Sqn	Spitfire VIII MT551 'W' left 1420, shot down by Flak at Mogliano, 1500; Lt G.E.Milborrow POW
28 SAAF Sqn	Dakota III KG498 during medivac mission crashed 10m SW Torretoria; Lt C.J.Jooste, five crew and 18 passengers KiA
US Casualties	
345th FS/350th FG	P-47D 44-19576 hit by Flak, belly-landed S Brescia 0915; 2/Lt Wayne P.Anderson KiA [10793]
345th FS/350th FG	P-47D 42-75737 *Hun Hunter* hit by Flak, pilot baled 300m from Castel Mella 0930; 2/Lt Michael L.Mangino POW [10792]
347th FS/350th FG	P-47D 42-28556 'red A-7C4' struck tree 3km S Bagnolo Mella 1100; 2/Lt Thomas H.Thompson KiA [10791]

Friday, 22 December 1944

On 22 December a patrol of Spitfire VIIIs from the Canadian-manned 417 Squadron, including JF880 'U' flown by Flg Off R.C.Webster, had a rare encounter with ANR Bf 109s.

A patrol from 417 Squadron over Verona was attacked by two Bf 109s of 2° Gruppo ANR, Cap Mario Bel-lagambi claiming a Spitfire shot down. Plt Off Gibson's Spitfire was damaged by the attack but reached base and landed safely. 417 Squadron did not make any claims, although M.llo Covre belly-landed his Bf 109 at Thiene after receiving 'combat damage'.

British Casualties	
417 Sqn	Spitfire VIII JF965 left 1305, attacked over Verona by two Bf 109s 1400, landed safely, Cat 2 dam; Plt Off A.D.Gibson safe
7 SAAF Sqn	Spitfire IXe PT820 left 1045, shot down by Flak, crashed 5m N Imola 1105; Capt R.N.Day KiA
7 SAAF Sqn	Spitfire IXe PT484 left 1045, shot down by Flak, crashed NE Imola 1110; Lt C.H.L.Paull POW
318 Sqn	Spitfire IX EN138 left 1400 on TacR of battle area, hit by Flak, crash-landed at base 1425; Flt Lt J.Preiba safe
40 SAAF Sqn	Spitfire IX left 1410 on Arty/R near Massa Lombarda, lost in cloud on return flight, pilot baled out 5m W Cesenatico; Lt C.Rose safe
293 Sqn	Walrus I K8592 lost a float landing in rough sea to pick up survivors, taken under tow by an HSL, abandoned and sank off Leghorn; Sgt F.A.Cail and crew safe
US Casualties	
438th BS/319th BG	B-25J 43-36062 *Jane* left 1257 to bomb Torre Beretti road and rail bridge, hit by Flak over target, crashed 1418; 1/Lt Charles J.Whelan and two KiA, three POW [10771]
438th BS/319th BG	B-25J 43-35968 left 1257 to bomb Torre Beretti road and rail bridge, hit by Flak over target, left engine damaged, crashed into sea 40m N Corsica 1455; 1/Lt LeRoy L.Miser and five KiA [10772]

Italian ANR Claims					
5ª Sq, 2° Gr C	Cap Mario Bellagambi	Bf 109G	Spitfire	nr Isola della Scala	1350

Italian ANR Casualties	
6ª Sq, 2° Gr C	Bf 109G damaged in combat, belly-landed at Thiene; M.llo Tullio Covre safe

Friday-Saturday, 22/23 December 1944

British Claims					
600 Sqn	Flg Off S.W.Rees/Flg Off G.Beaumont	Beaufighter VIf V8705	Ju 87 Damaged	N Forlì	2000
600 Sqn	Flg Off S.W.Rees/Flg Off G.Beaumont	Beaufighter VIf V8705	Ju 87	16m NW Forlì	2040
600 Sqn	Flg Off S.W.Rees/Flg Off G.Beaumont	Beaufighter VIf V8705	Ju 87	Forlì area	2120
US Claims					
414th NFS	1/Lt Albert L.Jones/Flt Off John Rudovsky	Beaufighter VIf	Ju 87	nr Asola	2130

German Casualties	
3./NSGr 9	Ju 87D-5 WNr 131434 E8+BL force-landed S Villafranca 1652; Obfw Herbert Schink WiA/gunner safe
2./NSGr 9	Ju 87D-5 WNr 140750 E8+JK shot down by night-fighter N Cremona 2130; Fhj Obfw Artur Heiland/Uffz Artur Ballok WiA
2./NSGr 9	Ju 87D-5 WNr 140747 E8+KK shot down by night-fighter nr Lugo; FhjFw Edgar Gerstenberger KiA/Gefr Hans Mechlinski WiA
2./NSGr 9	Ju 87D-5 WNr 130532 E8+FK shot down by night-fighter NW Bologna; Ofhr Hans Kolster/Gefr Gustav Leumann/KiA

Saturday, 23 December 1944

US Casualties	
346th FS/350th FG	P-47D 42-28827 '6D1' hit by Flak, crashed 5m E Piacenza 1010; 1/Lt John Diffendal KiA [14557]
1° Gr Caça/350th FG	P-47D 44-19665 'A6' hit by Flak, crashed nr Quistello 0850; 1° Ten Ismael da Motta Paes POW
84th BS/47th BG	A-20K 44-617 lost u/k cause, crashed into sea off Rosignano 0950; 1/Lt Elsworth Totten III and three MiA [10846]

Sunday, 24 December 1944

Eight P-47Ds of 347th Fighter Squadron attacked Thiene airfield.

US Casualties	
428th BS/310th BG	B-25J 43-27768 *Buffalo Gal* left Ghisonaccia 0715 on weather recce, crashed into mountain; 1/Lt Frank J.Folsom Jr and seven MiA [10725]
Italian ANR Casualties	
2° Gr C	14 Bf 109Gs destroyed by strafing at Thiene airfield

Monday, 25 December 1944

Twelve Marauders of 21 SAAF Squadron raided Treviso. Two aircraft lost formation and joined 24 SAAF and 30 SAAF Squadrons, a third aircraft developed a spin and the crew was ordered to bale out; two gunners did but pilot then recovered control, jettisoned bombs and returned to base.

US Casualties	
345th FS/350th FG	P-47D 42-27267 hit by Flak nr Piacenza, pilot baled 1115 and a/c crashed nr base; Lt Kenneth E.Clifton returned
346th FS/350th FG	P-47D 42-29017 '6A7' engine failure, belly-landed E Vicenza; 1/Lt Dempsey E.Ballard POW [10795]
German Casualties	
6.(F)/122	Ju 188D-2 WNr 150533 F6+GP failed to return; Uffz Hans Hartmann and crew MiA

Tuesday, 26 December 1944

Twelve Marauders of 30 SAAF Squadron set off to bomb Castelfranco Veneto marshalling yards at 1127 but lost a Marauder when its starboard engine caught fire. Unable to maintain height Lt Kippen attempted to crash land on the beach or ditch off the coast at Senigallia. Upon hitting the sea at 1135 the bomb load detonated and destroyed the aircraft, killing all the crew.

3 RAAF Squadron was on patrol at 8,500ft near Pordenone with Sqn Ldr Murray Nash leading a section of four and with a top cover section of three 1,500ft above. Ten Bf 109s of ANR 2° Gruppo bounced the latter section from out of the sun and Wt Off Jack Quinn who was lagging was shot down at about 1515. Nash had broken into the attack in time to see Quinn bale out. The 109s departed and no further combat ensued at this time. The six remaining Mustangs then flew around Aviano hoping to catch the Messerschmitts as they came into land. After ten minutes a Bf 109 was seen 4,000ft above and about a mile away at 9 o'clock. The Australian pilots climbed after it, and Blue 1, the leader of the top cover section, which was higher than Nash's Red Section, reached the level of the Italian fighter, which broke into the attack and made a head-on pass at Blue 1, then half rolled, dived straight through Red Section and continued down to the deck, being chased by Nash. The latter easily closed in on the Bf 109 despite it reaching some 400 mph at 30 to 50 feet. However, the pilot had difficulty in shooting because he was being bounced around in the slipstream. Eventually he hit the Messerschmitt in the port wing and both radiators which streamed glycol. As Nash put it in his combat report "we expected him to prang at any moment". Nash then pulled up hard to starboard both to get out of the way and to avoid the Flak he expected from Aviano airfield over which they were now flying. He saw Red 2 shooting at the 109 and then lost sight of both. Flg Off W.A.Andrews (Red 2) stated in his combat report:

"I closed in firing three long bursts from 150 to 30 yards 5 degrees astern. On first burst the starboard oleo leg fell down and on the second the port followed. He made no evasive action and I continued the attack as he flew over the southern boundary of Aviano aerodrome. Small pieces flew from the cockpit and port wing root and I was overtaking him very fast and I broke off the attack at 30 yards pulling up sharply and I did not see the e/a again. The aerodrome defences opened fire as I pulled away with light accurate 20 mill."

Flg Off Max Thomas was Blue 1 and stated:

"An aircraft was reported closing from 6 o'clock from out of the sun. Immediately after I saw a stream of tracers going past my port wing. I climbed sharply to the left and promptly spun. Recovering I saw an Me 109 on my left at 200 yards to which I gave a two-second burst from 8 o'clock – nil results. I then spun to the left evading tracers from a second Me 109 that attacked from the rear port quarter as I was making my attack. I recovered from the spin at about 5,000ft and jettisoned bombs and climbed above Red Section travelling west. Red leader then reported a single aircraft at 9 o'clock at about 1,000ft flying west. As I climbed up, he turned south towards our formation. I fired a short burst from 8 o'clock slightly below him – no strikes seen. He then peeled off into a vertical dive and flattened out just above the deck heading east. Red leader followed him down and came into range as he approached the southern boundary of Aviano aerodrome. I was flying a parallel course at 5,000ft and saw glycol streaming from the starboard side as a result of Red leader's attack. As Red leader broke away to the right, Red 2 continued the attack and finally broke away to the right. I then dived on the e/a which went into a gentle turn to the left around the perimeter of the aerodrome at about 100ft. I fired three two-second bursts closing from 300 yards to 50 yards from astern seeing strikes at the rear of the fuselage. No evasive action was taken. I overshot and pulled up to the right. Both port guns had jammed during this attack. I attacked again from astern firing three bursts from 300 yards to 150 yards when both starboard guns jammed also. When I broke away the e/a had made one-and-a-half circuits of the aerodrome at about 100ft and had maintained the same gradual rate of turn throughout. As I left glycol was still streaming from the a/c and I noticed damage to the port mainplane and fuselage."

Right: On Boxing Day Sqn Ldr Murray Nash, the commander of 3 RAAF Squadron, led a large patrol that had an engagement with ANR Bf 109Gs. Below: Several of these Mustangs of 3 RAAF Squadron parked at Fano were involved in the Boxing Day action including KH626 'Z' which suffered an undercarriage collapse on return. Next is KH616 '<>' in which Wt Off Quinn was shot down, while beyond is KH593 'A' flown by Flg Off Andrews, fire from whose aircraft damaged a Bf 109.

British Claims

3 RAAF Sqn	Sqn Ldr M.P.Nash	Mustang III KH716 'P'			
3 RAAF Sqn	Flg Off W.A.Andrews	Mustang III KH593 'A'	Bf 109 Damaged	Aviano a/f	1530
3 RAAF Sqn	Flg Off V.M.Thomas	Mustang III KH615 'B'			

British Casualties

3 RAAF Sqn	Mustang III KH616 '<>' shot down by Bf 109 4m SSW Pordenone 1550, pilot baled out; Wt Off J.F.Quinn POW
450 Sqn	Kittyhawk IV FX710 left 0900 after bombing pilot reported engine trouble, reached the sea and baled out; Wt Off L.G.Robinson seen next day by Walrus apparently dead
30 SAAF Sqn	Marauder III HD496 'G' left 1127 to bomb Castelfranco Veneto marshalling yards, after take-off fire seen from engine, ditched off Senigallia 1135, exploding on impact; Lt W.P.Kippen and five KiA

7 SAAF Sqn	Spitfire IX LF PT545 left 1215, hit by Flak, crashed SW Forlì 1255; Lt P.W.Nourse KiA
19 SAAF Sqn	Beaufighter X NV236 engine failure on take-off from Biferno, crashed into sea ½ mile off shore; Lt A.L.Hawkes KiA/Flg Off J.Treleaven safe
16 SAAF Sqn	Beaufighter X NE528 starboard engine caught fire, ditched 5m off Biferno; Lt L.F.H.Catherine KiA/Lt D.J.Driver safe, rescued
293 Sqn	Walrus I L2170 'Z' of B Flt from Falconara, abandoned and sunk after an ASR landing off Ravenna; Sgt R.T.Biche and crew safe

US Casualties

66th FS/57th FG	P-47D 42-75825 lost u/k cause N Piombino 1310; 1/Lt Donald G.Herdrich KiA

Italian ANR Claims

4ª Sq, 2° Gr C	Serg Magg Ernesto Keller	Bf 109G	P-51	1520
4ª Sq, 2° Gr C	Cap Ugo Drago	Bf 109G	P-51 (not confirmed)	1520

Italian ANR Casualties

4ª Sq, 2° Gr C	Bf 109G-14 Black 8 hit in combat, crash-landed; S.Ten Felice Squassoni safe

Wednesday, 27 December 1944

Four P-39s of 4° Stormo, led by the unit commander, Magg Luigi Mariotti, took off at 0915 on an armed reconnaissance mission over Kolasin-Prijepolje area. Mariotti's aircraft was hit by Flak and crashed, killing the pilot who was awarded a posthumous Medaglia d'oro. Magg Ranieri Piccolomini took temporary charge of 4° Stormo.

British Casualties

249 Sqn	Mustang III FB330 left 0915, hit by Flak strafing near Prijepolje, glycol leaked, pilot baled out near Niksic 1040; Flt Sgt M.Smith safe, linked up with a British SOE agent and returned in a few days
250 Sqn	Kittyhawk IV FX837 left 1300, exploded in bomb dive on railway near Padua, no Flak seen; Flg Off M.H.Sullivan KiA
253 Sqn	Spitfire IX MJ532 left 1150, shot down by Flak NE Tavidovic 40m SE Banja Luka 1320; Lt R.G.Cummings POW
145 Sqn	Spitfire VIII MT774 left 1115, hit by Flak, force-landed 3m NE Cesena in Allied lines; Sqn Ldr S.W.F.Daniel safe

Flt Lt Muir of 249 Squadron flying Mustang III KH561 'B' attacks German armoured cars on a snow-covered road near Plievlja in Yugoslavia on 27 December.

241 Sqn	Spitfire IXe PT613 left 1020, on Rover David mission, hit by intense light Flak 1050, force-landed in Allied lines, aircraft Cat E damaged; Flt Sgt L.M.Bailey safe
417 Sqn	Spitfire VIII JF452 left 1630 on weather recce, iced up, crashed on landing 1640; Flt Lt C.J.Malone safe
US Casualties	
345th FS/350th FG	P-47D 42-28321 hit by Flak, crashed 3m SE Somma Lombardo 1050, wreck captured by Germans; 2/Lt Dale H.Hargrove KiA [10796]
Italian Co-Belligerent Casualties	
73ª Sq, 12° Gr, 4° St	P-39 left 0915, hit by Flak, crashed 5km N Mojkovac; Magg Luigi Mariotti (Stormo CO) KiA

Wednesday-Thursday, 27/28 December 1944

British Casualties	
114 Sqn	Boston IV BZ493 left 0233 on armed recce, swung on take-off, crashed, writing off two Mosquitos of 256 Sqn and a USN Catalina; Sgt W.Absalom and three crew safe

Thursday, 28 December 1944

The Walrus amphibian adopted a unique role when on 28 December 624 Squadron was formed at Grottaglie under Sqn Ldr G.M.Gallacher for the mine-spotting role over the southern Adriatic. It became operational from Foggia in February 1945 tasked with flying mine reconnaissance over shipping routes looking out for German and Italian mines, which were often clearly visible from the air. The mine spotting was to allow clear passage into newly captured ports in support of the Royal Navy's 12th Minesweeping Flotilla. To conduct its specialised role 624 mounted detachments as far apart as Pisa and Hassani in Greece. In April it moved up the coast to Falconara and was there when the war ended, though it continued on its tasks on a reduced basis until disbanding in November.

British Casualties	
111 Sqn	Spitfire IX MH782 'B' left 0925 on escort to Baltimores, engine cut 15m NE Venice, hit by 20mm Flak as he crossed the coast, down in sea; Flt Sgt P.Taylor KiA
2 SAAF Sqn	Spitfire IXc MH557'E' left 1525, shot down by Flak SE Ravenna 1605, pilot baled out but parachute did not open; Lt M.Flynn KiA
93 Sqn	Spitfire IX LZ837 left 0925 on bomber escort, caught fire and crashed into sea off River Po mouth; Plt Off J.A.C.Strange KiA

Walrus Is L2201 'B', W2741 'E', Z1769 'A' and W3072 'C' of 624 Squadron that was formed at Grottaglie on 28 December for mine-spotting duties over the southern Adriatic.

12 SAAF Sqn	Marauder III HD649 'P' left 1035 to bomb marshalling yards at Udine, damaged by Flak; Lt W.P.Cohen and three safe, two WiA
30 SAAF Sqn	Marauder III HD484 'F' left 1230 to bomb marshalling yards at Udine, damaged by Flak, damaged further on landing; Lt G.B.Murray and five safe
30 SAAF Sqn	Marauder III HD584 'Q' left 1230 to bomb marshalling yards at Udine, damaged by Flak, damaged further on landing; Lt R.R.Truter and five safe

Thursday-Friday, 28/29 December 1944

Sqn Ldr K.G.Hart DFC, a former Battle of Britain fighter pilot, was killed on this day, when his Boston was shot down by Flak.

British Claims

256 Sqn	Flt Lt J.A.Porter/Flg Off G.S.Johnson	Mosquito XIII MM534	Ju 52/3m Damaged	3-4m NE Zenica	1750

British Casualties

18 Sqn	Boston IV BZ557 'Z' left 1642 on armed recce of Villafranca a/f, attacked a bridge over the Santerno river, shot down by Flak; Sqn Ldr K.G.Hart DFC and three KiA
114 Sqn	Boston IV BZ514 left 1930 on armed recce of Verona-Vicenza-Nervesa-Casarsa area, overshot landing, crashed into the sea off Falconara 2240; Flg Off B.R.Emmett and three KiA

US Claims

417th NFS	Lt Malcolm D.Campbell/2/Lt Robert J.McCullen	Beaufighter VIf --568 'V'	Ju 290	2130

Friday, 29 December 1944

12 SAAF Squadron on the way to attack targets in the Po Valley, passed over Udine where seven Flak trains were in the marshalling yards. The intense Flak here hit Lt C.Brichard's Marauder which blew up, causing damage to two others.

Flt Lt F.J.Lawrenson of 450 Squadron led an attack to dive bomb a road diversion. In his bomb dive the Flak hit his Kittyhawk, blowing off the hood and injuring him, though he managed to maintain control and landed at base. His total operational hours had reached 197.45 (a tour being 200 hours); and he was promptly declared tour expired. Nearly six years later, as a squadron leader, Frederick Lawrenson was serving with 77 RAAF Squadron in the Korean War when he was killed on Christmas Day 1952 being hit by ground fire in Meteor VIII A-77-852 which crashed and exploded.

Flg Off John Gardner of 249 Squadron was fortunate to survive when his Mustang III KH543 'F' crashed at Biferno when taking off for an armed reconnaissance on 29 December.

450 Sqn	Kittyhawk IV FX725 left 1400 to dive bomb a road diversion, a direct Flak hit blew off the hood and injured the pilot in the head and right arm 1505; Flt Lt F.J.Lawrenson WiA
601 Sqn	Spitfire IX PL352 left 0750 to bomb guns 1m NE Imola, hit by Flak, crash-landed at Pergola; Sgt I.Duffie WiA
249 Sqn	Mustang III KH543 'F' left Biferno on armed recce with two 250lb bombs on board but crashed after take-off; Flg Off J.W.Gardner safe
12 SAAF Sqn	Marauder III HD501 'S' blew up from direct Flak hit over Udine marshalling yards 1308; Lt C.J.P.Brichard and five KiA
12 SAAF Sqn	Marauder III HD620 'R' shot down by Flak over Udine marshalling yards 1308; Lt H.T.Funkey and five KiA
12 SAAF Sqn	Marauder III HD543 'V' shot down by Flak over Udine marshalling yards 1308; Maj H.Braithwaite and five POW
US Casualties	
525th FS/86th FG	P-47D 42-xx060 damaged by Flak 1110, pilot baled into Allied lines; 1/Lt John V.Jordan WiA
345th FS/350th FG	P-47D 42-28344 hit by Flak, crashed nr Castelnuovo Garfagnana 1430; Capt Eldon C.Baldwin KiA [14566]
346th FS/350th FG	P-47D 42-28333 lost u/k cause, possibly small-arms fire 1620; 1/Lt John W Phelan KiA [10946]
German Casualties	
2.(F)/122	Me 410B-3 WNr 190165 F6+GK crashed 30km SSW Modena; Obfhr Ernst Spöntjes/Uffz Schmauser KiA

Friday-Saturday, 29/30 December 1944

British Claims

256 Sqn	Flt Lt R.Smyth/Flg Off W.H.Palmer	Mosquito XIII HK412	Ju 88 Damaged	0255

Saturday, 30 December 1944

US Casualties

4th TCS/62nd TCG	C-47A 42-92680 on paradrop-resupply mission to partisan unit W Fornovo, crashed due to extreme turbulence, 1141; 1/Lt Don A.Ray and six KiA [10942]

Sunday, 31 December 1944

British Casualties

2 SAAF Sqn	Spitfire IXe MJ895 'S' left 1405 on sweep N Portomaggiore, shot down by Flak N Argenta 1505; Lt R.F.Bell evaded but wounded by land mine, reached Allied lines 26 January, also frostbitten
241 Sqn	Spitfire IXe PT767 left 1015 on bomber escort, force-landed at Cesenatico 1045; Flt Lt N.P.Michie safe
417 Sqn	Spitfire VIII MT656 left 0955 to bomb guns, engine cut 3m off Bellaria over the sea 1000, pilot baled out but not rescued; Wt Off K.S.Hanson KiA
318 Sqn	Spitfire IX NH262 left 0810 on Arty/R, damaged by Flak near Imola landed safely at base 0825; Flg Off R.Dusiecki WiA
US Casualties	
87th FS/79th FG	P-47D 42-29367 lost u/k cause 3m E Celje 1045; 1/Lt Albert V.Bratt Jr POW [10953]
87th FS/79th FG	P-47D 42-26370 *Dearest Dottie* shot down by Flak 8m SW Pola 1322; 1/Lt Richard P.Gorsuch MiA [10912]
527th FS/86th FG	P-47D 42-28132 '79' *Viv's Baby Shoes* damaged by own bomb blast nr Alfianello 1025; 2/Lt John E.Tompson POW [10794]

Sunday-Monday, 31 December 1944/1 January 1945

British Casualties

18 Sqn	Boston IV BZ508 'B left 2057 on armed recce of Po Valley, presumed to be a/c seen to ditch on fire E Venice, FTR; Flt Lt R.W.Gillham and three KiA

Thus 1944 came to an end, leaving Mediterranean Allied Tactical Air Force (MATAF) a much smaller organisation, though no less an effective one than it had been 12 months earlier. The MATAF Order of Battle at the close of the year was:

XII Tactical Air Command

27th Fighter Group	Three squadrons of P-47D Thunderbolts plus the attached 11 SAAF Squadron with Kittyhawks
57th Fighter Group	Three squadrons of P-47D Thunderbolts
86th Fighter Group	Three squadrons of P-47D Thunderbolts
350th Fighter Group	Three squadrons of P-47D Thunderbolts plus the similarly-equipped 1º Grupo de Caça (Brazilian)
8 SAAF Wing	Three squadrons of Spitfire IXs
47th Bomb Group (Light)	Four squadrons of A-20G Havocs
208 and 225 Squadrons	With tactical reconnaissance Spitfire IXs
414th, 415th, and 416th NFS	With Beaufighter VIfs and P-61 Black Widows (414th NFS only)

Desert Air Force

239 Wing	Four squadrons of Mustang IIIs and two squadrons of Kittyhawk IVs
244 Wing	Four squadrons of Spitfire VIIIs and one squadron of Spitfire IXs
7 SAAF Wing	Four squadrons of Spitfire IXs
324 Wing	Four squadrons of Spitfire IXs
285 Wing	Two squadrons of tactical reconnaissance Spitfire IXs
232 Wing	Four squadrons of Boston IVs and Vs
253 Wing	Three squadrons of Baltimore Vs
3 SAAF Wing	Four squadrons of Marauder IIIs
600 Squadron	With Beaufighter VIfs
256 Squadron	With Mosquito XIIIs

57th Bombardment Wing (Medium)

319th Bomb Group (Medium)	Four squadrons of B-25 Mitchells
321st Bomb Group (Medium)	Four squadrons of B-25 Mitchells
340th Bomb Group (Medium)	Four squadrons of B-25 Mitchells

3rd Photographic Reconnaissance Group

Three squadrons of Lockheed F-5 Lightnings

51st Troop Carrier Wing

Three groups of troop-carrying transports

ANOTHER NEW YEAR DAWNS

With the onset of good weather in late December, MATAF had returned to the attack on the lines of communication with a vengeance, joined once again on this occasion by the high-flying B-17s and B-24s of 15th Air Force. The north-eastern rail lines had all been cut in at least one key spot by the turn of the year, and the line through the Brenner Pass was attacked by everybody; no through traffic at all had been received there during the last five days of the year. Lines leading to the major routes were also bombed by both B-25s and fighter-bombers, while further heavy attacks were made on marshalling yards.

Raids in targets in Yugoslavia continued to be made by DAF units, particularly the 239 Wing Mustangs and 3 SAAF Wing Marauders. The continued presence over northern Italy of the Italian ANR 2º Gruppo Caccia caused the Spitfire and P-47 units to have to reduce the number of bomb-carrying sorties, and to allocate more time to the less-productive but vital task of escort. 244, 324 and 7 SAAF Wings all escorted 239 Wing's Kittyhawks during the month, while 324 Wing also escorted the South African Marauders.

By early 1945 to identify their aircraft to trigger-happy USAAF pilots the photo-reconnaissance Mosquito PR XVIs of 60 SAAF Squadron carried broad white stripes around the fuselage.

Most efforts of the fighters were to fly numerous Cab Rank sorties during the month. Transport of any sort was a favoured target as always, but the intention now was to try and create a 'transport desert' to deny all rapid movement to the Germans in the territory remaining in their hands.

Unlike other US night-fighter units that received the P-61, during January the 416th NFS at Rosignano replaced Beaufighters with the Mosquito XXX on which it continued night operations.

Monday, 1 January 1945

British Casualties	
43 Sqn	Spitfire IX PV137 'C' left 1030, shot down by 88mm Flak near Massa; Plt Off W.R.Dauphin KiA
241 Sqn	Spitfire IXe PT587 left 0900 on a Rover Paddy, crashed immediately after take-off 0905; Sgt R.Gill KiA
500 Sqn	Baltimore V FA632 'H' left 1000 to bomb Conegliano marshalling yards, hit by Flak approaching the target, crashed; Flt Sgt W.L.Frost and one KiA, two POW
US Casualties	
527th FS/86th FG	P-47D 44-80546 '91' hit high tension wires, crashed at Lodi 1110; Capt Boyd B.Chambers Jr KiA [15882]

Tuesday, 2 January 1945

British Casualties	
87 Sqn	Spitfire IX EN268 left 1230 to bomb guns, hit by 20mm Flak, damaged Cat II; Flt Sgt R.E.Micklam safe
US Casualties	
1° Gr Caça/350th FG	P-47D 42-26768 'B5' hit by Flak 0900; 1° Ten João Mauricio de Medeiros KiA
347th FS/350th FG	P-47D lost over Italy; 2/Lt Oliver B.Hays KiA

Wednesday, 3 January 1945

British Casualties	
2 SAAF Sqn	Spitfire IXe RR189 'H' left 1150, hit by Flak causing glycol leak, engine seized 2m S Migliarino SW Lake Comacchio; Lt A.Assad POW
7 SAAF Sqn	Spitfire IXe PT897 left 0850, hit by Flak, force-landed on return, Cat AC damaged; Maj R.H.C.Kershaw safe
7 SAAF Sqn	Spitfire IXe PT647 left 1000, engine failed after strafing, force-landed in Allied lines SW Ravenna; Lt D.H.Theron safe

B-25J Mitchell 43-28080 '6E' *Who Cares* of the 486th Bomb Squadron, 340th Bomb Group over the Tyrrhenian Sea en route to a target in northern Italy on 3 January 1945.

7 SAAF Sqn	Spitfire IXc MH657 left 1530, hit by Flak, got back to within 6m of Forlì, pilot baled out; Lt A.L.Basson safe
111 Sqn	Spitfire IX PT828 'F' left 1445, failed to return from attack on gun positions near Imola; Wt Off L.Rouke KiA
43 Sqn	Spitfire IX MK405 left 1200 shot down by ground-fired rockets, or blew up in bomb dive in Forlì area; Sgt D.V.Basso KiA
272 Sqn	Beaufighter X NV789 'V' left 2150 on armed recce to 25m NW Pola, attacking a tanker, FTR; Flg Off R.T.Greig/Flg Off B.D.Lilley KiA

US Casualties

65th FS/57th FG	P-47D 42-75640 '60' *Bomb Happy* shot down by Flak 0910 nr Torre Beretti; Maj Francis S.Manda POW [10950]
66th FS/57th FG	P-47D 42-29019 shot down by Flak NW Mantova 1245; 2/Lt Randolph W.Lee POW [10951]
527th FS/86thFG	P-47D 42-28036 '83' *Dal/Rosie* crashed 1m SE Ponte Oglio 1450; 2/Lt Clarence M.Thomas POW [10952]

Wednesday-Thursday, 3/4 January 1945

British Claims

256 Sqn	Plt Off A.H.Hounslow/Plt Off P.Lund	Mosquito XIII HK412	Ju 188	N Falconara	0323

German Casualties

Kdo Carmen	Ju 188A-2 WNr 170622 A3+TD lost; Gefr Albert Muhlhoff and four KiA

Thursday, 4 January 1945

British Casualties

40 SAAF Sqn	Spitfire IX left 1025, hit by Flak near Lugo, caught fire, crash-landed in Allied lines; Lt B.K.Ross safe
43 Sqn	Spitfire IX PT757 left 1020 to bomb houses in Senio area 1045, hit by Flak, force-landed at Forlì l/g 1100, Cat II damaged; Wt Off C.C.Hollingworth safe
145 Sqn	Spitfire VIII MT775 left 1000 on Rover Frank, engine cut after take-off, jettisoned bombs, belly-landed on a beach near Rimini 1005; Flt Lt D.I.S.Wood safe
417 Sqn	Spitfire VIII JF672 left 1330, engine failed after take-off, force-landed on the beach; Flg Off R.L.Cotram safe
213 Sqn	Mustang III KH665 left 1330, shot down by Flak while strafing a train in the Brod Doboj area; Flt Lt J.A.Mulcahy-Morgan KiA
253 Sqn	Spitfire VIII JF697 left 1205 on a sweep, lost formation in bad weather, FTR; Flt Sgt W.H.Aldercotte KiA
2 SAAF Sqn	Spitfire IXc MJ191 'Z' *Lady Bashful* left 1400, strafed near Cotignola, engine cut, force-landed in own lines N Forlì; Lt C.C.Hitchins safe
4 SAAF Sqn	Spitfire IX RR184 left 1120 on escort to Yugoslavia, engine trouble, crashed NW Cesenatico 1340; Lt J.J.Roelofse KiA
7 SAAF Sqn	Spitfire IXc MH891 'H' left 1550 to attack gun positions NW Cesena, shot down by Flak S Imola; Lt R.G.Whitehorn KiA
7 SAAF Sqn	Spitfire IXe PT900 left 1550 to attack gun positions NW Cesena, hit by Flak, crashed on landing at base; Capt K.A.Young safe
72 Sqn	Spitfire IX PT475 left 0840, hit by Flak 0910, nothing further heard; Flt Lt J.A.Gray POW

A Savoia S.82 of I° Gruppo, Raggruppamento Bombardamento e Trasporti. On 4 January six S.82s of this unit, escorted by four Spitfires of 51° Stormo, conducted a supply drop to partisans at Berane in Montenegro.

253 Sqn	Spitfire IX MA473 left 1100 strafing train near Sarajevo, hit by Flak, pilot baled Dolipolie NE Kaonth 1215; Plt Off W.Agnew POW
454 Sqn	Baltimore V FW643 'J' bombed San Alberto, on return bounced on landing, crashed into a sand dune; Sgt F.G.Lister and three WiA
US Casualties	
524th FS/27th FBG	P-47D 42-27346 crashed while strafing 1315; 2/Lt Bernard F.Quinlan KiA
523rd FS/27th FBG	P-47D 42-27973 shot down by Flak S Bassano 1415; 1/Lt Alexander R.Cattanach baled and evaded [10947]
87th FS/79th FG	P-47D 42-26808 *Mi Yukui* lost u/k cause nr Mokro, Yugoslavia 1220; 2/Lt William L.Harding KiA [10944]
87th FS/79th FG	P-47D 42-25296 shot down by Flak nr Stanghella 1330; 2/Lt Harry E.Bartley KiA [10949]
525th FS/86th FG	P-47D 44-20139 hit by Flak SE Bergamo 0930; 1/Lt John V.Connor Jr returned [10948]
346th FS/350th FG	P-47D 42-27004 '6CI' lost u/k cause, crashed 5km S Tortona 0900; 2/Lt John J.McFadden Jr KiA [14566]
428th BS/310th BG	B-25J 43-27666 *Sad Sack* shot down by Flak NE Arco; 1/Lt Robert G.McPherson and two KiA, two POW [10945]

Friday, 5 January 1945

British Casualties	
73 Sqn	Spitfire IX MJ992 'A' left 1000, FTR from a solo sweep near Athens; Flt Sgt H.J.O'Keefe KiA
94 Sqn	Spitfire Vb ER663 failed to pull out of a dive while strafing vehicles near Eleusis, Greece; Flt Sgt R.J.Andrews KiA
16 SAAF Sqn	Beaufighter X NV151 'H' left 1025 to attack coastal defence guns on Lussino Island, hit by Flak over target, crew baled out 1125, only one parachute seen to open landing on Cherso Island; Lt F.A.Lardner evaded/Lt L.E.Boughey KiA

Saturday, 6 January 1945

US Casualties	
526th FS/86th FG	P-47D 42-27928 hit by Flak off coast of Sestri Levante 1445; 2/Lt Kenneth D.Bostad KiA [11281]
523rd FS/27th FBG	P-47D 42-29291 shot down by Flak 0905; 2/Lt John V.Holbrook KiA

Monday, 8 January 1945

US Casualties	
66th FS/57th FG	P-47D 42-27070 dived into sea; Flt Off Walter C.McCollum K [16385]

Mosquito XIX TA428 YD-A was the first one delivered to 255 Squadron at Foggia during January 1945.

Tuesday, 9 January 1945

MATAF was ordered to give first priority to communications targets. XXII TAC was committed to the Brenner route and DAF to lower Tarvisio and Piedicolle rail route while 57th Bomb Wing was to attack river bridges and rail tracks in lower Brenner. This strategy was designed to prevent the Germans withdrawing units to reinforce other fronts elsewhere as much as to prevent supplies getting through to them. At this point, however, the weather deteriorated and few large-scale missions could be mounted. XXII TAC diverted its attacks from stretches of open track to bridges and diversions, managing to keep the greater part of the Brenner Pass blocked at a number of points throughout the month.

Within XXII TAC 8 SAAF Wing had finally moved to Pontedera at the start of January, 11 SAAF Squadron then joining the wing which continued operations against the command's targets alongside the resident 27th Fighter Group. Frequent duties for the Spitfires included escorts to the Kittyhawks and to C-47s dropping supplies at the front and to Italian partisan forces in Axis territory.

By night the activities of the intruders and interdicting Bostons continued. 55 Squadron had at last completed re-equipment to Bostons, and now the air echelon moved to Falconara to recommence operations. At Rosignano 255 Squadron was also converting to Mosquito XIXs and would shortly become fully operational on these aircraft with DAF.

British Casualties

3 RAAF Sqn	Mustang III KH615 left 1535, hit by 20mm Flak in dive-bombing attack on bridge at Alfonsine, crashed in flames SE of target; Flg Off V.M.Thomas KiA. Wreck and grave found on 13 May

---

Wednesday, 10 January 1945

Luftflotte 2 had by now shrunk to:

NAGr 11 *	Bf 109, FW 190	29	(23)
2.(F)/122	Me 410	4	(3)
4.(F)/122	Ju 88, Ju 188	8	(7)
6.(F)/122	Ju 188	4	(3)
NSGr 9	Ju 87	23	(14)

*Including the attached Seenot 20, which were the FW 190-equipped component.

British Casualties	
72 Sqn	Spitfire IX MJ203 shot down by Flak attacking rail targets at Canaro 1120; Flg Off D.G.Crawford baled out but hit aircraft, KiA
1 SAAF Sqn	Spitfire IXe PT791 left 1055, lost to Flak 10m E Porto Garibaldi, pilot baled out into sea; Lt M.H.L.Tweedie KiA
US Casualties	
345th FS/350th FG	P-47D 42-27276 '6C1' hit by Flak, damaged beyond repair in landing 1700; Maj Lee C.Wells safe

Thursday, 11 January 1945

Eleven Mustangs of 260 Squadron attacked Casarsa-Codroipo railway; three Bf 109s attempted to intercept without success. 244 Wing escorted 36 Baltimores from all three squadrons of 253 Wing to strike marshalling yards at Castelfranco.

British Casualties	
43 Sqn	Spitfire IX PT846 left 0905 to bomb artillery, hit by Flak and damaged Cat II; Flt Sgt H.Wilkinson WiA
111 Sqn	Spitfire IX MK513 'Y' left 1215, hit by Flak while strafing a ferry near Porto Garibaldi; landed at Bellaria a/f 1255; Plt Off A.J.McCallum safe
111 Sqn	Spitfire IX PT403 'C' left 1215, hit by Flak while strafing a ferry; crash-landed at Bellaria a/f 1255; Sgt K.Clappison safe
72 Sqn	Spitfire IX MJ200 left 0945, bombed guns 1010, damaged on landing, Cat II; Plt Off D.J.Gorham safe
112 Sqn	Mustang III FB255 'M' left 1420 to bomb rail bridge at Alfonsine, hit by Flak, crash-landed 1555; Wt Off J.S.Duncan POW
30 SAAF Sqn	Marauder HD569 'X' left 1134 from Jesi to bomb a bridge at Conegliano, swung on take-off, crashed and blew up, writing off Marauder HD516 'K' and damaging five more; Lt R.R.Truter and five KiA
US Casualties	
347th FS/350th FG	P-47D 44-19592 *Snotty Dotty* shot down by Flak 6m SE Piacenza 1040; 2/Lt Alexander Robertson POW [11279]
524th FS/27th FBG	P-47D 44-19586 shot down by Flak 1500; pilot returned
66th FS/57th FG	P-47D 42-29371 damaged Cat 2 by Flak 1000; pilot safe

Friday, 12 January 1945

US Casualties	
522nd FS/27th FBG	P-47D 42-26712 possibly shot down by Flak 0945; 1/Lt Silvio R.Vinciguerra KiA
346th FS/350th FG	P-47D 44-20106 '6C5' shot down by Flak 5m NE Vigevano 1430; 1/Lt Ernest D.Fahlberg rescued by partisans [11280]

Monday, 15 January 1945

Eight Mustangs of 112 Squadron led by Flt Lt Ray Hearn strafed Udine airfield and claimed a single-engine aircraft destroyed in flames, two others were hit and a petrol bowser burnt.

British Casualties	
260 Sqn	Mustang III FB274 shot down by Flak while strafing a train near Conegliano 1125; Capt G.MacG.Henderson KiA
417 Sqn	Spitfire VIII JF958 left 0925 escorting Kittyhawks, engine failed, last seen near Latisana; Wt Off R.J.Ashley KiA
19 SAAF Sqn	Beaufighter X 'Y' left 1110 to attack Lussin Piccolo Island, hit in port engine by Flak, ditched off Korna Island; Lt R.R. Campbell/Flg Off Davies rescued by a HSL from Vis after 5 hours in dinghy
US Casualties	
526th FS/86th FG	P-47D 42-27289 '48' *The Brat* lost u/k cause 4m W Caorle 1455; 1/Lt Lester L.Eastburn [11282]
German Casualties	
1./NAGr 11	Bf 109 destroyed by strafing at Udine

Tuesday, 16 January 1945

British Casualties	
252 Sqn	Beaufighter X NV377 following an engine fire, spun into the sea near Calino; Plt Off W.K.Ashley/Plt Off P.J.Gray KiA

Flt Lt E.Howey in Spitfire IX MH545 WU-F of 225 Squadron providing escort to a US B-25 during a reconnaissance on 17 January.

Wednesday, 17 January 1945

US Casualties

522nd FS/27th FBG	P-47D 42-29061 *Utah Undertaker* shot down by Flak 5m S Leno 1055; 1/Lt Wayne Wheeler evaded [11283]
64th FS/57th FG	P-47D 42-29002 damaged Cat 2 by bomb blast; pilot safe
64th FS/57th FG	P-47D 42-27656 flew through trees, damaged Cat 2; pilot safe
447th BS/321st BG	B-25J 43-36054 damaged by Flak, landed at base, salvaged; 1/Lt Louis C.Breckenridge and five safe
447th BS/321st BG	B-25J 43-36108 '70' left 1130 to bomb bridges at Ora, hit by Flak, landed at base; 1/Lt George R.Morrison Jr and four safe, one KiA

Thursday, 18 January 1945

British Casualties

145 Sqn	Spitfire VIII JF878 strafed building which exploded, destroyed by the blast; Flg Off A.G.P.Newman KiA
15 SAAF Sqn	Baltimore V FW826 left 1455 to bomb Massa Lombarda, port engine set on fire by Flak, observer baled out, crash-landed in the front lines near Pisignano; Lt Col L.H.G.Shuttleworth and two safe, observer Capt C.F.Marais POW

B-25J Mitchell 43-27649 *Stud* of the 379th Bomb Squadron, 310th Bomb Group going down in flames after being hit by Flak over Yugoslavia taking with it Capt Ellis J.McKanna and his crew, 18 January.

500 Sqn	Baltimore V FW455 'U' left 1505 to bomb fuel dumps at Massa Lombarda, damaged by heavy Flak; Sqn Ldr A.E.Bull and two safe, Plt Off M.C.Cook WiA
500 Sqn	Baltimore V FW772 'J' left 1505 to bomb fuel dumps at Massa Lombarda, damaged by heavy Flak, crash-landed at base; Flt Lt M.T.S.Davis and two safe, one WiA
24 SAAF Sqn	Marauder III HD601 'V' left 1226 to bomb a bridge at Pieris, port engine failed, had landing accident at Fano 1315; Lt G.H.Talbot and five safe
43 Sqn	Spitfire IX MK787 left 1445 to bomb barges S Chioggia, possibly damaged by Flak, crashed on landing 1600; Sgt D.Young safe
111 Sqn	Spitfire IX EN517 'X' left 1350 dive-bombed motor transports N Rovigo, hit by Flak, crash-landed on return; Flt Sgt A.A.Chapman safe
336 Sqn	Spitfire Vc JK374 left 0830 on recce of Eleusis-Thebes area, encountered bad weather, ran short of fuel, crash-landed on Evorra 1045; Flg Off P.Michelongonas safe
US Casualties	
522nd FS/27th FBG	P-47D 42-26422 'T' *Daisy Lee* shot down by Flak 5m S San Bonifacio 1235; 1/Lt John R.Adams KiA [11395]
27th FBG	6 P-47Ds damaged
525th FS/86th FG	P-47D 42-xx042 shot down by Flak 1500; 1/Lt Walter M.Bieber baled out and returned
379th BS/310th BG	B-25J 43-27649 *Stud* shot down by Flak over Yugoslavia 1214; Capt Ellis J.McKanna and six KiA [11392]
447th BS/321st BG	B-25J 43-4069 *Ruptured Duck* left 1115 to bomb RR bridge at Ala, shot down by Flak N Legnago 1350; 1/Lt Robert K.Murchland evaded, three POW, two KiA [11713]

Friday-Saturday 19/20 January 1945

British Casualties	
256 Sqn	Mosquito XIII MM582 'D' scrambled 0012, developed serious trouble, crashed into sea 1m W Nice a/d; Flg Off P.D.W.Brunt/Flg Off A.E.Harris KiA

Saturday, 20 January 1945

On the right of this group standing in front of a Bf 109G of the ANR's 2ª Squadriglia, 1° Gruppo Caccia is S.Ten Enrico Brini who was killed in an engagement with P-47Ds of the 350th Fighter Group.

British Casualties

500 Sqn •	Baltimore IV FA517 'J' left 1000 on bombing mission, aborted due to weather, damaged when undercarriage collapsed on landing 1145; Sgt R.G.Hibbins and three safe
417 Sqn	Spitfire VIII MT659 left 1255 to bomb a gun position W Imola, last seen N Pienza; Flt Lt J.Waslyk KiA
417 Sqn	Spitfire VIII MT688 left 1255 to bomb a gun position W Imola, last seen N Pienza; Flg Off R.Edge KiA

US Claims

346th FS/350th FG	1/Lt Elmer L.Belcher	P-47D	Bf 109	0815-1045

US Casualties

64th FS/57th FG	P-47D 42-75726 *Thunderbolt* wing hit ground during attack S Camisano 1045; 1/Lt James A.Graham KiA [11394]
525th FS/86th FG	P-47D 42-26577 *Miss Francis II* shot down by Flak 1345; 2/Lt Maurice Moran KiA [11393]
347th BS/340th BG	B-25J 43-4022 '7L' *Lil Jasper* shot down by Flak nr Trento 1330; 1/Lt Morris D.LaVine and three KiA, two POW [11835]

Italian ANR Claims

6ª Sq, 2° Gr C	Ten Alberto Volpi	Bf 109G	P-47	Verona	morning

Italian ANR Casualties

4ª Sq, 2° Gr C	Bf 109G hit in combat; S.Ten Enrico Brini KiA
6ª Sq, 2° Gr C	Bf 109G White 5 damaged; Ten Ermete Ferrero safe

Saturday-Sunday, 20/21 January 1945

Sqn Ldr George Coleman made 600 Squadron's last claims whilst flying Beaufighters, claiming two of NSGr 9's Stukas shot down. He had already been credited with three other successes when flying with Coastal Beaufighter units (46 and 272 Squadrons) and earlier with 256 Squadron in the UK and the Malta Night Fighter Unit.

British Claims

600 Sqn	Sqn Ldr G.B.S.Coleman/Flg Off N.Frumar	Beaufighter VIf V8734 'M'	Ju 87	7m NE Forlì	1748
600 Sqn	Sqn Ldr G.B.S.Coleman/Flg Off N.Frumar	Beaufighter VIf V8734 'M'	Ju 87	2m N Fusignano	1758

Flying Beaufighter VIf V8734 '6-M', Sqn Ldr George Coleman of 600 Squadron shot down two Ju 87s on this date. These were the unit's final claims with this type and 600 was to end the war as the RAF's top-scoring night-fighter squadron, being credited with around 180 victories.

British Casualties

55 Sqn	Boston V BZ592 left 1826 lost at Ferrara during an attack on road traffic; Sqn Ldr R.H.Stringer and three KiA
600 Sqn	Beaufighter VIf V8705 scrambled 1740, encountered Ju 87s 1803 shot at from behind, damaged and pilot wounded, returned to base, landed safely; Wt Off C.M.Ward WiA/Flt Sgt J.L.Richards safe

German Casualties

3./NSGr 9	Ju 87D-5 WNr 140717 E8+AL lost to night-fighter NE Fusignano; Obfhr Peter Stollwerk/Uffz Franz Fischer returned

Sunday, 21 January 1945

British Casualties

260 Sqn	Mustang III KH609 left 1410, hit by Flak, ditched in sea E Rimini 1515; Lt C.B.Susskind KiA

US Casualties

65th FS/57th FG	P-47D 42-28582 *Balls Out* destroyed by own bomb blast NW Cremona 1315; 2/Lt Clyde J.Casterline KiA [11714]
347th FS/350th FG	P-47D 42-29300 hit by Flak crash-landed at Pisa 1010; 2/Lt Edward S.Rock KiA
86th FS/79th FG	P-47D 43-25658 *Angel Puss* on fire, cause u/k 1445; 2/Lt Robert F.Hewitt POW [11708]
488th BS/340th BG	B-25J 43-27657 '8P' *Sweet Pea* collision 1230; 2/Lt William B.Pelton and four returned, one KiA [11711]
488th BS/340th BG	B-25J 43-4064 '8U' *L'il Critter From The Moon* collision 1230; 1/Lt William Y.Simpson and two KiA, three safe [11712]
448th BS/321st BG	B-25J 43-27652 *Out of Bounds* left 0945 to bomb RR diversion at Lavis, damaged by Flak, crashed on landing 1345, salvaged; 2/Lt Julius W.Rubin and five safe

German Casualties

1./NSGr 11	Bf 109G-6 WNr 230163 damaged on the ground by strafing at Orio al Serio
2./NSGr 9	Ju 87D-5 WNr 412082 crashed at Montichiari; Fhr Berndt Jungfer/Uffz Fritz Geide WiA

Italian ANR Casualties

2° Gr C	Bf 109 destroyed on the ground at Villafranca

Monday, 22 January 1945

During the month 5th Army units were also continuing to get good service from the British tactical reconnaissance units serving with them, as epitomised on 22 January by Sqn Ldr Donald Perrens, DFC, the second in command of 208 Squadron.

Perrens was spotting for some new 8in artillery which the Americans had recently introduced to service on this front. The target was an ammunition dump and Perrens stayed overhead in the face of fierce Flak for a full 40 minutes, allowing the gunners to register on, and destroy the target. He then stayed longer to direct fire onto the Flak batteries. But at this stage his Spitfire was hit and damaged. He was too low to bale out, so flew as far as possible towards Allied territory before carrying out a force-landing on a road. The aircraft struck the ground hard, and a vertebra in his spine was fractured. Unwittingly, he had come down right alongside the guns he had been serving, and he was helped from his cockpit by the gunners and removed to hospital where he was confined to a cast for two months. He received a DSO for his spirited performance on this date, and on recovery from his injuries was promoted to the post of wing commander flying, 285 Wing.

British Casualties

208 Sqn	Spitfire IX PT950 left 1200 on Arty/R, engine failed, attempted to reach base, crash-landed near 91st Div HQ 1300; Sqn Ldr D.F.Perrens WiA
601 Sqn	Spitfire IX JK884 left 1410 to attack 200 plus railway carriages between Mestre and Treviso, hit by Flak, 1545 pilot reported he was approaching the coast but not seen or heard from again; Flt Sgt J.L.Holland POW

US Casualties

523rd FS/27th FG	P-47D 44-20447 lost due to oil line failure; 2/Lt Jesse E.Shivers Jr baled safely [11533]
523rd FS/27th FG	P-47D 42-26715 hit by Flak, on fire, crash-landed at Pontedera 1610; Lt Trautwein safe
64th FS/57th FG	P-47D 42-25055 shot down by Flak nr Piacenza 1435; 2/Lt Louis E.Fraser POW [11709]
525th FS/86th FG	P-47D 42-28542 shot down by Flak at Castelfranco, pilot baled out N Padua 1025; 2/Lt Paul T.Jackson Jr POW [11707]
347th FS/350th FG	P-47D 42-28574 '6C5' *Lillian* shot down by Flak 5m NE Vigevano 1320; Maj Hugh D.Dow POW [11705]
1° Gr Caça/350th FG	P-47D 44-19666 'B6' shot down by Flak nr Milan 1415; 1° Ten Aurélio Vieria Sampaio KiA

Monday-Tuesday, 22/23 January 1945

British Casualties

256 Sqn	Mosquito XIII MM584 scrambled 0215, was following an e/a 0243 near Pedaso when plot faded, contact lost; Flt Sgt R.Roberts/Wt Off J.A.Hebdige MiA

The Spitfire IXs of 208 Squadron such as EN304 'Y' seen here at low level, provided vital tactical-reconnaissance information to the ground forces, often in the face of heavy ground fire.

Lt Col Jannie Blaauw (left) the officer commanding 208 Squadron, with his ground liaison officer, Maj Tim Bevan MC and Sqn Ldr Donald Perrens (right) who was awarded a rare immediate DSO for his actions on 22 January.

Tuesday, 23 January 1945

The anticipated movement northwards of German units now began, 356th Division being pulled out of the line, destined for the Eastern Front. Attacks on communications were at once intensified, and so effective were these that it took 15 days for the division even to reach the Italian frontier.

During the day, the pilots of five Spitfires of 417 Squadron were led by 244 Wing's new leader, Wg Cdr R.E.Bary, on an offensive patrol when they encountered 11 Bf 109s of the ANR's 2° Gruppo. The Messerschmitt pilots were described as making only a half-hearted attack on the Canadians. Bary and Flg Off J.T.Rose both fired at one Bf 109 which at once half rolled away. No claims were made but it seems that their shooting had been more effective than they realised for Italian pilot Ten Fausto Filippi had been shot down and killed.

5 SAAF Squadron sent ten Mustangs to dive bomb a railway bridge near Zagreb, no fewer than seven were hit by Flak, with two shot down, three receiving Cat II damage and two more Cat I damage.

Lt Cecil Boyd of 1 SAAF Squadron who had survived being shot down four times by Flak, was shot down again – this time he was killed.

British Casualties

40 SAAF Sqn	Spitfire IX left 1000, hit by Flak, pilot baled out S Mirano 16km W Venice; Capt D.C.Robinson evaded
1 SAAF Sqn	Spitfire IXc MH711 left 0710 on armed reconnaissance, hit by Flak, cockpit filled with smoke, crashed 10m NE Bologna 1055; Lt C.W.L.Boyd KiA
1 SAAF Sqn	Spitfire IXe PT541 left 0710 on armed reconnaissance, hit tree while strafing N Bologna, belly-landed; Lt H.J.Kritzinger evaded, returned to unit in April
112 Sqn	Mustang III FB280 'X' left 0950 to bomb rail bridge at Pjuj, hit by Flak, pilot baled out Pragersko 1110; Sgt P.L.Greaves safe
5 SAAF Sqn	Mustang IV KH717 left 1020 to bomb a railway bridge near Zagreb, shot down by Flak 1120; Capt B.G.S.Enslin KiA
5 SAAF Sqn	Mustang III KH587 'E' left 1020 to bomb a railway bridge near Zagreb, shot down by Flak 1120; Lt D.J.S.Jansen van Rends-berg KiA

Having previously been shot down several times, the luck of 20-year-old Lt Cecil Boyd of 1 SAAF Squadron finally ran out when he was killed near Bologna.

5 SAAF Sqn	Mustang III KH610 left 1020 to bomb a railway bridge near Zagreb, damaged Cat II by Flak; Lt P.Muir safe
5 SAAF Sqn	Mustang III KH533 left 1020 to bomb a railway bridge near Zagreb, damaged Cat II by Flak; Lt E.N.Lamberg safe
5 SAAF Sqn	Mustang IV KH692 'D' left 1020 to bomb a railway bridge near Zagreb, damaged Cat II by Flak; Capt H.J.E.Clarke safe
5 SAAF Sqn	Mustang III KH603 left 1020 to bomb a railway bridge near Zagreb, damaged Cat I by Flak; Lt N.J.E.Mathee safe
5 SAAF Sqn	Mustang III KB947 left 1020 to bomb a railway bridge near Zagreb, damaged Cat I by Flak; Lt L.Hingle safe
ME Comms Sqn	Beech Expeditor II HB271 disappeared flying from Rome to Brindisi; Wt Off J.W.McStay, Flg Off D.Hargreaves of 55 Sqn and members of the United Kingdom Parliament R.H.Bernays and J.F.Campbell KiFA

US Casualties

85th FS/79th FG	P-47D 42-26441 shot down by Flak 1330; Flt Off Wesley A.Stage POW [11710]
HQ 12th AF	C-47B 43-48313 on administrative flight from Algiers to Florence, lost possibly in bad weather; Maj Richard E.H.Lawrence and four MiA [11294]

German Claims

Flak	3./Feld-Ers Btl 198	e/a	near Altedo

Italian ANR Casualties

5ª Sq, 2° Gr C	Bf 109G-6 WNr 163466 Yellow 10 shot down, crashed nr S.Giorgio delle Pertiche; Ten Fausto Filippi KiA

Wednesday, 24 January 1945

British Casualties

213 Sqn	Mustang III KH596 left 1320 on anti-Flak escort to Beaufighters, became lost in cloud, returned to base, crashed on landing 1520; Flg Off F.A.E.Penson safe

Thursday, 25 January 1945

British Casualties

3 RAAF Sqn	Mustang III KH821 left 1355 on armed recce of railway from Gemona to Chiusaforte, lost coolant, ditched in River Po mouth; Flt Off D.B.Davies picked up by Walrus of 293 Sqn
US Casualties	
57th FG	P-47D 42-75718 *Billy Ritterhouse* crashed and blew up while strafing nr Nerviano 1100; Capt William R.Speirs, group ops officer, KiA [11706]
527th FS/86th FG	P-47D 42-27954 '90' shot down by Flak nr Milan 1115; 2/Lt Carlo A.Iavelli returned [11715]
346th FS/350th FG	P-47D 42-28580 lost u/k cause 1200; 2/Lt Robert L.Stringer KiA

Friday, 26 January 1945

Sgt Hibbins and his crew, who had crashed on landing six days earlier, were posted missing when their 500 Squadron Baltimore failed to return.

British Casualties

500 Sqn	Baltimore V FW794 'T' left 1425 on a mission to Argenta, failed to return; Sgt R.G.Hibbins and three KiA
213 Sqn	Mustang III FB312 left 1050 on armed-recce mission between Novska and Brod, lost leader in cloud; Flt Sgt A.W.Hearndon MiA

Saturday, 27 January 1945

British Casualties

24 SAAF Sqn	Marauder III HD585 'X' badly damaged by Flak while attacking Castelfranco Veneto marshalling yards, abandoned by crew, pilot drifted out to the sea and died from exposure before ASR arrived; Capt E.J.Jennings KiA, five safe
12 SAAF Sqn	Marauder III HD622 'S' left 1001 to bomb Castelfranco marshalling yards, damaged by Flak, landed at Rimini 1215; Flg Off L.A.N.Dickenson and five safe

The crew of 459 Squadron Baltimore V FW809 'V' at Berka after completing a leaflet raid on Kos and Leros on 26 January; left to right: Flt Lt R.H.Norman, Flg Off J.E.Aitken, Flg Off W.W.East, Flt Sgt J.H.Simmonds and the Met officer who went along for the ride.

250 Sqn	Kittyhawk IV FT949 left 1100, on return flight presumed engine failure, ditched off Ravenna; Flt Sgt P.Freeman KiA
US Casualties	
65th FS/57th FG	P-47D 42-26839 *Nell* shot down by Flak NE Viadana 1130; 1/Lt Fergus Meyer MiA, returned [11822]
64th FS/57th FG	P-47D 42-76012 hit by Flak, crash-landed 1510; pilot returned
64th FS/57th FG	P-47D 42-75966 hit by Flak, crash-landed at Grosseto 1510; pilot returned
447th BS/321st BG	B-25J 43-27506 *Rebel Devil* left 1215 on nickeling mission to Bassano, San Giovanni, Cento, Rovigo, Comacchio, engine failed, crew baled out over Allied lines 1400; 1/Lt William C.Morton Jr and five safe
447th BS/321st BG	B-25J 43-27718 left 1215 on nickeling mission to Bassano, San Giovanni, Cento, Rovigo, Comacchio, damaged by Flak, crashed on landing at base 1525, salvaged; 1/Lt Richard D.Appenzeller and five safe

Saturday-Sunday, 27/28 January 1945

British Casualties	
108 Sqn	Beaufighter VI ND181 'Y' left on intruder sortie to Maleme a/f, FTR; Flg Off E.F.J.Robinson/Flt Sgt A.S.Crystal MiA
US Casualties	
86th FS/79th FG	P-47D 42-76018 'X54' *Hossier Hotshot* damaged by bomb blast, 2.5km SW Merano 1135; 1/Lt James F.Hannon KiA [11812]
416th NFS	Mosquito MT475 lost on night-intruder mission over western Po Valley; Capt John A.Davies/2/Lt Hubbard P.Larsen KiA [11814]

Sunday, 28 January 1945

British Casualties	
7 SAAF Sqn	Spitfire IXc MA728 left 1425, engine trouble after bombing, crash-landed 3m NW Monselice 1515; Lt C.C.Schoombie POW

Monday, 29 January 1945

British Casualties					
241 Sqn	Spitfire IXE PT64 left 1100 on armed recce of Latisana-Sesana area, encountered severe weather, pilot reported instrument failure, no trace ever found; Flt Lt R.W.Henderson DFC MiA				
11 SAAF Sqn	Kittyhawk IV FX738 left 0805, caught fire while in bomb dive SW Bologna 0837; Lt L.J.Lithgow KiA				
US Claims					
346th FS/350th FG	2/Lt Richard P.Sulzbach	P-47D	Ju 87	5m SE Bologna, S Highway 9	1800
346th FS/350th FG	2/Lt Charles C.Eddy	P-47D	Ju 87 Probable	5m SE Bologna, S Highway 9	1800

P-47D Thunderbolt 44-19661 'D2' of 1° GAvCa moments before it was hit by Flak on this date forcing 1° Ten Josino Maia de Assis to bale out. He was initially rescued by partisans but was later captured by the Germans.

522nd FS/27th FBG	P-47D 42-26440 'red V' lost u/k cause 6m NW Rimini 1210; 2/Lt Donald J.Driessen KiA [11824]
522nd FS/27th FBG	P-47D 42-28575 'red O' shot down by Flak 6m S Bergamo 1705; 1/Lt Joseph E.Wisby POW [11833]
525th FS/86th FG	P-47D 42-75810 *Butch* shot down by Flak 1m S Brescia M/Y 1000; Flt Off Robert S.Bell baled and returned [11704]
1° Gr Caça/350th FG	P-47D 44-19661 'D2' shot down by Flak, crashed at Piacenza 0840; 1° Ten Josino Maia de Assis POW
486th BS/7th BG	A-20B 41-3267 '67' hit by Flak, crashed nr Villafranca a/d 1948; Maj John A.Tilton and three KiA [11825]

German Casualties

3./NSGr 9	Ju 87D-5 E8+AL damaged by small-arms fire nr Bologna; Obfhr Peter Stollwerk/Hptm Jahn safe
3./NSGr 9	Ju 87D-5 E8+FL damaged nr Monselice; Uffz Franz Fischer/Obgfr Heinz Staudt safe

Monday-Tuesday, 29/30 January 1945

British Casualties

55 Sqn	Boston V BZ583 left 0100 to bomb Camposanpiero, hit by Flak over Mestre, two crewmembers baled out, crash-landed; Lt R.C.Macintosh POW, navigator Lt M.P.Farrell DoW on 3 February, Flt Sgt N.J.Stebbings and Sgt J.D.Rowbottom evaded

US Casualties

416th NFS	Mosquito NF30 MM761 lost on night mission over Florence area; 1/Lt Frank H.Janish/2/Lt Eugene K.Franklin KiA [11813]

Tuesday, 30 January 1945

British Casualties

43 Sqn	Spitfire IX PT836 left 0835, hit by Flak, Cat II Damaged on landing 0955; Flt Lt I.G.Thompson WiA
43 Sqn	Spitfire IX PT534 left 1100 to attack barges N Adria, hit by Flak in bomb dive 1135; Flt Lt E.W.Creed POW
450 Sqn	Kittyhawk IV FT927 left 1250 to attack a bridge near Padua, hit by Flak in bomb dive, crashed in flames 1350; Flg Off E.A.Adams KiA
250 Sqn	Kittyhawk IV FX709 left 1130 to bomb bridge N Padua, shot down by Flak in bomb dive; Sgt D.G.M.Brettell KiA
5 SAAF Sqn	Mustang III KH603 left 1225, strafing, shot down by Flak 18m NW Trieste 1405, pilot baled out; Lt G.L.Redman POW
417 Sqn	Spitfire VIII MT546 left 1020 on armed recce, hit by Flak SE Vicenza, crashed on landing at Bellaria 1125; Flg Off T.R.Wilson WiA
92 Sqn	Spitfire VIII JF559 left 0820 bombing railway from Treviso to Casarsa, crashed on landing; Sgt S.Widdowsen WiA

US Casualties

86th BS/47th BG	A-20G 43-2619 '17' last seen SW Bologna 2158; 2/Lt Robert L.Luke KiA, two returned [11823]

Boston V BZ583 'L' of 55 Squadron was hit by Flak near Venice on 30 January and crash-landed in enemy-held territory.

Wednesday, 31 January 1945

A four-plane patrol from 72 Squadron had a bad day when the leader was shot down by Flak, and two of the other three Spitfires crashed on landing and were written off.

British Casualties	
72 Sqn	Spitfire IX PV123 'K' left 1135 on armed recce, shot down by 88mm Flak, tail broke off, crashed into Adige river; Plt Off R.Connen KiA
72 Sqn	Spitfire IX MA710 left 1135 on armed recce, crashed on landing at Rimini, Cat II damaged, w/o on 8 Feb; Flt Sgt T.M.Ninan safe
72 Sqn	Spitfire IX MK171 'O' left 1135 on armed recce, swung on landing at Rimini, hit an ambulance, Cat III damaged, w/o on 8 Feb; Flt Sgt W.D.Park safe
87 Sqn	Spitfire IX PT716 left 0805 to bomb Pavullo, shot down by Flak; Flt Sgt J.N.Harrison baled out, rescued by partisans
111 Sqn	Spitfire IX MK135 'Y' left 1215, hit in the engine by Flak, reached Allied lines S Russi 1245, pilot baled out; Flt Sgt A.J.Ellis safe
US Casualties	
525th FS/86th FG	P-47D 42-26698 struck high tension wires 5m SW Brescia 1120, bounced on the ground and exploded; 2/Lt Harold H.Locke KiA [12136]

Wednesday-Thursday, 31 January/1 February 1945

272 Squadron lost aircraft during shipping attacks, including their commanding officer, Wg Cdr Johnson.

British Casualties	
13 Sqn	Boston IV BZ495 'S' left 2230 on night intruder to Vigodarzere, N Padua; Flt Lt H.J.Cross and three KiA
114 Sqn	Boston IV BZ504 left 2355 on armed recce Nervesa-Mestre area, crashed on taking-off; Sgt R.P.Knight and three safe
272 Sqn	Beaufighter TFX NV570 attacked with rockets a ship in Gulf of Trieste, flew into the sea; Wg Cdr R.K.H.Johnson/Wt Off H.Roe KiA
272 Sqn	Beaufighter X NV495 'D' left 0615 on armed recce, engine failure on take-off from Falconara, could not maintain height and belly-landed; Flg Off D.A.F.Jackson/Plt Off J.V.Brick safe

FEBRUARY 1945

Good weather during the first two weeks of February allowed Balkan Air Force Spitfires, Mustangs and Hurricanes to enjoy a very active period over both the battlefield and against German communications. During the month the first unit of 281 Wing, 351 (Yugoslav) Squadron moved to Prkos on the mainland of Yugoslavia. Great efforts were being made by all elements of Mediterranean Allied Air Forces in this area and the Germans were finding their retreat increasingly hampered. Strategic Air Force bombers damaged the 4,200-ton minelayer *Kuckuck*, and she was then sunk in Fiume harbour by BAF Beaufighters, while Tactical and BAF units attacked bridges, marshalling yards and similar targets, also making shipping strikes in and around Trieste and Pola harbours. Strategic bombers were very active against the enemy railway system in support of the advancing Red Army.

Higher losses amongst 232 Wing's Bostons in recent weeks had led to the suspicion that Luftwaffe night-fighters might be about in the north. Thus from late February 255 Squadron would commence sending a pair of Mosquitos each night to patrol over possible Axis fighter airfields, while others patrolled over the mouth of the Po on the lookout for nocturnal reconnaissance machines.

At this period other changes in DAF included the arrival with 239 Wing of the first examples of the new Mustang IV (P-51D) with 'bubble' cockpit canopies, while in 601 Squadron the commanding officer, Sqn Ldr Turkington ended his second tour; Flt Lt C.T.Simpson, the B Flight commander, was promoted to replace him.

Early in the month the Allied Combined Chiefs of Staff met once more in Malta, their decision concerning Italy being to withdraw a further two infantry divisions and two fighter-bomber groups from the US forces still stationed there. The latter were scheduled to go first, and the 27th and 86th Fighter Groups would leave for France during the last week in February. It was understood that the whole 12th Air Force would eventually follow, but neither it nor the infantry units would leave until after Field Marshal Alexander's projected spring offensive. During February, however, the 16th SS Panzer Grenadier Division was also withdrawn from Italy. Once more MATAF was effective in slowing down this unit's move, 6,364 sorties being directed against the Brenner Pass and the Venetian Plain during this month.

The Auster IVs of 654 Squadron were active through February spotting for the guns of the 8th Army around Forlì.

To support this activity some of the 2nd Tactical Air Force Mosquito units occasionally landed in Italy having flown strikes into southern Germany and Austria before returning via another mission replicating the earlier Bomber Command shuttle missions.

Amongst the Allied units their other problems were exacerbated by thick snow which had fallen during late January, and this was to cut sortie rates until airfields could be adequately cleared. 2° Gruppo of the ANR was very active throughout early February however – far more so than for some time.

Friday, 2 February 1945

British Casualties	
249 Sqn	Mustang III FB308 missing in cloud SW Zagreb 1230; Lt R.V.Jacobs KiA
US Casualties	
346th FS/350th FG	P-47D 42-75879 collided with 42-25447 0800; 2/Lt Thomas E.Gomez KiA
346th FS/350th FG	P-47D 42-25447 collided with 42-75879 0800; 1/Lt Robert K.Morrow baled and returned
35th TCS/64th TCG	C-47 41-18683 crashed into mountain SW Montieri 1030; 1/Lt James D.Fitzgerald and two safe, 23 KiA [15386]
German Casualties	
2./NSGr 7	9 CR.42s WNrn 7206, 9168, 9224, 9776, 9885, 9828, 90804, 90886 and 9896 destroyed and 5 CR.42s WNrn 5695
	4X+VK., 7151, 8524, 8975 and 90887 20-25% damaged to a strafing attack by the 31st FG on Kurilovec a/f

Sunday, 4 February 1945

The 57th Fighter Group was providing an anti-Flak diversion for B-25s raiding a rail bridge at Piacenza when eight of the 66th Squadron were attacked from out of the sun by a formation identified as about 15 Bf 109s and FW 190s. Nine of these targeted the formation leader and his wingman, the latter claiming one damaged. However, 2/Lt Guilford Groendycke, the leader, was shot down, his aircraft being seen to crash and burn. Six more Axis fighters attacked the second element, the leader of which, 2/Lt Edward Palovich, pulled up to meet them, but he too failed to return. Pilots from a patrol of 24 Bf 109Gs from 2° Gruppo Caccia, which took off from Osoppo and Aviano airfields, reported encountering P-47s near Vicenza, Cap Bellagambi and Serg Benzi claiming one shot down each.

Mustang IVa KH681 'Z' of 5 SAAF Squadron became one of the first of this variant lost when it was shot down by Flak while attacking a bridge with the loss of Capt Peter Maguire.

British Casualties	
5 SAAF Sqn	Mustang IVa KH681 'Z' left 1145 to dive bomb rail bridge at Nervesa, shot down by Flak 1240; Capt P.G.Maguire KiA
93 Sqn	Spitfire IX LZ888 left 1415 to dive bomb target, hit by Flak crash-landed in Allied lines, damaged Cat III; Plt Off H.C.Fielding safe

US Claims					
66th FS/57th FG	2/Lt Carl J.Weisenberg	P-47D	Bf 109 Damaged	Padua-Venice	1205

US Casualties	
66th FS/57th FG	P-47D 42-29034 *Peggy II* shot down by fighters nr Vicenza 1205, crashed nr Valdagno, pilot baled; 2/Lt Edward J.Palovich POW [12087]
66th FS/57th FG	P-47D 42-29344 '78' shot down by fighters nr Vicenza 1205, crashed nr Thiene; 2/Lt Guilford D.Groendycke KiA [12088]
66th FS/57th FG	P-47D 42-20124 hit by Flak N Pontedera 1510, pilot baled; 1/Lt Louis O.Hays III safe
1° Gr Caça/350th FG	P-47D 42-26759 'B1' shot down by Flak, crashed at Castelfranco 1430; Cap Joel Miranda WiA, evaded
1° Gr Caça/350th FG	P-47D 42-26783 '2' shot down by Flak, crashed at Castelfranco 1430; 2° Ten Danilo Moura evaded

Italian ANR Claims					
5ª Sq, 2° Gr C	Cap Mario Bellagambi	Bf 109G	P-47	N Vicenza	1130-
4ª Sq, 2° Gr C	Serg Gualberto Benzi	Bf 109G	P-47	N Vicenza	1130-

Monday, 5 February 1945

British Casualties	
73 Sqn	Spitfire IX NH271 'V' left 1215 on sweep of road from Dubica to Novska, crash-landed nr Sanski Most 1330; Flt Lt R.H.Ball rescued by partisans

US Casualties	
525th FS/86th FG	P-47D 42-75663 *Slow Freight* shot down by Flak nr Montebello 0820; 1/Lt William P.Leahy KiA [12132]
486th BS/340th BG	B-25J 43-6098 '6M' hit by Flak 1245; 1/Lt Charles D.Ross DoW, six safe [12130]
97th BS/47th BG	A-20K 44-577 '83' *Hossier Gal* engine trouble, crashed E Pievepelago 2309; 1/Lt Robert K.Ritchie and one KiA, one evaded, one POW [12137]

Tuesday, 6 February 1945

A rather larger engagement than on the 5th took place between US P-47s and 16 ANR Bf 109Gs. Shortly after midday one flight of Messerschmitts engaged four Thunderbolts and made a diving attack on the Americans, following which one P-47 fell out of the formation and this was claimed shot down by Cap Drago. A second flight which was then attacked by the US pilots also claimed to have shot down a P-47, this being credited to Serg Magg Bianchini. Soon afterwards a lone B-25 was seen, and this was attacked by Ten Piolanti who reported that it blew up in the air. During this engagement one Bf 109 was lost.

US Claims

522nd FS/27th FG	2/Lt Robert E.Williams	P-47D	Bf 109	Vicenza area	1250
522nd FS/27th FG	Lt William J.Hay	P-47D	Bf 109	Vicenza area	1250
522nd FS/27th FG	Lt Jack A.Rudd	P-47D	Bf 109	Vicenza area	1250
522nd FS/27th FG	2/Lt Robert E.Williams	P-47D	2 Bf 109s Damaged	Vicenza area	1250
522nd FS/27th FG	Lt William J.Hay	P-47D	Bf 109 Damaged	Vicenza area	1250
522nd FS/27th FG	Lt Jack A.Rudd	P-47D	Bf 109 Damaged	Vicenza area	1250

US Casualties

447th BS/321st BG	B-25J 43-36204 *Maybe* left 1055 to bomb Rovereto marshalling yards, shot down by Flak, crashed nr Rovereto 1342;1/Lt Earl H.Remmel and one KiA, one evaded, four POW [12134]
447th BS/321st BG	B-25J 43-27730 *Katie* left 1055 to bomb Rovereto marshalling yards, shot down by Flak, crashed 7.5km E Rovereto 1350; 1/Lt Jackson R.Dodson and three POW, two evaded [12131]
447th BS/321st BG	B-25J 43-27542 *Superstitious Aloysius* left 1055 to bomb Rovereto marshalling yards, shot down by Flak crashed SW Riva del Garda 1350; 1/Lt Carl W.Cahoon and five POW. Liberated and returned to unit [12133]
310th BG	10 B-25s damaged in combat

Italian ANR Claims

4ª Sq, 2° Gr C	Cap Ugo Drago	Bf 109G	P-47	nr Vicenza	1245-
6ª Sq, 2° Gr C	Serg Magg Giacomo Bianchini	Bf 109G	P-47	nr Vicenza	1245-
5ª Sq, 2° Gr C	Ten Michelangelo Piolanti	Bf 109G	B-25	nr Vicenza	1245-

Italian ANR Casualties

5ª Sq, 2° Gr C	Bf 109G-6 WNr 160411 shot down by fighters; Serg Magg Fausto Fornaci KiA

Wednesday, 7 February 1945

A 2nd TAF shuttle mission by a Mosquito VI of 613 Squadron flown by Sqn Ldr A.G.Gardner returned to its base at A75-Cambrai/Épinoy in France.

British Casualties

351 Sqn	Hurricane IV KZ382 'V' left 1345, collided over Licki Osik with LE570 while strafing M/T, force-landed Sveti Rok, 20m NE Zara; Sgt Janez Antocić safe
351 Sqn	Hurricane IV LE570 N' left 1345 collided with KZ382 while strafing M/T force-landed Zemunik; Sgt Ljubomir Dvorski safe
351 Sqn	Hurricane IV LF455 left 1310 on sweep of Mostar-Sarajevo rail line, engine cut, belly-landed Zadvarje 1415; Sqn Ldr Aleksandar Cenić safe

US Casualties

66th FS/57th FG	P-47D 42-29317 hit by Flak, crashed nr Grosseto 1510, pilot baled; Capt Arno H.Heying safe
448th BS/321st BG	B-25J 43-4067 *The Big Swing* shot down by Flak nr Lavis 1315; 2/Lt Woodrow W.Sheffield and five interned and returned [12135]

Thursday, 8 February 1945

2° Gruppo Caccia was up in force intercepting a big formation of the 57th Bomb Wing's B-25s over the Tagliamento area. All three squadriglie together with the headquarters flight were led into an apparently highly effective attack by Magg Miani, no less than seven of the Mitchells being claimed shot down on this occasion, although no corresponding losses were reported by the Americans. 43 Squadron lost their Australian flight commander, Flt Lt Peter Hedderwick who was serving his second operational tour with the unit.

The impressive bomb log on B-25J Mitchell *Ave Maria* of the 447th Bomb Squadron, 321st Bomb Group that flew operations from Alesani, Corsica.

Ten CR.42s of Stab and 2.Staffel of NSGr 7 took off from their base at Agram-Gorica in Croatia for an anti-partisan mission. Several kilometres south-east of Agram-Gorica the CR.42 formation was jumped by P-38s of 14th Fighter Group. During the ensuing battle, the NSGr 7 suffered serious losses when four CR.42s failed to return (one reportedly by AA fire). According to American records, 1/Lt Bach of 37th Squadron claimed two biplanes, one probable and one damaged. However, the historian Csaba Becze's research has shown that the battle was not one-sided, since one of the NSGr 7's pilots claimed a P-38 during this dogfight as well. Unfortunately, his name is not known and nothing more remains about his identity in the existing documents. This combat seems to be the last biplane victory ever claimed.

Four Spitfires of 93 Squadron on a bombing operation were vectored onto an Me 410 flying along the coast which they chased from Porto Garibaldi northwards until 30 miles north of Venice where Lt Anderson claimed it damaged. It was later upgraded to a destroyed. On a technical note the squadron recorded that although they flew Mark IX Spitfires fitted with Merlin 70 engines they would not be supplied with gyro gunsights as only Spitfire squadrons with Merlin 66 engines had been so equipped.

In the evening a 72 Squadron Spitfire caught fire and the available fire-fighting appliances could not extinguish the flames, so it was left to burn out. Eventually the ammunition started to explode. One of 111 Squadron's truck drivers LAC B.Marshall was watching the fire from on top of a truck in the squadron's motor park a mile from the blaze, when a .303 round struck him in the eye, killing him.

British Claims					
93 Sqn	Lt H.P.Anderson	Spitfire IX PT470 'D'	Me 410	30m NE Venice	1330

British Casualties

72 Sqn	Spitfire IX caught fire 1830 and burnt out; LAC B.Marshall, 111 Sqn, killed by exploding ammunition
43 Sqn	Spitfire IX PT712 left 1430, shot down by Flak near Argenta, crashed 3-4m W Portomaggiore 1530; Flt Lt P.J.Hedderwick KiA
87 Sqn	Spitfire IX MH895 left 1435, bombed guns at Aulla, shot down by Flak 1500, crashed into the sea; Sgt W.F.Jones MiA
111 Sqn	Spitfire IX MK530 'B' left 1345, hit by Flak 1410 W Argenta, pilot reported he was wounded in the leg and could not open the cockpit cover, crash-landed 6m N Lugo in Axis lines; Plt Off G.Gray evaded
145 Sqn	Spitfire VIII MT663 left 1220, hit by Flak N Treviso 1300, glycol leaked, pilot pulled up to 6,000ft, rolled over to bale out but caught fire and crashed; Plt Off A.L.Briand DFC KiA
12 SAAF Sqn	Marauder III HD526 'L' left 1125 to bomb target at Gorizia, engine trouble, crash-landed at Rimini; Lt J.Annez de Taboada and one WiA, four safe
16 SAAF Sqn	Beaufighter X NT998 'W' left 1050 to attack marshalling yards at Dubova, hit by Flak over target 1246, crash-landed; Lt D.M.Bodley/Lt J.McClelland evaded
16 SAAF Sqn	Beaufighter X NV121 'D' left 1050 to attack marshalling yards at Dubova, hit by Flak over target 1246, ditched 4m NE Termoli; Maj H.E.Platt WiA/Capt C.Jenkinson MiA

US Claims

37th FS/14th FG	1/Lt Lawrence V.Bach Jr	P-38L	2 u/i biplanes	SE Agram-Gorica	1216-1232
37th FS/14th FG	1/Lt Lawrence V.Bach Jr	P-38L	u/i biplane Probable	SE Agram-Gorica	1216-1232
37th FS/14th FG	1/Lt Lawrence V.Bach Jr	P-38L	u/i biplane Damaged	SE Agram-Gorica	1216-1232
428th BS/310th BG	gunner S/Sgt Cecil A.O'Dell	B-25J 43-27566	} FW 190		1317
428th BS/310th BG	gunner S/Sgt Melvin W.Smith	B-25J			

US Casualties

524th FS/27th FBG	P-47D 42-26364 shot down by Flak 1300; 2/Lt Charles D.Young Jr KiA
524th FS/27th FBG	P-47D 42-27906 possible engine failure 1415; 2/Lt Donald W.Banner POW [12119]
523rd FS/27th FBG	P-47D 42-28353 engine trouble 1445; 1/Lt Wilbur H.Johnson returned [12117]
66th FS/57th FG	P-47D 42-29307 destroyed by explosion from ammo train nr Castelnuovo 1005; 2/Lt Alfred R.Lyth KiA [12124]
66th FS/57th FG	P-47D 42-27010 Leona hit by Flak nr Camporgiano 1110, pilot baled; 1/Lt Theodore Matula evaded [12121]
85th FS/79th FG	P-47D 42-27077 '30' Flying Gopher, Uncle Spud, Cousin Herb crashed while strafing 1155; 1/Lt George E.Keppler KiA [12120]
48th FS/14th FG	P-38L 44-25020 '2' shot down by small-arms fire 2km E Pochlarn 1245; Capt Kyle J.Pinney Jr KiA[12139]
HQ 14th FG	P-38L 44-25038 '7' shot down by Flak 2.5km SE Pochlarn 1246; 1/Lt Frederick R.Branscombe KiA [12138]
448th BS/321st BG	B-25J 44-28918 left 1150 to bomb Calliano railway bridge, shot down by Flak, crashed nr Calliano 1404; 2/Lt Charles F.Birkhead Jr and five KiA [12126]
446th BS/321st BG	B-25J 43-27496 Princess left 1150 to bomb Calliano railway bridge, damaged by Flak, crash-landed at Florence; 1/Lt Warren W.Chandler and five safe
447th BS/321st BG	B-25J 43-27498 '71' Ave Maria left 1150 to bomb Calliano railway bridge, hit by Flak; 1/Lt Wendell E.Marchant and five safe, bombardier KiA

NSGr 7	unknown	CR.42	P-38	SE Agram-Gorica	ca 1230

German Casualties

2.(F)/122	Me 410B-3 WNr 190096 F6+KK lost in combat 20km W Venice; Obfw Wilhelm Zimmermann/Uffz Wilhelm Lenecke KiA
2./NSGr 7	CR.42 WNr 90841 Black 1 shot down by P-38; Hptm Kurt Jacobs KiA
1./NSGr 7	CR.42 WNr 9832 White 1 shot down by P-38; Obfw Wolfgang Harnack KiA
Stab/NSGr 7	CR.42 WNr 90897 shot down by P-38; Hptm Eduard Jacob KiA
2./NSGr 7	CR.42 WNr 8864 Black 2 shot down by P-38; Gefr Hans-Heinrich Schreiber KiA

Italian ANR Claims

1° Gr C	S.Ten Franco Storchi	Bf 109G	B-25	over Adriatic	1220-
4ª Sq, 2° Gr C	Serg Magg Loris Baldi	Bf 109G	B-25	over Adriatic	1220-
4ª Sq, 2° Gr C	Serg Magg Sergio Mazzi	Bf 109G	B-25	over Adriatic	1220-
5ª Sq, 2° Gr C	Cap Mario Bellagambi	Bf 109G	B-25	over Adriatic	1220-
5ª Sq, 2° Gr C	S.Ten Michelangelo Piolanti	Bf 109G	B-25	over Adriatic	1220-
6ª Sq, 2° Gr C	Serg Magg Filippo Bonato	Bf 109G	B-25	over Adriatic	1220-
NC 2° Gr C	Cap Alberto Spigaglia	Bf 109G	B-25	over Adriatic	1220-

Italian ANR Casualties

5ª Sq, 2° Gr C	Bf 109G-6 WNr 10239 burnt on taking off; Ten Luigi De Masellis KiA
6ª Sq, 2° Gr C	Bf 109G-14 WNr 464469 damaged in combat; Serg Gino Poluzzi WiA

Friday, 9 February 1945

British Casualties

93 Sqn	Spitfire IX NH518 left 0700 on armed recce, hit by Flak, crash-landed in Allied lines 0815; Flt Sgt E.J.Jones safe
19 SAAF Sqn	Beaufighter X NV610 'Z' left 1042 to attack Banova Jaruga, hit by Flak, crash-landed near Kutina; Lt P.J.B.Kruger/Flg Off W.F.Younger evaded

US Casualties

86th FS/79th FG	P-47D 42-29038 *Smoky City* crashed 20m SW Parenzo 0815; 1/Lt Richard Ascenzi KiA [12118]

The Bf 109 G-10 flown by Serg Magg Loris Baldi of the ANR's 4ª Squadriglia, 2° Gruppo Caccia, was named 'Silva' after a girlfriend. He claimed a B-25 shot down over the Adriatic on 8 February.

Flg Off W R Johnson's crew take off for 458 Squadron's first anti-submarine patrol from Gibraltar in Wellington XIV NB890 'H' on 10 February.

German Casualties	
2./NSGr 7	CR.42 MM 9183 crash-landed after combat, 70% damaged; pilot safe

Saturday, 10 February 1945

British Casualties	
6 Sqn	Hurricane IV KX412 'A' left 0700 to attack a general's house, hit by Flak in engine, pilot baled out, landing in sea, got into dinghy, later 'bombed' by Flg Off J.C.Brand with food and comforts; Flg Off D.A.Blair safe
US Casualties	
526th FS/86th FG	P-47D 42-27965 *Lizzie* lost u/k cause E Caorle 1010; 2/Lt Robert V.Held KiA [12127]
1° Gr Caça/350th FG	P-47D 42-26775 'B6' shot down by Flak, crashed nr Rovigo 1440; 1° Ten Roberto Brandini POW

Sunday, 11 February 1945

Maj Swales, commanding officer of 4 SAAF Squadron, was rested on this date, his place being taken by Maj 'Dixie' Hilton-Barber from 7 SAAF Squadron.

US Casualties	
522nd FS/27th FBG	P-47D 42-26700 hit by Flak, last seen 1325; pilot unstated
522nd FS/27th FBG	P-47D 42-26438 *Libby* 'red D' hit by Flak 1m N Taglio di Po 1630; 1/Lt Glen H.Spencer POW [12122]
524th FS/27th FBG	P-47D 42-28568 hit by Flak 1700; 2/Lt William F.Alworth KiA
65th FS/57th FG	P-47D 42-29350 *Dear Helen II* hit by Flak N Padua 1440, pilot baled out; 1/Lt Lindsay R.Douglas Jr evaded [12123]
345th FS/350th FG	P-47D 42-28550 crashed M/Y at Fano 1045; 1/Lt Kenneth E.Clifton KiA [12985]
345th FS/350th FG	P-47D 42-27299 last seen entering cloud Forlì-Rimini sector 1049; 2/Lt Edmund J.Ozimek KiA [12365]

Sunday-Monday, 11/12 February 1945

British Casualties	
256 Sqn	Mosquito XIII HK160 scrambled at 0415, last plotted N of Cervia over the coast 0437; Flt Lt F.W.Price/Flg Off H.H.Hopkin MiA
German Casualties	
4.(F)/122	Ju 188D-2 WNr 150513 F6+AP lost at Grassobbio, near Bergamo a/f; Fw Biester and three KiA

Monday, 12 February 1945

Pilots of 2° Gruppo Caccia of ANR again reported intercepting B-25s, this time south-east of Verona. Cap Drago reported shooting down a B-25, but only managed to severely damage it.

The 310th Bomb Group reported that 12–15 Bf 109s and FW 190s attacked the second box of its formation on the bomb run on Legnago sugar refinery. Enemy aircraft flying in echelons of four made three aggressive attacks from 5–7 o'clock pressing to within 200 yards. Six B-25s were holed by machine-gun and cannon fire, one being severely damaged. 1/Lt R.L.McGinnis's aircraft bore the brunt of the attack, with the port engine and hydraulics shot out and one crew member, S/Sgt W.A.Linthicum being wounded; over 400 hits were counted after the aircraft landed at base. In return the bomber gunners, all from the damaged aircraft, claimed an initial four destroyed, actually destroying three Bf 109s and damaging others, including Drago's.

British Casualties						
93 Sqn	Spitfire IX MA534 left 1350 on armed recce, bombed barges in Loreo area, crashed Codigoro; Flg Off W.C.D.Slater KiA					
US Claims						
380th BS/310th BG	gunner Sgt Benjamin Hammond	B-25J 43-27717	Bf 109		W Legnago	1350
380th BS/310th BG	gunner Sgt Emil M.Strabac	B-25J 43-27717	Bf 109		W Legnago	1405
380th BS/310th BG	gunner Sgt Emil M.Strabac	B-25J 43-27717	Bf 109		W Legnago	1405
380th BS/310th BG	gunner S/Sgt W.A.Linthicum	B-25J 43-27717	Bf 109		W Legnago	1500
US Casualties						
380th BS/310th BG	B-25J 43-27717 damaged in combat; 1/Lt R.L.McGinnis and crew safe, one WiA					
Italian ANR Claims						
4ª Sq, 2° Gr C	Cap Ugo Drago	Bf 109G	B-25		Legnago area	1345-
Italian ANR Casualties						
6ª Sq, 2° Gr C	Bf 109G-14 WNr 464414 shot down; Ten Leandro Bonara KiA					
4ª Sq, 2° Gr C	Bf 109G-10 WNr 491320 Black 12 hit in combat, pilot baled out nr Carceri; Serg Magg Carlo Cavagliano safe					
6ª Sq, 2° Gr C	Bf 109G-6 WNr 160319 hit in combat, crash-landed nr Bovolone; Serg Giacomo Bianchini safe					
4ª Sq, 2° Gr C	Bf 109G damaged by return fire; Cap Ugo Drago safe					
6ª Sq, 2° Gr C	Bf 109G damaged by return fire; Ten Ermete Ferrero safe					

Tuesday, 13 February 1945

Nachtaufklärunggruppe 11's single-engined fighter types were seen more frequently now, and on this day pilots of 241 Squadron encountered a pair identified as FW 190s, Wt Off A.J.Ray claiming one shot down.

British Claims					
241 Sqn	Wt Off A.J.Ray	Spitfire IX FT639	FW 190	nr Lake Zignago	1500
British Casualties					
185 Sqn	Spitfire IX PT595 left 1000 to bomb ammo dump, hit by Flak, pilot baled out in enemy territory; Sgt C.D.Spruce POW/evaded				
213 Sqn	Mustang III KH461 left 0920 to bomb rail bridge, shot down by Flak in the Maribor area 1100, pilot baled out; Flt Lt G.P.Elliott POW				
US Casualties					
66th FS/57th FG	P-47D 44-20346 hit by Flak N Peschiera del Garda 1015; 2/Lt Donald C.Spalinger KiA [12144]				
486th BS/340th BG	B-25J 43-27670 '6Y' *Yankee Doodle Dandy* shot down by Flak N Bergamo 1055; 1/Lt Roman H.Figler and five POW [12092]				
486th BS/340th BG	B-25J 43-27505 '6W' *Idiots Delight* shot down by Flak N Bergamo 1055; 1/Lt Marshall W.Knighton and five POW [12093]				
86th BS/47th BG	A-20 lost over Italy; 2/Lt William B.Hart and one KiA, one safe				

Against a wintery Yugoslav backdrop, Lt S.J.Stevens of 19 SAAF Squadron unleashes a salvo of rockets from his Beaufighter against a target at Žužemberk on 13 February.

Flt Lt G.P.Elliot of 213 Squadron became the latest pilot to fall to Flak over the Balkans when he was shot down near Maribor in Mustang III KH461 'D'.

Wednesday, 14 February 1945

Sqn Ldr P.E.Vaughan-Fowler and his wingman Flg Off P.Donnelly (in KH794) left at 0800 on a weather recce of the Celje-Babin-Potok-Jablanac area in their new Mark IV Mustangs and reported the weather was clear. They then strafed and damaged a Ju 52 on Breg landing ground outside Loče, followed by some train strafing to the extent of "disabling" 11 locos and burning three rail cars with trucks on board, before returning safely. Later in the day all five of the squadron's available Mustangs shot up more locos and damaged a He 111 on Breg landing ground. Wt Off Heard who damaged the Heinkel was hit by Flak but reached Zara and landed safely. Another Mustang disappeared while strafing between Panikva and Loče.

British Claims					
213 Sqn	Sqn Ldr P.E.Vaughan-Fowler	Mustang IV KH671	Ju 52 Damaged on grd	Breg l/g	0800-1050
213 Sqn	Wt Off F.Heard	Mustang IV KH671	He 111 Damaged on grd	Breg l/g	1300-1600
British Casualties					
351 Sqn	Hurricane IV LF475 left 0927 on sweep Mostar Zenica area, hit by Flak strafing M/T, force-landed at Sarajevo a/f and overturned; Flt Lt M.Marinović safe				
213 Sqn	Mustang III HB875 left 1300, last seen while strafing in the Panikva-Loče area 1400-1430; Wt Off R.Thompson MiA				
Italian ANR Casualties					
2° Gr C	2 Bf 109Gs destroyed on ground at Lonate				

Thursday, 15 February 1945

72 Squadron was taken over by Sqn Ldr K.N.R.Sissons, formerly a flight commander in 43 Squadron.

US Casualties	
1° Gr Caça/350th FG	P-47D 42-26763 'B3' shot down by Flak 0850; Asp Raymundo da Costa baled and returned

Friday, 16 February 1945

324 Wing begins moving forward to Ravenna as the weather started to improve.

British Casualties	
213 Sqn	Mustang III KH518 left 1400 on armed recce Celje area, hit by Flak, engine failed SW Slunj 1515, pilot baled out; Flt Lt W.J.P.Straker evaded, was flying again by 20 March

318th FS/325th FG	1/Lt Walter K.Selenger	P-51	FW 190	12km S Grado	1340

German Casualties

Seenotst. 20	FW 190A-8 WNr 680124 lost in combat; Oblt Heinz Langer (St.Kpt) MiA

Saturday, 17 February 1945

Pilots of six Spitfires of 601 Squadron on a weather reconnaissance over the front encountered three Bf 109s in the Udine area, allowing Flg Off Proudman to claim a confirmed success.

The pilots of 2° Gruppo Caccia recorded their third engagement of the month, reporting intercepting B-25s escorted by British Spitfires near Lake Garda, heading for the Alps north of Tarvisio. No claims were submitted and MATAF recorded an attack by 10 to 15 Bf 109s at 1415 with no claims or losses. The B-25s had made their first Alpine penetration three days earlier when they flew north of Bolzano to attack a length of railway at Bressanone in the heart of the mountains and longer-range missions of this nature were frequently flown thereafter, but this date had seen the severest opposition to be encountered during these missions.

British Claims

601 Sqn	Flg Off H.G.Proudman	Spitfire IX PT641	Bf 109 in flames	Gemona, N Udine	0855
601 Sqn	Wt Off W.W.Stratton	Spitfire IX PT935	Bf 109 Probable	W Udine	0855

British Casualties

92 Sqn	Spitfire VIII MT562 'J' left 1245 from Bellaria, engine cut on take-off, crash-landed on adjacent beach; Flt Sgt J.Peacock safe
3 SAAF Sqn	Spitfire IXe PT709 last seen in bomb dive near Castelvecchio, WSW Bologna 1510; Lt J.S.Aberdein KiA
11 SAAF Sqn	Kittyhawk IV FT934 left 1210 to bomb locomotive repair sheds, on return caught fire, crashed 3m NNW Pontedera c1330, pilot baled out too low; Lt J.F.L.Burnard KiA

US Casualties

66th FS/57th FG	P-47D 42-26856 *Margie* hit by Flak SW Thiene 1410; 1/Lt James L.Moody KiA [12363]

French Casualties

GC 3/6	P-47D damaged by blast of own bombs, crashed nr Lantosque; Sous Lt Lecloux KiA

German Casualties

NAGr 11	Bf 109G-8 WNr 201439 shot down in combat, Udine area; Gefr Eberhard Croce WiA

Sunday, 18 February 1945

Mustangs of 112 Squadron strafed aircraft on Aviano airfield while returning from an attack on rail targets in northern Italy. A Breda-SAFAT 12.7mm machine gun rapidly manned by a 2° Gruppo ANR armourer opened fire and caught the aircraft of the long-serving Flt Lt Hearn who crashed in flames.

SAAF officers continued to provide a high proportion of squadron and flight commanders within RAF units and on 18 February Maj F.K.Weingartz DFC, was promoted from flight commander to take over from Sqn Ldr Peter Bagshawe as commanding officer of 250 Squadron when the latter's tour ended. In 324 Wing both 43 and 111 Squadrons lost one aircraft during the final week of the month but in the former unit Sqn Ldr Paddy Hemingway, DFC, arrived as a supernumerary; he was to take command of the unit on 6 March.

After a successful tour at the head of 250 Squadron, Sqn Ldr Peter Bagshawe handed over command on 18 February to Maj Felix Weingartz SAAF.

112 Sqn	Mustang IV KH820 'Q' left 1035, shot down in flames by ground fire at Aviano a/f 1220; Flt Lt R.V.Hearn KiA			

US Casualties

347th FS/350th FG	P-47D 44-20133 '7C1' engine failure, crashed Mantua area 1245; 2/Lt Andrew W.Freeborn POW [12364]			

Italian ANR Claims

2° Gruppo	Serg Magg Ernesto D'Ilario	Mustang	Aviano	1220

Sunday-Monday, 18/19 February 1945

US Claims

417th NFS	2/Lt Robert W.Condon/2/Lt Richard M.Cornwell	Beaufighter VIf	Me 210 or 410 Damaged	0230

Monday, 19 February 1945

British Casualties

12 SAAF Sqn	Marauder III HD505 'V' left 1457 on bomb raid on Conegliano, attacked at 1636, hit by Flak that killed one of the crew, damaged Cat A; Lt W.F.Harvey and four safe, 2/Lt B.M.Lindley KiA
12 SAAF Sqn	Marauder III HD526 'L' left 1457 on bomb raid on Conegliano, attacked at 1630, both engines damaged by Flak, one of the crew baled out; Lt Stewart* and five safe, Lt C.C.Bothma POW
	*There were two Lt Stewarts flying as pilots with 12 SAAF Sqn at this time, Lt W.Stewart and Lt J.B.Stewart, it is unknown as to which one was flying this aircraft

Italian ANR Casualties

5ª Sq, 2° Gr C	Bf 109G crash-landed due to engine failure; Ten Raul Di Fiorino safe

Monday-Tuesday, 19/20 February 1945

British Casualties

55 Sqn	Boston V BZ586 'K' left 1815 to bomb Vigodarzere marshalling yards, starboard engine set on fire by Flak, crash-landed SW Camisano Vicentino; Maj A.V.Johnson and three evaded, returned 2 May
114 Sqn	Boston V BZ607 on armed recce Padua-Mestre-Pordenone, hit by Flak over Nervesa della Battaglia, crashed nr Susegana; Wg Cdr R.R.Thomson (Sqn CO) and three KiA

Delivery of new fighters to the ANR continued with Bf 109K-4 W/Nr 330209 '3-17' seen at Lonate Pozzolo on arrival for 1° Gruppo Caccia.

Tuesday, 20 February 1945

Maj Tom Murray, the South African commanding officer of 111 Squadron, was leading an armed reconnaissance over the Padua-Monselice area when his aircraft suffered a direct hit from a 40mm shell as he dived on the target and his Spitfire crashed in flames. Murray had previously commanded 2 SAAF, 4 SAAF and 41 SAAF Squadrons, and had three confirmed and two probable aerial victories to his credit.

Flak was an increasing concern and new tactics were being developed to counter the menace. On this day 21 SAAF Squadron sent 11 Marauders on a bomb raid on the Rovigo marshalling yards, as per normal operations; sent along on this mission were the squadron's first dedicated anti-Flak aircraft, two Marauders with one more from 30 SAAF Squadron. Each aircraft was loaded with 192 20lb fragmentation bombs and flew about 70 seconds ahead of the main formation to bomb known Flak positions. When the first anti-Flak aircraft bombed gun positions from which heavy fire was coming, the fire ceased.

British Casualties	
30 SAAF Sqn	Marauder III HD 464 'E' left 0827 to bomb Rovigo, while forming up, dived into ground SW Jesi; Lt H.N.Lawless and five KiA
213 Sqn	Mustang III KH625 left 1340, crashed unknown cause 10m NE Naples 1430; Wt Off F.Heard KiA
111 Sqn	Spitfire IX MK476 'U' left 1045 on armed recce, attacked a train S Padua, hit by Flak, crashed and exploded 1125; Maj T.P.L.Murray KiA
1 SAAF Sqn	Spitfire IXc MA454 left 0700, hit by Flak, engine caught fire, pilot baled out S Udine 0820; Capt H.T.Snyman POW
2 SAAF Sqn	Spitfire IXe PT426 'T' burst into flames 1m W Copparo in bomb dive 0830, no Flak seen; Lt J.B.Miller KiA
3 SAAF Sqn	Spitfire IXc MH444 'H' last seen 20m NE Carrara in bomb dive 1430, possibly hit by Flak; Lt M.F.W.Austin KiA
4 SAAF Sqn	Spitfire IXe PT954 'X' left 0655 on weather recce, engine failed, pilot baled out over the Adriatic 0850; Capt T.A.Harris POW
US Casualties	
86th FS/79th FG	P-47D 42-29283 '46' shot down by Flak nr Casarsa 1525; 2/Lt Irvin C.Hoerr KiA [12362]
325th FS/86th FG	P-47 damaged by Flak at Casalecchio W Bologna, crash-landed at base; Lt Carl C.Baranek safe

Tuesday-Wednesday, 20/21 February 1945

British Casualties	
114 Sqn	Boston IV BZ460 left 0010, crashed into sea 24km N Falconara returning from night-intruder mission on Treviso-Mestre area; Sgt W.Absalom and three KiA

During the day a dozen Baltimores of 132° Gruppo of the Italian Co-Belligerent Air Force bombed Arsa but the aircraft flown by the commanding officer, Magg Massimilano Erasi, was shot down by Flak.

Wednesday, 21 February 1945

2° Gruppo Caccia encountered again 310th Bomb Group's Mitchells, escorted by Spitfires of 241 Squadron. Pilots of this unit reported sighting ten Bf 109s and FW 190s followed by about 24 more fighters, although the MATAF intelligence report limited the numbers to the initial ten and reported that six aggressive passes were made on the Mitchells. No losses were recorded by Allied aircraft on this occasion, although Serg Magg Ancillotti claimed to have probably shot down a Spitfire and a B-25. Ancillotti and Patton were hit by return fire and both baled out safely from their stricken Messerschmitts.

Speculation followed as to whether the sudden increase in sightings might be due to the arrival of Luftwaffe units at Klagenfurt in Austria. 232 Wing was ordered to mount a night attack forthwith, this being undertaken by six of 13 Squadron's Bostons. However, no aircraft were seen at Klagenfurt and further attacks did not follow.

British Claims

241 Sqn	Plt Off L.D.H.Jenner	Spitfire IXEe RK886	Bf 109 Damaged	Rimini	1240

British Casualties

3 RAAF Sqn	Mustang III KH617 left 0920 to dive bomb a rail diversion near Casarsa, probably hit by Flak, crashed and exploded; Wt Off I.Rennison KiA
5 SAAF Sqn	Mustang III HB947 left 1250 to bomb Dogna rail bridge, shot down by Flak NNE Udine 1415; Lt J.W.Potgieter KiA
112 Sqn	Mustang III KH636 'M' left 1330 to bomb bridge at Pieris, engine trouble, bombs fell off and exploded on touch down; Lt R.W.Strever WiA
7 SAAF Sqn	Spitfire IXc MH658 left 0630, hit by Flak NW Castel Bolognese, crash-landed on return to Forlì; Lt N.Bremner safe
450 Sqn	Kittyhawk IV FT858 left 0920 to bomb a rail diversion near Casarsa, lost port wing to 88mm Flak, crashed 1025; Wt Off R.A.Denholm KiA
43 Sqn	Spitfire IX EN296 left 0900, hit by Flak over Lake Comacchio, attempted to crash land, 500lb bomb still attached exploded on hitting the water 0930; Wt Off M.J.Mathers KiA
601 Sqn	Spitfire IX PT935 left 0825 on armed recce, strafed train 7m S Treviso, hit a tree, last seen S Chioggia at 7,500ft, crashed; Wt Off W.W.Stratton safe?
241 Sqn	Spitfire IX MH818 left 1115 on bomber escort, tyre burst on take-off, hit bank at runway end, burnt out; Flt Sgt A.B.Clarke safe

US Casualties

346th FS/350th FG	P-47D 44-19606 '6C6' *Sugar Tit* shot down by Flak, crashed SW Vicenza 0730; 2/Lt Everett L.Walling KiA [12566]
414th NFS	P-61B 42-39508 hit by Flak between Viareggio and Milan; 2/Lts Ky B.Putnam/John E.Marunovich baled and returned [12570]

Italian Co-Belligerent Casualties

281ª Sq, 132° Gr B	Baltimore FW851 shot down by Flak over Arsa harbour 1300; Magg Massimiliano Erasi (Gr CO) and three KiA

German Casualties

1./NAGr 11	Bf 109G-6 WNr 230164 lost in combat Padua-Vicenza; pilot safe
1./NAGr 11	Bf 109G-8 WNr 200620 engine failure over Adriatic, crashed at Salvore Point; pilot safe

Italian ANR Claims

6ª Sq, 2° Gr C	Serg Magg Rolando Ancillotti	Bf 109G	Spitfire Probable	nr Chiusaforte	1220-
6ª Sq, 2° Gr C	Serg Magg Rolando Ancillotti	Bf 109G	B-25 Probable	nr Chiusaforte	1220-

Italian ANR Casualties

6ª Sq, 2° Gr C	Bf 109G shot down by return fire; Serg Magg Rolando Ancillotti baled out safely
6ª Sq, 2° Gr C	Bf 109G White 6 *Idelma* shot down; Serg Renato Patton baled out, returned three days later

Wednesday-Thursday, 21/22 February 1945

British Casualties

114 Sqn	Boston IV BZ461 left 1930 on armed recce, strafed M/T on road beside Lake Comacchio, flew into the lake; Sgt B.Kelso and two evaded, one KiA
114 Sqn	Boston IV BZ496 left 2105 on armed recce, to attack bridges at Grisolera, FTR; Flt Sgt A.F.Barrett and three KiA
15 SAAF Sqn	Baltimore V FW822 'V' left 2035 to bomb a dump at Lake Comacchio; Lt A.MacD.Thomsen and three KiA
55 Sqn	Boston IV BZ532 left 2245 to bomb San Giovanni marshalling yards, shot down by Flak, crashed 4km W Mestre; Wt Off R.J.Graham and three KiA

| 55 Sqn | Boston V BZ606 left 2245 to bomb San Giovanni marshalling yards, presumably hit by Flak, crashed into the sea; Flt Sgt R.A.Lane and three KiA |
| 55 Sqn | Boston V BZ661 'W' left 2345 to bomb San Giovanni marshalling yards, caught fire in the air over San Donà di Piave, possibly due to flare igniting inside the aircraft; two crewmembers baled out, the pilot landed at Cesenatico 0345; Flt Lt F.Finney safe, one evaded, returned on 24 April, two KiA. Finney was awarded a DSO for his actions |

Thursday, 22 February 1945

US Casualties

| 66th FS/57th FG | P-47D 44-20140 hit by Flak 0835; 2/Lt Lincoln R.Sherwood safe [12463] |
| 97th BS/47th BG | A-20 lost over Italy; Flt Off William P.Naylor MiA |

Thursday-Friday, 22/23 February 1945

British Casualties

| 18 Sqn | Boston IV BZ507 'H' left 2000 to bomb marshalling yards at Cormons, FTR; Flg Off E.J.Cooper and three KiA |
| 18 Sqn | Boston IV BZ482 'M' left 2000 to bomb marshalling yards at Cormons, FTR; Sgt C.S.Drake and three KiA |

Friday, 23 February 1945

British Casualties

72 Sqn	Spitfire IX JK659 left 1220 to attack barges on River Po, crash-landed 1245 u/k cause in enemy territory; Flt Sgt T.M.Ninan POW
185 Sqn	Spitfire IX RK846 left 1500 on armed recce Parma-Fidenza area, possibly hit by Flak, pilot baled out into Allied lines near Viareggio 1545; Sgt P.S.Mayne safe
237 Sqn	Spitfire IX PT421 left 1545 on armed recce, strafed motor transports near Parma, hit by Flak, pilot baled out SW Parma; Flg Off J.V.Malloch kept safe by partisans and flown out back to Allied lines in April

US Claims

| 347th FS/350th FG | 2/Lt James H.Young | P-47D | Me 410 | 20m S Parma | 1030-1345 |
| 346th FS/350th FG | Flt Off William E.Hosey | P-47D | G.55 | 10km N Cittadella | 1515 |

Spitfire IX PT421 'M' of 237 (Rhodesia) Squadron flown by Flg Off Jack Malloch was shot down by Flak on 23 February though he was picked up by local partisans and eventually returned. Post war he became prominent in Rhodesian aviation and died flying a restored Spitfire on 26 March 1982.

German Casualties

1./NAGr 11	Bf 109G-6 WNr 230164 Black 10 shot down in combat 27km N Padua; Fw Ludwig Soukup KiA
1./NAGr 12	Bf 109G-6 WNr 410580 White 9 shot down by own Flak 5km E Fiume; Uffz Heinrich Voss KiA
1./NAGr 12	Bf 108 WNr 5119 GK+RK shot down by own Flak 40km NW Zagreb; Stfw Karl Neubauer/Uffz Karl-Ernst Wiborg KiA
2.(F)/122	Me 410B-3 WNr 190169 F6+NK shot down by P-47 3km SE Robecco; Lt Franz Girlich/Uffz Walter Kemna KiA
6.(F)/122	Ju 188D-2 WNr 159554 F6+CK crash-landed at Bergamo, 30% damaged; crew safe
1./NSGr 9	FW 190F-8 WNr 384549, mechanical trouble, 30% damaged; pilot safe

Friday-Saturday, 23/24 February 1945

British Casualties

55 Sqn	Boston IV BZ525 left to 'nickel' around Aviano, crashed near Donzella at the mouth of the River Po; Flt Sgt A.W.Peddell and two POW or evaded, one KiA
55 Sqn	Boston V BZ630 left 2110 to bomb Sacile and then armed recce of Pordenone-Treviso-Vicenza area, possibly lost near Casarsa; Flg Off B.G.Sherry and three MiA
114 Sqn	Boston IV BZ552 left 0100 on armed recce, crashed near Aquileia for unknown reasons; Capt F.G.Pratt and three KiA
114 Sqn	Boston V BZ618 left 2315 on armed recce of Pordenone-Udine-Monfalcone-Trieste area, FTR; Flg Off K.L.Cutts and three MiA

Saturday, 24 February 1945

At Osoppo T.Col Aldo Alessandrini, commanding officer of 2° Gruppo Caccia, handed over the command to Magg Carlo Miani.

British Casualties

11 SAAF Sqn	Kittyhawk IV FX805 left 0740 to attack dumps at Fogliano, engine failed in bomb dive, pilot baled out 1-2m E Castelvecchio; Lt I.J.Gow evaded
6 Sqn	Hurricane IV KX566 left 0620, missing from attack on Pag, Croatia 0650, reported crashed by partisans; Wt Off P.S.Rundle KiA

US Casualties

86th FS/79th FG	P-47D 42-75990 *Terry* lost u/k cause, last seen 0905; 2/Lt Arthur E.Burnap Jr KiA [12569]
86th FS/79th FG	P-47D 42-29270 hit by Flak, ditched into sea 1225; 1/Lt Thomas P.O'Brian MiA [12571]

Rocket projectiles fired from a 19 SAAF Squadron Beaufighter impact on the Italian freighter *Vittorio Locchi* (4,573 tons) in Fiume during an attack on 24 February.

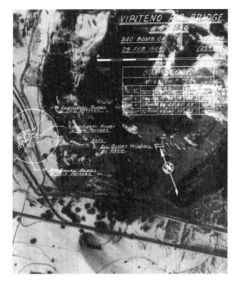

Left: During the 25th, the 340th Bomb Group destroyed the Vipiteno bridge that carried traffic from Austria into Italy. Below: Believed to be the only RAF pilot to hail from Fiji, Flg Off 'Mac' McCaig of 249 Squadron became a POW after being shot down when attacking enemy gunboats in the northern Adriatic near Pola.

Sunday, 25 February 1945

Eleven out of thirteen Marauders of 25 SAAF Squadron were hit by Flak during a bombing raid against the Arsa Channel coaling wharf during which it sustained its first casualty due to enemy action. 2/Lt N.de Gruchy the mid-upper turret gunner in Capt Sidelsky's aircraft, was wounded by shrapnel.

US medium bombers succeeded in knocking two spans out of a bridge at Vipiteno.

British Casualties

237 Sqn	Spitfire IX PT556 left 1635 on armed recce Genoa-Parma area, hit by Flak nr La Spezia, baled out off Viareggio into the sea 1710, parachute did not open; Flg Off P.W.Sutton KiA, body picked up by a Walrus
253 Sqn	Spitfire IX MJ990 left 1545 to bomb gun positions near Karlovac, shot down by Flak over Pag Island, pilot baled out; Flt Lt J.W.Patterson WiA, rescued by partisans and evacuated to Zara
4 SAAF Sqn	Spitfire IXe PT495 hit building while strafing 6m N Bondeno 1530; Maj G.Hilton-Barber KiA
5 SAAF Sqn	Mustang IVa KH800 left 1115 to bomb Stanghella road bridge SW Belluno, shot down by 40mm Flak 1230; Lt L.Hingle KiA

450 Sqn	Kittyhawk IV FX578 left 0930 to cut railway between Pordenone and Nervesa, exploded at 2,000ft when in bomb dive 1035, little Flak seen; Lt J.W.Bailey KiA
450 Sqn	Kittyhawk IV FX596 dive-bombed rail diversion near Casarsa, engine trouble, crashed on landing; Flt Lt D.L.Miller WiA
US Casualties	
489th BS/340th BG	B-25J 43-4000 '9X' shot down by Flak, crashed S Vipiteno 1300; 1/Lt Scott Herrin and four KiA, one POW [12567]
489th BS/340th BG	B-25J 43-27517 '9L' *Prop Wash* shot down by Flak, crashed nr San Leonardo 1300; 1/Lt James F.Matchette and two POW, three KiA [12573]
489th BS/340th BG	B-25J 43-4062 '9G' *Buvvies* hit by Flak, crash-landed nr Glurns, Italy, 1300; 1/Lt Gayle C.Gearhart and five POW [12707]

Monday, 26 February 1945

The German airfield at Malpensa was attacked by four Thunderbolts of the 350th Fighter Group at 1625; local Flak shot down the P-47 flown by 1/Lt Powers.

British Casualties	
249 Sqn	Mustang III HB912 'A' left 0625, shot down by Flak from E boats, pilot baled out 500 yds off Cherso Island 0734; Flg Off D.P.F.McCaig POW
253 Sqn	Spitfire IX MH704 left 1345 from Prkos on recce, shot down by Flak Bihac area, pilot baled out; Plt Off A.E.W.Day safe
5 SAAF Sqn	Mustang III KH533 left 1500 dive-bombing store houses NE Ferrara 1530, presumed shot down by Flak in bomb dive; Lt R.H.R.Flack KiA
241 Sqn	Spitfire IXe PT478 left 0825, shot down by Flak, pilot baled out, seen to land; Flt Sgt R.G.Williams evaded
241 Sqn	Spitfire IX MH586 left 0825, Flak damage and/or engine failure at Castelfranco, force-landed in Allied lines, Cat E damaged; Plt Off L.M.Bailey safe
352 Sqn	Spitfire Vc JK360 'A' on armed recce to Doboi, damaged by Flak, force-landed, hidden by partisans until the war's end; Zastavnik (Sgt) Mehmed Aljia Lošić rescued and returned
351 Sqn	Hurricane IV KX881 left 1450 on armed recce, crashed on landing at Canne 1615; Sgt N.Krsnik safe
US Casualties	
66th FS/57th FG	P-47D 44-20799 hit by Flak 8km N Verona 0930; 1/Lt Richard W.Kruse POW [12575]
347th FS/350th FG	P-47D 42-28339 *Virgin* hit by Flak, did not pull out of dive, crashed N Castano Primo 1645; 1/Lt John E.Powers KiA [12757]
German Claims				
Flak	6/925		P-47	1km N Fagnano	1625

Monday-Tuesday, 26/27 February 1945

British Casualties	
114 Sqn	Boston V BZ618, left 2105 to bomb a power station and an armed recce of the canals of the River Po delta, hit by Flak and crash-landed; Sqn Ldr G.Hampton and three crew POW

Tuesday, 27 February 1945

British Casualties	
87 Sqn	Spitfire IX MK473 left 1355, last seen dive-bombing near La Spezia, pilot baled out; Wt Off K.O.Brooks safe with partisans
185 Sqn	Spitfire IX PT543 left 1215 to bomb bridge S Vignola, hit by Flak, pilot baled out 1245, seen to land and wave; Flg Off C.W.R.Lord POW
US Casualties	
65th FS/57th FG	P-47D 42-75725 *Yin Fiss* hit by Flak 0915; 2/Lt William H.Anderson KiA [12572]
65th FS/57th FG	P-47D 42-76022 *Harsh-Hit* destroyed by own bomb blast over rail line Vicenza-Cittadella 1500; 2/Lt Paul W.Hughes KiA [12507]
66th FS/57th FG	P-47D 42-29321 hit by Flak 1140, Cat 2 damaged; pilot safe
345th FS/350th FG	P-47D 42-29006 *Hell's Angel* hit by Flak 10m W Spittal, Austria 0840; 2/Lt James C.Southard KiA [12563]
346th FS/350th FG	P-47D 44-19581 '6A6' *Curly Mohammed* damaged by target explosion, crashed S Lake Garda 1625; 1/Lt Maurice L.Asbury KiA [12562]
445th BS/321st BG	B-25J 43-36228 *Miss Bobby* left 0950 to bomb railway diversion bridges at Lavis, engine fire, cause u/k 1157; 2/Lt Jay DeBoer Jr interned, four POW, two evaded [12756]
448th BS/321st BG	B-25J 43-4076 left 0950 to bomb railway diversion bridges at Lavis, hit by Flak nr target 1200; 1/Lt Milford A.Smith and six POW [12708]

Above: Bombs dropped from Marauders of 39 Squadron explode in the marshalling yards at Sisak on the River Sava in central Croatia during an attack on 27 February. Below: A dozen Marauder IIIs of 39 Squadron attacked Sisak in the unit's second raid of the day.

Sisak was the final raid of the tour of 39 Squadron's Wg Cdr A.R.deL Inniss (left) who handed over command two days later.

On 28 February Field Marshal Alexander flew to meet Marshal Tito escorted by 213 Squadron Mustangs seen here parked at Zemun airfield, Belgrade, during the visit.

Wednesday, 28 February 1945

On this day Field Marshal Sir Harold Alexander, Supreme Allied Commander Mediterranean flew to Belgrade for consultations with Marshal Tito. His aircraft was escorted by Mustang IIIs of 213 Squadron to Zemun airport.

British Casualties	
337 Wing	Spitfire IX MA507 left on parade sweep over Salonika to mark the arrival of the Greek king, collided with Spitfire MA397, crashed in a bay nearby; Wg Cdr P.H.Woodruff KiA
336 Sqn	Spitfire Vc MA397 left on parade sweep over Salonika to mark the arrival of the Greek king, collided with Spitfire MA507, crash-landed; Flt Lt S.Baltazzis safe
336 Sqn	Spitfire V on return from above operation, engine cut on landing approach, force-landed; Flg Off C.Hatzilakos WiA
US Casualties	
65th FS/57th FG	P-47D 42-27948 *Miss 'D'* damaged by explosion of ammo dump 0905; 2/Lt Joseph G.Beesley KiA [12574]
64th FS/57th FG	P-47D 42-29361 hit by Flak 1105, Cat 2 damaged; pilot safe

Wednesday-Thursday, 28 February/1 March 1945

US Claims					
416th NFS	Capt Lawrence E.Englert/2/Lt Earl R.Dickey	Mosquito Mk 30 MM746	Ju 188	NW Cremona	2307
US Casualties					
416th NFS	Mosquito Mk 30 MM746 engine caught fire near base; Capt Lawrence E.Englert/2/Lt Earl R.Dickey baled out safely				
German Casualties					
4.(F)/122	Ju 188D-2 WNr 230412 lost in combat with night-fighter 15km NW Cremona; Lt Fritz Wöllert and three KiA, one WiA				
6.(F)/122	Ju 188D-2 WNr 15512 engine trouble, belly-landed at Bergamo; Uffz Heinich Happelt and one WiA				

Top: Ventura GR Vs of 22 SAAF Squadron, with 6463 'D' nearest, at Gibraltar from where they maintained watch against submarine incursions through the vital Straits. Above: Pending the arrival of Warwicks to replace Venturas, during February and March 27 SAAF Squadron used eight elderly Wellington VIIIs as interim equipment.

FEBRUARY SUMMARY

By the end of February 5 SAAF Squadron had lost three Mustangs and one flight commander. However, the losses of this and other DAF units remained fairly light compared with those suffered by the USAAF's 57th Fighter Group. During this one month this unit had suffered the loss of no less than 14 Thunderbolts, ten pilots failing to return.

Nonetheless, the Thunderbolt pilots of the 79th Fighter Group particularly, had been able to make good use of the better weather, flying fighter-bomber, reconnaissance and escort missions over the Villach and Klagenfurt areas. On one occasion 1/Lt Alfred C.Hearne of the 86th Squadron led a flight of aircraft to attack and destroy two locomotives, seven trucks, a lorry and two buildings, together with other targets damaged. He was awarded a British DFC by DAF for this performance.

Subsequently Maj Beck led the group over the Alps for its first attack on German soil from an Italian base, the Thunderbolts strafing locomotives in the Berchtesgaden area. On the 27th several hundred rail trucks, many fully loaded, were seen on the Villach-Lendorf line, and an estimated 75% were claimed destroyed or badly damaged. During this later part of the month anti-Flak attacks were also made, using rockets and 20lb fragmentation bombs, these sorties usually being flown in conjunction with attacks on bridges. Some very satisfactory – and satisfying – results were achieved. Late in the month the weather again turned foul, and once more activity slackened.

With 239 Wing's Mustangs and the 79th Fighter Group's P-47s now able to reach all targets, there was not the same need for day bombers. The activities of 232 Wing's intruders by night were still proving very effective in delaying, demoralising and generally upsetting the Axis forces, while shortage of ammunition now often caused them not to fire at single aircraft. In consequence, losses were reduced. The decision was therefore taken that 253 Wing's three Baltimore squadrons should also start undertaking these missions. After training during February, they were to begin operating in this new role in March. The intruders were now guided to their target areas by VHF radio beams. Once there, they cruised around dropping flares, attacking any unfortunate vehicles or other targets so illuminated.

February had also seen an attempt by the German commanders in Italy to negotiate a surrender. They were not, however, prepared to accept the unconditional terms upon which the Allies insisted, so no agreement was reached and hostilities continued.

CHAPTER 4

THE LAST RITES AND THE FINAL ALLIED OFFENSIVE

MARCH OVERVIEW

March 1945 heralded the start of spring as at last the weather introduced a more consistent spell of improved climatic conditions. Indeed, it was to allow 17 full days of operations plus 11 more when at least partial activities were possible; only three days were too bad for any flying. Rail targets remained the primary priority, and all Allied units were deeply involved. However, the Spitfires of DAF undertook a substantial number of escort missions to the Marauders of 3 SAAF Wing. Yugoslavia remained an area of significant importance for the South African bombers and for the Mustangs, and frequent sorties were made across the Adriatic, the latter aircraft operating from a new base at Cervia, to which 239 Wing had moved in late February.

Other units were also moving nearer to the front, 7 SAAF Wing joining 324 Wing at Ravenna, while the four Boston squadrons of 232 Wing all moved to Forlì. The Spitfires of 324 Wing were particularly involved in escorts during March, covering not only Kittyhawks and TacR Spitfires, but also US B-25s and A-20s. It was to be a month of particularly high losses for the wing, however.

In the face of the Russians' tremendous gains, the Germans now launched a strong counter-offensive in an effort to save the Hungarian oilfields and the industrial area of eastern Austria. However, by 17 March this had failed leaving elements of the German forces in Vienna cut off from those in Italy and Yugoslavia. In early March the German 7th SS Mountain Division 'Prinz Eugen' moved to clear the main route to Brod, and heavy fighting again flared. The Yugoslav partisan General Dropin now opened an offensive in Croatia with his newly formed 4th Yugoslav Army in an effort to clear the Gospić-Bihać area, and the coast and islands of North Dalmatia. The Balkan Air Force provided an air advisor at his headquarters and a liaison officer with each corps. On the opening day of his offensive, 19 March, Baltimores and Marauders of 254 Wing attacked strongpoints south-west of Bihać, the town being entered on the 25th, and taken on the 28th. Similar support was also given enabling the capture of Gospić, Senj and Ogulin. Strategic Air Force and Desert Air Force bombers maintained attacks against the road and rail system. The Germans suffered severe losses during the offensive with the partisans claiming 4,000 dead and 2,000 prisoners.

During this period, however, a group of some 2,000 refugees were surrounded in the Metlika area in southeast Slovenia. There were fears they would be killed by the German forces as they withdrew in reprisal for the Yugoslav attacks so Marshal Tito sent an urgent appeal to Allied AHQ for their evacuation. A suitable landing strip was identified at Griblje and between 21 and 26 March they were all flown out by a dozen C-47s of the 51st Troop Carrier Squadron, USAF. On one occasion German troops got within mortar range of the strip but were driven back by partisan forces. The day after the evacuation was completed, Croat Dornier Do 17 began bombing a dummy strip specially laid out as a decoy and continued to do so for the next week. The Luftwaffe had again appeared over Yugoslavia during March, albeit in very small numbers.

Thursday, 1 March 1945

British Casualties	
213 Sqn	Mustang IV KH861 ran short of fuel N Zagreb, pilot baled out S Karlovac; Flg Off A.G.R.Ashley evaded, returned on 18 March
249 Sqn	Mustang III HB851 left 0715, possibly hit by ground fire strafing a train, crashed near Varazdin 0830; Flt Lt J.R.Muir DFC KiA

Friday, 2 March 1945

British Casualties	
213 Sqn	Mustang IV KH846 left 0635, missing on weather recce in Zagreb area; Flg Off P.Donnelly MiA, probably evaded
1435 Sqn	Spitfire IX MH493 left 1030, lost in bad weather, crashed into sea 2m E Vis; Flg Off D.H.P.Lott KiA
11 SAAF Sqn	Kittyhawk IV FT872 'E' left 1600, engine failed in bomb dive 15m SW Parma 1654, pilot baled out; Lt R.A.Hartley evaded with partisan help, returned on 20 March

Friday-Saturday, 2/3 March 1945

British Casualties	
114 Sqn	Boston IV BZ563 lost on night interdiction to Argenta area; Plt Off S.Birch and two KiA

Saturday, 3 March 1945

Opposing fighters were encountered by pilots of 4 SAAF Squadron for the first time in many months when four Spitfires which were escorting 11 Marauders over Conegliano marshalling yards were attacked by a dozen fighters identified as both Bf 109s and FW 190s. The South African pilots, all new to air combat, engaged in a dogfight, claiming two Focke-Wulfs damaged, though one Spitfire was hit and the pilot had to bale out. The Italian intercepting force appears to have been drawn from 2° Gruppo Caccia, this unit losing two Bf 109s from the 22 which had taken off at 1030 from Aviano and Osoppo.

The Marauders of 12 SAAF Squadron faced a very determined attack by Bf 109s when attacking Conegliano marshalling yards. The squadron formation was a lead box of four, followed by two boxes of three. The third box of Marauders flown by Lt Dent, Lt Cohen and Lt Moolman, was attacked on the run-up to the target, the first and second boxes were attacked two minutes after bombing and a running fight ensued for about ten minutes. In all, five Marauders were damaged in the attack. Lt Richard Dent's aircraft was shot up so badly that it was almost cut in half by the only really determined fighter assault the unit was to suffer during this period. Despite this, the pilot held his position at the head of the box and led the formation back to base. Lt Dent received the award of an immediate DFC. Lt Moolman was attacked several times, but his gunners did not make a claim and one of them was wounded. The crew of Lt Cohen were attacked initially by three Bf 109s, one was claimed damaged by two of the gunners, and as it dived away it was chased by a Spitfire. They were then trailed to the coast by the other two Bf 109s, and just near the coast, Wt Off W.Wade threw out a bundle of propaganda pamphlets as one fighter approached, and it broke away as the pamphlet bundle broke open just in front of it. Ten Betti, who was following this lone aircraft out over the Adriatic, claiming hits, reported turning back; "…the bomber dissolved in a cloud of debris that I barely escaped!"

The ANR pilots claimed seven Marauders shot down, apparently made no claim for the Spitfire and lost four Bf 109s, one of which was shot down by German Flak returning to its base.

British Claims					
4 SAAF Sqn	Lt A.J.H.Pretorious	Spitfire IXe PL134 'P'	FW 190 Probable	Conegliano	1145
4 SAAF Sqn	Lt J.A.Neser	Spitfire HFIXe PL384 'E'	FW 190 Damaged	Conegliano	1145
12 SAAF Sqn	Wt Off C.F.Goedhals	Marauder III HD455 'J'	Bf 109 Damaged	Conegliano	1150
12 SAAF Sqn	Plt Off C.Menear	Marauder III HD612 'N' }	Bf 109 Probable	Conegliano	1150
12 SAAF Sqn	Plt Off H.H.Alcock	Marauder III HD612 'N' }			
12 SAAF Sqn	Sgt H.W.Day	Marauder III HD649 'P' }	Bf 109 Damaged	Conegliano	1150
12 SAAF Sqn	Sgt A.P.Bant	Marauder III HD649 'P' }			

British Casualties	
3 RAAF Sqn	Mustang III FB262 left 1415 on anti-Flak strike at Casarsa, hit by Flak, pilot baled out, a/c crashed in Bagnarola setting two houses on fire; Flg Off D.D.Tennant evaded, returned on 4 May
4 SAAF Sqn	Spitfire IXe SM149 'V' left 1035 on bomber escort to 12 SAAF Sqn, shot down by FW 190 over Oderzo 1145, pilot baled out; Lt M.F.Reim killed by Italian Fascists while evading
72 Sqn	Spitfire IX PT485 left 1555 to cut railway tracks Legnano area, struck power lines, crash-landed 1645, seen to be extracted from wreck by Italian civilians and carried to nearby farmhouse; Plt Off D.C.Degerlund POW
12 SAAF Sqn	Marauder III HD612 'N' badly damaged by Bf 109 Conegliano area 1150, landed on one engine at Cervia 1218, Cat B damaged; Lt R.G.Dent and five safe

12 SAAF Sqn	Marauder III HD649 'P' badly damaged by Bf 109 Conegliano area 1150, force-landed one engine out at Ravenna 1237, Cat B damaged; Lt H.W.Cohen and five safe
12 SAAF Sqn	Marauder III HD604 'Y' damaged by Bf 109 Conegliano area 1150, landed safely at base 1250, Cat A damaged; Lt H.J.Moolman and four safe, Wt Off D.Allington WiA
12 SAAF Sqn	Marauder III HD541 'G' damaged by Bf 109 Conegliano area 1150, landed at Rimini 1230 to get medical attention, Cat A damaged; Maj C.J.Ceuppens and four safe, 2/Lt J.H.Quilliam WiA
12 SAAF Sqn	Marauder III HD455 'J' damaged by Bf 109 Conegliano area 1150, landed safely at base 1250, Cat A damaged; Lt G.W.E.Nel and five safe
1435 Sqn	Spitfire IX JL136 engine failed, crashed in landing circuit at Falconara; Flt Sgt B.W.Smith KiFA

US Claims

347th FS/350th FG	1/Lt Sigmund F.Hausner	P-47D 42-27293	FW 190	20m N Bologna	1830-1835

US Casualties

64th FS/57th FG	P-47D 42-28047 hit by Flak 0845, Cat 2 damaged; pilot safe
66th FS/57th FG	P-47D 44-20991 lost u/k cause, crashed at Montecatini 1145; 1/Lt Gene Norris MiA
66th FS/57th FG	P-47D 42-26823 *Leona* hit by Flak 1155; 2/Lt Philip T.Lehman KiA [12565]
65th FS/57th FG	P-47D 42-29297 hit by Flak 1445, Cat 2 damaged; pilot safe
86th FS/79th FG	P-47D 42-29284 damaged by target explosion 1520; 1/Lt Zolton J.Angyal POW [12564]
347th FS/350th FG	P-47D 42-27293 hit by debris from FW 190, pilot lost control 5m SW Bologna and baled out 1835; 1/Lt Sigmund E.Hausner returned [12894]
85th BS/47th BG	A-20K 44-571 damaged by target explosion 2341; 2/Lt Samuel G.Clarke and one KiA, two POW [12876]

German Casualties

1./NSGr 9	FW 190F-8 WNr 583576 lost 10km S Bologna 1835; Hptm Willi Wilzopolski KiA

Italian ANR Claims

4ª Sq, 2° Gr C	S.Ten Felice Squassoni	Bf 109G Black 13	B-26	Conegliano-Adriatic	1044
4ª Sq, 2° Gr C	Ten Raffaele Valenzano	Bf 109G Black 3	B-26	Conegliano-Adriatic	1044
5ª Sq, 2° Gr C	Cap Mario Bellagambi	Bf 109G	B-26	Conegliano-Adriatic	1044
6ª Sq, 2° Gr C	Cap Guido Luccardi	Bf 109G	B-26	Conegliano-Adriatic	1050
6ª Sq, 2° Gr C	Ten Ermete Ferrero	Bf 109G	B-26	Conegliano-Adriatic	1050
5ª Sq, 2° Gr C	Serg Magg Guido Mazzanti	Bf 109G	B-26	Conegliano-Adriatic	1050
6ª Sq, 2° Gr C	Serg Ferdinando Zanardi	Bf 109G	B-26	Conegliano-Adriatic	1050

Italian ANR Casualties

6ª Sq, 2° Gr C	Bf 109G-6 WNr 160766 shot down by own Flak N Castelfranco; Serg Magg Vladimiro Zerini KiA
6ª Sq, 2° Gr C	Bf 109G-6 WNr 163842 Yellow 0 shot down in combat with B-26s S Fontanafredda; Serg Aurelio Cosmano KiA
6ª Sq, 2° Gr C	Bf 109G-6 WNr 163197 Yellow 15 force-landed at Aviano, 40% damaged; M.llo Italo Girace safe
6ª Sq, 2° Gr C	Bf 109G-10 WNr 490379 damaged in combat, belly-landed nr Aviano; M.llo Tullio Covre safe

Saturday-Sunday, 3/4 March 1945

British Casualties

256 Sqn	Mosquito XIII HK178 left 0355 from Forlì to attack Polesella pontoon bridge; Wg Cdr H.W.Eliot DSO DFC/Flt Lt W.T.Cox MiA

Sunday, 4 March 1945

British Casualties

73 Sqn	Spitfire IX MJ525 left 1050 on sweep of railways from Grosuplje to Trnje, pilot forced to bale out at Livinca; Plt Off J.W.Gilchrist safe, rescued by partisans
450 Sqn	Kittyhawk IV FX595 left 1350 to Vittorio Veneto area to bomb a bridge, shot down in flames SSE Belluno 1450; Lt J.B.Pyott KiA

US Casualties

87th FS/79th FG	P-47D 42-29299 *Smartin Up/Sei Kluge* engine failure, belly-landed S Rovigo 0945; 1/Lt Donald A.Montgomery POW [12709]
87th FS/79th FG	P-47D 42-25238 hit by Flak nr Nervesa 0945, ditched at sea; 1/Lt James D.Spraley rescued by 293 Sqn Walrus
64th FS/57th FG	P-47D 42-20126 hit by Flak 1000, pilot baled out; 1/Lt James L.Harp Jr returned

Sunday-Monday, 4/5 March 1945

British Casualties

114 Sqn	Boston IV BZ513 left 2103 on armed recce Ferrara-Padua-Castelfranco-Montebelluna and Treviso area, FTR, presumed crashed near Padua; Sgt A.G.Evans and three KiA

Monday, 5 March 1945

The Spitfire flown by Wt Off Harry Coates of 111 Squadron blew up, probably a Flak victim. His body was not found until 2017 and was eventually buried with full military honours.

Wt Off Harry Coates of 111 Squadron was shot down on this date and posted missing. He was buried with full military honours on 27 March 2019.

British Casualties

111 Sqn	Spitfire IX PT410 'R' left 0630, dive-bombed barges near Adria 0655, caught fire, believed from a Flak hit, crashed and blew up; Wt Off J.H.Coates KiA
93 Sqn	Spitfire HFIX NH362 left 1450 on sweep to Udine, dive-bombed barges near River Po, last seen in intense 20mm Flak; Plt Off P.Hunt KiA
2 SAAF Sqn	Spitfire FIXc EP891 'H' left 1300 to strafe rail targets, hit by Flak 5m SSW Casarsa 1355, pilot baled out; Lt W.R.Lawrie evaded with partisan help, returned on 4 May
40 SAAF Sqn	Spitfire FIX MA565 left 1700, shot down by 88mm Flak, pilot baled out 5m SW Argenta; Lt W.S.Parker POW
US Casualties	
87th FS/79th FG	P-47D 42-28558 shot down by Flak at Jesenica, Yugoslavia, 1130; 2/Lt Albert C.Mathias KiA [12561]

Monday-Tuesday, 5/6 March 1945

British Casualties

256 Sqn	Mosquito XIII HK229 scrambled at 0137, crashed into sea after take-off from Falconara; Wt Off J.S.Ely/Flg Off W.H.Palmer KiA

In the early hours of 6 March Mosquito XII HK229 'G' crashed shortly after taking off from Falconara. It was 256 Squadron's second loss in as many days.

Capt van Reenen of 11 SAAF Squadron evaded capture after having to bale out of Kittyhawk IV FX585 'G' during the afternoon.

Tuesday, 6 March 1945

In 324 Wing Sqn Ldr J.A.'Paddy' Hemingway DFC, who had arrived as a supernumerary with 43 Squadron at the end of February, became commanding officer on 6 March.

British Casualties	
1435 Sqn	Spitfire IX MK414 'F' left 1045 on armed recce, shot down by Flak, crashed at Malisana, pilot baled out; Plt Off J.Millward POW
43 Sqn	Spitfire IX PT774 'S' left 0845 on escort to Tac/R Spitfires, hit by Flak, crash-landed 5-6m W Adria 0935; Flt Sgt G.D.Howarth POW
72 Sqn	Spitfire IX PL128 left 0630 undertaking a 'Pineapple Sundae' operation 0700, strafed an object in a field nearby which blew up causing a severe high speed crash; Flt Lt D.M.Leitch KiA
417 Sqn	Spitfire VIII MT625 left 1445, entered a high speed stall strafing barge near Pordenone, crashed; Plt Off R.W.McKinnon KiA
11 SAAF Sqn	Kittyhawk IV FX585 left 1430 to bomb sugar refinery, engine trouble 30m NW Pistoia 1550, pilot baled out; Capt T.A.van Reenen evaded with partisan help, returned on 11 March
145 Sqn	Spitfire VIII MT660 left 1000 damaged by Flak, crash-landed at Castelfranco 1100; Plt Off J.A.Ulm POW
US Casualties	
87th FS/79th FG	P-47D 44-20858 *Dearest Dottie* shot down by Flak nr St Veit, Austria 1430; 1/Lt Arthur H.Pneuman Jr POW [12893]
64th FS/57th FG	P-47D 42-29021 hit by Flak 1315, damaged Cat 2; pilot safe
Italian ANR Casualties	
1° Gr C	Bf 109 destroyed on ground at Malpensa

Tuesday-Wednesday, 6/7 March 1945

British Casualties	
15 SAAF Sqn	Baltimore V FW768 'T' bombing stores sheds, on return to base pilot overshot approach, crashed into the sea off Cesenati-co 0049; Lt G.H.Ryland and three KiA
15 SAAF Sqn	Baltimore V FW597 left 0220 on armed recce to Codigoro, crashed on taking-off; 2/Lt A.F.Smith and three safe
272 Sqn	Beaufighter TFX NV137 left 1705 on armed recce, attacked shipping at Porto Nogaro, shot down by Flak, crashed at Malisa-na; Flt Sgt E.C.Berg/Wt Off H.F.Kirk KiA

Wednesday, 7 March 1945

3 RAAF Squadron lost one of its veterans, Flt Lt John Hodgkinson to Flak. He had served a previous tour on Kittyhawks with 77 Squadron in the Pacific, where he had claimed two Japanese aircraft shot down.

British Casualties	
3 RAAF Sqn	Mustang IV KH769 left 1410 to bomb Flak positions at Padua, hit by Flak in bomb dive, pilot baled out 3-4m E Corbola in the Po Valley; Flt Lt J.A.T.Hodgkinson POW
US Casualties	
65th FS/57th FG	P-47D 42-75972 *Miss-Mi-Lovin* hit by Flak 1025; 1/Lt Clarence L.Hewitt POW [12906]
65th FS/57th FG	P-47D 44-33070 hit by Flak 1025; 2/Lt Loye M.Copeland POW [12907]
65th FS/57th FG	P-47D 42-27643 hit by Flak 1025, damaged Cat 3; pilot safe
1° Gr Caça/350th FG	P-47D 42-26776 'A2' hit by Flak, crashed at Suzzara 1115; Cap Theobaldo Antonio Kopp evaded and returned
347th FS/350th FG	P-47D 44-20113 crashed into ground 7m NW Parma; Flt Off Andrew J.Langston [12919]
489th BS/340th BG	B-25J 43-35964 '9A' shot down by Flak; 1/Lt John C.Daniels and five POW, one KiA [12905]
German Casualties	
1./NAGr 11	Bf 109G-6 WNr 410531 lost near Latisana; pilot safe
1./NAGr 11	Bf 109G-6 WNr 230272 lost near Udine; pilot safe
Italian ANR Casualties	
5ª Sq, 2° Gr C	Bf 109G-6 WNr 161428 crashed at Osoppo; Serg Magg Ariosto Neri WiA

Wednesday-Thursday, 7/8 March 1945

British Casualties	
13 Sqn	Boston V BZ656 'S' left 2130 to bomb Migliarino, struck poles off end of Forlì runway, crashed and exploded; Wt Off J.B.Annand and three KiA

Thursday, 8 March 1945

Sqn Ldr Darby, the commanding officer – for little more than a week – of 111 Squadron, who had previously served as a flight commander with 87 Squadron, was killed during a close-support operation on this date, almost certainly by a faulty fuse. He was replaced by Sqn Ldr L.W.Farrow.

British Casualties	
111 Sqn	Spitfire IX SM170 'G' left 1350, blew up while diving on a factory near Miglioretto 1410; Sqn Ldr B.F.G.Darby KiA
21 SAAF Sqn	Marauder III HD477 'W' left 1445 to bomb Arsa, hit by Flak over target in starboard engine, crashed at Dignano, 7m N Pola 1645; Flg Off W.F.Blackwood and one KiA, four evaded
185 Sqn	Spitfire IX MH426 left 1150 to attack ammo dump SE Bologna, engine trouble, reached Allied lines near Pistoia, pilot baled out 1235; Flt Sgt R.J.Sleigh safe

Friday, 9 March 1945

At 0615 a Croatian Do 17Z of 3.LJ attacked Čemernica landing ground, dropping ten 50kg bombs. It turned to Sirač but near Petrinja, at 600 metres, it was attacked by a pair of 73 Squadron Spitfires on an early sweep in the Zagreb area, where Flg Off Letts has just shot down a Ca 313G of 19.ZJ near Lekenik village. Here Capt Maritz then sighted the Dornier and opened fire hitting the starboard engine, although the bomber escaped further damage and managed to return to base.

British Claims

73 Sqn	Flg Off R.R.Letts	Spitfire IX MK568	Ca 313	15m SE Zagreb	0620
73 Sqn	Capt W.F.Maritz	Spitfire IX MJ525	Do 17 Damaged	10m SE Zagreb	0620

British Casualties

250 Sqn	Kittyhawk IV FT982 collided in landing circuit 1615; Lt D.B.Tattersall KiA
250 Sqn	Kittyhawk IV FT965 collided in landing circuit 1615; Lt P.B.Somerset KiA
253 Sqn	Spitfire IX MJ644 left 0910 escorting 2 DC-3s to and from Sanski Most, engine trouble 1045, pilot baled out; Lt J.R.Cleverly flown back to Italy with military mission on 12 March

US Casualties

64th FS/57th FG	P-47D 42-28572 hit by Flak 1215, damaged Cat 2; pilot safe

Croatian Casualties

19.ZJ	Ca 313G 5436 shot down by 73 Sqn Spitfire near Lekenik
3.LJ	Do 17Z WNr 0402 attacked by 73 Sqn Spitfire, hit in starboard engine, landed at Borongai

Friday-Saturday, 9/10 March 1945

During a night Ranger sortie to the Venice area a Mosquito of 256 Squadron was damaged and ditched in the Adriatic, the navigator surviving the crash. However, the aircraft had ditched in a minefield but was located by an ASR Warwick of 293 Squadron that then co-ordinated the rescue. A Walrus of the same unit, flown by Flt Sgt R.J.Bickle alighted in the sea outside the minefield. The Warwick then dropped its airborne lifeboat which two of the Walrus crew recovered and sailed into the minefield to pick up the survivor before returning to the Walrus.

British Casualties

255 Sqn	Mosquito NFXIX TA427 intercepted an e/a, dived into the sea 70m NW of Cap Corse u/k cause; Flg Off K.Dutton/Plt Off J.D.Walker KiA
256 Sqn	Mosquito XIII MM527 left 1805 on Ranger patrol NE Venice, on firing cannon the nose blew off, fragments damaged starboard engine, ditched 1905, Wt Off R.E.Chamberlin WiA, rescued by Walrus of 293 Sqn, Flt Sgt N.Goodyear MiA
256 Sqn	Mosquito XIII MM579 left 1805 on Ranger NE Venice, damaged by Flak, belly-landed at Cesenatico 1922; Sqn Ldr D.Giles DFC/Plt Off W.R.Ford-Hutchison safe
15 SAAF Sqn	Baltimore V FW832 'R' left 0032 on armed recce Ferrara-Padua-Codigoro roads, crashed into mountain near Monselice 0102; Lt D.D.Davis and three KiA

The Warwick ASR Is of 293 Squadron like BV502 'N' parked at Pomigliano, were active throughout the campaign on air-sea-rescue duties, particularly over the Adriatic.

Saturday, 10 March 1945

Flt Lt Garry M.Blumer of 450 Squadron was awarded an immediate DSO for his actions on this day. Seriously wounded in the left leg and with multiple shrapnel wounds to both forearms, he managed to return to base and land. In a similar manner on this day, 2/Lt Richard Turner of 5 SAAF Squadron was wounded in the chest by ground fire; he also regained base, landed safely and received an immediate DFC.

Wg Cdr L.E.Leon left on one month special leave in South Africa and Sqn Ldr J.F.W.Elliot took temporary command of 55 Squadron.

British Casualties	
43 Sqn	Spitfire IX PL355 left 1435, shot down in bomb dive, crashed and exploded; Wt Off W.H.Hollis KiA
72 Sqn	Spitfire IX RK916 'H' left 1430 to bomb ammo dumps, exploded on bombing dive 1455; Flt Sgt P.S.Jennings KiA
450 Sqn	Kittyhawk IV FT874 left 1235, hit while attacking 12 barges nr Cavarzere 1310, belly-landed at base; Flt Lt G.M.Blumer WiA
5 SAAF Sqn	Mustang III KH610 left 1545 to attack dumps, hit by ground fire, landed safely at base; 2/Lt R.Turner WiA
6 Sqn	Hurricane IV KX583 left 1605, possibly hit by small-arms fire, crashed on a hillside nr Lussin, Croatia 1715; Flg Off I.J.MacGregor KiA
7 SAAF Sqn	Spitfire IXe PT897 left 1150 to bomb ammunition dumps, engine damaged by debris, pilot baled out 6m W Adria 1225; Maj R.H.C.Kershaw evaded

US Casualties	
65th FS/57th FG	P-47D 42-29035 hit by Flak 0845, damaged Cat 2; pilot safe
428th BS/310th BG	B-25J 43-27529 *Silver Slipper* hit by Flak Ora rail diversion bridge, dropped out of formation, starboard wing broke off 10m SE Ora 1210; 1/Lt Jordan E.Keister and five KiA [12920]
380th BS/310th BG	B-25J 43-27642 *Puss and Boots* shot down by Flak 1230; 1/Lt George F.Tilley and six baled and returned
428th BS/310th BG	B-25J 43-35957 hit by Flak Ora rail diversion bridge, crash-landed 6m S Parma 1245; 1/Lt George A Rorer Jr and three KiA, three safe [12817]
428th BS/310th BG	B-25J 43-27524 hit by Flak Ora rail diversion bridge, crew baled out 1245, crashed E Borgo Val di Taro; 2/Lt Joseph E.Anderson and four evaded (three returned to unit by 25 March), one POW [12971]
448th BS/321st BG	B-25J 43-27538 '87' *Down But Not Out* left 1150 to bomb Ceraino railway station, damaged by Flak, crash-landed at base, salvaged; 2/Lt Thomas S.Sculley and five safe

German Casualties	
1./NAGr 12	Bf 109G-8 WNr 200318 White 5 crashed at Zagreb; Obfw Wilhelm Koch KiA
2.(F)/122	Me 410A-3 WNr 120157 50% damaged by strafing at Ghedi
6.(F)/122	Ju 188D-2 WNr 150514 destroyed by strafing at Bergamo

Italian ANR Casualties	
1ª Sq,1° Gr C	Bf 109G-14 WNr 782474 '1-13' crashed on landing at Malpensa; Ten Giuseppe Rosati WiA
2ª Sq,1° Gr C	Bf 109G-10 WNr 491499 '2-10' crashed at Lonate, 80% damaged; Cap Camillo Barioglio (Sq CO) WiA
1° Gr C	Bf 109G-10 WNr 490688 75% damaged at Malpensa

Sunday, 11 March 1945

At 0610 on an early patrol of two Spitfires from 253 Squadron, pilots observed six Ju 52/3ms being loaded or unloaded on an airfield at Zagreb with the runway still lit. Flg Off W.Hindle strafed one through heavy Flak, claiming it probably destroyed.

The Marauders of 3 SAAF Wing were escorted to bomb Casarsa marshalling yards by eight P-47s. The fighter pilots reported seeing more than 20 Bf 109s, but no attack on the bombers was made.

British Claims					
253 Sqn	Flg Off W.L.Hindle	Spitfire IX MJ234	Ju 52 Probable (on ground)	Zagreb a/f	0610

British Casualties	
112 Sqn	Mustang III KH635 'F' left 0835 to bomb target W Padua on River Po, shot down by ground fire; Flt Sgt O.G.Jones KiA
213 Sqn	Mustang IV KH693 shot down by Flak at Cherso Bay 1200, pilot baled out, parachute did not open; Wt Off I.R.H.Iago KiA
213 Sqn	Mustang III KH598 left 1405, shot down by Flak strafing train near Nové Město, pilot baled out, parachute did not open; Wt Off P.M.Johnston KiA

US Casualties	
345th FS/350th FG	P-47D 42-28315 *Wendy* propeller failure, crashed 10m E Ferrara 1715; 1/Lt Lloyd F.Martin POW [12818]

85th BS/47th BG	A-20G 43-9620 hit tree and bridge 2102; Capt Gilman L.Leist KiA, two evaded [12981]
1° Gr Caça/350th FG	P-47D left to attack railway bridge at Casarsa, hit by Flak and by explosion of ammunition train crossing the bridge, belly-landed at Forlì a/f; Ten Rui Moreira Lima safe

Monday, 12 March 1945

An F-5E Lightning of the 32nd Photo Reconnaissance Squadron flown by Lt Clyde T.Allen was undertaking a sortie to check on bomb damage. Bf 109Gs of 2° Gruppo Caccia were scrambled to intercept. The US aircraft was attacked by Cap Drago, who saw it dive away, pouring white smoke, claiming to have shot it down. The Lightning had indeed been badly damaged, but Allen was able to increase power and escape into cloud. With the hydraulic system of his aircraft shot out which prevented him extending the undercarriage and with his fuel virtually exhausted, he successfully crash-landed on the runway of his home base at Florence.

British Casualties

225 Sqn	Spitfire IXe NH528 left 1345 on TacR, damaged by Flak Modena area, force-landed at Forlì a/f, Cat II; Flg Off B.A.Whitworth safe
213 Sqn	Mustang III HB951 struck a tree while strafing near Zagreb 1100, damaged Cat II, landed at base; Lt B.N.Chiazzari safe
73 Sqn	Spitfire IX MA796 (or MA731) left 1330 on sweep S of Karlovac; Lt W.H.Van Den Bos POW
7 SAAF Sqn	Spitfire IX MJ247 left 1330 to escort Kittyhawks, tyre burst on take-off, on return belly-landed on Ravenna beach; Lt J.C.C.Logan safe

US Casualties

32nd PRS	F-5E badly damaged by Axis fighter, crash-landed at base; Lt Clyde T.Allen
64th FS/57th FG	P-47D 42-26980 lost u/k cause, crashed 1.5km NNE Landriano 1520; 1/Lt Myers J.Reynolds III KiA [13007]

Italian ANR Claims

4ª Sq, 2° Gr C	Cap Ugo Drago	Bf 109G	F-5 Lightning	N Padua	1243

Italian ANR Casualties

6ª Sq, 2° Gr C	Bf 109G-6 engine trouble, crashed after combat; Serg Renato Quasso baled safely

Seen dispersed at Florence, the F-5E Lightnings of the 3rd Photo Reconnaissance Group roamed all over northern Italy locating targets for future attack.

Monday-Tuesday, 12/13 March 1945

British Casualties

256 Sqn	Mosquito XIII HK398 left 1820, damaged two barges on Villa Canal near Cavarzere, strafed trucks, damaged by return fire, belly-landed Forlì 1921, burnt out; Wt Off F.D.K.Southerden/Flt Sgt E.J.Lewington safe

Tuesday, 13 March 1945

The railway through the vital Brenner Pass between Austria and Italy is here under attack by Brazilian P-47s on 13 March.

British Casualties

73 Sqn	Spitfire IX PT668 'Y' left 1600, attacked shipping at Cherso Island, shot down by Flak, pilot baled out; Lt R.D.Collins rescued by ASR
73 Sqn	Spitfire IX EN135 'N' left 1520, hit by Flak, force-landed S Trieste 1700; Wt Off R.R.Willan safe, rescued by partisans
US Casualties	
66th FS/57th FG	P-47D 42-29356 hit by Flak 0845, damaged Cat 2; pilot safe

Wednesday, 14 March 1945

Spitfires of 111 Squadron escorted Marauders of 12 SAAF, 24 SAAF and 30 SAAF Squadrons to the Austrian border on this date; over Yugoslavia Mustangs of 3 RAAF Squadron attacked a train which had been brought to a halt following an attack by Wt Off J.M.Turkington; all 25 trucks were claimed destroyed.

On their first operational flight after their return from Germany, where the Italian pilots of 1° Gruppo Caccia were trained to fly the Bf 109G, 19 Messerschmitts took off from Lonate Pozzolo and Malpensa to intercept a formation of B-25s of 321st Bomb Group escorted by eight P-47Ds of 350th Fighter Group's 346th Squadron. The US bombers were intercepted over Lake Garda and a clash occurred with the escorting

---

Thunderbolts. Almost immediately 1/Lt John Bergeron hit M.llo Giuseppe Chiussi's aircraft, forcing the pilot to crash land. The unfortunate pilot ran into a wall and was killed. Then Flt Off Walter Miller shot down the Bf 109G flown by Serg Domenico Balduzzo who baled out too low to allow his parachute to open and died on impact with the ground. Magg Adriano Visconti, the Gruppo's commanding officer, decided for a determined frontal attack to the leader of the enemy formation, 2/Lt Charles Eddy. The two fighters flew head-on for a few seconds, firing all their guns. Visconti thought that some of his bullets reached the target but his own aircraft was hit in the cockpit by some splinters and he suffered wounds in the face and shoulder. Visconti baled out over the hills west of Lake Garda, was rescued by some local farmers and later taken to Gardone hospital, being discharged after a few days. Other Bf 109s were damaged during a following combat: Cap Cesare Marchesi crash-landed at Ghedi, while Serg Magg Isonzo Baccarini was forced to land at Orio, destroying his Messerschmitt, and M.llo Danilo Billi hit a wreck on landing at Malpensa, damaging his aircraft beyond repair. As a whole, a very hard blow for the Italian unit.

Above: Over Lake Garda the commander of I° Gruppo Caccia, Magg Adriano Visconti, led a determined frontal attack on a Thunderbolt, but was subsequently forced to bale out. Right: The Spitfire of Capt Wally Brunton of 4 SAAF Squadron was hit by Flak on this date, though he landed safely. He assumed command of the unit soon afterwards.

British Casualties

92 Sqn	Spitfire VIII MT768 left 1240 to bomb bridge on Pordenone-Casarsa railway, probably damaged by Flak, pilot baled out; Plt Off J.S.Ogg evaded, returned 30 April
213 Sqn	Mustang IV KH803 left 0900, hit by Flak at Wildon, force-landed at Zara l/g 1145; Flt Sgt N.Stevenson safe
87 Sqn	Spitfire IX MJ155 left 1400 to bomb fuel dumps near Bazzano, hit by Flak, crashed; Flt Sgt R.Pollock KiA
4 SAAF Sqn	Spitfire IXe PL377 'T' left 1415, hit by 40mm Flak, landed safely, Cat II damaged; Capt W.V.Brunton safe
7 SAAF Sqn	Spitfire IXe MJ901 left 1300, returned from operations with hung-up bomb, pilot ordered to bale out near base at Ravenna 1430; Lt J.C.C.Logan safe
7 SAAF Sqn	Spitfire IXc MJ670 'Y' left 1330 to escort Kittyhawks, burst tyre on take-off, propeller hit the runway, ordered to force land on the sand at Ravenna beach, Cat II damaged; Lt K.O.Embling safe

| 30 SAAF Sqn | Marauder III HD547 'S' left 1300 as anti-Flak a/c, bombed Flak positions S Pontebba marshalling yards, over target hit tail of HD461 at 1440, crashed; Capt L.F.L.Fewster and five POW |
| 30 SAAF Sqn | Marauder III HD461 'D left 1300 as anti-Flak a/c, bombed Flak positions S Pontebba marshalling yards, over target tail sliced off by starboard engine of HD547 at 1440, crashed; Lt L Badenhorst and four KiA, one POW |

US Claims

346th FS/350th FG	1/Lt John E.Bergeron	P-47D		Bf 109	SW Lake Garda	1000-1300
346th FS/350th FG	Flt Off Walter R.Miller	P-47D		Bf 109	SW Lake Garda	1000-1300
346th FS/350th FG	2/Lt Charles C.Eddy	P-47D		Bf 109	SW Lake Garda	1000-1300
346th FS/350th FG	2/Lt Robert G.Thompson	P-47D		Bf 109 Damaged	SW Lake Garda	1000-1300

US Casualties

| 347th BS/350th FG | P-47D 44-19664 *Little Sarah* lost to Flak NW Valeggio 1802; 1/Lt Leon E.Tracy POW [13047] |
| 65th FS/57th FG | P-47D 42-27644 hit by Flak, pilot baled out, parachute failed; 1/Lt Earle H.Evans KiA |

Italian ANR Claims

| NC 1° Gr C | Magg Adriano Visconti | Bf 109G-10 | | P-47 (unconfirmed) | Lake Garda | 1145- |

Italian ANR Casualties

3ª Sq, 1° Gr C	Bf 109G-10 WNr 491324 '3-1' take-off accident at Malpensa; Cap Guido Bartolozzi (Sq CO) DoW
NC 1° Gr C	Bf 109G-10 WNr 491356 hit in combat, pilot baled out W Lake Garda; Magg Adriano Visconti WiA
1ª Sq, 1° Gr C	Bf 109G-10 WNr 491485 '1-8', hit in combat, crashed nr San Vigilio; M.llo Giuseppe Chiussi KiA
3ª Sq, 1° Gr C	Bf 109G-10 WNr 491437 '3-7' hit in combat; Serg Domenico Balduzzo baled out, DoW
3ª Sq, 1° Gr C	Bf 109G-10 WNr 491407 '3-5' hit in combat, crash-landed at Ghedi; Cap Cesare Marchesi safe
3ª Sq, 1° Gr C	Bf 109G-10 WNr 491477 '3-9' hit in combat, crash-landed at Orio al Serio and turned over; Serg Magg Isonzo Baccarini safe
3ª Sq, 1° Gr C	Bf 109G-10 WNr 491325 '3-2' hit in combat, collided with wreck of Bartolozzi's aircraft on landing at Malpensa; M.llo Danilo Billi safe

Wednesday-Thursday, 14/15 March 1945

British Casualties

| 55 Sqn | Boston V BZ608 'T' left 1910 on armed recce Padua area, belly-landed 2355; Capt M Vracaric DFC and three safe |

Friday, 16 March 1945

Daytime road movement for the German army was virtually impossible due to Allied air superiority to which these wrecked SdKfz 7 half-tracks bear mute testimony.

British Casualties

417 Sqn	Spitfire VIII MT770 left 1435 to cut railway line Rovigo-Padua, not seen after bomb dive; Flg Off J.W.R.Weekes POW
249 Sqn	Mustang III HB859 left 1335 to bomb Rab Island, possibly damaged by Flak, engine failed over the Adriatic SE Ancona 1520, pilot baled out; Lt P.E.Hill KiA

US Casualties

488th BS/340th BG	B-25J 43-27551 '8H' lost u/k cause 1215; 1/Lt William B.Pelton and five KiA [14082]

Saturday, 17 March 1945

Above: Grp Capt Mike Pedley in his Spitfire Vc JK656 'MP'. The 337 Wing leader undertook a dive-bombing attack on Milos harbour on 17 March 1945 of which he noted: 'Huns obviously annoyed!'. Left: Grp Capt Mike Pedley of 337 Wing flew operationally for most of the war and was one of the few of his rank to regularly lead operations on a daily basis.

British Casualties

253 Sqn	Spitfire IX LZ915 hit by ground fire Rab Island SE Fiume, ditched after attack 1330; Wt Off H.I.Pinkerton KiA
1 SAAF Sqn	Spitfire FIXc MJ670 'A' left on weather recce, burst tyre on take-off, completed mission, crash-landed on return Cat II damaged; Lt L.N.Bulley safe

US Casualties

489th BS/340th BG	B-25J 43-27489 '9P' *Ooh Brother* hit by Flak 1210, crew baled out between Trento and Rovereto; 2/Lt Charles C.Parker taken prisoner and shot while trying to escape, three crew POW, two evaded helped by partisans [13073]
121st Liaison S	L-5B 44-17082 shot down by Flak over front line SW Pianoro 1200; S/Sgt Larquis W.Cunningham and B/Gen Gustav J.Braun KiA [12816]

Sunday, 18 March 1945

On this day 50 P-47s raided Campoformido airfield, finding only two twin-engined aircraft which the pilot described as being Ju 88-types, one of which was claimed damaged when the field was shot up. One Thunderbolt was shot down by Flak.

British Casualties

7 SAAF Sqn	Spitfire FIXc JL377 'B' left 1045 on armed recce, hit by Flak S Padua, damaged on landing 1240, Cat II; Lt M.H.Steyn safe
450 Sqn	Kittyhawk IV FT860 left 1320 to attack target S Ferrara 1400, hit by ground fire, belly-landed in Allied lines; Flt Sgt P.J.Jackman safe

US Casualties

85th FS/79th FG	P-47D 42-26431 lost to Flak 0830; 1/Lt Clarence E.Paff KiA [13272]
66th FS/57th FG	P-47D 42-27011 ditched 1645; Capt James C.Hare rescued
486th BS/340th BG	B-25J 43-4082 '6V' *Bottoms Up* lost u/k cause 1130; 2/Lt James C.Voelkers and five KiA [12980]
85th BS/47th BG	A-20G 43-9616 lost on night-intruder op, last seen 2310; 1/Lt Robert V.Smith and two KiA [12982]

Monday, 19 March 1945

British Casualties

225 Sqn	Spitfire FIX MA311 left 0945 on recce, probably hit by Flak, missing 1045 15m SE Merceto; Flg Off A.E.Joynt KiA
601 Sqn	Spitfire IX PL351 left 1500, hit by Flak, crash-landed 2m S Piove di Sacco; Wt Off G.H.Friis POW
2 SAAF Sqn	Spitfire IXc MJ272 'S' left 1515 on close support in Fusignano area, hit by ground fire, force-landed near Villanova 1600; Lt D.R.Phelan safe

US Casualties

66th FS/57th FG	P-47D 42-20107 hit by Flak 1335, damaged Cat 2; pilot safe
347th FS/350th FG	P-47D 42-74991 hit by Flak, crashed SW Cerea 1530; 2/Lt Walter F.Morrison POW [13275]

Tuesday, 20 March 1945

On this day pilots of 43 Squadron undertook 33 sorties in a total of eight separate operations all against rail targets, losing a flight commander, Flt Lt Manson, during one. 79th Fighter Group P-47s repeated the attack on Campoformido airfield which this time was found to be quite crowded; 21 Axis aircraft were claimed destroyed or damaged. On this occasion Me 262s (most probably Arado Ar 234s) were reported sighted near Udine, but these broke away.

This was a notable day for DAF as well, as Mustangs of 260 Squadron raided a factory at Copparo, attacking with 60lb rockets. This was the first occasion on which one of this command's fighter-bomber units had used these weapons in Italy and marked the culmination of several weeks of training by the squadron. Indeed, 260 was to remain the only unit to use rockets with the RAF in Italy until the close of hostilities.

In a combat near Sarajevo, the commander of 352 Squadron shot down a Hs 126.

British Claims

352 Sqn	Sqn Ldr H.Soic	Spitfire IX MH592	Hs 126	near Sarajevo	1015-1150

British Casualties

92 Sqn	Spitfire VIII MT689 left 1100 on recce, bombed barges on River Po, hit by Flak, pilot reached sea off River Po mouth and baled out; Capt R.H.Jacobs safe, rescued by ASR Catalina
43 Sqn	Spitfire IX MK549 'N' left 1430, last seen in bomb dive near Cavarzere 1500, shot down by Flak; Flt Lt C.G.R.Manson POW

601 Sqn	Spitfire IXe PT641 left 1210 to bomb barges, shot down by Flak, pilot baled out 3m E Porto Garibaldi; Sgt A.R.Charles rescued by Walrus
450 Sqn	Kittyhawk IV FX694 left 0800, attacked Torri rail bridge 0850, engine trouble, pilot baled out; Wt Off P.J.Jackman evaded
3 SAAF Sqn	Spitfire IXe PT458 damaged Cat II in hydraulic system by Flak; Lt M.G.Royston safe
4 SAAF Sqn	Spitfire FIXc MH556 'A' left 1250 to bomb railway line Monselice-Rovigo 1345, probably hit by Flak, pilot baled out; Lt D.J.Taylor safe
112 Sqn	Mustang IV KH793 'L' left 0615, shot down by Flak near Kranj while strafing train, pilot baled; Sqn Ldr G.L.Usher safe with partisans, held as prisoner due to total lack of identification for a month
249 Sqn	Mustang III KH619 'H' left 1450, strafed a train near Darvenja S Brod which exploded, pilot baled out; Flt Sgt W.J.Monkman evaded
19 SAAF Sqn	Beaufighter X NV122 'J' left 1045 attacked Cernik Castle, hit by Flak, crashed near Opatovac 1222; Capt R.F.Dickson KiA/ Flt Lt F.G.Brace evaded, back on 30 March
19 SAAF Sqn	Beaufighter X 'A' left 1045, attacked Cernik Castle, hit by Flak crash-landed at base; Lt Lindsay-Rae/Lt Huson safe
16 SAAF Sqn	Beaufighter X NV593 'P' left 1025 to attack Idrija, tyre burst after take-off, damaged on landing Cat B2; Lt T.S.Bailey/Lt D.A.Dyason safe
US Casualties	
486th BS/340th BG	B-25J 43-27487 '6B' *Devil's Helper* shot down by Flak nr Campo di Trens 1036; 1/Lt Edward V.Mack baled and POW, five KiA [13202]
488th BS/340th BG	B-25J 43-4038 '8X' shot down by Flak 5m W Mules 1036; 1/Lt John P.Wilkinson and five KiA [13205]
488th BS/340th BG	B-25J 43-27537 '8Z' shot down by Flak 1038, crashed 5m S Malè, crew baled out; 2/Lt James E.Jacobs and five POW (three possibly executed at Bolzano concentration camp) [13207]
German Casualties	
NSGr 7	Hs 126 lost; fate of crew unknown

Wednesday, 21 March 1945

A most unusual operation was undertaken with the codename 'Bowler'. Shipping had been noted by TacR aircraft of 318 Squadron in Venice harbour, and on the 18th it had been seen that the merchant vessel SS *Otto Leonhardt* was taking on stores. An attack was ordered. But as very careful and accurate bombing would be necessary, this was delayed by poor weather until the 21st. Air Vice-Marshal R.M.Foster, the commander of the Desert Air Force, coined the name for the raid when he advised his pilots that if any of Venice's historic buildings were hit, he, and probably all other senior officers involved in planning the attack, would be 'bowlerhatted' – i.e. retired from the RAF forthwith.

In the mid-afternoon a formation comprising three squadrons of Mustangs and one of Kittyhawks from 239 Wing and two squadrons of 79th Fighter Group P-47s, were led to the target by the 239 Wing leader, Wg Cdr G.H.Westlake, DFC and Bar. While 3 RAAF Squadron and the Thunderbolts acted in the Flak suppression role, the 48 fighter-bombers of 112, 450 and 5 SAAF Squadrons dived on the target. The *Otto Leonhardt* (ex-Greek of 3,682 tons) was hit and set on fire, going aground badly damaged. The motor torpedo-boat *TA 42* (ex-Italian *Alabarda*), a coaster and a number of barges were sunk, five warehouses demolished and 170 feet of the west quay were blown away. Only one bomb fell outside the harbour area, destroying a small building, but otherwise the attack was an unqualified success. So effective had the anti-Flak operations been that only one aircraft was badly hit. The pilot, Lt Senior, baled out into the sea just outside the harbour, where a waiting Catalina flyingboat at once landed to pick him up and return him to base just after the last fighter-bomber had landed. A photo-reconnaissance Spitfire which had followed the formation at higher altitude, photographed the whole attack in detail.

Another tactical innovation at this time was radar-directed bombing (Shoran) by formations of fighter-bombers, not only medium bombers. 11 SAAF Squadron on this date had four Kittyhawks directed by a ground station to release their bombs in level flight at 12,000ft.

Group Captain Beresford DSO DFC assumed command of 324 Wing.

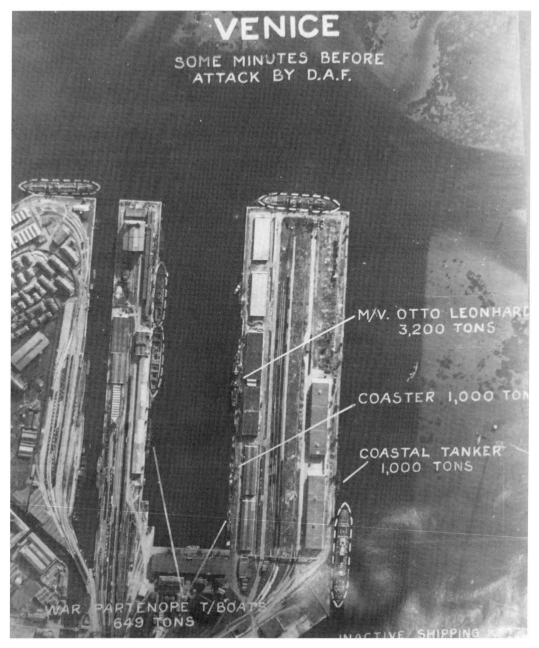

VENICE
SOME MINUTES BEFORE
ATTACK BY D.A.F.

M/V. OTTO LEONHARD
3,200 TONS

COASTER 1,000 TON

COASTAL TANKER
1,000 TONS

WAR PARTENOPE T/BOATS
649 TONS

INACTIVE SHIPPING

Venice harbour a few minutes before the Operation Bowler attack.

British Casualties

19 SAAF Sqn	Beaufighter X 'M' left 1255 to attack Podvinje N Brod, starboard engine hit by Flak, reached Zara l/g in Allied hands, crash-landed; Lt R.Brown/ Flg Off Corless safe
72 Sqn	Spitfire IX MA583 'S' left 1535 to dive bomb railway Treviso-Castelfranco, bomb exploded upon release, crash-landed 1605; Flg Off L.A.Frampton POW
87 Sqn	Spitfire IX PV306 left 1230 on armed recce of Reggio-Modena area, hit by Flak, pilot baled out; Flg Off A.M.Griffiths evaded
213 Sqn	Mustang IV KH804 crashed on landing at base 1310, written off; Flg Off A.G.R.Ashley WiA
213 Sqn	Mustang III KH614 shot down by Flak near Litija 1540; pilot baled out, seen to land safely; Flg Off P.B.Welch evaded
250 Sqn	Kittyhawk IV FX800 left 1445 to bomb shipping in Venice harbour, hit by Flak, pilot baled out S harbour; Lt B.A.Senior rescued by ASR Catalina

1435 Sqn	Spitfire IX MA790 left 1120, tyre burst on take-off, turned over and caught fire, pilot rescued by Wg Cdr G.M.Knocker and an American sergeant; Wt Off E.J.Skelton WiA

US Claims

380th BS/310th BG	gunner Sgt Blair L.Gardner	B-25J 4x-xx102	FW 190	Pordenone	
310th BG	gunner	B-25J	FW 190	Pordenone	1000
310th BG	gunner	B-25J	Bf 109	Pordenone	1000

US Casualties

66th FS/57th FG	P-47D 44-20873 *Sweetheart/Hell's Angel* hit by Flak, crashed nr Verona 0900, pilot baled; 1/Lt Miller A.Anderson POW [12983]
65th FS/57th FG	P-47D 42-26789 hit by Flak 1355, damaged Cat 2; pilot safe
79th FG	P-47D lost, pilot baled out; Lt Nicholas injured, rescued
97th BS/47th BG	A-20K 44-572 '91' damaged 0426; 1/Lt John L.Fields and two safe, one POW [12986]
446th BS/321st BG	B-25J 43-27747 *Spider's Frolic Pad* left 1105 to bomb railway bridge at Campo, shot down by Flak nr Ora 1347; 1/Lt Herman E.Everhart and one KiA, four interned in Switzerland [13203]
447th BS/321st BG	B-25J 43-35958 damaged by Flak, crash-landed at base; 1/Lt Lyle N.Brown Jr and five safe

Wednesday-Thursday, 21/22 March 1945

A pair of Ju 188 reconnaissance aircraft of 4./KG 200 were known to the Allied listening service to be operating over northern Italy. One of these landed at Udine but a second was still present in the air during the evening when an attempt was made to vector a 255 Squadron Mosquito after it. However, this aircraft was obliged to land as its fuel began to run out, but a second aircraft was scrambled after the intruder, this being vectored onto it. Contact was made in the Pola-Trieste area and the Junkers was shot down in flames, falling into the sea three miles offshore at 2245.

British Claims

255 Sqn	Flg Off J.Scollan/Flt Sgt E.Blundell	Mosquito XIX	Ju 188	between Pola-Trieste	2245

German Casualties

4./KG 200	Ju 188D-2 WNr 180444 MiA (possibly with the loss of Hptm Heinz Domack and crew of four)

Thursday, 22 March 1945

British Casualties

1 SAAF Sqn	Spitfire IXc MA801 'M' *Maud* strafed motor transports near Polesella, shot down by Flak NE Ferrara 1625; Lt W.A.Dowden POW
145 Sqn	Spitfire VIII JF897 left 1610 from Bellaria, engine cut, crash-landed on adjacent beach; Wt Off J.B.Ware safe
185 Sqn	Spitfire IX PT371 left 1515, last heard from 1555 in the Mirandola area; Flt Sgt R.J.Sleigh KiA
40 SAAF Sqn	Spitfire IX left 1345 on Arty/R, hit by Flak Massa Lombarda-Fusignano, crash-landed in Allied lines 1440; Lt S.Cooper safe
93 Sqn	Spitfire IX MA233 left 1005 on rail cut bombing Treviso-Nervesa, ran out of fuel, belly-landed short of runway at Ravenna; Flt Sgt J.E.Hartley safe

Thursday-Friday, 22/23 March 1945

A Ju 188 over the Adriatic was warned that there was Allied fighter activity at around 0215. Despite several more calls, this ceased to respond after 0412. It had been intercepted by a Mosquito of 255 Squadron and shot down as this RAF unit's final victory of the war. Its identity has not been discovered, however the loss was evidenced by the RAF's Wireless Interception Service.

British Claims

255 Sqn	Flt Lt W.R.Pertwee/Flt Sgt F.E.Smith	Mosquito XIX TA431 'N'	Ju 188	2m N River Po delta	0328

German Casualties

unknown	Ju 188 lost

Over the River Po during the early hours of 23 March a Mosquito XIX of 255 Squadron shot down a Ju 188 to claim the unit's final victory of the war.

Friday, 23 March 1945

Another combat was fought between Italian Messerschmitts and MATAF aircraft on this day, when a 2° Gruppo formation of six 4ª Squadriglia Bf 109s led by Cap Ugo Drago bounced over the Udine area P-47s from the 79th Fighter Group on a fighter-bomber mission at 0935. 2/Lt Jack Faires was hit and baled out just west of Fagagna, west of Udine. Capt Drago claimed a Bf 109 at this location and Serg Magg Loris Baldi another further to the north at Tarcento. Both appear to have claimed Faires for the loss of Baldi's Messerschmitt, the pilot surviving.

Half an hour later, 11 other Bf 109s from the headquarters flight and 6ª Squadriglia intercepted 25 B-25s of the 310th Bomb Group attacking the Pordenone bridge. The 310th reported 15–20 Bf 109s and FW 190s attacked the 380th Squadron box. Lt Summers in the lead aircraft, had his left engine shot out, the wheels dropped down and as it was leaving the formation three of the crew baled out. It was then attacked again by five to six Bf 109s and crashed. The bomber's gunners claimed seven Bf 109s, one seen to explode in the air and another going down in flames. This claim was apparently later reduced to two destroyed and two Bf 109s damaged. On this occasion the Italian pilots identified the bombers as Marauders, claiming two and a P-47 shot down, misidentified as a Spitfire. No Bf 109s were lost.

Other attacks on Aviano airfield destroyed an Arado Ar 234 jet reconnaissance-bomber. The Ar 234 was part of a detachment of these aircraft, based at Campoformido, that had recently arrived in Italy led by Oblt Erich Sommer.

The Ar 234 detachment was led by Oblt Erich Sommer who was one of the Luftwaffe's most experienced reconnaissance pilots.

At this time a handful of Arado Ar 234 jets were based in northern Italy for reconnaissance duties.

British Casualties

213 Sqn	Mustang III KH421 shot down by Flak strafing a train near Maribor 0735, pilot baled out but parachute did not open; Flt Lt J.H.M.MacKinnon KiA
250 Sqn	Kittyhawk IV FX842 left 1130, hit by 20mm Flak while strafing E Udine, undercarriage damaged, belly-landed; Lt M.A.Cousins WiA

US Claims

85th FS/79th FG	1/Lt Hollis B.Merrell	P-47D			
85th FS/79th FG	2/Lt Howard M.Moore	P-47D	Bf 109	Gorizia	0930
85th FS/79th FG	1/Lt Frank J.Ward	P-47D			
85th FS/79th FG	2/Lt Arthur R.Weand	P-47D			
379th BS/310th BG	Cpl Leo L.Gries	B-25J 43-36048	Bf 109	Pordenone	0950
380th BS/310th BG	Sgt Blair L.Gardner	B-25J	FW 190	NE Italy	0957
379th BS/310th BG	Sgt Samuel A.Blackwell	B-25J 43-27658	FW 190	5m S Pordenone	1000
379th BS/310th BG	S/Sgt Lewis A.Holloway	B-25J 43-4048	Bf 109	S Pordenone	1000
379th BS/310th BG	S/Sgt John T.Greenfield	B-25J 43-27775			
379th BS/310th BG	Cpl Edward B.Ely	B-25J 44-28949	Bf 109	Pordenone	1000
379th BS/310th BG	Sgt Charles G.Courbat	B-25J 43-27571			
379th BS/310th BG	Cpl Joseph A.Cahalane	B-25J	FW 190	5m S Pordenone	1000
379th BS/310th BG	Capt Peter J.Grant	B-25J 43-27582			
379th BS/310th BG	Sgt William M.Morris	B-25J 43-27567			
379th BS/310th BG	Sgt Sewell E.Brown	B-25J 43-27744	Bf 109	Pordenone	1010
379th BS/310th BG	Pvt Morris J.Williamson	B-25J 43-27582			

US Casualties

85th FS/79th FG	P-47D 42-29310 shot down by Bf 109 W Fagagna, W Udine, 0935; 2/Lt Jack Faires baled out, POW [13204]
380th BS/310th BG	B-25J 43-36238 *Sitting Pretty* shot down by e/a nr Motta di Livenza 0957; 2/Lt James J.Summers and five returned [13206]
380th BS/310th BG	B-25J damaged by fighters, force-landed at base; Capt Everett P.Robinson and six safe
379th BS/310th BG	B-25J 43-4048 damaged by fighters, returned; 1/Lt W.H.Poole and five safe

Italian ANR Claims

4ª Sq, 2° Gr C	Cap Ugo Drago	Bf 109G	P-47	Udine	0925
4ª Sq, 2° Gr C	Serg Loris Baldi	Bf 109G-10	P-47	N Tarcento	0935
6ª Sq, 2° Gr C	M.llo Tullio Covre	Bf 109G	P-47	Pordenone	1000
6ª Sq, 2° Gr C	Serg Magg Renato Patton	Bf 109G	B-26	Pordenone	1000
NC 2° Gr C	Cap Alberto Spigaglia	Bf 109G	B-26	Pordenone	1000

4ª Sq, 2° Gr C   Bf 109G-10 shot down nr Udine 0925; Serg Magg Loris Baldi safe

Friday-Saturday, 23/24 March 1945

US Casualties
16th TCS/64th TCG	C-47A 42-100954 lost over Italy, last seen 2030; 1/Lt Robert E.Wallin and six KiA [12897]
84th BS/47th BG	A-20K 44-336 *Friedsprat #2* left 0005 to Pordenone area, failed to return; Capt Bliss L.Mehr and three KiA [12984]

Saturday, 24 March 1945

This day was another example of many recent losses, most of which had been caused by the intense ground fire through which the fighter-bombers were required to fly. Although other wings did not suffer such heavy losses during the month as did 324, none were without casualties and the formation leaders continued to make up a disproportionate percentage of these. Sqn Ldr A.P.Q.Bluett had now left 112 Squadron, his tour having expired, but on the 20th his successor, Sqn Ldr G.L.Usher had been shot down over Yugoslavia while strafing, though on this occasion he was able to bale out. Sqn Ldr J.S.Hart then got the job. With 5 SAAF Squadron Maj Murdoch ended his tour also, Capt H.O.M.Odendaal, DFC, being promoted to take his place.

Four Mustangs from each of 213 and 249 Squadrons undertook an attack on Gornji Stupnik airfield near Zagreb, where initially they found a train, then spotted aircraft, two being claimed destroyed on the ground, but one of 213's Mustangs was lost to Flak.

British Claims
249 Sqn	Lt A.J.Malherbe	Mustang III KH594 'Y'	FW 190 on ground	Gornji Stupnik	1455
249 Sqn	Flg Off E.Geddes	Mustang III HB869 'W'	FW190 on ground	Gornji Stupnik	1455
249 Sqn	Lt A.J.Malherbe	Mustang III KH594 'Y'	FW 190 Damaged on grd	Gornji Stupnik	1455
249 Sqn	Flg Off E.Geddes	Mustang III HB869 'W'	Ju 88 Damaged on grd	Gornji Stupnik	1455

During an armed recce to the Zagreb area by 249 Squadron, Lt John Malherbe destroyed an FW 190 on the ground at Gornji Stupnik airfield.

British Casualties

16 SAAF Sqn	Beaufighter X NV567 'Y' left 1145 to attack Stocarska barracks, damaged by Flak, crash-landed on Drina river banks S Mravinjac 1315; Lt T.S.Bailey/Lt D.A.Dyason evaded, back on 11 April
92 Sqn	Spitfire VIII JG124 left 1420 on strafing recce, engine cut after take-off, force-landed 1m W Bellaria a/f, Cat II damaged; Sgt J.Doyle safe
237 Sqn	Spitfire IX MJ365 left 0600, strafed a train near Casalpusterlengo, N Piacenza, engine cut, crash-landed near Osteria Pietralunga; Plt Off L.P.Perason evaded
2 SAAF Sqn	Spitfire IXc MJ308 'Q' hit by Flak strafing NE Padua, crashed nearby; Lt L.de Klerk KiA
250 Sqn	Kittyhawk IV FT939 left 0720 dive-bombing a bridge at San Giorgio di Nogaro, engine cut, attempted to bale out N Venice, but parachute hung up on the tailplane; Flg Off F.D.Devlin (US) KiA
213 Sqn	Mustang IV KH809 shot down by Flak strafing a train N of Gornji Stupnik l/g, crashed 1445; Lt W.St.C.Thomson POW
US Casualties	
345th FS/350th FG	P-47D 44-33074 hit by Flak between Mantua and Reggio 0945; 1/Lt Albert M.Matthews rescued by partisans [13379]

Saturday-Sunday, 24/25 March 1945

British Casualties

55 Sqn	Boston IV BZ564 left 0045 on armed recce Treviso-Mestre area, engine trouble, ditched N Cesenatico 0115, seen to burn on the sea; Sgt A.M.Rogers and three KiA

Sunday, 25 March 1945

Another violent explosion killed an RAF pilot and totally destroyed his aircraft, the Spitfire of Flt Sgt Chapman of 111 Squadron blowing up while in its bombing dive. There was no Flak seen and Chapman became the third member of his squadron in March and another of the growing number of pilots lost to the continuing issue of faulty bomb fuses.

Maj Andrew Schindler, the commander of the 346th Fighter Squadron, was shot down on his 114th combat mission. He led a flight of eight P-47s to bomb a rail bridge but was hit by Flak pulling out of his bomb dive and lost oil pressure; soon his aircraft was on fire and he baled out but fractured his pelvis on landing. He was taken to Modena hospital and was there until the Germans pulled out and the town was liberated.

British Casualties

111 Sqn	Spitfire IX MA741 'X' left 1540 on a rail cut mission between Padua and Rovigo, blew up and disintegrated in bombing dive 1600; Flt Sgt A.A.Chapman KiA
US Casualties	
87th FS/79th FG	P-47D 42-29341 *Bad Penny/Jeannie* prop failure Villorba area 1520; 1/Lt Herbert L.Hanson returned [13209]
346th FS/350th FG	P-47D 44-20979 *Mike* '601' hit by Flak between Vicenza and Padua 1215; Maj Andrew R.Schindler WiA, POW, returned [13450]

Monday, 26 March 1945

British Casualties

73 Sqn	Spitfire IX MJ835 'P' left 1115 on armed recce, shot down near Ostrovac 1150, pilot baled but parachute failed; Flt Sgt D.L.Pratt KiA
US Casualties	
1° Gr Caça/350th FG	P-47D 42-26766 'B4' shot down by Flak, crashed nr Casarsa 0830; 1° Ten Othon Corrêa Netto evaded

Monday-Tuesday, 26/27 March 1945

British Casualties

13 Sqn	Boston V BZ558 'D' missing from night interdiction to Padua area; Wt Off E.A.Day and three KiA

Thursday, 29 March 1945

Lt Robert K.Morrow of 346th Squadron/350th Fighter Group led eight Thunderbolts on a mission during which they strafed Bergamo airfield claiming a Ju 88 destroyed and another damaged.

Parked at Kalamaki (Hassani) near Athens on 29 March, the Wellington XIIIs of 221 Squadron were used for bombing and supply drops in the fighting against the Greek communist insurgency.

British Casualties

237 Sqn	Spitfire IX PT960 left 1155 to attack stores depot near Pizzighettone 12m NW Cremona, bomb exploded at 6,000ft in bomb dive, some light Flak present; Flg Off H.E.C.Aylward KiA
3 SAAF Sqn	Spitfire IX PT455 'P' left 1010 on escort to C-47s supply dropping, engine failure, pilot baled out; Lt D.G.Nunan evaded, back on 4 April
11 SAAF Sqn	Kittyhawk IV FT945 'S' left 1125, engine cut on take-off at Pontedera a/f, crashed; 2/Lt D.C.Engelbrecht safe

US Claims

346th FS/350th FG	pilots	P-47s	Ju 88 on ground	Bergamo a/f
346th FS/350th FG	pilots	P-47s	Ju 88 Damaged on grd	Bergamo a/f

US Casualties

66th FS/57th FG	P-47D 44-33065 hit by fragmentation case 0850, damaged Cat 2; pilot safe

Friday, 30 March 1945

In late March both the Luftwaffe and ZNDH (Croatian air force) concentrated much of their effort to attempt to slow the advance of 4.Armija J in the region of Lika. Late in the afternoon four Croat Do 17Zs of 3.LJ, escorted by four Bf 109Gs of 2.ZJ, were sent to attack 4.JA positions near Gospić. They encountered three Spitfires of 73 Squadron led by Lt T.S.Harper that had left Prkos at 1710 to patrol over the Gospić-Zagreb area. Near Perušić at 1810 (local time) they engaged the Croat formation, identifiying the fighters as FW 190s, claiming one Do 17Z shot down and an FW 190 damaged; Vodnik (Vod: Sgt) Antun Pleše returned to Lučko with his Bf 109G-14 riddled. The pilot of a second Dornier was Stariji Vodnik (Str: Flt Sgt) Dragutin Žauhar, a prominent National Liberation Movement (NOP, the communist-led resistance movement) activist and in the melee his aircraft was attacked and slightly damaged but he escaped into cloud and headed to defect to the partisan airfield at Udbina, where he belly-landed nearby at Krbavsko Polje. The crew were captured and court-martialled but a partisan leader then vouched for Žauhar. However, the rest of his crew were less fortunate and were all executed. The Dornier was dismantled

Sqn Ldr 'Paddy' Hemingway took command of 43 Squadron during this period. At the time of writing (November 2020) he is the sole surviving Battle of Britain pilot.

and in mid-April was transported to Zemunik airfield for repairs; some ten days later it was flown to Zemun by Dragutin Žauhar. It is likely that this aircraft had been attacked by Lt Harper who recorded making "an ineffectual attack" and thus submitted no claim.

1/Lt Glenn L.Parish led a flight of four P-47s to bomb and strafe targets in the Po Valley. On the return journey Parish, on his first mission as a flight leader, located an ammunition dump near Aulla. On his second or third pass he strafed a field, where the Germans had stored ammunition away from the small huts that constituted the dump. There was a huge explosion leaving a mushroom cloud rising to 12,000ft and Parish was killed.

British Claims					
73 Sqn	Flg Off N.J.Pearce	Spitfire IX MJ349	Do 17	8m N Gospić	1745
73 Sqn	Plt Off J.W.Gilchrist	Spitfire IX JL239	FW 190 Damaged	8m N Gospić	1745
British Casualties					
352 Sqn	Spitfire Vc EF720, landed with hung-up bomb which exploded on landing at Vis; Plt Off Luigi Rugi (Italian) KiA				
40 SAAF Sqn	Spitfire IX PT566 left 1130, shot down by Flak near Lugo 1205, crashed inside Allied lines; Lt R.F.Krynauw KiA				
US Casualties					
346th FS/350th FG	P-47D 42-26947 *Buzzin Cuzzin* '6D4' damaged by target explosion E Aulla 0830; 1/Lt Glenn L.Parish KiA [13452]				
379th BS/310th BG	B-25J 43-27571 hit by Flak nr Rovereto 1500; 1/Lt Alexander McStea and one KiA, five returned [13451]				
488th BS/340th BG	B-25J 43-27708 '8V' *Battling Betty* hit by Flak W Venice 1500; 1/Lt Emmett W.Hughes and five POW [13704]				
486th BS/340th BG	B-25J 43-36107 '6D' damaged by Flak, crash-landed at base; 1/Lt L.J.Tremaine and five safe				
416th NFS	Mosquito NT249 lost u/k cause; 1/Lt Eldon W.Blake/2/Lt Max W.Galovich KiA [13453]				
Croatian Casualties					
3.LJ	Do 17Z-2 WNr 0401 shot down by Spitfire near Perušić; Sat Josepi Jortdanić and three KiA				
2.ZJ	Bf 109G-14 slightly damaged, returned to Lučko; Vod Antun Pleše safe				
3.LJ	Do 17Z-2 WNr 0411 slightly damaged, then the pilot defected, belly-landing near Udbina; pilot Str Dragutin Žauhar released but his crew court-martialled by partisans and executed				

Sqn Ldr Jack Slade of 94 Squadron led the patrol that shot down a Bulgarian Bf 109 over northern Greece and which was subsequently 'hushed-up'.

Above: Seen at Sedes in March 1945, Spitfire IX MJ730 'Y' was flown by Flg Off Rodney Simmonds to attack the Bulgarian Bf 109. This Spitfire survived the war, was later restored and remains airworthy in the United States. Left: Fw 200 C-3 Condor, G6+FY of Sonderstaffel Condor, subordinated to 14./TG 4, can be seen under the camouflage netting among the trees. It escaped detection during this strafing attack on Calato airfield, Rhodes by Beaufighters of 252 Squadron on 31 March.

Saturday, 31 March 1945

On this day a problem of identification occurred. According to Flg Off Rodney Simmonds, a pilot of 94 Squadron then based at Salonika:

"Four of us were returning from the Turkish/Bulgarian borders when we came across an Me 109 stooging along ahead of us at the same height. We couldn't believe our luck and the CO, without hesitation, led the attack. We all had a squirt and dispatched it in flames to mother earth. As it plunged down, I noticed instead of the usual German cross on the side of the fuselage it had something like an 'X'. At the debrief it was concluded that it was a Bulgarian air force machine. Regrettably our intel was not fully up to date for we had not been told that Bulgaria had capitulated to our allies, the Russians, two weeks previously and were no longer considered enemy. It was decided not to include the incident in any ORB report."

MARCH INTO APRIL

The rocket-armed Hurricanes of 6 Squadron had moved to Vis during March but in early April the rest of 281 Wing, 73, 253 and 352 Squadrons, moved to Yugoslavia, joining 351 Squadron at Prkos. All that now remained at Canne were some Italian Spitfire Vs and P-39s which had been operating with the wing; the move was codenamed Operation Bingham. Balkan Air Force now brought to a climax its support of the 4th Yugoslav army, flying more than 3,000 sorties during the month. Some 800 vehicles, 60 locomotives and 40 coastal vessels were strafed and the coastal defences were so effectively attacked that they offered little interference with the Yugoslav attacks which had cleared the coastline as far north as Kraljevica by mid month.

With so much practice the accuracy of the fighter-bombers of MATAF continued to improve. 7 SAAF Wing was really setting the pace here, and during March 2 SAAF Squadron achieved a remarkable 30% of bombs falling within the target area, while 1 SAAF Squadron was close behind with 28%. This latter unit was at this time starting to get the first examples of the new gyro gunsight to reach Italy. The pilots were disappointed with this, as it had been designed specifically with air combat in mind – and of this,

During March the rocket-firing Hurricanes of 6 Squadron had moved into an airfield on an island off the Croatian coast.

400

there was now precious little. For ground-attack work they preferred the old, tried and tested ring-and-bead sight better even than the reflector sight which had been standard throughout the war. Their preference was somewhat prejudiced in fact, for later very good results were to be achieved against ground targets with the gyro sight.

Over the western sector of the front the aircraft of 208 and 225 Squadrons remained active, spotting gun sites and convoy targets for the fighter-bombers of the 57th and 350th Fighter Groups, and 8 SAAF Wing. This latter unit made several attacks on the Cortemaggiore oil fields during the month, also carrying out a successful strike on an ammunition factory at Aulla.

By night the Mosquitos were now much in evidence. The intruder aircraft of 256 Squadron, now all fitted with the 'Gee' radar navigation aid, carried out many strafing attacks on barges on the Villa Canale. At the end of March they were given a change of role, being ordered to fly night-support sorties for the bombers of 232 and 253 Wings, and the Liberators of 205 Group, Strategic Air Force. These activities, which began on the 30th, were similar to those undertaken by 100 Group of Bomber Command from England. The Mark XII and XIII aircraft carried out patrols over possible night-fighter airfields in the Polesella area and also attacked troublesome Flak positions. Meanwhile, the aircraft of 255 and 600 Squadrons continued their defensive patrols, as did the increasing number of USAAF night-fighter units.

During the course of the month planning had been taking place for the spring offensive. It had been arranged that 8th Army would attack first, as in the previous August, to threaten the Axis left flank and draw off their reserves. When this had been accomplished, 5th Army in the centre would punch straight for Bologna. Planning for MATAF for such an operation was now very brief, for the whole organisation and its units were so experienced that little special training or arrangements were necessary.

At this time however, there were some considerable command changes on both sides of the lines. To the north, Feldmarschall Albert Kesselring was recalled to Germany to become the last commander of the German armies in the west. It was hoped that his great experience in staving off almost certain defeat might by some miracle delay the inevitable. The move was far too late, and conditions for defence in

In early April two YP-80A Shooting Star jet fighters were attached to the 94th Fighter Squadron, 1st Fighter Group and flown on familiarisation sorties.

Western Europe in the face of the overwhelming strength of the Allies, was a very different matter than in Italy. His place as commander of Armee Gruppe C was taken by General Heinrich von Vietinghoff, commander of 10.Armee. Armee Gruppe C still comprising 10. and 14.Armees, was still in quite good shape. It included some of the Wehrmacht's best divisions, and the inability to move units swiftly back to the Reich ensured that it had retained most of its heavy equipment. It now had to hand some 200 tanks, nearly as many as were in service on the whole Western Front. In the line facing the Allies were some 16 German and one Italian Fascist divisions, while in reserve were two more German mobile divisions. A further five German and four Italian divisions were involved in holding back the Yugoslav partisan army in the north-east, and in case of any breakthrough by the Allied armies in France, on the other side of the Alps.

It is a general precept of military strategy that a successful assault on a well-defended position requires a local superiority of attacking troops to defenders in the order of three to one. Alexander enjoyed no such superiority in Italy. Indeed, he was just able to match the strength of Armee Gruppe C in the line with 17 divisions composed of troops from no less than six nations – American, Brazilian, Canadian, British, New Zealander and Polish. These were backed up by four Italian Co-Belligerent combat groups, six armoured brigades and four infantry brigades including South African and Indian troops.

The preponderance of armour could still not be exploited, but the vastly powerful Allied air strength could. Apart from the handful of Bf 109s remaining to the ANR force, the Axis could offer no immediate defence, while their only support came from the few tactical and strategic reconnaissance aircraft of the Luftwaffe, and the remaining close-support aircraft of NSGr 9 – now reinforced by a small number of FW 190 fighter-bombers. The once-powerful Luftflotte 2 had ceased to exist even in name, the remaining 60 or so aircraft being under the command of Luftwaffe General Italien.

Now though, Allied aircraft flying over Austria, northern Yugoslavia, and targets beyond the Alps were faced with other German aircraft from Luftflotte 4, as this command retreated ever westwards with the southern part of the armies trying to hold back the Russian advance from the east. These new opponents were rarely encountered by MATAF units but they were frequently engaged by both 15th Air Force and Balkan Air Force, as the formations from these commands operated further from the Italian battlefront.

In Italy, however, Mediterranean Allied Air Force was seeing a considerable reshuffle of its own commanders. The commander-in-chief, General Ira Eaker, now left, as did his deputy, Air Marshal Sir John Slessor. The overall direction of Mediterranean aerial activities then passed to General Cannon, who was promoted from command of MATAF to take Eaker's place. MATAF and 12th Air Force were taken over by General Chidlaw, formerly commander of XXII TAC, and the latter position then went to Brig Gen Thomas C.Darcy. For his deputy, Cannon received Air Marshal Sir Guy Garrod, who had been acting commander-in-chief of Air Command, South East Asia until the new appointment was made. Thus, the spring of 1945 found DAF as the only major element of MATAF which had not changed hands. However, with the exception of Garrod, all the new commanders were long-serving MATAF men, and complete continuity was ensured.

The arrival of April found all preparation complete for Operation Wowser – the air forces' part of the Allied offensive. This time, to ensure an element of surprise, there was to be no sustained pre-assault attack to soften up the defences. Normal operations were to continue right up to zero hour on D-Day. Thereafter maximum air effort was to be co-ordinated with 15th Army Group during the initial stages of the attack. By this time the Combined Bomber offensive was virtually at a close, no worthwhile targets remaining in those shattered parts of Germany and Austria still in the hands of the Nazi regime. Consequently, the whole weight of the Strategic Air Force was to be thrown in alongside MATAF when the moment came.

Meantime the interdiction operations continued, the intention being to deny supplies to the defenders, and also to cut off their possible escape routes should they be forced into retreat. Assisted by the heavy bombers, the mediums and fighter-bombers were to cut every rail line north of the Po during early April, and also hammer away once more at the vital Po bridges. XXII TAC and DAF were both to concentrate primarily on supply dumps of fuel, ammunition and food behind the front.

Sunday, 1 April 1945
The month opened with the second of two raids by Marauders of 24 SAAF Squadron on ammunition dumps at Malcontenta. The attack was escorted by eight 79th Fighter Group P-47s, which blasted the defending Flak positions with rockets so effectively that defensive fire was stopped completely. Other Marauders of 25 SAAF Squadron bombed Okucani, Croatia.

The rescue of Flt Sgt Forster of 145 Squadron was the last of many such conducted by the venerable Walrus biplanes of 293 Squadron, some achieved in the most hazardous circumstances.

On 13 November 1944 Project Extraversion was approved to send four Lockheed YP-80A service-test examples of the US jet fighter to Europe, two of which went to Italy. The two YP-80As (44-83028 'A' and 44-83029 'B') arrived in Lesina on the Adriatic coast in late January 1945 and by March they had been assembled. In early April the jets were attached to the P-38J Lightning-equipped 1st Fighter Group where they were flown on local familiarisation sorties. Maj Ed LaClare, a 94th Fighter Squadron pilot, flew two operational sorties in a YP-80A without encountering any enemy aircraft. The jets were returned to the US in mid-June.

British Casualties

3 RAAF Sqn	Mustang IV KH851 left 1010, hit by Flak strafing trains in Maribor area 1130, pilot baled out; Flt Lt D.B.Davies POW
7 SAAF Sqn	Spitfire IXc MJ875 'R' left 1100 to bomb barges on River Po NW Ferrara, lost probably due to bomb exploding in bomb dive 1200; Lt K.O.Embling KiA
92 Sqn	Spitfire VIII JP356 left 0545 strafing E of Udine, possible ground fire caused engine to fail, pilot baled out over sea 0730; Flg Off C.Beasly rescued by an ASR Catalina 0945
92 Sqn	Spitfire VIII MT667 left 0800 on ASR escort for above loss, engine failed, pilot baled out off Porto Garibaldi; Sgt S.Widdowson rescued 1030 by 293 Sqn Walrus W2272 flown by Lt K.B.Walker
145 Sqn	Spitfire VIII JF838 left 0930, strafed a barge at mouth of River Piave, hit by Flak, FTR; Flt Sgt A.J.Stacey KiA
145 Sqn	Spitfire VIII JG247 left 0930, strafed a barge at mouth of River Piave, hit by Flak, pilot baled out 1m S of River Po delta; Flt Sgt W.B.Forster rescued 1230 by 293 Sqn Walrus X9482 flown by Flt Sgt R.J.Bickle/Flt Sgt A.S.Goldstein
25 SAAF Sqn	Marauder III HD669 'X' left 1100 to bomb Okucani, Croatia, starboard engine caught fire 30m W Split, crashed at Primosten, crew baled out, picked up by Yugoslav fishing boats, flown back by ASR OA-10 Catalina; Lt J.D.Phillips and six safe

Sunday-Monday, 1/2 April 1945

British Casualties

500 Sqn	Baltimore V FW786 'N' left 2044 on armed recce, crashed on landing 2035; Flt Sgt W.M.Burrell and three safe
500 Sqn	Baltimore V FW870 'G' left 2330 on armed recce, disappeared without trace; Flg Off F.Waterland and three MiA

Monday, 2 April 1945

It was on this date that one of the heaviest days of combat during the final weeks of the war in Italy occurred. This engagement has been analysed by our colleague Nick Beale and his Italian co-researchers and it is with considerable gratitude that we have received permission from him to summarise the events of this afternoon, detailed in his book *Air War Italy 1944-45* (Airlife, 1996). We feel this avoids unnecessary repetition of a single event common to, but equally important, to both our books.

It so happens that at about the same time of day two formations of B-25s, both from the 57th Bomb Wing, were dispatched to attack transport targets in the Brenner Pass area. Each bomber formation was escorted by P-47s of squadrons of the 350th Fighter Group. Initially ANR's 2° Gruppo appeared well placed to offer a fierce reception. At Aviano were 18 Bf 109s on alert comprising three from Nucleo Comando (HQ Flight), eight from 6ª Squadriglia and seven from 4ª Squadriglia. In Osoppo were seven of the 5ª Squadriglia and three from 4ª which had been transferred there a few days earlier. The rendezvous point for the whole 2° Gruppo was over Aviano. At 1345 the entire force was ordered to scramble, although four or five failed to do so for various technical reasons.

By 1415 the B-25s and 347th Fighter Squadron P-47s were about 35 miles south-east of Ghedi. Twenty-five Bf 109s of 2° Gruppo were just passing Verona, approaching Lake Garda. The 346th Squadron was 15 miles south-west of Villafranca; USAAF fighters had been warned at 1400 of bandits approaching from the Udine area. This advice, repeated at 1410 and 1415, was confirmed by Lt Richard Sulzbach of the 346th Squadron: "[he] did a fantastic job for us that day! Maj Gilbert's radio had malfunctioned and I was leading the formation. [Control] directed us so that we made contact with the enemy aircraft just as he told us we would." The 347th Squadron combat report continues: "…at 1420 hours, three miles east of Ghedi, a flight of 16 Me 109s sighted at 3 o'clock coming in from the east at 13,000ft the two bomber formation…"

The Italians were simultaneously spotted by the 346th Squadron; Lt Eddy: "I was observing a group of B-25s proceeding north 20 or 30 miles south of Brescia when I sighted 20 bandits at 2 o'clock at our same level heading west on a course that would cross our line of flight. I called them in to Green Leader." Maj Gilbert, the Green Leader, later reported: "… two or three miles west of Villafranca … at about 1420 hours, I observed about 16 bogeys at 2 o'clock headed west at the same level as my flight. Their course would place them at 12 o'clock to us about 1,200 yards away."

Meanwhile among the Italians (according to Serg Magg Cavagliano's diary): "Just after sighting the enemy bombers on our left 3,000 feet below us, we heard Miani curse … and tell Bellagambi to take the lead, as his airscrew pitch control had jammed, forcing him to abort. Miani turned sharply to the left and – I'll never understand why – all of the Nucleo Comando and 6ª Squadriglia followed him, disappearing from my sight."

Not all of 6ª Squadriglia aircraft had followed Miani (whose radio had meanwhile failed), however. There had been a heated exchange between Cap Spigaglia and Ten Alberto Volpi. The former wanted the Squadriglia to follow Miani and land at Villafranca but the latter, seeing no reason for this, refused to comply. Thus, while the Messerschmitts of Miani, Spigaglia, Caimi, Tampieri, Archidiacono and Moratti headed for Villafranca, Volpi and his section (Serg Patton and M.llo Fumagalli) prepared to attack. Cavagliano:

> "However, immediately after this impasse and while in a shallow dive to attack, Bellagambi throttled back abruptly and we heard him… say that suddenly a wash of oil over his windscreen had completely blinded him. His manoeuvre forced us to throttle back too, to avoid a collision. At that precise, confused moment, out of the corner of my eye I noticed the bombers passing below us, but also to our right – 1,500 feet higher than us – a 'cloud' of enemy fighters, four of which were diving into us… I screamed over the radio to Sarti to pull up and face their attack while ramming my throttle forward and starting the tightest possible turn to the right."

At this point eight P-47s of the 347th Squadron were just about to attack the 4ª Squadriglia head-on as four of the 346th Squadron Thunderbolts were closing on the tails of 5ª Squadriglia. The 347th combat report continues: "Midwood Black and Crimson Sections dropped all external fuel tanks and Black Section broke into the enemy aircraft closely followed by Crimson… as Black Section broke, the 109s started a climbing turn to the right, and by using full throttle and water (injection),our pilots were able to climb with the enemy…" The climbing Messerschmitts were those led by Drago who did the only thing possible: engage methanol injection and pull up.

The 346th Squadron P-47s reacted by splitting into pairs. Lt Sulzbach and his wingman, Flt Off Jennings, were first to close the pincers, turning left and diving onto the tail of the 'Red Devils', which were clearly disadvantaged by loss of speed. Maj Gilbert and his wingman, Lt Thompson, followed after a few seconds, enough to be left several hundred yards behind, Lts Barton and Eddy having meanwhile sighted six enemy aircraft above them and having become separated by Maj Gilbert's manoeuvre, climbed at full power to intercept. Also outdistanced, Lt Bergeron and Flt Off Miller turned right and tried to gain height.

By now battle had commenced in earnest, split into a series of 'duels' very difficult to follow. Sulzbach fell on Cavagliano's and Sarti's tails and though the former managed to evade, the latter was immediately hit by the American's fire. The shooting down of 'White 8' and death of Ten Sarti (crashed near Goito) was witnessed by Maj Gilbert: "The pursuing P-47, which I found later to be Lt Sulzbach, broke off the engagement while I continued to dive with the Me 109. I was closing rapidly, at about 5,000 feet when I observed him attempt an aileron roll but he did not pull out, crashing into the ground about twelve miles west of Villafranca."

While the 'Red Devils' and the three 6ª Squadriglia fighters scattered at Cavagliano's warning cry, the eight Bf 109s led by Drago were performing a deadly spiral with the four P-47s led by Capt Heckenkamp, closely followed by Lt Brandstrom's section. Heckenkamp closed on the Italian 'tail-end Charlie' (Ten Bruno Betti) and opened fire scoring hits which started 'Black 8' smoking. Betti's instrument panel suddenly exploded and smoke poured into the cockpit. After a last radio message to alert his comrades, he jettisoned the canopy and jumped.

Continuing his climb, Heckenkamp framed a second Messerschmitt in his gunsight and after one burst it too began to smoke heavily. In the earphones of the Italians flying for their lives echoed a desperate cry. Everyone recognised the voice of Ten Mario Giorio, whose 'Black 13' was seen out of control by Lts Taylor and Olson to crash and explode south of Villafranca.

The two 347th Squadron sections now split into pairs and continued fighting, while the Messerschmitts of 4ª Squadriglia, despite their losses, finally managed to climb away from the P-47s. Drago, gaining a momentary height advantage, suddenly executed a half roll and a dive onto the pursuing Americans. This broke up the Italian formation and only Serg Magg Loris Baldi, Drago's wingman, was able to follow. Of the others Ten Valenzano, Serg Magg Camerani and S.Ten Abba (on his first combat mission) regrouped and after quickly assessing the situation decided to head for Aviano. S.Ten Felice Squassoni, finding himself suddenly alone, continued climbing intending to escape the fighting.

Drago and Baldi did not notice that their dive had taken them past Heckenkamp and his wingman. With a sharp turn and steep dive the Thunderbolts were on the Italians' tails, Heckenkamp closing in for the kill and repeatedly hitting Bf 109 'Black 11' from which Serg Magg Baldi baled out, and despite wounds and a damaged parachute, he came down safely.

With the downing of Baldi, Heckenkamp had got three victories in 60 seconds. He could have gained a fourth if his ammunition had not run out moments later. In his sights was the unsuspecting Ten Volpi who had evaded the 346th's first attack, clearing a way between the enemy aircraft by firing at anyone crossing his path. Volpi had been hit in the engine, and it was while diving towards Villafranca airfield, trailing smoke, that the two P-47s caught him. After a few rounds Heckenkamp's guns quit. It was then the turn of Lt Taylor who overtook his leader. His eight 0.5in guns truncated the right wing of 'White 5' and with his engine on fire too, Volpi parachuted, landing safely near the airfield.

A second pair – after Wilkinson had regained position on Olson's wing – encountered Serg Margoni who had just escaped another Thunderbolt. Olson gave chase and hit the Messerschmitt which rolled over in flames and went straight in. Margoni's aircraft, like Baldi's, crashed near Pozzuolo sul Mincio. This victory appears to have been a 'double claim', Brandstrom and Wilson seeing it smoke, roll on its back, crash and explode in the same place as Margoni.

Meanwhile Maj Gilbert noticed that he was at 3,000ft over Villafranca airfield, just as Miani's group were about to land:

> "I looked again and saw six Me 109s preparing to land… They were at about 800 feet and circling to the left. It was very difficult to see them against the ground because they were camouflaged dark blue. I turned to the left and dived on them firing at each one in quick succession on the initial pass. I observed as I did so that all had their wheels and flaps down and that no Flak was being fired from the airdrome. As I pulled to the left for my second pass, I looked for my wingman but did not see him. On the second pass I again fired at each one in quick succession but concentrated mainly on the fifth one, giving him two to three short bursts from 400 to 200 yards range, decreasing deflection from 45 degrees to 25 degrees. Again, I broke hard left and came around for my third pass. I did not observe but four aircraft on this pass."

The fifth aircraft was M.llo Moratti's, hit by Gilbert in the landing pattern just as Miani's Bf 109 touched down. Although burned and wounded, Moratti survived. Gilbert continued:

> "…this time I concentrated on the number four. I gave him a good burst from a 45-degree overhead pass, observing strikes around the engine [which] ceased to function and his propeller started to windmill. Instead of turning left towards the field he continued on to the south-west while I continued on above him at 1,000 feet trying to reduce my speed. It appeared that he was going to crash land but made no effort to retract flaps or wheels. When about ten feet off the ground a P-47, later found to be my wingman, Lt Thompson, came in and gave him a short burst from 30 degrees on the port side. I observed strikes on the ground off to the Me's right wing. The Me 109 then crashed into a ploughed field two miles south south-west of Villafranca. His left wing was broken off by a tree. I did not see this aircraft burn nor the pilot get out."

Serg Archidiacono was badly wounded in the abdomen, causing him to die a few hours later. Three hours after the combat three of the Messerschmitts which had landed at Villafranca took off to return to Aviano, flown by Magg Miani, Ten Volpi and Serg Tampieri. Meanwhile two P-47s were undertaking a dusk patrol towards the same area; these were also from the 350th Fighter Group, but in this case from the unit's 345th Squadron. These Thunderbolts were first spotted by Volpi who rocked his wings in warning to Miani who led the trio in a climb but surprise was lost when Tampieri's belly tank refused to release, allowing the American pilots to engage. Lt Brooks recorded: "… as I pulled off a strafing pass I looked behind me and there were Me 109s turning in on us. We dropped the belly tanks, shoved it all forward and turned into them."

Top: A Bf 109 of the ANR's 5ª Squadriglia, 2° Gruppo Caccia which was involved in the fierce combat of 2 April 1945 during which the unit suffered severe losses. Above: During the day Maj Johnny Gasson, the officer commanding 92 Squadron, escaped injury when the Spitfire VIII MT648 he was flying was hit by Flak.

In a short dogfight Miani managed to disengage and reach Aviano but Volpi's aircraft was hit and he was forced to bale out for the second time in a few hours.

This final casualty brought the total of Messerschmitts lost by 2° Gruppo during this ill-fated day to 14 shot down or damaged beyond repair; this represented six pilots killed, two wounded and five baled out. The unit headquarters credited the 2° Gruppo with two B-25s shot down plus three P-47s unconfirmed. The thorough examination of all available documents appertaining to the day's claims and losses by those involved in this has persuaded the authors of *Air War Italy 1944-45* that no USAAF losses were suffered over Italy on this date.

The results for the 350th Fighter Group might have been classified as stupendous at this stage of the conflict, their claims for 14 aircraft shot down plus nine damaged coming so close to the actual losses of Italian aircraft lost as very rarely achieved in fighter combats anywhere and anytime.

On this day the 24 SAAF Squadron was out again, this time attacking battlefield targets close to the lines for the first time since September 1944.

Over Yugoslavia, near Lika, there was another dogfight on this date, when two pairs of Bf 109Gs set out to strafe ground targets near the village of Medak. En route, the second pair encountered 73 Squadron Spitfires which were undertaking a sweep during which Plt Off Pearce claimed a Messerschmitt destroyed. It appears that his victim was probably the aircraft flown by Porucnik (Por: Plt Off) Šerif Mehanović who crash-landed at around 1830 in no man's land near Primišlje from where he escaped back to Croat lines. He achieved several hits on the tail of the Spitfire that attacked him and claimed to have destroyed it. Partisans of 4.Corps later found wreckage from his Bf 109G. The second Bf 109G crash-landed at Lučko and was claimed probably destroyed by Lt T.S.Harper. Lt Harper noted that the Bf 109s had "dark-mottled camouflage with German markings and a large red and white indistinguishable patch behind the black cross on the fuselage". Their claim for one Bf 109 destroyed was the final air combat victory for the Balkan Air Force; Harper's was also the last claim by a SAAF pilot in the Mediterranean.

British Claims

3 RAAF Sqn	Flg Off A.F.Lane	Mustang IVa KH755 'W'	Fi 156	Mostar, Yugoslavia	0625
73 Sqn	Flg Off N.J.Pearce	Spitfire IX MJ349	Bf 109G	9m SW Karlovac	1830
73 Sqn	Lt T.S.Harper	Spitfire IX JL239	Bf 109 Probable	10m SW Karlovac	1830

British Casualties

185 Sqn	Spitfire IX MH892 burst into flames at start of bombing dive, no Flak seen, crashed NW Parma 1100; Lt E.W.Rosenstein* KiA
92 Sqn	Spitfire VIII MT648 'J' hit in port radiator by Flak, force-landed at base; Maj J.E.Gasson safe
260 Sqn	Mustang III KH592 left 0655, hit by Flak nr Graz, pilot baled over Adriatic; Lt R.H.Veitch safe, picked up by OA-10 Catalina
260 Sqn	Mustang III HB929 left 1315, shot down by ground fire SE Dravograd 1510, pilot baled out; Lt P.K Gibbings safe with partisans
5 SAAF Sqn	Mustang IVa KH705 left 1500, shot down by Flak near Leibnitz SW Maribor 1640 pilot baled out; Lt D.N.Boyd POW
6 Sqn	Hurricane IV KZ553 left 0700, hit by Flak, dived into sea and exploded nr Kikvenica, Croatia; Flt Sgt W.J.B.Jones KiA
112 Sqn	Mustang IV KM135 'K' left 0940, strafed motor transports 3m S Graz, hit by Flak, crashed and exploded; Flt Lt M.N.Matthias KiA
1435 Sqn	Spitfire IX MK238 'V' left 1500, shot down by Flak, crashed 4m NW Cittanova near Udine; Wt Off R.E.M.Thomas KiA
	* son of a WWI German fighter ace Willi Rosenstein, who left Germany in the 1930s being Jewish

US Claims

346th FS/350th FG	1/Lt Howard L.Barton	P-47D	Bf 109	Cittadella	1420
346th FS/350th FG	1/Lt Charles C.Eddy	P-47D	Bf 109	Cittadella	1420
346th FS/350th FG	1/Lt Howard L.Barton	P-47D	Bf 109 Damaged	15m SE Lake Garda	1420
346th FS/350th FG	1/Lt Charles C.Eddy	P-47D	Bf 109 Damaged	15m SE Lake Garda	1420
346th FS/350th FG	Maj Charles E.Gilbert II	P-47D	Bf 109	2m SSW Villafranca	1420
346th FS/350th FG	Maj Charles E.Gilbert II	P-47D	Bf 109	Villafranca a/f	1420
346th FS/350th FG	2/Lt Richard P.Sulzbach	P-47D	Bf 109	2m W Villafranca	1420
346th FS/350th FG	2/Lt Richard P.Sulzbach	P-47D	FW 190	Villafranca area	1420
346th FS/350th FG	Flt Off Walter R.Miller	P-47D	Bf 109 Damaged	nr Verona	1420
346th FS/350th FG	1/Lt John E.Bergeron	P-47D	FW 190 Damaged	nr Verona	1420
346th FS/350th FG	Flt Off Walter R.Miller	P-47D	Bf 109 Damaged	nr Verona	1420

347th FS/350th FG	Capt Frank W.Heckenkamp	P-47D	Bf 109	3m E Ghedi a/f	1430
347th FS/350th FG	Capt Frank W.Heckenkamp	P-47D	Bf 109	S Villafranca	1430
347th FS/350th FG	Capt Frank W.Heckenkamp	P-47D	Bf 109	3m E Ghedi a/f	1430
347th FS/350th FG	2/Lt Edward M.Olson	P-47D	Bf 109	Verona	1430
347th FS/350th FG	Flt Off Robert B.Taylor	P-47D	Bf 109	3m E Ghedi a/f	1430
347th FS/350th FG	2/Lt Rodney I.Brandstrom	P-47D	Bf 109 }	3m E Ghedi a/f	1430
347th FS/350th FG	1/Lt John W.Wilson	P-47D			
347th FS/350th FG	2/Lt Rodney I.Brandstrom	P-47D	Bf 109 Damaged	3m E Ghedi a/f	1430
347th FS/350th FG	1/Lt John W.Wilson	P-47D	Bf 109 Damaged	3m E Ghedi a/f	1430
347th FS/350th FG	2/Lt Oscar M.Wilkinson	P-47D	Bf 109 Damaged	E Ghedi	1430
345th FS/350th FG	1/Lt Horace W.Blakeney	P-47D	Bf 109 }	Verona area	1815-1950
345th FS/350th FG	1/Lt Darwin G.Brooks	P-47D			
345th FS/350th FG	1/Lt Horace W.Blakeney	P-47D	Bf 109 Damaged }	Verona area	1815-1950
345th FS/350th FG	1/Lt Darwin G.Brooks	P-47D			

US Casualties

87th FS/79th FG	P-47D 44-21039 shot down by Flak nr Moste, Yugoslavia 0925; 2/Lt Warren R.Bostick KiA [13449]

Italian Co-Belligerent Casualties

97ª Sq, 9° Gr, 4° St	P-39Q hit by Flak over Yugoslavia, crashed on return; Serg Mario Micheloni KiA

Italian ANR Claims

6ª Sq, 2° Gr C	Ten Aristide Sarti	Bf 109	B-25
4ª Sq, 2° Gr C	Ten Mario Giorio	Bf 109	B-25
5ª Sq, 2° Gr C	Serg Ettore Caimi	Bf 109	P-47 (unconfirmed)
6ª Sq, 2° Gr C	M.llo Mario Fumagalli	Bf 109	P-47 (unconfirmed)
5ª Sq, 2° Gr C	unstated	Bf 109	P-47 (unconfirmed)

Italian ANR Casualties

6ª Sq, 2° Gr C	Bf 109G White 8 hit in combat; crashed nr Goito 1420; Ten Aristide Sarti KiA
6ª Sq, 2° Gr C	Bf 109G Black 8 hit in combat, pilot baled out 1430; Ten Francesco Betti safe
5ª Sq, 2° Gr C	Bf 109G-10 Black 13 shot down in combat, crashed S Villafranca 1430; Ten Mario Giorio KiA
4ª Sq, 2° Gr C	Bf 109G-10 Black 11 hit in combat, crashed nr Pozzuolo sul Mincio, pilot baled 1430; Serg Magg Loris Baldi WiA
6ª Sq, 2° Gr C	Bf 109G White 5 hit in combat, pilot baled out 1430; Ten Alberto Volpi safe
5ª Sq, 2° Gr C	Bf 109G shot down in combat, crashed nr Pozzuolo sul Mincio; Serg Luigi Margoni KiA
6ª Sq, 2° Gr C	Bf 109G hit in landing pattern, crashed at Villafranca; M.llo Giuseppe Moratti WiA
6ª Sq, 2° Gr C	Bf 109G hit in landing pattern, crashed nr Villafranca; Serg Raffaele Archidiacono DoW
5ª Sq, 2° Gr C	Bf 109G Black 5 hit in combat, crashed nr Cittadella, pilot baled out; S.Ten Felice Squassoni safe
5ª Sq, 2° Gr C	Bf 109G shot down in combat nr Thiene; Ten Michelangelo Piolanti KiA
6ª Sq, 2° Gr C	Bf 109G hit in combat, force-landed at Treviso; M.llo Mario Fumagalli safe
5ª Sq, 2° Gr C	Bf 109G shot down by German Flak while taking off at Treviso; S.Ten Nando Spreca KiA
6ª Sq, 2° Gr C	Bf 109G hit in combat, pilot baled out 1730 (second time on same day); Ten Alberto Volpi safe
3° Gr C	Bf 109 hit in combat, crash-landed; M.llo Franco Fornasari safe

Croatian Claims

2.ZJ	Por Šerif Mehanović	Bf 109G	Spitfire	ca1830

Croatian Casualties

2.ZJ	Bf 109G crash-landed after combat with Spitfires near Primišlje; Por Šerif Mehanović escaped
2.LJ	Bf 109G crash-landed at Lučko; pilot safe

Tuesday, 3 April 1945

Psychological warfare was also being employed at this time, and during the first week of April 7,569,000 leaflets were dropped over northern Italy, nearly half of them by 24 SAAF Squadron. Even at this late stage, operations over Yugoslavia continued in support of Tito's partisan forces. Ground fire remained as fierce as ever here, DAF Mustangs suffering particularly, including the aircraft flown by the new commanding officer of 5 SAAF Squadron, Maj Odendaal, who was shot down on the 3rd. He was forced to bale out but survived to return safely to the unit immediately after the termination of hostilities a month later.

This day saw the final DAF success in the air during a midday sortie over the Maribor area when Flg Off Shannon shot down another Fi 156 which crashed in flames.

Flying Mustang IV KH794 'G' on a sweep near Maribor, Flg Off Shannon claimed an Fi 156 shot down; it was the final victory for 3 RAAF Squadron.

British Claims

3 RAAF Sqn	Flg Off A.F.Shannon	Mustang IVa KH794	Fi 156 in flames	Maribor area	1200 (1305)

British Casualties

92 Sqn	Spitfire VIII JG250 left 0720 to dive bomb guns, hit by light Flak, force-landed on the beach at Casal Borsetti; Maj J.H.Gasson safe.
3 RAAF Sqn	Mustang IV FB290 left 1205, shot down by Flak Maribor area 1315, pilot baled out; Wt Off W.J.F.McInerheney evaded, back on 5 May
3 RAAF Sqn	Mustang IVa KH621 left 1205, shot down by Flak SE Maribor 1305, pilot baled out; Wt Off A.Clark safe
601 Sqn	Spitfire IXe LF TA862 left 1030 to bomb a target near Ferrara, engine failed after take-off, bomb jettisoned, crash-landed; Flg Off A.G.R.Hallas WiA
112 Sqn	Mustang III FB288 'Z' left 0430 on armed recce, engine trouble, crashed near Graz; Sgt C.Walker KiA
5 SAAF Sqn	Mustang IVa KH805 left 1240, hit by Flak, pilot baled out near Celje 25m S Dravograd 1430; Maj H.O.M.Odendaal, DFC returned on 14 May

US Casualties

347th FS/350th FG	P-47D 42-28342 '7B1' hit by Flak, crashed near Sassuolo 1435; 1/Lt Norman K.Hubbard KiA [13636]
347th FS/350th FG	P-47D 42-28961 *Betty Jean* hit by Flak, pilot baled but parachute hit tail 1450; 1/Lt Wayne H.Smith KiA [13635]

Wednesday, 4 April 1945

The day saw the last sortie of 601 Squadron's Flg Off Proudman. He had survived being shot down on two previous occasions and had also been credited with shooting down on 17 February the first Bf 109 by an RAF unit of DAF in many months. He now went down in Axis territory when his new Spitfire IXe was hit by ground fire and was captured.

British Casualties

250 Sqn	Kittyhawk IV FX812 left 1555 attacking a bridge at San Giorgio di Nogaro, exploded in bombing dive; Flt Sgt G.V.Hall KiA
450 Sqn	Kittyhawk IV FX845 left 1700 to attack ferries at San Donà 1750, hit by 20mm light Flak, pilot baled out; Sgt K.R.Nash safe, picked up by Catalina
601 Sqn	Spitfire IXe HF RR244 left 1520, dive-bombed barges near Loreo N Lake Comacchio, hit by Flak, crash-landed; Flg Off A.G.Proudman POW

336 Sqn	Spitfire Vc ER194 on ASR patrol, engine failed on take-off, ditched near Kalamaki; Wt Off George Nicolopoulous KiA
6 Sqn	Hurricane IV LE510 shot down by ground fire nr Pag, Yugoslavia, pilot got out before it burst into flames; Sgt G.R.Oddie evaded and returned?

US Casualties

66th FS/57th FG	P-47D 44-33106 damaged Cat 2 1115; pilot safe
64th FS/57th FG	P-47D 42-29004 hit tension wires 1130, damaged Cat 2; pilot safe
65th FS/57th FG	P-47D 42-26789 hit by Flak 1320, damaged Cat 2; pilot safe
65th FS/57th FG	P-47D 42-20987 hit by Flak 1320, damaged Cat 2; pilot safe
486th BS/340th BG	B-25J 43-4033 '6J' *Lady's Delight* hit by Flak crew baled out 20m S Lake Garda; 1/Lt John L.Ellis and five POW [13705]
380th BS/310th BG	B-25J 43-27737 *Oklahoma/Betsy* collided with B-25 after bombing bridge at Drauburg; 1/Lt Donald E.Oliver and one KiA, five POW [13685]
380th BS/310th BG	B-25J 43-27552 *Pretzel* collided with B-25 after bombing bridge at Drauburg; 1/Lt Frank S.Miller Jr and five KiA [13682]

Thursday, 5 April 1945

Campoformido was raided by B-24s and their escort, causing the destruction of several German aircraft. On return from a reconnaissance mission in his Ar 234, Oblt Erich Sommer, leader of the Kommando bearing his name, recorded having attacked over Campoformido an enemy fighter, which he identified as a Spitfire, without visible results. A pilot of 1 SAAF Squadron reported a Me 262 over Venice and a pilot of an F-5 claimed that a Me 262 attacked but was driven off; both identifications clearly relate to the Kommando Sommer's Arados.

324 Wing was being supplied at this time with stocks of a dreadful new weapon – napalm. At first the highly volatile jellied petroleum cannisters were known to pilots as 'blazebombs', and the first to be used operationally by DAF were dropped by 111 and 93 Squadrons on 5 April.

Due to the ever-increasing shortage of Mark VIII Spitfires, another unit was informed on this day that it would change over to Mark IX Spitfires, this time 417 Squadron, who flew their last Mark VIII sorties on the 7th and their first Mark IX sorties on the 8th.

Just before the new offensive began, 7 SAAF Wing had a change of command. Col J.D.Human, DSO, DFC & Bar, ended his tour and was replaced by Col D.D.Moodie, DFC. Human had flown operationally from

As was common practice, Hannes Faure had his initials painted on his personal aircraft, in this case Spitfire IX MB973 which also carried his rank pennant beneath the cockpit.

the very start of the war, first in East Africa on Hartebeest biplanes, and subsequently on Tomahawks, Kittyhawks and Spitfires right through to 1945. He ended his final tour with five aerial victories to his credit, as well as his long leadership and direction of the wing's fighter-bomber operations. At the same time in 8 SAAF Wing Sqn Ldr G.W.Garton DFC was promoted from 87 Squadron to become wing leader, Sqn Ldr G.R.S.McKay from 601 Squadron replacing him.

Lt Veitch of 260 Squadron was shot down by Flak for the second time in four days and for the second time reached the sea from which he was again rescued by a Catalina.

There was also increasing evidence of the fault-line frictions as the forces of the Eastern and Western Fronts closed against each other with pilots of 249 Squadron increasingly meeting Soviet aircraft over Yugoslavia. On this day a U-2 army co-operation aircraft was encountered and a few days later a MiG 3 was chased.

The leader of 324 Wing during the final weeks of the war was the successful SAAF pilot, Lt Col Hannes Faure.

British Casualties	
260 Sqn	Mustang III FB214 left 0650, hit by Flak attacking communications near Ljubljana, pilot baled out off Trieste; Lt R.H.Veitch picked up next day by ASR OA-10 Catalina
450 Sqn	Kittyhawk IV FX693 left 1430 after rail targets in Udine-Grado area, burst into flames in bombing dive N Palmanova; Plt Off B.W.Brown KiA
213 Sqn	Mustang III HB881 struck a tree strafing near Vrhovine-Otocac 1100; Sgt E.P.Buchan KiA
87 Sqn	Spitfire IX MT533 left 1540, hit by Flak while strafing, baled out near Viareggio; Lt F.Steinhebel safe
351 Sqn	Hurricane IV KX414 left 0925, attacked target at Babin Potok SW Nis, failed to pull out of attack, crashed into a hill and exploded; Potporučnik Nikola Vemić KiA
1 SAAF Sqn	Spitfire IXe PT821 badly damaged by small-arms fire 10 NE Vicenza; Lt G.D.Doveton safe
German Casualties	
NAGr 11	3 Bf 109s destroyed and 9 damaged on the ground at Campoformido
NAGr 11	2 FW 190s damaged on the ground at Campoformido

Friday, 6 April 1945

British Casualties	
145 Sqn	Spitfire VIII JG166 left 0735, shot down in flames by Flak near Adria; Flg Off R.D.Franks KiA
237 Sqn	Spitfire IX NH267 left 1825 to escort RN ships, engine cut shortly after take-off, crashed; Sgt W.A.Maxwell KiA
2 SAAF Sqn	Spitfire IXe PL400 'D' hit in wing by Flak at Buia but continued, hit in oil cooler when strafing later, force-landed NE Dignano d'Istria, 12m N Pola 1530; Lt J.P.Hogan POW

Friday-Saturday, 6/7 April 1945

18 Sqn   Boston IV BZ489 left 2304 to attack ferry terminal E Pontelagoscuro, shot down by Flak, crashed into the sea off Porto Garibaldi 0020, pilot got out of the aircraft, found no trace of his crew, got into dinghy, drifted ashore in friendly territory a day later; Wt Off R.N.J.Whitwell safe, three KiA

Saturday, 7 April 1945

As the Wehrmacht forces were reorganised, the Luftwaffe General Italien had:

2./NAGr 11	FW 190 and Bf 109	24	(14)
Gruppe Stab/122	Ju 88, Ju 188	7	(-)
4.(F)/122	Ju 188	8	(6)
6.(F)/122	Ju 188	6	(6)
Kommando Sommer	Ar 234	3	(2)
NSGr 9	Ju 87, FW 190	38	(35)

Luftflotte 4 had amongst its units:

Nahaufklarungstaffel Kroatien	Hs 126, Bf 109	17	(16)

Sunday, 8 April 1945

Flg Off Roy Cotnam of 417 Squadron blew up in his bomb dive. The ORB recorded that this "gives us yet another inexplicable casualty as no Flak was encountered or seen". Such incidents would keep occurring.

92 Sqn   Spitfire VIII LV729 left 1900 to bomb mortars, pilot baled out; Flt Lt B.Garner safe

417 Sqn   Spitfire IX MK951 left 1755 to bomb target near Lendinara, exploded in bomb dive; Flg Off R.L.Cotnam KiA

6 Sqn   Hurricane IV KX826 left 0515, hit by Flak; pilot baled out near Prvic but did not survive; Sgt R.H.Davies KiA

21 SAAF Sqn   Marauder III left 1620 to attack Cavanella sugar refinery, hit by Flak at 1720, damaged on landing; Capt W.Spence and five safe

66th FS/57th FG   P-47D 42-29321 lost in mid-air collision 40m N Grosseto; 1/Lt Louis O.Hays III KiA [13706]

Sunday-Monday, 8/9 April 1945

256 Sqn   Mosquito XIII HK187 left 0010 on bomber support, lost over Yugoslavia; Wt Off R.J.Hedge/Flt Sgt J.Sanderson KiA

Monday, 9 April 1945

During the morning interdiction missions continued as usual until 1400 hours. At that point 825 B-17s and B-24s began the 15th Air Force Operation Wowser which, together with 234 B-25s and Marauders and 740 fighter-bombers from XII Bomber Command, DAF and XXII TAC, attacked the front-line positions facing 8th Army on the Senio river as it instigated its assault, Operation Buckland. The results were devastating, and the German defences were torn apart. As evening approached the infantry began their assault under an umbrella of fighter-bombers, troops of V Corps and Polish II Corps beginning the attack. The first large-scale use of napalm in Italy was registered when 48 Spitfires from 324 Wing dropped napalm cannisters on the Senio positions in support of the Poles. The squadrons shuttled backwards and forwards throughout the afternoon and evening, 93 Squadron for example, making no less than 40 sorties before darkness fell. To add to this sea of flame, troops used flamethrowers liberally to dispose of deep defences which were unaffected by the rain of high explosive from bombers and artillery. Every so often the barrage ceased for four-minute intervals to allow the Cab Rank of fighter-bombers to be called down on pinpoint targets.

Before darkness had fallen, V Corps and the Poles were across the river and had achieved their initial objectives, the infantry of the New Zealand Division then passing through their positions to take up the advance without suffering a single casualty. By night 205 Group heavy bombers and MATAF intruders continued the attack and next day the assault went on unabated.

After sustaining damage during an Operation Wowser mission, 1/Lt William Knight of the 428th Bomb Squadron, 310th Bomb Group had to land B-25J Mitchell 43-35982 *Angel of Mercy* at Fano with just the nosewheel extended.

While fighter-bombers concentrated on close support, the mediums attacked guns and troop concentrations, hitting the Santerno river defences and groups of men on each side of Highway 9 between the Senio and the Santerno. For these operations 3 SAAF Wing had been placed under the temporary control of the 57th Bomb Wing, the B-25s and Marauders operating jointly.

British Casualties

11 SAAF Sqn	Kittyhawk IV FT850 'M' left 0905 to dive bomb ammunition factory at Aulla, presumed hit by Flak over the target 0935, crashed 10m NE La Spezia; Lt J.R.Dekema KiA

US Casualties

85th FS/79th FG	P-47D 44-20849 lost u/k cause 1615: 1/Lt James H.McHenry KiA [13684]
1° Gr Caça/350th FG	P-47D 42-26784 'A1' shot down by Flak, crashed nr Padua 1850; 2° Ten Armando de Souza baled out safely
428th BS/310th BG	B-25J 43-35982 *Angel of Mercy* hit by bomb, crashed on landing; 1/Lt William T.Knight and five safe

Tuesday, 10 April 1945

During the day the town of Lugo was taken, and throughout the opening days of the attack many prisoners fell into Allied hands. Substantial proportions of these were dazed, bewildered and totally demoralized by the scale and weight of the assault. In the course of the first two days the mediums alone flew 624 sorties, while Strategic Air Force added a massive 1,673 more.

The fighter-bombers were continually over the front, attacking various targets requested by the army, or generally upsetting communications immediately behind the lines. XXII TAC concentrated for the moment on command posts and divisional headquarters, whereas DAF went after gun positions, tanks, houses, strongpoints, Nebelwerfer mortars, battalion and company headquarters and, particularly, vehicles. Even individual motorcycle dispatch riders were targeted, and indeed so thorough and concentrated was the level of attack that on occasions these latter unfortunate individuals could find themselves the object of pursuit by up to 15 aircraft!

While the tactical reconnaissance squadrons surveyed the devastation caused by the bombing, and searched for signs of substantial Axis movement, the air forces destroyed, damaged, or otherwise neutralised no less than 180 artillery pieces facing 8th Army. As on the Eastern Front, once denuded of their highly effective artillery support, the defences quickly crumbled away, and the ground forces were able to exceed their estimated rate of advance.

British Casualties

213 Sqn	Mustang III KH423 shot down by Flak 1145 strafing road in the Zenica-Brod area, pilot baled out; Lt E.Gardner safe
72 Sqn	Spitfire IX MJ632 'A' left 1040 on armed recce Po-Ferrara area, shot down by Flak 5m N of Portomaggiore 1120; Wt Off K.B.C.Williams KiA
72 Sqn	Spitfire IX RR259 left 1715 to attack artillery, hit by ground fire, force-landed in Allied lines 2m SW Fusignano, struck a tree and caught fire; Flt Lt H.King KiA
272 Sqn	Beaufighter X NV360 'U' left 1039, shot down by Flak, crashed into sea 2m W Salvore Point; Fl Lt P.C.Schaefer/Flg Off A.E.Easterbee KiA

US Casualties

346th FS/350th FG	P-47D 42-27068 *The Great Speckled Bird* '6C3' hit by Flak, belly-landed E Adria 0930; 2/Lt James M.Beck Jr POW [13774]
65th FS/57th FG	P-47D 42-29046 hit by Flak 0800, damaged Cat 2; pilot safe
66th FS/57th FG	P-47D 42-29264 hit by Flak 0830, damaged Cat 2; pilot safe
66th FS/57th FG	P-47D 44-20807 hit by Flak 0840, damaged Cat 2; pilot safe
66th FS/57th FG	P-47D 44-21024 hit by Flak 1200, damaged Cat 2; pilot safe

Wednesday, 11 April 1945

3 RAAF Squadron lost its only non-Australian pilot when Flt Lt James Edmonds was killed attacking a target near Imola. Later in the day Flt Lt A.F.Shannon was far more fortunate when returning from a mission and his Mustang began losing coolant. He managed to reach base and land safely, where it was discovered that an unexploded 37mm shell was lodged in the coolant system.

British Casualties

250 Sqn	Kittyhawk IV FX762 left 1105 to attack artillery, crashed near Argenta; Flt Sgt P.L.Hodder KiA
92 Sqn	Spitfire VIII MT801 left 1040, dive-bombed target nr Massa Lombarda, presumed hit by premature detonation of bomb, exploded; Plt Off C.P.K.Smith KiA
3 RAAF Sqn	Mustang IVa KH677 left 1335, crashed while attacking a building near Imola; Flt Lt J.T.Edmonds KiA
249 Sqn	Mustang III FB327 'S' left 1650, hit in the coolant system by small arms near Doboj, pilot baled out over Brac Island; Flg Off J.W.Gardner helped by locals, flown out by Dakota next day

US Claims

2nd FS/52nd FG	1/Lt Benjamin W.Hall III	P-51	Ar 234	Bologna	1330

US Casualties

445th BS/321st BG	B-25J 43-27545 *Maggie* left 0855 to bomb target nr Argenta, hit by Flak, last seen NE Argenta 0917; 1/Lt Louis M.Dentoni and three POW, two KiA [13748]
380th BS/310th BG	B-25J 43-99 damaged by Flak; 1/Lt Edward C.Rose and four returned, one KiA

German Casualties

Kommando Sommer	Ar 234B-2 WNr 140142 T9+DH shot down by US fighters, crashed 10m NW Alfonsine, pilot baled out; Lt Günther Gniesmer DoW

Italian ANR Casualties

2ª Sq, 1° Gr C	Bf 109G-10 WNr 490265 '2-1' damaged on landing; S.Ten Alessandro Gallone safe

Wednesday-Thursday, 11/12 April 1945

Nachtschlachtgruppe 9 claimed a Mosquito shot down near Ferrara, which is where the 256 Squadron Mosquito was lost. In the words of the squadron operations record book:

"At 0524, Flg Off R.A.Putnam, and his navigator, Flt Sgt J.H.Curley, were airborne in Mosquito 'V'. This aircraft failed to return and its crew, two of our best who had flown with the squadron since 14/9/44 have been reported missing. It is believed, although there is no information to verify it, that the aircraft that the crew of 'A' [Sqn Ldr Smith and Flg Off Wilmer] observed to be on fire SE of Ferrara was this Mosquito."

A 414th Night Fighter Squadron's Black Widow was also lost. After the war ended, 1/Lt Wayne Dorman was able to visit the P-61's crash site at Fontanella Grazioli (Mantova) where on pulling out of a strafing attack, it had struck a power line and hit a treetop, losing a wing, hitting the ground and careering to a halt about 800 metres south-east of the town. It broke up and caught fire.

British Casualties

256 Sqn	Mosquito XIII HK184 'V' left 0524 on armed recce of the River Po crossings from Ficarolo to the mouth, shot down by FW 190 and crashed at Palazzo Jaldi on the outskirts of Ravenna; Flg Off R.A.Putnam/Flt Sgt J.H.Curley KiA

US Casualties

414th NFS	P-61B 42-39515 *Frontdoor 50* last seen 2056 lost when it struck power lines and a tree strafing near Fontanella Grazioli; 2/Lt Lael M.Cheely and two KiA [13803]

German Claims

1./NSGr 9	Fw Werner Hensel	FW 190	Mosquito	nr Ferrara

Wg Cdr Ron Bary, the wing leader of 244 Wing, was killed during a fighter-bomber attack but was probably another victim of a premature bomb explosion.

Thursday, 12 April 1945

Four Kittyhawks of 450 Squadron dive-bombed various targets in the morning, each aircraft carrying three 500lb bombs. Red 1, Sqn Ldr Jack Doyle guided Red 4 Lt R.S.M.Wingfield on to a target near Medicina, and as the squadron ORB states was "close and nearby" to witness what happened. Just as Wingfield released his bombs one or more exploded, the largest bits of wreckage, a wing tip and the engine falling to earth. Here is a direct eyewitness account from a highly experienced pilot of a bomb exploding just as it was released. No Flak was seen at all. This issue affected Kittyhawks and Spitfires for nearly a year and appears to be a clear indication of occasional failure of the fuse causing the bomb to explode at the moment of release. Two hours later Wing Commander R.E.Bary, the Wing Commander Flying of 244 Wing, was killed when he too blew up in a dive-bombing attack in his Spitfire VIII, with a 93 Squadron Spitfire exploding in its bomb dive shortly afterwards.

It was at this time that it was brought to the attention of the more senior formation leaders that the long series of inexplicable mid-air explosions did indeed have a more specific and understandable cause. In his autobiography, *Flying Start*, Grp Capt 'Cocky' Dundas, commanding officer of 244 Wing, recorded:

"Very early on, when the success of the ground attack was still in the balance, I was faced with the need to make a terrible decision. Although I did not realize it at the time, it was foreshadowed by a curious and rather eerie incident a day or two before the campaign began. I was leading a dive-bombing sortie, had completed my own attack and was zooming up again, at the same time watching the others dive down. My eyes were on one of them, descending vertically towards the target, perhaps four or five hundred yards from me, when in a split second of time, that Spitfire just ceased to exist.

"I had never before seen anything like it. And although the memory of the incident has stayed clear in my mind right across the years, I have never been able to translate it adequately into words. At one moment there was the familiar, solid shape of a Spitfire, at the next a flash, as though the aircraft had been vaporized and turned into a million pieces of confetti. In reporting this incident, I expressed the view that the detonator on the bomb must have sustained a direct, flukish hit by enemy anti-aircraft fire.

"On 12 April Ron Bary was killed – a sad and terrible blow. The pilots who had been flying with him reported that his aircraft 'had exploded in the bomb dive'. Their description closely matched what I had seen two or three days earlier.

"Within hours I received a visit from an officer from Desert Air Force. He told me that a batch of suspect bombs had been recently delivered. A sample taken somewhere back up the supply line had shown that a very small proportion of fuses could lead to the bombs exploding in their dive. A number of these potentially lethal objects had been delivered to Desert Air Force, but the only ones actually sent on down to units in the field had come to 244 Wing. They were somewhere among several hundred bombs held by our squadrons – at the time we were using about a hundred and fifty bombs every day – and although in retrospect it seems surprising, there was no way of identifying them. There was, therefore, only one way of making absolutely certain that no more pilots would be blown to smithereens in their bomb dive. That was to suspend operations of our five squadrons at that critical moment. We must carry on.

"There was no further discussion of the matter, at any level – not between me and the squadron commanders, not with anyone at Desert Air Force. I do not know whether the AOC even knew about it. If he did, he never mentioned it to me. There is no written record of it in the Wing Log. Naturally, neither the squadron commanders nor I said anything to the pilots, or indeed to anyone else. A number of people, in the squadrons and in the wing armoury, must have known that there was a holus-bolus changeover of bombs taking place, but presumably some plausible reason was given and accepted.

"There were no more incidents such as I had witnessed. But for two or three days those of us who had sat in my house and had decided to carry on felt that a new dimension had been added to the always chancy business of dive-bombing."

The number of similar such events that have been recorded earlier in this volume must raise the question whether it was only 244 Wing which received an unwritten warning to maintain secrecy and ensure that the air offensive continued unabated in such a difficult situation. All wings suffered from the problem. Approximately 40 such instances are recorded in this book, and the rate of such fuses being faulty was at a low percentage,

As the 500lb bomb left Wg Cdr Bary's personal Spitfire VIII MT685 'RB', it apparently exploded, probably due to a faulty fuse.

During a strafing attack P-47D Thunderbolt 44-21023 '94' *Que Pasa* of the 66th Fighter Squadron, 57th Fighter Group hit a tree but returned safely to base.

although given the huge numbers of bombs dropped, it went with an extremely high fatality rate, with only one instance of a pilot surviving such an occurrence being known. It has been recorded that following similar such explosions within some of the Marauder bombers of 3 SAAF Wing, crews demanded that an investigation be undertaken by an officer of the unit who possessed prior legal experience. Apparently following this, the wing's personnel demanded that the bombs loaded on their aircraft be drawn from stocks manufactured in the US rather than in the UK.

British Casualties

93 Sqn	Spitfire IX TB197 left 0615 to attack a Pineapple Sundae target, hit by Flak, reached Allied lines, crash-landed near Villanova; Flt Sgt N.Simpson safe
93 Sqn	Spitfire IX PT929 left 1200 to bomb gun positions N Imola, exploded in bomb dive, crashed at Sasso Morelli 1245; Plt Off J.A.Allen KiA
253 Sqn	Spitfire IX MA581 left 1345, strafed motor transports, shot down by Flak near Zepce 1435; Plt Off H.B.Gray POW to Croatian forces
112 Sqn	Mustang III HB913 'S' left 1700 to bomb bridge at Bastia, hit by 20mm Flak, crashed NW of target; Lt E.N.Roberts KiA
112 Sqn	Mustang IVa KM127 'X' left 0800, pulled out of bomb dive, presumed shot down by intense light Flak E Medicina about 0900; Flt Sgt T.P.Roberts KiA
244 Wg	Spitfire VIII MT685 left 1143 on close-support mission NE Imola, blew up in dive on target 1215 (probably faulty bomb fuse), crashed at Bubano; Wg Cdr R.E.Bary KiA
450 Sqn	Kittyhawk IV FX553 left 0935 on armed recce, blew up in bomb dive near Medicina (probably faulty bomb fuse); Lt R.S.M.Wingfield KiA
185 Sqn	Spitfire IX NH581 left 0910 to bomb gun batteries at La Spezia harbour, shot down by Flak; Flg Off R.A.Bamford KiA
241 Sqn	Spitfire IXe MK859 left 0840, hit by Flak, ditched 1m NE Cervia 0910; Plt Off P.J.McNair KiA
417 Sqn	Spitfire IX MH454 left 1035 on a Rover Paddy, strafed a tank and other targets, engine failed, crash-landed 2m S Bagnacavallo; Flg Off A.White safe

US Casualties

66th FS/57th FG	P-47D 44-21023 hit tree while strafing 0900, damaged Cat 2; pilot safe	
64th FS/57th FG	P-47D 42-29264 hit tree while strafing 1120, damaged Cat 2; pilot safe	
345th FS/350th FG	P-47D 42-28319 caught fire 20m E mouth of River Po 1310; 2/Lt William W.Sumner KiA [13796]	
446th BS/321st BG	B-25J 43-4021 '31' *Lady Jane* left to bomb Maribor bridge, lost to Flak nr Solcava 1155; 1/Lt Allan A.Maki and three evaded helped by partisans, returned on 6 May, one KiA, one POW [13475]	

Thursday-Friday, 12/13 April 1945

454 Squadron called this night 'Black Friday', losing two crews with another crashing on landing.

British Casualties

454 Sqn	Baltimore Vc FW716 'Q' left 0135 on armed recce to Po crossing, shot down by Flak, crashed nr Medicina; Flg Off W. J.A.Duffy and three KiA
454 Sqn	Baltimore Vc FW740 'O' left 2300 to bomb Portonuovo 10m E Bologna, shot down by Flak near Argenta; Wt Off C.W. Evans and three KiA
454 Sqn	Baltimore Vc FW793 'G' crashed on landing on return from bomb raid; Wt Off I.Griffiths and three safe
500 Sqn	Baltimore V FW789 'B' left 0157 on armed recce Verona to Mestre, FTR; Flg Off S.R.Webber and three KiA

Friday, 13 April 1945

By the evening of the 13th the Santerno river had been reached on a three-division front, and the New Zealand infantry were already across. There was possibly another case of premature bomb detonation when a Spitfire of 7 SAAF Squadron was lost.

British Casualties

237 Sqn	Spitfire IX MJ983 left 1400 on bombing mission, engine cut 1450, crashed; Sgt J.H.Bennie KiA
72 Sqn	Spitfire IX MK687 left 0940 on a Rover David N Imola 1020, hit by light Flak, pilot baled out in enemy lines; Wt Off P.F.Schneider POW to 29 April, when he either escaped or was liberated
145 Sqn	Spitfire VIII JF954 'V' left 1650, hit by ground fire while strafing tanks S of Sesto Imolese, then struck overhead wires, crashed; Plt Off J.R.Moffat KiA
601 Sqn	Spitfire IXe HF PL489 left 1910 on armed recce of Medicina area, hit by Flak, pilot baled out, landed in Allied lines; Flt Lt O.H.E.Jones DFC safe
3 RAAF Sqn	Mustang III KH628 left 1355, not seen after dive-bombing target 5m S Medicina 1440; Wt Off T.K.Higgins WiA POW
1435 Sqn	Spitfire IX MJ289 'R' left 0905 on ASR search, crashed on landing 1045; Lt O.R.Tennant safe
417 Sqn	Spitfire IX MH371 left 1040 on Rover David, strafed motor transports, engine failed, crash-landed; Plt Off A.D.Gibson safe, returned
7 SAAF Sqn	Spitfire IXe MH944 'W' shot down in flames by 20mm Flak when in bombing dive attacking M/T near Massa Lombarda 0720; Lt N.Bremner KiA
7 SAAF Sqn	Spitfire IXe PY793 left 1325, blew up in bomb dive near Budrio, 10m ENE Bologna 1520; Lt G.F.McCormick KiA
US Casualties	
1° Gr Caça/350th FG	P-47D 44-20339 'D3' strafed ammunition depots near Spilimbergo 0900, a depot exploded, a/c crashed; Asp Frederico Gustavo dos Santos KiA

Friday-Saturday, 13/14 April 1945

During the evening of the 13th Sqn Ldr Hammond of 600 Squadron and his radar operator made the only definite interception of one of NSGr 9's aircraft to be achieved during April, shooting down one of the German unit's new FW 190 Jabos for the last aerial success of the war to be achieved by a DAF unit.

British Claims

600 Sqn	Sqn Ldr G.W.Hammond/Flg Off L.R.Moore	Mosquito XIX TA123 'H'	FW 190	Alfonsine area	2037
600 Sqn	Sqn Ldr G.W.Hammond/Flg Off L.R.Moore	Mosquito XIX TA123 'H'	FW 190 Damaged	Ferrara area	'2048

German Casualties

NSGr 9	FW 190 shot down by Beaufighter; pilot not identified

CASUALTIES MOUNT

At first the sheer weight of bombardment had prevented the German defences putting up much fire, but as they recovered from the initial shock, the amount of return fire reached unprecedented levels, and losses amongst the fighter-bombers rose to the highest suffered for many a long day. Flying debris was also a danger, as the pilots pressed home their attacks at minimum altitude, and many aircraft were to be hit by one or other of these hazards. The amount of 20mm and 40mm Flak was particularly intense and accounted for many of the losses suffered. 241 Squadron reported continual damage to its Spitfires, and by the end of the month virtually every aircraft on strength had been replaced because of this, though not one was actually shot down. Elsewhere in 244 Wing other units were not so fortunate, 601 Squadron having eight of its Spitfires shot down during the month, though three of the pilots were able to carry out crash-landings (one in Axis territory), and the pilots of four others baled out safely. Flt Lt O.H.E.Jones, DFC, actually baled out twice in a period of ten days. 145 Squadron lost six aircraft, with six more badly damaged; three pilots were reported missing and one wounded. As mentioned, on 12 April the wing leader, Wg Cdr R.Bary had been lost, his Spitfire being seen to blow up when in its bombing dive as he was leading 417 Squadron.

324 Wing also suffered quite severely, losing 13 aircraft, six of them belonging to 93 Squadron. At least seven of the pilots escaped injury, however, while two more were able to crash land, although wounded. Again, it was all too often the formation leaders who suffered the highest proportion of these losses; 43 Squadron lost three, one of which was the commanding officer, Sqn Ldr Hemingway, though he was able to bale out safely. On the 20th, however, Maj H.E.Wells, who had recently taken over 72 Squadron, was hit and wounded, though he managed to carry out a crash-landing. His place was taken on 1 May by Sqn Ldr E.Cassidy, DFC, who was posted in from 92 Squadron.

Losses in 239 Wing were no lighter, the Mustangs suffering particularly heavily. 5 SAAF Squadron lost eight aircraft during the month, two before the assault started, while 260 Squadron lost six and 112 Squadron three. Amongst the Kittyhawks, 250 Squadron lost six aircraft with many more damaged, though five of the pilots returned safely. Both Australian squadrons in the wing also suffered losses. In 5 SAAF Squadron Capt J.C.Coetzee, the senior flight commander, was killed on the 19th when two aircraft were lost, then on the 30th Lt Veitch of 260 Squadron baled out into the sea for the third time; he was picked up unharmed yet again.

During the month Capt H.J.E.'Nobby' Clarke, DFC, was promoted with 5 SAAF Squadron to the vacant post of commanding officer. Yet in comparison the squadrons of 7 SAAF Wing, which was just as heavily involved in operations as those already mentioned, survived with much lighter losses.

These losses were more than justified by the progress on the ground, and on 12 April 24 SAAF Squadron's crews were able to report that Allied tanks overran their target just as they were beginning their bomb run; the bombs had to be brought back. Next day the squadron dropped quantities of the deadly 20lb fragmentation bombs on a defended area near Argenta, while on the ground the army moved up Highway 9, pushing 10 Armee troops back over the Sillaro river to the east of Bologna. On the Adriatic coast Argenta was captured soon after the attack by the South African Marauders, and the victorious soldiers then poured through the Argenta Gap towards Ferrara, threatening to encircle the whole German east flank.

As these events were occurring and the 8th Army left flank was approaching the Idice river and Bologna, the signal was thereby triggered for 5th Army to commence its part of the offensive, and on the 14th, supported by another massive air bombardment and artillery barrage similar to those mounted on behalf of 8th Army on 9 April, US IV Corps resumed its advance on Bologna. Up to this point DAF had been accomplishing in excess of 500 sorties per day in support of 8th Army, while by night the Bostons and Baltimores were now attacking similar close-support targets as well as carrying on their campaign against road junctions, dumps, etc. Even these relatively safe night sorties were faced with a great increase in return fire at this stage, 15 SAAF Squadron for example, losing two of its Baltimores during the month, with 55 Squadron losing three Bostons, two of them in one night.

With the start of 5th Army's attack, the main weight of MATAF's effort was shifted to this sector of the front. Between the 15th and 18th over 2,000 heavy bomber sorties were to be made against targets between Bologna and the front lines. XXII TAC was now extremely active, its P-47s, Spitfires and Kittyhawks making 520 sorties in support of IV Corps' 10th Mountain Division on the 15th, though TacR Spitfires of 208 Squadron suffered three losses during 28 sorties on this date. The level of air support now being sustained was the heaviest ever achieved in the Mediterranean, despite the reduction in size of MATAF. It needs to be recalled,

Newly appointed to command 4 SAAF Squadron, Maj Wally Brunton usually flew Spitfire IX SM143 'T', adorned with the unit's badge on the nose.

however, that this was achieved to a large extent due to the commitment of virtually the whole of the great strength of 15th Air Force to these operations.

During the three days 16th–19th XXII TAC accomplished in excess of 1,500 sorties, and 57th Bomb Wing B-25s flew 274 in only two days, attacking reserve area and possible escape routes. The 57th Fighter Group provides a good example of the level of activity at this time. On the 14th 34 missions totalling 137 sorties were flown, similar levels of activity being achieved on each of the four days, the 17th proving to be the peak, with 36 missions totalling 152 sorties – approximately 50 per squadron. The last day of this tremendous effort was the 19th, following which operations then continued at a more normal level.

Saturday, 14 April 1945

Due to the demands of Desert Air Force, Mustangs were now in critically short supply, so on this date 249 Squadron handed its remaining aircraft to 213 Squadron. It then re-equipped once more with Spitfire IXs and moved to Prkos to join 281 Wing on attachment. A few days later, with few coastal targets still to attack, 272 Squadron, which had recently joined 287 Wing at Falconara, withdrew from operations and was disbanded by the end of the month.

British Casualties

72 Sqn	Spitfire IX MA537 left 0855 on armed recce, hit by 40mm Flak near Ferrara; crash-landed at base 1005; Plt Off H.L.S.Coulthurst WiA
3 RAAF Sqn	Mustang III FB299 left 1830, shot down in bomb dive 3m NW Castel San Pietro 1855, crash-landed, set on fire by German troops; Wt Off I.M.Redenbach POW, returned 8 May
43 Sqn	Spitfire IX RR246 'B' left 0640 on armed recce of Ferrara-Portomaggiore road, hit by Flak 0740 strafing a staff car, crash-landed; Wt Off A.G.Edwards WiA POW
93 Sqn	Spitfire IX RR258 left 1550 to bomb gun positions NW Imola, crash-landed at Ravenna; Flt Sgt B.E.Roberts safe
11 SAAF Sqn	Kittyhawk IV FX537 left 1620 to bomb command post at Formigine 1710, shot down by Flak, crash-landed SW Modena; Lt D.G.Boast WiA, found by partisans and evacuated

US Casualties

65th FS/57th FG	P-47D 44-20987 hit by Flak 0915, damaged Cat 2; pilot safe
64th FS/57th FG	P-47D 42-29002 hit by Flak 1010, damaged Cat 2; pilot safe
64th FS/57th FG	P-47D 42-75801 hit by Flak 1830, damaged Cat 2; pilot safe

Saturday-Sunday, 14/15 April 1945

British Casualties

500 Sqn	Baltimore V FW711 'H' left 2303 on armed recce, bombed a target, own bombs detonated prematurely badly damaging tail, starboard engine and hydraulics, scrapped on return; Flt Sgt L.J.Light and three safe

Sunday, 15 April 1945

Meteorological reconnaissance flights gathered weather data on which forecasts that were so critical to operational planning were based. In the Mediterranean this had been performed since 1943 by 520 Squadron that initially used Hudsons, but by this time flew the Halifax V with Hurricanes for shorter-range work.

208 Squadron lost three Spitfires in northern Italy which were the unit's last fatalities of WWII.

British Casualties

208 Sqn	Spitfire IX MA481 left 1030 on Tac/R N La Spezia, FTR; Flg Off J.N.F.Hanes KiA
208 Sqn	Spitfire IX MH423 left 1030 on Tac/R N La Spezia, FTR; Flg Off R.M.English KiA
208 Sqn	Spitfire IX MH794 left 1600 to escort Arty/R Spitfire over Bologna area, FTR; Plt Off F.S.Hughes KiA
87 Sqn	Spitfire IX MT533 left 1540 on Rover Joe, damaged by Flak, caught fire, pilot baled out near Viareggio into Allied lines; Lt F.Steinhebel safe
6 Sqn	Hurricane IV KX509 hit by 20mm fire during shipping recce W Albona 1945; Flt Lt J.C.Brand baled out, returned 17 April
2 SAAF Sqn	Spitfire IXc MJ533 'F' damaged by Flak attacking M/T, force-landed S Ferrara 1955; Lt H.P.S.Broome evaded and returned

US Casualties

64th FS/57th FG	P-47D 42-75986 shot down by Flak nr Marano sul Panaro 1255, pilot baled; 1/Lt William F.Berry returned [13807]
64th FS/57th FG	P-47D 42-29369 hit by Flak 1120, damaged Cat 2; pilot safe
346th FS/350th FG	P-47D 43-25653 *Jackson's Brat* '6A7' hit by Flak, crashed nr Vignola 1215; Flt Off Walter R.Miller KiA [13808]

Monday, 16 April 1945

On this date 3 SAAF Wing made its first radar bombing raid with the Shoran system, a small 'box' of four Marauders, led by Capt W.J.O. Musgrave in an aircraft of 21 SAAF Squadron, in an attack on a sugar refinery at Tresigallo. Several more such strikes were to be made during the rest of the month, these proving to be very accurate. On the same day the wing received a surprise visitor during the afternoon when a Croatian air force Bf 109G 'Black 4' flown by Narednik Josip Ceković landed at Jesi, while another Bf 109G 'Black 10' flown by Stražnik Vladimir Sandtner landed at Falconara and was seized by US troops. Both pilots had deserted from Lučko airfield in the Zagreb area.

During the day Messerschmitt Bf 109G-10, 'Schwartz 4' of the Croat 2. Avn Ftr Esc was flown to Falconara by Stražnik (Fw) Vladimir Sandtner who defected to the Allies.

British Casualties

3 RAAF Sqn	Mustang III KH710 left 1755, engine trouble on take-off, crash-landed with bombs on board; Wt Off D.J.Wells safe
92 Sqn	Spitfire VIII JF333 'A' left 1240 on ground-attack mission, shot down by Flak, crashed near Stradone 1305; Wt Off P.G.T.Hoolihan KiA
72 Sqn	Spitfire IX MJ420 left 1610, hit by Flak, crash-landed in own lines; Flg Off A.M.Graham safe
93 Sqn	Spitfire IX PT789 left 0620, hit by Flak strafing near San Nicolò, pilot baled out SE Consandolo 0700; Lt H.P.Anderson POW, escaped, returned by end of the month
93 Sqn	Spitfire IX TA806 left 0620, hit by Flak strafing near San Nicolò, landed safely at base, Cat II damaged; Flt Sgt A.B.Keith-Walker safe
93 Sqn	Spitfire IX MB807 left 1830, hit by Flak near Consandolo, returned Cat II damaged; Flt Sgt D.Hutton safe
213 Sqn	Mustang IV KB750 crashed on landing at Zara 1040, damaged Cat E; Lt I.D.Kenyon safe
73 Sqn	Spitfire IX PV120 'G' left 1530 on armed recce, shot down by Flak, force-landed 5m from Bihac; Flg Off R.R.Letts rescued by partisans, returned 18 April
73 Sqn	Spitfire IX PT498 'V' left 1530 on armed recce, shot down by Flak near Babin Potok, pilot baled out; Flg Off J.B.Baker rescued by partisans, returned 19 April
417 Sqn	Spitfire IX MJ293 left 1510 on a Rover Paddy patrol, last seen strafing motor transports; Flg Off J.T.Rose MiA
112 Sqn	Mustang IV KM133 'B' left 1710 on Cab Rank, engine cut after take-off, crash-landed; Flt Lt G.L.Hirons safe
6 Sqn	Hurricane IV LE268 spun in, hit the ground and exploded at Kraljevica 1910; Plt Off E.Tomlinson KiA
2 SAAF Sqn	Spitfire IXe RK890 'W' hit by Flak 12m E Bologna, force-landed; Lt D.W.Haines safe
145 Sqn	Spitfire VIII MT569 left 1040 on Rover David, hit by small-arms fire, strafing near bomb line, pilot baled near Castel San Pietro, broke leg when struck the tail baling out into Allied lines; Lt J.M.G.Anderson WiA, picked up by troops of 4th Polish Div, evacuated to casualty station

US Casualties

87th FS/79th FG	P-47D 44-21126 shot down by Flak nr Medicina 1640; 2/Lt James P.Moore Jr POW [13861]
345th FS/350th FG	P-47D 42-75000 engine failure or Flak, crashed 15m N Vergato 1510; 1/Lt Richard R.Poeton KiA [13811]

Monday-Tuesday, 16/17 April 1945

Two intruder bombers on this night were severely damaged by the premature explosion of their bombs on release, following on from another instance two nights earlier. Flg Off K.J.Hirsch's Boston had the starboard engine fail, the propeller was also unable to be feathered. He turned for base at Cesenatico, and on reaching Allied lines in a barely flyable condition ordered his crew to bale out, but the wounded gunner Flt Sgt R.J.Legge was unable to do so, so Hirsh kept heading for base where he carried out a successful crash-landing. The award of a DFC followed this example of courage and flying skill.

British Casualties

18 Sqn	Boston V BZ666 'M' left approximately midnight on night-interdiction sortie, shot down near Padua; Flt Sgt P.J.Lewis and three KiA
55 Sqn	Boston V BZ585 left 0345 to bomb target at Budrio, severely damaged by premature detonation of 40lb GP bombs, crash-landed, destroyed; Flg Off K.J.Hirsch and two safe, one WiA
500 Sqn	Baltimore V FW799 'U' left 0005 on armed recce Rovigo-Vicenza-Mestre-Padua, crashed near Lusiana N Vicenza; Flg Off L.M.Matthews and three KiA
454 Sqn	Baltimore V FW765 'U' left 0220 on armed recce, attacked ferry terminal at Polesella, damaged by premature detonation of own bombs, crash-landed at base; Wt Off F.W.J.Hogan and two WiA, one safe

Tuesday, 17 April 1945

Pilots of both 601 and 1 SAAF Squadrons reported chasing Me 262s during the day, but it is more likely that these were the Ar 234s of Kommando Sommer; in both cases they escaped unscathed.

Overall, the Desert Air Force flew over 1,000 sorties, the most it had done in one day in the Italian campaign. Maj 'Nobby' Clarke, the commander of 5 SAAF Squadron was heard to remark after landing his badly damaged Mustang: "They tell me the first twenty are the worst." He had now survived 21 times being shot up by Flak.

LCT-586 offloads the vehicles of 249 Squadron at Zadar, Croatia, during the unit's move to Prkos.

British Casualties

237 Sqn	Spitfire IX MJ643 left 1730 on armed recce of Milan-Brescia area, strafed train 1823, FTR; Flg Off M.C.Ward KiA
450 Sqn	Kittyhawk IV FX846 left 0810, engine trouble after bombing dive, belly-landed N Ravenna; Wt Off W.C.Bounds safe
250 Sqn	Kittyhawk IV FX580 left 1725 attacked target at Budrio, hit in bomb dive by Flak, pilot baled out into Allied lines; Sgt P.A.Morris safe
5 SAAF Sqn	Mustang IVa KM105 left 0605 on armed recce, wing struck a tree when strafing targets 10m SE Brescia 0711, crashed; Lt R.Sleep KiA
5 SAAF Sqn	Mustang III KH692 'D' left 1125 to bomb road bridge, hit by Flak, hydraulics damaged, hood jettisoned, landed at base, Cat II damaged; Maj H.J.E.Clarke safe
5 SAAF Sqn	Mustang III KH620 left 1435, dive-bombing bridge one wing shot off by Flak, pilot baled out but parachute only partly opened 1500; Lt G.C.A.van Dam KiA
241 Sqn	Spitfire IXE PT600 left 1245 to bomb bridge, hit by 20mm Flak in Malalbergo area, pilot baled out into Allied lines; Flt Sgt F.Stevens WiA
27 SAAF Sqn	Warwick GR V 741 PN754 'C' spun in and crashed at Gianaclis; Lt R.S.Douglas and seven KiA
2 SAAF Sqn	Spitfire IXc MH970 'V' damaged by Flak 11 miles NE Bologna 1615, returned to base; Lt J.E.Hartley safe
3 SAAF Sqn	Spitfire IXe PT962 'F' shot down by Flak in Sassuolo area 1800; Capt R.C.Egner POW, escaped and took surrender of 250 German troops, retuned to Sqn 1 May

US Casualties

66th FS/57th FG	P-47D 42-74988 destroyed by own bomb blast nr Formigine 0745; 2/Lt Vernon R.Peterson KiA [13810]
65th FS/57th FG	P-47D 42-26448 *Coxxet* shot down by Flak S Bazzano 1030; 2/Lt James L.Matt KiA[14074]
87th FS/79th FG	P-47D 42-27939 *Lady Thelma* shot down by Flak 1905; 1/Lt John C.Kittrell evaded [13749]
86th BS/47th BG	A-20B 41-3253 lost over Italy, last seen 0117; 1/Lt Lloyd W.Small and three KiA [13809]

Tuesday-Wednesday, 17/18 April 1945

British Casualties

15 SAAF Sqn	Baltimore V FW831 left 0120 on armed recce Brescia area, engine cut on approach 0315, a wing hit the ground and cartwheeled; Capt H.C.Murman and two crew KiA, one crew WiA

Wednesday, 18 April 1945

British Casualties

111 Sqn	Spitfire IX MJ190 'R' left 1340, hit by Flak near Budrio, crash-landed near base; Wt Off R.Prest WiA
145 Sqn	Spitfire VIII JF564 left 0705, hit by Flak, force-landed S Argenta; Sgt N.C.Reeves safe
450 Sqn	Kittyhawk IV FT928 'L' left 1640, damaged by Flak; Sqn Ldr J.C.Doyle safe
93 Sqn	Spitfire IX MB907 left 1240, hit by Flak strafing motor transports NW Budrio, crash-landed at Ravenna 1335; Plt Off A.W.Morris safe

Sqn Ldr Jack Doyle of 450 Squadron had a narrow escape when Kittyhawk FT928 'L' was damaged by Flak, though he flew it safely back to Cervia.

93 Sqn	Spitfire IX MJ955 left 1600 bombing target NW Budrio, engine caught fire, pilot baled out in Allied lines; Lt J.O.Connell safe
237 Sqn	Spitfire IX MK372 left 0945, bombed marshalling yards at Parma, on return flew into hill NE Pisa; Flt Lt J.F.Carlyle KiA
US Casualties	
65th FS/57th FG	P-47D 44-21043 hit by Flak 1115, damaged Cat 2; pilot safe
66th FS/57th FG	P-47D 42-75761 hit by Flak 1730, damaged Cat 2; pilot safe
345th FS/350th FG	P-47D 42-29008 *Rowdy* crashed into mountain 0800; 2/Lt Robert H.Clayton KiA [13805]
345th FS/350th FG	P-47D 44-21061 hit mountain while in cloud nr Castelmaggiore 0800; 1/Lt Kimber M.Middleton WiA [13806]
345th FS/350th FG	P-47D 42-75758 rocket tube caught fire nr Castelmaggiore 1700; 1/Lt Norbert J.Gorski KiA [13812]

Wednesday-Thursday, 18/19 April 1945

On this night the veteran strike Beaufighter Squadron, No. 272, flew its last operational sortie of the war.

British Casualties	
256 Sqn	Mosquito XIII HK508 'A' left 0515, pilot radioed navigator had baled out 5m S Copparo, then FTR; Sqn Ldr G.M.Smith DFC KiA/Flg Off H.J.Wilmer DFM POW
454 Sqn	Baltimore V FW834 'C' left 2346 on night-intruder mission to Po crossings, damaged by dropping bombs too low an altitude, but may well be by premature detonation of bombs; Sgt F.G.Lister and three KiA

Thursday, 19 April 1945

Firstly, during the later stages of the morning Bf 109s of 1° Gruppo were scrambled to intercept a single B-24 on a supply drop to partisans near the Swiss frontier. We consider that both participants fall within our classification of strategic operations which included aircraft of both categories involved – in this case three Bf 109s of 1° Gruppo were shot down by return fire from a specialist US 15th Air Force aircraft involved in just such activity, so we therefore intend to deal with the details within Volume 6.

A P-51D Mustang of the 325th Fighter Group provides close escort to a 340th Bomb Group B-25J Mitchell during the attack on the Ora bridge which was opposed by ANR Bf 109s.

Sqn Ldr George Milner Smith of 256 Squadron was killed when shortly before dawn his Mosquito was lost over the Po Valley east of Ferrara.

The day's second occasions were somewhat more difficult to work out. Soon after midday a formation of the 340th Bomb Group B-25s (Tactical Air Force) were being escorted by P-51s of the US 15th Air Force's 325th Fighter Group, to bomb the Ora bridge. During this raid the US fighter pilots claimed seven Bf 109s of 2° Gruppo C – five aircraft were actually lost, four of the pilots surviving. The pilot lost was Serg Renato Patton who therefore became the final pilot of his unit to be killed before the war ended. Here the escorts on an essentially tactical mission were being provided by a strategic unit, although Serg Patton was a member of the former. We decided that it would be appropriate to mention the action in Volume 5 – as we have done here – but to deal with it in more detail in Volume 6 in due course.

2° Gruppo, the main adversary of MATAF, had claimed 114 victories during its year of service, the majority of these claims being made against tactical aircraft, though some interceptions of 15th Air Force formations had occurred. The total claimed included some 23 P-47s and 58 twin-engined bombers of various types. The most successful pilots had been Cap Ugo Drago and Cap Mario Bellagambi, credited with ten apiece, and Serg Magg Attilio Sanson, with seven. The Gruppo's losses had totalled 55 aircraft while 38 pilots had been killed.

This very high percentage of fatal casualties to aircraft losses indicates the very much more difficult circumstances under which the Italians were operating than were the Allies. As a comparison, the Brazilian 1° Grupo de Caça, probably the least experienced of the XXII TAC fighter-bomber units, lost 17 P-47s on operations between September 1944 and April 1945, but the pilots of only five of these were killed.

British Casualties

92 Sqn	Spitfire VIII JG242 left 0715, hit by Flak, crash-landed in Allied lines near Castel San Pietro; Plt Off P.Davis safe
450 Sqn	Kittyhawk IV FX581 left 1720, failed to pull out of bomb dive, crashed near Imola 1750; Flg Off P.D.Allan KiA
93 Sqn	Spitfire IX RK912 left 0600, hit by Flak, crash-landed NW Argenta in Allied lines 0700; Flt Sgt J.E.Swales safe
5 SAAF Sqn	Mustang IVa KH713 left 1223, strafed guns 1305, shot down in flames by Flak, crashed into Allied lines 5m NE Argenta; Capt J.C.Coetzee KiA

Above: When flown by Ten Oddone Colonna, Messerschmitt Bf 109G-10 WNr 491333 '2-10' of 2ª Squadriglia, 1° Gruppo Caccia from Lonate Pozzolo was hit by return fire and damaged in this action on 19 April. Left: Having claimed the unit's final victory, the Bf 109G flown by Ten Aurelio Morandi was hit by return fire and he was killed.

5 SAAF Sqn	Mustang III FB264 left 1325, bombed and strafed strong point, shot down by Flak NW Portomaggiore 1400, pilot baled out; Lt D.R.Hattingh WiA, POW, escaped and evaded to Allied lines
7 SAAF Sqn	Spitfire IXe NH532 left 1120, damaged by Flak N Ferrara, pilot baled out nr San Alberto S Lake Comacchio 1230 in Allied lines; Maj D.M.Brebner returned
11 SAAF Sqn	Kittyhawk IV FX790 left 1840 bombing MT workshop, shot down by Flak near Cento 1920, dived straight into the target and exploded; Lt J.A.Topp KiA

US Claims

317th FS/325th FG	1/Lt Wendell B.Bagley	P-51	Bf 109	S Lake Garda	1235
317th FS/325th FG	1/Lt Woodrow P.Baldwin	P-51	Bf 109	Lake Garda	1235
317th FS/325th FG	1/Lt John Barrett	P-51	Bf 109	Lake Garda	1235
317th FS/325th FG	1/Lt Frank M.Bolek	P-51	Bf 109	S end Lake Garda	1235
317th FS/325th FG	1/Lt Frank M.Bolek	P-51	Bf 109 Damaged	S end Lake Garda	1235
317th FS/325th FG	1/Lt Frank W Schaefer	P-51	Bf 109	S Lake Garda	1235
317th FS/325th FG	1/Lt Woodrow P.Baldwin	P-51	Bf 109	Lake Garda	1240

US Casualties

346th FS/350th FG	P-47D 44-21005 '6D6' crashed into mountain in overcast 0910; 1/Lt Thomas Wilkinson Jr KiA [13998]				
347th FS/350th FG	P-47D 44-20981 hit by Flak WSW Monte S.Pietro, crashed 1605; 1/Lt Joseph F.Pickerel baled, returned on 21 April [14073]				
345th FS/350th FG	P-47D 44-21009 hit by Flak SW Bologna 1855; 1/Lt Burwell S.Palmer returned [13804]				
64th FS/57th FG	P-47D 44-33625 oil leak u/k cause, crashed nr Marano sul Panaro; pilot baled out 1745; 1/Lt Arthur C.Goettel evaded, returned next day [14067]				
66th FS/57th FG	P-47D 44-20116 hit by Flak 0915, damaged Cat 2; pilot safe				
428th BS/310th BG	B-25J 44-30335 lost to Flak, escorted by 15th AF fighters 1745; 1/Lt Donald A.McGilvray Jr and three POW, two KiA [14066]				
859th BS/2641st SG	B-24 42-50428 on special mission, shot down by e/a 1137, crew baled out; Capt Walter L.Sutton and three captured by Italians, two captured by Germans, copilot Lt Frank A.Stoherer and four taken to Switzerland by partisans [14028]				

Italian ANR Claims

2ª Sq, 1° Gr C	Ten Aurelio Morandi	Bf 109G	B-24	nr Swiss border	1140

Italian ANR Casualties

2ª Sq, 1° Gr C	Bf 109G shot down by return fire from B-24, crashed nr Cassina Rizzardi 1120; Ten Aurelio Morandi KiA
2ª Sq, 1° Gr C	Bf 109G-10 WNr 491333 '2-10' damaged by return fire from B-24; Ten Oddone Colonna safe
6ª Sq, 2° Gr C	Bf 109K-4 shot down in combat, crashed nr Ponti sul Mincio 1235; Serg Renato Patton baled out but parachute failed to open, KiA
6ª Sq, 2° Gr C	Bf 109K-4 shot down in combat 1km S Desenzano; Serg Magg Ferdinando Zanardi baled out safely
6ª Sq, 2° Gr C	Bf 109G Black 8 shot down in combat over Garda; Ten Bruno Betti baled out safely
6ª Sq, 2° Gr C	Bf 109G shot down in combat over Garda; M.llo Tullio Covre baled out safely
6ª Sq, 2° Gr C	Bf 109G White 12 damaged in combat over Garda; Ten Ermete Ferrero WiA

Friday, 20 April 1945

By now 5th Army had moved ahead fast, as had the 8th also; by this date US II Corps had taken Gesso, Casalecchio di Reno and Riale, while 10th Mountain Division had crossed Highway 9, thereby cutting the main lateral line of communication of Armee Gruppe C. The latter division then joined in 8th Army's advance up this highway towards Ferrara, putting the Germans in an increasingly perilous position.

Tanks were sometimes located by Auster AOP pilots such as on this day when Capt Barrow of 651 Squadron reported a tank in a barn near Portomaggiore. A Spitfire was handed over for him to control the attack that scored a direct hit. He then landed in an adjacent field to see the gory remains. Another Auster pilot of this unit landed to pick up a downed Spitfire pilot.

British Casualties

6 Sqn	Hurricane IV KX241 'N' left 1310 to attack E boats leaving Cherso Bay, hit by Flak and abandoned 1 mile off Balmazzinghi; Flg Off R.A.C.Kendle rescued
72 Sqn	Spitfire IX ML146 left 0600 on armed recce, hit by Flak, crash-landed 3m S Argenta; Maj H.R.Wells WiA
92 Sqn	Spitfire VIII MT676 left 1015, hit by Flak, crash-landed SW Argenta; Plt Off J.Parker safe
3 SAAF Sqn	Spitfire IX SM444 left 1430, damaged by Flak, crash-landed 1535; Lt M.H.Hartogh safe
111 Sqn	Spitfire IX MH974 'M' left 0920, hit by Flak, pilot baled out 3.5m E Argenta into Allied lines; Sgt E.A.Lord safe
112 Sqn	Mustang III KH467 'Z' left 0545 on armed recce, exploded in bomb dive attacking train S Trieste 0645; Lt J.H.Nixon KiA
601 Sqn	Spitfire IXe MJ909 left 1205, strafed gun positions 4m NE Bologna, hit by Flak, crash-landed in Allied lines; Sgt M.J.Hyett WiA
145 Sqn	Spitfire VIII MT634 left 0950, hit by small-arms fire, pilot baled out E Argenta 1040; Plt Off J.McV.Anderson safe, back to base with Capt A.N.Scott of 651 AOP Sqn
87 Sqn	Spitfire IX MH532 left 1810 on Rover Joe, bomb exploded on taking-off, destroyed; Plt Off L.R.John KiA
7 SAAF Sqn	Spitfire IXe MJ609 'B' left 1815 on armed recce, strafed armoured car S Po river, shot down by Flak 5m W Ostellato 1845, pilot baled out; Capt B.Guest POW, left behind when Germans pulled out of Rovigo on 27 April, liberated next day

US Casualties

66th FS/57th FG	P-47D 42-29264 *Greta I* shot down by Flak S Bologna 1340; 1/Lt Robert B.Orcutt MiA [14071]
346th FS/350th FG	P-47D 42.28299 '6B6' *Iron Mountain* shot down by Flak S Bologna 1340; 1/Lt R.C.Thompson MiA [14014]
346th FS/350th FG	P-47D 42-29048 '6D1' *Bach's Boche Bustin Bastard* hit by Flak NW Bologna 1415; 2/Lt Roger C.Ellis Jr baled out, returned [14075]
346th FS/350th FG	P-47D 44-33078 '6D6' shot down by Flak SE Castelfranco Emilia 1900; 1/Lt G.M.Fisher MiA [14007]

Italian ANR Casualties

2° Gr C	Bf 109G destroyed on ground at Orio al Serio

The dramatic and awful sight of Marauder III HD481 'S' after a direct hit by 88mm Flak over Ficarolo. Lt Oakes and his crew were the final losses for 24 SAAF Squadron.

Saturday, 21 April 1945

Elements of both 5th and 8th Armies entered Bologna from different directions, in consequence of which 10. and 14. Armees were split from each other. Heavy cloud and some ground fog prevented much air support being provided during the day. Finally, at 1600 46 P-47s from the 350th Fighter Group took off voluntarily under a solid overcast to fly in the most hazardous conditions through the mountains to give such aid as they could.

Breaking through into clearer weather over the Po Valley, the Thunderbolt pilots had a field day claiming 105 vehicles destroyed and 63 damaged, four Tiger tanks and three smaller tanks destroyed, 27 artillery pieces silenced, 82 horse-drawn vehicles immobilised, a barge sunk, three supply dumps left in flames, and a column of troops well-strafed. Nine P-47s were hit by Flak, one of these being shot down, but the pilot was able to evade capture and return safely to Allied lines.

Twelve Marauders of 24 SAAF Squadron were bombing pontoons over the Po north-west of Ferrara when accurate 88mm Flak struck one of them, blowing away the port wing and engine. The pilot was seen struggling with his controls, but the stricken bomber plunged straight down to crash, all the crew being killed. It was the squadron's final loss of the war.

British Claims

237 Sqn	Flg Off N.B.Mansell	Spitfire IX MK629	} Ju 188 on ground	Bergamo a/f	1200-1405
237 Sqn	Flt Sgt R.Morant	Spitfire IX PT624			

---

24 SAAF Sqn	Marauder III HD481 'S' left 0859 to bomb pontoon bridges over River Po near Ficarolo, direct Flak hit blew port wing off, crashed 12m NW Ferrara 1030; Lt K.T.Oakes and five KiA
213 Sqn	Mustang III HB853 shot down by Flak from a train SW Pakrac 0710; Flg Off D.E.Robertson WiA, evaded, flown by C-47 to Bari on 27 April
250 Sqn	Kittyhawk IV FX71 left 1040 to bomb bridge over River Reno, hit by Flak over target, crash-landed at base; Flt Sgt J.A.Morris safe
250 Sqn	Kittyhawk IV FX925 left 1610, strafed motor transports, hit by ground fire, belly-landed at base; Lt A.Reynolds safe
19 SAAF Sqn	Beaufighter X NV122 on return from strike, flew into ground near Canne; Lt A.R.D.Blacklaws/Lt C.L.Cowell KiA
7 SAAF Sqn	Spitfire IXe ML306 left 1130 on armed recce, hit by Flak 1230, landed safely at base; Lt E.R.Phelan slt WiA

US Casualties

66th FS/57th FG	P-47D 44-20342 hit by Flak 1805, damaged Cat 2; pilot safe
86th FS/79th FG	P-47D 42-75963 'X64' *Gow Job* lost u/k cause 0720; 2/Lt Loren H.Hintz KiA [14070]
346th FS/350th FG	P-47D 44-19723 *Sky Queen/Kitten* '6D4' hit by Flak, belly-landed between Castelfranco Emilia and Bologna; 2/Lt Richard P.Sulzbach picked up by 88th Division [14001]

Saturday-Sunday, 21/22 April 1945

British Casualties

18 Sqn	Boston V BZ590 'B' left 2054 to bomb River Po crossing at Taglio di Po, shot down by Flak, exploded on impact W Copparo; Sgt D.K.Raikes and three KiA

Sunday, 22 April 1945

It was now vital for Armee Gruppe C to withdraw if a disaster was to be averted, and Allied reconnaissance during the night of the 21st showed the whole length of the Po from Ostiglia to Crespino to be a mass of activity. Next day it became clear that the Germans were pulling out under cover of a sudden break in the weather. At once the whole fighter-bomber effort was shifted to the Po ferry crossings, while medium and strategic heavies concentrated on blocking routes to the north. Bridges over the Adige and Brenta rivers were destroyed, and in consequence many troops were trapped between the Po and the Adige. Now the effect of the continual Allied interdiction began to tell to a marked degree. The Germans were short of supplies and transport; the Po could be crossed only by ferry, and many of these had been sunk. Resistance was collapsing everywhere, and the retreat was fast becoming a rout.

Tremendous damage was inflicted by MATAF aircraft by day and night in the period 21–24 April. The 47th Bomb Group was much to the fore here, undertaking a continuous four-day series of round-the-clock attacks on German transport that were to earn the group a Distinguished Unit Citation. At this time, although still equipped mainly with A-20G Havocs, the group had begun introducing to action some A-26B Invaders which had started arriving in Italy during the previous month.

In this same period 239 Wing alone claimed some 500 vehicles destroyed, while Mosquitos of 256 Squadron were now active by night, destroying barges on the Po and other rivers, as the ferry sites and pontoons that had been thrown across were concentrated upon. 256 Squadron was receiving some Mosquito VI fighter-bombers at this time to increase the effectiveness of their attacks; the squadron had therefore converted one of its Mark XIII night-fighters to carry bombs as a preliminary to this new equipment.

The Brazilian 1º Grupo de Caça enjoyed its most successful day, flying 44 sorties over the Mantua area where 97 vehicles were claimed destroyed by its pilots. Not without cost as during the intense operations along the Po river the 350th Fighter Group, including the attached Brazilians, lost six Thunderbolts, four pilots being killed. A flight of four in the morning from the 345th Squadron was on an armed recce of the Po river between Ostiglia and Suzzara, when the number 4 disappeared after intense Flak was met at San Benedetto at 1045. The other three climbed to 5,000ft and then rocketed a target near the town, but on pulling away from the attack at 1100 the number 3 had also disappeared. Both pilots were killed. Later in the day at 1330 another pair from the squadron were out looking for the missing pilots and undertaking an armed recce, strafed two trucks when Lt Boettcher's engine started smoking badly; he called that his propeller was "out" and soon after crash-landed seven miles south of Parma at 1545; he was seen to get out and run for cover, the beginning of a successful evasion.

The American night-fighter squadrons at Pontedera were used on day armed-recce missions of the Po river crossings and two Mosquitos and a P-61 Black Widow were lost to Flak.

Top: At around this date at Pisa the 86th Bomb Squadron, 47th Bomb Group began receiving some A-26 Invaders, one of which was A-26C 43-22546 '63'. Above: Mosquito NF XXX MT482 was one of two aircraft of the 416th Night Fighter Squadron lost on armed-reconnaissance sorties during the day.

British Casualties

87 Sqn	Spitfire IX PT409 left 1425 on long-range strafing recce, strafed trucks Rondeno area, FTR; Sgt A.W.Ward KiA
417 Sqn	Spitfire IX MJ352 left 0710 on a Rover Paddy, attacked a tank 0745 under intense Flak; Flg Off F.A.Doyle evaded
250 Sqn	Kittyhawk IV FX820 left 0825, bombed a bridge N Ferrara, hit in dive by Flak, crash-landed near target; Lt B.B.McLeroth KiA
1 SAAF Sqn	Spitfire IXc MH605 on return swung into soft sand on landing and overturned; Lt I.Rowden safe

US Casualties

66th FS/57th FG	P-47D 42-28532 hit by Flak 1000, damaged Cat 2; pilot safe
66th FS/57th FG	P-47D 44-20847 hit by Flak 1000, damaged Cat 2; pilot safe
66th FS/57th FG	P-47D 44-20798 hit by Flak 1130, damaged Cat 2; pilot safe
65th FS/57th FG	P-47D 44-20118 *My Naked Ass* hit tree while strafing 1315; 1/Lt Earl A.Thompson KiA [14076]
64th FS/57th FG	P-47D 42-29011 hit by Flak 1545; pilot safe
65th FS/57th FG	P-47D 42-26789 hit by Flak 1620, damaged Cat 2; pilot safe
65th FS/57th FG	P-47D 42-29297 *Miss Criss/Smithy* hit by Flak 1700; 2/Lt Joseph J.Hauser KiA [14004]
66th FS/57th FG	P-47D 44-20798 hit by Flak 1700, damaged Cat 2; pilot safe
65th FS/57th FG	P-47D 42-26707 hit by Flak 1700, damaged Cat 2; pilot safe
64th FS/57th FG	P-47D 44-20866 hit by Flak 1800, damaged Cat 2; pilot safe
65th FS/57th FG	P-47D 44-20990 hit by Flak 1810, damaged Cat 2; pilot safe
85th FS/79th FG	P-47D 42-26819 *Chicago Kid II/Hey Chicken* hit by Flak, crashed NW Suzzara 1715; 2/Lt Glenn W.Faulkner KiA [14069]
1° Gr Caça/350th FG	P-47D 42-26773 'D6' lost to Flak (?) 1615; 2° Ten Marcos Coelho de Magalhães WiA, POW
345th FS/350th FG	P-47D 42-28564 *Mis Behavin'* lost to Flak nr Pegognaga 0950, crash-landed but broke up and overturned; 2/Lt Richard J.Greggerson KiA [14015]
345th FS/350th FG	P-47D 44-33099 left at 0930 on armed recce of Po Valley between Ostiglia and Suzzara, lost to Flak nr San Benedetto 1045; 2/Lt Charles R.Perryman KiA [14062]
345th FS/350th FG	P-47D 44-33553 left at 0930 on armed recce of Po Valley between Ostiglia and Suzzara, lost to Flak nr San Benedetto 1045; Flt Off Royce L.McCleskey KiA [14063]
345th FS/350th FG	P-47D 42-29001 left 1330 on armed recce, strafed trucks, hit by Flak, crash-landed 7m S Parma 1545; 1/Lt R.E.Boettcher evaded, returned [14072]
345th FS/350th FG	P-47D 44-19593 '6D3' left on armed recce, strafed M/T on road 10m SW Modena, E of Sassuolo, possibly hit by Flak 1630, crashed; 1/Lt Addison A.Bachman KiA [14005]
416th NFS	Mosquito XXX MT482 left Pontedera a/f 1110 on armed recce of Po Valley, FTR; 2/Lt Wesley Kangas/2/Lt Jack Herron KiA [14065]
416th NFS	Mosquito XXX NT248 'OG' left Pontedera a/f 1325 on armed recce of Parma-Piacenza-Mantua, shot down by Flak nr San Benedetto; Maj James D.Urso WiA/1/Lt Talmadge F.Simpson Jr MiA [14064]
414th NFS	P-61B-2 42-39486 *Gorgeous Geri* left base at Pontedera a/f at 1605 on armed recce of Modena-Mantua area, strafed M/T north of Oglio river 1645, hit by Flak E Cremona 1650, radar operator baled out, crashed; 2/Lt Frank F.Beaver KiA/Flt Off Stanley Kalan POW [14012]
84th BS/47th BG	A-20K 44-338 left base at 1045 on armed recce of Po river crossings NW Ferrara, hit by small-arms fire near Ostiglia, pilot WiA ordered crew to bale out, last seen 1045; 1/Lt Harold D.Moran KiA, three baled out, one shot on parachute, two POW, rescued within 48 hours [14008]

Monday, 23 April 1945

The 57th Fighter Group put in another big effort, 58 missions totalling 117 sorties being flown, but this time at a cost of six aircraft. Also Maj Carlton Chamberlain, commanding officer of the 64th Squadron, crash-landed in Allied territory.

During the late morning, in the Zagreb area two Croatian pilots, Satnik Ljudevit Bencetić and his wingman Porucnik Mihajlo Jelak, flying their Bf 109Gs, sighted two

Sat (Hptm) Ljudevit 'Lujo' Bencetić (left) and Por (Lt) Mihajlo Jelak (right) of the Croat 2 Lovacko Jato re-enact their combat with 213 Squadron Mustangs; the latter had crash-landed his aircraft after it was hit by Flt Lt 'Ginger' Hulse.

431

Above:: When he encountered the Croat Bf 109s Flt Lt Hulse was flying the further Mustang IV seen here, KH826 'G'. Left: Flt Lt Hulse of 213 Squadron made the RAF's final claim in the Mediterranean area when he believed he had damaged a Croatian Bf 109; in fact the aircraft crash-landed and was wrecked.

213 Squadron's Mustangs flown by Flt Lt G.S.Hulse and Flg Off F. J.Barrett. Diving on them Bencetić fired a burst from 80 metres at the Mustang flown by Barrett, setting its right wing and radiator on fire. Barrett tried to evade but was hit by a second burst from 50 metres and crashed near Velika Gorica. The leader Flt Lt G.S.Hulse scored hits on the engine of Jelak's aircraft, forcing him to crash land near Lučko adjacent to the Zagreb-Sisak railway line, from where he returned to base uninjured. Hulse made a claim for a Bf 109 damaged on his return, although in reality the Messerschmitt had been forced down. Either way this was the last air combat claim by a Commonwealth pilot in the Mediterranean. It also meant that Graham Hulse had registered claims against German, Italian, Bulgarian and Croatian aircraft to which he added claims against one or more of Russian, Chinese and North Korean-flown MiGs during the Korean War – a unique variety.

Sqn Ldr J.A.Hemingway of 43 Squadron was shot down by Flak and evaded with the help of Italian civilians.

During the early hours one of the last special duties operations in Italy was flown when Plt Off R.C.Dalzell of 148 Squadron in a Lysander IIIA infiltrated a two-man team near Udine. However, when landing at 0200 hours the aircraft wiped off its undercarriage and Dalzell joined the partisans until the arrival of Allied troops on 2 May.

British Claims

213 Sqn	Flt Lt G.S.Hulse	Mustang IV KH826 'G'	Bf 109 dam	nr Zagreb

British Casualties

318 Sqn   Spitfire IX MH702 left 0545 on TAC/R, damaged by Flak, crash-landed in Allied lines; Plt Off M.Sawicki safe

111 Sqn	Spitfire IX PL491 'T' left 1905, hit by Flak, crash-landed near base; Flg Off T.M.Colyer WiA
185 Sqn	Spitfire IX PL345 left 1020 strafing road near Aulla, failed to pull out of a dive, hit a house; Flt Lt F.T.Holliman KiA
213 Sqn	Mustang IV KH816 'G' shot down by Flak in Zagreb area 0805, crash-landed; Flt Sgt S.W.Farley POW?
213 Sqn	Mustang IV KH869 'J' shot down by Bf 109 SE Lučko nr Zagreb 1205; Flg Off F.J.Barrett KiA
601 Sqn	Spitfire IXe PT761 left 1930 to bomb guns near Ariano, hit by Flak W Portomaggiore, crash-landed in enemy territory; Flt Off P.C.Robson DoW
601 Sqn	Spitfire IXe PV300 left 1950 to bomb guns near Ariano, hit by Flak W Portomaggiore, pilot baled out into the front line (second time in ten days); Flt Lt O.H.E.Jones DFC safe
5 SAAF Sqn	Mustang III KH610 'C' left 1515 to dive bomb ferry terminals S River Po, crashed recovering from bombing dive, 20m SSW Venice; Lt P.Muir KiA
43 Sqn	Spitfire IX PT836 'A' left 0830, hit by Flak after bombing a truck near Rovigo 0900, hit again by Flak, pilot baled out NE Copparo; Sqn Ldr J.A.Hemingway evaded, assisted by partisans, returned that evening
7 SAAF Sqn	Spitfire IX MK189 damaged by light Flak when strafing; Lt P.A.Leslie safe
12 SAAF Sqn	Marauder III HD622 'S' left 0702 to bomb River Po ferry crossing, hit by Flak, force-landed at Rimini 0830, destroyed by fire; Lt B.Levin and three safe, two WiA
148 Sqn	Lysander IIIA V9707 crashed at 0200 on landing near Udine on agent drop; Plt Off R.C.Dalzell safe, joined partisans
US Casualties	
65th FS/57th FG	P-47D 44-21035 hit by Flak 0740; 2/Lt Lloyd J.Hayney WiA [14081]
64th FS/57th FG	P-47D 42-25288 hit by small-arms fire 0915 damaged Cat 2; pilot safe
66th FS/57th FG	P-47D 42-26752 hit by Flak 1035, damaged Cat 2; pilot safe
66th FS/57th FG	P-47D 42-20107 hit by Flak 1100, damaged Cat 2; pilot safe
64th FS/57th FG	P-47D 42-29369 hit by Flak 1155, damaged Cat 2; pilot safe
65th FS/57th FG	P-47D 44-20988 hit by Flak 1230, damaged Cat 2; pilot safe
64th FS/57th FG	P-47D 44-76024 hit by Flak 1300; 2/Lt Robert H.Reichelfelder KiA [14016]
64th FS/57th FG	P-47D 42-75713 hit by Flak 1330, damaged Cat 2; pilot safe
66th FS/57th FG	P-47D 44-20102 hit by Flak 1600, belly-landed, damaged Cat 2; pilot safe
65th FS/57th FG	P-47D 44-20866 *Schmaltize* hit by Flak 1840; 2/Lt Leonard R.Hadley MiA [14002]
346th FS/350th FG	P-47D 44-29028 '6A1' *The Ox* hit by Flak 1230; 1/Lt Martin S.Domin safe [14003]

On 23 April Lysander IIIA V9707 'G' of 148 Squadron flew into a field near Cortemilia, south of Asti in northern Italy to evacuate three wounded partisans. It was one of the last of such SOE support sorties.

345th FS/350th FG	P-47D 42-27321 hit by Flak 1500; 1/Lt William S.Marshall rescued [14003]				
97th BS/47th BG	A-26B 43-22441 crashed on taking-off 2145; 1/Lt Walter J.Fassett and two KiA [14013]				
16th TCS/64th TCG	C-47A 42-100954 lost over Italy on paradrop resupply mission; 1/Lt Robert E.Wallin and six KiA [12987]				
446th BS/321st BG	B-25J 43-4077 left 1735 to bomb Pontoon bridge, Guarda Veneta, hit by Flak 6m N Rimini, crashed on landing 1925; 1/Lt James E.Ratliff Jr and three safe, three WiA				
Croatian Claims					
2.Jl.Sk	Sat Ljudevit.Bencetić	Bf 109G Black 22	Mustang	nr Zagreb	ca 1200
2.Jl.Sk	Por Mihajlo Jelak	Bf 109G Black 27	Mustang Damaged	nr Zagreb	ca 1200
Croatian Casualties					
2.Jl.Sk	Bf 109G-14 Black 27 damaged in combat with Mustangs, crash-landed nr Velika Gorica; Por Mihajlo Jelak safe				

Tuesday, 24 April 1945

Lt Jack Filby of 5 SAAF Squadron was killed on 24 April when Mustang IVa KH808 'E' was lost near Padua during an armed reconnaissance.

British Casualties	
237 Sqn	Spitfire IX MK251 left 1355, presumed shot down by Flak at Trecella E Milan; Sgt J.K.Allan KiA
601 Sqn	Spitfire IXe TA817 left 1015, hit by Flak, crash-landed near Occomille 1125; Flt Lt T.E.Johnson safe
87 Sqn	Spitfire IX MK942 scrambled 1915 on interception, diverted to strafe motor transports S Pontremoli, struck a tree, returned to base Cat II damaged; Lt J.Steinhobel safe
93 Sqn	Spitfire HFIX PT465 left 0605 on armed recce, strafed a Flak position near Monselice which shot back, pilot baled out landing in enemy territory; Plt Off E.U.Fitzgerald evaded, returned on 3 May
93 Sqn	Spitfire IX RR188 left 0845 on armed recce, dive-bombed road bridge near Arquà, hit by Flak pilot baled out NW Copparo into Allied lines; Flt Sgt J.E.Swales safe
5 SAAF Sqn	Mustang IVa KH808 'U' left 0605 on armed recce, strafed M/T 12m W Padua 0650, crashed inverted into the ground; Lt J.E.Filby KiA
16 SAAF Sqn	Beaufighter X NV611 'U' left 1357 to attack Žužemberk, damaged by small-arms fire, overturned on landing 1655; Lt Ward-Able/Flg Off Hooley safe
1 SAAF Sqn	Spitfire IX NH467 badly damaged by Flak when strafing, force-landed Forlì, Lt F.P.de Wet safe
249 Sqn	Spitfire IX JG123 'G' crashed at Prkos after taking off for a strike; Lt A.J.Malherbe WiA
US Casualties	
87th FS/79th FG	P-47D 44-20080 *Zo-Zo* hit by Flak, crashed nr Guarda 1200; Capt Arthur E.Halfpapp KiA [13999]
65th FS/57th FG	P-47D 42-75724 hit by Flak 0810, damaged Cat 2; pilot safe
64th FS/57th FG	P-47D 42-29004 hit by Flak 0845, damaged Cat 2; pilot safe

Tuesday-Wednesday, 24/25 April 1945

Wednesday, 25 April 1945

Within two days of the fall of Bologna the bomb line on the 5th Army front had advanced beyond the range of 8 SAAF Wing's three Spitfire squadrons, only the Kittyhawks of 11 SAAF Squadron being able to maintain the attack. Consequently, on the 24th the wing moved forward to Bologna to resume operations. Losses so far had been relatively light, though 185 Squadron had been hardest hit, losing four pilots, two of whom were believed to have been killed.

The P-47s with their much greater range were able to carry on as before, and on the 24th and 25th occurred the 350th Fighter Group's proudest moments. Volunteers were called for to undertake a series of hazardous strafing attacks on an airfield at Ghedi in northern Italy where Axis aircraft had been spotted, which appeared to have just been moved in by the Luftwaffe in a desperate attempt to launch an air attack on Allied troops approaching the Po. During these attacks one pilot, 1/Lt Raymond Knight, carried out a number of sorties with such outstanding gallantry that he was awarded the Medal of Honor, America's highest award for bravery, and which was awarded to only two fighter pilots in the whole European and Mediterranean theatres throughout the war. A part of the citation for his award describes graphically the circumstances leading up to it:

"On the morning of 24 April he volunteered to lead two other aircraft against the strongly defended enemy airdrome at Ghedi. Ordering his fellow pilots to remain aloft, he skimmed the ground through a deadly curtain of anti-aircraft fire to reconnoitre the field, locating eight German aircraft hidden beneath heavy camouflage. He re-joined his flight, briefed them by radio, and then led them with consummate skill through the hail of enemy fire in a low-level attack, destroying five aircraft, while his flight accounted for two others.

"Returning to his base, he volunteered to lead three other aircraft in reconnaissance of Bergamo airfield, an enemy base near Ghedi and one known to be equally well defended. Again ordering his flight to remain out of range of anti-aircraft fire, Lt Knight flew through an exceptionally intense barrage, which heavily damaged his Thunderbolt, to observe the field at minimum altitude. He discovered a squadron of enemy aircraft under heavy camouflage and led his flight to the assault. Returning alone after this strafing, he made ten deliberate passes against the field despite being hit by antiaircraft fire twice more, destroying six fully loaded enemy twin-engined aircraft and two fighters. His skilfully led attack enabled his flight to destroy four other twin-engined aircraft and a fighter plane.

"He then returned to his base in his seriously damaged plane. Early next morning, when he again attacked Bergamo, he sighted an enemy plane on the runway. Again, he led three other American pilots in a blistering low-level sweep through vicious antiaircraft fire that damaged his plane so severely that it was virtually non-flyable. Three of the few remaining enemy

1/Lt Raymond Knight (right) and his crew chief with P-47D Thunderbolt 42-26785 '6D5' named *Oh Johnny* after his wife. This was the aircraft that he flew on his fatal final mission for which, combined with his earlier actions, he was posthumously awarded the Medal of Honor.

twin-engined aircraft at that base were destroyed. Realizing the critical need for aircraft in his unit, he declined to parachute to safety over friendly territory and unhesitatingly attempted to return his shattered plane to his home field. With great skill and strength, he flew homeward until caught by treacherous air conditions in the Apennine Mountains where he crashed and was killed."

The pilots of the 57th Fighter Group also put in another top-level effort, 46 missions going out totalling 106 sorties. This brought a further three losses, once again all the pilots being reported missing. During the day the Marauders of 24 SAAF Squadron undertook what was its last raid, successfully bombing the Montesanto marshalling yards to bring its activity for the month to 343 sorties amounting to 38 missions.

British Casualties	
2 SAAF Sqn	Spitfire IXe RK907 radiator hit by Flak 4m E Ferrara 1105, pilot baled out in Allied lines; Lt P.D.Leppan safe
2 SAAF Sqn	Spitfire IX PV260 strafing NE Ferrara 1325, crashed; Lt T.J.McD.Breakey KiA
237 Sqn	Spitfire IX PT624 left 1800, strafed motor transports at Vigevano, SW Milan, struck a house, crashed; Flg Off N.B.Mansell KiA
3 SAAF Sqn	Spitfire IX EN531 'L' left 0950, shot down by Flak, pilot baled out 1105; Lt N.P.G.Fisher evaded, back on 27 April
601 Sqn	Spitfire IXe MA538 left 1315 to bomb road 2m W Rovigo, hit by Flak, pilot baled out N Lake Comacchio into Allied lines 1415; Sgt M.Hall WiA
601 Sqn	Spitfire IXe PT708 left 1315 to bomb road 2m W Rovigo, hit by Flak, pilot baled out into Allied lines; Wt Off L.Brayshaw safe
601 Sqn	Spitfire IXe MJ618 left 1315 to bomb road 2m W Rovigo, hit by Flak, landing accident 1450; Sgt J.Dawson safe
417 Sqn	Spitfire IX PT474 take-off accident 1220, crashed, Cat III write off; Flg Off G.H.Slack safe
US Casualties	
65th FS/57th FG	P-47D 42-26789 *Dogie II* hit trees while strafing E Reggiolo 0900; 2/Lt Frank O'Rourke KiA [1400]
66th FS/57th FG	P-47D 42-28316 hit by Flak 0900; pilot safe
64th FS/57th FG	P-47D 44-21006 too low when strafing, crashed NW Parma 1250; 1/Lt Albert B.Nickels MiA [14011]
64th FS/57th FG	P-47D 44-21077 belly-landed NE Soragna 1710; 2/Lt Charles E.May returned [14009]
345th FS/350th FG	P-47D 44-33089 lost S Piacenza 1045; 1/Lt Ronald O.Bade returned [14017]
346th FS/350th FG	P-47D 42-26785 '6D5' *Oh Johnny* hit by Flak, crashed 5m NE Lucca; Lt Raymond L.Knight KiA [14088]
446th BS/321st BG	B-25J 43-4074 '27' left 0700 to bomb road bridge at Cavarzere, damaged by Flak, crash-landed at base; 1/Lt Roland B.Jackson and two safe, two WiA, one baled and KiA
German Casualties	
3./NSGr 9	Ju 87D-5 damaged by AA over Po crossing; Hptm Theodor Lindemann/Uffz Heinrich Leinberger safe
2./NSGr 9	Ju 87D-5 crashed nr Thiene; Oblt Friedrich Müller/Obgfr Lothar Görtz KiA

Wednesday-Thursday, 25/26 April 1945

British Casualties	
256 Sqn	Mosquito XII HK162 left 0120, shot down (or crashed) 0215; Flt Sgt R.J.G.Beard/Flt Sgt D.Maddock KiA

Thursday, 26 April 1945

On this day bad weather with heavy rain returned, but already targets were beginning to become scarce. However, during the morning two P-47s of the 66th Squadron, 57th Fighter Group, took off on the unit's 20th mission of the day to strafe various targets. While so doing, 2/Lt Roland Lee's aircraft struck a tree and suffered slight damage, but the two fighters were then attacked shortly after midday by a single Bf 109. This was described as being camouflaged in dark colours, having German crosses, together with yellow bands round the nose. This intrepid pilot made three separate passes at the Thunderbolts, but was then cut off by Lee's wingman, allowing Lee to get in a telling shot. The Messerschmitt was critically hit and the pilot baled out. This was the last engagement to be reported by any MATAF pilot before hostilities ceased. The description of its appearance, especially regarding the yellow nose bands, led the authors of *Air War Italy, 1944-45* to a strong conclusion that this had been an aircraft of 2./NAGr 11.

British Casualties	
7 SAAF Sqn	Spitfire IXe JL377 'B' left 1810, strafed motor transports 3m N Cavarzere, NE Rovigo, shot down by Flak 1845, crashed W Cavarzere; Lt P.B.During POW, persuaded his guards to surrender to him, returned on 30 April

Lt Peter During of 7 SAAF Squadron (third from right) with his German prisoners with whom he returned to Allied lines.

US Claims

66th FS/57th FG	2/Lt Roland E.Lee	P-47D	Bf 109	NE Verona	1310

US Casualties

66th FS/57th FG	P-47D 44-21108 hit by Flak, damaged Cat 2 1350; pilot safe
65th FS/57th FG	P-47D 44-20978 *Balls Out II* lost to Flak over Lake Garda 1400; 1/Lt Truman L.Allen KiA [14010]
64th FS/57th FG	P-47D 44-20341 pilot baled out in bad weather 1430; Capt Paul N.Hall safe
64th FS/57th FG	P-47D 44-33052 pilot baled out in bad weather 1430; Maj Robert A.Barnum safe
1° Gr Caça/350th FG	P-47D 44-21022 '2' strafed a train, lost to Flak, crashed Alessandria 0705; 1° Ten Luis Dornelles KiA

German Casualties

2./NAGr 11	Bf 109 lost in combat; pilot MiA

Friday, 27 April 1945

The Po crossings had proved to be virtually the end of Armee Gruppe C, for in the prevailing conditions all heavy equipment and much else vital to the further prosecution of the war was lost. By 25 April both Allied armies were already across the Po, and at this stage the Italian partisans rose openly, taking control of Genoa and Mantua. These towns, together with Ferrara, Piacenza, La Spezia and others were all in Allied hands by the 27th, 5th Army then closing in on Verona. The remaining German forces now had to rely mainly on their own feet, or on animal transport, but still the fighter-bombers were after them. An attempt to make a stand on the Adige was swept aside, and the Allied advance continued at increasing speed.

US Claims

15th TRS	1/Lt Haylon R.Wood	F-6C	Ju 87	Oberaudorf	1415
15th TRS	2/Lt Maxwell E.Chambers	F-6C			
15th TRS	1/Lt Haylon R.Wood	F-6C	Ju 87	Oberaudorf	1415

US Casualties

346th FS/350th FG	P-47D 44-20978 '603' *Philadelphia Philly-Torrid Tessie*, hit by Flak, belly-landed 6m W Ghedi; 1/Lt Homer J.St Onge picked up by partisans and returned [14089]

German Casualties

2./NSGr 9	Ju 87D E8-EK shot down by fighters over Inn Valley; Obfw Horst Rau/Obgfr Rudolf Ende safe
3./NSGr 9	Ju 87D E8+PL combat with American fighters over Inn Valley, belly-landed; Obfw Herbert Kehrer/Fw Alfons Heck safe

During an armed reconnaissance over the Po Valley P-47D 44-20978 '603' *Torrid Tessie* of the 346th Fighter Squadron, 350th Fighter Group was hit and belly-landed near Ghedi. 1/Lt Homer J.St Onge joined some partisans and was returned safely to Allied lines.

Friday-Saturday, 27/28 April 1945

British Casualties

15 SAAF Sqn	Baltimore V FW723 left 2345 on armed recce Padua-Venice road, exploded after bomb release 16km E of Padua 0035; Lt D.R.Bond survived blinded, picked up by partisans, three KiA

Saturday, 28 April 1945

British Casualties

260 Sqn	Mustang III KH459 shot down probably by Flak 32km SE Padua 1431; Lt D.C.Thompson returned 7 May

US Casualties

347th FS/350th FG	P-47D 42-28303 lost in bad weather, last seen 30m WSW Bologna 1450; 1/Lt Grant W.Bagley MiA [14158]
64th FS/57th FG	P-47D 44-21106 hit by Flak, damaged Cat 2 1230; pilot safe

Sunday, 29 April 1945

British Casualties

3 RAAF Sqn	Mustang KH755 left 1515 on armed recce, hit by Flak, belly-landed on the beach nr Venice; Wt Off D.S.Williamson safe, returned on 2 May
92 Sqn	Spitfire VIII MT559 left 1705 on recce E of Piave river, belly-landed on Portomaggiore l/g; Maj J.E.Gasson DSO DFC safe
249 Sqn	Spitfire IX MH980 left 1640 on armed recce, strafed M/T 10m SE Trieste, believed damaged by explosion of truck load of ammunition, headed for base leaking coolant, crashed 1750; Sgt E.Ramsbotham KiA
260 Sqn	Mustang III HB943 left 1710, shot down probably by Flak 16km ESE Padua 1815; Capt K.Foster returned 2 May
260 Sqn	Mustang III KH573 left 0715 on armed recce Trieste area, began streaming white smoke, did not respond to radio warnings, crashed into the Adriatic; Wt Off A.C.F.Klingner KiA.*
	*Klingner was the last RAAF fighter pilot lost on operations during the Mediterranean War

US Casualties

66th FS/57th FG	P-47D 44-19586 lost in bad weather 1040; 1/Lt Aikens V.Smith KiA [14079]
64th FS/57th FG	P-47D 42-75716 hit by Flak, damaged Cat 2 1200; pilot safe
525th FS/86th FG	P-47D 42-28604 *Dora Pat III* shot down by Flak 5m S Verona 1635; 2/Lt Lawrence L.Johnston POW [9039]

French Casualties

GC 2/6	P-39 hit by Flak nr Carmagnola, landed in liberated territory SE Turin; Maître Friot returned

Monday, 30 April 1945

At Bologna the newly arrived XXII TAC units were quickly bogged down in a sea of mud which prevented further flying. 225 Squadron moved to Villafranca di Verona, where conditions were better, and to here it was followed by 208 Squadron, followed by 8 SAAF Wing on the 30th. In the east other TacR units of 285 Wing were on the move, 318 and 40 SAAF Squadrons going to an airfield at Russi, near Ferrara. 318 Squadron had lost one aircraft during April, but this had crash-landed in an area just being occupied by Allied troops, and the pilot returned safely to the unit.

General von Vietinghoff had by this time realised that further hostilities would achieve nothing beyond the deaths of more of his men as they struggled northwards towards the Alpine passes. On 29 April he began negotiations with Field Marshal Sir Harold Alexander, the supreme commander of the Allied Forces Mediterranean, for the surrender of all his forces, and a ceasefire was agreed on 2 May.

Meanwhile, following the medium bombers, the night-intruders were the next to cease operations. 114 Squadron dispatched 12 Bostons during the night of 29/30 April to attack bridges and other targets of opportunity, and the next night aircraft of 55 Squadron dropped the last bombs on Italian targets when Plt Off M.Vracavic, a Yugoslavian pilot, attacked a road and rail crossing at Gemona at 2230.

Through April the elderly Hurricanes of 6 Squadron continued to be one of the most effective BAF units for inshore anti-shipping work, flying over 300 sorties during the month at a cost of three aircraft. During the final week of April, the 4th Yugoslav Army, closely supported by BAF, broke through north of Istria and reached the River Isonzo. Here it met the advancing spearheads of the British 8th Army from Italy at Monfalcone. This was the end for the Germans, and resistance began to fade away rapidly.

British Casualties

43 Sqn	Spitfire IX PV193 'D' left 1750 on armed recce, engine failed, crash-landed 4-5m SE Motta; Sgt A.S.Crookes safe, back on 9 May
92 Sqn	Spitfire VIII LV752 left 0700, strafed motor transports, hit by ground fire, crash-landed near Consiglio, 12m NE Vittorio Veneto 0820; Flg Off D.A.Stevenson evaded, back on 4 May
250 Sqn	Kittyhawk IV FX638 left 0920 to strafe motor transports in Udine area, shot down by Flak, pilot baled out in Allied lines; Lt H.E.Valentine safe
250 Sqn	Kittyhawk IV FX568 left 0920 to strafe motor transports in Udine area, shot down by Flak, pilot baled out in Allied lines; Flt Sgt D.Evans safe
260 Sqn	Mustang III HB880 hit by Flak over Udine; Lt R.H.Veitch baled in sea for third time in month, rescued next day by HSL
601 Sqn	Spitfire IXe NH231 left 1535, hit by Flak in the Conegliano area, engine damaged, crashed; Flg Off A.G.R.Hallas KiA
601 Sqn	Spitfire IXe PT504 left 1535, hit by Flak, crash-landed near Lake Comacchio; Flg Off T.J.Vose safe
241 Sqn	Spitfire IXE NH298 left 1640 on strafing recce Aviano-Udine, engine cut E Venice, pilot baled out into the Adriatic; Sgt C.R.Roberts rescued by 293 Sqn Catalina
253 Sqn	Spitfire VIII LV730 left 0645 on TacR to Ljubljana, engine cut, crashed into Adriatic off Goli Otok Island 0755; Flg Off W.L.Hindle KiA
93 Sqn	Spitfire HFIX TA806 left 1550, strafed motor transports near Miano, damaged by Flak, Cat II, landed at base; Flg Off J.B.Phillips safe

US Casualties

347th FS/350th FG	P-47D 44-20984 *The Reamer* hit steeple while strafing, crashed nr Possagno 0730; 2/Lt Stephen J.Verne KiA [14157]
1° Gr Caça/350th FG	P-47D 44-20338 'C6' hit by Flak N Lake Garda 0720; 2° Ten Renato Goulart Pereira baled out in Allied lines

Tuesday, 1 May 1945

On 1 May 6 Squadron flew its final mission over the Gulf of Trieste which had something of a comical twist. The four Hurricanes flown by Flt Lt Mould, Plt Off White, Wt Off Curtiss and Flt Sgt Hobbs were briefed to overfly enemy troopships leaving the port of Trieste. After the first pass the leading ship hoisted a white flag only for it to be immediately lowered. However, as the aircraft set up for an attack run, all the ships promptly

began hoisting white flags of surrender as the Hurricanes re-appeared resulting in the squadron claiming sixteen ships captured! 6 Squadron's long war was over. Twenty-five vessels in the Gulf of Trieste surrendered to rocket-firing Hurricanes of 281 Wing, following which few calls were made on the fighters.

Sadly, during the day the commanding officer of 5 SAAF Squadron was hit by Flak for the 22nd time, and on this occasion he was shot down and killed. Maj 'Nobby' Clarke was the last Commonwealth fighter pilot lost in action during the Italian campaign.

Already some of the fighter-bomber units had flown their last sorties, and those which operated on 1 and 2 May flew patrols only, poor weather and lack of targets, together with the pending ceasefire keeping activities to a minimum.

Maj 'Nobby' Clarke became the last Commonwealth fighter pilot killed in action in the Mediterranean when he was shot down near Trieste on 1 May.

British Casualties

5 SAAF Sqn	Mustang IVa KH692 'D' left 1415 on shipping strike Trieste-Grado, wing shot off by Flak 1505 20m W Trieste; Maj H.J.E. Clarke KiA

US Casualties

345th FS/350th FG	P-47D 42-26833 *Rapin Ravin* on armed recce of Udine area, shot down by light Flak NE Gorizia 1045; Maj Edward.J.Gabor, CO 345th FS, KiA [14087]
350th FG	P-47 lost; Maj Edward J.Byron Jr KiA

Wednesday, 2 May 1945

At 1400 German forces in Italy surrendered; all hostilities ceased officially, and the guns fell silent. A few sorties were flown in the next few days, dropping leaflets to German forces north of Genoa where surrender orders had not yet been received. A few of these troops shot at the Allied aircraft involved.

This Croat Saiman 200 was shot down by partisans in Yugoslavia shortly before the German surrender.

During a mission over Yugoslavia the two Spitfires of 7 SAAF Squadron lost were the last SAAF operational casualties of WWII.

British Casualties

7 SAAF Sqn	Spitfire IXc MJ521 engine failure during sweep over Yugoslavia, crash-landed 15m S Oqulin; Lt E.E.Stott picked up by partisans, returned on 6 May
7 SAAF Sqn	Spitfire IXc MH540 shot down by Flak 4m S Zagreb; Lt J.C.G.Logan POW, later released, returned late May

Thursday, 3 May 1945

324 Wing began moving to Rivolto and 244 Wing to Treviso, while 232 Wing moved to Aviano and 3 SAAF Wing to Udine. All units were now ready for operations over southern Germany and Austria, where fighting was still going on. Indeed, on this date the 57th Fighter Group dispatched its first mission over the Alps to this area.

British Casualties

351 Sqn	Spitfire Vc JL238 (borrowed from 352 Sqn) lost flying from Belgrade to base at Zemun, probably flew into Mt Dinara in bad weather; Kapetan Aleksandar Cenić (Sqn CO) MiA

The last raid over Yugoslavia by the Marauders of 25 SAAF Squadron sadly saw one of them shot down near Popovača.

Friday, 4 May 1945
The Marauder lost by 25 SAAF Squadron was the first and last Marauder lost by the squadron to enemy action. The crew were the final Commonwealth airmen killed by enemy action in the Mediterranean theatre.

25 SAAF Sqn	Marauder III HD 667 'P' left 0946 to bomb railway between Popovača and Dugo Selo, hit by Flak 1128, crashed near Zagreb; Lt L.J.van Rooyen and five KiA

The end! A wrecked Tiger tank carries the notice 'Destroyed by DAF' on its turret!

Saturday, 5 May 1945
On 5 May hostilities had ended in most of western Europe as well, and a few days later the war came to its close officially. However, the last two operational missions of the war in Italy were flown after the German surrender. A crew from 13 Squadron skippered by Flg Off Rankin were briefed to fly their Boston to Peretola, Florence, and left Forlì at 1050 arriving 45 minutes later. They were briefed by a senior officer that a pocket of about 200 Germans, probably Waffen SS, with tanks and anti-aircraft guns refused to believe the war was over and they were thought to be 'trigger-happy'. The crew was briefed to find them in a valley in the mountains near Tolmezzo-Pontebba and drop leaflets. On the first attempt on 4 May bad weather in the mountains forced a return so they made another attempt the following day, 5 May. This time they were successful and dropped the leaflets accurately onto the target area and encountered no enemy fire. Several days later Rankin's crew were told that they should count these as operational sorties despite their taking place two days after the war had ended.

Sunday, 6 May 1945
On the 6th the German withdrawal from Slavonica in eastern Slovenia was almost over and that evening all enemy troops north-west of Fiume surrendered.

Monday, 7 May 1945
The next day the Balkan Air Force flew its final sorties after which, for it, the war was over.

Thursday, 10 May 1945
When the war came to an end officially, 324 Wing became the first RAF unit to be based in Austria when on the 10th it began moving to Klagenfurt airfield.

Friday, 11 May 1945
In a portent of the difficult times ahead for the current Allies, three La 7 fighters of the Soviet Air Force 848 IAP led by 2/Lt N.N.Olejnik claimed two Jus shot down in flames in the vicinity of Graz. However, their victim was likely an Anson of the Desert Air Force Communications Flight, that was reported shot down by three 'Yaks', killing the crew.

DAF Comm Flight	Anson XII PH539 attacked by three Russian Yak fighters; force-landed nr Graz and struck tree; Plt Off Mervyn Ross Jacobs and two KiA

Above: A Beaufighter of 252 Squadron over the Acropolis during the victory flypast over Athens on 8 May. Below: Soon after hostilities ended RAF fighters like these Spitfires of 253 Squadron began patrolling the borders with Austria and Yugoslavia as friction with the Soviet-backed communists increased.

INTO THE PEACE

Despite seven days when bad weather had cut operations, April had been a record month, and a few examples can show the level of activity generally achieved. DAF had flown some 21,000 sorties, 3,020 of these being carried out by the 79th Fighter Group, the first time this unit had exceeded 3,000 in a month. Between the 9th and 26th, 300 close-support missions had been flown with exceptionally good results. In 244 Wing 601 Squadron had been particularly successful, claiming five tanks destroyed (including four Tigers) with six more damaged, five other armoured vehicles, plus 14 damaged, 13 guns destroyed and five damaged, 41 motor vehicles and 107 damaged, 12 trailers, 11 motorcycles, together with many other targets.

In 7 SAAF Wing 1 SAAF Squadron flew 670 sorties, claiming 98 vehicles destroyed, and 324 Wing had also been extremely busy. 93 Squadron flew 677 sorties in 154 operations, all of which were fighter-bomber or offensive patrols. 156 direct bomb hits were claimed, at 25% the highest percentage in the wing. 111 Squadron put in 668 sorties, Rover Jacks against artillery at first, spotter aircraft pinpointing the guns before calling in the Spitfires by radio, and then Rover Paddy sorties against the fleeing Axis troops after the 21st. In 43 Squadron 624 sorties were made, 55 buildings being claimed destroyed and 54 partially destroyed, 21 vehicles, 11 rail trucks, and a barge also being claimed, as well as 19 rail cuts, 12 road cuts, a pontoon bridge, and many other targets hit, including tanks, tank transporters and field guns.

With XXII TAC the really busy period had begun somewhat later, but by 26 April 11 SAAF Squadron's Kittyhawks had flown 430 sorties. When hostilities ceased the Brazilian 1º Grupo de Caça had acquitted itself very well, and since its introduction to operations the previous autumn had completed 2,560 sorties, attacking many ground targets, claiming among other things, two German aircraft on the ground, with damage to nine more. One pilot, Flt Lt Martinus Torres, had completed 99 sorties, the highest total for anyone in the unit.

During its eight months with XXII TAC, the 350th Fighter Group had claimed the destruction of prodigious quantities of Axis transport and material. Among the many targets attacked, claims included 3,068 motor transports destroyed, 339 locomotives, 1,270 items of rolling stock, 140 bridges, 890 armoured vehicles, and 288 artillery positions. Unfortunately, the unit's claims against opposing aircraft were fairly low. During its whole period of service in the Mediterranean, 50 were claimed shot down in combat, but a very large proportion of these were claimed earlier, during service in Tunisia and with Coastal Air Force. A further 108 aircraft were claimed destroyed on the ground, and many of these are believed to have been during the period with XXII TAC. In air combat the most successful pilots had been Capt Frank W.Heckenkamp, Capt Kitt R.McMaster Jr, both members of the 347th Squadron, and 2/Lt Richard P.Sulzbach of 346th Squadron, each of whom were credited with three confirmed victories. During the period with XXII TAC Flak damage was suffered very often, and by April eight aircraft were being hit for every 200 sorties flown. Throughout the eight months 53 aircraft had been shot down, or had crash-landed away from base, with another 469 damaged but able to return safely.

Final Orders of Battle of Mediterranean Allied Tactical Air Forces and Associated Units

255, 600 Squadrons	Mosquito XIX
216, 28 SAAF, 44 SAAF Squadrons	Dakota

Headquarters, Mediterranean Allied Air Forces

Desert Air Force
232 Wing

13, 18, 55, 114 Squadrons	Boston III, IV and V
256 Squadron	Mosquito VI

239 Wing

112, 260, 3 RAAF, 5 SAAF Squadrons	Mustang III and IV
250, 450 Squadrons	Kittyhawk IV

244 Wing
92, 145, 601 Squadrons   Spitfire VIII
241, 417 Squadrons   Spitfire IX

253 Wing
454, 500, 15 SAAF Squadrons   Baltimore
654, 655, 663 Squadrons   Auster AOP

285 Wing
208, 225, 318, 40 SAAF Squadrons   Spitfire IX

324 Wing
43, 72, 93, 111 Squadrons   Spitfire IX

3 SAAF Wing
12 SAAF, 21 SAAF, 24 SAAF, 30 SAAF Squadrons   Marauder III

7 SAAF Wing
1 SAAF, 2 SAAF, 4 SAAF, 7 SAAF Squadrons   Spitfire IX

XXII Tactical Air Command
8 SAAF Wing
87, 185, 3 SAAF Squadrons   Spitfire IX
11 SAAF Squadron   Kittyhawk IV

Balkan Air Force
254 Wing
39, 25 SAAF Squadrons   Marauder III
28°, 132° Gruppi   Baltimore V

281 Wing
73, 253, 352 Squadrons   Spitfire V, IX
6, 351 Squadrons   Hurricane IV
10°, 12° Gruppi   P-39
20° Gruppo   Spitfire V

283 Wing
213 Squadron   Mustang III
249 Squadron*   Spitfire IX
16 SAAF, 19 SAAF Squadrons   Beaufighter X
(* attached to 281 Wing)

Mediterranean Allied Coastal Air Force
286 Wing
38 Squadron   Wellington GR
624 Squadron   Walrus

287 Wing
237 Squadron   Spitfire IX
294 Squadron   Walrus, Warwick

Air Headquarters, Greece
337 Wing
335, 336 Squadrons   Spitfire
252 Squadron   Beaufighter X
13 (Hellenic) Squadron   Baltimore

Farewell! Air Marshal Sir Guy Garrod, the RAF C-in-C Mediterranean and Middle East, takes the final salute for the Desert Air Force at the victory flypast at Campoformido on the evening of 28 May 1945.

Air Headquarters, Eastern Mediterranean

32 Squadron	Spitfire IX
680 Squadron	Spitfire XI
	Mosquito XVI
221, 17 SAAF Squadrons	Warwick

Air Headquarters, Gibraltar

458 Squadron	Wellington GR
22 SAAF, 27 SAAF Squadron	Ventura

As the forces began to adjust their way of life to the new peace, initial efforts were directed towards staging a triumphant flypast by Desert Air Force. Carried out on 28 May over Udine, this was led by Lt Col C.S.Margo, DSO, DFC, the commanding officer of 24 SAAF Squadron, and one of the most highly decorated SAAF bomber pilots of the war, who had completed two tours. 8 SAAF Wing returned to take part in this event, so that a very large part of MATAF was involved.

It is worth noting that not included in the flypast were 255 and 256 Squadrons, and most of the rest of the units of XXII Tactical Air Command which might fairly be said to have been the full partners of DAF. These included 57th Fighter Group (64th, 65th and 66th Squadrons), 350th Fighter Group (345th, 346th and 347th Squadrons), the 1º Grupo de Caça, the 47th Bombardment Group (L) (84th, 85th, 86th and 97th Squadrons), and the 57th Bombardment Wing (M) (319th, 321st and 340th Bombardment Groups) plus

Mustang IIIs of 260 Squadron fly in formation over Campoformido during the victory flypast.

the two remaining US night-fighter squadrons (414th and 416th). The photo-reconnaissance and transport aircraft elements of MATAF were also not included. Also left out were the units of the Balkan Air Force and its associates of the Italian Co-Belligerent Air Force.

With the war in Europe at an end, the units of MATAF melted away much more quickly than did those of the tactical air forces in Germany. A few squadrons and groups remained for a little while as part of the occupation forces, but the strong and efficient organisation was soon little more than a memory. The true precursor of all Allied tactical air forces, at least insofar as Desert Air Force was concerned, MATAF and its progenitors had 'set the pace' all the way, providing the model on which other tactical air support was to be based throughout the Allied war fronts.

The long months of trial and error in Africa as the tiny air force with which the British Commonwealth there began the war, grew slowly in strength and efficiency, had frequently been both painful and traumatic. Indeed, it was almost inevitable in the circumstances that the forces in the Mediterranean area should make the mistakes from which they and others would learn. Despite this, a most formidable – and ultimately bat-tle-winning – weapon was forged in the harsh furnace of battle, upon which the armies in the field came to rely and trust. The degree of precision air support provided during the final offensive in Italy had seldom been equalled, while many of the lessons learned there were to prove of great assistance some years later when air power enabled a relatively small United Nations ground force to contain a huge Chinese Commu-nist army in Korea.

The memory of the general public is notoriously short and fickle, and the vagaries of the public relations machine have seldom allowed an even spread of credit where it is due. Not surprisingly, the blanket title of Mediterranean Allied Tactical Air Force did not prove a particularly memorable one, and it slipped swiftly into the mental backwaters of history.

Sadly, those who had served with such distinction in the two tactical air commands set up by the United States Army Air Force, soon found that their achievements were little-known at home, overshadowed by the publicity given to the more glamorous big battalions serving on the major fronts. After all, were they not the hand-maidens of the "D-Day Shirkers" decried by some members of parliament in London at the time of the invasion of Normandy?

For the British, despite this slur, posterity has been kinder – perhaps because for so long the earlier strug-gles in Africa had maintained so important a part of the British Commonwealth effort during the earlier years of the war culminating at El Alamein. For many years after the war the ex-airman who could proudly claim "I served with the Desert Air Force" enjoyed an accolade which almost carried as great a status as "I served during the Battle of Britain".

APPENDIX 1

ALLIED MEDITERANEAN NIGHT-FIGHTER ORGANISATION
JUNE–SEPTEMBER 1944

At the start of June 1944 the Allies had developed a highly effective night-fighter force covering the entire Mediterranean. The air defence sectors covered Palestine, the Nile Delta and the North African coast as far as Algeria as well as the Mediterranean islands and mainland Italy. This Appendix is to outline the deployment of these units from June to September 1944, and the subsequent reductions due to the lack of enemy activity.

In early June 1944 there were six RAF night-fighter squadrons in the Mediterranean, with 46, 153, 255, and 600 Squadrons flying the Beaufighter VIf whilst 256 was equipped with the Mosquito XII and XIII. 108 Squadron flew a mixture of both but its Mosquitos were withdrawn during July. The US 414th, 415th, 416th and 417th Night Fighter Squadrons (NFS) all used Beaufighters. In addition, at the end of May the Spitfire-equipped Gibraltar Defence Flight moved to Algeria as a counter to occasional daytime incursions. It was embedded as C Flight within 256 Squadron and later 153 Squadron. The flight was attached to these night-fighter units that provided administrative and operational support and was disbanded in early September.

The following breakdown highlights the areas of responsibility for the various units and some of the significant movements.

Eastern Mediterranean
Units based in this area were responsible for the defence of the Nile Delta and the vital Suez Canal, Cyprus and Palestine but also conducted some very successful offensive night-fighter and intruder operations over the Aegean.

With its HQ at Idku near Alexandria, 46 Squadron also had detachments at Tocra in Libya and St Jean, Palestine whilst at Idku 108 Squadron maintained a detachment of two Mosquitos to intercept high-altitude intruders. The whole squadron moved there in late July from where it moved to Greece three months later. To rationalise the various dispersed detachments in late July 108's Mosquito crews were transferred to 256 Squadron and four detached Beaufighter crews joined 153 Squadron. The 46 Squadron detachment at Tocra then joined 108 Squadron that was then earmarked to move to Aleppo as part of Force 438. This was to provide the night-fighter defence of the territory of neutral Turkey against the potential threat from overflight by German aircraft. In the event, this operation did not come to fruition. In early August the squadron assumed defence of the Nile Delta in concert with 46 Squadron. This released many of 46's crews for intruder work over the Aegean from a detachment in Cyprus, an activity that a 108 Squadron detachment at Gambut joined in September.

With little activity in the area, in October 108 Squadron moved to Greece and 46 Squadron gradually ran down and disbanded.

Central Mediterranean
Overflying the coast of North Africa from its main base at Reghaia near Algiers, 153 Squadron covered the port and shipping convoys. Further west at La Senia the Mosquitos of 256 Squadron and its Spitfires of C Flight covered Oran and adjacent shipping routes. This squadron's high-performance Mosquitos were also regularly detached east to Reghaia and also to Sardinia to where it moved in mid-August leaving a small element in Algeria. With the lack of threat, 153 Squadron was disbanded in September.

Mediterranean Islands

At the beginning of June 108 Squadron's main base was in Malta, with small detachments of Mosquitos located on Sardinia, Sicily and in Italy, but as outlined above, in late July it concentrated in Egypt. At this time the main night-fighter defence of Sardinia is best described as ad hoc comprising detachments from 108, 153 and 256 Squadrons and the US 414th NFS. The latter also operated detachments from two bases on Corsica supplementing the 417th NFS that were joined in early July by the 415th NFS. The night defences of Sardinia did not achieve an element of permanence until the arrival of 256 Squadron from Algeria in August. Its stay was relatively brief as it moved to Italy late the following month. September also saw the move of the 417th NFS to southern France to where the 415th had already moved following the Allied landings in August. The last dedicated night-fighter unit in the Mediterranean islands, the 414th NFS that moved to Italy in mid October.

Mainland Italy

On 1 June 255 Squadron was based at Foggia Main, with a detachment at Grottaglie as part of 323 Wing, 242 Group flying defensive patrols against Axis reconnaissance aircraft and night-attack Ju 87s. It also conducted regular intruder operations over Yugoslavia, including support to the RAF's night-mining campaign against traffic on the River Danube. No 255 was supplemented in early September by the arrival of ten crews from the disbanding 153 Squadron. These helped greatly as 255 Squadron was now maintaining an extensive network of detachments to cover south and central Italy.

The west coast of Italy was covered during this period by 600 Squadron based at Marcianise, near Naples though it too had several detachments. In June and early July the area was also covered by the 415th NFS from Pomigliano before it moved to Corsica, and the 416th NFS that also maintained detachments at Tre Cancello and Tarquinia. The 415th soon moved on but the 416th NFS remained in Italy moving north to Rosignano on the Tuscan coast on 1 September and on to Pisa a month later by which time the Mosquitos of 256 Squadron had arrived at Foggia on the east coast.

BRITISH AND COMMONWEALTH PERSONNEL AND THEIR UNITS

Baldwin, Flt Sgt E.W., 46 Sqn 12

Baldwin, Flt Sgt F.W.K., 46 Sqn 269, 271

Baldwin, Lt Cdr G.C., 4 Naval Fighter Wing 135

Balfour, Sqn Ldr T., attached 147ᵃ Sq RM 40, 53

Ball, Wt Off G., 47 Sqn 80

Ball, Flt Lt R.H., 73 Sqn 355

Ballantine, Plt Off P.S., 185 Sqn 180

Bamberger, Flt Lt C.S., 243 Sqn 126

Bamford, Flg Off R.A., 185 Sqn 417

Bamkin, Flt Lt E.G., 454 Sqn 11

Banks, Sgt A., 112 Sqn 238, 239

Banks, Sub Lt R., 881 Sqn 221, 222

Banner, Flt Lt F.S., 145 Sqn 264

Bannister, Sgt D.V., 603 Sqn 276

Bant, Sgt A.P., 12 SAAF Sqn 377

Barber, Plt Off G., 94 Sqn 309

Barker, Flt Lt F.R., 107 MU 196

Barnard, Flt Sgt D.T., 459 Sqn 12

Barnby, Lt Col M., 12 SAAF Sqn 161, 162

Barnes, Flt Lt D.S., 18 Sqn 160

Barnes, Flt Sgt N.E.J., 39 Sqn 130

Barnes, Flt Sgt R., 293 Sqn 284

Barnes, Sgt R.H., 260 Sqn 266

Barnett, Plt Off C.G., 38 Sqn 91

Barnett, Sqn Ldr J.S., 284 Sqn 134

Barnwell, Capt R.J., 1 SAAF Sqn 290

Barrett, Flt Sgt A.F., 114 Sqn 366

Barrett, Capt E.A., 16 SAAF Sqn 112, 113

Barrett, Flg Off F.J., 213 Sqn 432, 433

Barrett, Flg Off J.G., 252 Sqn 33

Barrett, Sub Lt J.G., 899 Sqn 216

Barrett, Flt Sgt R.A., 252 Sqn 151, 184

Barrett, Wt Off R.J., 47 Sqn 85

Barrett, Sgt T.J., 227 Sqn 24, 32, 43

Barrington, Flt Lt C.J., 600 Sqn 319

Barter, AF (E) S.T.C., HMS *Hunter* 225

Bartholomew, Lt D.V., 24 SAAF Sqn 266

Bartlett, Flg Off D.C., 600 Sqn 246

Barton, Sgt L.J., 252 Sqn 34, 78

Bary, Wg Cdr R.E., 244 Wing 348, 415, 416, 417, 419

Basso, Sgt D.V., 43 Sqn 339

Basson, Lt A.L., 7 SAAF Sqn 36, 38, 339

Bateson, Plt Off F.J., 33 Sqn 76

Batley, Lt, 21 SAAF Sqn 164

Battiste, Flt Sgt C.T.W., 46 Sqn 272, 273

Baxter, Wt Off L.J., 417 Sqn 255

Bayliss, Plt Off K.A., 208 Sqn 117

Bayly, Wt Off F.P., 454 Sqn 23

Bayly, Sqn Ldr R.H., 3 RAAF Sqn 140

Bays, Flt Sgt H.J., 46 Sqn 272, 273

Bazell, Flg Off H.E., 38 Sqn 34

Beach, Sgt R.W., 227 Sqn 103

Beard, Flt Sgt R.J.G., 256 Sqn 436

Beare, Flg Off B.J., 227 Sqn 46, 60, 61, 64

Beasly, Flg Off C., 92 Sqn 403

Beaton, Sqn Ldr D.C., 454 Sqn 95, 121

Beaumont, Flg Off G., 600 Sqn 185, 190, 235, 253, 330

Beaverbrook, Lord, Minister of Aircraft Production 20

Begbie, Lt F.W., 16 SAAF Sqn 125, 126

Begg, Lt C.G., 5 SAAF Sqn 304, 307, 323

Begg, Flt Sgt S., 76 OTU 89

Bell, Sgt A., 72 Sqn 294

Bell, Wt Off C.D., 127 Sqn 93

Bell, Sgt D.H., 213 Sqn 253, 262, 281, 328

Bell, Wt Off D.M., 87 Sqn 318

Bell, Lt G.R., 24 SAAF Sqn 95, 101

Bell, Maj J.E., 16 SAAF Sqn 102

Bell, Flt Sgt M.W., 46 Sqn 43

Bell, Lt R.F., 2 SAAF Sqn 336

Bennee, Lt P.W., 5 SAAF Sqn 181, 251

Bennett, Sqn Ldr D.B., 227 Sqn 96, 100

Bennett, Plt Off D.G., 241 Sqn 181

Bennie, Sgt J.H., 237 Sqn 418

Bennison, Sgt H.J., 243 Sqn 123

Beresford, Grp Capt T.B. de la P., 324 Wing 390

Bereżecki, Flt Lt W., 318 Sqn 198

Berg, Flt Sgt E.C., 272 Sqn 381

Berger, Lt A., 24 SAAF Sqn 101

Bernard, Flt Sgt P., 252 Sqn 43

Bernays, R.H., Member of Parliament, UK 349

Berry, Lt R.B., 16 SAAF Sqn 291

Bevan, Maj T., 208 Sqn 348

Bezencenet, Sqn Ldr P.M., 208 Sqn 269

Bezuidenhout, Lt J.N.H., 12 SAAF Sqn 207

Bignell, Flt Sgt P.G., 32 Sqn 240

Bignold, Flt Sgt T.R., 227 Sqn 96, 100

Billing, Wt Off W.H., 272 Sqn 240

Birch, Plt Off S., 114 Sqn 377

Bird, Flg Off G., 38 Sqn 56

Birtle, Sub Lt J., 809 Sqn 271

Blaauw, Lt Col J.P., 208 Sqn 348

Black, Flt Lt A.O., 293 Sqn 266

Black, Lt G.H., 19 SAAF Sqn 305

Blackburn, Sqn Ldr/Wg Cdr J.R., 46 Sqn/19 SAAF Sqn 93, 207

Blacklaws, Lt A.R.D., 19 SAAF Sqn 429

Blackwell, Wt Off G.W., 293 Sqn 316

Blackwell, Lt Col R.A., 24 SAAF Sqn 141

Blackwood, Flg Off W.F., 21 SAAF Sqn 381

Blair, Flg Off D.A., 6 Sqn 359

Blake, Sgt B.H.L., 227 Sqn 56

Bliss, Lt W.J.K., 41 SAAF Sqn 22

Blomley, Plt Off L.D., 454 Sqn 23

Bloomer, Lt Cdr A.W., 807 Sqn 235

Blow, Flt Sgt A.T., 603 Sqn 109

Bluck, Lt F., 17 SAAF Sqn 94

Bluett, Sqn Ldr A.P.Q., 112 Sqn 188, 395

Blumer, Flt Lt G.M., 450 Sqn 383

Blundell, Sgt/Flt Sgt E., 255 Sqn 151, 392

Blythe, Sgt P.J., 253 Sqn 290

Board, Flt Sgt R.J., 256 Sqn 322

Boardman, Flt Lt H.S., 153 Sqn 198

Boast, Lt D.G., 11 SAAF Sqn 420

Bodley, Lt D.M., 16 SAAF Sqn 357

Boffin, Flt Sgt C.A., 47 Sqn/19 SAAF Sqn 98, 207

Bond, Flg Off A.G., 47 Sqn 72

Bond, Lt D.R., 15 SAAF Sqn 438

Bond, Sqn Ldr H.StG., 46 Sqn 146

Boon, Sgt W.H., 252 Sqn 78, 80, 92

Booth, Flg Off R.B., 255 Sqn 124

Booyens, Lt J.G., 4 SAAF Sqn 217

Borcherds, Lt K.B., 2 SAAF Sqn 161

Borgen, Lt T.F., 17 SAAF Sqn 131

Borland, Lt E.R., 5 SAAF Sqn 303

Bosch, Lt D.C., 7 SAAF Sqn 313

Bosch, Lt J., 6 Sqn 169

Boshoff, Lt C.G., 94 Sqn 306

Bosman, Lt Col A.C., 7 SAAF Wing 243, 253

Boswell, Wt Off A., 46 Sqn 42, 58

Botherstone, Plt Off A.R., 213 Sqn 167

Bothma, Lt C.C., 12 SAAF Sqn 364

Bottle, Flt Sgt K.C., 46 Sqn 108, 257

Bottomley, Sgt E.B., 458 Sqn 12

Boughey, Lt L.E., 16 SAAF Sqn 340

Bounds, Wt Off W.C., 450 Sqn 423

Bouwer, Flt Sgt, 15 SAAF Sqn 90

Bowell, Wt Off D.W., 104 Sqn 86

Bowen, Sgt/Flt Sgt J.N., 603 Sqn 66, 72, 103

Bowen, Plt Off W.H., 38 Sqn 85

Bowles, Lt G.A., 24 SAAF Sqn 93, 101

Boxall, Wt Off S.E., 154 Sqn 123

Boy, Lt V., 92 Sqn 142

Boyd, Grp Capt A.H., 281 Wing 200

Boyd, Lt C.W.L., 1 SAAF Sqn 141, 256, 317, 348, 349

Boyd, Lt D.N., 5 SAAF Sqn 407

Boyd, Plt Off W.D.C., 38 Sqn 99

Boyer, Lt H.F.P., 7 SAAF Sqn 28

Boyle, Flt Lt A.R., 154 Sqn 91, 157

Boyle, Maj B.J.L., 4 SAAF Sqn 188

Boys, Lt N.G., 40 SAAF Sqn 192

Brace, Flg Off/Flt Lt F.G., 19 SAAF Sqn 281, 390

Bradford, Flg Of K.N., 252 Sqn 104

Bradley, Flt Lt A.J., 46 Sqn 273

Braill, Lt F.W., 21 SAAF Sqn 251

Braithwaite, Capt/Maj H., 24 SAAF Sqn/12 SAAF Sqn 101, 336

Brand, Lt A.McG., 250 Sqn 264

Brand, Flg Off/Flt Lt J.C., 6 Sqn 325, 359, 421

Brander, Sub Lt T.L.M., 881 Sqn 260

Bray, Wt Off F.R.W., 221 Sqn 194, 232

Bray, Flg Off H.J., 451 Sqn 142, 195

Brayshaw, Wt Off L., 601 Sqn 436

Breakey, Lt T.J.McD., 2 SAAF Sqn 436

Brebner, Capt/Maj D.M., 1 SAAF Sqn/7 SAAF Sqn 252, 426

Breet, 2/Lt J.A., 15 SAAF Sqn 94

Bremner, Flt Lt F.C., 73 Sqn 140

Bremner, Lt N., 7 SAAF Sqn 366, 418

Bremner, Lt T.D., 232 Sqn 123

Bretherton, Flg Off B.A., 255 Sqn 154, 155, 186, 192, 198

Brettell, Sgt D.G.M., 250 Sqn 352

Brewer, Sub Lt J.H., 807 Sqn 281

Brewer, Flg Off J.R., 600 Sqn 156, 237, 245

Brewis, Flt Lt A.G., 19 SAAF Sqn 250

Briand, Wt Off/Plt Off A.L., 145 Sqn 304, 357

Brichard, Lt C.J.P., 12 SAAF Sqn 335, 336

Brick, Plt Off J.V., 272 Sqn 353

Brierley, Sgt L.W., 213 Sqn 252

Brierley, Sub Lt R., 882 Sqn 213

Briggs, Lt R., 249 Sqn 144, 199

Brigham, Flt Sgt J.M., 243 Sqn 123

Briginshaw, Flt Sgt W., 46 Sqn 271, 275

Brink, Capt G.S., 24 SAAF Sqn 152

Brinton, Maj C.R., 15 SAAF Sqn 76

Bristol, Lt A.I., 4 SAAF Sqn 174

Brittain, Sub Lt G.H., 899 Sqn 216, 228, 281

Brittain, Sub Lt R., 881 Sqn 224, 228

Britton, Sgt B.C., 145 Sqn 259

Brittorous, Maj Gen F.G.R., 234 Inf Brigade 30

Brokensha, Lt P.B., 41 SAAF Sqn 159

Brooks, Flg Off J.W., 249 Sqn 78

Brooks, Wt Off K.O., 87 Sqn 370

Brooks, Sgt N.T., 450 Sqn 287

Brooksbank, Lt R.O.D., 24 SAAF Sqn 108

Broomfield, Sgt J.C., 462 Sqn 38

Brown, Plt Off B.W., 450 Sqn 411

Brown, Flt Sgt F.J., 454 Sqn 100

Brown, Sgt/Flt Sgt G.A., 227 Sqn 24, 25, 98

Brown, Sgt J., 185 Sqn 242

Brown, Mr J.D., Naval Historical Branch 208, 209

Brown, Sqn Ldr J.H., 6 Sqn 206, 235

Brown, Lt L.H., 1 SAAF Sqn 151

Brown, Flt Lt P.G., 178 Sqn 75

Brown, Lt R., 19 SAAF Sqn 391

Brown, Flt Sgt R.E., 46 Sqn 104

Brown-Gaylord, Flt Lt H., 145 Sqn 276

Browne, Flg Off J.P.J., 39 Sqn 153

Bruck, Sgt H.E., 46 Sqn 42, 54, 56

Brummer, Lt M.J.W., 14 Sqn 140

Brunt, Flg Off P.D.W., 256 Sqn 228, 344

Brunton, Capt W.V., 4 SAAF Sqn
386, 420

Buchan, Sgt E.P., 213 Sqn 411

Buchanan, Flg Off G.M., 185 Sqn
232

Buchanan, Wg Cdr J.K., 227 Sqn
84, 86, 87, 95

Budd, Flt Sgt W.C., 227 Sqn 24,
25, 29, 36

Buddell, Lt J.C., 7 SAAF Sqn 311

Bull, Sqn Ldr A.E., 500 Sqn 344

Bull, Flg Off C.F., 38 Sqn 101

Bulley, Lt L.N., 1 SAAF Sqn 389

Bullock, Flt Sgt F., 134 Sqn 18

Bullock, Flg Off J., 38 Sqn 13

Bulman, Sgt J.D., 252 Sqn 34

Bundock, Flt Sgt W.H., 87 Sqn 317

Bunn, Flt Sgt F.S., 603 Sqn 109

Bunting, Wt Off B., 93 Sqn 181

Bunting, Flg Off W.E.C., 72 Sqn 287

Bunyan, Flt Sgt/Plt Off J.E., 38 Sqn
92, 99

Bunyon, Plt Off R.W., 238 Sqn 11

Burden, Flt Lt R.H., 450 Sqn 240,
309

Burditt, Flg Off H.F., 293 Sqn 294,
295

Burger, Capt P.C.R., 4 SAAF Sqn
174

Burgess, Sgt A., 603 Sqn 82, 89

Burgess, Flg Off F.G., 272 Sqn 246

Burke, Flt Lt M.L., 243 Sqn 126

Burke, Sqn Ldr P.L., 600 Sqn 244,
245

Burl, Lt/Capt R.P., 7 SAAF Sqn/41
SAAF Sqn 32, 33, 34, 139, 159

Burleton, Wt Off J.L., 108 Sqn 272

Burls, Lt J.H., 243 Sqn 126

Burnard, Lt A.H., 15 SAAF Sqn 112

Burnard, Lt J.F.L., 11 SAAF Sqn 363

Burnet, Flt Lt J.B., 683 Sqn 41

Burnett, Lt A.E., 5 SAAF Sqn 323

Burnett, Flt Sgt T.W., 255 Sqn 124

Burniaux, Lt Col F.J., 12 SAAF
161, 228

Burrell, Flt Sgt W.M., 500 Sqn 403

Burrow, Wt Off F., 227/603 Sqn
56, 66

Busby, Wt Off W., 89 Sqn 34

Butler, Sqn Ldr I.B., 252 Sqn 150,
190

Butler, Wt Off R.T., 46 Sqn 269,
271, 273

Butterworth, Sgt W.H., 213 Sqn
281

Buxton, Plt Off D., 227 Sqn 132

Cail, Sgt F.A., 293 Sqn 330

Calder, Sub Lt G., 879 Sqn 216,
226, 228

Caldow, Flg Off L.A., 459 Sqn 95

Calveley, Flt Lt G.H., 19 SAAF
Sqn 239

Cameron, Lt D.M., 55 Sqn 242

Campbell, Lt F.R., 16 SAAF Sqn
208

Campbell, Sqn Ldr the Rev G.A.G.,
RAF 271

Campbell, Flg Off I.C., 55 Sqn 140

Campbell, J.F., Member of
Parliament, UK 349

Campbell, Lt R.R., 19 SAAF Sqn
342

Campbell, Flt Sgt S.S., 39 Sqn 122,
180, 250

Canter, Sub Lt P.J.M., 882 Sqn 213

Carlyle, Flt Lt J.F., 237 Sqn 424

Carr, Flt Sgt S., 46 Sqn 271

Carrick, Lt B.W.G., 253 Sqn 262

Carrick, Flt Lt G., 213 Sqn 37

Carruthers, Flt Lt J.D.R.B., 18 Sqn
192

Carter, Air Cdre Guy L., SASO of
the Balkan Air Force 168

Carter, Lt H.A., 4 SAAF Sqn 314

Carter, Sgt R.H., 227 Sqn 46

Cary, Sub Lt D.A., 899 Sqn 220

Cassidy, Lt A.J., 223 Sqn 161

Cassidy, Sqn Ldr E., 92 Sqn/72
Sqn 419

Catherine, Lt L.F.H., 16 SAAF Sqn
333

Cathro, Flt Sgt D.D., 39 Sqn 294

Catton, Lt Col E.G., 19 SAAF Sqn
249, 250

Caulfield, Flt Sgt T., 605 Sqn 282,
283, 284

Ceuppens, Maj C.J., 12 SAAF Sqn
378

Chamberlin, Wt Off R.E., 256 Sqn
382

Chambers, Sgt E.H., 46 Sqn 11

Champreys, Flt Lt B., 208 Sqn 169

Chandler, Flg Off L.A., 39 Sqn 164

Chapman, Flt Sgt A.A., 111 Sqn
344, 396

Chapman, Flt Sgt E.G., 46 Sqn
271, 275

Chapman, Lt H.G., 4 SAAF Sqn
164

Chapman, Maj W.J.B., 41 SAAF
Sqn 19

Chappell, Flg Off S., 213 Sqn 174,
200

Charles, Sgt A.R., 601 Sqn 390

Charles, Flt Lt I.D., 39 Sqn 153

Charles, Plt Off L., 46 Sqn 53, 70,
93

Charles, Sgt R., 600 Sqn 192, 216,
288

Chase, Sqn Ldr J.H., 73 Sqn 150

Cheesbrough, Sgt G., 260 Sqn 273

Cheesman, Lt A.E.F., 7 SAAF Sqn
31–33

Chessman, Lt D.G.C., 40 SAAF
Sqn 290

Chenery, Flt Sgt J.T., 600 Sqn 152

Chiazzari, Lt B.N., 213 Sqn 384

Chin, Maj D.E., 24 SAAF Sqn 106

Chippendale, Flt Sgt A., 19 SAAF
Sqn 240

Chrystall, Flt Lt C., 243 Sqn 117

Chumak, Flg Off W., 73 Sqn 287

Churchill, Maj R.F.E.S., MACMIS
168

Churchill, Winston S., Prime
Minister of United Kingdom 20,
29, 77, 168, 170

Clappison, Sgt K., 111 Sqn 342

Clark, Wt Off A., 3 RAAF Sqn 409

Clark, Lt B., 24 SAAF Sqn 243

Clark, Lt C.H., 16 SAAF Sqn 96

Clark, Flg Off E.C., 32 Sqn 298

Clark, Plt Off G.G., 112 Sqn 306

Clark, Plt Off J.D., 252 Sqn 190

Clark, Sgt P.J., 73 Sqn 260

Dowden, Lt W.A., 41 SAAF Sqn/1 SAAF Sqn 76, 77

Dowling, Sgt A.A., 213 Sqn 270

Downer, Lt G.H.W., 16 SAAF Sqn 217

Downes, Flg Off S., 18 Sqn 322

Doyle, Flg Off F.A., 417 Sqn 431

Doyle, Sgt J., 92 Sqn 396

Doyle, Sqn Ldr J.C., 450 Sqn 415, 423, 424

Drake, Sgt C.S., 18 Sqn 367

Drake, Sgt H., 223 Sqn 161

Driver, Lt D.J., 16 SAAF Sqn 333

Drown, Sgt P.A., 153 Sqn 216

Dryden, Flt Lt A.E., 249 Sqn 262, 264

Dryden, Lt A.T., 454 Sqn 92

Duberry, Flt Sgt C.D., 38 Sqn 58

Duchen, Lt M., 43 Sqn 275

Duckitt, Capt H van B., 31 SAAF Sqn 113

Duffey, Wt Off G., 6 Sqn 317

Duffie, Sgt I., 601 Sqn 336

Duffy, Flg Off W.J.A., 454 Sqn 418

Duke, Sqn Ldr N.F., 145 Sqn 119, 120, 234, 244, 264

Dummett, Lt Q.R., 94 Sqn 292

Duncan, Wt Off G.W., 458 Sqn 202

Duncan, Wt Off J.S., 112 Sqn 342

Duncan, Sgt W.H., 227 Sqn 42, 53

Dundas, Grp Capt H.S.L., 244 Wing 316, 415

Dunford, Flt Sgt J.B., 600 Sqn 318

Dunkerley, Capt R.K., 40 SAAF Sqn 117

Dunn, Flg Off/Flt Lt D.C., 154 Sqn/72 Sqn 126, 287

Dunning, Maj E.K., 3 SAAF Sqn 287

du Plessis, Lt J.H., 40 SAAF Sqn 184

du Preez, Lt H.T.R., 3 SAAF Sqn 99

During, Lt P.B., 7 SAAF Sqn 431, 432

Dusiecki, Flg Off R., 318 Sqn 336

Du Toit, Capt, SA Army 103

du Toit, Lt F.M., 145 Sqn 156

Du Toit, Lt L.W.M., 16 SAAF Sqn 103

du Toit, Lt P.J., 7 SAAF Sqn 305

du Toit, Col S.F., 8 SAAF Wing 258

Dutton, Lt H.C., 12 SAAF Sqn 167

Dutton, Flg Off K., 255 Sqn 382

Dyason, Lt D.A., 16 SAAF Sqn 390, 396

Dyer, Lt H.R., 24 SAAF Sqn 106

Eacott, Flt Sgt W.A., 603 Sqn 66

Eadon, Lt Cdr H.D.B., 809 Sqn 268, 269, 280

East, Lt, 12 SAAF Sqn 262

East, Sgt E.E., 243 Sqn 126

East, Flg Off W.W., 459 Sqn 350

Easterbee, Flg Off A.E., 19 SAAF Sqn/272 Sqn 285, 325, 414

Eaton, Grp Capt B.A., 239 Wing 188

Eaton, Lt B.J., 4 SAAF Sqn 317

Edbrooke, Sgt C.R., 38 Sqn 25

Edgar, Flt Sgt J.R., 603 Sqn 87, 88, 110

Edge, Flg Off R., 417 Sqn 345

Edmonds, Flt Lt J.T., 3 RAAF Sqn 414

Edwards, Wt Off A.G., 43 Sqn 420

Edwards, Flg Off D.L., 272 Sqn 289

Egner, Capt R.C., 3 SAAF Sqn 423

Eid, Flg Off G.E., 37 Sqn 306

Ekbery, Flg Off J.S., 145 Sqn 156

Eliav, LAC E., 227 Sqn 95

Eliot, Wg Cdr H.W., 256 Sqn 273, 277, 279, 378

Elliot, Sqn Ldr J.F.W., 55 Sqn 383

Elliot, AVM W., AOC Balkan Air Force 113, 114, 118, 128

Elliot-Wilson, Lt E.G., 21 SAAF Sqn 146

Elliott, Flt Lt G.P., 213 Sqn 360, 362

Elliott, Wt Off F., 14 Sqn 262

Ellis, Flt Sgt A.J., 111 Sqn 353

Ellis, Flg Off A.O., 450 Sqn 327

Ely, Wt Off J.S., 256 Sqn 379

Embling, Lt K.O., 7 SAAF Sqn 386, 403

Emmett, Lt T., 15 SAAF Sqn 87, 89

Emmett, Flg Off B.R., 114 Sqn 335

Encott, Flt Sgt W.A., 603 Sqn 65

Endler, Capt E.A., 15 SAAF Sqn 29

Engelbrecht, 2/Lt D.C., 11 SAAF Sqn 397

English, Flg Off D.G., 241 Sqn 139

English, Flg Off R.M., 208 Sqn 421

Enslin, Capt B.G.S., 5 SAAF Sqn 348

Etchell, Flt Sgt, 15 SAAF Sqn 92, 93

Etchells, Sgt K., 241 Sqn 194

Euler, Flg Off R., 47 Sqn 98

Evans, Sgt A.G., 114 Sqn 379

Evans, Plt Off C.W., 454 Sqn 418

Evans, Flt Sgt D., 250 Sqn 439

Evans, Flg Off D.D.S., 253 Sqn 290

Evans, Flg Off E., 32 Sqn 312

Evans, Flt Sgt J.A., 252 Sqn 43

Evans, Lt K.M., 807 Sqn 212, 213

Evans, Wt Off L.C., 73 Sqn 260

Evans, Flt Sgt L.J., 227 Sqn/19 SAAF Sqn 132, 249

Evans, Wt Off R.C., 32 Sqn 296

Everett, Flt Sgt L.A., 227 Sqn 104

Ewing, Wt Off H., 600 Sqn 152

Fairbairn, Flt Lt J.H., 213 Sqn 253, 255

Fairburn, Lt, 15 SAAF Sqn 76, 87, 88

Fairfield, Sgt W.H., 47 Sqn 85

Farfan, Flt Sgt F.W., 123 Sqn 22

Faria, Wt Off R., 3 RAAF Sqn 266

Farley, Sgt/Flt Sgt S.W., 213 Sqn 289, 433

Farmer, Flt Sgt K.R., 47 Sqn 58, 94

Farrell, Lt D.P., 1 SAAF Sqn 260

Farrell, Lt M.P., 55 Sqn 352

Farrow, Flt Sgt J., 134 Sqn 14

Farrow, Sqn Ldr L.W., 111 Sqn 381

Faulkner, Sqn Ldr K.L., 252 Sqn 28, 32

Faure, Maj/Lt Col J.H., 4 SAAF Sqn/324 Wing 188, 410, 411

Fawkner-Corbett, Plt Off R.V., 272 Sqn 318

Feeny, Plt Off D.P., 250 Sqn 306

Feight, Flg Off C.B., 227 Sqn 24, 25

Fell, Lt Cdr M.F., 800 Sqn 282

Fenton, Flt Sgt J., 227 Sqn 97

Fenton, Sgt R.H., 72 Sqn 246

Fereday, Flg Off C., 458 Sqn 202

Ferguson, Wt Off N.S., 603 Sqn 65, 68

Ferguson, Sgt R.A.W., 227 Sqn 86

Ferreira, Lt J.A., 12 SAAF Sqn 167

Fewster, Capt L.F.L., 30 SAAF Sqn 387

Field, Flt Sgt A.T., 3 RAAF Sqn 140, 152

Field, Lt R.G., 145 Sqn 240

Fielding, Sgt/Plt Off H.C., 93 Sqn 239, 355

Filby, Lt J.E., 5 SAAF Sqn 434

Filson-Young, Wg Cdr W.D.L., 47 Sqn 92

Finbow, Flt Sgt W.E., 47 Sqn 68

Findlay, Flg Off B., 603 Sqn 87

Finney, Flt Lt F., 55 Sqn 367

Firman, Flt Sgt D.E., 213 Sqn 248, 255, 281, 306

Fisher, Flt Sgt/Wt Off D., 255 Sqn 120, 246

Fisher, Lt D.R., 7 SAAF Sqn 32, 33, 38, 40

Fisher, Lt H.M., 1 SAAF Sqn 294

Fisher, Lt N.P.G., 3 SAAF Sqn 436

Fisher, Flg Off R.R., 93 Sqn 239

Fitzgerald, Plt Off E.U., 93 Sqn 434

Flack, Lt R.H.R., 5 SAAF Sqn 370

Flaherty, Sgt J.E., 203 Sqn 41

Fletcher, Flg Off J.B., 47 Sqn 57, 72

Flynn, Lt M., 2 SAAF Sqn 334

Foden, Flt Lt F.H., 272 Sqn 269

Foley, Sub Lt A.B., 809 Sqn, att 145 Sqn, 164, 290

Folkard, Sqn Ldr L.F., 454 Sqn 21, 22

Ford, Sub Lt A.C.B., 807 Sqn 281

Ford, Wt Off K.A.L., 213 Sqn 165

Ford-Hutchison, Plt Off W.R., 256 Sqn 382

Forrester, Flt Sgt J., 46 Sqn 273

Forster, Sgt W.B., 145 Sqn 403

Forsythe, Sqn Ldr C.R.A., 216 Sqn 31

Foskett, Sqn Ldr R.G., 94 Sqn 107, 117, 199, 298, 299

Foster, Flg Off C.H.A., 89 Sqn 42, 43

Foster, Sgt J., 603 Sqn 104

Foster, Capt K., 260 Sqn 438

Foster, AVM R.M., AOC Desert Air Force 390

Fountain, Flt Sgt R.E.R., 3 RAAF Sqn 126

Fowkes, Sgt G., 227 Sqn 58

Fowler, Flt Sgt L.A., 55 Sqn 435

Fowler, Flt Lt C.W., 252 Sqn 110, 266

Fox, Wt Off A.L., 249 Sqn 123

Foxcroft, Lt, 12 SAAF Sqn 224

Foxley, Sgt W.H., 603 Sqn 152, 180

Foxley-Norris, Wg Cdr C., 603 Sqn 276

Frampton, Flg Off L.A., 72 Sqn 391

Franck, Lt E.D.K., 4 SAAF Sqn 234

Franken, Lt C.J., 19 SAAF Sqn 282, 290

Franks, Flg Off R.D., 145 Sqn 411

Frearson, Sub Lt D.L.W., 881 Sqn 260

Freckelton, Flg Off H., 103 MU 15

Freeman, Sgt G.H., 47 Sqn 68

Freeman, Maj G.H.C., 25 SAAF Sqn 316

Freeman, Lt H.P., 1 SAAF Sqn 216

Freeman, Flt Sgt P., 250 Sqn 351

Freer, Flt Lt T.StB., 272 Sqn 25, 296

Frewer, Plt Off A.V., 232 Sqn 201

Friis, Wt Off G.H., 601 Sqn 287, 389

Frolich, Capt G., 24 SAAF Sqn 101

Frost, Sgt B., 454 Sqn 75

Frost, Flt Sgt W.L., 500 Sqn 338

Frumar, Flg Off N., 600 Sqn 345

Fry, Sub Lt A.O., 809 Sqn 213

Fry, Plt Off S.R., 92 Sqn 306

Fryer, Flt Lt J.M.J., 162 Sqn 26

Fryer, Flt Sgt W.P., 252 Sqn 28, 30, 33

Fuchs, Maj S., 16 SAAF Sqn 298

Fulton, Cpl, attached 147ª Sq RM 53

Funkey, Lt H.T., 12 SAAF Sqn 336

Funnell, Sgt J.V., 250 Sqn 321

Furstenberg, Lt, 15 SAAF Sqn 89

Gale, Flt Lt/Sqn Ldr W.W.B., 451 Sqn 96, 169, 187

Galitzine, Flt Lt E., 72 Sqn 192, 294

Gall, Sgt J.W., 37 Sqn 306

Gallacher, Flt Lt/Sqn Ldr G.M., 293 Sqn/624 Sqn 305, 334

Gantz, Flt Sgt B., 19 SAAF Sqn 220

Gardener, Flt Sgt A.C.A., 46 Sqn 70

Gardner, Sqn Ldr A.G., 613 Sqn 356

Gardner, Flt Sgt C., 46 Sqn 40

Gardner, Lt E., 213 Sqn 414

Gardner, Flg Off J.W., 249 Sqn 335, 336, 414

Garner, Flt Lt B., 92 Sqn 143, 412

Garnham, Plt Off G.L., 241 Sqn 228

Garrod, AM A.G.R., C-in-C RAF Mediterranean and Middle East 402, 446

Garth, Sgt A., 145 Sqn 196, 276

Garton, Wg Cdr G.W., 8 SAAF Wing 411

Garwood, Flg Off R.H., 213 Sqn 120, 255

Gaskell, Flg Off A.R., 18 Sqn 198

Gasson, Maj J.E., 92 Sqn 295, 406, 407, 409, 438

Gater, 2/Lt H.J., 450 Sqn 203

Gaydon, Flt Lt D.L., 272 Sqn 318

Gayner, Wg Cdr J.R.H., 153 Sqn 137

Geater, Lt H.A., 3 SAAF Sqn 99

Geater, Lt R.A., 19 SAAF Sqn 254, 255

Geddes, Flg Off E., 249 Sqn 395

Geere, Maj C.F., 19 SAAF Sqn 290, 298

Gelb, Lt H.R., 30 SAAF Sqn 246

Gelbhauer, Sgt M., 6 Sqn 252

Geldenhuys, Capt M., 3 SAAF Sqn 76, 77

Genillard, Flg Off A., 232 Sqn 142

Geoffrion, Plt Off L.P., 213 Sqn 61

George VI, King, 188

George, Lt C., 41 SAAF Sqn 22

George, Flt Sgt P.A., 238 Sqn 22

Gerrand, Plt Off N.H., 417 Sqn 180

Gibbard, Plt Off A.C., 227 Sqn 56

Gibbings, Lt P.K., 260 Sqn 407

Gibbon, Flt Sgt R.W., 46 Sqn 58, 70

Gibbons, Flt Lt N.J., 418 Sqn 284

Gibbs, Sgt R.W., 114 Sqn 240

Gibson, Plt Off A.D., 417 Sqn 330, 418

Gibson, Sub Lt D.A., 879 Sqn 213

Gibson, Sub Lt R.P., 881 Sqn 213, 260

Gilchrist, Plt Off J.W., 73 Sqn 378, 398

Giles, Sqn Ldr D., 256 Sqn 382

Giles, Plt Off R.M., 603 Sqn 63, 64, 66

Gill, Flt Sgt M.H., 108 Sqn 168

Gill, Sgt R., 241 Sqn 338

Gillham, Flt Lt R.W., 18 Sqn 336

Gittins, Flg Off/Flt Lt E., 227 Sqn 9, 10

Glass, Flt Sgt, 24 SAAF Sqn 98

Glass, Flg Off J.R., 208 Sqn 297

Glen, Plt Off R., 260 Sqn 180

Glynn, Plt Off P.F.L., 227 Sqn 24, 32, 43

Goedhals, Wt Off C.F., 2 SAAF Sqn 377

Golding, Lt C.A., 7 SAAF Sqn 41

Golding, Maj D.W., 73 Sqn 260

Goldman, Flt Lt W.E., 450 Sqn 153

Gooch, Sgt G.E.T., 32 Sqn 289

Goodes, Flt Sgt G.V., 252 Sqn 32

Goodman, 2/Lt A.E., 241 Sqn 122, 183, 184

Goodwin, Plt Off C., 603 Sqn 262

Goodwin, Sgt D.C., 112 Sqn 199

Goodwin, Flt Sgt I.D., 272 Sqn 304

Goodyear, Flt Sgt N., 256 Sqn 382

Gordon, Sgt A.W., 249 Sqn 200

Gorham, Plt Off D.J., 72 Sqn 342

Gosling, Flt Sgt R.T., 603 Sqn 105

Goss, Flt Sgt J.G., 600 Sqn 184

Gould, Flt Sgt C.J., 603 Sqn 105

Gould, Capt D.L., 15 SAAF Sqn 435

Gould, Flt Lt G.R., 241 Sqn 125, 126

Gow, Flt Sgt A., 603 Sqn 89

Gow, Lt I.J., 11 SAAF Sqn 368

Gowan, Sub Lt R.A., 879 Sqn 141, 226

Graham, Flg Off A.M., 72 Sqn 422

Graham, Flt Sgt H.W., 108 Sqn 272

Graham, Sub Lt L.D., 807 Sqn 235

Graham, Wt Off R.F., 46 Sqn 269, 271, 273, 274, 275

Graham, Wt Off R.J., 55 Sqn 366

Graham, Flt Lt T.C., 47 Sqn 63

Grainger, Sgt/Flt Sgt C.P., 252 Sqn 55, 133

Grandy, Grp Capt J., OC No. 210 Group 19

Gray, Plt Off G., 111 Sqn 357

Gray, Plt Off H.B., 253 Sqn 417

Gray, Flt Lt J.A., 72 Sqn 339

Gray, Flt Sgt L.W., 454 Sqn 232

Gray, Plt Off P.J., 252 Sqn 342

Gray, Capt R., 2 SAAF Sqn 122

Gray, Sqn Ldr R.G., 418 Sqn 284

Gray, Lt S.S.M., 40 SAAF Sqn 305

Greaves, Sgt P.L., 112 Sqn 348

Green, Flt Sgt A.D., 46 Sqn 271

Green, Flt Lt A.H., 38 Sqn 104

Green, Wt Off T.W., 232 Sqn 146

Green, Sgt T.W., 32 Sqn 289

Greenaway, Sgt J.R., 112 Sqn 243

Greenburgh, Flg Off P.H., 39 Sqn 132

Greene, Sgt T.W., 250 Sqn 287

Greenham, Lt C.F.G., 2 SAAF Sqn 222

Greentree, Flg Off A.G., 47 Sqn 66, 68

Gregory, Flg Off F.J., 47 Sqn 76

Greig, Flg Off R.T., 272 Sqn 339

Grennan, Wt Off G.B., 227 Sqn 36

Grewe, Sub Lt G.H., 800 Sqn 276, 277

Griessel, Lt S.P., 7 SAAF Sqn 243

Grieve, Flt Sgt P., 252 Sqn 89, 92

Grieve, Lt W.D.D., 72 Sqn 243

Griffin, Sgt C.B., 72 Sqn 326

Griffin, Wt Off D., 46 Sqn 271

Griffin, Flt Lt P., 162 Sqn 86

Griffiths, Flg Off A.M., 87 Sqn 318, 391

Griffiths, LAC H., 208 Sqn 275

Griffiths, Wt Off I., 454 Sqn 418

Griffiths, Flg Off J.L., 39 Sqn 122

Griffiths, Flt Lt R.V., 43 Sqn 193

Griffiths, Flt Sgt T.C., 255 Sqn 155

Grosse-Rasgado, Lt W.R.A., 12 SAAF Sqn 236, 240

Ground, Lt A.A., 7 SAAF Sqn 33, 38, 40

Grundy, Flt Lt J.W.E., 6 Sqn 281, 325

Grusd, Lt M.H., 250 Sqn 301

Guest, Flg Off A.W., 43 Sqn 240

Guest, Capt B., 7 SAAF Sqn 427

Hackett, Flt Sgt J., 237 Sqn 262

Haddon, Plt Off A.S., 252 Sqn 33

Hadley, Wt Off K.A., 256 Sqn 151

Haggarty, Flt Sgt S.J., 3 RAAF Sqn 266

Hall, Flg Off D.A.L., 252 Sqn 89

Hall, Lt E.W., 5 SAAF Sqn 323

Hall, Flt Sgt G.V., 250 Sqn 409

Hall, Flt Sgt J.I., 108 Sqn 273

Hall, Lt J.V., 16 SAAF Sqn 217

Hall, Wt Off K.G., 293 Sqn 139

Hall, Sgt M., 601 Sqn 436

Hall, Lt M.B., 15 SAAF Sqn 29

Hall, Flt Sgt M.F., 462 Sqn 53

Hallas, Flg Off A.G.R., 601 Sqn 409, 439

Halpin, Wt Off C.T., 3 RAAF Sqn 228

Hamankiewicz, Flt Lt J.R., 241 Sqn 242

Hamilton, Sgt J., 252 Sqn 80

Hammond, Wt Off, 15 SAAF Sqn 96

Hammond, Wt Off D.V., 46 Sqn 272, 273

Hammond, Sqn Ldr G.W., 600 Sqn 418

Hampton, Plt Off F.C., 73 Sqn 164

Hampton, Sqn Ldr G.L., 114 Sqn 370

Handley, Sqn Ldr D.S., 151 Sqn 203

Hanes, Flg Off J.N.F., 208 Sqn 421

Hannan, Flg Off J.N., 238 Sqn 124, 140

Hansel, Lt V.E., 24 SAAF Sqn 243

Hanson, Wt Off K.S., 417 Sqn 336

Harcourt, Flt Lt D.J., 294 Sqn 37

Harding, Lt J.D.H., 92 Sqn 128

Harding, Flt Sgt R.N., 145 Sqn 317

Hargreaves, Flg Off D., 55 Sqn 349

Harling, Flt Sgt J.R., 87 Sqn 261

Harman, Sgt/Plt Off E.G., 603 Sqn 83, 84, 110

Harnett, Flt Sgt G.W., 454 Sqn 23

Harper, 2/Lt A.H., 15 SAAF Sqn 112

Harper, Wt Off T.J., 603 Sqn (attached 47 Sqn) 61, 105

Harper, Lt T.S., 73 Sqn 397, 398, 407

Harrington, Flg Off F.H.W., 94 Sqn 111

Harris, Flg Off A.E., 256 Sqn 228, 344

Harris, Sgt A.W., 601 Sqn 244

Harris, Lt C.A., 55 Sqn 151

Harris, Sgt H.J., 227 Sqn 46

Harris, Capt T.A., 4 SAAF Sqn 365

Harrison, Sgt D., 603 Sqn 276

Harrison, Flt Sgt D.A., 46 Sqn 272, 273

Harrison, Lt H.B., 1 SAAF Sqn 141

Harrison, Lt H.L., 16 SAAF Sqn 285

Harrison, Flt Sgt J.N., 87 Sqn 314, 353

Harrison, Flt Sgt R.E., 24 SAAF Sqn 101

Harrison, Flt Sgt/Plt Off T.H., 253 Sqn 122, 262

Harrison, Flt Sgt W.G., 603 Sqn 109

Hart, Sqn Ldr J.S., 112 Sqn 395

Hart, Sqn Ldr K.G., 18 Sqn 335

Hart, Capt R.R., 601 Sqn 280

Hart, Lt T.F., 5 SAAF Sqn 323

Hartley, Flg Off G.S., 227 Sqn 97

Hartley, Flt Sgt J.E., 93 Sqn 392

Hartley, Lt J.E., 2 SAAF Sqn 423

Hartley, Flg Off R., 603 Sqn 112

Hartley, R.A. Lt 11 SAAF Sqn 377

Hartley, Sgt W.N., 47 Sqn 81

Hartogh, Lt M.H., 41 SAAF Sqn/3 SAAF Sqn 106, 427

Harvey, Lt W.F., 12 SAAF Sqn 364

Harwood, Flt Sgt L.H., 108 Sqn 273

Haslam, Wt Off P.C., 213 Sqn 55, 109

Hast, Flt Lt R.A., 450 Sqn 328

Hatsell, Flt Lt S.H., 605 Sqn 282, 283

Hattingh, Lt D.R., 5 SAAF Sqn 426

Haupt, Lt A.J., 16 SAAF Sqn 112, 113

Hawkes, Lt A.L., 19 SAAF Sqn 333

Hawkes, Flg Off W.D.C., 241 Sqn 183, 316

Haworth, Lt R.B., 899 Sqn 228

Hawthorne, Flt Sgt F., 252 Sqn 43

Hay, Plt Off G.L.L., 680 Sqn 57

Hay, Flg Off J.S., 94 Sqn 68, 70

Hayball, Sgt E., 13 Sqn 66

Hayden, Flg Off J.S., 47 Sqn 66

Haynes, Wt Off A.J., 601 Sqn 307

Hayter, Sqn Ldr J.C.F., 74 Sqn 19, 39

Hayter, Flg Off J.E., 47 Sqn 61

Hayward, Wt Off R.C., 87 Sqn 242, 243

Healey, Lt S.B., 2 SAAF Sqn 270

Heard, Wt Off F., 213 Sqn 362, 365

Heard, Sgt S.A., 462 Sqn 47

Hearn, Flt Lt R.V., 112 Sqn 251, 342, 363, 364

Hearndon, Flt Sgt A.W., 213 Sqn 350

Heaven, Lt C.W., 24 SAAF Sqn 101

Hebdige, Flt Sgt/Wt Off J.R., 256 Sqn 190, 318, 347

Hedderwick, Flt Lt P.J., 43 Sqn 356, 357

Hedge, Wt Off R.J., 256 Sqn 412

Hedger, Wt Off J.H., 3 RAAF Sqn 248

Hedley, Flt Sgt J.J., 500 Sqn 327

Hedon, Flt Lt D., 47 Sqn 63

Heher, 1/Lt C.G., 15 SAAF Sqn 81

Heide, Flg Off C.L., 603 Sqn 251, 259

Helm, Lt H.B., 213 Sqn 174, 183

Hemingway, Sqn Ldr J.A., 43 Sqn 363, 380, 397, 419, 432, 433

Henderson, Capt G.MacG., 260 Sqn 342

Henderson, Flt Lt R.W., 241 Sqn 351

Hendrick, Sgt E.J., 601 Sqn 243, 244

Hendry, Flg Off R.B., 72 Sqn 294

Henn, Flt Lt P.E., 216 Sqn 73

Henry, Lt A.R., 16 SAAF Sqn 285

Henry, Lt J.E., 19 SAAF Sqn 290, 301

Herd, Plt Off J.L., 241 Sqn 191

Herring, Sub Lt K., 809 Sqn 289

Hesseltine, Sgt A.J., 284 Sqn 120

Hewett, Lt W.A., 16 SAAF Sqn 234, 291

Hey, Flt Sgt J.P., 603 Sqn 47

Hibbins, Sgt R.G., 500 Sqn 345, 350

Hibbert, Flt Sgt L., 227 Sqn 103

Higgins, Wt Off T.K., 3 RAAF Sqn 418

Hill, Lt D.C., 800 Sqn 283

Hill, Lt P.E., 249 Sqn 388

Hilton-Barber, Maj G., 4 SAAF Sqn 359, 369

Hinchcliffe, Sgt D.A., 114 Sqn 273

Hinde, Flt Sgt G.W., 603 Sqn 152

Hindle, Flg Off W. L., 253 Sqn 383, 439

Hingle, Lt L., 5 SAAF Sqn 349, 369

Hirons, Flt Lt G.L., 112 Sqn 422

Hirsch, Flg Off K.J., 55 Sqn 422

Hissey, Flg Off G.S., 454 Sqn 92

Hitchins, Lt C.C., 2 SAAF Sqn 339

Hoare, Lt T.H., 800 Sqn 283

Hobbs, Flt Sgt A.R.B., 6 Sqn 439

Hodder, Flt Sgt P.L., 250 Sqn 414

Hodge, Plt Off A.K., 227 Sqn 10

Hodgkinson, Flt Lt J.A.T., 3 RAAF Sqn 381

Hodgson, Sgt J., 601 Sqn 325

Hodgson, Plt Off J.S., 33 Sqn 76

Hogan, Wt Off F.W.J., 454 Sqn 422

Hogan, 2/Lt J.P., 2 SAAF Sqn 411

Hogg, Flg Off M.C., 14 Sqn 133

Holdcroft, Sgt H., 253 Sqn 199

Holland, Flt Sgt J.L., 601 Sqn 347

Holland, Flg Off/Flt Lt J.S., 46 Sqn/227 Sqn 42, 54, 56, 100, 102

Holliman, Flt Lt F.T., 185 Sqn 433

Hollingworth, Wt Off C.C., 43 Sqn 339

Hollinshead, Flg Off E.V., 260 Sqn 273

Hollinshead, Sgt T.W., 272 Sqn 26

Hollis, Wt Off W.H., 43 Sqn 383

Holman, Flt Lt C.P., 272 Sqn 296

Holmes, Flt Sgt C., 46 Sqn 43

Holmes, Flg Off M.T., 14 Sqn 256

Holmes, Sgt N.M., 255 Sqn 216

Holt, Sgt L.A., 601 Sqn 199

Honeker, Flg Off H.R., 114 Sqn 324

Hooker, Flt Lt O., 46 Sqn 11

Hooker, Sub Lt R., 800 Sqn 283

Hooley, Flg Off, 16 SAAF Sqn 434

Hoolihan, Flt Sgt/Wt Off P.G.T., 92 Sqn 311, 422

Hooper, Sgt L.W.W., 260 Sqn 328

Hopgood, Sgt J.P., 252 Sqn 51

Hopkin, Flg Off H.II., 256 Sqn 360

Hopkin, Sgt/Flt Sgt L.E., 603 Sqn 84, 110

Hopkins, Plt Off K.I.E., 603 Sqn 63

Hopkins, Lt T.J.C., 1 SAAF Sqn 277

Horlock, Flg Off J.C., 272 Sqn 323

Hornshaw, Lt J.G., 879 Sqn 213

Horsfall, Flg Off J.A., 46 Sqn 42, 58, 70

Horsford, Flt Sgt J., 272 Sqn 249

Horsley, Sgt D.A., 134 Sqn 22

Horsley, Flt Lt W.A.H.J., 454 Sqn 78

Horter, Wt Off G.M., 417 Sqn 120

Horton, Lt E.H., 17 SAAF Sqn 204

Horwill, Flg Off E.E., 39 Sqn 287

Hoskin, Flt Sgt C.G., 227 Sqn 34

Hoskins, Flg Off W.H., 256 Sqn 183

Hounslow, Plt Off A.H., 256 Sqn 339

Hounsom, Lt A.E., 227 Sqn 42, 53

House, Flt Lt E.C., 238 Sqn 141

Howard, Flg Off K.A., 454 Sqn 232

Howarth, Flt Sgt G.D., 43 Sqn 380

Howarth, Maj R.H.F., 12 SAAF Sqn 224

Howes, Sgt R.C., 227 Sqn 10, 84, 86, 95

Howey, Flt Lt E., 225 Sqn 343

Howley, Flt Lt R.J., 94 Sqn 156, 309

Howson, Maj M.G., 15 SAAF Sqn 94

Hoyle, Lt J.C., 112 Sqn 232

Hubbard, Sqn Ldr H.G., 252 Sqn 33, 43, 78

Hughes, Plt Off E.T., 38 Sqn 192

Hughes, Plt Off F.S., 208 Sqn 421

Hughes, Sgt N.A.R., 260 Sqn 259

Hugo, Grp Capt P.H., 322 Wing 137

Huish, Sgt M.R., 241 Sqn 256

Hulse, Flg Off/Flt Lt G.S., 94 Sqn/213 Sqn 309, 431, 432

Hulse, Sgt R.J., 93 Sqn 240

Human, Col J.D., 7 SAAF Wing 410

Hume, Flg Off D.B., 47 Sqn 87

Hume, Flg Off G.McN., 454 Sqn 232

Humphrey, Flg Off T.H., 284 Sqn 120

Humphreys, Sgt C.E., 227 Sqn 46, 60, 61, 64

Humphreys, Sqn Ldr P.H., 111 Sqn 272

Hunt, Sgt A.F.W.W., 213 Sqn 289, 290

Hunt, Sub Lt E.W., 899 Sqn 213

Hunt, Plt Off P., 93 Sqn 379

Hunter, Lt D.M.A., 6 Sqn 178

Hunter, Flg Off J., 80 Sqn 15

Huson, Lt, 19 SAAF Sqn 390

Hutchinson, Sgt C., 601 Sqn 256

Hutchison, R.B. Flg Off 227 Sqn 87

Hutton, Lt, 16 SAAF Sqn 132

Hutton, Flt Sgt D., 93 Sqn 422

Hyatt, Flg Off W.J., 108 Sqn 275

Hyett, Sgt M.J., 601 Sqn 427

Hynd, Lt J.H., 7 SAAF Sqn 38

Hyslop, Flt Sgt R.I., 223 Sqn 180

Iago, Wt Off I.R.H., 213 Sqn 383

Ibbotson, Flt Lt D.R., 256 Sqn 277, 279

Ibbotson, Flt Lt D., 5 RFU 315, 316

Imrie, Sgt W.G., 94 Sqn 22

Ingalls, Flt Lt B.J., 417 Sqn 130, 131

Inggs, Lt V.C., 7 SAAF Sqn 37

Ingram, Flg Off A., 19 SAAF Sqn 290

Innis, Wg Cdr A.R.deL., 39 Sqn 372

Ipsen, Flt Lt I., 237 Sqn 123

Ironside, Lt D.E.J., 19 SAAF Sqn 290

Irvine, Flg Off C.A., 454 Sqn 23

Irwin, Flt Lt J., 46 Sqn 276

Jackman, Flt Sgt P.J., 450 Sqn 389, 390

Jackson, Flg Off D.A.F., 272 Sqn 353

Jackson, Sgt H., 227 Sqn 56

Jackson, Lt J.F., 72 Sqn 294

Jackson, Plt Off R., 213 Sqn 55

Jacobs, Plt Off M.R., DAF Comm Flight 442

Jacobs, Capt R.H., 92 Sqn 389

Jacobs, Lt R.V., 249 Sqn 354

Jacobsen, Flt Lt C.F., 249 Sqn 138

James, Wt Off C.V., 255 Sqn 196

James, Sub Lt D.D., 809 Sqn 221, 222, 281

James, Sub Lt D.E., 809 Sqn 290

James, Sgt E.C., 227 Sqn 61

James, Sgt E.W., 450 Sqn 245

James, Flt Sgt G.M., 127 Sqn 10, 11

James, Flt Sgt I.T.R., 32 Sqn 295

James, Flg Off T.H S., 451 Sqn 122

Jarmey, Sgt B.E., 250 Sqn 325

Jandrell, Sqn Ldr D.P., 260 Sqn 188

Jansen van Rensberg, Lt D.J.S., 2 SAAF Sqn/5 SAAF Sqn 184, 348

Jarvis, Flg Off H.E., 454 Sqn 104

Jeans, Sgt A.E., 185 Sqn 255

Jefferson, Lt C.E.H., 809 Sqn 234

Jefferson, Plt Off N.L., 600 Sqn 141, 192, 233

Jeffrey, Flg Off F.H., 600 Sqn 156

Jellie, Sub Lt J.H., 800 Sqn 283

Jenkins, Flg Off A.J., 114 Sqn 254

Jenkins, Lt B.D., 4 SAAF Sqn 194

Jenkinson, Capt C., 16 SAAF Sqn 357

Jenkinson, Flg Off D.K., 603 Sqn 180

Jenkison, Plt Off W., 227 Sqn/46 Sqn 25, 53

Jenner, Plt Off L.D.H., 241 Sqn 366

Jennings, Wt Off E.C., 3 RAAF Sqn 140

Jennings, Capt E.J, 24 SAAF Sqn 350

Jennings, Flt Sgt P.S., 72 Sqn 383

Jerromes, Sub Lt J.O., 809 Sqn 235

Jobling, Flt Sgt R.E., 227 Sqn 24, 25, 63

John, Plt Off L.R., 87 Sqn 427

Johns, Flg Off C.P., 272 Sqn 26

Johns, Sqn Ldr G.B., 260 Sqn 188

Johns, Plt Off N., 252 Sqn 150

Johnson, Maj A.V., 55 Sqn 364

Johnson, Lt E.C.K., 40 SAAF Sqn 244

Johnson, Flg Off G.C.N., 238 Sqn 140

Johnson, Flg Off G.S., 256 Sqn 335

Johnson, Wg Cdr M.A., 254 Wing 271

Johnson, Sqn Ldr/Wg Cdr R.K.H., 272 Sqn 325, 353

Johnson, Flg Off T.E., 255 Sqn 154, 155

Johnson, Flt Lt T.E., 601 Sqn 434

Johnson, Flg Off W.R., 458 Sqn 359

Johnston, Wt Off P.M., 213 Sqn 383

Johnstone, Plt Off J., 241 Sqn 139

Joiner, Flt Sgt J.H., 454 Sqn 66

Jolly, Flg Off J.F.H., 38 Sqn 109

Jones, Lt A.H., 112 Sqn 190

Jones, Sgt A.W., 112 Sqn 294

Jones, Sgt C.H., 250 Sqn 322

Jones, Flt Sgt E.J., 93 Sqn 358

Jones, Flg Off G.E., 252 Sqn 33, 43, 78

Jones, Flt Sgt G.L., 227 Sqn 91, 93

Jones, Flt Lt G.R., 451 Sqn 124

Jones, Flt Lt J.B.L., 241 Sqn 122

Jones, Flg Off J.W.A., 227 Sqn 113

Jones, Flt Sgt O.G., 112 Sqn 383

Jones, Flt Lt O.H.E., 601 Sqn 418, 419, 433

Jones, Flt Sgt R.H.G., 38 Sqn 200

Jones, Flg Off T.E., 47 Sqn 57

Jones, Sgt W.F., 87 Sqn 357

Jones, Flt Sgt W.J.B., 6 Sqn 407

Jooste, Lt C.J., 28 SAAF Sqn 329

Jooste, Lt R.J., 15 SAAF Sqn 112, 321

Joubert, Lt D., 9 SAAF Sqn 185

Joyce, Flt Sgt D., 603 Sqn 178

Joynt, Flg Off A.E., 225 Sqn 389

Joyson, Flg Off R.B., 256 Sqn 277

Judd, Capt D.R., 1 SAAF Sqn 151

Judd, Plt Off G.W., 600 Sqn 236, 237, 244, 245

Judd, Flg Off K.S., 227 Sqn 87

Judd, Sgt L.V., 253 Sqn 323

Jupp, Sqn Ldr A.H., 43 Sqn 118

Kallio, Sqn Ldr O.C., 417 Sqn 118

Karck, Sgt D.L., 93 Sqn 236

Kedie, Sgt J.R., 241 Sqn 294

Keeton, Lt L.S.J., 16 SAAF Sqn 291

Keith-Walker, Flt Sgt A.B., 93 Sqn 422

Kellar, Lt R.B., 17 SAAF Sqn 265

Kelly, Wt Off M.D., 293 Sqn 139

Kelly, Lt O.J., 7 SAAF Sqn 33

Kelsey, Capt K.C., 5 SAAF Sqn 302

Kelso, Sgt B., 114 Sqn 366

Kemp, Flg Off M.A., 451 Sqn 122

Kemp, Lt P.J., 24 SAAF Sqn 321

Kemp, Flg Off R.H., 252 Sqn 266

Kemp, Flt Lt/Sqn Ldr W.R., 227 Sqn 60, 61, 86

Kempnich, Flt Sgt A.W.J., 454 Sqn 100

Kenebel, Flt Sgt A.G., 55 Sqn 233

Kendall, Lt, 16 SAAF Sqn 234, 291

Kendall, Flg Off J.M., 227 Sqn 59, 61, 84

Kendall, Flt Sgt R., 227 Sqn 25

Kendle, Flg Off R.A.C., 6 Sqn 427

Kennedy, Flt Sgt P.S., 454 Sqn 35

Kent, Flt Sgt S.M., 46 Sqn 86

Kenyon, Lt A.M., 16 SAAF Sqn 105

Kenyon, Lt I.D., 213 Sqn 422

Kershaw, Maj R.H.C., 7 SAAF Sqn 338, 383

Keys, Flg Off M.G., 46 Sqn 93

Kilpin, Lt G.D., 5 SAAF Sqn 323

Kimber, Flg Off G.S., 417 Sqn 156

Kimberley, Flt Sgt E.R., 255 Sqn 155

King, Lt D.S.J.W., 7 SAAF Sqn 13

King, Flt Lt H., 72 Sqn 414

King, Flt Sgt H.G.C., 294 Sqn 106

King, Sgt J.F., 252 Sqn 23

King, Flg Off W.G., 603 Sqn 109

Kingcome, Grp Capt C.B.F., 244 Wing 316

Kingsford-Smith, Charles, pioneer aviator 303

Lorains, Sgt W., 47 Sqn 65

Lord, Flt Sgt A., 46 Sqn 120

Lord, Flg Off C.W.R., 185 Sqn 370

Lord, Sgt E.A., 111 Sqn 427

Lothian, Flt Sgt A., 600 Sqn 321

Lott, Flg Off D.H.P., 1435 Sqn 377

Lound, Sgt H.F., 94 Sqn 18

Louw, Lt J.A.S., 16 SAAF Sqn 95

Louw, Lt P.J.S., 242 Sqn 117, 184

Love, Wg Cdr R.C., 243 Wing 33

Lovell, Wg Cdr A.D.J., 322 Wing 126, 127

Lovell, Flg Off J.E., 47 Sqn 68, 72

Lovell, Sqn Ldr P.W., 127 Sqn 19

Lowe, Sgt A.B., 145 Sqn 242

Lowen, Flg Off I.L., 134 Sqn 22

Lowther, Flt Lt J.L., 43 Sqn 275

Lumsden, Flt Sgt T.R., 252 Sqn 28, 32

Lund, Lt J.R., 112 Sqn 295

Lund, Plt Off P., 256 Sqn 339

Lydford, Sgt P.F., 293 Sqn 194

Lynch, Flt Sgt/Wt Off E.T., 603 Sqn 65, 72, 105

Lyon, Plt Off C.B., 39 Sqn 294

Lyon, Lt R.V., 241 Sqn 178

Macartney, Sub Lt G.S., 809 Sqn 281, 290

MacDonald, Flg Off A., 600 Sqn 192

MacDonald, Sgt A.W., 70 Sqn 316

MacDonald, Flt Lt G.W., 603 Sqn 86

MacDonald, Flt Lt R.W., 418 Sqn 284, 285

MacDonald, Flt Lt W.A.R., 145 Sqn 156

MacFarlane, Sgt A., 213 Sqn 239

MacGlashan, Flt Lt P.D.K., 13 Sqn 229

MacGregor, Flg Off I.J., 6 Sqn 383

MacIntosh, Flg Off J.A.T., 252 Sqn 112, 190

Macintosh, Lt R.C., 55 Sqn 352

Mackay, Flg Off R., 227 Sqn 61, 84

MacKenzie, Lt B.G., 16 SAAF Sqn 277

Mackenzie, Lt Col B.R., 17 SAAF Sqn 229

Mackenzie, Lt D., 87 Sqn 247

Mackenzie, Flt Lt R.J., 601 Sqn 188

Mackenzie, Wg Cdr R.M., 227 Sqn 10, 20, 22

MacKinnon, Flt Lt J.H.M., 213 Sqn 394

Macklem, Flg Off J., 47 Sqn 92

MacLean, Brigadier F., MACMIS 113

MacLean, Petty Officer Pilot W.G., 800 Sqn 229, 232

MacLeod, Flt Sgt J.T., 417 Sqn 171, 182

MacLellan, Flt Lt E.H., 213 Sqn 290, 298

MacMurray, Maj T.C., 5 SAAF Sqn 310

Maconie, Flg Off, 203 Sqn 47

Maddison, Plt Off J., 260 Sqn 199

Maddock, Flt Sgt D., 256 Sqn 436

Maggs, Lt J.H.L., 151 Sqn 213

Maguire, Capt P.G., 5 SAAF Sqn 355

Maidment, Flt Sgt E.F., 38 Sqn 108

Main, Capt D.R.C., 680 Sqn 16

Mair, Lt B.D., 1 SAAF Sqn 327

Malherbe, 2/Lt A.J., 249 Sqn 265, 266, 395, 434

Malloch, Plt Off J.V., 237 Sqn 123, 367

Malone, Flt Lt C.J., 417 Sqn 334

Manktelow, Flt Sgt R.E.E., 272 Sqn 304

Manley, Flt Lt J.H., 252 Sqn 23

Mann, Sgt K.R., 112 Sqn 194

Manne, Lt E., 92 Sqn 178, 256

Manning, Sgt A.W., 249 Sqn 262

Manning, Wt Off C.H., 454 Sqn 98

Manning, Flt Sgt P., 153 Sqn 245

Manning, Lt R.W.P., 5 SAAF Sqn 302

Mansell, Flg Off N.B., 237 Sqn 428, 436

Manser, Flg Off W.A.P., 134 Sqn 22

Manson, Flt Lt C.G.R., 43 Sqn 389

Marais, Lt B.J., 55 Sqn 240

Marais, Capt C.F., 15 SAAF Sqn 343

Marais, Lt J.T., 93 Sqn 289

Maree, Maj D.W., 40 SAAF Sqn 153

Margo, Lt Col C.S., 24 SAAF Sqn 446

Margowski, Lt I., 12 SAAF Sqn 167

Maritz, Capt W.F., 73 Sqn 381, 382

Marquis, Flt Sgt A., 145 Sqn 327

Marsden, Flt Sgt J.G., 256 Sqn 318

Marsh, Flg Off E.S., 46 Sqn 38

Marsh, Flt Sgt K.E.M., 462 Sqn 53

Marshall, LAC B., 72 Sqn 357

Marshall, Lt R.D., 1 SAAF Sqn 242

Martin, Flg Off/Flt Lt G.A., 73 Sqn 287

Martin, Flt Sgt P.J., 252 Sqn 80

Mason, Flg Off C.H., 252 Sqn/19 SAAF Sqn 92, 259

Mathee, Lt N.J.E., 5 SAAF Sqn 349

Mathers, Wt Off M.J., 43 Sqn 366

Mathias, Maj M.W.P., 15 SAAF Sqn 435

Mathieson, Lt J.M., 17 SAAF Sqn 194

Matthews, Plt Off D.J.P., 154 Sqn 91

Matthews, Flg Off G.J., 227 Sqn 42

Matthews, Flg Off L.M., 500 Sqn 422

Matthews, Lt W.H., 7 SAAF Sqn 151

Matthias, Flt Lt M.N., 112 Sqn 402

Maxwell, Plt Off J.G.P., 94 Sqn 295, 296

Maxwell, Sgt W.A., 237 Sqn 411

May, Sgt A.D., 227 Sqn 10

May, Sqn Ldr G., 33 Sqn 19

Mayer, Sgt N., 46 Sqn 108

Mayes, Flt Lt G.H., 72 Sqn 140

Mayne, Sgt P.S., 185 Sqn 367

Mayo, Flt Sgt D., 46 Sqn 42

Mayor, Flt Sgt W.H., 46 Sqn 257

Morgan, Flt Sgt B.W.R., 272 Sqn 326

Morgan, Lt G., 40 SAAF Sqn 242

Morgan, Flg Off I., 293 Sqn 295

Morgan, Flg Off L.F., 227 Sqn 86

Morgan, Flt Sgt L.S., 39 Sqn 153

Morris, Flt Sgt J.A., 250 Sqn 429

Morris, Plt Off A.W., 93 Sqn 423

Morris, Wg Cdr E.J., 251 Wing 120, 121, 125, 126

Morris, Sgt F.W., 1435 Sqn 124

Morris, Sub Lt G.C., 809 Sqn 209, 213, 290

Morris, Sub Lt J.V., 807 Sqn 142

Morris, Plt Off J.W., 162 Sqn 95

Morris, Sgt/Flt Sgt P.A., 250 Sqn 423

Morrison, Sub Lt A.C.S., 809 Sqn 221, 222, 281, 290

Morrison, Maj R.L., 5 SAAF Sqn 255

Morton, Capt R.D.B., 4 SAAF Sqn 161

Mosedale, Flg Off H., 92 Sqn 316

Mostyn, Plt Off E.J., 38 Sqn 17

Moubray, Flg Off D.M., 237 Sqn 151

Mould, Sgt W.E., 213 Sqn 282

Mould, Flg Off C.E., 6 Sqn 439

Muir, Flt Lt G.A., 46 Sqn 100

Muir, Flt Lt J.R., 249 Sqn 333, 376

Muir, Capt K.G., 16 SAAF Sqn 132

Muir, Lt P., 5 SAAF Sqn 349, 433

Mulcahy-Morgan, Flt Lt J.A., 213 Sqn 328, 339

Mullens, Flt Sgt H.W., 39 Sqn 178, 255

Muller, Lt D., 242 Sqn 123

Muller-Rowland, Sqn Ldr S., 47 Sqn 68

Mumford, Sqn Ldr R.M., 256 Sqn 277

Munro, Flg Off K.R., 38 Sqn 85

Munton-Jackson, Maj R., 16 SAAF Sqn 132

Murdoch, Maj D.W., 5 SAAF Sqn 395

Murman, Capt H.C., 15 SAAF Sqn 423

Murray, Lt G.B., 30 SAAF Sqn 335

Murray, Lt G.C., 5 SAAF Sqn 289

Murray, Plt Off H.C., 417 Sqn 326

Murray, Capt P.N., 17 SAAF Sqn 99

Murray, Maj T.P.L., 111 Sqn 365

Musgrave, Maj W.J.O., 21 SAAF Sqn 421

Musto, Lt C.A., 13 Sqn 184

Myers, Flt Lt N.L., 242 Sqn 203

Nash, Sgt K.R., 450 Sqn 409

Nash, Sqn Ldr M.P., 3 RAAF Sqn 317, 331–332

Neal, Sub Lt W.A., 807 Sqn 235

Neighbour, Flt Sgt R.S., 227 Sqn 34

Neilson, Plt Off J.A., 19 SAAF Sqn 220

Nel, Lt G.W.E., 12 SAAF Sqn 378

Nel, 2/Lt T.C., 450 Sqn 151, 287

Nel, Lt Col W.A., 40 SAAF Sqn 153, 188

Neser, Lt J.A., 4 SAAF Sqn 377

Newman, Flg Off A.G.P., 145 Sqn 343

Newman, Wt Off F.R., 92 Sqn 236

Newsome, Sgt D., 293 Sqn 253

Newstead, Flt Sgt R., 55 Sqn 254

Newton, Flg Off R.H., 112 Sqn 164

Nice, Plt Off H.H., 238 Sqn 136, 140, 141

Nicholls, Plt Off B., 256 Sqn 318

Nicholls. Sqn Ldr J.H., 601 Sqn 188

Nicol, Flg Off D., 47 Sqn 80

Ninan, Sgt/Flt Sgt T.M., 256 Sqn/72 Sqn 151, 353, 367

Nisbet, Capt N.G., 7 SAAF Sqn 321

Nixon, Lt J.H., 112 Sqn 427

Noble, Flt Sgt A.C.B., 603 Sqn 87, 88, 96

Noble, Plt Off M., 255 Sqn 122

Noble, Flg Off/Flt Lt P.F., 249 Sqn 192, 271, 300, 301

Norman, Flg Off G.E.C., 46 Sqn 38

Norman, Flt Lt R.H., 459 Sqn 350

Normandale, Flg Off J., 38 Sqn 104

Northmore, Flg Off M.P., 94 Sqn 57

Norton, Flt Sgt D.A., 153 Sqn 216

Nottingham, Lt H.W., 203 Sqn 16

Nourse, Lt P.W., 7 SAAF Sqn 333

Nowak, Flg Off C.J., 241 Sqn 239

Nunan, Lt D.G., 3 SAAF Sqn 397

Nunneley, Lt C.W., 5 SAAF Sqn 228

Oakes, Flg Off A., 39 Sqn 132

Oakes, Lt K.T., 24 SAAF Sqn 428, 429

Oakes, Lt O.R., 800 Sqn 228

Oates, Wt Off/Plt Off A., 32 Sqn 278, 312

O'Connell, Wt Off J.B., 458 Sqn 202

O'Connor, Lt F.A., 4 SAAF Sqn 161

O'Connor, Flg Off M., 47 Sqn 63

Odd, Sgt A.C., 600 Sqn 245

Oddie, Sgt G.R., 6 Sqn 410

Odendaal, Maj H.O.M., 5 SAAF Sqn 395, 408, 409

Odendaal, Lt/Capt M.W.V., 4 SAAF Sqn 232, 313

Ogg, Plt Off J.S., 92 Sqn 386

Ogilvie, Sqn Ldr C.A., 47 Sqn 63

Ogilvy, Lt G., 879 Sqn 226, 228

Ogle, Lt D.S., 809 Sqn 288, 289

O'Keefe, Flt Sgt H.J., 94 Sqn/73 Sqn 292, 340

Oldfield, Flt Sgt E., 603 Sqn 63

O'Neil, Flg Off G.C.W., 451 Sqn 120

O'Reilly, Sgt J.T., 32 Sqn 278

Ord, Sgt M., 601 Sqn 174

Ormerod, Flt Lt J.A., 72 Sqn 175

Otto, Lt P.C.de B., 15 SAAF Sqn 96

Owen, Flg Off R.J., 227 Sqn 104

Pacquet, Wt Off R.A., 216 Sqn 34

Padden, Sgt C.T., 145 Sqn 317

Paddison, Flt Sgt J.E., 603 Sqn 110

Page, Sqn Ldr W.T., 126 Sqn 72

Pain, Sqn Ldr C.D., 603 Sqn 89

Paine, Sqn Ldr J., 451 Sqn 19

Painter, Flg Off H., 162 Sqn 159

Pallett, Sgt H.G., 249 Sqn 298

Palmer, Sgt S.G.C., 227 Sqn 36

Palmer, Flg Off W.H., 256 Sqn 336, 379

Parbury, Flt Lt C.R., 145 Sqn 136

Park, Wg Cdr G.R., 272 Sqn 289

Park, Flt Sgt W.D., 72 Sqn 353

Parker, Flg Off A.M., 74 Sqn 80

Parker, Flt Sgt H., 227 Sqn 103

Parker, Plt Off J., 92 Sqn 427

Parker, Sgt R.E.D., 111 Sqn 239

Parker, Lt W.S., 40 SAAF Sqn 379

Parkes, Flg Off R.W., 38 Sqn 91

Parry, Sgt I., 70 Sqn 316

Parsons, Lt, 12 SAAF Sqn 164

Parsons, Flt Sgt D.F., 603 Sqn 113

Passow, Flt Sgt L.J., 252 Sqn 33

Pate, Flt Sgt W.T.K., 134 Sqn 16

Paterson, Wt Off I.A., 284 Sqn 117

Patten, Sqn Ldr H.P.E., 255 Sqn 151

Patterson, Flg Off A.T., 39 Sqn 175

Patterson, Plt Off/Flt Lt J.W., 253 Sqn 263, 369

Pattison, Flg Off K.F., 221 Sqn 155

Paul, Flt Lt D.V., 454 Sqn 78

Paul, Flt Sgt W.D., 39 Sqn 63

Paull, Lt C.H.L.,7 SAAF Sqn 330

Payne, Sqn Ldr P.A.S., 39 Sqn 287

Peace, Flg Off R.T., 46 Sqn 101

Peacey, Plt Off J.S., 19 SAAF Sqn 259

Peachey, Lt C.P., 15 SAAF Sqn 97

Peacock, Flt Sgt J., 92 Sqn 363

Pearce, Flg Off N.J., 73 Sqn 398, 407

Peasley, Flg Off W.R., 46 Sqn 43

Peddell, Flt Sgt A.W., 55 Sqn 368

Pedley, Grp Capt M.G.F., 337 Wing 388

Peggram, Flt Sgt E.W., 47 Sqn 87

Peighton, Flt Sgt P.R., 38 Sqn 56

Pengelly, Flt Lt J.I., 605 Sqn 282, 283

Pennie, Flt Sgt E.F., 603 Sqn 152

Penny, Sgt R., 249 Sqn 152

Penson, Flg Off F.A.E., 213 Sqn 253, 349

Perason, Sgt/Plt Off L.P., 237 Sqn 396

Perrens, Sqn Ldr/Wg Cdr D.F., 208 Sqn, 285 Wing 346–347, 348

Perry, Sub Lt A.D., 809 Sqn 280

Perry, Flt Lt P.F., 208 Sqn 169

Perry, Sgt R.S., 249 Sqn 137

Pertwee, Flt Lt W.R., 255 Sqn 392

Peters, Lt J.V., 293 Sqn 177, 228, 232

Pettet, Lt G.F., 16 SAAF Sqn 203

Phelan, Lt D.R., 2 SAAF Sqn 389

Phelan, Lt E.R., 7 SAAF Sqn 429

Phelan, Wt Off T.K., 46 Sqn 269, 271

Philips, Plt Off T.J., 151 Sqn 204

Phillips, Flg Off A.J., 227 Sqn 9, 10

Phillips, Flg Off J.B., 93 Sqn 439

Phillips, Lt J.D., 25 SAAF Sqn 403

Phillips, Capt N.M., 2 SAAF Sqn 140

Philpott, Flg Off L.J., 250 Sqn 287

Philpott, Flt Sgt N., 153 Sqn 245

Phipps, Lt P.M.E., 16 SAAF Sqn 125, 126

Pickford, Wt Off S.G., 213 Sqn 248, 262

Piece, Flt Sgt A.W., 252 Sqn 50–51

Pienaar, Lt J.F., 12 SAAF Sqn 162

Pienaar, Capt J.M., 5 SAAF Sqn 282

Pienaar, 2/Lt S.W., 213 Sqn 183, 187, 193

Pierce, AF (E) W.G.P., HMS *Hunter* 225

Piercey, Sgt S.L., 145 Sqn 276

Pigot, Wt Off T.V., 1435 Sqn 81, 139

Piner, Flg Off S.W., 603 Sqn 72, 86

Pines, Flt Sgt R., 24 SAAF Sqn 101

Pinkerton, Wt Off H.I., 253 Sqn 389

Pinks, Flt Lt R.S., 255 Sqn 122

Pitman, Flg Off R.H., 39 Sqn 149

Pitt, Flt Sgt D.A., 252 Sqn 78

Pittard, Lt S.R.R., 1435 Sqn 295

Platt, Sgt C., RAF ME 40, 41

Platt, Maj H.E., 16 SAAF Sqn 357

Poate, Flg Off J.H., 451 Sqn 184

Pollard, Flg Off R., 19 SAAF Sqn 290

Pollock, Flt Sgt R., 87 Sqn 386

Pond, Fg Off K., 459 Sqn 144

Porter, Flg Off A.C., 272 Sqn 269

Porter, Flt Lt J.A., 256 Sqn 335

Postlethwaite, Flt Sgt C., 213 Sqn 294

Potter, Flt Sgt/Plt Off A.E., 252 Sqn/603 Sqn 110, 180, 276

Potts, Flt Sgt E.M., 39 Sqn/272 Sqn 149, 287, 323

Potvin, Wt Off E.F.F., 73 Sqn 197, 287

Poublon, Sub Lt C.A.M., 800 Sqn 217

Poulton, Sgt J., 252 Sqn 61

Powell, Wt Off A., 19 SAAF Sqn 281, 296

Powell, Lt E.R., 2 SAAF Sqn 185

Powell, Grp Capt J.A., 254 Wing 218, 220

Power, Flt Sgt A.H., 603 Sqn 89

Power, Wt Off J.R., 39 Sqn 63

Powers, Flg Off E.J., 227 Sqn 97

Pratley, Plt Off G.T., 80 Sqn 15

Pratt, Flt Sgt D.L., 73 Sqn 396

Pratt, Capt F.G., 114 Sqn 368

Preece, Sgt D.A., 249 Sqn 247

Preiba, Flt Lt J., 318 Sqn 330

Prendergast, Plt Off H.B., 74 Sqn 11

Prentice, Lt D.F., 112 Sqn 298

Prescot, Lt K.W., 7 SAAF Sqn 38

Prest, Wt Off R., 111 Sqn 423

Pretorious, Lt A.J.H., 4 SAAF Sqn 377

Price, Flt Lt F.W., 256 Sqn 360

Priest, Wt Off M.R., 458 Sqn 256

Pringle, Flt Lt A.P., 603 Sqn 87, 96, 103, 109

Pritchard, Plt Off W.B.P., 603 Sqn 65–66

Pritchett, Flg Off F.H., 603 Sqn 66

Proctor, Sqn Ldr J.E., 352 Sqn 219

Proudman, Flg Off H.G., 601 Sqn 171, 177, 257, 363, 409

Pugh, Flg Off R.H., 38 Sqn 90, 97

Pugh, Flt Lt R.M., 38 Sqn 11

Pumphrett, Lt T.W., 16 SAAF Sqn 239

Puntis, Lt H.A., 24 SAAF Sqn 97

Purdy, Flg Off G.H., 103 MU/451 Sqn 25, 96

Purnell, Flt Sgt J.G., 227 Sqn 131

Putnam, Wt Off R.A., 256 Sqn 414–415

Pygram, Flg Off J.R., 16 SAAF Sqn 203, 252

Pym, AM (2) E.F., HMS *Hunter* 225

Pyott, Lt J.B., 450 Sqn 378

Quick, Sgt, 19 SAAF Sqn 282

Quilliam, 2/Lt J.H., 12 SAAF Sqn 378

Quine, Flt Lt P., 32 Sqn 157, 178

Quinn, Wt Off J.F., 3 RAAF Sqn 331–332

Rachmann, Lt H.K., 249 Sqn 220, 296

Raikes, Sgt D.K., 18 Sqn 429

Railton, Flt Lt W., 454 Sqn 84

Rain, Flg Off J.B., 38 Sqn 115

Rainsford, Plt Off B., 237 Sqn 123

Rake, Flt Lt D.S.V., 32 Sqn 267, 313, 314

Raleigh, Lt J. B., 5 SAAF Sqn 260

Ralph, Wt Off F.A.O., 213 Sqn 328

Ramsbotham, Sgt E., 249 Sqn 438

Rapley, Wt Off F.H., 272 Sqn 323

Rashleigh, Flt Lt F.E.G., HQ RAF ME 40, 41

Rawbone, Sub Lt A.R., 809 Sqn 232, 281

Rawlings, Flt Sgt B.E., 454 Sqn 96

Ray, Wt Off A.J., 241 Sqn 360

Ray, Flt Sgt E., 249 Sqn 270

Ray, Sgt R.C., 252 Sqn 153

Rayment, Flt Sgt H.D.R., 238 Sqn 11, 22

Rayns, Flg Off J.F.A., 148 Sqn 317

Rayson, Flt Sgt R.M., 87 Sqn 306

Read, Flg Off F.W.T., 1435 Sqn 182

Redding, Capt B.L., 12 SAAF Sqn 162

Redenbach, Wt Off I.M., 3 RAAF Sqn 420

Redman, Lt G.L., 5 SAAF Sqn 352

Reece, Lt Cdr L.G.C., 807 Sqn 280

Rees, Flg Off S.W., 600 Sqn 246, 330

Reeves, Sgt N.C., 145 Sqn 423

Reid, Flg Off D.M., 252 Sqn 153

Reid, Wg Cdr G.A., 46 Sqn 19, 42, 43

Reid, Flg Off J.R.F., 19 SAAF Sqn 220

Reid, Sgt R.S., 227 Sqn 55

Reike, Flt Sgt D.M., 272 Sqn 314

Reim, Lt M.F., 4 SAAF Sqn 377

Rennison, Wt Off I., 3 RAAF Sqn 366

Reteif, Lt A.B., 9 SAAF Sqn 185

Reynolds, Lt A., 250 Sqn 429

Reynolds, Flg Off A.F., 272 Sqn 246

Reynolds, Flg Off C.L., 272 Sqn 194

Reynolds, Flg Off J.S.B., 241 Sqn 136

Reynolds, Flt Sgt J.S.L., 252 Sqn 80, 92

Reynolds, Flg Off/Flt Lt R.E., 255 Sqn 146, 156, 184, 190

Reynolds, Flt Lt T.W., 255 Sqn 318

Rhodes, Flt Sgt J.C., 603 Sqn 110

Ribbink, Capt F., 24 SAAF Sqn 98

Ribbink, Lt R., 16 SAAF Sqn 252

Richards, Flt Sgt J.L., 600 Sqn 346

Richards, Flt Lt K.A., 3 RAAF Sqn 189

Richards, Lt R., 16 SAAF Sqn 112

Richardson, Flg Off G.S., 93 Sqn (att 7 SAAF Sqn) 296

Riddell, Flt Lt R.D., 32 Sqn 157, 250

Rideout, Wt Off R.W., 417 Sqn 325

Ridley, Plt Off G.W., 227 Sqn 71, 75

Ridley, Lt W.P., 16 SAAF Sqn 95

Riley, Lt A.G., 293 Sqn 184

Rimes, Flt Sgt M.J., 232 Sqn 153

Rimington, Sgt J., 272 Sqn 287

Ringland, Flg Off A.H., 459 Sqn 100

Ritchie, Flt Lt J.M., 153 Sqn 103

Ritchie, Flg Off W., 73 Sqn 148

Robbs, Lt Col J.N., 24 SAAF Sqn 91

Robert, Flt Lt R.J., 451 Sqn 120

Roberts, Flt Sgt B.E., 93 Sqn 420

Roberts, Sgt C.R., 241 Sqn 439

Roberts, Lt E.N., 112 Sqn 417

Roberts, Flt Sgt R., 256 Sqn 190, 318, 347

Roberts, Flt Sgt T.P., 112 Sqn 417

Robertson, Flg Off D.E., 213 Sqn 429

Robertson, Flt Sgt/Wt Off D.H., 227 Sqn/19 SAAF Sqn 132, 249

Robinson, Capt D.C., 40 SAAF Sqn 348

Robinson, Sub Lt D.S., 807 Sqn 142

Robinson, Flg Off E.F.J., 108 Sqn 351

Robinson, Wt Off H.W., 203 Sqn 45

Robinson, Wt Off L.G., 450 Sqn 332

Robson, Flt Off P.C., 601 Sqn 433

Robson, Flt Sgt R.G., 39 Sqn 178, 255

Rochford, Capt J.V., 4 SAAF Sqn 296

Roe, Sgt/Wt Off H., 252 Sqn 78, 353

Roediger, Flt Lt I.H., 3 RAAF Sqn 162

Roelofse, Lt J.J., 4 SAAF Sqn 339

Roff, Sgt J.A.J., 227 Sqn 10

Rogers, Sgt A.M., 55 Sqn 396

Rogers, Flt Sgt M.H., 272 Sqn 195

Rogers, Flt Sgt J.J., 603 Sqn 180

Rogers, Lt Col R.H., 40 SAAF Sqn 188, 321

Rogers, Lt R.M., 800 Sqn 228

Roget, Wt Off K.V., 603 Sqn 63

Roll, Flt Sgt R.J., 227 Sqn 97

Roney, Flg Off J.W.J., 112 Sqn 312

Rooke, Plt Off D.C., 252 Sqn 92, 110

Rooks, Sgt/Flt Sgt A., 603 Sqn 66, 72, 87–88

Rorvik, Capt E.A., 7 SAAF Sqn 37, 39

Rorvik, 2/Lt R.E., 213 Sqn 249, 250, 252, 260, 290, 298

Rose, Lt C., 40 SAAF Sqn 330

Rose, Flg Off J.T., 417 Sqn 348, 422

Rosenstein, Lt E.W., 185 Sqn 407

Rosenstein, W., WWI aviator 407

Roskin, Sgt C.G., 227 Sqn 10

Ross, Flg Off A.E., 603 Sqn 87, 96, 110

Ross, Lt B.K., 40 SAAF Sqn 339

Ross, Flt Sgt H.F., 80 Sqn 18, 20

Ross, Lt J.B.S., 1 SAAF Sqn 252, 290

Rossner, Flg Off L., 47 Sqn 63

Rothwell, Flt Lt F., 232 Sqn 142

Rouke, Wt Off L., 111 Sqn 339

Rowbottom, Sgt J.D., 55 Sqn 352

Rowe, Flt Sgt A.D., 73 Sqn 113, 265

Rowe, Lt R.J., 185 Sqn 180, 260

Rowland, Flt Lt M., 103 MU 12

Rowlands, Flg Off/Flt Lt/Sqn Ldr H.R., 103 MU/213 Sqn/451 Sqn 15, 55

Rowley, Flt Sgt J.T., 46 Sqn 43

Roy, Lt G.A., 1 SAAF Sqn 242, 260

Royston, Lt M.G., 3 SAAF Sqn 390

Rudling, Flg Off R.E., 255 Sqn 318

Rundle, Wt Off P.S., 6 Sqn 368

Rushmere, Wt Off E.A., 1435 Sqn 165

Russell, Lt C.R., 16 SAAF Sqn 228

Rutland, Flg Off J.R., 272 Sqn 287, 323

Ryan, Lt K.T.F., 12 SAAF Sqn 162

Ryan, Lt T., 223 Sqn 156

Ryerse, Flg Off C.R., 267 Sqn 262

Ryland, Lt G.H., 15 SAAF Sqn 381

Salmon, Flt Sgt R.M.P.E., 114 Sqn 119

Sanders, Flg Off C.J., 255 Sqn 240

Sanders, Plt Off F.C., 3 RAAF Sqn 269

Sanderson, Flt Sgt J., 256 Sqn 412

Sanderson, Flg Off T.D., 134 Sqn 18

Saul, AVM R.E., AOC Air Defences, Eastern Mediterranean 19, 20, 36

Saunders-Knox-Gore, Flt Lt W.L., 13 Sqn 254

Sawicki, Plt Off M., 318 Sqn 432

Sawle, Flt Sgt L., 227 Sqn 87

Scade, Sqn Ldr T.P.K., 46 Sqn 42

Scanes, Sub Lt I.D., 800 Sqn 283

Scarlett, Flt Sgt/Wt Off L., 294 Sqn 145, 146

Scarlett, Flt Sgt R.F., 227 Sqn 97

Schaefer, Flt Lt P.C., 272 Sqn 414

Schneider, Wt Off P.F., 72 Sqn 418

Schneider, Lt S., 1 SAAF Sqn 228

Scholefield, Flt Lt H., 272 Sqn 235

Schonken, Lt H.A., 17 SAAF Sqn 88

Schoombie, Lt C.C., 7 SAAF Sqn 351

Scollan, Flg Off J., 255 Sqn 392

Scott, Lt A.G., 30 SAAF Sqn 326

Scott, Capt A.N., 651 Sqn 427

Scott, Flg Off F.N., 454 Sqn 100

Scott, Flt Sgt H.D., 19 SAAF Sqn 220

Scott, Flg Off J.M., 603 Sqn 89

Seares, Sgt A.J., 87 Sqn 239

Seel, Lt I.M., 7 SAAF Sqn 33, 34

Sefton, Flt Sgt J., 227 Sqn/19 SAAF Sqn 131, 242

Senior, Lt B.A., 250 Sqn 390, 391

Settle, Flg Off A.A., 39 Sqn 175

Seymour, Sgt H.C., 227 Sqn 55

Seymour, Flt Sgt J.D., 454 Sqn 100

Shannon, Flg Off/Flt Lt A.F., 3 RAAF Sqn 408, 409, 414

Shannon, Plt Off R.A., 417 Sqn 313, 325

Sharpe, Sub Lt A., 882 Sqn 222

Sharpe, Lt J.E., 601 Sqn 156

Shaw, Sub Lt A.I.R., 879 Sqn 226, 227, 228

Shaw, Flt Sgt J.G., 603 Sqn 175

Shaw, Wg Cdr M.J.A., 221 Sqn 85

Shearer, Sgt J.M., 73 Sqn 278

Sheldrick, Flt Sgt F.G.W., 227 Sqn/19 SAAF Sqn 112, 290

Shelver, Lt B.D., 2 SAAF Sqn 124

Shepherd, Lt A.M., 24 SAAF Sqn 96

Sherborne, Sub Lt F.T., 882 Sqn 221–222

Sherry, Flg Off B.G., 55 Sqn 368

Shields, 2/Lt W., 249 Sqn 255–256

Shone, Capt C.N., 2 SAAF Sqn 155

Shuttleworth, Capt A.F., 24 SAAF Sqn 98, 101

Shuttleworth, Lt Col L.H.G., 25 SAAF Sqn/15 SAAF Sqn 131, 239, 271, 323, 343

Sidelsky, Capt A., 25 SAAF Sqn 369

Sidney, Flg Off E.J., 451 Sqn 142

Sievwright, Lt K.D., 15 SAAF Sqn 234

Silberbauer, Lt J.C., 41 SAAF Sqn 106

Silvester, Sqn Ldr G.F., 32 Sqn 280

Simmonds, Flt Sgt J.H., 459 Sqn 350

Simmonds, Flg Off R.G.S., 238 Sqn/94 Sqn 158, 159, 399, 400

Simons, Wt Off G.G., 458 Sqn 327

Simpson, Sqn Ldr C.T., 601 Sqn 353

Simpson, Flt Lt D.G., 603 Sqn 109

Simpson, Flt Sgt N., 93 Sqn 417

Simpson, Lt T.J., 16 SAAF Sqn 95

Sissons, Sqn Ldr K.N.R., 72 Sqn 362

Sinclair, Flg Off/Flt Lt D., 185 Sqn/249 Sqn 167

Skelton, Wt Off E.J., 1435 Sqn 392

Skinner, Flt Lt A.P., 242 Sqn 123

Skinner, Wt Off, RAF attached 147ᵃ Sq RM 53

Skippen, Flt Sgt S.C., 252 Sqn 266

Slack, Flg Off G.II., 417 Sqn 436

Slade, Sqn Ldr J.W., 94 Sqn 398

Slade-Betts, Flt Lt/Sqn Ldr R., 253 Sqn/6 Sqn 263, 320

Slater, Wt Off J.A., 293 Sqn 194

Slater, Flg Off W.C.D., 93 Sqn 360

Sleep, Lt R., 5 SAAF Sqn 423

Sleigh, Flt Sgt R.J., 185 Sqn 381, 392

Slessor, AM Sir J.C., C-in-C Mediterranean Allied Air Forces, 113, 157, 219, 402

Sloan, Flg Off R.W., 93 Sqn 289

Smailes, Plt Off A.A., 213 Sqn 184

Small, Flt Lt/Sqn Ldr G.W., 238 Sqn/451 Sqn 140, 169

Smart, Flt Lt D.A., 13 Sqn 269

Smetherham, Lt, 15 SAAF Sqn 87

Smith, 2/Lt A.F., 15 SAAF Sqn 381

Smith, Flt Lt B., 216 Sqn 61

Smith, Flt Sgt B.W., 1435 Sqn 378

Smith, Flt Lt C.D.A., 213 Sqn 120, 248, 250, 252

Smith, Plt Off C.P.K., 92 Sqn 414

Smith, Wt Off D.B., 600 Sqn 318

Smith, Wt Off E., 92 Sqn 309

Smith, Sqn Ldr E.T., 237 Sqn 19

Smith, Flt Sgt F.E., 255 Sqn 392

Smith, Flt Sgt F.L., 256 Sqn 183

Smith, Sqn Ldr G.M., 256 Sqn 414, 424, 425

Smith, Wt Off G.R., 255 Sqn 115

Smith, Flt Lt H.R., 108 Sqn 125

Smith, Plt Off I.D., 237 Sqn 137

Smith, Sgt J.R., 252 Sqn 92

Smith, Flt Sgt M., 249 Sqn 333

Smith, Lt N.A., 16 SAAF Sqn 96

Smith, Sgt R.B., 603 Sqn 262

Smith, Flt Sgt R.V., 19 SAAF Sqn 290

Smith, Flg Off/Flt Lt T.H., 601 Sqn 244, 248

Smith, Sgt W.H., 600 Sqn 314

Smith, Sub Lt W.T.R., 881 Sqn 213

Smithes, Flt Lt J.H., 256 Sqn 159

Smyth, Flg Off K.C., 238 Sqn 123

Smyth, Flg Off M.W., 253 Sqn 262, 290

Smyth, Flt Sgt N., 252 Sqn 34

Smyth, Flt Lt R., 256 Sqn 336

Snape, Flg Off G.H., 227 Sqn 131

Snow, Flt Sgt A.J., 500 Sqn 327

Snyman, Capt H.T., 1 SAAF Sqn 365

Snyman, Sgt J.P., 24 SAAF Sqn 95

Snyman, Lt W.M., 16 SAAF Sqn 252

Sobey, Lt W.R., 40 SAAF Sqn 194

Somerset, Lt P.B., 250 Sqn 382

Somerville, Flg Off R., 47 Sqn 96

Southerden, Wt Off F.D.K., 256 Sqn 385

Speakman, Lt E.V., 807 Sqn 223, 225

Seear, Sgt S.A., 603 Sqn 262

Spence, Flt Sgt J.A., 39 Sqn 130

Spence, Capt W., 21 SAAF Sqn 412

Spence, Lt W.N., 5 SAAF Sqn 326

Spencer, Sub Lt C.D., 800 Sqn 228, 282, 283

Spencer, Plt Off E., 600 Sqn 141, 192, 233

Spencer, Lt J.R., 1 SAAF Sqn 141

Spencer, Flt Sgt K.R.E., 108 Sqn 168

Spooner, Flt Sgt/Wt Off P.G., 603 Sqn 66, 87, 88, 96

Spruce, Sgt C.D., 185 Sqn 360

Squires, Flt Sgt A.W., 252 Sqn 78, 80, 92

Stacey, Flt Sgt A.J., 145 Sqn 403

Stakes, Flg Off K., 227 Sqn 61, 63

Stanbury, Lt G.W., 16 SAAF Sqn 228

Standen, Wt Off A.R., 19 SAAF Sqn 240

Stanger, Sgt/Plt Off F.P., 252 Sqn 61, 92

Stapleton, Wt Off J.F., 454 Sqn 100

Staples, Sqn Ldr T.N., 13 Sqn 123

Starnes, Flt Lt R.F., 145 Sqn 136, 139

Stead, Lt N.H., 16 SAAF Sqn 102

Stebbings, Flt Sgt N.J., 55 Sqn 352

Steedman, Flt Lt A.M.S., 241 Sqn 137

Steele, Sqn Ldr J.L., 114 Sqn 324

Steenkamp, Lt W.F., 92 Sqn 138

Steinhebel, Lt F., 87 Sqn 411, 421

Stephen, Sgt J., 80 Sqn 31

Stephens, Plt Off S.C., 1435 Sqn 182

Stevens, Plt Off A.F.G., 293 Sqn 284

Stevens, Flt Sgt F., 241 Sqn 423

Stevens, Plt Off J.E., 27 SAAF Sqn 255

Stevens, Sgt R.F., 89 Sqn 12

Stevens, Lt S.J., 19 SAAF Sqn 361

Stevenson, Plt Off/Flg Off D.A., 92 Sqn 202, 203, 439

Stevenson, Flt Sgt D.A., 213 Sqn 294

Stevenson, Flt Sgt F.A., 252 Sqn 89

Stevenson, Flt Sgt N., 213 Sqn 386

Stewart, Lt A.R.L., 16 SAAF Sqn 106

Stewart, Sub Lt D., 807 Sqn 280

Stewart, Lt D.K., 16 SAAF Sqn 239

Stewart, Flg Off E.R., 93 Sqn 224

Stewart, Lt J.B., 12 SAAF Sqn 364

Stewart, Lt W., 12 SAAF Sqn 364

Steyn, Capt J.F.A., 16 SAAF Sqn 95

Steyn, Lt M.H., 7 SAAF Sqn 389

Stirling, Flg Off J.C., 145 Sqn 136

Stockden, Flg Off J., 238 Sqn 159

Stone, Flg Off J.C., 55 Sqn 435

Stopforth, Lt H.B., 16 SAAF Sqn 291

Stott, Flt Sgt A.E., 94 Sqn 41

Stott, Lt E.E., 7 SAAF Sqn 441

Straker, Flt Lt W.J.P., 213 Sqn 362

Strange, Plt Off J.A.C., 93 Sqn 334

Strange, Lt/Capt J.R.D., 16 SAAF Sqn 132, 250

Strange, Wt Off P., 73 Sqn 113

Stratton, Sqn Ldr W.H., 134 Sqn 19

Stratton, Wt Off W.W., 601 Sqn 363, 366

Strever, Lt R.W., 112 Sqn 366

Stringer, Sgt E.A., 213 Sqn 106

Stringer, Sqn Ldr R.H., 55 Sqn 346

Strutt, Flg Off P.C.J., 242 Sqn 203

Strydom, Lt, 15 SAAF Sqn 29, 30

Strydom, Lt J.H., 16 SAAF Sqn 132

Sturgess, Capt E.W., 4 SAAF Sqn 294

Styles, Wg Cdr L.H., 600 Sqn 236, 237, 276

Sullivan, Flt Lt J.M., 253 Sqn 294

Sullivan, Flg Off M.H., 250 Sqn 333

Summers, Flt Lt J., 255 Sqn 240

Susskind, 2/Lt C.B., 260 Sqn 304, 346

Sussmann Lt T.F., 24 SAAF Sqn 234

Sutton, Plt Off P.W., 237 Sqn 126, 369

Sutton, Flt Lt R.H., 451 Sqn 120–122

Swale, Wt Off T.R., 255 Sqn 216

Swales, Maj C.J.O., 4 SAAF Sqn 359

Swales, Flt Sgt J.E., 93 Sqn 425, 434

Swift, Sgt J.A., 227 Sqn 51, 63

Sykes, Sgt C.C., 603 Sqn 65, 72, 105

Sykes, Wt Off L.F., 603 Sqn 152, 180

Taffs, Plt Off H.S., 255 Sqn 115

Talbot, Lt G.H., 24 SAAF Sqn 344

Tame, Flg Off W., 603 Sqn 109

Tanner, Sgt J.R., 242 Sqn 126

Tattersall, Lt D.B., 250 Sqn 316, 382

Taylor, Flg Off A., 46 Sqn 101

Taylor, Flt Sgt A., 252 Sqn 80

Taylor, Flt Sgt A., 39 Sqn 287

Taylor, Flg Off A.D., 92 Sqn 232, 262

Taylor, Sub Lt C.B., 4 SAAF Sqn 154

Taylor, Lt D.J., 4 SAAF Sqn 390

Taylor, Flt Sgt D.W., 603 Sqn 153

Taylor, Flg Off E.A.T., 252 Sqn 102, 110

Taylor, Sgt E.S., 227 Sqn 34

Taylor, Wt Off E.W., 238 Sqn 141

Taylor, Sgt G., 6 Sqn 181

Taylor, Flt Sgt/Flg Off H.A., 38 Sqn 12, 23

Taylor, Capt I.N.L., 40 SAAF Sqn 124

Taylor, Lt J.W., 7 SAAF Sqn 31–33, 39

Taylor, Flt Sgt L.R., 38 Sqn 91

Taylor, Flt Sgt P., 111 Sqn 334

Tedder, ACM A., C-in-C Middle East Command, OC MAAF 6, 77

Tee, Sub Lt R.J., 800 Sqn 232

Te Kloot, Sqn Ldr J., 249 Sqn 134, 255, 260, 263–266, 271

Telford, Plt Off J.A., 600 Sqn 246

Temple-Murray, Plt Off P.T.P., 213 Sqn 37

Templeton, Sgt, Flt/Sgt J., 227 Sqn 42, 100, 102

Tennant, Flg Off D.D., 3 RAAF Sqn 377

Tennant, Sgt K.J., 603 Sqn 82, 89

Tennant, Lt O.R., 1435 Sqn 418

Terry, Flg Off G.A., 47 Sqn 59

Theron, Lt D.H., 7 SAAF Sqn 338

Thistleton, Lt H., 55 Sqn 185

Thom, Flg Off M.J.R., 603 Sqn 66, 72, 87–88

Thomas, Sgt A.G., 227 Sqn 87

Thomas, Flt Lt B.H., 43 Sqn 327

Thomas, Flg Off C.W., 19 SAAF Sqn 290, 301

Thomas, Sub Lt G.E., 807 Sqn 232

Thomas, Sgt H.E., 227 Sqn 10

Thomas, Flt Sgt K.F., 603 Sqn 178

Thomas, Flt Sgt K.G., 227 Sqn 58

Thomas, Sgt K.V., 47 Sqn 81

Thomas, Flg Off R.D., 418 Sqn 284–285

Thomas, Wt Off R.E.M., 1435 Sqn 407

Thomas, Flg Off R.H.V., 462 Sqn 38

Thomas, Flt Sgt R.J., 256 Sqn 322

Thomas, Flg Off V.M., 3 RAAF Sqn 331–332, 341

Thompson, Lt A., 41 SAAF Sqn 103

Thompson, Sgt C., 252 Sqn 89

Thompson, Flt Lt D.A., 600 Sqn 185, 190, 235, 253

Thompson, Lt D.C., 260 Sqn 438

Thompson, Sgt/Flt Sgt D.P., 47 Sqn 78, 81, 92

Thompson, Flt Lt E.H.G., 252 Sqn 113

Thompson, Flt Lt I.G., 43 Sqn 296, 352

Thompson, Grp Capt J.M., SASO, HQ, No 210 Group 137

Thompson, Flg Off K.R., 454 Sqn 317

Thompson, Wt Off R., 213 Sqn 362

Thompson, Lt W.M., 4 SAAF Sqn 246, 311

Thomsen, Lt A.MacD., 15 SAAF Sqn 366

Thomson, Wg Cdr R.R., 114 Sqn 364

Thomson, Lt W.St.C., 213 Sqn 396

Thornhill, Sub Lt J.E.M., 807 Sqn 235

Thornhill-Cook, Lt E.J., 24 SAAF Sqn 100

Thornton, Flt Sgt H., 272 Sqn 240

Thorogood, Sgt J., 227 Sqn 58

Thwaites, Flg Off W.W., 47 Sqn 68, 72

Tickner, Flt Sgt N.W., 94 Sqn 309

Tilley, Maj D.P., 19 SAAF Sqn 281, 296

Timmons, Flg Off J.P., 227 Sqn 36

Todhunter, Plt Off D., 454 Sqn 81

Tomlinson, Sgt/Plt Off E., 6 Sqn 277, 422

Tomlinson, Plt Off H.V., 38 Sqn 156

Tooze, Sgt A.R., 32 Sqn 280

Topp, Lt J.A., 11 SAAF Sqn 426

Towell, Sgt J., 600 Sqn 192

Towey, Wt Off A.M., 459 Sqn 165

Tozer, Flg Off A.W., 255 Sqn 155, 157

Treble, Flt Sgt F.E., 46 Sqn 114

Treleaven, Flg Off J., 19 SAAF Sqn 333

Tremlett, Flt Lt J.P., 227 Sqn 63

Treu, Lt J.W.M., 22 SAAF Sqn 328

Trevett, Sgt R.S., 89 Sqn 42, 43

Trigg, Flg Off L., 38 Sqn 184

True, Plt Off L., 232 Sqn/72 Sqn 186, 317

Truesdale, Flt Sgt T., 603 Sqn 63

Truscott, Lt, 15 SAAF Sqn 76

Truscott, Flt Sgt J.A., 252 Sqn 266

Truter, Lt R.R., 30 SAAF Sqn 335, 342

Tucker, Lt R.M., 15 SAAF Sqn 58

Tucker, Flt Sgt T.J., 256 Sqn 183

Turkington, Flt Sgt/Wt Off J.M., 3 RAAF Sqn 152, 385

Turkington, Flt Lt/Sqn Ldr R.W., 241 Sqn/601 Sqn 139, 174, 175, 178, 185, 188, 353

Turner, Lt A.G., 7 SAAF Sqn 33

Turner, Flg Off C.E., 227 Sqn 25, 27

Turner, Flt Sgt H.J., 603 Sqn 262

Turner, Flg Off J.S., 294 Sqn 256

Turner, 2/Lt R., 5 SAAF Sqn 383

Turner, Flt Sgt R.D., 256 Sqn 296

Tutill, Wt Off R.P., 232 Sqn 146

Tweedie, Lt M.H.L., 1 SAAF Sqn 342

Twomey, Flt Lt V.H., 73 Sqn 117

Tyrell, Sgt F.L., 227 Sqn 86

Udberg, Wt Off V., 293 Sqn 305

Ulm, Charles, pioneer aviator 303

Ulm, Wt Off/Plt Off J.A., 145 Sqn 303, 304, 380

Ulrich, Wt Off R.Y., 6 Sqn 165, 261

Underwood, Flt Sgt A., 252 Sqn 33

Underwood, Flt Sgt J.P., 108 Sqn 273

Unwin, Flg Off J.A., 47 Sqn 58, 94

Urwin, Flg Off C.B., 38 Sqn 26, 101

Usher, Sqn Ldr G.L., 112 Sqn 390, 395

Valentine, Lt H.E., 250 Sqn 439

van Amerongen, Lt A.J., 15 SAAF Sqn 92–93

Van Beerden, Lt, 15 SAAF Sqn 90

Vance, Flt Lt A.R., 19 SAAF Sqn 282

van Dam, Lt G.C.A., 5 SAAF Sqn 423

Van den Bergh, 2/Lt R.H., 73 Sqn 141

Van Den Bos, Lt W.H., 73 Sqn 384

van der Berg, Lt P.D., 16 SAAF Sqn 105

van der Merwe, 2/Lt P.J., 260 Sqn 304

Van Der Pol, Flt Sgt H., 38 Sqn 25

van der Spuy, Lt A., 2 SAAF Sqn 245

van der Walt, 2/Lt, 15 SAAF Sqn 89

van der Westhuizen, Lt R., 12 SAAF Sqn 164

van Deventer, Lt P.P., 7 SAAF Sqn 33

van Heerden, Capt C.S., 12 SAAF Sqn 207

van Niekerk, Lt, 21 SAAF Sqn 142

van Reenen, Capt T.A., 11 SAAF Sqn 380

Van Renan, Lt L.G., 15 SAAF Sqn 94

van Rensberg, Lt P.M., 238 Sqn 117, 136, 158, 159

van Rooyen, Lt L.J., 25 SAAF Sqn 442

Van Velzen, Capt P.A., 15 SAAF Sqn 58

van Vliet, Maj C.A., 7 SAAF Sqn 19, 38

Varese, Flt Sgt P., 38 Sqn 101

Varey, Sgt D., 260 Sqn 232

Vaughan, Flg Off D., 603 Sqn 112

Vaughan-Fowler, Sqn Ldr P.E., 213 Sqn 362

Veitch, Lt R.H., 260 Sqn 407, 411, 419, 439

Venter, Maj P.W., 92 Sqn 273

Vernon, Lt D.N., 5 SAAF Sqn 137

Vine, Sub Lt W.D., 800 Sqn 297

Viney, Sgt, 203 Sqn 44

Vintner, Flt Sgt J.F., 451 Sqn 278

Vorster, Lt V., 213 Sqn 120, 248, 250

Vos, Flt Lt C.S., 213 Sqn 174, 187, 234, 251, 253, 281

Vose, Flg Off T.J., 601 Sqn 439

Wade, Wt Off W., 12 SAAF Sqn 377

Wagstaffe, Flt Sgt J.W., 93 Sqn 250

Wait, Air Cdr C.H., 210 Group 19, 20

Waitman, Flt Sgt L.W., 600 Sqn 184

Walker, Flt Lt A.E., 6 Sqn 173, 174, 192

Walker, Sgt C., 112 Sqn 409

Walker, Plt Off J.D., 255 Sqn 382

Walker, Lt K.B., 284 Sqn/293 Sqn 154, 166, 403

Wall, Flg Off J.A., 32 Sqn 180

Wallace, Plt Off I.D., 39 Sqn 281, 283

Wallace, Lt T.E., 1 SAAF Sqn 252

Wallem, Lt A.E., 16 SAAF Sqn 106

Waller, Sgt G.N., 252 Sqn 190

Walley, Sgt J.M.S., 603 Sqn 66, 89

Walsh, Wt Off J., 255 Sqn 120, 246

Walton, Flg Off J.E., 241 Sqn 181, 217

Ward, Sgt A.W., 87 Sqn 431

Ward, Wt Off C.M., 600 Sqn 346

Ward, Flt Sgt D.G.R., 252 Sqn 43

Ward, Flg Off M.C., 237 Sqn 423

Ward-Able, Lt, 16 SAAF Sqn 434

Ware, Wt Off J.B., 145 Sqn 392

Warner, Flt Sgt H.J., 603 Sqn 180

Waslyk, Plt Off/Flt Lt J., 417 Sqn 322, 345

Waterhouse, Flg Off J.C.R., 80 Sqn 21, 22

Waterland, Flg Off F., 500 Sqn 403

Waters, Flt Sgt W.F., 601 Sqn 311

Wates, Capt G.H., 2 SAAF Sqn 259

Watford, Sgt B., 601 Sqn 247, 269

Watkins, Flt Lt H.E., 450 Sqn 232

Watkins, Wt Off J.G.P., 213 Sqn 177

Watson, Plt Off G.H., 46 Sqn 276

Watson, Flg Off J., 108 Sqn 139, 282

Watson, Wt Off J.C., 272 Sqn 249

Watters, Flt Lt J., 603 Sqn 56, 66

Watton, Plt Off A.J., 123 Sqn 11, 12

Watts, Flt Sgt P., 253 Sqn 296

Waugh, Capt E., Royal Marine Commando att MACMIS 168

Wayburne, Capt E., 1 SAAF Sqn 265

Weatherall, Flt Sgt F., 253 Sqn 326

Webb, Flg Off H.V., 39 Sqn 175

Webb, Lt J.C., 12 SAAF Sqn 162

Webber, Sgt E.A., 227 Sqn 58

Webber, Flg Off S.R., 500 Sqn 418

Webster, Flt Sgt A.M., 46 Sqn 114

Webster, Flg Off R.C., 417 Sqn 329

Webster, Flt Sgt W.D., 227 Sqn 34

Weeber, 2/Lt J.H., 112 Sqn 314

Weekes, Flg Off J.W.R., 417 Sqn 388

Weingartz, Maj F.K., 250 Sqn 363

Welch, Flg Off P.B., 213 Sqn 391

Wellington, Lt A.T., 16 SAAF Sqn 280

Wellington, Plt Off R.W., 227 Sqn 9

Wells, Wt Off D.J., 3 RAAF Sqn 422

Wells, Maj H.E., 72 Sqn 419, 427

Wells, Maj J.R.R., 274 Sqn/250 Sqn 19, 256

Welman, Lt P.J., 4 SAAF Sqn 148, 236

West, Flg Off C.N., 272 Sqn 246

West, Flt Lt J.G., 103 MU 25, 26

West, Sgt S.A., 603 Sqn 105

Westbrook, Lt L.D., 73 Sqn 277

Westlake, Wg Cdr G.H., 239 Wing 390

Westwell, Flt Sgt W., 600 Sqn 314

Whaley, Flt Lt L.F.S., 600 Sqn 245

Wheeler, 2/Lt H.D., 3 SAAF Sqn 304

White, Flg Off A., 417 Sqn 417

White, Sgt A.H., 454 Sqn 84

White, Plt Off A.J.B., 6 Sqn 439

White, Plt Off D.F., 241 Sqn 149, 199

White, Flg Off G.A., 55 Sqn 266

Whitehorn, Lt R.G., 7 SAAF Sqn 339

Whitehouse, Lt G.vd.H., 21 SAAF Sqn 255

Whitelaw, Flt Sgt J.McP., 216 Sqn 31

Whiteman, Flt Sgt N.V., 38 Sqn 71

Whiting, Sqn Ldr S.R., 213 Sqn 15, 165, 166, 176, 177, 183, 200, 251

Whitney, Sqn Ldr S.N.R., 213 Sqn 19

Whitten, Flt Sgt J.M., 458 Sqn 256

Whittingham, Capt R.T., 249 Sqn 262, 264, 289

Whitwell, Wt Off R.N.J., 18 Sqn 412

Whitworth, Flg Off B.A., 225 Sqn 384

Wickens, Flt Lt A.S., 16 SAAF Sqn 203, 252

Widdowsen, Sgt S., 92 Sqn 352

Wild, Flg Off B.J., 46 Sqn 58, 70, 268

Wilkinson, Flt Sgt H., 43 Sqn 342

Will, Flg Off A.H., 227 Sqn 87

Will, Lt/Capt I.G., 4 SAAF Sqn 276, 317

Willan, Wt Off R.R., 73 Sqn 385

Williams, Flt Sgt, 15 SAAF Sqn 90

Williams, Lt E., 4 SAAF Sqn 181

Williams, Plt Off D.E., 255 Sqn 233

Williams, Flg Off G., 227 Sqn 97

Williams, Wt Off K.B.C., 72 Sqn 414

Williams, Flg Off L.E.H., 225 Sqn 296

Williams, Flg Off R.A., 294 Sqn 248

Williams, Flt Sgt R.G., 241 Sqn 370

Williams, Mid R.G., 881 Sqn 260

Williams, Flt Sgt R.M.P., 145 Sqn 303

Williams, Flt Sgt S., 39 Sqn 178

Williams, Flt Sgt T.L., 151 Sqn 224

Williamson, Wt Off D.S., 3 RAAF Sqn 438

Willis, Sgt G.R., 47 Sqn 78, 81, 92

Willmott, Sqn Ldr T.W., 185 Sqn 146

Wilmer, Flg Off H.J., 600 Sqn 237, 276, 414, 424

Wilmot, Lt Col L.A., 239 Wing 189

Wilson, Sqn Ldr A., 238 Sqn 136

Wilson, Flt Lt A.F., 154 Sqn 174, 175

Wilson, Flg Off B.G., 603 Sqn 87

Wilson, Flt Sgt J.P., 18 Sqn 318

Wilson, Sgt K., 73 Sqn 157

Wilson, Sub Lt K.F., 800 Sqn 276

Wilson, Flg Off R.A.R., 227 Sqn 113

Wilson, Wt Off R.P., 253 Sqn 298

Wilson, Flg Off T.R., 417 Sqn 352

Wilson, Flt Sgt W.J., 74 Sqn 39, 40, 76

Wingfield, Lt R.S.M., 450 Sqn 415, 417

Wingham, Flg Off M.A., 255 Sqn 146, 156, 184, 190

Wint, Flt Sgt N., 600 Sqn 156, 157

Withers, Flt Sgt C.J., 203 Sqn 62

Wollaston, Lt C.D., 250 Sqn 266

Wolk, Lt, 15 SAAF Sqn 94

Wood, Flg Off A.G., 47 Sqn 76

Wood, Wt Off C.E.B., 72 Sqn 216

Wood, Flt Lt D.L.S., 145 Sqn 339

Wood, Capt F.E., 15 SAAF Sqn 141

Wood, Sgt F.J., 249 Sqn 321

Wood, Sub Lt N., 882 Sqn 226, 228

Wood, Flt Sgt N.W., 603 Sqn 87–88, 110

Wood, Sub Lt R.D., 809 Sqn 290

Woodhead, Lt G.L., 223 Sqn 161, 162

Woodier, Plt Off A.B., 603 Sqn 256

Woodruff, Sgt C.D., 73 Sqn 143

Woodruff, Wg Cdr P.H., 334 Wing/337 Wing 268, 295, 373

Woods, Lt A.W.R., 24 SAAF Sqn 149

Woods, Wg Cdr E.N., 249 Sqn 78

Woods, Lt E.V., 24 SAAF 193

Woods, Plt Off R.J.A., 253 Sqn 314

Woods, Sgt V., 253 Sqn 120

Wooler, Flt Lt J., 145 Sqn 136

Wootten, Sqn Ldr R.J.S., 178 Sqn 75

Worrall, Flt Sgt E.A., 603 Sqn 47

Worsley, Flt Sgt W.F., 18 Sqn 175

Worthington, Wg Cdr F.R., 38 Sqn 17

Wright, Flt Lt D., 92 Sqn 224

Wright, Wt Off K.F., 227 Sqn 91, 93

Wright, Flt Lt R., 89 Sqn 42, 43

Wright, Wt Off W., 154 Sqn 191

Wright, Flg Off W.H., 134 Sqn 22

Wroath, Plt Off P.M., 227 Sqn 60, 61, 63

Wyatt, Flt Lt C.A., 252 Sqn 151, 184

Wyles, Flg Off C.S., 227 Sqn 60, 61

Yaldwyn, Lt R.H., 15 SAAF Sqn 68

Yates, Flt Sgt M.B., 603 Sqn 66, 89

Yeats, Capt R.C., 3 SAAF Sqn 76, 77

Yorke, Flt Sgt H.E., 603 Sqn 175

Youl, Flg Off S.C., 450 Sqn 236

Young, Plt Off C.D., 92 Sqn 202

Young, Sgt D., 43 Sqn 344

Young, Flt Lt E.A.C., 252 Sqn 190

Young, Wg Cdr J.R.C., 153 Sqn/108 Sqn 103, 275

Young, Capt K.A., 7 SAAF Sqn 339

Young, Sgt M., 601 Sqn 260

Young, Flg Off N.F., 272 Sqn 246

Young, Plt Off W.J.T., 242 Sqn 137

Younger, Flg Off W.F., 19 SAAF Sqn 358

Youngleson, Lt F., 17 SAAF Sqn 181

Yurchison, Plt Off W., 227 Sqn 60, 61, 63

Zimmermann, Flg Off M.D., 38 Sqn 185

GREEK

Note: Spelling taken from RAF records. Current Greek spelling in brackets.

Angelidis, Flt Lt A., 13 (H) Sqn 184

Antonopoulis, Sgt A., 335 Sqn 104

Athanasakis, Wt Off E., 336 Sqn 22

Baltazzis, Flt Lt S., 336 Sqn 373

Calogeridis (Kalogeridis), Plt Off, 335 Sqn 302

Caridis, Flg Off E., 336 Sqn 70

Christakos, Flt Sgt K., 336 Sqn 110

Christakos, Plt Off S., 336 Sqn 84

Coskinas, Flg Off N., 13 (H) Sqn 57

Coundouris, Flg Off A., 335 Sqn 104

Diamantopoulos, Flt Lt S., 336 Sqn 65

Doucas, Flt Sgt V., 335 Sqn 22

Doukas, Sqn Ldr G., 335 Sqn 302

Economidis, Flg Off E., 13 (H) Sqn 200

Frangou (Fragou), Plt Off N., 335 Sqn 302

Frangoyannis, Flg Off P., 13 (H) Sqn 181

Georgakopoulos (Georgopoulos), Flt Lt E., 335 Sqn 302

Hatzakis, Flt Lt J.E., 13 (H) Sqn 290

Hatzilakos, Flg Off C., 336 Sqn 312, 373

Hadjioannou (Hatzioannou), Plt Off E., 335 Sqn 302

Karamolengos (Karamolegos), Flt Lt E., 335 Sqn 99

Katsaros, Flg Off J., 13 (H) Sqn 149

Kipouros, Flt Lt J., 336 Sqn 270

Kotas, Flt Lt E., 335 Sqn 284, 285

Leitmer, Flt Sgt M., 335 Sqn 22

Liakeas, Flt Lt G., 13 (H) Sqn 122

Mademlis, Sgt G., 336 Sqn 70

Margaritis, Flg Off J., 335 Sqn 280

Michaelidis, Flg Off G., 335 Sqn 302

Michelongonas, Flg Off P., 336 Sqn 344

Mitrakis, Flg Off E., 335 Sqn 280

Moulopoulos, Flg Off A., 336 Sqn 106

Nicolopoulous, Wt Off G., 336 Sqn 410

Panagalos, Sqn Ldr G., 335 Sqn 19

Papacostas, Flg Off J., 336 Sqn 103

Papaioannou, Plt Off G., 336 Sqn 270

Pleonis (Plionis), Flg Off G., 335 Sqn 145, 146

Psilolignos, Flg Off C., 336 Sqn 70

Sarsonis, Sgt D., 336 Sqn 25,70

Skantzikas, Wt Off S., 336 Sqn 22

Soufrilas, Wt Off/Plt Off D., 336 Sqn 25,106

Souvleros, Flg Off E., 336 Sqn 110

Stavropoulos, Sgt C.H., 336 Sqn 12

Tangalakis, Wt Off G., 335 Sqn 270

Tingos, Flt Lt E., 335 Sqn 323

Tsotsos, Flg Off G., 336 Sqn 106

Tzouvalis, Flt Sgt G., 336 Sqn 68

Vatimbellas, Sgt J., 335 Sqn 318

Vladousis, Plt Off, 335 Sqn 302

Volonakis, Flt Lt N., 335 Sqn 280

Voutsinas, Flt Lt D., 335 Sqn 302

Xanthacos, Wt Off G., 336 Sqn 25

Zafiropoulis, Flt Sgt B., 13 (H) Sqn 76

ROYAL YUGOSLAV AIR FORCE

Ankon, Plt Off L., 352 Sqn 266

Antocić, Sgt J., 351 Sqn 356

Beran, Capt I., 94 Sqn 70

Cenić, Sqn Ldr A., 351 Sqn 356, 441

Delic, Plt Off M., 352 Sqn 247

Djonlic, Capt M.M., 55 Sqn 119

Dvorski, Sgt L., 351 Sqn 356

Halambek, Flt Sgt Z., 352 Sqn 148

Jovanovic, Flt Lt R., 352 Sqn 232, 277

Karić, Flt Lt M., 351 Sqn 304

Klokocovnik, Plt Off J., 351 Sqn 307

Kluz, Plt Off F., 352 Sqn 256

Krsnik, Sgt N., 351 Sqn 370

Lošić, Sgt M.A., 352 Sqn 370

Manoljovic, Lt R., 94 Sqn 199

Marinović, Flt Lt M., 351 Sqn 362

Matejic, 2/Lt R., 94 Sqn 70

Nesterovic, 2/Lt R., 55 Sqn 273

Pesic, Sgt J., 351 Sqn 307

Popov, Flt Lt A., 352 Sqn 290

Protić, Sqn Ldr M., 352 Sqn 328

Rugi, Plt Off L., 352 Sqn 398

Soic, Sqn Ldr H., 352 Sqn 389

Stanic, Capt D., 94 Sqn 199

Vemić, Plt Off N., 351 Sqn 411

Vouk, Plt Off S., 351 Sqn 294

Vracaric, Capt M., 55 Sqn 387

Vukovic, Plt Off A., 352 Sqn 240

Zarkov, Capt S.D., 55 Sqn 140

YUGOSLAV MILITARY AND POLITICAL PERSONNEL

Ćetković, Gen-Maj Vlado, 290

Dropin, General, 376

Tito, Mshl Josip Broz, 29, 111, 113, 128, 150, 168, 176, 373, 376, 408

BRITISH AND COMMONWEALTH AIR FORCE UNITS

SQUADRONS

1 SAAF Sqn 141, 151, 163, 171, 172, 188, 216, 228, 242, 252, 256, 260, 265, 277, 290, 294, 314, 317, 327, 342, 348, 349, 365, 389, 392, 400, 410, 411, 422, 431, 434, 444, 445

2 SAAF Sqn 122, 124, 126, 140, 144, 147, 155, 161, 171, 172, 184, 185, 190, 222, 228, 245, 253, 254, 256, 259, 270, 334, 336, 338, 339, 365, 379, 389, 396, 400, 411, 421, 422, 423, 436, 445

3 RAAF Sqn 103, 126, 140, 152, 162, 172, 188, 189, 228, 248, 266, 269, 309, 317, 331, 332, 341, 350, 366, 377, 381, 385, 390, 403, 407, 409, 414, 418, 420, 422, 438, 444

3 SAAF Sqn 19, 76, 77, 98, 99, 117, 136, 141, 152, 156, 161, 171, 172, 188, 239, 258, 287, 298, 304, 318, 337, 363, 365, 376, 383, 390, 397, 413, 417, 421, 423, 427, 436, 441, 445

4 SAAF Sqn 141, 147, 148, 154, 161, 164, 171, 172, 174, 181, 188, 194, 217, 232, 234, 236, 239, 246, 276, 294, 296, 311, 313, 314, 317, 339, 359, 365, 369, 377, 386, 390, 420, 445

5 SAAF Sqn 137, 172, 181, 228, 243, 251, 255, 260, 265, 278, 282, 289, 298, 302–305, 307, 310, 317, 321–323, 326, 348–349, 352, 355, 366, 369, 370, 374, 383, 390, 395, 407–409, 419, 422–423, 425–426, 433, 434, 440, 444

6 Sqn 128, 129, 150, 154, 155, 165, 169, 173, 174, 178, 181, 192, 195, 200, 206, 218, 235, 252, 256, 261, 277, 281, 290, 302, 317, 318, 320, 325, 328, 359, 368, 383, 400, 407, 410, 412, 421, 422, 427, 439

7 SAAF Sqn 13, 19, 28, 30, 31, 32, 33, 34, 36, 37, 38, 39, 40, 41, 99, 130, 151, 172, 243, 256, 294, 296, 305, 311, 313, 321, 327, 330, 333, 338, 339, 351, 359, 366, 383, 384, 386, 389, 403, 418, 426, 427, 429, 433, 436, 437, 441, 445

9 SAAF Sqn 185, 253

10 SAAF Sqn 253

11 SAAF Sqn 258, 298, 337, 341, 351, 363, 368, 377, 380, 390, 397, 413, 420, 426, 435, 444, 445

12 SAAF Sqn 139, 161, 162, 163, 164, 167, 168, 196, 197, 205, 207, 216, 224, 228, 236, 240, 246 262, 335, 336, 350, 357, 364, 377, 378, 433, 445

13 Sqn 123, 154, 183, 184, 192, 223, 229, 254, 269, 353, 381, 396, 442, 444

13 (H) Sqn 24, 29, 118, 128, 129, 139, 149, 154, 165, 181, 184, 200, 238, 290, 445

14 Sqn 133, 140, 148, 149, 153, 194, 256, 262

15 SAAF Sqn 13, 26, 29, 30, 32, 41, 58, 68, 76, 81, 87, 88, 89, 90, 92, 93, 94, 96, 97, 101, 107, 110, 112, 120, 141, 172, 234, 321, 323, 343, 366, 381, 382, 419, 423, 435, 438, 445

16 SAAF Sqn 15, 91, 95, 96, 102, 103, 105, 106, 112, 113, 125, 126, 131, 132, 203, 204, 217, 228, 234, 236, 239, 250, 252,

253, 280, 285, 291, 298, 333, 340, 357, 390, 396, 434, 445

17 SAAF Sqn 88, 89, 91, 94, 99, 131, 181, 194, 204, 229, 242, 265, 273, 446

18 Sqn 160, 169, 175, 191, 192, 198, 273, 318, 322, 330, 335, 336, 367, 412, 422, 429, 444

19 SAAF Sqn 129, 207, 218, 220, 239, 240, 242, 249, 250, 254, 255, 281, 282, 285, 290, 294, 296, 298, 301, 305, 333, 342, 358, 361, 368, 390, 391, 429, 445

21 SAAF Sqn 136, 142, 146, 152, 164, 172, 251, 255, 331, 365, 381, 412, 421, 445

22 SAAF Sqn 320, 328, 374, 446

24 SAAF Sqn 91, 93, 95, 96, 97, 98, 100, 101, 105, 106, 107, 108, 112, 141, 149, 152, 164, 167, 172, 193, 207, 234, 243, 246, 266, 312, 321, 331, 344, 350, 385, 402, 407, 408, 419, 428, 429, 436, 445, 446

25 SAAF Sqn 131, 150, 238, 239, 270, 271, 285, 286, 287, 307, 316, 320, 323, 369, 402, 403, 441, 442, 445

27 SAAF Sqn 255, 321, 374, 423, 446

28 SAAF Sqn 329, 444

30 SAAF Sqn 246, 326, 331, 332, 335, 342, 365, 385, 387, 445

31 SAAF Sqn 110, 113, 114, 130

32 Sqn 129, 150, 154, 157, 178, 180, 234, 240, 243, 250, 268, 278, 280, 289, 291, 295, 296, 298, 311, 312, 313, 314, 446

33 Sqn 19, 76

36 Sqn 235, 256, 269

37 Sqn 306

38 Sqn 11, 12, 13, 17, 23, 25, 26, 34, 35, 56, 58, 64, 71, 78, 85, 86, 90, 91, 92, 93, 97, 99, 100, 101, 104, 108, 109, 113, 115, 152, 156, 180, 185, 192, 200, 320, 445

39 Sqn 63, 90, 122, 128, 129, 130, 132, 153, 164, 175, 178, 180, 250, 255, 281, 283, 287, 294, 320, 327, 371

40 SAAF Sqn 114, 117, 124, 153, 160, 161, 169, 171, 172, 184, 188, 192, 194, 242, 244, 256, 290, 296, 305, 310, 321, 330, 339, 348, 379, 392, 398, 439, 445

41 SAAF Sqn 19, 22, 76, 77, 103, 105, 106, 139, 159, 365

43 Sqn 118, 193, 231, 240, 275, 296, 308, 322, 327, 338, 339, 342, 344, 352, 356, 357, 362, 366, 380, 383, 389, 397, 419, 420, 432, 433, 439, 444

44 SAAF Sqn 444

46 Sqn 7, 10, 11, 12, 19, 25, 27, 30, 38, 40, 41, 42, 43, 53, 54, 55, 58, 67, 68, 69, 70, 84, 86, 91, 93, 99, 100, 101, 104, 108, 114, 120, 146, 257, 268, 269, 270, 271, 272, 273, 274, 275, 276, 449

47 Sqn 57, 58, 61, 62, 63, 65, 66, 68, 72, 76, 78, 80, 81, 84, 85, 87, 88, 89, 91, 92, 93, 94, 96, 98

55 Sqn 119, 140, 151, 167, 172, 185, 192, 233, 240, 242, 254, 266, 273, 341, 346, 349, 352, 364, 366, 367, 368, 383, 387, 396, 419, 422, 435, 439

72 Sqn 118, 136, 139, 140, 175, 192, 216, 243, 246, 287, 294, 317, 322, 326, 339, 342, 353, 357, 362, 367, 377, 380, 383, 391, 414, 418, 419, 420, 422, 427, 445

73 Sqn 113, 117, 128, 140, 141, 142, 143, 144, 148, 150, 154, 157, 164, 197, 260, 265, 277, 278, 287, 320, 340, 355, 378, 381, 382, 384, 385, 396, 397, 398, 407, 422, 445

74 Sqn 11, 19, 39, 40, 41, 74, 78,

77 RAAF Sqn 335

80 Sqn 15, 18, 19, 20, 21, 22, 30, 31

87 Sqn 128, 150, 194, 239, 242, 243, 247, 261, 306, 314, 317, 318, 338, 353, 357, 370, 381, 386, 391, 411, 421, 427, 431, 434, 445

89 Sqn 12, 34, 42, 43

92 Sqn 118, 126, 128, 135, 138, 142, 143, 175, 178, 188, 202,

203, 224, 232, 233, 234, 236, 248, 253, 256, 262, 273, 295, 306, 309, 311, 316, 327, 352, 363, 386, 389, 396, 403, 406, 407, 409, 412, 414, 416, 422, 425, 427, 438, 439, 445

93 Sqn 181, 200, 224, 236, 238, 239, 240, 250, 289, 296, 334, 355, 357, 358, 360, 379, 392, 412, 415, 417, 419, 420, 422, 423, 424, 425, 434, 439, 444, 445

94 Sqn 15, 18, 19, 22, 26, 41, 57, 69, 70, 101, 107, 110, 111, 112, 117, 156, 199, 292, 295, 296, 298, 299, 301, 306, 308, 309, 340, 398, 400

104 Sqn 86

108 Sqn 125, 139, 168, 190, 268, 272, 273, 275, 282, 287, 295, 351, 449

111 Sqn 210, 239, 272, 275, 321, 334, 339, 342, 344, 353, 357, 365, 379, 381, 385, 396, 423, 427, 433, 445

112 Sqn 137, 146, 164, 190, 194, 199, 203, 232, 238, 239, 243, 246, 251, 266, 285, 294, 295, 298, 305, 306, 312, 314, 342, 348, 363, 364, 366, 383, 390, 395, 407, 409, 417, 419, 422, 427, 444

114 Sqn 119, 197, 234, 240, 254, 273, 324, 334, 335, 353, 364, 365, 366, 368, 370, 377, 379, 439, 444

123 Sqn 11, 12, 19, 20, 22

126 Sqn 72, 150

127 Sqn 10, 11, 19, 89, 91, 93

134 Sqn 14, 16, 18, 19, 20, 22

145 Sqn 119, 120, 136, 139, 156, 164, 172, 188, 190, 196, 203, 210, 240, 242, 244, 252, 259, 264, 276, 280, 303, 304, 317, 327, 329, 333, 339, 343, 357, 380, 392, 403, 411, 418, 419, 422, 423, 427, 445

148 Sqn 129, 150, 317, 432, 433

151 Sqn 204, 210, 213, 224

153 Sqn 103, 104, 168, 198, 216, 234, 235, 245, 449

154 Sqn 91, 117, 123, 124, 126, 137, 157, 174, 175, 191

162 Sqn 26, 86, 95, 159

178 Sqn 36, 62, 75

185 Sqn 144, 146, 179, 180, 229, 232, 242, 255, 258, 260, 264, 360, 367, 370, 381, 392, 407, 417, 433, 435, 445

203 Sqn 16, 23, 41, 44, 45, 47, 62

208 Sqn 117, 119, 147, 169, 172, 188, 269, 275, 297, 337, 346, 347, 348, 401, 419, 421, 439, 445

213 Sqn 19, 28, 37, 55, 61, 94, 106, 107, 108, 109, 110, 112, 120, 128, 129, 165, 166, 167, 174, 176, 177, 183, 184, 187, 193, 199, 200, 207, 234, 239, 248, 249, 250, 251, 252, 253, 255, 259, 260, 262, 270, 281, 289, 290, 291, 294, 298, 306, 318, 326, 328, 339, 349, 350, 360, 362, 365, 373, 376, 377, 383, 384, 386, 391, 394, 395, 396, 411, 414, 420, 422, 429, 431, 432, 433, 445

216 Sqn 31, 32, 33, 34, 61, 73, 320, 444

221 Sqn 85, 111, 128, 150, 155, 194, 232, 397, 446

223 Sqn 118, 141, 156, 161, 162, 172, 180

225 Sqn 114, 119, 136, 172, 173, 202, 224, 254, 270, 296, 337, 343, 384, 389, 401, 439, 445

227 Sqn 7, 9, 10, 20, 22, 24, 25, 26, 27, 29, 32, 34, 36, 42, 43, 46, 51, 53, 55, 56, 57, 58, 59, 60, 61, 62, 63, 64, 71, 75, 84, 86, 87, 91, 93, 95, 96, 97, 98, 100, 102, 103, 104, 112, 113, 129, 131, 132, 218

232 Sqn 89, 123, 137, 142, 146, 153, 164, 173, 185, 186, 200, 201

237 Sqn 19, 22, 114, 122, 123, 125, 126, 137, 151, 173, 182, 262, 320, 323, 328, 367, 369, 396, 397, 411, 418, 423, 424, 428, 434, 436, 445

238 Sqn 10, 11, 19, 22, 117, 123, 124, 136, 140, 141, 158, 159, 173, 262

241 Sqn 122, 125, 126, 136, 137, 139, 147, 149, 172, 174, 175, 178, 181, 183, 184, 185, 188, 191, 194, 196, 199, 217, 228, 232, 239, 240, 242, 245, 256, 273, 294, 316, 334, 336, 338, 351, 360, 366, 370, 417, 419, 423, 439, 445

242 Sqn 117, 123, 126, 133, 137, 173, 184, 188, 203, 213, 217, 245

243 Sqn 117, 123, 126, 173

249 Sqn 75, 78, 123, 128, 129, 134, 137, 138, 146, 150, 152, 167, 192, 199, 200, 220, 247, 255, 256, 260, 262, 263, 264, 265, 266, 269, 270, 271, 281, 289, 292, 294, 296, 298, 300, 301, 321, 333, 335, 336, 354, 369, 370, 376, 388, 390, 395, 411, 414, 420, 423, 434, 438, 445

250 Sqn 172, 243, 256, 261, 264, 266, 287, 301, 306, 316, 321, 322, 325, 328, 333, 351, 352, 363, 382, 391, 394, 396, 409, 414, 419, 423, 429, 431, 439, 444

252 Sqn 14, 17, 23, 28, 30, 32, 33, 34, 36, 43, 50, 51, 55, 61, 76, 78, 80, 89, 92, 93, 102, 104, 110, 112, 113, 133, 150, 153, 184, 190, 191, 248, 266, 276, 342, 399, 443, 445

253 Sqn 117, 120, 122, 128, 129, 130, 150, 154, 172, 196, 199, 200, 262, 263, 278, 290, 294, 296, 298, 314, 323, 326, 333, 337, 339, 340, 369, 370, 382, 383, 389, 400, 417, 439, 443, 445

255 Sqn 115, 120, 122, 146, 147, 151, 154, 155, 156, 157, 173, 184, 186, 190, 192, 196, 198, 216, 233, 240, 246, 318, 341, 353, 382, 392, 393, 401, 444, 446

256 Sqn 151, 159, 164, 176, 177, 183, 190, 228, 272, 273, 277, 279, 285, 296, 318, 322, 334, 335, 336, 337, 339, 344, 345, 347, 360, 378, 379, 382, 385, 401, 412, 414, 415, 424, 425, 429, 436, 444, 446, 449, 450

260 Sqn 172, 180, 188, 191, 199, 202, 209, 232, 239, 250, 252, 257, 259, 266, 273, 304, 325, 328, 342, 346, 389, 407, 411, 419, 438, 439, 444, 447

267 Sqn 129, 168, 178, 262, 320

272 Sqn 24, 26, 194, 195, 235, 240, 246, 249, 250, 269, 287, 289, 296, 304, 312, 314, 318, 320, 323, 324, 325, 326, 339, 345, 353, 381, 414, 420, 424

283 Sqn 62

284 Sqn 117, 120, 126, 134, 154, 166, 256, 258

293 Sqn 117, 139, 177, 184, 194, 228, 232, 240, 253, 258, 266, 284, 294, 295, 305, 316, 330, 333, 350, 378, 382, 403, 439

294 Sqn 37, 106, 145, 146, 248, 256, 445

318 Sqn 136, 147, 169, 172, 188, 198, 330, 336, 390, 432, 439, 445

326 Sqn 125, 126, 159

335 Sqn 19, 20, 21, 22, 23, 98, 99, 104, 145, 146, 249, 261, 270, 280, 284, 285, 291, 302, 305, 318, 323, 445

336 Sqn 12, 19, 20, 22, 25, 65, 68, 69, 70, 84, 103, 106, 110, 270, 305, 312, 344, 373, 410, 445

351 Sqn 262, 294, 304, 307, 353, 356, 362, 370, 400, 411, 441, 445

352 Sqn 148, 200, 218, 219, 232, 235, 240, 247, 256, 266, 277, 290, 328, 370, 389, 398, 400, 441, 445

417 Sqn 118, 120, 130, 131, 132, 147, 151, 152 156, 171, 172, 180, 182, 199, 255, 313, 322, 325, 326, 329, 330, 334, 336, 339, 342, 345, 348, 352, 380, 388, 410, 412, 417, 418, 419, 422, 431, 436, 445

450 Sqn 141, 153, 172, 181, 203, 232, 236, 240, 245, 287, 305, 309, 313, 327, 328, 332, 335, 336, 352, 366, 370, 378, 383, 389, 390, 409, 411, 415, 417, 423, 424, 425, 444

451 Sqn 19, 96, 120, 121, 122, 124, 125, 142, 169, 173, 184, 187, 195, 259, 278

454 Sqn 7, 11, 13, 16, 20, 21, 22, 23, 35, 36, 54, 55, 64, 65, 66, 75, 76, 77, 78, 81, 84, 92, 95, 96, 98, 99, 100, 104, 113, 121, 131, 172, 232, 317, 340, 418, 422, 424, 445

458 Sqn 12, 202, 256, 320, 327, 359, 446

459 Sqn 12, 27, 28, 36, 87, 95, 100, 144, 165, 350

462 Sqn 35, 38, 43, 47, 53, 62, 75

500 Sqn 91, 101, 103, 104, 327, 338, 344, 345, 350, 403, 418, 421, 422, 445

600 Sqn 141, 147, 152, 156, 157, 173, 184, 185, 190, 192, 198, 216, 233, 235, 236, 237, 244, 245, 246, 253, 276, 288, 314, 318, 319, 321, 330, 337, 345, 346, 401, 418, 444, 449, 450

601 Sqn 130, 146, 147, 156, 157, 171, 172, 174, 177, 185, 188, 199, 243, 244, 247, 248, 256, 257, 260, 269, 280, 287, 307, 311, 316, 317, 325, 336, 347, 353, 363, 366, 389, 390, 409, 411, 418, 419, 422, 427, 433, 434, 436, 439, 444, 445

603 Sqn 46, 47, 61, 62, 63, 64, 65, 66, 68, 72, 82, 83, 84, 86, 87, 88, 89, 96, 103, 104, 105, 108, 109, 110, 112, 113, 152, 153, 175, 178, 180, 248, 251, 256, 258, 259, 261, 262, 276

613 Sqn 356

624 Sqn 150, 320, 334, 445

651 Sqn 427

654 Sqn 354, 445

655 Sqn 445

663 Sqn 445

680 Sqn 16, 27, 57, 94, 446

682 Sqn 94, 172, 264, 297

683 Sqn 41

700 Sqn 208

800 Sqn 208, 209, 217, 228, 229, 232, 276, 277, 282, 283, 293, 297, 298, 303, 304

807 Sqn 135, 142, 208, 212, 213, 216, 223, 225, 228, 232, 234, 235, 280, 281

809 Sqn 135, 164, 208, 209, 213, 216, 222, 228, 232, 234, 235, 268, 269, 270, 271, 280, 281, 288, 289, 290, 291

879 Sqn 141, 208, 209, 213, 216, 224, 226, 227, 228, 258, 298

881 Sqn 208, 213, 219, 221, 222, 226, 228, 232, 259, 260

882 Sqn 208, 213, 221, 222, 226, 228, 232

899 Sqn 208, 213, 216, 220, 228

1435 Sqn 81, 124, 138, 139, 150, 165, 181, 182, 249, 250, 295, 320, 377, 378, 380, 392, 407, 418

1586 Flight 129, 150

OTHER AIR FORCE UNITS

2 Balkan Air Terminal Service 128

4 ADU 197

5 RFU 315, 316

No.51 R&SU 197

76 OTU 89

103 MU 11, 12, 15, 25, 26, 30

107 MU 196

Belgian Congo Air Force 161, 228

DAF Comm Flight 442

Malta Night Fighter Unit 345

ME Comms Sqn 349

Wireless Interception service 392

WINGS

4 Naval Fighter Wing 135

D Naval Fighter Wing 208

3 SAAF Wing 136, 141, 152, 156, 161, 172, 337, 376, 383, 413, 417, 421, 441, 445

7 SAAF Wing 119, 136, 146, 161, 163, 171, 172, 188, 243, 301, 337, 376, 400, 410, 419, 444, 445

8 SAAF Wing 258, 287, 337, 341, 401, 411, 439, 445, 446

232 Wing 128, 172, 337, 366, 376, 441, 444

239 Wing 118, 138, 140, 156, 161, 163, 171, 172, 181, 188, 189, 337, 353, 376, 390, 419, 429, 444

243 Wing 33, 38, 41

244 Wing 118, 135, 136, 146, 163, 171, 172, 178, 185, 188, 208, 316, 337, 342, 348, 415, 416, 417, 419, 441, 444, 445

251 Wing 114, 118, 119, 120, 125, 126, 136, 137, 147, 157, 165, 169, 173, 187, 266

253 Wing 172, 337, 342, 375, 401, 445

254 Wing 128, 129, 156, 218, 238, 298, 320, 376, 445

281 Wing 128, 129, 200, 262, 353, 400, 420, 440, 445

285 (Reconnaissance) Wing 172, 337, 347, 439, 445

286 Wing 150, 320, 445

287 Wing 173, 320, 420, 445

322 Wing 114, 118, 125, 126, 127, 147, 157, 165, 173, 201, 245

323 Wing 128, 150, 320, 450

324 Wing 114, 118, 128, 139, 146, 147, 165, 173, 272, 275, 337, 362, 363, 376, 380, 390, 395, 410, 411, 412, 419, 441, 442, 444, 445

334 Wing 129, 150

337 Wing 373, 388, 445

GROUPS

100 Group 401

201 Group 7, 18, 19

205 Group 6, 7, 114, 130, 401, 412

209 Group 18, 19

210 Group 19, 20

212 Group 18, 19, 22

219 Group 18, 19, 22, 100

COMMANDS AND AIR FORCES

Combined Chiefs of Staff (CCS) 77, 113, 353

Air Command, South East Asia 402

Air Defences, Eastern Mediterranean (ADEM) 18, 19, 20, 36, 41

Balkan Air Force (BAF) 6, 77, 113, 114, 118, 128, 129, 149, 156, 167, 168, 200, 218, 238, 241, 250, 268, 287, 309, 320, 321, 322, 353, 376, 400, 402, 407, 439, 442, 445, 448

Bomber Command 401

Coastal Air Force (CAF) 6, 7, 29, 118, 150, 173, 188, 444, 445

Desert Air Force (DAF) 29, 105, 118, 119, 120, 128, 136, 141, 156, 163, 167, 168, 170, 171, 172, 173, 174, 188, 203, 208, 287, 337, 341, 353, 374, 376,

389, 390, 402, 408, 409, 410, 412, 413, 416, 418, 419, 420, 422, 442, 444, 446, 448

Forces Aériennes Françaises Libres (FAFL) 173

Mediterranean Air Command 6, 77

Mediterranean Allied Air Forces (MAAF) 7, 77, 118, 196, 353, 444

Mediterranean Allied Coastal Air Force (MACAF) 445

Mediterranean Allied Strategic Air Force (MASAF) 6, 7, 18, 29, 150, 320, 353, 376, 401, 402, 413

Mediterranean Allied Tactical Air Force (MATAF) 6, 55, 150, 170, 171, 173, 203, 265, 336, 337, 341, 353, 363, 366, 393, 400,

401, 402, 412, 419, 425, 429, 436, 444, 446, 448

Middle East Command, 6, 18, 101

North West African Coastal Air Force (NWACAF) 6

North West African Strategic Air Force (NWASAF) 6

North West African Tactical Air Force (NWATAF) 6

RAF Malta 7, 77

RAF Mediterranean and Middle East 157

RAF Middle East 6, 7, 18, 29, 40, 46, 77

RAF Regiment 31, 40

2909 Sqn RAF Regiment 33, 34, 35, 40

Special Operations Air Force 128

2nd Tactical Air Force 350, 354

ALLIED MILITARY UNITS

Allied Combined Chiefs of Staff 353

5th Army 118, 135, 147, 170, 189, 254, 287, 321, 346, 401, 419, 427, 435, 437

7th Army 170

8th Army 118, 135, 138, 140, 161, 163, 169, 170, 171, 172, 189, 233, 235, 254, 354, 401, 412, 413, 419, 427, 439

15th Army Group 77, 402

South African Army 189

4th Yugoslav Army 376, 400, 439

Military and Diplomatic Mission to Tito (MACMIS) 168

1st Armoured Division (French) 207

2nd New Zealand Division 412, 418

3rd Infantry Division (US) 207

10th Mountain Division 419, 427

36th Division (US) 207

45th Division (US) 207

234th Infantry Brigade 30

4th Parachute Regiment 265

40 Commando, Royal Marines 287

Long Range Desert Group 30

Special Boat Service 30

Canadian First Special Service Force 207

Greek Sacreda Squadron 61

9 (Field) Squadron Royal Engineers 40

II Corps (US) 427

II Corps (Yugoslavian) 129

II Corps (Polish) 171, 172, 412

IV Corps (US) 419

V Corps (US) 118, 135, 322, 412

VI Corps (US) 207, 218

XIII Corps (UK) 156, 171

French Expeditionary Corps 170

Adams, 2/Lt Billy E., 64th FS/57th FG 285

Adams, 1/Lt John R., 522nd FS/27th FG 344

Adams, Lt Col William A., 442nd BS/320th BG 214

Adler, 1/Lt W.Clifford, 527th FS/86th FG 328

Ainsworth, Lt Robert D., 524th FS/27th FG 239

Albury, 1/Lt Joseph L. Jr, 95th BS/17th BG 225

Alexander, 2/Lt Shuford M. Jr, 346th FS/350th FG 273

Allen, Lt Clarence, 100th FS/332nd FG 204, 207

Allen, Lt Clyde T., 32nd PRS/5th 384

Allen, 2/Lt Hyrum J., 417th NFS 293

Allen, 1/Lt Truman L., 65th FS/57th FG 437

Allison, Maj R.B., 379th BS/310th BG 196

Alston, Lt James M., VOF-1 225

Alworth, 2/Lt William F., 524th FS/27th FG 359

Anderson, Flt Off A.L., 344th BS/98th BG 14

Anderson, 2/Lt Beriger A., 526th FS/86th FG 319

Anderson, 1/Lt Douglas R., 448th BS/321st BG 307

Anderson, 1/Lt George W., 64th FS/57th FG 307

Anderson, 2/Lt James E. Jr, 86th FS/79th FG 307

Anderson, 1/Lt John P., 64th FS/57th FG 307

Anderson, 2/Lt Joseph E. Jr, 428th BS/310th BG 383

Anderson, 1/Lt Leslie E., 96th FS/82nd FG 79

Anderson, 1/Lt Miller A., 66th FS/57th FG 392

Anderson, 2/Lt Robert C., 417th NFS 320

Anderson, 1/Lt Robert L., 525th FS/86th FG 287

Anderson, 2/Lt Wayne P., 345th FS/350th FG 329

Anderson, 2/Lt William H., 65th FS/57th FG 370

Andrews, 2/Lt Franklin M., 414th NFS 268

Angyal, 1/Lt Zolton J., 86th FS/79th FG 378

Appenzeller, 1/Lt Richard D., 447th BS/321st BG 351

Arbuckle, Lt(jg) William N., VF-74 225

Armstrong, 1/Lt Joseph R., 442nd BS/320th BG 228

Arnold, 2/Lt Calvin J., 86th FS/79th FG 280

Arnsdorff, 1/Lt, 441st BS/320th BG 312

Arthur, 1/Lt Robert M., 10th TCS/60th TCG 312

Asbury, 1/Lt Maurice L., 346th FS/350th FG 370

Ascenzi, 1/Lt Richard, 86th FS/79th FG 358

Atkins, 2/Lt Damon E., 87th FS/79th FG 123

Attone, 2/Lt Jacob C., 414th NFS 268

Atwood, Lt Benjamin J., 65th FS/57th FG 325

Augspurger, Capt H.F., 415th NFS 271

Aynes, 2/Lt William, 316th FS/324th FG 167

Babcock, 2/Lt James F., 12th PRS/3rd PRG 256

Bach, 1/Lt Lawrence V. Jr, 37th FS/14th FG 357

Bachman, 1/Lt Addison A., 346th FS/350th FG 431

Bade, 1/Lt Ronald O., 345th FS/350th FG 436

Bagian, 2/Lt Philip, 87th FS/79th FG 236

Bagley, 1/Lt Grant W., 347th FS/350th FG 438

Bagley, 1/Lt Wendell B., 317th FS/325th FG 426

Baker, 1/Lt James M., 34th BS/17th BG 177

Baker, Lt Thomas M., 87th FS/79th FG 154

Baldwin, Capt Eldon C., 345th FS/350th FG 336

Baldwin, 1/Lt Woodrow P., 317th FS/325th FG 426

Ballard, 1/Lt Dempsey E., 346th FS/350th FG 331

Banker, 1/Lt Ernest H., 85th BS/47th BG 316

Banner, 2/Lt Donald W., 524th FS/27th FG 357

Baranek, Lt Carl C., 326th FS/86th FG 365

Barnum, Maj Robert A., 64th FS/57th FG 437

Barrett, 1/Lt John, 317th FS/325th FG 426

Barrons, 2/Lt William J., 414th NFS 184

Barryhill, 1/Lt Jesse W., 417th NFS 302

Bartlett, 2/Lt Stuart L., 86th FS/ 79th FG 122

Bartley, 2/Lt Harry E., 87th FS/ 79th FG 340

Barton, 1/Lt Howard L., 346th FS/350th FG 404, 407

Bass, Lt Cdr Harry B., VF-74 209, 223–224, 225

Bateman, 2/Lt William W., 65th FS/57th FG 220

Baughn, S/Sgt Harry J., 344th BS/98th BG 14

Beck, 2/Lt James M. Jr, 346th FS/350th FG 414

Beesley, 2/Lt Joseph G., 65th FS/57th FG 373

Beeson, 1/Lt Ellwood H., 447th BS/321st BG 62

Beaver, 2/Lt Frank F., 416th NFS 431

Bell, Lt, 84th FS/79th FG 117

Bell, Capt Donald W., 66th FS/57th FG 257

Bell, 1/Lt Robert B., 85th FS/79th FG 298

Caple, Maj Charles E., 325th FG 164

Carlson, Capt Zane E., 346th FS/350th FG 304

Carlyle, 1/Lt Lester C., 524th FS/27th FG 251

Carpenter, 2/Lt Elbert R., 347th FS/350th FG 133

Casey, 2/Lt Thomas V., 487th BS/340th BG 74, 137

Cassidy, Lt Benjamin B. Jr, 87th FS/79th FG 146

Castanedo, Lt(jg) Edwin W., VF-74 222–223

Casterline, 2/Lt Clyde J., 65th FS/57th FG 346

Castings, 2/Lt George Jr, 154th CMS 65

Cattanach, 2/Lt/1 Lt Alexander R., 523rd FS/27th FG 236, 340

Chalfield, 2/Lt Gene A., 97th FS/82nd FG 79

Chamberlain, Maj Carlton, 64th FS/57th FG 431

Chambers, Capt Boyd B. Jr, 527th FS/86th FG 338

Chandler, 1/Lt Warren W., 446th BS/321st BG 357

Chaplin, 2/Lt D.H., 523rd FS/27th FG 255

Chapman, 2/Lt Earl O., 95th FS/82nd FG 71

Chapman, Capt Franklin W., 414th NFS 311

Charpentier, 1/Lt Leonard A., 86th FS/79th FG 239

Cheely, 2/Lt Lael M., 414th NFS 415

Chiang, Gen. Kai-shek, 77

Chidlaw, Gen Benjamin W., XII AF 402

Childs, 1/Lt Ollie B., 95th BS/17th BG 316

Clark, 1/Lt Herbert V., 99th FS/332nd FG 216

Clark, 2/Lt William A. Jr, 314th FS/324th FG 236

Clark, 1/Lt William R., 97th FS/82nd FG 79

Clarke, 2/Lt Samuel G., 85th BS/47th BG 378

Claycomb, 1/Lt Donald E., 86th FS/79th FG 246

Clayton, 2/Lt Robert H., 345th FS/350th FG 424

Cleveland, 2/Lt Howard W., 66th FS/57th FG 147, 149, 154

Clifton, 2/Lt Emil G., 99th FS/332nd FG 239

Clifton, 1/Lt Kenneth E., 345th FS/350th FG 331, 359

Clifton, 1/Lt Leroy, 347th FS/350th FG 264

Coble, 1/Lt Truman R., 379th BS/310th BG 123

Coburn, Flt Off Julius H., 66th FS/57th FG 139

Cole, 2/Lt Truman C., 441st BS/320th BG 305

Coleman, S/Sgt Robert C., 343rd BS/98th BG 14

Collier, Sgt A.L., 512th BS/376th BG 45

Collins, 1/Lt Clifton A., 440th BS/319th BG 177

Collins, 1/Lt Harry L. Jr, 381st BS/310th BG 292

Condon, 2/Lt Robert W., 417th NFS 364

Connor, 1/Lt John V. Jr, 525th FS/86th FG 340

Cooke, 2/Lt Raymond K., 97th FS/82nd FG 71

Cooper, 2/Lt Donavon J., 525th FS/86th FG 234

Cooper, 2/Lt James E., 488th BS/340th BG 151

Copeland, 2/Lt Loye M., 65th FS/57th FG 381

Cordell, 2/Lt Dan B., 417th NFS 192

Core, Capt Jesse R. III, 527th FS/86th FG 325

Corning, Capt Clarence H., 97th FS/82nd FG 48

Cornwell, 2/Lt Richard M., 417th NFS 364

Correll, 1/Lt Carl E. Jr, 525th FS/86th FG 123

Cottle, 1/Lt Robert J. Jr, 448th BS/321st BG 240

Courbat, Sgt Charles G., 379th BS/310th BG 394

Coyne, Lt(jg) John H., VOF-1 228

Crabtree, 1/Lt Richard C., 523rd FS/27th FG 318

Craw, 2/Lt John I. Jr, 85th BS/47th BG 143

Crawford, Flt Off Harris F., 316th FS/324th FG 117

Criss, 2/Lt Donald A., 85th BS/47th BG 316

Crockett, Lt David D., VOF-1 225, 229, 230

Croskery, 1/Lt Keith S., 87th FS/79th FG 301

Cunningham, S/Sgt Larquis W., 121st LS 389

Curtin, 2/Lt William P., 525th FS/86th FG 196

Dailey, 1/Lt James B. Jr, 346th FS/350th FG 301

Danforth, Flt Off Samuel G. Jr, 414th NFS 285

Daniel, Flt Off William W., 523rd FS/27th FG 246

Daniels, 1/Lt John C., 489th BS/340th BG 381

Daniels, 2/Lt Robert H., 302nd FS/332nd FG 201

Darcy, Brig Gen Thomas C., XXII TAC 402

Davies, Capt John A., 416th NFS 351

Davis, 2/Lt Thomas D. Jr, 66th FS/57th FG 149, 242, 244

Davison, Capt Paul C., 12th TCS/60th TCG 252

Deakyne, 1/Lt Theodore A., 417th NFS 319

DeBoer, 2/Lt Jay Jr, 445th BS/321st BG 370

Deckert, 2/Lt George F., 66th FS/57th FG 120

Dehmer, 1/Lt Charles S., 66th FS/57th FG 323

DeMasters, Ens Marion F., VF(N)-74 226

Dentoni, 1/Lt Louis M., 445th BS/321st BG 414

Devlin, Lt, 445th BS/321st BG 62

DeVore, 2/Lt Jack, 417th NFS 313

Dexter, S/Sgt Harold H., 447th BS/321st BG 62

Dickey, 2/Lt Earl R., 416th NFS 373

Diemer, 2/Lt John E., 346th FS/350th FG 201

Diffendal, 1/Lt John, 346th FS/350th FG 330

Dillingham, ? 487th BS/340th BG 74

Dillon, 1/Lt Jack E., 441st BS/320th BG 132

Dilworth, 2/Lt George W., 314th FS/324th FG 247

Dinwiddie, 1/Lt Robert E., 441st BS/320th BG 229

Dodds, 1/Lt Wayne S., 66th FS/57th FG 323–324

Dodson, 1/Lt Jackson R., 447th BS/321st BG 356

Dolezal, 2/Lt Clarence, 96th FS/82nd FG 79

Domin, 1/Lt Martin S., 346th FS/350th FG 433

Donahue, 1/Lt Joseph M., 346th BS/99th BG 86

Donovan, 2/Lt Charles F., 487th BS/340th BG 273

Dossey, 1/Lt Vernon C., 448th BS/321st BG 294

Dorval, 2/Lt George J., 64th FS/57th FG 285

Doughty, 2/Lt Orville L., 96th BS/2nd BG 83

Douglas, 1/Lt Lindsay R. Jr, 65th FS/57th FG 359

Dow, Maj Hugh D., 347th FS/350th FG 347

Draughn, Flt Off Beverly D., 432nd BS/17th BG 225

Driessen, 2/Lt Donald J., 522nd FS/27th FG 352

Driscoll, 1/Lt Richard N., 444th BS/320th BG 232

Dunham, S/Sgt F.E., 512th BS/376th BG 45

Durante, 2/Lt Angelo M., G BS/321st BG 57

Durgin, Rear Adm Calvin T., TG 88.2 208, 233

Durland, 1/Lt Frederic E., 86th BS/47th BG 184

Eaker, Lt Gen/Gen Ira C., MAAF 75, 402

Eastburn, 1/Lt Lester L., 526th FS/86th FG 342

Eastman, 1/Lt Lawrence E., 523rd FS/27th FG 126, 178

Eckardt, Lt (Jg) Harold J., 111th TRS 128

Eddy, 2/Lt/1/Lt Charles C. Jr, 346th FS/350th FG 351, 386, 387, 403–404, 407

Edgar, Capt Thomas P. Jr, 34th BS/17th BG 126

Edwards, 2/Lt James T., 447th BS/321st BG 247

Eichorn, 2/Lt Benton F., 379th BS/310th BG 120

Eisenhower, Gen Dwight D., 46

Eldred, 2/Lt George F., 27th FS/1st FG 162

Ellis, 1/Lt Donald A., 347th FS/350th FG 277

Ellis, 1/Lt John L., 486th BS/340th BG 410

Ellis, 2/Lt Roger C. Jr, 346th FS/350th FG 427

Ely, Lt(jg) Curtis, M. VOF-1 235

Ely, Cpl Edward B., 379th BS/310th BG 394

Emerson, Capt Roy C., 66th FS/57th FG 218

Englert, Capt Lawrence E., 416th NFS 373

English, 2/Lt Edwin R., 96th FS/82nd FG 79

Ensley, Capt Arthur T., 380th BS/310th BG 314

Eschbach, 2/Lt Philip I. Jr, 95th BS/17th BG 234

Eshelman, T/Sgt Paul A., 343rd BS/98th BG 14

Estes, 1/Lt Russell G., 442nd BS/320th BG 255

Evans, 1/Lt Earle H., 65th FS/57th FG 387

Everhart, 1/Lt Herman E., 446th BS/321st BG 392

Ewing, Capt/Maj George W. Jr, 86th FS/79th FG 162, 182

Fahlberg, 1/Lt Ernest D., 346th FS/350th FG 342

Faires, 2/Lt Jack, 85th FS/79th FG 393, 394

Faison, 1/Lt Ronald M., 87th FS/79th FG 322

Fallon, Capt Paul J., 513th BS/376th BG 45

Fassett, 1/Lt Walter J., 97th BS/47th BG 434

Fast, Maj Robert D., 34th BS/17th BG 126

Faulkner, 2/Lt Glenn W., 85th FS/79th FG 431

Fields, 1/Lt John L., 97th BS/47th BG 392

Fierstein, Lt Stanley F., 111th TRS 231

Figler, 1/Lt Roman H., 486th BS/340th BG 360

Files, Capt Roger B., 86th FS/79th FG 236

Fischer, 2/Lt Roland J., 314th FS/324th FG 164

Fisher, 1/Lt Gene M., 346th FS/350th FG 427

Fisher, 1/Lt James B. Jr, 445th BS/321st BG 48

Fitzgerald, 1/Lt James D., 35th TCS/64th TCG 354

Fletcher, Flt Off Stephen E., 524th FS/27th FG 154

Flory, 2/Lt Laurence J. Jr, 522nd FS/27th FG 117

Folsom, 1/Lt Frank I. Jr, 428th BS/310th BG 330

Fontenot, T/Sgt V.L., 446th BS/321st BG 70

Ford, 1/Lt Claud E., 95th FS/82nd FG 48

Foss, 2/Lt Floyd P., 414th NFS 311

Foster, 2/Lt Lewis K., 526th FS/86th FG 255

Fournier, 2/Lt William J., 65th FS/57th FG 120

Fox, 2/Lt Billie J., 416th NFS 319

Frank, 1/Lt Robert R., 445th BS/321st BG 276

Franklin, 2/Lt Eugene K., 416th NFS 352

Fraser, 2/Lt Harry A. Jr, 447th BS/321st BG 62

Fraser, 2/Lt Louis E., 64th FS/57th FG 347

Freeborn, 2/Lt Andrew W., 347th FS/350th FG 364

Frierson, 2/Lt Edwin S., 64th FS/57th FG 317

Fromm, Capt Robert E., 522nd FS/27th FG 294

Fulton, 2/Lt Bruce W., 527th FS/86th FG 325

Gabor, Maj Edward J., 345th FS/350th FG 440

Galentine, 1/Lt Paul G. Jr, 381st BS/310th BG 314

Galovich, 2/Lt Max W., 416th NFS 398

Gardner, Sgt Blair L., 380th BS/310th BG 392, 394

Gary, 1/Lt Clarence A., 522nd FS/27th FG 201

Gearhart, 1/Lt Gayle C., 489th BS/340th BG 370

Gilbert, Maj Charles E. II, 346th FS/350th FG 403–405, 407

Gilmore, Lt Eugene O., 86th FS/79th FG 182

Gilmore, 2/Lt Samuel B., 348th BS/99th BG 52

Gimson, 1/Lt K.L., 381st BS/310th BG 180

Ginsberg, 2/Lt Erwin, 522nd FS/27th FG 139

Givens, S/Sgt John A., 344th BS/98th BG 14

Goettel, 1/Lt Arthur C., 64th FS/57th FG 427

Gogan, 1/Lt Harry L., 66th FS/57th FG 328

Gomez, 2/Lt Thomas E., 346th FS/350th FG 354

Gordon, 2/Lt Joseph E., 99th FS/332nd FG 201

Gorski, 1/Lt Norbert J., 345th FS/350th FG 424

Gorsuch, 1/Lt Richard P., 87th FS/79th FG 336

Goslin, Lt, 527th FS/86th FG 255

Gottlieb, Lt Abraham I., 523rd FS/27th FG 117

Grace, 1/Lt Lawrence G. Jr, 64th FS/57th FG 307

Graham, 1/Lt James A., 64th FS/57th FG 345

Graham, 2/Lt Joe S., 414th NFS 314

Granberg, Lt Martin J., 85th FS/79th FG 175

Grant, Capt Peter J., 379th BS/310th BG 394

Graves, 2/Lt William H., 97th BS/47th BG 153

Green, Maj Herschel H., 317th FS/325th FG 164

Green, 1/Lt William A., 448th BS/321st BG 124

Greene, 2/Lt James L., 85th FS/79th FG 192

Greenfield, S/Sgt John T., 379th BS/310th BG 394

Greggerson, 2/Lt Richard J., 345th FS/350th FG 431

Grey, 2/Lt Merril C., 316th FS/324th FG 252

Gries, Cpl Leo L., 379th BS/310th BG 394

Grinnell, 2/Lt William, 417th NFS 290, 313

Groendycke, 2/Lt Guilford D., 66th FS/57th FG 354, 355

Grossmith, 2/Lt Jared H., 428th BS/310th BG 308

Gugeler, 2/Lt Ivan W., 523rd FS/27th FG 124

Hacking, 1/Lt La Verle T., 379th BS/310th BG 308

Hadley, 2/Lt Leonard R., 65th FS/57th FG 433

Hain, 2/Lt Calvin S. Jr, 66th FS/57th FG 186

Hale, Lt Bruce H., 64th FS/57th FG 166

Halfpapp, Capt Arthur E., 87th FS/79th FG 434

Hall, 1/Lt Benjamin W. III, 2nd FS/52nd FG 414

Hall, 1/Lt/Capt Paul M., 64th FS/57th FG 301, 307

Hamilton, 1/Lt Robert D., 417th NFS 327

Hammond, Sgt Benjamin, 380th BS/310th BG 360

Hammond, Capt David Q. Jr, 444th BS/320th BG 306

Hammond, 2/Lt Jeremiah F., 314th FS/324th FG 128

Hancock, 1/Lt Charles T., 86th FS/79th FG 182

Hand, 2/Lt Stanley S., 96th FS/82nd FG 44

Hanes, Maj, 71st FS/1st FG 46

Hanna, 2/Lt Harry T., 37th FS/14th FG 50, 52

Hannon, 1/Lt James F., 86th FS/79th FG 351

Hansman, 2/Lt Ralph S., 523rd FS/27th FG 117

Hanson, 1/Lt Herbert L., 87th FS/79th FG 396

Hardin, 2/Lt William E., 345th FS/350th FG 247

Harding, 2/Lt William L., 87th FS/79th FG 340

Hardman, 1/Lt Albert F. Jr, 445th BS/321st BG 155

Hare, 1/Lt/Capt James C., 65th FS/66th FS/57th FG 155, 389

Hargrove, 2/Lt Dale H., 345th FS/350th FG 334

Harmer, Sgt Harry B., 447th BS/321st BG 62

Harp, 1/Lt James L. Jr, 64th FS/57th FG 378

Harris, 2/Lt Donald M., 522nd FS/27th FG 306

Harris, 2/Lt Jesse A. Jr, 522nd FS/27th FG 117

Hart, 2/Lt William B., 85th BS/47th BG 360

Hartmeister, 2/Lt Joel T., 445th BS/321st BG 48

Hartwick, 2/Lt George A. Jr, 15th CMS/5th PRG 240

Hauser, 2/Lt Joseph J., 65th FS/57th FG 431

Hausner, 1/Lt Sigmund E., 347th FS/350th FG 378

Hay, Lt William J., 522nd FS/27th FG 356

Hayney, 2/Lt Lloyd J., 65th FS/57th FG 433

Hays, 1/Lt Louis O. III, 66th FS/57th FG 355, 412

Hays, 2/Lt Oliver B., 347th FS/350th FG 338

Head, 1/Lt Billy M., 86th FS/79th FG 182

Hearne, 1/Lt Alfred C., 86th FS/79th FG 374

Hearne, Flt Off Theodore E., 417th NFS 175

Hearrell, Capt Dave C. Jr, 111th TRS 217

Heath, 2/Lt Ellis G., 522nd FS/27th FG 232

Hebbel, 2/Lt George T., 523rd FS/27th FG 251

Heckenkamp, Capt Frank W., 346th FS/350th FG 404–405, 408, 444,

Heinecke, 2/Lt Harold H., 417th NFS 155

Held, 2/Lt Robert V., 526th FS/86th FG 359

Hendrickson, Lt, 524th FS/27th FG 201

Henry, 2/Lt Lester J., 95th FS/82nd FG 162

Henry, S/Sgt William R., 447th BS/321st BG 62

Herdrich, 1/Lt Donald G., 66th FS/57th FG 333

Herman, 1/Lt Herbert, 439th BS/319th BG 325

Hernandez, 2/Lt Carl P., 525th FS/86th FG 154

Herreilers, S/Sgt Frederick H., 341st BS/97th BG 79

Herriges, 2/Lt Norbert W., 522nd FS/27th FG 201

Herrin, 1/Lt Scott, 489th BS/340th BG 370

Herron, 2/Lt Jack, 416th NFS 431

Hertel, Sgt Bob, 489th BS/340th BG 160

Hewitt, 1/Lt Clarence L. III, 65th FS/57th FG 381

Hewitt, Adm Henry K., 218

Hewitt, 1/Lt Robert F., 86th FS/79th FG 346

Heying, Capt Arno H., 66th FS/57th FG 356

Higginson, 2/Lt Benjamin A. Jr, 525th FS/86th FG 229

Hildebrandt, 1/Lt R.A., 95th BS/17th BG 269

Hilgard, 2/Lt Richard W., 86th FS/79th FG 182

Hill, 1/Lt George E., 527th FS/86th FG 295, 321

Hill, 2/Lt Thomas A., 417th NFS 155

Hill, Lt William R., 66th FS/57th FG 149

Hintz, 2/Lt Loren E., 86th FS/79th FG 429

Hipple, 1/Lt James H., 441st BS/320th BG 203

Hoerr, 2/Lt Irvin C., 86th FS/79th FG 365

Hoke, 2/Lt Robert E., 49th FS/14th FG 82

Holbrook, 2/Lt John V., 523rd FS/27th FG 340

Holder, Lt Bert E., 316th FS/324th FG 126, 156

Holloway, S/Sgt Lewis A., 379th BS/310th BG 394

Homan, 2/Lt John Jr, 97th FS/82nd FG 56

Hooper, S/Sgt Charles R., 343rd BS/98th BG 45

Hope, 2/Lt James T., 414th NFS 229

Horacek, Lt Leo Jr, VF-74 222

Hoschar, 1/Lt John P., 486th BS/340th BG 214

Hosey, FO William E., 346th FS/350th FG 367

Houser, 2/Lt Morris N., 10th TCS/60th TCG 179

Howard, 2/Lt Grover, 347th FS/350th FG 277

Howard, 1/Lt John M., 414th NFS 316

Howlett, 2/Lt D.G., 379th BS/310th BG 137

Hoy, 2/Lt Richard F., 111th TRS 229

Hubbard, 1/Lt Norman K., 347th FS/350th FG 409

Huff, 1/Lt Raymond J., 526th FS/86th FG 305

Hughes, 1/Lt Emmett W., 488th BS/340th BG 398

Hughes, 2/Lt Paul W., 65th FS/57th FG 370

Hughes, 2/Lt Thomas E., 37th BS/17th BG 285

Hulland, Ens Charles W.S., VF-74 223, 225

Hunger, 2/Lt Ned O., 522nd FS/27th FG 251

Hunt, 2/Lt Wesley H., 316th FS/324th FG 133

Hutchins, 1/Lt Sanborn B., 526th FS/86th FG 314

Hutton, 2/Lt David T., 66th FS/57th FG 273

Iavelli, 2/Lt Carlo A., 527th FS/86th FG 350

Ingley, Lt Harold J., 526th FS/86th FG 229

Inglis, 2/Lt Robert W., 417th NFS 175

Iverson, 1/Lt Harold G., 428th BS/310th BG 261

Jackson, 2/Lt Paul T. Jr, 525th FS/86th FG 347

Jackson, 1/Lt Roland B., 446th BS/321st BG 436

Jacobs, 2/Lt James E., 488th BS/340th BG 390

James, 2/Lt Arthur E., 526th FS/86th FG 328

Janish, 1/Lt Frank H., 416th NFS 352

Jefferson, 2/Lt Alexander, 302nd FS/332nd FG 201

Jefferson, 2/Lt Russell E., 525th FS/86th FG 154

Jefferson, 2/Lt Samuel, 100th FS/332nd FG 137

Jenkins, 2/Lt Harry E., 441st BS/320th BG 233

Jennings, Flt Off, 346th FS/350th FG 404

Jennings, Flt Off Russell K., 87th FS/79th FG 236

Jensen, 1/Lt Jerald B., 12th PRS/3rd PRG 234

Jerue, 1/Lt John P., 347th FS/350th FG 301

Johnson, 2/Lt Charles B., 100th FS/332nd FG 137

Johnson, 1/Lt John C., 154th TRS 328

Johnson, 1/Lt Langdon E., 100th FS/332nd FG 201

Johnson, 1/Lt Odell J., 314th FS/324th FG 252

Johnson, 2/Lt Richard L., 66th FS/57th FG 149

Johnson, 1/Lt Robert G. Jr, 345th FS/350th FG 328

Johnson, Lt Robert J., VF-74 218

Johnson, 1/Lt Wilbur H., 523rd FS/27th FG 357

Johnston, 2/Lt Lawrence L., 526th FS/86th FG 273, 439

Jones, 1/Lt Albert L., 414th NFS 330

Jones, Flt Off Alvin C., 47th BG 266

Jones, 1/Lt Edward C., 444th BS/320th BG 214

Jones, 2/Lt Edward F., 523rd FS/27th FG 130

Jones, 2/Lt Gordon H., 66th FS/57th FG 191

Jones, 1/Lt Russell W., 444th BS/320th BG 312

Jones, 1/Lt T.E., 488th BS/340th BG 166

Jordan, 1/Lt John V., 525th FS/86th FG 194, 336

Jorgensen, Flt Off Reginald M., 526th FS/86th FG 225

Joslin, 1/Lt James B., 525th FS/86th FG 314

Joyce, 2/Lt Paul R., 522nd FS/27th FG 166

Kalan, Flt Off Stanley, 416th NFS 431

Kamanski, Lt Charles W.P., 444th BS/320th BG 305

Kangas, 2/Lt Wesley, 416th NFS 431

Kapner, Flt Off Sylvan L., 527th FS/86th FG 169

Karlson, Lt, 111th TRS 124

Karrels, 1/Lt Clifford A., 525th FS/86th FG 305

Kazarian, 2/Lt Arthur S., 111th TRS 128

Keane, 1/Lt Robert E., 380th BS/310th BG 223, 256

Keister, 1/Lt Jordan E., 428th BS/310th BG 383

Keith, Flt Off Charles F., G BS/321st BG 57

Keller, 1/Lt Ralph H., 379th BS/310th BG 261

Keppler, 1/Lt George E., 85th FS/79th FG 357

Kienholz, 1/Lt Donald D., 94th FS/1st FG 82

Killian, 1/Lt Robert F., 381st BS/310th BG 137

King, 2/Lt Byron D., 488th BS/340th BG 304

King, 2/Lt J., 37th BS/17th BG 256

Kinley, 2/Lt Lloyd D., 527th FS/86th FG 240

Kirkendall, Capt James F., 314th FS/324th FG 162

Kittrell, 1/Lt John C., 87th FS/79th FG 423

Kleiderer, Lt Eugene L. Jr, 85th FS/79th FG 149

Klemme, 2/Lt Ardel, 526th FS/86th FG 264

Knight, 1/Lt Raymond L., 346th FS/350th FG 435–436

Knight, 1/Lt William T., 428th BS/310th BG 413

Knighton, 1/Lt Marshall W., 486th BS/340th BG 360

Knispel, 1/Lt Raymond C., 523rd FS/27th FG 244

Krasulak, 1/Lt Michael, 314th FS/324th FG 234

Kruse, 1/Lt Milford E., 448th BS/321st BG 308

Kruse, 1/Lt Richard W., 66th FS/57th FG 370

Kulik, 1/Lt Ernest J., 379th BS/310th BG 123

Kuykendall, 1/Lt William F., 524th FS/27th FG 239

LaClare, Maj Edward F., 94th FS/1st FG 206, 403

Lancaster, Lt Harold W., 65th FS/57th FG 156

Landan, 2/Lt Arnold, 527th FS/86th FG 200

Landers, 2/Lt Charles L., 87th FS/79th FG 117

Langston, Flt Off Andrew J., 347th FS/350th FG 381

Langston, 2/Lt Carroll N., 301st FS/332nd FG 120

Larkin, 2/Lt S.J., 381st BS/310th BG 195

Larsen, 2/Lt Hubbard P., 416th NFS 351

LaRue, 2/Lt Elmer H., 37th FS/14th FG 52

Larzelere, T/Sgt W.E., 513th BS/376th BG 45

Lavender, 2/Lt James F., 379th BS/310th BG 90

LaVine, 1/Lt Morris D., 487th BS/340th BG 345

Lawrence, 1/Lt Richard D., 526th FS/86th FG 325

Lawrence, Maj Richard E.H., 12th AF 349

Lawson, 2/Lt Elwood W., 345th FS/350th FG 328

Leader, Lt Douglas W., 526th FS/86th FG 322

Leahy, 1/Lt William P., 525th FS/86th FG 355

Lee, 1/Lt John E., 34th BS/17th BG 126

Lee, 2/Lt Randolph W., 66th FS/57th FG 339

Lee, 2/Lt Roland E., 66th FS/57th FG 437

Leeds, 1/Lt Oren E., 51st TCS/62nd TCG 310

Leek, 2/Lt Henry T. Jr, 66th FS/57th FG 317

Lefkow, 2/Lt Paul, 527th FS/86th FG 266

Lehman, 2/Lt Philip T., 66th FS/57th FG 378

Leist, Capt Gilman L., 85th BS/47th BG 384

Lemons, 2/Lt Leo E., 27th FS/1st FG 162

Lennon, 2/Lt Jerome J., 315th FS/324th FG 117, 200

Lenox, Flg Off Jack Jr, 49th FS/14th FG 82

Lent, 2/Lt Flamer S., 346th FS/350th FG 141

Lentz, 1/Lt Wilbur C., 487th BS/340th BG 292

Leverette, Maj William L., 37th FS/14th FG 49–52, 81

Levy, 1/Lt James K., 347th FS/350th FG 123

Ligon, 1/Lt Walton M., 446th BS/321st BG 307

Limberg, 2/Lt J.C., 95th BS/17th BG 269

Linthicum, S/Sgt W.A., 380th BS/310th BG 360

Lochowitz, 2/Lt Aloysius J., 525th FS/86th FG 360

Locke, 2/Lt Harold H., 525th FS/86th FG 353

Logsdon, 1/Lt James R., 444th BS/320th BG 305

Long, 1/Lt Richard W., 85th FS/79th FG 149

Longworth, 2/Lt Robert A., 71st FS/1st FG 213

Lord, 2/Lt James R., 66th FS/57th FG 199

Lovato, 1/Lt George C., 65th FS/57th FG 301

Lovely, 1/Lt Collis C., 111th TRS 203

Lown, 1/Lt Robert C., 66th FS/57th FG 324

Luce, 2/Lt Richard L., 32nd PRS/5th PRG 162

Luke, 2/Lt Robert L., 86th BS/47th BG 352

Lussier, 2/Lt Cedric S., 524th FS/27th FG 201

Lyth, 2/Lt Alfred R., 66th FS/57th FG 357

Mack, 1/Lt Edward V., 486th BS/340th BG 390

Mackey, 2/Lt John P., 523rd FS/27th FG 327

MacKinnon, 1/Lt John S., 443rd BS/320th BG 114

MacMullin, 1/Lt Robert J., 97th BS/47th BG 327

Macon, 2/Lt Richard D., 99th FS/332nd FG 201

MacRitchie, S/Sgt Wallace, 489th BS/340th BG 159

Magee, 1/Lt George M., 95th FS/82nd FG 48

Maki, 1/Lt Allan A., 446th BS/321st BG 418

Maleszewski, 2/Lt Francis P., 527th FS/86th FG 308

Maloney, 2/Lt Raymond L., 527th FS/86th FG 305

Maloney, Capt Thomas E., 27th FS/1st FG 213, 223

Mammarelli, 2/Lt Alfred D., 66th FS/57th FG 246

Manda, Maj Francis S., 65th FS/57th FG 339

Mangino, 2/Lt Michael L., 345th FS/350th FG 329

Manning, Sgt Hillard J., 445th BS/321st BG 70

Mapes, 2/Lt Douglas W., 315th FS/324th FG 244

Marchant, 1/Lt Wendell E., 447th BS/321st BG 357

Marcy, 1/Lt Richard P., 526th FS/86th FG 254

Margison, 2/Lt Robert L., 37th FS/14th FG 52

Markham, 2/Lt Joseph T., 65th FS/57th FG 185

Maron, 1/Lt Francis J., 27th FS/1st FG 85

Marple, 1/Lt George E., 438th BS/319th BG 177

Marsh, 2/Lt Glenn E., 525th FS/86th FG 317

Marshall, 1/Lt William S., 345th FS/350th FG 434

Martin, 1/Lt Lloyd F., 345th FS/350th FG 383

Martin, 2/Lt Samuel A., 64th FS/57th FG 143

Martone, 1/Lt Arthur E., 316th FS/324th FG 117

Marunovich, 2/Lt John E., 414th NFS 366

Masciullo, S/Sgt Carmen, 488th BS/340th BG 214

Master, 2/Lt Harry A., 526th FS/86th FG 277

Matchette, 1/Lt James F., 489th BS/340th BG 370

Mathias, 2/Lt Albert C., 87th FS/79th FG 379

Matt, 2/Lt James L., 65th FS/57th FG 423

Matthews, 1/Lt Albert M., 345th FS/350th FG 396

Matula, 1/Lt Theodore, 66th FS/57th FG 357

Mauck, Lt Warren R., 527th FS/86th FG 195–196

May, 2/Lt Charles E., 64th FS/57th FG 436

Maywald, 1/Lt Joe W., 381st BS/310th BG 197

McAllister, 1/Lt Lee A. Jr, 428th BS/310th BG 325

McArthur, 2/Lt Samuel C., 525th FS/86th FG 322

McCall, 1/Lt H.E., 347th FS/350th FG 266

McCargo, 1/Lt Forrest W., 346th FS/350th FG 324

McCleskey, Flt Off Royce L., 345th FS/350th FG 431

McCollum, Flt Off Walter C., 66th FS/57th FG 340

McCray, Maj Clarence R., 417th NFS 327

McCullen, 2/Lt Robert J., 417th NFS 335

McDaniel, 1/Lt Wallace S., 524th FS/27th FG 143

McDonald, 1/Lt E.W., 488th BS/340th BG 240

McDonald, 1/Lt G.K., 381st BS/310th BG 195

McDougal, 1/Lt Van W., 442nd BS/320th BG 214

McFadden, 2/Lt John J. Jr, 346th FS/350th FG 340

McGehee, Lt John R., 527th FS/86th FG 228

McGilvray, 1/Lt Donald A. Jr, 428th BS/310th BG 427

McGinnis, 1/Lt R.L., 380th BS/310th BG 360

McGowan, Capt Justin J., OSS 328

McGrath, 2/Lt Francis J., 82nd FG 71

McHenry, 1/Lt James H., 85th FS/79th FG 413

McKanna, Capt Ellis J., 379th BS/310th BG 344

McKeever, Ens William C., VOF-1 213, 214

McKenna, Sgt, 512th BS/376th BG 45

McKenzie, Maj Burton E., 49th FS/14th FG 81

McKenzie, 2/Lt Wilford P., 315th FS/324th FG 254

McMaster, Capt Kitt R. Jr, 347th FS/350th FG 444

McPherson, 1/Lt James F., 527th FS/86th FG 236

McPherson, 1/Lt Robert G., 428th BS/310th BG 340

McStea, 1/Lt Alexander, 379th BS/310th BG 398

Meek, 2/Lt Robert H., 487th BS/340th BG 292

Mehr, Capt Bliss L., 84th BS/47th BG 395

Menifee, 2/Lt James E., 86th FS/79th FG 281

Mercer, S/Sgt William R., 445th BS/321st BG 70

Merrell, 1/Lt Hollis B., 85th FS/79th FG 394

Metzger, 1/Lt William Jr, 514th BS/376th BG 79

Meyer, 1/Lt Fergus, 65th FS/57th FG 351

Michel, Capt Frederick H., 346th FS/350th FG 310

Middleton, 1/Lt Kimber M., 345th FS/350th FG 424

Miller, 1/Lt Frank S. Jr, 380th BS/310th BG 410

Miller, 2/Lt Gail G., 445th BS/321st BG 62

Miller, 1/Lt Jacob, 37th BS/17th BG 269

Miller, Flt Off Walter R., 346th FS/350th FG 386, 387, 404, 407, 421

Millican, 2/Lt Vincent I., 85th FS/79th FG 191

Milton, 2/Lt Lewis J., 314th FS/324th FG 197

Mingle, 2/Lt Carl R., 1st ERS 151

Minyard, S/Sgt W.T., 514th BS/376th BG 14

Miser, 1/Lt LeRoy L., 438th BS/319th BG 330

Mitchell, 2/Lt Harry W., 85th FS/79th FG 234

Mitchell, 1/Lt John L. Jr, 489th BS/340th BG 160

Moldrew, 2/Lt Lloyd G., 417th NFS 191

Montgomery, 1/Lt Donald A., 87th FS/79th FG 378

Moody, 1/Lt James L., 66th FS/57th FG 363

Moon, 2/Lt Earl C., 488th BS/340th BG 214

Mooney, Ens John A., VOF-1 230

Moore, 2/Lt Howard M., 85th FS/79th FG 394

Moore, 2/Lt James P. Jr, 87th FS/79th FG 422

Moran, 1/Lt Harold D., 84th BS/47th BG 431

Moran, 2/Lt Maurice, 525th FS/86th FG 345

Morris, Sgt William M., 379th BS/310th BG 394

Morrison, 1/Lt George R. Jr, 447th BS/321st BG 343

Morrison, 2/Lt Walter F., 347th FS/350th FG 389

Morrow, 1/Lt Robert K., 346th FS/350th FG 354, 396

Morton, 1/Lt William C. Jr, 447th BS/321st BG 351

Moschberger, 1/Lt Frederick J., 85th FS/79th FG 317

Mosher, 1/Lt Calvin D., 524th FS/27th FG 236

Moyer, Capt Luther K., 443rd BS/320th BG 247

Muffitt, 2/Lt Jack P., 94th FS/1st FG 71

Muir, 2/Lt Robert W., 95th FS/82nd FG 48

Mulhollen, 2/Lt Ralph D., 416th NFS 319

Murchland, 1/Lt Robert K., 447th BS/321st BG 344

Murphy, 2/Lt John F., 414th NFS 316

Muse, Maj Hugh M., 95th FS/82nd FG 54, 71

Mylly, Flt Off Rafael Y., 522nd FS/27th FG 187

Myrick, 1/Lt Frank E., 527th FS/86th FG 169

Nave, 2/Lt Leslie H., 523rd FS/27th FG 199

Naylor, Flt Off William P., 97th BS/47th BG 367

Neale, Flt Off Douglas V., 527th FS/86th FG 166

Neale, Lt Harold H. Jr, 524th FS/27th FG 228

Neely, 2/Lt Charles W., 314th FS/324th FG 199, 251

Nelson, Flt Off Alfred A., 522nd FS/27th FG 218

Neumann, 1/Lt Charles R., 64th FS/57th FG 313

Nevett, 2/Lt Richard K., 64th FS/57th FG 117

Newhouse, 2/Lt Ernest H., 64th FS/57th FG 120

Newman, 1/Lt John C., 523rd FS/27th FG 246

Nicholas, 1/Lt William E., 86th FS/79th FG 392

Nichols, Lt Lorn K., 347th FS/350th FG 327

Nicholson, 2/Lt Alvie H., 65th FS/57th FG 314

Nicholson, 1/Lt Hubert L., 111th TRS 218, 220

Nickels, 1/Lt Albert B., 64th FS/57th FG 436

Nielsen, 2/Lt Henry L., 524th FS/27th FG 239, 312

Nithman, Cpl Charles E., 379th BS/310th BG 69

Noesges, 2/Lt John C., 64th FS/57th FG 250

Norquist, 2/Lt T.E., 522nd FS/27th FG 318

Norman, 1/Lt Robert P., 87th FS/79th FG 305

Norris, 1/Lt Gene, 66th FS/57th FG 378

Novak, 1/Lt Harold T., 439th BS/319th BG 223

Noyd, 2/Lt Eugene L., 66th FS/57th FG 310

O'Brian, 1/Lt Thomas P., 86th FS/79th FG 368

O'Bryant, 1/Lt John L., 440th BS/319th BG 292

O'Dell, S/Sgt Cecil A., 428th BS/310th BG 357

Ogden, 2/Lt William W., 85th FS/79th FG 236

Oldham, Capt Richard G., 525th FS/86th FG 276

O'Leary, 2/Lt John D., 486th BS/340th BG 73, 74

Oliver, 1/Lt Donald E., 380th BS/310th BG 410

Olson, 1/Lt Charles J., 34th BS/17th BG 220

Olson, 2/Lt Edward M., 346th FS/350th FG 404–405, 408

Olson, Lt Norman A., 315th FS/324th FG 169

Olson, 1/Lt Orin E., 448th BS/321st BG 183

Olszewski, Ens Edward W., VOF-1 227, 228

O'Neil, 2/Lt Robert O., 100th FS/332nd FG 204–205, 207

Orcutt, 1/Lt Robert B., 66th FS/57th FG 427

O'Rourke, 2/Lt Frank J., 65th FS/57th FG 436

Ouellette, M/Sgt G.T., 514th BS/376th BG 14

Oyster, Sgt H.E., 439th BS/319th BG 325

Ozimek, 2/Lt Edmund J., 345th FS/350th FG 359

Paff, 1/Lt Clarence E., 85th FS/79th FG 389

Palmer, Lt Arthur J., 85th FS/79th FG 247

Palmer, 1/Lt Burwell S., 345th FS/350th FG 427

Palovich, 2/Lt Edward J., 66th FS/57th FG 354, 355

Pape, 2/Lt Garvin C., 345th FS/350th FG 310

Parish, 1/Lt Glenn L., 346th FS/350th FG 398

Parker, 2/Lt Charles C., 489th BS/340th BG 389

Patch, Gen Alexander M., 218

Patin, 1/Lt Robert L., 86th FS/79th FG 162

Patten, 2/Lt Roy E., 414th NFS 194

Patterson, Capt John E., 414th NFS 194

Patterson, 2/Lt William E., 345th FS/350th FG 287

Pavlovich, Ens Paul, VF-74 222

Pelton, 2/Lt William B., 488th BS/340th BG 346, 388

Peplinski, Flt Off James L., G BS/321st BG 57–58

Perkins, 1/Lt Robert E., 417th NFS 319

Pernicka, 2/Lt Louis J., 66th FS/57th FG 166

Perryman, 2/Lt Charles R., 345th FS/350th FG 431

Peters, 1/Lt Edgar N., 64th FS/57th FG 246

Peterson, 2/Lt Earl O., 439th BS/319th BG 266

Peterson, 1/Lt Frank, 380th BS/310th BG 137

Peterson, 1/Lt Frederick I., 446th BS/321st BG 283

Peterson, 2/Lt Vernon R., 66th FS/57th FG 423

Petry, 2/Lt A.G., 415th NFS 271

Petty, 2/Lt Charles, 515th BS/376th BG 45

Phelan, 1/Lt John W., 346th FS/350th FG 336

Phelps, 1/Lt Victor L., 87th FS/79th FG 283

Phillippi, Flt Off Carmen J., 414th NFS 229

Phillips, S/Sgt C.H., 514th BS/376th BG 14

Pickerel, 1/Lt Joseph F., 347th FS/350th FG 427

Pidcock, 1/Lt Manuel A., 527th FS/86th FG 327

Pike, 1/Lt R.W., 486th BS/340th BG 151

Pinney, Capt Kyle J. Jr, 48th FS/14th FG 357

Pirnie, Lt, 487th BS/340th BG 74

Pitts, 2/Lt Hiram C., 97th FS/82nd FG 74

Place, 2/Lt Richard L., 66th FS/57th FG 314

Playford, Capt, 332nd FG 122

Plutt, 2/Lt Stephen A., 95th FS/82nd FG 54

Pneuman, 1/Lt Arthur H. Jr, 87th FS/79th FG 380

Poeton, 1/Lt Richard R., 345th FS/350th FG 422

Pompay, Flt Off Alfred F., 315th FS/324th FG 132

Poole, 1/Lt W.H., 379th BS/310th BG 394

Porter, 2/Lt George L., 316th FS/324th FG 174

Porterfield, 2/Lt Josef A., 95th FS/82nd FG 80

Poucel, Lt Rene E.J., VOF-1 223

Powers, 1/Lt John E., 347th FS/350th FG 370

Pownall, 2/Lt William F., 414th NFS 308

Prasse, 2/Lt Charles W., 381st BS/310th BG 137

Prater, 2/Lt Robert E., 524th FS/27th FG 121

Prescott, 1/Lt John A., 414th NFS 285

Pridgeon, Lt Bobby J., 66th FS/57th FG 222

Pugh, 1/Lt R.C., 488th BS/340th BG 240

Purdum, Capt Lemuel W., 525th FS/86th FG 196

Putnam, 2/Lt Ky B., 414th NFS 366

Quattlebaum, 2/Lt Harrell O., 437th BS/319th BG 199

Quinlan, 2/Lt Bernard F., 524th FS/27th FG 340

Quitta, 1/Lt James V., 380th BS/310th BG 137

Rafael, 1/Lt Thomas E., 27th FS/1st FG 85

Ragsdale, 1/Lt Eual J., 86th BS/47th BG 290

Rahn, 2/Lt Claude G., 66th FS/57th FG 149

Ramey, 1/Lt Gordon A., 447th BS/321st BG 307

Ratering, 1/Lt Edwin G., 442nd BS/320th BG 121

Ratliff, 1/Lt James E. Jr, 446th BS/321st BG 434

Rawson, 1/Lt Paul E., 64th FS/57th FG 255

Ray, 1/Lt Don A., 4th TCS/62nd TCG 336

Ready, 2/Lt Walter W., 448th BS/321st BG 183

Redmon, 2/Lt William K. Jr, 347th FS/350th FG 326

Reichelderfer, 2/Lt Robert H., 64th FS/57th FG 433

Remley, S/Sgt Milton P., 343rd BS/98th BG 14

Remmel, 1/Lt Earl H., 447th BS/321st BG 356

Reynolds, 1/Lt Myers Jay III, 64th FS/57th FG 384

Rhodes, 2/Lt George M. Jr, 100th FS/332nd FG 204, 207

Rice, 2/Lt Dean H., 439th BS/319th BG 295

Richardson, 1/Lt John S., 445th BS/321st BG 261

Richmond, 2/Lt Robert L., 86th FS/79th FG 121

Richmond, 2/Lt William R., 316th FS/324th FG 252

Ricks, 2/Lt Gerald G., 315th FS/324th FG 216

Ridolphi, S/Sgt P.J., 515th BS/376th BG 45

Rielly, S/Sgt John R., 344th BS/98th BG 14

Ritchie, 1/Lt Robert K., 97th BS/47th BG 355

Ritger, 1/Lt Frederick C., 446th BS/321st BG 325

Ritter, Flt Off E.J., 488th BS/340th BG 197

Roberts, 1/Lt Floyd W., 440th BS/319th BG 292

Robertson, 2/Lt Alexander, 347th FS/350th FG 342

Robinson, Ens David E., VOF-1 223

Robinson, Capt Everett P., 380th BS/310th BG 394

Rochon, Sgt R., 439th BS/319th BG 325

Rock, 2/Lt Edward S., 347th FS/350th FG 346

Rock, 1/Lt John M., 380th BS/310th BG 252

Rodgers, 2/Lt Raymond, 417th NFS 302

Rogers, 2/Lt Cornelius G., 301st FS/332nd FG 122

Rohrig, 1/Lt David G., 96th BS/2nd BG 82

Roop, Flt Off Richard, 414th NFS 314

Roosevelt, Pres. Franklin D., 77

Rorer, 1/Lt George A. Jr, 428th BS/310th BG 383

Rose, 1/Lt Edward C., 380th BS/310th BG 414

Rose, Sgt J.W., 445th BS/321st BG 70

Rospo, 2/Lt Sam Jr, 86th FS/79th FG 159

Ross, 1/Lt Charles D., 486th BS/340th BG 355

Rossler, 1/Lt Donald H., 489th BS/340th BG 304

Rubin, 2/Lt Julius W., 448th BS/321st BG 346

Ruble, 2/Lt Roy C., 523rd FS/27th FG 255

Rudd, Lt Jack A., 522nd FS/27th FG 356

Rudovsky, Flt Off John, 414th NFS 330

Rusk, 2/Lt Leo J., 84th BS/47th BG 134

Russell, Capt Lawrence L., 445th BS/321st BG 276

Ryan, 1/Lt Edward H. Jr, 525th FS/86th FG 136

Ryan, 2/Lt Robert M. Jr, 86th FS/79th FG 162

Sandor, Lt Cdr John H., VOF-1 221, 223

Saunders, 1/Lt/Capt Jackson, 526th FS/86th FG 155, 264

Saunders, Flt Off LeRoy W., 316th FS/324th FG 246

Saunders, Lt/Capt Newton L., 527th FS/86th FG 195, 311

Sayre, 2/Lt Kenneth C. Jr, 524th FS/27th FG 121

Scates, 1/Lt Arthur J., 567th BS/389th BG 16

Schaefer, 1/Lt Frank W., 317th FS/325th FG 426

Schane, 1/Lt Charles W. Jr, 442nd BS/320th BG 304

Schindler, Maj Andrew R., 346th FS/350th FG 271, 396

Schneider, Capt W.J., 379th BS/310th BG 196

Schoener, 2/Lt Herbert C., 49th FS/14th FG 82

Schultz, 1/Lt Warren R., 64th FS/57th FG 307

Scott, 1/Lt Jack A., 353rd BS/301st BG 80

Sculley, 2/Lt Thomas S., 448th BS/321st BG 383

Seidman, 2/Lt Robert K., 49th FS/14th FG 82

Selenger, 1/Lt Walter K., 318th FS/325th FG 363

Sellars, 1/Lt, 526th FS/86th FG 155

Sennett, Sgt, 439th BS/319th BG 325

Sewell, 2/Lt George T., 526th FS/86th FG 327

Shank, 2/Lt Robert Earl, 95th BS/17th BG 199

Sharock, Lt M.W., 347th FS/350th FG 134

Sharp, Flt Off Harry E., 414th NFS 184

Shawver, 2/Lt James P., 95th FS/82nd FG 48

Sheffield, 2/Lt Woodrow W., 448th BS/321st BG 356

Sherwood, 2/Lt Lincoln R., 66th FS/57th FG 367

Shivers, 2/Lt Jesse E. Jr, 523rd FS/27th FG 347

Shovanek, 1/Lt Louis, 428th BS/310th BG 261

Shuttleworth, Lt David H., 87th FS/79th FG 146

Simmons, 2/Lt Alphonso, 100th FS/332nd FG 199

Simpson, 1/Lt Talmadge F. Jr, 416th NFS 431

Simpson, 2/Lt/1/Lt William Y., 488th BS/340th BG 313, 346

Slater, 2/Lt Edmund M., 379th BS/310th BG 90

Slatton, 2/Lt Jack L., 85th FS/79th FG 290

Slaughter, 2/Lt William A., 20th BS/2nd BG 82

Small, 1/Lt Lloyd W. Jr, 86th BS/47th BG 423

Smith, 1/Lt Aikens V., 66th FS/57th FG 439

Smith, Sgt Argyle H., 447th BS/321st BG 74

Smith, 2/Lt Eugene F., 66th FS/57th FG 325

Smith, 2/Lt Harold I., 95th FS/82nd FG 54

Smith, Maj Harry L. Jr, 97th FS/82nd FG 80

Smith, Capt James W., 65th FS/57th FG 244

Smith, 1/Lt Lewis C., 99th FS/332nd FG 121

Smith, S/Sgt Melvin W., 428th BS/310th BG 357

Smith, 1/Lt Milford A., 448th BS/321st BG 370

Smith, 1/Lt Robert V., 85th BS/47th BG 389

Smith, S/Sgt W.W., 514th BS/376th BG 14

Smith, 1/Lt Wayne H., 347th FS/350th FG 409

Snyder, Capt Robert H., 28th TCS/60th TCG 137

Sonnichsen, 1/Lt Noel, 87th FS/79th FG 190

Southard, 2/Lt James C., 345th FS/350th FG 370

Spaatz, Lt Gen Carl A., MAAF 77

Spackey, 1/Lt William G., 380th BS/310th BG 266

Spalinger, 2/Lt Donald C., 66th FS/57th FG 360

Sparks, Lt Oscar W., 314th FS/324th FG 160

Speirs, Capt William R., 57th FG 350

Spencer, 1/Lt Glen H., 522nd FS/27th FG 359

Spraley, 1/Lt James D., 87th FS/79th FG 378

Sprinkle, 2/Lt Homer L., 37th FS/14th FG 49–50, 52

St Onge, 1/Lt Homer J., 346th FS/350th FG 437, 438

Staehle, Capt D.L., 523rd FS/27th FG 306

Stage, Flt Off Wesley A., 85th FS/79th FG 349

Stahl, 2/Lt Kenneth L., 37th FS/14th FG 82

Stahl, 2/Lt Robert S. Jr, 86th FS/79th FG 281

Stalter, Lt William J., 85th FS/79th FG 175

Stearns, 1/Lt Albert D., 444th BS/320th BG 232, 235

Steiner, Lt Robert B., 86th FS/79th FG 182

Stephenson, 1/Lt Frederick H., 85th BS/47th BG 143

Stoherer, Lt Frank A., 859th BS/2641st SG 427

Stoutenborough, 2/Lt/1/Lt J.D., 95th FS/82nd FG 48, 79

Strabac, Sgt Emil M., 380th BS/310th BG 360

Stringer, 2/Lt Robert L., 346th FS/350th FG 350

Sturman, 1/Lt James F., 526th FS/86th FG 269

Sturmer, Lt, 438th BS/319th BG 228

Sullivan, 1/Lt John, Air Crew Rescue 328

Sulzbach, 2/Lt Richard P., 346th FS/350th FG 351, 403–404, 407, 429, 444

Summers, 2/Lt James J., 380th BS/310th BG 393, 394

Sumner, 2/Lt William W., 345th FS/350th FG 418

Surber, 1/Lt Louis L. Jr, 97th BS/47th BG 316

Sutton, Capt Walter L., 859th BS/2641st SG 427

Swartz, Flt Off William, 65th FS/57th FG 120

Taigan, 1/Lt Harland T., 85th BS/47th BG 290

Tallent, Lt Warren H., 86th FS/79th FG 183

Tarantino, 1/Lt Paul A., 347th FS/350th FG 306

Taylor, Lt, 71st FS/1st FG 46, 47

Taylor, Lt, 524th FS/27th FG 307

Taylor, Lt Col Oliver B., 14th FG 82

Taylor, Flt Off Robert B., 346th FS/350th FG 408

Taylor, Lt Walter C. Jr, 526th FS/86th FG 184

Tench, 1/Lt William C., 66th FS/57th FG 312

Tennery, 2/Lt John H., 95th FS/82nd FG 48

Theissen, 1/Lt Ralph A., 94th FS/1st FG 85

Thomas, 1/Lt Baxter, 489th BS/340th BG 214

Thomas, 2/Lt Clarence M., 527th FS/86th FG 339

Thompson, Lt, 347th FS/350th FG 404–405

Thompson, 1/Lt Earl A., 65th FS/57th FG 431

Thompson, 2/Lt Floyd A., 99th FS/332nd FG 143

Thompson, 2/Lt John E., 527th FS/86th FG 336

Thompson, 2/Lt Robert G., 346th FS/350th FG 387, 427

Thompson, 2/Lt Thomas H., 347th FS/350th FG 329

Thrasher, 2/Lt Thomas E., 523rd FS/27th FG 317

Throop, Sgt, 439th BS/319th BG 325

Tilley, 1/Lt George F., 380th BS/310th BG 383

Tilton, Maj John A., 86th BS/47th BG 352

Timmermann, Flt Off Nile F., 523rd FS/27th FG 177

Tomlinson, 1/Lt Robert C., 346th FS/350th FG 301, 310

Totten, 1/Lt Elsworth, 84th BS/47th BG 330

Tracey, S/Sgt Boyd F., 447th BS/321st BG 62

Tracy, 1/Lt Leon E., 347th FS/350th FG 387

Trautwein, Lt, 523rd FS/27th FG 347

Treadwell, 1/Lt Donald Jr, 440th BS/319th BG 292

Tremaine, 1/Lt L.J., 486th BS/340th BG 398

Tresville, Capt Robert B., 100th FS/332nd FG 137

Trunk, 1/Lt Paul E., 441st BS/320th BG 214

Turner, 2/Lt Aubry, 523rd FS/27th FG 124

Turner, 2/Lt Charles W., 66th FS/57th FG 120

Turner, 2/Lt Clements W., 95th FS/82nd FG 79

Turner, 2/Lt Wallace B., 524th FS/27th FG 326

Twedt, 2/Lt O.L.J., 381st BS/310th BG 195

Underwood, S/Sgt Edward H., 344th BS/98th BG 45

Underwood, 1/Lt Neil R., 97th BS/47th BG 217

Unger, S/Sgt G.R., 514th BS/376th BG 14

Urso, Maj James D., 416th NFS 431

Vaccaro, 1/Lt George W., 87th FS/79th FG 183

Valentine, Sgt C., 514th BS/376th BG 14

Van Dien, 2/Lt Fredrick L., 428th BS/310th BG 266

Van Houten, 1/Lt Eugene T., 85th FS/79th FG 306

Vantz, 2/Lt Vasil V., 85th BS/47th BG 143

Verne, 1/Lt Stephen J., 347th FS/350th FG 439

Vinciguerra, 1/Lt Silvio R., 522nd FS/27th FG 342

Voelkers, 2/Lt James C., 486th BS/340th BG 389

Wagner, 1/Lt Robert H., 92nd FS/81st FG 78

Wakeland, 1/Lt E.W., 439th BS/319th BG 223

Walker, 1/Lt Marion E., 447th BS/321st BG 256

Wallin, 1/Lt Robert E., 16th TCS/64th TCG 395, 434

Walling, 2/Lt Everett L., 346th FS/350th FG 366

Walsh, Lt Edward M., 86th FS/79th FG 120, 182

Ward, 1/Lt Frank J., 85th FS/79th FG 394

Ward, 2/Lt Walter R., 96th BS/2nd BG 82

Watson, 2/Lt Frederick W., 381st BS/310th BG 197

Watson, Lt James C. Jr, 527th FS/86th FG 228

Weand, 2/Lt Arthur R., 85th FS/79th FG 394

Weckesser, S/Sgt Clarence H., 344th BS/98th BG 45

Weier, 1/Lt Wilbert L., 444th BS/320th BG 232

Weisenberg, 2/Lt Carl J., 66th FS/57th FG 355

Welch, 2/Lt Howard F., 319th FS/325th FG 139

Welch, 1/Lt Oransdale R., 97th BS/47th BG 184

Welfley, 2/Lt Thomas L., 417th NFS 320

Welliver, 1/Lt Ruben Jr, 414th NFS 308

Wells, Maj Lee C., 345th FS/350th FG 342

Werling, 1/Lt T.J., 428th BS/310th BG 197

Wheeler, 1/Lt Wayne, 522nd FS/27th FG 343

Whelan, 1/Lt Charles J., 438th BS/319th BG 330

White, 2/Lt Forrest L., 111th TRS 217

Whiting, 2/Lt James R., 527th FS/86th FG 200

Whorlow, S/Sgt Paul A., 343rd BS/98th BG 45

Wiginton, Capt J.Maurice, 447th BS/321st BG 303

Wiginton, 1/Lt Murray B., 441st BS/320th BG 157

Wilcox, 2/Lt C.I., 34th BS/17th BG 185–186

Wilhelm, 2/Lt Richard D., 37th FS/14th FG 82

Wilkinson, 1/Lt John P., 488th BS/340th BG 390

US AIR FORCE AND NAVY AVIATION UNITS

US ARMY AIR FORCES

USAAF COMMANDS

USAAF FLYING UNITS

27th Fighter Group 117, 196, 201, 347, 353, 356

522nd Fighter Squadron 117, 139, 166, 187, 195, 196, 201, 218, 228, 232, 251, 294, 306, 318, 342, 343, 344, 352, 356, 359

523rd Fighter Squadron 117, 124, 126, 130, 177, 178, 192, 199, 236, 244, 246, 251, 255, 306, 317, 318, 327, 340, 347, 357

524th Fighter Squadron 121, 143, 154, 201, 236, 239, 251, 307, 312, 326, 340, 342, 357, 359

33rd Fighter Group 119

52nd Fighter Group 119, 414

2nd Fighter Squadron 414

57th Fighter Group 118, 119, 139, 140, 143, 146, 147, 148, 155, 174, 186, 202, 242, 307, 324, 337, 354, 374, 417, 420, 431, 436, 441, 446

64th Fighter Squadron 117, 120, 143, 153, 156, 166, 175, 202, 203, 228, 239, 246, 250, 255, 285, 301, 307, 313, 317, 343, 345, 347, 351, 373, 378, 380, 382, 384, 410, 418, 420, 421, 427, 431, 433, 434, 436, 437, 438, 439, 446

65th Fighter Squadron 120, 149, 155, 156, 164, 175, 185, 202, 203, 220, 236, 244, 247, 257, 283, 289, 301, 313, 314, 325, 339, 346, 351, 359, 370, 373, 378, 381, 383, 387, 392, 410, 414, 420, 423, 424, 431, 433, 434, 436, 437, 446

66th Fighter Squadron 120, 139, 140, 147, 149, 154, 166, 186, 191, 199, 202, 203, 216, 218, 222, 225, 234, 242, 244, 246, 251, 273, 305, 310, 312, 314, 317, 323, 325, 328, 333, 339, 340, 342, 354, 355, 356, 357, 360, 363, 367, 370, 378, 385, 389, 392, 397, 410, 412, 414, 417, 418, 423, 424, 427, 429, 431, 433, 436, 437, 439, 446

79th Fighter Group 117, 119, 131, 144, 146, 147, 148, 182, 187, 195, 203, 246, 374, 375, 389, 390, 393, 402, 444

85th Fighter Squadron 149, 175, 182, 191, 192, 203, 234, 236, 247, 290, 298, 306, 316, 317, 349, 357, 389, 394, 413, 431

86th Fighter Squadron 120, 121, 122, 159, 162, 175, 182, 183, 236, 246, 280, 281, 307, 346, 351, 358, 365, 368, 378, 429,

87th Fighter Squadron 117, 121, 123, 134, 136, 146, 154, 183, 190, 203, 214, 236, 283, 301, 305, 322, 336, 340, 378, 379, 380, 396, 408, 422, 423, 434

81st Fighter Group 119

92nd Fighter Squadron 78

82nd Fighter Group 44, 46, 47, 50, 54, 55, 56, 71, 73, 79, 80, 81, 173

95th Fighter Squadron 48, 54, 55, 56, 71, 79, 80, 162

96th Fighter Squadron 44, 55, 71, 79

97th Fighter Squadron 48, 52, 55, 56, 71, 74, 79, 80

86th Fighter Group 118, 119, 138, 155, 183, 195, 221, 276, 324, 337, 353

525th Fighter Squadron 123, 195, 196, 229, 234, 276, 281, 287, 295, 305, 314, 317, 322, 336, 340, 344, 345, 347, 352, 353, 355, 439

526th Fighter Squadron 155, 184, 185, 222, 225, 229, 254, 255, 264, 269, 273, 277, 305, 314, 319, 322, 325, 327, 328, 340, 342, 359

527th Fighter Squadron 166, 169, 195, 196, 200, 218, 223, 228, 236, 240, 255, 266, 276, 305, 308, 311, 321, 325, 327, 328, 336, 338, 339, 350

324th Fighter Group 114, 118, 169, 173, 202

314th Fighter Squadron 128, 162, 164, 167, 197, 199, 234, 236, 247, 251, 252

315th Fighter Squadron 117, 122, 169, 200, 216, 244, 254

316th Fighter Squadron 117, 126, 132, 133, 156, 160, 174, 246, 252

325th Fighter Group 317, 425

317th Fighter Squadron 164, 426

318th Fighter Squadron 363

319th Fighter Squadron 139

332nd Fighter Group 110, 119, 201, 204, 205

99th Fighter Squadron 121, 143, 201, 207, 216, 235, 239

100th Fighter Squadron 126, 137, 199, 201, 207

301st Fighter Squadron 120, 122, 240

302nd Fighter Squadron 201

350th Fighter Group 173, 278, 300, 309, 329, 337, 345, 370, 385, 396, 401, 403, 405, 407, 428, 429, 435, 438, 444, 446

345th Fighter Squadron 247, 260, 287, 310, 328, 329, 331, 334, 336, 342, 359, 370, 383, 396, 408, 418, 422, 424, 427, 431, 434, 436, 440, 446

346th Fighter Squadron 141, 201, 271, 273, 301, 304, 310, 324, 330, 331, 336, 340, 342, 345, 350, 351, 354, 366, 367, 370, 385, 387, 396, 397, 398, 403–405, 407, 414, 421, 427, 429, 433, 436, 437, 438, 444, 446

347th Fighter Squadron 123, 133, 134, 264, 266, 277, 301, 305, 306, 326, 327, 329, 330, 338, 342, 346, 347, 364, 367, 370, 378, 381, 387, 389, 403, 404, 408, 409, 427, 438, 439, 444, 446

1º Grupo de Caça 278, 305, 308, 330, 337, 338, 347, 352, 355, 359, 362, 381, 384, 396, 413, 418, 425, 429, 431, 437, 439, 444, 446

1ª Equadrilha de Ligação e Observação 279

1st Emergency Rescue Squadron 151, 289

Air Crew Rescue 328

111th Tactical Reconnaissance Squadron 118, 119, 124, 128, 146, 173, 188, 203, 208, 217, 218, 220, 229, 231

154th Tactical Reconnaissance
Squadron 328

414th Night Fighter Squadron 173,
184, 194, 229, 268, 285, 308,
311, 316, 321, 330, 337, 366,
414, 415, 431, 449, 450

415th Night Fighter Squadron 239,
241, 271, 337, 449, 450

416th Night Fighter Squadron 314,
317, 337, 338, 351, 352, 373,
398, 430, 431, 450,

417th Night Fighter Squadron 155,
175, 191, 192, 293, 302, 313,
319, 320, 327, 335, 364, 450

154th Combat Mapping Squadron 65

2nd Bomb Group (Heavy) 52,
81, 82

20th Bomb Squadron 82

96th Bomb Squadron 82, 83

17th Bomb Group (Medium) 185,
186, 224

34th Bomb Squadron 126, 177,
186, 220

37th Bomb Squadron 225, 256,
269, 285

95th Bomb Squadron 124, 199,
225, 234, 269, 316

432nd Bomb Squadron 225

47th Bomb Group (Light) 119,
142, 143, 147, 160, 173, 266,
337, 356, 429, 430, 446

84th Bomb Squadron 134, 316,
330, 395, 431

85th Bomb Squadron 143, 290,
316, 378, 384, 389

86th Bomb Squadron 184, 280,
290, 310, 352, 360, 423

97th Bomb Squadron 153, 184, 217,
316, 327, 355, 367, 392, 434

97th Bomb Group (Heavy) 52,
79, 81

341st Bomb Squadron 79

98th Bomb Group (Heavy) 14, 35,
44, 45, 71, 79, 80

343rd Bomb Squadron 14, 45

344th Bomb Squadron 14, 45

99th Bomb Group (Heavy) 46, 52

346th Bomb Squadron 86

348th Bomb Squadron 52

301st Bomb Group (Heavy) 52,
79, 80

352nd Bomb Squadron 52

353rd Bomb Squadron 80

310th Bomb Group (Medium)
66, 173, 175, 182, 186, 195, 196,
344, 356, 360, 366, 392, 393

379th Bomb Squadron 69, 90, 120,
123, 125, 137, 196, 261, 308,
344, 394, 398

380th Bomb Squadron 137, 223,
252, 256, 266, 314, 325, 360,
383, 392, 393, 394, 410, 414

381st Bomb Squadron 137, 180,
195, 197, 292, 314

428th Bomb Squadron 197, 261,
266, 308, 325, 330, 340, 357,
383, 413, 427

319th Bomb Group (Medium)
199, 291, 324, 337, 446

437th Bomb Squadron 199, 313

438th Bomb Squadron 124, 128,
177, 228, 330

439th Bomb Squadron 223, 266,
295, 325

440th Bomb Squadron 177, 269,
292

320th Bomb Group (Medium)
157, 230, 304, 307

441st Bomb Squadron 132, 157,
203, 214, 229, 233, 305, 312

442nd Bomb Squadron 214, 228,
255, 304

443rd Bomb Squadron 114, 247

444th Bomb Squadron 126, 214,
232, 235, 305, 306, 312

321st Bomb Group (Medium) 44,
46, 47, 50, 54, 57, 62, 246, 337,
356, 385, 446

445th Bomb Squadron 48, 62, 70,
155, 261, 276, 370, 414

446th Bomb Squadron 70, 283, 307,
325, 357, 392, 418, 434, 436

447th Bomb Squadron 62, 70, 74,
247, 256, 307, 343, 344, 351,
356, 357, 392

448th Bomb Squadron 124, 183,
240, 307, 308, 346, 356, 357,
370, 383

'G' Bomb Squadron 46, 50, 57, 58

340th Bomb Group (Medium) 71,
73, 153, 159, 306, 337, 339, 369,
425, 446

486th Bomb Squadron 74, 151,
166, 214, 305, 352, 355, 360,
389, 390, 398, 410

487th Bomb Squadron 74, 137,
153, 273, 292

488th Bomb Squadron 151, 166,
197, 214, 240, 304, 313, 346,
388, 390

489th Bomb Squadron 157, 158,
212, 300, 365, 376, 384, 398

376th Bomb Group (Heavy) 14,
35, 44, 47, 71, 79

512th Bomb Squadron 45

513th Bomb Squadron 45

514th Bomb Squadron 14, 45, 79

515th Bomb Squadron 45

389th Bomb Group (Heavy)

567th Bomb Squadron 16

2641st Special Group

859th Bomb Squadron 427

121st Liaison Squadron 389

3rd Photo Reconnaissance Group
337, 384

12th Photo Reconnaissance
Squadron 234, 256

15th Combat Mapping Squadron 240

32nd Photo Reconnaissance
Squadron 162, 384

60th Troop Carrier Group 128,
173

10th Troop Carrier Squadron 129,
179, 312

11th Troop Carrier Squadron 129

12th Troop Carrier Squadron 129, 252

28th Troop Carrier Squadron 129, 137

62nd Troop Carrier Group 173

4th Troop Carrier Squadron 336

51st Troop Carrier Squadron 310, 376

64th Troop Carrier Group 173

16th Troop Carrier Squadron 395, 434

35th Troop Carrier Squadron 354

US NAVY

USN Task Group 88.2 208

Observation Fighting Squadron (VOF-1) 208, 209, 213, 214, 221, 223, 225, 226, 227, 228, 230, 233, 234, 235, 236

Fighting Squadron (VF-74) 208, 209, 211, 218, 220, 221, 222, 223, 225, 236

Night Fighting Squadron (VF[N]-74) 208, 226

FRENCH AIR FORCE PERSONNEL AND THEIR UNITS

Allain, Sgt, GC 1/4 246

Ancelet, Sgt, GC 2/3 232

Auber, Cne Jean-Marie, GC 1/4 242

Baills, Sgt, GC 2/5 235

Bernard, Sgt Pierre, GC 2/5 133

Bouttier, Sous Lt Guy Antoine, GC 1/7 138

Bouvard, Lt Col Michel, 34 Esc Bomb 223

Bressieux, Adj Jérémie, GC 1/5 164

Chaboureau, Cne, GB 1/19 149

Cornet, Lt, GB 2/20 158–159

Courteville, Sgt-Chef, GC 2/7 159

de Chanterac, Lt, GC 2/3 195

de L'Espinay, Cne Pierre-Marie, GC 2/5 225, 234

de Montravel, Cne Jacques, GC 2/5 225, 234

de Saint-Exupéry Cdt Antoine, GR 2/33 186, 187

Demoulin, Cne Roger, GC 3/6 317

Despinoy Adj GB, 2/20 159

Doudies, Adj Jean, GC 2/7 198

Ducru, Lt Henry, GC 2/5 133

Dugit-Gros, Lt Henri, GC 2/3 197–198

Fanneau de la Horie, Lt Col, GC 1/4 233, 234

Faure-Doré, Cne Jean Clément, GC 2/3 197, 198

Fourlinie, Lt, GB 1/22 252

Friot, Maître, GC 2/6 439

Galano, Sgt Chef, GC 2/3 197–198

Gauthier, Sous Lt Georges, GC 3/6 132, 133

Gigot, Sgt Chef, GC 1/5 164, 176, 177

Giraud, Lt Gustave, GC 1/5 164, 176

Gouachon-Noireault, Cne Pierre, GC 2/5 132–133

Guillemard, Sous Lt Robert, GC 2/5 225, 234

Hallut, Sgt, GC 2/5 225

Hentges, Sgt-Chef Pierre, GB 2/20 159

Hoarau de La Source, GC 2/7 125–126

Jallier, Cne, GC 2/3 187

Lacassie, Sgt Laurent, GC 2/3 153

La Meslee, Cne Marin, GC 1/5 164

Lamy, Lt, GB 1/22 233

Lanier-Lachaise, Cne, GB 2/52 223

Lanier, Cdt, GB 2/52 223

Lanvario, Adj Jean, GB 2/20 252

Laurent, Sous Lt, GC 2/7 191

Leboucher, Sgt, GC 2/5 164

Le Guennec, Adj Alain, GC 2/3 197–198

Lenormand, Sous Lt, GB 1/22 124

Lesieur, Sgt Chef, GC 2/5 139

Lombardo, Lt, GC 2/3 153

Marill, Lt, GC 2/3 134

Marpaud, 2nd-Mtr, GC 3/6 138

Meunier, Lt, GB 1/19 220

Minot, Cne, GC 1/4 247

Racon, Lt, GC 1/4 246

Seeten, Sgt, GC 1/4 197–198

Seguin, Lt, GC 2/3 154

Simon, Sgt Chef, GC 1/5 164

Soubeirat, Lt Pierre, GC 1/4 234

Thierry, Cne, GC 2/5 139

Viala, Sous Lt, GB 2/20 159

Vincent, Sgt, GC 1/4 235

FRENCH UNITS

34 Esc Bomb 223

GB 1/19 'Gascogne' 149, 158, 220

GB 1/22 124, 184, 233, 252

GB 2/20 'Bretagne' 158–159, 252

GB 2/52 223

GC 1/4 'Navarre' 197–198, 225, 232, 233, 234, 235, 242, 246, 247

GC 1/5 'Champagne' 164, 177, 252

GC 1/7 'Provence' 138

GC 2/3 'Dauphiné' 134, 153, 154, 187, 195, 197–198, 232

GC 2/5 'La Fayette' 133, 138, 139, 164, 224, 225, 234, 235

GC 2/6 'Travail' 439

GC 2/7 'Nice' 125–126, 159, 191, 198

GC 3/6 'Roussillon' 133, 138, 317, 363

GR 2/33 187

GERMAN PERSONNEL AND THEIR UNITS

Abel, Uffz Lothar, Wekusta 27 306

Achilles, Uffz Werner, 9./KG 26 159

Ackermann, Uffz Erich, 2./NSGr 9 155

Adami, Uffz Alois, 1./NSGr 9 319

Ahrends, Lt Eberhard, 2./SAGr 126 78

Albert, Uffz/Gfr Gerhard, 8./JG 27 65–66

Albrecht, Obfw Otto, 3./SAGr 126 78

Albrecht, Ofhr, 6.(F)/122 198

Altnorthoff, Oblt Ernst-Georg, 12./ JG 27 16

Antes, Obgfr Franz, II./SG 10 305

Appel, Gefr Walter, 8./JG 27 92, 94

Armhorst, Obfw Emil, 15./TG 1 93

Arndt, Uffz Helmut, 2.(F)/123 106

Aschenbach, Gefr Arthur, 1./StG 3 43

Astheimer, Oblt Dietrich, 2./ SAGr128 204

Backenhausen, Uffz Kurt, 1.(F)/122 56, 102

Baierl, Uffz Otto, I./SG 3 66

Ballok, Uffz Artur, 2./NSGr 9 156, 330

Banke, Oblt Heinrich, Lw Kdo Südost 37

Bannwitz, Maj, Stab I./SAGr 126 198

Bantel, Fw Lorenz, Fl X FlK 37

Bartels, Fw Heinrich, 11./JG 27 41, 44, 45, 47, 48, 71, 74

Bartels, Uffz Ewald, 5./StG 3 35

Bauer, Lt Ludwig, 7./JG 27 78

Bauer, Uffz Rudi, 9./JG 27 44

Baumann, Hptm Lothar, Stab I./JG 77 139

Beck, Obfw Hans, 13./TG 1 103

Beck, Uffz Rudolf, 6.(F)/122 192

Becker, Kurt, II./KG 77 161

Begemann, Oblt Rolf, 1./NSGr 9 153, 154

Beise, Obfw, 1.(F)/123 141

Bell, Lt Kurt, 2./JGr 200 196

Bergmann, Lt Götz, 5./JG 51 176, 178

Berkemeyer, Uffz Artur, 1./NSGr 9 318

Berstecher, Lt Hans, 5./KG 6 40

Berstorff, Obstlt Georg, Lw Kdo Südost 37

Berthold, Obgfr Georg, 8./NJG 6 248

Beyer, Oblt Bernhard, 3.(F)/33 105

Bialucha, Fw Hans, 1./LG 1 72

Biester, Fw, 4.(F)/122 360

Binias, Uffz Manfred, 1./SAGr 126 35

Birkner, Obfw Hans, 4./StG 3 52

Bischofe, Obfw Franz, 1./NAGr 12 76

Blab, Obfw Rudolf, III./KG 100 216

Blaich, Major Theodor, NSGr 7 52

Blaschek, Uffz, 2.(F)/122 134

Bluschle, Uffz Herbert, 5./StG 3 52

Böckling, Lt, 4./SAGr 126 113, 132

Bollacke, Uffz Hans, 4./SAGr 126 105

Bordelle, Oblt Walter, II./TG 2 71

Bork, Obgfr Fritz von, 2./NSGr 9 156

Bormann, Obfw Walter, 2./NSGr 7 282

Borner, Fw Erich, 11./ZG 26 10

Bösler, Oblt Dietrich, 12./JG 27 33, 34, 52, 53

Böwing, Obfw Wilhelm, 3./NSGr 9 155, 245

Brädler, Obfw Walter, 8./TG 4 78

Braitsch, Obfw Emil, 6.(F)/122 156

Brandau, Fhr Johannes, 1./JGr 200 201

Braun, Ofhr Bruno-Georg, 2./NAGr 13 185

Bräustedt, Uffz Hans, 2.(F)/123 183

Brinkmann, Fw Otto, 3./NSGr 9 183, 237

Brunswig, Lt Friedrich, 2./SAGr 126 78

Büchner, Lt Werner, 7.Seenotst. 293

Buchholz, Obfw Helmut, 12./TG 1 90

Buckow, Ofhr Bernhard, 1./NSGr 9 318

Buder, Oblt Helmut, 8./NJG 6 248

Büge, Obfw Karl, 70.Seenotst. 279

Burger, StFw Leo, 6./Nav Flak Det 628 257

Burgstaller, Gefr Rudolf, 7./JG 77 246, 248

Burk, Oblt Alfred, 11./JG 27 47, 52

Burkhardt, Obfw Heinz, Wekusta 26 118

Büsen, Uffz Franz, 7./JG 27 87, 92

Busse, Uffz, 4./SAGr 126 113, 132

Buttner, Obgfr Walter 2./NSGr 9 149

Casper, Hptm Johannes, II./TG 4 34

Chalupka, Obfw Kurt, 4./SAGr 126 113

Christophe, Uffz Günther, 3./NSGr 7 287

Cöster, Fw Theodor, 8./LG 1 77

Cöster, Uffz Walter, 3./JGr 200 196, 198

Cremer, Hans, Seetransportst. 1 88

Croce, Gefr Eberhard, NAGr 11, 363

Culemann, Lt Hans-Gunnar, 7./JG 27, Stab III./JG 27 62, 73, 74, 92, 96, 97, 100, 101

Czibulski, Obfhr Josef, 1./JG 27 122

Daele, Oblt von der, 2.(F)/122 116, 134

Danders, Uffz Helmut, 2.(F)/123 26

Darbois, Uffz René, 3./JG 4 181

Dehl, Uffz Kurt, 1./SAGr 126 32

Deicke, Oblt Joachim, 6./JG 77 243

Delfs, Lt Klaus, 2.(F)/123 30

Denkmann, Oblt Georg, Eins.Gr Ju 88 52

Dess, Uffz, II./SG 10 302

Dettmar, Uffz Gustav, 10./JG 27 33

Deutsch, Fw Hans Joachim, 3./NSGr 9 183

Dickentmann, Fw Gustav, 13./TG 1 102

Dieroff, Uffz Christian, 2.(F)/123 22, 23

Dietrichkeit, Uffz Otto, 3./LG 1 73

Dietz, Fw Rudi, 7./JG 27 83

Dilcher, Wd Insp Kurt, Wekusta 27 13

Dittmann, Lt Karl, 2.(F)/123 37

Dittmann, Lt Kurt, II./TG 4 34

Dobrawa, Oblt Otto, 8./LG 1 66

Dolesal, Uffz Leopold, II./StG 3 13

Domack, Hptm Heinz, 4./KG 200 392

Döring, Obfw Günther, 2./KG 4 277

Dörrfeld, Obfw Günther, 13./TG 1 277

Drobinski, Fw Paul, II./LG 1 13

Dudeck, Maj Gerhard, TG 2 304

Düllberg, Maj Ernst, Stab III./JG 27 39, 40, 41, 44, 45, 71, 72, 79, 81, 82, 83, 97

Ebert, Gefr Gerhard, 7./JG 77 225

Eicker, Uffz Friedrich, 14./TG 1 95

Emmersdorfer, Oblt, 1./NAGr 12 311

Ende, Obgfr Rudolf, 2./NSGr 9 437

Enkel, Hubert, 4./SG 3 74

Epp, Fw Paul, Eins.Gr Ju 88 33

Erhard, Oblt Walter, 2./NAGr 13 126

Escher, Fw Hans, 70.Seenot 269, 273

Faber, Oblt Wolfgang, 6./KG 6 57

Fabijanović, Lt Šime, 15./KG 53 39

Fahrenberger, Fw Hans, 12./JG 27 16

Fahrmann, FhjFw Erich, 4./JG 77 139, 164

Faulhaber, Ofhnr Heinz, 5./TG 4 153

Fecht, Karl von der, Eins.Gr Ju 88 72

Feist, Fw Erich, II./TG 4 260

Fellerer, Hptm Leopold, Stab III./NJG 6 179

Fiebig, Gen Martin, LKS 9

Fietz, Uffz Herbert, 1./NSGr 9 192

Findeisen, Fw Heinz, FlK X K 31

Fink, Obfw Toni, 1./NSGr 9 237

Finke, Lt Andreas, 6.(F)/122 242

Firlus, Lt Alfons, 2./Eins.KG Ju 88 57

Fischer, Fw Karl-Heinz, 1./StG 3 32

Fischer, Hptm Gunther, 1./LG 1, Eins.Gr Ju 88 60

Fischer, Lt Gerhard, 2.(F)/122 214

Fischer, Lt Kurt, 2.(F)/123 99

Fischer, Obgfr Harry, 2./NSGr 9 240

Fischer, Uffz Erwin, II./LG 1 13

Fischer, Uffz Franz, 3./NSGr 9 308, 346, 352

Fischer, Uffz Kurt, Wekusta 26 14

Fischmann, Fw Rudolf, 1./StG 3 43

Forhne, Obfw Paul, LKS 4 272

Frank, Hptm Heinz, 6./LG 1 15

Francke, Fw, II./KG 77 161

Franke, Lt Martin, 5./KG 51 73

Franzmann, Obfhr Bernd-Heinz, 2./NAGr 11 128

Freiburg, Obfw Rudolf, 7./KG 100 217

Freisenhausen, Oblt Bodo, 6.(F)/122 287

Freudig, Obfw Erwin, 2.(F)/123 18, 20

Freybote, Uffz Herbert, 2./StG 3 28

Freytag, Lt Gerhard, 4.(F)/122 198

Frost, Maj Rupert, NSGr 9 311, 312

Funk, Uffz Fritz, 8./NJG 6 248

Gabauer, Obgfr Karl, 3./NSGr 9 183

Galle, Lt, 2.(F)/122 175

Gallina, Fw Walter, 16./TG 1 125

Gebhard, Fw Willi, 7.Seenotst. 9

Geide, Uffz Fritz, 2./NSGr 9 346

Geipel, Uffz Werner, 6./TG 3 228

Germann, Fw Helmut, III./KG 100 216

Gerstenberger, FhjFw Edgar, 2./NSGr 9 330

Gerstner, Lt, 2.(F)/122 175

Gerwins, Obfw Wilhelm, 1./SAGr 126 34

Geyer, Obfw Artur, 21./NAGr 12 138

Gieger, Obfw Otto, 3./NSGr 9 183

Giese, Uffz Hans, 7./JG 27 100

Girlich, Lt Franz, 2.(F)/122 368

Glaser, Lt Wilhelm, 1./Eis.Gr Ju 88 61

Gniesmer, Lt Günther, Kdo Sommer 414

Gniostko, Uffz Heinz, 2./NAGr 11 114

Görtz, Obgfr Lothar, 2./NSGr 9 436

Gosepath, Fw Ludwig, 7.Seenotst. 146

Gotthardt, Fw Reinhold, 13./TG 1 291

Götz, Fw Robert, 2.(F)/123 100

Graab, Obfhr Walter, 2./NAGr 11 236

Graf, Hptm Hans-Horst, 4./SG 4 151

Greller Uffz Heinz, 1./SAGr 126 35

Griebner, Oblt Hans, 16./TG 1 102

Grimmer, Uffz Erich, 1./Eins.Gr Ju 88 61

Gromotka, Obfw Fritz, 9./JG 27 38, 39, 44, 45, 48, 65, 66, 78, 79

Grone, Lt Volkmar von, 2./NSGr 9 245

Grosse, Lt Hans-Werner, 3./KG 77 118

Gruber, Obgfr Heinrich, 4./SAGr 126 252

Gruber, Uffz Franz, 11./ZG 26 90

Grundke, Gefr Helmut, 6./KG 100 71

Gründling, Obfw Heinz, 11./ZG 26 33

Grunert, Fw Walter, 4./StG 3 35

Gruttke, Lt Heinz, 2.(F)/123 29

Gummingen, Hptm Fhr Wolf von, LKS 9

Günther, Lt Helmut, 2./TG 4 69

Guth, Fw Herbert, 3./JGr 200 201

Gützmann, Lt Werner, 8./JG 27 48

Haarbauer, Oblt Hans, Wekusta 26 126

Hackl, Fw Heinz, 12./JG 27 71, 80, 82

Hagmann, Obfw Heinz, 2.(F)/123 107

Hahlbohm, Obfw, 2./SAGr 126 59

Hammel, Oblt Kurt, 8./JG 27/1./JG 77 41, 55, 56, 58, 164

Hanff, Uffz Gerhard, Stab/JG 77 164

Hanke, Uffz Heinz, 2.(F)/123 31

Hanneken, Gefr Johannes, II./StG 3 13

Happe, Gefr Wilhelm, 2./NSGr 9 152

Happelt, Uffz Heinrich, 6.(F)/122 373

Harder, Hptm Jürgen, I./JG 53 115

Harder, Obfw Emil, Seenotgr 70 262

Harings, Obfw Theodor, 1./SAGr 126 34

Harnack, Obfw Wolfgang, 1./NSGr 7 358

Hartmann, Uffz Hans, 6.(F)/122 331

Hassler, Obfw Heinrich, 2./NAGr 12 126

Hässler, Uffz, 4./SAGr 126 113

Haus, Lt, 1.Eins./NAGr 12 306

Hayessen, Lt Hans-Joachim, 7./JG 27 97, 101

Hecht, Lt Otto, 4./StG 3 52

Heck, Fw Alfons, 3./NSGr 9 437

Heckmann, Uffz Theo, 7./JG 27 44, 45, 48

Heene, Lt Gottfried, 6.(F)/122 256

Heichele, Ofhr Robert, 2./NAGr 13 216

Heidlauf, Obfw Helmut, 5.(K)/LG 1 118

Heidricks, Uffz Hans, 16./TG 1 98

Heiland, FhjObfw Artur, 2./NSGr 9 330

Helferich, Hptm, Liaison Officer ANR 187

Heller, Lt Richard, 1./JG 77 144

Hemmersbach, Fw Otto, 7./JG 27 95

Henkel, Oblt Claus-Wilhelm, 7./KG 27 275

Hensel, Fw Werner, 3./NSGr 9 191, 415

Hensel, Uffz Wilhelm, 7./JG 27 79

Herden, Fw Adolf, 7./TG 4 242

Hermanitz, Uffz Martin, 3./JGr 200 201

Hermann, Uffz Günter, 3./TG 4 271

Hermann, Uffz Siegfried, 4./KG 6 47

Herbstleb, Uffz Heinz, 6./TG 1 217

Herweg, Uffz Jacob, 9./JG 27 39, 44

Hess, Gefr Willi, 15./TG 1 93

Hesse, Fhr Richard, 2.(F)/122 203

Heydebrandt, Hptm Peter von, 5./StG 3 52

Hetzler, Lt Hans, 12./JG 27 33, 34, 74

Hientzsch, Fhj Uffz Manfred, 11./JG 27 33

Hiepe, Obgfr Georg, Seetransportst. 1 10

Hinz, Uffz Hans-Werner, 2./KG 26 223

Höchtl, Uffz Karl, 7./JG 27 64

Hoffmann, Obfw Robert, 3.(F)/33 328

Hoffmann, Uffz Günther, 3./TG 4 272

Hoffmann von Waldau, Gen Otto, LKS 9

Hofmeister, Uffz Josef, 2.(F)/123 33, 34

Högel, Uffz, 2./NAGr 13 216

Hohls, Lt Wolfgang, 11./JG 27 74

Holstein, Obfw Kurt, 1./NAGr 11 244

Holz, Uffz Walter, 2./JG 77 131

Holzapfel, Oblt Karl-Otto, 2./NAGr 11 167

Hoppe, Obfw Kurt, 8./JG 27 48

Hrdlicka, Hptm Franz, 5./JG 77 153, 154

Hubatsch, Fw Herbert, 8./NJG 6 248

Huberth, Obfw Anton, 1./NSGr 7 263

Hübner, Uffz Eberhard, 3./(F) 33 185

Hübner, Uffz Otto, 2./NAGr 11 133

Hug, Fw Oskar, 3./NSGr 9 245

Hupfeld, Lt Arnt-Richard, 1./JGr 200 196

Hürtner, Gefr Günther, II./SG 3 72

Hüssmann, Obgfr, 2./NSGr 9 240

Ibbs, Uffz Hans, 5./TG 1 225

Isken, Obfw Eduard, 2./JGr 200 196, 198, 200, 201, 207

Itzstein, Lt Fritz, 2./NSGr 9 155

Jackstadt, Obfw, 2.(F)/122 124, 252

Jacob, Hptm Eduard, Stab/NSGr 7 358

Jacobs, Hptm Kurt, 2./NSGr 7 358

Jägers, Uffz Adolf, 2./NSGr 9 152

Jahn, Hptm, 3./NSGr 9 352

Janicke, Fw Werner, Wekusta 27 13, 108

Janssen, Lt Kuno, 15./TG 1 272

Jantos, Obgfr Josef, 3./NSGr 9 245

Jäschke, Oblt Günther, 8./KG 27 276

Johnen, Oblt Wilhelm, 8./NJG 6 248

Jonas, Obfw Helmuth, 2.(F)/123 106

Jordt, Uffz Walter, II./TG 4 146

Jost, Uffz Ewald, 1./NSGr 7 287

Jungfer, Fhr Berndt, 2./NSGr 9 346

Kaeber, Oblt Hellmut, 2./NAGr 11 178

Kähn, Lt Kaspar, 1.(F)/33 180, 185

Kaiser, Uffz Josef, 9./JG 27 92

Kakarutt, Obgfr Max, 4./SAGr 126 109

Kämmerlig, Uffz Horst, 2./TG 4 262

Kannenberg, Uffz Heinz-Udo, 2.(F)/123 15

Kapahnke, Uffz Ewald, 2./NSGr 9 152

Karsch, Uffz Arthur, 2.(F)/122 200

Kasper, Uffz Hermann, 2./NSGr 9 155

Kaufmann, Obgfr Erwin, 3./NSGr 9 183

Kehrer, Obfw Herbert, 3./NSGr 9 437

Keich, Obfw Egon, 1./NAGr 11 184

Keil, Ofhr Jakob, II./StG 3 13

Keller, Fw Heinz, 11./JG 27 33

Kellner, Lt Friedrich, SAGr 126 75

Kemna, Uffz Walter, 2.(F)/122 368

Keser, Uffz Reinhold, II./StG 3 13

Kesselring, Feldmarshall Albert, 171, 189, 401

Killat, Uffz Max, II./LG 1 13

Kirschner, Hptm Joachim, Stab IV./JG 27 71–74

Kizina, Lt Horst, 7./JG 27 79

Klein, Lt Wolfgang, 3.(F)/33 110

Kleindick, Uffz Joachim, 16./TG 1 102

Kleinknecht, Uffz Walter, 4./SAGr 126 64, 65

Klemm, Uffz Rudolf, 4.(F)/122 192

Kley, Lt Werner, 3./Eins.KG Ju 88 57

Klindert, Lt Hans, 2./SAGr 126 58

Klinka, 2.(F)/122 253

Klose, Gefr Hans-Günter, 5./JG 77 243, 244

Kluck, Lt Hans, 2./SAGr 126 263

Klüsch, Uffz Max, 6./StG 3 28

Kluss, Uffz Alfred, 9./JG 27 46

Knapp, Obfw Helmut, 1.(F)/33 151

Kneissl, Gefr Walter, 1./StG 3 43

Kneschke, Gerhard, 14./TG 1 93

Kniestedt, Uffz Gunther, 2./JGr 200 207

Knittel, Obgfr Heinrich, 11./LLG 1 178

Knorth, Obfw Günther, 4./SAGr 126 113

Koch, Gefr Hermann, 1./NSGr 9 184

Koch, Oblt Wilhelm, 1./NAGr 12 383

Kocken, FhjUffz Alfred, 3./JGr 200 220

Köhler, Lt Ernst-Rudolf, 5./TG 4 181

Köhler, Lt Hermann, Flugber./LKS 9

Köhler, Uffz Günther, 6./KG 27 284

Köhlmann, Richard, 5./SG 3 68

Kolster, Ofhr Hans, 2./NSGr 9 330

Kolthoff, Oblt Bruno, Stab I./JG 77 139

Köntges, Oblt Günther, Stab/TG 30 68

Kornhoff, Obfw Heinz, I./KG 200 204

Korte, GenMaj Hans, Lw Griechenland 302

Koslowski, Obfw Paul, 16./TG 1 307

Krag, Uffz Wilhelm, III./KG 100 223

Krajacic, Hans, 4./StG 3 52

Krampf, Lt Hans-Karl, Stab/KG 26 202

Krause, Obfw Hubert, OKM Kurierstaffel 88

Krause, Uffz Helmut, Wekusta 26 146

Krieg, Fw Hans, 6.(F)/122 319

Kring, Uffz Albert, I./TG 4 43

Kröger, Obfw Ernst, 2./StG 3 52

Krüger, Fw Heinz, 8./NJG 6 248

Krüger, Uffz Helmut, Stab I./NSGr 9 192

Kruschel, Fw Hans, 3./NAGr 7 328

Kubeit, Kurt, 3./JGr 200 201

Küffner, Oblt Werner, 7./JG 27 44–45

Kühn, Uffz Günther, 11./JG 27 71, 74

Kuhlmann, Obmt, 3/31 Naval Flak 314

Kukeil, Lt Adolf, Eins.Gr Ju 88 23

Kunkel, Lt Richard, 11./JG 27 80

Kupfer, Obstlt Dr Ernst, Gen d.Schl.Fl 63

Kürschner, Obfhr Hubert, 1./NAGr 11 235

Kurth, Uffz Joachim, 1./SG 3 68

Kurz, Uffz Richard, 4./JG 77 158–159

Labus, Fw Erich, 2.(F)/123 289

Lacke, Oblt Günther, 8./KG 27 276

Lagemann, Obfw Wilhelm, Verb Kdo (S)1 38

Lange, Obfw Wilhelm, 7.Seenotst/70 Seenot 83, 275

Lange, Uffz Udo, 3./LG 1 69

Langendorf, Uffz Kurt, 9./KG 77 160

Langer, Fw Adalbert, 2.(F)/123 96

Langer, Oblt Heinz, Seenotst. 20 363

Langer, Uffz Hans, 5./JG 51 156

Lankes, Gefr Hans, 1./NSGr 9 158

Lässig, Uffz Gottfried, 2./NSGr 9 184

Laubis, Lt Ulrich, I./KG 26 223

Laufenberg, Uffz Franz, 3./NSGr 9 191

Lehr, Uffz Hermann, 1./NSGr 9 153, 154

Leifeld, Uffz Heinrich, 2./SAGr 126 58

Leinberger, Uffz Heinrich, 3./NSGr 9 436

Lenecke, Uffz Wilhelm, 2.(F)/122 358

Lenz, Gefr Heinrich, 2./NSGr 9 245

Leucht, Uffz Walter, 3./KG 26 218

Leumann, Flg/Gefr Gustav, 2./NSGr 9 184, 330

Lieber, Uffz Hans, 7.Seenotst. 59

Lilienthal, Uffz Karl-Heinz, 4./KG 6 56

Lindemann, Hptm Theodor, 3./NSGr 9 436

Lindemann, Oblt Justus, 2.(F)/123 11, 12

Lober, Obfw, 1./NAGr 11 181

Löffler, Uffz/Fw Hannes, 9./JG 27 38, 60, 61, 76, 77, 83

Löhr, GenObst Alexander, Army Group E 302

Loock, Uffz Max, 8./NJG 6 248

Lösch, Hptm Hans, 7.Seenotst. 32

Lube, Maj Paul, Ia Fl Führ N Balkan 282

Lübke, Obgfr Hugo, 15./TG 1 100

Lüdtke, Fw Joachim, 2.(F)/123 106

Ludwig, Uffz Hans, 3./JGr 200 214

Lührs, Oblt Dierk, *U-453* 91

Mader, Lt Josef, 4.(F)/122 194

Mahr, Lt, II./NJG 6 123

Maier, Uffz Christian, 7./JG 77 225

Malcher, Uffz Franz, II./KG 51 53

Malina, Fw Rudolf, 6./StG 3 52

Manger, Uffz Heinrich, 4./StG 3 52

Manz, Fw Alfred, II./TG 4 257

Marawitzek, Lt Norbert, II./KG 51 55

Markschlägel, Uffz, II./TG 4 55

Martens, Uffz Siegfried, 2./StG 3 52

Martin, Uffz Paul, 7./JG 27 64

Matlock, Obfw Robert, 13./TG 3 191

Mechlinski, Gefr Hans, 2./NSGr 9 330

Meidel, Uffz Josef, 4./SAGr 126 109

Meinecke, Obfw Heinz, 10./TG 2 242

Meister, Uffz Franz, 2.(F)/122 325

Meistring, Uffz Otto, 6./TG 1 217

Menzel, Hptm Paul, 1./NAGr 11 184

Merva, Uffz Gregor, 11./ZG 26 68

Merz, Fhr Walter, 16./FlVerb.G 2 272

Mett, Lt Hans-Georg, 2./NAGr 12 74

Metz, Lt Wilhelm, 1./NAGr 11 185

Metz, Uffz Konrad, 6.(F)/122 175

Metzger, Lt Rudolf, 4./StG 3 52

Meyer, Hptm August, Seetransportst. 1 269

Meyer, Hptm Otto, IV./JG 27 97

Michalek, Fw, 1./SAGr 126 10

Misch, 2.(F)/122 253

Möbius, Uffz Heinz, 1./NAGr 11 179

Möhrke, Obgfr Rolf, 3./NSGr 9 245

Mokrus, Uffz Erwin, 1./NSGr 9 156

Morath, Lt Werner, 4./KG 26 125

Morgenstern, Obfw Wilhelm, 10./JG 27 33

Moycis, Uffz Rudolf, 7./JG 27 44, 45, 84, 98, 100

Mühlbauer, Uffz Otto, 8./JG 27 39

Muhlhoff, Gefr Albert, Kdo Carmen 339

Müller, GenLt Friedrich-Wilhelm, 22 Inf Div 30

Müller, Lt Josef, 1./SAGr 126 10

Müller, Oblt Friedrich, 2./NSGr 9 436

Müller, Oblt Fritz, Stab(F)/122 179

Müller, Uffz Joachim, 1./NAGr 11 244

Müller, Uffz Michael, 5./KG 6 54

Nagler, Oblt Ernst, 1./NAGr 11 179

Napierski, Uffz Walter, 4./SAGr 126 65

Nawrocki, Obfw Bruno, 5./TG 4 103

Nawroth, Fw Johannes, 2./NSGr 9 155

Neff, Oblt Karl, 6./TG 4 102

Nehrenheim, Flg Karl-Friedrich, 5./JG 77 225

Nern, Uffz Kurt, IV./JG 27 32

Neubauer, Lt Gerhard, II./KG 6 53

Neubauer, Stfw Karl, 1./NAGr 12 368

Neumann, Gefr Franz, 6./StG 3 52

Neumann, Lt Kurt, 2.(F)/122 124, 325

Niederhöfer, Obfw Hans, 8./JG 27 48, 58

Nitsch, Obfw Alfred, 2.(F)/123 31

Nitzsche, Uffz Hermann, 3./SAGr 126 10

Nowotny, Uffz Joachim, Eins./KG 100 34

Obermeit, Uffz Walter, 2./StG 3 28

Oehler, Fw Wilhelm, 11./TG 4 260

Öhme, Fw, Werner, FlKomp/Ln 40 30

Ohnacker, Uffz Richard, 4./KG 6 37

Ortner, Obgfr Walter, 4./SG 3 74

Ospel, Obfw Hans, 7./KG 27 275

Ott, Uffz Eugen, 6./KG 27 277

Ottnad, Ofhr Alexander, 8./JG 27 58, 63, 71, 72

Pabst, Uffz Walter, Stab/KG 26 195

Paduch, Uffz, 4./SAGr 126 132

Paluweit, Obgfr Fritz, 6./TG 1 218

Panchyrz, Oblt Walter, 1.(F)/122 56

Pannhausen, FjFw Walter, 2./NAGr 12 126

Pata, Fw, 5./NJG 6 123

Pätz, Lt Wolf, 5./KG 51 68

Pauleweit, Obgfr Fritz, 6./TG 1 217

Pendel, Uffz Eugen, 2./NSGr 9 149

Penz, Uffz Johann, 7./JG 27 98

Perović, Oblt Marin, 15./KG 53 39

Peters, Lt Hans, 2.(F)/123 25

Peters, Lt Walter, 7./TG 4 179

Peters, Uffz Georg, 6./StG 3 52

Petzold, Oblt Heinz, I./TG 4 64

Pfaffendorf, Fw Josef, 7.Seenotst. 76

Pflüger, Uffz Werner, 7./JG 27 98

Pflugmacher, Oblt Edmund, 5./StG 3 35

Pfreng, Obfw Josef, 6./LG 1 15

Pfützner, Gefr Horst, 1./SAGr 126 88

Pfützner, Uffz Helmut, 6.(F)/122 198

Piasta, Obfw Otto, 7./LG 1 77

Pieper, Fw, 1./NSGr 9 153

Pietsch, Uffz Otto, 1./StG 3 32

Pieczkowski, Gfr Erich, 2./NAGr 11 133

Pink, Uffz Walter, 6./KG 100 69, 71

Pixberg, Oblt Helmut, 7./TG 2 304

Plattner, Lt Walter, 2.(F)/123 59, 61

Pleninger, Gefr Walter, 6./TG 4 96

Post, Uffz Hans, 13./TG 1 92

Pothmann, Gefr Heinrich, 8./JG 27 63, 65, 66, 72, 83

Potrafke, Lt Günther, 10./JG 27 79

Prenissl, Gefr Erfried, 4./StG 3 52

Pritsche, Obgfr Gottfried, 16./TG 1 149

Puff, Lt Karl, 3./NAGr 2 32

Quaet-Faslem, Kptlt Jürgen, TA 16 98

Radünz, Uffz Heinz, 5./KG 6 37

Raetz, Obfw Günther, 16./TG 1 276

Rahn, Lt Rudolf, 9./TG 2 254

Raspe, Lt Ernst, 2./NAGr 2 36

Rathgeber, Fw Rolf, 2./NAGr 11 234

Rathenow, Uffz Karl, 3./SAGr 126 181

Rau, Obfw Horst, 2./NSGr 9 437

Rauch, Fw Anton, 1./Eins.Gr Ju 88 52, 53

Rauer, Obfw Hellmuth, 2./NSGr 7 282

Rautenberg, Obfw Kurt, 6.(F)/122 293

Razinski, Fw Karl, 1./NSGr 9 192

Reeg, Obfw Willi, Gen d.Schl.Fl 63

Regel, Obfw Walter, 11./ZG 26 72

Reger, Obfw Arthur, 15./TG 1 95

Reggmann, Obfw Ernst, II./LG 1 13

Reich, Lt Klaus, II./StG 3 40

Reichel, Lt Wolfgang, 1./SAGr 126 88

Reinecke, Uffz Helmut, Seetransportst. 1 269

Reinhardt, Obfw Emil, 5./JG 51 156

Reisinger, Fw Hermann, Eins.Gr Ju 88 56

Resch, Flg Xaver, II./TG 4 62

Richert, Lt Fritz, 8./KG 26 191

Richter, Obfw Herbert, 2.(F)/123 31

Richter, Oblt, 2./SAGr 126 113

Rienth, Fw Ernst, 6./TG 4 239

Riepen, Fw Ernst, Stab/NAGr 12 254

Ringel, Uffz Martin, 2./NAGr 11 122, 235

Rippert, Obgfr Horst, 3./JGr 200 196, 198, 201

Risch, Stfw Walter, II./TG 4 57

Risken, Uffz Karl-Heinz, 2.(F)/122 76

Robbe, Uffz Siegfried, 13./SG 151 78

Robel, Lt Hans, III./StG 151 36

Rödel, Maj/Obstlt Gustav, JG 27 15, 44, 48, 52, 97

Rogge, Uffz Paul, SAGr 126 75

Röhrich, Obfw Lothar, 2.(F)/123 91

Rohwer, Oblt Klaus-Jürgen, 2./SAGr 126 248

Rose, Uffz Josef, 6./StG 3 52

Rosenberg, Obfw Gerhard, 1./TG 30 68

Rossbacher, Maj Rudolf, 24

Rössler, FhjFw Josef, 6./TG 4 154

Rössler, Obfhr Werner, 4./SAGr 126 252

Rössler, Obgfr Willi, 13./SG 151 78

Rüdiger, Uffz Horst, IV./JG 27 14

Ruhland, Lt Egon, 5./KG 6 54

Rumholz, Gefr, 2./NSGr 9 155

Rumpf, Uffz Wilhelm, II./LG 1 13

Rupp, Ofhr Friedrich, 2./SAGr 126 113

Rüssmann, Uffz Günther, 6.(F)/122 196

Rutter, Uffz Heinz, 1.(F)/123 121

Sahl, Uffz Fw Johann, III./JG 27 57

Schaaf, Uffz Karl, 6./TG 4 95

Schaar, Uffz Fritz, 1./SAGr 126 32

Schäfer, Oblt, 4./SAGr 126 113

Schafer, Uffz Walter, 3.(F)/123 13

Schafferus, Uffz Karl, 12./JG 27 16

Schaffhauser, Uffz Karl, 7./JG 27 46, 101

Scheibel, Hptm Horst, 2./NAGr 2 62

Scheibel, Lt Werner, Wekusta 26 151

Scheit, Obfw Johannes, 9./JG 27 38, 39

Scheller, Fw Georg, I./StG 3 46, 47, 52

Schellmann, Obstlt Karl-Heinz, Stab/TG 30 68

Schemel, Uffz Joachim, 5./JG 77 153, 154

Schertel, Gefr Erwin, 2./NSGr 9 245

Scherzer, Uffz Franz, 3./NSGr 9 237

Schiller, Lt Werner, 2.(F)/123 30

Schiller, Obfw Heinrich, 11./ZG 26 120

Schindler, Obfw Walter, 3./SAGr 126 78

Schink, Obfw Herbert, 3./NSGr 9 330

Schlang, Oblt Josef, Stab/JG 27 52

Schlichting, Gefr Günter, 1./NSGr 9 183

Schmauser, Uffz, 2.(F)/122 336

Schmidt, Fw Herbert, II./KG 51 53

Schmidt, Lt Karl-Georg, 4./KG 6 47

Schmidt, Uffz Fritz, 2.(F)/123 139

Schmidt, Uffz Hans, 11./ZG 26 90

Schmidt, Uffz Rudolf, 2.(F)/123 109

Schmidt, Uffz Werner, 2./SAGr 126 81

Schmitz, Obfw Günther, 10./TG 2 256

Schmuhl, Uffz Werner, 5./TG 1 187

Schneck, Obfw Wilhelm, 13./TG 1 275

Schneider, Uffz Hans-Joachim, 2./KG 4 271

Schneider, Uffz Herbert, 1./SAGr 126 32

Schneider, Uffz Mathias, 7.Seenotst. 55

Schofer, Lt Ernst, I./LG 1 13

Schott, Fw Karl, 5./KG 27 271

Schramm, Obfw, 2./SAGr 126 132

Schreiber, Gefr Hans-Heinrich, 2./NSGr 7 358

Schröder, Obfw Berthold, 13./TG 1 100

Schug, Oblt Peter, 2.(F)/123 31

Schüler, Hptm Helmut, Eins.Gr Ju 88 52

Schulze, Lt z.S Konrad, 2./SAGr 125 65

Schulze, Uffz Kurt, 6./FAGr 122 318

Schumacher, Obfw, Eins.Gr Ju 88 30

Schumann, Obfw Herbert, 2./SAGr 126 263

Schumm, Hptm Hans, 6. And 4./ KG 4 270, 295

Schummer, Uffz, II./JG 77 146

Schweigel, Oblt Hans, I./LG 1 13

Schwenken, Richard, II./StG 3 13

Schwobe, Uffz Richard, 1./NSGr 9 183

Seckel, Hptm Georg, 3./JGr 200 196, 198

Seegert, Obgfr Helmut, 2.(F)/122 203

Selhorn-Timm, Obfw Heinrich, Seetransportst. 1 88

Seutemann, Fw, 2./NAGr 12 107, 108

Sewald, Fhr, 2.(F)/122 311

Sicheritz, Oblt, II./KG 6 44

Siegling, Gefr Gerhard, 7./JG 27 90, 101

Siegmann, Uffz Waldemar, I./TG 4 17

Skambraks, Lt Horst, 6./StG 3 52

Sliwa, Fw Leo, 5./JG 77 144

Sölbrand, Obfw Christian, Seenot 3 214

Sommer, Oblt Erich, Kdo Sommer 393, 410

Sonnemann, Uffz Hans, 4./StG 3 52

Sonnenberg, Obgfr Paul, 3./NSGr 9 245

Sontowski, Obfw Adolf, 2./SAGr 125 65

Soukup, Fw Ludwig, 1./NAGr 11 368

Spielmann, Lt Heinz, 6./StG 3 52

Spöntjes, Obfhr Ernst, 2.(F)/122 336

Spörr, Obgfr Franz, 2./NSGr 9 184

Stämmler, Lt Dietrich, 2.(F)/122 200

Stark, Hptm Georg, NASt, Kroatien 282

Staudinger, Obfhr Michael, 15./TG 1 295

Staudt, Obgfr Heinz, 3./NSGr 9 352

Steinberg, Uffz Rolf, 9./JG 27 81, 82

Steinbrecher, Uffz Karl, 2./SAGr 126 78

Steinhoff, Obstl Johannes, Stab/JG 77 164

Steinig, Obfw Walter, 7.Seenotst. 84

Steinstrass, Obfw, 11./ZG 26 72

Stienkemeier, Obfw Karl-Heinz, 2./ SAGr 126 25

Stifter, Uffz Jordan, 1./StG 3 43

Stiller, Fw Hermann, 6./TG 1 225

Stock, Lt Franz, 2.(F)/123 15

Stockburger, Obfw Wilhelm, 2./ NAGr 13 144

Stoll, Uffz Friedrich, 11./ZG 26 89, 90

Stollwerk, Obfhr/Lt Peter, 3./NSGr 9 273, 308, 346, 352

Stölting, Obfw Hans, 2./NAGr 11 137

Stolzenberg, Lt Horst, SAGr 126 10

Strassburger, Uffz Fritz, 6./StG 3 35

Stratmann, Uffz Emil, Verb Kdo (S)1 38

Streb, Uffz Rudolf, Seenot 6 123

Strehl, Obfw Robert, 1.(F)/123 149

Striebel, Uffz Günter, 7./JG 27 96, 102, 105

Strulick, Uffz Walter, 15./TG 1 272

Stry, Hptm Herbert, 6./StG 3 35

Stuber, Fw Kaspar, 1./NSGr 9 319

Stübinger, Obgfr Alfred, 4./SAGr 126 105

Stückler, Fw Alfred, 8./JG 27 48, 63

Stumpf, Uffz Karl, III./JG 27 57

Sukowski, Lt Hans, 11./ZG 26 33

Sulz, Obfw Erich, 15./TG 1 272

Supsch, Obgfr, II./KG 77 161

Suwelack, Lt Gerhard, 10./JG 27 71

Tanck, Fw Karl, 5./JG 77 225

Tautz, Obgfr Rudolf, Flak 6./GR 522 98

Theusner, Met Dr Christian, Wekusta 27 30

Thomas, Obgfr, 8./NJG 6 248

Thomsen, Uffz Rolf, 1./NAGr 11 295

Thürner, Uffz Herbert, 1./SAGr 126 88

Till, Obgfr Franz, 3./NSGr 9 183

Tomschegg, Lt Hans, 1./JG 27 122

Torge, Uffz Walter, 10./JG 27 33, 34

Treichel, Obfw Siegfried, 16./TG 1 272

Trepper, Uffz Wilhelm, 7./KG 77 160

Tröster, Obgfr Ulrich, 2./NSGr 9 156

Trox, Kaptlt Hans-Georg, *U-97* 12

Tschirch, Obgfr Günter, 1./NSGr 9 192

Ubben, Maj Kurt, III./JG 27 97

Ugries, Uffz Karl-Heinz, 8./KG 26 187

Ullrich, FhjUffz/Gefr Friedrich, 8./ JG 27 58, 63, 81, 82

Ulrich, Fw Albert, 6./JG 77 158, 159, 160

Unsin, Fw Benno, 1./SAGr 126 32

Unverfehrt, Lt Werner, 5./KG 6 55

Urban, Uffz Kurt, 2./NSGr 9 184, 245

Urbanzyk, Obfw Alfred, 4./KG 26 223

Vaculka, Obgfr Franz, 4./StG 3 35

Vesely, Uffz Josef, II./LG 1 13

Vessen, Uffz Hans, 4.(F)/122 239

Vogelsang, Fw Johann, 4./KG 6 44, 61

Vogt, Uffz Robert, 16./TG 1 103

Voigt, Fw Günther, 6. and 1./TG 4
69, 253

Volke, FhjObfw Maximilian, 6./JG
77 246–248

Vorberg, Obfw Hans,
Seetransportst. 1 269

Voss, Obfw Max, 16./TG 1 296

Voss, Uffz Günther, 1./NSGr 9 236

Voss, Uffz Heinrich, 1./NAGr 12
306, 368

Wachtfeidl, Obgfr, 2.(F)/122 311

Wacker, Oblt Hermann, Wekusta
27 149

Wagner, Gefr Hans, 1./NSGr 9 156

Wagner, Lt Heinz-Hasso, 2./NAGr
12 114

Wagner, Uffz Gottfried, II./LG 1 13

Waissnor, Uffz Werner, 1./NSGr
9 184

Walcher, Obfw Josef, 4./KG 27 285

Walther, Uffz Heinz, 6./KG 6 56

Weber, Oblt, z.S *S 55* 80

Wehlam, Fw Wilhelm, 2./KG 100
62

Weigel, Lt Hans-Georg, 3./SAGr
126 181

Weil, Uffz Günther, Eins.2./NAGr
13 301

Weise, Lt Hans-Joachim, 5./KG
26 220

Weixelbaum, Hptm Helmut,
2.(F)/123 248

Wellmann, Lt Jürgen, 5./SG 3 68

Wendel, Lt Wolfgang, I./StG 3 46,
47, 52

Wenger, Uffz Reinhold, 5./TG 4 153

Wente, Fw Fritz, 6./StG 3 28

Wentzlaff, Uffz Franz, 6.(F)/122 191

Werfft, Lt Dr Peter, 9./JG 27 79, 83

Werner, Uffz Kurt, Seetransportst.
3 88

Westerwelle, Uffz Wilhelm, II./
StG 3 13

Wiborg, Uffz Karl-Ernst, 1./NAGr
12 368

Wiener, Obfw Stefan, 13./TG 1 293

Wilk, Gefr Hans, 3./NSGr 9 192

Wilzopolski, Hptm Willi, 1./NSGr
9 378

Witt, Lt, 2.(F)/123 271

Wittenberg, Uffz Helmut, 1./NAGr
12 262

Woldfarth, Lt Horst, 2.(F)7123 248

Wolff-Rothermel, Ofhr Klaus, 1./
NSGr 9 158

Wolfsen, Obfw Hans, 3./NSGr 9
192

Wolkersdorfer, Gefr Eduard, Stab
II./JG 51 178

Wöllert, Lt Fritz, 4.(F)/122 373

Wolters, Fw Fritz, Wekusta 27 30

Wolters, Fw Heinrich, 2./JG 77 144

Zacharias, Lt Wolfgang, 2./SAGr
126 25

Zantow, Obgfr Egon, 1./NSGr 9 237

Ziller, Obfw Horst, 10./JG 27 71

Zimmermann, Obfw Wilhelm,
2.(F)/122 358

Zimmermann, Uffz Karl, 1./SG 3 68

Zobel, Fw Gustav, 1./SAGr 126 88

Zschinger, Lt Herbert, I./LG 1 13

Zwarte, Lt Johann, 70.Seenotst. 291

LUFTWAFFE UNITS

Lw Griechenland 302

Lw Kdo Süd-Ost 9, 37, 97

N Balkan 282

Order of Battle 43, 93, 97, 102,
105, 107, 110, 218, 288

Fighter units

I./JG 4 (3 Staffel) 135, 181

Stab/JG 27 14, 15, 43, 44, 48, 52, 97

I./JG 27 (Stab, 1, 2 and 3 Staffeln)
120, 135

III./JG 27 (Stab, 7, 8 and 9 Staffeln)
37, 38, 39, 40, 41, 43, 44, 45, 46,
47, 48, 54, 56, 57, 58, 61, 62, 63,
64, 65, 66, 68, 69, 70, 71, 72, 73,
74, 77, 78, 79, 80, 81, 82, 83, 84,
85, 86, 87, 89, 90, 92, 93, 95, 96,
97, 98, 100, 101, 102, 105, 107,
110, 135

IV./JG 27 (Stab, 10, 11 and 12
Staffeln) 14, 16, 32, 33, 34, 36,
38, 41, 43, 44, 45, 47, 48, 52, 53,
71, 72, 74, 77, 80, 82, 135

13./JG 27 110

II./JG 51 (Stab, 4, 5 and 6 Staffeln)
135, 136, 156, 176, 178

I./JG 53 115, 135

III./JG 53 48

Stab/JG 77 139, 164, 239, 252

I./JG 77 (Stab, 1, 2 and 3 Staffeln)
122, 131, 133, 134, 135, 136,
139, 140, 142, 144, 151, 216

II./JG 77 (Stab, 4, 5 and 6 Staffeln)
126, 135, 136, 142, 144, 146,
151, 152, 153, 154, 158, 159,
160, 164, 210, 221, 225, 241,
243, 244, 246, 247, 248

III./JG 77 97, 135

JGr 200 (Stab, 1, 2 and 3 Staffeln)
136, 195, 196, 197, 198, 200,
201, 204, 207, 210, 214, 216,
220, 221, 223

II./NJG 6 (5 Staffel) 123

III./NJG 6 (Stab, 8 Staffel) 179, 248

11./ZG 26 10, 14, 31, 32, 33, 37,
43, 60, 61, 68, 72, 89, 90, 93, 97,
102, 105, 107, 120

Bomber units

2./KG 4 270, 271, 277

II./KG 4 (4, and 6 Staffeln) 270,
288, 295

II./KG 6 (Stab, 4, 5 and 6 Staffeln)
35, 37, 38, 40, 43, 44, 47, 52, 53,
54, 55, 56, 57, 61

KG 26 136, 195, 200, 207, 216, 218

I./KG 26 (Stab, 1, 2 and 3 Staffeln)
187, 191, 215, 216, 217, 218,
223

II./KG 26 (Stab, 4, 5 and 6 Staffeln)
125, 202, 203, 216, 217, 218,
220, 223

III./KG 26 (8 and 9 Staffeln) 159, 187, 191

II./KG 27 (Stab, 4, 5 and 6 Staffeln) 271, 275, 277, 284, 285

III./KG 27 (Stab, 7, 8 Staffeln) 273, 275, 276, 288, 296

II./KG 51 (Stab, 4, 5 and 6 Staffeln) 43, 46, 53, 54, 55, 58, 68, 73, 74

15./KG 53 39

KG 77 136, 207

I./KG 77 (2 and 3 Staffeln) 118, 202, 207

II./KG 77 161

III./KG 77 (7 and 9 Staffeln) 160

KG 100 43, 47, 136, 214

I./KG 100 (Stab, 1, 2 and 3 Staffeln) 62, 207

II./KG 100 (Stab, 4, 5 and 6 Staffeln) 34, 48, 61, 67, 69, 72, 75

III./KG 100 (Stab, 7, 8 and 9 Staffeln) 215, 216, 217, 218, 223

Eins./KG 100 14, 34, 48, 71, 75

I./KG 200 204

4./KG 200 392

LG 1 14, 43, 46, 136

I./LG 1 (Stab, 1, 2 and 3 Staffeln) 13, 14, 60, 69, 72, 73, 79

II./LG 1 (Stab, 4, 5 and 6 Staffeln) 13, 15, 118

III./LG 1 (Stab, 7, 8 and 9 Staffeln) 66, 72, 76, 77

IV./LG 1 13

III./LLG 176

11./LLG 1 178

Eins.Gr Ju 88 23, 30, 33, 52, 53, 56, 58, 61, 72

Dive-bomber units

NSGr 7 52, 263, 282, 287, 289, 354, 357, 358, 359, 390

NSGr 9 149, 152, 153, 154, 155, 156, 158, 183, 184, 191, 192, 198, 235, 236, 237, 240, 245, 273, 308, 311, 312, 314, 318, 319, 330, 341, 345, 346, 352, 368, 378, 402, 412, 415, 418, 436, 437

Stab/SG 3 72

I./SG 3 (Stab, 1, 2 and 3 Staffeln) 66, 68

II./SG 3 (Stab, 4, 5 and 6 Staffeln) 62, 63, 65, 68, 72, 74, 76

4./SG 4 151

SG 10 250, 304

II./SG 10 (Stab, 4, 5 and 6 Staffeln) 298, 301, 302, 303, 305

StG 3 46, 51

Stab/StG 3 43, 48

I./StG 3 (Stab, 1, 2 and 3 Staffeln) 14, 28, 32, 43, 46, 47, 49, 51, 52, 57

II./StG 3 (Stab, 4, 5 and 6 Staffeln) 13, 28, 35, 40, 43, 46, 51, 52, 53, 54, 57, 58, 62

III./StG 151 36

13./SG 151 78

Reconnaissance units

(F)/33 93, 105, 107, 109, 110, 151, 180, 185, 202, 203, 215, 218, 288, 328

(F)/122 43, 56, 76, 79, 93, 102, 118, 121, 124, 134, 156, 175, 179, 191, 192, 193, 194, 196, 198, 200, 202, 203, 210, 214, 239, 242, 252, 253, 256, 287, 293, 311, 319, 321, 324, 325, 331, 336, 341, 358, 360, 368, 373, 383, 412

(F)/123 11, 12, 13, 15, 18, 20, 22, 23, 25, 26, 28, 29, 30, 31, 33, 34, 37, 43, 53, 59, 61, 80, 86, 90, 91, 93, 96, 99, 100, 102, 106, 107, 109, 121, 139, 141, 181, 183, 248, 271, 288, 289

NAGr 2 32, 36, 43, 52, 62

NAGr 7 328

NAGr 11 54, 114, 122, 128, 133, 137, 155, 167, 178, 179, 181, 184, 185, 197, 234, 235, 236, 244, 248, 295, 314, 341, 342, 363, 366, 368, 381, 411, 412, 436

NAGr 12 48, 74, 75, 76, 107, 108, 114, 126, 138, 254, 262, 306, 311, 368, 383

NAGr 13 126, 144, 185, 206, 216, 301

NASt Kroatian 281

2./SAGr 125 25, 31, 43, 65, 81, 82

SAGr 126 (Stab, 1, 2 3 and 4 Staffeln) 9, 10, 32, 33, 34, 35, 43, 55, 58, 59, 62, 64, 65, 68, 75, 78, 81, 83, 84, 88, 93, 97, 98,

100, 101, 102, 105, 107, 109, 112, 113, 131, 132, 180, 181, 248, 252, 263

2./SAGr 128 204

Transport units

II./TG 1 (5 Staffel) 187, 210, 217, 218, 225

IV./TG 1 (Stab, 12, 13, 14, 15 and 16 Staffeln) 90, 92, 93, 95, 98, 100, 101, 102, 103, 104, 125, 149, 272, 275, 276, 277, 288, 291, 293, 295, 296, 307

TG 2 287

II./TG 2 (7 Staffel) 71, 74, 304

III./TG 2 (9 and 10 Staffeln) 242, 254, 256, 312

2./TG 3 318

6./TG 3 227, 228

IV./TG 3 (13 Staffel) 11, 191

I./TG 4 (Stab, 1, 2 and 3 and 4 Staffeln) 13, 17, 28, 37, 43, 53, 64, 66, 69, 72, 73, 74, 80, 82, 253, 256, 262, 271, 272, 288

II./TG 4 (Stab, 5, 6, 7 and 8 Staffeln) 9, 34, 55, 57, 62, 69, 71, 74, 78, 95, 96, 102, 103, 146, 152, 153, 154, 179, 181, 239, 242, 257, 260

11./TG 4 260

IV./TG 4 (14, and 15) 258, 278, 288, 399

TG 30 68

Seetransportst. 1 9, 10, 69, 88, 269

Seetransportst. 3 88

Flak units

1/1 Nav Mot Trasp Det. 319, 320

1/31 2 Platoon 317

3./Feld-Ers Btl 198 349

3.Flak Brigade 128, 294

3/22 MbFlak A 203

3/31 Naval Flak 298, 302, 310, 314, 316, 317

6./Naval Flak 257

6./720 Naval Flak 284 316

8./720 Naval Flak 298

III Brigade 301

III./FAS 2 138

278 Inf Div 138

Feld-Erg Btl 29 318

Flak 6./Gr 522 98

Flak 45 27

M Abt 720 277

Platoon TMiKW.A 320

Railway Trasport Det. 295

Miscellaneous units

2.Fliegerschuldiv. 324

3.(F)/2 93, 107

3.(Go)/Schlgr 1 251

3.Seenotst. 210, 214

6.Seenotst. 123

7.Seenotst. 9, 13, 28, 30, 32, 55, 56, 59, 76, 83, 84, 146, 293

20.Seenotst. 341, 363

70.Seenotst. 269, 273, 275, 279, 288, 291

16./FlVerb.G 2 82, 272

FlKomp/Ln 40 14, 30

Fl X FlK 31, 37, 92

Kdo.Fl.H.Ber. 7/VI 16

Kdo Carmen 339

Kdo Schumm 270

Kdo Sommer 393, 410, 412, 414, 422

OKM Kurierst. 88

Seenotgr 70 262

Stormkampf Staffel Kroatien 174

Verb Kdo (S)1 38

Wekusta 26 14, 30, 118, 126, 146, 151

Wekusta 27 13, 30, 43, 82, 108, 113, 149, 255, 306

ITALIAN PERSONNEL AND THEIR UNITS

Addonizio, Ten Luciano, 147ª Sq RM 31

Agostini, M.llo Serafino, FIAT test pilot 193

Alessandrini, T.Col Aldo, 2º Gr C ANR 368

Ancillotti, Serg Magg Rolando, 6ª Sq, 2º Gr C ANR 182, 183, 292, 293, 305, 366

Annoni, Cap Emanuele, 9º, Gr, 4º St C 36, 129

Archidiacono, Serg Raffaele, 6ª Sq, 2º Gr C ANR 404, 405, 408

Arrigoni, Serg Gianni, 3ª Sq, 1º Gr C ANR 140

Baccarini, Serg Magg Isonzo, 3ª Sq, 1º Gr C ANR 386, 387

Bacich, Magg Mario, 5º St Caccia 130

Bagajoli, Ten Arrigo, 386ª Sq, 21º Gr, 51º St C 130

Balboni Ten Giannino, Stormo Baltimore 322

Baldi, Serg Magg Loris, 4ª Sq, 2º Gr C ANR 305, 308, 316, 325, 328, 358, 393, 394, 395, 405, 408

Baldin, Serg Magg Filippo, 92ª Sq, 21º Gr, 51º St C 192

Balduzzo, Serg Domenico, 3ª Sq, 1º Gr C ANR 190, 386, 387

Ballista, Ten Alberto, 155º Gr, 51º St C 317

Barbasetti di Prun, Ten Silvio, 91ª Sq, 12º Gr, 4º St C 319

Barioglio, Cap Camillo, 2ª Sq, 1º Gr C ANR 383

Bartolozzi, Cap Guido, 3ª Sq, 1º Gr C ANR 387

Bartolozzi, Ten Osvaldo, 378ª Sq, 155º Gr, 51º St C 313

Bellagambi, Cap Mario, 5ª Sq, 2º Gr C ANR 142, 143, 144, 159, 291, 293, 295, 305, 324, 325, 330, 354, 355, 358, 378, 404, 425

Bentivoglio, Cap Giuseppe, 356ª Sq, 20º Gr, 51º St C 130

Benzi, Serg Gualberto, 4ª Sq, 2º Gr C ANR 354, 355

Beretta, Ten Alessandro, 3ª Sq, 1º Gr C ANR 149, 185, 186

Bernardi, Serg Magg Luigi, Gr AS 194

Betti, Ten Francesco, 6ª Sq, 2º Gr C ANR 377, 404, 408, 427

Biagiola, Ten Nazzareno, 253ª Sq, 132º Gr, St Baltimore 328

Bianchini, Serg Giacomo, 6ª Sq, 2º Gr C ANR 355, 356, 360

Biasi, Ten Tiberio, 6ª Sq, 2º Gr C ANR 300, 301

Biccolini, Cap Manlio, 155º Gr, 51º St C 130

Billi, M.llo Danilo, 3ª Sq, 1º Gr C ANR 386, 387

Bissoli, Ten Gioacchino, 93ª Sq, 8º Gr, 5º St C 130

Bolzoni, M.llo Romano, 6ª Sq, 2º Gr C ANR 144

Bonara, Ten Leandro, 6ª Sq, 2º Gr C ANR 360

Bonato, Serg Magg Filippo, 6ª Sq, 2º Gr C ANR 358

Boscaro, Serg Magg Luigi, 2ª Sq, 1º Gr C ANR 149

Brini, S.Ten Enrico, 4ª Sq, 2º Gr C ANR 345

Brombin, Serg Antonio, 395ª Sq, 154º Gr CT 24

Buscaglia, Magg Carlo Emanuele, 28º Gr, St Baltimore 148, 229, 232

Caimi, Serg Ettore, 5ª Sq, 2º Gr C ANR 404, 408

Camaioni, Ten Antonio, 4ª Sq, 2º Gr C ANR 305

Casalnuovo, T.Col Grimaldo, 90º Gr BT 13

Cavagliano, Serg Magg Carlo, 4ª Sq, 2º Gr C ANR 139, 157, 164, 305, 360, 404

Cavagnino, M.llo Giovanni, 4ª Sq, 2º Gr C ANR 175

Cella, Ten Silvio, 253ª Sq, 132º Gr, St Baltimore 256

Cerretani, Cap Umberto, 101º Gr, 5º St C 130

Chiussi, M.llo Giuseppe, 1ª Sq, 1º Gr C ANR 386, 387

Cimatti, Serg Magg Paolo, 2ª Sq, 1º Gr C ANR 191

Clauser, Ten Fabio, 90ª Sq, 10º Gr, 4º St C 304

Coletta, S.Ten Guido, 141ª Sq RM 33

Colonna, Ten Oddone, 2ª Sq, 1º Gr C ANR 426, 427

Cosmano, Serg Aurelio, 6ª Sq, 2º Gr C ANR 378

Covre, M.llo Tullio, 6ª Sq, 2º Gr C ANR 301, 330, 378, 394, 427

Cuomo, Cap Corv Alberto, *Monzambano* 28

Dagnino, S.Ten Aldo, 239ª Sq, 102º Gr, 5º St C 167

Dall'Asta, Ten Enzo, 84ª Sq, 10º Gr, 4º St C 318

De Bernardini, Serg Magg, 195ª Sq, 90º Gr, 30º St BT 11

De Ferrari, Ten Marco, 90ª Sq, 10º Gr, 4º St C 304

De Lieto, Ten Domenico, Gr AS ANR 194

De Masellis, Ten Luigi, 5ª Sq, 2º Gr C ANR 324, 325, 358

Desideri, M.llo Giuseppe, 6ª Sq, 2º Gr C ANR 160, 186

Dezzani, Cap Remo, 21º Gr, 51º St C 130

Di Fiorino, Ten Raul, 5ª Sq, 2º Gr C ANR 364

D'Ilario, Serg Magg Ernesto, 2º Gr C ANR 364

Donini, Serg Magg Mario, 356ª Sq, 20º Gr, 51º St C 304

Drago, Ten/Cap Ugo, 4ª Sq, 2º Gr C ANR 139, 164, 182, 183, 333, 355, 356, 360, 384, 393, 394, 404–405, 425

Erasi, Magg Massimiliano, 132º Gr, St Baltimore 148, 365, 366

Fagiano, S.Ten Amedeo, 4ª Sq, 2º Gr C ANR 310

Fanali, T.Col Duilio, 51º St C 129, 130

Feliciani, Serg Magg Luigi, 5ª Sq, 2º Gr C ANR 179

Ferazzani, Ten Giuseppe, 97ª Sq, 9º Gr, 4º St C 129

Ferrero, Ten Ermete, 6ª Sq, 2º Gr C ANR 345, 360, 378, 427

Filippi, Ten Fausto, 5ª Sq, 2º Gr C ANR 301, 348, 349

Fissore, Ten Alfredo, 4ª Sq, 2º Gr C ANR 160

Fornaci, Serg Magg Fausto, 5ª Sq, 2º Gr C ANR 292, 293, 356

Fornasari, M.llo Franco, 3º Gr C ANR 408

Franchini, Ten Giovanni, 351ª Sq, 21º Gr, 51º St C 130, 167

Fumagalli, M.llo Mario, 6ª Sq, 2º Gr C ANR 404, 408

Galetti, M.llo Artidoro, 6ª Sq, 2º Gr C ANR 146, 149, 292, 293

Gallone, S.Ten Alessandro, 2ª Sq, 1º Gr C ANR 414

Genitali, Serg Magg Francesco, 190ª Sq, 88º Gr 1857

Gensini, Ten Otello, 96ª Sq, 9º Gr, 4º St C 129

Gentile, Ten Francesco, 193

Giorio, Ten Mario, 5ª Sq, 2º Gr C ANR 325, 404, 408

Girace, M.llo Italo, 6ª Sq, 2º Gr C ANR 378

Giusto, Ten Raffaele, 90ª Sq, 10º Gr, 4º St C 320

Grasso, Ten Gennaro, 252ª Sq, 104º Gr AS 13

Graziani, Cap Giulio Cesare, 281ª Sq, 132º Gr, St Baltimore 148

Graziani, Ten Carlo, 208ª Sq, 101º Gr, 5º St C 260

Jannicelli, Ten Fiorenzo, 356ª Sq, 20º Gr, 51º St C 313

Jasinski, M.llo Enrico, Gr AS ANR 194

Keller, Serg Magg Ernesto, 4ª Sq, 2º Gr C ANR 333

Lalatta, Cap Ippolito, 8º Gr, 5º St C 130

Laurenti, Ten Arnaldo, 356ª Sq, 20º Gr, 51º St C 304

Leonesio, Ten Silvio, 239ª Sq, 102º Gr, 5º St C 167

Longhini, Ten Antonio 'Max', 4ª Sq, 2º Gr C ANR 310

Luccardi, Cap Guido, 6ª Sq, 2º Gr C ANR 378

Lunghi, Serg Magg Germano, 192ª Sq, 87º Gr, 30º St BT 24

Mancini, Cap Massimino, 6ª Sq, 2º Gr C ANR 148, 149

Mancini, Ten Giovanni, 6ª Sq, 2º Gr C ANR 146, 160

Manfredini, Ten Enrico, 361ª Sq, 155º Gr, 51º St C 130

Marchesi, Cap Cesare, 3ª Sq, 1º Gr C ANR 381, 382

Marescalchi, Cap Enrico, 253ª Sq, 104º Gr AS, 132º Gr, St Baltimore 9–10, 148

Margoni, Serg Luigi, 6ª Sq, 2º Gr C ANR 405, 408

Marin, Serg Luigi, 4ª Sq, 2º Gr C ANR 175

Marino, S.Ten Salvatore, 90º Gr BT 13

Mariotti, Magg Luigi, 4º St C 129, 333, 334

Marri, Ten Alessandro, 195ª Sq, 90º Gr, 30º St BT 11

Martinelli, Ten Tullio, 360ª Sq, 20º Gr, 51º St C 130

Matelli, Ten Luigi, 395ª Sq, 154º Gr CT 24

Mazzanti, Serg Magg Guido, 5ª Sq, 2º Gr C ANR 324, 378

Mazzi, Serg Magg Sergio, 4ª Sq, 2º Gr C ANR 175, 186, 358

Mecatti, Ten Mario, 91ª Sq, 12º Gr, 4º St C 129

Merani, Ten Adriano, Gr AS ANR 194

Mettimano, Ten Alessandro, 84ª Sq, 10º Gr, 4º St C 129

Miani, Magg Carlo, NC 2º Gr C ANR 182, 183, 291, 293, 356, 368, 404–407

Micheloni, Serg Mario, 97ª Sq, 9º Gr, 4º St C 408

Migliore, Ten Edoardo, 208ª Sq, 101º Gr, 5º St C 130

Minardi, Serg Guido, 5ª Sq, 2º Gr C ANR 295

Mingozzi, M.llo Renato, 4ª Sq, 2º Gr C ANR 144, 325

Moci, T.Col Paolo, 132° Gr, St Baltimore 229

Molteni, Serg Magg Natale, 90ª Sq, 10° Gr, 4° St C 319

Montuori, Cap Antonio, 209ª Sq, 102° Gr, 5° St C 130

Morabito, Serg Magg Tommaso, 2ª Sq, 1° Gr C ANR 181, 186

Morandi, Ten Aurelio, 2ª Sq, 1° Gr C ANR 426, 427

Moratti, M.llo Giuseppe, 6ª Sq, 2° Gr C ANR 404–405, 408

Morettin, S.Ten Fausto, 5ª Sq, 1° Gr C ANR 128

Morganti, Ten Giuseppe, 396ª Sq, 154° Gr CT 30

Morselli, Ten Luigi, Gr AS ANR 194

Moschi, M.llo Sesto, Gr AS ANR 187

Neri, Serg Magg Ariosto, 5ª Sq, 2° Gr C ANR 381

Neri, Ten Gianfranco, Gr AS ANR 187, 194

Nocera, Serg Magg Nicola, 260ª Sq, 28° Gr, St Baltimore 278

Noziglia, T.Col Giuseppe, St Baltimore 148

Nunnari, M.llo Francesco, 195ª Sq, 90° Gr, 30° St BT 11

Pacini, Serg Magg Luigi, 6ª Sq, 2° Gr C ANR 305, 307, 308

Palermi, Ten Elvio, 5ª Sq, 2° Gr C ANR 154

Pandolfo, Ten Francesco, Gr AS ANR 187

Parodi, Ten Mario, 238ª Sq, 101° Gr, 5° St C 130

Patton, Serg Renato, 6ª Sq, 2° Gr C ANR 366, 394, 404, 425, 427

Perina, Ten Marcello, Gr AS ANR 194

Pesce, Ten Giuseppe, 92ª Sq, 8° Gr, 5° St C 130

Pezzi, S.Ten Elio, 2ª Sq, 1° Gr C ANR 149

Piccolomini, Magg Ranieri, 10° Gr, 4° St C 129, 333

Piolanti, S.Ten Michelangelo, 5ª Sq, 2° Gr C ANR 355, 356, 358, 408

Pizzato, Leg Guido, Legione San Marco RSI 192

Poluzzi, Serg Gino, 6ª Sq, 2° Gr C ANR 358

Prampolini, Serg Magg Giordano, 252ª Sq, 104° Gr 13

Quasso, Serg Renato, 6ª Sq, 2° Gr C ANR 384

Raffone, S.Ten Dr Ubaldo, 147ª Sq RM 53

Rizzitelli, Ten Francesco, 91ª Sq, 12° Gr, 4° St C 320

Rosas, S.Ten Emanuele, 4ª Sq, 2° Gr C ANR 305, 325

Rosati, Ten Giuseppe, 1ª Sq, 1° Gr C ANR 383

Roveda, T.Col Renato, St Baltimore 148

Russo, S.Ten Giovanni, 147ª Sq RM 29

Saccomandi, Serg Primo, 195ª Sq, 90° Gr, 30° St BT 11

Sajeva, S.Ten Giovanni, 1ª Sq, 1° Gr C ANR 128

Saletti, Serg Renato, 2° Gr C ANR 155

Salvi, Cap Eugenio, 73ª Sq, 12° Gr, 4° St C 129

Sancristoforo, Serg Domenico, 2./SAGr 125 81, 82

Sanseverino, Ten Vittorio, 19ª Sq, 28° Gr, St Baltimore 148

Sanson, Serg Magg Attilio, 5ª Sq, 2° Gr C ANR 144, 292, 293, 295, 301, 425

Santuccio, Serg Magg Luigi, 5ª Sq, 2° Gr C ANR 165

Sarti, Ten Aristide, 6ª Sq, 2° Gr C ANR 404, 408

Scapellato, Cap Umberto, 260ª Sq, 28° Gr, St Baltimore 148

Scarinci, Ten Giuseppe, 378ª Sq, 155° Gr, 51° St C 130

Secchi, Serg Magg Pietro, 6ª Sq, 2° Gr C ANR 154

Sigismondi, S.Ten Vittorio, 386ª Sq, 21° Gr, 51° St C 256

Silvestro, Ten Mario, 195ª Sq, 90° Gr, 30° St BT 11

Spadaccini, Cap Paolo, 20° Gr, 51° St C 130

Spazzoli, M.llo Romano, 3ª Sq, 1° Gr C ANR 149

Spigaglia, Cap Alberto, NC 2° Gr C ANR 358, 394, 404

Spreafico, Cap Mario, 239ª Sq, 102° Gr, 5° St C 130

Spreca, S.Ten Nando, 5ª Sq, 2° Gr C ANR 408

Squassoni, S.Ten Felice, 4ª Sq, 2° Gr C ANR 333, 378, 405, 408

Stella, Serg Virginio, 6ª Sq, 2° Gr C ANR 146

Storari, M.llo Luciano, 147ª Sq RM 31

Storchi, S.Ten Franco, 1° Gr C ANR 358

Talin, Serg Leo, 5ª Sq, 2° Gr C ANR 159, 164, 292, 293

Tampieri, Serg Antonio, 6ª Sq, 2° Gr C ANR 404–405

Tommasi, Ten Carlo, 90ª Sq, 10° Gr, 4° St C 129

Torresi, Cap Giulio, 3ª Sq, 1° Gr C ANR 149

Valdes, M.llo Antonio, 192ª Sq, 87° Gr, 30° St BT 24

Valenza, Ten Vito, 239ª Sq, 102° Gr, 5° St C 33

Valenzano, Ten Raffaele, 4ª Sq, 2° Gr C ANR 157, 295, 325, 378, 405

Veronesi, Serg Magg, 1° Gr C ANR 149

Visconti, Magg Adriano, NC 1° Gr C ANR 183, 386, 387

Vitelli, Serg Magg Rolando, 190ª Sq, 88° Gr 187

Volpi, Ten Alberto, 6ª Sq, 2° Gr C ANR 345, 404–407, 408

Zanardi, Serg Magg Ferdinando, 6ª Sq, 2° Gr C ANR 378, 427

Zerini, Serg Magg Vladimiro, 6ª Sq, 2° Gr C ANR 378

Zorzut, Ten Arrigo, 195ª Sq, 90° Gr, 30° St BT 11

Zuccarini, Ten Gian Mario, 3ª Sq, 1° Gr C ANR 181

ITALIAN UNITS

Order of battle 129–130

Raggruppamento Bombardamento e Trasporti 340

4º Stormo Caccia 36, 129, 234, 304, 318, 319, 320, 333, 408

5º Stormo Tuffatori 33

5º Stormo Caccia 130

51º Stormo Caccia 130, 167, 192, 234, 256, 303, 304, 313, 317, 340

Stormo Baltimore 148, 232, 320

Stormo Notturno 150

1º Gruppo Trasporti Notturno 129

8º Gruppo (5º St C) 130

9º Gruppo (4º St C) 129

10º Gruppo (4º St C) 129, 304, 318, 319, 320, 445

12º Gruppo (4º St C) 129, 445

20º Gruppo (51º St C) 130, 257, 304, 445

21º Gruppo (51º St C) 130

28º Gruppo (St Baltimore) 148, 232, 278, 321, 322, 445

82º Gruppo RM 24

88º Gruppo Trasporti Notturno 129

90º Gruppo BT 12

93º Gruppo RM 24

101º Gruppo (5º St C) 130

102º Gruppo (5º St C) 130

104º Gruppo AS 9

132º Gruppo (St Baltimore) 148, 229, 238, 309, 328, 365, 366, 445

155º Gruppo (51º St C) 129, 130, 234, 313, 317

19ª Squadriglia (28º Gr, St Baltimore) 148

73ª Squadriglia (9º Gr, 4º St C) 129

84ª Squadriglia (10º Gr, 4º St C) 129, 318

90ª Squadriglia (10º Gr, 4º St C) 129, 304, 319, 320

91ª Squadriglia (12º Gr, 4º St C) 129, 319, 320

92ª Squadriglia (8º Gr, 51º St C) 130, 192

93ª Squadriglia (8º Gr, 51º St C) 130

96ª Squadriglia (9º Gr, 4º St C) 129

97ª Squadriglia (9º Gr, 4º St C) 129, 408

141ª Squadriglia RM 33

147ª Squadriglia RM 31, 35, 37, 53

190ª Squadriglia (88º Gr) 187

192ª Squadriglia (87º Gr, 30º St BT) 24

195ª Squadriglia (90º Gr, 30º St BT) 11

208ª Squadriglia (101º Gr, 5º St C) 130, 260

209ª Squadriglia (101º Gr, 5º St C) 130

238ª Squadriglia (101º Gr, 5º St C) 130, 266

239ª Squadriglia (102º Gr, 5º St C) 130, 167

252ª Squadriglia (104º Gr AS) 13

253ª Squadriglia (104º Gr AS/132º Gr, St Baltimore) 9, 148, 256, 328

260ª Squadriglia (28º Gr, St Baltimore) 148, 278

281ª Squadriglia (132º Gr, St Baltimore) 148, 366

351ª Squadriglia (21º Gr, 51º St C) 130, 167

356ª Squadriglia (20º Gr, 51º St C) 130, 304, 313

360ª Squadriglia (20º Gr, 51º St C) 130

361ª Squadriglia (155º Gr, 51º St C) 130, 234

378ª Squadriglia (155º Gr, 51º St C) 130, 313, 317

386ª Squadriglia (21º Gr, 51º St C) 130, 256

395ª Squadriglia (154º Gr Aut C) 24

396ª Squadriglia (154º Gr Aut C) 30

ANR

1º Gr C (NC, 1ª, 2ª e 3ª Sq) 128, 140, 141, 149, 181, 186, 190, 191, 358, 380, 383, 387, 414, 427

2º Gr C (NC, 4ª, 5ª e 6ª Sq) 137, 139, 144, 146, 149, 154, 155,

157, 159, 160, 164, 175, 179, 183, 186, 293, 295, 301, 305, 308, 310, 316, 325, 328, 330, 333, 337, 345, 346, 349, 355,

356, 358, 360, 362, 364, 366, 378, 381, 384, 394, 395, 408, 427

Gr Aerosiluranti 185, 187 194

Legione San Marco 192

OTHER NATIONALITIES

Brazilian

Brandini, 1º Ten Roberto, 1º Gr Caça/350th FG 359

Cordeiro e Silva, 2º Ten John R., 1º Gr Caça/350th FG 305

Corrêa Netto, 1º Ten Othon, 1º Gr Caça/350th FG 396

da Costa, Asp Raymundo, 1º Gr Caça/350th FG 362

da Motta Paes, 1º Ten Ismael, 1º Gr Caça/350th FG 330

de Magalhães, 2º Ten Marcos Coelho, 1º Gr Caça/350th FG 431

de Medeiros, 1º Ten João Mauricio, 1º Gr Caça/350th FG 338

de Souza, 2º Ten Armando, 1º Gr Caça/350th FG 413

Dornelles, 1º Ten Av Luiz Lopes, 1º Grupo de Caça/350th FG 437

dos Santos, Asp Frederico Gustavo, 1º Gr Caça/350th FG 418

Goulart Pereira, 2º Ten Renato, 1º Gr Caça/350th FG 439

Kopp, Cap Theobaldo, 1º Gr Caça/350th FG 381

Lafayette, Capt, 1º Gr Caça/350th FG 308

Lima, Ten Rui M., 1º Grupo de Caça/350th FG 384

Maia de Assis, 1º Ten Josino, 1º Gr Caça/350th FG 351, 352

Miranda, Cap Joel, 1º Gr Caça/350th FG 355

Moura, Ten. Cel Nero, 1º Gr Caça/350th FG 278

Moura, 2º Ten Danilo, 1º Gr Caça/350th FG 355

Pamplona, Capt, 1º Gr Caça/350th FG 308

Torres, Flt Lt Martinus, 1º Grupo de Caça/350th FG 444

Vieria Sampaio, 1º Ten Aurélio, 1º Gr Caça/350th FG 347

Bulgarian

Andonov, Por K.S., 2/6 Orlyak 296

Atanasov, Kpt K.A., 3/6 Orlyak 308, 310

Barev, Por A., 2/6 Orlyak 260

Bochev, Pod P.A., 3/6 Orlyak 278

Bonchev, Por N.D., 2/6 Orlyak 278

Damev, Por B.V., 3/6 Orlyak 284, 316

Georgiev, Por G.P., 2/6 Orlyak 296

Kafedieff, Lt S.S., 2 Stuka Pulk 303

Kalvachev, Por K.I., 2/6 Orlyak 306

Karalvamov, Kpt, 2 Stuka Pulk 303

Konstantinov, Pod M., 3/6 Orlyak 314

Kovachev, Kpt A.D., 3/6 Orlyak 314

Pavlov, Pod P.E., 3/6 Orlyak 264

Petrov, Kpt M.G., 2/6 Orlyak 260

Sotirov, Pod D.D., 3/6 Orlyak 264

Svetkov, Pod Martin, 2/6 Orlyak 252

Croats

Bartulović, Nar Bozidar, 2.LJ 281, 282

Bencetić, Sat Ljudevit, 2.J1 Sk 431–432, 434

Ceisberger, Ernest 281, 282

Ceković, Nar Josip, 421

Forkapic, Stanko, 15 Av Sq 249, 250

Hamader, Mirko, LPŠ 166

Jelak, Por Mihajlo, 2.J1 Sk 431, 432, 434

Jirasek, Josip, 15 Av Sq 249, 250

Jortdanić, Sat Josip, 3.ZJ 398

Jurković, Mate, 2.LJ 281, 282

Lojen, Nar, 281, 282

Mehanović, Por Šerif, 2.ZJ 407, 408

Petrović, Matja, 267, 268

Pleše, Vod Antun, 2.ZJ 397, 398

Romeo, Adum, 267, 268

Sandtner, Stražnik Vladimir, 421

Šintić; Puk Zlatko, 165

Vouk, Lt Albeiu, 1./Kroat Legion 186

Žauhar, Str Dragutin, 2.ZJ 397–398, 393

Hungarian

Hadnagy, Maj Domokos, 324

Szucs, Denes (Polish), 326

Yugoslav partisan

Ćetković, Gen-Maj Vlado, 8th Corps NOVJ 290

Lipošćak, Miljenko, 290

SHIPS

Abdiel (UK) 11

Achilles (Ger) 258, 281

Agathe (Ger) 96, 100, 101, 151

Aldenham (UK) 31

Anna (Ger) 285

Aspasia (Ger) 131

Athelmonarch (Ger) 12

Attacker (UK) 207, 208, 209, 213, 216, 226, 228, 258, 288, 296, 298

Aurora (UK) 59

Bayfield (US) 215

Beaufort (UK) 59

Bechelaren (Ger) 240, 241

PLACES